anniversary, birthday, jubil[ee]... ding, centenary, bicenten[ary]... Fourth of July, *special da[y]...*

Adj. *periodical*, periodic, ... tidal; measured, steady, ... constant, punctual, like clo[ck]... *lar*; breathing; beating; recurrent, intermittent, remittent; reciprocal, alternate; serial, successive, *continuous*.

seasonal, anniversary; paschal; hourly, daily, nightly, diurnal, biweekly, weekly, fortnightly, monthly; menstrual; yearly, annual, biennial, triennial; centennial, secular.

Vb. *be periodic*, recur; *come after*, turn, revolve, circle, *rotate*; return, come round again; take its turn, alternate; be intermittent; reciprocate; fluctuate, undulate, *oscillate*; beat, pulse, pulsate, throb; heave, pant, *breathe*; swing, sway, *hang*; ply, commute, *be wont*.

Adv. *periodically*, regularly; hourly, daily, weekly, monthly, yearly; every so often.

by *turns*, every other day.

137 Fitfulness: irregularity of recurrence

N. *fitfulness*, irregularity, *disorder*; spasm; remission; variability, *change*; April weather, *caprice*; staggering.

Adj. *fitful*, periodic, remittent, intermittent, stop-go, *discontinuous*; irregular; uneven, *unequal*; occasional, *infrequent*; inconstant, uncertain; variable; spasmodic, jerky; halting, desultory; erratic, eccentric, moody, *capricious*.

Adv. *fitfully*.

138 Change: difference at different times

N. *change*, alteration, variation, *difference*; mutation, permutation, declension; frequent change, variability; partial change, process, treatment, *qualification*; total change; sudden change, *revolution*; break, innovation, reformation; change of direction, shift, turn, *deviation*; change of position, transition, *passage*; translation, *interchange*; overthrow; change of mind.

transformation, transfiguration; metamorphosis; metabolism; transubstantiation; reincarnation; version, adaptation, translation, *interpretation*.

alterer; converter, transformer; catalyst, enzyme, ferment, leaven; editor; censor; chemist; decorator; magician, *sorcerer*; kaleidoscope; weathercock, renegade; new broom; bad influence; bad apple.

Adj. *changeable*, variable, mutable; fickle, *capricious*; affected, newfangled, *new*; provisional; alternative; *variegated*.

Vb. *change*, alter, vary; *grow*, *decrease*; change colour, change countenance, *lose colour*; vacillate, wobble, *be uncertain*; *be capricious*; turn, shift, veer, change course, *deviate*; make a transition, pass to, *pass*; take a turn; *get better*; submit to change, *conform*.

modify, alter, vary, modulate, diversify; superimpose, *add*; make a change, innovate; subvert, *invert*; reverse, turn back; rearrange, *arrange*; adapt, adjust; conform, *make conform*; remould, *form*; process, treat; revise, edit, correct, *rectify*; reform, *make better*; revamp, patch, darn, *restore*; pervert; mar, spoil, *impair*;

cause; affect, *influence*; transform, transfigure, transmute, transubstantiate, convert; digest; conjure, juggle, *deceive*.

Adv. *mutatis mutandis*.

139 Permanence: absence of change

N. *permanence*; *stability*; endurance, duration, perpetuity; fixity, fixity of purpose; rock, bedrock, foundation, solidity, *density*; sustenance, maintenance, conservation, *preservation*; law, rule; fixed law, entrenched clause, *fixture*; standing; tradition, custom, practice, *habit*; fixed attitude, conservatism; routine, *order*; static condition; conservative, reactionary, true blue, stick-in-the-mud, die-hard, *obstinate person*.

Adj. *permanent*, durable; persistent, unfailing, *perpetual*; inveterate, long-standing, *immemorial*; standing, entrenched, fixed, immutable; intact; living; conservative, reactionary, diehard, *obstinate*; stationary, static, immobile, *quiescent*; unaffected, *identical*.

Vb. *stay*, come to stay, *be stable*; abide, endure, subsist, outlive, survive, outlast, *last*; persist, hold, hold good; hold it, maintain, sustain; rest, remain, tarry, live, *dwell*; stand fast, *persevere*; stand pat, *stand firm*; stand still, resist change, *be quiescent*; grow moss, *be old*; allow to stand, let be, let alone, *permit*.

Adv. *as before*; at a standstill.

140 Cessation: change from action to rest

N. *cessation*; arrest, *restraint*; resignation.

stop, halt, dead stop; standstill, deadlock, stalemate, *draw*; checkmate, *defeat*; breakdown, *failure*; stoppage, stall; shutdown, *end*; hitch, check, *hindrance*; blockage, *closure*; walkout, *dissension*; closure of debate, guillotine, *silence*.

strike, resistance; general strike, 'national holiday'; work to rule; stoppage, walkout, sit-down strike, unofficial strike, mutiny; lockout, *exclusion*.

lull, interval, pause, remission; break, breather, rest, *refreshment*; holiday, leisure; interlude, breathing space, *interim*; abeyance, suspension; close season, respite, moratorium, truce, armistice, ceasefire, standstill, *delay*.

stopping place, port of call, port, harbour; stop, halt, pull-up, station; bus stop, terminus, terminal, *air travel*; dead end, blind alley, cul-de-sac; billet, destination, goal.

Vb. *cease*, stay, desist, refrain, hold; stop, halt; stand, rest, *repose*; have done with, end, finish, *terminate*; interrupt, *discontinue*; be mute; cease work, strike, *resist*; exclude; *be silent*; come to an end; *disappear*; end its run; collapse, *fail*, *be past*; withdraw, retire, resign; leave; *relinquish*; close; cease fire, *make peace*; call it a day, *be quiescent*, sleep.

halt, stop, put a stop to; arrest, check, stem, *obstruct*; cut short, call a halt, interrupt, *restrain*; cause a stoppage, stage a strike; bring to a standstill, freeze; checkmate, stalemate, thwart, *hinder*; check oneself, stop short, stop dead; grind to a halt, seize, stall, jam, stick, catch; brake, *retard*.

pause; hold back, hang fire; hesitate; wait awhile, suspend, adjourn, remit, *wait*; rest, *repose*.

Int. halt! hold! stop! enough! whoa! belay there! refrain! leave off! shut up! give over! cut it out! chuck it! drop it! knock it off! come off it! stow it!

141 Continuance in action

N. *continuance, continuity*; flow, *tendency*; extension; maintenance, *perpetuity*; progress, *progression*; break, run, rally, *series*; recurrence, *repetition*.

Adj. *unceasing*, continual, steady; nonstop, unremitting, incessant, *continuous*; *regular*, standing, *fixed*; undying, *perpetual*; unfailing, inexhaustible; invariable; persistent; haunting, recurrent.

Vb. *go on*, wag; keep going, proceed, advance, *progress*; never end, *be eternal*; pursue its course, trend, *tend*; endure, stick, hold, abide, rest, remain, linger, *stay*; obsess, haunt, frequent, *recur*; keep at it, persist, *persevere*; wait, *carry through*; *end*.

sustain, maintain, uphold, *support*; follow through, *continue*; keep alive, *preserve*; *repeat*; prolong, protract, *perpetuate*; let be, let alone, let things take their course, give scope, be lax.

Int. carry on! drive on! never say die! not out!

142 Conversion: change to something different

N. *conversion, production*; reduction, resolution; fermentation, ferment, leaven; chemistry, alchemy; mutation, transfiguration, *transformation*; sorcery; progress, *progression*, growth; course, lapse, flux, *course of time*; development, *increase*; evolution, *biology*; perversion; reformation; rebirth, *restoration*; loss of right; *influence*; *teaching, inducement*; *possibility*.

transition, transit, *passage*; movement, shift, translation, transfer; alteration, *change*; life cycle.

crucible, melting pot, retort, test tube; laboratory, foundry, *workshop*.

changed *person*, new man or woman; convert, neophyte, proselyte; renegade, turncoat; pervert, degenerate, *bad person*.

Adj. *converted*, affected; reborn, regenerate; becoming, *different*; convertible, impressionable, *changeable*.

Vb. *be turned to*, become, get; come to, turn to, ferment, *evolve*; *pass*; *be mixed*; mellow, *mature*; wax, *grow*; degenerate, *deteriorate*; suffer a sea change, *change*; enter a phase, enter a stage.

convert, reduce, process, ferment, leaven; reduce to, enchant, *bewitch*; transmute; render, make, mould, shape, *form*; brainwash, *influence*; *teach*; *convince*; regenerate, *revive*; pervert.

transform, transfigure; landscape, *decorate*; camouflage, disguise, *conceal*; render, *translate*; traduce, *misinterpret*; deform, *distort*; *modify*; reform, make something of, *make better*; remodel, redress, *restore*; assimilate; *exclude*.

Adv. *convertibly*.

143 Reversion

N. *reversion*, going back, return, regress, retreat, ebb; tracing back, *source*; *archaism*; throwback, *heredity*; retrospection, *remembrance*; retrospective action; reaction; repercussion, backlash, backfire, *recoil*; revulsion, revulsion of feeling, *regret*; counter-revolution, *revolution*; *relapse*; *restoration*; curvature; replacement, *restitution*; recovery, *acquisition*; taking back, *taking*; reply, feedback, *answer*; retort; turn, turning point, *crisis*; swing, *recurrence*; round trip; return journey, return ticket; *start*.

Adj. *reverted*, recessive, reflexive; reactive; reactionary, retroactive, *retrospective*; genetic.

Vb. *revert*, go back, turn, return, retrace, *regress*; reverse, face about, *invert*; ebb, retreat, withdraw, *recede*; kick back, rebound, *recoil*; slip back, backslide, *relapse*; retract, recant; hark back; start again, undo, *begin*; revive, *restore*; *liberate*; disenchant, *dissuade*; take back, recover, *retrieve*; resume, *acquire*; *retaliate*; give back, make restitution, reinstate, replace.

Adv. *reversibly*.

144 Revolution: sudden or violent change

N. *revolution*, full circle, circuit, *rotation*; radical change, clean slate, clean sweep; sudden change, catastrophe, surprise, *lack of expectation*; leap, plunge, jerk, start, *spasm*; shift, swing, switch, landslide; violent change, upset, overthrow; upheaval, eruption, explosion, cataclysm, *outbreak*; avalanche, crash, debacle, descent, havoc; revulsion, rebellion, counter-revolution, *reversion, revolt*; total change, abolition.

revolutionist, radical, revolutionary, Red; *agitator; destroyer*; idealist.

Adj. *revolutionary, new*; radical, thoroughgoing, *complete*; seismic, *violent*; subversive, red, *disobedient*; destructive.

Vb. *revolutionize*, subvert, overturn, *invert*; uproot, eradicate, make a clean sweep, obliterate, *demolish*; remodel; change beyond recognition, *transform*.

145 Substitution: change of one thing for another.

N. *substitution*; by-election, *vote*; commutation, exchange, switch, shuffle, *interchange*; replacement, transfer; self-sacrifice.

substitute, sub; proxy, alternate, agent, representative, *deputy*; dual representative; understudy, stand-in, *actor*; ghost, *author*; locum, *doctor*; reserve, twelfth man, *auxiliary*; supply, replacement, remount; relief, *successor*; double, changeling, *impostor*; mother figure, foster parent; synonym, doublet, *word*; metaphor, symbol, *representation*; prosthesis, artificial limb, pacemaker; transplant; alternative, second best, ersatz; scapegoat, sacrifice; makeshift, stopgap; *moderator*; expedient, *compromise*, good policy.

quid *pro quo*, equivalent; consideration, purchase money; value, worth, *price*; redemption, *offset*; replacement, change, *money*.

Adj. *substituted*; vicarious, *disinterested*; interchangeable, *equivalent*; dummy, plastic, mock, ersatz, counterfeit, *spurious*; makeshift, stopgap, provisional, acting, temporary, *ephemeral*.

Vb. *substitute*, commute; exchange, switch, *interchange*; compound, *compromise*; *deceive*; make do with, replace with; replace, succeed, *come after*; supersede, supplant, displace, oust, *eject*; replace.

Adv. *instead*.

146 Interchange: double or mutual change

N. *interchange*; exchange, *barter*, commutation, permutation, anagram; mutual transfer; all change, general post; shuffle; interplay, two-way traffic; rally (tennis); retort, repartee, *rejoinder*.

Adj. *interchanged*; mutual, two-way; reciprocal; intercontinental; interchangeable, convertible, *equivalent*.

Vb. *interchange*, exchange; change money, convert; barter, *trade*; permute, commute; switch, shuffle, castle (chess); *transpose*; *compromise*; reciprocate; requite, *retaliate*; bandy words, answer back, rejoin, *answer*.

Adv. *in exchange*.

147 Changeableness

N. *changeableness*, change; variability, variety; irregularity; instability, imbalance, unstable equilibrium, *inequality*; weak foundation; inquietude, disquiet; turning; flicker, flash; *caprice*; *inattention*; *aptitude*.

changeable *thing*, moon, chameleon; kaleidoscope; wax, clay; mercury, quicksilver, *fluid*; wind, weathercock; eddy; wheel; mobile, *motion*; fortune, wheel of Fortune; luck, *chance*; variable, variable quantity, *numerical element*; play of expression, mobile features, *appearance*; grasshopper mind, *inattention*; floating voter.

Adj. *changeful*, mutable, *changeable*; variant, variable; *iridescent*; *multiform*; quick-change, versatile, *skilful*; uncertain, *irresolute*; unaccountable; volatile, *different*; wayward, fickle, whimsical, *capricious*; giddy, dizzy, flighty, wanton, irresponsible; shifty, inconstant, unfaithful, disloyal.

unstable, unsound; rocky, rolling; mobile, restless, fidgety, desultory, spasmodic, *fitful*; *transient*; turning; gusty, *windy*; unsettled, loose, floating; erratic, rootless, *extraneous*; vagrant, rambling, wandering; tidal, *periodical*; yielding, impressionable, malleable, plastic, *soft*; flowing, running, melting, *fluid*.

Vb. *vary*, show variety; *change*; dodge, double, *avoid*; shuffle, be shifty, *be equivocal*; writhe, *wriggle*; dart, flit; leap, dance, flicker, gutter, *shine*; twinkle, flash; wave, flutter, flap, *hang*; shake, tremble; wobble, stagger, rock, reel, sway, swing, vibrate, *oscillate*; alternate, *fluctuate*; veer, tack, yaw, *deviate*, *navigate*; puff, *blow*; vacillate, waver, hesitate, float, drift, *be irresolute*; hover; be inconstant, *be capricious*.

Adv. *changeably*; now this now that.

148 Stability

N. *stability*, constancy; fixity; rest; steady state, stable equilibrium, balance, *equality*; nerve, aplomb, *resolution*; hardness;

solidarity, solidity, *density*; stiffening.

fixture, establishment, firm foundation; foundations, rock, bedrock, pillar, tower, pyramid; invariant, constant; fast colour, indelible ink; law, written constitution, entrenched clause.

stabilizer, fin, centreboard, keel; ballast, *offset*; buttress, *prop*.

Adj. *unchangeable*; stiff, inflexible, *obstinate*; *resolute*; predictable, reliable, *certain*; immutable; irreducible; changeless, irreversible; invariable, constant, *uniform*; steady, *regular*; durable, *permanent*; undying, perennial, evergreen, *perpetual*; imperishable, indestructible, inextinguishable, *invulnerable*. See *fixed*.

established, entrenched, settled; inveterate; irrevocable, irreversible; incontrovertible, of right; valid, confirmed.

fixed, steadfast, firm, secure, immovable; steady, stable, balanced; fast, ingrained, indelible; ineradicable, rooted, deep-seated, foursquare, well-founded; standing, pat; at rest, at anchor, run aground, stuck fast, stranded; immobile, frozen, like a statue, *still*.

Vb. *be stable*, stand, stick fast, hold, *stand firm*; show aplomb, show self-assurance; *outlast*; come to stay, *stay*; settle, *dwell*; strike root, strike deep, have long roots.

stabilize, root, found, establish, *perpetuate*; erect, *support*; float, set afloat; fix, set, stereotype; make valid, confirm, ratify, *endorse*; retain, retie; bind, make sure, make fast, *tie*; keep steady, retain equilibrium, balance.

149 Present Events

N. *event*, phenomenon; fact, *reality*; case, circumstance, *state*; occurrence, eventuality, incidence, happening; incident, episode, adventure, *occasion*; milestone, *juncture*; fortune, accident, casualty, contingency, *chance*; misadventure, mishap, *misfortune*; emergency, pass, *crisis*; coincidence; advent, *approach*; encounter, meeting; proceeding, *action*; result, product, consequence, issue, outcome, upshot, *effect*; denouement, solution, *evolution*; catastrophe, *end*.

affairs, doings, *deed*; agenda; concern, interests, *business*; world, life, situation, *circumstance*; *course of time*; vicissitudes, *adversity*.

Adj. *eventual*, consequential, resultant; circumstantial, contingent.

happening, incidental, accidental, occasional; doing, current, afloat.

eventful, stirring, busy, full of incident, *active*; momentous, critical, *important*.

Vb. *happen*, become, *be born*; *succeed*; take place, occur, come about, come to pass; befall, betide, *chance*; arise, *arrive*; present itself, *be present*; supervene, follow; issue, transpire, *result*; take its course, advance, *progress*; continue; *be past*; be so, prove, prove to be; bring about, occasion, *cause*.

meet with, incur, encounter, *meet*; find, *discover*; experience, pass through, have been through, *know*, *feel*; endure, undergo, *suffer*.

Adv. *eventually*, ultimately.

150 Destiny: future events

N. *destiny*, fate; horoscope, forecast, *prediction*; prospect, outlook, *expectation*;

futurity, intention; danger, *threat*; proximity, *approach*; future existence, hereafter, *future state*; next world, world to come, *heaven*; predestination, *necessity, certainty*.

Adj. impending, imminent; *preparatory*; destined, *fated*; forthcoming, forecast; inescapable, inevitable, going to be, bound to happen, *certain*; due, *necessary; probable; visible*; to come, *future*; at hand, close, *near*; instant, immediate, about to be; pregnant with; ready, *prepared; beginning*.

Vb. impend, *be to come*; hover, lour, loom, threaten; draw nigh, *approach*; front, face; *be near*; ripen, *mature*.
predestine, doom, preordain, foreordain, *necessitate*; foreshadow, presage, *predict*; have ready, *make ready*; plan, intend, *predetermine*.

Adv. *in the future*; eventually; whatever may happen; *probably*; soon, at any moment.

151 Cause: constant antecedent

N. *causation*; authorship; creation; invention; inspiration, *influence*; generation, provocation, *production*; impulsion, *motive*; cultivation, *agriculture*; temptation, *inducement*; opportunity, *occasion*.
cause, God; *existence*; creator, maker, *producer*; father, *parentage*; author, founder; agent, leaven; stimulus, *stimulant*; contributor, factor, moment, determinant; mainspring; *influence*; *destiny*; fate, *necessity*; force, *compulsion*.
source, fountain, *origin*; spring, fountainhead; mine, quarry, *store*; *home*; genesis, ancestry, lineage, descent, *parentage*; parent, ancestor, progenitor; loins; element, principle, first thing; nucleus, germ, seed, sperm, spore; egg, foetus, embryo; chrysalis, cocoon, *young creature*; bud, stem, stock; taproot, root, bulb, *plant*; radical, etymology, *linguistics*; foundation, bedrock, *base*; groundwork, spadework, *beginning*; raw material, ore.
seedbed, hotbed, *nest*; cradle, nursery, *origin*; breeding place, incubator, womb, fertile soil; hothouse, conservatory, *garden*.
causal *means*, appliance, *means*; pivot, hinge, lever, instrument, *tool*; dynamo, generator, battery, spark, *energy*; motor, engine, turbine, *machine*.
reason why, reason, cause; explanation, key, answer, *interpretation*; excuse, *pretext*; ground, basis, motive, idea, occasion.

Adj. *causal*, formative, effective, effectual; determinant, decisive, final, *ending*; seminal, germinal, *productive; beginning*; suggestive; answerable, responsible; *original*; explanatory; creative, inventive, *inimitable*.
fundamental, primary, elemental, ultimate; radical, basic, *intrinsic*; crucial, central, *important;* original, aboriginal, *first*; primitive, primordial, *primal*.

Vb. *cause*, originate, create, make, *produce*; beget, *generate*; invent, *discover*; underlie; be answerable, be responsible, be to blame; institute, found, inaugurate, *erect, elevate*; launch, set afloat, set afoot, set going, *begin*; open, broach, *initiate*; seed, sow, plant, water, *cultivate*; contrive, effect, effectuate, bring about, bring to

pass, *succeed*; procure, *find means*; stage-manage, engineer, *plan*; induce, precipitate, *hasten*; evoke, elicit, *attract*; provoke, arouse, *excite*; stimulate, *invigorate*; kindle, inspire, incite, tempt, *induce*; occasion, *motivate*; have an effect, show its result, make or mar, *influence*; *do*; determine, decide, *judge*; *prevail, predominate*.
conduce, tend to, *tend*; lead to, *come before*; contribute to, operate to, *be instrumental*; involve, imply, *be intrinsic*; entail, give rise to, *initiate*; promote, advance, encourage, foster, foment, abet, *aid*.

Adv. *causally*, because.

152 Effect: constant sequel

N. *effect*, consequent, consequence, corollary, *sequence*; result; derivative, precipitate, *remainder*; upshot, outcome, issue, denouement, *event*; final result; visible effect, mark, print, impress, *trace*; by-product, spin-off; aftermath, legacy, backwash, wake, repercussion, *sequel*; resultant action, response, *answer*; performance, *deed*; reaction, backlash; offspring, *posterity*; handiwork, *product*; karma, *fate*; moral effect, *influence*.
growth, development, *increase*; bud, blossom, fruit; ear, spike; produce, crop, harvest; profit, *gain*.

Adj. *caused*, due to; consequential; contingent, *subject*; resultant, derivative, descended; secondary; emergent, born of; *eventual*; done.
inherited, heritable, hereditary, Mendelian, *genetic*.

Vb. *result*, come of; accrue, *follow*; be due to; owe everything to, *borrow*; have a common origin, *be related*; take its source; issue, proceed, *emerge*; develop, unfold, *evolve*; bud, sprout, germinate, grow; show a trace, show an effect, receive an impression, *be plain*; *meet with*; happen; *produce*.
depend, *be subject*.

Adv. *consequently*; because of; of course, naturally, necessarily; *hence*.

153 Attribution: assignment of cause

N. *attribution*, assignment of cause; reference to, imputation; theory, hypothesis, model, assumption, conjecture, *supposition*; explanation, *interpretation*; enquiry; *reason why*; affiliation, *parentage*; *source*; attribute; credit, credit title.

Adj. *attributed*; relative; putative, *supposed*.

Vb. *attribute*, say of, assert of, predicate, *affirm*; accord, grant, allow, *give*; assign to, point to, trace to, connect with; *relate*; affiliate; charge with; make responsible, scapegoat, *accuse*; bring home to, *demonstrate*; credit, credit with, acknowledge.
account *for*, explain, *interpret*; assume, *suppose*.

Adv. *hence*, thence, therefore; whence, wherefore; since, because, thanks to, ergo, thus, so.
why! wherefore! whence! how! how come! cui bono!
somehow; somehow or other.

154 Chance: no assignable cause

N. *chance*; lot, fortune, *fate*; potluck; good fortune, luck; bad luck, *misfortune*; hap, hazard, accident, casualty, contingency, coincidence, *event*; chance hit, lucky shot, fluke; rare chance; chance meeting, chance encounter, *lack of expectation*; serendipity.

equal *chance*, fifty-fifty, *equality*; toss-up; lucky dip, random sample; lottery, raffle, tombola, sweepstake, premium bond; *divination*.

fair *chance*, *possibility*; half a chance; good chance, *opportunity*; long odds, odds, *advantage*; small risk, safe bet, *probability*.

calculation *of chance*, doctrine of chance; assurance, insurance, *undertaking*; *experiment*.

Adj. *casual*, fortuitous, chance, haphazard, random, stray; adventitious, accidental, incidental, contingent, *happening*; chancy, dicey, incalculable, *uncertain*.

causeless, groundless, indeterminate, *uncertain*; unaccountable, inexplicable.

Vb. *chance*, hap, so happen, *happen*; *meet with*, *discover*; risk it, chance it, leave it to chance, *gamble*; have small chance, *be unlikely*.

Adv. *by chance*; *at random*; perchance, perhaps; *possibly*.

155 Power

N. *power*, *authority*; control, sway; moral power, *influence*; spiritual power, charisma; witchcraft, *sorcery*; endurance, *stability*; driving force, *motive*; physical power, might, muscle, right arm, right hand, *strength*; dint, effort, endeavour; force, *compulsion*; stress, strain, shear; weight, *gravity*; weight of numbers, *greater number*; manpower, *personnel*; position of power, *advantage*; *truth*; emphasis; extra power, overdrive.

ability, capability, potentiality, *possibility*; competence, efficacy, *skill*; capacity, faculty, virtue, property; qualification, *fitness*; attribute; gift, *aptitude*; compass, reach, grasp, *range*; trend, *tendency*; permission.

energy, vigour, drive; internal energy, work, binding energy, mechanical energy, pedal power, engine power, horsepower; inertia; resistance, *friction*; force, *science of forces*; force of gravity, *gravity*; spring; pressure, head, charge, steam; full pressure; tension, motive power; *traction*; thrust, jet, jet propulsion, *propulsion*; momentum, impetus, *impulse*; *attraction*; *repulsion*; suction, *reception*; expulsion; potential function, potential; unit of work, erg, joule; calorie.

sources *of energy*, coal, gas, oil, *fuel*; wind power, solar energy; power station, hydroelectric station, *waterfall*; tidal barrage, tide mill; windmill; solar panel, solar battery, *heater*; generator, turbine, motor, *machine*.

electricity; lightning; induction, inductance, capacitance; resistance, conduction; frequency; electric charge, pulse, shock; electric current, circuit, electrode, anode, cathode; positive, negative; conductor, semiconductor, nonconductor, insulator; lightning conductor, earth, *safeguard*; live wire, *danger*.

electronics, electron physics, optics, *optics*; *radiation*; microprocessor, microelectronics; computer electronics; automation, *machine*; telegraph, telephone, television, radio, *telecommunication*; electrical engineering, electricity supply; power line, lead, flex, *cable*; distributor; pylon, grid, generator, magneto, dynamo; oscillator, alternator; transformer, commutator, power pack; battery, accumulator; cell, valve, tube, transistor; voltage, volt, watt, kilowatt; ohm; amp.

nucleonics, nuclear physics; fission, fusion, thermonuclear reaction; particle accelerator; Jet; atomic pile, nuclear reactor; moderator, coolant; radioactivity, fallout, *radiation*; *poison*; atomic bomb, *bomb*.

Adj. *powerful*, potent, *strong*; mighty, *great*; rising; prevalent, prevailing; almighty, omnipotent, irresistible, *supreme*; plenipotentiary, *authoritative*; virtual, potential, *possible*; competent, capable, able, adequate, equal to, *sufficient*; with resources, *rich*; *expert*; efficacious, effectual, effective; of power, of might, operative, workable; valid; cogent, compulsive; forcible, *violent*; bellicose, *warlike*.

dynamic, energetic, *vigorous*; high-tension, supercharged; *drawing*; locomotive, kinetic, *moving*; *mechanical*; electric, electrical, electronic; solid-state; live, charged; atomic, nuclear, thermonuclear; hydroelectric.

Vb. *be able*, can; be capable of; compass, manage, *do*; *suffice*; have power, control, *dominate*; force, *compel*; gain power, *prevail*.

empower, enable, endow; endow with power, arm, *strengthen*; electrify, charge; automate; power, drive.

Adv. *powerfully*.

156 Impotence

N. *impotence*, lack of power, power vacuum; *weakness*; inability; *failure*; *inaptitude*; decrepitude; disqualification; sterility, sterilization.

helplessness; *restraint*; impotent fury, *anger*; exhaustion, *fatigue*; collapse, breakdown, *failure*; faint, swoon, coma; *insensibility*; stroke, apoplexy, paraplegia, *disease*; torpor, *inaction*; atrophy; old age, *age*; loss of control; mental decay; mental weakness; minority; babyhood, infancy, *youth*; invalid, *sick person*, weakling.

eunuch; gelding, capon, bullock, steer, neuter; hermaphrodite.

ineffectuality; vanity; dead letter, scrap of paper; figurehead, dummy, man of straw, broken reed, *insubstantial thing*; bluster, empty talk.

Adj. *powerless*, impotent, unable; without authority; nominal, figurehead, constitutional, *insubstantial*; nugatory, invalid; *illegal*; *weak*; inoperative, unemployed; withdrawn; obsolete; kaput; unqualified, inept, dud, *useless*; inadequate, *insufficient*; ineffective, ineffectual, feeble; incapable, incompetent, inefficient.

defenceless, helpless, without resource; bereaved, bereft; orphan, *friendless*; weak, harmless, *innocent*; unarmed; indefensible, untenable; *vulnerable*.

impotent, powerless, feeble, *weak*; unsexed; sexless, neuter; sterile, barren, infertile; effete; senile; paralytic, stiff, *rigid*; unconscious, comatose, *insensible*; without self-control, incontinent; *supine*; nerveless, spineless, *irresolute*; *nervous*; helpless; waterlogged.

Vb. *be impotent*, be unable, cannot; *be useless*; avail nothing, fail; *fall short*; *be subject*; *submit*; feel helpless, shrug; *regret*; do nothing, *watch*; have a hopeless case; *disappear*, faint, swoon, *be insensible*; drop, collapse, *be weak*.

disable, incapacitate, *make useless*; disqualify; invalidate, *abrogate*; disarm, *weaken*; *counteract*; undermine, sap, *make concave*; exhaust, consume, *waste*; wind, prostrate, *strike*; paralyse; sprain, rick, wrench, twist, dislocate; cripple, lame, maim, hobble, nobble, hamstring, *hinder*, *impair*; stifle, throttle, suffocate, strangle, garrotte, *kill*; muzzle, deaden, *silence*; sabotage; deflate; unhinge, *disunite*.

unman, unnerve, enervate, paralyse, *frighten*; *weaken*; emasculate, castrate, neuter, spay, geld, *make sterile*.

157 Strength

N. *strength*, might, horsepower, HP, *power*; energy; force, *brute force*; spring; tone, temper; tensile strength; iron, steel, *hardness*; oak, heart of oak; endurance, grit, *stamina*.

vitality, *health*; vim, vigour, *life*; animal spirits; guts, nerve, backbone, *resolution*; physique, muscle, biceps, brawn, *size*; grip.

athletics, *sport*, *contest*; gymnastics, acrobatics, *exercise*; stadium, gymnasium, *arena*.

athlete, gymnast, tumbler, acrobat, contortionist, trapeze artist, circus rider, stunt man, *entertainer*; Blue, *contender*; heavyweight; strong man; champion; he-man, muscle man, *male*; strongarm man, bully, bruiser, tough guy, *desperado*; bouncer; amazon, virago, *woman*; matador, picador, toreador; Atlas, Titan, *giant*; tower of strength, *auxiliary*.

strengthening, reinforcement, *aid*; stiffening; tonic effect; *refreshment*; revival, *restoration*; emphasis, stress.

science *of forces*, dynamics, statics; thermodynamics; triangle of forces.

Adj. *strong*, lusty, vigorous, *young*; mighty, potent, armed, *powerful*; high-powered, high-tension; omnipotent, *superior*; incontestable, irresistible, victorious; sovereign, supreme, *ruling*; valid; *great*; *healthy*; heavy, *weighty*; strongarm, forceful, forcible, *severe*; urgent, pressing, compulsive; *assertive*; steely, *hard*; tough; deep-rooted, *firm*; solid, substantial, stable, *fixed*; stout, heady, alcoholic; neat, *whole*; entrenched, inviolable, *invulnerable*.

unyielding, staunch, *resolute*; stubborn, *obstinate*; persistent, *rigid*; solid, *dense*, impregnable, *invulnerable*; of iron nerve, indomitable, invincible; inextinguishable; unflagging, tireless, *industrious*; indestructible; proof, sound; waterproof, weatherproof, impermeable; fireproof, bulletproof.

stalwart, stout, sturdy, hardy, rugged, robust, doughty, *vigorous*; of good physique, able-bodied, muscular, brawny; sinewy, wiry, *active*; strapping, well-knit, well set-up, thickset, stocky, burly, beefy, husky, hefty, *large*; gigantic, colossal, Herculean, *huge*.

athletic, fit, *healthy*.

manly, masculine, *male*; virile, red-blooded, manful, *courageous*; grown-up.

Vb. *be strong*; pack a punch; *prepare*; overpower, overwhelm, *overmaster*; rally,

recover, revive; blow hard, *blow*.

strengthen, confirm, give strength to, lend force to, *augment*; underline, stress; reinforce, fortify; stuff, pad, line; buttress, prop, sustain, *support*; nerve, brace, steel, *give courage*; stiffen, toughen, temper, *harden*; act like a tonic, invigorate; animate, enliven, quicken, *excite*; *revive*; *refresh*; *cure*; *elevate*; *tighten*; power, engine, motor, *empower*.

Adv. *strongly*.

158 Weakness

N. *weakness*, lack of strength; delicacy, *sensibility*; *inequality*; weak foundation, instability; moral weakness, frailty; bodily weakness, *old age*; delicate health, *ill health*; *bulk*; weak state; anaemia; loss of strength, languor, torpor; exhaustion, collapse, *fatigue*; swoon, *insensibility*; decline, declension; *moderation*; relaxation; *mixture*; effect of weakness, crack, fault, gap; flaw, *blemish*; strain, sprain; weak point, *defect*.

weakling, effeminate, pansy; lightweight, *nonentity*; mollycoddle; old woman, invalid, *sick person*; lame dog, lame duck; infant, kitten, *young creature*; baby, *coward*; *favourite*; doormat, jellyfish, drip, weed, wet; victim, *sufferer*; gull, *dupe*.

weak *thing*, flimsy article, reed, thread, rope of sand; sandcastle, mud pie, house of cards, cobweb, gossamer, *insubstantial thing*; matchwood, eggshell, paper, glass, china; water, thin gruel.

Adj. *weak*, powerless, *impotent*; without force, invalid, *powerless*; helpless; harmless, *innocent*; babyish; effeminate, pansy, womanish, *female*; poor, feeble, slight, puny, small; lightweight, *light*; of poor physique, *little*; thin, *lean*; imbecile, *foolish*; sheepish, gutless, half-hearted, *irresolute*; nerveless, *nervous*; spineless, weak-kneed, submissive, yielding; *insubstantial*; *dry*; bloodless, anaemic, pale, *colourless*; limp, flaccid, flabby, floppy, *soft*; *hanging*; unstrung, slack, loose, *lax*; watery, wishy-washy, insipid, *tasteless*; low, quiet, faint; decrepit, old; too weak, past it; *capricious*; rickety, shaky, unstable; torpid, *quiescent*; only beginning, infant, *beginning*, new, *young*. See *flimsy*.

weakened, diminished, dissipated, spent, effete, *used*; laid low; bare; failing, weary; strained; weatherbeaten, worn, broken, tumbledown, *dilapidated*; rotten, *inert*.

weakly, infirm, delicate, sickly, *unhealthy*; groggy, rocky, seedy, poorly; underweight, skinny, *lean*; languid, listless; faint; sallow, wan, lacklustre, *colourless*.

crippled, *impotent*; halt, lame, game; knock-kneed, rheumatic, *imperfect*.

flimsy, gossamer, sleazy, tenuous, *insubstantial*; delicate, dainty; frail, fragile, brittle; shoddy, *useless*; rickety, ramshackle, shaky, wonky, crazy, tumble-down, *dilapidated*.

Vb. *be weak*, weaken; sicken, *be ill*; faint, fail, languish, flag; drop, fall, *tumble*; dwindle, *decrease*; decline, *deteriorate*; droop, wilt, fade, grow old; wear thin, crumble; yield, give way, sag, *soften*; split, *open*; dodder, totter, teeter, sway, reel, *oscillate*; tremble, shake; halt, limp, go lame; *be old*.

weaken, enfeeble, debilitate, enervate; unnerve, rattle, *frighten*; relax, slacken, loosen, *disunite*; shake, *soften*; strain, sprain, cripple, lame, *disable*; hurt, injure, *wound*; cramp, *obstruct*; effeminate; disarm, cushion, *blunt*; starve; rob; reduce, extenuate, thin, lessen, *abate*; dilute, water, adulterate, *mix*; eviscerate; *counteract*; decimate, *render few*; muffle, *mute*; invalidate, *abrogate*; damage, spoil, *impair*; sap, undermine; dismantle, *demolish*.

together, *join*; blend, *combine*; mine, quarry, *extract*; establish, found, constitute, institute, *initiate*; *arrange*; develop, exploit; automate; engineer, contrive, *plan*; perform, implement, execute, achieve, accomplish; bring about, effect, *cause*; unfold, develop, *evolve*; breed, hatch, rear, *breed stock*; sow, grow, farm, *cultivate*; bear young, *reproduce itself*; educate, *train*.

159 Production

N. *production*, creation; mental creation, *thought*; invention, original work; creative urge, productivity; effort, endeavour, *attempt*, *undertaking*; artistic effort, composition, authorship, *art*, *painting*, *sculpture*, *writing*; *musical skill*; doing, performance, output, throughput, turnout, *action*; execution, accomplishment, achievement; *preparation*; workmanship, *formation*; design, *plan*; *structure*, *arrangement*; tectonics, engineering, building, architecture; establishment, erection, *elevation*; making, manufacture, industry, *business*; process; assembly; assembly line, *continuity*, *machine*; factory, *workshop*; technology; mass production, automation; productivity deal; development, growth, *increase*, *abundance*; *scarcity*; farming, factory farming, *agriculture*; breeding, *animal husbandry*.

product, creature, creation, result, *effect*; output, turnout, printout; waste, slag; extract, essence; confection, compound, *a mixture*; handiwork; *manufacture*; article, thing, *object*; goods, wares, *merchandise*; gross national product; earthenware, *pottery*; stoneware, hardware; fabric, cloth, *textile*; production, work, opus, piece, *composition*; *masterpiece*; fruit, flower, blossom, berry; produce, yield, harvest, crop, vintage, *growth*; interest, increase, return, *gain*; mental product, brainchild, conception, *idea*; figment, fiction; offspring, young, egg, spawn, seed, *young creature*.

edifice, piece of architecture, building, structure, erection, pile, dome, tower, skyscraper, *high structure*; pyramid, *monument*; church, *temple*; mausoleum, *tomb*; habitation, mansion, hall, *house*; college, *school*; fortress, *fort*; stonework, brickwork, *building material*.

producer, creator, maker, Nature; founder, *cause*; *parentage*; creative worker, writer, *author*; composer, *musician*; painter, sculptor, *artist*; developer, architect, engineer; industrialist, *agent*; executive, *doer*; labourer, *worker*; artificer, *artisan*; grower, planter, cultivator, *farmer*; stock farmer, sheep farmer; miner; *stage manager*.

Adj. *productive*, creative, inventive, *imaginative*; constructive; industrial, *formative*; fruitful, *prolific*; *generative*.

produced, made; artificial, man-made, synthetic, cultivated; handmade; homemade, homespun; ready-made; begotten, *born*; grown; thought of.

Vb. *produce*, create, originate, make; invent, *discover*; conceive, *imagine*; write, design, *compose*, operate, *do*; frame, fashion, shape, *form*; knit, spin, *weave*; sew, tie; forge, chisel, carve, sculpture; cast; coin, *mint*; manufacture, fabricate, prefabricate, process, mill, *machine*; mass-produce, multiply, *reproduce*; construct, build, raise, rear, erect, *elevate*; put together, assemble, compose, cobble

160 Destruction

N. *destruction*, undoing, *reversion*; *extinction*; abolition; *silence*; *revolution*; precipitation, overthrow; dissolution; *separation*; *burning*; mass murder, massacre, genocide, *slaughter*; hatchet job; mischief, vandalism, *violence*; sabotage, *hindrance*; fire-raising, arson.

havoc, scene of destruction, disaster area, chaos, *confusion*, turmoil; wilderness, *desert*; carnage, shambles, *slaughterhouse*; upheaval, cataclysm, storm, *outbreak*; ravages; depredation, raid, *spoliation*; blitz, explosion, nuclear blast, *bombardment*; holocaust, hecatomb.

ruin, downfall, ruination, perdition; *adversity*; catastrophe, disaster, act of God, *misfortune*; collapse, landslide, *revolution*; breakdown, break-up, *failure*; crash, smash, smash-up, *collision*; wreck, shipwreck, wreckage, wrack; loss, Waterloo, *defeat*; knockout blow, KO, *knock*; slippery slope, road to ruin; apocalypse, doom, crack of doom, knell, *end*, *finality*; ruins.

Adj. *destructive*, internecine, *complete*; ruinous, *wasteful*; costly, *dear*; apocalyptic, *violent*; *furious*; merciless, *pitiless*; mortal, suicidal, cut-throat, *deadly*; subversive, *revolutionary*; incendiary, mischievous, pernicious; poisonous, *toxic*.

destroyed, undone, fallen; ground; lost, sunk, sunk without trace; had it, kaput; dilapidated; *ending*.

Vb. *destroy*, undo; abolish, annihilate, liquidate, exterminate, axe, *nullify*; devour, consume, *waste*; engulf, *absorb*; swamp, overwhelm, drown, *drench*; incinerate, gut, *burn*; wreck, shipwreck, sink (see *suppress*); end, put an end to, *terminate*; *kill*; poison, *murder*; decimate, *render few*; exterminate, spare none, *slaughter*, be pitiless; remove, extirpate, eradicate, uproot, *eject*; expunge, efface, erase, delete, cancel, *obliterate*; annul, revoke, *abrogate*; dispel, scatter, dissipate, *disperse*; dissolve, *liquefy*; evaporate; mutilate, deface, *deform*; make short work of, trounce, *defeat*; dish, sabotage, *obstruct*; play hell with, *bedevil*, *make*; ruin.

demolish, dismantle, *disunite*; level, raze, *flatten*; steamroller, bulldoze, *fell*; *slaughter*; subvert, overthrow, overturn, upset, *invert*; sap, *weaken*; undermine, mine, dynamite, explode, blow sky-high; bombard, bomb, blitz, *fire at*; wreck, smash, shatter, shiver, smash to smithereens, *break*; pulp, crush, grind; make mincemeat of; rend, *sunder*; *agitate*; batter, ram, *strike*; gut, strip bare, *uncover*.

suppress, quench, *extinguish*; cut short, abort, *discontinue*; quell, *oppress*; squelch, squash, *flatten*; quash, revoke, *abrogate*; blanket, stifle, smother, suffocate, strangle, *disable*; repress, *subjugate*; cover, *conceal*; drown, submerge, sink, scuttle, scupper, torpedo, sink without trace, plunge, *lower*.

lay *waste*, desolate, devastate, depopulate, *empty*; raid, ransack, *rob*; damage, spoil, mar, ruin, *impair*; ravage, deal destruction, run amok, make havoc, make a shambles, *be violent*; *waste*; *abase*; *burn*; defoliate, *make sterile*.

consume, devour; engulf, *absorb*; squander, run through, *waste*; cast before swine, *misuse*.

be *destroyed*, go west, be lost, *perish*; sink, *plunge*; have had it, *end*; fall, *tumble*; split; crumble, crumble to dust, *deteriorate*; succumb; go to pot, go to hell, go to blazes.

Adv. *destructively*, with a sledge hammer.

161 Reproduction

N. *reproduction*; *production*; *repetition*; mass production; multiplication, printing, *print*; *restoration*; *revival*; resurrection, resurgence; *recurrence*; *heredity*; reincarnation, *future state*; new edition, reprint, *edition*; copy, *duplicate*; Phoenix.

Adj. *reproduced*; *generative*.

Vb. *reproduce*, remake, reconstruct; rebuild; duplicate, clone, *copy*, *repeat*; take after, inherit, *resemble*; renovate, renew, *restore*; regenerate, resuscitate, reanimate, *revive*; reappear; resurrect; mass-produce, multiply; *print*; breed, *reproduce itself, be many*.

162 Propagation

N. *propagation*, *reproduction*; fertility; multiplication, *increase*; breeding, hatching, incubation, *animal husbandry*; eugenics, *biology*; sex; generation, genesis, *source*; parthenogenesis, virgin birth; spontaneous generation; AID; fertility drug, *fertilizer*; conception, pregnancy, gestation (see *obstetrics*); birth, nativity, happy event, *origin*; *failure*; birth rate; development, *growth*; fruition, flowering; puberty, maternity, paternity, *parentage*; donor; fertilizer; cultivator.

obstetrics; parturition, birth, childbirth, confinement; *anaesthetic*; labour, labour pains; delivery, breech delivery; waters, caul; placenta, afterbirth; maternity specialist, midwife; *nurse*; stork, gooseberry bush.

genitalia, loins, womb, *source*; genitals; male member, penis; scrotum; prostate; vulva, clitoris, vagina, uterus, ovary; ovum, egg; semen, seminal fluid, sperm, spermatozoa; seed, pollen.

Adj. *generative*, potent, virile; productive; fertile, fecund, *prolific*; germinal, seminal, genetic, *fundamental*; sexual, bisexual.

fertilized; breeding, broody, pregnant; heavy with, big with; with child; fallen; brought to bed of; *medical*; puerperal, maternity; antenatal; viviparous.

Vb. *reproduce itself*, yield, give increase, *be fruitful*; hatch, breed, spawn, multiply, teem, *be many*; germinate, sprout, burgeon, *grow*; bloom, flower, fruit, bear fruit, *mature*; seed, seed itself; conceive, get pregnant, fall; carry, bear; be brought to bed of, bring forth, give birth, have a baby; abort, *miscarry*; have young, have offspring, have progeny; drop, farrow, lamb, foal, calve, cub, pup, whelp, kitten, litter; *be born*.

generate, evolve, *produce*; give life to; beget, get, engender, spawn, father, sire; copulate, *unite with*; impregnate, inseminate,

pollinate; procreate, propagate; breed, hatch, incubate, raise, rear, *breed stock*; bud, graft, layer, *cultivate*.

163 Destroyer

N. *destroyer*; wrecker, vandal; raider; extinguisher; hatchet man, assassin; executioner; barbarian, Vandal, Hun; time, time's scythe, *course of time*; angel of death, *death*; destructive agency, locust, glutton; moth, woodworm, rust, erosion, *decay*; acid, mildew, blight, poison, *bane*; earthquake, fire, flood, *havoc*; *war*; instrument of destruction, sword, *weapon*; gunpowder, dynamite, *explosive*; blockbuster, *bomb*; juggernaut, bulldozer.

164 Parentage

N. *parentage*, paternity, maternity; fatherhood, motherhood; loins, womb, *source*; kinship, *family*; adoption, *protection*; parent, *humankind*; single parent, *divorce*; godparent, guardian, *protection*

genealogy, family tree, lineage, kin, *consanguinity*; race history, pedigree, heredity; line, blood, strain; blue blood, *nobility*; stock, stem, tribe, house, clan, *race*; descent, extraction, birth, ancestry, *origin*.

paternity, fatherhood; dad, pop, papa, pater, governor; grandfather, *old man*; ancestor, progenitor, forefather, forbear, patriarch, predecessor, *precursor*; father figure; adoptive father, father-in-law.

maternity, motherhood; maternal instinct, *love*; expectant mother, mother-to-be; mother, dam; mummy, mum; grandmother, gran; matron; *old woman*; mother substitute; mother-in-law; Mother Church, mother country.

Adj. *parental*, paternal; maternal, matronly; fatherly; motherly; family, patrilineal, matrilineal; hereditary, *genetic*; patriarchal, *immemorial*; ethnic.

165 Posterity

N. *posterity*, progeny, issue, offspring, young, *child*; breed, *race*; brood, seed, litter, farrow, spawn, *young creature*; *family*; succession, heritage; rising generation, *youth*.

descendant, son, daughter; infant, *child*; scion, shoot, sprout, *young plant*; heir, *beneficiary*; love child; branch, ramification, colony; graft, offset.

sonship, line, lineage, descent, *consanguinity*; indirect descent, ramification; irregular descent; succession, heredity; *priority*.

Adj. *filial*; descended; collateral; *prior*; adoptive; step-; hereditary, Mendelian, genetic.

166 Productiveness

N. *productiveness*, productivity, mass production, *production*; boom; superabundance, glut; fertility, Green Revolution, *plenty*; high birthrate, baby boom, population explosion; productive capacity; multiplication; *imagination*.

fertilizer, manure, dung, guano, compost, potash, lime; mulch, *agriculture*; semen, sperm, seed; fertility drug; fertility cult, phallus; Earth Mother.

abundance, wealth, riot, profusion, harvest, *great quantity*; teeming womb, mother earth, rich soil; hotbed, nursery, *seedbed*; cornucopia, horn of plenty; second crop, aftermath, *sequel*; rabbit warren, ant heap, *multitude*.

Adj. prolific, fertile, fecund; teeming, *generative*; fruitful; pregnant, heavy with; exuberant, lush, leafy, verdant, luxuriant, rich, fat; copious; creative, inventive, resourceful.

Vb. *make fruitful*; plant, water, irrigate, manure, compost, top-dress, *cultivate*; impregnate, inseminate; procreate, produce, propagate, *generate*.

be *fruitful*, flourish; burgeon, bloom, blossom; germinate; conceive, bear, give birth, *reproduce itself*; teem, proliferate, swarm, multiply, mushroom, *be many*; *augment*; populate.

167 Unproductiveness

N. unproductiveness, dearth, famine, *scarcity*; erosion; dying race, zero population growth, *decrease*; change of life, menopause; poor return, *loss*; waste of time, lost labour; slump, slack market.

contraception, birth control, family planning; contraceptive, pill, coil, loop, diaphragm, Dutch cap, French letter, condom, sheath; rhythm method, chastity, *restraint*; vasectomy.

desert, waste, lunar landscape; heath, moor, bush, wild, wilderness; dustbowl, *waste*; salt flat, *marsh*; *ice*; waste of waters, *ocean*.

Adj. unproductive; sparse, scarce, *insufficient*; waste, desert, desolate; bleak, gaunt, bare, *empty*; poor, stony, shallow; unprolific, barren, infertile, sour, sterile; rootless; arid, *dry*; fallow; impotent; without issue; celibate; fruitless; inoperative, *impotent*; ineffective; abortive.

Vb. *be unproductive*, - unprolific etc. adj. rust, stagnate, lie fallow; cease work, *cease*; hang fire, come to nothing, come to naught, *fail*; abort, *miscarry*; practise birth control.

make sterile, waste; castrate, geld; *lay waste*; addle, *decompose*; disinfect, *purify*.

168 Agency

N. agency, operation, work, working, doing, *action*; job, office, *function*; exercise, *use*; force, strain, stress, play, swing, *power*; *influence*; *management*; service; effectiveness; maintenance, support, *aid*; execution; process, treatment.

Adj. operative, effectual, efficient, efficacious; drastic, *severe*; executive, operational, functional; acting, working, at work, *doing, used*; active; live, potent, *dynamic, vigorous*; practical, workable, applicable, *advisable*; serviceable, *useful*.

Vb. operate, play; act, work, go, run, *do*; idle; serve, execute, perform, *function*; do its job; take effect, *cause*; have effect, *influence*; take action, strike, *be active*; maintain, sustain, *support*; crew, man; make operate; power, drive, *move*; process, treat; manipulate, handle, wield, *touch, use*; stimulate, excite, *invigorate*.

169 Vigour: physical energy

N. vigorousness, energy, vigour, life, *activity*; physical energy, pressure, force, impetus, *energy*; high pressure, *strength*; dash, *haste*; effort, *labour*; fervour, enthusiasm, *vigour*; gusto, relish, zest,

joy; spirit, vim, zip; fire, mettle, blood, *courage*; ginger, fizz, verve, snap, pep, drive, go; enterprise, initiative, *undertaking*; *violence*; oomph, thrust, push, kick, punch, *attack*; grip, bite, teeth, backbone, spunk, *resolution*; guts, grit, *stamina*; *vitality*; live wire, spark, dynamo, dynamite, quicksilver; rocket, jet; display of energy, *spurt*; show of force.

stimulation, tonic effect; boost, *increase*; excitement; stir, bustle, *activity*; ferment, fermentation; ebullience, *commotion*; froth, *bubble*; steam, *heating*.

keenness, acrimony; point, edge; zeal.

stimulant, booster; yeast, leaven, catalyst; stimulus, fillip, shot; spur, prick, prod, goad, lash, *incentive*; restorative, tonic, pep pill, *tonic*; aperitif, appetizer; seasoning, spice, *sauce*; liquor, alcohol, *alcoholic drink*; aphrodisiac, philtre, Spanish fly; pep talk, rousing cheer.

Adj. *vigorous*, energetic, *active*; *deadly*; forcible, forceful, vehement, *violent*; vivid, vibrant, *dynamic*; high-pressure, intense, strenuous, *industrious*; enterprising, go-ahead, *progressive*; aggressive; keen, *willing*; double-edged, potent, *powerful*; hearty, virile, full-blooded, *strong*; full of punch, full of pep, lusty, mettlesome, *lively*; blooming, bouncing, *healthy*; brisk, nippy, snappy; heady, racy; tonic, bracing, rousing, *exciting*; drastic, stringent, harsh, punishing, *severe*; *powerful*; lush, *prolific*.

keen, acute, sharp, incisive, trenchant, *forceful*; mordant, biting, poignant, pointed; virulent, caustic, *pungent*; acrid, acid, *sour*.

Vb. *be vigorous*, thrive, have zest, enjoy life, be healthy; burst with energy, *be strong*; show energy, *be active*; *exert oneself*; exert energy, drive, push, impel; bang, slam, wrench, cut right through; *force*; *accelerate*; be thorough, strike home, carry through; strike hard, hammer, dint, dent, *strike*; make an impression, *influence, impress*; *meddle*; show fight, *attack*.

invigorate, activate; electrify, intensify, double, redouble; boost, *strengthen*; rouse, kindle, inflame, stimulate, enliven, quicken, *excite*; act like a tonic, hearten, animate, *cheer*; intoxicate, *inebriate*; revive, *refresh*; give an edge to, *sharpen*; irrigate, *cultivate*.

Adv. vigorously, forcibly, hard, with telling effect; with a will; at full tilt, full steam ahead.

170 Inertness

N. inertness, inertia, inaction; languor, torpor, *insensibility*; rest, vegetation, passivity; apathy, sloth; passive resistance; vegetable, cabbage; extinct volcano.

Adj. inert, passive, dead; lifeless, languid, torpid, numb, *insensible*; heavy, sluggish, slow; *sleepy*; quiet, stagnant, *quiescent*; fallow; slack, *lax*; limp, flaccid, *weak*; apathetic, neutral, *indifferent, impassive*; pacific, *peaceful*; *powerless*; dormant, *latent*.

Vb. *be inert*, slumber, *sleep*; hang fire; smoulder, *lurk*; lie, stagnate, vegetate, *be quiescent*; just sit there.

Adv. inactively, at rest.

171 Violence

N. violence, frenzy, ferment; vandalism, destruction; turbulence, commotion; bluster, uproar, riot, row, roughhouse, rumpus, furore, turmoil; roughness; force, high hand, strong-arm tactics, terrorism; brute force; atrocity, outrage, torture, cruel act; barbarity, blood lust, inhumanity; ferocity; rage, hysterics, excitable state; fit, throes, paroxysm, spasm; shock, clash, collision; wrench, twist.

outbreak, outburst; flood, tidal wave, wave; cataclysm, earthquake, quake, tremor, revolution; eruption, volcano, furnace; explosion, blow-up, burst, blast, destruction; rush, onrush, assault, sortie, attack; gush, spurt, jet, torrent, stream.

storm, turmoil, turbulence; weather; squall, tempest, typhoon, hurricane, cyclone, gale; thunder; cloudburst, rain; blizzard; sandstorm, gale.

violent creature, brute, beast, dragon, tiger, wolf, mad dog; demon, devil, monster; savage, barbarian, vandal, iconoclast, destroyer; he-man, male; man of blood, assassin, executioner, butcher; homicidal maniac, madman; rough, tough, rowdy, thug, ruffian; hooligan, bully, bully boy, terror, tyrant; bravo, firebrand, incendiary, agitator; revolutionary, madcap, desperado; virago, termagant, Amazon; fury, scold, shrew.

Adj. violent, vehement, forcible, strong; acute, sharp; unmitigated; excessive, outrageous, extravagant, exorbitant; rude, abrupt, brusque, bluff, discourteous; extreme, severe, heavy-handed; primitive, barbarous, savage, brutal, bloody, cruel; hot-blooded, irascible; aggressive, bellicose, warlike; rampant; thrashing about, disorderly; rough, wild, furious, blustery, tempestuous, stormy, gale force, windy; rainy; uproarious, obstreperous, loud; rowdy, turbulent, tumultuous, boisterous, riotous; incendiary, revolutionary; intemperate, immoderate, unbridled, unrestrained; ungovernable, unruly, disobedient; irrepressible, inextinguishable, vigorous; hot, red-hot, inflamed, heated; inflammatory, flaming, fiery; volcanic, seismic, destructive; explosive; spasmodic; full of violence, disturbed.

furious, towering, mad, angry; impetuous, rampant; roaring, howling; headstrong, hasty; desperate, rash; savage, wild; vicious, fierce, ferocious, cruel; bloodthirsty, rabid, berserk, murderous; waspish, tigerish; frantic, hysterical.

Vb. be violent, break bounds, run wild, run riot, run amok, lay waste; tear, rush, dash, hurtle, hurl oneself, move fast; surge forward, stampede, mob, charge; raise a storm, riot, roughhouse, rampage; resort to violence, take to arms, go to war, revolt; see red, go berserk, be angry; storm, rage, roar, bluster, blow; ferment, foam, fume, run high, effervesce; flood, overwhelm, flow; explode, detonate, burst, fly, flash, flare; let fly, fulminate; erupt, struggle, strain, scratch, bite, kick, resist; savage, maul, wound; ride roughshod, oppress.

force, smash, break; tear, rend, sunder; bruise, crush, demolish; strain, wrench, pull, dislocate, sprain; twist, warp, deform, distort; force open, open; blow open, shock, shake, agitate; do violence to, abuse, misuse; violate, ravish, rape, debauch; torture, ill-treat.

make violent, stir, quicken, stimulate, excite; urge, goad, lash, whip, incite; inflame, kindle; heat; foment, exacerbate, exasperate, aggravate; whet, sharpen; irritate, infuriate, enrage; madden, make mad.

Adv. violently, forcibly; bodily; at one fell swoop; with a vengeance, like mad; slap bang, wham; head foremost, head first; like a bull at a gate.

172 Moderation

N. moderation, nonviolence; measure, golden mean; restraint, self-control, temperance; sobriety; middle way; mutual concession, compromise; relief; relaxation, remission; appeasement; quiet, calm, quietude; control, check, restraint.

moderator, remedy; balm; rose water, milk; sedative, lullaby; nightcap, barbiturate, soporific; opiate, opium, anaesthetic; dummy, stopper; wet blanket, damper; cold water, cold shower, extinguisher; brake, restraint; neutralizer; antidote; cushion; third force, peacemaker, mediator; rein.

Adj. moderate, reasonable, judicious, just; tame, gentle, harmless, mild, lenient; innocuous, innocent, weak; measured, limited, low-key, restrained; subdued, temperate, sober; cool, calm; still, quiet, tranquil; peaceable, pacific, peaceful; pink, neutral, indifferent.

lenitive, remedial; sedative, narcotic, soporific; smooth, soft; bland, emollient; refreshing.

Vb. be moderate, be halfway; go easy, keep within bounds, keep within reason, be temperate; settle, be quiescent; disarm, be at peace; remit, relent, show mercy; show consideration, be lenient; decelerate.

moderate, mitigate, temper; correct, adjust; tame, check, curb, control, chasten, govern, limit, restrain; lessen, diminish, slacken, abate; palliate, extenuate, qualify, weaken; blunt; cushion, support; soft-pedal, moderate language, purify; sober, dampen, damp, cool, chill, refrigerate, dissuade; blanket, smother, subdue, quell, extinguish.

assuage, ease, pour balm, mollify, soften; alleviate, lighten, relieve; counteract; allay, dull, deaden, render insensible; soothe, calm, comfort, still, quiet, hush, lull, rock, cradle, rock to sleep, bring to rest; sweeten; disarm, appease, pacify; slake, drink.

Adv. moderately, within bounds, within compass, within reason; at half speed; gingerly.

173 Influence

N. influence, capability, power, potentiality, ability; magnitude; upper hand, casting vote; footing, hold, grip; play, scope; purchase, pivot; clout, weight, pressure; pull, drag, attraction; repulsion; thrust, drive, propulsion; impact, impulse; leaven, contagion, infection; atmosphere, climate, circumstance; occult influence, magic, spell, sorcery; destiny, fate; fascination, hypnotism; malign influence, curse, ruin, bane; emotion, impulse, impression, feeling; persuasion, suggestion, impulsion, inspiration, motive; personality, charisma, leadership, credit, repute, prestige; hegemony, domination, tyranny, *authority*; sway, control, dominance, reign; sphere of influence, orbit; factor, vital role, leading part, *cause*; indirect influence, patronage, interest, favour, pull, friend at court, *aid*; strings, lever, *tool*; secret influence, Grey Eminence; force; lobby, pressure group, *inducement*; person of influence, uncrowned king or queen, big noise, big shot, bigwig; *government*.

Adj. *influential*, dominant, prevalent, prevailing, supreme; ruling, regnant, commanding; with authority, *authoritative*; rising; strong, potent, mighty, *great*, *powerful*; leading, busy, *active*; effective, *causal*; weighty, key, momentous, decisive, earth-shaking, *important*; telling, moving, emotional, *impressive*; appealing, attractive; gripping; irresistible; persuasive, suggestive; instructive, *educational*; catching, contagious, *infectious*; pervasive, *ubiquitous*.

Vb. *influence*, have a pull, carry weight, cut ice, *be important*; be well-connected; *command*; dominate, bestride; *be superior*; exert influence, make oneself felt, assert oneself; lobby, pull strings, *motivate*; gain a hearing, *attract notice*; have a voice; affect, tell; *impress*; *flatter*; urge, prompt, tempt, incite, inspire, dispose, persuade, convince, carry with one, *induce*; force, *compel*; sway; predispose, brainwash, prejudice, *bias*; appeal, allure, fascinate, *attract*; disgust, *repel*; *counteract*; make, *make better*; make or mar, change, *transform*; infect, leaven, colour, *modify*; contaminate, mar, *impair*; *work*, *operate*; play a part, guide, *direct*; *be an example*.

prevail, outweigh, override, *predominate*; overawe, overcome, subdue, subjugate; gain full play, master, *overmaster*; control, rule, *dominate*; hold, *retain*; gain a footing, take root, take hold, settle, *stay*; permeate, run through, colour, *pervade*; spread, rage, be rife, spread like wildfire.

Adv. *influentially*, to good effect.

174 Tendency

N. *tendency*, trend, tenor; tempo, rhythm, set, drift, *direction*; course, stream, main current, main stream; climate, *influence*; gravitation, affinity, *attraction*; polarity; *fitness*; gift, aptitude; proclivity, propensity, readiness, penchant, predilection, leaning, bias, prejudice; weakness; cast, bent, turn, grain; a strain of, *tincture*; vein, humour, mood; tone, quality, nature, characteristic, *temperament*; special gift, idiosyncrasy, *speciality*.

Adj. *tending*, conducive, leading to; working towards; *probable*; centrifugal; subservient, *liable*; apt to, prone to; ready to, about to, *prepared*.

Vb. *tend*, trend, verge, lean, incline; set, set towards, *approach*; affect, dispose, carry, bias, bend to, warp, turn, *influence*; point to, lead to; bid fair to, *be likely*; contribute to, *promote*.

175 Liability

N. *liability*, weakness, *tendency*; exposure; sensibility; potentiality, *possibility*; likelihood, *probability*; obligation, responsibility, *duty*.

Adj. *liable*, apt to; subject to, prey to, *subject*; open to, *vulnerable*; contingent; incident to, incidental; possible, *possible*; susceptible; answerable, responsible, amenable, accountable.

Vb. *be liable*, be responsible, *incur a duty*; incur, lay oneself open to; stand to gain, stand to lose; *be subject*; open a door to.

176 Concurrence: combination of causes

N. *concurrence*, joint effort; coincidence, *conformity*; concord, harmony, *agreement*; compliance, *consent*; concurrent opinion, consensus, *assent*; *submission*; concert, conspiracy, *plot*; league, alliance, *association*; conjunction, union.

Adj. *concurrent*; coincident, parallel; *corporate*; of one mind, at one with; joint; involved.

Vb. *concur*, acquiesce, *assent*; collude, connive, conspire, *plot*; agree, *accord*; hang together; contribute, help, aid, abet, serve, *minister to*; promote; go with, keep abreast of, run parallel to, *accompany*; unite, stand together, *cohere*.

Adv. *concurrently*, with one consent, with one accord.

177 Counteraction

N. *counteraction*; polarity; antagonism, antipathy, clash, conflict, *collision*; return action, reaction, repercussion; backfire, backlash, *recoil*; *resistance*, opposition; inertia, friction, drag, check, *hindrance*; interference, repression, *restraint*; *moderation*; cancellation, *destruction*; crosscurrent, headwind, *obstacle*; neutralizer, *antidote*; offset; *tactics*; deterrent, *defence*; preventive, *prohibition*.

Adj. *counteracting*, counter; *contrary*; hostile, *inimical*; recalcitrant; reactionary, reactive; preventive, contraceptive; *remedial*.

Vb. *counteract*, counter, cross, traverse, work against, *hinder*, react, *recoil*; agitate against, persecute, *be inimical*; resist, withstand, defend oneself, *oppose*; antagonize, conflict with, *be contrary*; clash, *collide*; interfere, *meddle*; repress, *suppress*; undo, cancel, *abrogate*; find a remedy, cure, *remedy*; recover, *retrieve*; obviate, prevent, inhibit, *prohibit*.

Adv. *although*, despite, notwithstanding; against, contrary to.

178 Space: indefinite space

N. *space*, expanse; extension, extent, surface, area; volume, cubic content; continuum, stretch, *continuity*; *time*; empty space; depth of space, abyss, *depth*; infinity; sky, outer space; world; terrain, open space, open country; lung, green belt, *plain*; prairie, steppe, *grassland*; outback, hinterland, *region*; wild, wilderness, waste, *desert*; everywhere, *presence*.

measure, proportions, dimension, *length*, *breadth*, *height*, *depth*; area, square measure, acreage; square inch, square yard, square metre, hectare, hide; volume, cubic content, *size*.

range, reach, carry, compass; coverage; stretch, grasp, span; radius, latitude, amplitude; sweep, spread, ramification; play, swing, *scope*; sphere, field, arena; *region*; prospect, *view*; perspective, *dis-*

tance; telescopic range; *optics*.

room, space, accommodation; capacity, stowage, storage space, *storage*; seating capacity, seating; standing room; margin, clearance; room to spare, elbowroom, room to swing a cat; room overhead, headroom, headway; sea room, seaway, leeway; opening, way, *open space*; living space.

Adj. spatial, space; cubic, three-dimensional; flat, superficial.

spacious, *extensive*; expansive, roomy, commodious; ample, vast, cavernous, capacious, broad, deep, wide; voluminous, baggy, *large*; *general*; far-flung, widespread, worldwide, global, world, *whole*; boundless, *infinite*, trackless.

Vb. extend, spread, range, cover; span, straddle, bestride; extend to, reach to, be *contiguous*; branch, ramify.

Adv. widely, everywhere, wherever; *throughout*; at every turn, here, there and everywhere.

179 Region: definite space

N. region, locality, *place*; sphere, orb, hemisphere; zone, belt; latitude, parallel, meridian; climate; tract, terrain, country, ground, soil, *land*; island, peninsula, continent; sea, *ocean*; Old World; Third World; compass, circumference, circle, circuit, *outline*; bounds, shore, confines, *limit*; pale, precincts, close, enclave, salient; corridor; *access*; area, field, theatre, *arena*; exclusive area.

territory, sphere, zone; beat, pitch, ground; lot, holding, claim; grounds, park, *estate*; domain, territorial waters; airspace, defensible space; possession, dependency, protectorate, dominion; colony, settlement; homeland, *home*; commonwealth, republic, kingdom, realm, state, empire.

district, purlieus, haunt, *locality*; quarter, division; state, province, county, shire, riding, lathe, hundred, rape; diocese, bishopric; parish, ward, constituency; borough, township, municipality; county, district; department, commune; hamlet, village, town, *abode*; *housing*; garden city, new town; suburb, suburbia, subtopia, dormitory suburb, stockbroker belt; green belt, *space*; golden circle; provinces, back of beyond; Wild West; outback, backwoods, bush, brush; countryside, *land*; hinterland.

city, metropolis, conurbation; West End, East End, City, Wall Street.

Adj. regional, territorial, insular; national, state; local, municipal, parochial, redbrick, *provincial*; suburban, urban, rural, up-country; district, town, country.

180 Place: limited space

N. place, site, location, position, *situation*; station, substation; quarter, locality, *district*; pitch, beat, billet, socket, groove; centre, meeting place, *focus*; dwelling place, fireside, *home*; place of residence, address, habitat, *locality*, *quarters*; premises, building, mansion, *house*; spot, dot; point, dot, pinpoint; niche, nook, corner, hole, pigeonhole, pocket, *compartment*; confines, bounds, baseline, crease (cricket); *limit*; prison, coffin, grave; precinct, bailey, paddock, compound, pen; close, quad, square; yard, area, courtyard, court, *open space*; farmyard, field, *farm*; stock farm.

Adv. somewhere, some place, wherever may be; locally, *near*.

181 Situation

N. situation, position, setting; scene; location, address, whereabouts; point, stage, milestone, *degree*; site, seat, base, *place*; habitat, range, *region*; post, station, standpoint, standing, ground, footing, *state*; side, aspect, attitude, posture, frontage; geography, topography; chart, *map*.

bearings, compass direction, declination; right ascension, *direction*; location.

Adj. situated, living at, to be found at, settled, set; local, topical.

Vb. be situated; be found at; be, lie, stand; live, live at, *dwell*; touch, be near.

Adv. in place, here, there; hereabouts, thereabouts; whereabouts.

182 Location

N. location, placement, disposition; radar; population; settlement, establishment; fixation, installation; deposition, *arrangement*; stowage, *storage*.

locality, quarters, purlieus, environs; environment, surroundings, milieu; neighbourhood, *district*; vicinity, *near place*; address, street, place of residence; habitat, abode; seat, site, *place*; meeting place, venue, haunt, *focus*; genius loci, spirit of place.

station, seat, site, position, *situation*; depot, base, colony, settlement; anchorage, *shelter*; lines, camp, temporary abode; hostel, *abode*; halting place, lay-by.

Adj. located, *situated*; rooted, settled, *fixed*; at anchor, *quiescent*; possessed.

Vb. place, assign a place, *arrange*; position, site, locate; base, centre; pinpoint; place right, aim well, hit, *aim*; put, lay, set, seat; station, post, park; install, ensconce, establish, fix; root, plant, implant, embed, graft, *insert*; bed, put to bed, cradle; accommodate, lodge, house, quarter, billet; impose; moor, tether, picket, anchor, *tie*; dock, berth, *bring to rest*; deposit, stand, erect, *elevate*; place with, transfer, bestow, invest, *assign*; array, deploy.

replace, put back, sheathe, bring back, reinstate, *restore*; repatriate, resettle, *transpose*.

stow; pocket, pouch, pack, bale, store; freight, load; *fill*.

place oneself, stand, anchor, *come to rest*, settle, strike root, gain a footing, *stay*; perch, alight, sit, squat, park; encamp, camp; stop at, lodge; hive, burrow, ensconce oneself, locate oneself, find a home; settle, populate, people, *dwell*; become a citizen.

183 Displacement

N. displacement; wrong place; shift, move, *motion*; red shift; aberration, *deviation*; transfer; mutual transfer, *interchange*; relief, replacement; removal, *extraction*; expulsion; exile; refugee, *wanderer*; misfit; docker, stevedore, removal man.

Adj. displaced, aberrant; unplaced; rootless, unsettled, roofless.

misplaced, *abnormal*; inappropriate, *irrelevant*; lost, missing, *absent*.

Vb. displace, disturb, disorientate, derail, dislocate; dislodge, unseat, *disunite*; expel, scatter, send flying, *disperse*; shift, remove, *move*; transport, *transfer*; change round; transpose, *interchange*; post, *send*; relegate, banish, exile, *dismiss*; set aside, supersede, *substitute*, *depose*; evict, *eject*; eradicate, uproot, *destroy*; discharge, unload, off-load; rake, sweep, *clean*; lift, raise, uplift, *elevate*; draw, *extract*.

isplace, mislay, lose, lose touch with, lose track of.

84 Presence

, *presence*, being there, existence; whereabouts, *situation*; being somewhere; being everywhere; physical presence, attendance, residence, occupation, sit-in, *possession*; visit, descent, stay; present moment, *present time*; spectator, bystander.

dj. *on the spot*, present, existent; resident; attendant, still there; ready, available, *prepared*; at home, at hand, within reach; *obvious*.

biquitous, omnipresent, pervasive, *universal*.

b. *be present*, exist, be, occupy, inhabit, *dwell*; hold, *possess*; stand, lie, *be situated*; witness, *watch*; resort to, frequent, haunt, meet one at every turn; occur, *happen*; stay, sojourn, summer, winter, *visit*; attend, assist at; take part, make one at, make one of; present oneself, *arrive*; face, confront, *defy*.

ervade, permeate, fill, *make complete*; impregnate, soak, run through; overrun, spread, meet one at every turn, *infiltrate*; *influence*.

dv. *here*, there, where, everywhere; aboard, at home; on the spot; before; personally.

85 Absence

l. *absence*; lack, *scarcity*; deprivation, *loss*; being nowhere, Utopia, *fantasy*; being elsewhere, alibi; leave of absence, furlough; absenteeism, French leave; absentee, truant; absentee landlord; postal voter.

mptiness, empty space, void, vacancy; blank, *gap*; nothing inside, shell; vacuum, air pocket; blank cartridge, blank paper, clean sheet; virgin territory; waste, *desert*; vacant lot, bomb site, *room*.

obody, nobody present.

dj. *absent*; gone, flown; lacking, wanting, missing; absent without leave; truant, absentee; lost, nowhere to be found.

mpty, vacant, vacuous, inane; void, devoid, bare, blank, clean; characterless, featureless; without content, hollow; vacant; desert; unsettled; godforsaken, lonely; bleak, desolate; uninhabitable.

Vb. *be absent*; absent oneself, cut, skip, take French leave, *avoid*; leave a gap; leave empty, evacuate, vacate; exhaust, *empty*.

o go, withdraw, leave, *depart*; make oneself scarce, retreat, *decamp*, *escape*; vanish, *disappear*; make room, vacate.

Adv. *without*, minus, sans.

not here; neither here nor there; elsewhere, somewhere else; nowhere.

186 Inhabitant

N. *dweller*, inhabitant, denizen; transient, visitant; migrant, expatriate, *foreigner*; insular, islander; water gipsy; highlander; commuter; provincial; peasant, *farmer*; bedouin; troglodyte; *poor person*. See *native*.

resident, householder; housewife, housekeeper; crofter; addressee, occupier, incumbent, possessor, *substitute*; tenant, lessee; inmate, in-patient; house surgeon, *doctor*; garrison, crew, *personnel*; lodger, boarder, guest, visitor; cuckoo, squatter; parasite, *bane*.

native, aboriginal, *precursor*; people, tribe, *nation*; local, local inhabitant; parishioner, city person, city slicker; cockney; yokel, rustic; fellow countryman or -woman, fellow citizen; national, patrial, citizen, burgess, voter; Briton; North Briton; Paddy; Northerner, Southerner; New Yorker, Parisian, *foreigner*; terrestrial; Martian.

settler, pioneer, *precursor*; colonist, colonial, creole; planter, *farmer*; resident alien, *foreigner*.

inhabitants, population, townspeople, country folk; populace, people, people at large, citizenry, yeomanry; suburbia, *housing*; household, *family*; settlement, stronghold; colony, commune, community.

Adj. *native*, vernacular, popular, national, ethnic; indigenous, aboriginal; earthbound, terrestrial; home, home-made; domestic, domiciliary; settled; resident.

occupied; manned.

187 Abode: place of habitation or resort

N. *abode*, habitat, haunt, station, *situation*; place of residence, *locality*; habitation, street, house, home, address, house number, number; domicile, residence; town, city, *district*; headquarters, base, seat, *focus*; temporary abode, camp, pad; weekend cottage, country seat, holiday home, seaside resort, hill station, *pleasure ground*; spa, sanatorium, *hospital*; lines, *station*; camp, caravan park.

quarters, accommodation, lodging, billet, berth, squat; barrack; rooms, chambers, digs; residential hotel, guest house, pension; boarding school, hostel, dormitory; hall of residence; convent, *monastery*.

dwelling, *roof*; prehistoric dwelling; tower, keep; cave, hut, kraal, igloo; wigwam, tepee, tent, *canopy*; lair, den, hole, form, burrow, warren, earth, *shelter*.

nest; branch, *tree*; perch, roost; covert, rookery, hatchery, aviary, apiary; anthill.

home, hearth, fireside, chimney corner, inglenook, roof; homestead, household; cradle, 'house where I was born', *origin*; native land, homeland, God's own country; native soil, native sod, native ground, native heath, home ground, home town; haunt, familiar territory, second home; household gods.

house, building, *edifice*; house of God, *temple*; home, residence, dwelling, dwelling house; country house, villa, detached house; prefab; ranch house, chalet, bungalow, seat, place, mansion, hall, stately home; palace, dome, castle, keep, tower, peel; manor house, manor, grange, lodge, priory, abbey; vicarage, *parsonage*; farmhouse, croft, hacienda, *farm*; official residence, Mansion House, White House, embassy, consulate.

small *house*, chalet, lodge, cottage, cot; cabin, hut, shanty; hovel, dump, hole, slum dwelling; box; shed, shack, lean-to, outhouse, outbuilding; shelter, tent, *canopy*; kiosk, booth, stall; houseboat, *boat*; mobile home, caravan, trailer, *vehicle*. See *flat*.

housing, *building material*; urban sprawl; asphalt jungle, urban blight; conurbation; town, burgh, suburb, *city*; housing estate, residential area, *district*; suburbia, subtopia; crescent, close, terrace, circus, square, avenue, street, *road*; block, court, row; inner city, ghetto, slum; shanty town; hamlet, village; scattered settlement.

flat, flatlet, penthouse; apartment, suite, chambers; bed-sitter, *chamber*; apartment block, mews.

stable, byre, cowshed; kennel, doghouse; sty, fold; dovecote, pigeon loft; stall, cage, coop, hutch, battery; stabling, mews, garage, carport, hangar; boathouse; marina, dock, basin, wharf, port, *shelter*; berth, quay, jetty, pier.

inn, hotel, hostelry, roadhouse, motel, bed and breakfast; doss-house, kip; hospice, night shelter; youth hostel; caravanserai, khan; rest house.

tavern, boozer; public house, pub, local; free house, gin palace, saloon; speakeasy, dive, joint; wine cellar, wine bar; beer cellar, beer hall, beer garden; bar.

café, restaurant, cafeteria; bistro, grill room, rotisserie; coffee bar, soda fountain; lunch counter, snack bar, sandwich bar; teahouse, tearoom; refreshment room, buffet, canteen, Naafi; take-away; coffee stall, pull-in.

meeting place, church; day centre, village hall; assembly rooms, club, night club, holiday camp, *place of amusement*; football ground, racecourse, dog track, *arena*; theatre, concert hall, stadium, stand; sports centre, gymnasium, drill hall, parade ground; quad, campus, village green; *focus; market*.

pleasance, park, grounds, green; walk, mall, avenue, parade, promenade, boulevard; national park, chase, *pleasure ground*.

pavilion, kiosk, bandstand, rotunda, folly, bower, grotto, *arbour*; arcade; tent, marquee, *canopy*.

retreat, sanctuary, refuge, asylum, ark, *shelter*; cubbyhole, den, sanctum, study, *chamber*; cell, hermitage; cloister, *monastery*; almshouse; workhouse, poorhouse; orphanage, home, hospice, halfway house, sheltered housing.

Adj. *residing*, abiding, dwelling, living; at home; residential.

urban, cosmopolitan, suburban.

provincial, parochial, local, domestic, vernacular; up-country, countrified, rural, rustic.

architectural; Gothic; classical, *olden*; brick, concrete, cob, half-timbered; modest, substantial, palatial, grand; detached; multistorey, high-rise.

Vb. *dwell*, inhabit, populate, people, *be present*; settle, *appropriate*; frequent, haunt, *visit*; reside, remain, abide, sojourn, live, *be situated*; take rooms, stay, keep, lodge, lie, sleep at; have an address; tenant, occupy, squat, *possess*; nestle, perch, roost, nest, hive, burrow, stable; camp, encamp, *place oneself*; tent, shelter, *seek refuge*; berth, dock, anchor, *come to rest*.

urbanize, develop.

188 Contents: things contained

N. *contents*, component; inventory, list; furnishings, equipment, *provision*; load, payload, cargo, freight, shipment; inside; stuffing, filling, wadding, lining; handful; *small quantity*, *great quantity*.

Vb. *load*, freight, charge, burden, stow; ship; weigh; pack, *insert*; pack tight; cram, stuff, *fill*; pad, wad, line; hide, conceal, *cover*.

189 Receptacle

N. *receptacle*, container, holder; frame, prop; hutch, cage, *prison*; folder, wrapper, envelope, cover, file; net, network; sheath, chrysalis, cocoon; *wrapping*; capsule, ampoule; pod, calyx, boll; mould, *form*; socket, mortise, *cavity*; groove, slot, furrow; hole, cave, cavity, *opening*; bosom, lap, *fold*; pin cushion; trap; well, reservoir, hold, repository, *store*; drain, cesspit, sump, *sink*; crockery, glassware, *pottery*.

bladder, airbladder; inner tube; football; balloon; sac, cyst, vesicle, blister, bubble, *swelling*; udder, teat, *bosom*.

maw, stomach, tummy; abdomen, belly, pot belly, paunch, *swelling*; gizzard, gullet, crop, jaws, mouth, *orifice*.

compartment, cell, follicle, ventricle; tray, cage, iron lung; cubicle, booth, stall; sentry box; box, *theatre; pew, church interior*; niche, nook, cranny, recess, bay; pigeonhole, cubbyhole; drawer, locker; shelving, rack, *shelf*; storey, floor, deck, *layer*.

cabinet, closet, commode, wardrobe, press; chest of drawers, tallboy; cupboard, unit; whatnot, dresser, china cabinet; buffet, sideboard, *stand*; freezer, *refrigerator*; cocktail cabinet, dumbwaiter; bureau, desk, console; bookcase.

basket; hamper, picnic basket; pannier; trug, punnet, rush basket, frail; crib, cradle, bassinet; laundry basket; workbasket; wickerwork; framework, crate; *frame; fortification*.

box, chest, ark; coffer, locker; case, canteen; safe, till, *treasury*; coffin, sarcophagus, *tomb*; tea chest; attaché case; suitcase, trunk, portmanteau; sea chest; hat box; ammunition chest, canister, caisson; *ammunition*; luggage, baggage; boot, luggage van.

small box; cardboard box, carton, packet; plastic box, airtight container; metal box, can, tin, canister; casket, *ritual object*; salt cellar, pepper mill; castor.

bag, sack, poke; handbag, vanity case, reticule, clutch bag; cornet, twist; survival bag; holdall, grip; haversack, rucksack; ditty bag, pouch, sling; pannier, saddlebag, nosebag; school bag, satchel, bundle; swag.

case, housewife; wallet, pocket book; spectacle case, compact; briefcase, portfolio; file, scabbard, sheath; pistol case, holster; arrow case, quiver, *store*.

pocket, fob, pouch; purse, sporran.

vat, butt, cask, barrel, tun, tub, keg; breaker; drum, *cylinder*; wine cask, pipe, hogshead, firkin; hopper, cistern, tank, *store*.

vessel, vase, urn, jar, amphora, crock, pot, pitcher, ewer, jug; *plant*; carafe, bottle; leather bottle; wine bottle, demijohn, magnum, jeroboam; flask, flagon, phial; crucible, retort, pipette, test tube; chamber pot, bedpan, *latrine*; pail, bucket;

churn, can, flowerpot; bin, dustbin, *sink*;
scuttle, hod; skip; bath, tub.

cauldron, *heater*; boiler, copper, kettle, skil-
let, pan, saucepan, steamer; girdle; casserole, Dutch oven; mess tin; tea urn,
teapot, samovar, coffeepot, percolator;
vacuum flask.

cup, eggcup, coffee cup, teacup, breakfast
cup; tea service, tea set; chalice, goblet,
beaker; horn, tankard, can, mug, stein,
noggin, schooner; tumbler, glass, wineg-
lass, brandy balloon, pony.

bowl, basin, pudding basin, punch bowl;
porringer; manger, trough; colander,
vegetable dish, tureen, gravy boat; rose
bowl, vase.

plate, salver, tray; platter, charger, dish;
palette; saucer; pan, scale; pallet; mortarboard, hod.

ladle, dipper, scoop; spoon, tablespoon,
dessertspoon, teaspoon; spade, trowel,
spatula, slice, shovel.

chamber, room, apartment, *flat*; cockpit,
cubicle, cab; cabin, stateroom; audience
chamber, throne room; cabinet, closet,
study, den, sanctum, *retreat*; library, studio, office, *workshop*; nursery; reception
room, drawing room, lounge, parlour,
salon, boudoir; bedroom, dormitory;
dressing room; bathroom, washroom;
mess, hall, refectory, canteen; smoking
room, bar, snug, *tavern*; galley, kitchen;
scullery, pantry, larder; dairy, laundry,
utility room, offices, outhouse; garage,
stable; storeroom, box room, glory hole,
storage; cloakroom, lavatory, *latrine*. See
compartment.

lobby, vestibule, foyer; corridor, passage,
hall; gallery, patio, balcony, portico,
porch, *doorway*; extension, lean-to.

cellar, vault, crypt, basement, *base*; coalhole, bunker, *storage*; hold, dungeon,
prison.

attic, loft; penthouse, garret, *summit*.

arbour, alcove, bower, grotto, summer-
house, gazebo, folly, pergola, *pavilion*;
sun lounge, conservatory, greenhouse,
glasshouse, *garden*.

Adj. recipient, capacious, voluminous,
spacious; hiding; baggy.

cellular, honeycombed, *concave*; marsupial;
ventral, *convex*.

capsular; vascular.

190 Size

N. size, magnitude, proportions, dimensions, *measure*; extent, expanse, area,
space; extension, *length*, *height*, *depth*;
width, amplitude, *breadth*; volume; girth,
circumference, *outline*; bulk, mass,
weight, *gravity*; capacity, intake, ton-
nage; measured size, calibre, *measurement*; real size, true dimensions; maximum; full size, life size; large size,
magnum; *chief part*; excessive size.

hugeness, enormity; towering proportions,
monstrosity; *height*.

bulk, mass, weight, avoirdupois, *gravity*;
lump, block, clod, boulder, *solid body*;
hunk, chunk, *piece*; mound, heap, *great
quantity*; mountain, pyramid, *high structure*; double chin, rotund figure, spare
tyre, *swelling*; muscle man, *athlete*; fat
person, tub, dumpling, mound of flesh,
tub of lard, hulk.

giant, colossus, *tall creature*; mountain of a
man or woman, young giant; ogre, monster; leviathan; whale, hippopotamus,
elephant, jumbo; mammoth, dinosaur;
Titan, Cyclops.

whopper, whacker, humdinger; a mountain
of a ◼ ▪ ◼ .

Adj. large, of size, big, *great*; large size,
jumbo; pretty large, considerable; bulky,
massive, *weighty*; ample, capacious,
voluminous, baggy; comprehensive,
broad; vast, extensive, *spacious*; monumental, towering, mountainous, *tall*;
fine, magnificent, thumping, thundering,
whacking, *whopping*; elephantine; megalithic; lusty, healthy, *strong*; so big, of
that order.

huge, immense, enormous, vast, mighty,
grandiose, stupendous, monstrous, *prodigious*; record size; colossal, mammoth,
gigantic, giant, mountainous; Herculean,
gargantuan; megalithic; outsize, *exorbitant*; limitless, *infinite*.

fleshy, meaty, fat, stout, obese, overweight;
plump, ample, chubby, podgy, *thick*;
squat, square, dumpy, chunky, stocky,
broad; tubby, portly, corpulent, pot-
bellied, *convex*; puffy, bloated, bosomy;
round, rotund, roly-poly, full, buxom,
jolly; strapping, lusty, burly, beefy,
brawny, *stalwart*.

unwieldy, cumbersome, hulking, gangling;
lumpy; too big, elephantine, overweight;
awkward, muscle-bound, *clumsy*.

Vb. *be large*, become large, expand; have
size, loom large, bulk, fill space, *extend*;
tower, soar, *be high*.

191 Littleness

N. littleness, small size, miniature quality;
lack of height.

minuteness, point, pinpoint, pinhead; crystal; atom, molecule, particle, electron,
neutron, proton, quark; nucleus, cell;
corpuscle; drop, droplet, dust, grain;
seed, *small thing*; bubble, button, molehill, *trifle*.

miniature, *picture*, microfilm, *photography*;
pocket edition, *edition*; epitome, *compendium*; model, microcosm; bubble car,
automobile.

dwarf, midget, pigmy; little people, elf; chit,
slip; mite, tot, tiddler, *child*; bantam,
small animal; pipsqueak, squirt, *nonentity*; doll, puppet; shrimp, runt, miserable
specimen.

microorganism, protozoan, plankton,
amoeba; bacteria, microbe, germ, virus;
algae, *plant*.

microscopy; microscope, micrometer.

microelectronics, *electronics*; chip, microprocessor.

Adj. little, *small*; petite, dainty, dolly; diminutive, pigmy; wee, tiny; toy, baby,
pocket, mini-; miniature, model; portable, handy, compact; snug, cosy, poky,
cramped, *narrow*; puny, *weak*; petty,
inconsiderable; one-horse.

dwarfish, *dwarf*, pigmy, undersized,
wizened; squat, dumpy, *short*.

exiguous, minimal, slight, scant, scanty,
small; thin, skinny, scraggy, *lean*; rudimentary, *beginning*; bitty, *fragmentary*.

minute, microscopic, infinitesimal; atomic;
powdery; imperceptible, intangible,
impalpable; *invisible*.

Vb. *be little*, contract, *become small*;
dwindle, *decrease*; require little space.

Adv. *in small compass*, in a nutshell; on a
small scale.

192 Expansion

N. *expansion*, increase of size, crescendo;
enlargement, *increase*; reinforcement,

addition; hyperbole, *exaggeration*; extension, spread; ribbon development, urban sprawl, *housing*; increment, accretion, *adjunct*; development, *growth*.

dilation; inflation, reflation, puff; dropsy, tumour, *swelling*.

Adj. *expanded*; widespread; expansive, *spacious*; flared, *broad*; wide open, *open*; tumescent, budding, flowering; full-blown; overblown, overgrown; obese, puffy, pot-bellied, bloated, fat; swollen, turgid; tight; varicose, *convex*.

Vb. *expand*, wax, increase, snowball, *grow*, widen, broaden, flare, splay, *be broad*; spread, extend, sprawl; deploy, take open order; spread like wildfire, overrun, mantle, straddle, *cover*; rise, gather, swell, distend, dilate; mushroom, balloon, belly, *be convex*; get fat, gain flesh; bud, burgeon, shoot, sprout, open, put forth, blossom, flower, blow, bloom, *be fruitful*.

enlarge; expand; leaven, *elevate*; bore, ream; widen, broaden; open; stretch, extend, *lengthen*; intensify, heighten, deepen; amplify, supplement, reinforce, *add*; double, redouble; develop, *augment*; distend, inflate, reflate, puff, *blow*; bulk, thicken; stuff, pad, *line*; cram, *fill*; fatten, *feed*; enlarge, *photograph*; magnify, exaggerate.

193 Contraction

N. *contraction*, reduction, deflation; decrease, shrinkage, diminuendo; abbreviation, *shortening*; *condensation*; *closure*; labour pains, *obstetrics*; consumption, atrophy; decline, retreat, recession, slump; neck, isthmus, bottleneck, hourglass; epitome, *compendium*.

compression, pressure, squeeze, strangulation.

compressor, mangle, roller; astringent; bandage, binder, tourniquet, *surgical dressing*; belt, band, garter, *girdle*; whalebone, stays, corset, *underwear*; straitjacket, iron boot, thumbscrew, *instrument of torture*; bear, python.

Adj. *contracted*, *small*; dense; compact; drawn tight, *narrow, closed*; contractile; wizened; *consumptive*.

compressive, astringent, binding.

Vb. *become small*, grow less, lessen, dwindle, wane, ebb, *decrease*; shrivel, wither, *decompose*; lose weight, lose flesh, *be light*; contract, shrink, narrow, taper, *be narrow*; condense, *be dense*; evaporate; draw together, *close*; pucker, purse, corrugate, wrinkle, *fold*.

make *smaller*, lessen, reduce, *abate*; contract, shrink, abridge, dwarf, stunt, *shorten*; diet, slim, *lighten*; taper, narrow, attenuate, thin, emaciate, *make thin*; puncture, deflate, rarefy, exhaust, drain, *empty*; evaporate; dehydrate, *dry*; cramp, constrict, pinch, nip, squeeze, bind, bandage, corset; draw tight, strain, *tighten*; draw together, clench, *close, join*; hug, crush, strangle; compress, compact, constipate, condense, *be dense*; huddle, crowd together; pack tight, cram, jam, *fill*; squash, *flatten*; cramp, restrict, *restrain*; limit, *circumscribe*; shave, shear, clip, trim, prune, pollard, *cut*; scrape, file, grind; crumple, *fold*; roll, press, flatten, *smooth*.

194 Distance

N. *distance*, light years, depths of space, *space*; measured distance, mileage, footage, *length*; elongation, aphelion, apogee; far distance, horizon, skyline, offing; background, *rear*; periphery, circumference, *outline*; drift, *deviation*; reach, grasp, compass, span, stride, *range*; far cry, long way, tidy step, long long trail, marathon.

farness, far distance; removal, *separation*; antipodes, pole; back of beyond; Far West, Far East; outpost; purlieus, outskirts; outer edge, frontier, *limit*; *absence*.

Adj. *distant*, distal, peripheral, terminal; far, farther; ulterior; ultimate, farthest, furthest, furthermost; long-range; yonder; outlying, peripheral; remote, aloof, far-flung, godforsaken; telescopic; lost to sight, lost to view, *invisible*; wide.

removed, inaccessible; beyond; overseas, transatlantic.

Vb. *be distant*, stretch to, reach to, extend to, spread to, go to, get to, carry to, *extend*; carry, range; outdistance, outdo; keep clear of, stand aloof, stand clear of, keep a safe distance, give a wide berth, *avoid*.

Adv. *afar*, far, far afield, way behind; yonder; at a distance; asunder, apart, abroad, afield; at arm's length.

beyond, further, farther; ahead; clear of, wide of.

too *far*, out of reach, out of range, out of bounds.

195 Nearness

N. *nearness*, proximity, propinquity, near distance, foreground, *front*; vicinity, neighbourhood, *surroundings*; brink, verge, *edge*; collision course; approximation, *approach*; location.

short distance, beeline, short cut; step, striking distance, close quarters; close range, earshot, gunshot; short span, inch, millimetre, *gap*; close-up, near approach; perigee, perihelion; close finish, near thing, *contest*.

near *place*, vicinity, neighbourhood, environs, suburbs, outskirts, *locality*; next door; second place, *sequence*.

Adj. *near*, proximate, proximal; very near, approximate; warm; about to meet; nearby, wayside, roadside, *accessible*; inshore; near at hand, at hand, handy, present; *shallow*; home, local; close to, next to, neighbouring, adjacent, *contiguous*; facing, *frontal*; close, intimate, inseparable; at close quarters; with nothing between; level; related, *akin*.

Vb. *be near*, be around, be about, *be present*; hang around, hang about, approximate; draw near, get warm, *approach*; meet, *converge*; neighbour, stand next to, adjoin, border, *be contiguous*; encroach; come close, skirt, graze, shave, brush, skim, hedge-hop; jostle, buzz, *obstruct*; follow close, shadow; come to heel, *follow*; clasp, cling to, hug, cuddle, *caress*; huddle, crowd, *congregate*.

bring *near*, approach, approximate; *juxtapose*.

Adv. *near*, locally, nigh, close to, at close range, at close quarters; close behind, within call, within hearing, within earshot, only a step; within reach, close at hand; face to face, eyeball to eyeball; next door, beside, alongside.

nearly, practically, almost, all but; more or less, near enough, roughly, around, somewhere around; about; hereabouts, thereabouts, circa; well-nigh; within an ace of, just about to.

196 Interval

N. *interval*, distance between, space; narrow interval, *short distance*; daylight, head, length; clearance, margin, freeboard, *room*; interval of time, *interim*; pause, break, truce, *lull*; hiatus; jump, leap; musical interval, tone, semitone, third, fourth, fifth, *musical note*.

gap, interstice, mesh, *network*; cavity, hole, *orifice*; pass, defile, *passage*; firebreak, *safeguard*; ditch, trench, *drain*; water jump, ha-ha, sunk fence, *partition*; ravine, gorge, chimney, crevasse, canyon, *valley*; cleft, crevice, chink, crack, rift, cut, gash, tear, rent, slit; flaw, fault, breach, break, split, fracture, rupture, fissure, chap, *separation*; slot, groove, *furrow*; indentation, *notch*; seam, join, *joint*; leak, *outlet*; abyss, chasm, *depth*; void; inlet, creek, *gulf*.

Adj. *spaced*, with an interval; split, cloven, cleft, cracked; *open*; far between.

Vb. *space*, interval, *set apart*; crack, split, start, gape, *open*; clear, show daylight between; lattice, mesh.

Adv. *at intervals*, now and again, every so often, off and on; with an interval.

197 Contiguity

N. *contiguity*, apposition, proximity; *touch*; continuity; contact; intercommunication; osculation; meeting, encounter; *union*; close contact, adhesion, cohesion, *coherence*; coincidence, *accompaniment*; tangent; border, fringe, *edge*; borderland, frontier, *limit*; buffer state.

Adj. *contiguous*; intercommunicating; tangential, end to end; adjacent, *continuous*; close, to, *near*.

Vb. *be contiguous*, overlap, *touch*; make contact, brush, rub, skim, scrape, graze, kiss; join, meet, *converge*; stick, adhere, *cohere*; lie end to end; adjoin, reach to, extend to, *extend*; sit next to, crowd, jostle, *be near*; border with, skirt, *hem*; coexist, coincide, *accompany*; intercommunicate, *connect*; contact.

juxtapose, range together.

Adv. *contiguously*; next, close; end to end.

198 Length

N. *length*, longitude; extent, extension; reach, long arm; full length, stretch, span, mileage, footage, *distance*; perspective, *depth*.

lengthening, extension, production; tension.

line, bar, rule, tape, strip, stripe, streak; spoke, radius; single file, line ahead, crocodile, queue, *sequence*; straight line; bent line, *curvature*.

long *measure*, measurement of length, *measurement*; unit of length, finger, hand, palm, span, cubit; arm's length, fathom; head, length; pace, step; inch, foot, yard; rod, pole, perch; chain, furlong; mile, knot, league; millimetre, centimetre, metre, kilometre; degree of latitude, degree of longitude; micron, wavelength; astronomical unit, light year, parsec.

Adj. *long*, lengthy, extensive, a mile long;

lank, *lean*; lanky, *tall*; interminable, *tedious*; *diffuse*; unabridged, full-length, *complete*.

longitudinal, oblong, linear.

Vb. *be long*, stretch; make a long arm; reach, stretch to, *extend*; drag, trail, drag its slow length along.

lengthen, stretch, elongate, *make thin*; spreadeagle, *expand*; sprawl, *be horizontal*; deploy, *disperse*; extend, unroll, unfold, *evolve*; produce, continue; prolong, protract; drawl, stammer.

look *along*; have a clear view, scan.

Adv. *lengthwise*; along; at full length, end to end, overall; head to foot, head to tail, stem to stern, top to toe.

199 Shortness

N. *shortness*, brevity; *brief span*; inch, centimetre, *short distance*; low stature; shrinkage; short hair, bob, crew cut; shorts.

shortening, abbreviation; *compendium*; cutback, cut, reduction; contraction.

shortener, cutter.

Adj. *short*, brief, *transient*; *little*; squat, dumpy, stumpy, stocky, thickset, stubby, *thick*; *low*; snub, blunt; scanty, *insufficient*; cut, topless, headless; shorn; sparing of words, terse, *concise*; potted, compact, *compendious*.

Vb. *be short*, fall short.

shorten, abridge, abbreviate; pot, *abstract*; recapitulate, *be concise*; compress, contract, telescope; reduce, diminish, *abate*; foreshorten, *distort*; kilt; behead, guillotine, axe, *sunder*; cut short, dock, curtail, truncate; cut back, slash, lop, prune; shear, shave, trim, crop, clip, bob, shingle, *cut*; mow, scythe; stunt, *retard*; scrimp, skimp, *make insufficient*.

Adv. *shortly*.

200 Breadth. Thickness

N. *breadth*, width, latitude; width across, span, wingspan; diameter, radius; gauge, bore, calibre; expanse, superficial extent, amplitude, *range*.

thickness, bulk.

Adj. *broad*, wide, expansive, *spacious*; full, flared, ample, baggy; wide-awake (hat); wide-angle (lens), *open*; stalwart; *general*.

thick, stout, dumpy, squat, *short*; thickset, tubby, stubby; thick-skinned, *strong*; *dense*; lumpy, to be cut with a knife.

Vb. *be broad*, get broad, broaden, widen, fatten, thicken; flare, splay, *expand*; straddle, bestride, span.

Adv. *broadways*; sideways.

201 Narrowness. Thinness

N. *narrowness*, narrow interval, tight squeeze, crack, chink, *short distance*; lack of breadth, line, strip, stripe, streak; vein, capillary, *filament*; knife-edge, tightrope, wire; narrow gauge; bottleneck, strait, *gulf*; ridge, col, saddle, *high land*; ravine, *valley*; pass, defile, *passage*; neck, isthmus, *bridge*.

thinness, *rarity*; consumption; scrag, skeleton; miserable specimen, scarecrow, rake, broomstick, shadow; lantern jaws, hatchet face; thread, paper, tissue, *transparency*; shaving, splinter, *small thing*; slip, wisp, *filament*.

narrowing, *contraction*; taper; neck, isthmus; stricture; waistline, waist, hourglass.

Adj. narrow, single track; strait, tight, close; fine, thin, transparent; spun, long; capillary, fibrous; slight, delicate, weak; attenuate, slender, slim, svelte; willowy; lanky, gangling.

lean, thin, spare, wiry; meagre, skinny; bony; cadaverous, haggard, gaunt, drawn, lantern-jawed; spindly, spidery; undersized, weedy, scrawny, scrubby, scraggy, exiguous; consumptive, wizened, peaky, sick; starveling; worn to a shadow, without an ounce of flesh to spare.

Vb. be narrow, narrow, taper, converge; become small.

make thin, contract, compress, pinch, nip; make oneself thin, starve, reduce, lose weight; slim; draw, spin, spin fine, lengthen; attenuate, rarefy.

202 Layer

N. layer, stratum, underlay, floor, base; outcrop, basset, projection; bed, course, range; row; zone, vein, seam, lode; thickness, ply; storey, tier, floor, landing; stage, planking, platform, frame; deck, quarterdeck, bridge, ship; film; bloom, dross, scum; patina, coating, coat, veneer, top layer, covering; scale, scab, membrane, peel, sheathe, bark, skin; level, water table; atmospheric layer, atmosphere.

lamina, sheet, slab, foil, strip; plate glass, plate, tinplate, sheet iron, sheet steel; plank, board, weatherboard, fascia; laminate, plywood; slat, lath, leaf; tablet, plaque, panel, pane; slab, flag, flagstone, slate; shingle, tile; slide, wafer, shaving, flake, slice, rasher; cardboard, sheet of paper, paper; card, platter, disc, circle.

stratification; bedding; overlap; Russian doll; onion skin; layer cake, sandwich, double-decker.

Adj. layered; flaky; slaty; scaly; filmy.

Vb. laminate, lay, deck, layer, shingle, overlap; zone, stratify, sandwich; plate, veneer, coat; split; whittle, skive, pare, peel, strip, uncover; shave, slice, make thin.

203 Filament

N. filament, flagellum, lash, eyelash, beard, hair; barb, plumage; flock, lock, shred of wool, lock of hair, wisp, curl; fringe, edging; stalk, tendril, plant; whisker, antenna, feeler; gossamer, cobweb, web, network; capillary, vein, conduit; ramification, branch; wire, element, wick, torch.

fibre, hair, Angora, mohair, cashmere, llama hair, alpaca; wool, merino; shoddy; silk, wild silk, floss; vegetable fibre, cotton, cotton wool, silk cotton, kapok; linen, flax; hemp; jute, sisal, coir; tow, oakum; raffia; worsted, yarn; spun yarn, thread, twine, twist, strand, cord, string, line, rope, cable; artificial fibre, rayon, nylon, textile; staple, denier, texture.

strip, fascia, band, bandage; braid, tape, strap, ribbon; fillet, girdle; lath, slat, batten, stave; shaving, wafer; splinter, shiver, shred, piece; streak, line.

Adj. fibrous; woolly, silky, downy, fleecy, hairy; wiry; capillary; narrow; stringy, thick.

204 Height

N. height, perpendicular length, vertical range, long way to fall; altitude, elevation, ceiling, pitch, summit; dizzy height; stature; eminence; sky, stratosphere, atmosphere.

high land, height, wold, moor, downs, rolling country; rising ground, rise, bank, slope, climb, incline; hill, eminence, mount, mountain; fell, scar, tor; mountain range, chain, sierra, cordillera; ridge, col, saddle, spur, headland, foothill, projection; crest, peak, pike, summit; precipice, cliff; crag, scar, bluff, steep, escarpment; gorge, canyon, ravine, valley; summit level; plateau, tableland.

small hill, hillock; hump, dune, moraine; barrow, tomb; mound, heap, earthwork; cairn, tell, monument; anthill, molehill, tussock, swelling.

high structure, column, pillar, turret, tower; pile, skyscraper; edifice; steeple, spire, belfry, church exterior; minaret; obelisk; dome, cupola, roof; colossus, sculpture; mausoleum, pyramid, tomb; pagoda, temple; ziggurat, Tower of Babel; mast, topmast; flagstaff; pole, maypole; lamppost, standard; pylon, radio mast; masthead, summit; watchtower, lookout, view; column of smoke, mushroom cloud.

tall creature, giraffe, elephant, mammoth, lamppost, grenadier, colossus, giant; poplar, pine, sequoia, tree.

high water, high tide, current; billow, tidal wave, wave; cataract, waterfall; flood, flood level.

altimetry, altimeter, meter, gauge.

Adj. high, sky-high; eminent, exalted, lofty, sublime, elevated; topmost; aerial, airborne, flying; towering, steep, dizzy.

tall, lanky, narrow; statuesque, Junoesque; colossal, gigantic, monumental, huge.

alpine; mountainous, hilly, highland; rolling.

overhanging; incumbent; aloft; prominent.

Vb. be high, tower, soar; surmount, clear, overlook, dominate, command, be superior; overhang, overshadow, cover; beetle; hover, hang; climax; mount, bestride; rise, ascend; lift oneself.

make higher, heighten, raise, hold aloft, elevate.

Adv. aloft; atop; above, overhead; above stairs, upstairs; upwards; breast high; throughout.

205 Lowness

N. lowness; sea level; marsh, steppe, plain; low elevation, molehill, pimple; gentle slope, slight gradient, incline; lower level, foothill; bottom, hollow, depression, valley; ocean; depths, cellar, well, mine, depth; floor, foot, base; nadir; low water, low ebb, low tide, current; low ball.

Adj. low, squat, short; oblique; recumbent, laid low, prostrate, supine; flat, at sea level, flat; low-level; lower, nether, inferior; sunken, concave; blunt; subterranean, underground, submarine, latent, deep; underfoot.

Vb. be low, lie low, lie flat, be horizontal; be beneath, underlie, lurk; slouch, crouch, stoop; crawl, wallow, grovel; depress, lower.

Adv. under, beneath, underneath; below; downwards; underfoot, underground, downstairs, below stairs; at a low ebb; below par.

206 Depth

N. *depth*, drop, fall; perspective, *length*; vertical range, profundity, nadir; deep water, *ocean*; unknown depths, *pitfall*; depression, bottom, *valley*; hollow, pit, shaft, mine, well, *cavity*; abyss, chasm, gap; vault, crypt, dungeon, *cellar*; cave, catacomb; pot-holing, *descent*; underworld, bottomless pit, *hell*; soundings, sound, probe, plummet, lead, lead line; sonar; bathyscaphe; submarine, submariner, frogman, *diver*; draught, displacement; *measurement*.

Adj. *deep*, steep, profound; abysmal, cavernous; deep-seated, deep-rooted, *fixed*; bottomless, fathomless; unfathomed, unfathomable; subterranean, underground; underwater, submarine; sunk; navigable; infernal.

Vb. *be deep*, gape, yawn; deepen, hollow, dig, *make concave*; fathom, sound, take soundings, plumb; drop, lower, *let fall*; go deep, touch bottom; plunge, founder.

Adv. *deeply*, profoundly.

207 Shallowness

N. *shallowness*; thin surface; veneer, thin coat, *skin*; surface injury, scratch, graze, *trifle*; shoal water, shallows; ford, *passage*; pond, puddle, *lake*; ripple, *wave*; light soil, stony ground, *soil*.

Adj. *shallow*, slight, superficial, *insubstantial*; surface, skin-deep; shoal; light, thin, narrow.

208 Summit

N. *summit*, sky, heaven, pole, top, peak, crest, apex, pinnacle, crown; maximum height, pitch; zenith, meridian, high noon, culmination, apogee; acme, *perfection*; limit; climax, turning point, *crisis*; divide, watershed, Great Divide, *partition*; coping, keystone; lintel, architrave; tympanum, capital, cornice; battlements, parapet, *fortification*.

vertex, apex, crown, cap, brow, head; tip, cusp, spike, nib, end, *extremity*; spire, *church exterior*; landing, *ascent*; fort; summit level, plateau, tableland, *high land*; gable; ceiling, *roof*; upper chamber, garret, *attic*; top storey; topside, upper deck, quarterdeck, hurricane deck, bridge, *ship*; topmast; masthead, *high structure*.

head, headpiece, pate, poll; nob, nut, noggin, conk, crumpet, bean, block, chump; upper storey, belfry; brow, dome, temple, forehead; loaf, brain, grey matter, *intelligence*; scalp, crown, skull, cranium, *cavity*; phrenology.

Adj. *topmost*, top, *high*; uppermost, supreme; polar; capital; head; meridian; tiptop, super, *best*.

Vb. *crown*, cap, head, top, tip, surmount, crest, *be high*; consummate, *climax*; take top place, *be superior*; *make complete*.

Adv. *atop*, on top, at the top; tiptoe.

209 Base

N. *base*, foot, toe, skirt; bottom, root; rock bottom, nadir, low water; footing, foundation, *basis*; fundamental, *origin*; groundwork, substructure, infrastructure, chassis, *frame*; pedestal, *stand*; floor, bed, bedrock, subsoil; ground, earth, foundations; footing, sill; damp course; basement, ground floor, *cellar*; flooring, pavement, hard standing, *paving*; carpet; wainscot, dado; keel; hold, bilge; sump, drain, *sink*.

foot, pedal extremities; sole, heel, instep, arch; toe, toenail, big toe; trotter, hoof, paw, pad; claw, talon, *nippers*; ankle, fetlock, pastern.

Adj. *undermost*, nethermost, bottom, *low*; basic, fundamental.

footed, pedal; shod.

Adv. *in the trough*; basically, fundamentally.

210 Verticality

N. *verticality*, upright carriage; *height*; right angle, square; elevation, azimuth circle; vertical line, plummet; vertical structure, hoist, upright, pole, stalagmite, *pillar*; sheer face, precipice, cliff, bluff, scarp, steep, *high land*; perpendicular drop, vertical height, rise.

Adj. *vertical*, upright, erect, standing; perpendicular; sheer, abrupt, steep, precipitous, *high*; straight, plumb; upstanding; bolt upright, unbowed; rampant.

Vb. *be vertical*, bristle; stand erect, stand upright, hold oneself straight; rise, stand, ramp, rear; keep standing.

make vertical, erect, rear, raise, pitch, *elevate*; up-end; stand.

Adv. *vertically*, upright; standing, all standing; at right angles; plumb.

211 Horizontality

N. *horizontality*; horizontal angle, azimuth; horizontal line, ruler, rule; horizontal course, strike; level, plane, dead level, dead flat, level plane; sea level, water table; stratum; slab, tablet, table, *layer*; level stretch, steppe, *plain*; marsh; platform, ledge, *projection*; terrace, esplanade; plateau, tableland, *high land*; bowling green, cricket ground, croquet lawn, *arena*; platter, *plate*; spirit level, *gauge*; horizon, horizon line, *limit*.

recumbency; lying down; prostration, proneness.

flattener, iron, mangle, press, rolling pin, roller, steamroller; bulldozer, juggernaut, *destroyer*.

Adj. *flat*, horizontal, level, plane, even, flush, *smooth*; trodden, trodden flat; smooth, calm.

supine; prone, prostrate; recumbent.

Vb. *be horizontal*, lie, lie flat, lie prostrate; recline, couch, sprawl, loll; grovel, *stoop*; become horizontal.

flatten, spread; lay flat, squash; make flush, level, even, grade, plane; iron, *smooth*; smooth down, prostrate, floor, ground, fell.

Adv. *horizontally*, flat; at full length.

212 Pendency

N. *pendency*; suspension, hanging, dangle, set, hang, drape.

hanging *object*, hanging ornament, drop, earring; tassel, tag, *trimming*; hangings, curtains, tapestry, *covering*; train, skirt; flap; pigtail, tail, *sequel*, *hair*; dewlap, lobe, appendix, *adjunct*; pendulum, bob, swing, hammock; chandelier, *lamp*; icicle, stalactite.

hanger, curtain rod, curtain ring, runner, rack; hook, peg, knob, nail, *prop*; suspender, braces, suspender belt, *underwear*; *cable*; clotheshorse; *frame*; davit, crane; spar, mast, *pillar*; gallows, gibbet, *pillory*.

Adj. hanging, pendent, pendulous; dependent, weeping; open-ended, loose; baggy, flowing.

Vb. hang, be pendent, drape, set; trail, flow; swing, sway, dangle, bob; nod, weep, loll, droop, sag, swag; stream, wave, float, ripple, flap; hover; overhang, lour; suspend, sling, hitch, fasten to, append, *join*; curtain, *cover*.

213 Support

N. support, aid; footing, ground; hold, foothold; life jacket, *safeguard*.

prop, support, bearing; carriage, carrier, chassis; buttress; bulwark, embankment, wall, shore, jack; flagstaff, stanchion, rod, bar, transom, brace, strut; stay, mainstay, guy, rigging; boom, spar, mast, yard, yardarm; *projection*; trunk, stem, stalk, *plant*; arch, *curve*; keystone, cornerstone; cantilever; pier (see *pillar*); bandage, jockstrap, truss, splint; stiffener, whalebone; corset, *underwear*; yoke, *hanger*, rest, headrest, stirrup; handrail (see *handle*); skid, chock, wedge, *obstacle*; staff, baton, stick, cane, crutch, crook; leg support, irons; bracket (see *shelf*); trivet, hob (see *stand*); arm, back, shoulder; shoulder blade, clavicle, collarbone; backbone (see *pillar*); Atlas; supporter, patron, *auxiliary*.

handle, holder, *receptacle*; hold, grip, hilt, pommel, haft; knob; lug, ear, loop; railing, handrail, rail, taffrail, balustrade; shaft, loom; tiller; crank; lever, trigger, *tool*.

basis, foundation, deck; raft, pallet, sleeper; *layer*; ground, groundwork, floor, bed, bedrock, rock bottom, *base*; flooring, pavement, *paving*; *land*; perch, footing, foothold.

stand, tripod, trivet, hob; table mat, coaster; anvil, block, bench; trolley; table, board; sideboard, dresser, *cabinet*; work table, desk, counter; pedestal; platform, gantry; footplate; landing, landing stage, pier; dais, pulpit, stage, *rostrum*; doorstep, threshold; altar step, *altar*; step, stair, tread, rung, round, *ascent*; stilt; shank, leg.

seat, throne, woolsack; bank, bench, form, settle; bucket seat, dicky; pew, *church interior*; stall, *theatre*; chair, armchair, easy chair; sofa, settee, divan, couch, ottoman, chesterfield, sociable; stool, footstool; saddle, pillion, pad, howdah; stocks, *pillory*; electric chair, hot seat; lap; mat.

bed, cot, crib, cradle, bassinet; marriage bed, bunk; couch; four-poster; pallet, airbed, shakedown; hammock, *hanging object*; sick bed, litter, hurdle, stretcher, *hospital*; bier, *funeral*; bedding, *coverlet*, bedstead, divan.

cushion, pillow; bolster, Dutch wife; mattress.

beam, joist, girder, rafter, tie beam, truss, *bond*; summer; *roof*; transom, crossbar, traverse; architrave, lintel.

pillar, shaft, pier, pile, pole, stake, stud, *structure*; post; king post, jamb; stanchion; banister; mullion; pilaster, column, caryatid; spinal column, spine, backbone; neck, cervix.

pivot, fulcrum, lever, purchase; hinge, *joint*; pole, axis; axle, swivel, spindle; bearing, gudgeon; rowlock; centreboard, keel.

shelf, ledge, offset, *projection*; corbel,

bracket, console; niche, *compartment*; sill, windowsill, mantelpiece, rack, dresser, *cabinet*; counter, plank, board, table, leaf, slab.

frame, skeleton; framework, scaffolding, *structure*; trellis; chassis, fuselage, body (of a car); undercarriage; trestle; easel, clotheshorse; housing; picture frame, sash, *outline*.

Adj. supporting; fundamental; spinal; holding.

Vb. support, sustain, bear, carry, hold, shoulder; uphold; prop, underpin, *elevate*; buttress, bolster, cushion; reinforce, *strengthen*; bandage, brace, truss, *tighten*; steady, stay; cradle, pillow, cup; maintain, *provide*; give support, *aid*; frame, set, mount, *enclose*; give foundations, bottom, ground, found, base, embed; stand, endure, *suffice*.

be *supported*; press; command support, have behind one.

Adv. astride, piggyback.

214 Parallelism

N. parallelism; parallel, *equality*; parallel lines, lines of latitude; rails, railway lines; parallelogram.

Adj. parallel, collateral, concurrent, concentric; equidistant, *equal*; corresponding, correspondent, *similar*.

Vb. be parallel, run together, run abreast, lie parallel; correspond, concur; parallel.

Adv. in parallel, alongside; abreast.

215 Obliquity

N. obliquity; oblique line, diagonal; oblique figure, rhomboid, *angular figure*; oblique angle; squint; curvature, camber, bend, humpback, *curve*; zigzag, chevron; switchback; oblique motion, swerve, lurch, stagger, *deviation*; splay, bias, twist, warp; leaning, list, tip, cant; slope, slant, tilt, pitch, rake; batter; bevel; inclined plane, ramp, chute, slide; leaning tower; *angular measure*.

incline, rise, ascent; ramp, gradient; hill, rising ground, *small hill*; fall, dip, downhill, *descent*; easy ascent, easy descent, gentle slope, escarpment, cliff, precipice; scarp, *fortification*; bank, scree, landslide.

Adj. oblique, inclined, bevel; tipsy, askew, skew, slant, aslant; leaning, recumbent; *angular*; wry, awry, wonky, crooked, cock-eyed, knock-kneed; diagonal, transverse; athwart, across; indirect, zigzag, herringbone, bent.

sloping, uphill, rising; downhill; steep, abrupt, sheer, precipitous, breakneck, *vertical*; easy, gentle, shelving.

Vb. be oblique, incline, lean, tilt; pitch, slope, slant, shelve, dip, decline, *descend*; rise, climb, *ascend*; cut, cut across, *cross*; lean, list, tip, bank, heel, cant; bend, sag, give; *stoop*; walk sideways, edge, sidle, sidestep; look sideways, squint; zigzag; dodge, swerve; diverge, converge.

make oblique, incline, lean, slant, slope, cant, tilt, tip, rake; splay, *deviate*; bend, crook, twist, warp, skew, *distort*; bevel; sway, bias, divert, *deflect*; curve, camber.

Adv. obliquely, across; askew; aslant; askance; crabwise, sidelong, sideways; at an angle.

216 Inversion

N. *inversion*, turning back to front, palindrome; turning backwards, *reversion*; turning inward; return; *interchange*; spoonerism.

overturning, upset, spill; somersault, cartwheel; *revolution*.

Adj. *inverted*, inverse; keel upwards; topheavy; topsy-turvy; flat, prone, *supine*; reverse, *contrary*, *opposite*.

Vb. *be inverted*, turn round, turn about, right about turn, *turn back*; capsize, turn turtle; *be oblique*; tumble; reverse, back, go backwards, *regress*.

invert, transpose, *interchange*; reverse; turn back; *fold*; introvert; upend, upturn, overturn, spill, upset, capsize; turn topsy-turvy.

Adv. *inversely*; contrariwise, other way round; back to front; topsy-turvy; face downwards.

217 Crossing: intertexture

N. *crossing*; crisscross, intersection; arabesque, *pattern*; braid, wreath, plait, *convolution*; entanglement, skein; crossroads, intersection, road junction, *road*; level crossing, *railway*; viaduct, flyover, *bridge*, traffic control.

cross, crux, crucifix, *ritual object*; pectoral, *heraldry*; swastika; *flag*; crossbar, transom, beam; scissors, nippers.

network, reticulation, netting, chicken wire; webbing, matting, wickerwork, trellis, wattle; honeycomb, lattice, grating, grid, grille; tracery, fretwork, filigree; lace, crochet, knitting, tatting, *needlework*; web, cobweb; net, drag-net, trawl; mesh.

textile, weave, web, loom; woven stuff, piece goods, bolt, roll, length, piece, cloth, stuff, material; broadcloth, fabric, tissue; batik; jute, hessian, canvas, duck; ticking, crash, towelling, candlewick; chintz, damask, brocade, rep, tapestry, *covering*; mohair, cashmere, alpaca, angora, *fibre*; wool, worsted; frieze, felt, baize; homespun, tweed, serge; flannel, swansdown; paisley, *pattern*; jersey, flannelette, winceyette; velvet, velveteen; corduroy; cotton, denim, drill, khaki; fustian, poplin, calico, gingham, seersucker; organdie; cheesecloth, muslin, mull, voile; cambric, lawn, linen; silk, georgette, chiffon; satin, taffeta, moire; shantung; tulle, net, gauze; lace; rayon, nylon, polyester, fibreglass, *fibre*.

weaving, texture; web, warp, weft, woof; nap, pile, *hair*; frame, loom, shuttle; weaver; knitting machine, distaff, whorl; spinner, spider.

Adj. *crossed*, crossing, cross, crisscross; diagonal, transverse, cross-eyed, *oblique*; crucial, forked, *angular*; *complex*; textile, woven; twill, herringbone; honeycombed, barred; striped, *variegated*.

reticular, webbed; micromesh.

Vb. *cross*, pass; intersect, cut, *be oblique*; splice, dovetail, link, *join*; mesh, net, knot; fork; *make angular*.

weave, loom; plait, braid; felt, twill, knit, crochet; spin.

enlace, interlace, interlink, interlock, intertwine, interweave, enmesh, engage gear; twine, entwine, wattle, twist, wreathe; mat, ravel, snarl, tangle, entangle, *derange*.

Adv. *across*, athwart; crosswise.

218 Exteriority

N. *exteriority*; *surroundings*; periphery, circumference, *outline*; exterior, outward appearance, *appearance*; surface, crust, cortex, shell, *skin*; outer side, face, facet, facade, *front*; other side; outside, open air; outer space, *distance*; *exclusion*; nonconformity; outsider, *nonconformist*.

Adj. *exterior*, outward, extra-; external; roundabout, peripheral; outer, outermost, outlying, extraterrestrial, *distant*; outside; outdoor, extramural; foreign, *extraneous*; *excluding*; *extrinsic*; centrifugal; eccentric; surface, superficial; skin-deep, *shallow*, facial, *frontal*.

Vb. *be exterior*, lie beyond, frame, enclose, *surround*; look outward, *be extrinsic*.

externalize, body forth, *make extrinsic*; project, extrapolate; expel, *eject*.

Adv. *externally*, outwardly, outwards; outside.

219 Interiority

N. *interiority*, interior, inside, indoors; inner surface; *skin*; sapwood, heartwood, *wood*; inmost being, soul; heart, centre, breast, bosom; inland, Midlands, hinterland, up-country; pith, marrow, *substance*; subsoil, *base*; *presence*; *interval*; cave, pit, *depth*; *marriage*; self-absorption, egoism, egotism; introvert; inmate, internee; *prisoner*.

insides, contents; inner man, interior man; viscera, vitals; heart, ticker; lights; liver, spleen; offal, *meat*; bowels, entrails, innards, guts, pluck, tripe; colon, rectum; abdomen, belly, paunch; womb, uterus; stomach, tummy; chest; gland; endocrine; cell, *organism*.

Adj. *interior*, internal, inward, *intrinsic*; inside, inner, *central*; inland, up-country; domestic, home, vernacular; intimate, familiar, *known*; indoor, intramural; inboard; endemic; deep-seated, ingrown, *fixed*; intravenous, subcutaneous; introvert, *intrinsic*.

Vb. *be inside*, lie within, lie beneath; show through, *be visible*.

hold *within*, hold, *comprise*; place within, embed, *insert*; keep inside, intern, *imprison*; enfold, *enclose*; absorb.

Adv. *inside*, within; at heart; indoors, at home.

220 Centrality

N. *centrality*; concentration, *condensation*; central position; midriff, waistline, parting, *partition*.

centre, centre of mass, centre of gravity, centre of pressure, centre of percussion; nerve centre, ganglion; centre of activity, *focus*; epicentre; storm centre, hotbed; heart, core, kernel, *essential part*; nub, hub; nucleus; navel; spine, backbone; marrow, pith; pole, axis, fulcrum, centreboard, *pivot*; centre point, *middle*; *heraldry*; eye, pupil; bull's-eye, target, *objective*.

Adj. *central*; nuclear; *middle*; concentric; geocentric; spinal; centripetal; chief, head, *supreme*.

Vb. *centralize*, centre, focus; concentrate, consolidate, *be dense*.

Adv. *centrally*, at heart, at the core, middle, midst.

221 Covering

N. *covering*; overlap; coating, *layer*; top layer, top dressing, mulch, topsoil, *soil*; topping, icing, frosting; cover, lid; gravestone, ledger, *tomb*; hatch, trapdoor; flap, shutter; film; glass, glass front, watch glass, crystal, *transparency*; cap, top, plug, bung, cork, *stopper*; plaster, *surgical dressing*; carapace, shell, tortoiseshell, *hardness*; mail, plate, *armour*; shield, cowl, cowling, bonnet, hood (of a car); scab; crust, fur, *dirt*; capsule, ferrule, sheath, envelope, *receptacle*; pillowcase; table cloth, chair cover, antimacassar; soft furnishings; hangings, curtains, *hanging object*; wallpaper, *lining*; mask, domino, *disguise*.

roof, cupola, *dome*; *vertex*; pantile, shingle, thatch, *building material*; eaves, *edge*; ceiling, deck; vault, *beam*.

canopy; tilt, awning, sunblind, *screen*; marquee, pavilion, big top; tent, bell tent, tepee, *dwelling*; canvas, tarpaulin, fly sheet; mosquito net, *network*.

shade, hood, eyelid, eyelash; blind; curtain, veil; umbrella, gamp, brolly; parasol, sunshade; sun hat, sun helmet; visor, eye shade, *screen*; peak (of a cap); dark glasses.

wrapping, wrapper, paper, cellophane, polythene; polystyrene, *lining*; blister pack, *receptacle*; bandage, roller, *girdle*; plaster cast, *surgical dressing*; book cover, binding, boards, dust jacket or cover; tunic, coat, *jacket*; mantle, *cloak*; scarf; life belt, life jacket, *safeguard*; lagging; cocoon, chrysalis; shroud, *grave clothes*.

skin; outer skin, epidermis, cuticle; true skin; peel, bark, crust, rind, coat, cortex; husk, hull, shell, pod, jacket; membrane, film; scalp, *head*; scale; pelt, fleece, fell, fur; leather, hide, rawhide; shagreen, patent leather; crocodile, alligator; pigskin, morocco, calf, kid, chamois, buff, buckskin; sheepskin, lamb, astrakhan; mink, sable, ermine; chinchilla, *fibre*; *plumage*.

paving, flooring, floor, parquet; deck, duckboards; pavement; paving stone, crazy paving; cobble, cobblestone; gravel, asphalt, tarmac, *road*.

coverlet, bedspread, counterpane, bedding, bedclothes, bed linen; sheet, quilt, eiderdown, duvet; blanket, rug; trappings; pall.

floor-cover, carpet, broadloom, pile carpet, mat, doormat, bath mat, rug; linoleum, vinyl; matting, red carpet, *formality*.

facing; veneer, coating, varnish, japan, lacquer, enamel, glaze; incrustation, roughcast, pebbledash; *building material*; stucco, rendering; wash, whitewash, distemper, emulsion, paint; stain, polish; coat of paint, *pigment*.

Adj. *overlying*, overlaying; overlapping.

covered, vaulted; *safe*; hooded; snowcapped; plastered.

dermal, cutaneous; scaly.

Vb. *cover*, superimpose; roof, cap, tip; ice, frost, decorate (a cake), spread, lay (a table), smother; insulate, lag, *line*; lap, enfold, envelope, *enclose*; blanket, shroud, mantle, muffle; hood, veil, *conceal*; case, bind, cover (books), box, pack; wrap, bandage, swathe, wrap round, dress, *doctor*; sheathe, encapsulate, encase, *insert*; garage.

overlie, overhang, overlap; overshadow; span, bestride, straddle, *be broad*; flood,
inundate, *drench*; crust, scab.

overlay, pave, floor, cement; roof, dome; vault, deck; tile, thatch; paper, wall paper, *line*; topdress, mulch; spread, smear; butter, anoint; powder, dust; sand; gravel, tarmac, metal.

coat, face, front; roughcast, encrust, shingle; stucco, plaster, render, decorate; veneer, varnish, lacquer, japan, enamel, glaze, size; paint, whitewash, distemper, emulsion, stain, *colour*; creosote; tar, pitch, pay; daub, bedaub, grease; gild, plate, silver; electroplate; waterproof, fireproof, *safeguard*.

222 Lining

N. *lining*, liner; coating, stuffing, wadding, padding; kapok, foam; lagging, insulation; backing, facing; upholstery; wall paper; panelling, wainscot; metal lining, bush; brake lining; *wrapping*; filling, washer.

Vb. *line*, encrust, *coat*; insulate, *cover*; inlay, back, face, paper, wallpaper; upholster, cushion; stuff, pad, wad; fill, pack; bush, *insert*.

223 Dressing

N. *dressing*, investment, investiture; clothing, covering, toilet; *fashion*; dress, garb, attire, rig; panoply, array; trim, harness, housing, trappings; paraphernalia, rig out, turn-out.

clothing, wear, apparel, raiment, linen; clothes, togs, gear, kit, clobber; outfit, wardrobe, trousseau; maternity wear, baby clothes; old clothes, tatters; working clothes; leisure wear, casual clothes; fine raiment; Sunday best; party dress, frippery, *finery*; fancy dress, masquerade; motley; colours; national costume.

garment, article of clothing; neck (see *neckline*); top, bodice, bosom; bib; waistline (see *belt*); bustle, train; crutch, codpiece; arms (see *sleeve*); fly, *opening*; patch pocket, *pocket*; gusset, gore, pleat, kick pleat; lapel, turn-up, *fold*; cuff, hemline, edging.

formal dress, formality; evening dress, morning dress; academic dress; mourning, black.

uniform, regimentals, *livery*; dress uniform, undress, mess kit; khaki; school uniform; clerical dress.

informal dress, undress, mufti; casual clothes, slacks, jeans; dishabille; dressing gown, bathrobe, wrapper, housecoat, smoking jacket.

robe, gown, drapery; sari; kimono; toga, cassock; shroud, *grave clothes*.

dress, frock, gown; creation, number, cocktail dress; chemise, shift, sack; shirt waister, pinafore dress, gymslip.

suit, outfit, ensemble; coordinates; lounge suit, costume, tweeds; leotard, body stocking; overalls, boiler suit, tracksuit; spacesuit.

jacket, coat, tail coat, dinner jacket, tuxedo; monkey jacket, blazer, reefer, sports jacket, riding habit, hunting pink; donkey jacket, parka, windcheater, anorak; bomber jacket; jerkin, tunic, tabard, waistcoat; bolero, matinee jacket.

jersey, pullover, woolly, jumper, sweater; polo neck, Fair Isle, cardigan, tank top; twin set.

trousers, trews; cords, flannels; bell bottoms; slacks, bags, plus fours;

breeches, jodhpurs, knickerbockers; chaps, dungarees, denims, jeans, shorts; bloomers, pantaloons, rompers.

skirt; dirndl, kilt, kirtle; sarong; straight skirt, culottes; ballet skirt, tutu; crinoline, hoop.

loincloth, dhoti, sarong; fig leaf, G-string, jockstrap; nappy or diaper.

apron, bib, pinafore, pinny, overall.

shirt, smock, angel top; polo neck, tee shirt, sweatshirt; blouse, camisole, top, sun top.

underwear, underclothes, undies, linen; lingerie, smalls; underpants, pants, boxer shorts; briefs, panties, French knickers, camiknickers, knickers, bloomers, drawers; combinations, thermal underwear; singlet, vest, chemise, slip, petticoat; foundation garment, corset, stays, girdle; brassiere, bra; suspender belt, braces.

nightwear, nightclothes; nightdress, negligee; nightshirt, pyjamas; bed jacket, nightcap.

beachwear, bikini; swimming costume, bathing suit, trunks.

overcoat, coat (see *jacket*): fur coat, *skin*; topcoat, greatcoat, frock coat; raglan; car coat, waterproof; mac, mackintosh, raincoat; trench coat; light coat, duster.

cloak, mantle; cape; domino, *disguise*; djellaba, shawl, plaid, poncho, Afghan.

neckwear, scarf; stole, boa; muffler; neckerchief, stock, cravat, tie, necklace; ruff, collar.

headgear; hat, cap, lid; headdress, mantilla; *finery*; coronet, tiara, *regalia*; fillet, snood; kerchief, headband, sweatband; turban; hood, cowl, wimple; veil, yashmak, *screen*; fez; busby, bearskin, helmet, *armour*; tin hat, crash helmet, skid lid, *safeguard*; woolly hat, sou'wester; cap, beret, tam-o'-shanter; deerstalker; Homburg, trilby, beaver, bowler, derby; slouch hat, stetson, sombrero, shovel hat, boater, panama, coolie hat, pith helmet, *shade*; bonnet, mob cap, cloche, pillbox; top hat, topper, silk hat, mortarboard.

wig; false hair, hairpiece, toupee; coiffure, *hair*.

neckline, boat neck, crewneck, cowlneck, poloneck, halterneck.

belt, waistband; cummerbund, sash; armband; *girdle*.

sleeve, arm, armhole; wristband, cuff.

glove, gauntlet; mitten, mitt, muff.

legwear, hosiery; nylons, tights; trunks, hose; leggings; *armour*, garter, suspender, *fastening*.

footwear, sock; slipper, mule; clog, sabot; creepers; brothel creepers; shoe, high heels, stiletto heels; slingbacks, lace-ups; boots, cowboy boots, wellingtons, wellies, gumboots.

clothier; tailor; *fashion*; seamstress; shoemaker; cobbler, *artisan*; hosier, hatter, milliner, draper, haberdasher; boutique, valet, *domestic*; dresser.

Adj. dressed, clad; shod.

tailored, tailor-made, bespoke, made-to-measure; single-breasted, one-piece, unisex; classic; skintight; buffant, *broad*; sartorial.

Vb. dress, clothe, array, apparel, garment, garb, attire; robe, drape, sheet, mantle; invest, uniform, equip, harness, *make ready*; deck, envelop, wrap, lap, enfold, swaddle, swathe, shroud, sheathe, *cover*.

wear, assume, don, clothe oneself; tie; change; carry, sport.

224 Uncovering

N. *uncovering*, exposure, *disclosure*; nudism, naturism; striptease, *stage show*; undress, dishabille, *informal dress*; moult; shaving, *havoc*.

bareness, decollete, bare neck, plunging neckline; nudity, nakedness; the altogether, state of nature, birthday suit; baldness, alopecia.

stripper, striptease artiste; flasher, streaker; furrier, peeler; depilatory; nude figure, nude.

Adj. uncovered; showing, *manifest*; undressed; topless; unshod; hatless; bare, naked, nude, raw; mother naked; stark, stark naked; starkers; threadbare, ragged, *poor*; drawn.

hairless, bald, smooth; threadbare; mangy; thin.

Vb. uncover, unveil, undress; strip, skin, scalp, flay; pluck, peel, bark, excoriate; hull, pod, shell, stone; bone, fillet, *empty*; denude, *lay waste*; expose, bare, lay open, *disclose*; draw (a sword); *extract*; unfold, unpack; *open*; abrade, rub.

doff, uncover; drop; change; shed, cast, cast a clout; moult, slough, cast its skin; scale; undress, disrobe, peel, strip; undo, untie, *disunite*.

225 Surroundings

N. *surroundings*; ambience, atmosphere, aura; medium, matrix; compass, circuit, circumference, periphery, perimeter, *outline*; milieu, environment, entourage; background, setting, scene, *situation*; neighbourhood, vicinity, *near place*; outskirts, environs, suburbs, green belt; purlieus, precincts, *housing*; outpost, border, *limit*; wall, fortification, *fence*; cordon, *girdle*.

Adj. circumjacent; atmospheric; peripheral; roundabout, *circuitous*; suburban, *near*.

Vb. surround, lie around, compass, encompass, lap, encircle, *circle*; girdle, *enclose*; wreathe around, embrace, hug, *caress*; contain, cloister, *circumscribe*; invest, blockade, *besiege*.

Adv. around, about, round about, all round; without, outside.

226 Interjacency

N. *interjacency*, presence; crossing; union; middle position, *middle*.

partition, curtain, *screen*; Great Wall of China; *exclusion*; wall, bulkhead, *fence*; divide, watershed, parting, *separation*; division, panel; septum, diaphragm, midriff, *centre*; field boundary, hedge, ditch, *gap*; common frontier, *limit*.

intermediary, medium, link, bond; go-between, broker, *mediator*; marriage broker, matchmaker, agent, *deputy*; middleman, retailer, *merchant*; advocate, *patron*; buffer, bumper, fender, cushion, *safeguard*; air lock, buffer state, halfway house, *middle*.

interjection; embolism, closure; interference, hindrance; episode, parenthesis, *adjunct*; insert, fly leaf, wedge, washer, lining.

interjector; interloper.

Adj. *interjacent*; intermediary; intrusive, *extraneous*; interplanetary, interstellar; intermediate; median, medium, mean, mediterranean, *middle*.

Vb. lie between, intervene, *be halfway*; permeate, *pervade*.

introduce, *admit*; sheathe; *insert*; *infuse*; splice, dovetail, mortise, *join*; insinuate, *infiltrate*.

put *between*, sandwich; cushion, *line*; interpose, interject; interpolate, intercalate; interleave, intersperse; interweave; bracket.

interfere, come between, intercept, *hinder*; intervene, intercede, *mediate*; interrupt; obtrude, *intrude*; invade, trespass, *encroach*; meddle.

Adv. *between*, 'twixt; among, amid, mid, midst; *while*.

227 Circumscription

N. *circumscription*; drawing round, circle, balloon; investment, siege, blockade, *attack*; confinement; ring, *fence*.

Adj. *circumscribed*; landlocked; *restrained*; limited, finite.

Vb. *circumscribe*, describe a circle, ring round, encircle, encompass; envelop, invest, blockade, picket, *besiege*; corral; enclose; box, cage, immure, cloister, *imprison*; frame, *surround*; encase, enfold, enshrine; edge, border, *limit*; clasp, hug, embrace, *caress*.

228 Outline

N. *outline*, circumference, perimeter, periphery; surround, frame, rim, *edge*; compass, circuit, *circle*; lines, features, *feature*; profile, relief, silhouette, skyline; *picture*; sketch, *plan*; figure, diagram; trace, tracing; skeleton, framework, *structure*; contour, contour line, shape, *form*; coastline, bounds, *limit*; circlet, band, *loop*; balloon, circle; ring, cordon, *barrier*.

Adj. *outlined*, framed; peripheral.

Vb. *outline*, describe a circle, construct a figure, *circumscribe*; frame, *surround*; delineate, draw, silhouette, profile, trace, *represent*; etch, *engrave*; map, sketch.

229 Edge

N. *edge*, verge, brim; outer edge, fly (of a flag); tip, brink, skirt, fringe, margin, *extremity*; inner edge, hoist (of a flag); confines, bounds, boundary, frontier, border, *limit*; littoral, coast, coastline, beach, strand, seaside, seashore, waterline, water's edge, front, waterfront, *shore*; wharf, quay, dock, *stable*; sideline, side, brim, kerb, wayside, roadside, bank; hedge, railing, *fence*; tyre, *wheel*; lip, ledge, cornice, rim, welt, flange, *projection*; horizon, skyline.

threshold, sill, doorstep, door, portal, porch, *doorway*; mouth, jaws, chaps.

edging, frame, *outline*; thrum, list; hem, hemline, border; *pattern*; binding, piping; fringe, frill, ruffle, flounce, valance, *trimming*; *notch*; wavy edge, purl, *coil*.

Adj. *marginal*, border; roadside, wayside.

Vb. *hem*, edge, border, trim, fringe, purl, mill, *notch*; bound, confine, *limit*.

230 Enclosure

N. *enclosure*, envelope, case, *receptacle*; wrapper, *wrapping*; girdle, ring, perimeter, circumference, periphery, *outline*; surround, frame, precinct, close; cloister, courtyard, *place*; reserve; lot, holding, claim, *territory*; fold, pen, sty, *cattle pen*; stockyard, croft, *farm*; park, *garden*; compound, yard, pound, paddock, field;

car park, *stable*; corral, kraal, stockade, lines; net, trawl, *network*; lobster pot, trap; cell, box, cage, *prison*.

fence, *network*; hurdle, wooden fence, haha, hedge, hedgerow; rails, balustrade, railing, taffrail; pale, wall, moat, ditch, trench, curtain wall.

barrier, wall, *partition*; *protection*; barricade, cordon, pale; balustrade, parapet; turnstile, *obstacle*; palisade, stockade, fort; portcullis, gate, door, bolt, bar, *closure*.

Vb. *enclose*, cordon, surround, wall; pen, hem, ring, *circumscribe*; cloister, immure, cage, *imprison*; wrap, lap, enfold, *fold*; hug, embrace, *caress*; frame, set, mount, box.

231 Limit

N. *limit*, *qualification*; definition; upper limit, ceiling, *summit*; lower limit, threshold, *base*; legal limit, Plimsoll line; saturation point; utmost, extreme, furthest point, farthest reach, *pole*, *extremity*; terminus, terminal, *end*; goal, target, touch, touchline, home, base, *objective*; turning point, crisis; Rubicon, *resolution*; limit of endurance, tolerance, capacity; physical limit, outside edge, perimeter, periphery, circumference, *outline*; tidemark, sea line, *shore*; landmark, boundary stone; milestone, *degree*; kerb, *road*; boundary, verge; frontier, border, *edge*; national frontier, state boundary; line, divide, parting, *partition*; horizon, equator; deadline, time limit, term, *period*; ultimatum, *threat*; speed limit; sound barrier.

Adj. *limited*, definite; finite; terminal; frontier, border, borderline, boundary.

Vb. *limit*, bound, border, edge, hem; top, crown; define, confine, condition, *qualify*; restrict, stint, *restrain*; encompass, *circumscribe*; demarcate; *mark*.

Adv. *thus far*, so far; on the borderline.

232 Front

N. *front*, forefront, *precedence*; forepart; prefix, frontispiece; forelock, *hair*; forecourt, entrance, *doorway*; foreground, proscenium; *priority*; front rank, first line, forward line, centre forward; avant-garde, vanguard, van, advance guard; spearhead, bridgehead; outpost, scout; forerunner, pioneer, *precursor*.

face, frontage; face of a coin, obverse, head; right side; front view, front elevation; *head*; brow, forehead; chin, features, visage, countenance, mug, mush, kisser, dial, clock, *feature*; prominent feature, nose, snout, conk, *protuberance*.

prow, nose, beak, rostrum, figurehead; bow; bowsprit; jib, forecastle, fo'c'sle, *ship*.

Adj. *frontal*, fore, forward, front, obverse; full frontal, head-on, oncoming, facing, *opposite*; anterior, *preceding*.

Vb. *be in front*, front, confront, face; be opposite; breast, stem, brave; *be oblique*; forge ahead, head, *precede*.

Adv. *in front*, before; ahead, *beyond*; far ahead, landward; face to face; head first, head foremost.

233 Rear

N. *rear*, rearward, back end, tail end, stern, *extremity*; heel; coda, *musical piece*; tail, brush, scut, pigtail, *sequel*; wake, train, *retinue*; last place, rear rank, back seat;

rearguard, *successor*; background, backdrop, *stage set*; hinterland, depths, far corner, *distance*; behind, backstage, back side; reverse side; reverse, other side, flip side; back door, back entrance, postern, *doorway*; backbone, spine, *prop*; nape, scruff; *head*.

buttocks, backside, behind, posterior; bottom, seat; bum, arse, ass, fanny; rear, stern, tail; hindquarters, croup; hunkers; rump, loin; dorsal region, lower back; anus.

poop, stern, quarter, counter, rudder, mizzenmast, *ship*.

Adj. *back*, rear, postern; posterior, after, hind, hinder, rearmost; bent back, *convex*; reverse, *opposite*; placed last, *inferior*; spinal, dorsal, lumbar; anal.

Vb. *be behind*, back; *aid*; follow, *come after*; lag, trail, drop behind, fall astern; tail, shadow, dog, *pursue*; follow at heel, *follow*; bend backwards, *be oblique*.

Adv. *rearward*, behind, back of; after; aft, astern; backward; above; overleaf; close behind; back to back.

234 Laterality

N. *laterality*; side movement; sidestep, *deviation*; sideline, side, bank, edge; coast, *shore*; siding, side entrance, side door; gable; broadside; beam; quarter, *poop*; flank; wing, fin, hand; cheek, jowl, chaps; side whiskers, *hair*; profile, side elevation; lee, lee side, leeward; windward, *direction*; east, Orient; west, Occident, *compass point*.

Adj. *lateral*, side, *marginal*; sidelong, glancing; manysided, multilateral, bilateral, trilateral, quadrilateral; collateral, *parallel*; moving sideways, edging; eastern, eastward, easterly, orient; west, western, westerly, westward.

Vb. *flank*, side, edge, skirt, border, *hem*; coast, move sideways, passage, sidle; sideslip, sidestep, *deviate*; extend sideways, deploy, outflank, *overstep*.

Adv. *sideways*, crabwise; askance; sidelong; abreast, alongside; aside, beside; *near*; to windward, to leeward.

235 Contraposition

N. *contraposition*, antithesis, opposition; antipodes; frontage, *direction*; opposite side, reverse, back, *rear*; polarity; crosscurrent, headwind, *opposition*; inverse.

Adj. *opposite*, reverse, inverse, *contrary*; facing, oncoming, *frontal*; diametrically opposite; polar; antarctic, arctic, northern, southern.

Vb. *be opposite*, stand opposite, subtend; face, confront; run counter, *counteract*; oppose.

Adv. *against*; facing, face to face; back to back; overleaf; contrariwise.

236 Dextrality

N. *dextrality*, right hand; right, offside, starboard; right-hand page, recto; right wing.

Adj. *dextral*; right-hand, starboard, offside; right-handed, ambidextrous, *skilful*.

Adv. *dextrally*, on the right; to the right, dextrad.

237 Sinistrality

N. *sinistrality*, left hand; left, near side, port; left wing; southpaw.

Adj. *sinistral*, sinister, left, left-handed; onside, nearside.

Adv. *sinistrally*, on the left; offside; sinistrad.

238 Form

N. *form*, idea; *whole*; essence, *substance*; significant form, *character*; art form, *art*, *verse form*; word form, *linguistics*; shape, turn, lines, architecture; formation, configuration, fashion, style, design, *structure*; contour, silhouette, relief, profile, frame, outline; figure, cut, set, trim, build, *feature*; face; look, expression, appearance, *mien*; posture, attitude, stance; get-up, turnout, rig; type, kind, pattern, stamp, cast, mould, blank, *prototype*; format, typeface, typography, *print*.

formation, creation, *production*; expression, *arrangement*; designing; knitting, *network*; needlework; pottery; moulding, *sculpture*; turning, joinery, *skill*; etymology, *linguistics*.

Adj. *formed*, receiving form, plastic; shaped; ready-made; ready, *prepared*; solid, concrete, *dense*.

formative, formal; plastic.

Vb. *form*, create, make, *produce*; shape, fashion, figure, pattern; blow (glass); turn, round, square; cut, tailor; silhouette, *outline*; sketch, draw, *represent*; model, carve, whittle, chisel; hew, *cut*; mould, cast; stamp, coin, mint; carpenter, mason; forge, smith; knead, work; construct, build, frame, *elevate*; express, formulate.

239 Amorphism: absence of form

N. *amorphism*, absence of form; prime matter; confusion, chaos, *disorder*; lack of shape; lack of definition; raw material; rough diamond; deformity.

Adj. *amorphous*, formless, inchoate; liquid, *fluid*; featureless, characterless; messy, chaotic; lacking definition, indistinct, nebulous, vague, fuzzy, *shadowy*; *beginning*; raw, *immature*; *incomplete*; rude, uncouth, barbaric, *artless*; rugged, *rough*; *unsightly*; malformed, misshapen, gnarled.

Vb. *deform*, destroy; dissolve, melt, *liquefy*; batter, *break*; grind, pulp; warp, twist, *distort*; deface, disfigure, *make ugly*; mutilate, truncate, *impair*; jumble, disorder, *derange*.

240 Symmetry: regularity of form

N. *symmetry*, proportion; balance, *equilibrium*; ramification; regular features, *beauty*; harmony, *agreement*; rhythm; finish, *perfection*.

Adj. *symmetrical*, balanced, equal; congruent; corresponding, *parallel*; similar; smooth, even, *uniform*; round, equilateral, *regular*; crystalline; formal, classic, comely, *shapely*; well set-up, *straight*; finished, *complete*.

241 Distortion: irregularity of form

N. *distortion*, disproportion, disproportionateness, want of symmetry; imbalance, *inequality*; projection, *map*; thrust, stress, strain, shear; bias, warp; buckle, bend, screw, twist, *convolution;* grimace, snarl, *gesture.*

deformity, monstrosity, abortion; *curvature;* clubfoot, rickets, *blemish, eyesore.*

Adj. *distorted,* irregular, asymmetric, scalene, disproportionate; weighted; grotesque; *amorphous;* gnarled, wry, awry, askew, crazy, crooked, cock-eyed, *oblique.*

deformed, ugly, *unsightly; imperfect;* misshapen, misbegotten; bandy, bow-legged, knock-kneed; round-shouldered; stumpy, *short;* haggard, gaunt, *lean;* bloated.

Vb. *distort,* disproportion, weight, bias; contort, screw, twist, knot, *twine;* bend, warp, *crinkle;* spring, buckle, crumple; strain, sprain, skew, wrest, torture, rack, *derange;* botch, *deform;* mangle, batter, *impair;* pervert, *misrepresent;* misconstrue, *misinterpret;* writhe, *wriggle;* wince, grimace, *gesticulate;* snarl, scowl, frown, *be sullen.*

242 Angularity

N. *angularity,* crotchet, bracket, crook, hook; bend, scythe, sickle, scimitar, *curvature;* chevron, zigzag; elbow, knee; shoulder blade, withers, *camber;* knuckle, ankle, groin, *joint;* crutch, crotch, fluke, *cross;* fork, *crossing;* corner, nook, niche, recess, *compartment;* nose, *protuberance;* wedge, arrowhead, *sharp point;* broad arrow, cusp; *fold;* indentation, *notch.*

angle.

angular *measure,* trigonometry; angular elevation, angular distance, angular velocity; zenith distance; second, degree, minute; altimeter; level, theodolite; transit circle; sextant, quadrant; protractor, set square.

angular *figure,* triangle; parallelogram, rectangle, square; quadrilateral, lozenge, diamond; rhombus, rhomboid; trapezium, trapezoid; polygon, pentagon, hexagon, octagon; cube, pyramid, wedge; prism.

Adj. *angular,* hooked, aquiline; crooked, zigzag, *oblique;* jagged, serrated; akimbo, knock-kneed; forked.

angulated, triangular, trilateral; cuneiform; square, foursquare, quadrilateral; trapezoid; multilateral.

Vb. *make angular,* angle, corner; hook, crook, bend; wrinkle, fold, *crinkle;* zigzag, *be oblique;* fork, branch, ramify, diverge; *deviate.*

243 Curvature

N. *curvature;* inward curve; outward curve; *fold;* sweep, *obeisance;* swerve, detour, *deviation;* downward bend, *descent;* curling, *convolution; deformity.*

curve, camber; elbow; turn, bend, U-turn; horseshoe; bay, *gulf;* figure of eight, *loop;* tracery, curl, *convolution;* festoon, swag, *pattern;* bow, rainbow, *arc;* arch, arcade, vault, *dome;* sickle, scimitar, crescent, meniscus, lens; trajectory, parabola, hyperbola, *caustic;* instep; swan neck.

Adj. *curved,* bent, *oblique;* bosomy, wavy; aquiline, *angular;* bent back; circumflex; vaulted; bow-legged; hooked; *round;* crescent, lunar.

Vb. *be curved,* curve, swerve, bend, loop, camber, arch, sweep, sag, swag, give, hang; *twine; leap.*

make *curved,* bend, crook, *make angular;* turn, round, *make round;* inflect; ben[...], back, *invert;* bow, incline, stoop; *fol[...] deflect;* arch; coil, *twine;* loop, curl, wav[...] crinkle; make figures of eight.

244 Straightness

N. *straightness; hardness;* chord, radiu[...] line; straight line, beeline; Roman roa[...] straight stretch, straight, reach; sho[...] cut, *short distance.*

Adj. *straight,* direct, even, right, true; lir[...] ear; rectilinear; perpendicular, *vertica[...]* stiff, inflexible, *rigid;* dead straigh[...] unswerving.

Vb. *be straight,* steer straight; go straigh[...] turn neither right nor left.

straighten, make straight; *flatten;* unbend [...] bow); *smooth;* stretch tight; *unrave[...]* unroll, unfold, *evolve.*

Adv. *straight on,* directly, *towards;* straigh[...] plumb.

245 Circularity: simple circularity

N. *circularity,* roundness, *rotundity.*

circle, circumference, *outline;* great circle[...] equator; orb; roundel; plate, sauce[...] round, disc, discus; coin, button, sequir[...] washer, hoop, ring; eye, iris; eyelet, loop[...] hole, *orifice;* circular course, circuit, cir[...] cus, roundabout; *zodiac;* fairy ring[...] smoke ring.

loop, figure of eight, *convolution;* bow, kno[...] ringlet, curl, *hair;* circlet, bracele[...] torque, *finery;* crown, coronet, *regalia[...]* corona, halo; wreath, garland; collar[...] necklace; band, cordon, sash, girdle, *bel[...] girdle;* lasso, halter.

wheel, pulley, castor; hub, tyre; rubber tyre[...] inner tube, roller.

arc, semicircle; crescent, rainbow, *curve[...]* sector, quadrant, sextant; ellipse, oval[...] ovule.

orbit, cycle, circuit, ecliptic; *circulation.*

Adj. *round,* circular, cyclic; annular; oval[...] elliptic, ovoid; spherical, *rotund.*

Vb. *be round,* make round, turn.

go *round,* girdle, encircle, *surround[...]* describe a circle, *outline;* move round[...] circulate, orbit, *circle.*

246 Convolution: complex circularity

N. *convolution;* torsion; reticulation, *net[...] work;* twine, twist, *fibre;* ripple, *wave[...]* wrinkle, *fold;* indentation, ragged edge[...] *notch;* undulation, *curve.*

coil, roll, twist; turban; spiral, helix; screw[...] worm, corkscrew; spring, whorl, ammo[...] nite; whirlpool, eddy, *vortex;* tendril[...] *plant;* scollop, *edging;* kink, curl; ringlet[...] *hair;* scroll, flourish, twirl, squiggle.

meandering; meander; *deviation;* labyrinth[...] maze; switchback, zigzag.

serpent, snake, eel, worm, *reptile.*

Adj. *convoluted;* cranky; sinuous, tortuous[...] ragged.

labyrinthine, serpentine; turning, *circu[...] itous.*

snaky, serpentine, vermiform.

undulatory, rolling; switchback; wavy[...] curly, frizzy; ragged; flamboyant.

coiled, spiral; wound.

intricate, involved, complicated, *complex.*

Vb. *twine,* twist, twirl, roll, coil, corkscrew[...] spiral, *rotate;* wreathe, entwine; bend.

rinkle, crimp, frizz, crisp, curl; wave, undulate, ripple; wrinkle, corrugate, *fold*; indent, scollop, *notch*; crumple, *distort*.
meander, loop, snake, zigzag, corkscrew. See *twine*.
wriggle, writhe, squirm, shake; worm.
Adv. in and out, round about.

247 Rotundity

N. *rotundity*, roundness; *circularity*.
sphere, globe, spheroid; hollow sphere, bladder; balloon, *airship*; soap bubble, *bubble*; ball, football, wood (bowls), marble, alley; cannonball, bullet, shot, pellet; bead, pill, pea, boll, puffball, globule; drop, droplet, blot; vesicle, bulb, onion, knob, pommel, *swelling*; boulder, rolling stone; hemisphere, hump, mushroom, *dome*; round head.
cylinder, roll, rolypoly; roller, rolling pin; round, rung; round tower, column; bole, trunk, stalk; pipe, drainpipe, *tube*; funnel, chimneypot; round box, pillbox; drum, barrel.
cone, shadow cone, penumbra; *dome*; cornet, horn, *cup*; top, pear shape.
Adj. round, rotund; spherical; globular, global; beady; ovoid; cylindrical; conical; *convex*; pot-bellied.
Vb. round, make spherical; sphere, globe, ball, bead; balloon, *be convex*; roll, *rotate*.

248 Convexity

N. *convexity*; *curvature*; bulge, bump; projection, protuberance, *prominence*; swelling; *bulk*; lens.
swelling, bump, lump, bulge, growth, excrescence, gall, knot, node, nodule; knuckle; emphysema; tumour; bunion, corn, wart, verruca; boil, carbuncle; pimple, blister, vesicle; polyp, adenoids, piles; proud flesh, weal, welt; cauliflower ear; drop, *sphere*; air bubble, *bubble*; boss, knob, nub; bulb, button, bud; belly, potbelly, corporation, paunch, *bulk*; billow, swell, *wave*.
bosom, bust, breast; boobs, bristols, knockers; nipple, pap, dug, teat, udder; thorax, chest; cuirass, breastplate.
dome, cupola, vault, *roof*; brow, forehead, *face*; skull, cranium, bald head, *head*; hemisphere, arch of heaven; mound; hillock, *small hill*; molehill, mushroom, umbrella.
earthwork, tumulus; tell, *monument*; barrow, hill fort; embankment.
camber, gentle curve, *curve*; arch, bow, rainbow; hump, humpback, hunchback, *deformity*; calf, elbow.
Adj. convex, rotund; lumpy; bosomy; ballooning, bouffant; swelling, swollen; bloated, potbellied; turgid, tumescent; *rough*.
arched, cambered, *curved*.
Vb. be convex, camber, arch, bow; swell, belly, bulge, bag, balloon; make convex, emboss, chase.

249 Prominence

N. *prominence*, eminence, *high land*; *visibility*; solar prominence, solar flare, tongue, tongue of flame.
projection, salient, salient angle, *angle*; forefinger, bowsprit, outrigger; tongue of land, spit, point, mull, promontory, headland, ness, *land*; peninsula, *island*; spur, foothill, jetty, mole, breakwater,

pier, *shelter*; outwork, *fortification*; pilaster, buttress, *prop*; shelf, sill, ledge, balcony; eaves, *roof*; overhang, rake; flange, lip, *edge*; nozzle, spout; tang, tongue; tenon, *joint*; snag, stump, outcrop; landmark, *high structure*.
protuberance, bump, *swelling*; prominent feature; nose, snout, conk; bill, beak, rostrum; muzzle, proboscis, trunk; antenna, *feeler*; chin, jaw, brow, beetle brow, *face*; figurehead, *prow*; horn, antler, *sharp point*.
relievo, relief, low relief; cameo, *sculpture*.
Adj. projecting, prominent, salient, bold; protuberant, pop-eyed; toothy; *rough*.
Vb. jut, project, protrude, pout, pop, *be visible*; roughen; expand; overhang, hang.

250 Concavity

N. *concavity, curvature*; depression, dint, dent; impression, stamp, imprint, footprint, *trace*; intaglio, *engraving*; furrow, indentation, *notch*; gap, *interval*.
cavity, hollow, niche, nook, cranny, recess, corner, *compartment*; hole, den, burrow, warren; chasm, abyss, *depth*; cave, cavern; grotto, alcove, *arbour*; bowl, cup, saucer, basin, trough, *vessel*; sump, *sink*; cell, follicle, pore, *orifice*; dimple, pockmark; saltcellar, armpit; honeycomb, sponge; funnel, tunnel, *tube*; groove, mortise, socket, pocket, *furrow*; sinus; bay, cove, creek, inlet, *gulf*; channel, riverbed, ditch, moat, canal, *conduit*; dip, depression, pothole, crater, pit.
valley, vale, dell, cwm, corrie, cirque, river valley; glen, dip, depression; ravine, gill, gorge, canyon, *gap*.
excavation, dugout, grave, *tomb*; opencast mining; shaft, well, mine, pit, colliery, quarry, *store*; gallery, sap, trench, burrow, warren; underground railway, tube, *tunnel*; dig, cutting, cut.
excavator, miner; dredger; sapper.
Adj. concave, hollow, cavernous; vaulted; sunk, sunken; cellular; honeycombed; spongy, porous.
Vb. be concave, retreat, retire; cup.
make concave, depress, stamp, impress; buckle, dent, dint; crush; excavate, hollow, dig, spade, delve, scrape, scratch, scrabble, trench, *groove*; mine, sap, undermine, burrow, tunnel, bore; honeycomb, perforate, *pierce*; *eject*; hole, pit, pockmark; indent, *notch*; sink a shaft, make a hole.

251 Sharpness

N. *sharpness*, acuity, sting; prickliness; suddenness.
sharp point, sting, prick, point, cusp, *vertex*; nail, tack, staple, *fastening*; nib, tag, pin, needle, stylus, bodkin, skewer, spit, broach; awl, gimlet, drill, auger; arrow, shaft, bolt, quarrel, arrowhead; barb, fluke, rapier, lance, pike, *spear*; fishing spear, gaff, harpoon; dagger, dirk, stiletto, *side arms*; spike, barbed wire; spur, goad, *incentive*; fork, prong, tine, pick, horn, antler; claw, talon, *nippers*; spire, steeple; peak, crag, *summit*.
prickle, thorn, bramble, thistle, nettle, cactus; bristle, *hair*; beard; porcupine, hedgehog; spine, needle, quill.
tooth, tusk, fang; first teeth; eyetooth, incisor, molar, premolar teeth; front teeth, set of teeth, denture, false teeth, plate, bridge; comb, saw; cog, ratchet, sprocket,

notch.

sharp edge, edge tool; jagged edge, broken glass; cutlery, steel, razor; blade, razor blade; share, ploughshare, farm tool; spade, mattock, trowel, shovel; scythe, sickle, hook, billhook; cutter, lawn mower; scissors, shears, clippers, secateurs, surgical knife, scalpel; chisel, plane, spokeshave, scraper; knife, carving knife; penknife, machete; chopper, cleaver, wedge; hatchet, axe, adze; battleaxe, axe; sword, broadsword, cutlass, scimitar, side arms.

sharpener, whetstone, grindstone; hone, steel, file, strop; emery, emery paper, sandpaper.

Adj. sharp, keen, acute; cutting, pointed; barbed; spiny, thorny; prickly, bristly, bearded; hairy; craggy, jagged, rough.
toothed; toothy; dental; serrated.

tapering, conical; horned.

Vb. be sharp, have a point, prick, sting; bristle with; have an edge, bite, cut; taper, come to a point, converge.

sharpen, edge, whet, hone, grind, file, strop; barb, spur, point; stud.

252 Bluntness

N. bluntness; lack of bite; blunt instrument, foil; blunt edge, blade, flat.

Adj. unsharpened; blunt, obtuse; rusty, dull; pointless; lacking bite; stubby, snub, square; round; flat, bluff.

Vb. blunt, make blunt, turn; dull, rust; be blunt, pull, scrape, tear.

253 Smoothness

N. smoothness, smooth texture; silk, satin, velvet; swansdown; smooth hair; smooth surface, mahogany, marble, glass, ice; dance floor, ice rink; lawn, plumb wicket, bowling green; tarmac, asphalt, paving; polish, varnish, gloss, glaze, finish; slipway, slide; smooth water, calm.

smoother, roller, steamroller; bulldozer; rolling pin; iron; mangle, wringer, press, plane, spokeshave, draw knife, sharp edge; rake, harrow; comb, brush, hairbrush; sandpaper, emery board; file; polish, varnish, enamel, facing; grease, oil, grease gun, lubricant.

Adj. smooth, uniform; slippery; greasy, buttery; shiny; soft, suave, bland; silky, silken, satiny; downy, woolly, fleecy; marble, glassy; bald, clean-shaven; sleek, slick, unruffled; plane, even, level, flush, flat; glassy, quiet, calm, still; blunt.

Vb. smooth, remove friction, streamline; oil, grease, butter, lubricate; plane, even, level; rake, comb; file, rub; roll, calender, press, iron, flatten; mow, shave, cut, shorten; unravel; starch, launder, clean; shine, burnish, make bright; buff, polish, glaze, wax, varnish, coat; pave, tarmac.
go smoothly, glide, float, roll, bowl along; slip, slide, skid; skate, ski; coast.

254 Roughness

N. roughness, asperity; broken ground; rough water, wave; rough air, turbulence, wind; broken glass, sharp edge; saw edge, notch; sierra, high land; rough going, dirt road; ripple, ripple mark, fold; rut, furrow; coarse grain; rough surface, washboard, grater, file, sandpaper, emery paper; rough texture, tweed, homespun, textile; gooseflesh; rough skin, chap, crack; undergrowth, wood; stubble, burr,

bristle, prickle.

hair, filament; thatch, fuzz, wool; crop, mop, mane, fleece; bristle, stubble, five o'clock shadow; locks, tresses, ringlet, tight curl; kiss curl; strand, plait, braid, pigtail, ponytail; topknot, forelock, dreadlocks; fringe, quiff, roll, French pleat, bun, chignon; false hair, hairpiece, switch, wig, toupee; thin hair, wisp; beard, beaver, goatee, imperial, Van Dyke; whiskers, face fungus, sideboards, moustache, toothbrush, handlebar; cilia; wool, fur, skin; tuft, flock; mohair, cashmere, Angora, fibre; pile, nap; velvet, plush; floss, fluff, fuzz, thistledown, lining.

plumage, pinion, wing; quill, barb, web; ruff, frill, plume, panache, crest; finery.

Adj. rough, uneven, broken; choppy; bumpy; chunky, crisp, roughcast; lumpy; stony, nodular; gnarled, cross-grained; coarse; cracked; craggy, jagged; scabrous, scaly; unkempt.

hairy; woolly, fleecy, furry; hirsute, shaggy, shagged, shock-headed; bristly, sharp; bearded; curly, frizzy, fuzzy, woolly.

downy; smooth; feathery, fledged.

fleecy, woolly.

Vb. be rough, bristle; creep (of flesh); scratch, catch; jolt, bump, jerk.

roughen, roughcast, mill, indent, notch; stud, boss; crisp, corrugate, wrinkle; ripple, crinkle; disorder, ruffle, tousle, derange; rumple, crumple, fold.

Adv. on edge.

255 Notch

N. notch, saw edge; indentation; nick, snip, cut, gash; gap; indent, dent, dimple; scollop, pattern; sprocket, cog, ratchet, cogwheel, saw, hacksaw, circular saw; tooth.

Adj. notched, jagged, sharp; serrated.

Vb. notch, tooth, cog; nick, blaze, score; scratch, scotch, scarify, bite, slice, cut; indent; jag, pink, slash; dent, mill; roughen; pinch, snip, crimp, fold.

256 Fold

N. fold; facing, revers, hem; lapel, cuff; turnup, dog's ear; plait, ply, pleat, tuck; gather, pucker, ruffle; flounce, frill; crumple, rumple, crease; wrinkle, ruck, frown, lines, age; crinkle; joint, elbow.

Adj. folded; dog-eared; turn-over.

Vb. fold, double, roll; crease, pleat; corrugate, furrow, wrinkle, groove; rumple, crumple, derange; curl, frizzle, frizz; crinkle; pucker, purse; ruffle, gather, frill, ruck, smock; tuck, kilt; hem, cuff; enfold, wrap, swathe, enclose; furl, reef.

257 Furrow

N. furrow, groove, chase, slot, slit, mortise; crack, chink, cranny, gap; trough, hollow, cavity; flute, fluting; gash, slash; scratch, score; streak, stripe; wake, rut, trace; gutter, runnel, ditch, trench, dugout, moat, channel, conduit; ravine, valley; corduroy, washboard; ripple, wave.

Adj. furrowed, striated; wavy, flowing.

Vb. groove, slot, rifle; chase; gash, scratch, score, incise, cut; claw, tear, wound; streak; grave, carve, etch, engrave; furrow, plough, channel, rut, wrinkle, line; corrugate, fold.

258 Opening

N. opening; yawn; splitting; hiatus, space, interval, gap; aperture, split, crack, leak; hole, potato; hollow, cavity; pocket.

perforation, piercing, puncture, acupuncture; bore, calibre; eyelet.

porosity, sponge; sieve, sifter, riddle, screen; strainer, colander; grater; honeycomb.

orifice, aperture, slot; oral cavity, mouth, gob, trap, jaws, muzzle; throat, gullet; sucker; mouthpiece, flue pipe, air pipe; nozzle, spout, vent, outlet; blower, blowhole; nasal cavity, nostril; inlet, outlet; small orifice; pore; hole, crater, pothole, cavity; manhole, armhole, buttonhole; punch hole, pigeonhole, compartment; eye, eye of a needle, eyelet; ring, loop.

window; shop window, glass front; loophole, fortification; lattice, grille; rose window, church interior; light, fanlight, skylight, sunshine roof; companion, cabin window, port, porthole; peephole; squint; car window, windscreen, windshield; window frame, sash, mullion, transom; window pane, transparency.

doorway, archway; doorstep, threshold, entrance; approach, drive, drive-in, entry; exit; passage, corridor, gangway, drawbridge, access; gate, portal, porch; door, lychgate; back door, postern, rear; small door, wicket; scuttle, hatch; trapdoor, companionway; stairwell; door jamb, gatepost, lintel; doorkeeper.

open space, space; yard, court, place; opening, clearing, glade; panorama, vista, view; rolling downs, landscape, open country, plain; alley, aisle, gangway, thoroughfare, passage; estuary, gulf.

tunnel; subway, underpass, underground railway, tube; Channel Tunnel; mine, shaft, pit, gallery; cave, cavity; bolthole, rabbit hole, dwelling; funnel, cone; sewer, drain.

tube, pipe, duct, conduit; pipette; tubing, piping, pipeline, hose; artery, vein, capillary; colon, gut; funnel, fistula.

chimney, chimneypot, chimney stack, smokestack, funnel; flue; volcano, furnace.

opener, key; handle; corkscrew, tin opener, purgative; password, open sesame; passport, safe conduct; pass, ticket, permit.

perforator; gimlet, corkscrew; auger, drill, burr, bit; probe; bodkin, needle, awl, bradawl, sharp point; pin, nail, fastening; skewer, spit, broach, stiletto, weapon; punch, stapler; dibble; pickaxe, pick.

Adj. open, patent, manifest; ajar; accessible; agape; opening; blooming.

perforated, perforate; honeycombed; shot through.

porous, spongy, leaky.

tubular; cylindrical, rotund; vascular, capillary.

Vb. open, unfold, unpack, undo; unlock, admit; uncover, bare, doff; unstop, uncork; unrip, disunite; lay open, show; force open, force; cut open, enlarge a hole, ream; fly open, split, gape, yawn; burst, explode; start, leak; space; deploy; separate, part, hold apart; bloom.

pierce, transfix, impale; gore, run through, stick, prick, lance, bayonet, spear, wound; spike, skewer, spit; prick, puncture, tattoo; probe, stab, poke; inject; perforate, hole, riddle, pepper, honeycomb; nail, drive, strike; punch; hull (a ship), scuttle; tap, drain, extract; bore, drill; burrow, tunnel, mine, make concave; cut through, penetrate, enter.

Adv. openly, patently.

259 Closure

N. closure; stoppage; contraction, strangulation; blockade; embolism, constipation; dead end, cul-de-sac, impasse, blank wall, road block, obstacle; blind gut.

stopper, cork, plug, bung, peg, spill, spigot; ramrod, piston; valve, wedge, wad, tampon; wadding, padding, stuffing, lining; dummy, gag, muzzle, fetter; shutter, screen; tight bandage, tourniquet, compressor; damper, choke, cut-out; tap, stopcock; top, lid, cap, cover, seal, covering; lock, key, bolt, bar, fastening; door, gate, doorway; cordon, fence.

doorkeeper, doorman, porter, janitor; commissionaire; sentry, night watchman, protector; warden, guard, keeper; jailer, turnkey.

Adj. closed; barred; impervious, impermeable, dense; impenetrable, impassable, impracticable, secluded; blank; drawn tight, drawn together.

sealed off; close, stuffy, muggy, fusty, insalubrious; staunch, tight, airtight, watertight, proof, waterproof, invulnerable.

Vb. close, shut, seal; clinch, fix, bind, make tight, tighten; cover; make all tight; clap to, slam, bang (a door); lock, fasten, snap, snap to; plug, caulk, cork, stopper; button, join; knit; clench (fist); block, dam, staunch, choke, throttle, strangle, smother, asphyxiate, obstruct; blockade, besiege; enclose, surround, circumscribe; trap, bolt, bar, imprison.

260 Motion: successive change of place

N. motion, change of position, change; movement, going, move, march; speed rate, speed, pace, tempo; locomotion, kinetic energy, motive power; forward motion, advance, progress, headway, progression; backward motion, recession; motion towards, approach; shift, deviation; egress; upward motion, rising, ascent; downward motion, descent, plunge; motion round, rotation, evolution; irregular motion, stir, bustle, unrest, activity; rapid motion, velocity; slow motion; regular motion, continuity; rhythm; preceding; motion after, following, pursuit; conduction; current, flow, flux, drift, stream; course, career, run; traffic, traffic movement, flow of traffic, passing along; transit, passage; transportation, transport; running, walking, riding; travel, land travel, water travel, air travel; gliding, rolling; manoeuvre, footwork; bodily movement, exercise, athletics; gesture; cinematography, motion picture, cinema; kinetics, dynamics.

gait, walk, port, carriage, conduct; tread, tramp, footfall, stamp; pace, step, stride; run, lope, jog, jog trot, dance step, hop, skip, jump, leap; skid, slide, waddle, shuffle, swagger, proud step, stalk, strut, goosestep, formality; march, double; trot, amble, canter, gallop.

Adj. moving, in motion, motor; mobile; progressive; locomotive; passing, restless, active; erratic, runaway; kinetic.

Vb. be in motion, move, go, hie, gang, wend, trail; gather way, navigate; budge, stir; flutter, wave, flap, hang; march, tramp, walk; tread; trip, dance, *leap*; shuffle, waddle; toddle, patter; run, *move fast*; roll, taxi; stream, drift, *flow*; paddle, row; skitter, slide, slither, skate, ski, toboggan, glide; fly, frisk, flit, dart, hover; climb, *ascend*; sink, plunge, *descend*; cruise, steam, chug, keep going, proceed; *progress*; pass through, *pass*; make a move, shift, dodge, duck, shift about, tack, manoeuvre, *deviate*; twist, *wriggle*; creep, crawl; hover about, *wait*; move house; *interchange*; make room; travel, stray, *wander*.

move, impart motion, set going, power; *operate*; stir, jerk, pluck, twitch, *agitate*; budge, shift, manhandle, trundle, roll, wheel, *displace*; push, shove, *impel*; drive, hustle, *hasten*; tug, pull, *draw*; fling, throw, *propel*; convey, transport, *transfer*; *send*; bring together; scatter, *disperse*; raise, uplift, *elevate*; drop, *let fall*; motion, gesture, *gesticulate*; transpose, *interchange*.

Adv. *on the move*, underway.

261 Quiescence

N. *quiescence*, subsidence, *cessation*; rest, pause, truce, standstill, *lull*; stand, stoppage, halt; fix, deadlock, lock; full stop, *stop*; embargo, freeze, *prohibition*; fixity, *hardness*; equilibrium, *stability*; trance, faint, *insensibility*.

quietude, quiet, hush, *silence*; peace; rest, *repose*; eternal rest, *death*; slumber, *sleep*; calm; dead quiet; armchair travel; *composure*; passivity; *pacifist*; *moderator*.

resting place, quarters; roof, *home, inn*; shelter, haven, *refuge*; place of rest, pillow, *bed*; *goal*; last rest, grave, *tomb*.

Adj. *quiescent*, quiet, still; asleep, *sleepy*; at rest, becalmed; at anchor; at a stand, at a standstill, idle; unemployed, *unused*; dormant, dying, *dead*; standing, stagnant, static, stationary, *inert*; sitting, sedentary; *supine*; housebound, *restrained*; settled, stay-at-home, *content*; *cautious*; unmoved, *indifferent*.

tranquil, secluded; peaceful, restful; easygoing, *leisurely*; uneventful, without incident, *uniform*; calm, airless, glassy, *smooth*; sunny, halcyon, *palmy*; at ease, comfortable; unruffled, serene.

still, flat, *tasteless*; immobile, motionless; expressionless, deadpan, *impassive*; steady; standing still, rooted, *fixed*; immovable, unable to move, stuck; stiff, frozen, *rigid*; benumbed, numb, *insensible*; quiet, *silent*; stock-still.

Vb. *be quiescent*, subside, *decrease*; *be silent*; stand still, keep quiet; stagnate, vegetate, *be inert*; stand, mark time, *wait*; stay put, sit tight, stand pat, remain, abide, *stay*; stand to, lie to, ride at anchor; tarry, *pause*; rest, take breath, *repose*; retire, go to bed, *sleep*; settle, *place oneself*; stay at home, *be unsociable*; ground, stick fast; catch, jam, lodge; stand fast, stand firm; be at a standstill, *cease*.

come *to rest*, stop, hold, stop short, freeze, *halt*; *decelerate*; anchor, alight, *land*; relax, rest, pause, *repose*.

bring *to rest*, quiet, quieten, quell, hush, *silence*; lull, soothe, *assuage*; lull to sleep, cradle, rock; let alone, let well alone, *avoid*; bring to a standstill, bring to, lay to, heave to; brake, *retard*; stay.

Adv. *at a stand*, at a halt.

Int. stop! stay! halt! whoa! hold! hold hard! hold on! hold it! don't move!

262 Land travel

N. *land travel*, travel; tourism; walking, riding, driving, motoring; journey, voyage, peregrination, odyssey; course, passage, sweep; pilgrimage; quest, expedition, safari, trek, field trip; reconnaissance, visit, trip, tour, circuit, turn, round, patrol; round trip; jaunt, hop, spin; trip, drive, lift, excursion, outing, airing, ramble, constitutional.

wandering, wanderlust; vagrancy; rambling, walkabout; migration, *egress*; transmigration, *passage*.

pedestrianism, walking, footing it; walkabout; walk, promenade, constitutional stroll, saunter, amble, ramble; hike, tramp, march, walking tour; run, cross-country run, jog, trot, lope, *gait*; paddle, foot race, marathon, *racing*; stalk, *chase*; somnambulism.

marching, campaign; advance, retreat; march, quick march, march past, parade, cavalcade, procession, *formality*; column, file, train, caravan.

equitation, manège, dressage, *skill*; point-to-point racing, *contest*; horse racing, riding, *athletics*; gait.

conveyance, lift, escalator; *foot*; horseback, mount, *horse*; bicycle, car, bus, train, coach, taxi, ambulance, *vehicle*; traffic, *passing along*.

leg, limb; shank, shin, calf; thigh, ham; knee, kneecap; *prop*; stump, wooden leg, *substitute*.

itinerary, route, *way*; march, course, *direction*; route map, plan, chart, *map*; guide, timetable; milestone, signpost; halt, *stop*; stopover; terminus.

Adj. *travelling*, vagrant, dusty, *dirty*; travelled; passing through, visiting, *passing*; nomad, floating, unsettled, restless; rootless, *extraneous*; footloose, errant, rambling, wandering; peripatetic; vagabond; walking, pedestrian; locomotive, *moving*.

legged, bow-legged, leggy, *tall*; spindly, lean.

Vb. *travel*, fare, journey; tour, visit, explore, *discover*; get around, knock about; pilgrimage; make a journey, trek; hike; fare forth, take wing, *depart*; migrate, emigrate, immigrate, settle, *place oneself*; shuttle, commute; go to, hie to, repair to, resort to; *arrive, visit*; go; wend, tread a path; plough through; *sustain*; course, race, post, *move fast*; proceed, advance, *progress*; coast, glide, slide, skate, ski, skim, roll along.

traverse, cross, range, pass through, *pass*; go round, *circle*; patrol; scout, reconnoitre, *scan*; scour, sweep, sweep through.

wander, migrate; rove, roam, bum around; ramble, amble, stroll, saunter, potter, dawdle, walk about, trail around; gallivant, hover, flit about; prowl, skulk, *lurk*; straggle, trail; *stray*.

walk, step, tread, pace, stride; *move fast*; strut, stalk, prance, mince, *be proud*; tread lightly, tiptoe, trip, skip, dance, *leap*; lumber, clump, stamp, tramp, stamp-sostep; toddle, patter, pad; totter, stagger, lurch, reel, stumble, *oscillate*; limp, hobble, waddle, shuffle, shamble, dawdle; paddle, wade; foot it, hoof it, hike, footslog; plod, stump, trudge, jog; go, perambulate; march, quick march, slow march; troop; file, file past, defile, *come after*; walk behind, *follow*; precede.

ride, mount, take horse, hack; trot, amble,

canter, gallop; prance, caper, passage; cycle, bicycle, bike, motorcycle; drive, motor; *fly*; take a lift, hitchhike.

Adv. *on foot*; en route; by road, by rail.

Int. come along! move along there! get along! get going! get out! git! go away! be off! buzz off! hop it! skedaddle! scram!

263 Traveller

N. *traveller*; adventurer, *mariner*; air traveller; pioneer, pathfinder, *precursor*; mountaineer, *climber*; pilgrim; globe-trotter, tourist, *spectator*; tripper; holidaymaker, visitor; roundsman, *pedlar*; commercial traveller, *seller*; messenger, *courier*; daily traveller, commuter.

wanderer, migrant, bird of passage, visitant, *bird*; floating population, nomad, bedouin, Romany, Bohemian; ranger; wandering minstrel, *entertainer*; rolling stone, drifter, vagrant, vagabond, tramp; hobo, bum, bummer; beachcomber; emigrant, refugee, deportee, exile, *foreigner*; runaway, fugitive; *solitary*; waif, stray, destitute, street beggar, *poor person*; Wandering Jew.

pedestrian, foot passenger; runner, *contender*; toddler; wader; *infantry*; sleepwalker.

rider; horseman, equestrian; *courier*; cavalier, knight, knight errant, *cavalry*; hunt, huntsman, *hunter*; jockey, show jumper, *contender*; breaker; cowboy; circus rider, trick rider, *athlete*; motor-cyclist, moped rider; passenger.

driver, drover, muleteer; coachman, whip; carter; car driver, chauffeur; joy rider; *beginner*; taxi driver; bus driver; train driver, stoker, fireman; guard, conductor, ticket collector; pilot.

264 Water travel

N. *water travel*; seafaring, nautical life; sailing; voyage, cruise, sail; course, run, passage, crossing; sea trip, breath of sea air, *refreshment*; way, headway, steerage way, seaway, *motion*; leeway, *deviation*; wake, track, wash, backwash, *eddy*; ocean track, steamer route, sea lane, *route*; boat, sailing ship, *ship*; sailor, *mariner*.

navigation; plane sailing, compass reading, dead reckoning, *measurement*; *skill*; nautical experience, weather eye; naval tactics, *tactics*.

aquatics, sailing; yacht racing, *racing*; surf riding, *sport*; swimming, floating, stroke, crawl, butterfly; *plunge*.

sailing aid, sextant, quadrant, *angular measure*; chronometer; log, line; lead, plummet, *depth*; anchor, *safeguard*; compass, needle, card; binnacle; radar; helm, wheel, tiller, rudder; sea mark, buoy, lighthouse, lightship, *signpost*; chart, *map*; nautical almanac.

propeller, screw, twin screw, blade, rotor; paddle wheel; oar, sweep, paddle, scull; pole, fin, flipper, *limb*; canvas, sail.

Adj. *seafaring*, sea, salty; nautical, naval, *marine*; sailing; at sea, afloat, waterborne, seaborne; rolling; seasick, green; seaworthy, tight, snug; navigable, deep.

swimming, floating, sailing; afloat; aquatic, like a fish; amphibian.

Vb. *go to sea*; become a sailor; live afloat; go sailing, boat, yacht; launch, launch a ship.

voyage, sail; take ship, book a passage, embark, put to sea, set sail; *traverse*; disembark, land, *arrive*; cruise; navigate, steam, ply, run, tramp, ferry; coast; roll, pitch, toss, tumble, wallow, *oscillate*.

navigate, man a ship, crew; put to sea, set sail; launch; weigh anchor; raise steam, hoist sail, spread canvas; carry sail; set a course; *orientate*; pilot, steer, captain, *direct*; stroke, cox; square; change course, veer, yaw, *deviate*; put about, wear ship, *turn round*; scud, *move fast*; fall to leeward; luff; beat to windward, tack, weather; round, double a point, circumnavigate, *circle*; be caught amidships; list, *be oblique*; turn turtle, capsize, overturn, *invert*; keep afloat, escape; seek refuge; lie to, lay to, heave to, *bring to rest*; take soundings, *measure*; await; tow, haul, warp, *draw*; ground, run aground, wreck, *destroy*; sight land, make a landfall, *approach*; make port; cast anchor, moor, dock, disembark, *land*; outmanoeuvre, *obstruct*; foul, collide; back, go astern, *regress*; surface, break water, *emerge*; dive, plunge; shoot, shoot a bridge, *pass*.

row; pull, stroke, scull; feather; catch a crab; punt; paddle, canoe; boat.

swim, float, sail, ride; scud, skim, skitter; surf, aquaplane; tread water; dive, plunge; bathe, dip, duck; wade, paddle, splash about, get wet, *be wet*.

Adv. *under way*, all aboard.

Int. ship ahoy! avast! belay there! all aboard! man overboard! yo-heave-ho! hard aport! hard astarboard! steady as she goes! land ahoy!

265 Mariner

N. *mariner*, sailor, seaman, seafaring man; salt; tar, Jack Tar, limey; landlubber; skipper, master mariner, master, mate, bosun; able seaman, *expert*; deckhand; cabin boy, *servant*; crew, complement, men, watch, *personnel*; trawler, whaler; privateer, buccaneer, sea king, Viking, pirate; sea scout, sea cadet; Ancient Mariner; Neptune, *sea god*.

navigator, pilot, sailing master, helmsman, steersman, quartermaster, cox, *leader*; lookout man; reefer; compass, binnacle, *sailing aid*.

nautical personnel, marine, submariner, naval cadet, rating, *naval man*; petty officer, midshipman, lieutenant, commander, captain, commodore, admiral, *naval officer*; Admiralty, Sea Lord; Trinity House, lighthouse keeper, coastguard, *protector*; river police, naval patrol.

boatman, waterman, wet bob; galley slave; oar, oarsman; gondolier; bargee; stevedore, docker, longshoreman; lock keeper.

Adj. *seamanlike*, like a sailor, *expert*; nautical, naval, *marine*.

266 Aeronautics

N. *aeronautics*, aerodynamics; ballooning; aerospace; rocketry, *rocket*; flight, *velocity*; aviation, flying; gliding, skydiving, free fall; flypast, formation flying, aerobatics, *ostentation*; vapour trail; spin, roll, side-slip; nose dive; crash dive, crash, *descent*; pancake, landing, *arrival*; takeoff.

air travel, air transport, airlift, *transport*; air service, airline; airlane, airway, air route, *route*; flight path, line of flight, *direction*; air space, *territory*; takeoff, landing, landing field, airbase; airstrip, runway, tarmac, airfield, aerodrome, airport, heliport; terminal, *goal*; hangar, *stable*; fear of flying.

space *travel*, space flight, *spaceship*; lift-off; orbit; space walk; reentry, soft landing.

aeronaut; glider, sky diver; *soldier*; aviator; astronaut, cosmonaut, space traveller; air traveller, air passenger, jet set, *traveller*; air hostess, *servant*; pilot, copilot; automatic pilot; navigator, air crew; pilot officer, *air officer*; aircraftman, *air force*; air personnel, ground crew, *personnel*; Mercury.

wing, pinion, wing feather, wing spread, *plumage*; aileron.

Adj. *flying, moving*; pinnate, aerial, *airy*; airworthy, airborne; airsick; aerospace.

Vb. *fly, wing*; soar, rise, *ascend*; hover, *hang*; flutter, flit; taxi, clear, climb, circle, *depart*; be airborne, have lift-off; glide, plane; float, drift, drift like thistledown, *be light*; stunt, spin, roll, side-slip; hedgehop, buzz, *be near*; stall, dive, spiral, *plunge*; crash, crash-land, pancake, ditch, tumble; *land*; jump, parachute, eject; orbit; *circle*.

Adv. *in flight*, on the wing.

267 Transference

N. *transference*, change of place; transfer; shift, drift, *deviation*; *interchange*; removal, expulsion; *displacement*; export, *trade*; mutual transfer, *barter*; importation, import; *reception*; logistics; provision; remittance; recall; *extraction*; recovery, *acquisition*; delivery; takeover, *purchase*; conveyance, transfer of property, *transfer*; committal, trust, *commission*; gaol delivery, release, *liberation*; transition; ferry, *passage*; transmigration, *transformation*; transmission, throughput; conduction, convection; communication, contact, *touch*; contagion, infection, *influence*; *translation*.

transport, transportation; conveyance, carriage, shipping, shipment, portage, porterage, haulage, draught; *traction*; cartage, air freight, airlift; means of transport, rail, road, *vehicle*; sea, canal, *ship*; pipeline.

thing *transferred*, jetsam, driftwood, drift, alluvium, detritus, scree, moraine, sediment, deposit; pledge, hostage, trust, *security*; legacy, *gift*; lease, *property*; cargo, load, payload, freight; black ivory, *slave*; shipment, *contents*; goods, luggage, baggage; container; passenger, rider, commuter, *traveller*.

transferrer, testator; sender; shipper, shipping agent, transporter; *merchant*; haulier, removal man, *carrier*; post office, post, *postal communications*; transmitter; vector, carrier (of a disease), *sick person*.

Adj. *transferable*, negotiable; portable; roadworthy, airworthy, seaworthy; conductive; communicable; contagious, *infectious*.

Vb. *transfer*, deliver, *assign*; devise, leave, *bequeath*; commit, *commission*; transmit; hand to, pass to; export, transport, convey, ship, airlift, fly, ferry, *carry*; infect, contaminate, *influence*; conduct; *add*; transfer itself to, adhere, stick, *cohere*.

transpose, shift, move, *displace*; transfer, switch, shunt, shuffle, castle (chess), *interchange*; detach, detail, draft; relegate, deport, expel, *eject*; drag, pull, *draw*; push, shove, impel; *load*; funnel,

transfuse, decant, *empty*; unloa[d], remove, *displace*; shovel, ladle, excavat[e], make concave; transliterate, *translate*.

send, remit, transmit; direct, consig[n], address; post, mail; readdress, forware[d]; order, *require*; detach, detail; send flyin[g], *propel*.

Adv. *in transit*.

268 Carrier

N. *carrier*, haulier, carter; shipper, tran[s]porter; lorry driver, *driver*; delivery va[n], lorry, truck, cart, goods train, *vehicle*; barge, cargo vessel, freighter, tram[p], *ship*; chassis, undercarriage, *prop*; palle[t], container; carrier bag, *bag*; escalator.

bearer, *retainer*, porter, coolie, stevedore[;] letter carrier, carrier pigeon, postman [or] -woman, special messenger, *courier*.

beast *of burden*, pack train; ass, donkey; o[x], bullock, *cattle*; sledge dog, husky; came[l], dromedary; elephant, *mammal*.

horse, equine species, quadruped; dobbi[n], gee-gee; nag; mount, steed; stallion, geld[-]ing, mare, colt, filly, foal; stud horse, brood mare, stud, stable; circus horse[;] roan, grey, bay, chestnut, sorrel, black[,] piebald, skewbald, dun, palomino.

thoroughbred; Arab, Barb; trotter; race[-]horse, stayer; fencer, jumper, hunter.

draught *horse*, punch, pit pony.

warhorse, remount; charger, steed, *ca[v]alry*.

saddle *horse*, cow pony; mount, hack; jade[;] screw, nag; pad; mustang, bronco.

pony, cob.

Adj. *bearing*, carrier, loaded.

equine, horsy; roan, asinine; mulish.

Vb. *carry*, bear, *support*; hump, heave, tote[,] shoulder; fetch, bring, reach; *transport*[;] cart, truck, rail, railroad; ship, waft, raf[t,] lift, fly, *transfer*; carry through, carr[y] across, ferry; convey, conduct, convoy[,] escort, *accompany*; have a rider; b[e] loaded with, be fraught, *be complete*.

269 Vehicle

N. *vehicle*, conveyance, public servic[e] vehicle, transport, vehicular traffic, peda[l] power; litter, stretcher, hurdle, crate[;] ambulance, fire engine; hearse; snow[-]plough, weasel; tractor, bulldoze[r,] amphibian, moon buggy; switchbac[k;] time machine.

sled, sledge, sleigh; bobsleigh, toboggan[;] coaster, ice yacht; surfboard; skate[;] skateboard; runner.

bicycle, cycle, bike, wheel, crate; veloci[-]pede, hobbyhorse, penny-farthing, Ordi[-]nary, Safety; sports model; tourist; tan[-]dem; tricycle, trike; moped; scoote[r;] motorcycle, motorbike, trail bike[;] motorcycle combination, sidecar; invali[d] carriage.

pushcart, perambulator, pram, baby buggy[,] pushchair; bath chair, wheelchair; bar[-]row, wheelbarrow, handcart, go cart[,] trolley, truck, float.

cart; dray, milk float; farm cart; prairi[e] schooner; caravan, trailer, horse-bo[x;] dustcart.

carriage, equipage, turnout, rig; chario[t,] coach; landau, phaeton; buggy; chaise[,] racing chariot; drag, brake; whisky; trap[,] gig, dogcart, governess cart.

war *chariot*, gun carriage, caisson; tank[,] armoured car, *cavalry*; jeep, staff car.

stagecoach, stage, mail coach; post chaise[,] omnibus. See bus.

ab, hackney carriage, hansom, fly; taxi.
us; omnibus, double-decker; motor coach,
coach, minibus.
-am, trolley.
utomobile, car, motor car; motor; limou-
sine; saloon, buggy; convertible; coupé,
sports car; racing car; hatchback, estate
car; jeep; police car, veteran car, vintage
car; banger, bus, jalopy, old crock; beetle,
bubble car; invalid car; minibus.
orry, truck, refuse lorry, dustcart; container lorry, juggernaut; tanker; car
transporter; van; electric van, float.
rain; express train, APT; slow train, goods
train, freightliner; milk train, night mail;
rolling stock, multiple unit; coach, carriage, compartment, smoker, nonsmoker; Pullman, sleeper; restaurant car;
truck, trolley; steam train, live rail; cable
railway, *railway*; Golden Arrow, Orient
Express.
ocomotive, iron horse; steam engine,
shunter, cab, tender; Rocket; traction
engine, steam roller.
onveyor; escalator, moving staircase, moving pavement; shovel, hod, *ladle*; fork,
trowel, *farm tool*; crane.
Adj. *vehicular*; automobile, locomotive;
non-stop, express, through; local.

270 Ship

N. *ship*, vessel, boat, craft; bark, barque;
great ship, little ship, cockleshell; bottom, keel, sail; hooker, tub, hull; hulk;
Golden Hind; steamer, motor vessel;
paddle steamer; passenger ship, liner,
ocean greyhound, floating palace; channel steamer, ferry; hovercraft, hydrofoil;
rotor ship; packet, dredger, hopper;
transport, hospital ship; tender, escort
vessel; pilot vessel; tug, launch; lightship,
weather ship; underwater craft, submarine, U-boat, *warship*.
galley; pirate ship, privateer, corsair;
Viking ship, longship; trireme.
merchant *ship*, merchantman; cog, galleon;
banana boat, tea clipper; slave ship,
slaver; cargo boat, freighter, tramp;
coaster; lugger; collier, tanker.
fishing *boat*, fishing smack, hooker; drifter,
trawler; factory ship; whaler.
sailing *ship*, sailing boat; windjammer, clipper, tall ship; barque; brig, brigantine,
schooner; frigate, corvette, *warship*; cutter, sloop, ketch, yawl; wherry; yacht,
sailing dinghy, smack; dhow, junk, sam-
pan.
rig, square rig.
sail, canvas; square sail, lug; course, main-
sail, foresail, royal; jib, spinnaker, balloon sail, rigging; mast, mainmast, mizzenmast, *prop*.
boat, skiff, lifeboat; tender, dinghy, pram;
longboat, jolly boat; cutter, gig; surf boat;
barge, lighter, pontoon; ferry; houseboat;
tugboat, tug; powerboat, motorboat,
motor launch; cabin cruiser.
rowing *boat*, galley; eight, shell; skiff,
dinghy, rubber dinghy; coracle; punt,
gondola; canoe, outrigger, dugout;
kayak.
raft, balsa, catamaran, trimaran; float, pontoon.
shipping, craft; fleet, flotilla, squadron,
navy; marine, mercantile marine, merchant navy; shipping line; flag of convenience, *flag*.
Adj. *marine*, maritime, naval, nautical, *seafaring*; sea-worthy, snug, tight, shipshape.

Adv. *afloat*, aboard.

271 Aircraft

N. *aircraft*, *aeronautics*; flying machine;
aeroplane, airplane, crate; plane, mono-
plane, biplane; amphibian; hydroplane,
flying boat; airliner, airbus, transport,
freighter; fighter, bomber, *air force*; jet
plane, jet, turbojet, turboprop; VTOL;
helicopter, chopper; hovercraft, *ship*;
glider; joystick, rudder; fin, tail; aileron,
wing; prop, *propeller*; cockpit, flight
deck; undercarriage, landing gear; parachute; test bed, wind tunnel; flight
simulator; aerodrome, *air travel*.
airship, balloon, captive balloon; dirigible,
Zeppelin; kite, parachute, chute; hang
glider; magic carpet; nacelle, car, gondola.
rocket, rocketry; step rocket, booster; nose
cone, warhead; *missile weapon*.
spaceship, spacecraft, space probe, space
capsule, space shuttle; lunar module;
space station, *satellite*; flying saucer,
UFO, unidentified flying object.
Adj. *aviational*, aerospace; airworthy, *flying*; supersonic; vertical take-off.

272 Velocity

N. *velocity*, celerity, speed, alacrity; speed of
thought; expedition; speed, tempo, rate,
pace, bat, *motion*; mach number; speed of
light, speed of sound, supersonic speed;
great speed, maximum speed, full steam;
utmost speed, press of sail, precipitation;
hurry, flurry, *haste*; reckless speed;
streak, streak of lightning, flash, flight;
gale, hurricane, tempest, torrent; electricity, telegraph, lightning; speed
measurement, speedometer, *gauge*; wind
gauge; log; speed trap, *trap*.
spurt, acceleration; burst, burst of speed,
burst of energy; thrust, drive, impetus,
impulse; jump, spring, bound, pounce,
leap; swoop, zip; dive, flying start, rush,
dash, scamper, run, sprint, gallop.
speeding, driving, racing; bowling along,
course, race, career, full speed, full lick;
pace, fair clip; quick march, double,
forced march, *haste*; quick retreat,
escape; race course, speed track, *racing*.
speeder, speed merchant, speed maniac,
scorcher, racing driver, *driver*; runner,
harrier; racehorse, *thoroughbred*; greyhound, cheetah, hare, deer, doe, gazelle,
antelope; ostrich, eagle, swallow; arrow,
bullet, cannonball, *missile*; jet, rocket;
clipper, *ship*; express, express train;
express messenger, Mercury, *courier*;
magic carpet.
Adj. *speedy*, swift, fast, quick, rapid,
nimble; dashing, lively, brisk, smart,
snappy, nifty, zippy, *vigorous*; expeditious, *hasty*; double-quick; prompt, *early*;
immediate; speeding, racing, ton-up;
running, runaway; flying; tempestuous;
breakneck, precipitate, *rash*; fleet, fleet of
foot; agile, nimble, slippery, evasive; like
quicksilver; like a bird; like an arrow; like
a flash; meteoric, electric, telegraphic,
supersonic.
Vb. *move fast*, move, shift, travel, speed;
drive, pelt, streak, flash, shoot; scorch;
scud; skim, nip, cut; bowl along; sweep
along, tear, rip, zip, rush, dash; fly, wing;
hurtle, dive; dash forward; plunge, lunge,
swoop; run, trot, double, lope, spank,
gallop; bolt, hotfoot it, leg it, scoot,
skedaddle, scamper, scurry, scuttle; hare,

run like mad; start, dart, flit; frisk, whisk;
spring, bound, leap, jump, pounce; ride
hard; hie, hurry, post, haste, *hasten*;
chase, chase, stampede, career, go full
tilt, go full pelt, go full lick, go full bat,
go full steam.

accelerate; gather momentum, spurt, sprint,
let it rip; quicken, give one his head,
drive, spur, urge forward; lend wings to,
expedite, *hasten*.

outstrip, overtake, overhaul; lap, outrun,
outdo; distance, outdistance, leave
behind, leave standing; lose; romp home,
be superior.

Adv. *swiftly*, apace; posthaste, with speed,
at full tilt; helter-skelter; presto, pronto,
like a shot; full speed ahead; like wildfire.

273 Slowness

N. *slowness*, languor; inertia; refusal to be
hurried, deliberation; *caution*; reluctance; working to rule, *strike*; drag, *friction*; brake, curb, *restraint*; time to spare,
leisurely progress, *leisure*; slow motion,
low gear; slow march, slow time,
andante; slow pace, crawl, creep, dawdle;
walk, amble, jog trot, *gait*; standing start,
lagging, lag, time lag, *delay*.

slowcoach, snail, slug, tortoise; funeral procession; slow starter, late developer; sleepyhead; *slacker*; drone.

Adj. *slow*; dripping; *clumsy*; halting, tardy,
dilatory, lagging, *late*; leisurely, *leisurely*; sedate, *formal*; deliberate, *patient*;
painstaking, *careful*; Fabian, *cautious*;
tentative; languid, slack, sluggish, *lazy*;
apathetic, phlegmatic, *insensible*; grad-
ual, imperceptible, invisible.

Vb. *move slowly*, go slow, amble, crawl,
creep, inch, inch along, ooze, drip,
trickle, dribble, *flow*; drift, *deviate*; hover;
shamble, slouch, shuffle, scuff; toddle,
waddle, take short steps, mince; plod,
trudge, tramp, lumber, stump, stump
along; wobble, totter, stagger, lurch;
struggle, toil, labour, chug, jolt, bump,
creak; limp, hobble, go lame; flag, falter;
trail, lag, fall behind, *follow*; hang fire,
drag oneself; tarry, be long about it, *be
late*; laze, maunder, idle; take it easy,
linger, stroll, saunter, dawdle, *walk*;
barely move, hardly beat; grope, *be tentative*; soft-pedal, hesitate, *be cautious*;
drawl, stammer.

decelerate, lose momentum; reduce speed;
relax, slacken, *pause*; lose ground, flag,
falter.

retard, check, curb, *moderate*; reef, shorten
sail, strike sail, *navigate*; brake, *restrain*;
backpedal, backwater, reverse, *regress*;
handicap, *hinder*.

Adv. *slowly*, leisurely; at half speed, with
leaden step; gingerly; adagio, largo.

gradatim, one at a time.

274 Impulse

N. *impulse*, impulsion, pressure; impetus,
momentum; boost, *stimulant*; *incentive*;
thrust, push, shove, heave; stroke; throw,
fling *propulsion*; lunge, kick, *attack*; percussion, beating; beat, *roll*; bang;
flick, clip, tap, *touch*; shake, rattle, jolt,
jerk, wrench; pulse, *spasm*; science of
forces, mechanics, dynamics.

knock, dint, dent; rap, tap, clap; dab, pat,
fillip, flip, flick; nudge, dig, *gesture*;
smack, slap; cuff, clout, clump, buffet;

blow; lash, stroke, hit, crack; cut, dri
(cricket); thump, biff, bang; punch, le
right, straight left, uppercut, jab, hoo
body blow; swipe; knock-out blov
stamp, kick; whop, swat; floggin
thrashing, beating; hiding, *corporal pu
ishment*; assault, *attack*; fisticuffs, *tu
moil*.

collision, encounter, meeting; head-on col
sion, bird strike; graze, scrape, *frictio*
clash; cannon; impact, bump, shoc
crash, smash, smashup, accident; brun
charge, force, *attack*; collision cours
multiple collision, pileup, *accum
lation*.

hammer; punch; beetle, maul, mallet; flai
bat, hockey stick, golf club; knocke
cosh, knuckle-duster, cudgel, club, mac
bicycle chain, sandbag, *weapon*; boxin
glove; pestle, anvil; beater.

ram, bulldozer; monkey; ramrod; cu
pusher.

Adj. *impelling*; dynamic.

Vb. *impel*, fling, heave, throw, *propel*; giv
an impetus, impart momentum; slan
bang, *close*; press; push, thrust, shov
tamp; pole, punt; hustle, prod, urg
spur, *accelerate*; fillip, flip, flick; jer
shake, rattle, shock, jog, jolt, jostle, *ag
tate*; shoulder, elbow, push aroun
deflect; expel, *eject*; frogmarch; drive fo
ward; goad, *incite*; drive, start, run, se
going, set moving, *operate*; raise, *elevat*
plunge, dip, *lower*.

collide, make impact, *touch*; encroach; co
verge; meet, encounter, clash; fenc
strike at; ram, butt, batter, dint, den
batter at, bulldoze, *demolish*; bun
against; graze, graze against, *rub*; bu
against; clash with, foul, fall foul of; ru
against, *charge*; clash against; trij
tumble; knock together.

strike, smite, hit, land a blow, aim a blov
lunge, lunge at, poke at, strike at; let fl
swing, flail; strike hard, slam, bang
knock; send flying; floor, *fell*; pat, patte
flip, fillip, tickle; tap, rap, clap; slaj
smack; clump, clout, clobber; box, spa
fight; buffet, punch, thump, whack
wham, pummel, trounce, belabour, soc
it to, let one have it; give one a black ey
or a bloody nose; pound, batter, blud
geon; biff, bash, dash, slosh, sock, slog
slug, cosh, cudgel, club, mug; sandbag
crown; concuss, stun, leave senseles
spank, wallop, thrash, lash, beat, whi
cane, *flog*; leather, strap, belt, give
hiding, *punish*; thresh, flail; hamme
drum; flap, squash, swat, *flatten*; pav
stroke, *caress*; scratch, maul, wound; ru
through, bayonet, pink, *pierce*; tear, cu
stone, pelt, snowball; head (a football
bat, strike a ball, swipe, drive, turr
glance, cut, crack, lift, lob, smash, volley
propel.

kick, spurn, boot, knee; trample; rid
roughshod; spur; heel, dribble, shoot (
football).

275 Recoil

N. *recoil*, revulsion, reaction, *reversion*
repercussion, echo; reflex, *reflectioi*
kick, kickback, backlash; ricochet, can
non; rebound, bounce, spring, sprin|
board, trampoline; volley, return (at ten
nis), boomerang; rebuff, repulse
repulsion; riposte, return fire.

Adj. *recoiling*, reactive; retroactive.

Vb. *recoil*, react, *counteract*; shrink, winc*
flinch, jib, shy, *avoid*; kick back, ricoche

cannon; spring back, rebound; return, swing back; reverberate, echo, *resound*; reflect, *shine*; boomerang, *retaliate*.

276 Direction

N. *direction*, bearing, compass reading, *bearings*; *situation*; set, drift, *current*; tenor, trend, *tendency*; aim; *course*, beam; beeline, straight shot, line of sight; course, tack; line, line of march, track, way, path, road, *route*; steerage; aim, target, *goal*; compass, *sailing aid*; signpost; direction finder, *gauge*; cross-country race, point-to-point.

compass *point*, cardinal points, half points, quarter points; quarter, North, East, South, West; azimuth.

Adj. *directed*; *parallel*; diagonal, *oblique*; sideways, *lateral*; facing, *opposite*; direct, unswerving, straightforward, one-way, *straight*; northbound, southbound; northern, northerly, southerly; western; eastern; directive.

Vb. *orientate*, orientate oneself, *navigate*; take a direction, bear; direct oneself; signpost, direct, *indicate*; pinpoint, locate, *place*; *be straight*; face, front, *be opposite*.

steer *for*, steer, make towards, go to, go towards; *be straight*.

point *to*, point, point towards, signpost, *indicate*; trend, trend towards, verge, dip, bend, *tend*.

aim, level, point; take aim, aim at; level at; cover; aim well, land, plant, *place*.

Adv. *towards*, versus, facing; through, via; straight, direct; point blank; directly, full tilt at; upstream, downstream; downwind; seaward, landward, homeward; cross-country; hither, thither; clockwise, anticlockwise,   counterclockwise; whither, which way!

277 Deviation

N. *deviation*, wrong course, wrong turning; aberration, deflection; shift, veer, slew, swing; declension; swerve, bend, *curvature*; detour, long way round; *circuit*; vagrancy, *wandering*; fall, lapse, *error*; wandering mind; drift, leeway; oblique motion, sidestep, sideslip; break, (googly cricket); yaw, tack; zigzag, slalom course.

Adj. *deviating*, aberrant, nonconformist, abnormal, deviant; eccentric; errant, wandering, rambling, vagrant, loose, footloose; random, erratic, *inexact*; desultory, *discontinuous*; abstracted; discursive, *irrelevant*; lost, stray, astray; wide; devious, roundabout, *circuitous*; indirect, crooked, zigzag, *oblique*.

Vb. *deviate*, digress, make a detour; *diverge*; turn, filter, turn a corner, turn aside, swerve, slew; step aside; alter course, change direction, yaw, tack; veer, (back wind); trend, bend, curve; zigzag, twine, twist, *meander*; swing, wobble, *oscillate*; steer clear of; sidle, passage; slide, skid, sideslip; break (cricket); glance, *be oblique*; shy, jib, sidestep, *avoid*.

turn *round*, turn about, about turn, wheel, wheel about; reverse, reverse direction, return; go back, *turn back*.

stray, err, ramble, rove, drift, straggle, *wander*; go astray, go adrift, get lost; *blunder*; lose track of.

deflect, bend, crook, *make oblique*; warp, skew; misdirect, *mislead*; avert, *parry*; divert; sidetrack, draw aside; bias, slice,

pull, hook, glance, bowl a break, bowl (wide cricket); shuffle, shift, switch, shunt, *interchange*; wear ship, *navigate*.

Adv. *astray*, adrift; right about; round about; all manner of ways; at a tangent, sideways; crabwise

278 Preceding: going before

N. *preceding*, priority, precedence; going before, leading, heading, flying start; preemption; pride of place, lead, leading role; pioneer, *precursor*; van, vanguard, avant-garde, *front*.

Adj. *foremost*, first.

Vb. *precede*, go before, herald; introduce; head, spearhead, lead; guide, conduct, direct; have a head start; preempt; get ahead of, lap, *outstrip*; be beforehand, be early; have right of way, *come before*.

Adv. *ahead*, before, foremost; primarily, first of all; age before beauty.

279 Following: going after

N. *following*, sequence; run, suit, *series*; pursuit, pursuance, *chase*; succession, reversion, *transfer*; last place, *rear*.

follower, attendant, hanger-on, camp follower, *dependant*; train, tail, wake, suite, *retinue*; following, party, adherent, supporter; satellite, moon, artificial satellite, space station, *spaceship*; trailer, caravan, cart; tender, *ship*.

Adj. *following*, subsequent.

Vb. *follow*, come behind, succeed, follow after, come to heel, *come after*; stick like a shadow, tag after; attend, *serve*; tag along, *accompany*; dog, shadow, trail, tail, track, *pursue*; drop behind, lag, trail, dawdle; *be behind*.

Adv. *behind*, rearward; after; one after another.

280 Progression: motion forwards

N. *progression*, going forward; procession, march, way, course, career; march of time, *course of time*; progress, forward march, *motion*; sudden progress, stride, leap, jump, *spurt*; irresistible progress, flood, tide, *current*; gain, advance, headway; *preceding*; next step, development, evolution, *ascent*, *continuity*; mystic progress, *piety*, *worship*; furtherance, promotion, advancement; rise, raise, lift, *elevation*;   enterprise,   *undertaking*; achievement, *success*; economic progress; progressive; go-getter, coming man or woman, upstart, *prosperous person*.

Adj. *progressive*, enterprising, forward-looking; *moving*, irreversible; advanced, *modern*.

Vb. *progress*, proceed; advance, go forward, take a step forward, develop, *evolve*; show promise, *get better*; do well, *prosper*; maintain progress, never look back; push forward, press onwards, *hasten*; make a good start, make initial progress; gain, gain ground, make headway, *move fast*; get ahead; distance, outdistance, leave behind, *outstrip*; gain height, rise, rise higher, *climb*; reach towards; recover lost ground, *recoup*; gain time.

promote, further, contribute to, advance, *aid*; prefer, upgrade, raise, lift, *elevate*; bring forward, push, force, develop, *invigorate*; *accelerate*; put ahead, put forward; favour, *cause*.

Adv. *forward*, onward, forth, ahead.

Int. *Forward! Forrard! En avant! Excelsior!*

281 Regression: motion backwards

N. *regression*, regress; reverse direction, backward step, *reversion*; retreat, *recession*; backing; decline, drop, fall, slump.

return, homeward journey; homecoming, *arrival*; reentry; going back, ebb, *current*; backing; relapse; U-turn, volte-face, about turn, *reversion*; turn, turning point, *crisis*; reflex, recoil.

Adj. *regressive*; reflex; backward; reactionary, *retrospective*; retroactive; backing, anticlockwise, counterclockwise; reverse; resilient, *elastic*; homing, homeward bound.

Vb. *regress*, recede, retrogress; retreat, retire, withdraw, fall back, turn tail; disengage, *resign*; backtrack, backpedal; give way, give ground, *disappear*; fall behind, fall astern; reverse, back, back water, go backwards; run back, flow back, regurgitate; slip back; ebb, slump, fall, drop, decline, *descend*; bounce back, recoil.

turn *back*; go back, go home, return; look back, hark back, *retrospect*; veer round, about face, execute a volte-face; double, double back; start back, jib, shrink, *avoid*; come back, come back again, come home.

Adv. *backwards*, back, astern.

Int. *back! hard astern! hands off!*

282 Propulsion

N. *propulsion*, drive; impulsion, push, *impulse*; projection; precipitation; cast, throw, chuck, toss, fling, sling, shy; pot shot, pot, shot, discharge, volley, *bombardment*; bowling, throw-in, full toss, yorker, lob (cricket); kick, punt, dribble (football); stroke, drive, swipe, *knock*; pull, slice (golf); rally, volley, smash (tennis); ballistics; archery; *skill*; gunshot, *distance*.

missile, projectile, shell, rocket, cannonball, ball, bullet, shot, pellet, brickbat, stone, snowball; arrow, dart, *missile weapon*; ball, football, rugby ball; bowl, wood, jack, puck, curling stone; discus, javelin; hammer, caber.

propellant, thrust, driving force, jet, steam, *energy*; spray, aerosol; pusher, *ram*; tail wind, *wind*; lever, treadle, pedal, oar, sweep, paddle; screw, blade, *propeller*; coal, petrol, *fuel*; gunpowder, dynamite, *explosive*; shotgun, rifle, *firearm*; revolver, *pistol*; airgun, pop gun, water pistol; blowpipe, pea-shooter; catapult, sling, bow, *missile weapon*.

shooter, gunman, rifleman, musketeer; gunner; archer, bowman, marksman, sharpshooter, shot, *proficient person*.

thrower; bowler, pitcher, curler.

Adj. *propulsive*, explosive, projectile, missile.

Vb. *propel*, launch, project; flight, throw, cast, deliver, heave, pitch, toss, cant, chuck, shy, bung; bowl, lob, york; hurl, fling, sling, catapult; dart, flick; pelt, stone, shower, snowball; precipitate, send flying; expel, pitchfork, *eject*; explode; serve, return, volley, smash, kill (tennis); bat, slam, slog, wham; sky, loft;

drive, cut, pull, hook, glance (cricket); slice, *strike*; kick, dribble, punt (football); putt, push, shove, shoulder, ease along, *impel*; wheel, pedal, roll, bowl, trundle, *rotate*; drive, hustle, *move*; sweep, sweep before one, drive like leaves; put to flight, *defeat*.

shoot, fire, open fire; volley, discharge, explode; let fly; cannonade, bombard, *fire at*; snipe, pot, pot at; pepper, pierce.

283 Traction

N. *traction*; *attraction*; haulage; draught, pull, haul; tug, tow; rake, harrow; trawl, dragnet; drawer, tower, haulier; square sail, *sail*; windlass; tug, tugboat, *ship*; tractor, traction engine, *locomotive*; loadstone, *magnet*; strain, tug of war, *contest*; thing drawn, trailer, *cart*.

Adj. *drawing*; retractile; attractive; ductile; drawn.

Vb. *draw*, pull, haul, hale; trice, warp, *navigate*; tug, tow; lug, drag, train, trail, trawl; rake, harrow; winch, lift, heave, *elevate*; *lower*; absorb; pluck, *extract*; wrench, *distort*; yank, jerk, twitch, tweak, pluck at, snatch at, *agitate*; pull towards, *attract*; pull back, retract.

Int. *yo-heave-ho!*

284 Approach: motion towards

N. *approach*, coming towards, advance, *progression*; near approach, approximation; flowing towards, *stream*; meeting, confluence; access, accession, advent, coming, *arrival*, presence; *pursuit*; onset, *attack*; advances, overture, *offer*; means of approach, *access*.

Adj. *approaching*, close, *near*; meeting; affluent, tributary; imminent, *impending*; coming, oncoming.

accessible, approachable, get-at-able; within reach, *possible*; available; wayside, roadside, nearby, *near*; inviting, sociable.

Vb. *approach*, draw near, be near; approximate, *bring near*; come within range, arrive; be visible; be drawn; come to close quarters, meet, *converge*; collide; near, move near; congregate; enter; accede, adhere, join, *accrue*; waylay, buttonhole; accost, greet; make overtures, court; nestle, caress; lean towards, incline, trend, *tend*; move towards; advance, *progress*; attack; close, *circumscribe*; hover; overtake, *outstrip*; follow hard, run one close; make a landfall, *land*; navigate.

Int. *this way! come closer! roll up! land ahoy!*

285 Recession: motion from

N. *recession*, retreat, leak; resignation; flight, *escape*, revulsion; recoil.

Adj. *receding*, retreating.

Vb. *recede*, retire, withdraw, fall back, retreat, regress; ebb, subside, shrink, decline, *decrease*; disappear; go, leave, evacuate, emigrate, depart; go outside, emerge; leak; move further, put space between, be distant; stand aside, make way, *deviate*; stray; flinch, *avoid*; flee; *escape*; go back, turn back; jump back, recoil; come unstuck, *separate*.

286 Attraction

N. *attraction*, pull, drag, draw, tug; drawing to; gravity, itch, *desire*; affinity, sympathy; allure, appeal, allurement, seduction, temptation, lure, bait, decoy, charm, siren song, *inducement*; siren; centre of attraction, cynosure, *favourite*.

magnet, coil magnet, solenoid; lodestar, *guide*.

Adj. *attracting*, attractive; siren; seductive; centripetal.

Vb. *attract*, pull, drag, tug, *draw*; exercise a pull, draw towards, appeal, charm, move, *impress*; lure, allure, bait, *tempt*; decoy, *ensnare*.

287 Repulsion

N. *repulsion*; repellent quality; reflection, recoil; *defence*; repulse, rebuff, snub, refusal.

Adj. *repellent*, off-putting; centrifugal.

Vb. *repel*, excite nausea, *cause dislike*; butt, head, *impel*; repulse, block, *parry*; dispel, *disperse*; reflect, *deflect*; be deaf to; *refuse*; rebuff, snub, *reject*; cold-shoulder, keep at arm's length, make one keep his distance; send one about his business; sack, *dismiss*.

Int. *be off! away with you! scram! hop it! get lost!*

288 Convergence

N. *convergence*, mutual approach, *approach*; collision course, *collision*; confluence, meeting, *union*; congress, concentration, resort, assembly, *assemblage*; pincer movement; *focus*; coming to a point, taper; tangent; perspective, *view*.

Adj. *convergent*; centripetal; concurrent; tangential; pointed, conical; knock-kneed.

Vb. *converge*; come together, *meet*; unite, gather together, congregate; *enter*; close with, intercept; *circumscribe*; pinch, nip; concentrate, focus; centre; taper, come to a point, *be narrow*.

289 Divergence

N. *divergence*, *difference*; going apart; moving apart, parting, *separation*; aberration, declination, *deviation*; spread; fork, crossroads, points, *crossing*; radiation, ramification; *star*.

Adj. *divergent*; radiant; centrifugal, centrifuge; aberrant.

Vb. *diverge*, *differ*; radiate; ramify; fork; part, part ways, part company, *separate*; change direction, switch; *deviate*; deploy, spread, scatter; straddle, spread-eagle; splay, splay apart.

290 Arrival

N. *arrival*, advent, accession, appearance, entrance, *approach*, presence; onset, *beginning*; coming, making; landfall, landing; meeting, encounter, *event*; greeting, handshake, *courteous act*; homecoming, *return*; reception, welcome, *celebration*; guest, visitor, visitant, new arrival, homing pigeon; finish, *contest*; last lap, home stretch.

goal, *objective*; native land, *home*; final point, terminus, *extremity*; stop, stopover, stage, halt; billet, landing stage, pier; port, harbour, haven, anchorage, *shelter*; dock, berth, *stable*; aerodrome, airport, heliport, terminal, *air travel*; terminus, railway station, depot, rendezvous, *meeting place*.

Adj. *arriving*, homing; terminal; *impending*.

Vb. *arrive*, come, reach, get there, *be present*; make land, sight, raise; make a landfall, make port; dock, berth, moor, drop anchor, *come to rest* (see *land*); park; home, *regress*; hit, make, win to, gain, attain; *carry through; enter*; make an entrance; appear, *visit*; stop at, stop, pause; *be early*; arrive at, find, *discover, prosper*; be brought, come to hand.

land, unload, discharge, *displace*; beach, ground, run aground, make a landing; step ashore, disembark, *emerge*; alight, perch, *descend*; dismount, set foot to ground.

meet, join, rejoin, see again; receive, greet, welcome, *be sociable*; go to meet; keep a date, rendezvous; encounter; hit, collide with, *collide*; gather, assemble, *congregate*.

Int. *welcome! welcome home! greetings! hullo! hi! pleased to meet you! aloha! shalom! salaam!*

291 Departure

N. *departure*, parting, removal; walk-out, exit, *egress; recession*; going back, *return*; migration, exodus; hop, flight, flit, getaway, *escape*; outset, *start*; takeoff, *ascent*; zero hour.

valediction, funeral oration, epitaph, obituary; last handshake, *courteous act*; sendoff, farewell address; last post, last words, parting shot; stirrup cup, nightcap.

Adj. *departing*, farewell; parting, outward bound.

Vb. *depart*, quit, leave, abandon, *relinquish*; retire, withdraw, *turn back*; remove, move house, leave home, emigrate, expatriate oneself; take wing; be going; bid farewell, say good night, part, part company; leave work, *cease*; go home, *emerge*; exit, *resign*; depart this life, *die*.

decamp, break camp, evacuate; make oneself scarce; take wing, *fly*; vamoose, skedaddle, beat it, hop it, scram, bolt, scuttle, skip, *move fast*; flee, take flight; flit, *disappear*; elope, abscond, *escape*.

start out, get going, begin; set forth, *emerge*; gird oneself, be ready to start, *make ready*; take ship, embark, *enter*; weigh anchor, set sail, *navigate*; mount, bit, bridle, harness, saddle, *ride*; emplane; catch a train, catch a plane, catch a bus.

Int. *goodbye! farewell! adieu! au revoir! auf Wiedersehen! a riverderci! be seeing you! cheerio! ciao! bye-bye! ta-ta! so long! pleasant journey! bon voyage! God be with you!*

292 Ingress: motion into

N. *ingress*, incoming, entry, entrance; reentry, *return*; influx, flood, *stream*; trespass; invasion, forced entry, inroad, raid, irruption, incursion, *attack*; osmosis; intake, *reception*; import, importation; right of entry, admission, admittance, access, *permission*; free trade, free market, *trade, scope*; ticket, pass, *permit, opener*.

way in, way, path, *access*; entrance, entry, door, *doorway*; mouth, opening, *orifice*; intake, inlet, *gulf*; channel, *conduit*; open door, free port, *market*.

incomer, newcomer; new arrival, new member, new face; new boy, *beginner*; visitant, visitor, caller, *sociable person*; migrant, colonist, settler, *foreigner*; raider; house-breaker, *thief*; entrant, competitor, *contender*; ticket holder, audience, house, gate.

Adj. *incoming*, inward, inward bound, homing; intrusive; penetrating.

Vb. *enter*; *come after*; *open*; gain admittance; call, *visit*; board, get aboard; insinuate oneself; *pierce*; notch; *tumble*; plunge; join, *be one of*; immigrate, *place oneself*; admit; insert; enter oneself, *contend*.

infiltrate, percolate, seep, soak through, penetrate, permeate, *mix*; taint, infect, *impair*.

burst in, force; flood, overflow, *flow*; congregate; invade, raid, break through, board, storm, *attack*.

intrude, trespass, gatecrash; interrupt, *derange*; burgle, *steal*.

293 Egress: motion out of

N. *egress*; exit; walkout, exodus; exile; issue; eruption, outburst, *outbreak*; sortie, *escape*; export, migrant, emigrant, *foreigner*; expatriate, colonist, *settler*; exile, remittance man.

outflow, effusion; emission; issue; weeping; bleeding, *haemorrhage*; perspiration, sweat; leak, escape, leakage, *waste*; drain, running sore, *loss*; discharge, drainage; overflow, spill, flood, *waterfall*; jet, fountain, spring, *source*; gush, squirt, *stream*; geyser; runny nose.

outlet, vent, chute; spout, nozzle, tap; pore, blowhole, *orifice*, *respiration*; sluice, floodgate, *conduit*; exhaust, exhaust pipe; spout, drainpipe, gargoyle; exit, path, *access*; *doorway*; escape, loophole, *means of escape*.

Adj. *outgoing*, outward bound; emergent; runny, leaky; running, bleeding; explosive, volcanic; spent.

Vb. *emerge*, project; *be visible*; surface, break water, *ascend*; transpire; egress, issue, debouch, sally, make a sortie; issue forth, *walk*; *leap*; evacuate, *decamp*; *emigrate*, *travel*; exit, *depart*; erupt, break through, *escape*.

flow out, *flow*; gush, spout, jet, emit; run, drip, dribble, trickle, ooze; rise, surge, overflow, spill, escape, leak, vent itself, debouch; *bleed*, weep; flood, inundate, *drench*.

exude, perspire, sweat, steam, *be hot*; ooze, seep, seep through, percolate, strain, filter, distil; run, dribble, drip, drop, drivel, drool, slaver, slobber, salivate, *be wet*; transpire, exhale, *breathe*.

294 Reception

N. *reception*, admission, admittance, access; invitation, *offer*; acceptance; open arms, welcome, *celebration*; initiation, baptism, *debut*; asylum, sanctuary, shelter, *protection*; introduction; importation, import; radio receiver, *telecommunication*; *respiration*; suction; digestion, absorption; fluid intake; intake, consumption, *waste*; infusion; interjection.

Adj. *admitting*, receptive; inviting, *accessible*; receivable, admissible, acceptable; absorbent, hygroscopic; digestive.

Vb. *admit*; receive, accept; grant asylum, afford sanctuary, shelter, *safeguard*; welcome; invite, *offer*; enlist, *employ*; give entrance or admittance to, allow access, give a ticket to; throw open, *open*; import, land, *transfer*; introduce, *come before*; *send*; initiate, *teach*; infiltrate, *insert*; take, be given, get, *receive*.

absorb, incorporate, engross, assimilate, digest; suck; sponge, blot, *dry*; ingest, imbibe; swallow, engulf, gulp, gobble, devour, *eat*, drink; inhale, *breathe*; sniff, snuff, *smell*; taste.

295 Ejection

N. *ejection*, expulsion; precipitation, *propulsion*; disqualification, *exclusion*; discharge, sack, boot, push; exile; *displacement*; deprivation; jettison; clean sweep, *destruction*; emission, effusion; libation; secretion; radioactivity, *radiation*; deportee, refugee, *outcast*.

ejector, bailiff, *substitute*; bouncer; emetic, *purgative*; *explosive*; volcano, *furnace*; radiator, radio transmitter, *telecommunication*; *aircraft*.

voidance, clearance, drainage, aspiration; eruption, *outbreak*; nausea, vomit, puke; gas, wind, burp, belch.

Adj. *expulsive*, explosive; sickening, emetic.

vomiting, sick, green; seasick, airsick.

Vb. *eject*, expel, *punish*; disbar, excommunicate, *exclude*; export, *transfer*; deport, expatriate, repatriate, resettle; exile, banish, transport, *seclude*; extrude, wash ashore; bounce, *propel*; precipitate, *propel*; *extract*; unearth, uproot, eradicate, *destroy*; eliminate, *obliterate*; get shot of; dispossess, expropriate, oust, evict, dislodge, turn adrift, *displace*; *hunt*; jettison, discard, throw overboard; blackball, *reject*; cut, cut dead, send to Coventry; supplant, supersede, replace, *substitute*.

dismiss, discharge, make redundant, drop; axe, sack, fire; send one about his business, *repel*; *frighten*; tell to go, *prohibit*.

empty, drain, void; evacuate, eliminate, excrete; vent, disgorge, discharge; decant, *transpose*; *drink*; aspirate; *open*; tap, broach, *pierce*; milk, bleed, let blood, *extract*; clear, make a clean sweep of, *clean*; unload, unpack, *displace*; disembowel, eviscerate, gut, clean, bone, fillet, *uncover*; *purify*; desolate, depopulate, render few.

emit, give vent to; *send*; *radiate*; emit a smell, exhale, perfume, scent, *smell*; vapour, fume, smoke, steam, puff; spit, spatter, sputter, splutter; pour, spill, shed, sprinkle, spray; spurt, squirt, jet, gush, *moisten*; bleed; drip, drop, ooze; dribble, drool, slobber, *exude*; sweat, perspire, *be hot*; secrete, *store*; pass, *excrete*; drop (a foal); lay (an egg); *generate*.

vomit, be sick, disgorge, retch, gag; spew, puke, cat, honk, poop; be seasick; feel nausea, heave.

eruct, belch, burp; break wind; cough, hawk, expectorate, spit, gob.

296 Food: eating and drinking

N. *eating*, taking food; nutrition; consumption; biting; digestion; table, diet; lack of appetite, anorexia; *bulk*; appetite, voracity, *hunger*; table manners, *practice*; vegetarianism; food chain, food web.

feasting, orgy, feast; reception, wedding breakfast, annual dinner, do, *celebration*; harvest supper; Christmas dinner, blowout, spread (see *meal*); loaded table; *plenty*; refectory.

dieting, dietetics, *therapy*; diet; regimen,

regime, course, diet sheet; meagre diet, poor table; malnutrition, *disease*; vitamin pill; nutrition expert.

gastronomy; good living; dainty palate, *discrimination*; epicure, gourmet.

cookery, cuisine, food preparation, dressing; domestic science, home economics, *provision*; baker, cook, chef; bakery, rotisserie, restaurant; kitchen, galley; oven, *furnace*; butter, margarine, oil; dripping, lard, *fat*; yeast, *leaven*; recipe, cookery book, *textbook*.

eater, feeder, consumer, picker, pecker; boarder; dainty feeder, connoisseur, gourmet, epicure; gourmand, *glutton*; carnivore; man-eater, cannibal; vegetarian, vegan, herbivore; omnivore, hearty eater, wolf, vulture, locust; teeth, jaws, *tooth*; mouth, pecker, gullet, stomach, belly, paunch.

provisions, stores, commissariat; foodstuff, groceries; keep, board, entertainment; sustenance, *provision*; home-grown food; commons, helping, *portion*; buttery, pantry, larder, cellar, *storage*; hay box, meat safe; freezer, fridge, *refrigerator*.

provender, animal food, fodder, feed, pasture, pasturage, forage; corn, oats, barley, grain, hay, grass, clover, lucerne, silage; dry feed, chicken feed, pigswill, cattle cake; saltlick.

food, meat, bread, staff of life; nutriment, nutrition, nurture, sustenance, pap; manna; daily bread, staple food, wheat, maize, rice; eats, victuals, grub, tuck, nosh, scoff; tack, biscuit, salt pork; heavy food, stodge; bad food, carrion, offal; health food; cheer, good food, good table; delicatessen; garnish, flavouring, sauce, *condiment*.

food content; roughage, bulk, fibre; calcium, iron; protein; fat, oil, cholesterol; starch; sugar, glucose, sucrose, lactose, *sweet thing*; additive, preservative, artificial flavouring.

mouthful, bite, nibble, morsel, *small quantity*; sop, sip, swallow; slice, titbit; sandwich, snack, crust; chocolate, sweet, popcorn; cud, quid, something to chew; tablet, pill, *drug*.

meal, refreshment, fare; light meal, snack, bite to eat; piece, sandwich, hamburger, hot dog; packed lunch, square meal, heavy meal; sit-down meal, repast, spread, feed, blowout, junket, *festivity*; picnic, barbecue; chance meal, potluck; breakfast, elevenses, lunch, brunch, tiffin; tea, five o'clock, high tea; dinner, supper; menu, bill of fare, diet sheet; list; cover, table, place; help, helping, *portion*; serving; self-service.

dish, course; main dish; salad; dessert, savoury; speciality; casserole, stew, hotpot, ragout, *a mixture*; goulash, curry; pilau, paella, risotto; pasta, ravioli, macaroni, spaghetti; pancake, pizza, pasty, pie, flan, quiche; fricassee; fry-up, mixed grill; egg dish; rehash.

hors-d'oeuvres, smorgasbord; starter; soup, broth, brew; stock, bouillon, bisque, chowder, puree; mulligatawny, minestrone; salami, pâté, galantine; salad, coleslaw; mayonnaise, *sauce*.

fish food, fish, fish pie, kedgeree; white fish, freshwater fish, trout, salmon, eel; cod, coley, rock salmon, dogfish, whiting, plaice, sole, skate, hake, halibut, haddock, turbot, mullet, mackerel, herring, whitebait; sardine, pilchard, tuna, tunny; seafood, shellfish, oyster, lobster, crayfish, crab, shrimp, prawn, scampi;

cockle, winkle, mussel, whelk, jellied eel; roe.

meat, flesh; human flesh, long pig; red meat, beef, mutton, lamb, veal, pork, venison, game; pheasant, chicken, *table bird, poultry*; meat substitute; roast meat, Sunday roast; haggis, black pudding; mince; sausage, banger, frankfurter; Cornish pasty; cut, joint, leg; baron of beef, sirloin; shoulder, hand of pork, skirt, scrag end, breast, brisket; shin, loin, flank, topside, silverside; cutlet, chop, escalope; steak, pork pie, ham, bacon, bacon rasher, gammon; tongue, knuckle, Bath chap, brawn, oxtail, tripe; offal, kidney, liver; suet, dripping, crackling; forcemeat, stuffing.

dessert, pudding, sweet; milk pudding, semolina, tapioca; rolypoly; jam tart, crumble, charlotte; stewed fruit, fool; fresh fruit, fruit salad; sorbet, mousse, sundae, trifle, blancmange, jelly, custard, *sweet thing*; cheese board.

sweets, confectionery; candy, chocolate, caramel, Turkish delight; acid drops, barley sugar, butterscotch, nougat; aniseed ball, lolly, lollipop, *sweet thing*; sweetmeat, bonbon; candy floss.

fruit, soft fruit, berry, gooseberry, strawberry, raspberry, loganberry, blackberry, bilberry, mulberry; currant, redcurrant, blackcurrant; stone fruit, apricot, peach, nectarine, plum, greengage, damson, cherry; apple, russet, pear; orange, grapefruit, lemon, lime, tangerine, mandarin; banana, pineapple, grape; rhubarb; date, fig; dried fruit, currant, raisin, sultana, prune; pomegranate, passion fruit, guava; mango, avocado; melon, honeydew; pawpaw; nut, coconut, pecan, peanut, groundnut, monkey nut; almond, walnut, chestnut, hazel nut; *sweet thing*.

vegetable, greens, *plant*; root vegetable, tuber, turnip, swede, parsnip, carrot; potato, yam; spud; green vegetable, cabbage, cauliflower, broccoli; spring greens; sorrel, spinach, asparagus, globe artichoke; leek, onion, marrow, courgette, pumpkin, squash; aubergine, eggplant, capsicum, pepper, chilli; lettuce, chicory; spring onion, radish, celery, beetroot; tomato; cucumber; cress, watercress; edible fungus, mushroom, truffle; edible seaweed; sauerkraut, ratatouille.

potherb, herb; marjoram, rosemary, sage, mint, parsley, thyme, basil, savory, tarragon, dill, fennel; coriander, caraway; caper; horse radish, *condiment*; borage.

cereals, wheat, buckwheat, oats, rye, maize, corn; rice, millet; breakfast cereal, cornflakes, muesli, oatmeal, porridge, gruel; flour, meal, wholemeal, wheat germ, bran; batter, dough; bread, crust, crumb; white bread, pumpernickel, toast, rusk; loaf, tin, farmhouse, bloomer, French stick; roll, croissant, crumpet, muffin, scone, teacake, oatcake, bannock; tortilla, waffle, wafer, cracker.

pastries, confectionery, pasty, turnover, dumpling; tart, flan, puff, pie; pastry, patisserie, gateau, cake, cheesecake; meringue, eclair, macaroon; bun, doughnut, flapjack, gingerbread, shortbread.

dairy product (see *milk*); cream, whey, junket; cheese, Cheddar, Caerphilly, Wensleydale, sage Derby; Gouda, Edam; Camembert, Brie; Parmesan; ripe cheese, Roquefort, Gorgonzola, Stilton, Danish blue.

drinking, fluid intake; potation; libation;

drinker; *drunkard*.

draught, drink, beverage, dram; gulp, sip, sup; bottle, bowl, glass, *cup*; cuppa; bumper; swig, nip, noggin, tot, slug; peg, double peg, snifter, chaser; long drink; short drink, short; quick one, snort; nightcap; loving cup; health, toast; mixed drink, cocktail, *mixture*; potion, infusion, *medicine*; divine drink, nectar.

soft *drink*; water, spring water, fountain; soda water, soda, soda fountain; table water, squash; milk, milk shake; ginger beer, ginger ale, fizz, pop, lemonade, orangeade; cordial, fruit juice, coconut milk; tea, char, pekoe, maté, *tonic*; coffee, black coffee, espresso; cocoa (see *milk*); sherbet, syrup, julep.

alcoholic *drink*, booze, wallop, tipple, poison; brew, alcohol, malt liquor, beer; draught beer, strong beer; ale, real ale; barley wine, stout, lager, bitter, porter, mild, home brew; shandy; scrumpy; perry, mead; wheat wine, rice beer, toddy, sake, tequila; spirits, firewater, hooch, moonshine, mountain dew, rot-gut, hard stuff; brandy, cognac; gin, schnapps, blue ruin; whisky, Scotch whisky, scotch; rye, bourbon, poteen; vodka; rum, demon rum, grog, punch, egg flip; cordial; cup, mixed drink, pink gin, mint julep; cocktail; aperitif; liqueur.

wine, red wine; vermouth; vino, plonk; table wine, sack, sherry, port, madeira; champagne, fizz, bubbly; claret, burgundy, Beaujolais; hock, Moselle, Bordeaux; retsina, chianti.

milk, cream; buttermilk, plant milk; milk drink, cocoa, chocolate; junket. See *dairy product*.

Adj.*feeding*; insectivorous; vegetarian, vegan; omnivorous; teetotal, *temperate*; *drunken*.

edible, eatable; kosher, drinkable; milky; palatable, succulent, dainty, delicious, tasty, savoury; cereal, wheaten; alcoholic, hard; soft.

nourishing, nutritious, rich, calorific; wholesome, *salubrious*.

culinary; done to a turn, well-done; underdone, red, rare, raw; burnt.

Vb.*eat*, feed, fare, board, mess; partake, taste; take a meal, have a feed, break bread; breakfast, lunch, have tea, dine, sup; feast, banquet, carouse, *revel*; eat well, have a good appetite, do justice to; drool, raven, *be hungry*; fall to, set to; stuff oneself, *sate*, guzzle; *expand*; take every course, leave a clean plate; *consume*; swallow, devour, bolt, wolf, make short work of; nibble, peck, lick, have a poor appetite; nibble at, peck at, sniff at; ingest, digest, *absorb*.

chew, masticate, champ, munch, crunch, scrunch; mumble, mouth, worry, gnaw, grind; bite, tear, rend, *cut*.

graze, browse, pasture, crop, feed; ruminate.

drink, imbibe, suck, *absorb*; quaff, drink like a fish, lap, sip; crack a bottle, booze, swill, swig, tipple, *get drunk*; knock it back; pledge, *toast*; have another; *replenish*; give to drink, wine, water; *provide*.

feed, nourish; nurture, sustain, board; give to eat, cater, purvey, *provide*; nurse, breast-feed, give suck; pasture, graze; fatten, *enlarge*; dine, feast, banquet, have to dinner, *be hospitable*.

cook, prepare a meal; bake, brown, roast, braise; broil, grill, barbecue, griddle, devil, curry; fry, scramble, poach, boil,

parboil; coddle, seethe, simmer, steam; casserole, stew; baste, lard, bard; whip, whisk, beat, blend, liquidize, stir; draw, gut, bone, fillet; stuff, dress, garnish; dice, shred, mince, grate; sauce, flavour, spice, *season*.

Int.bon appétit! here's health! here's mud in your eye! bottoms up! down the hatch! prosit! skol! cheers!

297 Excretion

N.*excretion*, discharge, secretion; effusion; egress; *respiration*; perspiration; *infection*; cold, catarrh, hay fever; cough; waterworks.

haemorrhage, bleeding, haemophilia, *blood*; menses, period, curse.

defecation, clearance; motion; constipation.

excrement, waste matter; faeces, stool, excreta, ordure, night soil; dung, cowpat, manure, muck; droppings, guano; urine, water; sweat, lather; spittle, spit, sputum; saliva, slaver, slobber, froth, foam; phlegm; catarrh, mucus, snot; matter, pus; afterbirth; slough, cast, pellet; *dirt*.

Adj.*excretory*; purgative, laxative; diuretic; menstrual; anal, urinary; watery; mucous; cast-off.

Vb.*excrete*, secrete; pass, move; defecate; relieve oneself; urinate, piddle, pee; have a pee, take a leak; make water, spend a penny; wet oneself; sweat, perspire, steam, glow, *be hot*; salivate, slobber, snivel; cough, spit; weep, *exude*; *be hungry*; be angry; cast, slough, *doff*.

298 Insertion: forcible ingress

N.*insertion*, parenthesis, *interjection*; *addition*; introduction; injection, shot, *perforation*; infusion, enema; insert, inset; stuffing, lining.

immersion; dip, bath, *plunge*; baptism, *Christian rite*; burial, burial at sea.

Adj.*inserted*, *additional*; intermediate.

Vb.*insert*, introduce; intrude; transfix, run through, *pierce*; load; pocket, stow, *impel*; inlay, inset, line; mount, frame, *circumscribe*; add; interpose, *put between*; *let fall*; putt; pot, hole; bury; sheathe, encapsulate, encase, *cover*.

infuse, instil, *mix*; impregnate, *infiltrate*; transfuse, decant, *transpose*; inject, *pierce*.

implant, plant, transplant, graft, engraft, bud; inoculate, vaccinate; embed, bury; impact, dovetail, *join*.

immerse, bathe, steep, souse, marinate, soak, *drench*; duck, dip, *lower*; submerge, flood; immerse oneself, *plunge*.

299 Extraction: forcible egress

N.*extraction*, removal, *displacement*; abortion; *destruction*; liberation, *deliverance*; forceps delivery; expression; suction, aspiration; pull, tug, wrench, *traction*; mining; fishery; essence, extract.

extractor; miner; wrench, forceps, pincers, pliers, tweezers, *nippers*; mangle; corkscrew, screwdriver, *opener*; lever, *pivot*; scoop, spoon, shovel; pick, pickaxe; rake; toothpick; vacuum cleaner; excavator; dredge, dredger; syringe; suction pump.

Adj.*extracted*.

Vb.*extract*, remove, pull, *draw*; elicit, educe; unfold, *evolve*; pluck; withdraw, excise, excavate, mine, quarry, unearth; dredge; expel, *eject*; extort; express, milk, tap; aspirate, suck, void, pump; eliminate, uproot, eradicate, extirpate, *destroy*; prune, *render few*; distil, extricate, unravel, free, *liberate*; unpack, unload, *displace*; eviscerate, gut, *empty*; *uncover*; select.

300 Passage: motion through

N. passage, transmission; transportation; transport; passing, passing through; *transition*; trespass; transit, traverse, crossing, journey, patrol, *land travel*; osmosis; egress; right of way, *access*; steppingstone, flyover, underpass, *bridge*; track, route, orbit, *path*; intersection, junction, *crossing*; channel, *conduit*.

passing *along*, passage, thoroughfare; traffic, road traffic, traffic movement, flow of traffic, circulation; walking, crossing, driving; traffic load, traffic density; traffic jam, procession, queue; *pedestrian, driver*; passerby.

traffic *control*, traffic engineering; highway code, *precept*; traffic lane, one-way street, dual carriageway, clearway, *road*; alternative route, *deviation*; white lines; street furniture, traffic lights, roundabout; pedestrian crossing, bollard, refuge, island; car park; lay-by; point duty, road patrol, speed trap; traffic police, traffic cop; traffic engineer; traffic warden, meter maid; lollipop man or lady.

Adj. *passing*.

Vb. pass, skirt, coast, *be near*; *move fast, be transient*; go past; pass along, circulate, weave; pass through, transit, traverse; shoot through, shoot a bridge, *navigate*; *emerge*; go through, percolate, permeate, *pervade*; patrol, beat, scour; penetrate, infiltrate, *enter*; bore, perforate, *pierce*; thread, thread through, string, *connect*; rake; open a way, force a passage; squeeze through, *progress*; cross, go across, make a crossing, *arrive*; wade across, ford; get through, get past, negotiate; pass beyond, *overstep*; *turn back*; cut across, *obstruct*; straddle, bestride; *bridge*, *cover*; carry across, transmit, *send*; pass to, hand, reach, *transfer*.

Adv. *en passant*, by the way.

301 Overstepping: motion beyond

N. overstepping, going beyond, *passage*; excursion, *deviation*; trespass, *guilty act*; infraction; *desire*; ribbon development; *exaggeration*.

Adj. surpassing, *superior*; too strong; excessive, *exorbitant*.

Vb. overstep, overpass; pass, leave behind; go beyond, go too far; exceed; overrun, override, overshoot, aim too high; overlap; surmount, *leap*; cross, *pass*; fill; overdo, *exaggerate*; strain, stretch, stretch a point; overestimate, *overrate*; *be intemperate*; oversleep, *be late*.

encroach, invade, *attack*; infringe, transgress, trespass, *be illegal*; poach, *steal*; squat, usurp, *appropriate*; *intrude*; overlap; erode, *impair*; infest, overrun; overflow, flood, *drench*.

outdo, exceed, surpass, outclass; transcend, rise above, *be superior*; go one better, outbid; outwit, overreach, *deceive*; outmanoeuvre, outflank; *move fast*; outrun, outdistance, *distance*; overhaul, overtake, shoot ahead; lap, leave standing, *outstrip*; leave behind, race, beat, beat

hollow, *defeat*.

302 Shortfall

N. shortfall; a minus, deficit, short measure, shortage, loss; leeway, drift, *deviation*; default; *lost labour*; *failure*; fault, defect, shortcoming, *blemish*; something missing, want, lack, need, *requirement*.

Adj. deficient, short, short of, minus, wanting, lacking, missing; substandard; undermanned, understaffed, below establishment; perfunctory, *incomplete*; inadequate, *insufficient*; failing, running short, *scarce*; below par, *imperfect*.

Vb. fall short; lack, want, be without, *require*; miss; lag, *be late*; stop short; fall behind, lose ground, slip back; slump, collapse, *regress*; fall through, come to nothing, fail, *miscarry*; *waste effort*; *disappoint*.

Adv. behindhand, in arrears; not enough; far from it; in vain.

303 Ascent: motion upwards

N. ascent, ascension, lift, upward motion; defiance of gravity; takeoff, lift-off; spiral; *aeronautics*; culmination, *summit*; rising, uprising, rise, upturn; upsurge, crescendo, *increase*; rising air, rising current, thermal; sunrise, dawn, *morning*; mountaineering; *attack*; jump, vault, pole jump, *leap*; bounce, *recoil*; rising ground, hill, *high land*; gradient, slope, ramp, *incline*; rising pitch, *musical note*; means of ascent, stairs, steps, stile, flight of stairs, staircase, landing; ladder, companionway; rope ladder; stair, step, tread, rung; lift, escalator; fire escape, *means of escape*.

climber, mountaineer; steeplejack; rocket, lark, skylark; geyser, fountain, *stream*.

Adj. ascending; rampant; floating, light; airborne; uphill, steep, *vertical*.

Vb. ascend, rise; defy gravity; become airborne, *fly*; gain height, mount, soar, spiral, climb; surface, break water; spring, vault, *leap*; bounce, *recoil*; grow; curl upwards; tower, aspire, spire, *be high*; gush, spout, jet, play; rear, ramp, *be vertical*; *lift oneself*; trend upwards, steepen, *be oblique*.

climb; mount; mountaineer; clamber, scramble, climb like a monkey; surmount, top, breast, conquer, scale, *be high*; *attack*; go upstairs, climb a ladder; mount (a horse).

Adv. up, uphill, upstairs; upwards, *aloft*; ever higher.

304 Descent

N. descent, declension, declination, *deviation*; cadence; landing; downward trend, spiral, decline, drop, slump, *decrease*; sunset; *comedown*; downfall, collapse, *ruin*; trip, stumble, lurch, capsize; tumble, crash, spill, fall; cropper; swoop, stoop, pounce; dive, header, plunge; nosedive, *aeronautics*; landing, arrival; subsidence, landslide, avalanche; *wind*; downpour, shower, *rain*; cascade, *waterfall*; slope, tilt, dip, *incline*; chute, slide, helter-skelter; precipice, sheer drop; mining; pot-holing; tumbler; plunger, *diver*; miner, sapper, *excavator*; soldier.

Adj. descending; tumbledown; submersible.

Vb. descend, decline, abate, ebb, *decrease*;

reach a lower level, slump, fall, drop, sink; sink like a lead balloon, *weigh; infiltrate;* touch bottom, *be low; be inferior;* precipitate, settle, set; collapse; subside, slip, give way; droop, sag, swag, *hang;* draw, have draught; submerge, dive, *plunge;* drown, *founder,* go underground; burrow, bore, tunnel, mine, sap, undermine, *make concave;* parachute; swoop, stoop, pounce; lose height, swing low; alight, light, perch, *land;* lower oneself; dismount, toboggan; fall like rain, shower, cascade, drip, *rain;* take a lower place, *regress;* dip, duck, *stoop;* flop, plop.

tumble, fall; topple, overbalance, capsize; slip, trip, stumble; stagger, totter, lurch, tilt, droop, *be oblique;* pitch, toss, roll; take a header, dive, *plunge;* take a running jump, precipitate oneself, *leap;* take a fall, come a cropper, *fall prostrate;* plop, plump; slump, sprawl; spiral, nosedive, crash.

Adv. *down,* downwards; downhill, downstairs, downstream.

305 Elevation

N. *elevation,* erection, uplift, upheaval; lift; hoist, boost; *aid;* exaltation, assumption; uprising, upswing, *ascent;* an elevation, eminence, high land, prominence; height above sea level, *height.*

lifter; yeast, *leaven;* lever, jack, *pivot;* dredger; crane, derrick, hoist, windlass; winch, capstan; forklift, elevator, dumb waiter, escalator, lift, cable railway; hot air, gas, hydrogen, helium; spring, springboard, trampoline; scaffolding, platform, *stand.*

Adj. *elevated,* exalted; erectile; upright, erect, upstanding, rampant, *vertical;* lofty, sublime, *high.*

Vb. *elevate,* heighten, *make higher;* swell, leaven, *enlarge;* raise, erect, build; lift; uplift; prop, *support; make vertical;* raise aloft, wave; hoist, trice; weigh, trip (anchor); *extract;* chair, shoulder, exalt, *honour;* mount, *crown; promote;* give a lift, *aid;* sky, loft, lob, *propel;* bristle, *be vertical.*

lift oneself, arise, rise, *ascend; be vertical.*

Adv. *on,* on tip toe; on the back of.

Int. upsy-daisy!

306 Lowering

N. *lowering,* depression, *impulse; plunge;* reduction; *revolution;* overthrow; overturn, upset; precipitation, *propulsion;* a depression, dent, dip, hollow, *cavity;* low pressure, *weather.*

obeisance, reverence, bow, salaam, kowtow, *courtesy;* bob, duck, nod, *courteous act; respect.*

Adj. *lowered,* at a low ebb, *low;* prostrate, *supine;* sedentary, sitting, sit-down; submersible.

Vb. *lower,* depress, *impel;* dose; *suppress;* lower, lower a flag, dip, half-mast, strike; deflate, puncture, flatten, squash, crush; let drop (see *let fall*); sink, scuttle, drown, *descend;* duck, souse, dip, *plunge; weigh;* capsize, tip, tilt, *invert;* crush, dent, hollow, *make concave.*

let fall, drop, shed; let go; pour, decant, *empty;* spill, slop, *moisten;* sprinkle, shower, scatter, dust, dredge; sow, broadcast, *disperse;* pitch or chuck overboard; precipitate, *propel.*

fell, trip, topple, tumble, overthrow; prostrate, spread-eagle, lay low, *flatten;* skittle, floor, drop, *impel;* raze, level, demolish; axe, *cut; blow;* undermine, wing, *shoot.*

abase, debase; demote, cashier, *depose;* humble, deflate, puncture, *humiliate;* crush, squash, *suppress.*

sit *down,* sit, squat; subside, sink, lower oneself; kneel, recline, *be horizontal;* roost, nest, *repose;* take a seat, seat oneself, park oneself; perch, alight, *descend.*

stoop, bend, bend forward, bend backward; lean forward; cringe, crouch, cower; slouch; bow, scrape, duck, bob; nod, make obeisance, salaam, prostrate oneself, kowtow, *show respect;* kneel, kneel to, genuflect.

307 Leap

N. *leap;* jump, hop, skip; spring, bound, vault; high jump, hop, skip and a jump; caper, gambol, frolic; kick, jeté; prance; springy step, light tread, *gait;* dance step; dance, reel, jig, Highland fling.

jumper; skipper, hopper; twister, rock 'n roller, *dance; entertainer;* kangaroo, goat, chamois, springbok; frog, grasshopper, flea; Jack-in-the-box, *plaything.*

Adj. *leaping;* skittish, frisky, fresh, *lively;* bouncing.

Vb. *leap,* jump, spring, bound, vault, hurdle, steeplechase; skip, hop, leapfrog, bob, bounce, rebound, buck, *oscillate;* trip, foot it, tread a measure, stamp, *dance;* caper, gambol, frisk, romp; prance, ramp, rear, plunge; cavort; start, give a jump; pounce; *ascend;* clear; flounce, flounder, jerk; writhe, *wriggle.*

Adv. *by leaps and bounds;* at a single bound.

308 Plunge

N. *plunge,* swoop, pounce, stoop, *descent;* nosedive, power dive, *aeronautics;* dive, header; swallow dive, dip; crash dive.

diver, frogman; dipper, *bird;* submariner; submarine; plunger, lead, plummet.

Vb. *plunge,* dip, duck, bathe, *be wet;* plump, plop; dive, make a plunge, take a header, go headfirst; welter, wallow, *souse,* immerse, drown; submerge, *descend;* sink, scuttle, *lower;* sound, fathom, *measure.*

founder, *descend;* drown, *be deep;* plummet, sink, sink like lead, *weigh.*

309 Circuition: curvilinear motion

N. *circuition,* circulation, wheeling, spiral, *rotation;* turning, turn, U-turn, *return;* orbit; lap; circuit, tour, round trip, full circle; figure of eight, *loop;* helix, *coil;* roundabout way, *circuit.*

circler; *mariner;* roundsman; patrol, patrolman or -woman; moon, satellite, *planet.*

Adj. *circuitous,* ecliptic; peripatetic; circumflex; devious, *roundabout.*

Vb. *circle,* circulate; compass, circuit, lap; tour; go round, skirt; circumnavigate; turn, round, double a point, round a corner, corner, revolve, orbit; wheel, spiral, come full circle, *rotate;* turn round, put about, *turn back;* draw a circle, describe a circle, *circumscribe;* curve, wind, twist, *meander;* make a detour, *circuit*.

310 Rotation: motion in a continued circle

N. *rotation*; revolution, full circle; circulation; spin; rolling, *progression*; spiral, roll, spin, turn, twirl, pirouette, waltz, *dance*; whirl, whirr; dizzy round, rat race; vertigo.

vortex, whirl; whirlwind, tornado, cyclone, *gale*; whirlpool, swirl, *eddy*; maelstrom, Charybdis; smoke ring, *loop*.

rotator, rotor, spinner; top, roundabout, merry-go-round; churn, whisk; lathe, circular saw; flywheel, wheel of Fortune, *wheel*; gyroscope, turntable; gramophone record, disc; wind pump, windmill, fan, sail; propeller, prop, screw; turbine; capstan; swivel, hinge; spit, jack; spindle, axle, axis, shaft, *pivot*; reel, roller, *cylinder*; rolling stone, planet, satellite, *wanderer*.

Adj. rotary; cyclic; dizzy.

Vb. *rotate*, revolve, orbit, *circle*; turn right round; spin, spin like a top, twirl, pirouette; corkscrew, *twine*; gyrate, waltz; whirl, whirl, whirr, hum, *resound*; mill around, swirl, eddy, *flow*; bowl, trundle; set rolling, roll, roll along; twirl, twiddle; churn, whisk, *mix*; turn, crank, wind, reel, spool, spin; slew, slew round, swing round, furl, *fold*; scroll.

Adv. round and round, clockwise, anticlockwise, counterclockwise.

311 Evolution: motion in a reverse circle

N. *evolution*, unrolling, unfolding; dénouement; development, *growth*.

Adj. evolving.

Vb. *evolve*, unfold, unroll, unwind, explicate, disentangle, *unravel*; develop, *become*; roll back, *open*.

312 Oscillation: reciprocating motion

N. *oscillation*; harmonic motion; vibration, tremor; rhythm; pulse, beat, throb; flutter; breathing, *respiration*; undulation, wave motion, frequency; frequency band, wavelength; *radiation*; sound wave, *wave*; seismic disturbance, earthquake, tremor, *violence*; seismology, seismograph; oscillator; pendulum, bob, yoyo.

fluctuation; shuttle service; rolling, roll, pitch, lurch, stagger, reel; shake, nod, wag, dance; springboard; swing, seesaw, rocker; shuttlecock, shuttle.

Adj. *oscillating*; vibrant; earth-shaking, seismic; pendulous; groggy; rhythmic, *periodical*.

Vb. *oscillate*; *radiate*; wave, undulate; vibrate, pulsate, pulse, beat, drum; tick, throb, palpitate; respire, pant, heave, *breathe*; play, sway, nod; swing, dangle, *hang*; seesaw, rock; lurch, reel, stagger, totter, teeter, waddle, wobble, wiggle, waggle, wag; bob, bounce, dance, *leap*; toss, roll, pitch, tumble, wallow; rattle, chatter, shake; flutter, quiver, shiver; flicker, *shine*; echo, *resound*.

fluctuate, alternate, reciprocate; shuttle; slosh about.

brandish, wave, wag, waggle, shake, flourish; pump; flutter, *agitate*.

Adv. to and fro; side to side; zigzag, seesaw; like a yoyo.

313 Agitation: irregular motion

N. *agitation*, irregular motion; broken water, rolling, *roughness*; flicker, twinkle, *flash*; sudden motion, start, jump, *lack of expectation*; hop, *leap*; shake, jig, jiggle; toss, *propulsion*; shock, jar, jolt, jerk, judder, bounce, bump, *impulse*; nudge, dig, jog, *gesture*; vibration, thrill, throb, pulse, flutter; shudder, shiver; quiver, quaver, tremor; fever; turning; rock 'n roll, *activity*; itch; twitch, grimace; disquiet, *worry*; trepidation, twitter, flap; shivers, jitters; aspen, aspen leaf.

spasm; twitch, tic; lockjaw, tetanus; cramp; pang; paroxysm, access, orgasm, *frenzy*; fit, epilepsy; pulse, throb; attack, seizure, stroke.

commotion, turbulence, tumult, *turmoil*; hurly-burly, hubbub; fever, flurry, rush, bustle, *haste*; racket, din; stir, ferment, fermentation, *bubble*; ground swell, heavy sea, *wave*; squall, tempest, thunderstorm, *storm*; whirlpool, *vortex*; whirlwind, *gale*; disturbance, atmospherics.

Adj. agitated; *active*; feverish, fevered, restless; scratchy, jumpy, all of a twitter, *nervous*; breathless; itchy; spasmodic, spastic; skittish, *lively*; flighty; shaky, tremulous.

Vb. be agitated; ripple, boil, bubble; stir, move, dash; shake, tremble, quiver, quaver, shiver; have a fever, throw a fit; writhe, squirm, twitch, *wriggle*; toss, turn, toss about, kick, plunge, rear, be violent; flounder, flop, wallow, roll, reel, pitch, *fluctuate*; sway, be oblique; pulse, beat, thrill, vibrate, judder, shudder; wag, waggle, wobble, stagger, lurch, dodder, totter, teeter, dither, *oscillate*; whirr, whirl, *rotate*; jig around, jump about, hop, bob, bounce, dance, *leap*; flicker, twinkle, gutter, sputter, *shine*; flap, flutter, twitter, start, jump; throb, pant, palpitate, miss a beat, be excited; bustle, rush, mill around, *rampage*; ramp, roar, be angry.

agitate, disturb, rumple, ruffle, *derange*; discompose, perturb, worry, *trouble*; ripple, puddle, muddy; stir, *mix*; whisk, whip, beat, churn, *rotate*; shake, wag, waggle, wave, flourish, *brandish*; flutter, fly (a flag), jog, jiggle, jolt, nudge, dig; jerk, pluck, twitch.

effervesce, froth, spume, foam, *bubble*; boil, seethe, simmer, sizzle, spit, be hot; ferment, work.

Adv. *jerkily*; by fits and starts with a hop, skip and a jump; spasmodically.

314 Materiality

N. *materiality*, empirical world, world of experience; material existence, world of nature; physical being, physical condition, *existence*; *world*; solidity, *density*; weight, *gravity*; personality, individuality, *speciality*; embodiment, incarnation, reincarnation; materialism, sensuality.

matter, stuff; prime matter; mass, material, fabric, body, frame, *structure*; substance; organic matter, flesh, plasma, protoplasm, *organism*; real world, world of nature, Nature.

object; inanimate object, still life; physical presence, body, real person, *person*; thing, gadget, something, commodity, article, item; *mineral*; raw material.

element, elementary unit; principle, *origin*; earth, air, fire, water; unit of being; factor, ingredient, *component*; chemical element, basic substance; isotope; physical element, atom, molecule; elementary particle, electron, neutron, proton, quark; nucleus; quantum; ion.

physics, physical science, science of matter; natural history, *biology*; chemistry, mechanics, theory of relativity; thermodynamics; atomic physics, nuclear physics; applied physics, technology, *skill*; natural philosophy, *science*; chemist, physicist.

Adj. *material*; real, natural; solid, concrete, palpable, tangible, sensible, weighty; physical; objective, impersonal, neuter; *substantial*; incarnate; corporal, bodily, carnal; worldly, *sensual*.

Vb. *materialize*, substantiate; make real, body forth; embody, incarnate, personify.

315 Immateriality

N. *immateriality*; idealism; spirituality; animism; spiritualism; other world, world of spirits, eternity, *perpetuity*; idealist, *philosopher*; ghost.

subjectivity, personality, myself, me, yours truly, *self*; ego, id; Conscious, Unconscious; psyche, higher self, *spirit*.

Adj. *immaterial*, without mass; incorporate; abstract, *mental*; shadowy, *insubstantial*; imponderable, intangible; disembodied; unearthly, transcendent; psychic; spiritual, otherworldly, *religious*; personal, subjective; illusory, *imaginary*.

Vb. *disembody*, spiritualize, dematerialize.

316 Universe

N. *universe*, whole; world, creation, sum of things, *matter*; cosmos, macrocosm, microcosm; outer space, void; big bang theory, *start*.

world; home of man; earth; middle earth, globe, sphere; biosphere; terrestrial surface, crust; plate tectonics, *land*; ocean; atlas, *map*; Old World, New World, *region*; geocentric system, personal world, *circumstance*.

heavens, sky, welkin, ether, hemisphere; firmament, vault of heaven; night sky, northern lights; *glow*.

star, heavenly body; sidereal sphere, host of heaven; constellation, Great Bear, Plough, Big Dipper, Orion, Southern Cross; starlight; main sequence; blue star, red star; double star, binary; multiple star; variable star; giant, red giant; dwarf, X-ray star, *radiation*; quasar, pulsar, neutron star, black hole; nova, supernova; Pole Star, North Star; Dog star; Milky Way, Galaxy; star cluster, galaxy, island universe; stellar motion, radial velocity.

nebula; cosmic dust, interstellar matter.

zodiac, ecliptic; house, mansion.

planet, asteroid; Mercury; Venus, morning star, Hesperus; Mars, red planet; Earth, Jupiter, Saturn, Uranus, Neptune, Pluto; comet, wandering star; *rotation*.

meteor, fireball; meteorite; meteoroid; meteor shower; radiant point.

sun, orb of day, eye of heaven; midnight sun; mock sun; sunlight; granule, sun spot, prominence, solar flare, corona; solar wind; Sol; solar system.

moon, satellite; new moon, mock moon; crater, mare; parish lantern; moonlight, moonshine.

satellite, moon; earth satellite, weather satellite; space station; space shuttle, *spaceship*; astronaut.

astronomy, star lore, stargazing; astrophysics; astrology, horoscope, *divination*; observatory, planetarium; *telescope*, astronomical telescope; transit instrument; radio telescope, dish; *photography*; celestial globe, astrolabe; astronomer, astrophysicist; stargazer.

uranometry; right ascension, declination; hour; hour circle, ecliptic; celestial pole; celestial equator; equinox, first point of Aries; solstice, galactic latitude or longitude; node; precession.

cosmography, cosmology.

earth sciences, geography, oceanography, geology.

Adj. *cosmic*, universal; interstellar, interplanetary; galactic.

celestial, heavenly; sidereal, stellar; solar, lunar; nebulous; geocentric; meteoric.

telluric, terrestrial; polar; worldwide, world, global, international, universal; *spacious*; worldly, earthly.

astronomic, astronomical, stargazing; telescopic.

geographic, geographical, oceanographic; geological; geodetic.

Adv. *under the sun*, here below.

317 Gravity

N. *gravity*, gravitation, force of gravity, gravity feed; weight, *bulk*; specific gravity; pressure, displacement, draught, load, freight; burden; ballast, *offset*; mass, lump, *solid body*; lump of, weight of, mass of; plummet, *diver*; weight, bob, lead, stone, millstone; statics.

weighing; equipoise; avoirdupois weight, grain, carat, scruple; ounce, pound, stone, quarter, hundredweight, ton; kilogram; megaton; axle load, laden weight.

scales; balance, pan, scale, weight; platform scale, weighbridge.

Adj. *weighty*, heavy, ponderous; leaden, cumbersome, *unwieldy*; massive, *dense*; pressing, incumbent; with a weight of, weighted, loaded, laden, charged; topheavy, *unequal*.

Vb. *weigh*, have weight, balance, *be equal*, compensate; outweigh, overbalance, *predominate*; wallow, sink, settle, *founder*, descend; weigh heavy, press, hang like a millstone, *lower*; load, *hinder*; *measure*; weigh oneself.

make heavy, weight; charge, burden, overweight, overload, *load*; gain weight, *be large*.

Adv. *weightily*, heavily; like a lead balloon.

318 Lightness

N. *lightness*; air, ether, *rarity*; defiance of gravity, *ascent*; feather, thistledown, cobweb, gossamer; fluff, dust, straw, *insubstantial thing*; cork, buoy; balloon, bubble; hot air, helium.

leaven; ferment, enzyme, yeast.

Adj. *light*, underweight, *deficient*; lightweight, featherweight; portable, handy, *little*; weightless, without weight, lighter than air; imponderable; sublime, airy, volatile, *rare*; doughy, barmy, yeasty; floating; feathery.

Vb. *be light*, defy gravity, surface, float,

swim; drift, waft, glide, be airborne, *fly*; soar, hover, *ascend*.

lighten, make light, make lighter, reduce weight, ease, *disencumber*; lighten ship, throw overboard, jettison, *empty*; gasify, *aerate*; leaven, work; raise, *elevate*.

319 Density

N. *density*, solidity, consistency; thickness, concentration; *hardness*; cohesion, *coherence*; relative density, specific gravity.

condensation, concentration; constipation; thrombosis; sedimentation; precipitation; condenser, compressor; gelatine, rennet, pepsin.

solid body, solid; block, mass, *matter*; knot, nugget, lump; condensation, nucleus, hard core; aggregate, conglomerate; concrete, cement; stone, crystal, *rock*; precipitate, deposit, sediment, silt, clay, cake, clod, clump; bone; gristle, cartilage; curd, clot, solid mass, phalanx, serried ranks; forest, thicket; wall, *obstacle*.

Adj. *dense*, thick, crass; close, heavy, stuffy (air); foggy, murky, to be cut with a knife; lumpy, consistent, monolithic; firm, knotty, gnarled; substantial, massive, *weighty*; concrete, solid, frozen, crystalline; compact, *full*; thickset, thick, bushy, luxuriant; serried; *rigid*; impenetrable, impermeable, impervious; indivisible, *strong*.

indissoluble, insoluble; sedimentary.

solidifying, binding; styptic, astringent.

Vb. *be dense*, become solid, solidify, consolidate; conglomerate, cement, *cohere*; condense, form a core or kernel; thicken; precipitate, deposit; freeze, *be cold*; set, jell; congeal, coagulate, clot, curdle; cake, crust; petrify, ossify, *harden*; compact, compress, contract, squeeze; pack, cram, *load*; mass, crowd, *bring together*; bind, constipate; precipitate, deposit.

320 Rarity

N. *rarity*, low pressure, vacuum; lack of substance; ether, gas, *air*; pressure reduction.

Adj. *rare*, tenuous, thin, fine, subtle; flimsy, slight, *insubstantial*; spongy, *elastic*; rarefied; void, hollow, *empty*; *light*; *immaterial*; straggly.

Vb. *rarefy*, expand, dilate; make a vacuum, exhaust, *empty*; attenuate, refine, thin; dilute, adulterate, *weaken*; gasify.

321 Hardness

N. *hardness*, resistance; rigour; temper; grit, stone, pebble; flint, silica, quartz, granite, marble, diamond, *rock*; adamant, metal; steel, iron, hardware, stoneware; cement, concrete; brick, block, board, heartwood; hardwood, teak, oak, *wood*; bone, gristle, cartilage; callus, corn; horn, ivory; crust, shell, hard core, hard centre; brick wall; stiffener, starch, wax; whalebone, corset, splint, *prop*.

hardening; stiffening, backing; sclerosis.

Adj. *hard*; *strong*; armoured; proof; iron, steel, steely; sun-baked; stony, rocky, flinty; gravelly, pebbly; crystalline, vitreous, glassy; horny; callous; bony; *tough*; icy, frozen, frozen solid.

rigid, stubborn, intractable; firm, inflexible, unbending; starchy; muscle-bound, *clumsy*; tense, taut, tight, set, solid; crisp, *brittle*; stiff, stark.

Vb. *harden*, steel, *strengthen*; temper;

toughen; crisp, bake, *heat*; petrify, ossify; calcify, *be dense*; freeze, *refrigerate*; stiffen, back, bone, starch, wax (a moustache), *tighten*.

322 Softness

N. *softness*; compliance; suspension; *marsh*; butter, grease, oil, wax, putty, paste, clay, dough, soap, plaster; padding, wadding, pad, *lining*; cushion, pillow, armchair, feather bed, *euphoria*; velvet, plush, fluff, fleece, *hair*; *plumage*; snow, snowflake.

Adj. *soft*, tender, *edible*; melting, *fluid*; yielding; springy, sprung, *elastic*; pneumatic, podgy; waxy, doughy; spongy, soggy, mushy, *marshy*; pithy; squashy, juicy; fleecy, *downy*; grassy; silky, *smooth*; limp; flaccid, flabby, floppy; unstrung, slack, loose; emollient.

flexible, whippy; pliable; ductile, malleable, tractable, plastic; lithe, willowy, supple, double-jointed; *athletic*.

Vb. *soften*, render soft; mellow, *mature*; oil, grease, *lubricate*; knead, massage, mash, pulp, squash; macerate, steep, *drench*; melt, thaw, *liquefy*; cushion, pillow; relax, *disunite*; yield, give, give way, relax, bend, unbend, *be elastic*.

323 Elasticity

N. *elasticity*, give, stretch; spring; suspension; bounce, *recoil*; rubber; guttapercha; whalebone; elastic; rubber band, rubber ball; gum.

Adj. *elastic*, stretchy, tensile; rubbery, springy, resilient; sprung, ductile, *soft*.

Vb. *be elastic* - tensile etc. adj. bounce, spring, spring back, *recoil*; stretch, give.

324 Toughness

N. *toughness*, *strength*; cohesion, *coherence*; leather, gristle, cartilage, *hardness*.

Adj. *tough*, durable; *strong*; tenacious, clinging, sticky; shockproof; weatherbeaten; hardboiled, overdone; stringy, sinewy, woody, fibrous; rubbery, leathery; indigestible, inedible; stubborn, *rigid*.

Vb. *be tough*, resist fracture; toughen, tan; temper, anneal, *strengthen*.

325 Brittleness

N. *brittleness*; frailty, *weakness*; bubble, eggshell, pie crust, matchwood, shale, slate; glass, porcelain, *pottery*; glasshouse, house of cards, sandcastle, *weak thing*.

Adj. *brittle*; *rigid*; fragile; papery, like parchment; shivery, crumbly, *powdery*; crisp, short, flaky; splitting, frail, delicate, flimsy, eggshell, *weak*; crazy, insubstantial; tumbledown, *dilapidated*; ready to break, ready to burst, explosive.

Vb. *be brittle*, fracture, *break*; crack, snap; star, craze; chip, split, shatter, shiver, fragment; splinter; burst, fly, explode; give way, crash, *tumble*; deteriorate; wear thin; crumble.

Int. fragile! with care!

326 Structure. Texture

N. *structure*, pattern, plan; complex, syndrome, *whole*; mould, shape, build, *form*; constitution, make-up, set-up, content, substance, *composition*; make, works, workings; architecture, tectonics; fabric, work, brickwork, stonework, woodwork; substructure, superstructure, *edifice*; scaffold, framework, chassis, shell, *frame*; cleavage; body, person, physique, anatomy, *organism*; bony structure, skeleton, bone, horn; science of structure, physiology, histology, *biology*.

texture, network, *crossing*; tissue, fabric, stuff, *textile*; staple, denier, *fibre*; web, weave; nap, pile, *hair*; grain, grit; *roughness*; surface; feel, *touch*.

Adj. *structural*, organic.

textural, textile, woven; silky, satiny, *smooth*; *rough*; fine, delicate, filmy; coarse, homespun, *hairy*.

327 Powderiness

N. *powderiness*; *dirt*; attrition; erosion; abrasion, *friction*; fragmentation; frosting.

powder, talc, chalk; pollen, spore; dust, soot, ash, *dirt*; flour; grist, meal, bran; sawdust, filings; powdery deposit; scurf, dandruff; debris, detritus; sand, grit, gravel, shingle; grain, seed, crumb, *piece*; granule, grain of powder, *small thing*; flake, snowflake; smut, smoke, smoke cloud, fog, smog, *cloud*; dust storm, dust devil, fen blow, *storm*.

pulverizer, miller; roller; mill, millstone, pestle; hand mill, grater, grindstone, file; abrasive, sandpaper, emery paper; molar, *tooth*; chopper, *sharp edge*; sledgehammer, *hammer*; bulldozer, *ram*.

Adj. *powdery*, dusty, smoky, sandy; *dry*; farinaceous, mealy; gravelly, flaky; ground; crumbly, *brittle*.

Vb. *pulverize*, powder, granulate; crush, mash, smash, shatter, fragment, disintegrate, *break*; grind, mill, mince, beat, bruise, pound, bray; knead; crumble, crumb, crunch, scrunch, *chew*; chip, flake, grate, scrape, rasp, file, abrade, *rub*; weather, rust, erode, *decompose*.

328 Friction

N. *friction*, drag; attrition, rubbing against, rubbing together, *collision*; erasure; abrasion; erosion, *destruction*; scrape, graze, scratch; rub; polish, elbow grease; shampoo, massage, facial; pumice stone; rubber; whetstone; masseur, *beautician*.

Adj. *rubbing*, grating; abrasive.

Vb. *rub*, rub against, strike (a match); gnash, grind; fret, fray, chafe, gall; graze, scratch, bark, *wound*; abrade; skin, flay; scuff, scrape, scrub, scour, burnish; brush, towel, curry, *clean*; polish, buff, *smooth*; erase, obliterate; gnaw, erode, *consume*; rasp, file, grind; knead, shampoo, massage; anoint, *lubricate*; wax, grate, be rusty, catch, stick, snag; stroke, *caress*; iron, *smooth*.

329 Lubrication

N. *lubrication*; an ointment, unction, oiling.

lubricant, graphite, black lead; wax, grease, *oil*; soap, lather, *cleanser*; saliva, spit, spittle; ointment, salve, *balm*; emollient, unguent.

Adj. *lubricated*; smooth-running, well-oiled; silent.

Vb. *lubricate*, oil, grease, wax, soap, lather; butter, *grease*; anoint, pour balm.

330 Fluidity

N. *fluidity*, liquidity; *water*; haemophilia; viscosity; hydraulics; fluid mechanics.

fluid, gas; liquid; water, *water*; drink, *draught*; milk, whey; juice, sap, latex; humour, mucus, saliva, *excrement*; serum, lymph, plasma; pus, matter; gore (see *blood*); dropsy, *disease*.

blood, claret; *life*; bloodstream, circulation; red blood, *vitality*; blue blood, *nobility*; gore; clot, *solid body*; corpuscle; lymph, plasma, serum, haemoglobin; blood group, Rhesus factor; blood count.

Adj. *fluid, amorphous*; liquid; clear; soluble, melting; viscous, fluent, running, *flowing*; runny, watery; succulent, juicy; squashy; pussy, *toxic*.

sanguineous; bloody, gory, bleeding.

331 Gaseousness

N. *gaseousness*, flatulence, *wind*; volatility; aerodynamics.

gas, vapour, elastic fluid; ether, *air*; miasma, *egress*; *wind*; fumes, reek, smoke; steam, water vapour, *cloud*; methane, *fuel*; marsh gas, *poison*; damp; *bladder*; balloon, airship; gasworks, gas plant, *workshop*; gasholder, *storage*; neon light, *lamp*; gas stove, *furnace*; gas meter, *meter*.

Adj. *gaseous*; volatile; aerial, airy; *air*; carbonated, *bubbly*; gassy, windy; pneumatic.

Vb. *gasify*, vapour, steam, emit vapour, emit; aerate.

332 Liquefaction

N. *liquefaction*; fusion, *mixture*; dissolution; thaw, melting, *heating*; solvent; flux; liquidizer.

solution, infusion; suspension; flux.

Adj. *liquefied*, molten; runny; solvent; soluble, *fluid*.

Vb. *liquefy*, liquidize, render liquid, clarify, *make flow*; dissolve, run, *flow*; thaw, melt, smelt, *heat*; fuse, render, clarify, leach; cast, found.

333 Vaporization

N. *vaporization*, atomization; exhalation, *cloud*; evaporation, distillation; steaming, volatility.

vaporizer; spray, aerosol; retort, still, distillery.

Adj. *vaporific*; gassy, smoky; volatile.

Vb. *vaporize*, evaporate; *gasify*; distil, sublime, sublimate, exhale, transpire, emit vapour, *emit*; smoke, fume, reek, steam, fumigate, spray; make a spray.

334 Water

N. *water*, HR_2O; heavy water DR_2O; hard water; drinking water, tap water, mineral water, soft *drink*; water vapour, steam, *cloud*; rain water, *rain*; spring water, *stream*; holy water; *ritual object*; weeping; sweat, saliva, *fluid*; high water, high tide, low water, *wave*; standing water, *lake*; sea water, brine, *ocean*; water cure, *therapy*; bath water, bath, shower, douche, splash, *ablutions*; lotion, lavender water, *cosmetic*; damp, wet; jug, ewer, *vessel*; tap, standpipe, hydrant, *conduit*; hose; water supply, waterworks, well, *store*.

Adj. *watery*, aqueous, aquatic, *fluid*; weak;

still; wet, moist, *humid*.

Vb. **add water**, water, adulterate, dilute, *weaken*; steep, soak, liquor; irrigate, drench, *moisten*; combine with water, hydrate; slake, *decompose*.

335 Air

N. **air**, gas; thin air, ether, *rarity*; cushion of air, air pocket; blast, *wind*; common air, oxygen, nitrogen, argon; welkin, blue, blue sky, *cloud*; open air, open, exposure, *space*; sea air, ozone; fresh air; airing; air-conditioning; ventilator, blower, fan, *refrigerator*; air-filter, *cleanser*; humidifier.

atmosphere, stratosphere, ionosphere; radiation layer; aerospace; greenhouse effect, *heating*.

weather; fair weather; dry spell, heat wave, *heat*; doldrums; atmospheric pressure, anticyclone, high pressure; cyclone, depression, low pressure; rough weather, *storm*, gale; bad weather, *rain*; cold weather; changeable weather; meteorology; weather forecast, *prediction*; isobar, millibar; glass, mercury, barometer; vane, weathercock; weather ship, weather station, rain gauge; climate; climatology.

pneumatics, aerodynamics; barometer.

Adj. **airy**, insubstantial; aerial; pneumatic; inflated; breezy, *windy*; fresh; atmospheric; high-pressure, *dense*, *rare*; climatic.

Vb. **aerate**; air, expose, *dry*; ventilate, *clean*; fan, winnow, make a draught, *blow*; *breathe*.

Adv. **alfresco** out of doors, in the open.

336 Moisture

N. **moisture**, humidity, sap, juice, *fluid*; dew point; condensation, rising damp; saturation, saturation point; rainfall, wet weather, *rain*; damp, wet; spray, froth, foam, *bubble*; mist, fog, fog bank, *cloud*; Scotch mist; drizzle, drip, dew, drop, raindrop, teardrop; wet eyes; saliva, slobber, spit, spittle, *excrement*; ooze, slime, mud, squelch, fen, *marsh*; sop.

moistening, saturation, deluge, *rain*; sprinkling, sprinkle, aspersion; overflow, flood, *waterfall*; wash, bath, *ablutions*; baptism, *Christian rite*.

irrigator, sprinkler; spray, rose; hose, syringe, squirt; pump, fire engine; swipe; water butt, dam, reservoir, *store*; sluice, water pipe, *conduit*.

hygrometry; rain gauge, *gauge*.

Adj. **humid**, wet, watery, rainy; damp, moist, dripping; dank, muggy, foggy, misty, *cloudy*; muddy, slimy, sloppy, squashy, *marshy*; fresh; juicy, *fluid*; gory, bloody.

drenched, sopping, soggy, sodden; wet through, sopping wet; waterlogged, awash.

Vb. **be wet**, be soggy, squelch, suck; slobber, salivate, sweat, perspire, *exude*; steam, reek, *emit*; percolate, seep, *infiltrate*; weep, bleed, stream; ooze, drip, leak; trickle, drizzle, rain, pour, *rain*; get wet; dip, duck, dive, *plunge*; bathe, wash; wallow; paddle, wade, ford.

moisten, wet, dampen; dilute, hydrate, *add water*; lick, lap, wash; splash, splatter; spill, slop; flood, spray, shower, spatter, sprinkle, syringe; dabble, baste, *infuse*.

drench, saturate; soak, deluge, wet through, make run with; leach; wash, bathe;

sluice, slosh, rinse, *clean*; baptize, *perform ritual*; plunge, dip, duck, submerge, drown, *immerse*; swamp, flood, inundate; dunk, souse, steep; macerate, marinate; pickle, brine, *preserve*.

irrigate, water, hose, pump; inundate, flood, overflow submerge; percolate, *infiltrate*; squirt, inject.

337 Dryness

N. **dryness**; thirst, *hunger*; drought, low rainfall, desert conditions; *desert*; dry climate, dry season; sun, *heat*.

desiccation; airing; drainage; heating; searing.

dryer; silica gel, sand, blotter; absorbent, absorbent material; mop, swab, sponge, towel, towelling; wringer, mangle; *hanger*; airing cupboard.

Adj. **dry**, thirsty, *hungry*; arid; sandy, dusty, *powdery*; bare, brown; desert; *colourless*; burnt, *hot*; sunny, fine, fair; waterproof; watertight, tight, snug, proof; dry-shod.

Vb. **be dry**, keep dry, wear waterproof clothing; keep watertight; evaporate; become dry.

dry, desiccate, freeze-dry; dehydrate; ditch, drain, suck dry, *empty*; mangle; spin-dry, air, evaporate; sun, expose to sunlight, sun-dry; smoke, kipper, cure; parch, scorch, bake, burn, *heat*; shrivel, bleach; mummify, *preserve*; *staunch*; blot, mop, sponge, *absorb*; swab, wipe, wipe dry.

338 Ocean

N. **ocean**, sea, blue, salt water, brine; waters, tide, *wave*; main, deep, deep sea; great waters; trackless deep, watery waste; herring pond, drink; sea lane, shipping lane; ocean floor, sea bed, sea bottom, ooze; Antarctic Ocean, Red Sea, Mediterranean, North Sea.

sea god, Neptune, Triton, Tethys; old man of the sea.

sea nymph, Nereid, siren; Calypso; mermaid; bathing beauty; water sprite, *fairy*.

oceanography; sea survey, Admiralty chart; bathyscaphe.

Adj. **oceanic**, pelagic; sea, marine, maritime; seaworthy, *seafaring*; submarine, underwater; *deep*.

Adv. **at sea**; afloat.

339 Land

N. **land**; earth, ground, crust, *world*; continent, mainland; hinterland; midland, inland, interior; delta, promontory, tongue of land, *projection*; isthmus, neck of land; terrain, high land; polder; steppe, *plain*; wilderness, *desert*; oasis, Fertile Crescent; isle, *island*; zone; country, district, tract, *region*; territory, estate; physical features; landscape, scenery; topography, geography, geology; land-lubber, islander.

shore, coastline, *outline*; coast, edge; strand, beach, shingle; seaboard, seashore, seaside; sea cliff, sea wall; lido; bank, river bank, lea, water meadow.

soil, arable land, *farm*; pasture, *grassland*; deposit, moraine, loess, silt, alluvium; topsoil, sand, dust, subsoil; mould, humus; loam, clay, bole, marl; china clay, kaolin, *pottery*; flinty soil, gravel; stone, pebble, flint; turf, sod, clod, *piece*.

rock, cliff, scar, crag; stone, boulder; reef;

stack; dyke, sill; igneous rock, granite, basalt; volcanic glass; magma, lava; sedimentary rock, sandstone, shale, limestone, chalk, conglomerate; schist, marble; massive rock, ore, *mineralogy*; precious stone, *gem*.

Adj. *territorial*, terrestrial, farming, *agrarian*; earthy, sandy; flinty, pebbly, gravelly, stony, rocky; marble; slaty; *seasonal*.

coastal, littoral, seaside; shore.

inland, midland, mainland, interior, central.

Adv. *on land*, overland, ashore.

340 Gulf: inlet

N. *gulf*, bay, cove, creek, reach, lagoon; natural harbour, road; inlet, outlet, fleet; sea loch; mouth, estuary, sound, strait, belt, gut, channel.

341 Lake.

N. *lake*, lagoon, land-locked water; loch, lough; fresh-water lake, inland sea, Dead Sea; broad; sheet of water, backwater; mud flat, wash, *marsh*; pool, tarn, mere, pond; stew; swimming pool, swimming bath; millpond; artificial lake, dam, reservoir, *storage*; well, *water*; basin, tank, cistern, sump, *sink*; ditch, *drain*; waterhole, puddle, splash, wallow.

Adj. *lacustrine*, land-locked.

342 Marsh

N. *marsh*, morass; flat, salt marsh; fen, moor; moss, bog, quagmire, quicksand; saltpan; wallow, slough, mire, mud, ooze; swamp, mangrove swamp.

Adj. *marshy*; moorish; boggy; squashy, spongy, *soft*; muddy, *dirty*; waterlogged.

343 Plain

N. *plain*; flood plain; river basin, *valley*; marsh; delta; waste, *desert*; tundra; ice plain, ice field, ice floe, *ice*; steppe, prairie, pampas; heath, common, wold, downs, moor, fell; plateau, tableland, *high land*; bush, range, open country, *space*; green belt, national park, *open space*.

grassland, pasture, pasturage, *animal husbandry*; field, meadow, mead, lea; chase, park, grounds; green, lawn, turf.

Adj. *campestral*, rural; flat, open, rolling.

344 Island

N. *island*, isle, islet; river island; lagoon island, atoll, reef, key; sandbank, bar; floating island, iceberg; peninsula; island continent; island universe, galaxy, *star*; archipelago; islander.

Adj. *insular*, sea-girt; isolated, marooned.

345 Stream: water in motion

N. *stream*, running water, watercourse, river, navigable river; tributary, branch, feeder; brook, burn, beck, gill, runnel; torrent, force; spring, fountain, fountainhead, *source*; jet, spout, gush; geyser, hot spring, well, *store*.

current, flow, set, flux, *progression*; egress; confluence; undercurrent, undertow, crosscurrent, rip tide; tide, tidal flow, tidal current; bore; race, millrace; tap,

standpipe, hydrant, *conduit*; bloodstream, circulation.

eddy, whirlpool, swirl, maelstrom, *vortex*; surge, *recession*; wash, backwash, wake, *sequel*.

waterfall, falls, cataract; cascade, force, shoot, weir; water power; flush, chute, spillway, sluice; overflow, spill; fresh; flood, spate, deluge, cataclysm.

wave, wash, backwash; ripple, *furrow*, swell, billow, roller, breaker, surf, spume; tidal wave; bore; rip; broken water, *roughness*; sea, angry sea; undulation.

rain, rainfall, *moisture*; precipitation; drizzle, Scotch mist; sleet, hail; shower, downpour, deluge, cloudburst, thunderstorm, *storm*; flurry, *gale*; wet spell, foul weather; rainy season, monsoon; patter; rain gauge.

Adj. *flowing*, runny, *fluid*; fluent, affluent; tidal; making, running, coursing, racing; rolling; choppy, *rough*; sluggish, *slow*; sheeting, lashing, driving, dripping; *outgoing*; *incoming*.

rainy, showery, drizzly; wet, *humid*.

Vb. *flow*, run, course, pour; ebb, regurgitate, *regress*; swirl, eddy, *rotate*; surge, break, dash, ripple, wrinkle; roll, swell; buck, bounce, *leap*; gush, rush, spout, spew, jet, play, squirt, splutter; well, issue, *emerge*; pour, stream; trickle, dribble, *exude*; drip, drop, *descend*; lap, wash, slosh, splash, *moisten*; purl, trill, murmur, babble, bubble, burble, gurgle; glide, slide; overflow, cascade, flood, inundate, deluge, *drench*; *enter*; discharge itself; flow through, leak, ooze, percolate, *pass*; ooze, wind, meander.

rain, shower, stream, pour, pelt; snow, sleet, hail; fall, rain hard, pour with rain; sheet; patter, drizzle, drip, drop, spit, sprinkle; be wet.

make *flow*, *emit*; make or pass water, *excrete*; broach, tap, *open*; pour, spill, *let fall*; transfuse, decant, *transpose*; *empty*; water, *irrigate*; clear, clarify, melt, liquefy.

staunch, *dry*; apply a tourniquet; stop a leak, plug, *close*; stem, dam, *obstruct*.

346 Conduit

N. *conduit*, water channel, riverbed; trough, basin, canyon, ravine, gorge, *valley*; canal system; canal, channel, watercourse; ditch; trench, moat, runnel; Irish bridge; gutter, mill race; duct, aqueduct; plumbing, water pipe, main, pipe, hose; standpipe, hydrant, tap, spout, funnel, *tube*; valve, sluice, weir, lock, floodgate, spillway; chute, *waterfall*; pipeline; gullet, throat; neck (of a bottle); blood vessel, vein, artery, aorta, carotid; capillary.

drain, gutter, gargoyle; scupper, overflow, drainpipe, *outlet*; culvert, drain pipe, ditch, sewer, *sink*; intestine, colon; catheter.

347 Wind: air in motion

N. *wind*, *air*; draught, thermal; weather; blast, blow (see *breeze*, *gale*); air stream, current, crosswind, headwind; tailwind, following wind; air flow, slip stream; air pocket; calm air, *quietude*; cold draught, cold wind, icy blast; hot wind, sirocco; seasonal wind, monsoon; regular wind; north wind; south wind; east wind; west wind, westerly, Zephyr; wind god.

anemometry, aerodynamics; wind rose;

wind gauge, weathercock, windsock.

breeze, zephyr; breath, breath of air, waft, whiff, puff, gust; light breeze, sea breeze.

gale, strong wind, blow, blast, gust, flurry, flaw; squall, sou'wester, hurricane, whirlwind, cyclone, tornado, twister, typhoon, *vortex*; thunderstorm, dust storm, dust devil, blizzard, *storm*; weather, gale force.

blowing, inflation; pump, bellows, windbag; woodwind, brass, *musical instrument*; blowpipe; exhaust pipe, exhaust, *outlet*.

ventilation, airing, *air*; draught; ventilator, air pipe; blower, fan, *refrigerator*.

respiration, breathing, expiration, inspiration; stomach wind, flatulence, belch; bellows; respirator, iron lung, oxygen tent; windpipe, *air pipe*; cough, croup, *respiratory disease*; sigh, sob, gulp, yawn; hard breathing; wheeze, rattle.

Adj. windy, airy, draughty, breezy, blowy; fresh; gusty; blustery, dirty, foul, stormy, tempestuous, boisterous, *violent*; windswept; storm-bound; gassy.

puffing; stertorous; breathless; pulmonary; chesty.

Vb. blow, puff, blast; blow hard, blow a hurricane, rage, storm, *be violent*; wail, howl, roar; screech, scream, whistle, pipe, *shrill*; hum, moan, mutter, sigh, *sound faint*; wave, flap, shake, flutter, *agitate*; draw, make a draught, ventilate, fan, *refrigerate*; blow along, waft, *propel*; veer, back, *deviate*; drop, abate.

breathe, respire, inhale; draw a deep breath; exhale; aspirate, puff, huff, whiff; sniff, sniffle, snuffle, snort; breathe hard, gasp, pant, heave; wheeze, sneeze, cough, *rasp*; sigh, sob, gulp, yawn; belch, burp.

blow up, inflate, dilate, *enlarge*; exhaust, *empty*.

348 Air pipe

N. air pipe, airway, air shaft, air well; wind tunnel, smoke tunnel; blowpipe, peashooter; windpipe, trachea, larynx; throat, gullet; nose, nostril, blowhole, nozzle, vent, mouthpiece, *orifice*; flue pipe, mouth organ, *organ*; gas main, gas pipe; tobacco pipe, pipe, briar, hookah, *tobacco*; funnel, flue, exhaust pipe, *chimney*; airbrick, air duct, ventilator, grating, louvre, air hole, *window*.

349 Semiliquidity

N. semiliquidity; thickness; emulsion, gore, albumen, mucus, phlegm, clot, *solid body*; pus, matter; juice, sap; soup, slop, gruel, cream; molten lava; oil slick; mud, slush, sludge, thaw, ooze, slime, silt, *marsh*.

thickening, *condensation*; starch, flour; gelatine, pectin.

viscosity, viscousness; coherence; glue, gluten, gum, *adhesive*; emulsion, size, paste, glaze, slip; gel, jelly; treacle, jam, syrup, honey, goo; wax, mastic, *resin*.

Adj. semiliquid; stodgy, starchy, thick, lumpy, *dense*; jellied, juicy, milky; mushy, sloppy, waterlogged, muddy, squashy, squidgy, *marshy*.

viscid, viscous, gummy, gooey; slimy, clammy, sticky, tacky; jammy, treacly, mucous.

Vb. thicken, congeal, *be dense*; coagulate, cohere; emulsify; gel, jelly, jell; starch, harden; curdle, clot; churn, mash, pulp; muddy, puddle, *make unclean*.

350 Bubble. Cloud: air and water mixed

N. bubble, suds, soapsuds, lather, foam, froth; head, top; sea foam, spume, surf, spray, *moisture*; mousse, meringue, candyfloss; yeast, *leaven*; scum, *dirt*; fermentation, fizz.

cloud, scud, rack; cloudbank; rain cloud, cumulus, cirrus; mackerel sky; vapour, steam; haze, mist, fog, smog; film; *nebula*.

Adj. bubbly, effervescent, frizzy; foaming, frothy, soapy; yeasty, *light*; scummy, *dirty*.

cloudy, overcast; nebulous; thick, foggy, hazy, misty, *dim*.

Vb. bubble, spume, foam, froth, cream, form a head; mantle, scum; boil, simmer, fizzle, gurgle, *effervesce*; work, ferment, fizz, sparkle; aerate; steam.

cloud, overcast; be cloudy, *be dim*.

351 Pulpiness

N. pulpiness; poultice, pulp, pith, paste, putty; porridge, pap, puree; mush, mash, squash; dough, batter, sponge; soft fruit, jam; mousse, *bubble*; ooze, slush; wood pulp.

Adj. pulpy; mushy, *soft*; succulent, juicy, squashy, ripe; flabby; doughy, pasty; soggy, spongy, *marshy*.

352 Unctuousness

N. unctuousness, oiliness, greasiness, soapiness, *lubrication*.

oil, animal oil, vegetable oil, mineral oil, petroleum; refined oil, fuel oil, paraffin, kerosene, petrol, gas, *fuel*; *lubricant*.

fat, grease, blubber, tallow; wax, beeswax; suet, lard, dripping, bacon fat, *cookery*; margarine, butter; cream; buttermilk; soap, *cleanser*.

unguent, salve, ointment; liniment, embrocation, lanolin; cream, cold cream, *cosmetic*.

resin, gum, gum arabic, myrrh, frankincense, camphor; amber, ambergris; pitch, tar, bitumen, asphalt; varnish, mastic, shellac, lacquer, japan; synthetic resin.

Adj. fatty, fat, adipose; sebaceous, waxy, waxen; buttery, milky, rich, *savoury*.

unctuous, greasy, oleaginous; dripping with oil; slippery.

resinous; tarry; gummy.

Vb. grease, oil, anoint, *lubricate*; baste; butter; resin.

353 Organisms: living matter

N. organism, organic matter; ecosystem; living matter, *life*; microscopic life, *microorganism*; cell, protoplasm, cytoplasm; nucleus; RNA, DNA; chromosome, gene, *heredity*; albumen, protein; enzyme; organic remains, *fossil*.

biology, microbiology; natural history, nature study; biochemistry, developmental biology, cytology; histology; anatomy, physiology, *structure*; *botany*; ecology; marine biology; genetics, eugenics, genetic engineering; evolution, natural selection; mechanism; naturalist.

Adj. organic; cellular.

biological, biogenetic; physiological, zoological.

354 Mineral: inorganic matter

N. *mineral*, mineral world, mineral kingdom; inorganic matter, *rock*; ore, metal, alloy, *a mixture*.

mineralogy, geology, petrology; metallurgy.

Adj. *inorganic*; inanimate; mineral; metallic.

355 Life

N. *life*, living, being alive, animate existence, being, *existence*; living being, being, soul, spirit; plant life, *vegetable life*; animal life; human life, *humankind*; gift of life, birth, nativity, *origin*; new birth, *revival*; life to come, *future state*; immortal life, *heaven*; animation; vitality, vital force, vital principle, life force; soul, *spirit*; beating heart, strong pulse; survival, longevity, *long duration*; animal spirits, animation, *moral sensibility*; wind, breath, breathing, *respiration*; vital air, breath of life; *essential part*; vital spark, vital flame; seat of life, heart, artery; vital necessity, staff of life, *food*; motherhood, fatherhood; sex, sexual activity; living matter, protoplasm, tissue; cell, *organism*; symbiosis, *association*; lifetime; life expectancy, life span, life cycle; viability, *possibility*.

Adj. *alive*, living, quick, live; breathing; *lively*; incarnate; above ground; tenacious of life; capable of life, viable; vital.

born, born alive; begotten; out of, by, *akin*, laid.

Vb. *live*, be alive, have life; respire, draw breath, *breathe*; exist, subsist, *be*; come to life, come to, quicken, revive; survive, *be left*; cheat death, have nine lives; *dwell*.

be born, begin; fetch breath, be begotten.

vitalize, give birth to, beget, conceive, support life, *generate*; enliven, bring to life, *invigorate*; reanimate, *revive*; support life, provide a living; keep alive, *feed*.

356 Death

N. *death*, extinction; process of death, dying (see *decease*); Dance of Death, mortality; sentence of death, doom, knell, execution, martyrdom; deathblow, quietus; *heaven*; *tomb*; hand of death, nether regions, Hades, *hell*; Death; Angel of Death; Pluto; autopsy, *inquest*; mortuary, morgue, *cemetery*.

decease, clinical death, end of life, extinction, exit, demise, curtains, *end*; passing; natural death, quiet end, euthanasia, *euphoria*; release, welcome end; loss of life, fatality, fatal casualty; sudden death, untimely end; watery grave; fatal disease, mortal illness, *disease*; dying day, last hour; deathbed, deathwatch, death scene; last agony, last gasp, last breath, swan song, death rattle, *finality*; passing bell.

the dead, forefathers, *precursor*; saint; ghost; dead body, corpse; next world, *future state*; world of spirits, underworld; Hades, Stygian shore; happy hunting grounds.

death roll, mortality, fatality, death toll, death rate; bill of mortality, casualty list; death register, *list*; death certificate, *record*; obituary, death notice.

Adj. *dying*, mortal, ephemeral, perishable, *transient*; moribund; had it; going; sick unto death, *sick*; fated to die, fey.

dead; gone, gone before; long gone; born dead, stillborn; lifeless, breathless, still; extinct, inanimate, bereft of life; stone dead, cold, stiff; kaput; beyond mortal ken; gone to Elysium; defunct, late, sainted, of sainted memory.

Vb. *die* (*see perish*); be dead, be gone, cease to be, cease to live; die young; die a natural death; decease; succumb, expire, stop breathing; fall asleep; pass; depart this life, *depart*; go to glory, reach a better world, awake to life immortal; croak, snuff it; cop it, have bought it; go west.

perish, become extinct; wilt, wither, come to dust, *decompose*; die hard; fall, be lost; become a martyr; die untimely; meet a sticky end, die a violent death; bleed to death; drown, *founder*; be put to death, suffer execution; commit suicide, *kill oneself*.

Adv. *post-obit*, post mortem.

357 Killing: destruction of life

N. *killing*, *destruction*; destruction of life; taking life, dealing death; blood sports, hunting, *chase*; blood-letting; selective killing, cull; mercy killing, euthanasia; murder, strangulation, hanging; ritual killing, sacrifice; martyrdom; crucifixion, execution, *capital punishment*; judicial murder, burning alive; deathblow, final stroke, quietus; violent death, fatal accident, fatal casualty, car crash, plane crash.

homicide, manslaughter; murder; regicide, parricide, patricide, matricide, fratricide; infanticide; genocide (see *slaughter*).

suicide; suttee, hara-kiri; mass suicide.

slaughter, bloodshed, carnage; wholesale murder, bloodbath, massacre, fusillade, holocaust; pogrom, purge, *destruction*; genocide, Final Solution; war, battle, *warfare*; Roman holiday, duel.

slaughterhouse, abattoir, shambles; bull-ring, *arena*; field of battle; battlefield; field of blood; gas chamber.

killer, man of blood; soldier, *combatant*; butcher, knacker; huntsman, *hunter*; trapper, rodent officer; toreador, picador, matador, *athlete*; executioner, hangman; lynch mob; homicidal maniac, psychopath; head-hunter, cannibal; beast of prey, man-eater; block, gibbet, axe, guillotine, scaffold, *means of execution*; insecticide, fungicide, pesticide, poison, bane.

murderer, homicide; assassin; thug; hatchet man, gangster, gunman, bravo, desperado, cutthroat, *ruffian*; parricide, regicide; suicide.

Adj. *deadly*, killing, lethal; fell, mortal, fatal; capital; malignant, poisonous, toxic; unhealthy, *insalubrious*; inoperable, incurable.

murderous, homicidal; suicidal; internecine, trigger-happy; ensanguined, bloody, gory, red-handed; bloodthirsty, cruel.

Vb. *kill*, slay, take life, *destroy*; put to sleep; hang, behead, guillotine, electrocute, *execute*; stone, stone to death; lynch; send one to his account; deal a deathblow, give one his quietus; shed blood, knife, sabre, spear, lance, bayonet, stab, run through, *pierce*; pistol, *shoot*; strangle, garrotte, choke, suffocate, smother, stifle, drown; bury alive; smite, brain, poleaxe, sandbag, *strike*; burn alive, *burn*; immolate, sacrifice; martyr;

condemn to death, *condemn*;

slaughter, butcher, poleaxe; massacre; decimate, scupper; spare none, *be pitiless*; annihilate, exterminate, liquidate, purge, commit genocide, *destroy*.

murder, assassinate, fix, settle; smother, suffocate, strangle, poison, gas.

kill *oneself*, commit suicide, suicide; commit hara-kiri, commit suttee; hang oneself; die Roman fashion; gas oneself; take poison, take an overdose; jump overboard, drown oneself; have a fatal accident, *perish*.

Adv. *in at the death*, in at the kill.

Int. no quarter! cry havoc!

358 Corpse

N. corpse, dead body, body; dead man or woman, victim; defunct, goner, stiff; cadaver, skeleton, death's-head, skull; mummy, mortal remains, relics; clay, dust, earth; tenement of clay; carrion; long pig, *meat*; organic remains, *fossil*; shade, *ghost*.

Adj. cadaverous; stiff, carrion.

359 Interment

N. interment, burial; urn burial; burial customs; myrrh; coffin, shell, casket, urn, sarcophagus; pyre, funeral pile, crematorium; mortuary, morgue; funeral parlour; sexton; undertaker, funeral director.

obsequies; mourning, wake; burial service; funeral solemnity, funeral procession; knell, passing bell; dead march, last post; memorial service, requiem, funeral hymn, funeral oration; elegy, dirge, *lament*; inscription, epitaph, obituary; sepulchral monument, tombstone, gravestone, ledger; brass; cross, war memorial; cenotaph, *monument*; monumental mason.

funeral, hearse, bier, pall, coffin; mourner, mute, pallbearer.

grave *clothes*, shroud, mummy wrapping.

cemetery, burial place; churchyard, graveyard, God's Acre; tower of silence; garden of remembrance.

tomb, vault, crypt; burial chamber, pyramid; mausoleum, sepulchre, pantheon; grave, narrow house, long home; common grave, mass grave, plague pit; grave pit, barrow, *earthwork*; dolmen, *monument*; shrine, memorial, cenotaph.

inquest, *enquiry*; autopsy, post-mortem.

Adj. buried, laid to rest, below ground, *dead*.

funereal, funerary; sombre, sad, *black*; mourning, mortuary, sepulchral; obituary; lapidary.

Vb. inter, bury; embalm, mummify; coffin; urn, entomb; consign to earth, lay to rest, put to bed with a shovel; cremate, incinerate, *burn*; go to a funeral; mourn, keen, hold a wake, *lament*.

exhume, disinter; unearth.

Adv. in memoriam, post-mortem; RIP.

360 Animality. Animal

N. animality, animal life, wild life; animal kingdom, fauna, brute creation; physique, flesh.

animal, living thing; creature, brute, beast, dumb animal; protozoon; *microorganism*; mammal, amphibian, fish, bird, reptile; worm, mollusc; crustacean, insect, arachnid; invertebrate, vertebrate; biped,

quadruped; carnivore, herbivore, omnivore, ruminant, man-eater; wild animal, game, big game; prey, beast of prey; pack, flock, herd, *group*; stock, livestock, *stock farm*; tame animal, household pet, goldfish, hamster, guinea pig, tortoise; young animal, *young creature*; draught animal, *horse, beast of burden*; blue whale, onyx; extinct animal, dodo, auk; prehistoric animal, pterodactyl, dinosaur, brontosaurus, tyrannosaurus rex, mammoth, mastodon; fabulous beast, unicorn.

mammal, viviparous animal; man, *humankind*; primate, ape, anthropoid ape, gorilla, chimpanzee, gibbon, baboon, mandrill, monkey; marmoset, lemur; marsupial, kangaroo, wallaby, wombat, koala bear, opossum; rodent, rat, mouse, dormouse, shrew, vole, porcupine, mongoose, chipmunk, skunk, polecat, squirrel; insectivorous mammal, ant-eater, mole; nocturnal mammal, bat, bush baby, badger, hedgehog, stoat, weasel, ferret; fox, vixen; jackal, lion (see *cat*); hare, rabbit, bunny; aquatic mammal, otter, beaver, water rat, water vole; marine mammal, walrus, seal, sea lion; cetacean, dolphin, porpoise, whale; pachyderm, elephant, rhinoceros, hippopotamus; bear; giant panda; giraffe, zebra (see *cattle*); deer, stag, hart, buck, doe, fawn; red deer; reindeer, caribou, elk, moose; gazelle, antelope, chamois, springbok, wildebeest, gnu; horse, donkey, *beast of burden*.

bird, fowl; fledgling, *young creature*; canary, budgerigar, parrot, macaw; songbird, songster, warbler, nightingale, lark, thrush, blackbird, linnet; curlew, plover, lapwing, peewit; dove, pigeon, woodpecker, jay, magpie, pie; jackdaw, rook, raven, crow; finch, goldfinch, chaffinch; tit, wren, robin, sparrow, wagtail, exotic bird; golden oriole; bird of passage, summer visitor, migrant, cuckoo, swallow, swift, martin; winter visitor, redwing, snow bunting; flightless bird, emu, ostrich, rhea, kiwi, penguin; owl; vulture, carrion crow; bird of prey, eagle; kite, kestrel, harrier, osprey, buzzard, hawk, falcon, hobby, shrike; fishing bird, pelican, kingfisher, gannet, cormorant, skua, gull, kittiwake, tern, oystercatcher, puffin, guillemot; ocean bird, albatross, petrel; marsh bird, wader, stork, crane, avocet, heron, bittern; ibis, flamingo; water bird, swan, cob, pen, cygnet; duck, drake, duckling; goose, gander, gosling; teal, mallard, widgeon; moorhen, coot, diver, dipper, grebe, dabchick.

table bird, woodcock, wood pigeon; peacock; grouse, ptarmigan, pheasant, partridge, quail; goose, duck, snipe; turkey; guinea fowl.

poultry, fowl, hen; cock, cockerel, rooster, Chanticleer; chicken, pullet; spring chicken, boiler, capon; bantam.

cattle, livestock, *stock farm*; bull, cow, calf, heifer, yearling; bullock, steer; beef cattle; dairy cattle, Jersey; ox; buffalo, bison; yak, musk ox; goat.

sheep, ram, ewe, lamb; Merino; mountain sheep.

pig, swine, boar, warthog; hog, sow, piglet, porker; Large White.

dog, canine; bitch, whelp, pup, puppy; cur, hound, mutt; mongrel, pariah dog, guide dog, bloodhound, mastiff; sheepdog, collie; bull terrier, bulldog, boxer; borzoi, Afghan hound, Dalmatian; greyhound, whippet; foxhound, beagle; basset, dachshund; gun dog, retriever, pointer, setter, terrier; spaniel, show dog, chihuahua; lap dog, pug; Welsh corgi; poodle, husky, sledge dog; wild dog, dingo; wolf, coyote.

cat, feline; puss, pussy, kitten, kit; tabby; mouser; big cat, lion; tiger, leopard, cheetah, panther, puma, jaguar, cougar, ocelot; wildcat, lynx.

amphibian, frog, bullfrog, tree frog; frogspawn, tadpole; paddock, toad; newt; salamander.

reptile, serpent, snake, viper, adder; cobra; puff adder, mamba, rattlesnake; anaconda, python; crocodile, alligator; lizard, slowworm; chameleon, iguana, monitor, gecko; turtle, tortoise, terrapin.

marine life; cetacean (see *mammal*); sea urchin, sea horse, sea anemone, coral, coral reef, jellyfish, Portuguese man of war, starfish; shellfish, mollusc, bivalve, clam, oyster, mussel, cockle; whelk, winkle, limpet; cuttlefish, squid, octopus; crustacean, crab, lobster, crayfish, shrimp; barnacle.

fish, swordfish, dogfish, shark; piranha, barracuda; stingray, electric ray; tunny fish, turbot, bass, *fish food*; coelacanth; pike, roach, perch, bream, carp; trout; salmon; eel, elver, lamprey; minnow, gudgeon, stickleback.

insect, larva, pupa; fly, bluebottle; mayfly; gnat, midge, mosquito; greenfly, aphid; ladybird; firefly, glow-worm; dragonfly, crane fly; butterfly, moth, bee, bumble bee, drone; wasp, hornet; beetle, cockroach; vermin, bug, bed bug, flea, louse, nit, mite, tick; woodworm, weevil, cockchafer, deathwatch beetle, *blight*; ant, termite; stick insect; locust, grasshopper, cicada, cricket.

creepy-crawly, grub, maggot, caterpillar; worm, earthworm, lugworm, wireworm; tapeworm, fluke; centipede; slug, snail; earwig, woodlouse; spider, tarantula; scorpion, *noxious animal.*

Adj. animal; beastly, bestial, feral, domestic; human, subhuman; vertebrate, invertebrate; warm-blooded; anthropoid; equine, asinine, mulish; bovine, ruminant; sheepish; elephantine; canine; feline, tigerish; foxy, aquiline; cold-blooded, fishy; amphibian, amphibious; saurian, serpentine.

361 Vegetable life

N. *vegetable life*, vegetable kingdom; flora, vegetation; biomass; flowering, blooming; *plenty, abundance*; Flora, Pan; faun, dryad, wood nymph, *nymph.*

wood, timber, lumber, softwood, hardwood, heartwood, sapwood; forest, jungle; bush, heath, scrub; woodland, coppice, spinney; thicket, brake, covert; park, chase, game preserve; plantation, arboretum; orchard, *garden*; grove, clump; clearing, glade; undergrowth, shrubbery, windbreak, hedge, hedgerow.

forestry, conservation; forester; lumberjack.

tree, shrub, bush, sapling, scion, stock; pollard; shoot, sucker, trunk, bole; limb, branch, bough, twig; conifer, fruit tree, mahogany, ebony, teak, walnut, oak, elm, ash, beech, sycamore, maple, plane, lime, linden; horse chestnut, copper beech; redwood, larch, fir, spruce, pine,

poplar, aspen, alder, sallow, willow; birch, rowan, mountain ash; crab apple, sweet chestnut; hazel, elder, spindle; hawthorn, may, blackthorn, sloe; privet, yew, holly, ivy, box, bay, laurel; rhododendron, camellia, azalea; magnolia, laburnum, lilac; wisteria; palm, mangrove; gum tree, eucalyptus, rubber tree *agriculture.*

foliage, greenery; umbrage; limb, branch, bough, twig, shoot; spray, sprig; leaf, frond, flag, blade; leaflet; pine needle, cotyledon; petiole, node, stalk, stem; tendril, prickle, thorn.

plant, herb, weed; root, tuber, rhizome, bulb, corm, *source*; cutting, *young plant* culinary herb; medicinal herb, *remedy* food plant, fodder, *vegetable, fruit* national plant, rose, leek, daffodil, thistle, shamrock; garden plant, pansy, carnation, lily; lavender, honeysuckle, wild plant, daisy, dandelion, buttercup, water plant, water lily, flag; desert plant, cactus, succulent; prickly plant, bramble, gorse; insectivorous plant, sundew, deadly nightshade, *poisonous plant* creeper, climber, vine; parasite, mistletoe; fern, bracken; moss, lichen, fungus, mushroom, puffball; mould, penicillin, seaweed, wrack; algae, *microorganism.*

flower, blossom, bloom, bud, burgeon, head, spike, catkin; petal, sepal; corolla, calyx; ovary, ovule, receptacle; pistil, style, stigma, stamen, anther, pollen, fruit, berry, nut; seed vessel, pod, capsule, cone; pip, spore, seed, *source* annual, biennial, perennial; house plant, exotic; garden flower, wild flower, flowerbed, seedbed; horticulture, *garden.*

grass, hay, pasture, pasturage, *grassland* turf, sod, lawn; meadow grass; sedge, rush, bulrush, reed, papyrus; Pampas grass, bamboo, sugar cane; grain plant, wheat, oats, barley, rye, millet, rice, grain, husk, chaff, stubble, straw.

Adj. vegetal, vegetable, botanical; evergreen; deciduous; hardy; floral, flowery, blooming; rank, lush, overgrown; weedy, leafy, verdant, *green*; grassy; herbaceous, herbal; composite; pinnate; fungous.

arboreal; timbered; woodland, woody, wooded; wild, scrubby, bushy.

wooden, wood, woody.

Vb. *vegetate*, germinate, sprout, shoot, grow; plant, garden, *cultivate*; forest, afforest.

362 Zoology: the science of animals

N. *zoology*; animal physiology, *structure* biology; anatomy; *anthropology*; ornithology, bird lore; entomology; taxidermy.

zoologist.

Adj. *zoological.*

363 Botany: the science of plants

N. *botany*; taxonomy; plant physiology, plant pathology; plant ecology; *forestry* mycology; botanical garden, *garden* herbal; herbalist.

Adj. *botanical.*

Vb. *botanize.*

364 Animal husbandry

N. *animal husbandry*, animal management; training, manège; breeding; veterinary science; dairy farming, *cattle*; sheep farming, poultry farming; veterinary surgeon, vet, horse doctor, *doctor*; ostler, groom, stable boy, *servant*; farrier, blacksmith; keeper, gamekeeper; game warden.

stock *farm*, stud; dairy farm, ranch; fish farm, hatchery; fish pond, fish tank; duck pond; pig farm; hive, apiary; pasture, *grassland*; poultry farm, chicken run, free range; battery, deep litter; factory farm.

cattle *pen*, byre, *stable*; hutch, coop; cowshed, pigsty; bird cage, aviary.

zoo, menagerie, circus; aviary, vivarium, aquarium; reptile house, monkey temple; bear pit; wildlife park, game park, game reserve.

breeder; cattle farmer; fancier.

herdsman; stockman; cowboy; shepherd; milkmaid; kennel maid.

Adj. *tamed*, broken; gentle, docile; domestic; thoroughbred.

Vb. *break in*, tame, domesticate, acclimatize; train, *teach*; back, mount, whip, spur, *ride*; yoke, harness, hitch, bridle, saddle; herd, corral, cage, *enclose*.

breed *stock*, breed, rear, raise, grow, hatch, culture, incubate, nurture, fatten; ranch, farm, *cultivate*.

groom, stable; tend, herd, shepherd; shear, fleece; milk; drench, water, fodder, *feed*.

365 Agriculture

N. *agriculture*, rural economy; cultivation; growth, harvest, produce, crop, vintage, *store*; cash crop, husbandry, farming; cattle farming, *animal husbandry*; cereal farming, hydroponics, tray agriculture, tank farming, tillage, spadework; horticulture; *forestry*; landscape architecture; water, dung, manure, *fertilizer*; fodder, winter feed; silage, *storage*.

farm, grange; arable farm, stock *farm*; ranch, hacienda; model farm; farmhouse; farmyard, barnyard; farm, kibbutz; arable land, fallow, *soil*; rice paddy; pasturage, pasture, *grassland*; demesne, manor farm, estate, holding, smallholding, croft; allotment, kitchen garden; market garden, nursery, garden centre; vineyard; fruit farm, orchard; tea garden, tea estate, sugar plantation.

garden, vegetable garden, cabbage patch, kitchen garden, allotment; fruit garden, orchard; arboretum, *wood*; patch, plot, grass, lawn, park; shrubbery, border, bed, flowerbed; seedbed, frame; cloche, conservatory, hothouse, greenhouse, glasshouse; flowerpot.

farmer, farm manager, bailiff; cultivator, planter; peasant; serf; villein; sharecropper, tenant farmer; gentleman farmer, yeoman; crofter; fruit grower, fruit farmer; farm hand, farm labourer; land girl; tractor driver, harvester; thresher; picker; farming community, peasantry, rustic.

gardener, flower grower; nurseryman or -woman; *forestry*; planter.

farm tool, plough, ploughshare; harrow, spade, fork, hoe, rake, trowel; dibble; drill; pitchfork; scythe, sickle, shears, secateurs, *sharp edge*; flail; winepress; thresher, binder, combine harvester;

tractor; haystack; elevator, barn, silo, *storage*.

Adj. *agrarian*, peasant, farming; bucolic, pastoral, rural, rustic; collective; arable, cultivable; dug.

horticultural, garden, topiary; herbal; cultured, forced, hothouse, exotic.

Vb. *cultivate*, *make fruitful*; farm, ranch, garden, grow; till, dig, delve, spade, dibble; seed, sow, broadcast, set, plant, transplant, plough, harrow, rake, hoe; weed, prune, *shorten*; graft, engraft, *implant*; layer, force, topdress, mulch, dung, manure, *invigorate*; sod; leave fallow; harvest, *store*; glean, reap, mow, cut, scythe, cut a swathe; bind, bale, sheaf; flail, thresh, winnow, sift, bolt, *separate*; crop, pluck, pick, gather; fence, *enclose*; ditch, drain, reclaim; water, *irrigate*.

366 Humankind

N. *humankind*, mankind, womankind; humanity, human nature; flesh, mortality; everybody, ourselves; human race, human species, man; human being, Eve, lords of creation; political animal; primitive humanity; early humanity; Australopithecus; bionic person, android; ethnic type, *race*.

anthropology, ethnology, ethnography, folklore, mythology; social anthropology, demography; social science, humanitarianism, *sociology*; humanism; anthropomorphism, pathetic fallacy.

person, individual, human being; creature, mortal, body, bod; a being, soul, God's image; one, somebody, such a one; party, customer, character, type, element; chap, fellow, *male*; girl, female, woman; personage, figure, person of note, VIP, *bigwig*; celebrity, star, *favourite*; *personnel*; unit, head, hand, nose.

social group, society, community, *group*; kinship group, *family*; primitive society, tribalism; community at large, people, folk; public, *generality*; population, populace, citizenry; upper class, aristocracy.

nation, nationality, nationalism; chauvinism, jingoism, imperialism, colonialism; civil society, body politic, people; state, realm, commonwealth; democracy, republic, *government*.

Adj. *human*, mortal; anthropoid; subhuman, *inferior*; ethnic; personal, individual.

national, state, civic, civil, public, general, communal, social; cosmopolitan, international.

367 Male

N. *male*, male sex, man, he, him; masculinity, manhood; male chauvinism; patriarchy; gentleman, sir, master; lord, his lordship; mister, monsieur, Herr, señor, don, signor, sahib; comrade; squire; Mac; mate, buddy, pal, *chum*; swain; gaffer, buffer, *old man*; fellow, guy, scout, bloke, chap, johnny; codger, card, cove, joker; blade, rake, gay dog; he-man, caveman; *weakling*; homosexual, *nonconformist*; eunuch; escort, beau, boy friend; bachelor, widower; bridegroom; married man, husband, *spouse*; family man, patriarch; father, *paternity*; uncle, brother, nephew; lad, boy, *youngster*; son; stag party, menfolk.

male animal, jack, cock, cockerel, rooster; drake, gander, cob; buck, stag, hart;

horse, stallion, entire horse, colt; bull, bullock, ox, steer; boar, hog; ram; dog, dog fox; gelding, capon, *eunuch*.

Adj. *male*, masculine, chivalrous; virile; mannish, butch.

368 Female

N. *female*, feminine gender, she, her; womanhood; feminism; matriarchy; effeminacy, *weakness*; gynaecology; obstetrics.

womankind, second sex; hen party; seraglio, harem.

woman, Eve, she; girl, *youngster*; virgin, maiden; nun, old maid; *spinster*, bachelor girl, career woman; sister; suffragette; bride, married woman, wife, squaw, widow, matron, *spouse*; dowager, *old woman*; mother, grandmother, *maternity*; working wife or mother, housewife; aunt, niece, sister, daughter; wench, lass, nymph; colleen, damsel; petticoat, skirt, doll, chick, bird; honey, baby; brunette, redhead; girl friend, sweetheart, moll, crumpet, bit of fluff; broad, courtesan, *loose woman*; lesbian, *nonconformist*; minx, hussy, baggage, jade; shrew, virago, Amazon; Venus.

lady; dame; her ladyship; madam, ma'am, mistress, Mrs, Ms, miss, madame, mademoiselle, Frau, Fraulein; signora, signorina, señora, señorita.

female *animal*, hen, pen, bitch; mare, filly; cow, heifer; sow, gilt; ewe; nanny goat; hind, doe; vixen, tigress.

Adj. *female*, she, feminine, petticoat, girlish, ladylike, maidenly, matronly; child-bearing, *generative*; lesbian; womanish, effeminate, pansy.

369 Physical sensibility

N. *sensibility*, sensitiveness, tenderness, soreness, sensitivity, touchiness; awareness, consciousness, *moral sensibility*; allergy; funny bone; aesthetics; aesthete, *people of taste*; touchy person, sensitive plant, thin skin.

sense; sensory apparatus, sense organ, nerve system; five senses; touch, hearing, taste, smell, sight, sensation, impression, *feeling*; effect, response, reaction, reflex; ESP; telepathy.

Adj. *sentient*, perceptive, sensitive, sensible, susceptible, sensory; sensuous, aesthetic, *feeling*; percipient, aware, conscious, *knowing*; acute, sharp, keen, *painful*; ticklish, itchy; tender, raw, sore; impressionable, alive, alive to, warm, responsive; hypersensitive.

striking, keen, sharp, poignant, acute, vivid, clear, lively; *exciting*; sudden, sensational, *impressive*.

Vb. *have feeling*, sense, become aware; perceive, *know*; be sensible of, *feel*; react, tingle, be sensitive; hear, see, touch, taste, smell; be alert.

cause feeling, stir, disturb, *agitate*; arouse, excite, make or produce an impression, *impress*; arrest, astonish, cause a sensation, *surprise*; sharpen, cultivate, *invigorate*; refine; hurt, *give pain*.

Adv. *to the quick*.

370 Physical insensibility

N. *insensibility*; mental insensibility; anaesthesia; analgesia; hypnosis, hypnotism; apoplexy, palsy; stupor, coma, trance; faint, swoon, blackout; narcolepsy, *dis-ease*; twilight sleep, *sleep*; Rip van Winkle.

anaesthetic, dope, *drug*; local anaesthetic, ether, chloroform, morphine, cocaine; gas, nitrous oxide; narcotic, knockout drops, draught, *soporific*; opium; pain killer, analgesic, *moderator*; acupuncture.

Adj. *insensible*, insensitive; obtuse, dull, oblivious; *deaf*; unseeing, *blind*; senseless, unconscious; inert, inanimate, dead, *quiescent*; numb, benumbed, frozen, paralytic; stoned, *dead drunk*; punch drunk; comatose; anaesthetic, analgesic, *soporific*.

unfeeling, cold, callous, thick-skinned, stony, proof, shockproof, *impassive*.

Vb. *be insensible*; have a thick skin, *be insensitive*; harden oneself, cease to feel; become insensible, faint, swoon.

render insensible, make insensible; blunt, deaden; paralyse; freeze, *refrigerate*; put to sleep, send to sleep; gas, chloroform, drug, dope; dull, stupefy; stun, concuss, brain, render unconscious, *strike*; pall, cloy, sate.

371 Physical pleasure

N. *pleasure*; thrill; sensuality; self-indulgence, hedonism; round of pleasure, rest, *refreshment*; treat, entertainment, *amusement*; feast; relish, *taste*; gusto, zest, keen appreciation; mental or spiritual pleasure, delight, ecstasy, *joy*.

euphoria, well-being, *content*; physical well-being, *health*; ease, convenience, comfort; luxury; lap of luxury, *wealth*; feather bed, velvet, cushion, pillow; peace, quiet, rest, *repose*; sleep; painlessness, euthanasia.

Adj. *pleasant*; pleasing; delightful; welcome, grateful, *refreshing*; genial, congenial, cordial, heart-warming; nice, agreeable, enjoyable; palatable, delicious, tasty; sugary, *sweet*; fragrant; *melodious*, lovely, *beautiful*.

comfortable, homely, snug, cosy, warm, restful; painless, peaceful, *tranquil*; convenient, easy, cushy; downy, *soft*; luxurious; happy, *content*; relieved.

sensuous, bodily, physical, *material*; voluptuous, *sensual*.

Vb. *enjoy*, relish, like, feel pleasure, *be pleased*; thrill to, *be excited*; *taste*; *prosper*; give pleasure, *please*.

Adv. *in comfort*; in clover, on a bed of roses.

372 Physical pain

N. *pain*, discomfort, malaise, inconvenience; distress, thin time, hell, *adversity*; exhaustion, strain, *fatigue*; hurt, bruise, sprain; cut, gash, *wound*; heartache, anguish, agony, *suffering*; slow death, torment, torture; crucifixion, martyrdom; rack, wheel, thumbscrew, *instrument of torture*; painful aftermath, hang over.

pang, throb, throes; stab, twinge, nip, pinch, stitch, crick, cramp, *spasm*; smart, sting, sharp pain, ache, headache, splitting head, migraine; toothache, earache, stomachache, bellyache, gripes, colic, collywobbles; neuralgia; arthritis, rheumatism; sciatica, lumbago, backache, *ill health*.

Adj. *painful*, excruciating, exquisite; harrowing; poignant; burning, biting, stabbing; sore, raw, tender; bitter, bittersweet, *sour*; disagreeable, uncomfortable, inconvenient, *unpleasant*.

...ained, hurt, suffering.

...b. give pain, ache, hurt, pain, sting; put to torture, lacerate, torment, *torture*; flog, crucify, martyr, vivisect, tear, lacerate, *cut*; prick, stab, *pierce*; gripe, nip, pinch, tweak, twinge, shoot, throb; devour, bite, gnaw, grind, grate, jar, fret, chafe, gall, *rub*; irritate, *aggravate*; *discord*; inconvenience, annoy, distress, *trouble*.

...eel pain, suffer; ache, smart, chafe; twitch, wince, flinch, writhe, squirm, creep, shiver, quiver; tingle; have a thin time, be a martyr, go through it, *have trouble*; shriek, yell, scream, howl, groan, *cry*; weep, *lament*.

373 Touch: sensation of touch

N. touch; feeling; massage, squeeze, pressure, *friction*; graze, contact; light touch; stroke, pat, caress; flick, flip, tap, *knock*; sense of touch, precision; delicacy, artistry, *skill*.

...ormication; gooseflesh; tingle; itch; rash, prickly heat, *skin disease*.

...eeler, organ of touch, antenna, whisker, tentacle; proboscis, tongue; digit, forefinger, thumb (see *finger*); hand, paw, palm, flipper, mitt.

...inger, forefinger, index, middle finger; thumb; big toe, *foot*; bunch of fives, bone sandwich; hand, fist, *nippers*; fingernail, talon, claw.

Adj. tactual, tactile; prehensile; tangible, palpable, *material*; light of touch, *clumsy*.

...handed; right-handed; left-handed; manual.

Vb. touch, make contact, graze, scrape, shave, brush, glance; kiss, be *contiguous*; overlap; hit, meet, *collide*; feel; finger, thumb, pinch, nip, massage, *rub*; palm, stroke, *smooth*; wipe, sweep, *clean*; touch lightly, tap, pat, dab, flick, flip, tickle, scratch; lip, lap, lick, tongue; nuzzle; paw, fondle, *caress*; handle, twiddle, fiddle with; manipulate, wield, ply, manhandle, *operate*; touch roughly, bruise, crush, *give pain*; fumble, grope, scrabble; *be tentative*.

...itch, tickle, tingle, creep, crawl, have gooseflesh; prick, prickle, titillate, scratch; thrill, excite, irritate, inflame, *cause feeling*.

374 Heat

N. heat; radiant heat; emission of heat; flame, glow, flush, blush; warmth, fervour, ardour; specific heat, sweat, swelter; fever heat, fever, hectic, *disease*; high temperature, white heat; torrid heat, high summer, flaming June; heat haze, *summer*; heat wave, scorcher; hot wind, sirocco; geyser, hot water, steam; tropics, torrid zone; sun, sunshine, solar heat, *heating*.

fire; bonfire, bale fire, *glow*; death fire, pyre; coal fire, *furnace*; Greek fire, *bomb*; conflagration, holocaust; heath fire, forest fire; fireball, blaze, flame, spark, flicker, arc, *flash*; flare, *torch*; eruption, volcano; pyrotechnics; arson; fire worship, *worship*; salamander, phoenix.

...thermometry, heat measurement, thermometer, thermostat; calorimeter; thermal unit, British Thermal Unit, therm, calorie; solar constant; thermodynamics.

Adj. hot, heated; inflamed, fervent, fervid; flaming, glowing, red-hot, like an oven; piping hot, *pungent*; feverish, febrile, fevered; sweltering; smoking; running with sweat, scalding, tropical, torrid, searing, *heated*; thirsty, burning, *dry*; running a temperature.

fiery, ardent, burning, flaming; smoking; ablaze, afire; incandescent, molten, glowing, aglow, *red*; igneous, lit, alight; volcanic.

warm, tepid, lukewarm; temperate, mild, genial, balmy; fair, sunny; summery; tropical, torrid, sultry; stuffy, close, muggy; *insalubrious*; snug, *comfortable*; at room temperature, at blood heat; calorific; thermal.

Vb. be hot, be warm; burn, kindle, catch fire, draw; blaze, flare, flame; glow, flush; smoke, smoulder, reek, fume, steam, emit; boil, seethe, *effervesce*; toast, grill, roast, sizzle, crackle, frizzle, fry, bake, burn; get burnt, scorch, boil dry; bask, sun oneself, sunbathe; get sunburnt, tan; swelter, sweat, perspire, glow; melt, thaw, *liquefy*; thirst, parch, be dry; stifle, pant; be feverish, have a fever, run a temperature; keep warm.

375 Cold

N. coldness, low temperature, cool; cold, zero temperature, zero; frigidity; sensation of cold, rigour, hypothermia, shivers, gooseflesh, frostbite; chill, catching cold; cold climate, Frigid Zone, North Pole, Arctic; snowline, permafrost; glacial epoch, Ice Age; polar bear, Eskimo.

wintriness, winter, cold snap; cold weather, cold front; arctic conditions, polar temperature; blizzard; frost, Jack Frost, rime, hoarfrost, white frost, sleet, hail, hailstone, silver thaw, black ice, freeze.

snow, snowfall, snowflake, snow crystal; avalanche, snow slip, snowdrift; flurry of snow; snowball, snowman, snowplough, snowshoe; winter sports, *sport*.

ice, ice cube; hailstone, icicle; ice cap, ice field, ice sheet, ice shelf, floe, iceberg, ice front, glacier; shelf ice, frozen sea; ice yacht; ice house, *refrigerator*; ice action.

Adj. cold, without heat, impervious to heat; cool, temperate, shady, chill, chilly, parky, nippy; fresh, raw, keen, bitter, nipping, biting, piercing; below zero; frigid; frosty, frostbound, snowy, icy; glacial; polar, arctic.

chilly, feeling cold; shivery; blue, blue with cold; perishing, frozen, frostbitten; like ice.

Vb. be cold, grow cold, lose heat; feel cold, chatter, shiver, tremble, shake, quake, quiver, shudder; freeze, starve, perish with cold; catch cold, get a chill; chill, *refrigerate*.

Adv. frostily, bitterly, coldly.

376 Heating

N. heating, increase of temperature; calorific value; keeping warm; space heating, district heating system, *heater*; melting; *cookery*; antifreeze mixture.

burning, combustion; kindling, ignition; conflagration, *fire*; roasting; suttee, *suicide*; holocaust; burner, *furnace*; caustic; hot iron, brand; match, *lighter*; stoker, fireman; burn mark, burn, brand, singe, scald, sunburn, tan.

incendiarism, arson, fire-raising, pyromania; incendiary, fire-bug; firebrand, revolutionary, *agitator*.

warm *clothes*, woollens, red flannel, thermal underwear; parka, wrap, muffler, muff; winter coat, *overcoat*; blanket, *coverlet*; padding, wadding, *lining*.

ash, volcanic ash, lava; carbon, soot, smut, lamp-black, smoke; product of combustion, clinker, charcoal, ember, cinder, coke, slag, dross, oxide.

pottery, ceramics; earthenware, stoneware, faience, porcelain; crockery, china, delft, willow pattern, terracotta; tile, brick, adobe; pot, urn, *vessel*.

Adj. *heated, hot*; lit; burnt; fused, molten; smoky; sunburnt.

heating, calorific, caustic, burning; oil-fired; incendiary, inflammatory; inflammable, *combustible*; antifreeze.

Vb. *heat*, warm; provide heating; thaw; inflame, foment, poultice; stew, stifle, suffocate; sun, parch, shrivel, sear, *dry*; toast, bake, grill, fry, roast, *cook*; melt, defrost, de-ice, *liquefy*; smelt; fuse, weld, cast, found.

kindle, ignite, light, set fire to, *fire*; fuel, stoke, rub two sticks together.

burn, gut; make a bonfire of; fire, set fire to; cremate, incinerate; boil dry, *dry*; corrode; coal, char, singe, scorch, tan; brand; scald.

377 Refrigeration

N. *refrigeration*, reduction of temperature; *ice*; *condensation*; *exposure*; air-conditioning; cold storage, *refrigerator*.

incombustibility, fire resistance; asbestos.

extinguisher, foam, water, hose, sprinkler, hydrant, standpipe; fire engine, fire brigade, fire station; *fireman*.

Adj. *cooled*; frozen; with ice, *cold*.

incombustible; fireproof.

Vb. *refrigerate*, cool, fan, *refresh*; ventilate, air, *aerate*; shade, shadow; *screen*; frost, freeze, congeal; freeze-dry; make ice, ice; chill, starve, nip, pinch, bite, pierce; frost-bite.

extinguish, quench, snuff, choke, stifle, smother, *suppress*; damp, stop burning.

378 Furnace

N. *furnace*; the stake, *means of execution*; volcano; gun barrel; forge, blast furnace, kiln; incinerator, crematorium; brazier, stove, oven, range; cooker, gas ring, burner, blowlamp, oxyacetylene lamp; fire, *fire*; brand, *lighter*; fireplace, grate, hearth; firedog; poker, tongs, shovel; hob, trivet, fireguard, fender; flue, *chimney*.

heater, radiator, solar panel; geyser, boiler, copper, kettle; hotplate; electric blanket; still, retort, crucible; blowpipe, bellows, damper; hot baths, Turkish bath, sauna, *ablutions*; hotbed, hothouse, conservatory, *garden*; sun trap, solarium; kitchen, galley; grill, saucepan; toaster, iron, curling tongs; heating agent, flame, sunlight, *heating*; gas, electricity, solar energy; steam, hot air; wood, coal, *fuel*.

379 Refrigerator

N. *refrigerator*; ventilator, fan; fridge, ice bucket; coolant, snow, ice; ice pack; rocks; cold storage, freezer.

380 Fuel

N. *fuel*, inflammable material, combustible; kindling; wood, faggot, log, biomass, *vegetable life*; turf, peat; cow dung, lignite, brown coal, charcoal; fossil fuel, coal, natural gas, petroleum, *oil*, *gas*; nuclear fuel, uranium, plutonium; petrol, four-star, juice; derv; paraffin, kerosene; alcohol, spirit, North Sea gas, acetylene, propane, butane, methane.

coal, black diamond, sea coal, anthracite; coal dust, slack; coal seam, coal deposit, coal measure, coalfield, *store*; cinders, *ash*; coke.

lighter, light, taper, spill, candle, *torch*; coal, ember, brand, firebrand; fire ship, incendiary bomb, *bomb*; wick, fuse, match, percussion cap, detonator; safety match; flint, steel, tinder, punk, spunk; tinderbox.

fumigator, incense, sulphur, brimstone.

Adj. *combustible*, inflammable, incendiary, explosive; carboniferous.

Vb. *fire*, stoke, feed, fuel; put a match to, *kindle*.

381 Taste

N. *taste*, savour; flavour, flavouring; smack, tang, twang, aftertaste; relish, gusto, zest, appetite; palate, tongue; tooth, stomach.

Adj. *tasty*, palatable, full of flavour, mouth-watering, appetizing, *savoury*; salty, peppery, *pungent*; spicy, racy, rich, strong, fruity, generous, mellow, vintage.

Vb. *taste*, find palatable, *enjoy*; savour, sample, try; sip, lick, sup, nibble, *eat*; have a taste, taste of, savour of, smack of, *resemble*; taste good, *make appetizing*.

382 Insipidity

N. *insipidity*, flatness, staleness, tastelessness; milk and water, water, pap.

Adj. *tasteless*, without taste, devoid of taste; vapid, insipid, watery; mild; with water; wishy-washy, sloppy; *unsavoury*; flat, stale.

383 Pungency

N. *pungency*, sting, kick, bite, edge; burning taste; hot taste; sharp taste, acerbity, acidity; roughness; strong taste, strength, tang, twang; bad taste; salt, brine, pepper, pickle, spice, *condiment*; *revival*; cordial, *stimulant*; dram, nip, tot, *draught*; hemp, *drug*.

tobacco, baccy, snout, nicotine; tobacco leaf; blend, smoking mixture; snuff; plug of tobacco, plug, quid, twist; flake; cigar, cheroot, Havana, corona; smoke, cigarette, fag; reefer, joint; filter tip, cork tip; butt, stub; tobacco pipe, churchwarden; briar, corncob; hookah; pipe of peace; bowl, stem; tobacco juice; snuffer; smoker, tobacconist, cigarette machine; snuff box, cigarette case, cigarette box, cigar box; pipe rack; pipe cleaner; tobacco pouch, tobacco jar; smoker, smoking compartment.

Adj. *pungent*, penetrating, strong, mordant, biting, *sharp*; caustic, burning, smoky; harsh, *rough*; bitter, acrid, tart, astringent, *sour*; heady; nutty, *tasty*; high; spicy; hot, peppery; piquant, *savoury*. salty, salt, brackish, saline.

Vb. *be pungent*, sting, set the teeth on edge, make the eyes water.

eason, salt, brine, marinade, souse, pickle; flavour, sauce; spice, pepper, devil, curry; smoke, kipper, *preserve*.

moke, use tobacco, indulge, smoke a pipe, pull, draw, suck, inhale; take a drag; puff; smoke like a chimney; chew a quid; snuff, take snuff, take a pinch.

384 Condiment

N. *condiment*, seasoning, flavouring, dressing, relish, garnish; aspic; salt, mustard, pepper, paprika, chilli, caper; black pepper, peppercorn; curry powder; turmeric; onion, garlic; spice, allspice, mace, cinnamon, ginger, nutmeg, clove, caraway seed, vanilla pod.

sauce, roux; gravy, stock; brown sauce; parsley sauce; apple sauce, *sweet thing*; tomato sauce, ketchup; chilli sauce, chutney, piccalilli; salad dressing, mayonnaise, vinaigrette.

Vb. *spice*, season.

385 Savouriness

N. *savouriness*, right taste; fine flavour; body, bouquet; savoury, relish, appetizer; delicacy, dainty, titbit, *mouthful*; game, venison, turtle; ambrosia, nectar.

Adj. *savoury*, nice, good, good to eat; spicy, *tasty*; done to a turn; appetizing, piquant, *pungent*; palatable, sweet; dainty, delicate; delectable, delicious, exquisite, choice; scrumptious; fresh, crisp; ripe, mellow, luscious, juicy, succulent; rich; racy, high; vintage.

Vb. *make appetizing*, spice, ginger, *season*; be savoury, smell good, taste good, taste sweet, *sweeten*; like, relish, savour, taste.

Int. yum-yum! mmm!

386 Unsavouriness

N. *unsavouriness*, nasty taste; roughness; acerbity; prison fare; rue; bitter pill; emetic, *poison*.

Adj. *unsavoury*, flat, *tasteless*; coarse, raw, undressed; overdone, burnt; inedible, stale, hard, leathery, *tough*; soggy, *soft*; rough, *pungent*; bitter, acrid, acid, *sour*; rank, rancid, putrid, rotten, high, stinking, *fetid*; nasty, foul, revolting, loathsome, *unpleasant*; sickly, mawkish; sickening, emetic, nauseous; poisonous, toxic.

Vb. *be unpalatable*, taste horrid; disgust, repel, sicken, nauseate, *cause dislike*; poison; lose its savour, pall.

Int. Ugh! yuk!

387 Sweetness

N. *sweetness*, sweetening; sweet tooth.

sweet *thing*, sweetening, honey, honeycomb, honeydew; honeysuckle; saccharin, sucrose, glucose, dextrose, lactose; sugar; molasses, syrup, treacle; sweet sauce, custard; sweet drink, julep, nectar, mead; conserve, preserve; candied peel; jam, marmalade, jelly; marzipan, icing, sugar coating; fudge, candy; lozenge, pastille; lollipop, ice cream, candyfloss, rock; confectionery, confection, cake, *dessert*.

Adj. *sweet*, honeyed, candied; sugary, saccharine; luscious, delicious, *pleasant*; savoury.

Vb. *sweeten*, sugar, candy, ice; sweeten wine, mull.

388 Sourness

N. *sourness*, acerbity; acidity; acid, tartar; lemon, vinegar; sloe, crab apple; alum; gall.

Adj. *sour*, acid; crabbed, tart, bitter; sharp, astringent, *pungent*; *unsavoury*; green, hard, rough, *immature*; dry.

Vb. *be sour*, sour, turn, turn sour; acidify; ferment.

389 Odour

N. *odour*, smell, aroma, bouquet, nose; sweet smell, perfume, essence; bad smell, stink, *stench*; smoke, fume, reek; breath, whiff, waft; strong smell; tang, scent, trail, *trace*; sense of smell; nostril, flair, protuberance; good nose, flair.

Adj. *odorous*, *fragrant*; strong, heady, heavy, *pungent*; smelly, redolent; malodorous, *fetid*; smelt; olfactory.

Vb. *smell*, have an odour; smell of, breathe of, reek of, reek; exhale; scent, nose, wind, get wind of, *detect*; get a whiff of; snuff, sniff, inhale, *breathe*; cause to smell, scent, perfume, incense, fumigate.

390 Inodorousness

N. *inodorousness*; absence of smell, inability to smell; lack of flair; deodorant, fumes, incense, pastille.

Adj. *odourless*, without smell; without sense of smell, without flair.

Vb. *have no smell*; ventilate, *purify*.

391 Fragrance

N. *fragrance*, sweet smell, sweet savour; aroma, bouquet, *odour*; violet, rose; flower garden, *garden*; buttonhole, nosegay.

scent, perfume; balm, myrrh, incense, frankincense; *condiment*; musk, ambergris, camphor; sandalwood, patchouli; essential oil, attar; lavender, thyme, spearmint, vanilla; frangipani; honeysuckle; toilet water; hair oil; face powder, *cosmetic*; mothball, lavender bag, sachet; pomander, potpourri, scent bottle, vinaigrette.

Adj. *fragrant*, redolent, *pleasant*; balmy; spicy, fruity.

Vb. *be fragrant*, smell sweet, smell like a rose, have a perfume, scent, perfume, fumigate; embalm.

392 Stench

N. *stench*, bad smell, bad odour; body odour; foul breath, halitosis; stink, pong, reek; noxious stench; fumes, miasma, *gas*; smell of death, taint, corruption, putrefaction, *decay*; *dirt*; stale air, fug; fungus, garlic; hydrogen sulphide, ammonia; skunk, polecat; stink bomb, bad egg; dung, *excrement*; latrine, sewer, *sink*.

Adj. *fetid*, heavy, strong; malodorous, smelly; stinking, rank, foxy, fruity, high; bad, rancid, putrid; stale, airless, musty, fusty, smoky, foul; noisome, noxious, *toxic*; acrid, burning, *pungent*; nasty, disagreeable, offensive, *unpleasant*.

Vb. *stink*, smell, reek, pong, hum; make a smell; have a bad smell, smell strong, smell offensive; smell bad, *decompose*; stink to high heaven; smell like a bad egg, smell like a drain; stink like a goat, stink like a polecat; overpower with stink.

393 Sound

N. sound, auditory effect; reception, hearing; audio, mono, monophonic sound, stereo; electronic sound, sound effect; sound track; noise, loud sound; low sound; quality of sound, tone, pitch, level, cadence; accent, intonation, twang, timbre, voice; tune, strain, melody, music; bang, roll, cry, discord; transmission of sound, telephone, radio, telecommunication; high fidelity, hi-fi; gramophone; loudspeaker, hearing aid; unit of sound, decibel; sonic barrier.

acoustics, phonics; phonetics; sound engineer.

speech sound, phone, syllable, polysyllable; consonant, liquid, sibilant; dental, nasal, guttural; aspiration, inspiration, expiration; rough breathing, stop, click; mute, aspirate, surd; glide, glide sound; vowel; diphthong, voice; rising diphthong; vowel gradation; umlaut; word; sound symbol, international phonetic alphabet, IPA, script.

Adj. sounding; sonic; supersonic; plain, audible, distinct; resounding, sonorous, resonant; stentorian, loud; auditory, acoustic; monophonic, mono; stereo, high fidelity, hi-fi; audio, audiovisual; phonetic; vocal; surd, voiceless.

Vb. sound; make a noise, be loud, resound; voice.

394 Silence

N. silence; hush, lull, rest, peace, quiet; solemn silence.

Adj. silent, still; calm, peaceful, quiet, quiescent; soft, faint; inaudible; soundproof; speechless, mute, voiceless; solemn, awful.

Vb. be silent, be taciturn; be mute; be still; become silent, be quiet.

silence, still, lull, hush, quiet, quieten, make silent; soft-pedal; stifle, muffle, gag, stop, muzzle, put to silence, make mute; drown.

Int. hush! sh! silence! quiet! peace! soft! whist! hold your tongue! keep your mouth shut! shut up! keep your trap shut! dry up! cut the cackle! stow it! mum's the word!

395 Loudness

N. loudness, sound; noise, high volume; broken silence, knock; burst of sound, report, sonic boom, slam, clap, thunderclap, burst, explosion, bang; siren, alarm, honk, toot, danger signal; prolonged noise, boom, rattle, roll; thunder, storm; dashing; fire, gunfire, artillery, blitz, bombardment; blast, blare, bray, fanfare, flourish; trumpet blast, clarion call, call; clang; peal, campanology; swell, crescendo, fortissimo, full blast, full chorus; clamour, outcry, roaring, shouting, whoop, shout, howl, shriek, scream, roar, cry; loud laughter, laughter; loud breathing, respiration; din, row, racket, crash, clash, clatter, hubbub, hullabaloo, ballyhoo, uproar, tumult, bedlam, pandemonium, all hell let loose, turmoil.

megaphone, amplifier, loud pedal; public address system, loudhailer, loudspeaker, speaker, microphone, mike; ear trumpet, hearing aid; loud instrument, whistle,

siren, hooter, horn, klaxon, gong; rattle, buzzer, bell, alarm, door knocker; trumpet, brass; stentorian voice, iron throat

Adj. loud, distinct, audible; at full volume, noisy, full of noise, uproarious, rowdy, rumbustious, disorderly; clamorous, shouting, crying; sonorous, deep, full, powerful, lusty, full-throated, stentorian, piercing; thundering, thunderous, crashing; shrill, strident; brassy; resounding, resonant; swelling, crescendo; fortissimo.

Vb. be loud; give tongue, call, catcall, caterwaul; scream, whistle, shrill; vociferate, shout, cry, laugh; clap, stamp, roar, bellow, howl; din, sound, boom, reverberate, resound; rattle, thunder, fulminate, storm, clash; ring, peal, clang, crash, bray, blare; slam, bang; burst, explode, detonate; knock, knock hard, hammer, drill; deafen, stun; swell; rampage.

Adv. loudly; aloud; full blast, full chorus; fortissimo, crescendo.

396 Faintness

N. faintness; less sound, low volume, reduction of sound; dull sound, thud, thump, bump; whisper; breath; undertone, undercurrent of sound; murmur, hum, drone, roll; sigh, moan; scratch, squeak, creak, pop; tick, click; tinkle, clink, chink; buzz, whirr; purr, purl, swish, burble, gurgle, rustle; patter; soft footfall, pad; soft voice, quiet tone, conversation level.

silencer, mute, damper, muffler, soft pedal; mute; cork; grease, oil, lubricant.

Adj. muted, distant, faint, inaudible, barely audible; just caught; weak, feeble; soft, low, gentle, piano, subdued; dull, deadbated, hoarse.

Vb. sound faint, whisper, breathe, murmur, mutter, speak low; sing low, hum, croon, purr, buzz, drone; purl, babble, ripple, lap, gurgle, flow; tinkle, chime; moan, sigh, blow; rustle, swish; tremble, melt, squeak, creak; plop, pop; tick, click, clink, chink; thud, thump, sound dead.

mute, soften, dull, deaden, dampen, soft-pedal; hush, muffle, stifle, silence.

Adv. faintly, with bated breath; aside; piano, pianissimo.

397 Bang: sudden and violent noise

N. bang, report, explosion, blast, blowout, backfire, sonic boom, peal, thunderclap, crash; crackling, crackle; smack, crack, snap; slap, clap, tap, rap; knock, slam; pop, plop; burst, burst of fire; volley, round, salvo; shot, cracker, banger, squib; bomb, grenade; gun, rifle, shot-gun, firearm.

Adj. rapping; banging, crashing; popping.

Vb. crackle; sizzle, fizzle, spit, effervesce; crack, split; click, rattle; snap, clap, rap, tap, slap, smack; plop, plonk.

bang, slam, wham, clash, crash, boom; explode, blast, detonate; pop, backfire; burst, be loud.

398 Roll: repeated and protracted sounds

N. roll, rumbling, grumbling; mutter, murmur, rhubarb rhubarb; din, rattle, clank, clack, clatter, chatter, clutter; clang, ping; tattoo; peal, carillon, campanology;

dingdong, cuckoo, *repetition*; trill, tremolo, vibrato, *musical note*; quaver; hum, whirr, buzz, drone; singing; barrage, cannonade, machine gun.

Adj. *rolling, resonant*; dingdong, monotonous.

Vb. *roll*, drum, tattoo, tap, thrum; chug; boom, roar; grumble, rumble, drone, hum, whirr; trill, chime, peal, toll; tick, beat, *oscillate*; rattle, chatter, clatter, clack; reverberate, clang, ping, ring, sing; quaver, shake, tremble, vibrate; patter, *sound faint*.

399 Resonance

N. *resonance*; vibration; reflection; echo, *recurrence*; twang; singing; peal, carillon; boom; clang; brass; peal, blare, bray, flourish; tinkle, jingle, chink, clink; ping, ring, chime; low note, *musical note*; low voice, bass, baritone, contralto.

Adj. *resonant*, vibrant; fruity, *loud*; sonorous; hollow, sepulchral.

Vb. *resound*, vibrate, reverberate, echo, *roll*; whirr; hum; sing; ping, ring; jingle, jangle, chink, clink, clank; tinkle; twang; thrum; gong, chime; tootle, toot, trumpet, blare, bray, *be loud*.

400 Nonresonance

N. *nonresonance*, dead sound, thud, thump, bump; plump, plop, plonk; cracked bell, *discord*; mute, damper, *silencer*.

Adj. *nonresonant*; dead, dull, heavy; cracked, *hoarse*; soundproof, *silent*.

Vb. *sound dead*; click, flap; thump, thud, bump, pound; soft-pedal, muffle, damp, stop, soften, deaden, stifle, silence, mute.

401 Sibilation: hissing sound

N. *sibilation*, hiss; sigma, sibilant; sputter, splutter; splash, rustle; squelch, swish, escape of air; goose, serpent.

Adj. *sibilant*.

Vb. *hiss*; snort, wheeze, snuffle, whistle; buzz, fizz, fizzle, sizzle, sputter, splutter, spit; splash, *effervesce*; swish; squelch, suck; rustle, *rasp*.

402 Stridor: harsh sound

N. *stridor*, cacophony, *discord*; roughness, harsh sound, aspirate, guttural; *friction*; scrape, scratch, creak, squeak; shriek, screech, squawk, yelp; high pitch, piping, wolf whistle; bleep; piercing note, *musical note*; high voice, soprano, treble, falsetto, tenor, countertenor; twang, drone; brass, blare; pipe, fife, piccolo, penny whistle, *flute*.

Adj. *strident*; grating, rusty, harsh, brassy, brazen, metallic; high, acute, shrill, piping; penetrating, piercing, tinny, *loud*; dry, reedy, squeaky, scratchy, cracked; sharp, flat, inharmonious.
hoarse, husky, throaty, guttural, raucous, rough, gruff; hollow, deep, sepulchral; stertorous.

Vb. *rasp*, stridulate, grate, crunch, scrunch, grind, saw, scrape, scratch, squeak; snore, snort; cough, hawk, choke, gasp, sob; bray, croak, caw, screech; grunt, burr, aspirate; crack, jar, clash, jangle, twang, clank, clink, *discord*.
shrill, stridulate, bleep; drone; trumpet, blare, *be loud*; pipe, flute, *play music*; whistle, catcall, caterwaul, *cry*; scream,

squeal, yelp, screech, squawk; buzz, hum, whine; go right through one, strain.

403 Human cry

N. *cry*, animal cry; human cry, exclamation, *voice*; *speech*; talk, chat, conversation; shouting, outcry, clamour, hullabaloo; yodel, song, chant, chorus, *vocal music*; shout, yell, whoop, bawl; howl, scream, shriek, *pain*; hail, *call*; tallyho, *chase*; cheer; laugh, giggle, *laughter*; hoot, boo, *disapprobation*; plaint, complaint; sob, sigh; caterwaul, squeal, wail, whine, boohoo; grunt, gasp, *respiration*; barker.

Adj. *crying*, clamorous, loud, vociferous; stentorian, full-throated, lusty; rousing, cheering.

Vb. *cry*, exclaim, ejaculate, *speak*; call, hail, *greet*; raise a cry, whoop; hoot, boo, whistle, *disapprove*; cheer, scream, screech, yowl, howl, groan, *feel pain*; snigger, giggle, *laugh*; caterwaul, squall, boohoo, whine, whimper, wail, fret, pule, *weep*; moan, sob, sigh, *lament*; mutter, grumble, *sound faint*; gasp, grunt, snort, snore, *breathe*; squeak, squawk, yap, bark.
vociferate, clamour, start shouting, shout, bawl, yell, holler; chant, chorus, *sing*; cheer, give three cheers, exult, *rejoice*; hiss, hoot, boo, *disapprove*; roar, bellow; yell, make oneself hoarse, *be loud*.

404 Ululation: animal sounds

N. *ululation*, animal noise, howling; drone; warble, call, cry, note; squeak, cheep, twitter; buzz, hum; croak, caw, coo, hiss, quack, cluck, squawk, screech; baa, moo, neigh, whinny; cock-a-doodle-doo, cuckoo; miaow, bark, yelp, yap, snap, snarl.

Adj. *ululant*; full-throated, *loud*; roaring.

Vb. *ululate*, cry, call, give tongue; squawk, screech; caterwaul, yowl, howl, wail; roar, bellow, bell; hum, drone, buzz; spit, *hiss*; woof, bark, bay; yelp, yap; snap, snarl, growl, whine; trumpet, bell; bray, neigh, whinny; bleat, baa; low, moo; miaow, purr; quack, cackle, gaggle; gobble, gabble, cluck, clack; grunt, snort, squeal; pipe, pule; chatter, sing, chirp, cheep, peep, tweet, twitter, chuckle, whirr, coo; caw, croak; hoot, honk, boom; grate, stridulate, squeak, *rasp*; sing like a bird, warble, carol, whistle, *sing*.

405 Melody: concord

N. *melody, music*; musical quality, tonality, euphony; chime, harmony, concord, concert, *agreement*; consonance, assonance; unison; resolution (of a discord); cadence, counterpoint, polyphony; thorough bass, figured bass, part, second, chorus; instrumentation; tone, tone colour; *musical skill*; phrase, passage, theme, coda; movement, *musical piece*.
musical *note*, note, keyboard, manual, pedal point; sharp, flat, double sharp, accidental, natural, tone, semitone; keynote, fundamental note; tonic, dominant, leading note; interval, second, third, fourth, fifth, octave, ninth; gamut, scale (see *key*); chord, arpeggio; grace note, grace, ornament, crush note, acciaccatura, mordent, turn, shake, trill, tremolo, vibrato, cadenza; tone, tonality, register,

pitch, high note; low note; undertone, harmonic, upper partial; monotone, drone; phrase, flourish, *tune*; bugle call, *call*.

notation, tonic solfa; written music, score; signature, clef, bar, stave, staff; line, space, brace; rest, pause, interval; breve, semibreve, minim, crotchet, quaver, semiquaver.

tempo, time, beat; rhythm, *prosody*; measure, timing; upbeat, downbeat; suspension, long note; rallentando, andante, adagio.

key, signature, clef, major key, scale, gamut, major scale, series, tone row; mode; Indian mode, raga.

Adj. *melodious*, musical, catchy; low, soft; sweet, velvet, mellifluous; clear; silvery; *resonant*; euphonious, true.

harmonious, consonant; matching, *similar*; monophonic; monotonous.

harmonic, chromatic; tonal, atonal, sharp, flat; modal, minor, major.

Vb. *harmonize*, concert, blend, chime, *accord*; chorus, *sing*; tune, pitch, string, *adjust*; compose, put to music, orchestrate, *compose music*; modulate, transpose; resolve a discord, restore harmony.

406 Discord

N. discord, dissonance, disharmony; tone row; imperfect cadence; preparation (of a discord); cacophony; Babel; row, din, noise, pandemonium, bedlam, tumult, racket, *turmoil*; atmospherics, wow, flutter.

Adj. discordant; *contrary*; grating, harsh, raucous, *strident*; inharmonious; cracked; sharp, flat; atonal, toneless, singsong.

Vb. *discord*, lack harmony, *disagree*; jangle, jar, grate, clash, crash; saw, scrape, *rasp*; be harsh; play sharp, play flat; thrum, drone, whine; prepare a discord.

407 Music

N. *music*, harmony; sweet music, *melody*; *musical skill*; writing music, composition; instrumental music, counterpoint, contrapuntal music; classical music, light music, pop; musical wallpaper, disco music; hot music, jazz, blue note, blues, mainstream jazz, trad, Dixieland, ragtime, swing, bop, stride piano; jive, rock 'n roll, rock music, heavy metal, new wave, punk; reggae; rhythm 'n blues, blue grass, folk; written music, score, performance, concert, prom; singsong; music festival, eisteddfod; school of music; Tin Pan Alley.

campanology, carillon, chime, peal; touch; hunting, making place; hunt, hunt forward, hunt backward, dodge; round; method, Plain Bob, Treble Bob; doubles; minor, major, royal; bell; treble bell, gong; church bell, *call*.

tune, melody, strain; theme song, signature tune; descant; reprise, refrain; air, aria, solo; peal, chime, carillon; flourish; phrase, passage, measure.

musical *piece*, composition, opus, work, piece of music; tape, recording, *gramophone*; instrumentation; arrangement, adaptation, setting; accompaniment, obbligato; voluntary, prelude, overture, intermezzo; incidental music, romance, rhapsody, extravaganza, impromptu, fantasia, caprice, divert-

imento, raga; medley, potpourri; study suite, fugue, canon, toccata; sonata, concerto, symphony; pastorale, scherzo rondo, jig, reel; gavotte, minuet, tarantella, mazurka, polonaise, polka, waltz *dance*; march, dirge; nocturne, serenade statement, exposition, development, variation; theme, motive, movement; passage, phrase; chord, *musical note* cadenza, coda.

vocal music, singing, lyricism; scat singing part, opera, operetta, light opera, musical comedy, musical, *stage play*; oratorio, cantata, chorale; descant, chant, plainsong; recitative; coloratura; singing practice, solfa; anthem, psalm, *hymn*; song lay, roundelay, carol, lyric, lilt; lieder ballad; folk song, top twenty, hit parade ditty, shanty, calypso; spiritual, blues; part song, glee, madrigal, round, catch canon; chorus, refrain, burden; choral hymn; boat song, barcarole; lullaby cradle song; serenade; love song, amorous ditty; song, bird call, dawn chorus, requiem, dirge, threnody, *lament*; recitative; words to be sung, libretto; psalter.

Adj. *musical, melodious*; philharmonic; vocal; recitative; lyric; choral; contrapuntal; set, set to music; instrumental; blue, cool; hot, jazzy, swinging, swung.

Adv. *adagio*, lento, largo, andante, moderato; allegro, allegretto; vivace, presto, prestissimo; piano, pianissimo, forte, fortissimo, sforzando; glissando, legato; staccato; crescendo, diminuendo, rallentando; tremolo, pizzicato, vibrato.

408 Musician

N. *musician*, artiste, virtuoso, soloist; *proficient person*; player, performer, concert artist; bard, minstrel, troubadour; street musician; composer; scorer; swinger; cat; music writer, librettist, song writer, psalmist; music teacher, music master, conductor (see *orchestra*); Pan; music lover, music critic.

instrumentalist, player, pianist, accompanist; keyboard performer, organist, concertina player; scraper; lyre player; piper, piccolo player, flautist; horn player; drummer, drummer boy, drum major; percussionist; hurdy-gurdy man.

orchestra; ensemble, strings, brass, woodwind, percussion; band, skiffle group, steel band; conductor, maestro; leader, first violin; orchestra player, bandsman.

vocalist, songster, warbler; Siren, mermaid; troubadour, minstrel; coloratura; treble, soprano, contralto, alto, tenor, countertenor, baritone, bass; songbird, nightingale, lark, thrush, blackbird, *bird*.

choir, chorus, waits, glee club; choir festival, eisteddfod; chorister, choirboy; cantor.

musical *skill*, musical ability, musical appreciation; performance, execution, fingering, touch, expression; *skill*.

Adj. *musicianly*, fond of music, knowing music, musical; minstrel; vocal, coloratura, lyric, choral; plain-song, *melodious*; instrumental, contrapuntal.

Vb. *be musical*, learn music, sight-read; have a good ear, have perfect pitch.

compose *music*, compose, write music, put to music, score, arrange, transpose, orchestrate, improvise.

play *music*, play, perform, execute, render,

interpret; conduct, beat time; syncopate; accompany; pedal, vamp, strum; harp; pluck; thrum, twang; fiddle, bow, scrape, saw; wind, blow, bugle, sound, trumpet, toot, tootle; pipe, flute, whistle; drum, tattoo, beat, tap, ruffle, *roll*; ring, ring a change; toll, knell; tune, string, set to concert pitch; practise, improvise, play a voluntary, prelude; give an encore.

sing, chant, hymn; intone, descant; warble, carol, lilt, trill, croon, hum, whistle, yodel; solfa; sing seconds; chorus, choir; sing to, serenade; minstrel; chirp, twitter, pipe; purr, *sound faint*.

409 Musical instruments

N. *musical instrument*, band, music, concert, *orchestra*; strings, brass, wind, woodwind, percussion; diaphragm, sound box.

harp; lyre, lute, sitar; zither, guitar, mandolin, ukulele, banjo, balalaika, zither; plectrum, fret.

viol, violin, fiddle, kit, crowd; viola or tenor violin, cello or violoncello; musical saw; bow; string, catgut; bridge; resin.

piano, grand piano, concert grand, upright piano, dulcimer, harpsichord, spinet, clavichord; player piano, pianola; keyboard, manual; loud pedal, damper.

organ; reed organ, harmonium, American organ; mouth organ, harmonica; comb; accordion, concertina; barrel organ, hurdy-gurdy; great organ, organ pipe, organ stop, manual, keyboard.

flute, fife, piccolo, flageolet; recorder; woodwind, reed instrument, clarinet, basset horn; saxophone, oboe, bassoon, ocarina; pipe, reed, straw; bagpipes; pan pipes; nose flute; whistle; mouthpiece.

horn, brass; bugle horn, bugle, trumpet, clarion; alpenhorn, French horn, sousaphone; euphonium, serpent; cornet, trombone, sackbut, tuba, bass tuba; conch, shell.

gong, bell; treble bell, church bell, alarm bell, *danger signal*; peal, carillon; rattle, clappers, castanets; xylophone, marimba, vibraphone; musical glasses, harmonica; glockenspiel; triangle; percussion instrument.

drum, timpani; war drum, tomtom; tabor, tambourine.

gramophone, record player, radiogram; tape recorder, hi-fi, stereo set, music centre; playback; recording, tape, cassette; gramophone record, disc, platter, LP, album, single; track, *registration*; musical box, jukebox; head, needle, stylus, pickup, cartridge; deck, turntable; amplifier, speaker, tweeter, woofer.

mute, damper, pedal, *silencer*.

410 Hearing

N. *hearing*, audition, *acoustics*; sense of hearing, good ear; reception, earshot, range, reach; something to hear, earful.

listening, *attention*; aural examination, *enquiry*; *interpretation*; sound recording, *record*; audition, *experiment*; interview, audience, hearing, *conference*; legal hearing, *legal trial*.

listener, hearer, audience, auditorium; stalls, pit, gallery, *spectator*; radio ham; disciple; monitor; little pitcher, *inquisitive person*.

ear, auditory apparatus, auditory nerve, acoustic organ; lug, lobe, auricle; aural cavity, cochlea, eardrum, tympanum;

auditory canal, labyrinth; hearing specialist.

hearing aid, deaf-aid, ear trumpet; hearing instrument, stethoscope; loudspeaker, loudhailer, tannoy, public address system, *publication*; microphone, mike, amplifier, *megaphone*; telephone, phone, blower; receiver, earpiece; walkie-talkie, *telecommunication*; sound recorder, sonar, *recording instrument*; radiogram, *gramophone*.

Adj. *auditory*, hearing, aural; audiovisual; acoustic; *attentive*; within earshot, audible.

Vb. *hear*, catch; list, listen; lip-read, *interpret*; prepare to hear; overhear, eavesdrop; intercept, bug, tap; hearken, give ear, give audience, interview, grant an interview, *interrogate*; hear confession, *confess*; *be attentive*; catch a sound; be told, hear it said, *be informed*.

be heard, become audible, *sound*; *be loud*; gain a hearing, have an audience; be broadcast.

Adv. *in earshot*, in one's hearing.

411 Deafness

N. *deafness*, hardness of hearing; inaudibility, *silence*.

Adj. *deaf*, dull of ear, hard of hearing; unable to hear; deaf to; deaf to music, tone-deaf; hard to hear; inaudible, silent.

Vb. *be deaf*, hear nothing, fail to catch; refuse to hear, *disregard*; turn a deaf ear to, *refuse*; be hard of hearing, use a hearing aid; lip-read, *translate*.

deafen, make deaf, stun, *be loud*.

412 Light

N. *light*, daylight, light of day, noon, broad day, *morning*; sunbeam, sunlight, sun; starlight, moonlight, moonshine; twilight; artificial light, candlelight, firelight, *lighting*; splendour; candle power, magnitude; sheen, shine, gloss, lustre (see *reflection*); blaze, blaze of light, glare, dazzle; flare, flame, *fire*; halo, nimbus, glory, corona; variegated light, spectrum, rainbow; coloration, riot of colour, *colour*; white.

flash; lightning, lightning flash; beam, stream, shaft, bar, ray, pencil; streak, meteor flash; sparkle, spark; glint, glitter, play, play of light; blink, twinkle, twinkling, flicker, glimmer, gleam, shimmer; spangle, tinsel; searchlight, *lamp*; firefly, *glow-worm*.

glow, flush, sunset glow, afterglow, dawn, sunset; steady flame, steady beam; aurora; northern lights; radiance, incandescence, *heat*; phosphorescence; will-o'-the-wisp, *glow-worm*.

radiation, emission, absorption; radioactivity; radioisotope; particle counter, fallout, mushroom cloud, *poison*; radiation belt, *atmosphere*; radio wave, *sound*; sky wave; wavelength; high frequency, VHF, UHF; interference, static, *electricity*; microwave; infrared radiation, radiant heat or energy; visible light; ultraviolet radiation; X-ray, cosmic radiation, cosmic noise; photoelectric cell; roentgen.

reflection, interference; polish, gloss, sheen, shine, lustre; glare, dazzle, blink, reflector, *mirror*; mirror image, *image*.

light contrast, tonality, chiaroscuro; value, half-tone, mezzotint.

optics, fibre optics; *photography*; radiology; magnification.

Adj. *luminous*, lucid; light, lit; bright, gay, resplendent, splendid, brilliant, flamboyant, vivid; colourful, *coloured*; radiant, refulgent; glaring, lurid, garish; incandescent, flaming, aflame, aglow, ablaze, *fiery*; glowing, *red*; fluorescent; soft; lustrous, shiny, glossy.

undimmed, clear, bright, fair, unclouded; sunny; starlit; glassy; lucid, pellucid, diaphanous, translucent, *transparent*.

radiating, radiant; cosmic; hot; reflective.

Vb. *shine*, be bright, burn, blaze, flame, flare, *be hot*; glow; shine full, glare, dazzle, blind; play, dance; flash, coruscate; glisten, lift, brighten; light, ignite, twinkle; glitter, shimmer, glance; scintillate, sparkle, spark; shine again, reflect; take a shine, gleam, glint.

radiate, beam, shoot, *emit*; reflect, refract; bombard; X-ray.

make *bright*, lighten, dawn, rise, wax (moon); clear, lift, brighten; light, ignite, *kindle*; show a light, shed lustre; flood with light, irradiate, illuminate; shine within, shine through, *be visible*; pass light through; polish, burnish, *clean*.

413 Darkness

N. *darkness*, dark; black; night, nightfall; dead of night, *midnight*; Stygian gloom; murk, gloom, dusk; shade, shadow, umbra, penumbra; silhouette, negative, radiograph, *photography*; dark place, darkroom; cavern, mine, dungeon, depths.

obscuration; blackout, fade; eclipse; extinction of light; sunset, sundown, *evening*; shading, hatching, chiaroscuro; dark lantern; snuffer; dip switch.

Adj. *dark*, sombre, swarthy, *black*; obscure, inky; cavernous; Stygian; murky; funereal, dreary, dismal, sombre; lurid, *dim*; shady, *shadowy*; all black; benighted; nocturnal; secret, *occult*.

unlit; unlighted; cloudy, *opaque*.

Vb. *be dark*; lour, gather; *be dim*; lurk; look black, gloom.

darken, black, brown; occult, eclipse, mantle, *cover*; curtain, shutter, veil, *screen*; obscure, obfuscate; dim; overcast, overshadow, spread gloom; spread a shade, cast a shadow; silhouette, *represent*; shade, hatch; *blur*; blacken.

snuff out, extinguish, quench, dip.

Adv. *darkling*; at night.

414 Dimness

N. *dimness*, blur, soft focus; loom; grey; lacklustre, lack of sparkle; matt finish; poor visibility; murk, gloom; fog, mist, *cloud*; shadow, shade, shadow of a shade; spectre, *visual fallacy*.

half-light, bad light; *evening*; twilight, dusk; daybreak, break of day, grey dawn; penumbra, partial eclipse.

glimmer, flicker, *flash*; 'ineffectual fire', firefly, *glow-worm*; side lights; candlelight, firelight, *light*; ember, hot coal; smoky light, tallow candle, dip; dark lantern, *lamp*; moonbeam, moonlight, starlight.

Adj. *dim*; dusky, dusk, twilight, crepuscular; wan, dun, grey, pale, *colourless*; faint; indistinct, bleary; glassy, dull, lacklustre, leaden; flat, matt; filmy, hazy, foggy, fogbound, misty, nebulous, *cloudy*; thick, smoky, muddy, *opaque*; dingy, rusty,

dirty.

shadowy, shady, overcast; vague, indistinct, obscure, fuzzy; deceptive; withdrawn, *invisible*; dreamlike, *insubstantial*.

Vb. *be dim*, be indistinct, loom; grow grey, fade, wane, pale, *lose colour*; lour, gloom; glimmer, flicker, gutter, sputter; *lurk*.

bedim, dim, dip; obscure, *blur*; smirch, smear, besmirch, sully; rust, mildew, muddy, dirty, *make unclean*; smoke, fog, mist, *make opaque*; overshadow, overcast; shade, shadow, veil, *cover*; hatch, *darken*.

Adv. *dimly*, vaguely, indistinctly.

415 Luminary: source of light

N. *luminary*, *light*; naked light, flame, *fire*; flare, source of light, orb of day, *sun*; orb of night, *moon*; starlight, *star*; bright star; evening star, Hesperus, Venus; morning star; fireball, *meteor*; galaxy, Milky Way; northern lights; lightning, lightning flash; spark, sparkle, *flash*.

glow-worm, *glow*; firefly; will-o'-the-wisp, Jack-o'-lantern; fireball; fiery dragon.

torch, brand, coal, ember; torchlight, link, match, *lighter*; candle, tallow candle, taper, spill, wick, dip, rushlight, nightlight, naked light, flare, gas jet, burner.

lamp, lantern, bull's-eye; safety lamp, oil lamp, gas lamp, gas mantle, mantle; electric lamp, flash gun, torch, flashlight, searchlight, arc light, floodlight; headlight, side light; tail light, reflector; bulb, flashbulb, electric bulb, filament; vapour light, mercury vapour lamp, Chinese lantern, fairy lights; magic lantern, projector; light fitting, chandelier, lustre; standard lamp, lamppost, standard; socket, bracket; candle holder, candlestick.

lighting, *light*; artificial lighting, indirect lighting; gas lighting, limelight, spotlight.

signal *light*, *danger signal*; traffic light, winker; Very light, rocket, star shell, parachute flare, flare; flare path, beacon, beacon fire, *signal*; lighthouse, lightship.

fireworks, illuminations, firework display, pyrotechnics; sky rocket, Roman candle, sparkler; banger, *explosive*.

Adj. *luminescent*, luminous, incandescent; fluorescent, neon; radiant; colourful, *coloured*; bright, gay.

Vb. *illuminate*, light, shine, make bright.

416 Screen

N. *screen*, shield, *protection*; covert, *shelter*; bower, *arbour*; shady nook; sunshade, parasol; sun hat, *shade*; awning, *canopy*; visor; lampshade; blinkers, eyelid, *eye*; dark glasses; partition, wall, hedge, *fence*; filter, *exclusion*; mask, *disguise*; hood, veil, mantle, *cloak*.

curtain, *shade*; window curtain, shade, blind, sunblind; shutter.

obfuscation; smoke screen; fog, mist, *moisture*; pall, cloud, dust, film, scale.

Adj. *screened*, sheltered; cool, *cold*; shady, *shadowy*; hooded, *blind*; impervious, impermeable.

Vb. *screen*, shield, shelter, *safeguard*; protect, *defend*; parry; blanket, *exclude*; veil, hood, *cover*; mask, hide, shroud, *conceal*; intercept, *obstruct*; blindfold, *blind*; shade, shadow, darken; curtain, canopy; *close*; cloud, fog, mist; smoke, frost, glaze, film, *make opaque*.

417 Transparency

N. *transparency*, transmission of light; clarity; transparent medium, water, ice, crystal, perspex, cellophane, glass, lens, eyepiece; pane, sheer silk, gossamer, gauze, lace, chiffon, *insubstantial thing*.

Adj. *transparent*, diaphanous, sheer, see-through; thin, fine, filmy, pellucid; translucent; liquid, limpid; crystal, crystalline, vitreous, glassy; clear, serene, lucid.

Vb. *be transparent*, transmit light, show through; shine through, pass light through, *make bright*; render transparent, clarify.

418 Opacity

N. *opacity*; thickness, solidity, *density*; frost; *dirt*; fog, mist, dense fog, smog, *cloud*; film, scale, *screen*; smoke screen.

Adj. *opaque*, thick, impervious to light, blank; cloudy, milky, filmy, turbid, muddy; foggy, hazy, misty, murky, smoky, *dim*; *dirty*.

Vb. *make opaque*, cloud, thicken; frost, film, smoke; obfuscate; *coat*; be opaque, *screen*.

419 Semitransparency

N. *semitransparency*; dark glasses; gauze, muslin, net; pearl, opal; horn, mica; tissue, tissue paper.

Adj. *semitransparent*, filmy, translucent, opalescent, milky, pearly; matt, misty, *dim*, cloudy.

420 Colour

N. *colour*, complementary colour, chromatic aberration; range of colour, chromatic scale; prism, spectrum, rainbow; mixture of colours, harmony, discord; colour scheme, palette; coloration, *painting*; colour photography, riot of colour, splash; tincture, metal, fur, *heraldry*.

chromatics, science of colour, spectrum analysis; prism.

hue, colour quality, saturation, tone, value; warmth; coloration, livery; pigmentation, colouring, complexion, natural colour; hue of health, flush, blush, glow; sickly hue, pallor; tint, shade, nuance, cast, dye; tinge, patina; half-tone, mezzotint.

pigment, colouring matter, rouge, *cosmetic*; dye, madder, cochineal, *red pigment*; indigo; woad; artificial dye, stain, fixative, mordant; wash, whitewash, distemper; paint, *art equipment*.

Adj. *coloured*, fast, constant; colourful, chromatic; *uniform*; prismatic; *variegated*.

florid, colourful, ruddy, *red*; intense, deep, strong; vivid, brilliant, *luminous*; warm, glowing, rich, gorgeous; gay, bright; gaudy, garish, showy, flashy; glaring, spectacular; harsh, stark, raw, crude; lurid, loud.

soft-hued, soft, quiet, tender, delicate, refined; pearly; light, pale, pastel; dull, flat, matt, dead; simple, sober, sad, *plain*; sombre, dark, *black*; drab, dingy; mellow; matching.

Vb. *colour*, crayon, daub, *paint*; rouge, *redden*; pigment, tattoo; dye, dip; woad, blue; tint, shade, shadow, *blacken*; tincture, tinge; wash, distemper, lacquer, *coat*; stain, run, discolour; tan, weather, mellow; illuminate, emblazon; white-wash, silver, *whiten*; yellow, *gild*; enamel.

bleacher, peroxide, bleach, lime.

421 Achromatism: absence of colour

N. *achromatism*; *photography*; pallor; anaemia; pigment deficiency; neutral tint; monochrome; albino, blond.

Adj. *colourless*, toneless, neutral; faint; albino, fair, blond, *yellow*; mousy; bloodless, anaemic; without colour; pale, pallid, *white*; ashy, ashen, livid, pasty, doughy, mealy, sallow, sickly, *unhealthy*; dingy, dull, leaden, *grey*; blank, glassy, lacklustre; lurid, ghastly, wan, *dim*; cadaverous, *dead*.

Vb. *lose colour*, be dim; pale, fade, bleach, blanch, turn pale, change countenance, *whiten*; run.

decolorize, fade, etiolate; blanch, bleach, peroxide, *whiten*; deaden, weaken; pale, dim; dull, tarnish, discolour, *make unclean*.

422 Whiteness

N. *whiteness*; lack of pigment; white light, *light*; white heat, *heat*; white man, white woman, white, paleface; albino.

white *thing*, alabaster, marble; snow, chalk, paper, milk, flour, salt, ivory, lily, swan; albino; silver, white metal, white gold, pewter, platinum; pearl, teeth; white patch, blaze.

whiting, white lead; whitewash, white paint, Chinese white.

Adj. *white*, candid, pure; light, bright, *luminous*; silvery, silver; alabaster, marble; snowy, snow-capped; frosty; white hot, *hot*; white like ivory; pure white; lacking pigment; *clean*.

whitish, pearly, milky; ivory, waxen, sallow, pale, *colourless*; off-white, mushroom, magnolia; ecru, *brown*; hoary, grizzled, *grey*; pepper-and-salt, *mottled*; blond, fair, Nordic; dusty, white with dust.

Vb. *whiten*, white, whitewash, wash, *clean*; blanch, bleach; pale, fade, frost, silver, grizzle.

423 Blackness

N. *blackness*; black, sable; pigmentation, pigment, dark colouring, colour; depth, deep tone; chiaroscuro, *chequer*; black man, black woman, black, Negro, Negress; coloured man or woman, coloured; blackamoor.

black *thing*, coal, charcoal, soot, pitch, tar; ebony, jet, ink, smut; bruise, black eye; blackberry, sloe; crow, raven, blackbird; black clothes, mourning.

black *pigment*, blacking, lampblack; ivory black; ink, japan; burnt cork.

Adj. *black*, sable; jetty; inky, *dark*; smoky, smutty, *dirty*; dark, brunette; coloured; sombre, mourning, *funereal*; deep; nocturnal.

blackish, rather black; swarthy, dusky, dark, coloured; livid; *dim*.

Vb. *blacken*, black, japan, ink; dirty, blot, smudge, smirch, *make unclean*; deepen, *darken*; singe, char, burn.

424 Greyness

N. *greyness*, neutral tint; hoary head; pewter, silver; gunmetal, slate; grey, oyster.

Adj. grey, neutral, dull, sombre, leaden, livid; cool, quiet; grizzled, hoary, silvery, pearly; mousy, dun, drab, steely; ashen, ashy, smoky; dapple-grey.

425 Brownness

N. brownness, brown, bronze, copper, amber; tobacco leaf, autumn colours; cinnamon, coffee, chocolate; butterscotch, caramel, burnt almond; walnut, mahogany; dark skin or complexion, suntan; brunette.
brown pigment, ochre, sepia, raw sienna, raw umber.
Adj. brown, bronze; sunburnt; dark, brunette; hazel; light brown, ecru, oatmeal, beige, buff, fawn, biscuit, mushroom; dun, drab; khaki; tawny, tan, foxy, bay, roan, sorrel, chestnut, auburn; russet, maroon; puce; dark brown, mocha, chocolate.
Vb. embrown, brown, bronze, tan, sunburn; singe, char, toast, burn.

426 Redness

N. redness, blush, flush, sunset, dawn, glow; warmth; bloom; high colour; red colour, crimson, scarlet, carnation, rose, geranium, poppy, cherry, tomato; burgundy, port, claret; gore, blood; ruby, garnet, cornelian; flame, fire; red ink, rubric; red planet, Mars; redskin, Red Indian; redhead.
red pigment, red dye, cochineal, carmine; vermilion; madder, crimson lake; red ochre, red lead; rouge, lipstick, cosmetic.
Adj. red; ruddy, sanguine, florid; warm, hot, fiery, glowing, red-hot, hot; fevered; bright red; carroty, sandy, auburn; russet, rusty, brown; pink, rosy, coral, carnation, damask; crimson, cerise, carmine; fuchsia, magenta, maroon, purple; sanguine; scarlet, vermilion, pillarbox red.
bloodstained, bloodshot; sanguine; ensanguined, bloody, gory.
Vb. redden; rouge; dye red, stain with blood; flush, blush, glow; mantle, colour, crimson, go red.

427 Orange

N. orange, gold, old gold; or, heraldry; copper, amber; sunflower, marigold; apricot, tangerine; marmalade; ochre, Mars orange, henna.
Adj. orange, ginger, tan; brassy.

428 Yellowness

N. Yellowness, yellow, brass, gold, old gold; topaz, amber, old ivory; sulphur, brimstone; buttercup, daffodil, primrose, dandelion; lemon, honey; saffron, mustard; jaundice, yellow fever; sallow skin, fair hair; blond.
yellow pigment, gamboge, cadmium yellow; yellow ochre, weld.
Adj. yellow, gold, tawny, sandy; fallow; pale yellow, jasmine, champagne; canary yellow, gilt, gilded; deep yellow, sallow, jaundiced.
gild, yellow.

429 Greenness

N. greenness, greenery; grass, moss, turf, green leaf, foliage; lime, greengage; jade, emerald, beryl, aquamarine; verdigris,
patina.
green pigment, vindian, bice; chlorophyll.
Adj. green, verdant; grassy, leafy; emerald blue; avocado, olive.

430 Blueness

N. blueness, blue, azure; blue sky, blue sea; sapphire, aquamarine, turquoise; blue bell, cornflower, forget-me-not.
blue pigment, blue dye, indigo, woad; ultramarine, cobalt, cobalt blue.
Adj. blue, azure; cerulean; turquoise; light blue, pale blue, sapphire, aquamarine; ultramarine, deep blue, navy; indigo; livid; cold, steely, blue with cold.
Vb. blue, turn blue; dye blue, woad.

431 Purpleness

N. purpleness, purple; imperial purple; amethyst; lavender, violet, heliotrope; heather, foxglove; plum, damson, aubergine; gentian violet; lilac, mauve.
Adj. purple; violet, mauve, lavender, lilac; fuchsia, magenta, puce; heliotrope; dark purple, mulberry; livid, purple with rage; blue.
Vb. empurple, purple.

432 Variegation

N. variegation, variety, diversity, difference; glancing, light; play of colour, shot colours; opal, mother-of-pearl; shot silk; moire; tricolour; colour; peacock, peacock butterfly, tortoiseshell, chameleon; motley, harlequin, patchwork; mixture of colour; kaleidoscope; rainbow, rainbow effect, band of colour, spectrum, prism.
chequer, check, pepper-and-salt; plaid, tartan; marquetry, inlay, inlaid work, mosaic, crazy paving, medley.
stripe; line, streak, band, bar; agate; zebra; tiger; mackerel sky; crack, craze, crackle; reticulation, network.
maculation; patch, speck, speckle, freckle; blemish; fleck, dot, blotch, splash; leopard, Dalmatian.
Adj. variegated; colourful, florid; tricolour; motley, random, crazy, of all colours, multiform; plaid, tartan; rainbow; prismatic; mosaic, tessellated, parquet.
iridescent, chameleon; mother-of-pearl; opalescent, pearly; shot, shot through with.
pied, pepper-and-salt, grizzled, piebald; skewbald, roan, check, dappled, patchy.
mottled, marbled; spotted, spotty, patchy; streaky, striated, barred, striped; brindled, tabby; cloudy, powdered, dusty.
Vb. variegate, diversify, fret, pattern; punctuate; chequer, check; patch, repair; embroider, work, decorate; braid, quilt; inlay, tile; stud, pepper, dot with; speckle, freckle, spangle, spot; sprinkle; powder, dust; tattoo, stipple; streak; stripe; craze, crack, be brittle; marble; vein, cloud, make opaque; stain, blot; discolour, make unclean; make iridescent; interchange colour, play.

433 Vision

N. vision, sight; eyesight; imagination; perception, recognition; acuity (of vision); good sight, short sight, dim sight; second sight; type of vision, double vision, mag nification; tired vision, blinking; oculist, optician, *optics*; dream, *visual fallacy*.

ye, visual organ, organ of vision, eyeball, iris, pupil, white, cornea, retina, optic nerve; optics; saucer eyes, eyelid, *screen*; naked eye, clear eye, weak eyes, *dim sight*; dull eye; evil eye, *sorcery*; hawk, eagle, cat, lynx; Gorgon.

ook, regard, glance, squint; glint, blink, flash; penetrating glance, gaze, watch; stare, glad eye, ogle, leer; wink, *hint*; grimace, dirty look, scowl, evil eye; peep, peek, glimpse, half an eye.

nspection, *visibility*; examination, autopsy, *enquiry*; view, preview, *manifestation*; oversight, *management*; survey; sweep, reconnaissance, reconnoitre; sight-seeing; look, once-over, rapid survey, rapid glance; second glance, double take; review; catching sight, view, first sight; espionage.

iew; vista, prospect, outlook, perspective; aspect, *appearance*; panorama, horizon, line of sight, line of vision; range of view, ken; field of view, amphitheatre; scene, setting, stage, *theatre*; angle of vision, slant, point of view, viewpoint, standpoint; lookout, watchtower, *high structure*; gazebo; observatory; stand, grandstand, stall; loophole, peephole, window.

Adj. seeing, visual, perceptible, *visible*; ocular, binocular; perspicacious, clear-sighted, vigilant, all eyes; visionary, *imaginative*.

Vb. *see*, behold; see truly; perceive, discern, distinguish, ken, *know*; see at a glance, be wise; descry, discover, *detect*; sight, espy, spy, spot, observe, *notice*; catch sight of, sight land; catch a glimpse of, glimpse; view, command a view of; witness, be a spectator, *watch*; dream, see things, *imagine*; have second sight, *foresee*; become visible, *be visible*.

gaze, regard, quiz, gaze at, look, look at; eye, stare, peer; stare at, stare hard, goggle, gape, gawk, gawp; focus; glare, glower, look black, *be angry*; glance, glance at; squint, look askance; wink, blink, *hint*; make eyes at, ogle, leer, *court*; gloat, *be pleased*; steal a glance, peep, peek, take a peep; notice, *be attentive*; look round; look ahead, *be cautious*; *be blind*; look at each other, make eye contact.

scan, inspect, examine, take stock of; contemplate, pore, *study*; look through, have or take a squint at, take a gander or a squint at; see; make a pilgrimage, go to see, *visit*; view, survey, sweep, reconnoitre; scout; peep, peek, *be curious*; spy, pry, snoop; observe, watch, *invigilate*; *await*; keep watch; peer; squint at; crane.

Adv. *at sight*, at first sight; *visibly*.

Int. look! view halloo! land ahoy!

434 Blindness

N. *blindness*, lack of vision; lack of light; darkness, *ignorance*; eye disease, cataract; *dim sight*; blind side, blind spot; tunnel vision; blind eye, *inattention*; dyslexia; glass eye, blind man or woman; *sleep*; Braille; white stick, guide dog.

Adj. *blind*, sightless, dark; unseeing; blindfold; benighted.

Vb. *be blind*; go blind; lose sight of; be tentative; wear blinkers; be blind to; ignore, have a blind spot; *disregard*; blink, wink, squint.

---

blind; dazzle, daze; darken, obscure, eclipse; blindfold, bandage, *screen*; hoodwink, bluff, *mislead*.

435 Dim-sightedness: imperfect vision

N. *dim sight*; weak eyes, eyestrain; myopia; long sight, double sight, double vision, cataract, film; swimming; conjunctivitis, pink eye; cast; squint, wink, blink; veil, curtain, *screen*; blind side, blind spot.

visual *fallacy*; refraction, *reflection*; aberration of light, *deviation*; false light; illusion, trick of light, phantasmagoria, mirage, *deception*; will-o'-the-wisp, glow-worm; phantom, spectre, wraith, apparition, *ghost*; vision, dream, *fantasy*; magic lantern.

Adj. *dim-sighted*, dark; short-sighted, long-sighted; colour-blind; cross-eyed; boss-eyed; blinking; *blind*; swimming, dizzy.

Vb. *be dim-sighted*, need spectacles, grope, peer, squint; blink; wink; see double, dazzle, swim; dim, fail.

blur, render indistinct, confuse; glare, dazzle, daze, *shine*; darken, dim, mist, fog, smoke, smudge; be indistinct, loom, *be dim*.

436 Spectator

N. *spectator*, seer, mystic, *visionary*; viewer; inspector, *manager*; waiter, attendant, *servant*; witness, eyewitness; passerby, bystander, onlooker; tourist, globetrotter, *traveller*; stargazer; train spotter, lookout; watchman, watch, sentry; patrolman, patrol; scout, spy, snoop, *detective*; *cinema*; viewer, TV addict; captive audience.

onlookers, audience, auditorium; box office, gate; house, gallery, gods, circle, pit, stalls; grandstand; crowd, *patron*.

Vb. *watch*, look at, view, *see*; witness, be present; follow, observe, attend, *be attentive*; eye, ogle, quiz; gape, gawk, stare; spy, scout, scan.

437 Optical instrument

N. *optical device*; glass, crystal, *transparency*; optic, lens, meniscus, eyepiece, ocular, objective; burning glass; *optics*; prism; kaleidoscope; stereoscope; light meter; visual display unit; projector, magic lantern, *cinema*; microfilm reader, slide viewer, *photography*.

eyeglass, spectacles, goggles, glasses, pince-nez, sunglasses, dark glasses, bifocals; thick glasses, contact lens, lorgnette, monocle; hand lens; oculist, optician.

telescope, reflector; terrestrial telescope, *astronomy*; sight, finder, viewfinder; periscope; spyglass, night glass; binoculars, field glasses.

microscope, electron microscope, microscopy, microphotography.

mirror, reflector; metal mirror; glass, full-length mirror.

camera; box camera, single-lens reflex camera, slr; cine camera, television camera; electric eye; shutter, aperture, stop; flashgun, *lamp*; film, *photography*.

438 Visibility

N. *visibility*; *appearance*; sight, exposure; clarity, definition, prominence; eyewitness, ocular proof, visible evidence, object lesson, *manifestation*; visual aid, *teaching*; scene, field of view, *view*; atmospheric visibility, high visibility, limit of visibility, ceiling, horizon, visible distance, *range*; landmark, *signpost*.

Adj. *visible*; perceptible; noticeable, remarkable; unmistakable, palpable; apparent; evident, showing, *manifest*; open, naked, sighted; telescopic, just visible.

obvious, showing, *shown*; plain, clear, clear-cut; definite; distinct; unclouded; spectacular, conspicuous, pointed, prominent, salient; striking, *luminous*; glaring, staring; *pronounced*; vivid; plain to see.

Vb. *be visible*, become visible, be seen, show, show through, *be transparent*; attract attention, *attract notice*; hit, strike; come to light; loom, show its face, *appear*; show up, *arrive*; arise, *begin*; surface, *ascend*; emanate, come out, *emerge*; project; show; develop; manifest itself, *be plain*; *enter*; come forward, advance; dazzle, glare; shine forth, *shine*; remain visible; make visible, expose, *manifest*.

Adv. *visibly*; on show, on view.

439 Invisibility

N. *invisibility*, *absence*; poor visibility; distance; *privacy*; hiding; mystery, *secrecy*; smoke screen, mist, fog, veil, curtain; blind spot, blind eye; blind corner, *pitfall*; *danger*; blank wall; black light, *radiation*.

Adj. *invisible*, imperceptible, indiscernible; indistinguishable; unseen; sightless; remote, *distant*; secluded; *latent*; shadowy, dark, secret, mysterious; dark.

indistinct, indefinite, indistinct, *dim*; faint, inconspicuous, microscopic, *minute*; vague, fuzzy, misty, hazy.

Vb. *be unseen*; hide, go to earth, *lurk*; escape notice, blush unseen, *be humble*; become invisible, pale, fade, die, *be dim*; be lost to view, vanish, *disappear*; make invisible, submerge, *conceal*; veil, screen, darken, eclipse.

Adv. *invisibly*.

440 Appearance

N. *appearance*, phenomenon; *visibility*; first appearance, rise, *beginning*; becoming, embodiment, presence, *existence*; showing, exhibition, display, view, preview, *manifestation*; *prediction*, *probability*; revelation; outside; appearances, look of things; visual impact, face value, first blush; impression, effect; image, pose, front, public face, *duplicity*; veneer, show, seeming, semblance; side, aspect, facet; phase, guise, garb, *dressing*; colour, light, outline, shape, dimension, *form*; set, hang, look; respect, light, angle, slant, point or angle of view, *view*; a *manifestation*; vision, *fantasy*; false appearance, mirage, hallucination, illusion, *visual fallacy*, apparition, spectre, *ghost*; reflection, image, *similarity*; mental image; likeness, *representation*; visual, *image*.

spectacle, effectiveness, impression, effect; vision, sight, scene; scenery, landscape; panorama, *view*; display, pageantry, pageant, parade, review, *ostentation*; revue, extravaganza, pantomime, floor show, *stage show*; television, video; illuminations; pyrotechnics; presentation, show, exhibition, exposition, *exhibit*; art exhibition, *picture*; visual entertainment, peep show, home movies; phantasmagoria, kaleidoscope; panorama, cyclorama; tableau, transformation scene; set, decor, setting, backcloth, background, *stage set*.

cinema, cinematography; big screen, Hollywood, film industry; film studio, film production, *photography*; direction, continuity, cutting, montage, projection; screenplay, scenario, script; special effects, animation; sound effects, sound track; projector; picture house, picture palace, circuit cinema, flea pit, *theatre*; film director, film star, *actor*.

film, pictures, movies, flicks, celluloid; 3-D; silent film, talkie; X certificate, big picture, short, newsreel, trailer; cartoon, travelogue, documentary, feature film, art film, new wave; epic, blockbuster, extravaganza, musical, box-office movie, thriller, cliffhanger, war film, blue movie, Western, horse opera, remake; rush, preview; general release.

mien, look, face; play of feature, expression, brow, countenance, looks; complexion, colour, cast; air, demeanour, carriage, bearing, deportment, poise, presence, gesture, posture, behaviour, *conduct*.

feature, trait, mark; lines, cut, shape, fashion, figure, *form*; outline, contour, relief, elevation, profile, silhouette; visage, *face*.

Adj. *appearing*, apparent, phenomenal; seeming, specious, ostensible; deceptive; outward, external, superficial, *exterior*; salient, showing, *visible*; visual, videoopen to view, hung, *shown*; impressive, effective, spectacular, *showy*; decorative; meretricious; showing itself, *manifest*; visionary, dreamlike, *imaginary*.

Vb. *appear*, show, show through, *be visible*; seem, look so, *resemble*; display oneself, cut a figure; exhibit, *manifest*; start, rise, arise; dawn, break, *begin*; happen; *arrive*, walk, *haunt*.

Adv. *apparently*, *visibly*; seemingly, to all appearances, at first sight, at first blush.

441 Disappearance

N. *disappearance*, loss; flight, *escape*; exit; dissolution; extinction; eclipse; thin air.

Adj. *disappearing*, evanescent, *transient*; dissipated; missing, *absent*; lost, lost to sight, lost to view, *invisible*; gone to earth; gone, *extinct*.

Vb. *disappear*, vanish; evaporate, dissolve, melt, *liquefy*; dwindle, *decrease*; fade, pale, *lose colour*; *be transient*; suffer an eclipse, *be dim*; disperse, dissipate, diffuse, scatter; absent oneself, fail to appear, play truant, *be absent*; go, be gone, depart, *decamp*; *escape*; hide, lie low, *lurk*; *conceal*; be lost to sight, *be unseen*; seclude oneself, *seclude*; become extinct; make disappear, erase, dispel, *obliterate*.

442 Intellect

N. *intellect*, mind, psyche, mentality; affect; *will*; understanding, conception; thinking principle, intellectual faculty; reasoning power; reason, *reasoning*; philosophy; *thought*; sense, *attention*; cognition, perception; insight; instinct, *intuition*; flair, *discrimination*; mental capacity, brains, senses, sense, grey matter, *intelligence*; great intellect, genius; mental evolution; seat of thought, brain, cerebellum, cortex, *head*; electroencephalograph; healthy mind.

spirit, soul, mind, inner sense; heart, breast, bosom, inner man, *essential part*; double, ba, genius, *self*; psyche, id, ego, self; personality; spiritualism.

psychology, science of mind; abnormal psychology; Freudian psychology, configuration theory; behaviourism; crowd psychology; psychiatry, psychotherapy, psychoanalysis, *therapy*; psychosurgery, *surgery*.

psychologist, psychiatrist, *doctor*; shrink.

Adj. **mental**, thinking, reasoning, *rational*; cerebral, intellectual, abstract; theoretical; *immaterial*; percipient, perceptive; cognizant, *knowing*; conscious, subjective.

psychic, psychological; psychosomatic; subconscious, subliminal; spiritual, otherworldly, *immaterial*.

Vb. **cognize**, perceive, *know*; sense, become aware of, become conscious of; note, *see*; advert, mark, *notice*; *reason*; understand, *be wise*; *think*; conceive, invent, *discover*; *imagine*; appreciate, *estimate*.

443 Absence of intellect

N. **absence of intellect**; brute creation; vegetation, *vegetable life*; inanimate nature; instinct, intuition; *absence of thought*; brain damage, unsound mind.

Adj. **mindless**; animal, vegetable; mineral, inanimate, *inorganic*; unreasoning, *unthinking*; brute; brainless, emptyheaded, *foolish*; moronic, wanting, *insane*.

444 Thought

N. **thought**, mental process, thinking; mental act; intellectual exercise, mental action, *intellect*; thinking cap; hard thinking, hard thought, concentration, *attention*; deep thought, profundity, *wisdom*; abstract thought, *idea*; conception; current of thought, reason, *reasoning*; brown study, reverie; invention, *imagination*; afterthought, *sequel*; retrospection, hindsight, *memory*; mature thought, *preparation*; forethought, *foresight*; telepathy.

meditation, *enquiry*; lateral thinking; reflection, consideration; absorption; introspection; retreat, mysticism, *piety*; deliberation, taking counsel, *advice*; examination, close study, concentration, application, *study*.

philosophy, metaphysics, ethics; philosophical thought, scientific thought, science, natural philosophy; philosophical doctrine, philosophical system, philosophical theory, *supposition*; school of philosophy, *opinion*; idealism; realism, *reasoning*; existentialism; determinism; mechanism; humanism, hedonism; utilitarianism; materialism; pragmatism; relativity; scepticism, *doubt*; nihilism, fatalism, *fate*; Scepticism; Marxism; Hinduism, Buddhism, Yoga, Zen, *religion*.

philosopher, man or woman of thought, *intellectual*; Academy, Garden, Porch; ascetic.

Adj. **thoughtful**; full of thought, pensive, ruminant, ruminative, reflective, introspective; dreamy, *abstracted*; concentrated, *attentive*; *studious*; considerate, prudent.

philosophic, metaphysical, speculative, abstract, systematic, rational.

Vb. **think**, *suppose*; conceive; fancy, *imagine*; think about, cogitate (see *meditate*); concentrate, *be attentive*; mull, *study*; think hard, worry at; think through, *reason*; invent, *discover*; devise, *plan*; entertain a notion, have an idea; believe; be mindful, *remember*.

meditate, ruminate, digest; wonder about, debate, *reflect*, contemplate, study; speculate; think about, consider; take stock of, ponder, weigh, *estimate*; revolve; reconsider, review, think better of; take counsel, advise with, *consult*; commune with oneself; brood, muse.

dawn upon, occur to, strike one; suggest itself.

cause *thought*, make one think, make an impression, *impress*; penetrate, obsess, *bias*.

engross, absorb, preoccupy; haunt, obsess, *bias*; fascinate, *bewitch*.

Adv. **in mind**; all things considered; after due thought; come to think of it.

445 Absence of thought

N. **absence of thought**, inability to think, absence of intellect; blank mind, *ignorance*; vacancy, abstraction; empty head; want of thought, *inattention*; gut reaction; instinct, intuition.

Adj. **unthinking**, **mindless**; incapable of thought; automatic; blank, vacant, empty-headed, *empty*; thoughtless, inconsiderate, *selfish*; irrational, *illogical*; stolid, stupid, wanting; inanimate, animal, vegetable, mineral.

unthought, inconceivable, unconsidered, *impossible*.

Vb. **not think**; be blank, be vacant; *disregard*; dream; misjudge.

446 Idea

N. **idea**, notion, abstraction, a thought; object of thought, abstract idea, concept; mere idea, theory, *supposition*; image, Platonic idea, archetype, *prototype*; conception, perception, apprehension, *intellect*; reflection, *thought*; impression, conceit, fancy, *imagination*; product of imagination, figment, fiction; complex; invention, brain-child; brain wave, happy thought; wheeze, wrinkle, device; view, slant, attitude, *opinion*; principle, leading idea, main idea; one idea.

Adj. **ideational**, thoughtful; theoretical; notional, ideal, *imaginary*.

447 Topic

N. **topic**, subject of thought; gossip, rumour, *news*; subject matter, subject; contents, chapter, section, head; what it is about, argument, plot, theme, message; text, commonplace, burden, motif; musical topic, statement, *musical piece*; concern, interest, matter, affair, situation, *circumstance*; shop, *business*; agenda, order paper, *policy*; motion, *request*; resolution; problem, headache, *question*; gist, pith; theorem, proposition, *supposition*; thesis, case, point, *argument*; issue, moot point, point at issue; field, field of enquiry, field of study, *study*.

Adj. **topical**; challenging; *uncertain*; thought about.

Adv. **in question**, in the mind, on-the-brain; on the agenda; before the house, under consideration, under discussion.

448 Curiosity: desire for knowledge

N. curiosity, study; interest, itch; zeal; wanting to know; question; sightseeing, land travel; morbid curiosity.

inquisitive person; busybody, gossip, gossip columnist; news reporter; globetrotter, spectator; snoop, spy, detective; interceptor.

Adj. inquisitive, curious, interested; searching, studious; ghoulish, prurient; agog, attentive; wanting to know, burning with curiosity; officious.

Vb. be curious, want to know, only want to know; seek, search; test, research, experiment; feel a concern, be interested, take an interest; show interest, show curiosity, be attentive; peep, peek, spy, scan; snoop, pry, enquire; eavesdrop, intercept, bug, listen, hear; interfere, meddle; quiz, question, interrogate; look, stare, gape, gawk, gaze.

Int. well! what news! what's going on! who! what! where! when! how! why! why on earth!

449 Incuriosity

N. incuriosity, lack of interest, mental inertia; insouciance; apathy, moral insensibility.

Adj. incurious, unthinking; without interest, uninterested; aloof, distant; unconcerned, indifferent; listless, inert, apathetic, impassive.

Vb. be incurious; be indifferent; be insensitive; see nothing, disregard.

450 Attention

N. attention, notice, regard, look; consideration, thought; heed, readiness, solicitude, observance; watch, guard, surveillance; caution; introspection; resolution; undivided attention, whole mind, concentration, application, close study, study; examination, scrutiny, checkup, review; close attention, attention to detail, pedantry; diligent attention, pains, trouble; exclusive attention, absorption, preoccupation, brown study, inattention; interest, inquisitive attention, curiosity; fixation, obsession, monomania, mania.

Adj. attentive, intent, diligent, assiduous, industrious; considerate, thoughtful, courteous; mindful, regardful, careful; alert, ready, with it; open-eyed, waking, wakeful, awake, awake to, alive to, sensitive; aware, conscious, thinking, thoughtful; observing, watchful, vigilant; rapt, missing nothing; all eyes; all attention; serious, earnest; eager to learn, studious; close, minute, nice, meticulous, particular, punctilious, accurate, fastidious; on the look-out, expectant.

obsessed, interested, inquisitive, single-minded, possessed; rapt; crazy.

Vb. be attentive, attend, give attention, look to, heed, mind, be careful; trouble oneself, care, take trouble, take pains, bother, exert oneself; listen; take seriously, make important; think; think of nothing else; concentrate, miss nothing; watch, be all eyes, gaze; hear; examine, inspect, vet, review, scan; overhaul, revise, make better; pore, mull, read, digest, study; pay some attention, glance at, flip through.

be mindful, be thinking of, remember; think of, regard, see; lend an ear to, hear; take care of, see to, look after; have regard to, have an eye to, intend; keep track of, pursue.

notice, note, register; mark, spot; review, reconsider, meditate; take account of, consider, weigh, judge; talk about, converse; mention, hint; recall, hark back, repeat; think worthy of attention, deign to notice, acknowledge, salute, greet.

attract notice, cut a figure; arouse notice, interest, impress; excite attention, be visible; make one see, show; bring forward, call attention to, advertise, publish; point to, indicate; stress, underline; occupy, tempt; fascinate, haunt, obsess, engross; alert, warn; call to attention, command.

Int. see! mark! lo! ecce! behold! lo and behold! look! look here! look out! look alive! look to it! hark! oyez! hey! mind out! nota bene! take notice! warning! cave! take care! watch your step!

451 Inattention

N. inattention, oblivion; oversight, aberration; lapse, error; lack of interest; detachment; disregard; want of thought; deviation; levity, caprice; unseeing eyes, blind spot, blind side; distraction, red herring, inducement; absence of thought; stargazer; scatterbrain, grasshopper mind, butterfly.

abstractedness, abstraction, wandering attention, absence of mind; stargazing; fit of abstraction, reverie, brown study; distraction, preoccupation.

Adj. inattentive, careless, negligent; unseeing, blind; deaf; inadvertent, unthinking; half asleep, only half awake; uninterested, indifferent; apathetic, impassive; oblivious, forgetful; inconsiderate, thoughtless, without consideration, regardless, rash; cavalier, offhand, cursory, superficial, shallow.

abstracted, absent-minded; absent; lost, rapt, stargazing; bemused, pensive, dreamy; sleepy.

distracted; otherwise engaged; nervous.

light-minded, wandering, desultory, trifling; frivolous, flippant; airy, volatile, flighty, giddy, dizzy, scatty, harebrained, featherbrained; wild, harum-scarum; crazy; inconstant, to one thing constant never, capricious.

Vb. be inattentive, hear nothing, be blind; be deaf; overlook, commit an oversight, blunder; let slip, catch oneself doing; lose track of, lose sight of; forget; dream, drowse, nod, sleep; trifle, play at; be abstracted, wander, imagine; muse, moon; idle, doodle; digress, stray; be rattled, be nervous; hinder (see distract); disregard, ignore, neglect; think nothing of, think little of, hold cheap.

distract, divert; make forget; entice, tempt; confuse, muddle, derange; disturb, interrupt, discontinue; disconcert, upset, perplex, discompose, fluster, bother, flurry, rattle, agitate; put one off his stroke, obstruct; daze, dazzle, blind; bewilder, flummox, puzzle; fuddle, addle, make mad.

escape notice, escape attention, blush unseen, lurk; meet a blind spot.

Adv. inadvertently; rashly, giddily.

452 Carefulness

N. carefulness, pains; heed, care, attention; anxiety, solicitude, worry; loving care, benevolence; *order*; attention to detail; nicety; pedantry; conscience, *probity*; readiness, *preparedness*; *caution*; fore-thought, *foresight*.

surveillance, *protection*; lookout, weather eye; vigil, watch, deathwatch; guard; *eye*; duenna, sentry, *protection, keeper*.

Adj. *careful*, thoughtful, considerate, considered, mindful, regardful, *attentive*; taking care, painstaking; solicitous, anxious; cautious, afraid to touch; loving, tender; conscientious, scrupulous, honest, *honourable*; diligent, assiduous, *industrious*; thorough, thorough-going; meticulous, minute, particular, circumstantial; nice, exact, *accurate*; perfectionist, *fastidious*; tidy, neat, clean, *orderly*; thrifty, *parsimonious*.

vigilant, alert, ready, *prepared*; watchful, wakeful, wide-awake; all eyes, open-eyed; prudent, provident, far-sighted; surefooted; circumspect, guarded, wary, *cautious*.

Vb. *be careful*, mind, heed, beware, *be attentive*; think twice, check, *be cautious*; keep a lookout, look right then left, *be tentative*; tidy, *arrange*; take pains, do with care, be meticulous; try, *exert oneself*.

look *after*, look to, see to, take care of, *manage*; take charge of; mind, tend, keep, *safeguard*; baby-sit; nurse, foster, cherish, *pet*; respect; keep an eye, monitor; escort, play gooseberry; serve, *minister to*.

invigilate, stay awake; keep vigil, watch; keep watch; keep a sharp lookout; mount guard, set watch, stand to, *safeguard*.

Adv. *carefully*; with care, gingerly.

453 Negligence

N. *negligence, inattention*; forgetfulness, *oblivion*; neglect, oversight; default; unguarded hour or minute; disregard; insouciance; *delay*; untidiness, *disorder*; trifling; botched job, loose ends, *failure*; trifler, slacker, waster; sloven, *slut*.

Adj. *negligent*, neglectful, careless; remiss; thoughtless, *unthinking*; oblivious, *forgetful*, *indifferent*; regardless, reckless, *rash*; casual, offhand, happy-go-lucky, *lax*; sloppy, slipshod, slaphappy, slapdash, perfunctory, superficial; hurried, *hasty*; inaccurate, *inexact*; slack, supine, *lazy*; late; untidy, *dirty*; unguarded, improvident, lapsed, *irreligious*.

neglected; unkempt, *dirty*; unguarded, unattended, left alone; lost sight of; unconsidered; *invisible*; put aside, *late*; unstudied; *undone*, perfunctory; *unused*.

Vb. *neglect*, omit; lose sight of, overlook; leave undone; botch, bungle, *be clumsy*; slur, skimp, scamp, *shorten*; skip, skim, jump, skim through, *conceal*; play with, trifle, *amuse oneself*.

disregard, ignore, dodge, shirk, blink, *avoid*; allow to pass, let pass, wink at, connive at, *be lax*; refuse to see, turn a blind eye to, dismiss, *be blind*; forbear, forget it, excuse, overlook, *forgive*; discount, *underestimate*, *deviate*; slight, cold-shoulder, cut, cut dead, *be rude*; turn a deaf ear to, *be deaf*; take lightly, *be indifferent*; pooh-pooh, *hold cheap*; exclude; desert, abandon, *relinquish*.

be *neglectful*, doze, drowse, nod, *sleep*; oversleep; drift, procrastinate, let slide, let slip; take it easy, let things go; shelve, pigeonhole, lay aside, push aside; make

neglectful, lull, *surprise*.

Adv. *negligently*; anyhow; any old how.

454 Enquiry

N. *enquiry*, challenge (see *question*); taking information, *information*; close enquiry, witch-hunt, spy mania (see *search*); inquisition, examination; visitation; checkup, medical; inquest, autopsy, audit, trial, *legal trial*; public enquiry, commission of enquiry, census, survey, market research; poll, *vote*; probe, test, check, trial run, *experiment*; review, scrutiny; introspection, self-examination; research, *study*; analysis; reconnaissance, reconnoitre, survey; airing, soundings, *conference*; philosophical enquiry, *philosophy*; *curiosity*.

interrogation, forensic examination; leading question, cross-question; quiz, brains trust; interrogatory; catechism; inquisition, third degree; dialogue; question time.

question, question mark, *punctuation*; query; questionnaire, *list*; question sheet, question paper, interrogatory; challenge; fair question, catch, cross-question, indirect question, feeler, leading question; moot point, point at issue, *topic*; crucial question, controversy, *argument*; problem, poser, headache.

exam, examination; interview, audition, *hearing*; practical examination, test, battery; intelligence test, IQ test; eleven-plus, entrance examination, common entrance; Certificate of Secondary Education, CSE, sixteen-plus, General Certificate of Education, GCE, O' level, A' level; tripos, finals; degree level, *respondent*; entrant, sitter.

search, probe, enquiry, quest, hunt, *pursuit*; domiciliary visit, house-to-house search; dig; potholing; search party; searchlight; search warrant.

police *service*, detection; detective work; third degree; CID, FBI, Interpol; secret police, Gestapo.

secret *service*, espionage, intelligence, MI5, SIS, CIA; informer, spy, undercover agent, cloak-and-dagger man; double agent, mole; spy ring.

detective; plain-clothes man; enquiry agent, private detective, private eye; hotel detective, amateur detective; Federal agent, CID man; sleuth, bloodhound, nose, spy, *informer*; handwriting expert.

enquirer; *news reporter*; student, *philosopher*; search party; talent scout; scout, spy, surveyor; inspector, visitor; scrutineer, censor; test pilot, research worker, analyst; sampler; *traveller*.

questioner; *inquisitive person*; question or quiz master; confessor; *clergy*.

Adj. *enquiring*, curious, inquisitive; quizzical; interrogatory, interrogative; searching, exploratory, empirical, tentative.

moot, questionable; problematic, doubtful, *uncertain*; knotty, *difficult*; undecided, left open.

Vb. *enquire*, ask, want to know, seek an answer; demand, *request*; agitate, air, ventilate, discuss, query, subject to examination, *argue*; seek (see *search*); pursue, probe, sound, take a look at, investigate, throw open to enquiry, hold or conduct an enquiry; try, hear, *try a case*; review, overhaul, audit, monitor, screen; analyse, dissect, parse, sift, winnow; research, *study*; consider, examine, *meditate*;

check; take soundings; fathom, X-ray, scan; peer, peep, peek, snoop, spy, pry, nose around, be curious; survey, reconnoitre, case; explore, be tentative; test, try, sample, taste, experiment.

interrogate, question; cross-question, cross-examine; badger, challenge, heckle; interview; examine, probe, quiz, grill; torture; pump, suck one dry; pose, propose a question, moot.

search, seek; conduct a search, rummage, ransack, comb; scrabble, forage, root about; scour, rake through; explore every inch; overhaul, frisk, fish, go fishing; explore every avenue, exert oneself; cast about, seek a clue, pursue; probe, explore, be tentative; dig, excavate, prospect, dowse.

be questionable, be open to question, arouse suspicion, challenge an answer, demand or require an explanation; be subject to examination, be open to enquiry.

Adv. on trial, under investigation.

in search of, on the track of.

455 Answer

N. answer, reply, response; reaction; return; official reply; returns, record; feedback, information; echo, respond, repetition; password, countersign, identification; open sesame; backchat, repartee; retort, riposte; dialogue; last word, final answer; clue, key, right answer, explanation, interpretation; solution, remedy; enigmatic answer, oracle, Delphic Oracle.

rejoinder, reply; defence, reply; refutation.

respondent, defendant; correspondent; candidate, applicant, entrant, sitter, contender.

Adj. answering, respondent, responsive; counter; corresponding, corresponding to; negative; conclusive, final.

Vb. answer, reply, write back, acknowledge, respond, be responsive, echo, repeat; react, answer back, flash back, come back at, retort, riposte, retaliate; rejoin, rebut, counter; field; parry, refuse to answer, avoid; contradict, negate; be respondent, defend; be expedient; interpret; settle, decide, judge; be expedient; answer to, correspond to.

Adv. in reply.

456 Experiment

N. experiment; probe; analysis, examination, enquiry; object lesson, proof; assay, estimate; check, test, test case; probation; practical test, trial, trial run, test flight, attempt; audition, voice test; ordeal, legal trial; pilot scheme, rough sketch, first draft; first steps, debut.

empiricism, guesswork, conjecture; tentative method; experience, practice, rule of thumb, trial; random shot, gamble; instinct, trial by nature, intuition; random sample, straw vote; feeler, question; trial balloon.

experimenter, research worker, analyst; chemist; test driver, test pilot; adventurer.

testing agent, criterion, touchstone; standard, yardstick, gauge; breathalyser; control; reagent, litmus paper, retort, test tube, crucible; wind tunnel; simulator, test track; laboratory.

testee, respondent; probationer, beginner; candidate, entrant, sitter, contender; subject of experiment, subject, patient; laboratory animal, guinea pig, rat, monkey.

Adj. experimental; provisional, tentative, speculative; trial, exploratory; empirical; venturesome; uncertain.

Vb. experiment; check, verify; prove; assay, analyse; research; dabble; vivisect, make a guinea pig of; test, enquire; try, try a thing once; give a trial to, attempt; give one a try; sample, taste; take a random sample, take a straw vote; put to the vote, vote; rehearse, practise, train; undergo a test.

be tentative, be empirical, seek experience; feel, touch; probe, grope, fumble; learn; fly a kite; fish, trawl; see how far one can go; speculate, gamble; venture, explore, prospect, undertake; probe, sound, enquire.

Adv. experimentally, on trial, on approval; by trial and error; on spec.

457 Comparison

N. comparison; check, enquiry; points of comparison, analogy, parallel, likeness, similarity; identification, identity; antithesis; contrast; simile, allegory, metaphor; standard of comparison, criterion, pattern, model, check list, control, prototype.

Adj. compared, set against; comparative, comparable; relative; figurative.

Vb. compare, collate, confront; bring together, juxtapose; draw a comparison, identify; parallel; contrast, differentiate; discriminate; match, pair, balance; view together, check with; institute a comparison, draw a parallel; compare to, compare with.

Adv. comparatively; relatively.

458 Discrimination

N. discrimination, distinction, discretion; insight, perception, flair, intelligence; appreciation, critique, critical appraisal, estimate; sensibility, moral sensibility; tact, delicacy, refinement, good taste; timing, sense of occasion; nicety; fine palate, taste; hair-splitting, reasoning; separation, selection, choice; nice difference, nuance, fine shade, difference.

Adj. discriminating, selective, judicious, discerning, discreet; sensitive, accurate, fine, delicate, nice, particular, fastidious; thoughtful, imaginative; critical, judicial; distinctive.

Vb. discriminate, distinguish, differentiate, compare; sort, sieve, sift; separate, set apart; select; exercise discretion, make a distinction, make an exception, qualify; refine, reason; appraise, taste, estimate; weigh, consider, judge; discern, have insight; know; give weight to, make important; attribute just value to, be just.

459 Indiscrimination

N. indiscrimination, lack of discrimination, generality; simplicity; want of consideration; insensibility, moral insensibility; lack of refinement, vulgarity, bad taste; loose terms.

Adj. indiscriminate; undistinguished, uniform; random; unmeasured, uncertain; promiscuous, haphazard, wholesale, blanket, general.

indiscriminating, uncritical; obtuse; insensitive, impassive; coarse, vulgar; indiscreet, rash; tone-deaf, deaf; colour-blind, blind;

inaccurate, *inexact*.
Vb. *not discriminate*, be indiscriminate, avoid precision, *be neutral*; *be foolish*; swallow whole; lump everything together, *bring together*; jumble, muddle, confuse, confound, *derange*; average.

460 Measurement

N. *measurement*; mensuration; dose, *finite quantity*; rating; appraisal, appreciation; estimation, *estimate*; calculation, computation, reckoning; dead reckoning; check; reading; *long measure*; trigonometry; second, degree, minute, quadrant, *angular measure*.

geometry; solid geometry; Euclidean geometry.

metrology, dimensions, length, breadth, height, depth, thickness, *size*; metric system, unit of measurement; axle load; linear measure, *long measure*; measure of capacity, volume, cubic contents, *measure*; liquid measure, gill, pint, quart, gallon, barrel, pipe, hogshead, *vessel*; litre; minim, dram; dry measure, peck, bushel, quarter; unit of energy, ohm, watt, *electricity*; horse power, *energy*; candlepower, *light*; decibel, *sound*.

coordinate, polar coordinates; grid reference.

gauge, measure, scale, time scale; balance; micrometer; yardstick, metre bar; yard measure, metal rule; chain, link, pole, perch, rod; lead, log; ruler, slide rule; T-square, set square, dividers, callipers, compass, protractor; sextant, quadrant, *sailing aid*; theodolite, astrolabe, *astronomy*; index, Plimsoll line, Plimsoll mark; tidemark, water line, *limit*; axis, coordinate; standard, criterion, *prototype*; milestone, *signpost*.

meter; altimeter; *depth*; thermometer; barometer; speed gauge, speedometer, *velocity*; *land travel*; time gauge, metronome, time switch; *micrometer*; seismograph.

surveyor, topographer.

appraiser, valuer, assessor, surveyor.

Adj. *metrical*; imperial, metric; cubic, linear.

measured; mensurable, measurable, calculable.

Vb. *measure*, survey; compute, calculate, count, reckon, *number*; quantify; tape, span; probe, sound, fathom, plumb, *plunge*; take soundings; pace, *time*; balance, *weigh*.

gauge, meter, take a reading, read; set a standard, *make uniform*; grade, calibrate, *graduate*; reduce to scale, map, *represent*.

appraise, gauge, value, cost, rate, *price*; evaluate, estimate, appreciate, assess, *estimate*; form an opinion, *judge*; tape.

mete out, weigh, divide, share, *participate*, *apportion*.

461 Evidence

N. *evidence*, data, case history; grounds; premises; hearsay, hearsay evidence, *report*; indirect evidence, circumstantial evidence, *circumstance*; constructive evidence, *supposition*; proof; corroboration; *certainty*; one-sided evidence, piece of evidence, fact, document, exhibit, *record*; clue, *hint*; sign; reference, quotation, citation; line of evidence; authority.

testimony, witness; statement, *information*; admission, confession, *disclosure*; plea,

pretext; word, assertion; Bible evidence; sworn evidence, deposition, affidavit, *oath*; word of mouth, oral evidence, documentary evidence, evidence to character; case record, dossier, *record*; written contract, *compact*; deed, testament, *security*.

credential; testimonial, chit, character, recommendation; seal, signature, docket; voucher, warranty, warrant, certificate, diploma, *security*; ticket, passport, visa, *permit*; authority, scripture.

witness, *spectator*; ear witness; indicator, telltale, *informer*; *signatory*; witness to character, referee; sponsor, *patron*.

Adj. *evidential*, offering evidence; suggestive, significant, *meaningful*; showing, indicative; indirect, secondary, circumstantial; firsthand, direct, seen; *probable*; constructive; cumulative; telling, damning; reliable, *certain*; demonstrative, conclusive, decisive, final; factual, documentary, *positive*; authentic, well-grounded, well-founded, *true*; weighty, authoritative; *orthodox*; spoken to, sworn to.

Vb. *evidence*, show, evince, furnish evidence; *give hope*; bespeak, *represent*; breathe of, tell of, declare witness to, *manifest*; lend colour to, *make likely*; tell its own tale, speak volumes; have weight, *influence*; suggest, *indicate*; argue, involve, *imply*.

testify, witness; swear, be sworn, *affirm*; bear witness, give evidence, speak to, depose, swear to; authenticate, certify, *make certain*; attest, subscribe, countersign, endorse, sign; plead, *argue*; admit, avow, acknowledge, *confess*; give a character reference.

corroborate, support, buttress, *strengthen*; sustain, *vindicate*; verify; confirm, ratify, establish, make good, *make certain*; lead evidence, document; collect evidence, concoct evidence, *fake*.

462 Counterevidence

N. *counterevidence*; evidence against, defence, *answer*; refutation; denial; oath against oath, one word against another; mitigating evidence, *qualification*; hostile witness, hostile evidence.

Adj. *countervailing*; cutting both ways, ambiguous, *equivocal*; converse, opposite, *contrary*; *negative*; telling against.

unattested; lacking proof, *uncertain*; *false*.

Vb. *tell against*; weigh against; contravene, traverse, run counter, contradict; rebut, oppose, *be contrary*; *counteract*; cut both ways, *be equivocal*; prove a negative, *negate*; fail to confirm, tell another story; weaken, damage, spoil; undermine, subvert, *destroy*; convict of perjury; contradict oneself, turn hostile.

Adv. *conversely*, on the other hand.

463 Qualification

N. *qualification*, specification, *speciality*; prerequisite, *requirement*; assumption, *supposition*; leaven, colouring, tinge; *change*; *moderation*; condition, *conditions*; proviso, reservation; exception, salvo, saving clause; demur, but, *opposition*; consideration, concession, allowance; redeeming feature, *offset*.

Adj. *qualifying*; colouring; contingent, provisional, *conditional*; saving; qualified; exceptional, exempt.

Vb. *qualify*, condition, limit, restrict,

restrain; colour, shade; leaven, alter, *modify*; temper, season, palliate, mitigate, *moderate*; adulterate, *weaken*; excuse, *extenuate*; grant, concede; lessen, *abate*; *exempt*; introduce new conditions; *require*; relax, be lax; take exception, object, demur, *deprecate*.

Adv. *provided*, provided always, subject to; with a pinch of salt; unless, *if*; though, although, even if.

nevertheless, even so, after all; despite; but, yet, still; whether.

464 Possibility

N. *possibility*, potentiality; capacity, *ability*; what is possible, *sufficiency*; what may be, *futurity*; what might be, *past time*; what one can do, best one can do; contingency, eventuality, a possibility, chance, *fair chance*; good chance, *opportunity*; bare possibility, ghost of a chance; likelihood, probability; credibility, *belief*; *good policy*; feasibility, *facility*; compatibility, *agreement*; risk of.

Adj. *possible*, potential, hypothetical; able, capable, viable; arguable, reasonable; feasible, practicable, negotiable, *easy*; workable; operable; approachable, accessible; available, still open; conceivable, thinkable, credible, imaginable; practical, *advisable*; allowable, permissible, legal; contingent, *future*; *probable*; only possible; liable.

Vb. *be possible*, may, might, maybe, might be; might have been, admit of, allow, *permit*; bear, be open to; be a possibility, depend, be contingent; stand a chance, *be likely*.

make *possible*, enable, *empower*; allow, *permit*; *facilitate*.

Adv. *possibly*, perhaps, perchance; within reach; peradventure, haply; may be, could be; if possible, if so be; God willing.

465 Impossibility

N. *impossibility*; what cannot be, what can never be; impasse, deadlock, *obstacle*; *prohibition*; impossible task, *hard task*.

Adj. *impossible*, hopeless; unnatural, against nature; unreasonable, contrary to reason, self-contradictory, *illogical*; *erroneous*; too improbable, incredible, inconceivable, unthinkable, unheard of; miraculous, *wonderful*; visionary, *imaginary*; irrevocable, beyond recall.

impracticable, insoluble, inextricable, too hard, beyond one, *difficult*; incurable, inoperable; insuperable, insurmountable, impassable; impenetrable; inaccessible; elusive.

Vb. *be impossible*, exceed possibility, defy nature.

make *impossible*, exclude, *prohibit*; set an impossible task; eat one's hat if, *negate*; attempt the *impossible*, *waste effort*; weave a rope of sand, skin a flint.

Adv. *impossibly*, nohow, no way.

466 Probability

N. *probability*, likelihood, *chance*; good chance, *possibility*; prospect, *prediction*; fair expectation, *expectation*; well-grounded hope, *hope*; safe bet, *certainty*; real risk, real danger, *danger*; natural course, *tendency*; presumption, *evidence*; likely belief, *belief*; good reason, colour; show of, semblance, *appearance*; theory of probability.

Adj. *probable*, likely, *liable*; natural; presumable; reliable, *certain*; hopeful, promising; impending; *vulnerable*; highly possible, *possible*.

plausible, specious; apparent, ostensible; reasonable, *rational*; convincing, persuasive, easy to believe, *credible*; well-grounded, well-founded, *true*; apt.

Vb. *be likely*, have a chance, stand a chance, *be possible*; bid fair to, *tend*; promise, *give hope*.

make *likely*, make probable; involve, *imply*; entail; promote, *aid*; lend colour to, point to, *evidence*.

assume, presume, flatter oneself, *believe*; conjecture, guess, dare say, *suppose*; think likely, *expect*; see ahead, *foresee*; be certain; gather, deduce, infer, *reason*.

Adv. *probably*; very likely, ten to one; seemingly, apparently, to all appearances; like enough.

467 Improbability

N. *improbability*, doubt; little chance, long shot; scarcely any chance; long odds, bare possibility; forlorn hope, poor prospect, *lack of expectation*; rare occurrence, rarity; implausibility, *falsehood*.

Adj. *improbable*, unlikely, more than doubtful, dubious, *uncertain*; unforeseen; hard to believe, fishy; rare, *infrequent*; unheard of, inconceivable, *impossible*; incredible, too good to be true.

Vb. *be unlikely*, have a bare chance, show little hope, offer small chance; be hard to believe, *cause doubt*; think unlikely.

Int. not likely! no fear! not on your life! not a hope! some hopes!

468 Certainty

N. *certainty*, certitude, certain knowledge, *knowledge*; certain issue, necessity; *fate*; reliability, *truth*; certainty of meaning; proof; *testimony*; making sure, check, *enquiry*; dead certainty, cert, sure thing, safe bet; fact; matter of fact, *event*; settled decision; gospel, Bible, *oracle*; dogma; dictum, axiom, *maxim*; court of final appeal, *tribunal*; last word, ultimatum, *conditions*.

positiveness, subjective certainty, assurance, confidence, conviction, persuasion, *belief*, *opinion*; fixity, obsession, *bias*; self-confidence.

doctrinaire; self-opinionated person, *obstinate person*; bigot, fanatic, zealot; oracle, Sir Oracle, knowall.

Adj. *certain*, sure, solid, well-founded, well-grounded, *substantial*; reliable, *trustworthy*; authoritative, official, *genuine*; factual, *true*; tried, foolproof, *safe*; infallible, unerring, *veracious*; self-evident, evident, apparent; unequivocal; unmistakable, clear, *obvious*; inevitable, irrevocable, inexorable, *fated*; bound, bound to be; inviolable, *invulnerable*; demonstrable.

positive, confident, assured, sure; opinionated; pontifical, *assertive*; doctrinaire, orthodox; set, fixed; clean-cut, definite, unequivocal, *intelligible*; convincing, *credible*; classified; affirmative, categorical, absolute, unqualified, unreserved, final, ultimate, conclusive, settled, without appeal.

undisputed, beyond doubt, without a shadow of doubt; undoubted, indubitable, unquestionable, incontrovertible,

incontestable, unimpeachable, undeniable, irrefutable.
Vb. *be certain*, stand to reason, *be reasonable*; be positive, be assured, satisfy oneself, feel sure, *believe*; understand, *know*; dismiss all doubt.
dogmatize, pontificate, *affirm*.
make *certain*, certify, authenticate, ratify, seal, sign, *endorse*; guarantee, warrant, assure; settle, decide, *judge*; remove doubt, persuade, *convince*; classify, *arrange*; make sure, ascertain, check, double-check, verify, confirm, clinch, *corroborate*; reassure oneself, take a second look, do a double take; insure against, *safeguard*; *be cautious*; ensure, make inevitable, *necessitate*.
Adv. *certainly*, definitely, to be sure, doubtless, of course; without fail, sink or swim, rain or shine, come hell or high water, come what may.

469 Uncertainty

N. *uncertainty*; mist, haze, fog; borderline case; query, question mark, *question*; open question, guesswork, *conjecture*; contingency, doubtful event, *chance*; gamble, toss-up, wager; bow at a venture, blind date; something or other, this or that.
dubiety, doubt; state of doubt, open mind, open verdict; suspense, *expectation*; doubt, indecision, hesitancy; seesaw, floating vote; embarrassment, perplexity, nonplus, quandary; dilemma, cleft stick.
unreliability, *error*; insecurity, touch and go, *danger*; variability, unpredictability, *lack of expectation*; Fickleness, *caprice*; lack of security, bare word, scrap of paper.
Adj. *uncertain*, doubtful, dubious; insecure, chancy; subject to chance; occasional, sporadic, *infrequent*; temporary, provisional, *transient*; fluid, *unstable*; contingent, *conditional*; indeterminate; random; indecisive, undecided, open; open to question, questionable, *moot*; arguable, disputable; suspicious, *improbable*; hypothetical, speculative; borderline; ambiguous, *equivocal*; *illogical*; enigmatic, cryptic, obscure; vague, hazy, misty, cloudy, *shadowy*; mysterious, *occult*; *complex*.
unreliable; treacherous, *dishonest*; unstable, variable, changeable; fickle, *capricious*; fallible, open to error, *erroneous*; precarious, ticklish.
doubting, doubtful, dubious, full of doubt; agnostic, sceptical; mistrustful, *cautious*; uncertain, diffident; hesitant, undecided, *irresolute*; unable to say, afraid to say; perplexed, distraught; brought to a standstill; lost, abroad, all at sea, adrift, astray, at a loss, at fault, clueless, *ignorant*.
uncertified, unchecked; unwarranted; unofficial, apocryphal; untold.
Vb. *be uncertain*, be contingent; *depend*; be open to question, be ambiguous, *be equivocal*; *doubt*; *await*; have a suspicion, suspect, wonder whether; dither, hover, float, sway, seesaw, waver, teeter, vacillate, shilly-shally, falter, pause, hesitate, *be irresolute*; avoid a decision, boggle, demur; flounder, drift, be at sea; grope, fumble, cast about, experiment, *be tentative*; get lost, *stray*; come to a standstill; be at a loss; could be wrong.

puzzle, perplex, confuse, maze, daze, bewilder, baffle, nonplus, flummox, stump, floor, *defeat*; mystify; bamboozle; fog, fox, *mislead*; *cause doubt*; make one think, demand reflection.
Adv. *in suspense*.

470 Reasoning

N. *reasoning*, force of argument; reason, lateral thinking, *intuition*; sweet reason; art of reasoning, logic; distinction, *discrimination*; induction, inductive reasoning, *philosophy*; set theory; *mathematics*; plain reason, simple arithmetic.
premise, postulate, basis of reasoning; principle; assumption, *supposition*; axiom, self-evident truth, *maxim*; data; hypothesis, provisional hypothesis.
argumentation, critical examination, analysis, *enquiry*; dialogue; formal logic; proposition, statement, thesis, theorem, problem; predicate; corollary; dilemma; QED; paradox.
argument, symposium, dialogue; controversy, debate, *dissent*; appeal to reason, set or formal argument, plea, thesis, case; submission; defensive argument, defence; aggressive argument, polemics; *peace offering*; war of words, paper war, *quarrel*; propaganda, *teaching*; hair-splitting; *dissension*; bad argument, *sophistry*; legal argument; parity of reasoning; same to you.
reasons, basis of argument, grounds; *cause*; pretext; case, case to answer; sound argument; point, clincher.
reasoner, *philosopher*; rationalist; disputant; proponent; *lawyer*; wrangler; argumentative person, sea lawyer, pedant; scholastic, *intellectual*.
Adj. *rational*, clear-headed, reasoning, reasonable; cogent, acceptable, admissible, pointed, well-grounded, *relevant*; sensible, fair, *just*; synthetic, consistent, systematic; discursive, inductive, universal; *certain*; *possible*.
arguing, appealing to reason; apologetic; argumentative; disputable, arguable, *uncertain*.
Vb. *be reasonable*, *be likely*; stand to reason, follow, hang together, hold water; appeal to reason; listen to reason, admit, concede, grant, allow, *assent*; have a case.
reason, think; apply reason, bring reason to bear; infer, deduce; explain, *interpret*.
argue; hold an argument, hold a symposium; discuss, *confer*; debate, dispute; quibble, chop logic; stress, strain, work an argument to death; plead; pamphleteer, *teach*; defend; attack; join issue, demur, cavil, *dissent*; analyse; overwhelm with argument, bludgeon; *demonstrate*; have words, wrangle, *bicker*; answer back, make a rejoinder, *answer*; start an argument; propose, moot.
premise, postulate, stipulate, assume, *suppose*.
Adv. *reasonably*, fairly; much less; consequently.

471 Intuition: absence of reason

N. *intuition*, instinct, association, automatic reaction, *absence of thought*; light of nature; telepathy; insight, second sight, clairvoyance; id, subconscious, *spirit*; direct apprehension; divination; inspiration, presentiment, impulse, *feel-*

ing; feminine logic; rule of thumb; hunch, impression, sense, guesswork; *bias*.

Adj. *intuitive*, impulsive; devoid of logic, *illogical*; impressionistic; subjective; involuntary, *spontaneous*; subconscious, *psychic*; above reason, independent of reason, unknown to logic, inspired, direct.

Vb. *intuit*; sense, have a funny feeling, have a hunch; somehow feel; dispense with reason, use feminine logic; guess, use guesswork.

Adv. *intuitively*, instinctively.

472 Sophistry: false reasoning

N. *sophistry*, feminine logic, *intuition*; double think; mental reservation; word fencing; subtlety; hair-splitting; claptrap, mere words, *empty talk*; quibble; chicanery, subterfuge, shuffle, dodge; evasion, *pretext*.

sophism, a sophistry, specious argument, exploded argument, fallacy; bad logic, loose thinking, solecism, flaw; circular reasoning; weak case.

sophist; devil's advocate.

Adj. *sophistical*, specious, plausible; evasive, insincere; hollow, empty; deceptive, illusory; pettifogging; sophisticated, tortuous.

illogical, contrary to reason, irrational, unreasonable; arbitrary; fallacious, fallible; inconsistent, incongruous; unwarranted, invalid, untenable; unsound; unfounded, groundless; inconsequential; incorrect, false, *erroneous*.

poorly *reasoned*, inconclusive; weak, feeble, frivolous, airy, flimsy; loose, woolly.

Vb. *reason badly*; talk at random, babble, burble, *mean nothing*.

sophisticate, mislead; mystify; quibble, cavil, *argue*; equivocate, *be equivocal*; dodge, shuffle, fence, *parry*; *be diffuse*; evade, *elude*; varnish, whitewash, cant; colour, *misrepresent*; pervert, misapply, *misuse*; pervert reason, torture logic; prove that white is black.

473 Demonstration

N. *demonstration*, evidence; proven fact, *truth*; proof, establishment, conclusive proof, *certainty*; *experiment*; argument, *reasoning*; exposition, *manifestation*; burden of proof, onus.

Adj. *demonstrating*, demonstrative; consequential, following, *relevant*; *affirmative*; convincing; conclusive, categorical, decisive, crucial; *educational*.

demonstrated, evident; undeniable, irrefutable, irresistible, incontrovertible, *certain*; capable of proof, demonstrable.

Vb. *demonstrate*, prove; show, evince, manifest, justify, *vindicate*, *corroborate*; document, substantiate, establish, verify, *evidence*; infer, deduce, draw, *reason*; satisfy, *make certain*; clinch an argument, *convince*.

be *proved*, prove to be true, emerge, follow, follow of course, stand to reason, *be reasonable*; stand, hold water, hold good, *be true*.

Adv. *of course*; QED.

474 Confutation

N. *confutation*, refutation; exposure; conviction; rejoinder, complete answer, *answer*; clincher, knock-down argument, retort, repartee, *witticism*; *ridicule*;

denial, denunciation; exploded argument.

Adj. *confuted*; refutable.

Vb. *confute*, refute, disprove, invalidate; rebut, retort, have an answer; negative, deny, contradict, *negate*; force to withdraw; confound, silence, floor, gravel, nonplus; expose; convict, *condemn*; blow sky-high, puncture, riddle, destroy, explode, *demolish*; have; overthrow, squash, crush, overwhelm, *defeat*; parry; stand; dismiss, override, sweep aside, *affirm*.

be *confuted*; have nothing left to say.

Adv. *in rebuttal*; on the other hand.

475 Judgment: conclusion

N. *judgment*, discretion, *discrimination*; lack of discretion; *authority*; verdict, finding; sentence, *punishment*; pronouncement; decision, award; order, ruling; *decree*; decree nisi; decree absolute; irrevocable decision; settled decision; result, upshot; moral, *maxim*; *intuition*; corollary, *reasoning*; wisdom; unclouded eye, *justice*; referendum, plebiscite, poll, vote.

estimate, estimation, view, opinion; *philosophy*; calculation, *measurement*; consideration; *comparison*; appreciation, appraisal, *interpretation*; criticism, *aid*; destructive criticism, *hindrance*; critique, review, notice, comment, *article*; survey; *report*; favourable report, *approbation*; unfavourable report, censure, *disapprobation*; legal opinion, *advice*.

estimator, judge; umpire, referee; surveyor, valuer; inspector, reporter, ombudsman; counsellor, *adviser*; censor, critic, reviewer; commentator; juror, assessor, jury; voter, elector, *electorate*.

Adj. *judicial*, judicious; shrewd, *wise*; dispassionate, *just*; juridical; conclusive; moralistic, sententious; expressive of opinion; censorious; critical, appreciative; advisory.

Vb. *judge*, arbitrate, referee; hear, try, *hold court*; rule, pronounce; find, find against; decree, award, adjudicate; decide, settle, conclude; confirm, make absolute; sentence, doom, *condemn*; vote; judge well, see straight; deduce, infer, *reason*; gather, collect; recapitulate; *teach*.

estimate, measure, calculate, make, *gauge*, value, evaluate, appraise; rate, rank; conjecture, guess, *suppose*; take stock, account; consider, weigh, ponder, *meditate*; examine, investigate, vet, *enquire*; express an opinion, commentate, comment, review; survey, *scan*; censor, censure, *disapprove*.

Adv. *sub judice*, under trial, under sentence.

476 Misjudgment. Prejudice

N. *misjudgment*, wrong impression, *error*; loose thinking, misconstruction; wrong verdict, miscarriage of justice, *injustice*; deception; fantasy; false dawn.

prejudgment; preconceived idea; hangup, fixation, monomania, *mania*.

prejudice, prepossession, predilection; partiality, favouritism, *injustice*; bias, jaundiced eye; blind spot, blind side; party spirit, *party*; sectionalism; chauvinism, my country right or wrong; class war, class prejudice; sexism, sex prejudice; racialism; colour prejudice; colour bar, apartheid, segregation, discrimination, exclusion; anti-Semitism, *hatred*.

narrow *mind*, narrow sympathies; closed mind; pedantry; *positiveness*; pedant, stickler, *perfectionist*; *crank*; zealot, bigot, fanatic, *doctrinaire*.

bias, unbalance, *inequality*; warp, bent, slant, *tendency*; angle, point of view, private opinion, *opinion*; obsession; fad, craze, *whim*.

Adj. *misjudging, mistaken*; fallible, gullible, *foolish*; wrong, wrong-headed; unseeing, *blind*; short-sighted; subjective, visionary, impractical; whimsical, *crazy*; besotted, infatuated, *enamoured*.

narrow-minded, narrow, cramped, hidebound; parochial, provincial, insular; donnish, *severe*; literal, matter-of-fact; hypercritical, fussy, *fastidious*; stiff, unbending, *obstinate*; *positive*; opinionated; *proud*.

biased; jaundiced; prejudiced, closed; clannish, *sectional*; one-sided, *sectarian*; prepossessed, preconceived; unreasoning, unreasonable, *illogical*; discriminatory; illiberal, intolerant; fanatic, *obstinate*; *blind*.

Vb. *misjudge*, miscalculate, miscount, *blunder*; reckon without; *underestimate*; overestimate, *overrate*; guess wrong, misconceive, *misinterpret*; overreach oneself; *be foolish*; *reason badly*.

prejudge, judge beforehand, *predetermine*; presuppose, presume; *be rash*.

bias, warp, twist, bend; jaundice, prejudice, predispose, *influence*; haunt, obsess, *engross*.

be biased, be one-sided, see one side only, show favouritism, favour one side, *do wrong*; lean, favour, hold it against one, discriminate against, *oppress*; pontificate; blind oneself to, have a blind side, have a blind spot, *be blind*.

477 Overestimation

N. *overestimation*, overestimate; *exaggeration*; *boast*; ballyhoo, *publicity*; panegyric, gush, hot air, *empty talk*; much ado about nothing; megalomania, vanity, *pride*; egotism; optimism; unnecessary pessimism, defeatism; *hope*; prophet of doom, Jonah; barker.

Adj. *optimistic*, upbeat, sanguine; raving. overrated; overdone.

Vb. *overrate*, overestimate; rave, think too much of; make too much of, *exaggerate*; strain, overdo, inflate, magnify, *enlarge*; boost, puff, *praise*; whitewash.

478 Underestimation

N. *underestimation*, underestimate; conservative estimate, modest calculation, *moderation*; understatement, meiosis; euphemism, prudery, *humility*; irony, *affectation*; pessimism; cynic.

Adj. *depreciating*, derogatory, pejorative; conservative, *moderate*; modest, *humble*; despairing, *hopeless*; affected.

undervalued, underrated; slighted, neglected.

Vb. *underestimate*, underrate; discount, *cheapen*; depreciate, disparage, slight, pooh-pooh, *hold cheap*; do less than justice, *misjudge*; understate; soft-pedal; *disregard*; make little of; deflate, make light of, belittle; think too little of, *despise*; set at naught, scorn, *ridicule*.

479 Discovery

N. *discovery*, finding; invention; potholing; *search*; detective instinct, nose, flair, *pursuit*; detection; *location*; *certainty*; exposure, revelation, *manifestation*; serendipity; an inversion, an inspiration; strike, find, treasure trove; eye-opener, *lack of expectation*; solution, explanation, interpretation; key, open sesame, *opener*.

detector, probe; spy satellite, *spaceship*; sonar; early warning system; radar, radar trap; finder, *telescope*; sensor; *meter*; spotter, scout; *traveller*.

Adj. *discovering*, exploratory; on the scent, on the track, warm.

Vb. *discover*, invent, explore, find a way, *experiment*; hit it, have it; strike, hit; meet, encounter, *meet with*; tumble to, awake to, *understand*; find, locate, *place*; identify, *know*; verify, ascertain, *make certain*; unearth, uncover, disinter, bring to light, *manifest*; elicit, *search*; get wind of, *be informed*.

detect, expose, *show*; find a clue, see daylight; descry, discern, perceive, notice, spot, sight, catch sight of, *see*; sense, trace; smell a rat; nose, scent, wind; follow, trace, *hunt*; trap, *ensnare*.

Int. eureka! got it!

480 Belief

N. *belief*, suspension of disbelief; credence, credit; state of belief, assurance, conviction, persuasion; strong feeling, firm impression; confidence, reliance, trust, faith; religious belief, *religious faith*; full belief, full assurance; uncritical belief, *credulity*; implicit belief, *certainty*; obsession, blind belief, *prejudice*; *intuition*; subjective belief; expectation, *hope*; folklore; public belief, public opinion; *probability*; *probity*; token of credit, pledge.

creed, credo; dogma; principles, articles; catechism, articles of faith; rubric, canon, rule, *maxim*; declaration of faith, professed belief, profession, confession, confession of faith, *disclosure*; doctrine, system, school, *philosophy*; theology.

opinion, sentiment, mind, view; point of view, viewpoint, stand, position, attitude, angle, *view*; impression, *feeling*; conception, concept, thought, *idea*; thinking, way of thinking, way of thought, *philosophy*; assumption, presumption, principle; theory, hypothesis, *supposition*; surmise, guess, *conjecture*.

Adj. *believing*, holding, confident, assured, reliant, secure, *certain*; sure, cocksure, *positive*; possessed; wedded to; confiding, trustful, unquestioning; loyal, pious, *orthodox*; opinionated.

credible, plausible, reasonable, *possible*; likely, *probable*; reliable, trustworthy, trusty; worthy of credence, persuasive, convincing, impressive; held; supposed, putative, hypothetical.

credal, taught, confessional; orthodox, authoritative; of faith; sacrosanct; undeniable, absolute.

Vb. *believe*, be a believer, *be orthodox*; credit, give faith to; hold, hold to be true; maintain, declare, *affirm*; profess, confess; receive, accept, admit, agree, *assent*; buy, swallow, swallow whole; assume; be certain; rest assured, confide, trust, take one at his or her word; be told, understand, know, *be informed*; come to believe; *discover*; grant, allow.

opine, think, conceive, fancy; have a hunch, surmise, guess, *suppose*; suspect, *feel*; deem, esteem, apprehend, assume, presume, take it, hold; embrace an opinion, get hold of an idea; have a point of view, account; hold an opinion, express an opinion, *affirm*; *recant*.

convince, make believe, assure, persuade, satisfy; bring home to, *demonstrate*; make confident; convert, bring round; propagate a belief, indoctrinate, *teach*; sell an idea to, put across; *influence*; compel belief, obsess, haunt; come round to, convince oneself.

be *believed*; carry conviction; find credence, pass current, pass for truth.

Adv. *credibly*; faithfully.

481 Unbelief. Doubt

N. *unbelief*, disbelief, discredit; disagreement, *dissent*; inability to believe; denial, denial of assent; contrary belief, *opposition*; want of faith; infidelity, *heresy*; scorn, mockery, *ridicule*; change of belief, loss of faith.

doubt; critical attitude; misgiving, distrust, mistrust; scepticism; reserve, reservation, *qualification*; demur, *opposition*; scruple, qualm, suspicion.

unbeliever; heathen, infidel, *heretic*; atheist, sceptic, agnostic; dissenter; lapsed believer; denier; cynic.

Adj. *unbelieving*, incredulous, sceptical; heathen, infidel; unfaithful, lapsed; doubtful, undecided; suspicious, shy, shy of, *nervous*; slow to believe, mistrustful; impervious, hard to convince; hardboiled.

unbelieved, exploded; incredible, unbelievable, *impossible*; inconceivable, staggering, *wonderful*; hard to believe, hardly credible; untenable; open to suspicion, open to doubt, suspect, suspicious, questionable, disputable, far-fetched; socalled, pretended.

Vb. *disbelieve*, be incredulous, find hard to believe, discredit, refuse credit, greet with scepticism, withhold assent, disagree, *dissent*; mock, scoff at, *ridicule*; deny, deny outright, *negate*; refuse to admit, ignore; retract, lapse, relapse, *recant*.

doubt, *be uncertain*; demur, object, cavil, question, scruple, boggle, stick at, *qualify*; pause, hesitate, waver, *be irresolute*; treat with reserve, distrust, mistrust, suspect, *be nervous*; be shy of, shy at; be sceptical, take leave to doubt; smell a rat, scent a fallacy; hold back.

cause doubt; render suspect; discredit, *defame*; shake; stagger, startle, *surprise*; pass belief, *be unlikely*; argue against, deter, tempt, *dissuade*; impugn, attack.

Adv. *incredibly*, unbelievably; in utter disbelief.

doubtfully, with a pinch of salt.

482 Credulity

N. *credulity*; simplicity; rash belief, uncritical acceptance, *belief*; will to believe, blind faith, unquestioning belief; dotage; superstition; *conformity*; sucker, mug, dupe.

Adj. *credulous*, amenable; *gullible*; simple, unsophisticated, green; childish, silly, soft, stupid, *foolish*; infatuated; confiding, trustful.

Vb. *be credulous*; kid oneself; *reason badly*;

believe every word, buy it, *believe*; accept, *absorb*; swallow, swallow anything, swallow whole, swallow hook; touch wood; *overrate*.

483 Assent

N. *assent*, yes, yea, amen; hearty assent, welcome; agreement, *consent*, acceptance; *submission*; recognition; admission, clean breast, plea of guilty; confession, *disclosure*; declaration of faith, profession; sanction, nod, go-ahead, green light; *permission*; approval, *approbation*; concurrent testimony, accordance, corroboration, *evidence*; seal, signature, mark, cross; visa, pass, *permit*; stamp, *label*; favour, sympathy; support, *aid*; *flattery*.

consensus, same mind, *agreement*; concordance, harmony, unison, *concord*; solid vote, general consent, universal agreement, universal testimony; popular belief, public opinion, general voice; chorus, single voice; thinking alike, same wavelength, mutual sympathy, *similarity*; understanding, bargain, compact.

assenter, follower; fellow traveller; yesman; willing voter; supporter; *patron*; subscriber, *signatory*; party; professor.

Adj. *assenting*; party to; sympathetic, *friendly*; unanimous, solid, with one voice; acquiescent, *willing*; pleased.

assented; unanimous, confirmed; bipartisan.

Vb. *assent*, concur, agree with, *accord*; welcome, hail, cheer, acclaim, *applaud*; be certain; accept, buy it; concede, admit, own, acknowledge, grant, allow, *be reasonable*; plead guilty, avow, *confess*; signify assent, nod, say aye, say yes, agree to, go along with, *consent*; sanction, *permit*; ratify (see *endorse*); see eye to eye; echo, ditto, say amen, say hear hear; chorus; defer to, *respect*; be a yes-man, rubber-stamp, *flatter*; reciprocate, be *friendly*; accede, adhere, side with, *join a party*; collaborate, go along with; tolerate (see *acquiesce*); covenant, come to an understanding, have a mutual agreement, *contract*.

acquiesce, accept, *obey*; tolerate, suffer, endure, wear it; *submit*; yield, defer to; allow, *permit*; let it happen, *watch*; conform.

endorse, second, support; subscribe to, attest, *sign*; seal, stamp, rubberstamp, confirm, ratify, sanction, *consent*; authenticate, *make certain*; countersign.

Adv. *consentingly*, willingly; in full agreement, all the way, on all points.

unanimously, with one accord, with one voice, with one consent, to a man.

Int. amen! amen to that! hear, hear! aye, aye!

484 Dissent

N. *dissent*, amicable dissent, agreement to disagree; difference, confirmed opposition, *opposition*; difference of opinion, contrary view, controversy, *dissension*; party feeling, party spirit, faction, *party*; popular clamour, *anger*; discontent, *disapprobation*; schism; alternative life style, nonconformity; walkout, *strike*; reluctance; denial, lack of consent, *refusal*; doubt; cavil, demur, reservation, *qualification*; protest, protestation; challenge, *defiance*; passive resistance, sedition.

dissentient, critic; dissident, dissenter, protestant; *sectarian*; *schismatic*; rebel; dropout, **nonconformist**; *malcontent*; minority; splinter group, cave, faction, *party*; *opposition*; *opponent*; agitator, firebrand, revolutionary.

Adj. *dissenting*, dissident; agnostic, sceptical; schismatic, *sectarian*; nonconformist; malcontent; *deprecatory*; recusant; disinclined, reluctant; obstructive; challenging, *defiant*; intolerant.

unadmitted, denied, *negative*.

Vb. *dissent*, differ, *disagree*; beg to differ, combat an opinion; demur, object, cavil, boggle, scruple, *qualify*; protest, *deprecate*; resist, *oppose*; challenge, *defy*; show reluctance; withhold assent, *refuse*; be indifferent; *prohibit*; negative, contradict, *negate*; repudiate; never intend to, *reject*; look askance at, *disapprove*; secede, withdraw, *relinquish*; recant, retract; argue, wrangle, bicker, *quarrel*.

Adv. *no*, on the contrary; at issue with; under protest.

Int. God forbid! not on your life! not on your nelly! over my dead body! ask me another! tell that to the marines! never again! not likely!

485 Knowledge

N. *knowledge*, ken; knowing, cognition, recognition; apprehension, comprehension, perception, understanding, grasp, *intellect*; conscience; insight, *intuition*; precognition, *foresight*; *revelation*; lights, enlightenment, *wisdom*; learning, folk wisdom, folklore; occult lore, *sorcery*; education, background; experience, acquaintance, acquaintanceship, familiarity; private knowledge, *information*; public knowledge, notoriety, common knowledge, open secret, *publicity*; complete knowledge; partial knowledge, sidelight, glimpse, inkling, suggestion, *hint*; suspicion, scent; sensory knowledge, impression, *feeling*; introspection, detection, clue; expert knowledge, savvy, know-how, expertise, *skill*; smattering, science of knowledge.

erudition, lore, wisdom, scholarship, literature, *learning*; academic knowledge; solid learning, profound learning; smattering; reading, pedantry; information, mine of information, store of knowledge, *library*; department of learning, faculty, *academy*; scholar, *intellectual*.

culture, *literature*; education, instruction, *teaching*; literacy; liberal education; cultivation.

science; natural philosophy, scientific knowledge, applied science, technology; tree of knowledge.

Adj. *knowing*, omniscient, *wise*; cognizant, *mental*; conscious, aware, mindful of, *attentive*; alive to, sensible of; experienced, at home with, familiar with; intimate, privy to, wise to, *informed*; fly, canny, shrewd; conversant, practised, proficient, *expert*.

instructed, informed of, *informed*; taught; literate; numerate; learned, bookish, literary; erudite, scholarly, *studious*; well-read, well-informed, knowledgeable; donnish, scholastic; highbrow, intellectual, cultured, cultivated, sophisticated, blue-stocking; professional, *expert*.

known, seen; certain; noted, celebrated, famous; public, notorious, well-known; familiar, intimate, dear; too familiar, hackneyed, stale, trite; proverbial, household, commonplace, corny, *usual*; current, prevalent, *general*; *intelligible*.

Vb. *know*, savvy, ken; have knowledge; apprehend, conceive, catch, grasp, twig, click, have, get, *understand*; possess, comprehend, master; come to know; get to know, know again; appreciate; be conscious of, be aware, be cognizant; discern, *discriminate*; perceive, *see*; examine, study, *scan*; mull, con, *be attentive*; know well, see through, read one like a book; *be certain*; know of, have knowledge of, know something; *be informed*; know backwards, have it pat, be master of, *be expert*; have a little knowledge of; experience, *learn*; be omniscient; *be wise*.

be known; be public knowledge.

Adv. *knowingly*, with knowledge.

486 Ignorance

N. *ignorance*, unknowing; lack of news; unawareness, unconsciousness, *insensibility*; incomprehension; obstacle to knowledge; false knowledge, superstition, *error*; blind ignorance, lack of knowledge; lack of education; blank mind; inexperience, lack of experience; simplicity; lack of information, general ignorance; moral ignorance, *folly*; Age of Ignorance; imperfect knowledge, ignorant person, illiterate, *ignoramus*; layman, amateur; Philistine.

unknown *thing*, obstacle to knowledge; unknown quantity, matter of ignorance; prehistory, *antiquity*; Greek; Dark Continent, unknown country, virgin soil; dark horse, mystery, *secret*; unidentified flying object, UFO; unidentified body; unknown person.

sciolism, smattering, a little learning; glimpse, *hint*; unreal knowledge, *error*; affectation of knowledge, pedantry, bluff, *affectation*.

Adj. *ignorant*, unknowing, blank; unwitting, unconscious, oblivious, *insensible*; unseeing; a stranger to; *uncertain*; clueless, without a clue; *blind*; tentative; lay, amateurish, unqualified, inexpert; unversed, green, raw; innocent of, *innocent*; simple, *artless*; gauche, awkward; unenlightened, benighted; savage; pagan; backward, dull, dense, dumb; empty-headed, foolish; dark; old-fashioned, *retrospective*; *forgetful*; regardless; indifferent.

uninstructed, uninformed; vague about, *uncertain*; unschooled; illiterate, uneducated; lowbrow; Philistine; simple, dull, dense, dumb (see *ignorant*).

unknown, unbeknown, untold, unheard; unsaid; unseen, never seen, *invisible*; dark, enigmatic, mysterious, *occult*; strange, new, unprecedented; *anonymous*; unidentified; unfathomed; virgin, novel, *new*; *future*; unknown to fame, unheard of, obscure, humble; lost, missing, *absent*.

dabbling, smattering; unqualified, quack, *affected*; half-baked, shallow, superficial, dilettante.

Vb. *not know*, be ignorant, lack information; be innocent of, be green; cannot say; can only guess, *suppose*; know nothing of; *be deaf*; be at a loss, *be uncertain*; have everything to learn; misunderstand; misconstrue, *misjudge*; half know, know a little; half guess, guess, suspect, wonder, *doubt*; forget; lack interest; refuse to know, ignore, *disregard*; make ignorant; mystify, *keep secret*; profess ignorance, *be indifferent*; want to know, ask, *enquire*; grope, fumble, *be tentative.*

Adv. *ignorantly*, unawares.

487 Scholar

N. *scholar*, savant, learned person, man or woman of learning; don, reader, professor, pedagogue, *teacher*; doctor, clerk, scribe, pedant, bookworm; prodigy of learning, mine of information; student, serious student; graduate, qualified person, professional, specialist, *proficient person*; world of learning, senior common room.

intellectual, academic, scholastic, *philosopher*; brain worker; mastermind, brain, genius, prodigy, *sage*; know-all; highbrow, egghead, bluestocking; man or woman of science; boffin; academician, Immortal; patron of learning.

collector, connoisseur, dilettante, *people of taste*; librarian, curator, *keeper*; antiquary, *antiquarian*; collector of words, compiler, *linguist.*

488 Ignoramus

N. *ignoramus*, illiterate, lowbrow; philistine, *vulgarian*; duffer, wooden spoon, dunce; goof, goose, *fool*; greenhorn, novice, raw recruit, *beginner*; babe, innocent, *dupe*; bigot, *narrow mind.*

sciolist, pedant; dilettante; quack, charlatan, *impostor.*

489 Truth

N. *truth*, verity, intrinsic truth; basic truth; truism, *axiom*; consistency, accordance with fact; honest truth, sober truth, light, light of truth, gospel, Holy Writ, Bible, *revelation*; nature, *world*; *existence*; actuality, *reality*; fact; home truth, candour, *probity*; naked truth; appearance of truth, *probability.*

authenticity; it, *identity.*

accuracy, attention to fact; realism, local colour; fidelity, precision, *measurement*; mot juste, aptness, *adaptation*; meticulousness, *attention*; pedantry, rigour; *meaning*; true report, statistics, *evidence.*

Adj. *true*, veritable; correct, right, so; real, tangible, *substantial*; actual, factual; well-grounded, well-founded; literal, truthful, *veracious*; true to scale, likely, *probable*; certain; unquestionable; consistent, reasonable, *rational*; natural, true to life, true to nature, faithful; realistic, objective; candid, honest.

genuine; authentic, veritable, valid, official, pukka; sound, solid, reliable, honest, *trustworthy*; natural, pure, sterling; trueborn; rightful, legitimate; unadulterated, unsophisticated, unvarnished.

accurate, exact, precise, definite, direct, straight; unerring, constant, regular, *uniform*; punctual, right, correct, true; never wrong, infallible; close, faithful, representative; fine, nice, delicate, sensitive; scientific, electronic; scrupulous, punctilious, meticulous, strict, severe, *attentive*; literal; rigid, just so, *fastidious.*

Vb. *be true*, be so, be just so, happen, exist, be; hold, hold true, hold good, hold water, wash, ring true; conform to fact, prove true, hold together, be consistent; have truth, omit nothing, *be truthful*;

look true, seem real, come alive, cop nature, *represent*; square, set, trim *adjust*; substantiate, corroborate; prove *demonstrate*; be right, be correc *detect.*

Adv. *truly*, verily, really, indeed; *actually* sic; exactly, precisely, plumb, right, to a inch, to a hair, to a nicety, to a turn, jus right.

490 Error

N. *error*; untruth; *deviation*; fallacy; super stition, *ignorance*; subjective error; mis understanding, misconstruction, cross purposes; bad memory, *oblivion*; *false hood*; illusion, hallucination, mirage, *visual fallacy*; false light, false dawn; menta error, delusion; dream, *fantasy*; fals impression, wrong idea (see *mistake*) prejudice, *bias.*

inexactness; systematic error, *generality* loose thinking, *sophistry*; *anachronism* misreport; misuse of language, mala propism, *solecism.*

mistake, bad idea (see *error*); inappropriat move; blunder; wrong impression, mis taken identity, wrong person, wron address; glaring error, bloomer, clanger howler, gaffe, bull; loose thread, over sight, *inattention*; bosh shot, *failure* bungle, slip-up, boob, goof; fluff, muff slip, spoonerism, *solecism*; clerical error misprint, erratum, corrigendum; trip stumble; bad tactics, wrong step; sol ecism, *bad taste*; blot, flaw, *blemish.*

Adj. *erroneous*, wrong; *unreal*; aberrant unsound, self-contradictory, *illogical improbable*; baseless, unfounded exploded; *fallacious*; apocryphal unorthodox; untruthful, lying, *false* fake, *spurious*; illusory, deceptive; subjective, *imaginary*; wild, crackpot, *absurd* fallible, liable to error, wrong-headed, perverse, prejudiced; *ignorant.*

mistaken; misread; *clumsy*; wandering; wide; at fault, cold, at sea, *uncertain.*

inexact, inaccurate; free; broad, *general*; incorrect; erratic, wild, hit or miss; insensitive, clumsy; maladjusted; slow, fast, faulty; misread.

Vb. *err*, commit an error, go wrong, mistake; be mistaken; delude oneself, *misjudge*; receive a wrong impression, be at cross-purposes, misunderstand, misconceive, misapprehend, get it wrong; miscount, *overrate*, *underestimate*; go astray, *stray*; gain, be fast, *be early*; lose, be slow, stop, be late.

blunder, trip, stumble, miss, fault, *be clumsy*; slip, drop a brick, drop a clanger, boob, goof; betray oneself, *disclose*; blot, flaw; fluff, muff, botch, bungle; blow it, fail; miscount, *misjudge*; misread, misquote, misprint, misapprehend, *misinterpret.*

mislead, misdirect, *deflect*; misinform, lead astray, pervert, cause to err; beguile, lead one a dance, *deceive*; give a false impression, falsify, garble, *dissemble*; whitewash, *conceal.*

491 Maxim

N. *maxim*, gnome, adage, saw, proverb, byword, aphorism; dictum, tag, saying; truth; epigram, *witticism*; wise maxim, sage reflection; truism, commonplace, platitude, hackneyed saying, trite remark; motto, watchword, slogan, catchword; formula; text, rule, *precept*;

gloss, comment, note, remark, *commentary*; moral, fable, cautionary tale, *narrative*; book of proverbs; folklore.

axiom, self-evident truth, truism, tautology; principle, postulate, theorem, formula.

Adj. aphoristic, sententious, proverbial, *wise*; piquant, pithy, terse, snappy, *concise*; enigmatic; common, banal, trite, corny, hackneyed, commonplace, stock, *usual*.

Adv. proverbially, to coin a phrase.

492 Absurdity

N. *absurdity*; false logic, *sophistry*; silly season, *folly*; *lost labour*; nonsense verse; rot, rubbish, nonsense, jargon, twaddle, *silly talk*; rhapsody, romance, fustian, bombast, *exaggeration*; Irish bull, malapropism, howler, *mistake*; paradox, *lack of expectation*; spoonerism, joke, *witticism*; pun; riddle; quibble; anticlimax, bathos; sell, catch.

foolery, antics, tomfoolery, *revel*; whim; extravaganza; escapade, scrape, *predicament*; practical joke, monkey trick, piece of nonsense; drollery; burlesque, parody, caricature, *ridicule*; farce, pretence, *affectation*; ostentation.

Adj. absurd, inept, ludicrous, laughable, comical, grotesque, *ridiculous*; rash, silly, asinine, *foolish*; nonsensical, senseless, *meaningless*; preposterous, without rhyme or reason, *illogical*; wild, overdone, extravagant; pretentious, *affected*; frantic, mad, crazy, crackpot, hare-brained, *erroneous*; fanciful, fantastic, *imaginative*; futile, fatuous, *useless*; inconsistent, *irrelevant*; punning, *equivocal*.

Vb. *be absurd*, act like a fool, behave like an idiot, *be foolish*; fool, fool about, lark about, monkey around, *amuse oneself*; be a laughingstock, *be ridiculous*; clown, burlesque, parody, caricature, mimic, guy, *ridicule*; talk like a fool, talk rot, *mean nothing*; rant, rave, *be insane*; romance, *exaggerate*.

493 Intelligence. Wisdom

N. *intelligence*, thinking power, *intellect*; brains, brain, grey matter, head, headpiece, loaf, upper storey; wit; lights, understanding, sense, savvy, gumption, knowhow; quick thinking, readiness, ability, capacity, mental grasp; calibre, intelligence quotient, IQ; high IQ; aptitude; talent, genius; inspiration, *intuition*; brainwave, bright idea, *idea*.

sagacity, discretion, *discrimination*; perception, clear thought, clear thinking; acumen, acuity; practical mind; balance; forethought, *foresight*; subtlety, craft, *cunning*; worldly wisdom, oneupmanship, *skill*; policy, tact, *tactics*.

wisdom, wise understanding; grasp of intellect, profundity of thought, *thought*; depth, depth of mind, experience, ripe knowledge, *knowledge*; tolerance, catholic outlook; mental poise, mental balance, sobriety, enlightenment.

Adj. *intelligent*, brainy, clever, forward, bright, brilliant, of genius, *gifted*; capable, able, practical, *skilful*; apt, ready, quick, receptive, acute, sharp, alive, aware, with it, *attentive*; astute, shrewd, fly, smart, canny, all there; knowing, sophisticated, worldly-wise; clever clever; sagacious, provident, prudent, watchful, *careful*; farsighted, clearsighted; discerning; penetrating, perspicacious, clear-headed, calculating; subtle, crafty, wily, foxy, artful, *cunning*; politic.

wise, sage; thinking, *thoughtful*; reasoning, *rational*; knowledgeable; highbrow, intellectual, profound, deep; sound, sensible, reasonable, *sane*; staid, sober, *serious*; reliable, responsible, *trustworthy*; experienced, cool, collected, unflappable; proof against flattery; balanced, realistic, objective; judicious, impartial, *just*; tolerant, enlightened; unprejudiced; broad, broad-minded; politic, *cunning*; well-advised, *advisable*.

Vb. *be wise*; accumulate experience, have a fund of wisdom, *know*; have brains, sparkle, scintillate, shine, *be good*; see with half an eye, see at a glance; know a thing or two, know how to live, get around; be realistic; show foresight, *foresee*; be prudent, take care, *be cautious*; grasp, fathom, *understand*; discern, see through, penetrate, *see*; distinguish, *discriminate*; have sense, listen to reason, *be reasonable*; plan well, be politic, *plan*; have tact, *be cunning*; repent, *be penitent*.

494 Unintelligence. Folly

N. *unintelligence*, lack of intelligence, want of intellect, *absence of intellect*; poverty of intellect; weakness of intellect, lack of brains, low IQ, low mental age; Down's syndrome, mongolism, mental deficiency; mental handicap; idiocy; poor head; simplicity.

folly, act of folly, *foolery*; trifling, levity, frivolity, *inattention*; sophistry; *lost labour*; idiocy, lunacy, utter folly; blind side, obsession; second childhood, dotage, *old age*; conceit, vanity.

Adj. *unintelligent*, lowbrow; incompetent, clumsy, dull; subnormal; undeveloped, immature; backward, retarded, moronic, imbecile, *insane*; deficient, wanting, vacant, a button short; limited, weak; slow; stupid, obtuse, dense, thick, crass, gross, heavy, stolid, bovine; dumb, dim; cracked, barmy, *crazy*; impenetrable, impervious; prosaic, literal, matter-of-fact; wrong-headed.

foolish, silly, imbecile, asinine, apish; nonsensical, senseless, fatuous, futile, inane, *absurd*; ludicrous, laughable, *ridiculous*; like a fool, fallible, *gullible*; simple, artless; *ignorant*; gauche, awkward, soft, wet, soppy, goody-goody, *innocent*; gormless, goofy, gawky; childish, babyish, puerile, infantile; senile, besotted, fond; amorous, sentimental, *enamoured*; maudlin, *drunk*; mindless, witless, shallow, superficial, frivolous, feather-brained; eccentric, unstable, extravagant, wild, madcap; scatty, nutty, dotty, daft, *crazy*.

unwise, unenlightened; unscientific, *ignorant*; unreasoning, irrational, *illogical*; indiscreet; injudicious; unseeing, shortsighted, *blind*; thoughtless, *unthinking*; impatient, *hasty*; foolhardy, reckless, *rash*; prejudiced, intolerant, *narrow-minded*; inconsistent; unreasonable, against reason; inept, incongruous, unseemly, improper, *inexpedient*; ill-advised, *mistaken*.

Vb. *be foolish*, maunder, drivel, babble, burble, *mean nothing*; go haywire, *be insane*; never learn; invite ridicule, look like a fool, look foolish, *be ridiculous*; make a fool of oneself, *be absurd*; misbehave, *amuse oneself*; *waste effort*; err; miscalculate, *misjudge*.

495 Sage

N. *sage*; learned person, *scholar*; wise man, wise woman; elder statesman or -woman, counsellor, consultant, authority, *adviser*; expert, *proficient person*; genius, master mind; master, mentor, guide, guru, pundit, *teacher*; *religious teacher*; seer, prophet, *oracle*; yogi, *ascetic*; leading light; master spirit, great soul; doctor, *philosopher*; egghead, boffin, highbrow, *intellectual*; wizard, witch doctor, *sorcerer*; magus, Magi; learned judge; Nestor; Grand Old Man.

wiseacre, wise guy, know-all, *vain person*; brains trust; wise fool.

496 Fool

N. *fool*, *madman*; buffoon, clown, comic, jester, zany, harlequin, *entertainer*; perfect fool, complete idiot, ass, jackass, donkey, goose, cuckoo; idiot, born fool, natural; mongol, cretin, moron, imbecile; half-wit, stupid, silly; stooge, butt, *laughingstock*; madcap, *desperado*; incompetent, twit, clot; flibbertigibbet; trifler; crackpot, eccentric, odd fellow, *crank*; gaffer; babbler; old man.

ninny; noodle, nincompoop, muggins, booby, sap, big stiff, stick, dizzy, dope, jerk, goof; greenhorn, *beginner*; wet, weed, drip, mollycoddle, goody-goody, *weakling*; child, babe, *innocent*; sucker, mug, *dupe*.

dunce, dullard; duffer, dolt, dumb cluck, *ignoramus*; fathead, bonehead, pinhead, dunderhead; nitwit, dimwit; chump, clot, clod, clodhopper, oaf, lout, booby, bumpkin; block, stock, stone.

497 Sanity

N. *sanity*; reason; balance, mental equilibrium; sobriety, common sense; coherence; lucid interval, lucid moment; proper mind, senses; sound mind; mental hygiene, mental health.

Adj. *sane*, normal; of sound mind, all there; rational, reasonable; sober; fully conscious; coherent, *intelligible*; lucid, clearheaded; balanced, cool, calculating, *judicial*; sane enough.

Vb. *be sane*; be of sound mind, become sane, see sense.

make *sane*, bring to their senses or their right mind; sober, bring round.

Adv. *sanely*; reasonably, like a reasonable human being.

498 Insanity

N. *insanity*, lunacy, madness; mental sickness, mental illness; mental instability, intellectual unbalance; abnormal psychology; loss of reason, sick mind, brain damage; mental decay, dotage, *age*; mental deficiency, idiocy, mongolism, Down's syndrome; autism, aberration; *prejudice*; psychiatry, *psychology*; psychotherapy, *therapy*; psychiatrist, *doctor*.

psychopathy, personality disorder; identity crisis; emotional disturbance; neurosis, anxiety neurosis, nerves, nervous disorder; hysteria; attack of nerves, nervous breakdown, brainstorm; shellshock, combat fatigue; obsession, compulsion, claustrophobia, *phobia*; paranoia; split personality, schizophrenia; psychosis; confusion; hypochondria; depression; blues, *melancholy*; manic depression, elation. See *mania*.

mania, megalomania, kleptomania; homicidal mania.

frenzy, furore, frenetic condition; ecstasy, delirium, raving, hysteria; distraction; *alcoholism*; epilepsy, fit, paroxysm, spasm; brain fever, sunstroke; vertigo.

eccentricity; strange behaviour; oddity, twist, kink, craze, fad; a screw loose; fixation, hangup, repression; complex, obsession, monomania, ruling passion, fixed idea, *bias*; hobbyhorse, *whim*.

lunatic *asylum*, mental home, mental hospital, madhouse, Bedlam; nuthouse, funny farm; *hospital*.

Adj. *insane*, mad, lunatic, moon-struck; of unsound mind, demented; certifiable, mental; abnormal, sick; maladjusted; psychotic; neurotic, hysterical; paranoid, schizoid; manic; imbecile, moronic, subnormal; raving mad, declared insane.

crazy, wandering, bemused, *abstracted*; demented; infatuated, possessed; fond, besotted, *enamoured*; touched, wanting, *foolish*; crackers, cracked, scatty, screwy, nutty, nuts, batty, bats, cuckoo, barmy, bonkers; daft, loony, potty, dotty; cranky, wacky, eccentric, erratic, funny, queer, odd, peculiar, *abnormal*; crotchety, whimsical, *capricious*; dizzy, giddy.

frenzied, rabid; furious, *angry*; haggard, wild, distraught, *suffering*; possessed, possessed with a devil; frantic, frenetic, demented, like one possessed, beside oneself; berserk, running amok, running wild, *violent*; hysterical, raving, rambling, wandering, incoherent, fevered, *sick*.

Vb. *be insane*, have a screw loose; drivel; *be foolish*; ramble, wander, babble, rave; see things.

go *mad*, go crackers, become a lunatic; go berserk, run amok, see red, *get angry*.

make *mad*, drive insane, madden; craze, derange; *excite*; unhinge, unbalance; infuriate, make one see red, *enrage*; possess, obsess.

499 Madman

N. *madman*, lunatic, mental case; nut, nutcase, loony; abnormal character, psychopath, psycho; neurotic; psychotic; schizoid; manic-depressive; raving lunatic, maniac; *drunkard*; dope addict, dope fiend; drug addict; idiot, natural, cretin, moron, *fool*.

crank, crackpot, nut; eccentric, oddity, oddball, *laughingstock*; freak, *nonconformist*; fad, fanatic, lunatic fringe; seer, dreamer, *visionary*; knight errant.

enthusiast, *busy person*; zealot, *obstinate person*; devotee, aficionado, addict, fiend, nut, freak, bug, buff; fan, supporter, *patron*; connoisseur, fancier, *people of taste*; radio ham, opera buff; *collector*.

500 Memory

N. *memory*; tenacious memory, collective memory.

remembrance, exercise of memory, recollection, recall; rehearsal, *repetition*; *learning*; reminiscence, reminiscent vein, retrospection, review, retrospect, hindsight; flashback, recurrence; afterthought, *sequel*; nostalgia, regrets, *regret*; memoirs; history, narration, *narrative*; fame, notoriety.

reminder, memorial, testimonial, celebration; token of remembrance, souvenir, keepsake, relic, memento, autograph; trophy, bust, statue, *monument*; prompter; *witness*; memorandum, memo, chit, note, notebook, diary, album, scrapbook; leading question, prompt, suggestion, cue, *hint*; mnemonic, aid to memory.

mnemonics, art of memory; mnemonic device, artificial memory, electronic brain; data bank, *store*.

Adj. *remembered*; green, fresh, of recent memory; of blessed memory; memorable, unforgettable; haunting, persistent, undying; deep-rooted, deep-seated, indelible; *known*.

remembering, mindful; evocative, memorial; reminiscent; unable to forget; mnemonic.

Vb. *remember*, mind, know again, *know*; recollect; *retain*; never forget, recall, call to mind, think of; *be mindful*; reminisce; remind oneself, make a note of.

retrospect, recollect, recall, recapture, reflect, review, think back, retrace, hark back, bring back to memory, *look back*; recapture old times; make an effort to remember.

remind, take one back; drop a hint, prompt, suggest, *hint*; haunt, obsess; *excite*; make one think of, commemorate, raise a memorial, toast, *celebrate*; relate, recount, recapitulate, *repeat*; petition, *request*; write history, narrate, *describe*.

memorize, commit to memory, get to know, con, *know*; *learn*; *repeat*.

be remembered; recur; ring a bell; haunt; make history, leave a name, *have a reputation*; be eternal.

Adv. in memory, lest we forget.

501 Oblivion

N. *oblivion*; loss of memory, amnesia, blackout, total blank, mental block; hysterical amnesia, fugue state; insensibility; *ingratitude*; dim memory, hazy recollection; short memory, decay of memory, memory like a sieve; waters of oblivion; good riddance.

amnesty; pardon, absolution, *forgiveness*.

Adj. *forgotten*, beyond recall; left; repressed.

forgetful, oblivious; insensible; unable to remember; mindless, *negligent*; absentminded, inclined to forget, *abstracted*; willing to forget, *forgiving*; ungrateful.

Vb. *forget*; consign to oblivion, be oblivious, amnesty, let bygones be bygones, *forgive*; efface, *obliterate*; remember nothing; be forgetful, have a short memory; lose sight of, leave behind, overlook; be absentminded; dry (up); have a short memory, have a memory like a sieve; almost remember, draw a blank.

be forgotten; escape notice.

502 Expectation

N. *expectation*, expectancy, *attention*; *intention*; confident expectation, reliance, confidence, trust, *certainty*; presumption; foretaste; optimism, cheerful expectation; eager expectation, *desire*; ardent expectation, *hope*; suspense; pessimism,

dread, apprehension, *fear*; anxiety, worry; *probability*; reckoning, calculation, *estimate*; prospect, lookout, outlook, forecast, *prediction*; contingency, *possibility*; destiny, *fate*; *practice*.

Adj. *expectant*, sure, confident, *certain*; anticipatory, ready, *prepared*; *vigilant*; tense, *excited*; agog; hopeful, sanguine; apprehensive, anxious, *nervous*; *hopeless*; open-eyed, curious, *inquisitive*.

expected; *probable*; prospective, future, *impending*.

Vb. *expect*, face; contemplate, promise oneself, *intend*; reckon, calculate, *estimate*; predict, forecast, *foresee*; see it coming; think likely, presume, dare say, *assume*; be confident, be certain; anticipate, forestall, *prepare oneself*; be careful; hang around (see *await*); apprehend, dread, *fear*; look forward to, hope, *desire*; flatter oneself, *believe*.

await; *wait*; mark time, stand to attention; lead one to expect, *cause desire*.

Adv. expectantly, with bated breath.

503 Lack of expectation

N. *lack of expectation*; false expectation; resignation; lack of interest, apathy; unforeseen contingency, unusual occurrence; *error*; lack of warning, surprise; surprise packet, Jack-in-the-box; windfall, *benefit*; shock, start, jolt, turn; blow, thunderclap, bombshell; revelation, eyeopener; culture shock; paradox; astonishment, *wonder*; anticlimax.

Adj. *unexpected*; unforeseen; *improbable*; unannounced; without warning, surprising; staggering, amazing, *wonderful*; shocking; sudden; like a bombshell; contrary to expectation, *equivocal*; unprecedented, *unusual*; freakish, *abnormal*; whimsical, *capricious*; unaccountable.

inexpectant, unguarded, uninformed, *ignorant*; thunderstruck; *hopeless*; apathetic, *indifferent*.

Vb. *not expect*, think unlikely, *be unlikely*; despair; get a shock, have a jolt, start, jump; receive a revelation, goggle, stare.

surprise; catch, trap, ambush, *ensnare*; catch unawares; startle, jolt, make one jump, give one a turn; stagger, stun; strike one all of a heap; *disappoint*; give one a surprise; astonish, amaze, astound, be wonderful; shock, electrify, *impress*; derange; come like a thunderclap.

Adv. unexpectedly; all of a sudden, without warning, without notice, unawares.

504 Disappointment

N. *disappointment*, regrets, *regret*; false expectation; bad news, *news*; *discontent*; mirage, false dawn; shock, blow, setback; hitch; partial success, near failure; bad luck, trick of fortune, *misfortune*; anticlimax, *lack of expectation*; comedown, letdown; damp squib; *failure*.

Adj. *disappointed*, crestfallen; disgruntled; *hopeless*; heartbroken, *dejected*.

disappointing, *insufficient*; abortive; deceptive.

Vb. *be disappointed*, fail; *fall short*; expect otherwise; *regret*; listen to a false prophet; be crestfallen, look blue, look blank; be sick at heart, be without hope, *despair*.

disappoint, *fall short*; disillusion; serve badly, fail one; foil, thwart, frustrate, *hinder*; amaze, *surprise*; disconcert, humble, *humiliate*; betray, play one false, *be dishonest*; play one a trick, jilt; discontent, dissatisfy, sour, *cause discontent*; refuse, deny, reject.

Adv. *disappointingly.*

505 Foresight

N. *foresight,* prevision; foretaste; precognition, foreknowledge, second sight; premonition, presentiment, foreboding, *omen*; prognosis, *prediction; certainty*; programme, prospectus, *plan*; forethought, vision; providence, *caution*; readiness, provision, *preparation.*

Adj. *foreseeing,* prospective, prognostic; prescient, farsighted, sagacious, *wise*; provident, prudent, *cautious*; anticipatory, *expectant.*

Vb. *foresee,* divine, prophesy, forecast, *predict*; forewarn, *warn*; have second sight; have prior information, *be informed*; see ahead, see it coming, scent; *expect*; be beforehand, anticipate, forestall, *be early*; make provision, *prepare*; surmise, make a good guess, *suppose*; *predetermine*; plan ahead, *plan; look ahead; be wise*; keep a sharp lookout, *be attentive*; provide, provide against, *be cautious.*

506 Prediction

N. *prediction,* prophecy; apocalypse, *revelation*; forecast, prognosis; presentiment, foreboding, *foresight*; presage, programme, prospectus, *plan*; announcement, notice, *publication*; warning, warning shot, *danger signal*; prospect, *expectation*; shape of things to come, horoscope, fortune; type, *prototype.*

divination; augury; astrology; necromancy.

omen, portent, presage; prognostic, symptom, sign; augury; caution, *warning*; harbinger, herald, *messenger*; type; *danger*; black cat, *talisman*; portent of bad luck, broken mirror; bird of ill omen, owl, raven.

oracle, consultant, *sage*; calamity prophet, doom merchant; prophet, seer; soothsayer, *sorcerer*; medium; Delphic oracle; Sibyl; cards, dice, lot; tripod, crystal ball, mirror, tea leaves, palm; Bible.

diviner; tipster; fortune-teller, gipsy, palmist; augur.

Adj. *predicting;* apocalyptic; foreboding, *cautionary.*

presageful, significant, ominous, portentous, big with fate, pregnant with doom; auspicious, promising, fortunate, favourable, *prosperous*; inauspicious, sinister, adverse.

Vb. *predict,* forecast, make a prediction, prognosticate, make a prognosis; foretell, prophesy, forebode, bode, augur, spell; presage, portend; foreshadow, shadow forth, herald, *come before*; point to, typify, signify, *indicate*; announce, give notice, notify, *advertise*; forewarn, give warning, *warn*; look black, lour, menace, *threaten*; promise, augur well, bid fair to, *give hope.*

divine; cast a horoscope, cast a nativity; *gamble.*

507 Supposition

N. *supposition,* notion, *idea*; fancy, conceit, pretence, *affectation*; presumption, assumption, postulate; condition, *conditions*; proposal, proposition, *offer*; sub-

mission, *argument*; hypothesis, theory, model, theorem, *topic*; thesis, position, stand, attitude, standpoint, *opinion*; suggestion, *hint*; basis of supposition, clue, data, *evidence*; suspicion, hunch, inkling (see *conjecture*), instinct, intuition; *thought, possibility.*

conjecture, guess, surmise, suspicion; mere notion, bare supposition, vague suspicion, rough guess, crude estimate; shrewd idea, *intuition*; guesswork; gamble, shot.

theorist, research worker; academic, critic, armchair detective; *doctrinaire*; *philosopher*; boffin.

Adj. *suppositional,* notional, hypothetical, theoretical, armchair, speculative, academic, of academic interest; gratuitous; suggestive.

supposed; *topical*; given; putative; pretended, so-called; *unreal*; imaginable, *imaginary.*

Vb. *suppose,* pretend, fancy, dream, *imagine*; think, conceive, opine; divine, have a hunch; surmise, conjecture, guess, suppose so, dare say; persuade oneself, *believe*; presume, assume, presuppose; assert, *affirm*; take, take it, postulate, *reason*; speculate, have a theory, *meditate*; sketch, draft, outline, *plan*; gamble.

propound, propose, *offer*; moot, move, propose a motion, *request*; put a case, submit, *argue*; put forth, make a suggestion, venture to say, put forward a notion, *advise*; suggest, *hint*; urge, *motivate.*

Adv. *supposedly,* seemingly.

508 Imagination

N. *imagination;* skill; fantasy, understanding, insight, empathy, sympathy, *moral sensibility*; frenzy, ecstasy, inspiration, fancy, imagery; artistry, creative work.

ideality, conception, thought; ego ideal; mental image, projection, *appearance*; concept, image, conceit, fancy, notion, *idea*; whim; *caprice*; figment, fiction, *falsehood*; work of fiction, story, *novel*; science fiction, fairy tale; imaginative exercise, flight of fancy, romance, fantasy, extravaganza, rhapsody, *exaggeration*; *poetry*; shadow boxing.

fantasy; vision, dream, nightmare; phantom, *ghost*; shadow, vapour; mirage, *visual fallacy*; delusion, hallucination, *error*; reverie, brown study; trance, somnambulism, *insensibility*; sick fancy, delirium, *frenzy*; *sophistry*; make-believe, daydream, golden dream, *desire*; romance, stardust; romanticism, escapism, idealism; Utopia; Happy Valley; Shangri-la, Middle Earth; wonderland; cloud-cuckoo-land, dream world; good time coming, millennium, *future state*; idle fancy, myth, *fable.*

visionary, seer; dreamer, *inattention*; idealist, Utopian, *philanthropist*; ostrich; *romantic*; crank; creative worker, *artist.*

Adj. *imaginative,* creative, lively, original, inventive, fertile, ingenious, resourceful, skilful; *romantic*; fictional; Utopian; extravagant, grotesque, bizarre, whimsical, preposterous, impractical, *absurd*; visionary, otherworldly, quixotic.

imaginary, unreal, *insubstantial*; subjective, notional, chimerical, illusory, *erroneous*; dreamy, visionary, ideal; cloudy, *shadowy*; fictitious, fabulous, mythological; fanciful; hypothetical; pretended, make-

believe.
Vb. *imagine*, *think*; fancy, dream; think of; devise, invent, originate, create, have an inspiration, *improvise*; coin, hatch, concoct, fabricate, *produce*; envisage, *see*; conceive, form an image of; figure to oneself, paint, capture, recapture, *represent*; *exaggerate*; pretend, make-believe, daydream; *understand*.
Adv. *imaginatively*; with imagination.

509 Meaning

N. *meaning*, substance, essence, spirit, sum, gist, pith; contents, text, matter, *topic*; deep structure, sense, value, drift, tenor, purport, import, implication, colouring; force, effect; bearing, scope; expression, diction, *style*; semantics, *linguistics*.
connotation, significance, reference, application; *interpretation*; context; original meaning, *source*; range of meaning, comprehension; extension; intention, main meaning, leading sense; idiom, *speciality*; usage, acceptance, *practice*; single meaning; double meaning; same meaning, equivalent meaning, convertible terms; synonym, *identity*; opposite meaning, antonym; level of meaning, literal meaning; *metaphor*, esoteric sense; constructive sense.
Adj. *meaningful*, significant, of moment, *important*; substantial, pithy, meaty, full of meaning, pregnant; indicative; telling, *expressive*; pointed; suggestive, evocative, implicit; express, explicit, *plain*; *affirmative*.
semantic, *linguistic*; literal, verbal, *plain*; *figurative*; *intelligible*; ambiguous, *equivocal*; *identical*; tantamount, equivalent, *similar*, *contrary*; idiomatic, *special*; obscure; clear; constructive, *tacit*; nonsensical, *absurd*; without meaning, *meaningless*.
Vb. *mean*, have a meaning, bear a sense, mean something; convey a meaning, get across, *communicate*; typify, *indicate*; signify, denote, connote, *represent*; import, purport, intend; point to, spell, involve, *imply*; convey, express, declare, assert, *affirm*; bespeak, tell of, speak of, breathe of, speak volumes, *evidence*; mean to say, be driving at, really mean; *be identical*; repeat; coincide, *accord*; *disagree*; draw a meaning, infer, *understand*.
Adv. *significantly*, with meaning; so to speak.

510 Lack of meaning

N. *lack of meaning*, absence of meaning; truism, platitude, *maxim*; mere words; *sophistry*; dead letter; scribble, *script*; daub; empty sound, meaningless noise; jargon, rigmarole; abracadabra, hocus-pocus; gabble, double dutch, Greek, Babel; raving, delirium, *frenzy*; double-talk; *flattery*.
silly *talk*, nonsense; stuff, balderdash, rubbish, rot; drivel, twaddle, fiddle-faddle, bosh, tripe, bilge, bull.
empty *talk*, wind, gas, hot air, verbiage; rant, bombast, fustian; eyewash; claptrap, poppycock; *fable*; humbug, *falsehood*; moonshine, bunkum, bunk, boloney, hooey; flannel, flummery, blarney, *flattery*; patter, spiel; talk, chatter, prattle, babble, gabble, jabber, jabber jabber, yak yak, rhubarb rhubarb, *chatter*.
Adj. *meaningless*, without meaning; non-sense, nonsensical, *absurd*; senseless, null; insignificant, inane, empty, trivial, trite; fatuous, trashy, trumpery; windy; incoherent, raving.
unmeant, involuntary; insincere.
Vb. *mean nothing*, scribble, scratch, daub, strum; talk bunkum, talk like an idiot, *be absurd*; talk, babble, prattle, prate, gabble, gibber, jabber, *be loquacious*; talk double dutch, doubletalk; rant, *exaggerate*; gush, rave, drivel, drool, waffle, twaddle; vapour, talk hot air, gas, *be foolish*; blarney, *flatter*; make nonsense of, *misinterpret*; be Greek to, *puzzle*.
Int. Rubbish! what rot! nonsense! fiddle-sticks!

511 Intelligibility

N. *intelligibility*, clarity, coherence; precision, *certainty*; simplicity, straightforwardness, plain speech; plain words, plain English, mother tongue; paraphrase, *facility*; *interpretation*.
Adj. *intelligible*, coherent, *sane*; audible, distinguishable, unmistakable; *known*; explicable; unequivocal, *meaningful*; explicit, positive, *certain*; distinct, clear-cut, precise, *definite*; well-spoken, articulate; downright, forthright, *plain*; straightforward, simple, *easy*; obvious, self-explanatory, easy to understand, easy to grasp, made easy; popular; clear, limpid, *transparent*; pellucid, lucid; readable, legible; luminous, *visible*.
expressive, telling, striking, vivid, graphic, highly coloured, forceful, strong.
Vb. *be intelligible*, come alive; be readable, read easily; make sense, *be reasonable*; tell its own tale, *evidence*; *be visible*; get across; clarify, elucidate, *interpret*; make easy, simplify, *facilitate*; recapitulate, *repeat*.
understand, comprehend, apprehend, *know*; master, *learn*; have, hold, retain, *remember*; have understanding, be wise; see through, penetrate, fathom, *detect*; spot, descry, discern, distinguish, see at a glance, see with half an eye, *see*; *be certain*; grasp, get hold of, seize, dig; register; be with one, follow, savvy; collect, get, twig; get wise to, tumble to, rumble; begin to understand, see it all; get to know, be told, *be informed*.
Adv. *intelligibly*, plainly, simply.

512 Unintelligibility

N. *unintelligibility*, perplexity, difficulty; *lack of meaning*; double dutch; jargon, foreign tongue, private language, *dialect*; slang; *speech defect*; scribble, scrawl, lettering; Greek, *secret*; hard saying, paradox, knotty point, obscure problem, crux, riddle; mysterious behaviour.
Adj. *unintelligible*, incomprehensible, inconceivable, inexplicable, unaccountable; *unknown*; unfathomable, inscrutable, impenetrable, blank, expressionless, *impassive*; inaudible, unreadable, illegible, crabbed; *invisible*; occult; cryptic, obscure; esoteric, *private*; enigmatic.
puzzling, hard to understand, complex, *difficult*; hard, beyond one, abstruse, elusive; enigmatic, mysterious, *occult*; nebulous, misty, hazy, dim, obscure, *shadowy*; ambiguous, *equivocal*; of doubtful meaning; fishy, strange, odd, *abnormal*; without a solution, insoluble; *uncertain*.
inexpressible, unspeakable; unutterable,

ineffable; incommunicable; profound, deep; mystic, transcendental.

Vb. *be unintelligible*, be hard, be difficult, present a puzzle, *puzzle*; *be equivocal*; talk double dutch, *mean nothing*; speak badly, *stammer*; write badly, scribble, scrawl; *cause doubt*; perplex, complicate, entangle, confuse, *bedevil*; require explanation; be too deep; escape one; pass comprehension, baffle understanding.

not *understand*, make nothing of, make neither head nor tail of; find too difficult; wonder, be at sea, *be uncertain*; have a blind spot, *be blind*; misunderstand one another, be at cross-purposes, *blunder*; get one wrong, *misjudge*.

513 Equivocalness

N. *equivocalness*; double meaning; doubletalk, weasel word, *lack of meaning*; conundrum, riddle, oracle; mental reservation; white lie, *untruth*; quibble, *sophistry*; ornament; pun, *witticism*; anagram, acrostic; *analogue*.

Adj. *equivocal*, ambiguous, ambivalent; double, two-edged; left-handed, facing both ways; vague, evasive.

Vb. *be equivocal*, cut both ways; pun; have a second meaning, *mean*; *be contrary*; fudge, waffle, stall, *avoid*; equivocate, prevaricate, weasel, *dissemble*.

514 Metaphor: figure of speech

N. *metaphor*; allusion, application; allegory; *interpretation*; fable, parable, *teaching*; symbol; symbolism, imagery, *imagination*; simile, likeness, *comparison*; personification.

trope, figure, figure of speech, flourish; manner of speech; irony, sarcasm, *satire*; *ornament*; hyperbole, *exaggeration*; stress, emphasis; euphuism, euphemism, *affectation*; contrast, antithesis, *comparison*.

Adj. *figurative*, tropical; comparative; *affected*; colloquial, *plain*; hyperbolic; satirical; flowery, florid, *ornate*.

Vb. *figure*, image, embody, personify; typify, *represent*; fable; apply; contrast, *compare*; employ metaphor, *ornament*.

Adv. *metaphorically*; so to speak.

515 Interpretation

N. *interpretation*, definition, explanation, exposition; light; illustration, *example*; resolution, solution, key, clue, *answer*; *amendment*; application, particular interpretation, twist, turn; construe, reading, *meaning*; *metaphor*; usual text; alternative reading, criticism, appreciation, *literature*; critique, review, *estimate*; critical power; insight, feeling, sympathy, *moral sensibility*.

commentary, comment; gloss, footnote; inscription, caption, legend, *phrase*; motto, moral, *precept*; exposition, *dissertation*; critical edition; glossary, lexicon, *dictionary*.

translation, version, rendering, free translation, loose rendering; faithful translation, construe; key, crib; paraphrase; epitome, *compendium*; adaptation.

hermeneutics, science of interpretation; *linguistics*; phrenology; prophecy, *divina-*

tion.

interpreter, exponent, *teacher*, *religious teacher*; rationalist; editor; commentator; critic, reviewer; medium, *spiritualism*; polyglot, *linguist*; *antiquarian*; spokesman, mouthpiece, representative, *delegate*; public relations officer; performer, *musician*; player, *actor*; poet, painter, sculptor, *artist*.

guide, precedent, *example*; lamp, light, star, courier, *director*; showman, demonstrator.

Adj. *interpretive*, constructive; explanatory; *literary*; definitive; illuminating, exemplary; editorial; polyglot; equivalent, *equal*; literal, strict, *accurate*; faithful; free, *inexact*.

interpreted; cracked.

Vb. *interpret*, define, clarify, make clear; explain, unfold, expound, elucidate, *be intelligible*; illustrate, *exemplify*; demonstrate, *show*; show round; edit, annotate, compose a commentary, gloss; read, spell; adopt a reading, accept an interpretation, construe, give a sense to, make sense of, *understand*; illuminate, enlighten, *inform*; deduce, *reason*; be spokesman; typify; simplify, *facilitate*.

translate, make a version, make a key, make a crib; render, English; rehash, reword, paraphrase; abridge, amplify, adapt; transliterate, transcribe; encode; lipread.

decipher, crack, decode; read, piece together; solve, resolve, unravel, disentangle.

Adv. *in plain words*, plainly; that is, to wit, namely, to make it plain, to explain.

516 Misinterpretation

N. *misinterpretation*, misunderstanding, misconstruction, misapprehension; cross-purposes, *mistake*; wrong explanation; misconstrue; wrong interpretation; twist, turn, perversion; strained sense; false reading; false colouring, dark glasses; *exaggeration*; parody, travesty, *ridicule*; abuse of language, *solecism*.

Adj. *misinterpreted*, mistaken; misread.

Vb. *misinterpret*, misunderstand, misapprehend, misconceive, *misjudge*; get wrong, get one wrong, *blunder*; misread, misspell, *err*; misconstrue; give a twist or turn, pervert, wrench, twist, *distort*; equivocate, weasel, *be equivocal*; add a meaning, *add*; suppress, subtract; misquote; falsify, garble, *misrepresent*; travesty, parody, caricature, guy, *ridicule*; overrate; underestimate, inflate, *exaggerate*; traduce, misrepresent, *defame*.

517 Manifestation

N. *manifestation*, revelation, daylight, exposure, *disclosure*; expression; proof, *evidence*; *comparison*; presentation, production, projection, *representation*; sign, token, *signal*; *omen*; preview, *view*; showing, exhibition; display, *ostentation*; proclamation, *publication*; *publicity*; candour, plain speech, home truth; prominence, *visibility*; apparition, vision, *appearance*; glory; incarnation.

exhibit, specimen, sample, *example*; piece of evidence, quotation, citation, *evidence*; model, mock-up, *image*; show piece, antique, curio; display, show, mannequin parade, *spectacle*; scene, view; showplace, showroom, showcase, placard, hoarding, *advertisement*; sign, *label*; shop window, museum, gallery, *collection*; retrospective, exhibition, exposition; fair, *market*.

xhibitor, publicist; demonstrator; showman; impresario, *stage manager*; peacock, *vain person*; model, mannequin.

Adj. manifest, apparent, ostensible; plain, clear, *definite*; *intelligible*; showing, *visible*; conspicuous, noticeable, notable, prominent, pronounced, signal, marked, striking, *obvious*; open, patent, evident; gross, crass, palpable; self-evident, unmistakable, incontestable, *certain*; public, famous, notorious, *well-known*; showy; arrant, glaring, stark staring, flagrant, loud.

ndisguised, overt, explicit, express, *affirmative*; public; unreserved, open, candid, heart-to-heart, *veracious*; free, frank, downright, forthright, straightforward, outspoken, blunt, *plain*; honest to goodness, honest to God; bold, daring, *defiant*; brazen, shameless, immodest, barefaced, *impure*; bare, naked.

hown, declared; showing, *visible*; brought forth; brought face to face; worn.

Vb. manifest, reveal, divulge, *disclose*; evince, *evidence*; bring to light, unearth, *discover*; explain, make plain, make obvious, *interpret*; expose, lay bare, unroll, *uncover*; throw open, *open*; elicit, draw forth, *extract*; invent, bring forth, *produce*; shadow forth, incorporate, incarnate, personify, typify, exemplify, *indicate*; accentuate, enhance, develop, *augment*; *illuminate*; highlight, spotlight; express, formulate, *affirm*; bring, mention, cite, quote; *make important*; bring to notice, produce, proclaim, *publish*; solve, elucidate, *decipher*.

how, exhibit, display; expose to view, dangle; wave, flourish, *brandish*; sport, *wear*; flaunt, parade; make a show of, affect, *be affected*; present, feature, enact, *represent*; stage, release; televise; stage an exhibition, hang (a picture); demonstrate, *teach*; show round, draw attention to, bring to notice, *indicate*; confront, bring face to face; reflect, image, mirror, *imitate*; expose, *disclose*.

be plain, unveil, *doff*; *speak plainly*; tell its own story, *be intelligible*; be obvious, stand to reason, go without saying; be conspicuous, *be visible*; be seen, *attract notice*; loom large, *be near*; rear its head, transpire, come to light, *appear*.

Adv. manifestly, plainly, openly; at first blush; honestly; before God, before all.

518 Latency

N. latency; treachery, *perfidy*; dormant condition, potentiality, *possibility*; mysticism; ambiguous advice, *oracle*; symbolism, allegory, *metaphor*; implication; mystery, *secret*; dark; deceptive appearance; *danger*; dark horse, mystery man; mole, *pitfall*; strings, friend at court, *influence*; Freemasonry; secret influence; something rotten; innuendo, suggestion, *hint*; undercurrent, undertone, aside; secret society, cabal, intrigue, *plot*; *ambush*; code, invisible writing, cryptography.

Adj. latent; dormant, passive, *quiescent*, inert; potential, undeveloped, *possible*; *unknown*; subterranean, *deep*; undercover; unseen, *invisible*; murky, obscure, *dark*; impenetrable, *secluded*.

tacit, unsaid, untold of, unsung; unde-

clared; implicit; suggestive.

occult, mysterious, mystic; *figurative*; cryptic, esoteric; covert; indirect, crooked, *oblique*; clandestine, secret, kept quiet; insidious, treacherous; underhand; hushhush, top-secret; *private*.

Vb. lurk, hide, be latent; burrow, stay underground; lie low, lie doggo, *be quiescent*; avoid notice, *be unseen*; evade detection, escape recognition; *dissemble*; creep, slink, tiptoe; stage-manage, underlie, *cause*; smoke, smoulder, be inert.

imply, insinuate, whisper, murmur, suggest, *hint*; understand, infer; connote, carry a suggestion, involve, spell, *mean*.

519 Information

N. information, communication of knowledge; data base; tradition, hearsay; enlightenment, instruction, *teaching*; intercommunication; communication; mass media; telling, narration, *narrative*; notification, announcement, annunciation, warning, advice, notice, mention, tip, tip-off (see *hint*); advertisement, circular, *publicity*; common knowledge, general information, gen, info; factual information, background, documentary, *truth*; material, literature, *reading matter*; inside information, dope, lowdown, private source, confidence, *secret*; earliest information, scoop; stock of information, acquaintance, *knowledge*; file, dossier, *record*; piece of information, word, report, intelligence, *news*; a communication, wire, telegram, cable, *message*; flood of information, spate of news; leak, *disclosure*.

report, review; *enquiry*; paper, Green Paper, account, *narrative*; statement, return, *statistics*; specification, *estimate*; progress report, bulletin, handout, press release, *news*; representation, presentation, case; memorial, petition, *entreaty*; round robin.

hint, whisper, aside; indirect hint; broad hint, signal, nod, wink, look, nudge, kick, *gesture*; prompt, cue; suggestion, lead, leading question; caution, *warning*; tip, tip-off (see *information*); word, verb. sap., *advice*; innuendo, *calumny*; clue, symptom, *interpretation*; sidelight, glimpse, inkling, *glimmer*; suspicion, guess, *conjecture*; good tip, wheeze, dodge, wrinkle.

informant, teller, *narrator*; *speaker*; mouthpiece, representative, *delegate*; harbinger, herald, *messenger*; witness; authority, source; quarter, channel, circle, grapevine; go-between, contact, *intermediary*; information centre; news agency; correspondent, reporter, commentator, columnist, gossip writer, *news reporter*; tipster, *adviser*; guide, topographer; little bird.

informer, spy, snoop, sleuth, *detective*; inside agent, mole; stool pigeon, nark, snitch, sneak, nose, blabber, grass; telltale, talebearer, gossip.

guidebook; travelogue, topography; handbook, manual, ABC; timetable; itinerary, route map, chart, plan, *map*; gazetteer, *reference book*; nautical almanac; telephone directory, phone book; catalogue, directory; courier, *guide*.

Adj. informative, communicative, chatty; instructive, documentary, *educational*; expressive, *affirmative*; *written*; oral, verbal, spoken; advisory; *cautionary*; explicit, clear, *definite*; candid, *plain*;

indiscreet, *loquacious*.
informed, *knowing*; told, genned-up.
Vb. **inform**, certify, advise, intimate, impart, convey (see *communicate*); apprise, have one know, give to understand; brief, instruct, *teach*; let one know; enlighten, fill with information, *educate*; *indicate*; insinuate (see *hint*); confide, get confidential; put one wise, put right, correct, disillusion; be specific, state, name, signify, *specify*; mention, speak of, *speak*; gossip; be indiscreet, talk, be *loquacious*; leak information, reveal, *disclose*; tell, blab, split, grass, snitch, peach, squeal, *confess*; rat, implicate an accomplice; betray one; report against; inform against, lay an information against, shop, denounce, *accuse*.
communicate, transmit; *correspond*; report, cover, make a report, report progress, post; get through, get across; contact; convey, bring word, write, *correspond*; flash news, flash, beam; send a message, speak, semaphore, *signal*; wire, telegraph, telex, radio; telephone, phone, call, dial, ring, give one a ring or a tinkle or a buzz; disseminate, broadcast, televise; announce, notify, give notice, *advertise*; carry a report, *publish*; retail, recount, narrate, *describe*; commune, *converse*; exchange information.
hint, suggest; prompt, *remind*; caution, *warn*; *advise*; wink, nudge, *gesticulate*; insinuate, breathe, whisper, just mention, let fall, imply, leave one to gather, intimate.
be informed, *know*; be told, receive information; get to hear of, overhear, *hear*; get wind of, scent, *discover*; gather, infer, *understand*; come to know, get a report, *learn*; become alive to, be *attentive*; *enquire*; have information, have something to tell; claim to know, *affirm*.
Adv. *reportedly*, as stated, from what one can gather.

520 Concealment
N. **concealment**, confinement; hiding; burial, cache; disguise, camouflage, *deception*; masquerade; incognito; smoke screen, *screen*; reserve, discretion; secret thought, mental reservation, ulterior motive; lack of candour, evasion; white lie; subterfuge; D notice; *untruth*; duplicity.
secrecy, *silence*; mystery, *secret*; seal of secrecy; secret society, Freemasonry; clandestine behaviour; low profile; underhand dealing; conspiracy, *plot*; cryptography, cryptogram, code; invisible ink.
Adj. **concealed**, hiding, lost; *latent*; incommunicado; mysterious; cryptic, *occult*; private, *secluded*; privy, confidential; secret, top secret, hush-hush, inviolable; ex-directory; untold; *anonymous*; covert; hooded; clandestine, undercover, underground, subterranean, *deep*.
disguised; incognito, *anonymous*; unknown.
stealthy, silent, furtive, sneaking, like a thief; clandestine, hugger-mugger, cloak-and-dagger; underhand, surreptitious, *dishonest*.
reticent, reserved, withdrawn; noncommittal, cagey, evasive; vague, discreet, silent, *taciturn*; tight-lipped; close, secretive; *unsociable*.
Vb. *conceal*, hide, secrete, ensconce, confine, *seclude*; *store*; hide underground, bury; whitewash, *cover*; varnish; *obliterate*; slur, *disregard*; smother, stifle, *suppress*; veil, muffle, mask, disguise; camouflage; shroud, *screen*; shade, obscure, eclipse, *darken*; obfuscate; assume a mask, masquerade, *dissemble*; code, encode.
keep secret, keep it dark, keep close; look blank, keep a straight face, keep mum, be *taciturn*; be discreet, neither confirm nor deny; keep back, reserve, withhold; *suppress*; keep a low profile; blindfold, bamboozle, *deceive*.
be stealthy, hugger-mugger, conspire, *plot*; snoop, sneak, slink, creep; glide, steal; steal along, steal past; tiptoe, pussyfoot; prowl, skulk, loiter; be anonymous, stay incognito; wear a mask, assume a disguise, *dissemble*; lie doggo, *lurk*; evade, shun, dodge, *avoid*; play hide-and-seek; take cover, go to earth; go underground; vanish, *disappear*; bury oneself, be *unsociable*; lay an ambush, *ambush*.
Adv. *secretly*, hugger-mugger; with bated breath; between ourselves; aside, to oneself; without beat of drum; incognito.
stealthily; underhand.

521 Disclosure
N. **disclosure**, revelation, apocalypse; daylight, cold light of day; denouement, catastrophe, *event*; *publication*; exposure, *manifestation*; showdown; communication, leak, *hint*; giveaway; cloven hoof, tell-tale sign, blush; admission, confession; confessional; clean breast, whole truth, *truth*.
Adj. **disclosed**, *shown*; showing, visible; confessed, avowed; *open*; laid bare.
disclosing, opening; apocalyptic; *transparent*; explanatory; communicative; leaky; indiscreet, garrulous, *loquacious*; telltale, indicative; confessional, penitent.
Vb. *disclose*, reveal, expose, *manifest*; bare, denude, *doff*; unfold, unroll, unpack, *uncover*; unveil; *open*; lay open, *discover*; detect; be *transparent*; betray; unmask; expose oneself, *blunder*; declare oneself; correct, set right, disillusion, *inform*.
divulge, declare, be open about, express; vent, give vent to, *speak*; ventilate, air; *publish*; speak of, talk, must tell; utter; breathe; leak, *communicate*; let drop, let fall, *hint*; speak plainly; unbosom oneself; confide; report, tell, *accuse*; split, peach, squeal, blab, *inform*; rat.
confess, admit, avow, acknowledge; concede, grant, allow, own, *assent*; implicate oneself, plead guilty; talk, sing, sing like a canary; come across with, come clean; tell all, admit everything, be *truthful*; make a clean breast of it, go to confession, be *penitent*.
be disclosed, break, *appear*; come to light, show its face, show its true colours, be *plain*; transpire, become known, be *known*; emerge; show, be *visible*; show through, be *transparent*.

522 Hiding. Disguise
N. **hiding-place**, hide, hideaway, hole, *refuge*; lair, den, *retreat*; cache, secret place; crypt, vault, *cellar*; closet, secret drawer, safe place, safe, safe deposit, *storage*; recess, corner, nook, cranny, niche; secret passage, cover, underground, *shelter*.
ambush; *trap*; catch, *pitfall*; decoy, stool pigeon, *impostor*.

disguise, blind, masquerade, *deception*; camouflage, protective colouring, *mimicry*; dummy, *sham*; veneer, *covering*; mask, visor, veil, domino, *cloak*; fancy dress; cloud, smoke screen, cover, *screen*.
ider; *impostor*.

b. *ambush*, lurk; *ensnare*; assume a disguise, wear a mask; obfuscate; waylay.

523 Publication

N. *publication, disclosure*; proclamation; edict, ban, *decree*; call-up, summons; cry, bugle call, *call*; beat of drum; press conference, press release, advance publicity (see *advertisement*); notification, public notice, official bulletin; announcement, pronouncement, manifesto, programme, platform; book trade, *book; telecommunication*; broadcast, newscast, *news; rumour*; circulation, circular, encyclical.

publicity, limelight, spotlight, public eye; common knowledge, *knowledge; manifestation*; open secret, open scandal; notoriety, fame; currency, circulation, sale, extensive sales; readership, audience; public relations, PR, propaganda, display, showmanship, window dressing, *ostentation*; sensationalism, ballyhoo, *exaggeration*; advertising; medium of publicity, television, radio; public address system, loudspeaker, *hearing aid*; public comment, journalism, coverage, report, *enquiry*; newsreel, newsletter, *news*; open letter; editorial, *article*; pulpit, platform, hustings, soapbox, *rostrum*; printing press, *print*; blaze of publicity.

advertisement, notice, advert, ad, personal column; headline, streamer, spread; puff, blurb, ballyhoo; handout, handbill; bill, poster, *exhibit*; billboard, hoarding, placard, sandwich board; advertising copy, slogan, jingle; plug, trailer, commercial; hard sell, subliminal advertising.

the press, fourth estate, Fleet Street, newspaper world, news business; newspaper, newssheet, sheet, paper, rag, tabloid, comic; serious press, organ, journal, daily paper, daily, broadsheet, heavy; morning paper, issue, edition, extra; magazine section, supplement, leaflet, handbill, pamphlet, brochure, open letter, newsletter.
journal, review, magazine, periodical, daily, weekly, monthly, quarterly, annual; gazette, trade journal, house magazine, trade publication, *reading matter*.

publicizer; herald, trumpet, *messenger*; barker, tout; bill sticker, bill poster; publicist, publicity agent; copywriter, blurb writer, commercial artist, public relations officer, PRO, propagandist, pamphleteer; printer, publisher; reporter, *news reporter*.

Adj. *published*; passing round, current; public, *known*; open; broadcast; mixed media.

publishing.

well-known, public, celebrated, famous, notorious, crying, flagrant, blatant, glaring, sensational, *manifest*.

Vb. *publish*, make public, carry a report, *communicate*; report, cover; write an open letter, reveal, *divulge*; highlight, spotlight; radio, broadcast, televise; relay, diffuse, *inform*; spread, circulate, distribute, disseminate; ventilate, discuss, *argue*; pamphleteer, propagate, *teach; print*; syndicate, edit, sub; issue, release,

send forth; bring to public notice, let it be known; spread a rumour, fly a kite; rumour, noise abroad, talk about, retail, pass round, put about, *be loquacious*; voice, broach, talk of, speak of, utter, emit, *speak*.

proclaim, announce, herald, promulgate, notify; ban, denounce, *accuse*; pronounce, declare, *affirm*; make a proclamation, issue a pronouncement, publish a manifesto; celebrate, sound, noise, trumpet, blaze abroad, cry, shout, scream, thunder, *be loud*; declaim.

advertise; insert a notice, bill, placard, post; headline, splash; spotlight, promote; make much of, feature; sell, boost, puff, extol, *overrate*; din, plug, *repeat*.

be *published*, become public; acquire notoriety; circulate, pass current, pass round, get about, spread abroad, spread like wildfire, fly about; find a publisher; have a circulation, sell well, go like a best-seller, *be sold*.

Adv. *publicly*, openly.

524 News

N. *news*, bad news; tidings, gospel, *religion*; intelligence, report, word, advice; piece of information, something to tell, titbit, *information*; bulletin, handout; newspaper report, press notice; news item, news flash, *broadcast*; fresh news, sensation, scoop, exclusive; old news, copy; yarn, story, newscast, newsreel, *publicity*; news value.

rumour; flying rumour, fame; hearsay, gossip, talk, tittle-tattle, *chat*; scandal, *calumny*; whisper, buzz, noise; false report, hoax; grapevine, bush telegraph.

message, word of mouth, word, advice, tip, *information*; communication, *signal*; wireless message, radiogram, cable, telegram, wire, *telecommunication*; postcard, *postal communications*; ring, phone call; errand, embassy, *commission*.

news *reporter*, reporter, correspondent, *author*; press representative; *gossip*; retailer of news; newsagent, newsvendor, newspaper boy or girl.

messenger, forerunner, *precursor*; harbinger, *omen*; ambassador, minister, legate, spokesman or -woman, *envoy*; apostle, emissary; herald, trumpet; *law officer*; go-between, contact, contact man, *intermediary*.

courier, runner, express; postman, *postal communications*; telegraph boy, page, commissionaire; carrier pigeon, *carrier*; Iris, Mercury.

Adj. *rumoured*; going about, passing round; rife, afloat; full of news, chatty; newsworthy.

Vb. *rumour*, fly a kite; *correspond*. See *inform, disclose, publish*.

525 Secret

N. *secret*, secret lore, mystery; confidential matter, hush-hush subject, top-secret file, state secret; confidential communication, confidence; sphinx, man or woman of mystery, enigmatic personality; dark horse, unknown quantity; unmentionable thing; unknown country, *unknown thing*.

enigma, mystery, puzzle; problem, poser, teaser; hard nut to crack, hard saying, knotty point, crux, *difficulty*; code, cryptogram; anagram, acrostic, crossword;

riddle, conundrum, rebus; labyrinth, maze.

526 Communications

N. *telecommunication*, telephony; semaphore, *signal*; cable, telegram, wire, *message*; bush telegraph, *rumour*; radar; telex, teleprinter, tape machine, ticker; intercom, walkie-talkie; microphone, *megaphone*; *hearing aid*; telephone; line, telephone exchange, switchboard; wireless operator, radio ham, telephonist.

postal *communications*, Postal Union, GPO; post, mail; surface mail, parcel post, postcode, postage stamp; pillarbox, postbox, letterbox; post office, mailbag; postmaster or -mistress, postman or -woman, *messenger*; pigeon post.

broadcasting, *publicity*; BBC; ITA; independent radio or television; transmitter, booster, communications satellite; aerial, antenna; AM, FM, *radiation*; radio station, television channel, network; wireless, radio, crystal set; portable, transistor, tranny; television, telly, TV, small screen; colour television; *camera*; videotape, *recording instrument*; autocue; *information*; Open University; viewer, spectator.

broadcast, transmission, relay, *publication*; recording, repeat, *record*; programme, phone-in, quiz, chat show, music, *amusement*; news, news roundup, *news*; time signal; talk, feature, documentary, *report*; soap opera, *drama*; cartoon, film, *cinema*; commercial, *advertisement*.

broadcaster, commentator, newscaster, compere, question master; disc jockey, DJ; media personality, *person of repute*.

527 Affirmation

N. *affirmation*; proposition; saying, dictum, *maxim*; statement; submission, thesis, *supposition*; voice, choice, suffrage, ballot, *vote*; expression; written statement, prepared text; declaration, profession; assertion, say-so; admission, confession, *disclosure*; corroboration, assurance, warrant, *testimony*; *vigour*; stress, accent, emphasis; *repetition*; challenge, provocation, *defiance*; protest; appeal, representation, *entreaty*; remark, interjection, *speech*; comment, criticism, *estimate*; self-assertion, push, thrust, drive; *positiveness*.

oath, deposition, affidavit, *testimony*; word of a gentleman, word of honour, pledge, promise, warrant, guarantee, *promise*.

Adj. *affirmative*, positive; predica'tive; valid; committed; earnest, meaning; solemn, sworn, formal.

assertive, saying, telling; assured, confident, *positive*; trenchant, incisive, pointed, decisive, decided, *forceful*; distinct, *definite*; express, peremptory, categorical, absolute, insistent; vehement, thundering, *violent*; flat, broad, round, blunt, strong, outspoken, *plain*; pontifical, of faith, unquestionable; challenging, provocative, *defiant*.

Vb. *affirm*, state, express, formulate; declare, pronounce, deliver, enunciate, *proclaim*; give expression to, voice, *speak*; remark, comment, observe, say; state with conviction, be bound, dare swear, *opine*; vow, protest; make a statement, make an assertion, assert, predicate; maintain, hold, contend, *argue*; demonstrate; advance, urge, *propound*; represent, submit; appeal, adjure, claim, *request*; allege, asseverate, aver; bear witness, *testify*; certify, confirm, warrant, guarantee, *corroborate*; commit oneself, pledge, engage, promise; *offer*; profess, avow; admit, *confess*; *stand firm*; challenge, *defy*; repudiate, *negate*; say outright, assert roundly, *speak plainly*; be assertive, shout; claim to know, say so, pontificate.

swear, be sworn, swear an oath, attest, *corroborate*; *negate*; *testify*.

emphasize, stress, accent, accentuate, underline; shout, thunder, fulminate, *be loud*; be urgent, be earnest, urge, enforce, insist, *command*; say with emphasis, drive home; plug, labour, *repeat*; highlight, enhance, *make important*.

Adv. *affirmatively*, positively.

Int. As I stand here! As God is my witness! Cross my heart and hope to die!

528 Negation

N. *negation*, negative, nay; denial, *refusal*; refusal of belief, disbelief; *dissent*; contrary assertion, appeal, *rejoinder*; refutation; challenge, *defiance*; qualification; protest; disclaimer; negative attitude; inability to confirm; refusal of consent, *prohibition*; cancellation.

Adj. *negative*; *contrary*; *disobedient*; *deprecatory*; recusant; denied.

Vb. *negate*, negative; contravene, *disobey*; deny, belie, contradict, deny flatly, contradict absolutely; *make impossible*; repudiate, disavow, disclaim, disown, *reject*; refuse to corroborate; be indifferent; demur, object, *qualify*; disagree, *dissent*; dissociate oneself, *oppose*; traverse, impugn, question, refute, rebut, disprove; refuse credence, *disbelieve*; protest, appeal against, *deprecate*; challenge, *defy*; thwart, *obstruct*; refuse; prohibit; revoke, invalidate, *abrogate*; renounce, *relinquish*; abjure, recant.

Adv. nay, no.

Int. never! a thousand times no! nothing of the kind! quite the contrary! far from it! anything but! no such thing!

529 Teaching

N. *teaching*, pedagogy, private teaching, education, schooling, upbringing; tutelage, leading strings; direction, guidance, instruction, edification; direct method; induction, *reasoning*; tuition, preparation; seminar, teach-in, clinic, workshop, tutorial; initiation, introduction; training, discipline, drill, *exercise*; persuasion, conviction; propaganda, *publicity*.

education, *culture*; classical education, moral education, moral training; technical training, coeducation, progressive education, kindergarten method; elementary education, grounding; day release; sandwich course; physical education, gymnastics.

curriculum, course of study, *learning*; core curriculum, common core; ABC, *beginning*; foundation course; set books, text book; set task, project, exercise, homework, prep; liberal arts; grammar, rhetoric, logic; arithmetic, geometry, astronomy, music; night school, *school*.

lecture, talk, reading, discourse; sermon, oration; lesson, parable; problem play, stage play; readership, chair; lecturer, teacher.

Adj. *educational*, tutorial; scholastic, schoarly, academic; audiovisual, instructive; didactic, hortative; primary, comprehensive; set; extramural, intramural; extracurricular; redbrick, Oxbridge, Ivy League; humane, scientific; practical, utilitarian.

. educate, edify (see teach); breed, rear, nurse, nurture, develop, form, mould, shape; put to school, have taught; tutor, teach, school; ground, coach, cram, prime, prepare; guide, direct; instruct, inform; enlighten; stuff with knowledge, indoctrinate, impregnate, infuse, instil, implant, engraft; chasten, sober.

.ch, be a teacher, take a class; lecture; tutor, impart instruction; dictate; preach, harangue; discourse, hold forth; point a moral; elucidate, expound, interpret; indoctrinate, inoculate; pamphleteer, disseminate propaganda, condition, brainwash, influence.

.in, coach, prepare; initiate, tame; nurse, foster, cultivate; inure; drill, exercise, practise, make second nature, accustom; make fit, qualify; teach manners, teach how to behave.

30 Misteaching

. misteaching; false intelligence; false name; mistake; ignorance; false teaching, propaganda, falsehood; perversion; false logic, sophistry.

.dj. misteaching, propagandist; ignorant, mistaken.

.. misteach; misinform, misdirect, misguide, mislead; corrupt, make wicked; pervert, distort; misrepresent; cry wolf, deceive; lie, be false; suppress knowledge; brainwash.

31 Learning

. learning, lore, wide reading, scholarship; acquisition of knowledge; intellectual curiosity, curiosity; tutelage, apprenticeship, initiation, preparation; first steps, beginning; aptitude; culture, cultivation, late learning; learned person, scholar.

.udy; application; grind; class; homework, prep, preparation; further reading, further study; reading, attention; research, research work, enquiry.

.lj. studious, academic; partial to reading, bookish, well-read, scholarly, erudite, learned, scholastic, knowing; sedulous, diligent, industrious; receptive, docile, willing; attentive.

.b. learn, get oneself taught, go to school, attend college, read, take a course; acquire knowledge, gain information, assimilate learning, imbibe, know; apprentice oneself, serve an apprenticeship, article oneself, prepare oneself; train, practise, exercise, be wont; master; graduate.

.udy, apply oneself; do; enquire; swot, cram, grind, mug; revise; read, peruse, wade through; thumb, browse, skip; be studious.

.dv. studiously.

32 Teacher

. teacher, mentor, guide; minister, pastor; guru, sage; tutor, coach; governor, governess, keeper; educationist, pedagogue; pedant; beak, schoolmarm; master or mistress, school teacher, year tutor; house master or mistress; assistant teacher, deputy head, head teacher, head,

headmaster or -mistress, principal; pupil teacher, usher, monitor; prefect; dean, don, fellow; lecturer, demonstrator, exponent; reader, professor; consultant, adviser; teaching staff, faculty, senior common room.

trainer, coach; disciplinarian.

preacher, pastor; orator, speaker; evangelist; apostle, missionary, pioneer, precursor; seer, prophet, oracle; pamphleteer, propagandist.

Adj. pedagogic, educational.

533 Learner

N. learner, disciple, follower; proselyte, convert, initiate; bookworm, scholar; pupil, scholar, schoolboy or -girl; day pupil, boarder; classmate, fellow student; gifted child; late developer, remedial pupil; old boy, old girl.

beginner, young idea, novice; new boy or girl, greenhorn, tenderfoot, neophyte; rabbit, amateur, lay person; recruit, rookie; colt, cadet, trainee, apprentice; probationer.

student; undergraduate; former student; commoner, pensioner; prize boy; honours student; graduate, fellow; mature student, research worker, specialist.

class, form, grade, remove, shell; set, band, stream; age group, vertical grouping, house; lower form, art class, study group, workshop; conference; seminar, teaching.

Adj. studentlike, young; undergraduate, collegiate; scholarly, studious; preschool; rudimentary.

534 School

N. academy, institute, institution, college, gymnasium; school of music, ballet school, academy of dramatic art; charm school; university, university college, campus; Open University; redbrick university, Oxbridge, varsity; college of further or higher education; polytechnic, poly; school of philosophy, Academy.

school, playgroup, kindergarten; infant school, private school, preparatory school; primary school; boarding school; convent school, special school; community home; Borstal; remand home, detention centre; blackboard jungle.

training school, nursery, training ground, arena; training ship, training college, tech; college of commerce, seminary; law school, medical school, medical college, teaching hospital; military college, staff college; West Point.

classroom; study; lecture room, lecture hall, auditorium, amphitheatre; resources area, library; workshop, laboratory, lab, language lab; gymnasium; campus; desk; reader, primer, crib, textbook; slate, copybook, workbook, exercise book, record; visual aid, blackboard, spectacle.

rostrum, tribune, dais, forum; platform, stage; hustings, soapbox; chair, lecture; pulpit, lectern; microphone; leader page, column, publicity.

Adj. scholastic, educational.

535 Veracity

N. veracity; nothing but fact, fidelity, fidelity to fact, realism; candour, manifestation; honour bright; love of truth, probity; simplicity; plain dealing; plain words, home truth, unvarnished tale, true statement, honest truth, *truth*; clean breast, true confession, unqualified admission, *disclosure*; gate of horn; true prophet.

Adj. *veracious*, truthful, *true*; reliable, *trustworthy*; factual, bald, unvarnished, scrupulous, exact, just, *accurate*; full, particular, circumstantial, *diffuse*; simple, ingenuous, *artless*; meant; unaffected, unpretentious, open, aboveboard; candid, unreserved, forthcoming; blunt, free, downright, forthright, outspoken, straightforward, honest to goodness, honest to God, *plain*; *intelligible*; honest, sincere, *honourable*; truly spoken; infallible.

Vb. *be truthful*, swear true, *swear*; be true; mean it, really mean, *be serious*; keep nothing back, *show*; come clean, make a clean breast of it, *confess*; *disclose*; *predict*; say truly, *demonstrate*.

Adv. *truthfully*, *truly*; without fear or favour; exactly.

536 Falsehood

N. *falsehood*; treachery, bad faith, *perfidy*; lying, perjury, *untruth*; fiction, forgery, *deception*; invention, *imagination*; evasion, double-talk, fencing; economy of truth; *sophistry*; *exaggeration*; perversion; false colouring; *ostentation*; humbug, bunkum, boloney, hooey, *empty talk*; cant, eyewash, hogwash (see *duplicity*); euphemism, blarney, soft soap, *flattery*; liar.

duplicity; false conduct, double life; guile; front, facade, outside, show, *ostentation*; pretence, bluff, act, fake, counterfeit, *sham*; hypocrisy; acting, simulation, cant; lip service, cupboard love; false piety; show of sympathy; Judas kiss; fraud, legal fiction; cheat, sharp practice, frame-up, *foul play*; *pretension*; low cunning, *cunning*.

Adj. *false*, without truth; untruthful, lying, mendacious; treacherous; artful, *cunning*; disingenuous, dishonest, ambiguous, evasive, *equivocal*; meretricious; overdone; counterfeit, fake, sham, snide, quack, bogus, *spurious*; deceptive, deceitful; packed.

hypocritical, hollow, empty, insincere; pretended, seeming; make-believe, acting, double, two-faced, shifty, sly, treacherous, designing, Machiavellian; sanctimonious; plausible, smooth, creepy, goody-goody; mealy-mouthed, *affected*.

Vb. *be false*, perjure oneself, bear false witness, swear that black is white; lie, utter a falsehood; strain, tell a tall story, *exaggerate*; tell a fib, tell a whopper, lie hard; invent, make believe, romance, *imagine*; *misinterpret*; garble, doctor, falsify, *distort*; overstate, understate, *misrepresent*; misreport, misquote, misinform, cry wolf; lull, soothe, *flatter*; play false, play a double game, *be dishonest*; break faith, betray.

dissemble, dissimulate, disguise, *conceal*; simulate, counterfeit, *imitate*; assume, affect, play a part, make a show of, *act*; feign, sham, pretend; malinger, *deceive*; lack candour, be less than honest; keep something back, fail to declare; prevaricate, shuffle, dodge, trim, *be equivocal*.

cant, *be affected*; colour, varnish, paint, embroider; act a part.

fake, fudge, fabricate, coin, forge, counterfeit, *imitate*; frame; manipulate, fiddle,

wangle, rig, pack (a jury); spin, wea▮ cook, concoct, hatch, invent, *plot*.

Adv. *falsely*.

537 Deception

N. *deception*; credulity; *folly*; fallacy, soph▮ try; illusion, delusion, hallucinatio▮ error; false appearance, mockery, mira▮ will-o'-the-wisp, *visual fallacy*; sho▮ paint (see *sham*); false reputatio▮ bubble; deceit, lie, pious fraud, *falseho▮ guile, craft, *cunning*; hypocris▮ duplicity; treachery, perfidy; mach▮ nation, hanky-panky, jiggery-poke▮ *plot*; fraudulence, cheat.

trickery, shenanigan; sharp practice, chic▮ nery; swindle, ramp, racket, wang▮ fiddle, diddle, swiz, sell, fraud, che▮ *foul play*; trick, confidence trick, fast on▮ wiles, ruse, shift, dodge, fetch, blir▮ feint, *stratagem*; wrinkle; bait, gimmic▮ red herring, tub to a whale; hoax, blu▮ spoof; game, sport, joke, rag, *witticis▮ sleight, pass, hocus-pocus, illusion, ventr▮ oquism; juggle, googly; magic, *sorcery▮ trap, *ambush*; catch; plant, frame-up, f▮ play; hook, noose, snare, gin, spring gu▮ man trap; net, web; blind, decoy, dec▮ duck, bait, lure, sprat to catch a mac▮ erel; flypaper; booby trap, mine, pit, p▮ *fall*; trapdoor, false bottom, *secret*; fal▮ gift, Trojan horse.

sham, false front, veneer, *duplicity*; lip se▮ vice; make-believe, pretence, *affectatio▮ paint, whitewash, varnish, gloss; man▮ straw, paper tiger; *impostor*; dumm▮ scarecrow; facsimile, *copy*; film s▮ *insubstantial thing*; mockery, counterfe▮ forgery, fake; masquerade, mask, cloa▮ disguise, false colours; shoddy, *rubbis▮ tinsel, paste; Mosaic gold; German s▮ ver.

Adj. *deceiving*, deceitful, lying; deceptiv▮ *latent*; illusory; specious, glib, slick, sl▮ pery, *smooth*; treacherous, insidiou▮ *false*; pretended; prestigious; trick▮ crafty, wily, artful, *cunning*.

spurious, false, fake; sham, counterfe▮ *false*; make-believe, mock, ersatz, bogu▮ so-called; artificial, plastic, paste, c▮ tured; shoddy, *useless*; tinsel, meret▮ cious, flash, catchpenny, *cheap*; car▮ board, pasteboard, *brittle*; sophisticate▮ *mixed*; underweight, *light*.

Vb. *deceive*, delude, dazzle, beguile; give▮ false impression, belie; *disappoint*; blin▮ fold, *blind*; kid, bluff, bamboozle, hoo▮ wink, hoax, humbug, *mislead*; spoo▮ mystify; play false, betray, two-tim▮ double-cross, *be dishonest*; intrig▮ against, *plot*; circumvent, overreach, ou▮ wit, outmanoeuvre, *outdo*; forestall, ▮ *early*; pull a fast one, outsmart, *be cu▮ ning*; trick, cheat, con, swindle, sel▮ rook, do; diddle, gyp, fleece, pluc▮ shortchange, *defraud*; juggle, conjur▮ force a card, fob; practise chicanery, p▮ rymander, tinker with, fiddle, wang▮ *dissemble*; whitewash, cant; counterfe▮ fake.

befool, fool, make a fool of, make an ass o▮ make one look silly; mock, make fun o▮ *ridicule*; rag, make an April fool of, ▮ *absurd*; sport with, jilt; have, dupe, gu▮ outwit; trick, trap, take advantage of▮ manipulate; kid, spoof, bamboozle, ▮ along (see *deceive*); cajole, get round, lu▮ soothe, *flatter*; *disappoint*; *mislead*.

ensnare, snare, trap, entrap, lime; enmes▮ entangle, net; trip, catch, hook; bai▮

dangle a bait, lure, decoy, entice, *tempt*; waylay, *ambush*; nab, nick, kidnap, shanghai, *steal*.

Adv. *deceptively*.

538 Untruth

N. untruth, *falsehood*; understatement, *exaggeration*; lie, fib, whopper; false statement; broken word, breach of promise, *perfidy*; perjury, false oath; false evidence, frame-up, *evidence*; fiction, invention, false excuse; perversion; gloss, varnish; lie factory, propaganda machine; gate of ivory.

mental *dishonesty*, economy of truth, pious fraud, mental reservation, *qualification*; show, make-believe; pretence, profession, false plea, excuse, *pretext*; evasion, subterfuge, shift, shuffle; irony, backhanded compliment, *affectation*; sham, empty words, *duplicity*; Judas kiss, *perfidy*; mask, *disguise*.

fable, invention, fiction, imaginative exercise; story, tale, *narrative*; tall story, shaggy dog story, *exaggeration*; fairy tale, romance, tale, yarn, story; claptrap, gossip, *rumour*; myth, mythology; moonshine, farce, sell, swiz, hoax, humbug, flummery, *empty talk*.

Adj. untrue, lying, mendacious, *false*; nothing less true; mythological, fabulous, unfounded, empty; fictitious, makebelieve; artificial, synthetic; bogus, socalled, *spurious*; *boastful*; evasive, surreptitious, equivocal; *affected*; satirical.

Vb. be untrue; be unlikely; lie, be a liar, *be false*; spin a yarn, *exaggerate*; makebelieve, *imagine*; pretend, sham, counterfeit, forge, falsify, *dissemble*.

539 Dupe

N. dupe, fool, *laughingstock*; *ninny*; gudgeon; easy prey, easy target, sitting duck, soft touch, pushover, cinch; fair game, victim, fall guy, stooge, mug, sucker, gull, pigeon; greenhorn, innocent, *beginner*; puppet, pawn, *instrument*; vulnerable public.

Adj. gullible; had, done, sold a pup; innocent, green, silly, *foolish*.

Vb. be duped, be had, be done; rise, nibble; catch a Tartar.

540 Deceiver

N. deceiver; practical joker, Puck, *humorist*; actor, hypocrite, canter, Pharisee; false friend, jilt; turncoat, rat; double agent; traitor, Judas, *knave*; serpent; forger, *imitator*.

liar; story-teller; imaginative person; traveller; *exaggeration*; false witness, *falsehood*.

impostor, adventurer; pretender, charlatan, quack, mountebank; fake, fraud, humbug; front man.

trickster; cheat; cardsharp, rook; shyster; shark; slicker; twister, jobber, rogue, *knave*; confidence trickster, con man; decoy, stool pigeon; wily bird, fox.

conjuror, illusionist; quick-change artist; magician, *sorcerer*.

541 Exaggeration

N. exaggeration, inflation, magnification, enlargement; optimism; stretch, strain; extremism; overkill, excess, violence; ostentation; sensationalism, ballyhoo, publicity; hyperbole; adulation, *flattery*; colouring, *ornament*; embroidery, *addition*; disproportion; caricature, burlesque, *satire*; big talk; rant, tirade; excessive loyalty, chauvinism, *prejudice*; tall story, yarn, *fable*; flight of fancy, *imagination*; fuss, pother, excitement, much ado about nothing, *commotion*; *liar*.

Adj. exaggerated; strained, overdone, inflated; histrionic; melodramatic; swelling, *boastful*; tall, fanciful, steep, egregious, preposterous, outrageous, farfetched, *absurd*; lofty, extravagant, excessive; violent, immoderate, *exorbitant*; fulsome, inordinate, *superfluous*.

Vb. exaggerate, magnify, expand, inflate, *enlarge*; add to, *add*; enhance, heighten, add a flourish, embroider, decorate; overdo, overdraw, overcharge, overload; overweight, *make important*; puff, oversell, *overrate*; make much of, make too much of, *flatter*; stretch, strain, distort; caricature; protest too much; overact; rant, talk big, *boast*; run riot; go too far, *overstep*; spin a yarn, *be false*; intensify, exacerbate, *aggravate*.

542 Indication

N. indication, drawing attention, showing, *manifestation*; meaning; notification, *information*; symbolism, *representation*; symbol, x, *letter*; secret symbol, hieroglyph; sacred symbol, cross, crescent; magic symbol, *talisman*; natural symbol, image, type, figure; token, emblem, figurehead (see *badge*); symptom, sign, *evidence*; tell-tale sign, blush, *disclosure*; nudge, wink, *hint* (see *gesture*); omen; clue, scent, whiff; noise, footfall, *sound*; pointer, finger, forefinger, index finger (see *indicator*); guide, index, *directory*; key, *interpretation*; contour lines; marker, mark; blaze; nick, scratch, *notch*; stamp, print, impression; stigma; prick, tattoo mark, *perforation*; scar, *blemish*; line, score, stroke; note, catchword (see *punctuation*); legend, caption, *description*; inscription, epitaph; motto, monogram; love token, favour. See *badge*.

identification, nomenclature, *classification*; means of identification, brand, earmark, trademark, imprint (see *label*); autograph, signature, hand, *script*; fingerprint, footprint, spoor, track, trail, *trace*; secret sign, password, open sesame, watchword, countersign, shibboleth; colour, colouring, characteristic, trait, outline, form, shape, *feature*; personal characteristic, trick, trick of speech; mole, scar, birthmark, strawberry mark, *blemish*; litmus paper; mark, note.

symbology, code, *secrecy*; picture writing, *script*.

gesture, sign language; sign, *hint*; pantomime, dumb show, mime; stage business; body language; demeanour, *mien*; motion, move; tic, twitch, *spasm*; shrug; nod, beck, wink, twinkle, glance, ogle, leer, grimace, *look*; smile, laugh, *laughter*; touch, kick, nudge, jog, *knock*; hug; handshake, grip; push, shove, *impulse*; signal, wave; excitable state; *resolution*; snap; *defiance*; flag-waving, *celebration*; clap, cheer, *applause*; hiss, boo, catcall, raspberry, *disapprobation*; frown, scowl, pout, *discontent*.

signal, *message*; sign, symptom, *manifestation*; flash, rocket, Very light, maroon;

railway signal, heliograph, semaphore; telegraph, *telecommunication*; signal lamp, *lamp*; warning light, beacon, beacon fire, *fire*; warning signal, red flag, warning light, green light, all clear, *signal light*; alarm, warning signal, SOS, *danger signal*; whistle, siren, hooter, buzzer, knocker, *gong*; bell, doorbell, alarm bell, angelus, carillon; time signal, pip, minute gun, dinner gong, dinner bell; passing bell, knell.

indicator, index, pointer, arrow, needle, arm, finger, hand; Plimsoll line, *gauge*; traffic indicator, winker; direction finder, radar; white line, *traffic control*; weathercock, wind sock, *weather*.

signpost, direction post; milestone; lighthouse, lightship, buoy, *safeguard*; compass, *sailing aid*; lodestar, cynosure, Southern Cross, *star*; landmark; cairn, *earthwork*; monument, memorial; tidemark, *limit*.

call, proclamation, ban, *publication*; shout, hail; invitation; call to prayer, church bell, *worship*; summons, word, word of command, *command*; distress call, Mayday; bugle, trumpet, reveille, assemble, charge, advance, rally, retreat; last post; peal, flourish; drum, tattoo, *roll*; call to arms, fiery cross; battle cry, slogan, catchword, watchword, shibboleth; challenge, countersign.

badge, token, emblem, symbol, sign, insignia (see *heraldry*); roundel; badge of sovereignty, throne, sceptre, orb, crown, *regalia*; mark of authority, badge of office, Black Rod, mace, *badge of rule*; baton, *badge of rank*; medal, gong, cross, order, star, garter, sash, ribbon; badge of merit, laurels, wreath, fillet, chaplet, garland, *trophy*; colours, blue, cap, oar; badge of loyalty, favour, rosette, love knot; badge of mourning, black, *clothing*.

livery, dress, *uniform*; tartan, tie, blazer; chevron, wings; flash, cockade, rosette.

heraldry; Roll of Arms; coat of arms; achievement; shield, escutcheon; crest, wreath, helmet, crown, coronet; motto; field, quarter, sinister, chief, base; charge, device, bearing, ordinary, bar, label, pale, bend, bend sinister, chevron, pile, cross; lozenge; quartering; animal charge, lion, unicorn, eagle, falcon; floral charge, cinquefoil, trefoil; badge, rebus, antelope, portcullis; national emblem, rose, thistle, leek, daffodil, shamrock; device, spread eagle, bear; swastika; colour, azure, sable; metal, or; fur, ermine, potent; College of Arms, Earl Marshal, King of Arms, herald, herald extraordinary, Rouge Dragon, Portcullis.

flag, ensign, red ensign, Red Duster; jack, flag of convenience; colours, King's Colour, standard, banner; pennon, streamer, pennant, triple tail; bunting; yellow flag; white flag, *submission*; eagle, tricolour; Union Jack; Old Glory; Red Flag; black flag, Jolly Roger; hoist, fly; flagpole, flagstaff.

label, mark of identification, tattoo, caste mark (see *identification*); ticket, bill, docket, chit, counterfoil, stub, duplicate; tally, counter, chip; tick, letter, number, check, mark; sticky label, sticker; tab, tag; name tape, fascia; sign, bush, *exhibit*; plate, trade sign, trademark, hallmark, cachet, rebus; earmark, brand, stigma, broad arrow; seal, signet, stamp, impress, impression; masthead, caption, heading, title, superscription, rubric; imprint,

watermark; name; card, birth certificate, identification papers, identity card; passport, pass, *permit*; witness, signature, hand, sign manual, autograph, mark, cross, monogram; fingerprint, footprint, *trace*.

punctuation, punctuation mark, point, stop, period; comma, colon, semicolon; apostrophe; exclamation mark, question mark; crotchet, crook, brace; hyphen; dash, dot, blank; reference mark, asterisk, star; dagger, squiggle; hand, index; accent, diaeresis, cedilla; vowel point, breve, umlaut; stroke, mark of abbreviation, paragraph; plus sign, decimal point; italics, bold type.

Adj. *indicating*, indicative; expressive, suggestive, *meaningful*; typical, representative, token, nominal; telltale; characteristic, personal, individual, *special*; demonstrative, explanatory, exponential; ominous.

heraldic; sinister; azure, sable, or, ermine, rampant.

marked; spotted, *mottled*; indelible.

Vb. indicate, point, *point to*; exhibit, *show*; blaze, signpost; register, *record*; name, identify, classify, *specify*; index, reference; guide, *direct*; signify, denote, connote, suggest, imply, involve, spell, bespeak, argue, *mean*; typify, *represent*; declare, *affirm*; highlight; evince, give evidence of, attest, testify, witness to, *evidence*; intimate, smack of, smell of, hint; betray, reveal, *disclose*; inform against, *inform*; forebode, presage, *predict*.

mark, demarcate, *limit*; label, ticket, docket, tag, tab; earmark, designate; note, annotate, line, score, underline, underscore; number, letter, page; tick; nick, scribe, *notch*; chalk; scratch, scribble, cover, write; blot, stain, blacken, *make unclean*; scar, disfigure, *make ugly*; punctuate, dot, dash, cross, asterisk; blaze, brand; prick, tattoo, *pierce*; stamp, seal, punch, impress, emboss; imprint, *print*; etch, *engrave*; emblazon; impale, quarter, difference; marshal, charge.

sign, ratify, countersign, *endorse*; autograph; subscribe; initial.

gesticulate, pantomime, mime, mimic, *imitate*; wave, wag, waggle, *agitate*; wave to, *greet*; stamp, *applaud*; gesture, motion, sign; point, thumb, beckon, *attract notice*; nod, beck, wink, shrug; jog, nudge, poke, prod; look, look volumes, glance, leer, ogle, *gaze*; twinkle, smile, *laugh*; *disapprove*; *lament*; *be resolute*; *be angry*; snap, bite, *be sullen*; grimace, pout, scowl, frown; *despise*; shuffle, pat, stroke, *caress*.

signal, speak, *communicate*; semaphore, heliograph; thumb; wave through; dip, half-mast, salute; alert, dial 999, *raise the alarm*; fire a warning shot, *warn*.

Adv. symbolically.

543 Record

N. *record*, recording; memoir, chronicle, annals, history, *narrative*; case history, *biography*; photograph, portrait, sketch, *representation*; file, dossier; public record, gazette, official journal, Hansard; official publication, blue book, White Paper; minutes; memorandum; returns, *report*; tally, scoreboard; form, document; voucher, certificate, diploma, charter; birth certificate, marriage lines, *title deed*; copy, *duplicate*; archives, papers; record, book, roll, register, registry; tablet, table, notebook, logbook, log, diary, journal, commonplace book, scrapbook, album; ledger, *account book*; index, *list*; card, microfilm, *miniature*; tape; pressing, *gramophone*; inscription, legend, caption, heading; wall writing, graffiti; *script*.

registration, registry; recording, engraving; reservation; entry, book-keeping, accountancy.

monument, memorial; mausoleum, *tomb*; statue, bust, *image*; brass, tablet, slab, inscription; funerary achievement, *heraldry*; pillar, column, memorial arch, obelisk, *spectacle*; idol; ancient monument, dolmen, megalith, *antiquity*; cairn, barrow, tell, *earthwork*; testimonial, cup, ribbon, *trophy*.

trace, vestige, relic, remains; track, footstep, footprint, pug, tread; spoor, slot; scent, smell; wake, wash, trail, furrow, swathe, path; thumb impression; fingerprint, *evidence*; mark, tidemark, stain, scar, scratch, weal, welt, *blemish*.

Adj. *recording*; monumental.

recorded; *written*; extant.

Vb. *record*, tape, videotape; film, *photograph*; paint, *represent*; document; docket, file, index, catalogue; inscribe, cut, carve, grave, incise, *engrave*; commit to writing, *write*; *print*; note, mark, make a note of; minute, calendar; chronicle, *describe*.

register, tally, score; tabulate, table, enlist, *list*; enter, post, book, *account*; reserve, inscribe; log, *remember*.

Adv. on record.

544 Recorder

N. *recorder*, registrar, *notary*; scribe; secretary, receptionist; writer; clerk; record clerk, *accountant*; *engraving*; draughtsman, *artist*; cameraman, *photography*; record room, Record Office; Recording Angel.

chronicler, diarist, historian, biographer, *narrator*, *antiquarian*; reporter, columnist, *news reporter*; candid camera.

recording instrument, recorder, tape recorder; record, disc, *gramophone*; teleprinter, tape machine, *telecommunication*; cash register, till, checkout; turnstile; seismograph, speedometer, *gauge*; flight recorder, black box; stopwatch; camera; pen, pencil, *stationery*.

545 Obliteration

N. *obliteration*, erasure; blue pencil; cancellation, cancel; burial, oblivion, *amnesty*; blot, stain, *dirt*; clean slate, clean sweep, *revolution*; rubber, duster, sponge; abrasive.

Adj. *obliterated*; intestate.

Vb. *obliterate*, cover, conceal; deface, make illegible; efface, eliminate, erase, abrade, *rub*; expunge, blot, cancel, delete; score through; censor; raze, *demolish*; bury, cover; *forget*; submerge, *lower*, drown, silence; *disappear*.

546 Representation

N. *representation*, personification, incarnation, embodiment; conventional representation, diagram, *writing*; presentation, *manifestation*; performance, doing, *acting*; therapy; mimicry, dumb show; characterization, *description*; drawing, illustration, *painting*; creation, work of art, *product*; impression, likeness, identikit, *similarity*; exact likeness, double, facsimile, *duplicate*; trace, tracing, *outline*; reflection (see *image*); pictorial equivalent, true picture, striking likeness, realism, *picture*; bad likeness; reproduction, lithograph, *printing*; etching, engraving; design, blueprint, draft, cartoon, sketch, outline, *plan*; projection.

image, *duplicate*; mental image, *idea*; projection, silhouette, *reflection*; visual, visual aid, *spectacle*; idol; cherub; statuary, statue, colossus; statuette, bust, torso, head, *sculpture*; effigy, figure, figurine, figurehead; gargoyle; wax figure; dummy, lay figure; model, doll; marionette, puppet, snowman, gingerbread man; scarecrow, guy; robot, automaton; type, symbol.

art, architecture, *formation*; fine arts; graphic art, *painting*; plastic art, *sculpture*; classical art, Baroque, Rococo; modern art, abstract art; classicism, realism; Surrealism, Expressionism, *school of painting*; op art, kitsch, *bad taste*; functional art; calligraphy, tapestry, embroidery, pottery.

photography, radiography; telephotography; cinematography, *cinema*; photograph, photo, picture, snapshot, snap; plate, film, exposure, negative, print, slide, transparency; frame, still; reel, spool, cassette; filmstrip, microfilm, movie, *film*; radiograph, X-ray, *radiation*; photocopy, *copy*; *printing*; shot, take, close-up, mug shot, pan, cover shot, dissolve, fade; lens, *camera*; cameraman.

map, chart, plan, outline, *statistics*; sketch map; Admiralty chart; ground plan; elevation, projection, atlas, globe; *astronomy*; cartography.

Adj. *representing*, representative; pictorial, graphic, vivid; figurative; representational, realistic; primitive, impressionistic; abstract; artistic; photogenic.

represented, drawn, fairly drawn; being drawn.

Vb. *represent*, denote, mean; type, typify, incarnate, embody, personify; impersonate, *deceive*; pose, model, *be an example*; present, enact, perform, do; project, shadow forth, suggest; reflect, image; mimic, mime, copy, *imitate*; depict, *describe*; delineate, draw, picture, portray, figure; illustrate, emblazon, *paint*; catch a likeness, catch, capture, register, *record*; make an image, carve, cast; cut, engrave; mould, shape, *form*; design, blueprint, draft, *plan*; diagram, construct a figure, describe a circle, *outline*; sketch, scrawl, doodle, *improvise*; map, chart, survey, plot.

photograph, photo; snapshot, snap, take, shoot, film; X-ray, radiograph; expose, develop, process, print, enlarge, reduce.

547 Misrepresentation

N. *misrepresentation*; false light, *falsehood*; bad likeness, *injustice*; travesty, parody, *exaggeration*; caricature, burlesque, guy, *ridicule*; flattery, *art*; bad art; daub, botch, scrawl.

Adj. *misrepresented*; flat, cardboard.

Vb. *misrepresent*; deform, *distort*; give a twist or turn, *flatter*; *exaggerate*; overdraw, caricature, guy, burlesque, parody, travesty; daub, botch, splash; lie, *be* *false.*

548 Painting

N. *painting*, graphic art, colouring; finger painting; washing; drawing, *representation*; artistry, composition, design, technique; line, perspective, golden section; treatment, tone, atmosphere, ambience; highlight, local colour, shading, contrast; monotone, monochrome, *colour*; chiaroscuro.

art *style*, style of painting, grand style, grand manner, *form*; intimate style, genre painting (see *art subject*); pastiche; scene painting, oil painting, watercolour, tempera, gouache; fresco painting.

school *of painting*, Mannerism, Baroque, Rococo, Realism, Romanticism, Impressionism, Symbolism, Cubism, Expressionism, Surrealism, Abstract Expressionism, action painting; minimal art, *art*.

art *subject*, landscape; scene, prospect, panorama, *view*; interior, conversation piece, still life, pastoral, nocturne, nude; crucifixion, nativity.

picture, pictorial equivalent, *representation*; tableau, mosaic, tapestry; collage, montage; brass rubbing; painting, pastiche; triptych, panel; fresco, mural, wall painting, poster; canvas, daub; drawing, sketch, outline, cartoon; oil painting, gouache, watercolour, pastel, wash drawing, design, pattern, doodle; cartoon, caricature, silhouette; miniature; old master, masterpiece; study, portrait, head, profile; studio portrait, snap, pinup, *photography*; reproduction, halftone; woodcut, *engraving*, print, plate; illustration, fashion plate, picture postcard, cigarette card, stamp, transfer, scrap, sticker; picture book, scrapbook, photograph album, *book*.

art *equipment*, palette, palette knife, spatula, paintbrush, paint tube; oils, oil paint, tempera, distemper, gouache, varnish, *facing*; ink, crayon, pastel, chalk, charcoal, heelball; pen, pencil; *paper*; canvas, easel, picture frame, mount; studio, art museum, picture gallery; model, sitter, poser, subject.

Adj. *painted*, graphic, pictorial, scenic, picturesque, decorative; pastel, *coloured*; linear, chiaroscuro; *grey*.

Vb. *paint*, wash, *colour*; tint, retouch, daub; *coat*; paint a picture, do a portrait, portray, draw, sketch, cartoon, *represent*; illuminate; ink, chalk, crayon, pencil, stencil, shade, stipple.

549 Sculpture

N. *sculpture*, plastic art, *representation*; *formation*; carving, stone cutting, wood carving; moulding; rock carving; *school of painting*; mobile; kinetic art; statuary; group; statue, colossus; statuette, figurine, bust, torso, head; model, cast, death mask, *image*; ceramics, *pottery*; medallion, cameo, intaglio; relief, bas-relief; stone, marble, bronze, clay, wax, plasticine; armature; chisel.

Adj. *glyptic*, statuary, statuesque, marmoreal; plastic.

Vb. *sculpt*, sculpture, *form*; cut, carve, whittle, chisel, chip; chase, engrave, emboss; model, mould, cast.

550 Engraving. Printing

N. *engraving*, etching, line engraving; gem cutting, gem engraving; glass engraving; mezzotint; wood engraving, woodcut; steel plate, stone, block, chisel, burr, needle, style.

printing, *print*; plate printing, colour printing; fabric printing, batik; stereotype; impression; die, punch, stamp.

Vb. *engrave*, grave, incise, cut, undercut; etch, stipple, scrape; bite; sandblast; impress, stamp; lithograph, *print*; mezzotint.

551 Artist

N. *artist*, craftsman or -woman, *artisan*; architect, *producer*; draughtsman or -woman; fashion artist; drawer; illustrator, commercial artist; painter; amateur, Sunday painter; pavement artist; miniaturist; portrait painter, Academician, old master, primitive; Impressionist, action painter, *school of painting*; art historian.

sculptor, statuary, monumental mason, moulder.

engraver; lapidary, chaser; *printer*.

552 Language

N. *language*, tongue, speech, idiom, parlance, talk; parole; spoken language, patter, lingo, *dialect*; personal language; mother tongue, vernacular, common speech, vulgar tongue; colloquial speech, *speech*; correct speech; creole, pidgin, pidgin English; sign language, *gesture*; International Scientific Vocabulary, Basic English; artificial language, Esperanto; official language, Mandarin, Standard English, BBC English; machine language; learned language, Latin, Greek, Sanskrit; polyglot medley; Babel, babble, *confusion*.

language *type*, language group, Indo-European, Celtic, Romance.

linguistics, language study, philology, comparative grammar, syntax, *grammar*; phonetics, *pronunciation*; lexicography, *etymology*; semantics, *meaning*; nomenclature; linguistic geography; speech community; genius of a language, sense of idiom.

literature, written language, creative writing, *reading matter*, classics, arts, humanities; PEN, *author*; literary genre, fiction, nonfiction, *narrative*, *description*; lyricism, poetry, *poem*; *drama*; criticism, *estimate*; literary criticism, *interpretation*; literary style, *metaphor*; literary movement, Classicism, Romanticism, Symbolism, Idealism, Expressionism, Surrealism, Realism; literary history; history of literature; Golden Age, *era*; compendium of literature, *anthology*; digest, reader, *textbook*.

linguist, language student, *etymology*; grammarian, *grammar*; acoustics; student of literature, *scholar*; classical scholar, *antiquarian*; polyglot, bilingual.

Adj. *linguistic*, grammatical; monosyllabic; tonal; correct, pure; written, literary, standard; spoken, living, idiomatic; vulgar, colloquial, vernacular; local; current, common; bilingual; multilingual, polyglot.

literary, written, polite; classical, romantic; futuristic; learned; formal; critical.

53 Letter

. *letter*; sign, symbol, character, *writing*; alphabet, ABC, criss-cross row; initial teaching alphabet, International Phonetic Alphabet, IPA; *speech sound*; Chinese character, ideogram; cuneiform, hieroglyph, *lettering*; Greek alphabet, lettering, black letter, Gothic; ampersand; big letter, cap; small letter, minuscule; block letter; cursive; type.

itials, first letter; monogram; anagram, acrostic, acronym.

oken *letter*, phone; consonant, vowel, syllable, *voice*; guttural, liquid, *speech sound*.

elling; orthography; spelling game, spelling bee; *translation*.

dj. literal; Cyrillic; cuneiform, *written*; Gothic, roman; large, capital, initial; small, minuscule; phonetic, *vocal*.

b. spell, read, syllable; transliterate; letter, write; initial, sign.

dv. alphabetically.

54 Word

. *word*; expression, *phrase*; term, *name*; syllable, *speech sound; meaning*; synonym, *identity*; pun, weasel word; antonym; root; folk etymology; derivative, doublet; stem; part of speech, *grammar*; diminutive, pejorative, intensive; contraction, abbreviation, acronym, portmanteau word; catchword, vogue word; *similarity*; swearword, *malediction*; hard word, long word, polysyllable; short word, monosyllable; many words, verbiage.

ictionary, lexicon, word list, glossary, vocabulary; thesaurus, *store*; compilation, concordance, index.

ymology, philology, *linguistics; meaning; pronunciation*; terminology, *nomenclature*; lexicography; compiler.

dj. verbal, literal; titular, nominal; lexical; derivative, conjugate, cognate; wordy, verbose.

dv. verbally; verbatim.

55 Neology

. *neology*, neologism; coinage, new word, catch phrase; loan word, loan translation, *word*; newfangled expression, technical language, jargon, technical term; hybrid, hybrid expression; corruption, telegraphese; baby talk; doubletalk; affected language, archaism, *affectation*; abuse of language, abuse of terms, malapropism, *solecism*; spoonerism, *witticism*; *speech defect*.

alect, idiom, lingo, patois, vernacular, *language*; burr, brogue, accent, *pronunciation*; cockney, Doric; broken English; pidgin; hybrid language; anglicism, Americanism, gallicism; *speech defect*; *linguistics*.

lang, vulgarism; jargon, argot, cant, patter; gipsy lingo, Romany; back slang, pig Latin; backchat, scurrility; *empty talk*.

dj. neological, newfangled; barbaric, barbarous, hybrid, corrupt, pidgin; foreign, archaic, obsolete; irregular.

ialectal, vernacular; Doric, Cockney, broad; guttural, nasal; provincial, local; homely, colloquial; nonstandard, cant; technical, special.

b. neologize, coin words, invent vocabulary; talk slang, cant; talk cockney, speak with an accent, burr, *voice*.

556 Nomenclature

N. *nomenclature*; terminology; description; appellation, denomination; apostrophe; baptism, *Christian rite*.

name, first name, forename, Christian name; middle name(s), surname; maiden name, appellation; nickname, pet name, diminutive; epithet, description; handle, style, *title*; heading, caption; signature, *label*; term, trade name; same name, namesake, synonym; pen name, pseudonym, *misnomer*; noun, *part of speech*; place name.

nomenclator.

Adj. named, titled; alias; so-called; nominal, titular; what one may fairly call.

naming.

Vb. name, call, give a name, christen, *perform ritual*; give a handle to, surname, nickname, dub; give one his title, sir; title, entitle, style, term, *specify*; distinguish, *discriminate*; define, mark; announce; blacklist, *reprobate*.

be *named*; answer to.

Adv. by name; namely.

557 Misnomer

N. *misnomer*; malapropism, *solecism*; wrong name, alias; pen name; stage name, pseudonym; nickname, pet name, *name*.

no *name*; anon, certain person, so-and-so; N or M, sir or madam; Miss X; this or that; some, any.

Adj. misnamed, self-styled, would-be, so-called.

anonymous, unknown, faceless, nameless, without a name; incognito; a certain, certain, such; some, any, this or that.

Vb. misname, miscall; nickname, dub; *name*; assume an alias; be anonymous; dissemble.

558 Phrase

N. *phrase*, form of words; clause, sentence, period, paragraph; expression; idiom, mannerism, *speciality*; fixed expression, formula; set phrase, set terms; euphemism, metaphor; catch phrase, slogan; hackneyed expression, well-worn phrase, commonplace, *habit*; saying, motto, moral, epigram, *maxim*; lapidary phrase, epitaph; inscription, legend, caption, *record*; words, compliments, *empty talk*; terminology, *nomenclature*; surface structure, diction, wording, choice of words, choice of expression; roundabout phrase, periphrasis, circumlocution; paraphrase, *translation*; written phrase, *script*.

Adj. phraseological, periodic; idiomatic.

Vb. phrase, word, articulate, syllable; reword, *translate*; express, formulate, state, *affirm*; put words together, turn a sentence, round a period, *show style*.

Adv. in terms.

559 Grammar

N. *grammar*, philology, *linguistics*; analysis; accidence, case, declension; conjugation, mood, voice, tense; number, gender, *punctuation*; umlaut, attraction, *etymology*; syntax, word order, ellipsis, apposition; bad grammar, *solecism*; good grammar, correct style, Standard English.

part *of speech*, noun, pronoun; adjective;

verb, adverb, preposition, copula, conjunction, interjection; subject, object; article, particle, affix, suffix, prefix; formative; diminutive, intensive.

Adj. grammatical, correct; irregular, anomalous; masculine, feminine, neuter; singular, dual, plural; predicative; verbal; comparative, superlative.

Vb. parse, analyse, inflect, conjugate, decline; punctuate; construe, interpret.

560 Solecism

N. solecism, bad grammar; faulty syntax; ornament; irregularity, dialect; malapropism, bull, slip, mistake; speech defect.

Adj. ungrammatical; irregular, abnormal; faulty, improper, incongruous.

Vb. be ungrammatical, violate grammar, commit a solecism; mispronounce, stammer; misspell, blunder.

561 Style

N. style, fashion, mode, tone, manner, vein, strain, idiom; idiosyncrasy, mannerism, speciality; mode of expression, diction, parlance, phrase; choice of words, vocabulary, literary style, command of language or idiom, power, vigour; sense of language; literary charm, grace; word magic, oratory; weak style; severe style; elaborate style, ornament; clumsy style.

Adj. stylistic, mannered, literary; elegant, ornate; expressive, eloquent, fluent; racy, idiomatic; plain, forceful.

Vb. show style, style, express, phrase.

562 Perspicuity

N. perspicuity, clarity, transparency; limpid style; definition.

Adj. perspicuous, lucid, limpid, transparent; clear, intelligible; explicit, clear-cut, definite; exact, accurate; direct, plain.

563 Imperspicuity

N. imperspicuity; abstraction; involved style, ornament; hard words, difficulty; profundity, depth; ellipsis; cloud of words, verbiage.

Adj. unclear, cloudy, opaque; cloudy, obscure, dark; mysterious, enigmatic; abstruse, profound, deep; indirect, latent; vague, indefinite, uncertain; ambiguous, equivocal; tortuous, involved, complex; harsh, crabbed, stiff, inelegant; hard, full of long words, difficult.

564 Conciseness

N. conciseness, brevity, soul of wit; pithy saying, maxim; aphorism, epigram, witticism; economy of words, few words; telegraphese; ellipsis, abbreviation, contraction, shortening; epitome, outline, brief sketch, compendium; portmanteau word; nutshell.

Adj. concise, brief, short; laconic, monosyllabic, sparing of words, taciturn; irreducible, succinct; crisp, brisk; trenchant, incisive; terse, curt, brusque; ungracious; compendious, compact, pithy, pregnant, sententious, neat, exact, pointed; elliptic, telegraphic; summary, cut short.

Vb. be concise, need few words, cut a long story short; telescope, compress, condense, contract, abridge, abbreviate, shorten; outline, sketch; resume, abstract;

be short with, cut short; be sparing with words, be taciturn.

Adv. concisely; to cut a long story short.

565 Diffuseness

N. diffuseness, amplitude; blow-by-blow account; fertility, output, productivity; inspiration, vein, flow; abundance, redundancy; rich vocabulary, wealth of terms, verbiage, flatulence; epic length, repetition; tedium; gush, rigmarole, waffle, empty talk; effusion, tirade, harangue; sermon, oration; descant, dissertation.

pleonasm, redundancy; tautology; circumlocution, periphrasis; padding, expletive, extra; episode.

Adj. diffuse, verbose, nonstop, loquacious; profuse, copious, ample, rich; fertile, abundant, voluminous, prolific; inspired; flowing, fluent; exuberant, redundant; circumstantial, minute; effusive, windy; turgid; ornate.

prolix, of many words, long-winded, wordy, prosy; made to last; tedious; lengthy, epic, long; discursive, rambling; incoherent; desultory, pointless, irrelevant; indirect, roundabout.

pleonastic, redundant, excessive, superfluous; repetitious.

Vb. be diffuse, dilate, amplify, detail, expand; descant, discourse at length; repeat, repeat oneself; pad, protract, lengthen; gush, flow; let oneself go, rant; harangue; use long words; spin a long yarn; be tedious; be loquacious; wander, waffle, digress, deviate; ramble, maunder, drivel, yarn, never end; be equivocal.

Adv. diffusely, at great length.

566 Vigour

N. vigour, power, strength, vitality, drive, force, oomph, energy; decision; vim, punch, pep, guts; sparkle, verve, panache; spirit, fire, ardour, glow, warmth, fervour, enthusiasm, passion, feeling; bite; strong language, stress, emphasis; repetition; solemnity, gravity, weight; elevation, grandeur; rhetoric.

Adj. forceful, powerful, strong; energetic, vigorous; racy, idiomatic; bold, dashing, spirited, vivacious, lively; warm, glowing, fiery, ardent, impassioned, fervent; vehement, insistent, positive, affirmative; cutting, incisive, trenchant, sharp; pointed, pungent, mordant, salty; grave, sententious, serious; heavy, meaty, solid, weighty, forcible, cogent; vivid, graphic, effective; flowing, inspired, eloquent, lofty, grand, sublime, impressive.

Adv. forcefully, with conviction.

567 Feebleness

N. feebleness, weakness; weak style, frigidity; poverty; lack of force, lack of sparkle, lack of conviction; lack of style; anticlimax.

Adj. feeble, weak, thin, flat, vapid, insipid, tasteless; wishy-washy, watery; sloppy, sentimental; meagre; wan, colourless, bald, plain; languid, flaccid, nerveless, tame, conventional; ineffective, cold, frigid, prosaic; monotonous, prosy, pedestrian, dull, dry, tedious; hackneyed, stale, pretentious; forced; inane, empty, juvenile, childish; careless, slipshod, lame, poorly reasoned; limp, loose, lax, inexact, disconnected, disjointed, ram bling; poor, trashy, *vulgar*.

568 Plainness
N. *plainness*, simplicity; plain prose, *prose*; plain words, plain English; homespun, household words; rustic flavour, vernacular; common speech, vulgar parlance; idiom; Anglo-Saxon monosyllable.

Adj. *plain*, simple, *artless*; austere, severe; bald, spare, stark, bare; neat, *clean*; pure, unadulterated; unvarnished, *veracious*; unassuming, unpretentious, *modest*; chaste, restrained; unaffected, honest, natural, straightforward; homely, homespun, vernacular; prosaic, sober, *serious*; dry, stodgy, *tedious*; humdrum, workaday, everyday, commonplace, *usual*; *prosaic*.

Vb. *speak plainly*, call a spade a spade, use plain English, *be intelligible*; say outright, tell it like it is, tell one straight or to his or her face; talk turkey.

Adv. *plainly*, simply; directly, pointblank.

569 Ornament
N. *ornament*, colour, embroidery, frills; *phrase*; euphuism; euphemism; rhetoric, purple patch or passage; figure of speech; alliteration, assonance; metaphor, simile, antithesis.

magniloquence, high tone, *vigour*, hyperbole, *exaggeration*; flatulence, inflation; affectation, *ostentation*; highfalutin, bombast, rant, fustian, *empty talk*; long words.

phrasemonger, fine writer; orator, *speaker*.

Adj. *ornate*, rich, luxuriant, florid, flowery; precious; pretentious, *affected*; meretricious, flashy, flamboyant, *showy*; brassy, sonorous, *loud*; tropical, *figurative*; stiff, stilted.

rhetorical, *eloquent*; resonant, sonorous, *loud*; orotund; highfalutin; grandiose, stately; pompous, fustian; grandiloquent; inflated, turgid, swollen; *figurative*.

Vb. *ornament*, beautify, grace, adorn, enrich, *decorate*; charge, overload; elaborate, load with ornament.

570 Elegance
N. *elegance*, style, grace, *beauty*; refinement, taste, *good taste*; propriety, restraint, distinction, dignity; clarity; purity, simplicity; classicism; harmony, euphony, balance, proportion, *symmetry*; rhythm, ease, flow, readiness, felicity; polish, finish; *ornament*.

stylist, stylish writer; classical author, classic, purist.

Adj. *elegant*, stately, *beautiful*; graceful; stylish, polite, refined, *tasteful*; distinguished, chaste, *pure*; good, correct, idiomatic; sensitive, expressive, clear; simple, natural, unaffected, *plain*; ready, easy, smooth, flowing, fluent, tripping, mellifluous, euphonious; balanced; neat, felicitous, happy, right; artistic, wrought, elaborate, artificial; finished; restrained; *perfect*; classic, classical, Attic.

Vb. *be elegant*, show taste, *have taste*; have a good style, write well, have a light touch; elaborate, polish, refine, *perfect*; turn a period, point an antithesis, *show style*.

571 Inelegance
N. *inelegance*; roughness; lack of finish, lack of polish; cacophony, *discord*; lack of flow, *hardness*; bad grammar, *solecism*; speech defect; vulgarism, vulgarity, *bad taste*; mannerism, affectation; exhibitionism, *ostentation*; sham; lack of restraint, excess.

Adj. *inelegant*, graceless, *ugly*; faulty, incorrect; crabbed, tortuous; long-winded, *diffuse*; *imperfect*; bald, *plain*; coarse, crude, rude, doggerel, uncouth, barbarous, *artless*; impolite, tasteless, *vulgar*; impure, meretricious; unrestrained, immoderate, excessive; turgid, pompous, forced, artificial, unnatural, mannered, *affected*; ludicrous, grotesque, *ridiculous*; offensive, grating; heavy, ponderous, insensitive; rough, harsh, uneasy, abrupt; halting, cramped; clumsy, awkward, gauche; wooden, stiff, stilted, *formal*.

572 Voice
N. *voice*, vocal sound, *sound*; *speech*; singing voice, *vocal music*; powerful voice, lung power; tongue, vocal cords; bellows; larynx, voice box; vowel, diphthong, open vowel, syllable, *speech sound*; delivery, attack; articulate sound, *cry*; exclamation, gasp; mutter, whisper; tone of voice, timbre, pitch, tone, intonation.

pronunciation, elocution, stress, emphasis; thesis; accent, pure accent, native accent, burr, brogue, drawl, twang, *dialect*; trill; aspiration, rough breathing, glottal stop; stammer, speech defect; solecism.

Adj. *vocal*, oral, aloud; phonetic; articulate, distinct, clear; well-spoken, *melodious*; pronounced, spoken, read aloud; *hoarse*; tonal, guttural, *hoarse*; shrill, *strident*; sibilant.

Vb. *voice*, pronounce, syllable, *speak*; mouth, give tongue, give voice, express, utter, enunciate, articulate; inflect, modulate; breathe, aspirate; trill, roll, burr; accent, stress; whisper, exclaim; ejaculate, *cry*; drone, intone, chant, warble, carol, hum, *sing*; bellow, shout, vociferate, *be loud*; mispronounce, lisp, drawl, *stammer*.

573 Voicelessness
N. *voicelessness*; thick speech; *silence*; harsh voice; childish treble, falsetto; sob; undertone, low voice, whisper, bated breath; surd; voiceless speech, sign language, *gesture*; return.

Adj. *voiceless*; surd; inaudible; mute, dumb; speechless; inarticulate, tongue-tied; silent, mum, *taciturn*; dry, hollow, sepulchral, cracked, *hoarse*; breathless.

Vb. *be mute*, keep mum, *be taciturn*; be silent, *keep secret*; check oneself; be struck dumb; *gesticulate*; *stammer*.

make mute, strike dumb, rob one of words; muffle, hush, deaden, *mute*; muzzle, gag, stifle, *suppress*; cut one short; still, hush, put to silence, put to sleep, *silence*.

speak low, whisper, *sound faint*; hint.

Adv. *voicelessly*, with bated breath.

574 Speech
N. *speech*, tongue, *voice*; parlance, *language*; oral communication, word of mouth, *report*; spoken word, *word*; verbal intercourse, *discourse*, conversation, talk, palaver, prattle, chinwag; address,

apostrophe; ready speech; effusion; cultivated speech, elocution, voice production; mode of speech, delivery, *pronunciation*; ventriloquism; speech without words, sign language, *gesture*; thing said, speech, dictum, remark, comment, interjection; fine words, *empty talk*; spiel, patter.

oration, speech, effusion; public speech, discourse, address, talk; *celebration*; panegyric, eulogy; farewell address, funeral oration; toast, vote of thanks; broadcast, commentary, *lecture*; recital, reading; set speech, sermon; harangue, earful, mouthful; tirade, diatribe, invective; monologue, *soliloquy*; written speech, paper, screed, *dissertation*; preamble, prologue, narration, peroration.

oratory, rhetoric, stump oratory; elocution, rant; vituperation, invective; soapbox, *rostrum*.

eloquence, eloquent tongue; command of words, *style*; power of speech, power, *vigour*; elocution, good delivery, impressive diction, torrent of words, peroration, purple passage.

speaker; orator, public speaker, toastmaster; soap-box orator, tub-thumper, demagogue, *agitator*; lecturer; prologue, narrator, chorus, *actor*; mouthpiece, spokesman or -woman, *delegate*; advocate, mediator, *intermediary*; patter merchant, *seller*.

Adj. *speaking*, able to speak; bilingual, polyglot; articulate, fluent, outspoken, talkative, *loquacious*; oral, *vocal*; well-spoken, audible, spoken, verbal; fruity, *resonant*.

eloquent; grandiloquent, *forceful*; rousing, *exciting*.

Vb. *speak*, mention, say; utter, articulate, voice; pronounce, declare, *affirm*; come clean, *divulge*; whisper, breathe, *hint*; talk, *converse*; emit, deliver oneself of; break silence; gossip, prattle, chatter, *be loquacious*; patter, jabber, gabble; tell a thing or two, *be diffuse*; recite; read, read aloud, dictate; speak a language; *gesticulate*.

orate; declaim, deliver a speech; hold forth, spout; rise to speak; preach, harangue; lecture, address, *teach*; invoke, *speak to*; mouth, rant, rail; speak like an angel, spellbind, be eloquent; talk to oneself; ad-lib, *improvise*.

575 Speech defect

N. *speech defect*, loss of speech; stammer, stutter, lisp; drawl, slur; thick speech, cleft palate; burr, brogue, *dialect*; accent, twang, *pronunciation*; affectation; speech therapy.

Adj. *stammering*, nasal; indistinct, thick, inarticulate; tongue-tied; breathless, *voiceless*.

Vb. *stammer*, stutter; drawl, hesitate, falter, quaver; mumble, mutter; lisp; snuffle, snort, sputter, splutter; drone; gabble, slur; blubber, sob; mispronounce.

576 Loquacity

N. *loquacity*; runaway tongue, flow of words; spate of words, inexhaustible vocabulary; patter, spiel; garrulous old age, *remembrance*.

chatter, gabble, jabber, palaver; clack, quack, cackle, babble, prattle; small talk, gossip, tittle-tattle; waffle, gush, gas, hot air, *empty talk*.

chatterer, rapid speaker; chinwag, rattle, chatterbox; gossip, blabber, *new reporter*; magpie, parrot, jay; windbag.

Adj. *loquacious*, talkative, garrulous; communicative, chatty, gassy, windy, verbose, long-winded; nonstop, voluble, fluent, glib, ready, effusive.

Vb. *be loquacious*, have a long tongue, chatter, rattle; gossip, tattle, *converse*; clack, quack, gabble, jabber, *mean nothing*; talk, jaw, yak, prate, prose, gas, waffle, haver, twitter, drone, maunder, drivel, shoot; be glib; talk at length; gush, spout; *be diffuse*; filibuster; talk oneself hoarse, talk shop, bore, *be tedious*; buttonhole.

Adv. *loquaciously*.

Int. rhubarb rhubarb! blah blah! yak yak█

577 Taciturnity

N. *taciturnity*, silent habit, *silence*; incommunicativeness, reserve, *secrecy*; few words; economy of words; person of few words; clam, oyster, statue; Trappist.

Adj. *taciturn*, mute, mum, *silent*; sparing of words, saying little, monosyllabic; short, curt, laconic, brusque, gruff, *concise*; incommunicative; withdrawn, reserved, guarded, *reticent*; close, tight-lipped; discreet, *cautious*; inarticulate, tongue-tied, *voiceless*; deaf.

Vb. *be taciturn, be concise*; say nothing, have little to say; observe silence; refuse comment, neither confirm nor deny; *keep secret*; fall silent, *cease*; be speechless, be mute; omit, *disregard*.

Int. hush! shut up! mum's the word! no comment! verb. sap. a word to the wise!

578 Allocution

N. *allocution*, apostrophe; address, lecture, talk, speech, pep talk, *oration*; greeting, salutation, hail; appeal, interjection, aside; audience.

Adj. *vocative*.

Vb. *speak to*, speak at; address, talk to, lecture to; turn to; appeal to, pray to, invoke; sir; approach, accost; hail, call to, salute, say good morning, greet; parley with, *converse*; take aside, buttonhole.

579 Interlocution

N. *interlocution*, parley, converse, conversation, talk; dialogue; exchange, repartee, banter, badinage; *quarrel*; verbal intercourse; commerce, communion, communication, intercommunication, *information*.

chat, chinwag, natter; chit-chat, talk, prattle, gossip, *rumour*; tattle, tittletattle, *chatter*; fireside chat, cosy chat, heart-to-heart.

conference, talks, parley, pow-wow, palaver; debate, forum, symposium, seminar, teach-in; controversy, polemics, *argument*; high-level talks, summit meeting, summit; *treaty*; convention, meeting, gathering, *assembly*; working lunch, reception, party, *social gathering*; audience, interview, audition; huddle, council, *advice*.

interlocutor; *respondent*; partner; gossip, news reporter.

Adj. *conversing*, chatty, *loquacious*; communicative; advisory.

Vb. *converse*, parley, talk together (see *confer*); buttonhole, bandy words, question, answer; chat, have a chat or a natter or a a good talk; have a cosy chat, *speak*; buzz, natter, chinwag, gossip, tattle, be *loquacious*; commune with, get confidential with; whisper together.

confer, take counsel, hold a council of war, pow-wow, palaver; discuss, debate, *argue*; parley, negotiate, hold talks; consult with, *consult*.

580 Soliloquy

N. *soliloquy*, monologue; interior monologue; apostrophe; aside.
soliloquist.

Adj. *soliloquizing*, thinking aloud.

Vb. *soliloquize*, talk to oneself, say to oneself, say aside, think aloud; pray aloud; address an empty house, have an audience of one.

581 Writing

N. *writing*, composition, authorship, journalism, itch to write, *description*; literary output, *literature*; script, copy, writings, works, books, *reading matter*; Grub Street; paperwork, *record*; ways of writing, handwriting; longhand; shorthand writing, shorthand, stenography; stereotype; *print*; braille; secret writing, code, *secret*; picture writing; *advertisement*; carving, cutting, *engraving*; study of handwriting.

lettering, stroke, down-stroke; line, dot, point; flourish, squiggle, scroll, *convolution*; handwriting, hand, fist; calligraphy, penmanship; fair hand, cursive hand, script, copperplate; printing; clumsy hand, illegible writing, scribble, scrawl; alphabet, *letter*; ideogram; hieroglyph; cuneiform, arrowhead.

script, written matter; specimen; writing, screed, scrawl, scribble; manuscript, *book*; original, autograph; signature; copy, transcript, fair copy, *duplicate*; typescript, stencil; newsprint; *letter*, epistle, written reply; inscription, *record*; superscription, caption, heading.

stationery; stylus, reed, quill, pen, nib; pencil, crayon, chalk; papyrus, parchment, vellum; foolscap, *paper*; writing paper, notepaper, wove paper, notebook, pad; slate, blackboard; inkstand, inkwell; penknife; blotter; typewriter, ribbon; stencil.

calligrapher; scribbler; writer, scribe, clerk, *recorder*; subscriber, signatory; creative writer, *author*; letter writer, *correspondent*; handwriting expert.

stenographer, shorthand writer, typist.

Adj. *written*; manuscript, autograph; cursive, copybook, copperplate; cuneiform; Gothic, roman, *literal*; perpendicular, upright, bold, spidery.

Vb. *write*, be literate; engrave, inscribe; letter, block, print; flourish, scroll; write well, write a clear hand; write badly, scribble, scrawl, blot, erase; commit to paper, note, *record*; transcribe, copy, make a fair copy, engross; type; draft, formulate; compose, concoct; pen, pencil; *correspond*; *sign*; put pen to paper, spill ink; be an author, write books, *describe*; write poetry.

582 Print

N. *print*, printing, *writing*; typography, block printing, offset process, web offset; *printing*; *photography*; cold type; composition, make-up; stereotype; plate, shell.

letterpress, print, impression; printout; copy, pull, proof, page proof, revise; imprint, *edition*; dummy, trial copy, off-print.

print-type, type, stereotype, plate; matrix; broken type, pie; upper case; face, typeface, boldface, bold, old face, bastard type; roman, Gothic, black letter, *letter*; body, bevel, shoulder, shank, beard; lead, rule, em; space, quad; type bar, slug.

type *size*, type measure, type scale; brilliant, diamond, pearl, ruby, nonpareil, minion, bourgeois, elite, long primer, great primer.

press, printing works; rotary press, offset press; galley, chase; roller, web.

printer, compositor, type-setter.

Adj. *printed*; set; solid, tight, crowded.

Vb. *print*, stamp; compose; register, justify; make ready, impose, machine; collate; lithograph, offset, stereotype; put to bed; proofread, correct; *publish*.

583 Correspondence

N. *correspondence*; communication, *information*; mail, post, postbag, *postal communications*; letter, epistle, missive, bulletin; love letter, Valentine, *endearment*; postcard, card; air letter, air mail, sea mail; business letter, bill, account; open letter, *publicity*; circular, round robin, chain letter; note, line, chit; answer; envelope, cover, stamp, seal; postcode.

correspondent, letter writer, poison pen; recipient, addressee; foreign correspondent, contributor, *news reporter*; contact.

Adj. *epistolary*, postal.

Vb. *correspond*, correspond with, *communicate*; write to, send a letter to, drop a line; report, *inform*; acknowledge, reply, write back, answer, *publish*; write again; forward, mail, airmail; stamp, seal, frank, address.

Adv. *by letter*.

584 Book

N. *book*, title, volume, tome, roll, scroll, document; manuscript, MS; script, typescript; publication, best-seller, potboiler; remainder; work, classic; major work, magnum opus; slim volume; booklet; picture book, *picture*; magazine, periodical, rag, *journal*; brochure, pamphlet; bound book, hardback, paperback (see *edition*).

reading matter, writing; papers, *record*; script, copy; text, libretto, lyrics, scenario, screenplay, book of words; proof, revise, pull; writings, prose literature, *prose*; *poetry*; classical literature, *literature*; history, biography, travel, *description*; work of fiction, *novel*; memoirs, *biography*; oration; essay, tract, treatise, *dissertation*; piece, *article*; *poem*; *anthology*; early works; posthumous works, literary remains; complete works; newspaper, magazine, *journal*; issue, number, part, instalment, serial, sequel.

textbook, school book, reader, *classroom*; primer, grammar; text; selection, *anthology*; standard text, handbook, manual; pocket book (see *reference book*).

reference *book*, work of reference; lexicon, dictionary; gazetteer, yearbook, annual, directory; calendar, *chronology*; guide; notebook, diary, album, *record*; bibliography, reading list.

edition, impression, issue, run; series, set, collection, library; bound edition, complete works; first edition, reprint; rehash; adaptation, *compendium*; book production, layout, format; house style; front matter, preface; dedication; title, title page, *label*; table of contents; appendix, supplement, index, bibliography; caption, heading, headline, footnote; guide word, catchword; margin, gutter; page, leaf; sheet, signature, quire; chapter, division, part, section; paragraph, clause, passage, excerpt, inset; plate, print, illustration, halftone, line drawing, *picture*.

bookbinding, binding, casing; case, cover, jacket, *wrapping*; boards, *paper*; cloth, linen, leather, pigskin, calf, morocco, vellum, parchment; spine, headband.

library, book collection; national library, book club; bookcase; bookstall.

bookperson, literary person; reader, bookworm, *scholar*; book lover, book collector; librarian, library assistant; stationer, book dealer; publisher, printer; editor; book reviewer, reviewer.

author, writer; literary person; historian, biographer, *narrator*; prose writer; verse writer, *poet*; playwright, librettist; script writer, *dramatist*; freelance; copywriter; *news reporter*; editor, subeditor, copy editor, contributor, correspondent, columnist, gossip writer, diarist; scribbler, hack, potboiler; ghost, ghost writer.

Adj. *bibliographical*; bound, hardback, paperback; loose-leaf; marbled, gilt; antiquarian.

585 Description

N. *description*, account, statement, summary, *report*; brief, abstract, inscription, caption, legend, *compendium*; narration, relation, rehearsal, recital, version (see *narrative*); nonfiction, documentary account; specification, characterization, *list*; portrait, sketch, profile, *representation*; psychic profile, case history, *record*; faction, documentary drama; local colour; picture, realism; travelogue; cameo; *poem*; eulogy, *praise*; parody, *satire*; obituary, epitaph, lapidary inscription.

narrative, plot, subplot, scenario, *stage play*; episode, *event*; complication; dramatic irony, comic relief; fantasia, *fantasy*; imaginary account, fiction, story, tale, romance, folk tale; tradition, legend, mythology, myth, saga, epic; ballad, *poem*; allegory, parable, cautionary tale; yarn, *fable*; anecdote, reminiscence, *remembrance*; annals, chronicle, history, *record*.

biography, human interest; life, life story or history; obituary; personal account, autobiography, memoirs, *remembrance*; diary, *record*.

novel, fiction, tale; fictional biography; short story, novelette; light reading, *reading matter*; romance, love story, Western, science fiction; gothic novel, ghost story; novel of low life, picaresque novel; crime story, whodunit; cliffhanger, thriller, penny dreadful, horror comic; paperback, pulp literature; potboiler, trash; popular novel, blockbuster, best-seller, *book*.

narrator, reporter; raconteur; storyteller, mythologist; fiction writer, *author*; biographer; memoir writer, diarist; historian, *recorder*; Muse of History.

Adj. *descriptive*, representational; graphic,

colourful, vivid; sharp; realistic, convincing; picturesque, striking; impressionistic, suggestive, evocative, emotive, moving, *exciting*; mythological, *figurative*; epic, heroic, romantic, cloak-and-dagger; picaresque; narrative, autobiographical; full, circumstantial, *diffuse*; factual, documentary, nonfiction, *accurate*; fictitious, fictional, imaginative, *imaginary*; *literary*.

Vb. *describe*, delineate, draw, picture, depict, paint, *represent*; evoke, bring to life, make one see; detail, descend to, *specify*; sketch, *outline*; relate, recount, rehearse, recite, report, give an account, *communicate*; write, write about, *record*; narrate, tell, tell a story, yarn, unfold a tale; construct a plot; romance, *imagine*; review, recapitulate, *repeat*; reminisce, *retrospect*.

586 Dissertation

N. *dissertation*, treatise, tract; exposition, summary, *compendium*; theme, thesis, *argument*; essay, examination, survey, *enquiry*; discourse, descant; memoir, paper, monograph, study; screed, harangue, sermon, *lecture*; commentary, textbook.

article, column; leading article, leader, editorial; essay; literary composition, set piece, comment, review, notice, critique, criticism, write-up, *estimate*.

dissertator; pamphleteer, publicist; editor, leader writer; writer, contributor, *author*; reviewer, critic, commentator, pundit.

Adj. *discursive*; critical.

Vb. *dissertate*, treat, handle, write about, deal with, do justice to; descant, *argue*; pursue a theme, develop a thesis; survey; discuss, ventilate; notice; write an essay, do a paper; annotate, commentate, *interpret*.

587 Compendium

N. *compendium*, epitome, summary, brief; contents, analysis; abstract, gist; digest; synopsis, survey; review, recap; rundown; draft, minute, note, *record*; sketch, outline, skeleton; blueprint, *plan*; syllabus, prospectus, *list*; abbreviation, *shortening*; contraction.

anthology, treasury, garland; *textbook*; collection, compilation, miscellany; gleanings, leaves; album, scrapbook, notebook, commonplace book.

epitomizer; cutter.

Adj. *compendious*, pithy, *concise*, abstracted, *short*; potted; collected.

Vb. *abstract*, resume; reduce, abbreviate, abridge, *shorten*; summarize; docket, *record*; condense, pot, *be concise*; consolidate, compile, *list*; collect, *bring together*; combine; excerpt, glean, select; sketch, outline.

Adv. *in sum*; at a glance.

588 Poetry. Prose

N. *poetry*, song; verse, rhyme, numbers.

poem; lines; narrative verse, heroic poem, epic; dramatic poem, lyric drama, verse drama, Greek tragedy, Greek comedy, trilogy, *drama*; light verse, lyric verse, ode; dirge, elegy; occasional poem; song, hymn, shanty, lay, ballad, *vocal music*; love song; *anthology*; canto, fit; cycle, sequence.

doggerel, lame verse; jingle, ditty, nursery

rhyme; nonsense verse; limerick; mock epic, burlesque, satirical verse.

verse *form*, sonnet, sestet; burden, refrain; couplet; triplet, quatrain; rhyme royal; concrete poetry; verse, stanza, stave; broken line.

prosody, metre, measure, numbers, scansion; rhyme, rhyme scheme; assonance, alliteration; cadence, rhythm, metrical unit, foot; iamb, trochee, spondee; blank verse; heroic couplet, thesis, beat, stress, accent; caesura, diaeresis.

poet, poet laureate; Lake poet; bard, minstrel; troubadour; epic poet, bucolic poet; librettist.

prose, prose rhythm; prose poem; everyday language; prose writer, *author.*

Adj. *poetic*; heroic, Homeric; lyrical; lyric; bucolic; *literary*; doggerel; metrical, measured.

prosaic, pedestrian; matter-of-fact, *plain.*

Vb. *poetize*, sing; scan; rhyme, chime, jingle; versify; compose an epic, write a lyric, write a sonnet; lampoon.

write *prose*, stick to prose.

589 Drama. Ballet

N. *drama*; West End; silver Screen, Hollywood, *cinema*; show business, dramatic entertainment; straight drama, legitimate theatre; repertory, rep; theatricals, masque, dumb show, tableau, *representation*; tragic mask, sock; Tragic Muse; Comic Muse.

dramaturgy, dramatic form, *narrative*; theatricals, dramatics; good theatre, good cinema; play writing, histrionic art, action, movement, plot, subplot, *narrative*; characterization, *representation*; production, revival; casting; rehearsal, direction, stage management; showmanship; stage directions; dialogue, soliloquy, stage whisper, aside, cue; business; entrance, exit (see *acting*); prologue, chorus; act, scene; curtain, blackout; epilogue; curtain call, encore; interval, intermission, break; performance, preview, first night, first house, road show; sellout, hit, long run.

stage *play*, play, drama, work; piece, show, vehicle; libretto, scenario, script, text, book of words, prompt book; part, lines, *speech*; dramatic representation, *representation*; sketch, skit; double bill; intermezzo; monologue; masque; mystery play, miracle play; Greek drama, trilogy, cycle; melodrama; tragedy, tragicomedy; comedy, comedy of manners, Restoration comedy; black comedy, farce, slapstick, burlesque, extravaganza; pantomime; musical comedy, musical, light opera, grand opera, *vocal music*; radio drama, television play, *broadcast*; screenplay, *cinema*; shadow play, puppet show.

stage *show*, spectacle; ice show, circus, amusement; variety, music hall, vaudeville; review, revue, leg show, floor show, cabaret; act, turn; star turn, transformation scene, set piece, tableau.

ballet, dance; choreography; classical ballet, modern dance; toe dance, *dance*; solo; arabesque; pirouette, *rotation*; jeté, leap.

stage *set*, set, setting, scenery, scene, *spectacle*; drop curtain, drop, backdrop, backcloth, cyclorama; screen, wings, flat; background, foreground, front stage, upstage, stage, boards, apron, proscenium, proscenium arch; gauze, curtain,

trap, prompt box (see *theatre*); costume, make-up, greasepaint.

theatre, amphitheatre, stadium, *arena*; circus, hippodrome; fleapit, picture house, *cinema*; Greek theatre, pier, pavilion; big top; playhouse, opera house, music hall, vaudeville theatre, night club, cabaret; stage, boards, proscenium, wings, flies (see *stage set*); dressing room, footlights, spotlight, spot, limelight, floodlight, flood; auditorium, orchestra; seating, stalls; pit; box, circle, mezzanine; gallery, balcony, gods; front of house, foyer, bar, box office, stage door.

acting, *representation*; interpretation, impression, pantomime, *mimicry*; repertoire; character, personage, role, part, cameo; stock part, heavy father, merry widow, stage villain; principal boy or girl; Harlequin, Columbine, Pierrot, Pantaloon; pantomime dame; chief part, hero, antihero; stage fever; stage fright.

actor, actress; mimic, mime, *imitator*; player, trouper, ham; rep player, character actor; star, star actor or actress, film star, starlet, *favourite*; comedian, comedienne, comedy actor or actress; ballerina; protagonist, lead, leading man, leading lady, juvenile lead; understudy, stand-in, *substitute*, *analogue*; super, extra, bit player; chorus; troupe, company, cast; narrator; prologue, *speaker.*

entertainer, performer, artiste, artist; impressionist; troubadour, minstrel; street musician; *vocalist*; comic, comedian, comedienne, humorist; acrobat, *athlete*; clown, buffoon, *fool*; pierrot, Punch; show girl.

stagehand; prop man, stage carpenter, scene painter; electrician, machinist; special effects man, continuity girl; wardrobe mistress, make-up artist; prompter; programme seller, usher, usherette, doorman.

stage *manager*, producer, director; manager, press agent; impresario, showman; backer, sponsor, angel.

dramatist; tragic poet, *poet*; playwright, scenario writer, librettist; gag man, *humorist.*

playgoer; film fan, opera buff; audience, house, sell-out; stalls, pit, circle, gods, gallery, balcony; *spectator*; dramatic critic, play or film reviewer.

Adj. *dramatic*; scenic, theatrical, stagy; live, legitimate; histrionic, mimetic; tragic; comic, burlesque, knockabout, slapstick, *funny*; melodramatic, sensational, *exciting*; avant-garde; showing, running, *shown*; acting, cast, miscast; stage-struck.

Vb. *dramatize*, be a dramatist; make a play of; do a play, stage, mount, produce, direct, stage-manage; rehearse, cut; cast, typecast, give a part, assign a role; star, feature, bill; present, release, *show*; open.

act, perform, enact, play, do a play, *represent*; personify, impersonate, *mime*, pantomime, *imitate*; create a role, play a part; play opposite, support; star, co-star, upstage; ham, overact, *exaggerate*, rant, roar; underact; understudy, *substitute*; rehearse; fluff, dry; ad-lib, gag.

Adv. *on stage*, upstage, downstage; backstage.

590 Will

N. *will*, willing, volition; disposition, mind, preference; act of will; strength of will,

willpower, determination, *resolution*;
self-control, *temperance*; intent, purpose,
intention; decision; *command*; *desire*;
self-will; *caprice*; free will, self-
determination; free choice, option, discretion, *choice*; unprompted will, *voluntary work*; primacy of will.

Adj. *volitional*, willing; unprompted, spontaneous, original, *voluntary*; optional;
minded; wilful, *obstinate*; arbitrary,
authoritarian; independent, *free*; determined, *resolute*; decided, intentional.

Vb. *will*; *command*; *be free*; be so minded,
see fit, think best, *choose*; purpose, determine, *intend*; wish, *desire*; be independent, *please oneself*; *judge*; *be obstinate*;
be resolute; volunteer, offer, *be willing*;
originate, *cause*.

Adv. *at will*, at pleasure, ad lib.

591 Necessity

N. *necessity*; last shift, last resort, *predicament*; what must be, *destiny*; determin-
ism, fatalism; force of circumstances, act
of God, fatality, *event*; physical necessity,
law of nature; force, *compulsion*; logic,
proof; legal necessity, force of law, *law*;
moral necessity, obligation, conscience,
duty; a necessity, a necessary, a must,
requirement; want, lack, *poverty*; reflex
action, reflex, instinct, impulse, *intuition*.

fate, lot, cup, portion; weird, karma; doom,
predestination, election, *destiny*; book of
fate, God's will, will of Allah, will of
heaven; fortune, *chance*.

fatalist; pawn, tool, automaton, robot,
machine.

Adj. *necessary*, indispensable, requisite;
demonstrable, *imperative*, compulsive;
overriding, irresistible, *superior*; compulsory, mandatory, binding, *obligatory*;
with force of law, *legal*; inevitable, inescapable, inexorable, *certain*.

involuntary; unconscious, unthinking,
unwitting, blind, impulsive, *spontaneous*;
reflex, automatic, mechanical.

fated, fatal; appointed, destined; elect,
chosen; foredoomed; bound, *subject*.

Vb. *be forced*, *submit*; be fated, bow to fate;
needs must; make a virtue of necessity; be
unable to help it, be made that way; be
subject to impulse, *be subject*.

necessitate, dictate, impose, oblige, *compel*;
doom, *predestine*; insist; demand,
require.

Adv. *necessarily*, of necessity, of course,
perforce; willy-nilly.

592 Willingness

N. *willingness*; free choice, option, *choice*;
disposition, mind; leaning, bent, bias,
penchant, propensity, *tendency*; facility,
aptitude; readiness, right mood, favourable humour, receptive frame of mind;
good will, *benevolence*; *assent*; compliance, *consent*; cheerful consent, alacrity,
zeal, ardour, enthusiasm; initiative; devotion, dedication, sacrifice; loyalty; *submission*.

voluntary *work*, voluntary service, *philanthropy*; honorary employment, labour of
love; gratuitous effort; *gift*.

volunteer, willing horse; *busy person*; do-
gooder, *philanthropist*.

Adj. *willing*, acquiescent; compliant, agreeable, content; receptive, favourable,
inclined, disposed, amenable; gracious,
genial, cordial; happy, pleased, glad;

ready, *prepared*; prompt, quick, *active*;
forward; zealous, eager, dedicated; impatient; dependable, reliable; earnest; helpful, docile, biddable, easy-going; loyal,
obedient; submissive; obsequious, *servile*;
dying to; would-be; meaning, meaning
to.

voluntary, unprompted, *spontaneous*; self-
imposed; open to choice, optional,
chosen; *offering*; gratuitous, free, honorary.

Vb. *be willing*, have half a mind to; feel like,
have a good mind to, *will*; yearn to,
desire; mean to, *intend*; agree, acquiesce,
assent; show willing, comply, *consent*;
hearken, lend a willing ear, be found
willing, *obey*; try, *attempt*; show zeal;
collaborate; anticipate, meet halfway;
swallow, jump at, leap at; can't wait;
stomach; choose freely, *choose*; volunteer, sacrifice oneself, *offer oneself*.

Adv. *willingly*, with a will, readily; *at will*;
readily, like a shot; with open arms, with
a good grace, without demur; with
pleasure.

593 Unwillingness

N. *unwillingness*, reluctance; *dissent*;
demur, *qualification*; protest; *opposition*;
refusal; *hindrance*; abstention, *absence*;
want of alacrity, lack of zeal; *caution*;
scruple, qualm of conscience, *doubt*;
repugnance, *dislike*; recoil, aversion;
grudging service; shelving, *delay*;
neglect.

slacker; forced labour, *slowcoach*.

Adj. *unwilling*, indisposed, reluctant,
averse; adverse, irreconcilable; *deprecatory*; squeamish; full of regrets, with
regret; hesitant, *cautious*; shy, bashful,
modest; half-hearted, lukewarm; backward, *slow*; fractious, restive, recalcitrant, *disobedient*; perfunctory, remiss,
negligent; grudging, *sullen*; forced.

Vb. *be unwilling*, *dislike*; disagree, stick,
boggle, scruple, *dissent*; object, demur,
protest, *deprecate*; resist, *oppose*; reject,
refuse; recoil, blench, fight shy, duck, jib,
shirk, *avoid*; skimp, scamp, *neglect*; hold
back, hang back, hesitate, hang fire, go
slow; slack; dissociate oneself, abstain,
obstruct; grudge, begrudge, grimace, *be
sullen*; drag oneself, do with regret, have
regrets, *regret*; depart.

Adv. *unwillingly*, with a bad grace; with
regret, with a heavy heart.

594 Resolution

N. *resolution*, determination, zeal; resolve,
decision, drive, vigour, energy, *activity*;
fixity of purpose, concentration, iron
will, willpower, *will*; strength of character, self-control, self-possession; aplomb,
mettle, daring, dash, *attack*; guts, pluck,
spunk, grit, backbone, spirit; fortitude,
stiff upper lip, moral fibre, *courage*; devotion, dedication; firm principles, reliability, constancy, *stability*; pressure, *compulsion*; *hardness*; iron, steel, rock;
bulldog breed; stamina.

Adj. *resolute*, determined, *willing*; desperate; serious, earnest, concentrated; insistent, pressing, urgent, driving, forceful,
energetic, heroic, *vigorous*; zealous, thorough, *attentive*; steady, firm, staunch,
reliable, constant; strong-minded, decisive, decided, unbending, immovable,
inflexible, uncompromising, intransigent, *obstinate*; stern, grim, inexorable,

implacable, relentless, ruthless, merciless, *pitiless*; iron, steely, *hard*; undaunted; steadfast, unflinching, game, tenacious; indomitable; armoured, proof; *temperate*; purposeful, single-minded, whole-hearted, devoted, dedicated.

Vb. *be resolute*, steel oneself, take a resolution, will, resolve, determine, purpose, *intend*; decide, fix, seal, conclude, finish with, *terminate*; accept responsibility, *will*; insist, press, urge; cut through, override; mean business, stick at nothing; see it through, *carry through*; face, *face danger*; outface, dare, *defy*; endure, *suffer*; bring to a head; be single-minded, commit oneself, give oneself to; set to, buckle to, go to it, strain, *exert oneself*.

stand *firm*, stay put; never despair, stand fast, persevere; endure, *suffer*, die hard, die game.

Adv. *resolutely*; at any price; like a man; come what may, come hell or high water; live or die, neck or nothing.

Int. Here goes! Alea jacta est!

595 Perseverance

N. *perseverance*; constancy, *resolution*; singleness of purpose, concentration, *attention*; application; hard work; endurance, patience, fortitude, *suffering*; maintenance; *repetition*.

stamina, *strength*, grit, backbone, pluck; bulldog courage, *courage*; hard core, diehard, old guard, *obstinate person*; trier, stayer, willing worker, *worker*.

Adj. *persevering*, persistent, tenacious, stubborn, *obstinate*; game, plucky; patient, dogged, *industrious*; strenuous, *laborious*; steady, unfaltering, unflagging, untiring, indefatigable; sleepless, *vigilant*; unfailing, unremitting, constant; indomitable; undaunted, *resolute*.

Vb. *persevere*, persist, keep at it; never say die, *hope*; endure, *suffer*, try, *attempt*; maintain, *sustain*; plod, slog, work at, *work*; continue, rally, keep going; cling, hold fast, *retain*; stick with it, see it through; survive, *be left*; *be obstinate*; *stand firm*; work till one drops; *exert oneself*; complete, *carry through*.

Adv. *persistently*, never say die; sink or swim.

596 Irresolution

N. *irresolution*, loss of nerve; broken resolve, broken promise; indecision, floating vote; *caution*; levity, *caprice*; lack of willpower, lack of drive; passivity; good nature, compromise; apathy; weak will, *weakness*; *submission*.

waverer; shuttlecock, butterfly, feather, *changeable thing*; floating voter; weathercock, chameleon, turncoat.

Adj. *irresolute*, undecided, indecisive; uncertain; squeamish; gutless, timid, tremulous, faint, nerveless; *nervous*; half-hearted, lukewarm, *indifferent*; infirm, infirm of purpose; characterless, featureless, *inert*; weak-kneed, spineless, *weak*; suggestible, flexible, *soft*; easygoing, good-natured, *lax*; inconstant, variable, temperamental; whimsical, *capricious*; emotional, restless, without ballast, *unstable*; uncommitted, irresponsible, giddy, feather-brained, light; fidgety, impatient; superficial; unfaithful.

Vb. *be irresolute*, blink, jib, shy, shirk, *avoid*; shuffle, shilly-shally, *be equivocal*; fluctuate, vacillate, seesaw, wobble,

waver, sway, hover, teeter, dither, *oscillate*; *be uncertain*; keep undecided, delay; dally, dilly-dally, *wait*; debate, balance, *argue*; hesitate, *be cautious*; falter, grow weary; *relinquish*; make a compromise, *compromise*; yield, give way, *submit*.

Adv. *irresolutely*; seesaw.

597 Obstinacy

N. *obstinacy*; determination, will, *resolution*; self-will; *hardness*; hard line; constancy, fixity, *stability*; stiff neck, *resistance*.

opinionatedness, *positiveness*; ruling passion, obsession, *bias*; blind side; *ignorance*; old school.

obstinate *person*, stubborn fellow, mule; stick-in-the-mud; hard core; fanatic, stickler, pedant, zealot, bigot, *narrow mind*; sticker, stayer; die-hard, *stamina*; crank.

Adj. *obstinate*, stubborn; pig-headed, mulish; pertinacious, firm, determined, *resolute*; dogged, tenacious; stiff, wooden, rigid; adamant, inflexible, unbending; obdurate, uncompromising, intransigent; unmoved, immovable; inexorable, implacable, merciless, *pitiless*; set, wedded to, hidebound; impervious, blind, deaf; opinionated, *positive*; dour, grim, sullen; stiff-necked, *impenitent* (see *wilful*); perverse, incorrigible, bloody-minded, plain cussed; possessive; irreversible; persistent, incurable, chronic.

wilful, wayward, arbitrary; headstrong, perverse; unruly, restive, refractory; irrepressible, ungovernable, intractable, *disobedient*; incorrigible; cross-grained, crotchety, *irascible*.

Vb. *be obstinate*, persist, *persevere*; *be impenitent*; stay put, *stand firm*; insist; please oneself; cling to custom, *be wont*; *be rash*; become chronic, *last*.

Adv. *obstinately*, like a mule.

598 Tergiversation

N. *tergiversation*, change of mind; afterthought, *sequel*; change of allegiance; change of purpose, alteration of plan, new resolve; good resolution; revulsion, *recoil*; *relapse*; change of direction, *deviation*; U-turn, volte-face, *return*; treachery, *perfidy*; *schism*; change of mood, temperament; coquetry, *caprice*.

recantation, apology; *oath*; disclaimer, denial; recall.

tergiversator, turncoat, rat; weathercock, *changeable thing*; Vicar of Bray; double-dealer, two-faced person; jilt, flirt, coquette, *caprice*; renegade; traitor, *knave*; quisling, fifth columnist; lost leader, quitter; tell-tale, *informer*; strike-breaker, blackleg, scab; *schismatic*; runaway; recidivist; convert, proselyte.

Adj. *tergiversating*, *equivocal*; slippery, supple, versatile, treacherous; reactionary, going back; fickle, *capricious*; *irresolute*; renegade; recidivist; false, unfaithful, disloyal.

Vb. *tergiversate*, think again, think better of it, *be irresolute*; *vary*; scratch, withdraw, resign; crawl; change front, change round, swerve, tack, wheel about, *turn round*; *turn back*; repent, *be penitent*; reform, *get better*; fall back, backslide, *relapse*; trim, shuffle, face both ways, *be equivocal*; ditch, jilt, desert; forsake, abandon, *relinquish*; turn against, play false.

apostatize; switch; desert, defect; blackleg, rat; betray, collaborate, be dishonest.

recant; eat humble pie; take back, backpedal, backtrack, do a U-turn; withdraw; retract, disavow, disclaim, repudiate, deny, negate; renounce, abjure; recall, revoke, rescind, abrogate.

599 Caprice

N. caprice; bias; variability, levity.

whim, caprice, fancy, fantastic notion, weird idea; passing fancy, impulse; sweet will, humour, mood, fit, crotchet, maggot, quirk, kink, fad, craze, freak; escapade, prank, foolery; coquetry, flirtation.

Adj. capricious, purposeless; whimsical, fanciful, fantastic; eccentric, temperamental, crotchety, freakish, fitful; hysterical, mad, crazy; mischievous, wanton, wayward, perverse; particular, fastidious; arbitrary, unreasonable; fretful, moody, contrary, irascible; refractory, wilful; erratic, uncertain; volatile, skittish, giddy, frivolous; inconsistent, inconstant, variable, unstable; irresponsible, fickle, feckless; flirtatious, playful.

Vb. be capricious, submit to a whim; be fastidious; vary; be fickle, vacillate, be irresolute; be absurd; flirt, coquette, amuse oneself.

Adv. capriciously, now this, now that.

600 Choice

N. choice, election, discrimination; selection; adoption; appointment, commission; right of choice, option; freedom of choice, discretion, pick; deliberate choice, decision; preference, predilection, partiality, leaning, bias, tendency; taste; offer; range of choice, selection, list, possible choice, alternative; difficult choice, dilemma; limited choice; only choice; blind choice; better choice, greater good, lesser evil, good policy; favour, fancy, first choice, top seed; thing chosen, selection, gleanings; literary selection, anthology; bad bargain; favouritism, injustice.

vote, voice, opinion; representation, cumulative vote; ballot, open vote, card vote; vote of confidence; division, poll, plebiscite, referendum; suffrage, franchise, right of representation; ballot box; polling; straw vote, election, by-election; indirect election, primary; hustings, candidature; return; suffragette.

electorate, elector, electoral college; quorum; electoral roll; constituent, constituency, borough, polling booth, ballot box; slate, ticket, manifesto.

Adj. choosing, optional; showing preference, preferential; selective, eclectic; elective, electoral.

chosen; preferable, better, advisable; select, choice, excellent; assorted; elect, designate; special, favourite, fancy, pet; God's own.

Vb. choose, have a voice, have free will, will; shop around; accept; elect, co-opt, adopt, approve; would like, favour, fancy, like best; incline, lean, have a bias, tend; prefer, have a preference, like better, would rather; might do worse; think fit, think it best to, decide, judge; commit oneself; be resolute; range oneself, side, back, support, embrace, espouse; wed.

select, pick, pass, approve; nominate, appoint, commission; designate, mark; earmark, reserve, set apart; recommend, propose, second; excerpt, cull, abstract; glean, winnow, sift, discriminate; separate; skim, cream; be fastidious.

vote, have a voice; poll; cast a vote, divide; elect, return; reject; electioneer; accept a candidature, stand, offer oneself; take a poll, hold a referendum; hold an election.

Adv. optionally, at pleasure; alternatively; rather; à la carte.

601 Absence of Choice

N. no choice, necessity; compulsion; any; justice; apathy; moral apathy; equality; indecision, open mind; floating vote; refusal to vote, abstention; disqualification.

Adj. choiceless, without alternative, necessary; without a preference, unable to choose, happy either way, neutral; open to conviction, undecided, irresolute; uninterested, apathetic, indifferent; morally neutral, amoral; disinterested; without favouritism, impartial, just; without a vote; nothing to offer, featureless, characterless.

Vb. be neutral, abstain; waive, stand aside, relinquish; stand between, be halfway; be irresolute; be indifferent.

have no choice, take it or leave it, make a virtue of necessity, be forced.

Adv. neither.

602 Rejection

N. rejection; disapprobation; denial; rebuff, repulse, frozen mitt, cold shoulder, refusal; spurn, kick; electoral defeat, lost election, defeat; exception, exclusion; disuse; discard, reject, wallflower.

Adj. rejected, ineligible; sent back; inexpedient.

Vb. reject, decline, rebuff, repulse, spurn, refuse; return, send back, return with thanks, disapprove; ignore, disregard; vote against, dissent; scrap, discard, ditch, junk, throw aside; revoke, abrogate; set aside, supersede, depose; expel, eject; eliminate; except, exempt, exclude; blackball, cold-shoulder, be rude; disclaim, disavow, deny, negate; repudiate, recant; scout, scorn, disdain, laugh at, mock, deride, ridicule; sniff at, hold cheap.

603 Predetermination

N. predetermination, predestination, necessity; destiny; decree, will; resolve, project, intention; preparation; order paper, agenda, business; frame-up, packed jury, plot; closed mind, prejudice.

Adj. predetermined, appointed, fated; deliberate, aforethought; with a motive, studied, measured; considered; contrived; packed, prepared.

Vb. predetermine, appoint, foreordain, predestine; premeditate, resolve beforehand, intend; agree beforehand; settle, fix; contrive a result, cause; contrive, arrange, prearrange, plan; frame, pack a jury, fake.

604 Spontaneity

N. spontaneity; impromptu; reflex, impulse, intuition; snap decision; spurt, burst of confidence, disclosure; inspiration, sudden thought, hunch, flash, idea.

improviser; creature of impulse.

Adj. *spontaneous*; offhand, extemporaneous, sudden, snap; makeshift; impromptu; unprompted, unprovoked; *voluntary*; unguarded, *rash*; natural, involuntary, automatic; *artless*; impulsive, emotional, *feeling*.

Vb. *improvise*, vamp, ad-lib; obey an impulse, *be capricious*.

Adv. extempore, impromptu, offhand.

605 Habit

N. *habit*, disposition, habit of mind, *temperament*; force of habit; familiarity, second nature; study, occupation; addiction, confirmed habit, constitutional; trait, idiosyncrasy; knack, trick, mannerism; instinct, leaning, *tendency*; bad habit; usage, long habit, custom, use, wont; prescription, *long duration*; tradition, law, precedent; way, ways, way of life; beaten track, groove, rut; fixed ways, round, daily grind; run, routine, drill, system, *order*; red tape, conservatism, old school, *conformity*.

practice, usual custom, usual policy, matter of course; *conformity*; mores, social usage; institution, ritual, observance, *rite*; religious observance, *cult*; mode, vogue, craze, *fashion*; convention, protocol, done thing; drill, form, *etiquette*; manners; standing order, routine, *conduct*, *order*.

habituation, training, *teaching*; seasoning; association, reflex, fixation, complex; drill, *repetition*.

habitué, creature of habit, addict, dope fiend; customer, regular, client; devotee, fan.

Adj. *habitual*, customary, familiar, *known*; routine, *regular*, conventional, *orthodox*; inveterate, time-honoured, permanent; haunting, besetting, clinging; ingrained, dyed-in-the-wool, *intrinsic*; rooted, deep-seated, *fixed*.

usual, accustomed; natural; household, familiar, well-known, *known*; trite, trodden, beaten, well-worn, hackneyed; banal, commonplace, common, ordinary; *general*; set, stock, *typical*; prevalent, widespread, current, *universal*; monthly, daily, everyday, of everyday occurrence, *frequent*; practised, done; right, settled, professional, official; invariable; *fashionable*.

habituated, accustomed to, known to; given to; dedicated, devoted to, wedded to; used to, familiar with, *knowing*; inveterate, confirmed; practised, *prepared*; tame.

Vb. *be wont*, love to, be known to, be used to, use to; be a creature of habit; go daily, haunt, frequent; make a habit of; never vary, observe routine, cling to custom; become a habit, stick; settle, take root; obtain, hold good, *prevail*.

habituate, accustom oneself, get used to; take to; catch oneself doing; practise, *repeat*; accustom, inure, season, harden, *train*; domesticate, tame; acclimatize, implant, *teach*; condition, brainwash, *influence*.

Adv. *habitually*, regularly; of course.

606 Desuetude

N. *desuetude*, disuse, rust, decay; lost habit, lost skill, lack of practice; *oblivion*; new custom; *nonconformity*; want of habit, inexperience, *ignorance*.

Adj. *unwonted*; unpractised; unnecessary; bad form, non-U, *vulgar*; old-fashioned, defunct, *past*; against custom; unprecedented, *original*.

unhabituated, unaccustomed; undomesticated; *immature*; new to, new, raw, fresh, green; rusty.

Vb. *disaccustom*, cure of, *cure*; break a habit, outgrow; slough, shed.

be *unpractised*; try a thing once; offend custom, infringe protocol; lapse, *be old*; rust, *deteriorate*.

607 Motive

N. *motive*, cause of action, what is behind it, *cause*; grounds, *reason why*; driving force, impetus, spring, mainspring; intention, *objective*; ideal, principle, lodestar, direction; aspiration, *hope*; ambition, desire; calling, call, *vocation*; conscience, honour, *duty*; shame, *fear*; ulterior motive; impulse, inspiration.

inducement, pressure, press; *influence*; indirect influence, side pressure; provocation, inspiration; support, *aid*; invitation, *request*; temptation, allurement, seduction, fascination, charm, sex appeal, *attraction*; flattery; *endearment*; persuasion, sales talk; pep talk, trumpet call, *call*; *lecture*; advocacy, *advice*; propaganda; advertising, soft sell, *advertisement*; graft, reward; honeyed words, siren song.

persuadability; *moral sensibility*; credulity.

incentive, inducement; stimulus, fillip, tickle, prod, spur, goad, lash, whip; rod, big stick, *threat*; tonic, provocative, carrot, sop, *stimulant*; charm, *spell*; attraction, *magnet*; will-o'-the-wisp, *visual fallacy*; lure, decoy, decoy duck, bait, *trap*; loss leader, special offer; profit, *gain*; cash, gold, *money*; pay, salary, perks, pay increase, rise, raise, bonus, *payment*; handout, *gift*; gratuity, tip, bribe, hush money, slush fund, *reward*; pork barrel; golden apple, forbidden fruit; offer one cannot refuse, *offer*.

motivator, manager, *influence*; tactician; prompter; counsellor, *adviser*; vamp, siren; orator, *speaker*; advocate, salesman, propagandist; ringleader, *leader*; firebrand, *agitator*; lobby, pressure group.

Adj. *inducing*; incentive, provocative, persuasive; directive; tonic, challenging, rousing, *exciting*; inviting, attractive; irresistible; *habitual*.

induced; inspired; *excited*; receptive, tractable, docile, *willing*.

Vb. *motivate*, motive, move, manipulate, operate; *influence*; weigh, count, be a consideration, sway, *prevail*; override, predominate; appeal, challenge; infect, inject with, *educate*; interest, intrigue, *impress*; charm, fascinate, captivate, spellbind, *bewitch*; pull, *attract*; push, *impel*; force, enforce, *compel*; bend, incline, dispose; predispose, prejudice, *bias*; predestine, *predetermine*; lead, direct, *manage*; lead astray, *mislead*; give a lead, set an example, *precede*.

incite, stimulate, *invigorate*; encourage, *give courage*; inspire, animate, provoke, rouse, rally, *excite*; evoke, call forth, challenge; exhort, invite, urge, insist, press, exert pressure, lobby; nag, needle, goad, prod, jog, jolt; spur, prick, tickle; whip, lash, flog; drive, hurry, *hasten*; instigate, prompt, abet, *aid*; insinuate, suggest, *hint*; advocate, recommend, counsel, *advise*; start, kindle, *initiate*.

induce, instigate, bring about, *cause*; persuade, carry with one, *convince*; browbeat (see *motivate*); compel; bring round, talk round, *convert*; procure, enlist, engage; cajole, *flatter*; conciliate, appease, *pacify*; entice, seduce (see *tempt*).

tempt, try; entice; tease; allure, lure, ensnare; coax, wheedle, pet; *facilitate*.

bribe, offer an inducement, *offer*; suborn, seduce, corrupt; square; oil; tip, *reward*.

be *induced*, yield, succumb, *submit*; concede, *consent*.

608 Dissuasion

N. *dissuasion*, contrary advice; caution, *warning*; setback, *hindrance*; reproof, admonition; rebuff, *resistance*; disincentive; deterrent, *danger signal*; cold water, damper, wet blanket; killjoy, spoilsport.

Adj. *dissuasive*; reluctant; *deprecatory*; warning against, *cautionary*.

Vb. *dissuade*, persuade against; caution, *warn*; remonstrate, castigate, *reprove*; expostulate, deprecate; shake, stagger, give one pause, *cause doubt*; intimidate, *threaten*; deter, daunt, cow, *frighten*; turn one aside, *deflect*; hold one back, keep back, *restrain*; render averse, disenchant, disillusion; set against, repel, disgust, fill with distaste, *cause dislike*; dishearten, discourage, dispirit, *depress*; crush, squelch, dampen, quench, cool, chill; *blunt*; calm, quiet, *moderate*.

609 Pretext

N. *pretext*, ostensible motive, statement, profession, claim; plea, excuse, defence, apology; loophole, alibi, *means of escape*; *prop*; shallow pretext, thin excuse; quibble, salvo, proviso, *qualification*; subterfuge, *stratagem*; false plea, pretence, previous engagement, *untruth*; blind; smoke screen, cloak, cover, *screen*; makeshift, *substitute*; colour, gloss, guise, *appearance*; bluff.

Adj. *ostensible*, pretended; specious, plausible; seeming.

excusing, apologetic.

Vb. *plead*, allege, claim, profess, *affirm*; pretext, make a plea of, *argue*; offer an excuse, excuse oneself, *justify*; palliate, *extenuate*; find a loophole, *escape*; bluff; varnish, colour; blind; pretend, affect, *dissemble*.

Adv. *ostensibly*.

610 Good

N. *good*; supreme good; public weal, common weal, common good; balance of interest, greater good, lesser evil, utilitarianism, *good policy*; weal, well-being, welfare; riches, *wealth*; luck, fortune, happy ending; blessing, world of good (see *benefit*); benediction, *benevolence*.

benefit, advantage, interest; service, convenience, behalf, *utility*; crop, harvest, return, *acquisition*; profit, increment, *gain*; edification; boon, *gift*; good turn, *kind act*; favour, blessing; godsend, windfall, piece of luck, treasure trove, find, prize; good thing, desirable object.

Adj. *good*, fine, blessed, beatific, *happy*; gainful; advantageous, heaven-sent, *beneficial*; worthwhile, *valuable*; helpful; praiseworthy; moral, *virtuous*.

Vb. *benefit*, favour, bless; do good, help, serve, avail, be of service, *be useful*; edify, advantage, profit; pay, repay; do one a power of good, *make better*.

flourish, thrive, do well; rise, *prosper*; arrive, *succeed*; improve, *get better*; turn to good account; make a profit, *gain*; make money, *get rich*.

Adv. *well*, aright.

611 Evil

N. *evil*, evil conduct, disservice, injury, dirty trick, *foul play*; wrong, injury, outrage, *injustice*; crying evil, shame, abuse; curse, scourge, poison, pest, plague, sore, *bane*; ill; sad world; bale, trouble, *adversity*; affliction, misery, distress, *suffering*; grief, woe, *sorrow*; malaise, discomfort, *worry*; nuisance; hurt, bodily harm, wound, bruise, cut, gash, *pain*; blow, buffet, stroke, *knock*; outrageous fortune, calamity, bad luck, *misfortune*; casualty, accident, *event*; fatality, *death*; catastrophe, *ruin*; tragedy, sad ending; mischief, harm, damage, *loss*; ill effect, bad result; disadvantage, drawback, *defect*; setback, hitch; evil plight, *predicament*; *poverty*; sense of injury, grievance, *discontent*; cause of evil.

Adj. *evil*, wicked, *vicious*; black, foul, shameful, *wrong*; bad, too bad; inauspicious, sinister, *adverse*; insidious, prejudicial; *maleficent*; fatal, fell, mortal, *deadly*; ruinous, *destructive*; calamitous, tragic, *unfortunate*; all wrong, awry.

Adv. *amiss*, wrong, all wrong, awry, sour; unfortunately; worse luck!

612 Intention

N. *intention*, intent, meaning, calculation, *estimate*; purpose, determination, resolve, *resolution*; mind, *intellect*; criminal intent, *guilt*; *benevolence*; view, prospect; future intention, proposal; constant intention, study, pursuit, occupation, *business*; project, design, *plan*; enterprise, *undertaking*; ambition, *desire*; decision; final decision, ultimatum, *conditions*; bid, *attempt*; engagement, *promise*; solemn threat, *threat*; final intention, destination, *end*; final cause; *reason why*; trend, *tendency*.

objective, destination, object, end, aim; axe to grind; mark, butt, target; target area, bull's-eye, *centre*; tape, *goal*; place of pilgrimage, Mecca, *focus*; quarry, game, prey, *chase*; prize, crown, wreath, *trophy*; dream, aspiration, vision.

Adj. *intending*, hell-bent, *resolute*; intentional, deliberate, voluntary; serious, minded, disposed, inclined, *willing*; prospective, would-be, ambitious.

intended; deliberate, intentional, studied, purposeful, aforethought.

Vb. *intend*, purpose, propose; have an eye to, contemplate; study, meditate; calculate, *expect*; *foresee*; mean to, really mean, have every intention, *be resolute*; have a purpose, harbour a design; resolve, determine, premeditate, *predetermine*; project, design, *plan*; shoulder, *undertake*; engage, *promise*; threaten to, *threaten*; predestine; earmark, *mark*.

aim at; go after, drive at, strive after, *pursue*; make a bid, endeavour, *attempt*; be after, promise oneself, propose to oneself, nurse an ambition, aspire to, dream of, think of, talk of, *desire*; take aim, point at, level at, aim high, *aim*.

Adv. *purposely*; designedly, advisedly, knowingly; with malice aforethought; with a view to, with an eye to.

613 Nondesign. Gamble

N. *nondesign, chance*; instinct; coincidence, *accompaniment*; accident, fluke, luck, *event*; good luck, windfall; bad luck, *evil*; lottery, *equal chance*; divination; lot, wheel of Fortune, *fate*; mascot, amulet, charm, *talisman*.

gambling, taking a chance; plunge, risk, hazard, Russian roulette, *danger*; gamble, potluck, *chance*; venture, flutter, *experiment*; shot, blind bargain; bid, throw; toss of a coin, turn of a card; wager, bet, stake, psychic bid; last throw, desperate bid; dice, die; element of risk, game of chance; bingo; fruit machine; roulette; turf, horse-racing, *racing*; football pool, pools; draw, lottery, raffle, tombola, sweepstake, premium bond; futures.

gaming-house, hell; casino, pool room, bingo hall, amusement arcade; racecourse, turf; tote.

bourse, exchange, bucket shop.

gambler, player; better, layer, backer; turf accountant, bookmaker, tout, tipster; enterprising person; gentleman of fortune, adventurer, undertaker, entrepreneur, *undertaking*; plunger; bear, bull, stag.

Adj. *unintentional*, inadvertent, *involuntary*; *spontaneous*; accidental, fortuitous, *casual*.

designless, aimless, purposeless; happy-go-lucky; *indiscriminate*; random, haphazard; wandering, footloose.

speculative, *uncertain*; hazardous, chancy, dicey; venturesome, adventurous, enterprising.

Vb. *gamble*, game, play; throw, dice, bet, stake, wager, lay; play high, offer odds, make a book; back, punt; cover a bet, cover, hedge, *seek safety*; speculate, have a flutter, *experiment*; hazard, risk, tempt Providence; buy blind, *be rash*; venture, chance it, tempt fortune, trust to chance; raffle, draw, spin a coin.

Adv. *at random*, incidentally; at a venture.

614 Pursuit

N. *pursuit*, pursuance, follow-up, *sequence*; hunting, quest, *search*; *following*; witchhunt; prosecution, execution; *business*.

chase, run; steeplechase, *racing*; hunt, hunting, tally-ho; beat, drive, beating; hunting, *sport*; blood sport, fox hunt; fishing, angling; fly fishing, whaling; coursing; fishing tackle, bait, fly; *firearm*; *trap*; dragnet; game, quarry, prey, victim, *objective*; catch, *acquisition*.

hunter; search party; trailer, shadow; huntsman, huntress; whip; beater; sportsman, *player*; gun, shot, marksman or -woman; headhunter; poacher; trapper, rodent officer; falconer; fisherman, trawler, whaler; field, pack, hound, foxhound, bloodhound, *dog*; hawk, *bird*; beast of prey, man-eater, *mammal*; mouser, *cat*.

Adj. *pursuing*, after; *following*; hunting; fishing, piscatorial.

Vb. *pursue*, seek; *search*; send after; stalk, prowl after, shadow, dog, track, trail, tail, *follow*; *discover*; witch-hunt, harry, persecute, *oppress*; chase, hunt, whoop,

hark; rush at, tilt at, ride full tilt at, charge at, *charge*; leap at, jump at, *leap*; snatch at, *take*; *aim at*; run after, woo, *court*; mob; be after, *intend*; busy oneself; persist, *persevere*; *hasten*; *progress*.

hunt, go hunting; go fishing, fish, angle; trawl; whale; shrimp; net, catch, *ensnare*; mouse, stalk, fowl, hawk; course; start game, flush, beat, start; poach.

Adv. *pursuant to*, after.

Int. Halloo! View halloo! Yoicks! Tallyho!

615 Avoidance

N. *avoidance, hindrance*; abstinence, abstention, *temperance*; forbearance, *moderation*; refusal, inaction, cop-out; passivity; evasive action, dodge, duck, sidestep; centrifugal force; retreat; evasion, flight, *escape*; shy, *fear*; wide berth, safe distance, *distance*; revulsion, recoil; defence mechanism, defensive reaction, *defence*; repression, prohibition; *absence*; escapism.

avoider; trickster; quitter, coward; slacker; truant, renegade; runaway, fugitive, refugee; *visionary*; ostrich.

Adj. *avoiding*; evasive, elusive, slippery, hard to catch; wild; shy, *modest*; blinking, *nervous*; backward, reluctant; non-committal, *taciturn*; passive, inert; uncommitted, *neutral*; centrifugal; fugitive, runaway, fly-by-night; hiding, *latent*.

avoidable.

Vb. *avoid*; bypass, circumvent, *deviate*; turn aside, cold-shoulder; hold aloof, stand apart, shun, eschew, leave, let alone, have nothing to do with; give a miss; fight shy, draw back, *recede*; stand aloof, give a wide berth, sup with a long spoon, *be distant*; keep clear; forbear, spare; refrain, abstain, deny oneself, do without, *be temperate*; *moderate*; hold back; shelve, postpone; funk, shirk, *neglect*; shrink, flinch, start aside, jib, refuse, shy, blink, blench, *be nervous*; take evasive action, lead one a dance, play hide-and-seek; sidestep, dodge, duck; deflect, *parry*; get round, obviate, skirt round; fence, hedge, pussyfoot, *be equivocal*; evade, escape, *elude*; skulk, cower, hide, *lurk*; disown, deny, *negate*; repress, suppress, *prohibit*; *plead*; prevent, foil, *hinder*.

run away, desert, play truant, jump bail, take French leave; abscond, welsh, flit, elope, *escape*; absent oneself, *be absent*; withdraw, retire, retreat, turn tail, *turn round*; flee, flit, fly, take to flight; bolt, run, beat it, make oneself scarce, scoot, scram, skedaddle, *move fast*; part company, decamp; scuttle, do a bunk.

Int. hands off! keep off! beware! forbear!

616 Relinquishment

N. *relinquishment*; going; dereliction; schism; walk-out, *strike*; cop-out; yielding, *transfer*; waiver, *resignation*; disuse; cancellation; world well lost.

Adj. *relinquished*, cast-off, castaway.

Vb. *relinquish*, drop, let go, leave hold of; surrender, resign, yield; waive; *be humble*; cede, transfer, *assign*; forfeit, *lose*; renounce, recant; forget it, *forget*; wean oneself; deny oneself, abstain, *avoid*; shed, slough, *doff*; drop, discard; lose interest, have other fish to fry, *be indifferent*; abdicate, scratch, withdraw, retire, *resign*; *submit*; leave, quit, vacate, evacuate, *depart*; forsake, abandon, leave stranded, desert; play truant, *be absent*; strike, *cease*; secede; rat; ditch, jilt, *deceive*; shelve, postpone; annul, cancel, *abrogate*.

617 Business

N. *business*, interests; main business, occupation, concern, care; aim, ambition, *intention*; case, agenda; enterprise, venture, undertaking, pursuit, *activity*; routine, round, *practice*; business life, daily work; business world, City; art, technology, industry, commerce, big business; business company, *corporation*; agriculture; cottage industry, industrialism, industrial arts, manufacture, *production*; trade, craft, handicraft, *skill*; guild, union, business association, *association*; employment, work, avocation (see *vocation*); sideline, hobby, pastime, *amusement*.

vocation, calling, life work, mission, *commission*; life, walk of life, career, chosen career, labour of love, self-imposed task, *voluntary work*; living, livelihood, daily bread; profession, craft, trade; line, line of country (see *function*); exacting profession, high calling; religious profession, ministry; cloth, veil, habit; military profession, arms, *war*; naval profession, sea; legal profession, *law*; teaching profession, education, *teaching*; medical profession, medicine, practice; business profession, industry, commerce, *trade*; government service, civil service, *management*; public service, public life; social service, *sociology*.

job, *activity*; work, task, set task, exercise, *labour*; duty, charge, commission, mission, errand, quest, *mandate*; employ, service, employment, working day, manhour; occupation, situation, position, berth, incumbency, appointment, post, office; regular employment, full-time job; temporary job; opening, vacancy; labour exchange, employment agency, Job Centre, Department of Employment.

function, what one has to do; capacity, office, duty; area, realm, province, orbit, sphere; scope, field, terms of reference, *range*; beat, round; department, line, line of country; role, part; business, job; responsibility, concern, care, look-out, baby, pigeon.

Adj. *businesslike*, efficient, *skilful*; industrious, busy, *active*; vocational, professional, career; industrial, commercial, mercantile; *functional*; official; routine, systematic, *orderly*; workaday, *habitual*; freelance; *preparatory*.

Vb. *employ*, busy, occupy, keep one engaged; give employment, engage, recruit, hire, enlist, appoint, post, *commission*; pay; give a situation to, offer a job to, fill a vacancy, staff with, staff.

busy *oneself*, work, *serve*; have a profession, do a job, earn a living; earn an honest crust, turn an honest penny, *acquire*; take a situation; be doing, bustle, *be busy*; concern oneself with, *meddle*; work at, ply; turn to; have to do, *incur a duty*; amuse oneself.

function, work, go, *operate*; fill a role; officiate, act; substitute; hold office, hold a portfolio, hold a place, have a job, serve (see *busy oneself*).

do *business*, transact, negotiate, *make terms*; ply a trade, ply a craft, exercise a profession, follow a calling, work at a job;

have a business, drive a trade, keep shop; do business with, *trade*; transact business, be an employer, be an industrialist; open a shop.

Adv. *professionally*.

618 Plan

N. *plan*, scheme, design; *order*; programme, project, proposal, *intention*; proposition, suggestion, motion, resolution (see *policy*); master plan, scale drawing, blueprint, *map*; diagram, flow chart, *statistics*; sketch, outline, draft, memorandum; skeleton, roughcast; model, pattern, pilot scheme, prototype; proof, revise, proof copy, *copy*; drawing board, back room, headquarters, base.

policy, forethought, *foresight*; *wisdom*; course of action, plan of attack, procedure, strategy, *tactics*; operational research, *enquiry*; address, approach, attack, *way*; steps, *action*; stroke of policy, coup, *deed*; scenario, forecast, *prediction*; programme, prospectus, platform, plank, ticket, slate; line, formula, *rule*; schedule, agenda, *business*.

contrivance, expedient, resource, recourse, resort, card, *means*; recipe, nostrum, *remedy*; loophole, alternative, answer, *means of escape*; artifice, device, gimmick, dodge, ploy, shift, flag of convenience, *stratagem*; wangle, fiddle, *foul play*; knack, trick, *skill*; stunt, wheeze; inspiration, happy thought, bright idea, *idea*; notion, invention; tool, weapon, contraption, gadget, *instrument*; makeshift, *substitute*; feat; bold move, stroke, masterstroke, *deed*.

plot, intrigue; web, web of intrigue; cabal, conspiracy, inside job; scheme, racket, game, *stratagem*; frame-up, machination; *motive*; secret influence; *defence*.

planner, projector; founder, author, architect; boffin, *expert*; brains, mastermind; tactician; statesman or -woman, politician, Machiavellian; go-getter, *busy person*; spinner, spider; cabal.

Adj. *planned*, schematic, *prepared*; *orderly*.

planning, resourceful, ingenious, *cunning*; purposeful; involved; Machiavellian.

Vb. *plan*, resolve, *intend*; approach, approach a problem, make a plan, design, draft, blueprint; frame, shape, *form*; revise, *rectify*; project, programme; shape a course, schematize, *order*; schedule, phase, adjust; invent, *discover*; conceive a plan, *imagine*; find a way, make shift to; contrive, devise, engineer; hatch, concoct, mature, *prepare*; arrange, prearrange, *predetermine*; calculate, think ahead, *be wise*; have a policy, follow a plan, work to a schedule; do everything with a purpose, have an axe to grind.

plot, scheme, have designs; manipulate, pull strings, *influence*; cabal, conspire, intrigue; concoct, brew; hatch a plot, *be cunning*; undermine, *ensnare*; work against, frame, *fake*.

619 Way

N. *way*, route, *itinerary*; manner, wise, guise, fashion, style, *form*; method, mode, line, approach, address, attack; procedure, process, way of, way of doing things, *tactics*; operation, treatment; working arrangement, *compromise*; usual way, routine, *practice*; technique, knowhow, *skill*; going, gait, *motion*; way forward, progress, *progression*; royal road, primrose path; way of life, behaviour, *conduct*. See route.

access, right of way, communications; way to, direct approach, *approach*; entrance, door, *doorway*; drive, gangway; porch, hall, corridor, vestibule, *lobby*; way through, pass, defile, *passage*; intersection, junction, crossing; zebra crossing, *traffic control*; strait, sound, *gulf*; channel, fairway, canal, *conduit*; lock, stile, turnstile, tollgate; stairs, ladder, *ascent*.

bridge, brig; footbridge, flyover, aqueduct; suspension bridge, viaduct, span; railway bridge; pontoon bridge, drawbridge; causeway, stepping-stone, gangway, gangplank, catwalk, duckboards; ford, ferry, *passage*; underpass, *tunnel*; isthmus, neck.

route, direction; line, course, march, tack, track, beat; trajectory, orbit; lane, *traffic control*; air lane, sea-lane, seaway, fairway, *conduit*; trade route; short cut, bypass; detour, roundabout way, *circuit*; line of communication, line of retreat, line of advance.

path, footpath, pavement; towpath, ride; byway, lane, track, rabbit run, trail, right of way, public footpath; glade, walk, promenade, esplanade, parade, front, avenue, drive, boulevard, mall; pedestrian precinct, arcade, aisle, cloister; racetrack, running track, *arena*; fairway, runway.

road, highway; main road, A road, cinder track; switchback; toll road; thoroughfare, through road, artery, bypass, ring road; motorway; clearway; acceleration lane; crossroads, junction, T-junction, turn-off; intersection, roundabout; crossing, *traffic control*; roadway, carriageway, central reservation, crash barrier; cycle track; street, alley; close, avenue, *housing*; pavement, kerb; paving, paving stone; hard shoulder, verge; macadam, tarmac, asphalt, road metal; surface, road building, traffic engineering.

railway, railroad, line; permanent way, track, lines, third rail; main line; monorail, cog railway, funicular, ropeway; overhead railway, subway, tube, metro, *train*; light railway, narrow gauge, junction, crossover, level crossing, tunnel, cutting, embankment; siding, turntable; station, halt, stop, platform; signal, gantry, signal box, cabin; rails, points, frog, ballast.

Adj. *communicating*, *accessible*; through, main, arterial, trunk; tarmac; lit; busy, trodden, beaten.

Adv. *via*.
how.

620 Middle way

N. *middle way*, middle course, via media; balance, golden mean, happy medium, *average*; intermediate technology; central position, halfway, halfway house, *middle point*; slack water, half tide; direct course, straight line, short cut, beeline; short circuit; noncommittal, *moderation*; mutual concession, *compromise*.

moderate; neutral, uncommitted person, uncommitted nation.

Adj. *neutral*, impartial, *just*; noncommittal, uncommitted; detached, *indifferent*; moderate, *central*; lukewarm, *irresolute*; grey.

undeviating, unswerving, *central*; direct, *straight*; halfway, midway, intermedi-

ate.

Vb. *be midstream*, steer a middle course, go straight, look neither to right nor to left.

be halfway, go halfway, *compromise*; balance; *be uncertain*.

621 Circuit

N. *circuit*, roundabout way, circuitous route, bypass, detour, loop, loop line, *deviation*; *convolution*; circulation, orbit, round, lap; circumference, *circle*; full circle.

Adj. *roundabout*, circuitous, indirect; *diffuse*.

Vb. *circuit*, round, lap, go round, make a circuit, *circle*; make a detour, *deviate*; turn, bypass, short-circuit, *avoid*; lead one a dance; encircle, embrace, encompass, *surround*; skirt, edge round.

Adv. *round about*.

622 Requirement

N. *requirement*, essential, a necessary, a must, *necessity*; needs, necessaries; indent, order, requisition; prerequisite, prior conditions, *conditions*; want, lack, need; gap, *absence*; demand, *purchase*; consumption, input, intake; shortage, *shortfall*; balance due, *debt*; claim, request; ultimatum, injunction, *command*.

needfulness, case of need, occasion; want, pinch, *poverty*; exigency, emergency, *crisis*; *important matter*; obligation, *duty*; bare minimum.

Adj. *required*, requisite, prerequisite, needful; necessary, essential, vital, indispensable; reserved; lacking, missing, *absent*.

necessitous, lacking, deprived of; destitute, *poor*.

demanding, crying, imperative, urgent, instant, pressing; compulsory.

Vb. *require*, need, want, lack; be without; miss; need badly, crave, *desire*; claim, *request*; find necessary, find indispensable, be unable to do without, must have; consume, take, *waste*, *use*; create a need, render necessary, necessitate, oblige, *compel*; *demand*; stipulate, *give terms*; order, indent, requisition; reserve, book, earmark.

Adv. *in need*; necessarily; of necessity, at a pinch.

623 Instrumentality

N. *instrumentality*, operation, *agency*; occasion, *cause*; result, *effect*; pressure, *influence*; efficacy, *power*; occult power, magic, *sorcery*; help, *aid*; support; interference, *activity*; medium, *means*; use, employment, application, *utility*; use of machinery, instrumentation, automation, *machine*.

instrument, hand, organ, lackey, slave, *servant*; agent, midwife, medium, help, assistant; go-between, *mediator*; catalyst; vehicle; pawn; robot, *machine*; stooge, puppet, creature, *auxiliary*; weapon, implement, appliance, lever, *tool*; magic ring, *spell*; key, skeleton key, passkey, *opener*; open sesame, watchword, password; passport, safeconduct, warrant, *permit*; stepping-stone, *bridge*; channel, high road, highway, *road*; push button, switch; device, expedient, makeshift, gadget; card, trump.

Adj. *instrumental*, working, *operative*; manual; automatic, push-button, *mechanical*; effective, efficient, efficacious, effectual, *powerful*; telling, weighty; magic, *magical*; conducive, *causal*; practical, applied; serviceable, employable, handy, *useful*; ready, available, *willing*; helpful; functional, subservient; intermediate.

Vb. *be instrumental*, work, act, *operate*; perform, do; serve, lend oneself or itself to, *minister to*; help, assist, *aid*; advance, promote; *participate*; cause; *be useful*; intermediate, interpose, intervene, *mediate*; pull strings, *influence*; effect, *cause*; tend; achieve, *carry through*.

Adv. *through*, per, thanks to.

624 Means

N. *means*, wherewithal; power, capacity, *ability*; strong hand; facilities; *tool*; technology, *knowledge*; technique, knowhow, *skill*; wherewithal, equipment, supplies, stock, munitions, ammunition, *provision*; resources, raw material; *machine*; labour resources, pool of labour, manpower, *personnel*; *wealth*; liquidity, *money*; capital, *instrument*; stock-intrade, *property*; investment portfolio; revenue, income, receipts, *receipt*; line of credit, *credit*; stand-by, *safeguard*; freedom of choice, alternative, *choice*; method, steps, *way*; cure, specific, *remedy*; expedient, device, resort, recourse; makeshift, *substitute*; *means of escape*; desperate remedy, last resort, last hope, last throw.

Vb. *find means*, supply, find, furnish, *provide*; equip, *make ready*; finance, promote, float; *be able*; contrive, be resourceful; find a way, *plan*; beg, borrow or steal, *acquire*.

Adv. *by means of*, with; through.

625 Tool

N. *tool*, implement, *instrument*; apparatus, appliance, utensil; weapon, arm, *arms*; device, contraption, gadget; screw, screwdriver, drill; wrench, spanner; pliers, tweezers, *nippers*; chisel, wedge, *sharp edge*; rope, *cable*; peg, nail, *hanger, support*; lever, jemmy, crowbar, jack, *pivot*; grip, lug, haft, shaft, tiller, helm, rudder, *handle*; pulley, *wheel*; switch, stopcock; trigger; pedal, pole, *propulsion*; ram, *hammer*; prehistoric tool, flint.

machine, mechanical device; machinery, mechanism, works; clockwork; *component*; spring, mainspring, hairspring; automatic gear change; motor, engine, turbine, dynamo; servomechanism, servomotor; robot, automaton; computer.

mechanics, engineering; *electronics*; cybernetics; automatic control, automation; mechanical power, mechanical advantage; technology.

equipment, furniture; gear, tackle, harness; fixture, *adjunct*; outfit, kit; upholstery; trappings, *dress*; paraphernalia, *property*; wares, stock-in-trade, *merchandise*; plant, *workshop*.

machinist, operator, operative; driver, *agent*; engineer, technician, mechanic, fitter; craftsman, *artisan*.

Adj. *mechanical*; automatic, *instrumental*.

626 Materials

N. *materials*, resources, *means*; material, stuff, staple, stock, *substance*; raw material, grist; meat, fodder, *food*; oil, *fuel*; ore, mineral, metal, ingot; clay, adobe, china clay, gypsum, *soil*; glass, transparency; plastic, polythene, polystyrene, latex, celluloid, fibreglass; rope, yarn, wool, *fibre*; leather, hide, *skin*; timber, log, faggot, stick, *wood*; rafter, board, *beam*; plank, planking, plywood, lath, stave; stuffing, *lining*; cloth, fabric, *textile*.

building material, building block, brick, *pottery*; cob; *structure*; thatch, slate, tile, shingle, *roof*; stone, marble, flint, masonry; rendering, *facing*; composition, cement, concrete; paving material, flag, cobble, *paving*; hard core, gravel, tarmac, asphalt, *road*.

paper, pulp, newsprint; card, cellophane; cardboard, pasteboard, chipboard, hardboard, plasterboard; sheet, foolscap, quire, ream; notepaper, *stationery*.

627 Store

N. *store*, mass, heap, load, stack, stockpile, *accumulation*; packet, bagful, bagful, *quantity*; harvest, crop, vintage, mow, *acquisition*; haystack; stock, stock-intrade, *merchandise*; capital, holding, investment, *property*; fund, backlog; savings, savings account, nest egg; deposit, hoard, treasure, cache; bottom drawer, hope chest, trousseau, *provision*; pool, kitty; common fund, community chest, *joint possession*; quarry, mine, natural resources, natural deposit, coalfield, oilfield; coal mine, colliery, working, shaft; coalface, seam, lode; pipe, pipe vein; vein, bonanza, strike; well; fountain, *source*; supply, stream; tap, pipeline; treacle well, cornucopia, abundance, *plenty*; repertoire, range (see *collection*).

storage, stowage, gathering, *accumulation*; conservation, *preservation*; safe deposit; *protection*; stabling; storage, storage space, space, accommodation, *room*; loft, hold, bunker, *cellar*; supply base, storehouse, storeroom, stockroom; warehouse, goods shed, godown; depository, depot; dock, wharf, garage, *stable*; magazine, arsenal, armoury; treasure house, *treasury*; exchequer, vault, coffer, till, safe, bank; data bank; *memory*; hive, honeycomb; granary, barn, silo; water tower, reservoir, cistern, tank, gasholder; battery, garage, petrol station, petrol pump; dump, sump, drain, sewage farm, *sink*; pantry, larder, buttery, *chamber*; cupboard, shelf, cabinet; refrigerator, fridge, deep freeze; portmanteau, holdall, box; container, holder, quiver, *receptacle*.

collection, set, archives, file, *record*; folder, bundle, portfolio, *accumulation*; museum, *antiquity*; gallery, library, thesaurus, *dictionary*; menagerie, aquarium, zoo; waxworks, exhibition, *exhibit*; repertory, repertoire.

Adj. *stored*; held; available; spare.

Vb. *store*, stow, pack, bundle, *load*; dump, garage, stable, warehouse; barn; gather, harvest, reap, mow, pick, glean, *cultivate*; stack, heap, pile, amass, accumulate, *bring together*; panic buy, stockpile, *augment*; fuel, coal, bunker, *provide*; fill, refill, refuel, *replenish*; save, keep, hold, file, *retain*; bottle, pickle, conserve, *preserve*; leave, set aside, keep back, reserve; fund, bank, deposit, invest; hoard, treasure, hive, bury, cache, *conceal*; husband, make a nest egg; equip oneself, *prepare oneself*; pool.

628 Provision

N. *provision*, logistics, equipment; service, delivery; self-service; entertainment, maintenance; supply, feed; pipeline; commissariat, supplies, stores, *store*; reinforcement, refill; food, *provisions*; helping, portion, *meal*; produce, *product*; increase, return, *gain*; conservation, resource management, *economy*; budget; possible need, *preparation*.

provider, donor; creditor, moneylender; wet nurse, feeder; purser, *treasurer*; steward, butler; quartermaster, victualler; provision merchant, grocer, greengrocer, baker, poulterer, fishmonger, butcher, vintner, wine merchant; retailer, middleman, shopkeeper; pimp.

caterer, hotelier, restaurateur; landlord, landlady, mine host, publican; housekeeper, housewife; cook, chef; confectioner.

Adj. *provisioning*; self-service; *sufficient*; provided, all found; well-appointed, three star; available.

Vb. *provide*, afford, offer, lend, *give*; provision, find; equip, furnish, arm, man, *make ready*; supply, maintain supply; yield, *produce*; cater, purvey; procure, pimp; service, service an order, *sell*; deliver; hand round, serve; feed, board, maintain, keep, clothe; stock, budget, make provision, *store*; fuel, coal, bunker; gather food, forage, water, tap, draw, milk, *extract*; export, import, *trade*.

replenish, reinforce, make good; refill, *fill*; refuel, reload.

629 Waste

N. *waste*, wastage; leakage, ebb; consumption; intake, *requirement*; outlay, expense, *expenditure*; exhaustion, drainage; melting; damage, *loss*; lack of economy, unnecessary expenditure; useless expenditure, *misuse*; vandalism, wilful destruction, sabotage, *destruction*; waste product, refuse, *rubbish*.

Adj. *wasteful*, extravagant, unnecessary, uneconomic, *prodigal*; throwaway, *superfluous*; *destructive*.

wasted; gone to waste; fruitless; futile.

Vb. *waste*, consume, swallow, devour, *eat*; spend, *expend*; take, exhaust, deplete, drain, suck dry, *empty*; dissipate, scatter, *disperse*; abuse, overwork, impoverish, milk dry, *misuse*; erode, damage, *impair*; misapply; *waste effort*, be extravagant, squander, run through, be prodigal; be careless, slop, spill; be destructive, ruin, destroy, sabotage, *lay waste*; suffer loss, decay, *decrease*; leak, run low; melt, liquefy; evaporate, gutter, *burn*; run to seed, *deteriorate*; run to waste.

630 Sufficiency

N. *sufficiency*, right amount; qualification; right number, quorum; enough; adequate income, competence, living wage; exact requirement; minimum, bare minimum, least one can do; *possibility*; full measure, satisfaction, content; fulfilment; bellyful.

plenty, cornucopia, *abundance*; flood, spate, *stream*; lashings, galore, *great quantity*; amplitude; riches, *wealth*; luxury, loaded table, feast, banquet; orgy, riot, profusion; fat; fertility, productivity; harvest, bumper crop; rich vein, bonanza, ample store, endless supply, store; more than enough, too much, superabundance.

Adj. *sufficient*; self-sufficient, *complete*; enough, adequate, competent; enough to go round; equal to, *equal*; satisfactory; measured, commensurate; just right; barely sufficient, only just enough; makeshift, provisional.

plenteous, ample, more than enough, *superfluous*; openhanded, generous, lavish, *liberal*; extravagant, prodigal; wholesale, without stint, unsparing, unmeasured, inexhaustible, *great*; luxuriant, riotous, lush, rank, fertile, fat, *prolific*; profuse, abundant, copious, *redundant*; rich, opulent, affluent.

filled, flush, *full*; chock-full, replete, ready to burst; *content*; teeming, *multitudinous*.

Vb. *suffice*, be enough, do, answer, be *expedient*; just do, work, serve; qualify, reach; pass, pass muster, wash; do all that is possible; stand, *support*; saturate, fill, refill, *replenish*; prove acceptable, satisfy, *content*; more than satisfy, satiate, give one his bellyful, *sate*; make adequate provision, *provide*.

abound, proliferate, teem, swarm, bristle with, *be many*; riot, *be fruitful*; flow, shower, snow, pour, stream, sheet, *rain*; brim, overflow; *be rich*.

have enough, be content; eat; drink; have had enough; *afford*.

Adv. *enough*, tolerably; ad lib.

631 Insufficiency

N. *insufficiency*; discontent; little enough, nothing to spare; somewhat, *small quantity*; too few; deficiency; defect; deficit; failure, weakness, *shortfall*; pittance, dole, mite; *parsimony*; short allowance, short commons, starvation diet; fast day; malnutrition, vitamin deficiency, *disease*.

scarcity; dearth, seven lean years; drought, famine, starvation; shortage, *shortfall*; power cut, *decrease*; none to spare, short supply; deprivation, *poverty*; lack, want, need; ebb, low water.

Adj. *insufficient*; inadequate, too little; scant, scanty, slender; too small, *small*; deficient, lacking, *incomplete*; wanting, poor, *inferior*; incompetent, unequal to; weak, thin, watery, *insubstantial*; stingy, *parsimonious*.

unprovided, vacant, bare, *empty*; emptyhanded, insatiable; cramped; *poor*; understaffed, undermanned, shorthanded; *absent*.

underfed; starving, spare, scurvy, thin, skinny, *lean*.

scarce, rare, *infrequent*; sparse, *few*; short, at a premium, hard to get.

Vb. *not suffice*, be insufficient, be *imperfect*; *restrain*; want, lack, need, require, leave a gap, *require*; fail, *disappoint*; fall below, be *inferior*; come short, default, *fall short*; tinker.

be unsatisfied, come again, take a second helping, still feel hungry, be *hungry*; spurn an offer, reject with contempt, *reject*; miss, want, feel something is missing, *require*; be unable to have enough of.

make insufficient, ask too much, expect too much; overwork, impoverish, damage, *impair*; exhaust, deplete, squander, *waste*; grudge, hold back, stint, skimp, ration, be *parsimonious*; disinherit.

Adv. *insufficiently*; failing; at a low ebb.

632 Redundance

N. redundance, overspill, overflow, flood;
abundance, superabundance, riot, profusion, plenty; bonanza, store; upsurge,
increase; avalanche, spate, great quantity;
too many, mob, crowd; saturation, saturation point; excess, waste; too much,
exaggeration; overweight; burden, load,
overload, last straw, gravity; more than is
fair, main part; more than enough, bellyful, sufficiency; fat; disease.
superfluity, luxury, frills, luxury article;
overkill; bonus, cash crop, spare cash,
money to burn, extra; margin, overlap,
excess, surplus, balance, remainder;
excrescence, accessory, fifth wheel, parasite; padding, expletive; tautology;
redundancy, unemployment; activity; too
much of a good thing, glut; inflation;
surfeit, overdose.
Adj. redundant, too many, many; over-
much, excessive, immoderate, exorbitant;
overdone; full; flowing; tedious; replete;
bloated.
superfluous; needless, unnecessary, useless;
excessive, wasteful; luxury, luxurious;
surplus, extra; spare, to spare, additional;
dispensable, expendable.
Vb. superabound, riot, abound; run riot, be
fruitful; bristle with, meet one at every
turn, be many; overflow, ooze at every
pore, be complete; stream, flood, inundate, deluge, overwhelm, flow; engulf,
absorb; overstep; overlap, extend; soak,
saturate, drench; stuff, gorge, cram, fill;
congest, choke, suffocate; overdose, glut,
cloy, satiate, sicken, sate; pamper oneself,
be intemperate; do more than enough;
oversell; overstock; overdo, exaggerate;
overload; overcharge, surcharge; lavish,
be liberal; be lavish, make a splash, be
prodigal; crawl with, stink of, be rich.
be superfluous, be left; duplicate; take a
sledgehammer to crack a nut, waste
effort; be useless.
Adv. redundantly, too much, overly,
beyond measure.

633 Importance

N. importance, primacy, priority, precedence; supremacy; import, consequence,
significance, weight, gravity, solemnity;
substance, pith, moment; interest, consideration, concern, business; mark,
prominence, distinction, eminence,
repute; influence, prestige; size, magnitude; rank, high standing, degree; value,
merit, goodness; use, utility; stress,
emphasis.
important matter, vital concern; turning
point, crisis; breath of life; grave affair;
notable point, memorandum; big news,
news; great doings, exploit, deed; landmark, milestone; topic; red day.
chief thing, issue, crux, topic; bedrock, fact,
reality; essential, requirement; priority,
first choice, choice; gist, meaning; substance, essential part; highlight, main feature; best part, cream, salt, pick, elite;
keynote, cornerstone, mainstay, kingpin;
head, spearhead; heart, core, kernel,
nucleus, nub, centre; hub, pivot; cardinal
point, main part; chief hope, trump card,
main chance.
bigwig, personage, notable, personality,
heavyweight, somebody, person of repute;
local worthy; great man or woman, VIP,
brass hat; big gun, big shot, big noise, big
bug, big wheel, big chief; leading light,

master spirit, sage; kingpin, key person,
expert; first fiddle, star, lion, catch,
favourite; uncrowned king or queen,
head, chief, superior; superior person,
lord of creation; aristocrat; magnate,
mogul, mandarin; baron, tycoon, autocrat; top brass, top people, establishment,
authority; influence.
Adj. important, weighty, grave, solemn,
serious; pregnant, big; of consequence, of
consideration, of concern; considerable,
worth considering; earth-shaking,
momentous, critical, fateful, timely;
chief, capital, cardinal, staple, major,
main, paramount, supreme; crucial,
essential, material, relevant; central;
basic, fundamental, bedrock, radical; primary, prime, foremost, leading; overriding, uppermost, superior; worthwhile,
valuable; necessary, vital, indispensable,
irreplaceable, key; helpful, useful; significant, telling, trenchant, meaningful;
imperative, urgent; overdue, late; high-
level, summit, topmost; top-secret, latent;
high, grand, noble, great.
notable, of mark, egregious, remarkable;
memorable, signal, unforgettable; first-
rate, outstanding, superior; ranking, top-
flight, excellent; conspicuous, prominent,
eminent, distinguished, exalted, august,
noteworthy; imposing, commanding,
impressive; formidable, powerful; newsworthy, front-page; eventful, stirring,
breath-taking, earth-shaking, seismic.
Vb. be important, matter, be a consideration, bulk large, motivate; weigh, carry,
tell, count, cast a long shadow, influence;
import, signify, mean; concern, interest,
affect, be related; have priority, come
first, predominate; come before; be something, be somebody, command respect;
deserve notice, make a stir, create a sensation, cut a figure, cut a dash, attract
notice.
make important, give weight to; enhance,
highlight; stress, underline, labour; headline, splash, advertise; bring to notice,
proclaim; celebrate; magnify, enlarge;
make much of, exaggerate; lionize, honour, glorify, exalt, show respect; make a
fuss about, make a stir, make much ado;
value, esteem, make much of, think
everything of, respect; overestimate, overrate.
Adv. importantly, primarily; largely, above
all, to crown all.

634 Unimportance

N. unimportance; lack of substance;
nothingness; frivolity; red herring.
trifle, inessential, technicality; nothing, parish pump; accessory, secondary matter,
side-show; nothing to speak of, nothing
to boast of, nothing to worry about; tithe,
fraction, part; bagatelle, fig, damn, straw,
chaff, pin, button, feather, dust; cobweb,
gossamer; small item, tuppence, small
change, small beer; paltry sum, peanuts,
chickenfeed, fleabite; scratch; nothing to
it, easy thing; jest, joke, farce, amusement; peccadillo, venial sin; trivia, detail;
whit, jot, trickle, small quantity; cent,
brass farthing, small coin; nonsense,
fiddle-faddle, drivel, empty talk.
bauble, toy, rattle, plaything; gewgaw, bric-
a-brac, novelty, trinket; tinsel, trumpery,
frippery, trash; froth, foam, bubble.
nonentity, nobody; man of straw, insubstantial thing; figurehead; trifler; lightweight,
small beer; small fry, small game; banana

republic; other ranks, lower orders; second fiddle, *inferior*; underling, *servant*; pawn, stooge, puppet, *instrument*; poor relation, *poor person*; pipsqueak, whippersnapper, squirt, trash, *object of scorn*.

Adj. *unimportant*, immaterial, *insubstantial*; ineffectual, inconsequential; insignificant, *meaningless*; *irrelevant*; inessential, fringe; unnecessary, dispensable, expendable; small, petty, trifling, nugatory, flimsy, paltry, *inconsiderable*; negligible; weak, puny, powerless, *impotent*; measly, miserable, pitiful, pitiable, pathetic; mean, sorry, shabby, *poor*; obscure; beneath notice, beneath contempt; jumped-up, potty; low-level, of second rank, secondary, minor, subsidiary, peripheral, *inferior*.

trivial, trifling, fiddling, niggling; pettifogging, nit-picking, technical; footling, frivolous, puerile, childish, *foolish*; windy, airy, *insubstantial*; superficial, *shallow*; slight, *small*; lightweight, *light*; venial; parish-pump, small-time; one-horse, second-rate, potty, grotty, trumpery, trashy, tawdry, catchpenny, shoddy, *bad*; *cheap*; *useless*; toy, token, nominal; mediocre, nondescript, commonplace, ordinary, uneventful, *usual*.

Vb. *be unimportant*, signify little; *disregard*; *hold cheap*; humiliate.

Int. no matter! never mind! so what! too bad!

635 Utility

N. *utility*, use; efficacy, *ability*; sufficiency; *good policy*; readiness, *presence*; avail, help, good stead, *aid*; value, worth, merit, *goodness*; virtue, function, capacity, *power*; advantage, commodity; productivity; profit, mileage, *gain*; convenience, benefit, public utility, common weal, public good, *good*; utilitarianism; employment, *use*.

Adj. *useful*, of use, helpful, of service; sensible, practical, applied, functional; versatile, all-purpose, of all work; practicable, commodious, convenient, expedient, *advisable*; handy, ready, at hand, available; serviceable, disposable, adaptable, applicable; employable; good, valid, current; subsidiary, subservient, *instrumental*; able, competent, efficacious, effective, effectual, efficient, *powerful*; conducive; adequate, *sufficient*; pragmatic, utilitarian.

profitable, remunerative, *gainful*; prolific, fertile, *productive*; beneficial, advantageous, worthwhile, *good*; invaluable, priceless, *valuable*.

Vb. *be useful*, avail, prove helpful, be of value; have some use, perform a function; function, work, *operate*; perform, *do*; serve, answer, *suffice*; *be expedient*; help, advance, promote, aid; do service, *serve*; tend; benefit, profit, advantage, *do good*; bear fruit, *be fruitful*; pay, make a use.

find *useful*, employ, make use of, *use*; turn to good account; *gain*; *get better*.

Adv. *usefully*.

636 Inutility

N. *inutility*; vanity; inability; inconvenience; disservice, mischief, damage, detriment, *loss*.

lost *labour*, *failure*; waste of breath, waste of time, dead loss; lost trouble; blind alley, obstacle.

rubbish, good riddance, trash, stuff; waste, refuse, lumber, junk, scrap, litter; wastage, waste paper; chaff, bran; scraps; offal, carrion; dust, muck, debris, slag, clinker, dross, scum, *dirt*; peel, dead wood, stubble, weeds; old clothes; reject; midden, rubbish heap, slag heap, dump.

Adj. *useless*, purposeless, pointless; futile, *absurd*; impracticable; redundant, *superfluous*; expendable, dispensable, unnecessary; inapplicable, *inexpedient*; unqualified, inefficient, incompetent; unable, ineffective, feckless, ineffectual, *impotent*; inoperative, dud; invalid; unserviceable; effete, past work, obsolete, outmoded, *antiquated*; hopeless, vain.

profitless; wasteful; vain, abortive; thankless; fruitless, barren, sterile; idle, *lazy*; trashy, *bad*; dear at any price, *dear*.

Vb. *be useless*; *hinder*; *fail*; refuse to work; *be superfluous*.

make *useless*, disqualify, disarm, *disable*; castrate, emasculate; cripple, lame, impair; dismantle; sabotage, *obstruct*; undo, *disunite*; deface, *abrogate*; devalue, *cheapen*; pollute, contaminate, lay waste, *make sterile*.

waste *effort*; talk to a brick wall; *be superfluous*; flog a dead horse; tinker; *be absurd*.

Adv. *uselessly*.

637 Good policy

N. *good policy*; answer, *utility*; fitness, propriety; high time, opportunity, *occasion*; convenience, pragmatism, utilitarianism, opportunism; profit, advantage, *benefit*; facilities, *means*; an expedient.

Adj. *advisable*; better to, desirable, worthwhile, *beneficial*; acceptable; suitable, *fit*; fitting, seemly, proper, *right*; due; well-timed, auspicious, opportune, *timely*; prudent, politic, judicious, *wise*; expedient; advantageous, *useful*; convenient, workable, practical, pragmatic, practicable, negotiable; qualified; applicable, handy, effective, effectual.

Vb. *be expedient*, befit; help, *aid*; forward, advance, promote, *be useful*; answer; wash, work, do, serve, be better than nothing, *suffice*; *succeed*; fit, *accord*; profit, advantage, benefit, *do good*.

Adv. *expediently*, well.

638 Inexpedience

N. *inexpedience*; bad policy, counsel of despair, *error*; inaptitude; *wrong*; disqualification, disability, handicap, *obstacle*; inconvenience, disadvantage, detriment; doubtful advantage, mixed blessing; last resort, *necessity*.

Adj. *inexpedient*, undesirable; ill-advised, impolitic, imprudent, injudicious; inappropriate, malapropos, unseemly, *undue*; improper, objectionable, *wrong*; ineligible, inadmissible, unhappy, infelicitous, inept, inopportune, untimely, *ill-timed*; *insufficient*; inconvenient; hurtful, unhealthy, *insalubrious*; useless; untoward, *adverse*; awkward, clumsy, cumbersome, hulking, *unwieldy*.

Vb. *be inexpedient*, come amiss, won't do, won't wash; *be useless*; bother, discommode, incommode, put to inconvenience, *trouble*; disadvantage, hurt, *harm*; work against, *obstruct*; embarrass, be difficult.

639 Goodness

N. goodness, health; skill; quality, vintage; long suit, good points; merit, desert, title to fame; eminence, virtue, worth, value, price; perfection; quintessence, essence; benevolence; virtuous character, virtue.

elite, chosen few, chosen people; pick, prime, flower; cream, meritocracy; crack troops; top people, bigwig; top drawer, upper crust, aristocracy, upper class; choice bit, titbit, prime cut; plum, prize, trophy.

exceller, nonpareil, nonesuch; prodigy; genius; superman, wonder, prodigy; paragon; grand fellow, good person; treasure, favourite; jewel, pearl, ruby, diamond, gem; pearl of price, gold, masterpiece; best-seller, best ever, absolute end; winner, humdinger, wow, knockout, hit, a beauty; star, idol, favourite; best of its kind; top seed; champion, victor.

Adj. excellent, fine; exemplary; good, virtuous; above par, preferable, better, superior; very good, first-rate, alpha plus; prime, quality, fine, most desirable; God's own, superlative; rare, vintage, classic, perfect; choice, select, exquisite, chosen; exclusive, pure; worthy, meritorious; admirable, estimable, praiseworthy, creditable; famous, great; lovely, beautiful; glorious, splendid, magnificent, marvellous, wonderful, terrific, sensational, superb.

super, fantastic, way-out, fabulous, groovy; spot-on, bang-on; top-notch, top-flight (see best); lovely, glorious, gorgeous, heavenly, prodigious; smashing, stunning, topping, swell, great, grand, famous, capital, dandy; scrumptious, delicious, juicy, jammy.

best, optimum, A1, champion, tiptop, top-notch, nothing like it; first, first-rate, crack; a cut above, second to none, supreme; unequalled, unparalleled, unmatched, peerless, matchless, perfect; record; capital, cardinal, important.

valuable, of value, invaluable, inestimable, priceless, above price, costly, rich, of price; irreplaceable, unique, rare, precious, golden, worth a king's ransom; sterling, gilt-edged, sound, solid.

beneficial, wholesome, healthy, salutary, sound, salubrious; refreshing, worthwhile, advantageous, useful; favourable, kind, propitious, prosperous; harmless, inoffensive, innocuous, innocent.

not bad, tolerable, passable, respectable, standard, fair, satisfactory, sufficient; nice, decent, pretty good, all right; sound, fresh; unexceptionable; indifferent, middling, mediocre, ordinary, fifty-fifty, average, median.

Vb. be good, have quality; have merit, deserve well, deserve; qualify, pass, pass muster, suffice; challenge comparison, vie, rival, be equal; excel, transcend, be superior.

do good, have a good effect, edify; do a world of good, be salubrious; make a man of, make better; help, benefit; favour, prosper; do a favour, do a good turn, confer an obligation.

Adv. aright, well, rightly, properly, famously.

640 Badness

N. badness; demerit; low quality, low standard; flaw; poor make; taint, decay, corruption; confusion, disorder, disease; ill,

hurt, harm, injury, detriment, damage, mischief, evil; poison, blight, cancer, bane; pestilence, sickness, plague; centre of infection, plague spot, hotbed, infection; affair, scandal, slur; abomination, filth; sewer, sink; gall; sting, ache, pang, pain; anguish, suffering; cruelty, spite; depravity, vice; sin, guilt; bad influence, evil genius; evil spirit, demon; ill wind, evil star, misfortune; black magic, evil eye, hoodoo, jinx, sorcery; curse, malediction; bad character.

Adj. bad, arrant, vile, base, evil; gross, black; irredeemable; bad of its kind, poor, mean, grotty, measly, execrable; awful, inferior; shoddy, tacky, crummy, punk, pathetic, useless; faulty, imperfect; bad at, incompetent, inefficient, unskilled; clumsy, badly done; scruffy, dirty; foul, noisome, gone bad, rank, unsound, affected; corrupt; septic; irremediable, incurable; vicious, accursed, wicked; heinous, sinful, guilty; mean, shabby, dishonest; wrongful, wrong; sinister; shameful, scandalous, disgraceful, discreditable; sad, melancholy, lamentable, pitiable, pitiful, woeful, grievous, sore; intolerable; heavy, onerous, burdensome; too bad.

harmful, hurtful, prejudicial, inexpedient; deleterious, destructive; pernicious, fatal, deadly; costly, dear; ruinous, calamitous, adverse; noxious, malign, malignant, unhealthy, noisome, infectious, insalubrious; poisonous, toxic; sinister, ominous, dire, dreadful, baleful, accursed, evil; mischievous, malicious, malevolent; puckish, impish, unkind; bloody, bloodthirsty, inhuman, cruel; outrageous, rough, furious, violent; harsh, intolerant; monstrous, exorbitant.

not nice, obnoxious, nasty, beastly, horrid, horrible, terrible, gruesome, grim, ghastly, awful, dreadful, scruffy, disreputable; foul, rotten, lousy, putrid, stinking, sickening, revolting, nauseous; loathsome, abominable, hateful; vulgar, sordid, low, indecent, improper, gross, obscene, impure; shocking, reprehensible, monstrous, horrendous; miserable.

damnable, confounded, blinking; execrable, accursed, cursed, hellish, infernal, diabolic.

Vb. harm, do one a harm, do one a mischief, hurt; cost one dear, be dear; disagree with, make one ill; injure, damage, pollute, impair; corrupt, pervert; play havoc with, derange; be useless; worsen, make things worse; do evil, do wrong; molest, pain, torment; plague, vex, trouble; spite, be unkind, be malevolent.

ill-treat, maltreat, mishandle, abuse, misuse; burden; persecute, oppress, wrong, do wrong; distress, torment; outrage, violate, force, be violent; savage, maul, bite, scratch, tear, wound; stab, pierce; batter, bruise, buffet, strike; rack, crucify, torture; spite, be malevolent; crush, destroy.

Adv. badly, amiss, wrong, ill.

641 Perfection

N. perfection, finish, classic quality; nothing wrong with, mint condition; quintessence, essence; peak, pinnacle, summit; height or pitch of perfection, extreme, last word; masterpiece.

paragon, nonesuch, nonpareil, flower, a beauty, prince of; ideal, saint, classic, pattern, pattern of perfection, standard, norm, model, mirror, *prototype*; phoenix, rarity; superman, demigod, *prodigy*.

Adj. *perfect*, finished, brought to perfection; ripe; just right, ideal, impeccable, infallible; correct, irreproachable; immaculate; spotless, without blemish, without a stain; pure; *innocent*; sound; tight, watertight, seaworthy; whole, entire, one hundred per cent; complete, intact; beyond praise, *excellent*, consummate, *supreme*; brilliant, masterly, *skilful*; pattern, standard, model, classic, classical.

undamaged, with a whole skin, unscathed; without loss, whole, entire, *intact*; *healthy*.

Vb. *perfect*, consummate, bring to perfection; ripen, *mature*; correct, *rectify*; *crown*; complete, *carry through*.

Adv. *perfectly*, to perfection, to a turn.

642 Imperfection

N. *imperfection*; possibility of perfection; *error*; bit missing; lack, want, *requirement*; deficiency; failure, failing, weakness, *shortfall*; low standard, pass degree; inferior version, poor relation; second best, makeshift, *substitute*; *average*; loss of fitness, *fatigue*; *mixture*.

defect, fault, *error*; flaw, rift, leak, loophole, crack, *gap*; deficiency, *shortfall*; lack, foible, screw loose; weak point, soft spot, vulnerable point, tragic flaw; *weakness*; scratch, taint, stain, spot, smudge, *blemish*; drawback, catch, snag, *obstacle*.

Adj. *imperfect*, less than perfect; fallible; uneven, patchy; faulty; cracked; leaky; rickety, *flimsy*; unsound, *vulnerable*; marked; past its best; below par; stale; *unhealthy*; inadequate, deficient, wanting, lacking, *insufficient*; *incomplete*; partial, broken, *fragmentary*; undermanned, short-handed, below strength; perfunctory; overwrought, overdone; lame; undeveloped, raw, crude, scratch, *immature*; makeshift, provisional, secondary; second-rate, *inferior*; poor, negative, *bad*; ordinary, much of a muchness, so-so, middling, average, *median*; moderate; nothing to boast of; only passable, tolerable, bearable, better than nothing.

Vb. *be imperfect*, fall short of perfection, have a fault; *fall short*; lie open to criticism, dissatisfy; barely pass, scrape through; fail to gain approval, *incur blame*; be weak.

Adv. *imperfectly*, to a limited extent, barely, almost, all but.

643 Cleanness

N. *cleanness*, absence of dust, *purity*; shine, polish; cleanliness.

cleansing, clean, washing; sprinkling; airing; sanitation, drainage, sewerage, plumbing, *hygiene*; water closet, flush, *latrine*.

ablutions, washing; hygiene, douche, flush; wash; bathing; shampoo; dip, *plunge*; bath, tub; hipbath, bidet; washbasin, washstand; hot bath, sauna; shower, bathroom, washroom, public baths; plunge bath, swimming bath, swimming pool; wash, laundry; washboard, dolly; copper, boiler, washing machine, launderette.

cleanser; disinfectant, deodorant, soda, detergent, soap; water, shampoo; mouth wash, gargle; lotion, dentifrice, toothpaste; pumice stone; polish, blacking;

wax, varnish; whitewash, paint, *whiting*; *black pigment*; *purgative*; sewer, drainpipe, *drain*; waterworks.

cleaning utensil, broom, mop, sponge, swab, scourer; duster, whisk; brush, nailbrush, toothbrush, toothpick, dental floss; comb, hair brush, waste bin, dustbin; carpet sweeper, vacuum cleaner; doormat; squeegee; pipe cleaner; screen, sieve, riddle, strainer; filter, blotter; rake, hoe; sprinkler; dishwasher.

cleaning cloth, duster; dishcloth, tea towel; leather, chamois; flannel, facecloth, towel, handkerchief, tissue; bib, apron, napkin, serviette; place mat, tablemat, tablecloth; mat; cover, dustsheet, *coverlet*.

cleaner, refiner, distiller; dry cleaner, laundress, washerwoman; fuller; scrubber; dish-washer, scullion; charwoman, cleaner, help, home help; sweeper, dustman, refuse collector; lavatory attendant, sanitary engineer; chimneysweep; window cleaner; barber, hairdresser, beautician; picker; crow, vulture.

Adj. *clean*; snowy, *white*; clean, bright; cleanly, dainty, nice, *fastidious*; fresh; shorn; spruce, natty, neat, tidy, well-groomed, *orderly*; antiseptic, hygienic, sterile, *salubrious*; pure, refined, immaculate, spotless, stainless, *perfect*; blank; kosher, *edible*.

cleansing; disinfectant; hygienic, sanitary, purgative, purgatory; detergent.

Vb. *clean*, spring-clean; groom, valet, spruce, trim, *arrange*; wash, wipe, wash clean, dry, wring; sponge, mop, swab, scrub, scour; flush; sandblast, scrape, *rub*; launder, starch, iron; bleach, dry-clean; soap, lather, shampoo; bathe, dip, dunk, rinse, sluice, douche, shower, *drench*; dust, whisk, sweep, beat, vacuum; brush; comb, rake, buff, polish; shine, black, *make bright*; whitewash, *whiten*; erase, *obliterate*; strip, pick, pick clean, clear, make a clean sweep, *eject*.

purify, purge; expurgate; sublimate, elevate, *make better*; cleanse; purify oneself; ventilate, fan, fumigate; decontaminate, disinfect, chlorinate; refine, distil, clarify, rack, skim, scum; strain, filter, percolate, leach; sift, sieve, *eliminate*; flush, drain, *make flow*.

644 Uncleanness

N. *uncleanness*; *marsh*; squalor, *poverty*; *disorder*; stink, *stench*; pollution; corruption, taint, putrefaction; *infection*; abomination; dirty linen.

dirt, filth, stain, patch, blot; muck, mud, sludge, slime; quagmire, bog, *marsh*; night soil, dung, droppings, ordure, faeces, *excrement*; snot, mucus; dust, mote, *powder*; cobweb, grime, smut, smudge, soot, smoke; grounds, dregs, lees; sediment, sedimentation, deposit, precipitate, fur; scum, dross, froth; cinders, clinker, slag, *ash*; drainage, sewerage; cast skin, slough; scurf, dandruff; tartar, plaque; pus, matter; refuse, garbage, litter, *rubbish*; rot, rust, mildew, mould, fungus, *decay*; carrion, offal; vermin, flea, nit, *insect*.

swill, hogwash; bilge; sewage, drainage; wallow, slough.

latrine, privy, bog, loo; closet, long drop, water closet, WC; cloakroom, powder room, washroom, lavatory, toilet; urinal, public convenience, comfort station; commode, bedpan, chamber pot, potty, jerry.

sink, sink of corruption; kitchen sink; cesspit, sump, septic tank; gutter, sewer, main, cloaca, *drain*; midden, rubbish heap, dustbin, *vessel*; coalhole, *cellar*; pigsty, den; slum, tenement, *housing*; shambles, *slaughterhouse*; *infection*; spittoon.

dirty *person*, sloven, slattern, drab, *slut*; litter lout; street arab; beast, pig.

Adj. *unclean*, unholy, *profane*; smutty, obscene, corrupt, *impure*; coarse; septic, poisonous, *toxic*; *infectious*; sordid, squalid, insanitary, *insalubrious*; foul, offensive, nasty, grotty; abominable; noisome, nauseous, stinking, malodorous, *fetid*; beastly; grubby, scruffy, lousy; high; flyblown, carrion.

dirty; dusty, smoky; thick with dust; unkempt, sleazy, bedraggled; black, dingy; greasy; messy, mucky, muddy, slimy, *marshy*; thick, turbid; musty, fusty; mouldy, rotten, *dilapidated*.

Vb. *be unclean*, get dirty, collect dust, clog; rust, mildew, moulder, fester, rot, go bad, addle, *decompose*; grow rank, smell, *stink*; wallow.

make unclean, foul; dirty, soil; grime, cover with dust; stain, blot, sully, tarnish; make a mess; daub, smirch, besmirch, smut, smudge, blur, smoke; spot, patch; streak, smear, grease; cake, clog, muddy, rile; spatter, splash, slobber, slaver, *moisten*; poison, taint, infect, corrupt, pollute, contaminate, *impair*; defile, profane, desecrate.

645 Health

N. *health*, good constitution, *vitality*; fitness, condition, pink of condition; bloom, ruddy complexion; *well-being*, *euphoria*; whole skin; *goodness*; long life, longevity, ripe old age, *age*; hygiene, healthy state, clean bill of health.

Adj. *healthy*, healthful, wholesome, hygienic, sanitary, *salubrious*; fresh, blooming, ruddy, rosy, florid; lusty, bouncing, strapping, hale, hearty, sound, fit, well, fine, bonny, *vigorous*, of good constitution, never ill, robust, hardy, strong, vigorous, *stalwart*; feeling fine, feeling great; A1; a picture of health, feeling good; pretty well.

Vb. *be healthy*, look after oneself; feel fine, bloom, thrive, flourish, enjoy good health; have never felt better; wear well, look young; keep fit, keep well; have a clean bill of health.

get healthy, recuperate, be well again, return to health; mend, convalesce, take a fresh lease of life, become a new man or woman, *revive*.

646 Ill health. Disease

N. *ill health*, delicacy, weak constitution; *weakness*; loss of condition; chronic complaint, allergy, hay fever, catarrh; chronic ill health, hypochondria; nerves.

illness, loss of health; affliction, disability, handicap, *weakness*; sickness, ailment, complaint, complication; condition, history of; bout of sickness, visitation; attack, spasm, stroke, seizure, apoplexy, fit; shock; nausea; vertigo; headache, migraine, *pain*; sign of illness, symptom; temperature, fever, shivers, shakes, *spasm*; hypothermia; delirium, *frenzy*; breakdown, collapse; *insensibility*; coma;

terminal disease, fatal illness, *decease*; sickbed, deathbed.

disease, malady, distemper, disorder; epidemic disease, infectious disease; alcoholism, drug addiction; deficiency disease, malnutrition, kwashiorkor, pellagra, rickets, scurvy; atrophy; traumatic disease, trauma; organic disease, epilepsy; endocrine disease, diabetes; cancer; respiratory disease; virus disease; febrile disease; dropsy; brain disease.

plague, pest, scourge, *bane*; pestilence; infection, contagion; epidemic, pandemic; Black Death.

infection, contagion, bug; miasma, pollution, taint; gangrene, sepsis, *poison*; plague spot, hotbed; vector, carrier, host; parasite, worm, *bane*; virus, bacteria; germ; botulism; gastroenteritis, infectious disease, cold, influenza, flu; diphtheria, pneumonia; tuberculosis; measles, German measles, rubella; mumps; smallpox; scarlet fever; fever, malaria (see *tropical disease*); typhus, jail fever; typhoid; polio; meningitis; sleepy sickness, tetanus, lockjaw; rabies, hydrophobia.

tropical disease, fever, malaria; cholera; yellow fever; dumdum fever; leprosy; kwashiorkor.

digestive disorders, indigestion, dyspepsia; nausea; colic, gripes; stomach ache, guts ache; stomach upset, collywobbles; lurgy; gastroenteritis; dysentery, cholera; typhoid; botulism; flatulence, wind; heartburn; hiatus hernia; ulcer, enteritis; peritonitis; appendicitis; jaundice; hepatitis, cirrhosis, cystitis, kidney failure; piles; constipation.

respiratory disease, cough, cold, sore throat; catarrh; adenoids; laryngitis, croup; bronchitis; emphysema, asthma; pleurisy, pneumonia; pneumoconiosis; silicosis; diphtheria; lung cancer; pulmonary tuberculosis, consumption.

cardiovascular disease; gallop rhythm; murmur, valve lesion, valvular lesion; heart condition, bad heart, heart trouble; congenital heart disease; rheumatic heart disease, heart failure; coronary thrombosis, coronary; cerebral thrombosis, brain haemorrhage, stroke; blood pressure; low blood pressure; vascular disease; arteriosclerosis; thrombosis, clot, embolism.

blood disease, anaemia, leukaemia; haemophilia; bleeding, haemorrhage.

cancer, growth; tumour; rodent ulcer.

skin disease, skin lesion; mange; leprosy; prickly heat; herpes, shingles; dermatitis; eczema; ringworm; itch; thrush; rash, eruption; acne; pustule, pimple; cyst; blister, wart, verruca, *swelling*; mole, freckle, birthmark, pockmark, *blemish*.

venereal disease; syphilis; venereal ulcer.

ulcer, gathering; lesion, *wound*; scald, burn; sore, boil, abscess, fistula; cyst; chilblain; corn, *swelling*; gangrene, rot, *decay*; discharge, pus, matter.

rheumatism, rheumatics; rheumatic fever; muscular rheumatism; frozen shoulder; tennis elbow; arthritis, gout, *pang*; lumbago, sciatica.

nervous disorders, nervous breakdown; brain tumour; brain haemorrhage; stroke, seizure, paraplegia; atrophy; *insensibility*; palsy; involuntary movements, tremor, tic, *spasm*; epilepsy; polio; multiple sclerosis.

animal disease, distemper, swine fever; myxomatosis; anthrax; liver fluke; thrush; fowl pest; hard pad; mange; rabies.

...ck *person*, sufferer; patient, case, mental case, *madman*; invalid, martyr to ill health; consumptive; addict, alcoholic; spastic, paralytic; crock, cripple, *weakling*; sick list.

...athology, diagnosis, prognosis; bacteriology, *therapy*.

adj. *unhealthy*, unsound, sickly; infirm, decrepit, *weak*; delicate, of weak constitution, liable to illness, always ill; mangy; peaked; sallow, pale, anaemic, *colourless*; *green*; jaundiced, *yellow*; invalid.

...ick, ill, unwell, indisposed, below par; queasy, poorly, seedy, squeamish, groggy, grotty, queer; feverish; bedridden; prostrate; *insensible*; critical, serious, comfortable; chronic, incurable, inoperable; mortally ill, moribund, *dying*; peaky.

...iseased, pathological; affected; rotten; morbid; psychosomatic, *mental*; infectious, contagious; poisonous, purulent, *toxic*; consumptive; anaemic; bloodless; rheumatic, rheumatoid; rickety, paralytic, spastic; venereal; swollen; bronchial, throaty, full of cold; febrile, fevered, feverish; sore, tender; inflamed; spotty; mangy.

...b. *be ill*, enjoy poor health; ail, suffer, undergo treatment; have a complaint or an affliction, be a chronic invalid; complain of; feel sick, *vomit*; sicken, fall sick, fall ill; catch, catch an infection, catch a bug, contract a disease; be stricken; have a stroke, collapse; languish, pine, peak, droop; flag, flag, lose strength, get worse, sink, *deteriorate*; grow weak, *be weak*.

Adv. *morbidly*.

647 Salubrity

N. *salubrity*, state of health; well-being, *health*; whole food, health food; fresh air, ozone, *air*; sunshine, outdoors; benign climate, health resort.

...ygiene, sanitation, cleanliness; preventive medicine, prophylaxis, *prophylactic*; quarantine, *protection*; sanatorium, spa, *hospital*; therapy; keeping fit, constitutional, *exercise*.

...nitarian, sanitary inspector, public health inspector; sanitary engineer; medical officer.

adj. *salubrious*, healthful, healthy, wholesome; pure, fresh, *clean*; tonic, bracing, refreshing, *restorative*; hygienic, sanitary, sterile, antiseptic; prophylactic, protective, *remedial*; salutary, *beneficial*; nutritious; harmless, benign; innocuous; immune, *invulnerable*.

...b. *be salubrious*, agree with one; have a good climate; prevent disease; keep fit, *be healthy*.

...nitate, disinfect, boil, chlorinate; inoculate, vaccinate, *quarantine*, isolate, *seclude*; ventilate, *aerate*; *purify*; cleanse, *clean*; drain, *dry*; conserve, *preserve*.

Adv. *healthily*.

648 Insalubrity

N. *insalubrity*; lack of hygiene, lack of sanitation; unhealthy conditions; slum; bad air, bad climate; smoke haze, smog; sewer, *sink*; infectious person, carrier, vector; germ, microbe, *microorganism*; miasma, contagion, *infection*; pollution, radioactivity, fallout; *bane*.

Adj. *insalubrious*, unhealthy; insanitary, *unclean*; bad, nasty, noxious; *marshy*, stagnant, foul, inedible; indigestible;

unsound, stale, gone bad; airless; stuffy.

infectious; contagious, catching, taking, communicable; pestilent; epidemic, pandemic, endemic; sporadic; *dirty*.

toxic, poisonous; venomous; gathering, septic, pussy, purulent; lethal, *deadly*.

Adv. *unwholesomely*.

649 Improvement

N. *improvement*; uplift; good influence, *influence*; transfiguration, transformation; new leaf; revival, recovery, *restoration*; evolution, development; advance, onward march, march of time, progress, *progression*; furtherance, advancement, promotion; kick upstairs, rise, raise, lift, jump, *ascent*; upswing, *elevation*; *increase*.

amendment, *repair*; *arrangement*; reformation, reform, Borstal, *school*; rectification; red ink, blue pencil; *edition*; revise, proof; review; *sequel*; polish.

civilization; culture; black culture; civility, refinement, *good taste*; training, proper upbringing, *education*; cultivation, polish, *culture*; exercise.

reformism, idealism; socialism; radicalism; extremism, revolution, sedition; social engineering, *sociology*.

reformer, restorer; editor; progressive; Fabian, *moderate*; liberal, radical, revolutionary, *agitator*; socialist, Red; New Dealer; idealist, Utopian, *visionary*; social worker, philanthropist.

Adj. *improved*; *superior*; better; *wise*.

improving, reformatory, remedial, *restorative*; progressive, radical; perfectionist, Utopian; perfectionist, *fastidious*.

Vb. *get better*, improve, mend; rally, revive, recover; make progress, make headway, advance, develop, evolve, *progress*; mellow, ripen, *mature*; bear fruit, *be fruitful*; rise, *ascend*; graduate, *succeed*; better oneself, *prosper*; reform, go straight, be penitent; improve oneself, *learn*; take advantage of.

make better, better, improve, ameliorate, reform; polish, elaborate, enrich, enhance; do one a power of good, *do good*; transfigure, *transform*; make, have a good influence, leaven, *influence*; uplift, regenerate; refine, elevate, sublimate, *purify*; teach manners; mend, *repair*, restore, cure; recruit, revive, *refresh*; soften, mitigate, palliate, *moderate*; forward, advance, upgrade, promote; foster, encourage, bring to fruition, *mature*; *use*; develop, reclaim; till, weed, dress, water, *cultivate*; tidy, *arrange*; *clean*; renovate, refurbish, renew, give a face lift; *beautify*; embellish, adorn, ornament, *decorate*.

rectify, put right, set right, straighten, *adjust*; mend, patch, *repair*; correct, proof-read; revise, edit, amend, emend; rewrite, remould, remodel, recreate, reform; streamline; review, reconsider, think again, think better of.

650 Deterioration

N. *deterioration*; reversion to type, throwback, *heredity*; decline, ebb, *decrease*; twilight; slump, depression, recession; *poverty*; exhaustion, *waste*; corruption, perversion, prostitution, loss of morale, decadence, depravity; downward course, primrose path, *descent*; setback, *relapse*; bad ending, tragedy, *misfortune*.

dilapidation, collapse, ruination, *destruction*; lack of maintenance, disrepair, neglect; slum, back street, *poverty*; ravages of time, erosion, rust, rot, canker, corruption, putrefaction, *decay*; mildew, blight; *old age*; atrophy, *disease*; ruin, wreck.

impairment, *misuse*: detriment, damage, waste, *loss*; patina; pollution; *infection*; mixture; assault, insult, outrage, *attack*; ruination, *destruction*; injury, mischief, harm, *havoc*; *weakness*; sprain, strain; sabotage.

wound, injury, trauma; open wound, bloody nose; sore, *ulcer*; lesion; cut, gash, abrasion, nick, snick, scratch; stab, prick, jab, puncture, *perforation*; bruise, bump, black eye, thick ear, *swelling*; burn, scald; rupture, hernia; broken head, fracture; scar, mark, *blemish*.

Adj. *deteriorated*; hurt, effete, *useless*; stale, gone bad, rotten, *bad*; flat, *tasteless*; tired; worse, far gone; failing, senile, senescent; at low ebb; backward; lapsed, recidivist; degenerate, corrupt, *vicious*; *poor*.

dilapidated; broken, cracked; weather-beaten; decrepit, ruinous, ramshackle, shaky, rickety, tumbledown, run-down; worn, shabby, tatty, dingy; worn to a shadow, *useless*; seedy, *poor*; rusty, rotten, moth-eaten, dog-eared.

Vb. *deteriorate*, worsen, get worse; slip, slide, go downhill; *relapse*; slump, decline, wane, ebb, sink, fail, *decrease*; slip back, *regress*; lapse; degenerate, let oneself go, ruin oneself, run to seed; *be wicked*; disintegrate, fall apart, collapse, fall, totter, droop, stoop, *tumble*; contract, shrink, *become small*; age, *grow old*; fade, wither, wilt, shrivel, perish, crumble, moulder, mildew, grow moss; weather, rust, rot, decay, *decompose*; spoil, stale, lose its taste, lose its flavour, go flat, go sour, turn; go bad, smell, *stink*; corrupt, putrefy, rankle, fester, suppurate, gangrene, *decompose*; sicken, *be ill*; do worse, make things worse, *aggravate*.

pervert, deform, warp, twist, *distort*; abuse, prostitute, *misuse*, deprave, *debauch*; vitiate, corrupt, *make wicked*; lower, degrade, debase, *abase*; *transform*; brainwash.

impair, damage, hurt, injure, *harm*; jumble, play havoc with, *derange*; dismantle; spoil, maul, mar, botch, *be clumsy*; touch, tinker, meddle with, *meddle*; worsen, deteriorate, exacerbate, embitter, *aggravate*; kill with kindness, *be foolish*; degrade, lower, coarsen; devalue, debase, *cheapen*; blacken, blot, spot, stain, *make ugly*; scar, mark, wrinkle, *blemish*; deface, disfigure, deform, warp, *distort*; corrupt, vitiate (see *pervert*); mutilate, maim, lame, cripple, *disable*; scotch, pinion, cramp, hamper, *hinder*; castrate; expurgate, eviscerate; curtail, dock, *shorten*; cream, skim; adulterate, alloy, *mix*; subvert, shake, sap, mine, undermine, *weaken*; honeycomb, bore, gnaw, fret, erode, corrode, rust, rot, mildew, *decompose*; blight, blast; ravage, waste, scorch, overrun, *lay waste*; wreck, ruin, *destroy*; crumble, fray; exhaust, consume, *waste*; infect, contaminate, poison, ulcerate; taint, canker, foul, pollute, *make unclean*; defile, desecrate, profane.

wound, scotch, draw blood, tear, rend, lacerate, mangle, rip, *disunite*; maul, savage, *be violent*; bite, scratch, claw; gash, hack,

incise, *cut*; scarify, score, *groove*; nick, notch; sting, prick, pink, stab, gore, run through, *pierce*; bruise, contuse, buffet, *strike*; crush, grind; chafe, *rub*; smash, *break*; graze, pepper, wing.

651 Restoration

N. *restoration, restitution*; redress, amends, reparation, reparations; finding again; recovery, *taking*; recall, replacement; rescue, salvage, redemption, ransom, salvation, *deliverance*; reformation; *amendment*; reaction; return to normal, reinforcement; *provision*.

repair, reparation; rectification; restoration; making like new; mending, darning, clout, patch, darn, reinforcement; new look, face-lift.

revival, recovery, *refreshment*; resurgence, recovery, rally, comeback; fresh spurt, new energy; economic recovery, economic miracle, boom; artificial respiration; second youth, Indian summer; face-lift, new look; rebirth, renaissance, new birth; new life, resurrection; resurrection day, *future state*.

recuperation, recovery, cure; mending; restoration to health, *remedy*; moderation, *relief*; psychological cure, catharsis.

mender, painter, decorator, rectifier, restorer; cobbler; tinker, plumber, handyman; *doctor*; psychiatrist.

Adj. *restored*; like new; born again; reborn, healthy; better; back to normal, oneself again; operable; found.

restorative, recuperative, medicinal, remedial.

Vb. *be restored*, recover, come round, come to, revive, rally; pull through, get well, convalesce, recuperate; *get better*; survive, live through; live again, resurrect, come to life again; reappear, make a comeback; be oneself again, bounce back; return to normal; resume, start again, begin; look like new.

restore, give back; make amends, atone; put back, replace; recall, rehabilitate; reconstitute, reconstruct, reform, *make better*; valet, *clean*; renovate, renew, rebuild, remake, redo; overhaul, service, refit, refurbish, make like new; make whole, reafforest, reclaim; recycle; reinforce, *strengthen*; *replenish*; rally, bring together; redeem, ransom, rescue, salvage, *deliver*; release, *liberate*.

revive, resuscitate, regenerate, recall to life, resurrect, reanimate; rejuvenate; recruit, *refresh*.

cure, heal, make well, cure of, break of; nurse, medicate, *doctor*; bandage; nurse through, work a cure, restore to health (set a bone); close, knit together; right itself, put itself right, work its own cure.

repair, amend, emend, right, set to rights, put right, remedy, *rectify*; overhaul, mend, fix; cobble, heel; retread, recover; thatch, *cover*; line; darn, patch; stop, fill (teeth); retouch, revamp; seal, stop a gap, plug a hole, *staunch*; caulk, *close*; splice, bind, *tie*; piece together, refit, *join*; give a face-lift, refurbish, recondition, renovate, renew, remodel, reform.

retrieve, get back, recover, regain, recapture; find again, reclaim, claim back; compensate oneself, *recoup*.

652 Relapse

N. *relapse*, lapse; throwback, return, *reversion*; fall; recurrence, fresh outbreak.

b. *relapse*, slip back, throw back, return, retrogress, *regress*; degenerate, *deteriorate*; backslide, lapse; have a relapse, suffer a recurrence.

653 Remedy

N. *remedy*, succour, help, *aid*; *moderator*; remedial measure, *amendment*; redress, amends, *restitution*; cure; medicinal value; sovereign remedy, specific, answer, solution; prescription, recipe, formula, nostrum; quack remedy, patent medicine; sovereign remedy, panacea, cure-all; elixir.

medicine, pharmacopoeia; vegetable remedy, herb, simple; balm, balsam; medication, medicament, patent medicine, proprietary drug, placebo; pill, tablet, tabloid, capsule, lozenge; draught, potion, elixir; infusion; dose, drench; drops, drip; injection, jab, shot; preparation, mixture, powder, linctus; plaster (see *surgical dressing*); spray, inhaler; medicine chest, medicine bottle.

prophylactic, preventive; sanitation, sanitary precaution, quarantine, *hygiene*; prophylaxis; vaccine, TAB; quinine; antiseptic, disinfectant, germicide, insecticide, *poison*; dentifrice, toothpaste, tooth powder, *cleanser*; mouthwash, gargle; fluoride.

antidote; quinine; antigen, antibody; antibiotic; sedative; antacid, analgesic, painkiller. See *drug*.

purgative, purge, laxative; castor oil; diuretic; emetic; digestive, dill water; douche, enema.

tonic, restorative; cordial, tonic water, tonic wine; *stimulant*; caffeine, nicotine, alcohol; spirits; infusion, herb tea; vitamin tablet, iron pill.

drug, synthetic drug, antibiotic; penicillin; streptomycin, insulin; hormone, steroid, progesterone; contraceptive pill, *contraception*; analgesic, aspirin, codeine, *anaesthetic*; sedative; barbiturate, *soporific*; narcotic, dope, morphine, opium, cocaine; stimulant; lotus.

balm, balsam, oil, emollient, *moderator*; salve, ointment; cream, *cosmetic*; lanolin, liniment, embrocation; lotion, wash; eyewash; placebo.

surgical dressing, dressing, lint, gauze; swab; bandage, roller, sling, splint, cast; tourniquet; fingerstall; patch; application, plaster, poultice, compress; tampon, tent, roll; pessary, suppository; traumatic.

medical art, therapeutics; medical advice, practice; nature cure; medicine, acupuncture; radiography; diagnosis, prognosis, *pathology*; Christian Science; gynaecology, *obstetrics*; geriatrics, paediatrics; ophthalmology, neurology, dermatology, ear; bacteriology, microbiology, virology; pharmacology; veterinary medicine.

surgery, general surgery, plastic surgery, prosthesis; operation, op; bleeding, blood-letting; transplant; mastectomy, vasectomy; drawing, filling; massage, chiropody, pedicure, manicure; electrolysis.

therapy, therapeutics, medical care; treatment, nursing, bedside manner; first aid; course, cure; regimen, diet; osteopathy;

hormone therapy; chemotherapy; physiotherapy; heat treatment; shock treatment; mental treatment, clinical psychology; child psychology; psychotherapy, psychiatry, psychoanalysis, *psychology*; group therapy, acupuncture; intravenous injection.

hospital, infirmary, general hospital, mental hospital, *lunatic asylum*; dispensary, clinic, nursing home, hospice; leper asylum, leper colony; hospital ship, hospital train; stretcher, ambulance; ward, sick bay, sickroom, sickbed; hospital bed, tent, iron lung; respirator, incubator, intensive care unit; x-ray machine, scanner; dressing station; consulting room, surgery, clinic, community health centre; sanatorium, spa; pump room, baths; solarium, sun lamp.

doctor, physician; leech, quack, charlatan, veterinary surgeon, vet; herbalist, herb doctor; witchdoctor, medicine man, *sorcerer*; medic, medical student; houseman, intern, registrar; medical practitioner, GP; locum; surgeon; medical officer, sanitary inspector; medical adviser, consultant, specialist; psychiatrist; anaesthetist; midwife; radiotherapist; masseur; optician, oculist; dentist, dental surgeon; medical profession, National Health Service; Red Cross.

druggist, apothecary, chemist, pharmacist; pharmacy.

nurse, sister, matron; SEN; SRN; special nurse, district nurse, health visitor; nursing auxiliary, ward orderly, dresser, medical attendant, stretcher-bearer; almoner, hospital social worker, *sociology*; lady with a lamp.

Adj. *remedial*, restorative; helpful, *beneficial*; therapeutic, medicinal, hygienic, *salubrious*; specific, sovereign; emollient, analgesic, narcotic, anaesthetic, *insensible*; peptic, digestive, emetic, laxative; prophylactic, disinfectant, antiseptic; tonic.

medical, pathological; herbal; surgical; traumatic; clinical; operable.

Vb. *remedy*, fix, put right, correct, *restore*; succour, help, *aid*; apply a remedy, treat, heal, work a cure, *cure*; palliate, soothe, *relieve*.

doctor, practise, have a practice; treat, prescribe, advise; attend, *minister to*; tend, nurse; give first aid, *revive*; put to bed; medicate, drench, dose, purge; inject, give a jab; dress, bind, swathe, bandage; apply a tourniquet, *staunch*; poultice, plaster, foment; set; drug, dope; operate, cut open, amputate; bleed; transfuse; massage, rub, manipulate; draw, extract, pull, stop, fill, crown; pedicure, manicure; vaccinate, inoculate; disinfect.

654 Bane

N. *bane*, cause of injury, malevolent influence; curse, plague, pest, scourge, ruin, *evil*; malady, *disease*; weakness, bad habit, besetting sin, *vice*; hell, cup, visitation, affliction, *adversity*; woe, funeral, *sorrow*; cross, trial; bore, *tedium*; bugbear; burden, white elephant; stress, strain, perpetual worry, constant anxiety, torment, *worry*; running sore, *ulcer*; acid, gall; emetic; bite, sting, poison dart, fang, briar, nettle, *sharp point*; source of trouble, *pitfall*; viper, adder, serpent, *reptile*; snake; parasite, leech, tapeworm, insect, *creepy-crawly*; mosquito, wasp, *noxious animal*; locust, *destroyer*; holy terror, *tyrant.*

blight, rot, mildew, mould, rust, fungus; moth, woodworm, canker, cancer, *decay;* visitation, *plague;* frost, nip, cold; drought.

poison; bad food, bad water, pollution; bacteria, salmonella, germ, virus, *infection;* carcinogen; chemical weapon, venom, toxin; deadly poison, germicide, insecticide, pesticide; fungicide, DDT; acid; hemlock, arsenic, strychnine, cyanide; nicotine, *tobacco;* poison gas, mustard gas; choke damp; foul air, miasma, sewer gas; atmospheric pollution, smog; lead pollution; uranium, plutonium; radioactivity, mushroom, fallout, strontium 90, *radiation;* dope, opium, heroin, *drug; alcoholism;* lethal dose, overdose.

poisonous *plant,* hemlock, deadly nightshade, henbane.

poisoning, *homicide; infection;* botulism; germ warfare, *warfare.*

Adj. baneful, pestilent, noisome; virulent, poisonous, venomous, *toxic;* cursed, accursed, *evil.*

655 Safety

N. *safety,* security; *multitude;* secure position, permanent post, safe job; social security, welfare state, *sociology;* safe distance, wide berth; all clear, danger past; guarantee, warrant, *certainty;* sense of security, assurance, confidence, *courage;* safety valve, *means of escape;* close shave, narrow escape, *escape;* rescue, *deliverance.*

protection, conservation, *preservation;* insurance, surety, *caution;* patronage, auspices, aegis, fatherly eye, *aid;* protectorate, tutelage, custody, *restraint;* safekeeping, keeping, charge, grasp, grip, embrace; ward, *surveillance;* safeguard, precaution, preventive measure, *defence;* sanitary precaution, prophylaxis, quarantine, *hygiene;* segregation; cushion, buffer; screen, cover; umbrella, *shelter;* means of protection, deterrent, *weapon;* safe-conduct, passport, pass, *permit;* escort, convoy, guard, *armed force;* defence, bastion, bulwark, tower of strength; haven, sanctuary, asylum, *refuge;* anchor, *safeguard;* moat, ditch, palisade, stockade, *fence;* shield, breastplate, panoply, armour plate, *armour.*

protector, guardian, tutor; guardian angel, patron saint, liege lord, *patron;* preserver, shepherd; bodyguard, lifeguard, strong-arm man, bouncer; vigilante; custodian, curator, warden; warder, guard, coast-guard; duenna, governess, nanny, *keeper;* lookout, watch, watchman; firewatcher, fire fighter, fireman; policeman or -woman, police constable, police sergeant, sheriff; copper, cop, *police;* private eye, *detective;* sentry, garrison, security forces; watchdog, guard dog, *dog; surveillance.*

Adj. safe, without risk; assured, secure, sure, snug; with a whole skin, intact; insured; hygienic, *salubrious;* at anchor; above water; clear; sheltered; held; reliable, *trustworthy;* benign, harmless, *good.*

invulnerable, immune, impregnable, sacrosanct; defensible, *strong;* proof, fool-proof; weatherproof, waterproof, fire-proof; bulletproof; snug, tight, seaworthy, airworthy; armoured.

tutelary, guardian, protective; *disinterested;* watchful, *vigilant;* fail-safe; doubly sure;

keeping; antiseptic, disinfectant, *salubri- ous.*

Vb. *be safe,* find safety, come through, *escape;* keep a whole skin, have nine lives, be snug, nestle, stay at home; *lurk;* keep a safe distance, give a wide berth, *avoid.*

safeguard, keep safe, guard, protect; spare, *show mercy; defend;* shield; champion; grant asylum, afford sanctuary; keep, conserve, *preserve;* treasure, hoard, store, *imprison;* ward, mother; nurse, foster, cherish; have charge of, take charge of, *look after;* hide, *conceal;* cushion, cocoon, *support;* insulate, earth; cover, shroud, cloak, shade, *screen;* garage, house, shelter; ensconce, enfold, embrace, *enclose;* make safe, secure, fortify, *strengthen;* fence round, *circumscribe;* arm, armour; shepherd, convoy, escort; flank, support; garrison, mount guard; inoculate, vaccinate; chlorinate, disinfect; warrant, guarantee, *make certain;* keep order, police, patrol.

seek safety, play safe, *be cautious;* lie low, *lurk; escape; move fast;* live to fight another day, think better of it; shorten sail, take refuge, *seek refuge.*

Adv. *under shelter;* with impunity.

656 Danger

N. *danger,* peril; shadow of death; parlous state, forlorn hope, *predicament;* emergency, *crisis;* jeopardy, risk, hazard, ticklish business; black spot, snag, *pitfall;* trap, ambush; daring, venture, *undertaking;* slippery slope, road to ruin; sword of Damocles, menace, *threat;* sense of danger, apprehension; rocks ahead, *danger signal;* narrow escape, close shave, near thing, *escape.*

vulnerability, danger of; security risk; exposure; instability; easy target, sitting duck; vulnerable point, *weakness;* tender spot; human error.

Adj. *dangerous,* perilous, fraught with danger, treacherous; unfrequented; hazardous, venturesome, dicey, dodgy, chancy, *speculative;* serious, ugly, nasty, critical; at stake; ominous, foreboding; toxic, poisonous; unhealthy, infectious, *insalubrious;* inflammable, explosive.

unsafe, slippery, treacherous; insecure, unsound, precarious, dicky; top-heavy, *unstable;* shaky, ramshackle, rickety, frail, dilapidated; crazy, *weak;* leaky, waterlogged; critical, ticklish.

vulnerable, *liable;* open to, wide open, naked, bare; helpless; unguarded.

endangered, facing death; at bay.

Vb. *be in danger, be liable;* totter, slip, slide, *tumble;* get lost, *stray.*

face danger, face death, dice with death; *be courageous;* expose oneself, lay oneself open to; *defy;* face heavy odds; challenge fate, tempt providence, court disaster; *be rash;* venture, dare, risk it, take a chance, *gamble.*

endanger, spell danger, face with, imperil; hazard, compromise; risk, stake, venture, *gamble;* threaten danger, loom, forebode, bode ill, menace, *threaten;* run one hard, overtake, *outdo.*

657 Refuge. Safeguard

N. *refuge,* sanctuary, asylum, retreat, safe place; traffic island, zebra crossing; last resort, bolthole, foxhole, burrow; trench;

dugout, earth, hole, den, lair, covert, nest, lap, hearth, *home*; defensible space, privacy; sanctum, *chamber*; cloister, cell, hermitage, ivory tower, *retreat*; temple, ark, citadel; wall, rampart, bulwark, bastion; stronghold, fastness, *fort*; keep, ward; secret place; dungeon, *prison*; rock, pillar, tower, tower of strength, mainstay, *prop*.

shelter, cover, roof; covert, earth, hole; fold; lee; lee wall, windbreak, hedge, *fence*; camp, stockade; shield, wing; fireguard, fender, bumper, mudguard, windscreen, *screen*; umbrella; sun helmet, sunglasses, goggles; protective clothing, overalls; haven, harbour, port; anchorage, quay, jetty, marina, dock, *stable*; *lunatic asylum*; halfway house, sheltered housing; almshouse, charitable institution, hospice; Welfare State.

safeguard, means of safety, protection, *safety*; *hindrance*; crush barrier, guardrail, railing; mail, *armour*; arms, deterrent, *weapon*; respirator, gas mask; safety device, safety catch, safety valve; lightning conductor, fuse, earth; crash helmet; parachute; safety net; lifeboat, rubber dinghy, life raft, *raft*; life belt, life jacket, lifeline, breeches buoy; rope, plank, *means of escape*; anchor, grapnel, drogue; lead, brake, *fetter*; bolt, bar, lock, key, *stopper*; ballast, *offset*; mole, breakwater, sea wall, embankment; lighthouse, lightship, *sailing aid*; jury mast, *extra*.

Vb. seek refuge, take refuge, *seek safety*; turn to; claim sanctuary, seek political asylum; make port, reach safety, reach home, find shelter.

658 Pitfall: source of danger

N. pitfall, pit, catch; snag, *obstacle*; booby trap, firetrap, minefield, *trap*; surprise, *lack of expectation*; *ambush*; thin ice; quagmire, *marsh*; sandbar; shoal, shoal water, shallows; reef, rock; lee shore; steep, chasm, abyss, crevasse, precipice, *high land*; crosscurrent, undertow, *current*; vortex, maelstrom, whirlpool, eddy; tidal wave, flash flood, *wave*; storm, squall, hurricane, *gale*; volcano, *furnace*; dynamite, time bomb, powder keg, *explosive*; *danger*; hotbed, *infection*; source of trouble, hazard, *bane*.

troublemaker, stirrer, wrecker; *enemy*; firebrand, *agitator*; ugly customer, undesirable, delinquent, *ruffian*; *influence*; yellow peril, Nemesis.

659 Warning

N. *warning*, caution; example, lesson, notice, *information*; word, tip, tip-off, wink, nudge, *hint*; *publication*; final warning, final notice, ultimatum, *demand*; admonition, *reprimand*; deterrent; protest; warning shot; foreboding, premonition, *prediction*; voice, voice of conscience, warning voice, *conscience*; alarm, siren, foghorn, fog signal, alert, red alert, *danger signal*; stormy petrel, bird of ill omen, *omen*; gathering cloud, war cloud, *danger*; symptom, sign; knell; beacon, light, *signal*, *indicator*; menace, *threat*.

warner, adviser; prophet; signaller; watchman, lookout, watch, *surveillance*; scout, spy; picket, sentry, *protector*; advanced guard, rearguard; watchdog.

Adj. *cautionary*, warning; *deprecatory*; exemplary, instructive; prognostic;

ominous; deterrent.

warned, *cautious*; *expectant*; *prepared*.

Vb. warn, caution; give fair warning, give notice, notify, *inform*; drop a hint, *hint*; counsel, *advise*; remind; admonish, reprove; spell danger, forewarn, *predict*; forearm, alert, *prepare*; lour, menace, *threaten*; advise against, *dissuade*; remonstrate, protest, *deprecate*.

be warned, receive notice; beware, take heed, *be careful*; be taught a lesson.

Int. look out! watch out! cave! mind your step! look where you are going!

660 Danger signal

N. *danger signal*, note of warning, *warning*; murmur, *discontent*; black cap, evil omen, *omen*; storm cone, gale warning; warning sound, alarm clock, alarm bell, burglar alarm, fire alarm, fire bell, foghorn, fog signal, bell buoy, motor horn, klaxon, bicycle bell, police whistle; blast, honk, toot; alarm, church bell, curfew, siren, alert, tattoo, beat of drum; *call*; war cry; fiery cross; warning light, beacon; red flag, distress signal, SOS, *signal*; sign of alarm, start, tremor, sweat, *fear*.

false alarm, cry of 'wolf', scare, hoax; bugbear, nightmare, bad dream; blank cartridge; *untruth*; alarmist.

Vb. raise the alarm, dial 999, alert, arouse, scare, startle, *frighten*; honk, toot; cry blue murder, *proclaim*; give a false alarm, cry wolf, cry too soon; sound a warning, toll, knell.

661 Preservation

N. *preservation*, safekeeping, keeping alive; safe conduct, *protection*; saving, salvation, *deliverance*; conservation, conservancy; upkeep, maintenance, support, *provision*; service; insulation; *storage*; reservation, *economy*; self-preservation; game reserve, bird sanctuary, conservation area; taxidermy; cold storage; *hygiene*; preventive medicine, quarantine.

preserver, saviour, *deliverance*; amulet, charm, mascot, *talisman*; preservation order; preservative, ice, amber, formaldehyde; camphor, mothball, lavender; spice, pickle, brine, aspic, *condiment*; freezer, *refrigerator*; silo; safety device, seat belt, gas mask, *safeguard*; incubator, respirator, iron lung, life support system.

Adj. *preserving*; preservative, conservative, prophylactic, protective, preventive, hygienic, *salubrious*.

preserved, kept, fresh, intact, whole, *perfect*; frozen; potted; *safe*.

Vb. preserve, conserve, keep alive, keep fresh, freeze, *refrigerate*; embalm, mummify, stuff; pickle, salt, *season*; souse, marinate; cure, smoke, kipper, dehydrate, sun-dry, *dry*; pot, bottle, tin, can; protect, paint, varnish, whitewash, creosote, waterproof; maintain, service, *repair*; support; keep alive, feed, sustain, provision, supply, *provide*; keep safe, garage, *safeguard*; store, reserve, save; nurse, tend, *doctor*; cherish, treasure, *look after*; hug, hold, *retain*; keep going, prolong; save, save alive, rescue, *deliver*.

662 Escape

N. escape, leak, leakage, loss, egress; delivery, rescue, deliverance; riddance, relief; getaway; flight, flit, French leave; retreat; runaway; evasion; narrow escape, close shave, close call, narrow squeak, near thing, danger; discharge, reprieve, acquittal; setting free, liberation; impunity; escapism.

means of escape, exit, back door, secret passage, egress; ladder, fire escape, escape hatch; drawbridge, bridge; vent, safety valve, safeguard; dodge, device, trick; loophole, escape clause, qualification.

escaper, runaway; truant; fugitive, refugee; survivor.

Adj. escaped, flown; truant; fugitive, runaway; slippery, elusive; free, at large; relieved; exempt.

Vb. escape, find or win freedom, achieve liberty; make a getaway, break gaol; abscond, jump bail, flit, elope, skip, take French leave; make oneself scarce, beat a hasty retreat, decamp; slip through, break loose, get free; emerge; secure an acquittal, go scot-free; scrape through, survive; be exempt; find relief, be relieved; leak.

elude, evade, welsh, abscond, dodge, avoid; lie low, lurk; escape notice, be found to be missing, be absent.

663 Deliverance

N. deliverance, delivery, extraction; riddance, relief; emancipation, liberation; rescue; salvage, restoration; salvation, redemption, divine function; ransom, purchase; release, amnesty; discharge, reprieve, acquittal; day of grace, respite, delay; truce, standstill, cessation; escape; dispensation.

Adj. extricable.

Vb. deliver, save, rescue, throw a lifeline; extract; extricate, unravel; untie, disunite; disencumber; relieve; release, unlock; emancipate, free, set free, set at large, liberate, acquit; deliver oneself, escape; save oneself; redeem, ransom, purchase; salvage, retrieve, recover, bring back, restore; spare, excuse, exempt.

Int. to the rescue! all hands to the pump! help!

664 Preparation

N. preparation, making ready; clearance; preliminary step, priming; preliminary course, trial run, trial, experiment; practice, rehearsal, brief; training, teaching; beginning; study, prep, homework, learning; spadework, labour, groundwork, foundation, basis; scaffold, scaffolding, frame; rough sketch, first draft, outline, blueprint, scheme, plan; shadow cabinet, shadow factory; arrangement; advice, forethought, foresight; bottom drawer, nest egg, store.

fitting out, logistics, provision; appointment, commission, equipment, array, armament; promotion; debut.

maturation; seasoning; hatching, gestation, incubation, sitting, nursing, nurture; cultivation, tillage, agriculture; bloom; fruition.

preparedness, readiness, maturity; puberty; fitness, shipshape condition, height of training, pitch of perfection, perfection.

preparer, coach; pioneer, precursor; packer;

stevedore; fitter, provider; cultivato planter, farmer; brewer, cook, cookery.

Adj. preparatory, preliminary, precedin provisional, stopgap; hatching; forth coming, impending; learning, studious.

prepared, ready, alert, vigilant; made ready all set, ready to go; qualified, practised, a concert pitch, word-perfect; informe tight, snug; armed, fully armed, armed a all points; well-appointed, provided ready to hand; operational.

matured, ripe, mellow, mature; trieed experienced, veteran, expert; adul grown, fledged, grown-up; flowerinng well-done; wrought; deep-laid.

ready-made, ready to use; instant.

Vb. prepare, take steps; make ready, bridg pioneer, come before; predispose, incline cultivate; set to work, address oneself t begin; sketch, outline, blueprint, plar plot, concert, prearrange, predetermine forearm, guard against, insure, see safety; anticipate, expect.

make ready, ready, stow, pack, store; com mission, tune, adjust, arrange; array bring together; set, cock, prime, load raise steam, crank; equip, crew, man; fi furnish, dress; arm, provide with arms provide with teeth, provide; improvise rehearse, drill, groom, exercise, traiir inure, acclimatize; coach, brief, inforrm

mature, mellow, ripen, bring to fruitioon perfect; force, invigorate; bring to a heaad climax; stew, brew, cook; hatch, incu bate, breed, breed stock; grow, farm, cuu tivate; nurse, nurture, elaborate, carrr through; season, weather, smoke, drr cure; temper, season, harden.

prepare oneself, qualify oneself, serve a apprenticeship; study, brief onesellf train, exercise, rehearse, practise, learr shoulder arms; be prepared, stann ready.

Adv. in preparation; on the stocks.

665 Nonpreparation

N. nonpreparation, lack of preparation; pot luck; lack of training, want of practicee disqualification; crudity; neglect; rushh haste; impromptu, snap answer; surprisee lack of expectation.

undevelopment; state of nature, native statee virgin soil; raw material, rough diamondd late developer; rough copy; embryoo abortion.

Adj. unprepared, backward, behindhandd late; makeshift; without preparation, a lib, impromptu, snap, spontaneouss unstudied, artless; rash, careless, neglii gent; rush, hasty; unguarded, vulnerablee caught unawares; shiftless, improvidennt thoughtless, happy-go-lucky; scratchh unpractised; fallow, virgin, unused.

immature, green; callow; adolescent, juvee nile, girlish, young; undeveloped, hallf baked, raw, imperfect; backward, latee unborn, rudimentary, beginning; roughh hewn, uncut; before time, prematuree abortive; apprentice, undergraduatee unskilled; crude, coarse, rude, savagee artless; forced, precocious.

uncooked, raw, red, rare, underdone; hallf baked, cold; undressed; indigestiblee inedible, tough.

unequipped, undressed; deficient; unqualii fied.

Vb. be unprepared, lack preparation, bb incomplete; lie fallow, rust, deterioratee want practice, need training; offer pott luck, improvise; let tomorrow take care oo itself; be premature, *be early*; catch unawares, *surprise*.

Adv. *unreadily*, extempore, off-hand.

666 Attempt

N. *attempt*, essay, bid; step, move, gambit, *deed*; endeavour, struggle, strain, effort; tackle, try, some attempt; good try, valiant effort; best effort, best one can do; random effort; determined effort, go at, shot at, stab at, jab at, crack at, whack at, bash at; first attempt, first go, first shot, first offence, *debut*; final attempt, last bid, last throw; venture, adventure, quest, operation, exercise, *undertaking*; aim, goal, *objective*; high endeavour.

trier; fighter, *contender*; idealist, *perfectionist*; activist; undertaker, contractor, entrepreneur, jobber.

Adj. *attempting, willing*; game, *resolute*; searching; tentative; ambitious, venturesome, daring, *enterprising*.

Vb. *attempt*, essay, try; seek to, aim, *intend*; seek, *search*; offer, bid, make an attempt, make shift to, do something about; endeavour, struggle, strive, try hard, *be resolute*; *exert oneself*; pull hard, strain, sweat, *work*; tackle, have a go, give it a try, give it a whirl, have a shot at, have a crack at, have a stab at, *undertake*; make a go of; take a chance, tempt providence, venture, speculate, *gamble*; test, make trial of, *experiment*; fly a kite, *be tentative*; be ambitious, attempt too much, *fail*.

Int. Here goes!

667 Undertaking

N. *undertaking*, job, task, assignment; self-imposed task, labour of love, pilgrimage, *voluntary work*; contract, engagement, obligation, *promise*; operation, exercise; programme, project, design, *plan*; tall order, big undertaking, *hard task*; enterprise; quest, search, adventure, *enquiry*; venture; occupation, *business*; struggle, effort, campaign, *attempt*.

Adj. *enterprising*, adventurous, venturesome, daring; go-ahead, progressive; alive to opportunity; ambitious; *rash*; responsible.

Vb. *undertake*, apply oneself to; tackle, *attempt*; go about; set forward, set going, *initiate*; proceed to, fall to, set to, buckle to, *begin*; *be courageous*; assume responsibility, take charge of, *manage*; execute; *busy oneself*; assume an obligation, *incur a duty*; engage to, commit oneself, *promise*; get involved, volunteer, *be willing*; be busy; show enterprise, pioneer, venture, dare, *face danger*; apprentice oneself, *prepare oneself*.

668 Use

N. *use*, disposal, *possession*; employment, application, appliance; exercise, *practice*; resort, recourse; mode of use, treatment, good usage, proper treatment; hard usage, wrong use, *misuse*; effect of use, wear; exhaustion, consumption, *waste*; reuse; benefit, service, *good policy*; utility; office, purpose, point, *function*; long use, wont, *habit*.

Adj. *used*, applied; worn, threadbare, second-hand, dog-eared, well-worn, *dilapidated*; beaten, *known*; hackneyed, stale; practical, utilitarian, *advisable*;

makeshift, provisional; subservient, *instrumental*; available, employable, convertible, *useful*; disposable.

Vb. *use*, employ, exercise, practise; apply, exert, bring to bear, administer; give to, consecrate to, dedicate to; assign to, allot (see *dispose of*); make use of, convert, convert to use, *find useful*; reuse, recycle, exploit; milk, drain, *extract*; put to good use, turn to account, use to advantage, make hay with; make play with; make a tool or handle of; take advantage of; put to use, wear, consume, *waste*; handle, thumb, *touch*; tread, follow, beat (a path); work, drive, manipulate, *operate*; wield, ply, brandish; overwork, tax, task, *fatigue*; mould, *form*.

avail *oneself of*, adopt, try; resort to, run to, have recourse to; make do with.

dispose *of*, command; control; allot, assign, apportion; spare, requisition; set going, deploy, *motivate*; enjoy, *possess*; consume, expend, absorb, *waste*.

669 Nonuse

N. *nonuse*, abeyance, suspension, *inaction*; *absence*; unemployment; forbearance, abstinence; savings, *store*; disuse, superannuation; waiver, surrender; cancellation; write-off.

Adj. *unused, absent*; useless, *inexpedient*; reserved; spare, extra; untapped, lying idle or fallow; *new*; left to rot; unnecessary, redundant; free, vacant; unemployed, idle.

disused, derelict, cast-off; done with; retired; obsolete, *antiquated*.

Vb. *not use*, abstain, forbear, do without, *avoid*; dispense with, waive, *relinquish*; overlook, disregard, *neglect*; spare, save, reserve, *store*; decline, *reject*.

stop *using*, disuse, *cease*; outgrow; leave to rust, dismantle, *make useless*; have done with, lay aside; discard, dump, ditch, scrap; jettison, throw overboard, *eject*; slough, *doff*; relinquish, resign; suspend, withdraw, cancel, *abrogate*; discharge, make redundant, *dismiss*; drop, supersede, replace, *substitute*; be unused, rust, *deteriorate*.

670 Misuse

N. *misuse*, abuse, wrong use; maladministration; malpractice, perversion; prostitution; *impiety*; pollution; *waste*; force, *violence*; outrage, injury, *evil*.

Vb. *misuse*, abuse; put to bad use, misdirect; divert, manipulate, misappropriate, *defraud*; violate, desecrate, *profane*; prostitute, *pervert*; pollute, *make unclean*; do violence to, *force*; strain, *distort*; take advantage of, exploit, *use*; manhandle, knock about, ill-treat; maltreat, *oppress*; misgovern, misrule, mishandle, mismanage; overwork, overtax, *fatigue*; work hard, *impair*; squander, *waste*; misapply, use a sledgehammer to crack a nut, *waste effort*.

671 Action

N. *action*, doing, performance; steps, move, *policy*; commission; execution, accomplishment; procedure, routine, *practice*; behaviour, *conduct*; movement, play, swing, *motion*; operation, working, evolution, *agency*; force, pressure, *influence*; work, labour, drama, *activity*; occupation, *business*; manufacture, *production*;

employment, *use*; effort, endeavour, campaign, crusade, *attempt*; *management*.

deed, act, action, exploit, feat, achievement, *prowess*; bad deed, crime, *foul play*; stunt, *ostentation*; gesture, measure, step, move, *policy*; manoeuvre, evolution, *tactics*; stroke, blow, coup; job, task, operation, exercise, *undertaking*; proceeding, deal, doings; work, handiwork, workmanship, *skill*; *masterpiece*; drama, scene; acts, *narrative*.

doer, man *or* woman of action, activist, *busy person*; practical person; hero, *brave person*; practitioner, *expert*; stunt man *or* woman, player, *actor*; performer; criminal; operator, *agent*; contractor, undertaker, entrepreneur; executor, executive, administrator, manager, *director*; hand, workman, operative, *worker*; craftsman, *artisan*; creative worker, *artist*.

Adj. *doing*, acting, red-handed; working, at work, *operative*; industrious, busy, *active*; *habitual*.

Vb. do, act, perform; *operate*; *influence*; manipulate, *motivate*; use tactics, twist, turn, manoeuvre, *be cunning*; do something, lift a finger; proceed, proceed with, get going, move, take action, take steps; try, *attempt*; tackle, *undertake*; adopt a measure, enact, legislate, *make legal*; perpetrate, commit, achieve, accomplish, complete, *carry through*; take care of, execute, implement, fulfil; *observe*; make history, win renown, *have a reputation*; practise, exercise, discharge, prosecute, pursue, wage, ply, employ oneself, *busy oneself*; officiate, *function*; transact, proceed, *do business*; administer, manage, control, *direct*; have to do with, *deal with*; sweat, labour, campaign, *work*; exploit, *use*; intervene, *aid*; participate; *meddle*; conduct oneself, *behave*; play about, lark around, *be absurd*; stunt.

Adv. *in the act*, redhanded; while one is about it.

672 Inaction

N. *inaction*, nothing doing, inertia; inability to act; failure to act, neglect; abstention; passive resistance, *defiance*; suspension, abeyance; deadlock, stalemate, *stop*; *insensibility*; passivity, vegetation, doldrums, quiet, calm; *leisure*, rest, *repose*; unemployment; sinecure; Fabian policy, *delay*; lack of progress; defeatism.

Adj. *nonactive*, inoperative, idle; passive, dull, sluggish, *inert*; *leisurely*; Fabian; *hopeless*; stationary, motionless, immobile, *quiescent*; cold, extinct; without a sign of life, *dead*; unemployed, without employment, *unused*; incapable of action, *impotent*; benumbed, *insensible*; apathetic, phlegmatic, *impassive*; neutral, *indifferent*; *deaf*.

Vb. *not act*, hang fire; refrain, abstain, *avoid*; watch; *wait*; procrastinate; let it rip, let things take their course, let well alone; stay neutral, *be indifferent*; do nothing, tolerate, turn a blind eye, *disregard*; sit tight, *be inert*; drift, slide, coast; *despair*; let pass, leave alone, give it a miss, *neglect*; stay still, keep quiet, *be quiescent*; sit back, relax, *repose*; *be useless*; have nothing to do, *have leisure*; pause, desist, *cease*; rust, lie idle, lie fallow; lie dead, *die*.

Adv. *without action*, without movement; nothing doing.

673 Activity

N. *activity*, action; interest; social activity; *motive*; movement, *sedition*; life, stir, *motion*; alacrity; readiness; expedition, *velocity*; spurt, burst, fit, *spasm*; hurry, flurry, hustle, bustle, frantic haste, *haste*; fuss, bother, ado, to-do, tumult, frenzy, *turmoil*; whirl, scramble, rat race, maelstrom, *vortex*; drama, great doings, much ado, thick of things; plenty to do, *business*; press of business; pressure of work; high street, heavy traffic; press; hum, hive, hive of industry, *workshop*.

restlessness, fiddling, aimless activity, *inattention*; fever, fret, *frenzy*; enthusiasm, ardour, fervour, abandon, *warm feeling*; vigour, energy, enterprise, initiative, push, drive, go, pep; spirit, animation, vitality, *life*; insomnia.

assiduity, application, concentration, *attention*; industry, drudgery, *labour*; determination, *resolution*; painstaking.

overactivity, excess; displacement activity, *lost labour*; *commotion*; interference; intrigue, *plot*.

busy person, new broom; zealot, fanatic, *obstinate person*; hard worker, *worker*; factotum, housewife, drudge, dogsbody, fag, slave, Trojan; horse, beaver, ant, bee; eager beaver, busy bee, workhorse; man *or* woman of action, activist, militant, *doer*; sharp fellow, live wire, dynamo, go-getter, pusher.

meddler, stirrer, officious person, spoilsport, busybody, *inquisitive person*; *adviser*; fusspot, nuisance.

Adj. *active*, stirring, *moving*; going, working, incessant; expeditious, *businesslike*; able, able-bodied, *strong*; quick, brisk, nippy, spry, smart, *speedy*; nimble, tripping; energetic, forceful, *vigorous*; up-and-coming, *enterprising*; frisky, coltish, dashing, sprightly, spirited, mettlesome, live, vivacious, *lively*; eager, ardent, *fervent*; fierce, desperate, *resolute*; zealous; prompt, instant, ready, *willing*; awake, alert, watchful, wakeful, *vigilant*; sleepless, restless, feverish, fretful, fidgety, jumpy, fussy, nervy, frantic; *excitable*; involved; aggressive, militant, *warlike*.

busy, lively, eventful; stirring, astir, afoot; hard at work, hard at it, fully engaged; at work.

industrious, studious, sedulous, assiduous; *laborious*; unflagging, tireless, indefatigable; efficient, workmanlike, *businesslike*.

meddling, officious, pushy, intrusive.

Vb. *be active*, show interest, trouble oneself, *participate*; be stirring, stir, *move*; run riot, *rampage*; rouse oneself; hum, thrive, *prosper*; make progress, *progress*; keep moving; push, shove, thrust, drive, impel; be vigorous; rush, surge, flow; roar, rage, bluster, *blow*; explode, burst, *be violent*; dash, fly, run, move fast; *attempt*; take pains, be attentive; buckle to, *exert oneself*; persist, persevere; make short work of; jump to it, show zeal, make things hum, *do*; burn with zeal, *be willing*; anticipate, wake, watch, *be careful*; assert oneself, react, show fight, *defy*; protest, agitate, demonstrate, *deprecate*.

be busy, busy oneself; bustle, hurry, scurry, hasten; go all ways at once; waste effort; rise early, go to bed late; fuss, fret, fume, *be excitable*; have other things to do, have other fish to fry, *be engaged*; slave, slog, *work*; overwork, overdo it, make work, make heavy weather of, never stop;

affect zeal, *be affected*.

meddle, interpose, intervene, interfere, be officious; *intrude*; pester, bother, dun, annoy, *trouble*; be bossy, boss, boss one around, *oppress*; tinker, touch, *impair*.

Adv. *actively*; full tilt, whole hog.

Int. Wakey wakey! rise and shine! shake a leg! get going!

674 Inactivity

N. *inactivity*, inaction; inertia, torpor, lull, suspension, *cessation*; slack period, doldrums, grave, morgue; rust; slump, recession, *decrease*; unemployment, shutdown; absenteeism; *delay*; *leisure*.

sluggishness, lethargy, sloth; slow progress; *weakness*; languor, *moral insensibility*; stupor, torpor, *insensibility*; apathy; phlegm; *submission*.

sleepiness, *fatigue*; tired eyes; *fantasy*.

sleep, slumber, kip; deep sleep; drowse; light sleep, nap, catnap, shut-eye, snooze, doze, siesta, *repose*; winter sleep; coma, trance, hypnosis, *insensibility*; somnambulism; sleepy sickness, *disease*; gate of ivory; Land of Nod; cot, cradle, pillow, bed.

soporific, nightcap; sedative, barbiturate; opiate, poppy, opium, morphine, *anaesthetic*; lullaby.

idler, drone; slacker, clock-watcher; sleepyhead; *slowcoach*; hobo, bum, tramp, *wanderer*; mendicant, *beggar*; parasite; layabout, good-for-nothing, ne'er-do-well, wastrel; drifter; dummy, passenger, absentee landlord; idle rich; dreamer, sleeper; dormouse, hedgehog; Rip van Winkle.

Adj. *inactive*, motionless, stationary, at a standstill, still, extinct, *quiescent*; inanimate, lifeless, *inert*; torpid, benumbed, unconscious, *insensible*; sluggish, stiff, rusty; listless, lackadaisical, *dejected*; tired, faint, languid; dull, heavy, leaden, stolid, *impassive*; supine, submissive; uninterested, apathetic, *indifferent*; *absent*; idle, empty, *leisurely*.

lazy, slothful, sluggish, work-shy, indolent, idle, bone-idle; *leisurely*; *slow*; tardy, dilatory, *late*; slack, remiss, careless, *negligent*.

sleepy, tired; somnolent, stupid with sleep; drowsy, dozy, groggy; asleep, fast asleep; unconscious; dormant, comatose.

soporific, sedative.

Vb. *be inactive*, do nothing, rust, stagnate, vegetate, smoulder, hang fire; delay; take it easy, let things go, *be neglectful*; hang about, *wait*; slouch, lag, loiter, dawdle, dally, *be late*; stand, sit, lie, lollop, loll, lounge, laze, rest, take it easy, *repose*; slack, skive, shirk, *avoid*; sit around; have nothing to do, loaf, idle; waste time, trifle, dabble, fiddle-faddle, piddle, potter, putter, *waste effort*; come to a standstill, *decelerate*, dilly-dally, hesitate, *be uncertain*; droop, faint, fail, languish, slacken, *come to rest*; slump, *decrease*; be still, *be quiescent*; discontinue, stop, come to an end, *cease*; tire.

sleep, slumber, snooze, nap, catnap; hibernate; sleep well, sleep like a log, sleep like a top, sleep like a little child; dream; snore; go to sleep, fall asleep, take a nap, have a kip; feel sleepy, yawn, nod, doze, drowse; go to bed; roost, perch.

make *inactive*, put to sleep, put to bed; send to sleep, lull, rock, cradle; soothe, *assuage*; deaden, paralyse, dope, drug, *render insensible*; stiffen, cramp, *fetter*;

dismantle, *make useless*; *dismiss*.

675 Haste

N. *haste*, hurry, scurry, hustle, bustle, flurry, whirl, scramble, *activity*; flap, flutter, fidget, fuss; rush, rush job; feverish haste, race against time; immediacy; push, drive, expedition, *velocity*; acceleration, forced march, dash, *spurt*; inability to wait.

Adj. *hasty*, impetuous, impulsive, *rash*; feverish, impatient, ardent, *fervent*; boisterous, furious, *violent*; precipitate, breathless, breakneck, *speedy*; expeditious, prompt, without delay; making speed; hotfoot, running, racing; unable to wait; hurried, slapdash, cursory, *negligent*; forced, rush; urgent, immediate, *important*.

Vb. *hasten*, expedite; urge, drive, spur, goad, whip, lash, flog, *incite*; rush; be hasty, be precipitate, *be rash*; haste, make haste; post, race, run, *move fast*; overtake, *outstrip*; spurt, dash, make a forced march, *accelerate*; hurry, scurry, hustle, bustle, fret, fume, fidget, *be active*; act without ceremony, brush aside; rush through, dash through, make short work of; work against time or to a deadline; *be late*; make every minute count; make oneself scarce, *decamp*.

Adv. *hastily*, helter-skelter, pell-mell, feverishly, post-haste, hotfoot, apace; with all haste, at short notice; immediately.

Int. hurry up! be quick! buck up! look lively! look sharp! get a move on! get a wiggle on! step on it! quick march! at the double!

676 Leisure

N. *leisure*, spare time, convenience; time to kill; sinecure; holiday, break, vacation, leave, furlough; time to spare, ample time; rest, ease, relaxation, *repose*; *resignation*.

Adj. *leisurely*, deliberate, *slow*; at any odd moment; at leisure; at a loose end, at ease; retired.

Vb. *have leisure*, have time enough, have plenty of time, have time to spare; spend, pass; want something to do; take a holiday, *repose*; retire, *resign*; save labour.

677 Exertion

N. *exertion*, effort, struggle, *attempt*; strain, stress; tug, pull, stretch, heave, lift, throw; drive, force, pressure, applied energy, *energy*; ergonomics; ado, trouble; muscle, elbow grease; pains, taking pains; overwork; extra work, overtime; battle, campaign, fray.

exercise, practice, drill, training, work-out, *preparation*; physical education, PE, keeping fit, constitutional; gymnastics, *athletics*; yoga; games, sports, *sport*.

labour, industry, work, long haul; spadework, donkeywork; manual labour; housework, daily grind, toil, drudgery, slavery, sweat, fag, grind, strain, treadmill, grindstone; hack work; bull; penal work, hard labour, *penalty*; forced labour, *compulsion*; fatigue, fatigue duty, *duty*; piecework, homework, outwork; task, chore, job, operation, exercise, *deed*; shift, trick, stint, stretch, bout, spell of work, *period*; job of work; working life, working day.

Adj. *labouring*, born to toil; working, hard

at it, *busy*; laborious, *industrious*; strenuous, energetic, *active*; painstaking, thorough, *attentive*; taking exercise; athletic.

laborious, full of labour; killing; gruelling, punishing; troublesome, weary, wearisome, painful, burdensome; heroic, Herculean; arduous, hard, warm, heavy, uphill, *difficult*; thorough, painstaking; elaborate, artificial, fiddling; *useless*.

Vb. *exert oneself*, apply oneself, make an effort, try, *attempt*; struggle, strain, strive, sweat blood; trouble oneself, bestir oneself; turn every stone, do all one can; strain every nerve, use every muscle, *be active*; *be willing*; drive through, hammer at, slog at, *persevere*; battle, campaign, take action, *do*.

work, labour, toil, drudge, fag, grind, slog, sweat; sweat blood; pull, haul, tug, shove, hump, heave; dig, spade, lumber; set about, set to, *begin*; keep at it, plod, *persevere*; work hard, work overtime, moonlight, work double shift, *be busy*; slave, work like a galley slave, work like a horse, work like a Trojan; work oneself to death; overdo it, make work; serve, *minister to*; put to work, overwork, task, tax, *fatigue*.

Adv. *laboriously*.

678 Repose

N. *repose*, rest; ease, comfort, *euphoria*; sweet sleep, *sleep*; relaxation, breathing space, breather, *refreshment*; pause, respite, recess, break, *lull*; interval, *interim*; holiday, vacation, leave, furlough, sabbatical year, *leisure*; day of rest, Sabbath, Lord's day.

Adj. *reposeful*, restful; carefree, casual, at ease, *content*; snug, *comfortable*; peaceful, quiet, *tranquil*; sabbatical, holiday, *leisurely*.

Vb. *repose*, rest, take a rest, take it easy, sit back; recline, loll, lounge, laze, sprawl, *be horizontal*; perch, roost; couch, go to bed, go to sleep, *sleep*; relax, unwind, unbend, forget work; breathe, take a breather; *come to rest*; take a holiday, *have leisure*.

Adv. *at rest*.

679 Fatigue

N. *fatigue*, languor, lethargy; physical fatigue; mental fatigue; distress; limit of endurance, exhaustion, collapse; strain; hard breathing, *respiration*; faint, swoon, blackout, *insensibility*.

Adj. *fatigued*, tired, *sleepy*; spent; done, fagged; stupid with fatigue, dull, stale; strained; dog-tired, tired to death, ready to drop, dead beat, beat, whacked, knackered, more dead than alive, prostrate; stiff, sore; footsore; haggard, worn; faint, languid; still tired; tired of; jaded.

panting, breathless.

fatiguing, gruelling, punishing, *laborious*; tiresome, wearisome; wearing, exacting, demanding; irksome, *tedious*.

Vb. *be fatigued*, overdo it; get weary, gasp, pant, puff, blow, grunt, *breathe*; languish, droop, drop, sink, flag, fail, *be weak*; stagger, faint, swoon, feel giddy; yawn, nod, drowse, *sleep*; succumb, drop, collapse; must have a rest; overwork, get stale, need a rest, need a break, need a change, need a holiday.

fatigue, tire, wear, exhaust, fag, whack,

prostrate; wind; demand too much, task, tax, strain, work, drive, overdrive, flog, overwork, overtax; enervate, drain, distress, harass, irk, jade, *trouble*; tire to death, weary, bore, send to sleep, *be tedious*.

680 Refreshment

N. *refreshment*, breather, breath of air, repose; break, recess, *lull*; recreation, restoration; revival; *relief*; *stimulant*; refreshments, *food*; wash.

Adj. *refreshing*; cool, *cold*; bracing, recreational, *restorative*.

refreshed.

Vb. *refresh*, clean; air, fan, ventilate, *aerate*; shade, cool, *refrigerate*; brace, stimulate, invigorate; recruit, recreate, revive, reanimate, recuperate, *restore*; ease, *relieve*; allow rest, give a breather; offer food, *feed*.

be refreshed, breathe, draw breath; respire; come to; revive; renew oneself, take a breather; have a change, have a rest, *repose*.

681 Agent

N. *agent*, operator, actor, performer, player, practitioner; *doer*; minister, tool, *instrument*; functionary, *officer*; representative, *delegate*; spokesman, *deputy*; proxy, *substitute*; executor, executive, administrator, dealer; middleman, *merchant*; employer, industrialist, *producer*.

worker, volunteer; social worker, philanthropist; independent worker, freelance, self-employed person; drudge, dogsbody, fag, hack; menial, factotum, domestic servant, *servant*; beast of burden, *slave*; ant, beaver, *busy person*; professional person, business man, business woman, breadwinner, wage slave, employee; brain worker, boffin; clerical worker, girl Friday, man Friday; shop assistant, *seller*; charwoman, dustman, *cleaner*; labourer, farm worker, *farmer*; working man or woman, working girl, workman, hand, operative, factory worker, factory hand; navvy, roadman; plate-layer; docker, stevedore, packer, porter, coolie.

artisan, artificer, tradesman, technician; master, *proficient person*; journeyman, apprentice; craftsman or -woman, potter, turner, joiner, carpenter, cooper; wheelwright; shipwright; architect, master mason, mason, bricklayer, plasterer, painter, decorator; forger, smith, blacksmith, goldsmith, silversmith, gunsmith, locksmith; tinker; collier, miner; mechanic, machinist, fitter; engineer; plumber, electrician; weaver, spinner, tailor, cutter, needlewoman; jeweller; glassblower.

personnel, staff, force, company, gang, squad, crew, complement, cadre, *band*; *actor*; mate, colleague, associate, partner, *colleague*; men, payroll; labour, labour pool, labour force, manpower, proletariat.

682 Workshop

N. *workshop*, studio; study, library; laboratory, plant, installation; works, factory, workshop, yard; sweatshop; mill, loom; sawmill, paper mill; foundry; steelworks; blast furnace, forge, smithy, *furnace*; power station, gasworks, *energy*; quarry, mine, *store*; colliery, coalmine, pit, coalface; tin mine; mint; arsenal, armoury; dockyard, shipyard; wharf, dock, *stable*; refinery, distillery, brewery; shop, bench, production line; nursery, *farm*; dairy, *stock farm*; kitchen, laundry; office, bureau, business house, firm, company; offices, secretariat, Whitehall; hive of industry, *activity*.

683 Conduct

N. *conduct*, behaviour, deportment; bearing, carriage, port; demeanour, attitude, posture, *mien*; aspect, look, *appearance*; tone, tone of voice, delivery, *voice*; motion, action, *gesture*; mode of behaviour, fashion, style; manner, guise, air; poise, dignity, presence; good manners, *courtesy*; bad manners, *discourtesy*; pose, *affectation*; mental attitude, outlook, *opinion*; mood, *feeling*; good behaviour, *virtue*; misconduct; democratic behaviour, common touch; past behaviour, record, history; reward of conduct, deserts; way of life, morals, principles, customs, manners, *habit*; line of action, *policy*; career, course, race, walk, walk of life, *vocation*; observance, routine, *practice*; procedure, process, method, *way*; treatment, direction, *management*; velvet glove; jackboot, iron hand; *deed*; behaviourism.

tactics, strategy, campaign, programme, *plan*; line, *policy*; political science, politics, realpolitik; gamesmanship, one-upmanship, *cunning*; *skill*; *advantage*; *delay*; manoeuvre, shift; move, gambit, *deed*; game, *stratagem*.

Adj. *behaving*; psychological; political, businesslike.

Vb. *behave*, act, *do*; behave well, *be virtuous*; behave badly, misbehave, *be wicked*; deserve well of, deserve ill of; gesture, gesticulate; posture, pose, affect, *be affected*; conduct oneself, set an example, lead a good life, *be active*; *participate*; pursue, *busy oneself*; follow a course; *be free*; employ tactics, manoeuvre, jockey, twist, turn; behave towards, treat.

deal with, have to do with, *do*; handle, manipulate, *operate*; conduct, run, *manage*; see to, cope with; transact, enact, execute, carry through; *plan*; work at, work through, *work*; go through, read, *study*.

684 Management

N. *management*, conduct, running; agency, commission; care, charge, control, authority; oversight, *surveillance*; patronage, *protection*; art of management, tact, way with, *skill*; business management, work study, operational research; *policy*; housekeeping, husbandry, economics, political economy; government; regimen, regime, dispensation; regulation, *legislation*; ministry, cabinet, staff work; bureaucracy, civil service; secretariat, government office, *workshop*.

directorship, direction, responsibility, control, *command*; dictatorship, leadership; guidance, steerage; pole star, lodestar, *guide*; helm, rudder, wheel, tiller, joystick; needle, compass, binnacle; *sailing aid*; beam, radar, *direction*; remote control.

Adj. *directing*, leading, directional; authoritative; *authoritarian*; managerial; executive, administrative; legislative;

high-level, *important*; economic, political; official.

Vb. *manage*, manipulate, manoeuvre, *influence*; *know*; handle, conduct, run; minister, administer, prescribe; supervise, superintend, oversee, *invigilate*; nurse, *look after*; have charge of, *motivate* (see *direct*); keep order, police, regulate; legislate, *make legal*; control, govern, sway, *rule*; know how to manage, have a way with.

direct, lead, pioneer, precede, *come before*; boss, dictate, *command*; hold office, hold a responsible position, have responsibility; mastermind, have overall responsibility; *incur a duty*; preside; head, captain, skipper, stroke, pilot, cox, steer, *navigate*; point, *point to*; *indicate*; shepherd, guide, conduct; introduce; escort, *accompany*; channel, funnel; route, train, lead, lead through.

Adv. *in control*.

685 Director

N. *director*, governor; cabinet, *council*; board, chair; staff, brass, management; manager; employer, capitalist, boss, *master*; headman, chief, head of state, *superior*; principal, head, rector, moderator, dean, vice-chancellor, chancellor; president, chairman, speaker; premier, prime minister; captain, skipper, stroke, cox, master, *mariner*; steersman, helmsman, *navigator*; pilot, *guide*; forerunner, *precursor*; drill sergeant; *teacher*; *adviser*; king-maker; *influence*.

leader, judge (Old Testament), *governor*; messiah; spearhead, centre forward; shepherd, drover, *herdsman*; pacemaker; toastmaster, MC; high priest; conductor, first violin; drum major; *autocrat*; ringleader, demagogue, *agitator*; captain.

manager, responsible person; key person, kingpin, *bigwig*; administrator, executive, executor; *doer*; statesman or - woman, politician; housekeeper, housewife; steward, bailiff, farm manager, reeve, agent, factor, *consignee*; superintendent, inspector, foreman or - woman, gaffer; warden, house master or mistress, matron, nurse, tutor, *protector*; disciplinarian; party manager, whip; custodian, caretaker, curator, librarian, *keeper*; huntsman; circus manager, ringmaster.

official, tin god; marshal, steward; shop steward; government servant, *servant*; officer of state, high official, vizier, minister, secretary of state, secretary-general, secretary, bureaucrat, Eurocrat, mandarin, *officer*; judicial officer, magistrate, *position of authority*; commissioner, prefect; consul, proconsul, praetor; first secretary, counsellor, envoy; alderman, mayor, councillor, functionary, party official, clerk; school prefect, monitor.

686 Advice

N. *advice*, counsel; words of wisdom, *wisdom*; *therapy*; criticism, *estimate*; moral injunction, prescription, *precept*; caution, *warning*; recommendation, proposition, proposal, motion, *supposition*; suggestion, submission; tip, *hint*; guidance, instruction, *information*; charge, *legal trial*; taking counsel, deliberation, huddle, powwow, parley, *conference*; reference, *council*; advice against.

adviser, counsellor, consultant, troubleshooter; professional consultant, *expert*; referee, arbiter; advocate, prompter; medical adviser, therapist, *doctor*; legal adviser, counsel, *lawyer*; guide, mentor, *teacher*; monitor; Nestor, Dutch uncle; oracle, wise man, *sage*; busybody; committee of enquiry, *council*.

Adj. advising, advisory; hortative; warning, *cautionary*; didactic; moral.

Vb. advise, give advice, counsel, think best, recommend, prescribe, advocate, commend; propose, move, put to, submit, suggest, *propound*; prompt, *hint*; press, urge, exhort, *incite*; advise against, *dissuade*; admonish, *warn*; enjoin, charge, dictate, *command*; be expedient.

consult, seek advice; hold a public enquiry; take advice, listen to; accept advice, follow advice; advise with, hold a council of war, deliberate, parley, sit round a table, *confer*.

687 Council

N. council, council board, round table; council chamber, board room; Star Chamber, court, *tribunal*; Privy Council; Curia; vestry; cabinet, panel, quango; think tank, board, Royal Commission; congregation, *assembly*; convocation, *synod*; convention, congress, meeting, summit; durbar, diet; moot; federal council, Security Council; municipal council, soviet; sitting, session, audience, hearing, *conference*.

parliament, Upper House, House of Lords, another place'; Lower House, House of Commons; senate; legislative assembly; National Assembly; Supreme Soviet; Congress, Senate; quorum, division.

councillor, privy councillor; peer, life peer; Lords Spiritual; representative, deputy, congressman or -woman, member of Parliament, MP, *delegate*; lobby fodder; parliamentarian; municipal councillor, mayor, alderman, *official*.

Adj. parliamentary.

688 Precept

N. precept, firm advice, *advice*; direction, instruction, injunction, charge, *command*; commission, *mandate*; order, writ, *warrant*; prescription, ordinance, regulation, *decree*; canon, form, norm, formula, rubric; *rule*; principle, rule, moral, *maxim*; recipe, receipt, *remedy*; commandment, statute, act, code, *legislation*; tenet, article, constitution; ticket, party line; canon law, *law*; rule of custom, convention, *practice*; technicality, nice point; precedent, leading case, text, *example*.

Adj. preceptive, mandatory, binding; statutory, *legal*; customary, conventional, *usual*.

689 Skill

N. skill; grace, style; address; ease, *facility*; competence; faculty, capability, capacity, *ability*; all-round capacity; touch, grip, control; mastership, prowess, *goodness*; strong point, forte, major suit; attainment, accomplishment, experience, expertise, professionalism; technology, science, know-how, technique, technical knowledge, *knowledge*; practical ability; art, artistry, delicacy, fine workmanship; finish, execution, *perfection*; craft, *cunning*; worldly wisdom; finesse, tact, dis-

cretion, *discrimination*; feat of skill, trick gimmick, dodge; tightrope walking; *tactics*; skilful use, *use*.

aptitude, innate ability; bent, *tendency* faculty, gift, flair; turn, knack; talent genius; fitness, qualification.

masterpiece, a beauty; magnum opus; work manlike job, stroke of genius, master stroke, feat, exploit, hat trick, *deed*; ace trump, clincher; work of art, curio.

Adj. skilful, good, good at, top-flight, first rate, *excellent*; crack; apt, handy, dexter ous, ambidextrous, deft, slick, adroit agile, nimble, neat; surefooted; cunning clever, quick, shrewd, smart, ingenious politic, *wise*; adaptable, flexible resourceful, ready; many-sided, versatile sound, able, competent, efficient; wizard masterful, masterly, like a master, magis terial, accomplished, finished, *perfect*.

gifted.

expert, experienced, veteran, tried; prac tised, *prepared*; finished; proficient qualified, competent; efficient, pro fessional, *businesslike*.

well-made; deep-laid; finished; happy; artis tic, artificial, sophisticated, stylish *elegant*; cunning; shipshape, workman like.

Vb. be skilful, be good at, do well, *be good* shine, excel, *be superior*; show aptitude know just when to stop; exploit, *use*; tak advantage of; get round, *be wise*; exercis discretion, *discriminate*.

be expert, turn professional; qualify oneself *learn*; have experience, be an old hand know backwards, *know*; play with, dem onstrate, stunt.

Adv. skilfully, well, with skill, like a master like a machine; naturally.

690 Unskilfulness

N. unskilfulness, want of skill; lack of prac tice; inexperience, *ignorance*; inability disqualification; *pretension*; booby prize wooden spoon.

bungling, travesty; bungle, botch, dog's breakfast, shambles; poor performance poor show, bad job, flop, *failure*; fumble muff, fluff, miss, slice, bosh shot, over throw, misfire, own goal, *mistake*; *inat tention*; *misuse*; misrule, maladministra tion; misconduct, antics; much ado abou nothing, lost labour.

Adj. unskilful, stick-in-the-mud; inept unable, incapable, *impotent*; incompe tent, inefficient, ineffectual; impolitic stupid, foolish; thoughtless; wild, giddy happy-go-lucky; feckless, futile; inad equate, *insufficient*.

unskilled, raw, green, undeveloped, *imma ture*; unqualified, inexpert, scratch ignorant, unversed; ham, lay, amateur ish, amateur; unsound, charlatan, quack specious, pretentious, *affected*.

clumsy, awkward, gauche, uncouth *discourteous*; maladroit; left-handed ungainly, hulking, gangling; stiff, rusty *unused*; unaccustomed, unpractised slapdash, *negligent*; tentative; graceless *inelegant*; top-heavy, lop-sided, *unequal* cumbersome, ponderous, ungainly unwieldy; inexact.

bungled, badly done, faulty, *imperfect*; ill advised; unhappy, infelicitous; crude amateurish, home-made, *artless*; slap dash, superficial, perfunctory; half baked.

Vb. be unskilful, tinker; catch a Tartar mishandle, mismanage, misconduct, misrule, misgovern; misapply, *misuse*; misdirect, *blunder*; *forget*; ham, overact, underact; go rusty; come a cropper, come unstuck, *fail*; *be nervous*.

act *foolishly*, make a fool of oneself, *be absurd*; become an object lesson; *lose a chance*; *blunder*; *waste effort*.

be *clumsy*, lumber, bumble, hulk; trip, stumble, *blunder*; stutter, *stammer*; fumble, grope, flounder, *be tentative*; muff, fluff; pull, slice; overthrow, overshoot, *overstep*; give a catch, give a chance; spill, slop, drop, drop a catch, drop a sitter, *let fall*; catch a crab; bungle, drop a brick, *blunder*; botch, spoil, mar, blot, *impair*; fool with, *meddle*; make a mess of it, make a hash of it, *miscarry*; do a bad job, make a poor fist at, *fail*.

691 Proficient person

N. *proficient person*, sound player, expert, adept, dab hand; handyman, *paragon*; Renaissance man; master, graduate; intellectual, mastermind, *sage*; genius, wizard, *prodigy*; magician; maestro, virtuoso; *musician*; first fiddle, champion, black belt, ace; white hope; crack shot; acrobat, gymnast, *athlete*.

expert, practitioner; professional, pro, specialist, authority, doyen, professor, *teacher*; pundit, savant, *scholar*; veteran, old hand, old soldier, sea dog; practised hand, practised eye; knowing person, smart customer, cunning fellow; sharp, *trickster*; cosmopolitan, man or woman about town, career woman; tactician, politician; artist, craftsman or -woman; technician, *artisan*; experienced hand, key man or -woman; consultant, *adviser*; boffin; connoisseur, fancier.

692 Bungler

N. *bungler*, failure, *loser*; incompetent; muff, butterfingers; lump, lout, clumsy clot, hulk, swab; duffer, stooge, clown, buffoon, booby, clot, clod, stick, oaf, ass, *fool*; slob, sloven, slattern, *slut*; scribbler, bad hand, bad shot; amateur; novice, greenhorn, colt, raw recruit, *beginner*; quack, *impostor*; landlubber, fair-weather sailor, horse marine; *misfit*.

693 Cunning

N. *cunning*, craft, *skill*, lore, *knowledge*; *imagination*; guile, gamesmanship, subtlety; stealth; chicanery, *foul play*; finesse; *deception*; *duplicity*; *flattery*; disguise; *tactics*; policy, diplomacy, real-politik; underhand dealing, sharp practice; *influence*; intrigue, *plot*.

stratagem, ruse, art, artifice, resource, resort, device, wrinkle, ploy, shift, dodge; machination, game, *plot*; subterfuge, evasion; excuse, *pretext*; white lie; cheat, *deception*; trick; feint, catch, net, web, ambush, Trojan horse, *trap*; ditch, pit, *pitfall*; web of cunning, web of deceit; blind, flag of convenience, *sham*; manoeuvre, move, *tactics*.

slyboots, crafty fellow, wily person, serpent, snake, fox; fraud, hypocrite; cheat, *trickster*; glib tongue; tactician.

Adj. *cunning*, learned, knowledgeable, *wise*; crafty, artful, sly, wily, subtle, serpentine, foxy, feline; tricky; secret; Machiavellian; knowing, fly, slick, smart, sophisticated, urbane; canny, pawky, sharp, astute, shrewd, acute; cagey, *reticent*; experienced, *skilful*; resourceful, ingenious; deep-laid; insidious; shifty, slippery, *equivocal*; deceitful; crooked, devious, *dishonest*.

Vb. *be cunning*, try a ruse, finesse, shift, dodge, juggle, manoeuvre, jockey, double-cross, twist, turn, *wriggle*; lie low, *lurk*; intrigue, scheme, play a deep game, spin a web, weave a plot, have an axe to grind, *plot*; contrive, wangle, devise, *plan*; monkey about with, tinker, gerrymander; circumvent, overreach, pull a fast one, trick, cheat, *deceive*; blarney, *flatter*; outsmart, outwit, go one better, know a trick worth two of that, *outdo*; waylay, undermine, *ambush*.

Adv. *cunningly*.

694 Artlessness

N. *artlessness*, simplicity; inexperience; candour; truth, *probity*; *ignorance*; vulgarity, crudity, *bad taste*.

ingenue, ingenuous person; child of nature, savage; lamb, *innocent*; ninny; greenhorn, novice, *beginner*; rough diamond, plain man, Philistine; simple soul, pure heart; provincial, yokel, rustic, country cousin.

Adj. *artless*, without art, without artifice, unstudied; *simple*; unvarnished, *plain*; native, natural, homespun, homemade; *unskilled*; wild, savage, primitive, backward, *ignorant*; unsophisticated, ingenuous, childlike, *innocent*; born yesterday, simple-minded, callow; guileless, confiding; unaffected, unreserved, uninhibited, *spontaneous*; candid, frank, open, straightforward, *veracious*; single, true, honest, sincere, *honourable*; aboveboard; blunt, outspoken; transparent; prosaic, matter-of-fact, literal, *accurate*; shy, inarticulate, unassuming, unpretentious, *modest*; Philistine; tone-deaf, *deaf*; uncouth, *vulgar*; *ill-bred*.

Vb. *be artless*, be *innocent*; eschew artifice; confide; call a spade a spade, *speak plainly*; *be truthful*.

Adv. *artlessly*, without art, without affectation; openly, with an open heart.

695 Difficulty

N. *difficulty*, hardness; nonstarter; perplexity; complication; inconvenience, embarrassment; drag, *friction*; rough ground, hard going, bad patch, *roughness*; quagmire, slough, *marsh*; knot, coil; problem, crux, hard nut to crack, poser, teaser, puzzle, headache; handicap, obstacle, snag, rub, *hindrance*; hitch; maze, crooked path, *convolution*; cul-de-sac, dead end, impasse, blank wall, *closure*; deadlock, standstill, stoppage, *stop*; stress, brunt, burden, *fatigue*; trial, ordeal, temptation, tribulation, *suffering*; trouble, *adversity*; difficult person, handful; hot potato.

hard task, test, trial of strength; Herculean task; task, job, hard row to hoe; handful, tall order, tough assignment, stiff job, hard work, uphill struggle, *labour*.

predicament, embarrassment, false position, delicate situation; nonplus, quandary, dilemma, cleft stick; borderline case; catch-22 situation; fix, jam, hole, scrape, hot water, trouble, fine kettle of fish, pickle, stew, imbroglio, mess, muddle; pinch, strait, straits, pass, slippery slope, sticky wicket, tight corner, ticklish situation, hot seat, *danger*; critical situation, exigency, emergency, *crisis*.

Adj. *difficult*, hard, tough, formidable; steep, arduous, uphill; inconvenient, onerous, burdensome, irksome, *laborious*; exacting, demanding, big, insuperable, impracticable, *impossible*; offering a problem, problematic, more easily said than done; delicate, ticklish, tricky; awkward, unwieldy, hard to cope with; intractable, refractory, *disobedient*; stubborn, perverse, *obstinate*; naughty, *wicked*; clueless, obscure, knotty, complex, complicated, inextricable, *intricate*; impenetrable, impassable, trackless; thorny, rugged, craggy, *rough*; sticky, critical.

in *difficulties*; clueless; *suffering*; hard pressed, hard put to it; at bay; stuck, stuck fast, aground.

Vb. *be difficult*, make things difficult; complicate, *bedevil*; inconvenience, bother, irk, plague, lead one a merry dance, *trouble*; set one a problem, pose, perplex, baffle, nonplus, stump, *puzzle*; encumber, clog, hamper, obstruct, *hinder*; make things worse, *aggravate*; lead to an impasse, create deadlock, *make impossible*; go hard with, run one hard, *endanger*.

be *in difficulty*, have a problem; *be tentative*; have more than one can cope with, *be busy*; be at a loss, *be uncertain*; be put to it, be put to trouble, have trouble with; strike a bad patch; cop it, catch a packet, catch a Tartar; have a hard time of it, *have trouble*; *suffer*; have more than enough; invite difficulty, make a problem of, make heavy weather of, flounder; stick, come unstuck, *miscarry*; swim upstream, struggle, fight, *contend*; have to face it, *face danger*.

Adv. *with difficulty*, with much ado, hardly; uphill; despite; at a pinch.

696 Facility

N. *facility*, ease, convenience, comfort; capability, capacity, *possibility*; making easy, *liberation*; free hand, full play, full scope, clean slate, *scope*; facilities, *aid*; leave, *permission*; simplicity; straightforwardness; easy going; fair wind, clear coast, clear road, *opportunity*; straight road, highway, primrose path, *road*; downhill, *descent*.

easy thing, a pleasure; soft option, short work, light work, cushy number, sinecure; picnic, doddle, *amusement*; chickenfeed, piece of cake; easy money, fast buck; smooth sailing, easy ride; nothing to it, sitter, easy target, sitting duck; easy meat, soft touch; pushover, walkover, *victory*; cinch, sure thing, dead cert, *certainty*.

Adj. *easy*, facile, cushy; effortless, painless; light, short; *smooth*; *simple*; foolproof; easily done, feasible, *possible*; helpful; downhill, downstream; convenient, *comfortable*; approachable, within reach, *accessible*; open to all, *open*; *intelligible*.

tractable, manageable, easy-going, *willing*; submissive; yielding, malleable, ductile, *flexible*; handy, manoeuvrable.

facilitated, made easy; light; unfettered, unrestrained; given a chance; at home, quite at home, at ease, *comfortable*.

Vb. *be easy*; be open to all; have a simple answer, *be intelligible*; run well, go like clockwork.

do *easily*, make nothing of, make light of, make short work of; carry all before one,

win at a canter, have a walkover, *win*; sail home; be at ease, be at home, take to like a duck to water; take it easy; *submit*; spare effort, save oneself trouble.

facilitate, ease, make easy; *smooth*; grease, oil, *lubricate*; explain, simplify, *interpret*; enable, *empower*; leave it open, allow, *permit*; give a chance to, *make possible*; help, speed, expedite, *aid*; pioneer, blaze a trail, *come before*; give full play to, leave open, leave a loophole, *give scope*.

disencumber, free, liberate, *deliver*; clear, weed, *clean*; cut through red tape; disengage, disentangle, extricate, *unravel*; untie, *disunite*; *cut*; ease, lighten, unload, unburden, alleviate, obviate, *relieve*.

Adv. *easily*, readily, like clockwork; swimmingly; without difficulty, just like that; without a hitch, without let or hindrance, freely.

697 Hindrance

N. *hindrance*, rub; fixation, hangup, block; blockage, *closure*; blockade, siege, *attack*; control, squeeze, *restraint*; arrest, *detention*; check; drag, *friction*; interference; sabotage, *opposition*; countermeasure, lockout; defence, *resistance*; disincentive; hostility, *disapprobation*; blacking, boycott; prophylaxis, sanitation, *hygiene*; birth control, *contraception*; ban, embargo, *prohibition*; nuisance value.

obstacle, hindrance, nuisance, drawback, inconvenience, handicap, *difficulty*; bunker, hazard; bottleneck, blockage, road block, traffic jam; a hindrance, tie, tether, *bond*; previous engagement; red tape; snag, block, stop, stymie; hurdle, hedge, ditch, moat; jump, barrier, bulkhead, wall, boom, dam, weir, embankment, *safeguard*; bulwark, breastplate, buffer, parapet, portcullis, barbed wire; fence, blockade; curtain, iron curtain, *partition*; stile, gate, turnstile, tollgate; crosswind, headwind, crosscurrent; impasse, deadlock, stalemate, vicious circle, catch-22; cul-de-sac, blind alley, dead end.

hitch, snag, catch, lightning strike, *strike*; repulse, rebuff, *refusal*; spot of trouble; technical hitch, breakdown, failure, engine trouble; puncture, flat; leak, burst pipe; fuse, short circuit; stoppage, holdup, setback, *stop*; something wrong, screw loose.

encumbrance, handicap; drag, clog, shackle, chain, *fetter*; baggage, lumber; cross, millstone, dead weight, *gravity*; pack, burden, load, overload, last straw; onus, incubus; mortgage, *debt*.

hinderer, hindrance; red herring; wet blanket, damper, spoilsport, killjoy; interceptor, fielder; filibuster; interloper; poltergeist, gremlin; *opponent*, rival, competitor, *contender*.

Adj. *hindering*, obstructive; cross, contrary, unfavourable, *adverse*; restrictive; prohibitive, preventive; prophylactic; offputting, intrusive, obtrusive, *extraneous*; inconvenient, *inexpedient*; hard, rough, *difficult*; onerous, burdensome, *weighty*; tripping; disincentive; defensive.

hindered, waterlogged, cramped, overgrown; held back, stuck, becalmed, *restrained*; single-handed; stranded.

Vb. *hinder*, hamper, obstruct, impede; bother, annoy, inconvenience, *trouble*; embarrass, disconcert, upset, disorder, *derange*; trip; tangle, entangle, enmesh, *ensnare*; come between, intervene, interpose, *meddle*; intercept, undermine, nip, stifle, choke; gag, muzzle, *make mute*; suffocate, repress, *suppress*; quell, kill stone dead, *kill*; hamper, burden, encumber; press, *weigh*; load with, *load*; cramp, handicap; shackle, trammel, *fetter*; restrict, circumscribe, *limit*; check, brake, hold back, *restrain*; set one back, *retard*; lame, cripple, hobble, hamstring, paralyse, *disable*; scotch, wing, *wound*; discountenance, *shame*; intimidate, deter, *frighten*; discourage, dishearten, *dissuade*; mar, spoil, *impair*; damp; snub, rebuff, *refuse*.

obstruct, intervene, interpose, interfere, *meddle*; obtrude, *intrude*; stymie, snooker, *lie between*; buzz, jostle, crowd, squeeze; *follow*; stop, intercept, block, *close*; jam, jam tight, cause a stoppage, bring to a standstill; bandage, bind, *staunch*; dam; divert, *mislead*; parry; barricade, enclose; fence, blockade, *circumscribe*; deny access, *exclude*; prevent, inhibit, ban, bar, *prohibit*.

be obstructive, give trouble, *be difficult*; stall; baffle, foil, stymie; counter, *counteract*; check, thwart, frustrate; object, *oppose*; interrupt, interject, heckle, barrack; refuse a hearing, *be loud*; take evasive action, *avoid*; filibuster, *be loquacious*; protract; strike, *halt*; picket, molest; sabotage.

698 Aid

N. aid, help, helping hand, lift, boost; succour, rescue, *deliverance*; comfort, support, backing; reinforcement; willing help; service, ministry, ministration, *kind act*; interest, good offices; custom, *purchase*; patronage, auspices, countenance, suffrage, favour, *protection*, *influence*; good will, charity, sympathy, *benevolence*; advocacy, championship; good advice, constructive criticism, *advice*; promotion, furtherance, advancement; nursing; first aid, *medical art*; relief, *refreshment*; preferential treatment, favourable conditions, favourable circumstances; fair wind, *propulsion*; facilities, magic carpet, magic wand, *facility*; self-help.

subvention, economic aid, monetary help; *gift*; charity, *philanthropy*; social security, benefit, loan, temporary accommodation, *credit*; subsidy, hand-out, bounty, grant, allowance, expense account; stipend, bursary, scholarship, *reward*; supplies, maintenance, support, keep, upkeep, *provision*; manna, *food*.

aider, help, assistant, lieutenant, henchman, aide, right-hand man, man Friday, stand-by, support, mainstay; tower of strength, rock, *protector*; district nurse, social worker, counsellor, *adviser*; good neighbour, Good Samaritan; ally; reinforcements, *auxiliary*; benefactor; sponsor, *patron*; booster, friendly critic; factor, useful ingredient, *component*; springboard, *instrument*.

Adj. aiding, helping, obliging; kind, well-disposed, well-intentioned; neighbourly, *friendly*; favourable, propitious; of service, of help, *useful*; constructive, well-meant; assistant, auxiliary, subsidiary, ancillary, accessory; contributory; subservient, *serving*; *instrumental*.

Vb. aid, help, assist, lend a hand, give a helping hand; give a lift to; spoonfeed; be kind to, do one a good turn; see one through; oblige, accommodate, lend money to, *lend*; facilitate, speed, lend wings to, further, advance, boost, *promote*; abet, instigate, foment, nourish, *induce*; contribute to, be accessory to; lend support to, bolster, *support*; comfort, sustain, hearten, give heart to, encourage, rally, embolden, *give courage*; succour, send help to, relieve, *deliver*; reinforce, fortify, *strengthen*; ease, *refresh*; *restore*.

patronize, favour, *be auspicious*; sponsor, back, guarantee; recommend; propose, second; countenance, give countenance to, connive at, protect, *safeguard*; join; contribute to, subscribe to, *endorse*; befriend; side with, champion, *defend*; vote; give moral support to, intercede; *defray*; entertain, keep, cherish, foster, nurse, mother, *pet*; *purchase*.

minister to, help, oblige, *serve*; give first aid to, nurse, *doctor*; squire, valet, mother; be of service to, make oneself useful to, be *useful*; be willing; toady, humour, *flatter*; slave, *work*; be assistant to, *be instrumental*.

Adv. in aid of; thanks to.

699 Opposition

N. *opposition*, antagonism, hostility, enmity; conflict, friction, lack of harmony, *dissension*; repugnance, *dislike*; denial; challenge, *defiance*; firm opposition, stand, *resistance*; revolt; going against, *disapprobation*; walkout, *dissent*; physical opposition, headwind, crosscurrent, *obstacle*; mutual opposition, tug of war; faction, competition; political opposition, underground, alternative society, *nonconformity*.

opposites; *contender*.

Adj. opposing; against; hostile, *inimical*; unfavourable, *adverse*; cross; *contrary*; cussed, bloody-minded, *obstinate*; refractory, recalcitrant, *disobedient*; at odds with; militant; facing, face to face, eyeball to eyeball, *frontal*; *opposite*; rival, *jealous*.

Vb. *oppose*, go against, *be contrary*; side against, *resist*; reject; object, kick, protest, protest against, *deprecate*; collide; vote against, *disapprove*; dissociate oneself; contradict, belie, *negate*; counter; work against, *counteract*; thwart, baffle, foil, *be obstructive*; challenge, dare, *defy*; set at naught; *hold cheap*; flout, *disobey*; rebuff, spurn, *refuse*; emulate, rival, match oneself with, compete with, bid against, *contend*; set against.

withstand, confront, face, *face danger*; rise against, *revolt*; meet, encounter, *fight*; struggle against, breast, stem; cope with, *be active*; *stand firm*; *resist*.

Adv. in opposition, against, versus; despite.

700 Opponent

N. *opponent*; adversary, antagonist, foe, *enemy*; assailant; opposite camp; independent party; diehard, irreconcilable; reactionary, counter-revolutionary; dissident, *malcontent*; agitator; rival, competitor, runner-up; fighter; entrant, *contender*; wrangler; common enemy, universal foe, outlaw.

701 Cooperation

N. *cooperation*; symbiosis; duet, double harness, tandem; joint effort; team work, working together, concerted effort; relay, relay race, team spirit; lack of friction, agreement, *concord*; party spirit; *inducement*; conspiracy, *plot*; complicity, sympathy; fraternity, solidarity, fellowship, freemasonry, fellow feeling, comradeship; common cause, helping one another; mutual concession, *compromise*; mutual advice, *conference*.

association, coming together; *joint possession*; pool, kitty; membership, affiliation; tie-up, *relation*; ecosystem; combination, *union*; solidarity, *whole*; *unity*; fusion, merger; voluntary association, coalition, alliance, league, federation, confederacy; axis, united front, *political party*; an association, fellowship, college, club, fraternity, *community*; set, clique, cell, *party*; trade union, chapel; business association, company, syndicate, combine, consortium, trust, cartel, ring, *corporation*; housing association, economic community, commune, *community*.

Adj. *cooperative*, helpful; married; bipartisan; federal, *corporate*.

Vb. *cooperate*, collaborate, work together; join forces, *participate*; show willing, play ball, reciprocate, respond; lend oneself to, espouse; take part; rally round, *aid*; hang together, stand shoulder to shoulder, sink or swim together; make common cause with; network, band together, associate, league, ally; coalesce, merge, unite, *be mixed*; combine, make common cause, club together; understand one another, think alike; conspire, *plot*; *consult*; collude, connive; treat with, negotiate, *make terms*.

Adv. *cooperatively*.

Int. All together now!

702 Auxiliary

N. *auxiliary*, relay, recruit, fresh troops, reinforcement; second line, paramilitary formation; ally, assistant, helpmate, helping hand; right-hand man, second, tower of strength; adjutant, lieutenant, aide-de-camp; secretary, clerk; midwife; dogsbody, *servant*; server; best man, bridesmaid; *friend*; hanger-on, satellite, henchman, follower, *dependant*; disciple, adherent, *sectarian*; loyalist; stooge, puppet, *instrument*; shadow, familiar; jackal, running dog, creature.

collaborator; fellow traveller, fifth column, fifth columnist.

colleague, associate, fellow, brother, sister; partner; comrade, companion, playmate; alter ego, second self, faithful companion; mate, chum, pal, buddy, crony, *friend*; helpmate, better half, *spouse*; standby, stalwart; ally; accomplice, accessory.

patron, guardian angel, *protector*; well-wisher; champion, advocate, friend at court; supporter, sponsor, backer, guarantor; voter; aficionado, fan, *lover*; good friend, Jack at a pinch; rich uncle, *benefactor*; founder; patron of art, collector; customer, client.

703 Party

N. *party*, movement; group, class, *classification*; confession, communion, denomination, church, *sect*; faction, cabal, cave, splinter group; circle, kitchen cabinet; set, clique, caucus, junta, politburo, committee, club, cell, cadre; ring, closed shop; team, eight, eleven, fifteen; crew, complement, *personnel*; troupe, company, *actor*; gang, knot, bunch, outfit, *band*; horde, *crowd*; side, camp.

political *party*, right, left, centre; Conservative, National Front; Labour; Greens; coalition, popular front, bloc; comrade, Red, commie, Trot; socialist, Fabian; rightist, true blue; leftist; populist, democrat; moderate; party worker, party member, politician; militant, activist, *doer*.

society, coalition, combination, combine, *association*; league, alliance, axis; federation, confederacy; economic association, union, EEC, Common Market, free trade area; private society, club, *focus*; secret society, Freemasonry, lodge, cell; friendly society; chapel; group, division, branch, youth movement, Cubs; fellow, associate, member; party member, comrade; corresponding member, affiliate, *component*.

community, fellowship, brotherhood, body, congregation, fraternity; guild; race, tribe, clan, sect, *family*; order, *classification*; social class, *social group*; state, nation.

corporation, body; incorporated society, body corporate, *council*; company, firm, concern; house, establishment, institute; trust, combine, monopoly, cartel, syndicate, conglomerate, *association*; trade association, chamber of commerce, guild.

Adj. *corporate*, incorporate; joint, bonded, federal; allied; social, *sociable*; fraternal, *friendly*; communal.

sectional, Masonic, *sectarian*; clannish, exclusive; class-conscious; rightist, true-blue; right of centre, leftist, pink, red; Tory; radical, conservative.

Vb. *join a party*, subscribe; join, become a member; enlist; *enter*; belong to, make one of; side with, range oneself with; club together, associate, ally, league; cement a union, merge; found a party.

Adv. *in league*, shoulder to shoulder, back to back; all together.

704 Dissension

N. *dissension*, dissent; *opposition*; disharmony, dissonance, jar, jangle, *discord*; recrimination; odds, friction, tension; *resentment*; hostility, *hatred*; disunity, internal dissension; rift, cleavage, cleavage of opinion, separation; split, faction, *schism*; misunderstanding; breach, rupture, severance of relations; challenge, *defiance*; ultimatum, declaration of war, *war*.

quarrelsomeness; warlike behaviour; *defiance*; sharp tongue, *scurrility*; mischief, spite; apple of discord, spirit of mischief, Ate, Mars.

quarrel, feud, vendetta, *revenge*; war, *warfare*; strife; conflict, clash, *collision*; legal battle; controversy, dispute, wrangle; paper war, *argument*; wordy warfare, words, stormy exchange, altercation, set-to, abuse, *scurrility*; jar, spat, tiff, squabble, jangle, wrangle, hassle, squall; rumpus, hubbub, racket, row, commotion, scrimmage, fracas, brawl, fisticuffs, *turmoil*; gang warfare, riot, *fight*.

casus belli; tender spot, sore point; apple of discord, bone to pick; point at issue.

quarreller, wrangler; rival, *contender*; scold, bitter tongue, *shrew*; aggressor.

Adj. *quarrelling*, contrary; at odds, at loggerheads, *inimical*; schismatic; rebellious, *disobedient*; sore; awkward, cantankerous, *irascible*; *sullen*; implacable; quarrelsome, bellicose, *warlike*; pugnacious, combative, aggressive, militant; abusive, shrewish, scurrilous; argumentative, contentious.

Vb. *quarrel*, disagree, *dissent*; clash, conflict, *collide*; misunderstand, pull different ways, have a bone to pick, *differ*; recriminate, *retaliate*; part company, split, break with; declare war, *go to war*, go to law, take it to court, *litigate*; dispute; have a feud with; sulk, *be sullen*; oppose.

make *quarrels*, pick a fight, start it; make something of it, challenge, *defy*; irritate, provoke, *enrage*; have a bone to pick, have a crow to pluck; cherish a feud, enjoy a quarrel; embroil, entangle, estrange, set at odds, *excite hate*; create discord, *discord*; sow dissension, make mischief, make trouble; divide, draw apart, disunite, come between, *sunder*; *aggravate*; set against, match with; incite, *motivate*.

bicker, spat, tiff, squabble; nag, jar, spar, spar with; jangle, wrangle, dispute with, *argue*; scold, *cuss*; have words with, row, row with; brawl, *rampage*.

705 Concord

N. *concord*, harmony, *melody*; unison, unity, duet, *agreement*; *consensus*; lack of friction, understanding, rapport; solidarity, team spirit; sympathy, fellow feeling, *love*; amity, *friendship*; rapprochement, reunion, reconciliation; good offices; happy family, *peace*; goodwill, honeymoon period.

Adj. *concordant*; eye to eye, unanimous, of one mind, bipartisan; compatible, united, bonded, allied; fraternal, loving, amicable, *friendly*; happy, peaceable, pacific, at peace, *peaceful*.

Vb. *concord*; pacify; agree, *accord*; see eye to eye, play a duet, pull together; reciprocate, respond, run parallel, *concur*; *be friendly*; remain at peace, *be at peace*.

706 Defiance

N. *defiance*, dare, daring, challenge, gauntlet; bold front, brave face, *courage*; war dance, war cry, war whoop, war song, battle cry; *threat*; display, *ostentation*.

Adj. *defiant*, challenging, provocative, bellicose, militant, *warlike*; saucy, *insolent*; rebellious, *disobedient*; greatly daring, *courageous*; stiff-necked, *proud*; reckless, trigger-happy, *rash*.

Vb. *defy*, challenge, *dissent*; *oppose*; caution, warn; demand satisfaction; dare, beard; brave; *face danger*; laugh to scorn, set at naught; *hold cheap*; bid defiance to; show fight, *threaten*; *be proud*; look big, show a bold front; wave a banner, *brandish*; march, demonstrate, stage a sit-in; *be insolent*; shout, *triumph*; crow, bluster, brag, *boast*.

Adv. *defiantly*.

Int. do your worst! come on if you dare!

707 Attack

N. *attack*, best method of defence; aggression, *injustice*; *foul play*; assault, grievous bodily harm, *violence*; armed attack, offensive, drive, push, thrust, pincer movement, *tactics*; run at, dead set at; onslaught, onset, rush, shock, charge;

sally, sortie, breakthrough; counterattack; shock tactics, surprise; invasion, incursion, irruption; raid, foray; blitz, air raid, air attack, night attack; storm; boarding; investment, siege, blockade, *surroundings*; challenge, tilt.

terror *tactics*, war of nerves; bloodbath, *slaughter*; havoc.

bombardment, cannonade, barrage, strafe, blitz; broadside, volley, salvo; fire, gunfire, fusillade, burst of fire; antiaircraft fire, flak.

lunge, thrust, pass; cut, stab, jab; bayonet, cold steel; punch, swipe, kick, *knock*.

attacker, assailant, aggressor; hawk, militant; spearhead, storm troops, strike force; fighter pilot, air ace, bomber, *armed force*; sharpshooter; raider.

Adj. *attacking*, pugnacious, combative, aggressive, *warlike*; militant, hostile, *inimical*; boarding.

Vb. *attack*; start a fight, declare war, *go to war*; assault, assail, make a dead set at, have at; savage, maul, draw blood, *wound*; let fly at, let one have it; surprise, blitz, overwhelm; invade, *encroach*; raid, foray, overrun, infest; show fight; counterattack, *retaliate*; thrust, push, *impel*; erupt, sally, make a sortie, break through, *emerge*; board, lay aboard; storm, carry, capture, *overmaster*; ravage, make havoc, scorch, burn, *lay waste*; harry, drive, beat, corner, bring to bay, *hunt*; challenge, *defy*; *oppose*; break a lance, *fight*.

besiege, lay siege to, invest, surround, blockade, *enclose*; sap, mine, undermine, spring a mine.

strike *at*; lay about one, swipe, flail, hammer, *strike*, kick; go berserk, run amok, *be violent*; have at, have a fling at, fetch a blow, have a cut at; mug; clash, ram, *collide*; make a pass at, lunge; close with, come to close quarters, fight hand to hand; push, butt, thrust, poke at, thrust at; stab, spear, lance, bayonet, run through, *pierce*; strike home, lay low, abase; *be dishonest*.

charge, advance against; rush, mob, *rampage*; make a rush, rush at, run at, dash at, tilt at, ride full tilt at; ram, shock, *collide*.

fire *at*, shoot at; fire a shot at, take a potshot, pop at, snipe, *shoot*; torpedo, sink; strafe, bombard, blitz, cannonade, shell, fusillade, pepper; bomb, plaster; open fire, let fly, volley; rattle, blast, rake, straddle; take aim, level, *aim*.

lapidate, stone, throw a stone, heave a brick; shy, sling, pelt; hurl at, *propel*.

Adv. *aggressively*.

708 Defence

N. *defence*, self-defence, *resistance*; art of self-defence, boxing, *pugilism*; judo; counter, parry; posture of defence, guard; defensive alliance, balance of power; safekeeping, *preservation*; *protection*; a defence, rampart, bulwark, screen, buffer, fender, bumper, *safeguard*; deterrent, *weapon*; munitions, *ammunition*.

defences, lines, fieldwork; outwork; earthwork, embankment, mound; mole, boom; wall, barricade, fence, *barrier*; palisade, stockade; moat, ditch; trench, dugout; booby trap, *trap*; barbed wire; spike; Great Wall of China; bunker, *shelter*; barrage, antiaircraft fire, flak; barrage balloon; minefield, mine; smokescreen, *screen*.

fortification (see *fort*); bulwark, rampart, wall; parapet, loophole; scarp; curtain, bastion; outwork; buttress.

fort, fortress, stronghold, fastness; citadel, capitol, *refuge*; castle, keep, ward, tower, turret, donjon; portcullis, drawbridge; gate, postern, sally port; peel, pillbox; blockhouse, strong point; Roman camp; British camp, *earthwork*.

armour, harness; full armour, panoply; mail, scale armour, armour plate; breastplate; cuirass; hauberk, coat of mail; helmet, helm; visor, beaver; siege cap, steel helmet, tin hat; bearskin, busby; gauntlet; shield, target; protective clothing, riot shield, gas mask, *safeguard*.

defender, champion, *patron*; loyalist, patriot; bodyguard, lifeguard, Praetorian Guard, *soldier*; watch, sentry; patrol, patrolman; garrison, picket, guard, escort, rearguard; Home Guard, militia, thin red line; fireman, firewatcher; Civil Defence; guardian, warden, *protector*, warder, custodian, *keeper; deliverance*.

Adj. *defending*; defensive, protective, anti-aircraft.

defended, armoured; *prepared*; castellated; entrenched; defensible, proof, bulletproof, *invulnerable*.

Vb. *defend*, guard, protect, keep, watch, ward, *safeguard*; fence, hedge, moat, *circumscribe*; palisade, barricade, *enclose*; block, *obstruct*; cushion, pad, shield, curtain, cover, *screen*; cloak, *conceal*; provide with arms, arm, *make ready*; harness, armour; reinforce, fortify, *strengthen; stand firm*; garrison, man; champion, *vindicate*; rescue, *deliver*.

parry, counter, riposte, fence, fend, hold or keep at bay, keep at arm's length, *avoid*; turn, avert, deflect; play, play with; stall, block, *obstruct*; fight a defensive battle, stalemate; fight back, show fight, give a warm reception to, *resist*; repulse, *repel; withstand; avail oneself of; turn back*; survive, scrape through, live to fight another day, *escape*.

Adv. *defensively*, at bay.

709 Retaliation

N. *retaliation*, reprisal, revenge; requital, recompense, comeuppance, *reward*; desert, deserts; punitive action, retribution, Nemesis, *punishment*; reaction, boomerang, backlash, *recoil*; counter; counterattack, sally, sortie, *attack*; recrimination, riposte, retort, *rejoinder*; a game at which two can play; deterrent.

Adj. *retaliatory*; punitive; reciprocal.

Vb. *retaliate*, recoup; *punish*; counter, riposte, *parry*; make a requital, be quits, get even with, *avenge*; requite, *reward*; serve rightly, teach one a lesson; reciprocate; return, retort, cap, answer back, *answer*; recriminate, *accuse*; react, boomerang, *recoil*; kick back, *resist*; hoist one with his own petard.

be rightly served, serve one right; get what was coming to one.

Adv. en revanche.

Int. it serves you right! take that! *put that in your pipe and* smoke it! the laugh's on you! now who's laughing!

710 Resistance

N. *resistance*, stand, brave front, *opposition*; reluctance; repugnance, *dislike*; demur, *qualification*; protest, passive resistance; rising, insurrection, resistance movement, backlash, *revolt*; self-defence, *defence*; repulsion, repulse, rebuff, bloody nose, *refusal*; refusal to work, *strike*.

Adj. *resisting*, standing firm against; reluctant; recalcitrant, *disobedient*; stubborn, *obstinate*; indomitable; tough, proof, bulletproof, waterproof; *repellent*.

Vb. *resist*, offer resistance, give a warm reception, stand against, *withstand*; obstruct, *hinder*; challenge, defy; confront, outface, *face danger*; struggle against, contend with, *oppose*; kick, protest, *deprecate*; demur, object, *qualify*; cease; engineer a strike, *halt*; mutiny, rise, *revolt*; make a stand, keep at arm's length, *parry*; make a fight of it, *contend; stand firm*; endure, *suffer*; be proof against, repel, rebuff, *refuse*; resist temptation; last, *outlast*.

Int. No surrender!

711 Contention

N. *contention*, strife, tussle, conflict, clash, running battle, *dissension*; combat, war, *warfare*; debate, dispute, controversy, polemics, paper warfare, *argument*; altercation, words, *quarrel*; stakes; competition; gamesmanship, rat race; cutthroat competition; sports, athletics, *sport*.

contest, trial, trial of strength, test of endurance, marathon, pentathlon, decathlon, tug-of-war; tussle, struggle, *attempt*; bitter struggle, needle match; equal contest, dingdong fight; close finish, *short distance*; competition, free-for-all; knockout competition, tournament, joust, tilt; prize competition, stakes; match, rally; event, handicap; heat, final, semifinal, quarterfinal, Cup tie; set, game, rubber; sporting event, wager, bet, *sport*; field day, *amusement*; Derby day (see *racing*); athletics, gymnastics; gymkhana, rodeo; games, Highland Games; Lords, *arena*.

racing, speed contest, *speeding*; race, sprint, dash; road race, marathon, slalom, obstacle race; relay race, horse racing, sport of kings; point-to-point, steeplechase, sticks, *leap*; motor race, motor rally, speedway, motocross; cycle race; dog racing, boat race; regatta; racecourse, track, stadium, *arena*.

pugilism, noble art of self-defence, boxing, fisticuffs; boxing match, prizefight; mill, spar, clinch, in-fighting; round, bout; *sport*.

wrestling, judo, karate; catch, hold; wrestle.

duel, affair of honour; single combat, tournament; fencing, swordplay, quarterstaff; bullfight; cockfight; bullring, cockpit, lists, *arena*.

fight, hostilities, appeal to arms, *warfare*; battle royal, free fight, free-for-all, roughhouse, horseplay, scuffle, scrum, scrimmage, scramble, dogfight, fracas, uproar, rumpus, *turmoil*; gang warfare, street fight, riot, rumble; brawl, broil, *quarrel*; fisticuffs; affray, set-to, tussle; running fight, close quarters; combat, fray, clash, conflict, *collision*; encounter, dustup, scrap, brush; skirmish; engagement, action, stand-up fight, shoot-out, *battle*; deed of arms, *deed*; campaign, struggle; death struggle; field of battle, battlefield.

contender; fighter; gladiator, *combatant*; fencer, swordsman; candidate, entrant; competitor, rival; runner-up, finalist;

front runner, favourite, top seed; starter, also-ran; runner, *athlete*.

Adj. *contending*, rival, racing; *sporting*; running; athletic; contentious, quarrelsome; irritable, *irascible*; aggressive, combative, pugnacious, bellicose, *warlike*; at loggerheads, at odds, at war; keen, cutthroat; hand-to-hand, close, at close quarters; dingdong.

Vb. contend, combat, strive, struggle, battle, fight, tussle, wrestle, *attempt*; oppose, *resist*; make a point of, insist; contest, compete, challenge, stake, wager, bet; play, play against, match oneself, vie with, race, run a race; emulate, rival, *be jealous*; *outdo*; enter; tilt with, try a fall, *strike at*; have a hard fight, fight to a finish.

fight, have a fight, scuffle, row, scrimmage, scrap, set to, *be violent*; *attack*; lay about one, *strike at*; mix it; box, spar, pummel, jostle, hit, kick, scratch, bite, *strike*; fall foul of, join issue with, *quarrel*; duel, give satisfaction; encounter, have a brush with, skirmish; engage, *give battle*; come to close quarters, close with; fence, fight hand to hand, use cold steel; appeal to arms, *go to war*; combat, campaign, *wage war*; fight hard, *be resolute*.

712 Peace

N. *peace*, a quiet life; harmony, *concord*; piping times of peace; peacetime; universal peace; *order*; end of hostilities, *cessation*; truce, armistice, *lull*; *moderation*; cordial relations, *friendship*; pacifism, peace at any price, nonviolence; pipe of peace; league of peace, peace treaty, *treaty*; *amnesty*.

pacifist, man or woman of peace, dove; peace party, *moderator*; neutral, civilian, noncombatant; peacemaker, *mediator*.

Adj. *peaceful*, quiet, halcyon, *tranquil*; piping, *palmy*; without war, without bloodshed, bloodless; harmless, *innocent*; easygoing, *amiable*; peaceable, law-abiding, pacific; pacifist; unarmed, noncombatant, civilian; passive, submissive; at peace; neutral; peacetime.

Vb. *be at peace*, be pacific, *be innocent*; avoid bloodshed; *mediate*.

Adv. *peacefully*; without violence.

713 War

N. *war*, arms; appeal to arms, undeclared war; paper war, *quarrel*; war of nerves; gunboat diplomacy; police action; real war, internecine war, war of revolution; holy war, crusade, jihad; aggressive war; limited war; major war, total war, atomic war, push-button war; war of attrition; chivalry; martial music, bugle, trumpet; call to arms, bugle call, *call*; battle cry, war whoop, war song, *defiance*; god of war, Mars.

belligerency, state of war, state of siege; resort to arms, declaration of war, hostilities; wartime, wartime conditions, time of war.

bellicosity, war fever; love of war, military spirit; militarism; jingoism, chauvinism, *prejudice*.

art *of war*, strategy, *tactics*; *fortification*; *skill*; ballistics; drill, training, *teaching*; logistics, *plan*; military experience, *knowledge*.

war *measures*, war footing, *preparation*; call to arms, clarion call, fiery cross, *call*; war effort, war work, call-up, national ser-

vice, military duty; blackout.

warfare, war, warpath, making war, bloodshed, *violence*; active service; military service, *bombardment*; investment; aerial warfare, economic warfare, blockade, attrition; psychological warfare, propaganda; offensive warfare, *attack*; defensive warfare, *defence*; mobile warfare; campaign, expedition; incursion, invasion, raid; order, word of command, orders, *command*; password, watchword; battle cry, slogan, *call*; plan of campaign, battle orders, *plan*.

battle, battle royal, *fight*; line of battle, array; line, front, battle station; armed conflict, action, scrap, skirmish, brush, collision, clash; offensive, blitz, *attack*; defensive battle, stand, *defence*; engagement, sea fight, dogfight; arena, battlefield, field of battle, theatre of war, area of hostilities.

Adj. *warring*; at war, militant; armed, *prepared*; embattled; engaged, at loggerheads.

warlike, bellicose; militant, aggressive, pugnacious, combative; fierce, *cruel*; bloodthirsty; military, paramilitary, martial, veteran; chivalrous; military, naval; operational.

Vb. *go to war*, resort to arms; declare war, open hostilities; appeal to arms, *fight*; take to arms, rise, rebel, *revolt*; call to arms; arm; recruit, conscript; enlist, take a commission.

wage *war*, march to war, war, war against; campaign; shoulder a musket, smell powder; soldier; invade, *attack*; *stand firm*; *defend*; manoeuvre, march; blockade, besiege, invest, *surround*; shed blood, *slaughter*; ravage, burn, scorch, *lay waste*; demolish.

give *battle*, battle, join battle; engage, provoke an engagement; combat, *fight*; take a position, rally, stand, *resist*; *charge*; open fire, *fire at*; skirmish, brush with, contend.

Adv. *at war*.

714 Pacification

N. *pacification*; appeasement, *moderation*; reconciliation, rapprochement; accommodation, *agreement*; *compromise*; good offices, convention, entente, understanding, peace treaty, SALT, *treaty*; suspension of hostilities, truce, armistice, ceasefire, *lull*; forced reconciliation, *compulsion*.

peace *offering*, *moderator*; appeasement; olive branch, overture, peaceful approach, hand of friendship; flag of truce, white flag, pipe of peace, *peace*; blood money, *restitution*; fair offer, easy terms, *moderation*; amnesty; mercy, *forgiveness*.

Adj. *pacificatory*; friendly; happy, *content*.

Vb. *pacify*, make peace, give peace to; allay, mollify, soothe, *assuage*; heal, *cure*; return a soft answer, coo like a dove, *be friendly*; conciliate, propitiate, disarm, reconcile, placate, appease, satisfy, *content*; bring to rest; restore harmony; bring to terms, meet halfway, *compromise*; accommodate, *adjust*; bring together, mediate; show mercy, *be lenient*; grant a truce, grant an armistice, grant peace, give terms; be at peace.

make *peace*, cry quits, *cease*; let bygones be bygones, *forget*; come to an understanding, agree to differ; make a truce, suspend hostilities, disarm.

715 Mediation

N. *mediation*, good offices; diplomacy; parley, *conference*.

mediator, common friend, middleman, matchmaker, go-between, *intermediary*; umpire, referee; representative, attorney, agent, *delegate*; peace party, *moderator*; troubleshooter, ombudsman; marriage guidance counsellor, *adviser*, peacemaker, dove.

Adj. *mediatory*. propitiatory.

Vb. *mediate*, intervene, *meddle*; put oneself between, interpose, *put between*; propitiate; be a go-between; bring together, negotiate; arbitrate, umpire, *judge*; *pacify*.

716 Submission

N. *submission*; *servitude*; compliance, consent, *assent*; peace at any price, line of least resistance, resignation, fatalism; yielding, white flag, surrender; deference, humble submission, *humility*; act of submission, homage, *loyalty*; kowtow, *obeisance*; quitter; mouse, doormat, *coward*.

Adj. *submitting*, quiet, meek, law-abiding, *peaceful*; submissive, *obedient*; resigned, acquiescent; malleable, *soft*; weak-kneed, supine, prostrate; *humble*.

Vb. *submit*, yield; defer to; bow to, make a virtue of necessity, yield with a good grace, admit defeat; resign oneself, be resigned, *acquiesce*; accept, *assent*; be indifferent; withdraw, *turn back*; cease resistance, cry quits, have had enough, surrender; capitulate; yield oneself; renounce authority.

knuckle *under*, succumb, collapse; sag, wilt, faint, drop; be submissive, do homage, *be subject*; eat humble pie, eat dirt, *be humble*; take it, digest, stomach, *suffer*; bend, bow, kneel, kowtow, crouch, cringe, crawl, *stoop*; grovel; *ask mercy*.

717 Combatant. Army. Navy. Air Force

N. *combatant*, fighter, *contender*; aggressor, assailant; shock troops; warrior, brave; bodyguard; gunman, strongarm man; bully, bravo, rough, rowdy, *ruffian*; swashbuckler; swordsman, fencer, sword, gladiator, *athlete*; toreador, matador, picador; competitor, *contender*; champion, champ; knight, *patron*; wrangler; barrister, advocate.

pugilist, pug, boxer, bruiser; flyweight, bantamweight, featherweight, welterweight, middleweight, heavyweight; *pugilism*.

militarist, militant, warmonger, hawk; Samurai; professional soldier, freelance, mercenary (see *soldier*); soldier of fortune, adventurer; freebooter, pirate, privateer, buccaneer.

soldier, army man; military man, long-term soldier, regular; troops (see *armed force*); conquistador; old soldier, veteran; warrior, brave; man-at-arms, centurion; colour escort, colour sergeant, ensign, cornet; sharpshooter; auxiliary, territorial, Home Guard; yeomanry, yeoman; irregular, irregular troops; raider, freedom fighter; underground fighter; *elite*; *protector* (see *armed force*); volunteer; pressed man; conscript, recruit, rookie; serviceman, GI, Aussie, sepoy; woman soldier, female warrior, Amazon, Wren, WRAC.

soldiery, cannon fodder; gallant company, merry men, private, private soldier, man-at-arms; archer, bowman; lancer; musketeer, rifleman, grenadier, bombardier; gunner; pioneer, sapper, miner, engineer; signalman; corporal, sergeant, lieutenant, *army officer*.

army, host, camp; phalanx, legion, horde, mass, *multitude*; warlike people, martial race; general levy; National Guard, militia, yeomanry; regular army, draft; armed forces, air arm, fleet air arm, fleet.

armed force, forces, troops, effectives, men, personnel; armament, armada; ceremonial troops, household troops; Household Cavalry; spearhead, expeditionary force, flying column; parachute troops, paratroops, commando, task force; combat troops, field army, line, first echelon; wing, van, vanguard, rear, rearguard, centre, main body; second echelon, base troops, reinforcements, draft, levy, *auxiliary*; base, staff; detachment, picket, party, detail; patrol, night patrol, night watch, sentry, *protector*; garrison, occupation troops, army of occupation.

formation, array, line; square, phalanx; legion, cohort, century; column, file, rank; unit, group, detachment, corps, division, brigade, artillery brigade, battery; regiment, squadron, troop; battalion, company, platoon, section, squad, detail, party, *band*.

infantry, foot regiment, foot soldier, foot; mountain infantry.

cavalry, yeomanry; heavy cavalry, horse, cavalry regiment; horseman, rider; horse artillery; horse soldier, yeoman; trooper; chivalry, knight; man-at-arms, lancer, hussar, dragoon; armour, armoured car, armoured personnel carrier; tank, Panzer; charger.

navy, sea power, admiralty; sail; fleet, flotilla, naval armament, armada; fleet, flotilla.

naval man, naval service, navy, senior service; admiral, Sea Lord, *naval officer*; sailor, *mariner*; able seaman, rating, pressed man; powder monkey; cabin boy; gob, swab; marine, jolly, limey; submariner, *nautical personnel*; Royal Navy, RN; Wavy Navy.

warship, war vessel, war galley, trireme, galleon, *ship*; raider, privateer, pirate ship; armoured vessel, capital ship, battleship; monitor; cruiser, frigate, corvette; mosquito boat, gunboat, motor torpedo boat; destroyer; fire ship; minelayer, minesweeper; submarine, U-boat; aircraft carrier, landing craft, duck, amphibian; transport, troopship; tender, store ship, flagship, flotilla leader.

air force; Royal Air Force Volunteer Reserve; air arm, flying corps, air service, fleet air arm, squadron, flight, group, wing; *aircraft*; battle plane, bomber, fighter, interceptor; flying boat, patrol plane, scout; transport plane; Zeppelin, captive balloon, *airship*; air troops, airborne division; parachute troops; aircraftman, ground staff; fighter pilot, navigator, air crew.

718 Arms

N. *arms* (see *weapon*); armament, munitions; arms race; nuclear deterrent, *defence*; arms traffic; ballistics, rocketry, archery.

arsenal, armoury, gun room, gun rack,

ammunition chest; arms depot, *storage*; magazine, powder barrel, powder keg, powder flask, powder horn; caisson, ammunition box; cartridge belt; quiver; scabbard, sheath; holster, *receptacle*.

weapon, arm, deterrent; deadly weapon, armour, plate, mail, *defence*; offensive weapon, *attack*; conventional weapon, *warfare*; secret weapon, death ray, laser; germ warfare, gas, *poison*; natural weapon, teeth, *sharp point*.

missile *weapon*, javelin, harpoon, dart; lasso; boomerang; arrow, shaft, bolt, quarrel; arrowhead, barb; stone, brick, brickbat; shot, ball, bullet, pellet, shell, shrapnel, rocket, bow, longbow, crossbow, catapult, sling; blowpipe; bazooka, cruise missile, ICBM, *missile*.

club, mace, *hammer*; ram; bat, staff, stave, stick, switch, quarterstaff; bludgeon, truncheon, cudgel, sandbag, knuckleduster, cosh, bicycle chain.

spear, harpoon, gaff; lance, javelin, pike, assegai; bill, halberd, *sharp point*.

axe, battleaxe, tomahawk, hatchet, halberd; bill; poleaxe, chopper, *sharp edge*.

sidearms, sword; cold steel, broadsword, claymore, two-edged sword, cutlass, hanger, short sword, swordstick; sabre, scimitar; blade; rapier, tuck; fencing sword, épée, foil; dagger, bayonet, dirk, poniard, dudgeon, stiletto, *sharp point*; machete; knife, *sharp edge*.

firearm, small arms, hand gun; flintlock, musket; blunderbuss; rifle, sporting gun, shotgun; bore, calibre; muzzle; trigger, lock; magazine; breech, butt; sight; ramrod.

pistol; six-shooter, colt, revolver, repeater, rod, automatic.

gun, ordnance, artillery, horse artillery; battery, broadside; artillery park, cannon, bombard, swivel, petard; mortar; piece, field piece, field gun, great gun, cannon royal, heavy metal; howitzer, trench gun; antiaircraft gun, ack-ack, bazooka; assault gun, pom-pom, Maxim, machine gun, flamethrower; caisson; rocket site, silo.

ammunition, live shot; round of ammunition, round; shot, buckshot; ball, cannonball, bullet, projectile, *missile*; slug, stone, pellet; shell, shrapnel; flak, ack-ack; wad, cartridge, spent cartridge, dud; cartridge belt, cartridge clip; cartridge case.

explosive; powder, gunpowder; saltpetre, high explosive, gun cotton, dynamite, gelignite, TNT; cap, detonator; fuse; priming, charge, warhead.

bomb, explosive device; shell, bombshell; grenade, pineapple; megaton bomb, A-bomb, H-bomb; mushroom cloud, fallout; blockbuster; cluster bomb, incendiary bomb, Greek fire; mine, landmine; limpet; booby trap, *trap*; depth charge, torpedo, tin fish; flying bomb, V-1, V-2; rocket bomb; time bomb, infernal machine.

719 Arena

N. arena, field, field of action; ground, terrain; centre, scene, stage, theatre; hustings, platform, floor; amphitheatre, stadium, stand, grandstand; campus, parade ground, forum, *focus*; hippodrome, circus, course, racecourse, turf; track, ring, bullring, ropes; rink, gymnasium, gym; range; playground, beach, lido, pier, fairground, *pleasure ground*;

recreation ground, pitch, court, bowling alley, lists; cockpit; bridge table; auction room; examination hall.

battleground, battlefield, field of battle; field of blood; theatre of war, combat zone; front, front line; sector, salient, bulge, pocket; beachhead, bridgehead; *battle*.

720 Completion

N. completion, finish, end; terminus, goal; issue, upshot, *event*; result, end product, *effect*; fulfilment, *sufficiency*; maturity, fruition, readiness, *preparedness*; culmination, *perfection*; attention; roofing; top, crown, superstructure, *summit*; missing link, *requirement*; last touch, last stroke, clincher; achievement, work done, last straw, *limit*; climax, payoff; resolution, solution, catastrophe, last act, final curtain, *finality*.

effectuation; execution, discharge; performance, *action*; accomplishment, achievement, *success*.

Adj. completive, perfective; topmost; conclusive, final, last, *ending*; thorough, thoroughgoing, *resolute*.

completed, full, full-blown, *complete*; done, highly wrought, elaborate, *perfect*.

Vb. carry through; drive home, clinch, seal; dispose of; complete, consummate, *make complete*; elaborate, *perfect*; ripen, bring to a head, *mature*; get through, get shot of, dispose of, bring to its close, *terminate*; set at rest, *bring to rest*.

carry out, see through, effect, enact, *do*; execute, discharge, implement, effectuate, compass, bring about, accomplish, fulfil, consummate, achieve, *succeed*; make short work of.

climax, cap, crown all, *crown*; reach its peak; come to a crisis; touch bottom; come to its end, come to fruition, *arrive*; have enough of, be through with, *have enough*.

721 Noncompletion

N. noncompletion, failure; neglect; deficiency, deficit, *shortfall*; lack; continuity; *inattention*; work undone; lack of finality, drawn game; stalemate, deadlock.

Adj. uncompleted, partial, fragmentary, incomplete; undone; half-baked, underdone, *immature*; perfunctory, superficial; left hanging; lacking finish, inchoate, sketchy, *imperfect*; continuous.

Vb. not complete, hardly begin, leave undone, leave hanging, *neglect*; skip, scamp, tinker; *wound*; *fail*; defer, postpone.

Adv. on the stocks.

722 Success

N. success, glory; success all round, happy outcome, happy ending, favourable issue; success story, progress, steady advance, time well spent, *progression*; fresh advance, breakthrough; run of luck, good fortune; advantage, lead, first blood, *advantage*; momentary success; exploit, feat, achievement, *deed*; accomplishment, goal; a success, triumph, hit, triumphant success; good hit, good shot, *skill*; lucky stroke, fluke; hat trick, stroke of genius, masterstroke, *masterpiece*; trump, trump card; pass, qualification.

victory, beating, *defeat*; conquest; *attack*;

honours of battle; win; outright win, complete victory, checkmate; narrow win; easy win, runaway victory, love game, walkover, pushover, picnic, *easy thing*; slam, kill, knockout, KO; upper hand, advantage, edge, certain victory, *advantage*; stalemate, *draw*; celebration of victory, triumph, ovation, *celebration*.

victor, winner, champion, medallist; first; conquistador; beater; master, mistress; a success, self-made man or woman, man or woman to watch, rising star, *prosperous person*.

Adj. **successful**, effective, efficacious; efficient; sovereign, *remedial*; fruitful; happy, lucky; felicitous, masterly, *skilful*; surefire, foolproof; unerring, infallible, surefooted, *certain*; victorious, *excellent*; leading, *superior*; rising, sitting pretty, *prosperous*; triumphant; victorious; glorious.

unbeaten, unbowed, *resolute*; invincible.

Vb. **succeed**, effect, accomplish, achieve, compass, *carry through*; make a success of, make a go of, make short work of; make good, rise, do well, get promotion, *prosper*; pass, qualify, graduate, give a good account of oneself, *be superior*; advance, break through, make a breakthrough, *progress*; strive to some purpose; have a success, make a hit, make a kill; score a point, arrive, be a success, get around, click.

be *successful*, be efficacious, be effective; answer; do oneself proud; compass, manage, *do*; work, act, work like magic, act like a charm, *operate*; take effect, tell, pull its weight, *influence*; bear fruit, be *fruitful*; get it, hit it; be surefooted; be irresistible, *do easily*; be *resolute*; avoid defeat, *stand firm*.

triumph, celebrate; crow, boast; score; contrive a success, manage, make it, win through; surmount; find a loophole, *escape*; make headway against, *resist*; gain.

overmaster, *be superior*; master, overcome, overpower, overthrow, overturn, override, *outdo*; prevail, *predominate*; checkmate, trump, ruff; conquer, vanquish, quell, subdue, subject, suppress, crush, *subjugate*; capture, carry, take, storm, *attack*.

defeat (see *overmaster*); discomfit, dash; repulse, rebuff, *repel*; confound, dismay, *frighten*; best, *be superior*; worst, outplay, outpoint, outflank, outmanoeuvre, outclass, *outdo*; disconcert, trip, *obstruct*; baffle, gravel, nonplus, *puzzle*; defeat easily; beat, lick, thrash, whip, trounce, swamp, overwhelm, crush, drub, trample underfoot; beat hollow, rout, put to flight, scatter, *disperse*; silence, *suppress*; flatten, crush; run hard, corner, check, *endanger*; put an end to, settle, fix, dish, *destroy*; sink, *plunge*; break, bankrupt, *impoverish*.

win, achieve victory, be victorious; carry all before one, romp home, have a walkover, *do easily*; scrape home, survive; become champion, *be superior*.

Adv. **successfully**, swimmingly; to some purpose, with good result, with good effect, beyond all expectation; with flying colours.

723 Failure

N. **failure**, lack of success, negative result; *misfortune*; hindrance; vain attempt,

futile effort, *lost labour*; mess, muddle; bungle; abortion, miscarriage; hopeles; failure, damp squib, washout, fiasco; flop; bosh shot, misfire, slip, *mistake* dead stop, halt, *stop*; engine failure, electrical fault, breakdown, hitch; collapse; fall, stumble, trip, *descent*; weakness, anticlimax; *loss*.

defeat; nonplus, deadlock, stalemate, *stop* lost battle, repulse, rebuff, bloody nose; check, reverse; checkmate, mate, beating hiding, thrashing; retreat; *flight* recession; stampede, panic, *fear*; rou; landslide; fall, downfall, collapse; wreck; perdition, graveyard, ruin; lost cause; deathblow, quietus; utter defeat, Water loo; conquest.

loser; also-ran, nonstarter; has-been, extinc; volcano; misery; dud, failure, flop; lemon; sacrifice, victim, prey, *dupe*; bor; loser; underdog, *inferior*; dropout, *misfi*; bankrupt, insolvent.

Adj. **unsuccessful**, ineffective, pale; inglori; ous, obscure, empty-handed; *unfortu* nate; vain, negative, fruitless; dud, hang ing fire; stillborn, abortive, premature unplaced, failing; tripping, wandering *uncertain*.

defeated, beaten, worsted; *inferio* whacked; unplaced; scattered, put t; flight; sunk; kaput, brought low, faller; made a prey.

grounded, stranded; brought low; bank rupt.

Vb. **fail**; muddle, botch, bungle, *blunder* flunk, be found wanting; fail one, *dis; appoint*; lose a chance; misdirect, go wide; miss, *deviate*; draw a blank, retur; empty-handed, *waste effort*; lose; over reach oneself, come a cropper, fall, col; lapse, slide, *tumble*; malfunction, come; unstuck; falter, stall, seize; stop, come t; a dead stop, come to a dead end; stick; *cease*; come to a sticky end, *deteriorate* run aground, ground, sink, *founder* make a loss, crash, bust, break, go bank rupt.

miscarry, be stillborn, abort; misfire, hang fire; fall, crash, *tumble*; come to naught; come to nothing, be *useless*; fail to suc ceed, fall flat, come to grief; burst, bust; explode; flop, prove a fiasco; go wrong; go amiss, go awry, take an ugly turn; make things worse, aggravate; *dis; appoint*.

be *defeated*, lose, suffer defeat, take a beat ing; just lose, just miss; fall, succumb, *b; subject*; fall a prey to; retreat, los; ground, *recede*; take to flight; admi; defeat, had enough, cry quits, *submit*; g; downhill, deteriorate.

Adv. **unsuccessfully**.

724 Trophy

N. **trophy**, sign of success; war trophy; spoils, capture, *booty*; scalp, head; *wound*; memorial, memento; *monumen*; triumph, ovation, *celebration*; prize, ben; efit, benefit match; prize, wooden spoon; *reward*; sports trophy, cup, pot, plate; shield; award, Golden Rose; laurels; crown, chaplet, garland, wreath, palm; palm of victory; favour, love token; *badge*; flying colours, *ostentation*; glory; *repute*.

decoration, honour, *title*; *honours*; citation; rosette, ribbon, sash; athletic honour; blue, oar; medal, gong, star, cross, garter; order; service stripe, VC, Iron Cross; Distinguished Service Cross, Medal o;

Honour; Legion of Honour, civic crown.

725 Prosperity

N. prosperity, success; well-being, welfare, weal; boom; roaring trade, favourable trade balance; luxury, Easy Street, wealth; golden touch, plenty; favour, godsend, good; bonanza, luck, break, chance; glory, renown, prestige.

palmy days, heyday, prime; summer, sunshine, fair weather, Indian summer, pipping times, peace; easy times, clover, velvet, euphoria; golden times, Golden Age; expansive times, Elizabethan Age.

prosperous person, man or woman of substance, man or woman of property, rich person; rising man or woman; child of fortune, lucky fellow, lucky dog; upstart, profiteer; celebrity, hero, person of repute; lion, favourite.

Adj. prosperous; rising, doing well; well set-up, well-to-do, well-off, affluent, comfortable, fortunate, lucky; at ease, happy; fat, sleek.

palmy, balmy, halcyon, golden, rosy; pipping, blessed; providential, favourable, promising, auspicious, propitious, clear, fine, fair, glorious, expansive; agreeable, cosy, comfortable.

Vb. prosper, thrive, flourish; do well, have a good time of it, enjoy; make hay, have it easy, have it made, 'never have had it so good'; grow fat, feed well, eat; blossom, bloom, flower, be fruitful; win glory, have a reputation; boom, drive a roaring trade; profiteer, gain; go far, make it, arrive, succeed; make money, make a fortune, strike it rich, get rich; keep afloat.

have luck, have a lucky break, have a run of luck; strike lucky, strike oil, strike a rich vein.

be auspicious, promise, promise well, augur well, set fair; favour, prosper, profit, benefit; bless; water; take a good turn, do good; glorify, honour.

Adv. prosperously, swimmingly.

Int. Good luck! all the best! best of British!

726 Adversity

N. adversity, adverse circumstances, misfortune, mixed blessing (see misfortune); continual struggle, weary way, difficulty; hardship, hard life, tough time, suffering; pain; bad times, iron age, evil; burden, load, pressure; event; worry; misery, dejection; bitter cup, bitter pill; cross, sorrow; curse, blight, blast, plague, scourge, visitation; bane; cold wind, draught, chill, cold, winter; gloom; ill wind, blow, opposition; setback, check, rebuff, reverse, defeat; rub, pinch, plight, funeral, predicament; poor lookout, trouble ahead; trough, bad patch, rainy day; slump, recession, depression; threat; decline, fall, downfall, ruin; broken fortune, want, need, distress, extremity, poverty.

misfortune, bad fortune, bad luck, hard luck; failure; evil dispensation, evil star, malign influence; hard case, raw deal, rotten hand; hard lot, hard fate, hard lines; ill hap, mishap, mischance, misadventure, accident, casualty, chance; disaster, calamity, catastrophe.

unlucky person, poor unfortunate, constant loser, poor risk; star-crossed lover, sport of fortune, plaything of fate, Jonah; down-and-out, loser; underdog, inferior; new poor, poor person; lame dog, lame duck, weakling; scapegoat, victim, wretch, sufferer; prey, dupe.

Adj. adverse, hostile, ominous, sinister, inauspicious, unfavourable; bleak, cold, hard; cross, thwart, contrary, untoward; malign; dire, dreadful, ruinous, destructive; calamitous; too bad, bad.

unprosperous, inglorious; unwell; poor.

unfortunate, ill-fated, star-crossed; fraught, futureless; luckless, hapless, poor, forlorn, miserable, undone, unhappy; stricken, accursed; accident-prone.

Vb. have trouble, go through it, be hard pressed, fall foul of; strike a bad patch, suffer; come to grief, miscarry; be poor; go downhill, decline, deteriorate; sink, founder; come to a bad end, fail; go hard with, be difficult.

Adv. in adversity; unfortunately.

727 Averageness

N. averageness, average; golden mean, neither too much nor too little; common lot, mixed blessing; average circumstances, a modest competence; plain living, moderation; middle class, bourgeoisie; Main Street, suburbia, subtopia; common man, commoner.

Adj. middling, average, mediocre; neither good nor bad, middlebrow; ordinary, commonplace, median; common, representative, typical; moderate; decent, quiet, modest; undistinguished, inglorious, nothing to boast of; minor, secondrate, second best, inferior; fair, fair to middling; so-so, all right, adequate; tolerable, passable, fifty-fifty, much of a muchness; medium, middle, colourless, grey, neutral.

Vb. be middling, pass muster, suffice; manage well enough, avoid excess, be halfway; be imperfect.

728 Authority

N. authority, power; 'they', master; Whitehall, director; right, prerogative; law, rightful power, lawful authority; legislative assembly, parliament; regency, committee, commission; office of authority, office, place (see position of authority); portfolio, jurisdiction; vicarious authority, influence; indirect authority, patronage, prestige, credit; leadership, hegemony; supremacy; pride of place, priority, precedence; majesty, royalty, crown, nobility; dignity; purse strings; sea power, admiralty, trident; acquisition of power, succession, accession; seizure of power.

governance, rule, sway, direction, command; control, hold, grip, clutches; domination, whip hand; effective control, reach, long arm; dominion, sovereignty, raj, supremacy; reign, regency, dynasty; foreign rule, empire; imperialism, colonialism, neocolonialism; white supremacy, black power; regime, regiment, regimen; state control, paternalism; bureaucracy, civil service, red tape.

despotism, paternalism, tyranny; dictatorship, absolutism, autocracy, absolute monarchy; state socialism, state capitalism; police state, rule of terror, brute force.

government, direction, management; form

of government, state system; politics, politicking; constitutional government, rule of law; *anarchy*; theocracy; monarchy; federalism; tribalism; patriarchy; paternalism; squirearchy, aristocracy, meritocracy, oligarchy, minority rule, elitism; triumvirate; rule of wealth, plutocracy; representative government, party system, *political party, vote*; democracy; popular will; majority rule, one man one vote; collectivism; communism, Maoism; party rule, Fascism, National Socialism; committee rule; army rule, military government, martial law; mob rule, mob law; syndicalism, socialism; bureaucracy, technocracy; self-government, autonomy, home rule; puppet government, *instrument*; caretaker government, regency, interregnum; sphere of influence, mandate.

position *of authority*, post, place, office, office of power, office of dignity; royalty; regency; emirate, lordship; sultanate; consulate, prefecture; headship, presidency; mastership; government post, Cabinet seat; seat of government, capital, metropolis, palace, White House, Kremlin, Number Ten, Whitehall; secretariat, *workshop*.

political *organization*, body politic; state, commonwealth; country, realm, kingdom, republic, city state, city; temple state; federation; principality, duchy, dukedom; empire, dominion, colony, dependency, protectorate, mandate, *territory*; free world, Third World, *region*; banana republic; buffer state; province, county, *district*; body politic, constitution.

Adj. *authoritative*, competent; magisterial, official; mandatory, binding, compulsory; masterful; commanding, lordly; imperious, bossy; peremptory, arbitrary, absolute, totalitarian, *authoritarian*; powerful, *strong*; leading; preeminent, preponderant, dominant, paramount, *supreme*.

ruling, regnant; sovereign; royal, regal, queenly, princely, lordly; imperial; magisterial.

governmental, political, constitutional; administrative, official; patriarchal, feudal, democratic, popular, classless, republican; *independent*.

Vb. *rule*, hold sway, reign, reign supreme; govern, control, *command*; manage, hold office, *direct*; have a place, occupy a post, have authority, rule absolutely, *oppress*; dictate; plan; keep order, police.

take *authority*, take office, take command; assume authority, form a government; gain power, take control; seize power, usurp.

dominate; preponderate, *predominate*; boss, command; overmaster; *influence*; regiment, discipline, drill, drive, *be severe*; dictate, coerce, *compel*; subjugate; override, overrule, overawe; *be free*.

be *governed*, have a constitution, owe fealty, owe loyalty, *be subject*.

Adv. *by authority*.

729 Laxity: absence of authority

N. *laxity*; *scope*; lack of ceremony; relaxation, *liberation*; *permission*; indulgence, toleration, licence; line of least resistance, *submission*; weak will, feeble grasp, *weakness*; inertia; surrender of control,

resignation; concession, *compromise*; King Log.

anarchy; free-for-all; disorder, chaos, *tumoil*; licence, indiscipline; anarchism, nihilism; interregnum, power vacuum; misrule; mob law, reign of terror; defiance of authority; deposition.

Adj. *lax*, loose, slack; feeble, soft, *weak*; slipshod, remiss, *negligent*; *indifferen•*; informal; happy-go-lucky; permissive; tolerant, easy, gentle, *lenient*; weak-kneed, *irresolute*; lacking authority.

anarchic; unbridled; insubordinate, *insolent*; rebellious, *disobedient*; disorderly; unruly, *riotous*; *illegal*; lawless.

Vb. *be lax*; hold a loose rein, give one their head, give rope enough, *give scope*; stretch a point, connive at; tolerate, su•fer; *permit*; spoonfeed, indulge, spoil, *b•* lenient; *compromise*; relax, *disunite*; los• control, *be impotent*; renounce authority, *relinquish*; abdicate, resign; misrule, mis• govern, mismanage, reduce to chaos, *derange*.

please *oneself*, let oneself go, indulge oneself, *be intemperate*; be a law unto oneself, defy authority, resist control, *dis-obey*; act without authority; arrogate, usurp authority, *be undue*.

unthrone, unseat, overthrow, force t• resign, *depose*; usurp.

730 Severity

N. *severity*; pedantry; *hardness*; discipline, firm control, strong hand, tight grasp; *authority*; rod of iron, heavy hand; rig•our, extremity; pound of flesh; *restrain•*; prudery; visitation, inquisition, harassment; spite, *revenge*; lack of mercy; hars• treatment, cruelty, *inhumanity*; self-denial.

brute *force*, rule of might, gunboa• diplomacy, *power*; *compulsion*; *violence* arbitrary power, absolutism, autocracy dictatorship; tyranny; Fascism; militar• ism; martial law, iron rule, iron hand jackboot; bludgeon.

tyrant, pedant, stickler; petty tyrant; disc•plinarian, martinet, sergeant major; jack boot; hanging judge; heavy father, Dutc• uncle; Big Brother, authoritarian, des• pot, dictator, *autocrat*; boss, commissar• bully, hard master, taskmaster; blood-sucker, publican, predator, harpy; vul• ture, octopus; ogre, brute, *monster*; Kin• Stork.

Adj. *severe*, austere, Spartan, *ascetic*; stric• extreme; strait-laced; donnish; hyper-critical, *fastidious*; intolerant, censorious• unbending, rigid, *hard*; hard-headed• hard-boiled, flinty, dour; inflexible• obdurate, uncompromising, *obstinate*• inexorable, relentless, merciless, unspar•ing, implacable, *pitiless*; heavy, stern• stiff; punitive, stringent, Draconian• drastic, savage.

authoritarian, masterful, lordly, arrogant• haughty, *insolent*; absolute, unfettered• arbitrary, totalitarian, Fascist; impera• tive, compulsory; fussy, bossy.

oppressive, harsh; exacting, grasping, extor• tionate, predatory, searching, unsparing• high-handed, overbearing; heavy• handed, rough, bloody, *violent*; brutal• cruel.

Vb. *be severe*, be cruel to be kind; exer• authority, discipline; deal hardly with *restrain*; put a stop to, *suppress*; per• secute, *pursue*; ill-treat, mishandle• abuse, *misuse*; treat rough, get tough•

with; visit with, chastise, *punish*; wreak vengeance, *avenge*; *retaliate*; *be illegal*; be extreme; *be pitiless*; *slaughter*.

oppress, take liberties, *please oneself*; assume, arrogate, *be undue*; domineer, lord it; overawe, intimidate, *frighten*; bludgeon, *compel*; shove around; bully, bait, harass, plague, annoy, *torment*; persecute, spite, *be malevolent*; break, tame; task, tax, drive, *fatigue*; overtax, exploit, extort, suck, squeeze, grind; trample, tread underfoot, *suppress*; enslave, *subjugate*; ride roughshod, injure, *do wrong*; misgovern, misrule; rule with a rod of iron; whip, scourge, rack, *torture*; shed blood, *murder*; be heavy, burden, crush, *weigh*.

Adv. *severely*.

731 Leniency

N. *leniency*; forbearance, soft answer, *patience*; pardon, *forgiveness*; quarter, mercy, clemency, compassion, *pity*; humanity, kindness, *benevolence*; favour, sop, concession; indulgence, toleration; sufferance, allowance, leave, *permission*; complaisance; justice with mercy, *moderation*; light rein, light hand, velvet glove; wet, liberal.

Adj. *lenient*, soft, gentle, mild; tolerant; complaisant; easy, easy-going, *lax*; forbearing, longsuffering, *patient*; clement, merciful, *forgiving*; tender; too soft.

Vb. *be lenient*, show consideration, go easy, *moderate*; featherbed, spoonfeed, spoil, indulge, humour, *pet*; gratify, favour, *flatter*; tolerate, allow, connive, *permit*; stretch a point, *be lax*; concede, *consent*; refrain, forbear, *be patient*; pity, spare, give quarter, *show mercy*; pardon, *forgive*; amnesty, *forget*; relax.

732 Command

N. *command*, invitation, summons; commandment, ordinance; injunction; bidding, behest; dictum, say-so; charge, commission, appointment, *mandate*; brief, *information*; directive, order; word of command, word; beck, nod, sign, *gesture*; signal, bugle call, *call*; whip, categorical imperative, dictate, *compulsion*; negative command, taboo, ban, embargo, *prohibition*; countermand.

decree, edict, fiat; law, canon, *precept*; bull, papal decree; circular, encyclical; ordinance; decree nisi, decree absolute; decision; act, *legislation*; plebiscite, electoral mandate, *vote*; dictate.

demand, claim; requisition, *request*; notice, final demand, ultimatum; blackmail; threat; levy, tax demand, *tax*.

warrant, commission, written authority, passport, *permit*; writ, summons, subpoena, citation, *legal process*.

Adj. *commanding*, imperative, categorical; mandatory, obligatory, peremptory, compulsive; *authoritative*; decisive, conclusive, final; demanding, insistent, vocal.

Vb. *command*, bid, invite; order, tell, issue a command, give an order, signal, call, nod, beck, motion, sign, *gesticulate*; wink, *hint*; direct, give a directive, instruct, brief; rule, enjoin; give a mandate, charge, *commission*; impose, set a task, make obligatory, *impose a duty*; detail; call together, convene, *bring together*; summon; cite, subpoena, issue a writ, *litigate*; send back, remand; dictate,

compel; countermand, *abrogate*; lay an embargo, ban, taboo, proscribe, *prohibit*.

decree; promulgate, *proclaim*; declare, say, say so, *affirm*; prescribe, ordain, appoint, *predetermine*; enact, make law, legislate, *make legal*; rule, give a ruling, *judge*.

demand, require, requisition, *require*; order, indent, *request*; send a final demand, give final notice, present an ultimatum, blackmail, *threaten*; reclaim, *claim*; demand payment, dun, bill, invoice; charge, *price*; exact, levy, *tax*.

Adv. *commandingly*.

733 Disobedience

N. *disobedience*, indiscipline; delinquency; refusal to obey orders, *defiance*; disregard of orders; infraction, crime, sin, *guilty act*; passive resistance, *resistance*; opposition; hindrance, *discontent*; mafia.

revolt, mutiny; direct action, *strike*; faction, dissension; schism; explosive situation; sabotage, *destruction*; disturbance, disorder, riot, gang warfare, tumult, barricades, *turmoil*; rebellion, insurrection, rising, uprising, *outbreak*; putsch; resistance movement, *resistance*; *revolution*; terrorism; civil war, *war*; regicide, *homicide*.

sedition; cabal, intrigue, *plot*; terrorism, anarchism, nihilism; treason, lese-majesty, *perfidy*.

revolter, awkward person, difficult character, handful, *difficulty*; naughty child, scamp, little monkey, *bad person*; rebel; demonstrator, striker, *opponent*; splinter group, *schismatic*; dissident, *malcontent*; blackleg, scab, *nonconformist*; maverick, lone wolf; traitor, Quisling, fifth columnist; regicide; insurgent; resistance, underground; Black Panther, Black Muslim; Provisional; red, red republican; counter-revolutionary, reactionary, White Russian; mafia, bandit.

agitator; demonstrator; tub-thumper, demagogue; firebrand; red, commie; suffragette; ringleader.

rioter, rowdy, *ruffian*; wrecker; secret society.

Adj. *disobedient*; naughty, mischievous; awkward, difficult, wayward, restive, impatient of control, vicious, unruly, *violent*; intractable, ungovernable; insubordinate, rebellious, bloody-minded; contrary, nonconformist; recusant; recalcitrant; challenging, *defiant*; refractory, perverse, *obstinate*; subversive, revolutionary, reactionary; disloyal; intrusive; wild, feral, savage.

riotous; rumbustious, rowdy, unruly, wild, *disorderly*; *lawless*; rebellious.

Vb. *disobey*; be disobedient, misbehave; flout authority; disobey orders, *defy*; oppose; commit a crime, *be illegal*; violate, infringe, transgress, trespass, *encroach*; turn restive, kick, chafe, fret; bolt, take French leave, be a law unto oneself, *please oneself*.

revolt, rebel, mutiny; strike, *cease*; sabotage, *obstruct*; undermine, work underground; secede; betray; agitate, demonstrate, protest, *desperate*; start a riot, stage a revolt, lead a rebellion, *resist*; rise, renounce allegiance, *achieve liberty*; overthrow, upset.

734 Obedience

N. *obedience*, compliance, *observance*; goodness; readiness; *submission*; passivity; morale, discipline, *duty*; deference; *slave*.
loyalty, constancy, devotion, fidelity, good faith, *probity*; allegiance, fealty, homage, service, deference, submission; vote of confidence.

Adj. *obedient*, compliant; loyal, faithful, true-blue, steadfast, constant; devoted, dedicated, sworn; offering homage, submissive; law-abiding, *peaceful*; complaisant, amenable, docile; good; filial; ready, *willing*; acquiescent, resigned, passive; meek, biddable, dutiful; manageable, tame; respectful, subservient, obsequious, slavish, *servile*.

Vb. *obey*, comply, do to order, *observe*; come to heel, *conform*; assent, *consent*; listen, hearken, heed, mind, obey orders; observe discipline; hold oneself ready, *be willing*; vote to order; follow, *serve*; be loyal, owe loyalty, bear allegiance, pay homage, *keep faith*; pay tribute, *be subject*; make oneself useful, do Trojan service, *minister to*; yield, defer to, bow, bend, stoop, *be submissive*, *submit*; grovel, cringe, *be servile*; play second fiddle, *be inferior*.

Adv. *obediently*, to order; yours to command, at your service.

735 Compulsion

N. *compulsion*, spur of necessity, *necessity*; law of nature, *law*; act of God; moral compulsion, *conscience*; blackmail, *threat*; negative compulsion, *restraint*; sanction, *penalty*; duress, force, main force, big stick, bludgeon, strong arm, strongarm tactics, *brute force*; pressgang, call-up, draft; extortion, *taking*; slavery, forced labour, labour camp, *servitude*; command performance, *command*.

Adj. *compelling*, compulsive, involuntary, of necessity, inevitable, *necessary*; imperative, peremptory, *commanding*; compulsory, mandatory, binding, *obligatory*; urgent, pressing, overriding; omnipotent, irresistible, *powerful*; forcible, forceful, cogent; high-pressure, sledgehammer, strongarm.

Vb. *compel*, constrain, coerce, *force*; enforce; dictate, necessitate, oblige; bind; order, *command*; impose, *impose a duty*; make one; impress, draft, conscript; drive, dragoon, regiment, discipline; bulldoze, steamroller, railroad, pressgang; bludgeon, *oppress*; requisition, commandeer, extort, exact, *take*; apply pressure, squeeze, *torture*; blackmail, hijack, hold to ransom, *threaten*; be peremptory, insist, make a point of, press, urge; *affirm*; compel to accept, foist; force-feed; hold back, *restrain*.

Adv. *by force*, perforce, of necessity, forcibly; at gunpoint.

736 Master

N. *master*, mistress; master or mistress of, captor, possessor; sire, lord, lady, dame; liege, lord, lord paramount, lord's lord, suzerain; *protector*, *patron*; seigneur, squire, laird, *aristocrat*; *male*; landlady, *lady*; senator, plutocrat; sir, madam, *title*; patriarch, *parentage*; senior, head, principal, provost, *superior*; schoolmaster or -mistress, *teacher*; president, speaker, director; employer, captain of industry, capitalist, boss, governor, *manager*; leader, lord of creation, bigwig; ruling class, ruling party, dominant interest; 'them', Whitehall, Pentagon, *government*; staff, High Command.
autocrat, absolute ruler, absolute monarch; despot, tyrant, dictator, Big Brother; tycoon, boss, *bigwig*; petty tyrant, commissar, tin god, *official*.
sovereign, suzerain; Majesty, Highness; dynasty, house, royal line, royal blood; royalty, monarch, king, queen, rex, regina; divine king, Pharaoh; emperor, empress; Kaiser; prince, princess, Dauphin, Crown Prince or Princess, Great King, King of Kings, Shah; khan, Great Khan; Celestial Emperor; Mikado; Mogul, Sultan, Sultana; pope, pontiff.
potentate, ruler; chief, chieftain, headman; prince; emir, begum; archduke, duke, duchess, Elector; regent, Prince Regent.
governor, High Commissioner, Governor-General, Crown Representative, viceroy; proconsul; grand vizier, bey, pasha; Prince Bishop; patriarch, archbishop, cardinal; imam, *leader*.
officer; functionary, mandarin, nabob, bureaucrat, *official*; civil servant, *servant*; commissar; chief officer, prime minister, grand vizier, vizier, chancellor; constable, marshal, seneschal, warden; mayor, mayoress, alderman, provost, city father, councillor, dignitary, local worthy, *person of repute*; sheriff, bailiff; justice, *judge*; magistrate; president, doge; consul, proconsul, praetor; prefect, district officer; commissioner, revenue officer, collector, headman; mace-bearer, beadle; tipstaff, *law officer*; sexton, verger, *church officer*; courier, *messenger*; party official, whip.
naval officer, Sea Lord; admiral, commodore, captain, commander, lieutenant, petty officer, leading seaman, *nautical personnel*.
army officer, staff, High Command, staff officer, brass hat; marshal, general, brigadier, colonel, major, captain, lieutenant; ensign, cornet; warrant officer, NCO, sergeant major, sergeant, corporal, lance corporal; adjutant, aide-de-camp, quartermaster, orderly officer; military tribune, legate, centurion; war minister, warlord, commanding officer, commander, commandant; military rank, *degree*.
air officer, air marshal, air commodore, group captain, wing commander, squadron leader, flight lieutenant, flying officer, flight sergeant, *air force*.

737 Servant

N. *servant*, *official*; fag, slave; general servant, factotum, *busy person*; humble servant, menial; orderly, attendant, verger, *church officer*; subordinate, underling, *inferior*; assistant, secretary, right-hand man; paid servant, mercenary, hireling, employee, hand; handyman, labourer, *worker*; hack, drudge, dogsbody; farmhand, *farmer*; shepherd, milkmaid, *herdsman*; shop assistant, *seller*; steward, stewardess, cabin boy; waiter, head waiter, barman, pot boy, *tavern*; ostler, groom, stable boy or lad; errand boy, messenger, runner, *courier*; doorman, commissionaire, janitor, *doorkeeper*; porter, *bearer*; page boy, bellboy; sweeper, *cleaner*; caretaker, housekeeper (see *domestic*); occasional servant, help, daily, char, charwoman; universal aunt; nurse, *keeper*; companion.

domestic, staff, *personnel*; domestic servant, manservant, man, footman, lackey; servant girl, maid, parlour maid, housemaid, chambermaid; domestic drudge, maid of all work, skivvy; kitchen maid, kitchen boy, scullion, housekeeper, butler, cook; steward, chaplain, governess, tutor, nurse, nanny; personal servant, page, squire, valet, batman; gyp, scout; outdoor staff, groom, coachman, chauffeur, *driver*.

retainer, follower, following, suite, train, *retinue*; court, courtier; attendant, usher; bodyguard, henchman, squire, page, page of honour, household staff, chamberlain, equerry, steward, bailiff, seneschal; housekeeper; butler; chaplain; lady-in-waiting, companion; governess, nurse, nanny, *keeper*.

dependant, client; hanger-on, parasite; satellite, camp follower, creature, jackal, *follower*; stooge, puppet, *instrument*; subordinate, *inferior*; minion, lackey, man, henchman, vassal; pensioner; apprentice, ward, charge, foster child.

subject, national, citizen, *native*; liege, vassal; people, citizenry; subject population, dependency, colony, satellite.

slave, thrall, slave girl; helot; serf, villein; galley slave, *worker*; temple prostitute; eunuch; chattel, puppet, pawn; machine, robot, *instrument*; captive, *prisoner*.

Adj. *serving*; menial; working; *obedient*; subject.

Vb. *serve*, minister to; *accompany*; follow, obey; tend, squire, valet, dress; char, oblige; do service, make oneself useful, *be useful*; *function*.

738 Badge of rule

N. *regalia*, royal trappings, emblem of royalty, crown, orb, sceptre; coronet, tiara, diadem; rod of empire, sword of state, *authority*; robe of state, royal robe; ermine, royal purple; throne, royal seat, seat of kings; ensign, *flag*; royal standard, royal arms, *heraldry*; lion, eagle.

badge *of rule*, emblem of authority, staff, wand, wand of office, verge, rod, Black Rod, baton, truncheon, gavel; signet, seal, ring; sword of state, sword of justice, mace; pastoral staff; woolsack, chair, bench; sartorial insignia, triple crown, mitre; cap of maintenance, cap of dignity; robe, mantle, toga.

badge *of rank*, sword, belt, sash, tab, *badge*; uniform, *livery*; brass, star, crown; gold braid; chevron, stripe, anchor, curl; garter, order.

739 Freedom

N. *freedom*, liberty, being at large; freedom of action, initiative; free will, *will*; free thought, free speech; rights, civil rights; privilege, prerogative; licence, excess of freedom, indiscipline; free love, *illicit love*; isolationism; emancipation, setting free, *liberation*; franchise, secret ballot, *vote*.

independence, freedom of action; freedom of choice, *choice*; floating vote; freedom of thought, emancipation, *nonconformity*; individualism, individuality, *speciality*; self-determination, national status, *nation*; autonomy, self-government, *suf-*

ficiency; freehold, *property*; independent means, competence, *wealth*.

scope, play, range; swing, rope; field, room, living space, elbowroom, wide berth, leeway, margin, clearance, *room*; latitude, liberty, Liberty Hall; permissive society; fling, licence, excess; *opportunity*; facilities, free hand, blank cheque; free-for-all, free field, free enterprise, free trade, free port, free market; open country.

free person, freeman, burgess, citizen, voter; freedman; free agent, freelance; independent; neutral, *moderate*; freethinker, liberal; bohemian, *nonconformist*; lone wolf, solitary.

Adj. *free*, freeborn; scot-free; at large; *liberated*; footloose, go-as-you-please; exempt, immune; *plain*; broad, broad-minded, unprejudiced, independent, *just*; all things to all men, *sociable*; loose, unbridled, incontinent, wanton, *impure*; at leisure, retired; at home, at ease, *leisurely*; free of cost, gratis; unreserved, *accessible*.

unconfined, unfettered, unbridled; unchecked, unrestrained; uninhibited, informal, casual; free-range, wandering, random.

independent; unilateral, *spontaneous*; detached, *indifferent*; free to choose, uncommitted; *neutral*, *unsociable*; irrepressible; self-sufficient, self-supporting, self-contained; ungovernable; self-employed, free-lance; unofficial, cowboy, wildcat; single, bachelor.

unconditional, without strings; free-for-all; absolute; open, wide open; arbitrary; freehold.

Vb. *be free*, enjoy liberty; go free, save oneself, *escape*; take French leave, *disobey*; be free of, range, have scope, have play, have a free hand, have elbowroom; have plenty of rope; feel at home, make oneself at home; feel free, be oneself, let oneself go, *repose*; cut loose, *please oneself*; drift, wander, roam, *stray*; go it alone, stand alone; will, have a free mind, be independent; *defy*; be self-sufficient, *suffice*; take liberties, make free with, presume, *be insolent*; dare, venture, make bold to, permit oneself.

give scope, allow initiative, give one his head, allow full play, give free rein to, allow enough rope; *be lax*; give a free hand, *facilitate*; release, set free, enfranchise, *liberate*; let, charter, *permit*; let alone; leave it open.

Adv. *freely*, liberally, at will.

740 Subjection

N. *subjection*; subordinate position, inferior rank, inferior status; dependence, tutelage, apron strings, apprenticeship, *learning*; mutual dependence, symbiosis; allegiance, nationality; conquest, colonialism; loss of freedom, *submission*; discipline, restraint; yoke, *fetter*.

service, employ, employment; tribute; vassalage, *loyalty*; compulsory service, forced labour, *compulsion*.

servitude, slavery, bondage, yoke.

Adj. *subjected*; subdued; deprived of freedom, *restrained*; underprivileged; *serving*; downtrodden, underfoot, henpecked; brought to heel; submissive; subservient, slavish, *servile*.

subject; satellite; bond, bound, tributary, colonial; liege, vassal, feudal, *obedient*; subordinate, of lower rank, junior, cadet, *inferior*; dependent; subject to, liable to,

liable; a slave to; voiceless; *servile*; paid.
Vb. *be subject*, pay tribute, *obey*; vote to order; *be inferior*; be a doormat; serve, be a slave; *submit*; pawn, mortgage, *assign*; be a tool, *be instrumental*; cringe, fawn, *be servile*.
subjugate, subdue, reduce, subject, *overmaster*; annex; take captive, *triumph*; take, capture, lead captive, reduce to servitude, enslave; fetter, bind, *imprison*; rob of freedom, disfranchise; treat like dirt, *oppress*; repress, *suppress*; captivate, *impress*; enchant, *bewitch*; dominate, *influence*; discipline, regiment; tame, quell; bring to heel; *dispose of*.

741 Liberation

N. *liberation*, setting free, release, discharge, *acquittal*; free expression, catharsis, *feeling*; *separation*; riddance, *relief*; rescue, redemption, salvation, *deliverance*; emancipation; parole, bail; relaxation (of control); absolution, *forgiveness*; deed of release.
Adj. *liberated*; relieved; set free.
Vb. *liberate*, rescue, save, *deliver*; dispense, *exempt*; pardon, *forgive*; discharge, absolve, *acquit*; make free, emancipate; enfranchise; grant equal rights, end discrimination; release, free, set free, set at liberty; parole, *give terms*; unlock, *open*; loosen, loose, untie, disentangle, extricate, disengage, clear, *unravel*, unstop, uncork; unleash; let loose, leave to wander, turn adrift; charter; give play to, *give scope*; vent, give vent to, *empty*; leave hold, let go; relax, *be lax*; lift, *relieve*; *abrogate*; disband, send home, *disperse*; unload, *disencumber*.
achieve liberty, breathe freely; assert oneself, claim freedom of action; *revolt*; free oneself, shake oneself free; break loose, *escape*.

742 Restraint

N. *restraint*, self-control, *temperance*; reserve; repression, *compulsion*; cramp, check, *hindrance*; curb, drag, brake, snaffle, bridle, *fetter*; arrest, veto, ban, bar, embargo, *prohibition*; legal restraint, *law*; control, discipline, *authority*; *penalty*.
restriction, *limit*; speed limit; curfew; squeeze, duress, pressure, *compulsion*; control; restrictive practice, restraint of trade, exclusive rights, *exclusion*; monopoly, price ring, cartel, closed shop; ring, circle, protection, protectionism, mercantile system, tariff, tariff wall; *economy*; economic pressure, freeze, price control, credit squeeze; blockade.
detention, custody, *protection*; arrest; keeping, keep, care, charge, ward; quarantine, remand, refusal of bail; duress; bondage, slavery, *servitude*; burial; confinement, sentence, time, a stretch, porridge; penology.
Adj. *restraining*, restrictive, conditional, with strings; keeping, hidebound; straitlaced, unbending, strict, *severe*; stiff, *rigid*; tight, *narrow*, close; poky; protective.
restrained, *temperate*; reserved, shy; *obedient*; limited, scant, tight; cramped; bound; fogbound, snowbound.
imprisoned; landlocked; kept close, incommunicado; *captive*; inside; serving a sentence, doing time, doing porridge.

Vb. *restrain*, hold back, arrest, check, curb brake, *retard*; cramp, clog, hamper, *hinder*; swathe, bind, *tie*; call a halt, stop, put a stop to, *halt*; inhibit, veto, ban, bar *prohibit*; bridle, discipline, control, *be severe*; subdue, *subjugate*; restrain oneself; grip, hold, pin, *retain*; fight back restrict, tighten, limit, keep within bounds, *circumscribe*; assuage, *moderate* repress, *suppress*; muzzle, gag, silence *make mute*; censor, *obliterate*; restrict access, *exclude*; restrict supplies, withhold, keep back, stint; restrict consumption, ration, be sparing, retrench; try to stop, resist, *oppose*; police, patrol, keep order.
arrest, apprehend, catch, cop, nab, collar pinch, nick; handcuff, take, make a prisoner, take prisoner, capture, lead captive kidnap, seize, take hostage; take charge of, hold.
fetter, manacle, bind, pinion, handcuff; pillory, tether, picket, *tie*; shackle, trammel, hobble; enchain, chain; make conditions, attach strings.
imprison, confine, immure, quarantine intern; hold, detain, gate; keep close hold incommunicado; cloister, *seclude* entomb, bury; cage, kennel, impound corral, herd, pen, cabin, trap, *enclose* incarcerate, remand, jug; keep prisoner refuse bail.

743 Prison

N. *prison*, open prison, halfway house; penitentiary, reformatory, Borstal; remand home, sin bin; prison ship; dungeon, black hole, limbo; Tower; Fleet; Sing Sing; criminal lunatic asylum.
gaol, jail, clink, jug, can, stir, big house; glasshouse, brig.
lockup, nick, police station; roundhouse; cell, Death Row; dungeon cell, dungeon, torture chamber; prison van; dock, bar; pound, pen, cage, coop, kennel; ghetto, reserve; stocks, pillory, lock, padlock bolt, bar, barred window.
prison *camp*; concentration camp; labour camp; penal settlement or colony Botany Bay.
fetter, shackle, trammel, bond, chain, irons. hobble; manacle, pinion, handcuff bracelet; straitjacket, corset; muzzle, gag. bit, bridle, snaffle, halter; rein; yoke, collar, harness; curb, brake, skid, clog, drag *hindrance*; lead, tether, rope, leading string, apron strings, *halter*.

744 Keeper

N. *keeper*, custodian, curator; record keeper, *recorder*; charge officer; caretaker, housekeeper; seneschal, warden, ranger, gamekeeper; guard, escort, convoy; garrison; watchdog, sentry, lookout, watchman, watch, coastguard, lighthouse keeper, *protector*; tutor, duenna, governess, nurse, nanny, *domestic*; foster parent, guardian, probation officer, *philanthropist*.
gaoler, jailer, turnkey, warder, prison guard, prison officer, screw; prison governor.

745 Prisoner

N. *prisoner*, captive, capture, prisoner of war; close prisoner; political prisoner, prisoner of conscience; detainee, prisoner of state; defendant, accused, *accused person*

son; Borstal boy; old lag, jailbird; gaol inmate, guest of Her Majesty; convict; lifer; trusty; chain gang, galley slave, *slave*; hostage, kidnap victim, *security*.

Adj. *captive*; inside; without bail.

746 Commission: vicarious authority

N. *commission*, vicarious authority; committal, delegation; devolution; deputation, legation, mission, embassy, *envoy*; regency, *authority*; representation, proxy; card vote; agency, trusteeship, *management*; public service, bureaucracy, *government*.

mandate, trust, charge, *command*; commission, assignment, appointment, office, task, errand, mission; enterprise, *undertaking*; return, election, *vote*; translation, transfer; investment, investiture, installation, induction, ordination, coronation; power of attorney, written authority, charter, writ, *warrant*; diploma, *permit*; terms of reference, *conditions*; responsibility, care, ward, charge.

Adj. *commissioned*; vicarious, representational.

Vb. *commission*, empower, charge, sanction, charter, *permit*; post, accredit, appoint, collate, assign, name, nominate; engage, hire, staff, *employ*; invest, install, ordain; enthrone, crown, anoint; commit, leave it to; consign, trust with; delegate, depute, return, elect, give a mandate, *vote*.

Adv. *by proxy*.

747 Abrogation

N. *abrogation*; vacation; cancellation; recall, repeal; abolition, dissolution; suspension, disuse, dead letter; undoing, *reversion*; countermand; reprieve.

deposal, deposition; discharge, sack, removal; *punishment*; deprivation; replacement; recall, transfer, relief.

Adj. *abrogated*, set aside, void; dead; dormant, *unused*.

Vb. *abrogate*, annul, cancel; scrub, *obliterate*; invalidate, abolish, dissolve, nullify, void, vacate; quash, set aside, reverse, overrule; repeal, revoke, recall; rescind; undo; countermand; disclaim, disown, deny, *negate*; repudiate, retract, *recant*; ignore, *disregard*; call a halt, *restrain*; suspend, discontinue, make a dead letter of; wish undone, *regret*; *relinquish*.

depose; unseat; disbar, *exclude*; disestablish; suspend, cashier, *dismiss*; oust, *eject*; demote, degrade, recall, relieve, supersede, replace, remove, *transfer*.

748 Resignation

N. *resignation*; pension, golden handshake, *reward*; waiver, surrender; disclaimer; *leisure*; feeling of resignation, *submission*; quitter; pensioner.

Adj. *resigning*; outgoing, former, retired, one-time.

Vb. *resign*; be relieved, vacate, vacate office; stand aside, leave it to; declare (cricket); scratch, withdraw, surrender, *submit*; quit, chuck it; *assign*; abdicate, abandon, renounce, *relinquish*; retire; decline to stand again, refuse battle; waive, disclaim, abjure, *negate*; retract, *recant*.

749 Consignee

N. *consignee*, committee, panel, quango, *council*; counsellor, wise man, working party, *adviser*; stakeholder; nominee, licensee; trustee, executor, *agent*; factor, bailiff, steward, *manager*; caretaker, curator, *keeper*; representative (see *delegate*); legal representative, attorney, counsel, advocate, *law agent*; proxy, *deputy*; middleman, broker, stockbroker, *intermediary*; underwriter, insurer; purser, bursar, *treasurer*; rent collector; secretary of state, *officer*, functionary, *official*.

delegate, shop steward; nominee, representative, member; official representative, commissioner; correspondent, *correspondent*; emissary, special messenger, *messenger*; plenipotentiary (see *envoy*); delegation, mission.

envoy, emissary, legate, permanent representative, resident, ambassador, High Commissioner; ambassador at large; minister; consul, first secretary, attaché; embassy, legation, mission, consulate, High Commission; plenipotentiary.

750 Deputy

N. *deputy*, surrogate, alternate, proxy; scapegoat, substitute, understudy, stand-in; pro-, vice-, viceroy, vice-chancellor; proconsul; vicar; deputy prime minister, *officer*; right-hand man, lieutenant, secretary; alter ego; caretaker government; heir, heir apparent, successor designate, *beneficiary*; mouthpiece, herald, *messenger*; second, advocate, champion, *patron*; agent, factor, attorney, *consignee*.

Adj. *deputizing*; vice-, pro-; plenipotentiary; intermediary.

Vb. *deputize, function*; represent, be executor, *manage*; negotiate, replace, *substitute*.

Adv. *on behalf*, pro.

751 Permission

N. *permission*, liberty, *freedom*; leave, sanction, clearance; accordance, grant; licence, warrant; allowance, sufferance; tolerance, toleration, indulgence; passive consent, *consent*; connivance, *aid*; blessing, approval, *approbation*; grace, *benevolence*; concession, dispensation; release, *liberation*.

permit, express permission, authority, law, *warrant*; commission, *mandate*; grant, charter, patent, pass, password; passport, visa, safe-conduct; ticket, chit; licence, free hand, blank cheque; *scope*; leave, leave of absence, furlough, holiday; parole, ticket of leave; clearance, all clear, green light, go-ahead.

Adj. *permitting*, permissive, complaisant, tolerant, *lenient*.

permitted, *legal*; patent; open, optional, without strings, *unconditional*; permissible, allowable; printable.

Vb. *permit*, let, *make possible*; give permission, grant leave, grant, accord, vouchsafe, *give*; nod, say yes, *consent*; bless; *offer*; sanction, pass, *approve*; entitle, warrant, charter, patent, enable, *empower*; ratify, *make legal*; restore permission; lift, lift a ban, dispense, release, *exempt*; clear, give clearance, *liberate*; concede, allow, *assent*; give one a chance, let one try; favour, privilege, indulge, *facilitate*; leave the way open, open the door to *open*; foster, encourage; humour, *be patient*; suffer, tolerate, brook, *be lenient*; connive, wink at, *be lax*; allow a free hand, issue a blank cheque, *give scope*; permit issue of, *please oneself*.

ask *leave*, beg permission, ask if one may; seek a favour, petition, *request*; get leave, have permission; receive a charter.

Adv. *by leave*, with permission, underlicence; legally, legitimately.

752 Prohibition

N. *prohibition*, injunction; countermand; interference; interdict, veto, ban, embargo; curfew, *restraint*; taboo, Index; *refusal*; *disapprobation*; prohibition of drink, *temperance*; *economy*; repression; abolition, cancellation, suspension; blackout; forbidden fruit, contraband article.

Adj. *prohibiting*, prohibitory, forbidding, prohibitive, excessive, *impossible*; penal, *punitive*; hostile, *inimical*, exclusive, *excluding*.

prohibited, forbidden; barred; contraband, illicit, unlawful, *illegal*; taboo, untouchable; unmentionable, unprintable.

Vb. *prohibit*, forbid; veto, refuse permission, refuse leave, *refuse*; withdraw permission, cancel leave; countermand, revoke, suspend, *abrogate*; inhibit, prevent, *hinder*; restrict, stop, *restrain*; ban, interdict, taboo, proscribe, outlaw; black; impose a ban; bar, *exclude*; excommunicate, *eject*; repress, stifle, kill, *suppress*; censor, *obliterate*; *be severe*; *disapprove*; discourage, *dissuade*; clip, narrow, pinch, cramp, *circumscribe*; block; intervene, interpose, interfere.

753 Consent

N. *consent*; agreement, *assent*; compliance, *observance*; concession, grant, accord; acceptance, entertainment, allowance, *permission*; sanction; partial consent, compromise.

Adj. *consenting*, agreeable, compliant, ready, ready enough, *willing*; yielding.

Vb. *consent*, say yes, nod; give consent, ratify, confirm, *endorse*; sanction, pass, *permit*; *approve*; tolerate, allow, connive, *be lenient*; agree, accede, *assent*; acquiesce; come round; force oneself; yield, give way, *submit*; comply, grant a request; grant, accord, concede, vouchsafe, *give*; deign, condescend, *be courteous*; listen, hearken, *hear*; turn a willing ear, go halfway to meet, *be willing*; *content*; accept, jump at; clinch a deal, close with, settle, *make terms*.

754 Offer

N. *offer*, proffer; improper offer, bribe, *inducement*; tender, bid, declaration, motion, proposition, proposal; approach, overture, advance, invitation; tentative approach, feeler; present, presentation, offering, gratuity, sacrifice, *gift*; dedication; candidature, application, *request*.

Adj. *offering*, inviting; *shown*; open, available; to let; open to bid.

Vb. *offer*, proffer, make an offer, bid, tender; present, *give*; dedicate, consecrate; sacrifice to; introduce, broach, move, propose, make a proposition, put forward, suggest, *propound*; approach, approach with, make overtures, make advances; induce, *bribe*; invite, send an

invitation, *be hospitable*; hawk, hawk about, *sell*; auction; cater, *provide*; make available, make a present of, *make possible*; pose, confront with.

offer *oneself*, stand, be a candidate, compete, enter, *contend*; volunteer, come forward, *be willing*; apply, *request*.

755 Refusal

N. *refusal*; denial, negative answer, nay; uncompromising answer, flat refusal, *defiance*; repulse, rebuff, *repulsion*; denial policy, *resistance*; protest; self-denial; restraint, *temperance*.

Adj. *refusing*, recusant; *deprecatory*; deaf to.

refused, inadmissible; *impossible*.

Vb. *refuse*; excuse oneself; disagree, *dissent*; deny, negative, repudiate, disclaim, *negate*; decline, spurn, *reject*; repulse, rebuff, *repel*; *dismiss*; resist persuasion, be unmoved, *be obstinate*; turn a deaf ear, *be deaf*; hang fire, hang back; have nothing to do with, shy at, jib at, *avoid*; *exclude*; look askance at, dislike, disfavour, discountenance, *disapprove*; refuse permission, *prohibit*; *resist*; oppose, *withstand*; kick, protest, deprecate; grudge, begrudge, withhold, *retain*; deny oneself, waive, renounce, *relinquish*; go without, be ascetic.

Adv. *denyingly*, with a refusal, without acceptance; never, nothing doing.

756 Request

N. *request*, humble petition; negative request; *sale*; strong request, forcible demand, requisition; last demand, ultimatum, *demand*; blackmail, *threat*; claim; consumer demand, *requirement*; postulate, proposition, proposal, motion, suggestion; overture, approach, *offer*; bid, application, suit; petition, memorial, round robin; prayer, appeal, plea (see *entreaty*); pressure, instance, *compulsion*; clamour, cry; invitation, temptation; flag day, bazaar, charity performance; advertising, *advertisement*; small ad; wish, want, *desire*.

entreaty; submission; prayer; appeal, apostrophe; solemn entreaty; incantation.

Adj. *requesting*, inviting, mendicant; *offering*; demanding; insistent; clamorous, importunate, pressing, urgent, instant. supplicatory.

Vb. *request*, ask, invite, solicit; make overtures, approach, accost, *offer*; woo, *court*; seek, *search*; need, require; crave, make a request, prefer an appeal, beg a favour, ask a boon, have a request to make, make bold to ask, *desire*; apply, make application, bid, apply to, appeal to, run to, address oneself to; tout, hawk, solicit orders, *sell*; petition; press a claim, expect, *claim*; *demand*; blackmail, *threaten*; be instant, insist; urge, persuade, *induce*; coax, wheedle, cajole; importune, ply, press, dun, besiege; demand entrance; touch, *borrow*; requisition, *take*; raise money, tax, *levy*; send an ultimatum, *give terms*.

beg, cadge, crave, sponge, bum, scrounge; thumb a lift, hitchhike; make a collection, *levy*, require.

entreat, make entreaty, beg hard; pray, implore, beseech, append, conjure, adjure; invoke; appeal to, *speak to*; pray to, *offer worship*; kneel to; *acquire*.

757 Deprecation: negative request

N. *deprecation*, negative request, contrary advice; *request*; murmur, cheep, squeak, complaint, *discontent*; exception, demur, protest, *opposition*; reaction, backlash; gesture of protest, *disapprobation*; open letter, round robin; march, *refusal*.

Adj. *deprecatory*; protestant; vocal.

Vb. *deprecate*, advise against, have a better idea, dissuade; touch wood, *practise sorcery*; intercede, mediate; pray, appeal, *entreat*; *ask mercy*; show embarrassment, *disapprove*; remonstrate, expostulate, *reprove*; jeer, groan, stamp; murmur, beef, complain; object, take exception to; demur, jib, kick, squeak, protest against, cry blue murder, *oppose*; demonstrate, strike, *cease*.

758 Petitioner

N. *petitioner*, supplicant; pretender; aspirant, expectant; solicitor; customer; suitor; tout, barker; dun; pressure group, lobby; applicant, candidate, entrant; competitor, runner, *contender*.

beggar; mendicant, mendicant friar, fakir; tramp, bum, *wanderer*; parasite, *toady*.

759 Promise

N. *promise*, *offer*; undertaking, commitment; engagement, *marriage*; troth, plight, word, parole, word of honour, sacred pledge, vow, *oath*; declaration; declared intention, *intention*; profession, fair words; assurance, pledge, credit, honour, warrant, warranty, guarantee, insurance, *security*; voluntary commitment, *compact*; covenant, bond, promise to pay, *debt*; obligation, debt of honour, *duty*; firm date, *undertaking*; party, *signatory*.

Adj. *promissory*, promising.

promised; engaged, bespoke, reserved; committed; bound.

Vb. *promise*, say one will, *affirm*; proffer, *offer*; make a promise, vow, *swear*; warrant, guarantee, assure, confirm, secure, insure, underwrite, *give security*; pledge, stake; engage, give a firm date, *undertake*; commit oneself, bind oneself, be bound, covenant, *contract*; accept an obligation, accept responsibility, *incur a duty*; promise to pay, incur a debt of honour, *borrow*; bespeak, reserve, *intend*; *wed*.

take *a pledge*, demand security, *make certain*; adjure, swear, *testify*; make one promise, parole, *believe*; expect, *be certain*.

Adv. *as promised*, duly; truly.

760 Compact

N. *compact*, contract, bargain, agreement, mutual undertaking, *undertaking*; deed of honour, *promise*; mutual pledge; engagement, *marriage*; covenant, bond, *security*; league, alliance, cartel; pact, convention, understanding, *agreement*; private understanding, something between them; secret pact, conspiracy, *plot*; *conditions*; deal, *compromise*; composition, arrangement, settlement; *assent*; seal, signet, signature; deed of agreement, indenture, *title deed*.

treaty, international agreement; peace treaty; convention, concordat, protocol;

signatory, subscriber; *witness*; adherent, party; contractor; *mediator*.

Adj. *contractual*, conventional; bilateral, multilateral; sworn; signed, sealed and delivered.

Vb. *contract*, engage, *undertake*; *promise*; covenant, make a compact, strike a bargain, sign a pact, do a deal, adhere; league, ally; treat, negotiate, *bargain*; *compromise*; stipulate, *give terms*; agree, come to an agreement, arrive at a formula, come to terms, *make terms*; conclude, close, settle; indent, execute, sign, subscribe, ratify, attest, confirm, *endorse*; insure, underwrite, *give security*.

761 Conditions

N. *conditions*, making terms, diplomacy, horse-trading, *barter*; formula, terms; final terms, ultimatum, time limit, *threat*; *compulsion*; condition, set of terms, frame of reference; articles, articles of agreement; provision, clause, proviso, strings, reservation, exception, small print, *qualification*; essential clause, *requirement*; rule, *precept*; contractual terms, *treaty*; terms of reference, *mandate*.

Adj. *conditional*; subject to terms, contingent, provisional; guarded, entrenched; binding, obligatory.

Vb. *give terms*, propose conditions; condition, bind, attach strings; *demand*; stipulate, *require*; be severe; insert a proviso, leave a loophole, *qualify*; add a clause.

make *terms*, negotiate, treat, parley, *confer*; deal with, make overtures, *be tentative*; haggle, *bargain*; proffer, *offer*; yield a point, *compromise*; negotiate a treaty, do a deal, *contract*.

Adv. *on terms*; conditionally, provisionally, subject to, with a reservation; strictly, to the letter; necessarily, sine qua non; for the last time.

762 Security

N. *security*, precaution, *caution*; guarantee, warranty, writ, *warrant*; word of honour, *promise*; patronage, *protection*; surety, bail, caution, parole; pledge, pawn, hostage; stake, stake money, deposit, earnest, token, instalment; token payment, *payment*; indemnity, insurance, *safety*; transfer of security, mortgage, *transfer*; collateral, collateral security, sponsor, underwriter, *patron*.

title *deed*, deed, instrument; unilateral deed, deed poll; bilateral deed, indenture; charter, covenant, bond, *compact*; receipt, IOU, voucher; certificate, marriage lines; seal, stamp, signature, acceptance; valuable security, treasury note, note of hand, bill, treasury bill, bill of exchange; blue chip, gilt-edged security; portfolio, share, debenture; mortgage deed, policy, will, testament, codicil; certificate of probate; archives, *record*.

Adj. *pledged*, pawned, deposited; on lease, on mortgage.

secured, insured; gilt-edged.

Vb. *give bail*, go surety, take bail; *take a pledge*.

give *security*, offer collateral, mortgage; pledge, pawn, pop, hock, *borrow*; guarantee, warrant, *make certain*; authenticate, verify, *corroborate*; execute, endorse, seal, stamp, sign, countersign, subscribe, *endorse*; accept, grant a receipt, write an IOU, *receive*; *promise*; secure, indemnify, insure, assure, underwrite, *safeguard*.

763 Observance

N. *observance*, *practice*; full observance, fulfilment, satisfaction, *sufficiency*; adherence to, attention to; performance, discharge, acquittal, *action*; compliance; *conformity*; attachment, fidelity, faith, *loyalty*; sense of responsibility, reliability, *probity*.

Adj. *observant*, *doing*; watchful, careful of, attentive to, *attentive*; conscientious, diligent, earnest, religious, punctilious; perfectionist, *fastidious*; literal, exact, *accurate*; responsible, reliable, dependable, *trustworthy*; loyal, true, compliant, *obedient*; adherent to; faithful, *honourable*.

Vb. *observe*, heed, respect, regard, have regard to, pay respect to, acknowledge, pay attention to, attend to, *be attentive*; keep, practise, adhere to, cling to, follow, be loyal to, *conform*; comply, *obey*; fulfil, discharge, perform, execute, *do*; satisfy, *suffice*.

keep *faith*, be faithful to, have loyalty to, *be honourable*; *pay*; give one his due.

Adv. *with observance*, faithfully; literally, meticulously, according to the spirit of.

764 Nonobservance

N. *nonobservance*; inattention; *nonconformity*; anarchism, *anarchy*; shortcoming; protest; disregard, discourtesy, *disrespect*; bad faith, breach of promise, *perfidy*; denial; failure; *penalty*.

Adj. *nonobservant*, lapsed; nonconformist; neglectful, *negligent*; unprofessional; maverick, cowboy; indifferent, informal, *lax*; *disobedient*; unlawful; disloyal, unfaithful.

Vb. *not observe*, abhor, *reject*; discard; set aside, *abrogate*; omit, ignore, skip, *neglect*; disregard, slight; stretch a point, *be lax*; violate, do violence to, trample underfoot, *force*; transgress, *overstep*; *disobey*; desert; fail; break faith, dishonour, *negate*; cancel; *be dishonest*; cut, shirk, dodge, evade, elude, *avoid*; shuffle, quibble, equivocate, *be equivocal*; forfeit, incur a penalty.

765 Compromise

N. *compromise*, concession; mutual concession, formula, *compact*; composition, commutation; second best, half a loaf; working arrangement, *way*; *average*; halfway, middle way.

Vb. *compromise*, find a formula, find a basis; meet one halfway, *be halfway*; stretch a point, *be lax*; strike an average, go Dutch; compound, commute, *substitute*; arbitrate; *pacify*; make a virtue of necessity.

766 Acquisition

N. *acquisition*; collection, *assemblage*; *sale*; transfer, *avarice*; heap, stack, pile, pool, scoop, jackpot, *accumulation*; finding; finding again, recovery, *restoration*; redemption, *purchase*; appropriation, *taking*; theft; find, windfall, treasure, treasure trove; free gift, *gift*; legacy; gratuity, baksheesh, *reward*; benefit match, prize, plum, *trophy*; gravy, *benefit*; easy money, *facility*; pelf, lucre, *money*; plunder, *booty*.

earnings, income, wage, salary, screw, pay

packet, productivity bonus, *pay*; pay scale, differential, pension, superannuation, 'golden handshake'; emolument, *reward*; allowance, expense account; perquisite, perks; salvage; commission, rake-off, *discount*; return, receipts, proceeds, turnover, takings, revenue, *receipt*; harvest, vintage, crop, aftermath, gleanings; output, produce, *product*.

gain, thrift, savings, *economy*; credit side, profit, capital gain, winnings; dividend, share-out; usury, interest, *increment*; lucrative deal; pay increase, rise, raise, *increase*; advantage, benefit; selfish advantage, personal benefit.

Adj. *acquiring*, acquisitive, accumulative; *prosperous*; hoarding, saving.

gainful, lucrative, remunerative, *rewarding*; advantageous; fruitful, fertile, *productive*; paid.

acquired, had, got; ill-gotten.

Vb. *acquire*, get; earn, gain, obtain, procure, get at; find, strike, come across, *discover*; get hold of, get possession of, annex, *appropriate*; win, capture, catch, land, net, bag, take; pick, tot, glean; gather, reap, crop, harvest; draw, tap, milk, mine, *extract*; collect, accumulate, heap, *bring together*; scrape together, collect funds, raise, levy; save, hoard, *store*; buy, preempt, *purchase*; reserve, book, engage, *be early*; get somehow, beg, borrow or steal; get a living, turn an honest penny, *busy oneself*; get money, draw a salary, draw a pension; have an income, have a turnover, gross, take, *receive*; convert, cash, clear, make; get back, recover, salvage, recycle, regain, redeem, recapture, *retrieve*; take back, resume, reclaim; compensate oneself, *recoup*; break even; attain, reach; catch; incur.

inherit, be left, receive a legacy; succeed, succeed to.

gain, profit, earn a dividend; make, win; make money, *prosper*; make a fortune, make a killing, turn a pretty penny, *get rich*; scoop, win; sell at a profit.

be profitable, profit, repay, be worthwhile, *be useful*; pay, pay well; gross, yield, *produce*; pay a dividend, show a profit, *prosper*; accrue.

767 Loss

N. *loss*, deprivation, privation; sacrifice, forfeit, lapse, *penalty*; hopeless loss, perdition, *ruin*; setback, check, reverse; loss of profit, overdraft, failure; consumption, *expenditure*; wastage, leakage, *waste*; drain, *decrease*; riddance, *liberation*; defeat.

Adj. *losing*; prodigal; deprived; shorn of, bereft, bereaved; minus, without, lacking; quit of; set back, broke, bankrupt, insolvent; *disinterested*.

lost, gone; missing; lost, stolen or strayeds; absent; wanting, lacking, short, *deficient*; irrecoverable, irretrievable, irredeemable; spent; forfeit.

Vb. *lose*, mislay, *misplace*; miss, let slip, lose a chance, squander, *waste*; deserve to lose, forfeit, sacrifice; spill, allow to leak; throw good money after bad, *expend*; *aggravate*; be a loser, *have trouble*; be set back, sell at a loss; be unable to pay, break, go broke, go bankrupt; overdraw, be minus.

be lost, be missing, *be absent*; lapse, go to pot; *disappear*; be a good riddance, *relieve*.

768 Possession

N. *possession*, rightful possession; hold, grasp, grip; *possessor*; a possession, *property*; tenancy, holding, *estate*; tenure, fee, fief, feud; long possession, prescription, *habit*; exclusive possession, monopoly, corner, ring; preemption; future possession, appropriation, *taking*.

Adj. *possessing*, holding, propertied, landed; possessed of; exclusive, possessive.

possessed, had; proper, personal, *special*; *private*, reserved, engaged; inherent.

Vb. *possess*, be possessed of, own, have; die possessed of, *bequeath*; hold, grip, *retain*; have absolute disposal of, command, *dispose of*; boast of, *claim*; contain, include, *comprise*; fill, occupy, squat, inhabit; enjoy, *use*; have all to oneself, hog, corner; *get*, take possession, *take*; recover, *retrieve*; preoccupy, preempt, reserve, book, engage, *be early*; succeed, *inherit*.

belong, belong to; go with; be subject to, owe service to, *be subject*.

Adv. *possessively*; in one's own right, by right of possession.

769 Nonownership

N. *nonownership*, vacancy; tenancy, temporary lease; dependence; *poverty*; loss of possession; deprivation, *loss*.

Adj. *not owning*, dependent, *subject*; destitute, penniless, *poor*; lacking, minus, without.

unpossessed; international, common; vacant, *empty*; derelict.

770 Joint Possession

N. *joint possession*; joint tenancy; common land, common, global commons; public property, public domain, *property*; joint government; joint stock, common stock, pool, kitty, *store*; socialism, communism, collectivism; collective farm, collective, commune, kibbutz, *farm*.

participation, membership, affiliation; co-op., *association*; Dutch treat, bottle party, dividend, share-out; share, lot, whack, *portion*; complicity, sympathy; fellow feeling, sympathetic strike, joint action.

participator, member, partner, co-op., *colleague*; shareholder, stockholder, *possessor*; housing association; sharecropper, *farmer*; socialist; contributor, *patron*.

Adj. *sharing*, joint; common, communal, international, global; collective; involved, *corporate*; sympathetic.

Vb. *participate*; partake of, take a share, share, go shares, go halves, go fifty-fifty, *apportion*; go Dutch, *defray*.

communalize; pool; hold in common.

Adv. *in common*, share and share alike; jointly.

771 Possessor

N. *possessor*, holder; captor; squatter; lodger, occupier, incumbent; trustee; lessee; tenant, householder, franklin, yeoman; vassal, *dependant*; peasant, serf, villein, *farmer*; subtenant.

owner, monarch; master, mistress, proprietor; buyer; lord, lord paramount; landed gentry, landed interest; squire, laird, *aristocracy*; man or woman of property, shareholder, stockholder, landlord, land-

lady; testator.

beneficiary; *recipient*; incumbent; expectant, successor, successor apparent; next of kin; heir apparent; crown prince, *sovereign*; joint heir.

772 Property

N. *property*; possession; stake, venture; personal property, church property; chattel, real property, personal estate, belongings, paraphernalia, effects, baggage, things; cargo, *contents*; goods, wares, stock, stock-in-trade, *merchandise*; plant, furniture.

estate; circumstances, what one is worth; resources, *means*; substance, capital, *wealth*; revenue, income, *receipt*; portfolio; stake, holding, investment; copyright, patent; claim, demand; right, title, interest; living; lease, tenure, freehold, fee, fee simple, fee tail; tenement.

lands, land, acreage, grounds; estate, property, real estate, real property; tenement, holding, tenure, freehold, fief, feud, manor, honour, lordship, domain, demesne; plot, *territory*; farm, ranch, hacienda; common land, common, *joint possession*; dependency, dominion.

dower, dowry, dot, portion, marriage settlement; allotment, allowance, pin money; alimony, birthright; heritage; legacy; heirloom; remainder, reversion; entail.

Adj. *proprietary*; immovable, real, personal; propertied, landed, feudal, freehold, leasehold; hereditary, heritable, limited.

Vb. *dower*, endow, possess with, *give*; devise, *bequeath*; grant, allot, *assign*; possess, *commission*; establish, found.

773 Retention

N. *retention*; clinging to; foothold, *support*; bridgehead, beachhead, *advantage*; clutches, grip, gripe, grasp, hold, stranglehold; squeeze; clinch, lock; hug, embrace, clasp, cuddle, *endearment*; keep, ward, *detention*; refusal; holding action, pincer movement; plug, stop, *stopper*; ligament, *bond*.

nippers, pincers, pliers, wrench, tongs, forceps, vice, clamp, *fastening*; talon, claw, *sharp point*; tentacle, hook, tendril, *feeler*; teeth, *tooth*; paw, hand, *finger*; fist.

Adj. *retentive*, tenacious, prehensile; vice-like; clinging, adhesive, sticky, gummy, gooey; firm; tight; tight-fisted, *parsimonious*; shut fast, *closed*.

retained; fast, bound, held; kept; reserved, engaged; kept back; esoteric, incommunicable, *occult*; inalienable.

Vb. *retain*, hold; grab, buttonhole, hold back, *obstruct*; catch, steady, *support*; hold fast, hold tight, keep a firm hold of; cling to, stick to, adhere; grip, gripe, grasp, clinch, clench, lock; hug, clasp, clutch, embrace; pin, throttle, strangle, *restrain*; detain, *imprison*; contain, *enclose*; keep to oneself, keep back, withhold, *keep secret*; *store*; save, keep, *preserve*; keep back, withhold, *refuse*.

774 Nonretention

N. *nonretention*, parting with, disposal, alienation, *transfer*; *sale*; release, *liberation*; dispensation; dissolution (of a marriage), *divorce*; cancellation; disuse; leak.

derelict, jetsam, *rubbish*; cast-off, slough;

waif, stray, orphan, maroon, outcast, pariah.

Adj. *not retained*; disposed of; left behind; *liberated*; made redundant; derelict; heritable; available.

Vb. *not retain*, part with, alienate, transfer, *assign*; dispose of, *sell*; be open-handed, *be prodigal*; free, let go, let slip, leave hold of; unlock, *open*; untie, disentangle, *disunite*; forego, dispense with, do without, spare, waive, abandon, cede, yield, *relinquish*; renounce, abjure, *recant*; cancel, revoke, *abrogate*; lift, *liberate*; supersede, replace, *substitute*; disown, disclaim, *negate*; dissolve (a marriage), *divorce*; disinherit, *impoverish*; *marry*; ditch, jettison, throw overboard, *eject*; abandon, maroon; retire; discharge, give notice to quit, *dismiss*; drop, discard; withdraw, *resign*; estrange; sit loose to, *be indifferent*; leak, emit.

775 Transfer (of property)

N. *transfer*, transmission, consignment, delivery; settlement; conveyancing, conveyance; assignment; alienation; demise, *devise*, *gift*; lease, let, rental, hire; *sale*; trade, *barter*, exchange, *interchange*; changeover; devolution, delegation, *commission*; succession, reversion; pledge, pawn, hostage.

Adj. *transferred*; lent; negotiable; heritable.

Vb. *assign*, convey; grant, *give*; let, rent, hire, *lease*; alienate, *sell*; negotiate, barter, *trade*; *substitute*; exchange, convert, *interchange*; confer, invest with; commit, delegate, *commission*; *marry*; deliver, give delivery, transmit, pass to, *transfer*; pledge, pawn, *lend*; withdraw a gift, give to another; disinherit, *impoverish*; dispossess, expropriate, relieve of.

bequeath, will, devise, demise; grant, assign; leave, will a legacy; make a will, add a codicil; leave a fortune, *be rich*; have something to leave.

change hands, pass to another; pass, shift; circulate, *circle*; succeed, inherit, *acquire*.

776 Giving

N. *giving*; charity, *philanthropy*; generosity, *liberality*; subscription to; presentation, award, *reward*; delivery, commitment, consignment, conveyance, *transfer*; settlement; grant, accordance; investment, investiture.

gift, keepsake, token; present; Christmas box, whip-round, tip, fee, baksheesh, gratuity, drink money, *reward*; fee, consideration; bribe, *inducement*; prize, award, presentation, *trophy*; benefit, benefit match, benefit performance; alms, dole, charity, *philanthropy*; food parcel, free meal; *bounty*, manna; largesse, hand-out; bonus, bonanza; something extra; perks, expense account; grant, allowance, subsidy, aid; boon, grace, favour, service, labour of love, *voluntary work*; free gift; piece of luck, windfall, *acquisition*; conscience money, *payment*; forced loan, benevolence, tribute, *tax*; legacy, *transfer*.

offering, dedication; *piety*; peace offering, collection, sacrifice; Easter offering; subscription, flag day; stake.

giver, donor; testator; subscriber, contributor; tributary, *subject*; almoner, blood donor, *benefactor*; distributor of largesse,

Lady Bountiful, rich uncle, Fathe Christmas.

Adj. *giving*, tributary, *subject*; contributor charitable; generous, bountiful, *liberal*. given, gifted; gratuitous, gratis, free; allow able.

Vb. *give*, bestow, lend, render; afford, pro vide; vouchsafe, favour with, sho favour, grant a boon, *be lenient*; gran accord, *permit*; gift, donate, make present of; *leave*, *bequeath*; endow enrich; give a prize, present, awar *reward*; confer, vest, invest with; ded cate, consecrate, vow to, *offer*; immolate sacrifice, *offer worship*; give a presen gratify, tip, consider, remember; *bribe* bestow alms, give to charity; give freely lavish, *be liberal*; spare, give free; stanc treat, entertain, *be hospitable*; dispense allot, *apportion*; contribute, subscribe pay towards, help, help with money, *aic* have a whip-round; *participate*; pa with, *pay*; share, share with, impart, *com* municate; give one his due; pay tribute cede, yield, *relinquish*; deliver, *assign* commit, consign, *commission*; send.

777 Receiving

N. *receiving*, admittance, reception; *acqu* sition; acceptance, assumption; suc cession; collection, receipt of custom; receipt, windfall, *gift*; toll, tribute, due receipts, proceeds, winnings, takings *earnings*; receiving end.

recipient; receiver; trustee, *consignee* addressee, *correspondent*; buyer; license lessee; heir, successor, *beneficiary*; payee pensioner; remittance man, *dependan* winner, scholar; object of charity, *beggar* *sufferer*.

receiver, liquidator, *treasurer*; payee, collec tor, publican; customs officer; share holder.

Adj. *receiving*, recipient; receptive impressionable, *sensitive*; paid; giver favoured.

Vb. *receive*, be given; get, *acquire*; collec levy, toll, *take*; gross, net, pocket, pouch accept, *admit*; draw, be paid; have a income, draw a pension; inherit, succee to; receipt, acknowledge.

be *received*, be drawn; *accrue*; come t hand.

778 Apportionment

N. *apportionment*, appointment, assign ment, allotment, appropriation; division partition; shares, deal, dispensation *limit*; place, seat, station, *degree*; publi sector.

portion, share, share-out, cut, split; divi dend, allotment; lot, contingent; propor tion, ratio; quantum, quota; halves, *part* deal, hand (at cards); dole, mess, modi cum, pittance, allowance; ration, ratio book, coupon; dose, measure, dollop whack, helping, slice, *piece*; rake-of commission, *discount*; stake; task, stin *labour*.

Vb. *apportion*, allot, allocate, appropriate appoint, assign; assign a part, cast; assig a place, detail, billet; partition, zone demarcate, *limit*; divide, split, cut; halve bisect; go shares, *participate*; share, dis tribute, spread around; dispense, admin ister, serve, deal, *give*; measure, ration dose; get a share.

Adv. *pro rata*; respectively, each to each per head.

779 Lending

N. *lending*; usury, *credit*; investment; mortgage; advance, loan, accommodation; lease, let, sublet.

pawnshop, bank, credit company, finance corporation, building society, International Monetary Fund, World Bank.

lender, creditor; harsh creditor; financier, banker; moneylender, usurer, loan shark; pawnbroker, uncle; lessor; backer, angel; tallyman.

Adj. *lending*; extortionate; lent, loaned, on credit

Vb. *lend*, loan; advance, accommodate, allow credit, give one a loan, *credit*; back, finance; invest, sink; *speculate*.

lease, let, demise; sublet.

Adv. *on loan*, on credit, on advance; on security.

780 Borrowing

N. *borrowing*; loan application; mortgage, *debt*; credit account, credit card; hire purchase, HP, instalment plan; joyride; loan; forced loan, benevolence, *tax*; *deception*.

Vb. *borrow*, touch, *request*; mortgage, pawn, pledge, pop, hock, *give security*; take a loan, exact a benevolence; use a credit card, get credit, get accommodation; *purchase*; promise to pay, raise a loan, float a loan; invite investment; beg, borrow, or steal, *acquire*; cheat, crib, infringe, *copy*.

hire, rent, farm, lease, charter.

781 Taking

N. *taking*; seizure, capture, rape; taking hold, grasp, apprehension; taking possession, appropriation, assumption; requisition, compulsory purchase, *acquisition*; compulsory saving; taxation, levy, *tax*; taking back, recovery; removal, *displacement*; furtive removal; bodily removal, press gang; raid, *spoliation*; take, haul, catch, capture, prize, plum, *booty*; receipts, takings, winnings, gleanings, *earnings*.

expropriation; forcible seizure, attachment; distress; expulsion; takeover, deprivation; *transfer*; capital levy; extortion; swindle, rip-off.

rapacity; thirst, *hunger*, greed, *avarice*; extortion, blackmail.

taker, remover; raider; press gang; slaver; captor, *master*; locust, *destroyer*; bloodsucker, leech, parasite, vampire, harpy, vulture, wolf, shark; beast of prey, predator; *receiver*.

Adj. *taking*; grasping, extortionate, rapacious; voracious, ravenous, *hungry*; predatory; acquisitive, possessive.

Vb. *take*, accept, be given, *receive*; take back (see *appropriate*); admit; anticipate, be early; take hold, clutch, grip, cling, *retain*; seize, snatch, grab, pounce, spring; snatch at, reach, make a long arm; grasp at, clutch at, grab at, make a grab, capture, rape, storm, *overmaster*; conquer, captive, *subjugate*; catch, overtake, intercept, *outstrip*; apprehend, make an arrest, nab, nobble, collar, *arrest*; make sure of, fasten, pinion, *fetter*; hook, trap, snare, lime, *ensnare*; net, land, bag, pocket, pouch; gross, have a turnover, *acquire*; gather, accumulate, collect, *bring together*; cull, pick, pluck; reap, crop, harvest, glean, *cultivate*;

scrounge, tot, ransack, *search*; snaffle; help oneself, *steal*; pick clean, strip, uncover, remove, deduct, *subtract*; unload, *displace*; draw, milk, tap, mine, *extract*.

appropriate, annex; pirate, *copy*; take possession; assume, *possess*; succeed, *inherit*; place oneself; overrun, people, populate, occupy, settle; win, conquer; take back, recover, resume, repossess, recapture, *retrieve*; reclaim, *claim*; commandeer, requisition, *demand*; usurp, arrogate, trespass, squat, *be undue*; make free with; hog; engulf, swallow, *absorb*; devour.

levy, raise, extort, exact, *extract*; compel to lend, *borrow*; exact tribute, make pay, collect a toll; *tax*; overtax, suck dry (see *fleece*); exhaust, drain, *empty*; wring, squeeze, *oppress*; divert resources.

take *away*, remove, shift, unload, *displace*; send; lighten, *disencumber*, abstract, relieve of, *steal*; remove bodily, escort, *accompany*; kidnap, crimp, shanghai, press, impress, abduct, ravish; *decamp*; raid, loot, plunder, *rob*.

deprive, bereave, orphan, widow; denude, strip, uncover, depose; dispossess, usurp; oust, evict, expel, *eject*; expropriate, confiscate, foreclose; disinherit.

fleece, pluck, skin, shear, gut; strip, strip bare, *uncover*; swindle, cheat, *deceive*; blackmail; bleed, bleed white, sponge, suck, suck like a leech, suck dry; soak, sting; *defraud*; devour, *eat*; bankrupt, leave one without a penny or cent, *impoverish*.

782 Restitution

N. *restitution*, return, reversion; *restoration*; redemption, ransom, rescue, *deliverance*; recovery; refund, indemnity, damages, *penalty*; amends, reparation.

Adj. *restoring*.

Vb. *restitute*, make restitution, *restore*; return, render, give back; *pay*; refund, repay, recoup, reimburse; indemnify, pay an indemnity, pay damages, compensate; make reparation, make amends, *atone*; bring back, repatriate; ransom, redeem, *deliver*; reinstate, rehabilitate, restore one to favour; recover, *retrieve*.

783 Stealing

N. *stealing*, theft, larceny; robbery; robbery with violence, holdup; rape, hijack; abstraction, removal, *taking*; literary theft; joyride; act of theft; job, fiddle.

brigandage banditry, piracy, buccaneering; privateering; raid, foray, *attack*.

spoliation, pillage; sack; rapine, *havoc*.

peculation, breach of trust; blackmail, extortion, protection racket; daylight robbery, rip-off; tax evasion, fraud, fiddle, swindle; confidence trick, skin game, *deception*.

thievishness, kleptomania; intention to steal.

Adj. *thieving*; with intent to steal; predatory; *dishonest*.

Vb. *steal*, lift, thieve, pilfer, shoplift, help oneself; pick locks, blow a safe; burgle, rob, relieve of; rifle, sack; swipe, nobble, nick, pinch, pocket, bone, prig, snaffle, snitch, *take*; forage, scrounge; lift cattle, rustle; abduct, kidnap, shanghai; abstract, purloin, filch; crib, copy, infringe copyright, pirate, *copy*; smuggle, run, bootleg, poach, hijack.

defraud, embezzle, peculate, misappropri-

ate, purloin; fiddle, commit breach of
trust; con, swindle, cheat, diddle, chisel,
deceive; rook, pigeon, gull, dupe; pluck,
skin, *fleece*.

rob, rob with violence, mug; commit highway robbery, *pirate*, buccaneer, filibuster, maraud, raid, foray, forage,
scrounge; strip, gut, ransack, rifle; plunder, pillage, loot, sack, ravage, spoil, *lay
waste*; make a prey of, blackmail; extort,
screw, squeeze, *oppress*.

784 Thief

N. *thief*, swell mob; crook; petty thief;
sneaker, sneak thief; pickpocket, dip;
cattle thief, rustler; burglar, house-
breaker; poacher, runner; slaver; fence,
receiver of stolen property; pirate.

robber; brigand, bandit, outlaw, Robin
Hood; highwayman; thug, *ruffian*; gangster, racketeer; gunman; pirate, buccaneer, corsair, filibuster, privateer; raider,
freebooter; wrecker.

defrauder; cheat, shark, con man, *trickster*;
forger.

785 Booty

N. *booty*, spoil, spoils; spoils of war, *trophy*;
plunder, loot, pillage; prey, victim,
quarry; find, strike, prize, purchase,
haul, catch, *gain*; stolen article, stolen
goods, swag; moonshine, hooch, bootleg,
contraband; graft, blackmail; pork barrel.

786 Barter

N. *barter*, exchange, *interchange*; exchange
of goods, truck, truck system; traffic,
dealing; horse-trading.

trade, commercial intercourse; visible
trade, foreign trade, protection; free
trade, open market, *market*; traffic, slave
trade; black market; retail trade, *sale*;
capitalism, free enterprise, *scope*; free
market economy; mutual profit; dollar
diplomacy, *inducement*; commerce, *business*; private enterprise, private sector,
venture, *undertaking*; deal, bargain, *compact*; clientele, custom, *purchase*.

Adj. *trading*; commercial, mercantile;
wholesale, retail; *speculative*.

Vb. *trade*, exchange, *interchange*; barter,
truck; open a trade, merchant, *do business*; handle; fence; *sell*; trade with,
finance, back, promote; have an eye to
business.

speculate, venture, risk, *gamble*; invest;
racketeer, profiteer; go bust; operate,
bull, bear, stag.

bargain, negotiate, haggle, dicker, *make
terms*; make a bid, make a takeover bid,
preempt; outbid, *offer*; *overrate*; *underestimate*; charge, *give terms*; take; drive a
bargain, do a deal, *contract*.

Adv. *in trade*, in business; across the counter.

787 Purchase

N. *purchase*; takeover, preemption;
redemption, ransom, *deliverance*; hire
purchase; *expenditure*; mail order; custom, patronage, consumer demand,
requirement; *inducement*; bid, *offer*; first
refusal, right of purchase; a purchase,
buy, bargain.

purchaser, buyer; consignee; buyer of
labour, employer; customer, patron, cli-

ent, clientele; consumer; redeemer;
share-buyer, bull, stag.

Adj. *bought*, paid for, redeemed, purchased,
bribed.

buying, marketing; preemptive, bidding.

Vb. *purchase*, buy, *acquire*; shop, market;
require; make a good buy; buy outright;
borrow; store; preempt, corner; make a
take-over bid; square, suborn, *bribe*; buy
back, redeem, ransom, *deliver*; *defray*;
speculate; buy service, rent, *hire*; bid,
offer; buy shares, bull, stag.

788 Sale

N. *sale*; marketing; disposal; clearance, sell-
out; clearance sale, sale of work, bazaar;
sale of office; exclusive sale, monopoly,
oligopoly, *restraint*; public sale, auction,
Dutch auction; good market; sales,
boom; bad sales, *adversity*; service, sales
talk, pitch, sales patter, spiel; hard sell,
advertisement; market research, *enquiry*;
thing sold, seller, *merchandise*.

seller; bear; barrow boy, costermonger, *pedlar*; shopkeeper, dealer; retailer; sales
representative, rep; traveller; agent, tout;
shop assistant, shop girl, salesman; clerk;
ticket agent; roundsman, milkman.

Adj. *salable*; sold; sought after; available.

Vb. *sell*, make a sale; flog, dispose of; market, vend; bring to market, dump; hawk,
peddle, push; tout; *provide*; auction;
wholesale; retail; *trade*; sell at a profit,
gain; sell at a loss, *lose*; undercut,
cheapen; remainder; *cease*; clear stock,
hold a sale; sell again; sell forward.

be *sold*; sell, have a sale, have a market,
meet a demand, sell well, boom; be a
best-seller; sell badly.

789 Merchant

N. *merchant*, merchant prince; livery company, guild, chamber of commerce, concern, firm, *corporation*; business person,
man or woman of business; entrepreneur,
operator; fence; slaver; wholesale merchant; dealer; middleman, broker, stockbroker; estate agent, financier; banker;
money-changer.

tradespeople; tradesman, retailer, middleman, tallyman; shopkeeper, *seller*; iron-
monger, haberdasher, grocer, provision
merchant.

pedlar, *seller*; street seller, cheapjack; costermonger, barrow boy.

790 Merchandise

N. *merchandise*, article of commerce, line,
staple; article, commodity, stock, stock-
in-trade; range, repertoire, *store*; freight,
cargo, *contents*; stuff, supplies, wares,
goods; shop goods; perishable goods;
sundries.

791 Market

N. *market*, mart; open market, free trade
area, Common Market, Comecon; free
market, *trade*; black market, underground economy, market cross, forum,
focus; street market, Petticoat Lane; auction room; fair, motor show; exhibition,
exposition, shop window, *exhibit*; corn
market, wheat pit, corn exchange;
exchange, Change, kerb market, bucket
shop; Wall Street; toll booth, custom
house.

emporium, free port, depot, warehouse,

storage; wharf, quay; general market, bazaar, arcade, pedestrian precinct.

shop; store, emporium, bazaar, boutique, bargain basement, supermarket, hypermarket; concern, firm, establishment, house, corner shop, stall, booth, stand, kiosk, barrow, counter, shop window, window display; premises, place of business, *workshop*.

792 Money

N. money, Lsd; pelf, *wealth*; lucre, root of all evil; medium of exchange, cash nexus; currency; sound currency, honest money, legal tender; money of account, sterling, precious metal, gold, silver, ready money, cash, change, *small coin*; pocket money, paltry sum, chickenfeed, peanuts.

shekels, brass, tin, dough, lolly, sugar, bread; swag, loot, gravy; soap, palm oil, *incentive*.

funds, hot money; liquidity; account; wherewithal, *means*; ready nexus; finances, exchequer, cash flow, cash supplies; treasure, *provision*; remittance, *payment*; capital; sum of money, amount, figure, sum, quid, smacker; fiver, tenner, pony, monkey, grand; mint of money, pile, packet, *great quantity*; purse, *store*.

finance, world of finance; money power, purse strings, almighty dollar; money market, exchange, *market*; exchange rate, parity, par, *equality*; snake; floating pound; rising exchange rate, strong pound; gold standard; green pound; deficit finance, inflation, inflationary spiral; deflation; reflation.

coinage, issue; metallic currency, coin, piece; monetary unit, monetary denomination; guinea, sovereign, pound, quid; crown, florin, shilling, bob, sixpence, tanner, penny, copper, halfpenny, farthing; decimal coinage, fifty p, ten p, five p, two p, one p, half p; dollar, buck; half dollar, quarter, dime, nickel, cent; eagle; franc, mark; guilder, krona, krone, lira, peseta, rupee, rand, yen; talent, shekel, ducat, angel, noble, real, piece of eight; change, centime, pfennig, cash, *small coin*; shell money, wampum; numismatics.

paper money; wad; note, treasury note, bill, buck; bill of exchange, negotiable instrument; draft, order, check, cheque, letter of credit; note of hand, IOU; coupon, warrant, certificate, bond, *security*.

false money, base coin, snide; forgery; dud cheque, *nonpayment*.

bullion, bar, ingot, nugget; solid gold, solid silver; precious metal, platinum, gold, silver.

minter, mint master; forger; moneychanger, mint master; cashier, *treasurer*; financier, capitalist; *rich person*.

Adj. monetary; pecuniary, fiscal; sterling, sound, solvent, *rich*; inflationary, deflationary; withdrawn.

Vb. mint, coin, stamp; issue, circulate; pass, utter; forge, counterfeit.

demonetize, withdraw; clip; devalue, depreciate, inflate, *cheapen*.

draw money, cash, cash a cheque, *pay*.

793 Treasurer

N. treasurer, bursar, purser; cashier, teller, croupier; stakeholder, trustee, steward, *consignee*; liquidator; *receiver*; *accountant*; banker, financier; paymaster, almoner; mint master; bank, *treasury*.

794 Treasury

N. treasury, treasure house, thesaurus; exchequer, public purse; fund, *store*; custom house; bursary; bank; savings bank, building society; coffer, chest, *box*; treasure chest, depository, *storage*; strongbox, safe, safe deposit, cash box, stocking, mattress; till, cash register, cash desk, slot machine; receipt of custom, box office, gate, turnstile; purse, purse strings, *pocket*; wallet, wad, rouleau, *case*.

795 Wealth

N. wealth, lucre, pelf, brass, *money*; golden touch; riches, *plenty*; luxury; ease, comfort, easy circumstances, *euphoria*; credit; solidity, substance; competence, *sufficiency*; high income, surtax bracket, *receiving*; gain; resources, capital, *means*; bank account; limitless resources, bottomless purse; nest egg, *store*; tidy sum, power of money, pile, packet, cool million, *great quantity*; fortune, *property*; bonanza, mine, king's ransom; plutocracy, capitalism.

rich person, man or woman of means; baron, tycoon, oil magnate, nabob, millionaire; moneymaker, moneyspinner, fat cat, capitalist, plutocrat, heir to riches, poor little rich girl, *beneficiary*; jet set; new rich, self-made man, *prosperous person*; plutocracy.

Adj. rich, lush, fertile, *prolific*; abundant, luxurious, plush, slap-up; wealthy; opulent, affluent, *prosperous*; well-off, well-to-do, *comfortable*.

moneyed, propertied, worth a lot, worth a packet; made of money, rolling, dripping, loaded; stinking rich; flush; solvent, sound, able to pay; all straight.

Vb. be rich, turn all to gold; have money, have means, draw a large income; be flush, have credit, command capital, have money to burn; die rich, *bequeath*.

afford, be able to pay, be solvent, *have enough*.

get rich, inherit; prosper; enrich oneself, make money; make a packet, make a pile, make a bomb, make a fortune, strike it rich, *gain*; seek riches.

make rich, enrich, leave one a fortune, *bequeath*; enhance, *augment*; improve, *make better*.

796 Poverty

N. poverty, Lady Poverty; voluntary poverty; Queer Street; loss of fortune, beggary; utter poverty, penury; privation, necessity, need, want, pinch, *requirement*; bare cupboard, empty larder, *scarcity*; famine; light pocket, empty purse, insufficient income, slender means, meagre resources, low water; straits, distress, *suffering*; hand-to-mouth existence, poorness; general poverty, recession, slump, depression; squalor, slum, substandard housing; workhouse, poorhouse.

poor person, broken man or woman, bankrupt, insolvent; hermit, *ascetic*; pauper, indigent, poor beggar, vagrant, tramp, down-and-out, *beggar*; underdog; new poor; *object of scorn*; poor white, white trash; poor relation, *inferior*; Job.

Adj. *poor*; underprivileged; impecunious, short, short of funds, short of cash; skint, bust, broke, bankrupt, insolvent; broken; deprived; poverty-stricken; needy, indigent, *necessitous*; hungry; straitened, hard put to it; penniless, destitute; without a bean, without a cent, without a sou, without prospects.

beggarly, starveling, shabby, seedy, tattered, threadbare, tatty, *dilapidated*; scruffy, squalid, mean, *dirty*; poverty-stricken.

Vb. *be poor*, earn little or nothing, scratch a living, scrape an existence; be unable to afford; starve, *be hungry*; want, lack, *require*; become poor, go broke; *deteriorate*; claim supplementary benefit.

impoverish, reduce to poverty, leave destitute, beggar; ruin, *destroy*; rob, strip, *fleece*; dispossess, disinherit.

797 Credit

N. *credit*, repute, reputation, *prestige*; sound proposition; trust, confidence, reliability, *probity*; limit of credit; line of credit, tick; credit card, credit note; credit balance, *receipt*; account, score, tally, bill; national credit, floating debt, *debt*; loan, mortgage; vote.

creditor, dun; depositor.

Vb. *credit*, grant a loan, *lend*; grant, vote; await payment; take credit, open an account, keep an account with, *borrow*.

798 Debt

N. *debt*; obligation, commitment; mortgage, *security*; debit, charge; national debt, promise to pay, debt of honour, *promise*; bad debt, write-off, *loss*; good debt, *gain*; tally, account; deficit, overdraft, balance to pay, *shortfall*; inability to pay; frozen balance, *nonpayment*; *credit*; overdue payment, arrears, back pay, back rent.

interest, usury, pound of flesh; premium, rate of interest, bank rate.

\debtor, loan applicant; bad debtor, insolvent.

Adj. *indebted*, indebted, liable, committed, responsible, answerable, bound; unable to pay, insolvent.

owed, due, overdue; outstanding; chargeable, payable, returnable, bearing.

Vb. *be in debt*, owe, have to repay; owe money, pay interest; accept a charge, be liable; get credit, *borrow*; use a credit card, keep an account with; welsh, do a moonlight flit; make oneself responsible, *incur a duty*.

799 Payment

N. *payment*; discharge, release, satisfaction, clearance, settlement; *receipt*; cash payment, ready money, *money*; first payment, earnest, earnest money, deposit; instalment, standing order; hire purchase; due payment, subscription, tribute, *tax*; voluntary payment, collection, *offering*; composition, indemnity, *restitution*; remittance, *expenditure*.

pay, payoff, pay packet, pay day, wages bill, wages, salary, *earnings*; grant, subsidy; salary, pension, annuity, emolument, fee, garnish, bribe, *reward*; cut, commission, *discount*; something paid, subscription, collection, tribute, *tax*; damages, indemnity, *penalty*; redundancy pay, golden handshake; paymaster, purser, cashier,

treasurer.

Adj. *paying*; paying in full, paying cash; o of debt, owing nothing.

Vb. *pay*, disburse, *expend*; contribute, giv barter, *trade*; make payment; com across; pay a high price; pay back, repa reimburse, compensate; *bribe*; pay wage remunerate, tip, *reward*; pay cash, hon our (a bill); meet, satisfy, redeem, di charge, get a receipt; clear, liquidat settle, settle an account, *account*; settle score; *retaliate*.

defray; buy a round, stand treat, treat, *giv* go Dutch, *participate*.

Adv. *cash down*; cash on delivery, C.O.D with ready money.

800 Nonpayment

N. *nonpayment*, default; stoppage, *penalt* moratorium, embargo, freeze; refusal pay, protest, *refusal*; tax evasion; hi purchase; *false money*.

insolvency, inability to pay; crash, failur failure of credit; nothing to pay wit overdraft; *debt*.

nonpayer; failure, lame duck; bankrup insolvent debtor.

Adj. *nonpaying*, behindhand; unable to pa insolvent, bankrupt; *indebted*; *poor*.

Vb. *not pay*, default, embezzle, swindl *defraud*; get behindhand; stop paymen freeze, block; refuse payment, protest bill; practise tax evasion, *be dishones* divert; dishonour, repudiate; becom insolvent, go bankrupt; sink, fail, brea go bust, crash; welsh, *deceive*; absconc *decamp*; be unable to pay, *be poor*, l *parsimonious*; cancel a debt, discharge bankrupt, *abrogate*.

801 Expenditure

N. *expenditure*, *payment*; cost of livin outgoings, overheads, expense accoun expense, outlay, investment; fee, tac *pay*.

Adj. *expending*; generous, *liberal*; extrava gant, *prodigal*.

expended, spent, paid.

Vb. *expend*, spend, buy, *purchase*; inves sink money; afford, stand, disburse, *pa* give money, donate, *give*; do it proud, b lavish, *be liberal*; fling money arounc blow, *be prodigal*; consume, run throug *waste*.

802 Receipt

N. *receipt*, voucher; revenue, royalty, due customs, *tax*; turnover, takings, pr ceeds, returns, receipts, gate money, gat income, privy purse; emolument, regula income, pay, salary, wages, *earning reward*; pension, annuity, tontine; allow ance, pocket money, inadequate allow ance, pittance; alimony, maintenanc scholarship, *acquisition*; interest, retur rake-off; winnings, capital gain, *gai* bonus, premium, *extra*; prize, *troph* draw, legacy.

Adj. *received*, paid, acknowledged.

Vb. *acquire*, receive, take.

803 Accounts

N. *accounts*, accountancy, commerci arithmetic; book-keeping, entry, aud account, balance sheet; budget, *provisio* running account, statement of accoun statement, bill, invoice, manifest, *lis* account paid, account settled, *payment*; reckoning, computation, score, tally.

account *book*, journal, ledger, register, books, *record*.

accountant, cost accountant; cashier, *treasurer*; actuary.

Adj. *accounting*, bookkeeping; reckoning; accountable.

Vb. *account*; budget, cost, value, *estimate*; book, enter, post, debit, credit, *register*; prepare a balance sheet; prepare a statement, present an account, charge, bill, invoice; overcharge, surcharge, undercharge, *price*; fiddle, garble, doctor, *defraud*; audit; take stock, inventory, catalogue, *list*.

804 Price

N. *price*, rate; piece rate, high rate, ceiling; low rate, floor; price control, fixed price, *restraint*; value, worth, what it will fetch; scarcity value, famine price; price list, tariff; quotation, price charged; amount, figure; ransom, fine, *penalty*; demand, dues, charge, surcharge, supplement, *extra*; overcharge, excessive charge, extortion, ransom; fare, hire, rental, rent, fee, entrance or admission fee; commission, rake-off; salvage; postage; cover charge; bill, invoice, reckoning, shot.

cost, damage, *expenditure*; overheads; wages, wage bill; damages, *penalty*; cost of living, cost of living index.

tax, dues; taxation, tax demand, *demand*; rating, *estimate*; rate, levy, toll, duty; charge, forced loan, aid, benevolence; *compulsion*; forced savings; punitive tax, *penalty*; tribute, blackmail, ransom, *payment*; tithe; national insurance; poll tax, estate duty, death duty; direct taxation, income tax, PAYE, surtax, supertax, company tax, capital levy; indirect taxation, excise, customs, tariff; local tax; purchase tax, VAT; salt tax; feudal *tax*.

Adj. *priced*, charged, fixed; chargeable, dutiable; paid.

Vb. *price*, cost, assess, value, rate, *estimate*; raise a price, ask a price, charge, require, *demand*; bill, invoice.

cost, be worth, fetch; amount to, come to; bear a price.

tax, impose a tax; fix a tariff, levy a rate, value; toll, excise, subject to duty, make dutiable; take a toll, *levy*; take a collection, *beg*; fine, *punish*.

805 Discount

N. *discount*, reduction, rebate, cut; stoppage; concession, allowance, margin, special price; tare; drawback; cut price, cut rate, special offer, loss leader, *incentive*; bargain price, bargain sale; percentage; commission, rake-off.

Vb. *discount*, deduct, *subtract*; allow a margin, tare; reduce, depreciate, abate, rebate, *abate*; offer a discount, cut, slash, *cheapen*; take a discount.

Adv. *at a discount*, below par.

806 Dearness

N. *dearness*; value, high worth; famine price; scarcity value, rarity, dearth, *scarcity*; extortion, rip-off; overcharge, excessive charge, bad value, bad bargain, high price, cost, pretty penny; ruinous charge; cheap money, inflation, inflationary pressure.

Adj. *dear*, expensive; costly; extravagant; exorbitant, excessive, extortionate, preposterous, steep, stiff, sky-high; prohibitive, more than one can afford; dear at any price, *useless*; rising, inflationary.

of value, of worth, *valuable*; priceless, beyond price; invaluable, *useful*; inestimable, worth a king's ransom, worth a fortune; precious, rare, scarce, like gold dust, *infrequent*; at a premium.

Vb. *be dear*, cost a lot, cost a packet, cost a pretty penny, harden; appreciate, escalate, soar, mount, climb; get too dear; prove expensive, cost one dear, cost a fortune.

overcharge, sell dear, oversell, ask too much; profiteer, soak, sting, bleed, skin, extort, short-change, hold to ransom, *fleece*; bull, auction, *sell*.

pay too much, be stung, be had, be done; pay high, pay dear, buy a white elephant; ruin oneself.

Adv. *dearly*, dear, at a price, at great cost, at huge expense.

807 Cheapness

N. *cheapness*; good value, snip, bargain; sale goods, seconds; low price, reasonable charge; cheap rate, excursion fare, *discount*; nominal price, peppercorn rent, easy terms; Dutch auction; fall, slump; deflation; glut, *plenty*.

no charge, gift; labour of love, *voluntary work*; free trade, free port; free entry, free admission, free pass, free ticket; free quarters, free board, free service, free delivery.

Adj. *cheap*, inexpensive, moderate, reasonable, fair; cheap to make; substandard, shop-soiled; economical, economy, economy size; worth its price; low, going cheap; cut-price; easy to buy; worth nothing, cheapjack, catchpenny, *useless*.

uncharged, gratuitous, complimentary; gratis; free, free of charge; honorary, *voluntary*; given; free.

Vb. *be cheap*, cost little, be economical; cost nothing, be without charge, be free; cheapen, depreciate, decline, sag, fall, drift, slump, plunge, plummet.

cheapen, lower, keep cheap, cut, slash; undercharge, underrate, sacrifice, make a present of, *give*; undercut, undersell; dump, unload; glut; bear.

Adv. *cheaply*; at cost price, at prime cost, at a discount.

808 Liberality

N. *liberality*, munificence, generosity; open heart, open hand, open purse, hospitality, open house; free hand, blank cheque, *scope*; cornucopia, *plenty*; bounty, largesse; *gift*; handsome offer, *offer*; charity, *kind act*.

good giver, liberal donor; Lady Bountiful, Father Christmas, rich uncle, *benefactor*.

Adj. *liberal*, free, free-handed, lavish, *prodigal*; large-hearted, *disinterested*; bountiful, charitable; hospitable, *sociable*; handsome, generous, splendid, slap-up; lordly, princely, royal, right royal; unsparing, unfailing; abundant, ample, bounteous, flowing, full; *redundant*.

Vb. *be liberal*, lavish, shower largesse, *give*; overpay, pay well, keep open house, be *hospitable*; do one proud; give a blank cheque, *give scope*; spend freely, *be prodigal*.

Adv. *liberally*, with open hand.

809 Economy

N. *economy*, thrift; care; husbandry, good housekeeping; good management, credit squeeze; economy drive; time-saving; saving, sparing; savings, *store*, conservation; *niggard*; good housewife, careful steward.

Adj. *economical*, time-saving; chary of expense, *parsimonious*; thrifty, careful, prudent, canny, frugal, saving, sparing; spare; meagre, Spartan, sparse; marginal, with nothing to spare.

Vb. *economize*, be economical, waste nothing, recycle, reuse; keep within compass; cut back, retrench; pinch, scrape, *be parsimonious*; save, spare, hoard, *store*; plough back, make every penny work, *get rich*.

Adv. *sparingly*, economically, frugally.

810 Prodigality

N. *prodigality*, profusion; idle display, idle expenditure, conspicuous consumption, *ostentation*; wasteful expenditure, *waste*; deficit finance; misuse of funds, *misuse*. prodigal, prodigal son, waster, wastrel, profligate, spendthrift.

Adj. *prodigal*, lavish, *liberal*; profuse; extravagant, regardless of cost, wasteful, profligate; uneconomic, spendthrift, improvident, reckless, dissipated.

Vb. *be prodigal*, splash money around; spend money like water; blow everything, squander, *waste*; dissipate; misspend, throw good money after bad; spend more than one has, overdraw; save nothing.

Adv. *prodigally*; like a prodigal, like a spendthrift.

Int. hang the expense a short life and a merry one easy come, easy go

811 Parsimony

N. *parsimony*; credit squeeze, *economy*; false economy; cheese-paring; grudging hand, closed purse.
avarice, cupidity; rapacity, greed, *desire*.
niggard, skinflint, screw, scrimp, scraper, tightwad; miser, money-grubber; squirrel, magpie; churl, codger, curmudgeon; usurer; Scrooge.

Adj. *parsimonious*, careful, *economical*; too careful, frugal to excess; mean, mingy, stingy, near, close, tight; tight-fisted, grudging, churlish, illiberal, ungenerous, uncharitable, empty-handed; chary, sparing, shabby, small-minded.
avaricious, grasping, *selfish*; possessive, acquisitive; hoarding, saving; covetous, rapacious, extortionate; mercenary, venal, sordid.

Vb. *be parsimonious*, retain; grudge, begrudge, withhold, keep back, *refuse*; stint, skimp, starve, spare, *make insufficient*; scrape, scrimp, pinch; screw, skin a flint, *fleece*; starve oneself, live like a pauper; hoard wealth, never spend a penny; grudge every farthing, haggle, *bargain*; cadge, beg, borrow; hoard, *be selfish*.

Adv. *parsimoniously*, niggardly, sparingly, on a shoestring.

812 Affections

N. *affections*; emotional life; nature, disposition, *character*; spirit, temper, tone, grain, mettle, *temperament*; cast of mind, trait, *state*; personality, psychology, mentality, outlook, *heredity*; being, breast, bosom, heart, soul, core, inmost soul, inner man, *essential part*, spirit; attitude, frame of mind, vein, strain, humour, mood; predilection, turn, bent, bias, *tendency*; passion, *prejudice*; heartstrings, *feeling*; force of character; anthropomorphism, pathetic fallacy.

Adj. *with affections*, affected, cast; instinct with, inborn, inbred, congenital, *genetic*; deep-rooted, *intrinsic*; emotional, demonstrative, *feeling*.

813 Feeling

N. *feeling*, experience, emotional life, affect, sensation, sense of, *sense*; emotion, sentiment; true feeling; impulse; intuition, instinct; response, reaction, fellow feeling, sympathy, empathy, appreciation, understanding, *knowledge*; impression, deep feeling, deep sense of, *moral sensibility*; religious feeling, *piety*; benevolence; *love*; resentment; thrill, kick, spasm, shock, turn, *lack of expectation*; pathos, *suffering*; release of feeling; romanticism; manifestation of feeling; expression, play of features, *gesture*; blush, flush; gooseflesh, tremor, quiver, flutter, flurry; stew, ferment, *commotion*; swelling heart; control of feeling, endurance, stiff upper lip, *patience*.
warm *feeling*, glow; full heart, hot heart; fervour, ardour, enthusiasm, dash, fire, vigour, zeal, *activity*; mania, *prejudice*; emotion, passion, ecstasy, inspiration; elevation, *excitable state*.

Adj. *feeling*, sensible, sensory, *sentient*; spirited, vivacious, lively, *sensitive*; sensuous, *sensual*; living, bearing, *suffering*; sensitive, vibrant, responsive; involved, sympathetic; tenderhearted; emotional, passionate, full of feeling; unctuous, soulful; intense, tense, *excited*; cordial, hearty; effusive; sentimental, romantic, mawkish, maudlin, treacly, soppy, sloppy.
impressed, affected; touched, excited; struck, awestruck, struck all of a heap; rapt, ecstatic; lyrical, raving, *excitable*.
fervent, fervid, passionate, ardent, tense, intense; eager, breathless; impassioned, vehement, earnest, zealous; exuberant, warm-blooded, impetuous, impatient, *excitable*; warm, fiery, glowing, burning, red-hot, flaming, *hot*; hysterical, overwrought, feverish, hectic; strong, furious, *violent*.
felt, experienced; heartfelt, cordial, hearty, warm, sincere, *veracious*; deep-seated, profound, *deep*; stirring, heart-warming, emotive, strong, *impressive*; smart, acute, keen, poignant, piercing, trenchant, sharp; caustic, burning, pungent; penetrating, absorbing; ecstatic; pathetic, affecting.

Vb. *feel*, sense, receive an impression; entertain, take to heart, *be sensitive*; experience, live, live through, taste; bear, endure, undergo, smart, *suffer*; suffer with, share, *participate*; respond, react; tingle, warm to, fire, kindle, catch, be inspired, *be excited*; cause feeling, *impress*.
show *feeling*; demonstrate, *manifest*;

enthuse, *be pleased*; *get angry*; turn colour, look blue, look black; go livid, go purple, *blacken*; look pale, blench, turn pale, go white, *whiten*; colour, blush, flush, glow, mantle, turn red, turn crimson, *redden*; quiver, tremble, wince; flutter, shake, quake; tingle, thrill, vibrate, throb, *oscillate*; palpitate, pant, heave, draw a deep breath, *breathe*; reel, lurch, stagger; stutter, *stammer*.

Adv. *feelingly*, earnestly, heart and soul; with a full heart; heartily, devoutly, sincerely.

814 Sensibility

N. *moral sensibility*, soul; thin skin, soft spot, tender spot; sore point, *resentment*; affection, *love*; spirit, verve, *vigour*; ebullience; *discrimination*; temperament; *sensibility*; touchy person, sensitive plant, bundle of nerves.

Adj. *impressible*, malleable, plastic, *soft*; sensible, aware, conscious of, awake to, alive to, responsive, *sentient*; touched; impressionable, *excitable*; susceptible; romantic, sentimental; soppy, wet; emotional; soft, tender, tender-hearted.

sensitive, sore, raw, tender, *sentient*; aesthetic, fastidious, particular; hypersensitive, all feeling, *excitable*; touchy, irritable, impatient, thin-skinned, easily stung, *irascible*.

lively, alive, vital, vivacious; skittish, *merry*; irrepressible; mettlesome, spirited, alert, aware, *attentive*; impatient; nervous, highly-strung, overstrung, temperamental; mobile, changeable; impassioned, *fervent*; fanatic; expressive, racy, *forceful*.

Vb. *be sensitive*, have a soft heart, take it to heart, *pity*; tingle.

Adv. *on the raw*, to the quick, where it hurts most.

815 Insensibility

N. *moral insensibility*; lack of sensation, stupor, *insensibility*; inertia; lethargy; vegetation; *inattention*; insouciance, detachment, apathy; phlegm, sangfroid; repression, repression of feeling, *patience*; poker face, deadpan expression; thick skin, rhinoceros hide; cold heart, frigidity; *hardness*; lack of feeling, dry eyes, heart of stone, heart of marble, *inhumanity*; *tedium*; *lack of wonder*.

unfeeling *person*, iceberg, icicle, cold fish, cold heart, cold-blooded animal; stoic, ascetic; stock, stone, block, marble.

Adj. *impassive*, unconscious, *insensible*; insensitive; phlegmatic, stolid; wooden; bovine; dull, slow; proof, proof against, ascetic; unconcerned, aloof, distant, detached, *indifferent*; unaffected, calm, *tranquil*; steady, unruffled; imperturbable, without nerves, cool; inscrutable; blank, expressionless, deadpan; unseeing, *blind*; *deaf*; impersonal, dispassionate, without warmth, reserved, stony, frigid, frozen, icy, cold, cold-blooded, coldhearted; unfeeling, heartless, soulless, inhuman.

apathetic; unmoved; half-hearted, lukewarm, *indifferent*; uninterested; nonchalant, careless, regardless, neglectful, *negligent*; spiritless, lackadaisical; stagnant, *quiescent*; sluggish, supine; passive, *inert*; torpid, numb, benumbed, comatose, *insensible*.

thick-skinned; impenetrable, impervious; blind to, deaf to, dead to, closed to;

obtuse, insensitive; callous, tough, *hard*; hard-bitten, hard-boiled; shameless, unblushing, amoral.

Vb. *be insensitive, be insensible*; be blind to, *be blind*; lack animation, lack spirit, lack verve; harden oneself, *be pitiless*; *be indifferent*; be a Philistine; *despise*; ignore, *disregard*; *be temperate*; stagnate, vegetate; *be resolute*.

make *insensitive*, *render insensible*; render callous, steel, toughen, *harden*; sear, *dry*; deafen, *silence*; *blind*; *pervert*; stale, coarsen; satiate, cloy, *sate*; deaden, *blunt*.

Adv. *in cold blood*, with dry eyes, without emotion, with steady pulse; without enthusiasm.

816 Excitation

N. *excitation*, rousing; possession, inspiration; calling forth; animation, invitation, appeal, *inducement*; provocation, irritation; impression, image, impact, *influence*; fascination, *sorcery*; rapture, *joy*; emotional appeal, human interest, sentiment, pathos, sensationalism, melodrama; excitement, high pressure, tension, *energy*; state of excitement, ebullience; shock, thrill, *spasm*; stew, ferment, tizzy, flurry, furore, *commotion*; pitch of excitement, fever pitch, orgasm, *frenzy*; climax, *crisis*, excited feeling, passion, emotion, enthusiasm, lyricism, *feeling*; fuss, drama, *excitable state*; temper, fury, rage, *anger*; interest, *curiosity*; *wonder*; awe, *fear*.

excitant, tub-thumper, *agitator*; sob sister; headline, *publicity*; fillip, ginger, tonic, *stimulant*; upper, pep pill; sting, prick, goad, spur, whip, lash, *incentive*; fan.

Adj. *excited*, busy, astir, *active*; *bubbly*; tense; feverish, hectic; frantic; glowing, *fervent*; heated, *hot*; red-hot with excitement, violent, *furious*; wild, mad, livid, roaring, *angry*; avid, eager, agog; *feeling*; all of a flutter; restless, restive, overwrought, distraught; beside oneself, hysterical, running amok, a prey to passion; crazy about, *enamoured*; inspired, possessed, impassioned, lyrical, raving, *excitable*.

exciting, heady, exhilarating, provocative, piquant; salty, spicy, appetizing; evocative, emotive, suggestive; hair-raising; moving, affecting; heating, kindling, rousing, stirring; cheering, rousing, sensational, dramatic, melodramatic; stunning, mind-blowing; gripping, absorbing.

impressive, imposing, grand, stately; regal, royal, queenly, *noble*; awe-inspiring, sublime; picturesque, scenic; striking, dramatic; telling, forceful.

Vb. *excite*, affect, infect, *influence*; *cheer*; touch, move, *sadden*; strike a chord, startle, electrify; raise to fever pitch, *heat*; inflame, kindle, draw a spark, *burn*; sting, pique, irritate, *enrage*; tease, *torment*; *hurt*; *incite*; enthuse, inspire, possess; stir, rouse, arouse, wake, evoke, call forth; thrill, exhilarate, intoxicate; transport, send, *delight*.

animate, enliven, quicken, revive, resuscitate, *restore*; inspire; encourage, hearten, *give courage*; give an edge, whet, *sharpen*; urge, nag, spur, goad, lash, *accelerate*; jolt, jog; fillip, give a fillip to, stimulate, ginger, *invigorate*; cherish, foster, foment, *strengthen*; fuel, intensify, fan.

impress, leave an impression; project or

present an image; interest, hold, grip, absorb; intrigue, rouse curiosity; strike, claim attention, *attract notice*; affect, *influence*; bring home to, drive home; come home to, penetrate, pierce, *be intelligible*; arrest, shake, smite, stun, amaze, astound, stagger, *surprise*; stupefy, petrify, *be wonderful*; dazzle, fill with admiration; inspire with awe, humble; overwhelm; oppress, perturb, disquiet, upset, unsettle, distress, worry, *trouble*.

be excited; flare, flame, burn, *be hot*; sizzle, seethe, boil, explode, *effervesce*; thrill to, *feel*; tingle, tremble, *be excitable*; quiver, flutter, palpitate; mantle, flush, *show feeling*; squirm, writhe, *wriggle*; dance, stamp, ramp; jump, *leap*; be unable to sleep.

Adv. *excitedly*; all agog, with beating heart.

817 Excitability

N. excitability; instability, temperament; hot blood, hot temper; *bias*; headstrong behaviour; *haste*; turbulence; nerves, flap.

excitable state, elevation, elation, abandon; thrill, transport, trip, high, ecstasy, inspiration, lyricism, *feeling*; fever, fever of excitement, fret, fume, trepidation, bother, fuss, flurry, whirl; warmth, *heat*; ferment, pother, stew; gust, storm, tempest, *gale*; outburst, outbreak, explosion, scene, *commotion*; brainstorm, hysterics, delirium, fit, agony, *frenzy*; distraction, madness; mania, passion, rage, fury, *violence*; temper, rampage, *anger*.

Adj. excitable, raw, *sensitive*; passionate, emotional; susceptible, romantic; suggestible, inflammable, like tinder; unstable, impressionable; variable, temperamental, volatile; fitful, *capricious*; restless, nervy, fidgety, edgy; highly-strung, nervous, skittish, mettlesome, *lively*; irritable, fiery, hot-tempered, *irascible*; impatient, trigger-happy, *hasty*; impetuous, impulsive, madcap, *rash*; savage, fierce, vehement, boisterous, rumbustious, tempestuous, turbulent, stormy, uproarious, clamorous, *violent*; restive, *riotous*; volcanic, explosive, ready to burst; intolerant; rabid, *furious*; feverish, febrile, frantic, hysterical; tense, electric; inspired, raving, lyrical, *excited*.

Vb. be excitable, fret, fume, stamp; shuffle, chafe, fidget; show excitement, show temperament, *show feeling*; tingle with; have nerves, flap; start, jump, *be nervous*; have a temper, *be irascible*; foam, froth, have hysterics, *go mad*; abandon oneself, let oneself go, go wild, run riot, run amok, see red; storm, rush about, *rampage*; ramp, rage, roar, *be violent*; explode, create, *get angry*; kindle, burn, smoulder, catch fire, *be excited*.

818 Inexcitability

N. inexcitability, good temper; composure; cool, sangfroid, frigidity, *moral insensibility*; unruffled state, *quietude*; peace of mind, *content*; equanimity, balance, poise, even temper, philosophy, balanced mind, *equilibrium*; self-possession, self-control, *temperance*; repression; detachment; gravity, sobriety; *courtesy*; lack of spirit, lack of mettle; *moderation*.

patience, patience of Job; forbearance, endurance, longsuffering; tolerance, toleration; resignation, *submission*.

Adj. inexcitable, dispassionate, cold, frigid, heavy, dull, *impassive*; stable; cool, imperturbable, unflappable; steady; moderate, *temperate*; inscrutable, deadpan; deliberate, *slow*; even, level, equable, *uniform*; even-tempered, easy-going, sunny; staid, sedate, sober, demure, reserved, grave, *serious*; quiet, *quiescent*; placid, unruffled, calm, serene, *tranquil*; sweet, gentle, mild, meek, *innocent*; *moderate*; peaceful; easy, easygoing, *lenient*; comfortable, *content*; *indifferent*; acquiescent, resigned, submissive, *obedient*; spiritless, lackadaisical, torpid, passive, *inert*; tame; earthbound, *prosaic*.

patient, meek, armed with patience; tolerant, longsuffering, forbearing; stoic, philosophical.

Vb. keep calm, be collected; compose oneself, keep cool, keep a cool head; *be insensitive*; relax, take things easy, *repose*; resign oneself, have patience, be resigned, *submit*.

be patient, show patience, show restraint, forbear; stand, tolerate, bear, endure, support, sustain, suffer, abide; resign oneself; brook, take, swallow, digest, stomach, pocket; *forgive*; be tolerant, condone, be lenient; turn a blind eye, overlook, *be lax*; allow, *permit*; ignore provocation, *be at peace*; coexist, *compromise*.

tranquillize, steady, moderate, *assuage*; calm, rock, lull, *bring to rest*; compose, *pacify*; *relieve*; control, repress, *restrain*.

819 Joy

N. joy, *pleasure*; great pleasure, sensation of pleasure, thrill, kick; delight, rapture, exaltation; ecstasy; unholy joy, malice; life of pleasure; honeymoon.

happiness, felicity, good fortune, wellbeing, comfort, ease, *euphoria*; unalloyed delight, rose without a thorn; golden age, age of Aquarius; bliss; cloud nine, nirvana, Paradise, Elysium, Garden of Eden, Arcadia, *fantasy*; happy valley, bower of bliss, home sweet home.

enjoyment, satisfaction, fulfilment, *content*; delectation, relish, zest, gusto; indulgence; full life, hedonism; glee, merrymaking, lark, frolic, gambol, *merriment*; fun, treat, excursion, outing, *amusement*; refreshment, good cheer.

Adj. pleased, glad; receiving with open arms; happy, *content*; loving it; *merry*; exalted, overjoyed, *jubilant*; cheering, shouting; ecstatic, raving.

happy; blithe, joyful, joyous, *merry*; radiant, starry-eyed; felicitous, lucky, fortunate, *prosperous*; blessed; at ease, made comfortable, *comfortable*.

Vb. be pleased; feel or experience pleasure, hug oneself, purr, purr with pleasure, be cheerful; laugh, smile, rejoice; rave, rave about, *show feeling*; solace oneself with, wallow, spoil oneself, *enjoy*; have fun, amuse oneself; gloat; savour, appreciate, relish, taste; take a fancy to, like, *love*; think well of, *approve*.

820 Suffering

N. suffering, heartache, *melancholy*; nostalgia, *desire*; discontent; *fatigue*; nightmare, incubus; *affliction*, distress, anguish, angst, agony, torture, torment, *pain*; twinge, stab, smart, sting, thorn, pang; bitter cup; Passion, Crucifixion, Calvary, martyrdom; rack, *punishment*;

purgatory, hell, damnation; *difficulty*; inconvenience, discomfort, malaise; trial, ordeal; shock, blow, visitation, tribulation, *bane*; extremity, *illness*; living death, fate worse than death, *evil*; unhappy times, iron age, *adversity*.

sorrow, grief, gloom, *dejection*; dole, woe, misery, despair; valley of woe, *adversity*; heavy heart, displeasure, *discontent*; chagrin, remorse, regret.

worry, discomfort, disquiet, inquietude, fret; dismay, distress; phobia, hangup; anxiety, concern, solicitude, thought, care; responsibility, load, burden; strain, tension; a worry; trouble, *evil*; bother, irritation, pest, death of, *bane*; *bore*; something to worry about, lookout, funeral; headache, teaser, puzzle, problem.

sufferer, victim, scapegoat, sacrifice; prey, shorn lamb, *dupe*; willing sacrifice, martyr; object of compassion, wretch, misery; patient, *sick person*.

Adj. *suffering*, ill, sick; bleeding, *pained*; uncomfortable, ill at ease; anxious, unhappy about, apprehensive, *nervous*; sick with worry; longsuffering, downtrodden; made a prey; stricken; careworn, woeful, woebegone, haggard.

unhappy, infelicitous, accursed, *unfortunate*; despairing, *hopeless*; pitiable, poor, miserable; sad, melancholy, despondent, disconsolate; heart-broken, sick at heart; woebegone, *dejected*; weeping, tearful; pained; sorry.

Vb. *suffer*, undergo, endure, go through, experience, *feel*; bear, endure; bear pain, bleed; hurt oneself, be hurt, smart, chafe, ache, *feel pain*; wince, flinch, writhe, squirm, *wriggle*; become a martyr, sacrifice oneself; *stand firm*; have a thin time, go through it, have trouble enough, *have trouble*; trouble oneself, fuss, worry, worry to death, fret; mind, take it badly, take it to heart; sorrow, passion, grieve, weep, sigh, *lament*; pity oneself, be despondent, *be dejected*; have regrets, kick oneself, *regret*.

821 Pleasurableness

N. *pleasurableness*, amenity, sunny side, appeal, *attraction*; *flattery*; charm, fascination, *beauty*; honeymoon, *joy*; something nice, a delight, a treat, a joy; novelty, pastime, fun, *amusement*; interest, melody, harmony, *music*; spice, zest, relish; dainty, titbit, sweet; balm, *refreshment*; *plenty*; peace, *quietude*, *leisure*; fantasy.

Adj. *pleasurable*, pleasant, nice, good; pleasing, agreeable, grateful; acceptable, welcome; wonderful, marvellous, splendid, *excellent*; painless, *comfortable*; refreshing; peaceful, quiet, *tranquil*; luxurious, voluptuous, *sensuous*; genial, warm, sunny, *cheering*; delightful, delectable, delicious, exquisite, choice; luscious, juicy; delicate, tasty, *savoury*; sugary, *sweet*; musical, *melodious*; picturesque, scenic, lovely, *beautiful*; amiable, dear, endearing; attractive, appealing, seductive, inviting; enchanting, ravishing, Siren; haunting, heart-warming, *exciting*; homely, cosy; pastoral; heavenly; beatific, blessed, *happy*.

Vb. *please*, give pleasure, agree with; make things pleasant, *flatter*; lull, soothe, *assuage*; comfort, *cheer*; put at ease, make comfortable, *relieve*; sugar, sweeten; stroke, pat, pet, baby, coddle, nurse, *caress*; indulge, be lax; charm, interest, *amuse*; rejoice, gladden, make happy; gratify, satisfy, *content*; bless.

delight; rejoice, exhilarate, elate, elevate, uplift; thrill, intoxicate, ravish; transport, send, *excite*; *flatter*, excite love; *make appetizing*; refresh; tickle, tickle one to death, titillate, tease; entrance, enrapture; enchant, charm, *bewitch*; *impress*; allure, seduce, *attract*.

822 Painfulness

N. *painfulness*, painful treatment, roughness, harassment; *evil*; *eyesore*; friction, irritation; *pain*; sore subject, sore point, rub, soft spot, *moral sensibility*; sore, ulcer, *bane*; shock, *lack of expectation*; disgust, nausea; bitter cup, bitter draught, bitter pill, vinegar; bread of affliction, *adversity*; tribulation, ordeal, cross, *suffering*; trouble, care, *worry*; pathos; sorry sight, sad spectacle, object of pity; heavy news, *sorrow*; hot water, *predicament*.

annoyance, death of, pest, curse, plague, *bane*; embarrassment, *worry*; interference, nuisance; burden, drag; grievance, complaint; hardship, *evil*; last straw, limit; offence, affront, insult, provocation, *indignity*; displeasure, *resentment*; menace.

Adj. *paining*, sore, tender; dolorous, *painful*; scathing, searing, scalding, burning, sharp, biting, nipping, gnawing, caustic, vitriolic; harsh, hard, rough, cruel, *severe*; gruelling, punishing, searching, exquisite, excruciating, extreme; hurtful, poisonous.

unpleasant, disagreeable; uncomfortable, joyless, dreary, dismal, *cheerless*; hideous, *ugly*; thankless; distasteful, *unsavoury*; foul, nasty, beastly, horrible; malodorous, stinking, *fetid*; bitter, sharp, *sour*; invidious, obnoxious, offensive, objectionable, undesirable, odious, hateful, loathsome, nauseous, slimy, revolting, repellent; execrable, accursed.

annoying, too bad; troublesome; wearisome, irksome, tiresome, *tedious*; burdensome, onerous, *weighty*; unfortunate, untoward, *adverse*; awkward, impossible; importunate; provoking, maddening; biting.

distressing, grievous; moving, affecting; harrowing, heartbreaking, heart-rending; pathetic, tragic, sad, woeful, mournful; pitiful, lamentable, *pitiable*; ghastly, grim, dreadful, shocking, appalling.

intolerable, insufferable, impossible, insupportable, unbearable, *exorbitant*; past bearing; extreme, enough to make one mad, enough to make a parson swear, enough to provoke a saint.

Vb. *hurt*, injure, *harm*; pain, *give pain*; bite, cut, tear, rend, *wound*; gall, plague, nettle, mortify, *huff*; touch a soft spot, grieve, afflict, distress, *sadden*; corrode, embitter, exacerbate, gnaw, chafe, rankle, fester, *aggravate*; offend, insult, affront.

torment, martyr; harrow, rack, *torture*; give one a bad time, maltreat, bait, bully, rag, persecute, assail, *oppress*; be offensive, snap at, bark at, *be rude*; importune, dun, besiege, *demand*; haunt, obsess; annoy, tease, pester, plague, nag, badger, worry, try, harass, harry, heckle; molest, bother, vex, provoke, ruffle, irritate, needle, sting, chafe, fret, bug, gall, irk, rile, *enrage*.

trouble, discomfort, disquiet, disturb, agitate, discompose, disconcert, upset, incommode, *derange*; worry, embarrass, perplex, *puzzle*; exercise, tire, *fatigue*; weary, bore, *be tedious*; obsess, haunt, bedevil; *depress*; infest, thwart, *obstruct*.

displease, *incur blame*; grate, jar, disagree with, give one a pain; disenchant, disillusion, *disappoint*; dissatisfy, *cause discontent*; offend, shock, horrify, disgust, revolt, repel, sicken, nauseate, make one sick, make one vomit, *cause dislike*; appal, *frighten*.

823 Content

N. *content*, satisfaction, complacency; self-satisfaction, *vanity*; measure of content, ray of comfort, resignation, *quietude*; ease of mind, nothing left to worry about, *euphoria*; reconciliation; comfort, sitting pretty; *consent*; resignation, *submission*.

Adj. *content*, *happy*; *peaceful*; cosy, snug, *comfortable*; at ease; *cheerful*; *pleased*; *disinterested*; without desire, without passion; resigned, acquiescent; fairly content; easily pleased, easygoing, *lenient*; secure, *safe*; thankful, *grateful*.

contenting, satisfactory, *sufficient*; tolerable, bearable; passable, acceptable; desirable.

Vb. *be content*, purr, purr with content, *be pleased*; be thankful, *be grateful*; *prosper*; congratulate oneself, *rejoice*; be at ease, be at home, sit pat, sit pretty, *enjoy*; *make peace*; take comfort, *be relieved*; rest content; complain of nothing, have nothing to grouse about; acquiesce, *submit*.

content, satisfy, gratify, *please*; meet with approval; make happy; grant a boon, *give*; *sate*; comfort, *cheer*; bring comfort to, speak peace to, *relieve*; be kind to, lull, set at ease, set at rest; propitiate, disarm, reconcile, conciliate, appease, *pacify*.

Adv. *contentedly*, with satisfaction.

824 Discontent

N. *discontent*; displeasure, pain, *disapprobation*; cold comfort; irritation, chagrin, pique, bile, spleen, *resentment*; disquiet, *worry*; grief, *sorrow*; strain, tension; unrest; *commotion*; nit-picking; ill will, *envy*; competition; grievance, grudge, complaint, *quarrel*; melancholy, ennui, *dejection*; dirty look, grimace, scowl, frown; groan, curse, *malediction*; cheep, squeak, murmur.

malcontent, grouch, Jonah; plaintiff; critic; person with a grievance, angry young man; dissident, dropout; *agitator*; irreconcilable, diehard, *opponent*; hard taskmaster, *tyrant*.

Adj. *discontented*; malcontent, dissident; obstructive; restless, restive, *disobedient*; disgruntled, weary, *unhappy*; sad, unrelieved, disconsolate, *dejected*; grudging, jealous, envious; bitter, *sour*; peevish, testy, cross, *sullen*; grumbling; *deprecatory*; sore; fretful, querulous, petulant; hard to please, hard to satisfy, exacting, *fastidious*; critical, hypercritical, censorious; irreconcilable, hostile, *inimical*.

discontenting, *insufficient*; sickening; *tedious*; obstructive.

Vb. *be discontented*, be critical, crab, carp, find fault, *be fastidious*; lack, miss, feel something is missing, *require*; sneer, groan, jeer, *disapprove*; mind, take offence, take amiss, take ill, take to heart, *resent*; sulk, *be sullen*; look blue, look glum, make a wry face, *be dejected*;

moan, mutter, murmur, whine, bleat, beef, protest, complain, object, cry blue murder, *deprecate*; bellyache, grumble, grouse, croak, snap; wail, *lament*; be aggrieved, have a grievance; *oppose*; *revolt*; grudge, envy; *quarrel*; make a meal of it; return, *reject*; *regret*.

cause *discontent*, dissatisfy; *disappoint*; *depress*; dishearten, discourage, *dissuade*; sour, embitter; upset, chafe, fret, niggle, bite, irritate, *huff*; mortify, *humiliate*; offend, cause resentment, *displease*; shock, *incur blame*; nauseate, sicken, disgust, *cause dislike*; arouse discontent, make trouble, agitate, *revolt*.

825 Regret

N. *regret*; *resentment*; futile regret; soul-searching, remorse, contrition, compunction, regrets; disillusion, *sequel*; nostalgia, *desire*; sense of loss, *demand*; matter of regret, pity of it.

Adj. *regretting*, missing, homesick, wistful; *retrospective*; bitter; irreconcilable, inconsolable; sorry, full of regrets, apologetic, soul-searching, penitent.

regretted; regrettable, too bad, a shame.

Vb. *regret*, rue, deplore; never forgive oneself; wish undone, *lament*; hark back, *retrospect*; look back; miss, miss badly, want back; hanker after, be homesick, *desire*; express regrets, feel compunction, feel remorse, be sorry, *be penitent*; ask mercy; deplore, deprecate, lament, *disapprove*; *resent*.

826 Relief

N. *relief*, rest, refreshment; *moderation*; good riddance; *deliverance*; solace, comfort, silver lining, *hope*; feeling better, sigh of relief; *revival*; lullaby, cradle song; salve, *balm*; painkiller, analgesic, *anaesthetic*; sedative, *soporific*; pillow, *cushion*; ray of sunshine.

Adj. *relieving*, *refreshing*; analgesic; restorative, *remedial*.

Vb. *relieve*, ease, soften, cushion; relax; temper, *moderate*; lift, raise, lighten, unburden, *disencumber*; spare, *exempt*; save, *deliver*; console, solace, comfort; give hope; encourage, hearten, *cheer*; shade, cool, fan, ventilate, *refresh*; restore, repair, *cure*; bandage, poultice, *doctor*; calm, soothe, nurse, pour balm, pour oil, palliate, mitigate, moderate, alleviate, *assuage*; *smooth*; stroke, pat, *caress*; cradle, lull, put to sleep, *sleep*; render insensible; *pity*.

be relieved, relieve oneself, obtain relief; feel relief, draw a long breath, breathe again; console oneself, take comfort, feel better, smile again, *be cheerful*; come to, be oneself again, pull oneself together; rest content, *be content*.

827 Aggravation

N. *aggravation*, irritation; *increase*; making worse; complication, *difficulty*.

Adj. *aggravated*; complicated; unrelieved, unmitigated, make worse.

Vb. *aggravate*, intensify, *strengthen*; enhance, heighten, deepen; increase, *augment*; worsen, make worse, *deteriorate*; add insult to injury; exacerbate, embitter, further embitter, sour, inflame, *excite*; exasperate, irritate, *enrage*; complicate, make bad worse.

Adv. *aggravatedly*, worse and worse, from

bad to worse, out of the frying pan into the fire.

it. so much the worse! tant pis!

28 Cheerfulness

N. *cheerfulness*, alacrity; optimism, *hope*; *joy*; good humour; vitality, spirits, *life*; light heart, carefree mind, *content*; sparkle, animation, elevation, *excitable state*; party spirit.

merriment; cheer, high spirits, abandon; gaiety, glee, mirth, hilarity, *laughter*; levity, frivolity, *folly*; merry-making, fun, sport, *amusement*; jubilation, jubilee, *celebration*.

Adj. *cheerful*, cheery, blithe, *happy*; hearty, genial, convivial, *sociable*; sanguine, sunny, bright, radiant; breezy, of good cheer; upbeat, hopeful, resilient, irrepressible; carefree, light-hearted, happy-go-lucky, debonair, bonny, buxom, bouncing; pert, jaunty, perky, chirpy, spry, spirited, sprightly, vivacious, vital, full of pep, *lively*; *willing*.

merry, joyous, joyful, waggish, jocular, gay, light, frivolous; playful, sportive, frisky, frolicsome; arch, sly; merry-making, jovial, jolly, singing; wild, shouting, roaring with laughter, hilarious, uproarious, rip-roaring, rollicking.

jubilant, overjoyed, *pleased*; triumphant, cock-a-hoop; riotous.

cheering, exhilarating, exhilarating, *exciting*; tonic, like a ray of sunshine; balmy, palmy, bracing, *salubrious*.

Vb. *be cheerful*, keep cheerful, *hope*; *be resolute*; take heart, *be relieved*; brighten, let oneself go, abandon oneself; radiate good humour, smile, beam, sparkle; dance, sing, carol, lilt, chirp, whistle, laugh, *rejoice*; whoop, cheer, *celebrate*; have fun, frisk, frolic, romp, gambol, sport, have a good time, *amuse oneself*; throw a party, make whoopee, *be sociable*.

cheer, gladden, warm, *content*; comfort, console, *relieve*; *please*; inspire, enliven, *animate*; exhilarate, elate, *delight*; encourage, hearten, jolly along, bolster, *give courage*; act like a tonic, *invigorate*.

Adv. *cheerfully*; airily; allegro.

29 Dejection. Seriousness

N. *dejection*, low spirits, dumps, doldrums; disillusion; defeatism, pessimism, despair, death wish, suicidal tendency; exhaustion, *fatigue*; heartache, misery, *sorrow*; grey dawn; gloom, dejected look, long face; funereal aspect, downcast countenance, lacklustre eye; cause of dejection, sorry sight, *bore*; care, thought, trouble, *worry*.

melancholy, hypochondria; neurosis; depression, black mood, blues, horrors, sigh; spleen, bile, *discontent*; disgust of life, angst, nostalgia; *suffering*.

seriousness; gravity, solemnity, sobriety; straight face, dead pan; heavy stuff; earnest.

moper, Jonah, *malcontent*; sourpuss, bear with a sore head; damper, wet blanket, killjoy, spoilsport; misery; death's-head.

Adj. *dejected*, joyless, dreary, cheerless, unhappy, despondent, downbeat, despairing, *hopeless*; beaten, overcome; nervous; *suffering*; downcast, downhearted, *low*; sluggish, listless, spiritless, lackadaisical; lacklustre, *dim*; crestfallen,

ready to cry; subdued, piano.

melancholic; blue, feeling blue; jaundiced, sour; thoughtful, pensive, full of thought; melancholy, sad; heavy, heavy-hearted, sick at heart, heart-sick, *unhappy*; sorry; mournful, doleful, woeful, tearful; cheerless, joyless, dreary; forlorn, miserable, unrelieved, disconsolate; moody, *sullen*; dull, dismal, morose, glum; woebegone; wan, haggard, careworn.

serious, sober, solemn, sedate, stolid, staid, demure, grave, stern, *severe*; sour, dour, Puritan, grim, dark, forbidding, saturnine, *sullen*; inscrutable, deadpan; prim; heavy, dull, solid, *tedious*.

cheerless; unrelieved, dreary, dull, flat, *tedious*; dismal, lugubrious, funereal, dark, forbidding; drab, grey, sombre, overcast, murky; cold.

Vb. *be dejected*, lose heart, admit defeat, *despair*; succumb; languish, sink, droop, sag, wilt, flag; look downcast, look blue, pull a long face; mope, brood, *think*; lay to heart, sulk, *be sullen*; yearn, long, desire; sigh, grieve, groan, *suffer*, weep, *lament*; regret.

be serious, keep a straight face; look grave, look glum; lack sparkle, lack humour, be a bore, *be tedious*; sober, chasten.

sadden, grieve, bring grief, bring sorrow; impress; annoy, pain, *cause discontent*; deny comfort, render disconsolate, drive to despair; crush, overcome, overwhelm, prostrate; orphan, bereave.

depress; dismay, dishearten, discourage, dispirit, unnerve, *frighten*; cast a shadow, *darken*; damp, dampen, be a wet blanket, throw cold water, *dissuade*; *disappoint*; disgust, *displease*; strain, weary, *fatigue*; bore, *be tedious*; chasten, sober, *teach*.

830 Rejoicing

N. *rejoicing*, manifestation of joy, *festivity*; jubilation, jubilee, triumph, *celebration*; shout, yell, *applause*; cheers, hosanna, *praise*; thanksgiving, *thanks*; psalm, *hymn*; elation, *joy*; *revel*; merrymaking, abandon, *merriment*.

laughter; loud laughter, roar of laughter; *ridicule*; laugh, guffaw; chuckle, chortle, gurgle, cackle, crow, coo; giggle, snigger, titter; smile, simper, smirk, grin, twinkle; humour, *wit*; comedy, farce.

laugher, giggler, cackler, sniggerer; grinner; mocker, derider; god of ridicule; comic muse.

Adj. *rejoicing*, rollicking, cheering, shouting, *jubilant*; lyrical, ecstatic.

laughing, humorous, laughable, risible, derisory, *ridiculous*; comic, comical, funny, *absurd*.

Vb. *rejoice*, be joyful, dance, skip, *leap*; clap, whoop, cheer, *applaud*; shout, yell oneself hoarse, *vociferate*; carol, sing; *praise*; exult, crow, *celebrate*; felicitate, *congratulate*; bless, give thanks, *thank*; abandon oneself, let oneself go, riot, *rampage*; make merry, *be cheerful*; have a good time, frolic, frisk, *revel*; have a party, celebrate, *be sociable*; feel pleased, congratulate oneself, gloat, *be pleased*; purr, coo, gurgle.

laugh, laugh outright, bubble with laughter, hoot, chuckle, chortle, crow, cackle, giggle, snigger, titter; laugh at, mock, deride, *ridicule*; shake, fall about, roll around, burst with laughter, laugh fit to burst.

smile, grin; grimace; smirk, simper; twinkle, beam, flash a smile.

Int. cheers! three cheers! huzza! hurrah! hooray! hosannah! hallelujah! glory be! hail the conquering hero!

831 Lamentation

N. *lamentation,* wail, wail of woe, weeping; mourning; black; cypress, willow; crying, greeting, *dejection;* melting mood, *pity;* wet eyes; breakdown, hysterics; cry, tear, teardrop; sob, sigh, groan, moan, whimper, whine, grizzle, bawl, boo-hoo.

lament, plaint, complaint, dirge, knell, requiem, threnody, elegy, death song, swansong, funeral oration; keen, wake, *condolence;* howl, shriek, scream, outcry; tale of woe; show of grief, *sham.*

weeper; mourner, mute, *funeral; malcontent;* dying duck, dying swan.

Adj. *lamenting;* tearful; with moist eyes; ready to cry; mourning, mournful, doleful, lugubrious, *unhappy;* woeful, woebegone, haggard, *dejected;* plaintive; *funereal;* at half-mast; fretful, querulous, with a tale of woe; pathetic, pitiful, lamentable, *pitiable.*

Vb. *lament,* grieve, sorrow, sigh, *suffer;* deplore, *regret; pity;* bemoan; sing a requiem; mourn, wail, keen; *express grief;* take it badly; complain, beef, bellyache, grouse.

weep, wail, greet; be ready to cry; cry, cry like a child, cry like a baby, boo-hoo, bawl; howl, squall, yell, clamour, scream, shriek; sob, sigh, moan, groan, *suffer;* snivel, grizzle, blubber, pule, whine, whimper; get ready to cry, weep without cause.

Adv. *tearfully.*

832 Amusement

N. *amusement,* pleasure, interest, delight; entertainment, dramatic entertainment, happening, *drama;* radio, television; *pastime,* hobby, labour of love, *voluntary work;* solace, recreation, *refreshment;* relaxation, *repose;* holiday, *leisure;* gala day, *special day;* play, sport, fun, good cheer, *merriment;* occasion, do, show, junket, Gaudy night, *celebration;* outing, excursion, jaunt, pleasure trip; treat, picnic (see *festivity*); garden party, flower show, gymkhana, jamboree, *assembly;* game, game of chance, game of skill; whist drive, bridge party (see *card game*); round games.

festivity; visiting, *social round;* fun, *laughter;* social whirl, round of pleasure, round of gaiety; high life, good time; festival, fair, funfair, carnival, fiesta, gala; masque; merrymaking, *merriment;* high day, *special day;* wassail, wake; housewarming, party, *social gathering;* orgy, carouse; bust, binge, blowout; barbecue, bump supper, dinner, banquet, *meal.*

revel, rout, rave-up, whoopee, fun, high old time; spree, junket, horseplay; bonfire, pyrotechnics, Fifth of November; play, game, romp, frolic, lark, escapade, antic, prank, rag, trick, *foolery.*

pleasure ground, park, chase, grouse moor; green, common; arbour; seaside, lido, bathing beach, holiday camp; playground, recreation ground, links, golf course; rink, tennis court, bowling green, croquet lawn, *arena;* circus, fair, swing, roundabout, merry-go-round, scenic railway, switchback, big wheel, big dipper, tunnel of love, ghost train; dodgems; seesaw, slide, helter-skelter.

place of amusement, fairground, funfair, amusement arcade; skittle alley, concert hall, vaudeville, hippodrome; picture house, *cinema;* playhouse, *theatre;* dance floor; dance hall, disco; cabaret, night club, clip joint; bingo hall, casino.

sport, outdoor life; sportsmanship, gamesmanship, *skill;* sports; games, gymnastics, *athletics,* leap, contest, racing, *pugilism;* outdoor sports, rambling; running; riding, pony-trekking; archery, hunting, shooting and fishing, *chase;* water sports, swimming, bathing; sailing; rock-climbing, mountaineering, *ascent; descent;* winter sports, ice hockey; curling; flying, gliding, *aeronautics;* tourism, *land travel.*

ball game; King Willow, cricket, baseball, softball, rounders; tennis, pingpong; badminton; squash; handball, volleyball; fives; netball, basketball; football, soccer; Rugby football; lacrosse, hockey, polo, water polo; croquet, golf, skittles, bowls, curling; marbles; quoits, hoop-la; billiards, snooker, pool; bagatelle, pinball, bar billiards.

indoor game; quiz; charades; word game, spelling bee; paper game; darts, dominoes, jigsaw puzzle.

board game, chess, draughts, checkers; backgammon; ludo, go.

children's games, swinging; leapfrog, hopscotch, *leap;* touch, tag, he, chain he, hide-and-seek.

card game, cards, game of cards, rubber of whist, rubber of bridge; whist, auction bridge, nap; écarté, loo, cribbage, quadrille; rummy, canasta, casino, cheat; solo, solitaire, patience; snap, old maid, racing demon; bingo; pontoon, black jack; brag, poker, banker.

gambling game, dice; roulette; raffle, tombola, sweepstake, football pool.

dancing, dance, ball; masquerade; fancy dress dance; tea dance, square dance; hop, jam session, disco; *ballet;* choreography.

dance, war dance; shuffle; solo dance; clog dance, fan dance; cancan; belly dance; gipsy dance, flamenco; country dance, hay; hornpipe, keel row; folk dance, polonaise, mazurka; jig; fling, reel, Dashing White Sergeant; tarantella, bolero, gavotte, quadrille, minuet, polka; valse, waltz; foxtrot, turkey trot, quickstep; Charleston, black bottom, blues, tango, rumba, samba, conga, conga line, cha-cha; Palais Glide; stomp, bop, jive, rock 'n' roll, twist; snowball; ballerina, *actor; entertainer; jumper.*

plaything, bauble, souvenir, trinket, toy, *bauble;* rattle, Jack-in-the-box, doll; top, yo-yo; marbles; ball, balloon, *sphere;* hoop, tricycle, skateboard, surfboard; popgun, airgun, water pistol; toy soldier, model, model yacht, model aeroplane, clockwork train, model railway; magic lantern, peep show, toy theatre, *exhibit;* puppet show, *image;* pintable; card, cards, pack, stack, deck; domino, tile; draught, counter, chip; chess piece, pawn, knight, bishop, castle or rook, queen, king.

player, sportsman or -woman, sporting man or woman; competitor, *contender;* forward, striker, defence, goalkeeper; batsman, fielder, bowler; marksman, archer; chess tiger, chess rabbit; fellow sportsman or -woman, playmate, *colleague.*

reveller; drinker, drunk, *drunkard;* eater; *sociable person;* playboy; holidaymaker, tourist, *traveller*; Lord of Misrule, MC, toastmaster.

adj. *amusing*, entertaining, sportive, full of fun, *merry*; pleasant; laughable, ridiculous, *funny*; recreational, *refreshing*; festive, holiday.

amused, *pleased*; festive, sportive, rollicking, playful, waggish, jolly, jovial; horsy, sporty, sporting, *athletic*; at play; easy to please.

vb. *amuse*, entertain, entertain, beguile, divert, tickle, make one laugh; titillate, please, *delight*; recreate, *refresh*; solace, enliven, *cheer*; treat; raise a smile, wake laughter, wow, slay, *be ridiculous*; humour; give a party, *be hospitable*; be a sport, be great fun.

amuse oneself, kill time, *have leisure*; play, play at, have fun, enjoy oneself, drown care, *be cheerful*; make holiday, have an outing, have a field day, have a ball; sport; dally, toy, wanton; frisk, frolic, romp, gambol, caper; lark around, skylark, fool about, *be absurd*; jest; play cards, take a hand; game, dice, *gamble*; play games, be devoted to sport; camp, picnic; sail, yacht, fly; hunt, shoot, fish; play golf; ride, trek, hike, ramble; run, race, jump; bathe, swim, dive; skate, ski, toboggan.

dance, waltz, foxtrot, Charleston, tango, rumba, jive, stomp, bop, twist, rock 'n' roll; whirl, *rotate*; cavort, caper, jig about; shuffle, hoof, trip, tread a measure, *leap*.

revel, make merry, make whoopee, celebrate, *rejoice*; make it a party, have a good time; let oneself go; junket, roister, drown care; feast, banquet, quaff, carouse, wassail; *drink*; *get drunk*; never go home till morning.

int. carpe diem! eat, drink and be merry!

833 Tedium

N. *tedium*, ennui, *melancholy*; lack of interest; languor, *fatigue*; too much of a good thing; disgust, nausea, *dislike*; sameness; *repetition*; time to kill.

bore, irk, drag, bind, chore; dull work, beaten track, daily round, *habit*; grindstone, treadmill, *labour*; pub bore; drip, wet blanket, killjoy, misery; frump; too much of a good thing.

adj. *tedious*, devoid of interest; uneventful; slow, leaden, heavy; dry, arid; flat, stale, insipid, *tasteless*; bald, *plain*; humdrum, soulless, suburban, dreary, stuffy, bourgeois, dull; stodgy, prosaic, unreadable; prosy, long, long-winded, drowsy, *soporific*; binding, wearisome, tiresome, irksome; wearing, chronic, mortal; repetitious; same, invariable, monotonous, *uniform*; too much; nauseous.

bored; stale, weary, jaded, blue, world-weary, weary of life; uninterested, *indifferent*; sick of.

vb. *be tedious*, pall, lose its novelty, cloy, glut, jade, satiate, *sate*; nauseate, sicken, disgust, *cause dislike*; bore, irk, try, weary, *fatigue*; bore to death, bore stiff; weary to distraction, stay too long; fail to interest, make one yawn, send one to sleep; drag; never end; prove monotonous, *repeat oneself*; buttonhole, *be diffuse*.

Adv. *boringly*, to death; ad nauseam.

834 Wit

N. *wit*, point; ready wit, verbal readiness; *sequel*; salt; sparkle, *intelligence*; humour, wry humour, drollery, pleasantry; *merriment*; trifling, *inattention*; fun, tomfoolery, funny business, *foolery*; comic turn, laugh a minute; broad humour, vulgarity, *bad taste*; farce, knockabout comedy, slapstick, ham, high camp; fancy, *whim*; cartoon, comic strip, caricature; biting wit, cruel humour, satire, sarcasm, *ridicule*; irony, *affectation*; black comedy, gallows humour; *sophistry*.

witticism, piece of humour, stroke of wit, sally; spoonerism; epigram, conceit; pun; feed line, banter, chaff, badinage; retort, repartee, backchat, *answer*; sarcasm, *satire*; joke, jest, good one; quip, quirk, crank, gag, crack, wisecrack; old joke; stale jest, chestnut; practical joke, hoax; broad jest, dirty joke, story, limerick.

humorist, wit; card, character, wag, joker; funny man; teaser; practical joker; comedian, comedienne, comic, *entertainer*; comic writer; *imitator*; raconteur; jester; motley fool, clown, buffoon, stooge, *fool*.

Adj. *witty*, quick; Attic, *elegant*; pointed; brilliant, smart, clever; salty, racy, piquant; fruity; snappy, biting, pungent, keen; sharp; ironic, dry, sly, pawky; facetious, flippant, jocular, waggish; lively, pleasant, gay, *merry*; comic, funny ha-ha, *funny*; comical, humorous, droll; whimsical, *capricious*; playful, sportive, *absurd*.

Vb. *be witty*, scintillate, sparkle, flash; jest, joke, quip, gag, wisecrack; tell a good story, raise a laugh, *amuse*; pun, equivocate, *be equivocal*; fool, *be absurd*; play with, tease, chaff, rag, banter, twit, make merry with, make fun of, poke fun at, *ridicule*; mock, caricature, burlesque; retort, flash back, come back at, *answer*; have a sense of humour, enjoy a joke.

Adv. *in jest*.

835 Dullness

N. *dullness*, dejection; *tedium*; lack of sparkle, lack of inspiration; lack of humour, inability to see a joke, impenetrable gravity; prose, matter of fact.

Adj. *dull*; straight; deadly dull; stuffy, dreary, deadly; pointless, meaningless, *tedious*; colourless, drab; flat, bland, vapid, insipid, *tasteless*; derivative, superficial; stupid; without laughter, grave, prim, *serious*; graceless, lacking wit, *inelegant*; heavy, ponderous, sluggish, *slow*; stodgy, prosaic, matter-of-fact, pedestrian, unreadable; stale, banal, commonplace, trite, *usual*.

Vb. *be dull*, bore, *be tedious*; prose; never see a joke, not see the point.

836 Beauty

N. *beauty*, pulchritude; ripe perfection, *perfection*; grandeur, nobility; splendour, *light*; transfiguration; polish, gloss, ornament; scenic beauty, scenery, view, landscape, *spectacle*; form, fair proportions, regular features, *symmetry*; physical beauty; attraction, charm; appeal, glamour, sex appeal; graces; good looks, handsome features, pretty face; eyes of blue, pearly teeth, trim figure, vital statistics; grace, chic, style, dress sense, *fashion*;

delicacy, refinement, *good taste*; appreciation of beauty, aesthetics.

a *beauty*, thing of beauty, work of art; garden, beauty spot; masterpiece; jewel, pearl, treasure, *paragon*; peacock, swan, flower, rosebud, rose, lily; fair one, lady bright; belle, raving beauty, toast, idol, *favourite*; dream girl; beauty queen, Miss World, bathing belle, pin-up girl, cover girl; pin-up, cheesecake; hunk; fine figure of a man or woman; blond(e), brunette, redhead; English rose; dream, vision, poem, picture; angel; stunner, knockout; doll, dolly bird, cookie; glamour puss, glamour girl or boy; heartthrob, dreamboat; vamp, siren, witch; scorcher, lovely, honey, peach, dish; fairy; Grace, Venus; Narcissus.

Adj. *beautiful*, beauteous, of beauty; lovely, fair, bright, radiant; comely, bonny, pretty; sweet, pretty-pretty, nice, good enough to eat; *photogenic*; handsome, good-looking, well-favoured; husky; tall, dark and handsome; gracious, stately, statuesque, Junoesque; adorable, divine; lovely to behold; picturesque, scenic; artistic, cunning, curious, quaint; aesthetic, *tasteful*; exquisite, choice, *chosen*; *perfect*.

splendid, sublime, heavenly, superb, fine, *excellent*; grand, *noble*; glorious, ravishing, rich, gorgeous, *florid*; bright, resplendent, radiant, glowing; glossy, magnificent, specious, *showy*; ornate.

shapely, regular, classic; buxom, bosomy, clean-limbed, straight, slender, slim, svelte, willowy, *lean*; graceful, elegant, chic; petite, dainty, delicate; *perfect*.

personable, prepossessing, agreeable; comfortable, buxom; attractive, dishy, appealing; sexy, cute; enchanting; winsome; clean-cut, wholesome, lusty, blooming, ruddy, *red*; rosy; sightly, becoming, fit to be seen, passable; presentable, proper, decent, neat, natty, tidy, trim; spruce, snappy, dapper, glossy, sleek; smart, stylish, classy, *fashionable*; elegant, dainty, delicate, refined, *tasteful*.

Vb. *be beautiful*, *bewitch*; beggar all description; be photogenic, photograph well; have good looks, have bright eyes; bloom, glow, dazzle, *shine*; do one credit, win a beauty contest.

beautify, trim, improve; brighten, *make bright*; tattoo, *decorate*; set (a jewel); grace, suit, fit, become, go well, flatter; transfigure; give a face-lift; prank, powder, rouge.

837 Ugliness

N. *ugliness*; lack of beauty; want of symmetry; lack of form, *deformity*; *blemish*; squalor, filth; plain features, ugly face; a face to stop a clock; wry face, snarl, forbidding countenance, grim look; haggard look; dim eyes, hand of time, *age*.

eyesore, blot, botch, patch, *blemish*; aesthetic crime; ugly person, fright, frump; scarecrow, horror, death's-head, gargoyle, grotesque; monster, abortion; harridan, witch; toad, gorilla, baboon, crow; ugly duckling; satyr; Gorgon; Beast.

Adj. *ugly*, lacking beauty; hideous, foul, *unclean*; frightful, shocking, monstrous; repellent, odious, loathsome; beastly, nasty; homely, plain, without any looks; mousy; forbidding, ill-favoured, grim, saturnine, *sullen*.

unsightly, worn; unseemly; imperfect; formless, irregular, *amorphous*; grotesque; badly made, disproportionate, misshapen, misbegotten; dumpy, squat; bloated; *colourless*; ghastly, wan, grisly, gruesome.

graceless, *inelegant*; squalid, dingy, poky, dreary, drab; lank, dull, mousy; dowdy; garish, gaudy, gross, indelicate, coarse, *vulgar*; rude, crude, rough, rugged, uncouth, *artless*; clumsy, awkward, ungainly, cumbersome, hulking, *unwieldy*.

Vb. *be ugly*, lack beauty, fade, wither, age, *grow old*; look ill, look a wreck, look a mess, look a fright.

make ugly, fade, discolour; wither, *deteriorate*; soil, sully, *make unclean*; spoil, deface, disfigure, mar, blemish, blot; *deform*; pull a face, grimace, *be sullen*; torture, twist, *distort*; mutilate, *impair*.

838 Beautification

N. *beautification*; transfiguration, *transformation*; plastic surgery, face-lift, *surgery*; beauty treatment; face mask, face pack, facial; massage, manicure; pedicure, chiropody; sun lamp; toilet, make-up; painting; *ablutions*.

hairdressing, scalp massage; shaving, clipping, trimming; cutting, haircut; shave, hair cut, clip, trim, singe; hair style, coiffure, crop, bob, shingle, urchin cut, curling, setting; hairdo, set, wave, perm; curl, *coil*; bang, fringe, ponytail, chignon, bun; Afro, *hair*; false hair, hairpiece, toupee, switch, *wig*; curling iron, tongs, curl papers; comb, hairpin, hairgrip, slide; hairnet, snood.

hairwash, shampoo, rinse, colour tone; bleach, dye, henna, peroxide; hair spray, lacquer, grease; hair-restorer.

cosmetic, aid to beauty, patch, beauty spot; make-up, paint, greasepaint, rouge, cream, lanolin, *unguent*; lipstick, lip gloss; nail polish, nail varnish, powder, kohl, mascara, eye shadow, eyeliner; hand lotion, bath oil, bath essence, bubble bath, *cleanser*; antiperspirant, deodorant; scent, perfume, essence, cologne, lavender water, cologne stick; eyebrow pencil; powder puff, compact, vanity case, manicure set, nail file, nail scissors, clippers; shaver, razor, depilatory; toiletries.

beauty *parlour*, beauty salon; boudoir, dressing room, health farm.

beautician, beauty specialist; plastic surgeon; make-up artist; barber, hairdresser.

Adj. *beautified*; powdered; bouffant; *beautiful*.

Vb. *primp*; ornament, *decorate*; prank; preen; rouge, paint, shadow, highlight, powder; wear scent; shave; curl, wave, have a hairdo, have a facial, have a manicure, *beautify*.

839 Ornamentation

N. *ornamentation*, adornment, garnish, ornate style, *ornament*; baroque, rococo, gilt, *ostentation*; setting, background; silver, china, glass; flower arrangement, wreath, garland, bouquet, nosegay, posy, buttonhole; object d'art, bric-a-brac, curio.

ornamental *art*; architecture, building, painting; statuary, *sculpture*; frieze, dado; capital; pilaster, caryatid, figurehead; boss, cornice, corbel, gargoyle; moulding, beading, fluting; tracery; *facing*; panelling; gilt, gold leaf; lettering, illustration, *art*; batik; *heraldry*; etching, *engraving*; work, handiwork, handicraft, woodwork, fretwork; pokerwork; filigree; carving; intaglio; inlay, inset, mosaic, marquetry; metalwork; setting; cut glass, wrought iron.

pattern, motif, print, design, composition, *structure*; detail, geometrical style, rose window, cusp, trefoil; tracery, scrollwork, arabesque, flourish, *coil*; swag, festoon; weave, diaper, *texture*; paisley, *textile*; chevron, key pattern; check, *chequer*; pin-stripe, *stripe*; spot, dot; herringbone, zigzag; watermark, *identification*.

needlework, tapestry; cross-stitch, sampler; patchwork; open work, embroidery, smocking; crochet, lace; tatting, knitting, *network*; stitch, purl, plain, stocking stitch, chain stitch, French knot.

trimming, piping, valance, border, fringe, frieze, frill, flounce, *edging*; binding; trappings; braid, frog, lapel, star, rosette, cockade, *badge*; bow, *fastening*; pompom; tassel, bead, bugle; ermine, fur, *hair*; feather, osprey, plume, panache, *plumage*; streamer, ribbon.

finery, togs, Sunday best, *clothing*; frippery, chiffon, trinket, gewgaw; tinsel, spangle, sequin, glass, paste, rhinestone, *bauble*.

jewellery; diadem, tiara, *regalia*; drop, locket, *hanging object*; crucifix; amulet, charm, *talisman*; rope, string, necklace, choker, chain, *loop*; torque, bracelet, wristlet, bangle; ring, earring, signet ring, *circle*; cameo, brooch, clasp, fibula, badge, crest; stud, pin, collar stud, *fastening*; medal, medallion.

gem, jewel, stone, uncut gem; brilliant, sparkler, diamond, rock, ice; solitaire; carbuncle, ruby, pearl, opal; sapphire, turquoise, emerald, beryl, aquamarine; garnet, amethyst, topaz, cornelian, agate, onyx; heliotrope, moonstone, hyacinth; coral, ivory, mother of pearl, jet, amber, jade.

Adj. ornamental, decorative, fancy; intricate, elaborate, quaint; picturesque, pretty-pretty; scenic, landscape, topiary; Doric, Ionic, Corinthian, Romanesque; baroque, rococo.

ornamented, luxuriant; *ornate, variegated*; mosaic, inlaid; overdone, *vulgar, florid*; luscious, plush, gilt, gilded, *rich*; gorgeous, garish, flashy, gaudy, meretricious, showy.

bedecked, wearing, sporting; looking one's best, in one's Sunday best; in one's best, in one's Sunday best; looking one's best, in one's Sunday best; beribboned, festooned.

Vb. decorate, adorn, embellish, enhance, enrich; grace, set, *ornament*; paint; *beautify*; garnish, trim, shape; array, deck, bedeck, *dress*; prank, preen; furbish, burnish, *clean*; garland, crown, *honour*; stud, spangle; whitewash, varnish, grain, japan, lacquer, *coat*; enamel, gild, silver; emblazon, illuminate, illustrate, *paint, colour*; border, trim, hem; work, embroider, tapestry; pattern, inlay, engrave; encrust, emboss, bead, mould; fret, carve, *groove, notch*; wreathe, festoon, trace, scroll, *twine*.

840 Blemish

N. blemish; scar, weal, welt, mark, pockmark; injury, flaw, crack, defect; deformity; stigma, spot, *eyesore*; graffiti; blur, blotch, smudge; smut, patch, smear, stain, tarnish, rust, patina, *dirt*; spot, speck, speckle; freckle, mole, birthmark, strawberry mark; excrescence, pimple, blackhead, carbuncle, wart, *swelling*; acme, eczema, *skin disease*; harelip, cleft palate; cast, squint; cut, scratch, scald, bruise, black eye, cauliflower ear, broken nose, *wound*.

Adj. blemished, cracked, *imperfect*; fly-blown, *dirty*; shop-soiled; marked; spotted; spotty; knock-kneed, bandy; crooked.

Vb. blemish, flaw, crack, injure, damage, *impair*; blot, smudge, stain, smear, sully, soil, *make unclean*; brand, *mark*; scar, pit, pockmark; mar, spoil, *make ugly*; deface, disfigure, *deform*.

841 Good Taste

N. good taste, taste, restraint, simplicity; best of taste, *goodness*; refinement, delicacy, euphemism, *purity*; fine feeling, nice appreciation, palate, *discrimination*; *etiquette*; tact, consideration, natural courtesy, dignity, manners, breeding, civility, social graces, *courtesy*; propriety, decorum; grace, polish, finish, gracious living; cultivation, culture; aesthetics, criticism; artistry, flair, *skill*.

people *of* taste; connoisseur, amateur, dilettante; epicure, gourmet, epicure; aesthete, critic; arbiter of taste, *fop*; purist, *obstinate person*; prude.

Adj. tasteful, gracious; choice, exquisite, *excellent*; simple, *plain*; graceful, Attic, classical, *elegant*; chaste, refined, delicate, *pure*; aesthetic, artistic, *sensitive*; discerning; nice, dainty, finicky, *fastidious*; critical, appreciative, *judicial*; decent, seemly, becoming, *apt*; proper, correct, *fashionable*; well-bred.

Vb. have taste, discriminate; appreciate, value, *judge*; be fastidious.

Adv. tastefully, properly, agreeably.

842 Bad Taste

N. bad taste, poor taste; bad art, kitsch; international airport plastic; prostitution of talent; yellow press, vulgarism, vandalism; vulgarity; shoddy, frippery, tinsel, glitter, paste, ersatz, *bauble*; lack of feeling; bad joke, untimely jest; frump, dowdy, square.

ill-breeding, vulgarity; bad form; bad manners, *discourtesy*; rough behaviour, *disorder*.

vulgarian, snob, social climber, cad, bounder; rough diamond; proletarian, *commoner*; Vandal, Philistine; barbarian, savage; punk.

Adj. vulgar, *inelegant*; tasteless, gross, crass, coarse; philistine, barbarian, *artless*; commercial; tawdry, cheap, catchpenny, gingerbread, ersatz; flashy, meretricious, *showy*; obtrusive, blatant, loud, gaudy, garish, raffish; shameless; fulsome, excessive; shabby genteel, *affected*; common, low, gutter, sordid, *disreputable*; improper, indelicate, indecorous; going too far, scandalous, indecent, ribald, obscene, *impure*.

ill-bred; non-U, *plebeian*; loud, hearty; insensitive, blunt; impolite, unmannerly, *discourteous*; dowdy, rustic, provincial, countrified, gone native; crude, rude, churlish, uncouth, *ignorant*; unsophisticated, *artless*; barbaric; awkward, gauche, *clumsy*; rowdy, riotous, *disorderly*; superior, *affected*.

Vb. *vulgarize*, cheapen, coarsen, debase, lower; show bad taste.

843 Fashion. Etiquette

N. *fashion*, style, mode, cut, *form*; method, *way*; vogue, cult, *habit*; prevailing taste, current fashion, *modernism*; rage, fad, craze, cry, furore; new look, latest fashion; last word; extreme of fashion, dash, ostentation; ton, flair, chic; dress sense, fashion show, mannequin parade, *exhibit*; *affectation*; world of fashion, Vanity Fair, passing show.

etiquette, *formality*; protocol, convention, custom, *practice*; snobbery, done thing, good form; appearances; decorum, propriety, right note, *good taste*; *courtesy*; breeding, polish; ladylike behaviour; manners, best behaviour; grand air, poise, dignity, savvy, *conduct*.

beau monde, society; town, best end of town; court, drawing room, salon; top drawer, right people, smart set, upper ten, *nobility*; cream, upper crust, cream of society, *elite*; gilded youth, beautiful people, jet set; fashionable person, glass of fashion; man or woman about town, man or woman of fashion, classy dame; slave to fashion; socialite, playboy, cosmopolitan, *sociable person*.

fop, fine gentleman, macaroni, buck, pearly king; fine lady, belle, pearly queen; debutante; dandy, exquisite, beau; peacock, clothes-horse, fashion plate; coxcomb, puppy; swell, nob, Lady Muck; Corinthian, spark, blood, blade, lad, gay dog; lounge lizard, carpet knight, gallant; ladykiller.

Adj. *fashionable*, modish, stylish; correct; à la mode, chi-chi; exquisite, chic, elegant, well-groomed, *tasteful*; dressy; dashing, snazzy, flashy, *showy*; dandy, smart, classy, swank, swell, swish, posh; newfangled, *modern*; hip, groovy, trendy, with it; *affected*; conventional, done, *usual*.

well-bred, thoroughbred, *noble*; cosmopolitan, sophisticated, urbane; polite, housetrained; U, ladylike, *genteel*; civil, wellspoken, *courteous*; courtly, stately, *formal*; poised, easy, smooth, correct, decorous, proper, decent; considerate, *amiable*; punctilious, *honourable*.

Vb. *be in fashion*, be done, be wont; get with it, *conform*; *be sociable*; entertain, *be hospitable*; observe decorum; cut a dash, cut a figure, give a lead; look right, pass; have an air, have style; show flair, dress well.

Adv. *fashionably*, in style, à la mode.

844 Ridiculousness

N. *ridiculousness*; drollery, wit; *nonconformity*; bathos, anticlimax; *boast*; bombast, *exaggeration*; comic interlude, light relief; light verse, doggerel, limerick, *witticism*; spoonerism, malapropism, bull; comic turn, comedy, farce, burlesque, slapstick, knockabout, *stage play*; paradox, *lack of expectation*.

Adj. *ridiculous*, ludicrous, preposterous, monstrous, grotesque, fantastic, cockeyed, inappropriate, *absurd*; awkward,

clumsy; silly, *foolish*; derisory; laughable, risible; bizarre, rum, quaint, odd, queer, *unusual*; strange, outlandish, *extraneous*; mannered, stilted, *affected*; inflated, extravagant; crazy, crackpot, fanciful, *imaginary*; whimsical, *capricious*.

funny, *abnormal*; comical, droll, humorous, waggish; rich, priceless, side-splitting, hilarious, a real hoot; light, comic; satirical; burlesque; doggerel; slapstick, knockabout.

Vb. *be ridiculous*, make one laugh, excite laughter, raise a laugh; tickle; entertain, *amuse*; look silly, be a figure of fun, cut a ridiculous figure, be a laughingstock, fool, *be absurd*; descend to bathos; make an exhibition of oneself; poke fun at, make one a laughingstock, *ridicule*.

845 Affectation

N. *affectation*, cult, fad, *fashion*; *ostentation*; assumption of airs, *airs*; striking attitude, high moral tone; pose, public image; mannerism, trick, literary affectation, esoteric vocabulary; euphuism, *ornament*; pout, grimace, *gesture*; coquetry, *caprice*; conceit, *vanity*; euphemism, false shame; irony, backhanded compliment, *ridicule*; *duplicity*.

pretension, artifice, sham, humbug, *deception*; shallow profundity; *formality*; pedantry; *prudery*.

affecter, humbug, quack, charlatan, *impostor*; *actor*; hypocrite; coquette, flirt; mass of affectation, poser, *vain person*; *humorist*; coxcomb, dandy, *fop*; purist, pedant; know-all, *wise guy*; prig, puritan, goodygoody, *prude*; bluestocking.

Adj. *affected*, full of affectation, self-conscious; studied, mannered, precious, chichi, *ornate*; artificial, unnatural, stilted, stiff, starchy, *formal*; prim, mealy-mouthed, sanctimonious, self-righteous, smug, demure; arch, sly, *merry*; coy, cute, twee; *boastful*; shallow, hollow, specious, pretentious, fulsome, stagy, theatrical; camp; striking an attitude, *vain*; *ill-bred*; bogus, *false*; insincere; overdone.

Vb. *be affected*, affect, wear, assume; pretend, feign, make a show of, bluff, *dissemble*; *imitate*; affect zeal, *be busy*; perform, act a part, *act*; overact, ham, *exaggerate*; posture, pose, prance, mince, ponce about; swank, *be vain*; *know*; be elegant; brag, talk big, *boast*; pout, simper, smirk, *smile*; coquette, flirt, languish, *excite love*; cant; save appearances.

846 Ridicule

N. *ridicule*, mockery, *disrespect*; *laughter*; raillery, ribbing, banter, badinage, chaff; horseplay, practical joke, *foolery*; grin, snigger, laugh, scoff, mock; irony, sarcasm, barbed shaft, backhanded compliment; catcall, hoot, hiss, *censure*; insult, *indignity*; *witticism*.

satire, denunciation; parody, burlesque, travesty, caricature, cartoon; skit, spoof, send-up, take-off, *mimicry*; squib, lampoon.

laughingstock, object of ridicule, figure of fun, butt, common jest, by-word; sport, game, Aunt Sally; April fool, buffoon, clown, zany, *fool*; stooge, butt, foil, feed, straight man; guy, caricature, travesty, mockery of; eccentric, *crank*; original, card, caution, queer fish, geezer, museum piece, back number, square; fall guy, victim, *loser*.

adj. *derisive*, flippant; sardonic; quizzical; satirical; ribald, *vulgar*; burlesque.

vb. *ridicule*, deride, laugh at, grin at, smile at, smirk at; snigger; banter, chaff, rally, twit, rib, tease, roast, rag, poke fun, make merry with, make fun of, make sport of, make a monkey of, kid, fool, make a fool of, make an April fool of; mock, scoff, jeer; turn to a jest, make a joke of, turn to ridicule, *hold cheap*; deflate, make one look silly, *humiliate*.

satirize, lampoon; mock; mimic; *imitate*; parody, travesty, spoof, burlesque, caricature, guy, *misrepresent*; expose, denounce, pillory, *accuse*.

847 Hope

N. *hope*, assumption, presumption, *expectation*; sanguine expectation, conviction, *belief*; reliance, trust, confidence, faith, assurance, *certainty*; eager hope, *probability*; *relief*; safe hope, security, anchor, mainstay, staff, *support*; final hope, last throw; ray of hope, *possibility*; good omen, favourable auspices, promise, fair prospect, *omen*; blue sky, silver lining; optimism, enthusiasm; rosy picture.

aspiration, ambition, purpose, *intention*; pious hope, vision, pipe dream, *fantasy*; land of promise, utopia, millennium, *objective*.

hoper, aspirant, candidate; hopeful, expectant, heir apparent, *beneficiary*; prisoner of hope; utopian; *visionary*.

Adj. *hoping*, starry-eyed; ambitious, would-be; *imaginative*; hopeful, *expectant*; sanguine, confident, *certain*; airy, uncritical; *jubilant*; reasonably confident.

promising, full of promise, favourable, auspicious, propitious, *prosperous*; bright, fair, golden, rosy; hopeful; plausible, likely, *probable*; utopian; *illogical*; visionary, *imaginary*.

vb. *hope*, trust, confide, have faith; rest assured, feel confident, *believe*; presume, *assume*; speculate, look forward, *expect*; dream of, aspire, promise oneself, soar, aim high, *intend*; have a hope; feel hope, take heart, take hope, *be relieved*; remain hopeful, *stand firm*; hope against hope, keep hope alive, never say die; catch at a straw, *be cheerful*; persevere; be hopeful; flatter oneself, *reason badly*; anticipate, *be early*; dream, *imagine*.

give hope, encourage, comfort, *cheer*; promise, promise well, bid fair, *be likely*; paint a rosy picture, *predict*.

Adv. *hopefully*; without despair; airily, lightly.

int. nil desperandum! never say die! while there's life, there's hope!

848 Hopelessness

N. *hopelessness*, loss of hope, defeatism, dismay, *dejection*; pessimism, despair, last hope gone; resignation, *lack of expectation*; vain hope, *fantasy*; message of despair, wan smile; poor lookout; hopeless case, dead duck; hopeless situation, bad job, bad business, *predicament*; counsel of despair, misery.

adj. *hopeless*, bereft of hope, without hope, despairing, desperate, suicidal; inconsolable, disconsolate, *dejected*; desolate, forlorn; undone, without resource, *unfortunate*.

unpromising, hopeless, without comfort,

cheerless; desperate; inauspicious, *adverse*; ominous; irremediable, incurable, inoperable; past cure, beyond hope, past recall; incorrigible, irreparable, irrecoverable, irrevocable, irredeemable; irreversible, inevitable; impracticable, *impossible*.

Vb. *despair*, lose heart, lose hope; give way to despair, *be dejected*; *submit*.

leave no hope, drive to despair, *disappoint*; be incurable.

849 Fear

N. *fear*, dread, awe, *respect*; abject fear, fright, funk, blue funk; terror, state of terror, trepidation, alarm, shock, flutter, flap, flat spin; fit, fit of terror, scare, stampede, panic, *spasm*; flight; horror, cold sweat, blood turning to water; consternation, dismay; defence mechanism, repression, escapism.

nervousness, want of courage, lack of confidence; bluster; loss of nerve, mistrust, apprehension, disquiet, solicitude, anxiety, care, *worry*; depression, *dejection*; defeatism, pessimism; trepidation, flutter, tremor; nerves, willies, collywobbles, shivers, jitters, heebie-jeebies; goose-flesh.

phobia, claustrophobia, agoraphobia; fear of death; antisemitism, *hatred*; spy mania.

intimidation, war of nerves, war cry, fee, faw, fum; *threat*; caution, *warning*; terror, terrorism, reign of terror; sword of Damocles, *punishment*; deterrent, *weapon*; object of terror, goblin, hobgoblin, *demon*; spook, spectre, *ghost*; Gorgon, scarecrow, nightmare; bugbear, ogre, *monster*.

alarmist, scaremonger; defeatist, pessimist, doom merchant.

Adj. *fearing*, afraid, frightened, funky; *respectful*; panic-stricken; hysterical; frozen; aghast, awestruck, frightened to death; more frightened than hurt.

nervous, defensive, tense, uptight; despairing, *hopeless*; timid, timorous, shy, diffident, self-conscious, *modest*; coy, wary, *cautious*; doubtful, suspicious, windy, *irresolute*; disturbed; apprehensive, uneasy, fearful, anxious, *unhappy*; highly-strung, jumpy, nervy; tremulous, shaky; breathless.

frightening, shocking, formidable, redoubtable; hazardous, hairy; tremendous, dreadful, fearsome, *impressive*; grim, grisly, hideous, ghastly, lurid, frightful, revolting, horrible, terrible, awful, appalling, mind-blowing; hair-raising, blood-curdling; weird, eerie, creepy, gruesome, macabre, sinister, portentous, ominous; roaring, *loud*.

Vb. *fear*, funk, be afraid, dread, *respect*; flap; take fright, take alarm, flap, panic, stampede, take to flight, fly; start, jump, flutter; faint, collapse.

quake, shake, tremble, quiver, shiver, shudder, stutter, quaver; shake like a jelly, be frightened to death; change colour, blench, pale; wince, flinch, shrink, shy, jib, *avoid*; quail, cower, crouch, skulk, come to heel; stand aghast, freeze, freeze with horror.

be nervous, feel shy, *be modest*; suspect, distrust, mistrust, *doubt*; shrink, shy, quail, funk it; be anxious, dread; hesitate, think twice, think better of it, *be cautious*.

frighten, fright, grimace; scare, panic, stampede; intimidate, menace, *threaten*; alarm, cry wolf; scare stiff, scare half to death; make one jump, give one a fright, give one a turn, startle, flutter, flurry, *agitate*; start, flush, *hunt*; disquiet, disturb, perturb, haunt, obsess, *trouble*; make nervous, rattle, shake, unnerve; make a coward of; strike with fear, awe, overawe, *impress*; quell, subdue, cow, *overmaster*; amaze, shock, stagger, flabbergast, stun, *surprise*; dismay, confound, abash, disconcert, *derange*; daunt, deter, discourage, *dissuade*; institute a reign of terror, *oppress*; browbeat, bully, *torment*; terrify, horrify, harrow, make aghast; chill, freeze, paralyse, petrify, rivet, turn to stone, *render insensible*; appal.

850 Courage

N. *courage*, valour, derring-do; moral courage, *probity*; VC courage, heroism, gallantry, chivalry; self-confidence, self-reliance, ignorance of fear, daring, nerve; defiance of danger, hardihood; spirit, mettle, dash, go, panache; enterprise, *undertaking*; bulldog courage; high morale, fortitude, determination, *resolution*; pluck, spunk, guts, heart, heart of oak, backbone, grit, *stamina*; sham courage, pot valour; desperate courage, courage of despair; brave face, bold front, *defiance*; fresh courage, animation, *inducement*.

manliness, manhood, *probity*, virtue, chivalry; morale, devotion to duty; endurance, stiff upper lip, *resolution*.

prowess, derring-do, chivalry, heroism, heroic achievement, gallant act, act of courage; feat, feat of arms, exploit, stroke, *deed*; desperate venture; heroics.

brave *person*, hero, VC; knight; good soldier, stout fellow, brave, warrior, *soldier*; man, man or woman of mettle, man or woman of spirit, plucky fellow, game dog, bulldog; daredevil; bully, bravo, *desperado*; Amazon; gallant knight; gallant company; forlorn hope, *elite*; lion, tiger, bulldog.

Adj. *courageous*, brave, valiant, gallant, heroic; chivalrous, martial, *warlike*; stout, doughty, tall, bonny, manful, tough, red-blooded; militant, bellicose, aggressive; fierce, bloody, savage, *cruel*; bold, *defiant*; dashing, hardy, audacious, daring, venturesome, *rash*; adventurous, *enterprising*; mettlesome, spirited, lionhearted; full of courage, full of fight, full of spirit, full of spunk; full of Dutch courage; unbowed, firm, steady, dogged, indomitable, never say die; desperate, determined, *resolute*; of high morale, game, plucky, sporting, unflinching, *willing*.

unfearing, intrepid, nerveless, with nerves of steel or of iron; sure of oneself, confident; fearless; undaunted, unabashed, unconcerned.

Vb. *be courageous*, show spirit; *fight*; venture, adventure, *undertake*; dare, *face danger*; show fight, brave, face, outface, beard, affront, *defy*; confront; *affirm*; show a bold front, *stand firm*; charge; laugh at danger, *be rash*; show prowess, show valour; *keep calm*; endure, *suffer*.

take courage, take heart of grace, nerve oneself; show fight, *be resolute*; rally, stand, *stand firm*.

give *courage*, animate, hearten, nerve, make a man of; embolden, encourage, inspire, *incite*; rally, *cheer*; preserve morale; reassure, give confidence.

Adv. *bravely*, courageously; as bold as brass.

851 Cowardice

N. *cowardice*, abject fear, funk, *fear*; craven spirit; want of courage, lack of daring, absence of morale; defeatism; white feather, yellow streak, low morale, faint heart, chicken liver; Dutch courage; discretion, better part of valour; safety first, *caution*.

coward; funk, craven; sneak, rat, tell-tale, *informer*; runaway; coward at heart, bully, braggart; baby, *weakling*; quitter, cur, chicken, rabbit, mouse, jellyfish, invertebrate, doormat; *alarmist*.

Adj. *cowardly*, coward, craven; pusillanimous, timid, timorous, fearful, unable to say boo to a goose, *nervous*; soft, womanish, babyish, *weak*; spiritless, without grit, without guts, chicken; sneaking, yellow, abject, base, vile; lacking morale, *hopeless*; prudent, discreet, *cautious*; bashful, shy, coy, *modest*; easily frightened, funky, unstable, infirm of purpose, *irresolute*.

Vb. *be cowardly*, lack courage, be irresolute, be nervous; shrink, funk, *avoid*; hide, slink, skulk, sneak; quail, cower, cringe; show a yellow streak, show fear, turn tail, panic, stampede, scuttle, desert; show discretion, live to fight another day, be *cautious*.

852 Rashness

N. *rashness*, lack of caution, *inattention*, neglect; *folly*; lack of consideration, frivolity, levity; indiscipline; temerity, presumption; *haste*; game of chicken; courage of despair, *courage*; needless risk, *danger*; reckless gamble, last throw; reckless expenditure.

desperado, daredevil, madcap, hothead, adventurer, plunger; harum-scarum, ne'er-do-well; one who sticks at nothing, gunman; bully, bravo, *ruffian*.

Adj. *rash*, ill-advised, harebrained, foolhardy, wildcat, injudicious, indiscreet, imprudent; careless, slapdash, accident-prone, *negligent*; thoughtless, inconsiderate; light, frivolous, airy, breezy, flippant, giddy, harum-scarum, slaphappy, trigger-happy; irresponsible, reckless, regardless, foolhardy, lunatic, wanton, wild, cavalier; bold, daring, audacious, madcap, daredevil, neck or nothing, breakneck, suicidal; overweening, presumptuous, arrogant, *insolent*; precipitate, hell-bent, desperate, *hasty*, unchecked, headstrong, *wilful*, *ignorant*, impulsive, impatient, hot-blooded, furious, *excitable*; venturesome, *speculative*, adventurous, *enterprising*; improvident, *prodigal*.

Vb. *be rash*, lack caution; expose oneself, charge at, rush at, *hasten*; plunge, *gamble*; waste; *be prodigal*; play with fire, dice with death, *face danger*; play a desperate game, court disaster, tempt providence; anticipate, aim too high.

Adv. *rashly*, lightly.

853 Caution

N. *caution*, care, heed; doubt; instinct of self-preservation; *secrecy*; calculation, careful reckoning, safety first; nothing left to chance, *preparation*; deliberation, mature consideration, sobriety, balance, discretion, worldly wisdom, *wisdom*; insurance, precaution, *safeguard*; forethought, *foresight*; Fabian policy, *patience*; going slow, one step at a time; *delay*.

Adj. *cautious*, wary, watchful, *attentive*; *careful*; doubtful, suspicious, *nervous*; insured; guarded, secret, secretive, incommunicative, cagey, *reticent*; experienced, twice shy, *prepared*; circumspect, gingerly, tentative; conservative, *safe*; responsible, *trustworthy*; prudent, prudential, discreet, *wise*; noncommittal, *neutral*; frugal, economical; canny; timid; slow, deliberate, Fabian, *patient*; sober, cool; cold-blooded, calm.

Vb. *be cautious*, beware, take good care, *be careful*; play safe; *be wise*; go slow; *conceal*; *keep secret*; hide, lurk; look, scan; *be tentative*; tread warily, pussyfoot; look twice, *be mindful*; calculate, reckon, *judge*; know when to stop; let well alone, keep aloof, *avoid*; *predict*; *look ahead*; *estimate*; assure oneself, make sure, *make certain*; cover oneself, insure, hedge, *seek safety*; leave nothing to chance, *prepare*.

Adv. *cautiously*, with caution, gingerly.

854 Desire

N. *desire*, wish, *will*; summons, call, cry, *command*; dun, *demand*; wanting, want, need, exigency, *requirement*; claim; nostalgia, *regret*; hankering; thinking, daydream, *fantasy*; ambition, aspiration, *hope*; yen, urge, *impulse*; itch; intellectual curiosity, *curiosity*; zeal; passion, ardour, warmth; rage, fury, *frenzy*; monomania, *mania*; appetite, hunger, thirst, hungry look (see *hunger*); cupidity, *avarice*; greed; voracity; lust (see *libido*); inordinate desire.

hunger, famine, empty stomach; appetite, thirst; burning thirst, dipsomania, *alcoholism*.

liking, fancy, *love*; stomach, appetite, zest; relish, tooth, *taste*; leaning, penchant, propensity, trend, *tendency*; weakness, partiality; affinity, sympathy; mind, *intention*; predilection, favour, *choice*; whim, *caprice*; hobby, craze, fad, mania, bias; fascination, allurement, attraction, temptation, seduction, *inducement*.

libido, life instinct, sexual urge; sexual desire, passion, rut, heat; lust.

desired object, wish, desire, desirable thing, *requirement*; catch, prize, plum, *trophy*; lion, idol, cynosure, *favourite*; forbidden fruit; envy, temptation; magnet, lure, draw, *attraction*; aim, goal, star, ambition, aspiration, dream, *objective*; ideal, *perfection*.

desirer; *lover*; glutton; fancier, amateur, dilettante, *collector*; devotee, idolater; well-wisher, *patron*; aspirant; pretender; candidate, parasite; ambitious person.

Adj. *desiring*, unable to resist; oversexed, lustful, rutting, must; wanting, *demanding*; missing; inclined, minded; ambitious; would-be, wistful, hankering; demanding more; curious, solicitous, sedulous, anxious; eager, keen, burning, ardent, agog, breathless, impatient; vocal; avid; fond, partial to.

greedy, acquisitive, possessive, *selfish*; ambitious; voracious, omnivorous; insatiable; rapacious, grasping; exacting, extortionate.

hungry; empty; peckish, ravenous; thirsty, dry.

desired; desirable, enviable; acceptable, welcome; appetizing; catchy, attractive, appealing; *voluntary*.

Vb. *desire*, want, miss, require; *demand*; call, summon, *command*; invite, *be hospitable*; wish, pray; wish otherwise, *regret*; covet, envy; promise oneself, have a mind to, aim at, have at heart, *intend*; *plan*; aspire, dream of, dream, daydream, *hope*; want a lot, aim high; expect, *claim*; intercede, invoke; wish ill, *curse*; wish one well; welcome, be glad of, jump at, catch at, grasp at, clutch at, *take*; lean towards, *tend*; favour, prefer, select, *choose*; crave, hanker after; long, yearn, pine, languish; can't wait, must have; like, affect, *love*; take to, warm to, moon after, burn; ogle, make eyes at, solicit, woo, *court*; make a dead set at, run after, chase, *pursue*; lust, lust after, *be impure*; rut.

be *hungry*, hunger, famish, starve, have an empty stomach, be ready to eat a horse; have a good appetite, *eat*; thirst; be dry.

cause *desire*, incline, *motivate*; arouse desire, excite love; stimulate, *excite*; smell good, *make appetizing*; parch, raise a thirst; dangle, tease, titillate, *tempt*; allure, seduce, draw, *attract*; *give hope*.

Adv. *desirously*, with appetite, hungrily, thirstily, greedily.

855 Indifference

N. *indifference*; lack of interest, want of zeal; faint praise, two cheers; *lack of wonder*; nothing between them; anorexia; inertia, apathy; insouciance; *inattention*; open mind, equity, *justice*; middle way; neutral, *moderate*; *slacker*; wallflower.

Adj. *indifferent*, unconcerned; uninterested; lukewarm, half-hearted; impersonal, phlegmatic, *impassive*; calm, cool, cold; nonchalant, careless, perfunctory; *negligent*; supine, lackadaisical, listless; easy-going, *lax*; unmoved, insensible to; loveless; impartial, inflexible, *just*; noncommittal, moderate, *neutral*; promiscuous; amoral.

unwanted; unprovoked; loveless; all one to; insipid, tasteless, *unsavoury*; undesirable.

Vb. *be indifferent*, see nothing wonderful; damn with faint praise; *dislike*; take it or leave it; shrug, dismiss, let go, make light of, *hold cheap*; take neither side, *be neutral*; grow indifferent; fail to move, leave one cold, *make insensitive*.

Int. Never mind! what does it matter! who cares! so what!

856 Dislike

N. *dislike*; reluctance; displeasure, *resentment*; discontent; *dissent*; aversion; antipathy, allergy; rooted dislike, distaste, disrelish; repugnance, repulsion, disgust, abomination; horror, *fear*; phobia; prejudice, *bias*; animosity, bad blood, ill feeling, mutual hatred, *hatred*; nausea, turn, vomit; object of dislike, pet aversion, Dr Fell.

Adj. *disliking*, disinclined; squeamish, queasy; averse, hostile, *inimical*; shy; loveless; *indifferent*; sick of.

disliked, undesirable; grating, bitter; *repellent*; revolting, abhorrent, loathsome, *hateful*; abominable; nauseous, sickening, fulsome, foul, stinking, *unsavoury*; disagreeable, insufferable, *intolerable*;

loveless; *ugly*.

Vb. *dislike*, disrelish; *reject*; object, *deprecate*; mind, *resent*; take a dislike to; react against, *recoil*; feel sick at, want to heave, *vomit*; shun, *avoid*; look askance at, *disapprove*; sniff at, sneer at, *despise*; make a face, grimace, *be sullen*; be unable to abide, can't stand, detest, loathe, abominate, abhor, *hate*; shudder at, *fear*; wish undone, *regret*.

cause *dislike*, deter, *frighten*; antagonize, *enrage*; set against, set at odds, make bad blood, *excite hate*; satiate, pall, jade, *sate*; disagree with, upset, *disagree*; revolt, *repel*; offend, grate, jar, *displease*; *torment*; disgust, nauseate, sicken, make one sick; *shock*, make a scandal, *incur blame*.

Adv. *ad nauseam*.

Int. ugh! horrible! yuk! revolting!

857 Fastidiousness

N. *fastidiousness*, nicety, delicacy; *discrimination*; refinement, *good taste*; idealism, artistic conscience, *conscience*; nit-picking, pedantry, hair-splitting; *prudery*.

perfectionist, idealist, purist, fusspot, pedant, stickler, hard taskmaster; gourmet, epicure.

Adj. *fastidious*; nice, dainty, delicate; perspicacious, discerning; particular, demanding, finicky; scrupulous, meticulous, squeamish, *attentive*; punctilious, painstaking, conscientious, critical, hypercritical, fussy, pernickety, hard to please, censorious; donnish, precise, exacting, difficult, *severe*; prim.

Vb. *be fastidious*; choose; refine, *argue*; *discriminate*; find fault; fuss, say ugh!, feel superior, disdain, *despise*; keep oneself to oneself, *be unsociable*.

858 Satiety

N. *satiety*; stuffing, saturation, saturation point; glut, surfeit, too much of a good thing, *tedium*; overdose, excess.

Adj. *sated*, replete; sick of; jaded.

Vb. *sate*, satiate; satisfy, quench, slake, *suffice*; saturate, *fill*; soak, *drench*; stuff, gorge, glut, surfeit, cloy, jade, pall; overdose; sicken, *cause dislike*; spoil, kill with kindness; bore, weary, *be tedious*.

859 Wonder

N. *wonder*, state of wonder, wonderment; admiration, hero worship, *love*; awe, fascination; cry of wonder, gasp of admiration, whistle, exclamation, exclamation mark; *silence*; open mouth; shock, surprise, *lack of expectation*; astonishment; stupor, consternation, *fear*.

thaumaturgy, magic, *sorcery*; wonderful works; stroke of genius, feat, exploit, *deed*; transformation scene.

prodigy, portent, sign, eye-opener, *omen*; something incredible, quite something; phenomenon, miracle, marvel, wonder; drama, sensation; object of wonder or admiration, wonderland, *fantasy*; sight, *spectacle*; infant prodigy, genius, man or woman of genius, *proficient person*; wizard, *sorcerer*; hero, wonder boy, dream girl, bionic man, *paragon*; freak, sport, curiosity, oddity, monster, monstrosity; puzzle.

Adj. *wondering*, awestruck; rapt; pop-eyed, agape; dumb, inarticulate, speechless, breathless, left without words, *silent*; struck all of a heap, thunderstruck; aghast.

wonderful, to wonder at, wondrous, marvellous, miraculous, monstrous, prodigious, phenomenal; stupendous, fearful; admirable, exquisite, *excellent*; *best*; striking, awe-inspiring, breathtaking, *impressive*; dramatic, sensational; shocking; rare, exceptional, extraordinary, unprecedented, *unusual*; remarkable, noteworthy; strange, odd, very odd, weird, unaccountable, mysterious, enigmatic; exotic, outlandish, unheard of, *extraneous*; fantastic, *imaginary*; impossible, hardly possible, too good or bad to be true, *improbable*; unbelievable, incredible, inconceivable, indescribable; unutterable, unspeakable, ineffable, *inexpressible*; surprising; mind-blowing, amazing; magic, *magical*.

Vb. *wonder*, marvel, admire, whistle; gasp, gasp with admiration; *love*; stare, goggle at, gawk, gape, look aghast; be awestruck, *fear*; be silent.

be *wonderful*; surpass belief, *cause doubt*; beggar all description, beat everything; spellbind, enchant, *bewitch*; dazzle, strike with admiration, *excite love*; strike dumb, awe, electrify, *impress*; stagger, stun, daze, stupefy, petrify, confound, astound, astonish, amaze, flabbergast, *surprise*; baffle, bewilder, *puzzle*; startle, *frighten*; shock, *incur blame*.

Adv. *wonderfully*; wondrous strange, strange to say, wonderful to relate.

Int. Amazing! incredible! I don't believe it! well I never! blow me down! did you ever! gosh! wow! how about that! bless my soul! 'pon my word! goodness gracious! whatever next!

860 Lack of wonder

N. *lack of wonder*, lack of astonishment; composure, quietude; cold blood, *moral insensibility*; lack of imagination; disbelief; matter of course, just what one thought, nothing to wonder at.

Adj. *unastonished*; accustomed; calm, collected; phlegmatic, impassive, *apathetic*; unmoved, *indifferent*; cold-blooded; blind to, *blind*; expectant.

unastonishing; customary, common, ordinary, nothing wonderful, *usual*.

Vb. *not wonder*, see nothing remarkable, be *insensitive*; *disbelieve*; see through, *understand*; see it coming, *expect*; *keep calm*.

Int. no *wonder*; nothing to it; of course; quite so, naturally.

861 Repute

N. *repute*, reputation, report, title to fame, name, character, *credit*; regard, esteem, *respect*; opinion, good odour, favour, popularity, vogue, *fashion*; acclaim, applause, approval, cachet, *approbation*.

prestige, aura, mystique, magic; glamour, dazzle, lustre, splendour; prowess, glory, honour, kudos, esteem, estimation, account, worship; face, caste; degree, rank, ranking, standing, footing, status, *serial place*; condition, position; precedence; prominence, eminence, *visibility*; distinction, high rank, majesty, *nobility*; dignity, solemnity, grandeur; name to conjure with; *influence*; hegemony, primacy, *authority*; leadership; snob value.

famousness, title to fame, celebrity, renown,

stardom, fame, name, note; household name; glory, *success*; notoriety, *disrepute*; *publicity*; posthumous fame, *memory*; undying name; remembrance.

honours, honour, blaze of glory, crown, halo, nimbus, glory; laurels, wreath, garland, favour; feather, *trophy*; order, star, garter, ribbon, medal; sword, shield, arms, *heraldry*; an honour, distinction, accolade, award, *reward*; compliment, flattery, incense, eulogy, *praise*; memorial, statue, bust, picture, portrait, niche, plaque, temple, monument; title of honour, dignity, handle, *title*; patent of nobility, peerage, academic honour, degree, diploma, certificate, *academic title*; source of honour, College of Arms; honours list, birthday honours, roll of honour, *list*.

dignification; coronation, *celebration*; dedication; promotion, advancement, *progression*; exaltation, *elevation*; *restoration*.

person *of repute*, gentle reader; worthy, sound person, good citizen, loyal subject, pillar, pillar of society; man or woman of honour, *honourable person*; knight, dame, peer, *person of rank*; somebody, great man, great woman, big shot, big noise, big name, big wheel, VIP, *bigwig*; notable, celebrity, figure, champion; lion, star, rising star; popular hero; idol, *favourite*; cynosure, model, mirror, *paragon*; cream, cream of society, *elite*; choice spirit, leading light, *leader*; grand old man, *sage*; noble army, great company, bevy, galaxy, constellation, band.

Adj. reputable, reputed, of repute, of good or sound reputation, of credit; *trustworthy*; *honourable*; worthy, creditable, meritorious, prestigious, *excellent*; respectable, well thought of; moral, *virtuous*; popular, modish, *fashionable*.

worshipful, reverend, honourable; admirable, *wonderful*; heroic, *courageous*; imposing, august, stately, grand, sublime, *impressive*; lofty, high, *elevated*; mighty, *great*; lordly, princely, queenly, royal, regal, *noble*; glorious, full of honours, titled; time-honoured, ancient, *immemorial*; sacrosanct, sacred, holy.

noteworthy, notable, remarkable, extraordinary, *unusual*; fabulous, *wonderful*; of mark, of distinction, distinguished, *important*; conspicuous, prominent, public, *obvious*; eminent, preeminent, peerless, foremost, *superior*; ranking, leading, commanding; brilliant, bright, lustrous, *luminous*; illustrious, splendid, glorious.

renowned, celebrated, sung; of renown, of glorious name, of fame; famous, historic, illustrious, great, noble, glorious, *excellent*; notorious, *disreputable*; well-known, *known*; of note, noted (see *noteworthy*); resounding; evergreen, imperishable, deathless, immortal, eternal, *perpetual*.

Vb. have a reputation, wear a halo; have a good name, have a name to lose; rank, stand high, have status or standing, have a position, enjoy consideration, *command respect*; stand well with, do oneself credit, win honour, win renown, gain prestige, gain recognition, build a reputation, earn a name, acquire a character; be somebody, *prosper*; graduate, *succeed*; cut a figure, cut a dash, cover oneself with glory; rise to fame, flash to stardom; shine, excel, *be good*; eclipse, overshadow, *be superior*; have precedence,

play first fiddle, star, *come before*; have fame, have a great name; make history.

seek repute; *be proud*; flaunt, *feel pride*; lord it, queen it, prance, strut; brag, *boast*.

honour, revere, regard, respect; fear; *worship*; know how to value, appreciate, prize, value, tender, treasure, *love*; show honour, pay respect, pay due regard, *show respect*; be polite to, *be courteous*; compliment, *flatter*; grace with, dedicate to, inscribe to; praise, glorify, acclaim, *applaud*; deck with laurels, make much of, lionize, chair; credit, *thank*; glorify, commemorate, *remember*; celebrate, renown, *proclaim*; reflect honour, lend distinction or lustre to, do credit to, be a credit to.

dignify, glorify, exalt, deify, consecrate, dedicate, *sanctify*; install, enthrone, crown, *commission*; distinguish, *indicate*; advance, upgrade, *promote*; honour, *decorate*; bestow a title, create, elevate, ennoble; dub, knight; give one his or her title, sir, *name*; take a title.

862 Disrepute

N. disrepute, bad reputation, bad name, bad character, shady reputation, past; *disrespect*; notoriety, infamy, ill repute, ill fame; bad odour, ill favour, disfavour, discredit, black books, bad light, *odium*; dishonour, disgrace, shame (see *slur*); smear campaign; ignominy, loss of honour, loss of reputation; loss of face, loss of rank; comedown.

slur, reproach, *censure*; imputation, aspersion, reflection, slander, abuse, *calumny*; slight, insult, *indignity*; scandal, disgrace, shame, pollution; stain, smear, smudge, dirt; stigma, brand, mark, spot, blot, tarnish, taint, *blemish*; dirty linen; bar sinister, badge of infamy, scarlet letter.

object of scorn, scandalous person, reproach, byword, contempt, discredit, *bad person*; reject; poor relation, *nonentity*; failure, *loser*.

Adj. disreputable, shifty, shady; notorious, of ill fame, nefarious; arrant, *bad*; doubtful, dubious, questionable, objectionable; ribald, improper, indecent, obscene, *impure*; characterless; petty, pitiful; outcast; base, abject, despicable, odious, *hateful*; mean, cheap, low, *vulgar*; shabby, squalid, dirty, scruffy, *unclean*; poor, *dilapidated*.

discreditable; ignoble; improper, inexpedient; *dishonest*; despicable; shameful, disgraceful, scandalous, shocking, outrageous, unmentionable; too bad.

degrading, ignominious; derogatory; beneath one.

inglorious, without repute, without prestige, without note; without a name, nameless, *anonymous*; servile; *modest*; unknown to fame, unheard of, obscure, *unknown*; unseen, unheard, *invisible*; unsung; *plebeian*; sunk low, shorn of glory.

Vb. have no repute, have a past; rank low; play second fiddle, take a back seat, *be inferior*; blush unseen, *be unseen*.

lose repute; fall, sink, *descend*; fade, wither; incur discredit, incur dishonour, incur disgrace, achieve notoriety, *incur blame*; disgrace oneself, *fail*; lose prestige, lose face; admit defeat, crawl, crouch; look silly, look foolish, cut a sorry figure, *be absurd*; be brought to book.

demean oneself, condescend, stoop, marry beneath one; make oneself cheap,

cheapen oneself; forfeit self-respect.
shame, pillory, expose, post; scorn, mock, *ridicule*; snub, *humiliate*; discompose, disconcert, deflate; degrade, downgrade, demote, cashier, disbar, strip, *punish*; blackball, *exclude*; vilify, malign, disparage, *defame*; taint; sully, mar, blacken, tarnish, stain, blot, smear, *make unclean*; debase, defile, desecrate, profane; brand, tar, *mark*; dishonour, disgrace, discredit, give a bad name; be a public scandal, *incur blame*; trample, tread underfoot, outrage, *oppress*; disdain, *despise*; make one blush, *debauch*.

863 Nobility

N. *nobility*, distinction, rank, station, order, *degree*; royalty, majesty, prerogative, *authority*; birth; descent, ancestry, line, lineage, pedigree, *genealogy*; noble family, noble house, dynasty, *family*; blood, caste, badge of rank, patent of nobility, coat of arms, crest, *heraldry*.
aristocracy, patrician order; nobility; lordship, lords, peerage, House of Lords; dukedom; landed interest, squirearchy; county family, county set, gentry, gentlefolk; great folk; life peerage.
upper *class*, upper ten, upper crust, top layer, top drawer; best people, better sort, chosen few, *elite*; high society, social register, high life, fashionable world; ruling class, *authority*; rich person; salaried class.
aristocrat, patrician, Olympian; person of high caste, Brahman; thoroughbred; senator, magnate, dignitary; don; gentleman; squire, laird; emperor, king, queen, prince, *sovereign*; nob, swell, *fop*; superior person, *bigwig*.
person *of rank*, titled person, noble, noble lord or lady, seigneur; lordship; peer, peeress; princess royal, duke, archduke, duchess; marchioness, count, countess; earl, viscount, viscountess, baron, baroness, thane, baronet, knight; bey, begum, emir, khan, *potentate*, governor.
Adj. *noble*, chivalrous; ladylike (see *genteel*); royal, regal, every inch a king or queen; queenly, princely, lordly; ducal; of royal blood, of high birth, of good family; thoroughbred; of rank, titled; haughty, high, exalted, grand, *great*.
genteel; patrician; Olympian; superior, high-class, classy, posh, U, highly respectable; of good breeding, *wellbred*.

864 Commonalty

N. *commonalty*, commons, third estate, bourgeoisie; citizenry, democracy; silent majority, grass roots; general public; people at large, populace, vulgar herd; mass of society, proletariat; rag.
rabble, mob, horde, *crowd*; rout; riffraff, scum, dregs of society, cattle, vermin.
lower *classes*, lower orders, *inferior*; common sort, small fry, humble folk; working class, steerage, steerage class, lower deck; proletariat; slum population; white trash; underworld, low company, low life.
middle *classes*, bourgeoisie; Brown.
commoner, bourgeois(e) plebeian; citizen, mere citizen; democrat, republican; proletarian; working man or woman, *worker*; native; little man, common type, *common man*; common person, *inferior*; private; underling, *servant*; upstart,

social climber, Philistine, *vulgarian*; a nobody, *nonentity*; outcaste; Untouchable; villein, serf, *slave*.
country-dweller, countryman or -woman, yeoman, rustic, swain, gaffer, peasant, cultivator, *farmer*; boor, churl; yokel, hind, clod, clodhopper; bumpkin, country cousin, provincial, hillbilly; village idiot, *ninny*.
low *fellow*, fellow, cad; *poor person*; guttersnipe, street arab, ragamuffin; down-and-out, tramp, bum, vagabond, *wanderer*; beggar; low type, bully, ugly customer, plug ugly, ruffian, rowdy, rough, *ruffian*; rascal, knave; gangster, hood; criminal, delinquent; barbarian, savage, Vandal.
Adj. *plebeian*, common, simple, without rank; ignoble; *middling*; mean, low, low-down, *disreputable*; lowly, base-born, low-born, of low origin, of mean parentage, of mean extraction; servile; humble, of low estate, of humble condition, *inferior*; non-U, proletarian; homely, homespun, *plain*; obscure, inglorious; coarse, uncouth, *ill-bred*; cockney, bourgeois, Main Street, suburban, provincial, rustic; *vulgar*; churlish, *ungracious*.
barbaric, barbarous, barbarian, wild, savage; without arts, primitive, neolithic, *artless*.

865 Title

N. *title*, title to fame, claim; title of honour, courtesy title, handle; honour, distinction, order, *honours*; royal we, editorial we, *formality*; mode of address, Royal Highness, Excellency, Grace, Lordship, Ladyship, noble, my liege, my lord, my lady, dame; Right Honourable; Reverend, Monsignor, His Holiness; padre; your reverence, your honour, your worship; sire, sir, madam, ma'am, master, mister, mistress, miss, Ms; monsieur, madame, mademoiselle; don, señor, señora, señorita; signora, signorina; Herr, Frau, Fraulein; sahib; comrade.
academic *title*, doctor; doctor of philosophy, PhD; doctor of literature, doctor of divinity; doctor of medicine, MD; doctor of music; bachelor of arts, BA; bachelor of literature; bachelor of science; bachelor of law; bachelor of music; master of arts, MA; master of science, MSc; Professor; reader, lecturer.

866 Pride

N. *pride*, proud heart; proper pride, self-esteem; self-respect, self-confidence; conceit, swank, side, *vanity*; snobbery, *affectation*; false pride, *moral sensibility*; dignity, reputation, *prestige*; hauteur, disdain, *contempt*; overweening pride, hubris; swelling pride, pomp, show, display, *ostentation*; *prejudice*; object of pride, boast, joy, *favourite*; cynosure, pick, flower, *paragon*.
proud *person*, snob; mass of pride, pride incarnate; swank; lord of creation, *bigwig*; fine gentleman, *fop*; turkey cock; *rich person*; class-conscious person, *aristocrat*.
Adj. *proud*, elevated, haughty, lofty, sublime, *high*; showy, fine, grand, *fashionable*; grandiose, stately, statuesque, *impressive*; royal, queenly, lordly, *noble*; self-respecting, *courageous*; high-spirited, *lively*; stiff-necked, *obstinate*; mighty, *great*; imperious, commanding, *authoritative*; high-handed, overweening,

overbearing, arrogant, *insolent*; brazen, unblushing, unabashed.

rideful, full of pride, inflated, swelling, swollen; stuck-up; upstage, uppish; haughty, disdainful, superior, supercilious, hoity-toity; standoffish, aloof, distant, stiff, starchy, unbending, *ungracious*; feeling pride, proud of; *boastful*; pleased with oneself; cocky, bumptious, *vain*; pretentious, *affected*; pompous, showy.

b. be proud, stand erect, refuse to stoop; give oneself airs, think it beneath one, be too proud to, be too grand to; be stuckup, swank, swagger, strut; condescend; disdain, *despise*; display hauteur, *be insolent*; lord it, queen it, *oppress*.

eel pride, boast of, *boast*; hug oneself, be pleased; flatter oneself, think a lot of oneself, be vain.

867 Humility. Humiliation

N. humility, humble spirit; resignation, *submission*; courtesy; humble person, mouse, violet.

umiliation, letdown, climbdown, comedown, *indignity*; rebuke, *reprimand*; shame, disgrace, *disrepute*; sense of shame, sense of disgrace, blush, confusion; shamefaced look, hangdog expression; hurt pride, *resentment*.

dj. humble, lowly; meek, submissive, resigned; self-effacing, *disinterested*; courteous; harmless, inoffensive, *innocent*; unassuming, unpretentious, without airs, without side, *modest*; mean, low; of lowly birth, *plebeian*.

umbled; crestfallen, sheepish, *dejected*; ashamed; *inglorious*; brought low.

b. be humble, humble oneself, *demean oneself*; play second fiddle, *be modest*; *be disinterested*; condescend, unbend, *be courteous*; stoop, crawl, sing small, eat humble pie; stomach, pocket, *forgive*.

humbled; receive a snub, *be ashamed*; be ashamed of oneself, feel shame; blush, *redden*; feel small.

umiliate, humble, chasten, abash, disconcert; lower, deflate; make one feel small, make one sing small, teach one his place, make one crawl; snub, cut, crush, squash, *be rude*; slight; mortify, put to shame, *shame*; make a fool of, make one look silly; *outdo*; daunt, *frighten*; *overmaster*.

868 Vanity

N. vanity, vain pride, *pride*; conceit, self-importance, megalomania; swank, side; assurance, good opinion of oneself, self-esteem; self-satisfaction; narcissism, egotism; exhibitionism, *ostentation*; Vanity Fair.

irs, affectation; swank, *ostentation*.

ain person, Narcissus; self-centred person, coxcomb, *fop*; peacock; know-all, big-head; Miss Clever; pompous twit, *insubstantial thing*.

dj. vain, overweening, stuck-up, proud; egocentric, self-centred, self-complacent, full of oneself, *selfish*; smug, pleased with oneself; opinionated, clever clever; bumptious, cocky, perky, *insolent*; immodest, blatant; *boastful*; pompous, pretentious, so-called; *affected*.

b. be vain; have a high opinion of oneself; *boast*; admire oneself, plume oneself, *feel pride*; swank, strut, talk big, push oneself forward; get above oneself, give oneself airs, *be affected*.

make *conceited*, fill with conceit, inflate, *flatter*.

Adv. conceitedly, vainly, swankily.

869 Modesty

N. modesty, lack of ostentation, retiring disposition; *prudery*; blush; chastity, *purity*; *humility*; unassuming nature; reserve; modest person, shy thing, mouse.

Adj. modest, without vanity; self-effacing, unobtrusive, unseen, unheard, *humble*; quiet, unassuming, unpretentious; moderate, mediocre; shy, retiring, timid, diffident, *nervous*; awkward, constrained, inarticulate; bashful, rosy; shamefaced, sheepish; reserved, demure, coy; *affected*; chaste, *pure*.

Vb. be modest, show moderation, ration oneself, *be temperate*; efface oneself, yield precedence, *be humble*; play second fiddle, take a back seat; blush unseen, *escape notice*; retire, shrink, hang back, be coy, *avoid*; feel shame, blush, colour, crimson, mantle, *redden*; be virtuous.

Adv. modestly; without fuss, without ceremony, without beat of drum.

870 Ostentation. Formality

N. ostentation, display, parade, show, *manifestation*; exhibitionism, *publicity*; splendour; self-importance, *vanity*; fuss, swagger, pretension, *airs*; swank, side, strut; bravado, heroics, *boast*; dramatics, sensationalism, *exaggeration*; bonhomie; showmanship, effect; solemnity (see *formality*); grandeur, dignity; rhetoric; flourish, big drum, *publication*; pageantry, pomp, circumstance, pride, panache, flying colours, dash, splash, *finery*; frippery, glitter, tinsel; idle pomp, idle show, false glitter, mockery; tomfoolery, *foolery*; travesty, *mimicry*; exterior, gloss, veneer, polish, varnish; pretence, profession, *pretext*; lip service, *deception*.

formality, state, dignity; royal we, editorial we, *title*; ceremony, ceremonial, *ritual*; drill; protocol, form, *etiquette*; *attention*; routine, *practice*; solemnity, formal occasion, function, red carpet, *celebration*; full dress, regalia, finery, *formal dress*; correct dress, *uniform*.

pageant, show, *exhibit*; fete, gala, gala performance, tournament, tattoo; field day, great doings, *celebration*; *spectacle*; set piece, tableau, scene, stage effect, *stage set*; display, stunt; pyrotechnics; carnival, *festivity*, *revel*; procession, promenade, flypast; turnout, review, parade, array, *assembly*.

Adj. ostentatious, showy, pompous; prestige; specious, seeming, hollow, *spurious*; consequential, pretentious, would-be, *affected*; *vain*; inflated, turgid, orotund, windy; grand, highfalutin, splendid, brilliant, magnificent, grandiose, posh; superb, royal, *liberal*; sumptuous, luxurious, costly, expensive, *dear*.

showy, flashy, dressy, *fashionable*; colourful, lurid, gaudy, gorgeous, *florid*; tinsel, garish, *vulgar*; flaming, flagrant, blatant, public; brave, dashing, gallant, gay, jaunty, sporty; spectacular, scenic, dramatic, histrionic, theatrical, stagy; sensational, daring.

formal, solemn, stately, grand, fine; ceremonious, punctilious, correct, precise, stiff, starchy; of state, public, official; ceremonial, ritual.

Vb. *be ostentatious*; cut a dash, make a splash, make a figure; glitter, dazzle, *shine*; flaunt, sport, *wear*; wave, flourish, *brandish*; trumpet, *proclaim*, *defy*; demonstrate, exhibit, *show*; make a display; stage-manage; polish, veneer, *coat*; shoot a line, *boast*; *attract notice*; put oneself forward, advertise oneself, *be affected*; prance, promenade, swan around; parade, march, march past, fly past; peacock, strut, swank, *be vain*; make an exhibition of oneself, make people stare.

871 Celebration

N. *celebration*, performance, *action*; *remembrance*; observance, *ritual*; ceremony, function, occasion, do; formal occasion, coronation, installation, presentation, *commission*; debut, *beginning*; reception, welcome, *formality*; official reception, *applause*; festive occasion, fete, jubilee, *festivity*; jubilation, cheering, ovation, triumph, salute, salvo, tattoo, roll, fanfare, flying colours; illuminations; firework display; bonfire, *fire*; *trophy*; harvest home, thanksgiving, *thanks*; health, toast.

special *day*, day to remember, great day, *holy day*; Armistice Day, D-Day, Remembrance Sunday; Fourth of July, birthday; wedding anniversary, silver wedding, centenary, bicentenary, *anniversary*.

Adj. *celebratory*, observing; occasional, anniversary, centennial, *seasonal*; festive, jubilant; triumphant.

Vb. *celebrate*, perform, *do*; hallow, keep holy, keep sacred, *sanctify*; commemorate, *remember*; honour, observe, keep, maintain; make it an occasion, make much of, welcome, do one proud, *be hospitable*; do honour to, fete; chair, *elevate*; mob, rush, *rampage*; garland, wreathe, crown, *reward*; lionize, beat a tattoo, fire a salute, fire a salvo; cheer, triumph, *rejoice*; make holiday, *revel*; present, inaugurate, launch, install, *commission*; *begin*.

toast, pledge, clink glasses; drink to, drain a bumper, drink a health, *drink*.

Adv. *in honour of*, in memory of, in celebration of, on the occasion of.

872 Boasting

N. *boasting*; *ostentation*; swagger, swank, bounce, *vanity*; advertisement, *publicity*; fine talk, *empty talk*; heroics, bravado; chauvinism, jingoism, *bias*; bluster; *threat*.

boast, brag, puff, *advertisement*; flourish, bravado, bombast, rant, fustian, tall talk, *exaggeration*; hot air, gas, bunkum, *empty talk*; bluff, bounce, *deception*; presumptuous challenge, *defiance*; big talk, big drum, bluster, idle threat, *threat*.

boaster, braggart, brag, loudmouth, charlatan, pretender, *impostor*; bouncer, liar; swank, *vain person*; swashbuckler, Pistol; hot air merchant.

Adj. *boastful*; braggart; *vain*; bellicose, *warlike*; hollow, pretentious, empty, *spurious*; grandiloquent; triumphant, cock-a-hoop.

Vb. *boast*, brag, talk big, shoot a line, bluff, bluster, shout; bid defiance, *defy*; vapour, prate, rant, gas, *mean nothing*; enlarge, magnify, *exaggerate*; trumpet, parade, flaunt, *publish*; puff, *advertise*; sell oneself; flourish, wave, *brandish*; *threaten*; strut, swagger, prance, swank, *be vain*; gloat, hug oneself, *be pleased*; boast of, *be proud*; *triumph*; exult, *rejoice*.

873 Insolence

N. *insolence*, hubris, *pride*; tyranny, bravado, *defiance*; bluster, *threat*; disdain, *contempt*; sneer; *scurrility*; assurance, self-assertion; presumption; hardihood, effrontery; face, front, brazen face.

sauciness, disrespect; nerve, gall, brass, cheek, neck; lip, mouth, sauce, V-sign, *gesture*; taunt, personality, insult affront, *indignity*; throwaway manner, *discourtesy*; defiance, answer, provocation, backchat, *rejoinder*; raillery, banter, *ridicule*.

insolent *person*, impertinent, cheeky devil; minx, hussy, baggage, madam; whipper-snapper, pup, puppy; upstart, tin god, *nonentity*; braggart; *proud person*; bully, hoodlum, swashbuckler, desperado, *ruffian*.

Adj. *insolent*, bellicose, *warlike*; rebellious, *defiant*; scurrilous, lofty, supercilious, disdainful, contemptuous; haughty, snooty, up-stage, *proud*; arrogant, presumptuous; brash, bumptious, bouncing, *vain*; flagrant, blatant; shameless, lost to shame, unblushing, unabashed, brazen; bold, hardy, audacious, *rash*; overweening, overbearing, imperious, magisterial, lordly, arbitrary, high-handed, harsh; *boastful*.

impertinent, pert, forward, fresh; impudent, saucy, cheeky, brassy, cool, jaunty, perky, cocky, cocksure, flippant, flip; cavalier, offhand, familiar, breezy, airy; impolite, rude, *discourteous*; defiant; provocative, offensive; personal.

Vb. *be insolent*, get personal, *be rude*; have a nerve, cheek, sauce, give lip, taunt, provoke, *enrage*; retort, answer back, *answer*; get above oneself; presume, arrogate, assume, make bold to, make free with, get fresh; *be proud*; sneer at, *despise*; banter, rally, *ridicule*; express contempt, sniff, snort; *be indifferent*; send to blazes, *defy*; outlook, outface, take a high tone, lord it, queen it; bully, browbeat, treat with a high hand, *oppress*; swank, swagger, swell, look big, *be vain*; brag, talk big, *boast*; be a law unto oneself, disobey; defy nemesis, tempt providence.

Adv. *insolently*, impertinently, pertly; outrageously.

874 Servility

N. *servility*, abject spirit, lack of self-respect, *submission*; compliance; *humility*; bent back, bow, scrape, duck, bob, *obeisance*; *flattery*; *service*; servile condition, slavery, *servitude*.

toady, yes-man, rubber stamp; creep; hypocrite, spaniel, courtier; sycophant, parasite, leech; jackal, hanger-on, *dependant*; lackey, *retainer*; born slave slave; lapdog, poodle; tool, creature *instrument*.

Adj. *servile*, dependent, *subject*; slavish, mean, abject, base, tame; subservient submissive; compliant, supple, *obedient*; prostrate, sneaking, creepy, obsequious, unctuous, slimy.

Vb. *be servile*, stoop to anything, *demean oneself*; squirm, roll, sneak, cringe crouch, creep, crawl, grovel; bow, scrape, bend, bob, duck, kowtow, make obeisance, kneel, *stoop*; *be humble*; toady to, spaniel, fawn, ingratiate oneself, pay court to, curry favour, *flatter*, squire, attend, *serve*; comply, *obey*; *be instrumental*; whine, wheedle, *beg*; sponge; *conform*.

Adv. *servilely*, cap in hand.

875 Friendship

N. *friendship*, amity, *concord*; friendly relations, relations of friendship, friendly intercourse; companionship, togetherness; fellowship, comradeship, brotherhood, *association*; solidarity, support; acquaintanceship, acquaintance, familiarity, *knowledge*; fast friendship, *love*; introduction, recommendation, commendation; overtures, rapprochement, *approach*; reconciliation.

friendliness, kindness, *courtesy*; warmth, *benevolence*; camaraderie; hospitality; greeting, welcome, open arms, handshake, hug, *courteous act*; regard, *respect*; goodwill, fellow feeling, sympathy, response; understanding, same wavelength, entente, honeymoon, *concord*; partiality, *prejudice*; favouritism, *injustice*; support, *aid*.

friend, girlfriend, boyfriend; acquaintance, lifelong friend, crony, neighbour, fellow countryman or -woman; cousin, clansman; well-wisher, backer, *patron*; second, *protector*; fellow, sister, brother, partner, associate, *colleague*; ally, *auxiliary*; guest, frequent visitor; young friend, host, *sociable person*; former friend.

close friend, soul mate, kindred spirit; best man, bridesmaid; dear friend, intimate, bosom friend, bosom pal; alter ego, other self, *shadow*; comrade, companion, happy family.

chum, crony; pal, mate, cobber, buddy; fellow, comrade, roommate, stable companion, *colleague*; playmate, classmate; pen friend, pen pal.

xenophile, Anglophile, *philanthropist*.

Adj. *friendly*, amicable, devoted, *loving*, loyal, faithful, staunch, fast, firm, tried, *trustworthy*; fraternal, sisterly; natural, easy; compatible, congenial, sympathetic, understanding; well-meaning, well-intentioned; hearty, cordial, warm, hospitable, *sociable*; effusive, demonstrative; matey; friendly with, *knowing*; intimate, inseparable, thick.

b. *be friendly*, have neighbourly relations, hobnob, keep company with, go about together, be inseparable, *be sociable*; have a large acquaintance; embrace, *greet*; welcome, entertain, *be hospitable*; *understand*; like, warm to, become fond of, *love*; mean well.

befriend, acknowledge, know; favour, protect; overcome hostility; make welcome; strike an acquaintance, knit friendship; make overtures, *approach*; court; take to, warm to, click with; hobnob, make known to each other, introduce, present, commend; renew friendship, *make peace*.

Adv. *amicably*.

876 Enmity

N. *enmity*, hostility, antagonism, *opposition*; antipathy, *dislike*; *hatred*; animosity, spite, grudge, ill feeling, ill will, bad blood; *envy*; *ice*; alienation,

strain, tension, *dissension*; rancour, *resentment*; *perfidy*; breach, breach of friendship, *quarrel*; hostile act; conflict, hostilities, state of war, *belligerency*; vendetta, feud.

enemy; traitor; bad neighbour; antagonist, opposite side, *opponent*; competitor, rival, *contender*; open enemy, foe, hostile force, *combatant*; aggressor; fifth column, Trojan Horse; public enemy, outlaw, pirate; personal enemy, arch enemy; misogynist, *misanthrope*; Anglophobe, *narrow mind*; pet aversion, *hateful object*.

Adj. *inimical*, disaffected; disloyal, unfaithful; aloof, distant, *unsociable*; cool, chilly, frigid, icy, *cold*; incompatible; hostile; irreconcilable; bitter, rancorous; jealous, grudging, *envious*; *malevolent*; at feud, at enmity, at loggerheads; aggressive, militant, at war with; intolerant; venomous, deadly, fell.

Vb. *be inimical*, show hostility; bear ill will, bear malice, *be malevolent*; grudge, *envy*; hound, persecute, *oppress*; chase, *hunt*; battle, *fight*; make war, *wage war*; take offence, take umbrage, *resent*; *quarrel*; be incompatible, conflict, collide, clash, *be contrary*; withstand, *oppose*.

make enemies, be unsociable; get across, cause offence, antagonize, irritate, *enrage*; estrange, alienate, make bad blood, set at odds.

877 Sociality

N. *sociality*, membership, membership of society, *association*; making one of, being one of; team spirit; fellowship, comradeship, companionship, society; camaraderie; social intercourse, familiarity, togetherness, *friendship*; social circle, *friend*; social ambition; society.

sociability, social activity, *conformity*; sociable disposition; social success, popularity; social tact, common touch; social graces, good manners, *courtesy*; *good taste*; ability to mix; readiness to chat; welcome; greeting, glad hand, handshake, embrace, *courteous act*; hospitality, entertaining, open house, Liberty Hall, pot luck, *liberality*; good company, good fellowship, bonhomie; merrymaking, gaiety, *revel*; cheer, *food*; social board, loving cup.

social gathering, meeting, *assembly*; reunion, get-together, social; reception, at home; entertainment, *amusement*; singsong, camp fire; party; housewarming, house party, social meal, feast, banquet; communion, love feast, agape, *ritual act*; coffee morning, tea party, bun fight, cocktail party, picnic, barbecue, bottle party, *festivity*; dance, ball, hop, disco.

social round, social whirl, season, social entertainment; visiting, calling; stay, visit, call, visiting terms, haunting, *friendship*; engagement; rendezvous, assignation, date, meeting place, club, pub, local, *focus*.

sociable person, active member, caller, visitor; convivial person, good fellow; good mixer, good company; social success, catch, lion, *favourite*; jolly person, boon companion, club woman; good neighbour, *friend*; hostess, host, guest; parasite; social butterfly; socialite, ornament of society, social climber.

Adj. *sociable*, gregarious, social, outgoing, fond of company; companionable, affable, chatty, fond of talk; cosy; neighbourly, matey, *friendly*; hospitable, cordial, warm, hearty; convivial, festive, jolly, jovial, *merry*; lively; urbane, *courteous*; easy.

welcomed, entertained; welcome; popular, liked.

Vb. *be sociable*, enjoy society, like company, *star*; love a party; hobnob, mix with, *be friendly*; mix well, be a good mixer, get around, know how to live, gate-crash; have fun, *amuse oneself*; get together, make it a party, club together, go Dutch, share, go shares, *participate*; take pot luck, *eat*; *drink*; pledge, *toast*; carouse, *revel*; make oneself welcome, make oneself at home; relax, unbend, *repose*; chat to, *converse*; date, make a date; make friendly overtures, *befriend*; introduce oneself; write to, *correspond*.

visit, see people, go visiting, sojourn, stay, weekend; call; leave a card.

be *hospitable*, keep open house, *be liberal*; invite, have round, be at home to, receive; welcome, welcome with open arms, hug, embrace, *greet*; preside; do proud, *celebrate*; have company, entertain, *feed*; give a party, *revel*; accept, provide entertainment, *provide*.

Adv. *sociably*.

878 Unsociability. Seclusion

N. *unsociability*; autism; refusal to mix, keeping oneself to oneself; home life, domesticity; singleness; *parsimony*; distance, lonely pride, *pride*; cut, cut direct, *discourtesy*; silence, lack of conversation; boycott, *exclusion*; blacklist.

seclusion, privacy, private world; island universe, *star*; *quietude*; home life, domesticity; solitude; retreat; confinement; division, *separation*; segregation, quarantine, exile, *exclusion*; reserve, reservation, ghetto, native quarter, harem; gaol, *prison*; godforsaken hole, back of beyond; island, desert, wilderness; hideaway; den, study, sanctum, cloister, cell, hermitage, *retreat*; ivory tower, private quarters, shell; backwater.

solitary, unsocial person, iceberg; lonely person, lonely heart; loner, lone wolf, rogue elephant; island; introvert; stay-at-home; troglodyte; recluse, anchorite, hermit; pillar monk; maroon, castaway, *derelict*.

outcast, pariah, leper, outsider; outcaste, untouchable; expatriate, alien, *foreigner*; exile, deportee, evacuee, refugee, outlaw, bandit; vagabond, *wanderer*; waif, stray, derelict; reject, *rubbish*.

Adj. *unsociable*, unsocial, antisocial, introverted, morose; foreign, *extraneous*; stay-at-home, quiet, domestic; inhospitable, forbidding, hostile; distant, aloof, unbending, stiff; stand-offish, haughty; frosty, icy, cold, *sullen*; close, silent, *taciturn*; cool, impersonal, *indifferent*; solitary, lonely, lone, *alone*; shy, retiring, withdrawn, afraid of company; wild, feral; celibate.

friendless, forlorn, desolate; lonely, lonesome, solitary; without company, *alone*; sent to Coventry.

secluded, private, *latent*; quiet, lonely; remote, godforsaken, unfrequented; unseen, *unknown*; desert, desolate, empty.

Vb. *be unsociable*, keep oneself to oneself, shun company, talk to nobody; go it alone, play a lone hand; immure oneself,

remain private, stand aloof, *avoid*; stay at home, bury oneself, vegetate, *be quiescent*; retire, make a retreat.

make *unwelcome*, *disapprove*; repel, keep at arm's length, make one keep his distance, ignore, cut, cut dead, *be rude*; cold-shoulder; rebuff; expel, *eject*; boycott, send to Coventry, blacklist, blackball, *exclude*; refuse to meet, refuse to mix with, have nothing to do with, *avoid*, excommunicate, banish, exile, outlaw, ban, *punish*.

seclude, island, isolate, quarantine, segregate; confine, *imprison*.

879 Courtesy

N. *courtesy*, chivalry, gallantry; deference, *respect*; consideration, *humility*; civility, manners, good behaviour, good breeding, *good taste*; diplomacy; *formality*, amenity, kindness, *benevolence*; easy temper, good humour, complaisance, common touch, social tact; smooth tongue, *flattery*.

courteous *act*, act of courtesy, polite act, graceful gesture, courtesy, civility, favour, charity, kindness, *kind act*; soft answer; compliment; kind words, *endearment*; introduction, presentation, welcome, reception, invitation; recognition, nod, salutation, salute, greeting, smile, kiss, hug, squeeze, handshake, *respects*; salaam, kowtow, bow, *obeisance*; terms of courtesy, respects, regards, duty, love; farewell, *valediction*.

Adj. *courteous*, chivalrous, generous, *noble*; courtly, gallant, correct, *formal*; polite, civil, urbane, gentle, ladylike, *well-bred*; gracious, *humble*; *respectful*; anxious to please, *attentive*; obliging, complaisant, kind; sweet; agreeable, suave, bland, smooth, well-spoken; obsequious, *servile*.

amiable, nice, sweet; affable, friendly, *sociable*; considerate, kind; inoffensive, harmless, *innocent*; gentle, easy, mild, *lenient*; unruffled; good, *obedient*; pacific, peaceable, *peaceful*.

Vb. *be courteous*, show courtesy, treat with deference, *respect*; give one his or her title, call sir, call madam; oblige, *aid*; condescend, *be humble*; notice, *be attentive*; conciliate, speak fair, *pacify*; make oneself agreeable, be all things to all men; return a soft answer, *be patient*; become courteous, express regrets, *atone*.

pay *one's respects*; pay compliments, *flatter*; drink to, pledge, *toast*; homage, kneel; *show respect*; honour, crown, wreathe; garland, chair, *celebrate*.

greet, flag, *signal*; accost, *approach*; acknowledge, *notice*; hail, *vociferate*; nod, wave, smile, blow a kiss; bid good morning, *speak to*; salute, make salutation; uncover; bend, bow, bob, duck, salaam; make obeisance, prostrate oneself, kowtow, *stoop*; advance to meet, *show respect*; escort, *accompany*; make a salute, present arms, parade, *celebrate*; receive, welcome, welcome home, *be sociable*; welcome with open arms, *be pleased*; embrace, hug, kiss, *caress*; usher, present, introduce, *admit*.

Adv. *courteously*, with respect, with all due deference.

880 Discourtesy

N. discourtesy, bad manners, failure of courtesy, want of chivalry, lack of manners, scant courtesy; misconduct; want of consideration.

rudeness, acerbity, acrimony, asperity; roughness; inattention; short answer; sarcasm, ridicule; unparliamentary language, rude words, scurrility; rebuff, insult, indignity; sauce, lip, cheek; shouting; black look, scowl, frown; a discourtesy, piece of bad manners.

rude person; savage, barbarian, brute, lout, boor, loudmouth, insolent person; curmudgeon, crab, bear; sourpuss, malcontent.

Adj. discourteous; unceremonious, impolite, rude; unmannerly, uncouth, beastly, savage, barbarian, ill-bred; insolent, impudent; cheeky, saucy, pert, forward, impertinent; unpleasant, disagreeable; cool, indifferent; cavalier, airy, breezy, inconsiderate.

ungracious, grim, serious; gruff, sullen; peevish, testy, irascible; difficult, surly, churlish, unsociable; grumbling; rough, rugged, harsh, brutal, severe; bluff, free, frank, blunt; brusque, short, concise; tart, sharp, biting, pungent; abusive; offensive, truculent.

Vb. be rude, want manners, flout etiquette; be artless; display bad manners, show discourtesy, be insolent; be beastly to, snub, cold-shoulder, cut, ignore, look right through, cut dead; eject; cause offence, huff; insult, abuse; take liberties, make free with, make bold; stare, ogle, gaze; make one blush, shame; shout, interrupt; get angry; curse, swear, damn, cuss; snarl, growl, frown, scowl, lour, pout, sulk, be sullen.

Adv. impolitely, discourteously, like a boor.

881 Congratulation

N. congratulation, compliments; happy returns; salute, toast; welcome, official reception, celebration; thanks, gratitude.

Adj. congratulatory, complimentary; triumphal, welcoming.

Vb. congratulate, felicitate, compliment; wish one joy, give one joy, wish many happy returns; sanction a triumph, accord an ovation, give three cheers, clap, applaud; fete, mob, rush, lionize, celebrate; congratulate oneself, be pleased; thank Heaven, be grateful.

882 Love

N. love, affection, friendship, charity; agape, true love, real thing; natural affection; possessive love; conjugal love; sentiment, feeling; kindness, benevolence; Platonic love, friendship; mutual love, mutual affection, mutual attraction, sympathy, fellow feeling, understanding; predilection, tendency; preference, choice; fancy, caprice; attachment, devotion, loyalty; courtly love, gallantry; moral sensibility; power of love, fascination, sorcery; desire; lust, libido; regard, respect; admiration, wonder; dawn of love, crush; madness; worship; romantic love, passion, fire of love, enthusiasm, rapture, ecstasy, transport, excitable state; abnormal affection; love psychology, narcissism.

lovableness, popularity, gift of pleasing; charm, fascination, appeal; coquetry; sentimental value.

love affair; romance; flirtation, amour, entanglement; free love; intrigue, seduction, illicit love; something between them; course of love; engagement, marriage; broken engagement, broken romance, broken heart.

love-making, endearment; courtship; pursuit of love, coquetry; gallantry.

love-nest, abode of love, bower, Bower of Bliss; honeymoon cottage, nuptial chamber; harem, seraglio.

lover, love, sweetheart; young man, boyfriend; swain, beau, gallant, spark, cavalier, squire, escort, date; steady; suitor, follower, captive, admirer; aficionado, fan, devoted following, fan club; gigolo, lady-killer; paramour; flirt, coquette; vamp.

loved one, beloved, love, true love, soul mate, darling; intimate, close friend; favoured suitor, lucky man, spouse; conquest, girlfriend, girl, bird, honey, baby, sweetie; angel, princess; sweetheart, valentine, flame, idol, hero; heartthrob, dream man, dream girl; favourite, mistress, concubine, kept woman.

lovers, loving couple, love-birds; starcrossed lovers.

love god, goddess of love, Venus; Cupid, blind boy.

love emblem, turtledove; Cupid-s bow, Cupid's dart golden arrow; bleeding heart, bjroken heart, love token.

Adj. loving, sisterly; loyal, disinterested; making love; affectionate, demonstrative; tender, motherly, conjugal; gallant, romantic, sentimental, lovesick; lovelorn, dejected; fond of, fond; possessive, jealous; devoted, flirtatious, capricious; amatory, amorous, ardent, passionate, fervent; lustful.

enamoured, inclined to; struck with, caught, hooked; infatuated, besotted, crazy about, crazy; happy; ecstatic, excited.

lovable, congenial, sympathetic; winsome, amiable; sweet, divine, adorable; lovely, graceful, good-looking, beautiful; attractive, seductive; prepossessing, appealing, engaging, endearing, irresistible; desirable; enchanting; beloved, dear, darling, pet, fancy, favourite.

erotic, aphrodisiac, erogenous; sexy, impure; amatory, excited.

Vb. love, like, care, quite like, be partial to; be fond of; be susceptible, have a heart, bear love towards, hold dear, cherish, cling to, embrace; appreciate, value, prize, treasure, regard, admire, revere, respect; adore, worship; burn with love, make love, unite with; make much of, spoil, pet, fondle, caress.

be in love, burn, sweat, faint, die; burn with love, glow with ardour, flame with passion, love to distraction, be insane; take a fancy to, take a shine to, take to, warm to, dig; desire; form an attachment, get infatuated, have it bad; go mad; woo, sue, sigh, court; chase, pursue; honeymoon, wed.

excite love, arouse desire, cause desire; warm, inflame, heat; rouse, stir, flutter, enrapture, excite; dazzle, charm, enchant, fascinate, bewitch; allure, draw, attract; make oneself attractive; lure, bait, seduce, tempt; flirt, coquette, philander; toy, vamp, caress; smile, leer, make eyes, ogle, wink, court; attract

notice; make a hit, *make mad*; make a
conquest, captivate, *subjugate*; catch,
wed; be amiable, make oneself a favourite; steal every heart; curry favour, *flatter*.

Adv. *affectionately*, kindly; madly.

883 Hatred

N. *hatred*, hate; revulsion of feeling, disillusion; aversion, antipathy, allergy, nausea,
dislike; intense dislike, repugnance,
abomination; disfavour, displeasure (see
odium); alienation, *dissension*; hostility,
antagonism, *enmity*; animosity, ill feeling, bad blood, acrimony, rancour,
resentment; malice, ill will, evil eye, spite,
grudge; *envy*; wrath, *anger*; hymn of hate,
malediction; scowl, snap, snarl; phobia,
anti-Semitism, racialism, colour prejudice, *prejudice*.

odium, disfavour, *disapprobation*; discredit,
bad odour, black books, *disrepute*.

hateful *object*; bitter pill; abomination; filth;
enemy; bugbear, Dr Fell; pest, menace,
good riddance, *bane*; rotter, *cad*; heretic,
blackleg; scab.

Adj. *hating*, loveless; set against; averse,
abhorrent, hostile, *inimical*; envious,
malicious, full of malice, malignant,
malevolent; bitter, rancorous; full of hate,
implacable; vindictive; virulent.

hateful, odious, invidious, obnoxious,
beastly, nasty, horrid; abhorrent, loathsome, abominable; accursed, execrable,
cursed; offensive, repellent, nauseous,
revolting; bitter, sharp, *sour*.

hated; loveless; lovelorn.

Vb. *hate*, bear hatred; loathe, abominate,
detest, abhor; *avoid*; recoil at, *recoil*; can't
bear, can't stand, *dislike*; find loathsome,
find obnoxious; refuse, *reject*; spurn, *despise*; execrate, hold accursed, denounce,
curse; bear malice, *be malevolent*; feel
envy, *envy*; bear a grudge, *resent*; scowl,
growl, snap, snarl, *be sullen*; insult, be
insolent; turn to hate.

excite hate, grate, jar, *repel*; disgust, nauseate, *cause dislike*; shock, horrify, *incur
blame*; antagonize, destroy goodwill,
estrange, alienate, sow dissension, create
bad blood, turn friendship, turn all to
hate; poison, embitter, exacerbate, *aggravate*; exasperate, incense, *enrage*.

884 Endearment

N. *endearment*, blandishments, compliments, *flattery*; loving words, pet name;
affectionate behaviour; osculation;
caress, embrace, clasp, hug, cuddle,
squeeze, pressure, salute, kiss, smacker;
nibble, bite; stroke, tickle, slap, pat,
pinch, nip, *touch*; familiarity, advances,
pass.

wooing; play, lovemaking; wink, glad eye,
come hither look, ogle, amorous glance,
fond look, sigh; flirtation, coquetry, gallantry, courtship, suit, advances, *love-
making*; serenade, love song, love lyric,
amorous ditty; love letter; love poem,
sonnet; proposal, engagement, *marriage*.

love *token*, favour, ribbon, glove; ring, valentine, love letter; posy; arrow, heart,
love emblem; tattoo.

Adj. *caressing*, clinging, demonstrative,
affectionate, *loving*; soppy; flirtatious.

Vb. *pet*, pamper, spoil, spoonfeed, mother,
smother, kill with kindness; cosset,
coddle; make much of; treasure, *love*;

cherish, foster, *safeguard*; nurse, lap,
rock, cradle, baby; sing to; coax,
wheedle, *flatter*.

caress, love, fondle, dandle; play with,
stroke, smooch, pat, paw; kiss; embrace,
enfold, lap; clasp, hug, hold one tight,
cling, *retain*; squeeze, press, cuddle;
snuggle, nestle, nuzzle, nibble; play,
romp, wanton, toy, trifle, dally, spark;
make love, spoon, pet, neck, snog,
smooch; vamp, *excite love*; fawn, rub
oneself against; (of a crowd) mob, rush,
snatch at.

court, make advances; make eyes, ogle, leer,
eye, *gaze*; become familiar, get fresh,
make a pass; gallivant, philander, flirt,
coquette, *excite love*; run after, chase,
pursue; squire, escort, *accompany*; hang
round, *follow*; date, make a date; go
steady; sue, woo, pay court to, pay suit
to; serenade, caterwaul; sigh, pine, languish, *love*; propose, propose marriage,
become engaged, make a match, *wed*.

885 Darling. Favourite

N. *darling*, dear, my dear; dear friend; dear-
est, dear one, only one; love, beloved;
heart, sweetheart, fancy, valentine; sweetie, sugar, honey; precious, jewel, treasure; angel, angel child, cherub; poppet,
moppet; pet, lamb, chick, chicken,
duck.

favourite, darling; cosset; jewel; good man,
good chap, fine fellow, marvellous
woman; brick, sport, first choice, front
runner, top seed, only possible choice;
boast, pride; national figure, favourite
son, Grand Old Man, *person of repute*;
idol, hero, golden girl or boy; media
personality, star, general favourite, cynosure; pinup girl, *a beauty*; centre of
attraction, cynosure, *attraction*; catch
lion.

886 Resentment. Anger

N. *resentment*, displeasure, *discontent*; ill
humour; rancour; slow burn; umbrage,
offence, huff, tiff, pique; bile, spleen, gall
acerbity, acrimony, bitter resentment
hate, *hatred*; animosity, grudge, bone to
pick, crow to pluck, *enmity*; spite
revenge; malice; hot blood; cause o
offence, red rag to a bull, sore point
irritation; provocation, insult, affront
last straw, *indignity*; wrong, injury, *injustice*.

anger, irritation; dudgeon, wrath; rage
fury, passion, *excitable state*; temper
tantrum, tizzy, paddy, fume, fret, pet, fi
of temper, burst of anger, outburst
explosion, storm, stew, ferment, taking
paroxysm; rampage; shout, roar; angr
look, glare, frown, scowl; growl, snarl
bark, bite, snap, asperity; warmth, heat
high words, *quarrel*; *indignity*; fisticuffs
fight.

Adj. *resentful*, stung, miffed; stung, hurt
sore; pained, hurt; warm, indignant; bit
ter, full of hate, rancorous, virulent; ful
of spleen, *malevolent*; full of revenge
vindictive; jealous, green with envy, *env*
ous; grudging.

angry, stern, *serious*; impatient, cross
waxy, ratty, wild, mad, livid; irate; stung
hot; angry with, mad at; indignant
beside oneself with rage; shirty; warm
burning; speechless, crying with rage
savage, violent, *furious*; apoplectic, rabid
berserk; roaring, glaring, *sullen*; red wit

anger, bloodshot, red; pale with anger; fierce, irascible.

b. resent, find intolerable, be unable to stomach, suffer; feel, mind, feel resentment; take amiss, take ill; take offence, take umbrage, take exception to, quarrel; jib, get sore; burn, smoulder, sizzle, simmer; express resentment, be malevolent; take to heart, let it rankle, remember an injury, cherish a grudge, bear malice; go green with envy, envy.

t angry, get cross, get wild, get mad; get sore, go spare; kindle, grow warm, grow heated, colour, redden, flush with anger; take fire, ramp; bridle, bristle; lose patience, forget oneself; throw a tantrum, stamp, shout; let fly, explode; see red, go berserk, go mad, be excitable.

e angry, interrupt, chafe, fret, fume, fuss, flounce, dance, ramp, stamp, champ; create, perform, make a scene, make a row, rampage; turn nasty; rage, rant, roar, bellow, bluster, storm, thunder, fulminate, be loud; look like thunder, look black, glare, glower, frown, scowl, growl, snarl, be sullen; spit, snap; weep with rage, shake with passion, swell with fury, stamp with rage, dance with fury, be excited; let fly, be violent.

uff, pique, sting, nettle, rankle, smart; wound, hurt; antagonize, get across, give umbrage, offend, cause offence, embitter, excite hate; cause dislike; affront, insult, outrage.

rage, upset, discompose, ruffle, irritate, rile; annoy, vex, pester, bug, bother, trouble; do it to annoy, tease, bait, needle, torment; bite, fret, nag, gnaw; exasperate; push too far; anger, incense, infuriate, madden, drive mad; goad, sting, taunt, invite a quarrel; make one see red; cause resentment, embitter, poison; exasperate, aggravate; embroil, set at loggerheads.

dv. angrily, bitterly; in anger, in fury, in the treat of the moment.

87 Irascibility

. irascibility; asperity, gall, bile, vinegar; moral sensibility; readiness to take offence; temperament; uncertain temper, hot temper, limited patience; hot blood, inflammable nature; bad temper.

rew, scold, fishwife; termagant, virago, vixen, battleaxe, harridan, fury; Tartar, hornet; bear, misanthrope; mad dog; fiery person, redhead.

dj. irascible, impatient, choleric, irritable, peppery, testy, crusty, peevish, crotchety, cranky, cross-grained; prickly, touchy, thin-skinned, sensitive; inflammable, like tinder; hot-blooded, fierce, fiery, passionate, excitable; quick, warm, hasty, trigger-happy, rash; shrewish, vixenish; petulant, cantankerous, querulous; bitter, sour; liverish; scratchy, snappy, snappish, waspish; tart, sharp, short; uptight, edgy; fractious, fretful, moody, temperamental, changeable; gruff, grumpy, ratty, like a bear with a sore head; cross, stroppy, sullen.

b. be irascible, have a temper; snort, bark, snap, bite, be sullen; get angry.

88 Sullenness

. sullenness; ill humour; vinegar; pout, grimace, discontent; discourtesy; ill temper; spleen, bile, liver; dumps, grouch, temperament; melancholy; black look, glare, glower, lour, frown, scowl; snort, growl, snarl, snap, bite.

Adj. sullen, forbidding, ugly; saturnine, overcast, cloudy, dark; stern, grim, serious; cross, unsociable; surly, morose, crabbed, crusty, cross-grained; difficult; snappish, shrewish, vixenish, cantankerous, quarrelsome, stroppy; refractory, disobedient; grumbling, grumpy; acid, tart, sour; gruff, rough, abrupt, brusque, discourteous; temperamental, moody; jaundiced; blue, melancholy; petulant, peevish, shirty, irascible; sultry.

Vb. be sullen, gloom, glower, glare, lour; look black, scowl, frown; spit; snap, snarl, growl, snort; make a face, grimace, pout, sulk, be unsociable; mope, be dejected; grouch, grouse, carp, crab, complain, grumble, mutter, smoulder.

Adv. sullenly, with a bad grace.

889 Marriage

N. marriage, matrimony, one flesh; wedlock, wedded state, state of matrimony, wedded bliss; match, union, alliance; conjugal knot, nuptial bond, marriage tie, marriage bed, life together; banns, marriage certificate, marriage lines; marriage god, Hymen.

type of marriage, monogamy, bigamy, polygamy, polyandry; second marriage; marriage of convenience; mixed marriage, mixture; misalliance, free union, free love; compulsory marriage, forcible wedlock, shotgun wedding.

wedding, match, engagement; ring; marriage ceremony; wedding service, nuptial mass, nuptial benediction, Christian rite; church wedding, civil marriage, runaway match; solemn wedding, torch of Hymen, nuptial song; wedding day; marriage feast, wedding breakfast, reception; honeymoon; silver wedding, wedding anniversary, special day.

bridal party, best man, maid or matron of honour, bridesmaid, page; attendant, usher.

spouse; marriage partner, man, wife; married couple; bride, young matron; bridegroom; consort, partner, mate, helpmate, better half, affinity; married man, husband, man, old man; henpecked husband; married woman, wedded wife, lady, matron; woman, old dutch, rib, grey mare, Duchess of Fife, joy of my life; squaw; faithful spouse; second husband, second wife, common-law husband or wife.

polygamist, Mormon; bigamist.

matchmaker, go-between; marriage bureau, personal column; marriage guidance counsellor, mediator.

nubility, marriageable age; good match, suitable party, welcome suitor, lover.

Adj. married; wedded, united, made one; just married, newly-wed.

marriageable, nubile, of age, eligible, suitable; engaged, bespoke.

matrimonial, marital, connubial; premarital; nuptial; conjugal, matronly.

Vb. marry, match, mate; make a match, betroth, espouse; join, couple, splice, hitch.

wed, marry, espouse; take a wife, find a husband; court; get married, mate with, marry oneself to, unite oneself with, accept a proposal, become engaged; say 'I do', be made one, unite with; mate, couple, honeymoon, cohabit; marry well, make a good match; make a bad match, repent at leisure; make a love match;

elope; contract marriage, make an honest woman of, go through a form of marriage; marry again; commit bigamy; intermarry.

Adv. *matrimonially.*

890 Celibacy

N. *celibacy,* singleness, single state; maidenhood, *purity.*

celibate, bachelor; confirmed bachelor; enemy of marriage, misogynist, *misanthrope;* monastic, *monk;* hermit, solitary; monastic order, *holy orders.*

spinster, bachelor girl; debutante; maid, maiden; maiden aunt, old maid; *nun;* Amazon.

Adj. *unwedded;* single; free, *independent;* maidenly, virgin, virginal, *pure;* spinster; bachelor; celibate, *monastic.*

Vb. *live single;* refuse marriage, *be free;* live like a hermit, *be unsociable;* take orders.

891 Divorce. Widowhood

N. *divorce,* dissolution of marriage; divorce decree, decree nisi, decree absolute; separation; consanguinity, affinity; living apart, separate maintenance, alimony; broken marriage, broken engagement; divorce court, divorce case; divorcee, nor wife nor maid; corespondent; single parent.

widowhood; widows' weeds *formal dress;* widower, widow, widow woman, relict; dowager, dowager duchess; war widow, grass widower, Merry Widow.

Adj. *divorced,* separated, living apart.

widowed, husbandless, wifeless.

Vb. *divorce,* separate, live apart, desert, *relinquish; disunite;* file a divorce suit; get a divorce; put asunder, dissolve marriage, grant a divorce, pronounce a decree absolute.

be *widowed.*

widow, bereave, make a widow or widower.

892 Benevolence

N. *benevolence,* good will; benignity, kindly disposition, heart of gold; bonhomie; milk of human kindness, goodness of nature, warmth of heart, kindness, charity, *love;* godly love, fraternal feeling, *friendship;* consideration; understanding, concern, fellow feeling, empathy, sympathy, *feeling;* condolence, *pity;* decent feeling, humanity, humanitarianism, *philanthropy; utilitarianism, sociology;* hospitality, generosity, magnanimity, *liberality;* tolerance, toleration; mercy, *forgiveness;* God's love, grace of God; blessing, benediction.

kind *act,* kindness, favour, service; good deed, charity, relief, alms; good offices, good turn, helpful act, *aid;* labour of love, *voluntary work.*

kind *person,* Christian; good sort, good neighbour, good Samaritan, well-wisher, friend; patron; idealist, do-gooder, philanthropist.

Adj. *benevolent,* well meant, well-intentioned, *friendly;* to oblige; good of one, so good of; sympathetic; kindly disposed, benign, kindly, kind, good, human, decent, Christian; affectionate, *loving;* fatherly, paternal; motherly, maternal; fraternal; sisterly; good-humoured, good-natured, easy, sweet,

gentle, *amiable;* merciful, *forgiving;* to[l]erant, *lax;* humane, considerate, *lenien[t]* soft-hearted, tender; pitiful; genial, ho[s]pitable, *sociable;* bounteous, bountif[ul] *liberal;* generous, *disinterested;* benef[i]cent, charitable, humanitarian, doir[g] good; obliging, accommodating, helpf[ul] complaisant, gracious, gallant, chiva[l]rous, *courteous.*

Vb. *be benevolent;* show concern; unde[r]stand; *forgive;* wish well, bless, bestow benediction; bear good will, mean we[ll]; look with a favourable eye, favour; ben[e]fit, *do good;* be a good Samaritan, do [a] good turn, render a service, oblige, *ai[d];* reform, *make better.*

philanthropize, do good, go about doin[g] good, do good works, have a social con[cern?] science, show public spirit, care; g[et] involved, *be active;* reform, improv[e] visit, nurse, *minister to;* mother, pet.

Adv. *benevolently,* kindly; to oblige.

893 Malevolence

N. *malevolence,* ill will, *enmity;* evil inten[t] bad intention, cloven hoof; spite, ga[ll] despite, malice, malice aforethought; ba[d] blood, hate, *hatred;* venom, *ban[e]* acrimony, acerbity; rancour, splee[n] *resentment;* unholy joy, *envy;* evil ey[e] spell.

inhumanity, lack of humanity, lack of co[n]cern; lack of charity; hardness of hea[rt] heart of marble, heart of stone; *hardnes[s]* cruelty, barbarity; ferocity; sadism; va[n]dalism, *destruction.*

cruel *act,* cruel conduct; ill usage, *misus[e]* disservice, ill turn; foul play, bloodshe[d] *violence;* excess; act of inhumanity, inh[u]man deed, atrocity, outrage; cruelty, to[r]ture, barbarity; murder, *homicide;* ma[ss] murder, genocide, *slaughter.*

Adj. *malevolent,* meaning harm; il[l] natured, churlish, *sullen;* nasty, blood[y] minded, bitchy, cussed, *wilful;* maliciou[s] catty; mischievous, baleful, malig[n] malignant; vicious, venomous, *dead[ly]* full of spite; jealous, *envious;* disloya[l] treacherous; bitter, rancorous, impla[c]able, merciless, *pitiless;* vindictive; ho[s]tile, fell, *inimical;* intolerant.

maleficent, hurtful; poisonous, venomou[s] virulent, caustic; working evil, *bad.*

unkind, ill-natured, *sullen;* unchristia[n] cold, hostile, *inimical;* inhospitab[le] *unsociable;* ungenerous, uncharitab[le] mean, nasty; rude, harsh, gruff, beastl[y] *ungracious;* unfeeling, insensib[le] unmoved, *impassive;* stern, *severe;* toug[h] hardboiled, hardbitten, *hard;* inhuma[n] unnatural.

cruel, grim, fell; steely, hard-hearted, ca[l]lous, cold-blooded; heartless, ruthles[s] merciless, *pitiless;* bloodthirsty, *murde[r]ous;* bloody, *violent;* savage, extrem[e] outrageous; feral, tigerish; unnatur[al] subhuman; brutal, rough, trucule[nt] fierce, ferocious; savage, barbarous, wil[d] inhuman, fiendish, demoniacal, satan[ic] hellish, infernal.

Vb. *be malevolent,* bear malice, cheris[h] grudge, *hate;* show ill will; show env[y] *envy;* spite, do one a bad turn; *be pitile[ss]* gloat; bully, maltreat, *ill-treat;* mole[st] hurt, injure, annoy, *harm;* malign; teas[e] harry, hound, persecute, torture, oppre[ss] raven, *slaughter;* rankle, fester, poiso[n] create havoc, blight, blast, *lay wast[e]* bewitch.

Adv. *malevolently,* with evil intent; spit[e]

fully, out of spite.

poor relief, benefit, dole; Welfare State; community service, social service, social work, good works.

patriotism, public spirit; nationalism, chauvinism, my country right or wrong; Zionism.

philanthropist, *benefactor*; humanitarian, do-gooder, social worker, *kind person*; community service worker, Peace Corps, *volunteer*; champion, knight, knight errant; Messiah, *leader*; missionary, person with a mission, dedicated soul; idealist, flower people, *visionary*; utilitarian, Utopian; cosmopolitan, internationalist.

patriot, lover of one's country; nationalist.

Adj. philanthropic, humanitarian, humane, human; charitable; enlightened, liberal; cosmopolitan, international; *disinterested*; visionary, dedicated; utilitarian.

patriotic; loyal, true, true-blue.

Vb. be charitable.

Adv. pro bono publico.

894 Malediction

N. *malediction*, curse; evil eye, *spell*; denunciation, *threat*; onslaught, *attack*; thunder; ban; bell, book and candle.

scurrility, vulgarity; bad language; naughty word, expletive, swearword, oath, swear, damn, curse, cuss, invective, vituperation, abuse, mutual abuse, stormy exchange; vain abuse, empty curse, more bark than bite, *threat*; aspersion, reflection, slander, *calumny*; cheek, sauce; epithet, insult, *indignity*; scorn, *contempt*; *reproach*.

Adj. cursing, damning; profane, unparliamentary, scurrilous, ribald, *vulgar*; blue; abusive, vitriolic.

cursed; accursed, execrable; under a spell.

Vb. curse, bewitch; wish ill, *be malevolent*; wish one joy of; curse with bell, book and candle; execrate; fulminate, thunder against, *reprove*; denounce, *accuse*; excommunicate, damn, *condemn*; confound, send to blazes; abuse, vituperate, revile, rail, chide, heap abuse, *reprobate*; throw mud.

cuss, curse, swear, damn, blast; blaspheme; swear like a trooper; slang, abuse, blackguard, *reprobate*; rail at, scold.

Int. curse a curse on! a plaque on! woe to! woe betide! ill betide! confusion seize! confound it! devil take it! blast! damn! dang! darn! drat! hang! the deuce! the dickens!

895 Threat

N. *threat*, menace; *malediction*; challenge, dare, *defiance*; blackmail, *demand*; battle cry, war whoop, war of nerves; deterrent, big stick, *weapon*; black cloud, *omen*; secret weapon, *pitfall*; impending danger, sword of Damocles, *danger*; danger signal, fair warning, *warning*; bluster, idle threat, *boast*; bark, growl, snarl.

Adj. threatening; defiant, *boastful*; grumbling, *sullen*; portentous, ominous, foreboding; *impending*; ready to spring, *angry*; abusive; deterrent; nasty, unpleasant.

Vb. threaten, menace, blackmail, *demand*; hijack, hold to ransom; frighten, deter, intimidate, bully, *frighten*; roar, bellow, vociferate; fulminate, thunder, *curse*; bark, talk big, bluster, *boast*; shake, wave, flaunt, *brandish*; make a pass, *defy*; snarl, growl, mutter, *be sullen*; bristle, spit, grow nasty, *get angry*; hold at gunpoint; cover, *aim*; gather, mass, lour, hover; bode ill, presage, disaster, promise trouble, spell danger, *predict*; serve notice, caution, forewarn, *warn*; breathe revenge.

Adv. threateningly, menacingly, on pain of death.

896 Philanthropy

N. *philanthropy*, humanitarianism, humanity, *benevolence*; humanism, internationalism; altruism; idealism, *virtue*; universal benevolence, utilitarianism; common good, socialism, communism; chivalry; dedication, nonconformist conscience, good works, mission; Holy War, jihad, crusade, campaign, cause, voluntary agency, charitable foundation, charity, *aid*.

sociology, social science, social engineering;

897 Misanthropy

N. *misanthropy*, hatred of mankind; inhumanity; egotism.

misanthrope, misogynist; cynic; unsocial animal, *solitary*; bear, malcontent.

Adj. misanthropic, inhuman, antisocial, unsociable.

Vb. *misanthropize*, become a misanthrope, lose faith in human kind.

Adv. misanthropically, cynically.

898 Benefactor

N. benefactor, *philanthropist*; Lady Bountiful, Father Christmas; guardian angel, good genius, *protector*; founder, supporter, *patron*; *patriot*; saviour, redeemer, *deliverance*; champion; Good Samaritan, *kind person*; good neighbour, *friend*; saint, *good person*.

899 Evildoer

N. *evildoer*, malefactor; villain, blackguard, bad lot; scamp, monkey, imp of mischief, little devil, holy terror; gossip; traitor, wrecker, Vandal, Hun, iconoclast, *destroyer*; incendiary.

ruffian, blackguard, rogue, scoundrel, *knave*; lout, hooligan, hoodlum, *low fellow*; yobbo, punk; bully, terror; rough, tough, rowdy, ugly customer, bruiser, thug; bravo, desperado, assassin, cutthroat, hatchet man, gunman, butcher; genocide; plague, scourge, *bane*; petty tyrant, *tyrant*; brute, beast, savage, barbarian, caveman; cannibal, head-hunter; homicidal maniac, *madman*.

offender, black sheep, *bad person*; suspect; culprit, guilty person, law-breaker; criminal, villain, crook, malefactor, felon; delinquent; recidivist, lag, convict, jailbird; lifer; probationer; mobster, gangster, racketeer; housebreaker, *thief*; forger; bloodsucker; outlaw, public enemy, *enemy*; criminal world, underworld, Mafia.

hellhag, fiend, devil incarnate; bitch, virago, *shrew*; fury, harpy, siren; ogre, witch, vampire, werewolf, *monster*.

noxious *animal*, brute, beast, beast of prey, predator; tiger, man-eater, wolf, jackal, fox; kite, vulture, *bird*; snake, serpent, viper, *reptile*; salamander; scorpion, wasp, hornet; pest, locust, *insect*; rat, *bane*; wild cat, mad dog, rogue elephant.

900 Pity

N. pity; remorse, compunction, *regret*; charity, compassion, humanity, *benevolence*; soft heart; melting mood, *sorrow*; *dejection*; sympathy, empathy, understanding, fellow feeling (see *condolence*); self-pity.

condolence, sympathetic grief, sympathy, fellow feeling; comfort, *relief*; professional condolence, keen, wake, lament.

mercy, quarter, grace; second chance; clemency, forbearance, longsuffering, *forgiveness*; light sentence, *penalty*; *acquittal*.

Adj. pitying, sympathetic, understanding, merciful, clement, full of mercy, *lenient*; melting, tender, tender-hearted, soft, soft-hearted; weak, *lax*; easily touched; disposed to mercy, *forgiving*; humane, charitable; forbearing, *patient*.

pitiable, pitiful, piteous, pathetic, heart-rending; challenging sympathy.

Vb. pity, show compassion, show pity; feel with, *participate*; sorrow, grieve, *lament*; console, comfort, *cheer*; have pity, have compassion, melt, thaw, relent, *forgive*.

show *mercy*, spare, give quarter; commute (a sentence); pardon, amnesty; forgive; be slow to anger, forbear; give one a break, give one a second chance, *be lenient*; relent, unbend, show consideration; be cruel to be kind.

ask *mercy*, cry mercy; excite pity, move to compassion, propitiate, disarm, melt, thaw, soften, *pacify*.

Int. alas! poor thing! for pity's sake! for mercy's sake! for the love of God! have mercy! have a heart!

901 Pitilessness

N. pitilessness, lack of pity; rigour; hardness of heart, *inhumanity*; *hardness*; pound of flesh; short shrift.

Adj. pitiless, unfeeling, *impassive*; unmoved; hard-hearted, callous, tough, *hard*; harsh, intolerant, *severe*; brutal, *cruel*; merciless, ruthless, heartless; indisposed to mercy, unrelenting, relentless, inflexible, inexorable, implacable; vindictive.

Vb. be pitiless, turn a deaf ear; spare none; be deaf to appeal; persecute, *be severe*; take one's revenge, *avenge*.

902 Gratitude

N. gratitude, grateful heart, feeling of obligation, grateful acceptance, appreciation.

thanks, thankyou; thanksgiving, eucharist, benediction, blessing; *celebration*; grace; thankyou letter; credit, credit title, recognition, full praise; tribute, *praise*; parting present, tip, *reward*; requital, return.

Adj. grateful, thankful, appreciative; showing appreciation, blessing; beholden, indebted.

Vb. be grateful, have a grateful heart, overflow with gratitude; praise Heaven; feel an obligation, cherish a favour, never forget; receive with open arms.

thank, give thanks, praise, bless; acknowledge, credit, *attribute*; appreciate, show appreciation, tip, *reward*; return a favour, requite, repay, repay with interest; return with thanks.

Adv. gratefully, with gratitude, with thanks, with interest.

Int. thanks! many thanks! much obliged! thank you! thank goodness! thank

Heaven! Heaven be praised!

903 Ingratitude

N. ingratitude, lack of gratitude, lack c appreciation; grudging thanks; *oblivion* thankless task, thankless office; thankles person, ungrateful wretch.

Adj. ungrateful, discourteous; forgetfu incapable of gratitude, *apathetic*.

unthanked, thankless, without credit; unre quited.

Vb. be ungrateful, show ingratitude; grudg thanks; forget a kindness.

Int. thank you for nothing! no thanks to

904 Forgiveness

N. forgiveness, pardon, reprieve, amnesty indemnity, grace, indulgence, *mercy* cancellation, remission, absolution *acquittal*; excuse; mutual forgiveness reconciliation; forgiving nature, pity longsuffering, forbearance, *patience*.

Adj. forgiving, merciful; willing to forgive lenient; forbearing, longsuffering patient; reluctant to punish.

forgiven; pardonable, venial, excusable.

Vb. forgive, pardon, reprieve, amnesty, for get; remit, absolve; cancel, obliterate relent, unbend, accept an apology, b lenient; be merciful, show mercy; bea with, forbear, tolerate, be patient; pocke stomach; forget an injury, ignore wrong, overlook; connive, wink at, cor done, *disregard*; excuse, justify; inter cede, *mediate*; exculpate, exonerate acquit; be ready to forgive, let bygones b bygones, be friendly; restore to favou celebrate.

beg pardon, ask mercy; propitiate, placate atone.

Adv. forgivingly, without resentment.

905 Revenge

N. revengefulness; spite; deadly rancou resentment.

revenge; vengeance, day of reckoning, pur ishment; reprisal, punitive expeditior vendetta, feud, enmity.

avenger; Nemesis, Eumenides, avengin furies.

Adj. revengeful, breathing vengeance taking vengeance; at feud, inimica implacable, unrelenting, relentless, pit less; vindictive, malevolent; rancorous.

Vb. avenge, avenge oneself, take vengeance exact retribution, repay, square a account; get back at, retaliate; gloat.

be revengeful, be malevolent; bear malice promise vengeance, hate; harbour grudge, have a crow to pluck, be inim cal; let it rankle, remember an injury refuse to forget, resent.

906 Jealousy

N. jealousy; jaundiced eye; distrust, mis trust, doubt; resentment; envy; hate hatred; competition; love; eterna triangle, revenge; competitor, rival.

Adj. jealous, jaundiced, envious; possessive loving; suspicious; rival.

Vb. be jealous, scent a rival, suspect, mis trust, distrust, doubt; view with a jaun diced eye, envy; resent competition.

907 Envy

N. envy, envious eye, desire; ill-will, spite, spleen, bile; grudging praise.
Adj. envious, green with envy, jealous; covetous, longing; grudging.
Vb. envy, cast envious looks, resent; covet, crave, lust after, desire.

908 Right

N. right, fitness, what ought to be, what should be; obligation, duty; propriety, etiquette; conformity; precept; morality, good morals, morals; virtue; rectitude, honour, probity; deserts, claim.
justice; redress; reform; tardy justice, overdue reform; even-handed justice; retribution, reward; detachment, equality; equity; fair deal, fair treatment, fair play; equal opportunity; good law; Nemesis.
Adj. right, rightful, proper; fitting, suitable, fit; good, ethical; put right; normal, standard, classical.
just, upright, righteous, right-minded, virtuous; disinterested, unprejudiced, unswerving, neutral; detached, impersonal, dispassionate, objective; equal, egalitarian, impartial, even-handed; fair, square, equitable, reasonable, fair enough; unimpeachable; legitimate, legal; sporting, honourable; due; overdue.
Vb. be right, behove, be due; have justice, have good cause.
be just, be honourable; do justice, hand it to; see justice done, see fair play, judge; temper justice with mercy, show mercy; right a wrong, redress, remedy, mend, reform, put right, rectify; serve one right, retaliate; try to be fair; hide nothing.
Adv. rightly, with justice; like a judge, equally, without distinction, without fear or favour, fairly, without favouritism.

909 Wrong

N. wrong, something wrong; something rotten, curse, bane, scandal; disgrace, shame, dishonour, slur; bad taste; guilt; vice, sin; irregularity, crime; misdoing, trespass; misdeed, offence, guilty act; a wrong, injustice, mischief, outrage, foul, foul play; sense of wrong, complaint, charge; grievance, resentment; bad person.
justice; miscarriage of justice, wrong verdict; corrupt justice, packed jury, bias; inequity; discrimination, partiality, leaning, favouritism, favour, nepotism; preferential treatment, positive discrimination; party spirit, old school tie, prejudice; justice denied; inequality; foul play.
Adj. wrong, bad; odd, queer, suspect, abnormal; unseemly, improper, vulgar; wrongheaded, unreasonable; inadmissible; irregular, foul, unwarranted; wrongful, illegitimate, illicit, criminal, illegal; culpable, offside, guilty; inexcusable, objectionable, reprehensible, scandalous; mischievous; dishonest, sinful, vicious, immoral, wicked.
unjust, uneven, weighted, unequal; inequitable; hard, severe; foul; discriminatory, one-sided, leaning to one side, partial, prejudiced; venal; illegal.
Vb. be wrong, go wrong, err, deteriorate.
do wrong, wrong, hurt, injure, do an injury, harm; be severe; commit a foul; commit a crime, be illegal; transgress, infringe, trespass, encroach; wink at, connive at; do less than justice, withhold justice; weight; lean, lean to one side, discriminate against, show partiality, show favouritism, discriminate; favour; go too far; commit, perpetrate.
Adv. wrongly; unjustly, illegally; with criminal intent.

910 Dueness

N. dueness, what is due; responsibility, obligation, duty; bare minimum; dues, payment; debt; tribute, credit, recognition, thanks; qualification, deserts, right; claim, title, right; birthright; interest, legal right, prescription, ancient lights; human rights, freedom; constitutional right, civil rights; privilege, prerogative, privilege; charter, warrant, licence, permit; liberty, franchise; bond, security, title deed; patent, copyright; recovery of rights, restoration, restitution; possessor; heir, beneficiary; plaintiff; person with a grievance.
Adj. due, payable; coming to one; lawful; constitutional, entrenched, untouchable, unimpeachable, inviolable; confirmed, inalienable; legitimate, rightful, of right, legal; heritable, reserved; fit, fitting, right; proper, advisable.
deserving, worthy of, worthy, meritorious.
Vb. be due, ought, ought to be, should be, should have been; be due to, have it coming; behove, befit.
claim, lay claim to, take possession, appropriate; claim unduly, arrogate; levy; reclaim, retrieve; sue, demand redress, request; enforce a claim, exercise a right; establish a right, patent, copyright.
have a right, expect, claim; have a claim to, demonstrate; justify, substantiate, vindicate; get a favourable verdict.
deserve, merit, be worthy; earn, have it coming to one, have only oneself to thank.
grant claims, give every man his due, be just; assign, credit, attribute; hand it to, acknowledge, thank; allow a claim, warrant, permit; admit a right, acknowledge a claim, honour, meet an obligation, honour a bill, pay; privilege, give a right, give one a title; allot, prescribe, apportion; make legal; confirm, endorse.
Adv. duly, by right, by law, by divine right.

911 Undueness

N. undueness, lack of expectation; bad taste; demerit, vice; ingratitude; absence of right, want of title; gratuity, bonus; too much; main part; breach, infraction; impiety.
arrogation, assumption, presumption; tyranny; inroad, trespass.
loss of right, disqualification; loss; deprivation; seizure, robbery; cancellation; waiver.
usurper, tyrant; pretender, impostor; squatter.
Adj. undue; gratuitous; inappropriate, improper, unseemly, inexpedient; preposterous, absurd.
unwarranted; illicit, illegitimate, illegal; stolen; excessive, presumptuous, insolent; wrong; invalid, weak; forfeit; false, bastard, spurious; fictitious, would-be, affected.
unentitled, without title, uncrowned; unqualified, without qualifications,

incompetent; underprivileged, without rights; deprived, bereft.

Vb. *be undue*; show bad taste; presume, arrogate, *be insolent*; usurp, borrow, *steal*; trespass, squat, *encroach*; infringe, break, violate, *be illegal*; desecrate, profane.

disentitle, *depose*; disqualify, disfranchise; invalidate, *abrogate*; *prohibit*; dispossess, expropriate; forfeit, defeat a claim; make illegitimate, *make illegal*; debase, *impair*.

Adv. *unduly*; without desert.

912 Duty

N. *duty*, what ought to be done, obligation, onus, responsibility; fealty, allegiance, loyalty; sense of duty; discharge of duty, performance, acquittal, discharge, *observance*; call of duty, bond, tie, engagement, commitment, word, pledge, *promise*; task, office, charge, *commission*; walk of life, station, profession, *vocation*.

conscience, categorical imperative, inner voice, 'still, small voice'.

code *of duty*, code of honour; *precept*.

morals, morality, *virtue*; honour, *probity*; moral principles, ethics, ethical philosophy, moral science, idealism, humanism, utilitarianism, behaviourism, *philosophy*.

Adj. *obliged*; beholden; bound, sworn, committed, engaged; liable, chargeable, answerable, responsible, accountable; answerable to God; conscientious; dutiful, *obedient*.

obligatory, incumbent; binding, compulsory, mandatory, peremptory, operative; inescapable; strict, unconditional, categorical.

ethical, moral, *virtuous*; honest, decent, *honourable*; moralistic; utilitarian.

Vb. *be one's duty*, be incumbent, behove, become, befit, *be due*; belong to, fall to; rest with.

incur *a duty*, accept responsibility, make oneself liable, commit oneself, *promise*; owe it to oneself.

do *one's duty*, *obey*; discharge, acquit, perform, *do*; *observe*; discharge an obligation, redeem a pledge; honour, meet, *pay*.

impose *a duty*, require, oblige, look to; call to office, offer a post, post, *commission*; assign a duty, saddle with, detail, order, enjoin, decree, *command*; tax, task, *fatigue*; exact, *be severe*; expect it of one, *expect*; bind, condition, *give terms*; take security, *take a pledge*.

Adv. *on duty*; with a clear conscience.

913 Undutifulness

N. *undutifulness*, default, want of duty, neglect; *disrespect*; evasion of duty, copout; *oblivion*; want of alacrity; absenteeism, *absence*; *escape*; infraction, breach of orders, indiscipline, mutiny, rebellion; sabotage, *hindrance*; treachery, *perfidy*; *schism*; escapism; truant, absentee; slacker; traitor; rebel; *schismatic*.

Adj. *undutiful*; rebellious, *disobedient*; disloyal, treacherous; irresponsible; truant, absentee, *absent*.

Vb. *fail in duty*, neglect; *disregard*; oversleep, *sleep*; blink, *disappoint*; shirk, evade, malinger, *avoid*; *be exempt*; play truant, *be absent*; abscond, *escape*; quit, scuttle,

scarper, *decamp*; abandon, desert, *relinquish*; break orders, *disobey*; mutiny, rebel, *revolt*; be disloyal, prove treacherous, betray; sabotage, *obstruct*; with draw, secede.

914 Nonliability

N. *nonliability*, dispensation; conscience clause, *qualification*; impunity, privilege special treatment, benefit of clergy; fran chise, charter; liberty, *freedom*; licence leave, *permission*; *permit*; excuse, *acquittal*; absolution, pardon, amnesty, *forgiveness*; discharge, release, *liberation*; evasion of responsibility, escapism resignation.

Adj. *nonliable*, unaccountable; scot-free exempt, immune; unaffected; indepen dent, free-born, *free*.

Vb. *exempt*, set apart, set aside; eliminate exclude; excuse, exonerate, exculpat acquit; grant absolution, absolve, pardo *forgive*; spare, *show mercy*; privileg charter, *permit*; dispense, give dispensation, grant impunity; amnesty, forge enfranchise, set at liberty, release, *liberate*; stretch a point, *be lenient*.

be *exempt*; enjoy impunity, *be free*; exemp oneself, excuse oneself, absent onesel take leave; *transfer*; *escape*.

915 Respect

N. *respect*, regard, consideration, esteem approbation; high standing, honou favour, *repute*; polite regard, attention courtesy; due respect, deference humility; humble service, devotio loyalty; admiration, awe, *wonder*; terro fear; reverence, adoration, *worship*.

respects, regards, duty, kind regards, cou teous act; red carpet, guard of honou address of welcome, salutation, salaam nod, bob, duck, bow, scrape, kowtov *obeisance*; reverence, homage; salut honours of war.

Adj. *respectful, humble*; obsequious, servil submissive; awestruck; polite, *courteou* ceremonious; prostrate; showing respec rising, standing, all standing.

respected, *reputable*; respectable, reveren venerable; time-honoured; imposin *impressive*.

Vb. *respect*, think well of, rank hig esteem, regard, value; admire, *wonde* reverence, venerate, exalt, magnify, *ho our*; adore, *worship*; revere, *fear*; defer t submit; pay tribute to, *praise*; do homag to, make much of, lionize, *celebrate*.

show *respect*, render honour, pay homag welcome, hail, salute, present arm greet; cheer, drink to, *toast*; bob, duc bow, kneel, kowtow, prostrate onese stoop; observe decorum, stand, ris uncover; humble oneself, condescend, *é humble*.

command *respect*, awe, overawe, impos impress; enjoy a reputation, rank hig *have a reputation*; compel respect, con mand admiration, *be wonderful*; dazzl receive respect, gain honour, gain a rep tation.

Adv. *respectfully*, with all respect; savin your grace, saving your presence.

916 Disrespect

N. *disrespect*, want of respect, discourtes dishonour, disfavour, *disapprobatio* neglect; low esteem, *disrepute*; *scurrili* scorn, *contempt*; mockery, *ridicule*; *impiety*.

indignity, affront, insult, slight, snub, outrage; V-sign; taunt, jeer, *contempt*; quip, sarcasm, mock, flout, *ridicule*; hiss, hoot, boo, catcall, brickbat, *disapprobation*.

Adj. *disrespectful*, neglectful, *negligent*; insubordinate, *disobedient*; irreverent, *profane*; outspoken, *plain*; rude, impolite, *discourteous*; airy, breezy, offhand, cavalier, familiar, cheeky, saucy, *impertinent*; outrageous, *insolent*; satirical; scurrilous; pejorative; supercilious, disdainful.

unrespected, *disreputable*.

Vb. *not respect*; be unable to respect, *disapprove*; underrate, *underestimate*; have a low opinion of, disdain, scorn, *despise*; denigrate, disparage, *defame*; toss aside, *reject*; show disrespect, lack courtesy, push aside, crowd, jostle, *be rude*; ignore, *disregard*; snub, slight, insult, affront, outrage, *humiliate*; dishonour, disgrace, put to shame, *shame*; trifle with, treat lightly, *hold cheap*; cheapen, lower, degrade; desecrate, profane; abuse, *curse*; taunt, twit, *be insolent*; laugh at, guy, scoff, mock, flout, deride, *ridicule*; jeer, hiss, hoot, heckle, boo, point at, spit at, *reprobate*; mob, hound, chase, *pursue*; pelt, stone, heave a brick.

Adv. *disrespectfully*.

917 Contempt

N. *contempt*, scorn, disdain, *pride*; *affectation*; superior airs, smile of contempt, snort, sniff; slight, *indignity*; sneer, dig at; *ridicule*; snub, rebuff, *discourtesy*.

contemptibility; byword of reproach, *object of scorn*.

Adj. *despising*, full of contempt, contemptuous, disdainful, snooty; haughty, lofty, airy, supercilious, *proud*; impertinent, *insolent*.

contemptible, despicable, beneath contempt; abject, *bad*; petty, paltry, little, mean, *small*; trifling, pitiable, futile.

Vb. *despise*; consider beneath one, *be proud*; disdain, spurn, sniff at, snort at, *reject*; snort; snub, *be rude*; scorn, whistle, hiss, boo, point at, *reprobate*; laugh at, have a dig at, laugh to scorn, scoff, scout, flout, jeer, mock, deride, *ridicule*; *oppress*; disgrace, *shame*.

hold *cheap*, have a low opinion of; ignore, dismiss, discount, *disregard*; belittle, disparage, fail to appreciate, underrate, *underestimate*; decry; think nothing of, think small beer of, laugh at, pooh-pooh; slight, trifle with, treat lightly, treat like dirt, lower, degrade, *humiliate*.

Adv. *contemptuously*, with contempt, with disdain.

contemptibly, miserably.

918 Approbation

N. *approbation*, approval; satisfaction, *content*; appreciation, recognition, *gratitude*; good opinion, kudos, credit, *prestige*; regard, admiration, esteem, *respect*; good books, good graces, grace, favour, popularity, affection, *love*; adoption, acceptance, welcome, favourable reception, *reception*; sanction, *permission*; nod of approval, blessing; nod, wink, consent, *assent*; countenance, patronage, championship, advocacy, *aid*; friendly notice, favourable review, *estimate*; good word, testimonial, reference, commendation, recommendation.

praise, benediction, blessing; compliment, encomium, eulogy, panegyric, adulation, *flattery*; hero worship, *wonder*; faint praise, two cheers; shout of praise, hosanna, alleluia; song of praise; tribute, credit, due credit, *thanks*; complimentary reference, bouquet, accolade, citation, honourable mention, commendation, glowing terms; official biography; puff, blurb, *advertisement*.

applause, acclaim, enthusiasm, excitement; warm reception, *celebration*; acclamation, cheering, clap, three cheers; thunderous applause, ovation, encore, curtain call; bouquet.

commender; clapper; friendly critic, admirer, fan club; advocate, supporter, *patron*; booster; agent, tout, barker; electioneer, election agent.

Adj. *approving*, content; appreciative, *grateful*; favourable, friendly; complimentary, laudatory, lyrical; lavish, generous; fulsome, uncritical; thunderous, *loud*; ecstatic, *excited*.

approvable, admissible, permissible, acceptable; worthwhile, *useful*; meritorious, laudable, estimable, worthy, praiseworthy, creditable, admirable, unimpeachable, beyond all praise, *perfect*; enviable, desirable.

approved, tried; blessed; popular, thought well of, *reputable*; favoured, *chosen*.

Vb. *approve*, see nothing wrong with, sound pleased, think highly of, *respect*; like well, *love*; think well of, admire, esteem, value, prize, treasure, cherish, *honour*; appreciate, give credit, salute, hand it to; think good, think perfect; think desirable, *envy*; see to be good, mark with approbation; accept, pass, tick; nod, wink, *assent*; sanction, bless, *permit*; ratify, *endorse*; commend, recommend, advocate, support, back, favour, countenance, give one a reference or a testimonial.

praise, compliment, pay compliments, *flatter*; speak well of, speak highly; bless, *thank*; salute, pay tribute to, hand it to; commend, give praise, exalt, extol, glorify, magnify; wax lyrical; *exaggerate*; puff, inflate, overestimate, *overrate*; lionize; trumpet, boost, *advertise*; praise oneself.

applaud, receive with applause, welcome, hail, hail with satisfaction; acclaim, receive with acclamation, clap, give a big hand, stamp, whistle; cheer, give three cheers, give three times three; welcome, congratulate, garland, chair, *celebrate*; drink to, *toast*.

be *praised*, get a citation; recommend oneself, *seek repute*; find favour, win praise, gain credit, *have a reputation*; get a compliment, receive a tribute, get a hand, get a clap, get a cheer; receive an ovation, *triumph*; deserve praise; pass, do, pass muster.

Adv. *approvingly*, with admiration, with compliments; without demur.

commendably, admirably, wonderfully; to satisfaction, to approval.

Int. bravo! well done! hear hear! encore! bis! three cheers! hurrah! hosannah!

919 Disapprobation

N. *disapprobation*, discontent; return; *refusal*; disfavour, displeasure, *dislike*; low opinion, *disrespect*; bad books, *disrepute*; niggling; hostility, *enmity*; exception, cavil, *qualification*; complaint, clamour, outcry, protest; *anger*; hiss, boo, whistle, catcall, *ridicule*; boycott, bar, ban, *exclusion*; blackball, blacklist, Index.

censure, blame; home truth, criticism, stricture; hostile attack, onslaught, *attack*; bad press, critical review; open letter, tirade, diatribe, *opposition*; conviction; *false charge*; slur, slander, innuendo, *calumny*; brand, stigma.

reproach; *quarrel*; invective, vituperation, *scurrility*; *malediction*; aspersion, reflection, *indignity*; taunt, sneer; sarcasm, irony, satire, biting wit, biting tongue, dig, cut, hit, brickbat, *ridicule*; hard words, silent reproach.

reprimand; stricture; censure, rebuke, reproof, snub; rocket, raspberry; expression of displeasure, black mark; *punishment*; admonition, rating, roasting, wigging; lecture.

disapprover; damper, wet blanket, spoilsport, misery; pussyfoot, puritan, *prude*; *opponent*; critic, knocker; censor; misogynist, *misanthrope*; malcontent.

Adj. *disapproving*, unable to approve; sparing of praise, grudging; silent, *taciturn*; unfavourable, hostile, *inimical*; clamorous, *deprecatory*; critical; hypercritical, niggling; caustic, sharp, bitter, venomous, trenchant, mordant; sardonic; censorious; damning.

disapproved; found wanting, *insufficient*; fallen foul of; henpecked; *disreputable*.

blameworthy, too bad; exceptionable, open to criticism, *bad*; reprehensible, *discreditable*; reprobate,.culpable, to blame.

Vb. *disapprove*, fail to appreciate, think little of, take a dim view of; think ill of, *despise*; fail, plough; return, *reject*; *prohibit*; cancel, *abrogate*; censor, *obliterate*; withhold approval, look grave, *dissent*; disfavour, reprehend, lament, deplore, *regret*; abhor, reprobate, *dislike*; disown, look askance, avoid, ignore; keep at a distance, ban, bar, blacklist, *exclude*; protest, remonstrate, object, take exception to, demur, *deprecate*; discountenance, exclaim, hoot, boo, bay, heckle, hiss, whistle; throw mud; hound, chase, mob, lynch; make a face, spit; look black, be sullen; *be angry*.

dispraise, damn with faint praise, damn, *condemn*; fault, niggle, crab, cavil, depreciate, belittle; oppose, tilt at, shoot at, *attack*; let fly, savage, maul, slash, slate, scourge, flay; thunder, fulminate, storm against, *rampage*; cry shame, slang; gird, rail, revile, abuse, execrate, *curse*; vilify, blacken, *defame*; brand, pillory; expose, denounce, recriminate, *accuse*; sneer, twit, taunt.

reprove, reprehend, reproach, rebuke, snub; call to order, caution, *warn*; book, give one a black mark; censure, reprimand, take to task; carpet; remonstrate, expostulate, admonish, castigate, chide, correct; lecture, read one a lecture, give one a wigging, trounce, roast, browbeat, chastise, *punish*.

blame, find fault, carp; get at, *bicker*; reprehend, hold to blame, hold responsible; incriminate, complain against, impeach, charge, *accuse*; recriminate, *retaliate*; *condemn*.

reprobate, reproach; upbraid, slate, rate, berate, rail, strafe, revile, abuse, blackguard, *curse*; scold, lash.

incur *blame*, catch it; be held responsible; be open to criticism; get a bad name, *lose repute*; stand accused; be an example, be a scandal, shock, revolt, *cause dislike*.

Adv. *disapprovingly*, reluctantly, against one's better judgment, underprotest; reproachfully.

920 Flattery

N. *flattery*, blarney, blandishments, sweet talk; flannel, soft soap, salve, incense, adulation; honeyed words, *endearment*; compliment; coquetry; euphemism, hypocrisy, *sham*.

flatterer; coquette; tout, booster; courtier, yes-man; creep, sycophant, parasite, minion, hanger-on, *toady*; fair-weather friend, hypocrite.

Adj. *flattering*, overdone; complimentary, full of compliments; fulsome; sugary, saccharine; mealy-mouthed; bland; smooth, unctuous, slimy, smarmy, obsequious, courtly, *servile*; specious, plausible; false, insincere.

Vb. *flatter*, compliment, *praise*; overdo it; puff, boost, *overrate*; burn incense to, assail with flattery; soft-soap; blarney, flannel; sugar; wheedle, coax, cajole, coo; lull, soothe, beguile, *deceive*; humour, jolly along; make things pleasant, tell people what they want to hear; smooth; make much of, *caress*; fawn, cultivate, court, pay court to; smirk, *smile*; curry favour; toady to, *be servile*; insinuate oneself; flatter oneself, *be vain*.

Adv. *flatteringly*.

921 Detraction

N. *detraction*, faint praise, two cheers, understatement; criticism, bad review, bad press, *disapprobation*; onslaught, *attack*; hatchet job; exposure, bad light, *disrepute*; scorn, contempt; *malediction*; abuse, invective, *scurrility*; *untruth*; spite, aspersion, reflection, snide remark (see *calumny*); whisper, innuendo, imputation; smear campaign; brand, stigma, *lack of wonder*.

calumny, slander, libel, false report, *untruth*; smear, dirty word, *slur*; offensive remark, personality, insult, taunt, dig at, brickbat, *indignity*; scoff, sarcasm, *ridicule*; sneer, sniff; caricature; skit, lampoon, squib, *satire*; scandal, scandalous talk, malicious gossip, bad mouth.

detractor; cynic; censor; candid friend, candid critic; critic, knocker; Philistine, *vulgarian*.

defamer, hatchet man; gossip columnist, gutter press; scold, *shrew*; poison pen.

Adj. *detracting*, derogatory, pejorative, contemptuous; scandalous; abusive, scurrilous; shrewish, caustic, bitter, venomous; snide; catty, *malevolent*; candid, *plain*.

Vb. *detract*, depreciate, disparage, sell short; deflate, puncture; *underestimate*, belittle, slight, *hold cheap*; sneer at, sniff at, *despise*; decry, damn with faint praise, fail to appreciate, *disapprove*; find nothing to praise, knock, slam, fault, slash, slate; caricature, guy, *misrepresent*; lampoon; scoff, mock, *ridicule*; whisper, insinuate.

defame, dishonour, damage, compromise, degrade, lower, put to shame, *shame*; give a dog a bad name; denounce, expose, pillory, brand, *accuse*; calumniate, libel, slander, traduce, malign; vilify, denigrate, blacken, tarnish, sully; speak ill of, speak evil, gossip, make scandal, talk about, backbite; discredit, *cause doubt*; smear, smirch, besmirch, spatter, throw mud, fling dirt, *make unclean*; hound, witch-hunt, *hunt*; smell evil, muckrake, *pursue*.

922 Vindication

N. vindication, restoration, *restitution*; triumph of justice, right triumphant; clearance, *acquittal*; good grounds, just cause, every excuse; self-defence, defence, alibi, plea, excuse, whitewash, gloss, *pretext*; fair excuse, *truth*; partial excuse, *qualification*; reply, rejoinder, recrimination; true bill; just punishment, *punishment*.

vindicator; advocate, champion; character witness, *witness*; defendant, *accused person*.

Adj. vindicating; apologetic.

vindicable, defensible, arguable; specious, plausible; allowable; excusable, pardonable, venial; *innocent*; *true*.

Vb. vindicate, revenge, avenge; do justice to; set right, restore, rehabilitate; maintain, advocate, *argue*; undertake to prove, confirm, make good, prove, *demonstrate*; champion, *defend*; support, offer moral support.

justify, warrant, furnish an excuse, give a handle, give one cause; clear, exonerate, exculpate, *acquit*; give colour to, colour, whitewash, varnish, gloss; justify oneself, *plead*; plead ignorance.

extenuate, excuse; palliate, mitigate, soften, soft-pedal, slur, gloss, varnish, whitewash; be lenient.

923 Accusation

N. accusation, complaint, charge, home truth; censure, blame, stricture, *reproach*; challenge, *defiance*; recrimination, *rejoinder*; twit, taunt, *indignity*; imputation, information, denunciation; plaint, suit, action; prosecution, citation, summons; true bill; substance of a charge, case, case to answer; particular charge, count, *evidence*.

false *charge*, frame-up; false information, hostile evidence, counterfeit evidence, plant; illegal prosecution, lie, libel, slander, scandal, stigma, *calumny*.

accuser, plaintiff; charger; grass, nark, *informer*; common informer; prosecutor; hostile witness, *enemy*.

accused *person*, prisoner; defendant, respondent, corespondent; culprit; suspect, victim of suspicion, marked man; victim.

Adj. accusing, accusatory; incriminating, pointing to, condcriminatory; calumnious, defamatory; suspicious.

accused, informed against, suspect; charged.

accusable; chargeable, liable to prosecution; inexcusable, indefensible; without excuse, without defence, *heinous*; *vulnerable*.

Vb. accuse, challenge, *defy*; taunt, twit, be insolent; point, point a finger at, reproach, *reprove*; brand, pillory, gibbet, calumniate, *defame*; charge with, hold against, hold responsible, hold to blame, bring home to, *blame*; point at, expose, name, *divulge*; denounce, inform against, tell, blab, *inform*; involve, implicate, incriminate; recriminate; make one a scapegoat; accuse oneself, plead guilty, *confess*; involve oneself, lay oneself open.

indict, impeach, arraign, inform against, lodge a complaint, lay information

against; complain, charge, bring a charge, *litigate*; book, cite, summon, prosecute, sue; bring an action, bring a suit, bring a case; *attack*; lie against, *be false*; frame, *fake*.

Adv. accusingly.

924 Probity

N. probity, rectitude, goodness, sanctity, virtue; *purity*; good character, moral fibre, integrity; high character, nobility; tender conscience, *honour*, principles; *observance*; reliability, sense of responsibility; candour; good faith, *truth*; fidelity, faith, troth, constancy, *loyalty*; sportsmanship, *justice*; *repute*; chivalry; principle, point of honour, code, code of honour, *right*; court of justice, court of honour.

honourable *person*, man of honour, woman of her word, sound character, trusty soul, *good person*; true lady, perfect gentleman, true knight; fair fighter, fair player, good loser, sportsman, sport, good sport, trump, brick, good sort, true Brit.

Adj. honourable, upright, erect, of integrity, of honour, *virtuous*; correct, strict; lawabiding, honest; principled; scrupulous, conscientious, soul-searching; incorruptible; immaculate, *innocent*; stainless, clean; noble, high-minded, *pure*; ingenuous, guileless, *artless*; good, straight, square, one hundred per cent; fair, equitable, impartial, *just*; sporting; chivalrous; respectable, *reputable*; pious.

trustworthy, reliable, dependable, tried, proven; trusty, true-blue, sure, staunch, constant, faithful, loyal, *obedient*; responsible, dutiful; conscientious, religious, scrupulous, meticulous, punctilious, *careful*; candid, frank, open, openhearted, transparent, ingenuous, without guile, *true*; straightforward, truthful, *veracious*.

Vb. be honourable, behave well, behave like a gentleman, *be virtuous*; play fair, shoot straight, *be just*; be a sport, be a brick; fear God, *be pious*; keep faith; hate a lie, *be truthful*; go straight, reform, *get better*.

925 Improbity

N. improbity; lack of probity, lack of conscience, lack of principle; *inattention*; opportunism; *falsehood*; partiality, *injustice*; corruption, graft, nepotism; disgrace, dishonour, shame, *disrepute*; villainy, roguery; crime, complicity.

perfidy, infidelity, *untruth*; bad faith; Judas kiss, *duplicity*; treachery, sell-out; treason, *sedition*; fifth column, Trojan horse; breach of faith, broken word, broken faith, broken promise, scrap of paper; cry of treason.

foul *play*, dirty trick, foul, *wrong*; professional foul; trick, shuffle, chicanery; practice; dirty work, job, deal, ramp, racket; fiddle, wangle, hanky-panky, monkey business; tax evasion; crime, felony.

Adj. dishonest, wrong; unprincipled, unscrupulous; shameless, dead to honour, lost to shame; immoral, *wicked*; shaky; supple, flexible; disingenuous, untruthful; two-faced, insincere; tricky, artful, slippery, foxy, *cunning*; shifty, *equivocal*; designing; sneaking, underhand, *latent*; indirect, bent, crooked, devious, oblique, tortuous; insidious, dark, sinister; shady, fishy, suspicious, doubtful, questionable; *spurious*; illicit, *illegal*; foul, *bad*; unclean, *dirty*; mean, shabby, *disreputable*; derogatory; inglorious, ignominious; ignoble.

rascally, criminal, *lawless*; picaresque; blackguard; scurvy, arrant, low, low-down, base, vile; mean, shabby, paltry, pettifogging, abject.

venal, hireling, mercenary, *bought*; corrupt.

perfidious, treacherous, unfaithful, inconstant, faithless, *false*; disloyal, disloyal, *disobedient*; insidious, dark, Machiavellian; *spurious*.

Vb. *be dishonest*, yield to temptation, be lost to shame; lead a life of crime, *be illegal*; fiddle, wangle, gerrymander, start a racket, racketeer; peculate, *defraud*; cheat, swindle, *deceive*; betray, play false; play double, double-cross, *dissemble*; fawn, *flatter*; break faith, *be false*; shuffle, dodge, prevaricate, *be equivocal*; lose repute; smell fishy.

Adv. *dishonestly*, by fair means or foul, treacherously.

926 Disinterestedness

N. *disinterestedness, justice*; unselfishness, selflessness, *humility*; self-control, self-denial, self-sacrifice, martyrdom; rising above oneself, heroism, *courage*; elevation of soul, idealism, elevation, nobility, magnanimity; chivalry, generosity, liberality, *benevolence*; purity of motive, dedication, labour of love; loyalty, faith, *probity*, *philanthropy*; altruism, consideration, kindness, *courtesy*; compassion, *pity*; charity, *love*.

Adj. *disinterested*, impartial, without self-interest, *just*; *temperate*; incorruptible, honest, *honourable*; self-effacing, modest, *humble*; selfless; devoted, dedicated; loyal, faithful; heroic, *courageous*; thoughtful, considerate, kind, *courteous*; pure; quixotic, high-minded, lofty, elevated, sublime, noble, chivalrous; generous, liberal, unsparing.

Vb. *be disinterested*, sacrifice, sacrifice oneself, put oneself last, take a back seat, *be humble*; rise above oneself; have nothing to gain.

927 Selfishness

N. *selfishness*, narcissism, *vanity*; self-pity, self-indulgence, ego trip; self-absorption; egoism, egotism, individualism; self-preservation; axe to grind, personal advantage, selfish benefit; self-seeking, self-interest; I'm all right, Jack; cupboard love; *parsimony*; greed, *avarice*; *injustice*; selfish ambition, power politics.

egotist, self-centred person, *vain person*; go-getter, adventurer; money-grubber, miser, *niggard*; hog.

Adj. *selfish*, egocentric, self-centred; personal; self-seeking; *intemperate*; *vain*; with an interest; uncharitable, cold-hearted, *unkind*; mean, petty, paltry; illiberal, ungenerous, *parsimonious*; acquisitive, mercenary; venal, *dishonest*; covetous, *envious*; possessive, *jealous*; designing; mundane, worldly, earthly, worldly-wise.

Vb. *be selfish*, put oneself first, think only of oneself, take care of number one; love oneself, have only oneself to please; hang onto, hog, *retain*; have an axe to grind.

Adv. *selfishly*; on the make; far one's own

sake.

928 Virtue

N. *virtue*, moral strength, moral tone; goodness, holiness, spirituality, odour of sanctity, *sanctity*; *justice*; rectitude, character, integrity, honour, *probity*; perfect honour; morality, ethics, *morals*; sexual morality, temperance, chastity, *purity*; virtuous conduct, good behaviour, duty done; good conscience, conscious rectitude.

virtues; faith, hope, charity; justice, temperance, fortitude; saving quality, saving grace; a virtue, good fault; worth, merit, desert; *perfection*; magnanimity, altruism; idealism; self-control, *temperance*.

Adj. *virtuous*, moral, *ethical*; good, *excellent*; stainless, *pure*; *innocent*; irreproachable, impeccable, above temptation, *perfect*; holy; principled, right-minded, *right*; righteous, *just*; upright, sterling, honest, *honourable*; dutiful, *obedient*; *disinterested*; generous, well-intentioned; sober, *temperate*; chaste, virginal; proper, exemplary; elevated; meritorious, worthy, praiseworthy.

Vb. *be virtuous, be good*; behave; practise virtue, resist temptation, *be temperate*; rise superior to, have a soul above; go straight, *be honourable*; love good, hate wrong, *be just*; edify, set a good example, *do good*.

Adv. *virtuously*, well, with merit; purely.

929 Wickedness

N. *wickedness*, principle of evil; Devil, cloven hoof, *Satan*; fallen nature; iniquity, sin, *wrong*; *guilt*; *impiety*; ignorance of good; hardness of heart; bad behaviour; loose morals; vice, corruption, depravity, bad character; villainy, roguery, *foul play*; want of principle; crime; *inhumanity*; devil worship; shame, scandal, abomination, enormity, infamy, *disrepute*; delinquency, wrongdoing, wicked ways, course of crime; primrose path, slippery slope; low life, criminal world, underworld; den of vice, sink of iniquity, *sink*.

vice, fault, demerit; human weakness, frailty, foible, *weakness*; shortcoming, defect, deficiency, failing, flaw, weak point, weak side; trespass, injury, outrage, enormity, *wrong*; sin, pride, lust, anger, envy, sloth; venial sin, small fault, peccadillo, scrape; *bad taste*; offence, *guilty act*; crime, felony, deadly crime.

Adj. *wicked*, immoral, amoral, *indifferent*; lax, unprincipled, unscrupulous, *dishonest*; unblushing, callous, shameless, brazen; ungodly, irreligious, profane; evil, *bad*; evil-minded, *malevolent*; *maleficent*; bad, naughty, *disobedient*; weak (see *frail*); sinful, full of sin, *guilty*; graceless, reprobate; hopeless, incorrigible, irredeemable; accursed, godforsaken; hellish, infernal, fiendish, satanic, *diabolic*.

vicious, good-for-nothing, ne'er-do-well; hopeless; punk, graceless; miscreant; improper, unseemly, indecent, *vulgar*; without morals, immoral; intemperate; profligate, characterless, lost to virtue, lost to shame, *disreputable*; corrupt, degenerate, sick, rotten; brutal, *cruel*.

frail, infirm, feeble, *weak*; human, *lax*; suggestible, *vulnerable*; fallen, *imperfect*.

heinous, heavy, grave, serious, deadly;

black, scarlet; abysmal, hellish, infernal; sinful, immoral, *wrong*; criminal, nefarious; monstrous, flagrant, scandalous, shameful, disgraceful, shocking, outrageous, obscene; gross, foul, rank; base, vile, abominable, accursed; mean, shabby, despicable, *bad*; culpable; reprehensible, indefensible, *unwarranted*; brutal, *cruel*; inexcusable, inexpiable.

Vb. *be wicked*, scoff at virtue; lapse, relapse, backslide; *deteriorate*; do wrong, transgress, misbehave, be naughty; trespass, offend, sin, err, stray, slip, trip, stumble, fall; *be weak*.

make *wicked*, render evil, corrupt, *pervert*; mislead, lead astray, seduce, *tempt*; set a bad example.

Adv. *wickedly*, wrongly, sinfully; viciously, vilely; unforgivably, irredeemably.

930 Innocence

N. *innocence*; clear conscience; nothing to declare, nothing to confess; every excuse; *acquittal*; ignorance of evil, *ignorance*; inexperience; purity of heart, state of grace, *virtue*; *purity*; *probity*; *perfection*; golden age.

innocent, babe, newborn babe, babe unborn; child; lamb, dove; angel, pure soul; goody-goody; innocent party.

Adj. *innocent*, pure, stainless, spotless, immaculate, *clean*; sinless, unerring, impeccable, *perfect*; green, *ignorant*; guileless, *artless*; well-meaning, well-intentioned; innocuous, harmless, inoffensive, playful, gentle, child-like; goody-goody.

guiltless; bloodless; irreproachable, above suspicion; unexceptionable, unimpeachable, with every excuse; pardonable, excusable, venial.

Vb. *be innocent*, be honourable; be virtuous; have every excuse, have a clear conscience, have nothing to be ashamed of, have nothing to confess or declare; *be artless*; stand free of blame, stand above suspicion; acquit oneself.

Adv. *innocently*; with a clear conscience.

931 Guilt

N. *guilt*; delinquency; original sin; complicity; burden of guilt; blame, censure, *reproach*; guilt complex; conscious guilt, guilty conscience, guilty behaviour; suspicious conduct, blush, stammer, embarrassment; confession, *disclosure*; twinge of conscience, remorse, shame.

guilty *act*, sin, *vice*; misdeed, wicked deed, misdoing, trespass, offence, crime; misdemeanour, felony; misconduct, malpractice; peccadillo; scrape; lapse, slip, blunder, *mistake*; fault, failure, dereliction of duty; injustice, injury, *wrong*; enormity, atrocity, outrage, *cruel act*.

Adj. *guilty*; thought guilty, made responsible; responsible, *liable*; at fault, to blame, culpable, chargeable; shameful, reprehensible; without excuse, inexcusable; inexpiable, mortal, deadly, *heinous*; sinful, *wicked*; criminal, *illegal*; *murderous*; red-handed; hangdog, sheepish, shamefaced, ashamed.

Vb. *be guilty*, be at fault; be caught red-handed; plead guilty, *confess*; trespass, transgress, sin, *be wicked*.

Adv. *guiltily*; without excuse; red-handed, in the vary act, flagrante delicto.

932 Good Person

N. *good person*, fine human being, sterling character, *honourable person*; pillar of society, model of virtue, perfection, *paragon*; Christian, saint; great saint; angel, *innocent*; heart of gold, *kind person*; good neighbour, Good Samaritan, *benefactor*; idealist, *philanthropist*; *favourite*; hero, *brave person*; goody, good guy, good sort, stout fellow, brick, trump, sport; rough diamond, ugly duckling.

933 Bad Person

N. *bad person*, limb of Satan; fallen angel, recidivist, lost sheep, lost soul, one without morals; reprobate, good-for-nothing, ne'er-do-well, black sheep; scallywag, scamp; rake, profligate; wanton, hussy, *loose woman*; wastrel, waster, prodigal son, *prodigal*; scandalous person, reproach, outcast, dregs, riffraff, trash, scum, *object of scorn*; nasty type, ugly customer, undesirable, bad 'un, wrong 'un, thug, bully, *ruffian*; bad lot, bad egg, bad hat, bad character, bad guy, villain; bad influence, bad example; bad child, terror, whelp, monkey, little devil.

knave, vagabond, wretch, rascal, rapscallion, *low fellow*; rogue; criminal; thief, pirate, freebooter; villain, blackguard, scoundrel, miscreant; cheat, liar, crook; impostor, twister, *trickster*; sneak, grass, rat, *informer*; renegade; traitor, Quisling, Judas; animal, dog, hound, swine, snake, serpent, viper, reptile, vermin, *noxious animal*.

cad, nasty bit of work, scoundrel, blackguard; rotter, blighter, bastard, bounder, jerk, heel, slob, scab, son of a bitch; skunk, dirty dog; pimp, pervert, degenerate; cur, hound, swine, rat, worm; louse, insect, vermin; pig, beast, cat, bitch.

monster, horror, unspeakable villain; monster of cruelty, brute, savage; ogre, *tyrant*; Juggernaut; public enemy number one; monster of iniquity or depravity, fiend, demon, ghoul, *devil*; fury; devil incarnate, gorilla, terror, nightmare.

934 Penitence

N. *penitence*, contrition, attrition, compunction, remorse, *regret*; humble confession, *disclosure*; confession, *Christian rite*; humility; voice of conscience, *guilt*; white sheet, *penance*; apology; grudging apology.

penitent; prodigal son; reformed character.

Adj. *repentant*, contrite, sorry, apologetic, full of regrets; ashamed; weeping; penitent, penitential, penitentiary, doing penance; regenerate, born again.

Vb. *be penitent*, repent, show compunction, feel shame, feel sorry, express regrets; reproach oneself, go to confession, *confess*; do penance, wear a white sheet, *atone*; *lament*; scourge oneself; eat humble pie; rue, have regrets, wish undone, *regret*; think again, think better of; *learn*; reform, *get better*, recant.

Adv. *penitently*, like a penitent, in sackcloth and ashes.

Int. sorry! mea culpa! repent! for pity!

935 Impenitence

N. *impenitence*, lack of contrition; refusal to recant; hardness of *heart*, *hardness*;

despair of, *bad person*.
Adj. *impenitent*, recusant; obdurate, inveterate, stubborn, *obstinate*; without regrets; unrelenting, relentless; without compunction, without a pang, heartless, *cruel*; unmoved; hard, unblushing, brazen; incorrigible, irredeemable, hopeless, lost, *wicked*.
unrepented, unregretted, unatoned.
Vb. *be impenitent*, would do it again; refuse to recant, *be obstinate*; *be pitiless*.
Adv. *impenitently*; without compunction.

936 Atonement

N. *atonement*, making amends, amends, apology, satisfaction; reparation, indemnity, blood money, conscience money, *restitution*; quits; composition, *compromise*.
propitiation, satisfaction, reconciliation; redemption, *divine function*; sacrifice, offering; scapegoat, *substitute*.
penance, shrift, confession; sacrament of penance, penitential exercise; purgatory; penitent form, anxious seat, corner, *pillory*; white sheet.
Adj. *atoning*, making amends; apologetic; *offering*; penitential, penitentiary, doing penance, *punitive*.
Vb. *atone*, make amends, make reparation, indemnify, compensate; *beg pardon*; propitiate, conciliate, *pacify*; give satisfaction; sacrifice to, offer sacrifice; expiate; *be disinterested*; reclaim, redeem.
do *penance*, pray, fast, flagellate oneself, suffer purgatory; go to confession, *confess*.

937 Temperance

N. *temperance*, *moderation*; self-denial; self-control, self-discipline, *restraint*; continence, chastity, *purity*; *sobriety*; forbearance; abstinence, abstention, total abstinence; prohibition; vegetarianism; *economy*; plain living, simple life; frugal diet.
abstainer, *sober person*, pussyfoot; nonsmoker; vegetarian, vegan; dropout; enemy of excess, Spartan, *ascetic*.
Adj. *temperate*, within bounds, measured, *moderate*; plain, Spartan, sparing, economical, frugal, *parsimonious*; forbearing, abstemious; dry, teetotal, *sober*; vegan, vegetarian, continent, *restrained*; chaste, *pure*; ascetic.
Vb. *be temperate*, moderate, temper, keep within bounds, avoid excess, *avoid*; know when one has had enough, know when to stop, *be moderate*; keep sober, *be sober*; forbear, refrain, abstain, *avoid*; control oneself, *restrain*; deny oneself, *be ascetic*; go dry; ration oneself, *starve*; diet, make *thin*.

938 Intemperance

N. *intemperance*, want of moderation, abandon; excess, luxury; too much; waste, consumer society; want of self-control, indiscipline; indulgence; addiction, bad habit, *habit*; drug habit; high living; hangover.
Adj. *intemperate*, immoderate, excessive, *redundant*; unmeasured; wasteful, extravagant, profligate, spendthrift, *prodigal*; luxurious, *superfluous*; unrestrained, lacking self-control, *riotous*; incontinent; *drunk*; animal, *sensual*.
Vb. *be intemperate*, plunge, wallow; lack self-control, want discipline, lose control, *be lax*; deny oneself nothing, indulge oneself, *please oneself*; *be prodigal*; run to excess, run riot, exceed, *overstep*; stick at nothing, *waste*; *revel*; drink like a fish, drink to excess, *get drunk*; eat to excess, gorge, pig it, make oneself sick; be incontinent, grow dissipated, *be impure*; addict oneself, become a slave to habit, *be wont*.
Adv. *intemperately*, with abandon; without moderation, without control.

939 Sensualism

N. *sensualism*, materialism; sensuality, sexuality; love of pleasure, hedonism, *pleasure*; luxury; full life, life of pleasure, high living, wine; abandon; indulgence; orgy, debauch, *revel*.
sensualist, animal, pig, swine, hog; playboy; sybarite, voluptuary; epicure, gourmet, gourmand, *glutton*; hard drinker, *drunkard*; loose liver, profligate, rake; drug addict; degenerate.
Adj. *sensual*, earthy, gross, *material*; carnal, bodily; sexual, venereal, *erotic*; animal, bestial, beastly; voluptuous; luxurious; incontinent, *intemperate*; dissipated, impure; riotous, *drunken*.
Vb. *be sensual*, live well, *prosper*; indulge oneself, do oneself proud; run riot, *be intemperate*.
Adv. *sensually*.

940 Asceticism

N. *asceticism*; *penance*; ascetic practice, yoga; holy poverty, *poverty*; plain living, simple fare, Spartan fare; fast day, *fast*; self-denial, *temperance*; *economy*; hair shirt.
ascetic, spiritual athlete, yogi, fakir, dervish; hermit, anchorite, recluse, *solitary*; Cynic; *penitent*; sober person; Puritan; spoilsport, killjoy, pussyfoot.
Adj. *ascetic*; austere, *severe*; Spartan, *temperate*; *sober*; plain, wholesome, *salubrious*.
Vb. *be ascetic*, live like a Spartan; fast, *starve*; live like a hermit, wear a hair shirt; walk through fire.
Adv. *ascetically*, simply, plainly.

941 Fasting

N. *fasting*; anorexia, *ill health*; keeping fast, strict fast; spare diet; short commons, *scarcity*; starvation, *hunger*.
fast, fast day, Friday, Good Friday, Lent, Ramadan; day of abstinence; hunger strike, *strike*.
Adj. *fasting*; *temperate*; keeping fast, keeping Lent; without food, empty; *lean*; wanting food, *hungry*; sparing, frugal, *economical*; scanty, *scarce*; meagre, thin, poor, Spartan.
Vb. *starve*, famish, *be hungry*; macerate, waste with hunger; have nothing to eat, *be poor*; fast, go without food; keep Lent, keep Ramadan; eat nothing; eat less, diet, reduce, *abate*; make a little go a long way, *be temperate*; keep a poor table, *be parsimonious*.

942 Gluttony

N. *gluttony*, greed, voracity; insatiable appetite, *hunger*; good living, indulgence; belly worship, *gastronomy*; bust, blowout, masses of food.

glutton; locust, wolf, vulture, cormorant, pig, hog; vampire, blood-sucker; good eater, *eater*; coarse feeder; gourmand, gourmet, epicure.

Adj. *gluttonous*, rapacious; voracious; omnivorous, insatiable, never full, *hungry*; stuffing.

Vb. *gluttonize*; guzzle, bolt, wolf, gobble, devour; fill oneself, gorge, cram, stuff; glut oneself, *eat*; have a good appetite; eat like a trooper, eat like a horse, eat like a pig, make a beast of oneself; make oneself sick; keep a good table.

Adv. *gluttonously*; at a gulp, with one bite.

943 Sobriety

N. *sobriety, temperance*; state of sobriety, clear head; dry area.

sober *person*, moderate drinker; Band of Hope, temperance society; pussyfoot.

Adj. *sober*, abstemious; *temperate*; teetotal, pussyfoot dry; clear-headed, with a clear head; without a hangover; unfermented, unalcoholic, soft.

Vb. *be sober*, drink water; never touch drink, *be temperate*; become teetotal; go dry; keep a clear head.

Adv. *soberly*, with sobriety.

944 Drunkenness. Drug-taking

N. *drunkenness*; influence of liquor, inspiration; Dutch courage, *courage*; blackout; thick speech, *speech defect*; staggering; drop too much; potation; flowing bowl, booze, liquor, *alcoholic drink*, *wine*; jag, lush, blind, binge, spree, *revel*.

crapulence; hangover, thick head, sick headache.

alcoholism, alcoholic addiction, dipsomania, *mania*; delirium tremens, D.T.'s, heebiejeebies; red nose.

drug-taking, smoking; hard drug, joint, reefer, roach; shot, fix; narcotic, dope; nicotine, *tobacco*; cannabis, hemp, hashish, hash, pot, grass; cocaine, coke, snow; heroin, horse, smack; morphine, opium, *drug*; stimulant, pep pill, speed; LSD, acid, peyote; drug addiction, drug abuse, drug dependence, habit; cold turkey; drug addict, dope fiend, freak; head.

drunkard, inebriate, drunk, lush; slave to drink, alcoholic, pathological drunk; drinker, boozer, old soak, souse, sponge; thirsty soul; Bacchanal.

Adj. *drunk*, merry, happy, high, elevated, *excited*; mellow, full; *disorderly*.

tipsy, squiffy, tight, pissed; stewed, smashed, sloshed, sozzled, soused, plastered; maudlin, tearful; drunken, muzzy, woozy; dizzy, giddy, staggering.

dead *drunk*, stoned, blind drunk, blind, blotto; paralytic; gone, shot, stiff.

crapulous, with a hangover, with a thick head; dizzy, giddy, sick.

drugged, high, zonked; stoned, *insensible*.

drunken, inebriate, *intemperate*; always tight, never sober; sodden, vinous, stinking of liquor; thirsty, bibulous, fond of a drink; bloodshot, liverish; given to drink, alcoholic.

intoxicating, poisonous; exhilarating, heady like wine, *exciting*; stimulant; opiate, narcotic; psychedelic, mind-blowing; alcoholic, vinous; hard, potent, *strong*; neat.

Vb. *be drunk*, have had too much; have a weak head, succumb, be overcome; stutter, *stammer*; see double, lurch, stagger, reel, *oscillate*.

get *drunk*, have too much, drink deep, drink hard, drink like a fish, drink to get tight; crack a bottle, knock back a few, lush, bib, tipple, fuddle, booze, guzzle, swig, swill, soak, souse, *drink*; quaff, carouse, wassail, *revel*.

drug *oneself*, smoke, sniff, snort, inject oneself, shoot, mainline; take a trip.

inebriate, exhilarate, elevate, *excite*; fuddle, befuddle, stupefy; make drunk.

945 Purity

N. *purity, perfection*; moral purity, morals, morality; propriety, delicacy, *good taste*; shame; chastity, continence, *temperance*; frigidity, *moral insensibility*; honour, maidenhood, maidenhead.

prudery; false shame; gravity; *affectation*; euphemism.

virgin, maiden, maid, old maid, spinster, *celibate*; religious celibate, *monk, nun*; virtuous woman.

prude, prig, Victorian; Puritan; guardian of morality, censor, Watch Committee.

Adj. *pure, perfect*; sinless, *innocent*; maidenly, virgin, virginal; rosy, *modest*; coy, shy; chaste, continent, *temperate*; impregnable, incorruptible, *honourable*; unfeeling, *impassive*; frigid, *cold*; immaculate, spotless, snowy, *white*; good, moral, *virtuous*; Platonic, elevated; decent, decorous, delicate, refined, *tasteful*; printable, quotable, clean.

prudish, squeamish, Victorian; prim, *affected*; straitlaced, narrow-minded, puritan; holy, sanctimonious.

946 Impurity

N. *impurity; bad taste*; exhibitionism; loose talk, blue story; smut, dirt, filth, obscene literature; pornography, soft porn; blue film, skin flick.

unchastity; easy virtue; permissive society; vice, sexual delinquency; lust, *libido*; sexuality; licence, gallantry; seduction.

illicit *love*, forbidden fruit; criminal conversation, unlawful carnal knowledge; incest, perversion, buggery; infidelity; eternal triangle, intrigue, amour, seduction, *love affair*; free love, irregular union, *type of marriage*.

rape, indecent assault, grope; gang bang; sex crime, sex murder.

social *evil*, prostitution, indecent exposure; white slave traffic; vice squad.

brothel; house of ill fame, house of ill repute.

Adj. *impure*, unclean, nasty, *dirty; insalubrious*; indelicate; vulgar, coarse, gross; ribald, broad, free, loose; strong, racy, bawdy, Rabelaisian; suggestive, provocative, piquant; spicy, juicy, fruity; immoral, equivocal; naughty, wicked, blue; unmentionable, unprintable; smutty, scabrous, stinking, rank, offensive; indecent, obscene, lewd, salacious; prurient, erotic; sexual, sexy, hot.

unchaste, *vicious*; susceptible, *frail*; fallen, of easy virtue, of loose morals, amoral, immoral, incontinent, light, wanton, loose, fast, naughty; wild; immodest, daring; unblushing, shameless, scarlet, meretricious; promiscuous.

lecherous, carnal, voluptuous, *sensual*; lustful, prurient, rampant, rutting; hot, randy; oversexed; bestial; lewd, free, loose; dissolute, dissipated, profligate, vicious.

extramarital, irregular; unlawful; homosexual, Lesbian, *abnormal*; unfaithful.

Vb. *be impure*, be immoral; be unfaithful; be dissipated, *be intemperate*; fornicate, whore, wench; keep a mistress, have a lover; lust, rut, be hot, *desire*; be promiscuous, sleep around; become a prostitute; pimp, procure, keep a brothel.

debauch, defile, smirch, *make unclean*; proposition, seduce, lead astray; take advantage of; dishonour, deflower, wreck, ruin, disgrace, *shame*; prostitute, make a whore of; lay, bed, lie with, *unite with*; rape, ravish, violate, molest, abuse, outrage, interfere with, assault.

Adv. *impurely*.

947 Libertine

N. *libertine*; gay bachelor; flirt; loose fellow, fast man, gay dog, rip, rake, profligate; lady-killer, gallant, gigolo; false lover, *lover*; corespondent, adulterer; wolf, stud; lecher, flasher, satyr, goat, dirty old man; sex maniac; male prostitute; pervert, *nonconformist*.

cuckold, deceived husband, injured husband.

loose *woman*, wanton, easy lay; fast woman, hot stuff; woman of easy virtue; flirt, piece, bit, wench, jade, hussy, minx, miss, sex kitten; baggage, trash, trollop, drab, slut; tart, chippy, scrubber, pick-up; vamp, adventuress, scarlet woman; *other woman*.

kept *woman*, mistress, paramour, concubine, unofficial wife; bit of fluff, moll.

prostitute, pro; white slave, fallen woman; harlot, trollop, whore, strumpet; broad, hooker, scrubber; pick-up, casual conquest; courtesan; temple prostitute, *slave*.

bawd, go-between, pimp, ponce, madam; white slaver.

948 Legality

N. *legality*, formality, form, formula, rite, due process; form of law; good law; *justice*.

legislation; regulation; plebiscite, *vote*; popular decree; law, statute, ordinance, order, decree; canon, rule, edict, *precept*.

law; body of law, constitution, charter, institution; statute book, legal code; penal code, written law, personal law, international law; law of commerce, commercial law, law of contract, law of crime, criminal law; legal process, *jurisdiction*; writ, summons, lawsuit, *legal trial*.

jurisprudence, science of law, legal learning; legal advice.

Adj. *legal*, lawful, *just*; law-abiding, *obedient*; legitimate, competent, permissible, allowable; statutory, constitutional; legislative; made law, ordered; liable or amenable to law.

Vb. *be legal*, legitimate etc. adj.

make *legal*, confirm, ratify, *endorse*; vest, establish; legislate, pass, enact, ordain, enforce, *decree*.

Adv. *legally*, by law, by order.

949 Illegality

N. *illegality*, bad law, legal flaw, loophole, irregularity, error of law, wrong verdict; miscarriage of justice, *injustice*; prohibition.

lawbreaking, breach of law; trespass, offence, civil wrong; malpractice, *foul play*; guilt; criminal activity, criminal offence, crime, misdemeanour, felony; wrongdoing, *wrong*; criminology, criminal statistics; criminal.

lawlessness; crime wave, *anarchy*; summary justice; kangaroo court, gang rule, mob law, riot, rebellion, *revolt*; arbitrary rule, martial law; jackboot, *brute force*.

bastardy, bar or bend or baton sinister; bastard, illegitimate child, spurious offspring.

Adj. *illegal*, illegitimate, illicit; contraband, hot; incompetent, without authority, informal, unofficial; unlawful, wrongful, *wrong*; irregular, contrary to law; punishable.

lawbreaking, *wicked*; *guilty*; criminal; shady, *dishonest*.

lawless, without law, chaotic; ungovernable, *riotous*; violent, summary; arbitrary, irresponsible, unaccountable; unofficial, cowboy.

bastard, illegitimate, spurious; misbegotten, baseborn; without a father, without a name, without benefit of clergy.

Vb. *be illegal*, be lawless, *do wrong*; encroach, *please oneself*.

make *illegal*, outlaw; *prohibit*; *punish*; suspend, annul, cancel, *abrogate*.

Adv. *illegally*, illicitly, unlawfully, criminally.

950 Jurisdiction

N. *jurisdiction*, portfolio, *function*; judicature; competence, legal authority, *authority*; Home Office; local jurisdiction, local authority, corporation, municipality, county council, *council*; *tribunal*; office, bureau, secretariat, *workshop*; legal authority, competence, *mandate*.

law *officer*, legal administrator, Lord Chancellor, Attorney General, Lord Advocate, Solicitor General; Crown Counsel, public prosecutor; judge advocate, district attorney, *judge*; mayor, sheriff, *position of authority*; court officer, tipstaff, bailiff; beadle, mace-bearer, *official*.

police, police force; constabulary, military police, police officer, policeman or -woman, constable, copper, cop, patrolman or -woman; police sergeant, police inspector, police superintendent, commissioner of police, chief constable, provost marshal; watch; special patrol group; plain-clothes man, *detective*.

Adj. *jurisdictional*, competent; executive, administrative, directive; judiciary, juridical; subject to jurisdiction.

Vb. *hold court*, administer justice, *judge*; *try a case*; take judicial notice.

951 Tribunal

N. *tribunal*, seat of justice, woolsack, throne; bar, bar of justice; court of conscience, tribunal of penance, confessional; forum, *council*; public opinion, electorate; bench; board; judicial assembly.

lawcourt, court, court of law, court of justice, criminal court, Federal Court, High Court; District Court, County Court; Supreme Court, Court of Appeal; Court of Exchequer, Star Chamber; House of Lords, *parliament*; High Court of Justice, Court of Criminal Appeal; Admiralty Division; Probate Court, Court of Chancery, court of equity; circuit court; assizes; Court of Session, sessions, Central Criminal Court, Old Bailey; court of record, court baron; guild court, hustings; court-martial, drumhead court.

ecclesiastical *court*, Curia; Inquisition, Holy Office.

courtroom, court-house; bench, woolsack, jury-box; dock, bar; witness box.

Adj. *judicatory*, judicial

952 Judge

N. *judge*, justice, your Lordship; Lord Chancellor, Lord Chief Justice, Lords of Appeal; military judge, Judge Advocate General; chief justice, recorder; sessions judge, district judge, magistrate, coroner; honorary magistrate, JP; bench, judiciary; hanging judge.

magistrate, his or her Worship, his or her Honour; arbiter, umpire, referee, assessor, Ombudsman; Recording Angel, *recorder*.

jury, twelve just men; grand jury, jury list; juror, juryman or -woman.

953 Lawyer

N. *lawyer*, legal practitioner, man or woman of law; common lawyer, barrister, advocate, counsel, junior barrister, stuff gown, junior counsel; senior barrister; silk gown, silk, leading counsel; circuit barrister; *expert*; shyster, crooked lawyer.

law agent, attorney, attorney at law; solicitor, legal adviser, legal representative, legal agent, advocate; equity draftsman.

notary, notary public; *law officer*.

jurist, legal adviser, legal expert, legal light, master of jurisprudence, pundit; student of law, law student.

bar, English bar, Inner Temple, profession of law, legal profession; advocacy.

Adj. *jurisprudential*, called to the bar, at the bar; forensic.

Vb. *do law*; take silk; accept a brief, take a case, advocate, plead; practise law.

954 Litigation

N. *litigation*, going to law; legal dispute, quarrel; issue; lawsuit, suit at law, suit, case, cause, action; prosecution, charge; test case, *experiment*; claim; plea, petition, *request*; affidavit, written statement.

legal process, proceedings, legal procedure, course of law, *jurisdiction*; citation, subpoena, summons, search warrant, *warrant*; arrest, apprehension, detention, committal, *restraint*; bail, surety, security, injunction, stay order; writ.

legal trial, trial, justice seen to be done; sessions, inquest, inquisition, examination, *enquiry*; hearing, prosecution, defence; hearing of evidence, *evidence*; examination, *testimony*; *reasoning*; rejoinder; proof; ruling, finding, decision, verdict; majority verdict, hung jury; favourable verdict, *acquittal*; unfavourable verdict; *punishment*; appeal, retrial; precedent, case law; cause list; case record, dossier, *record*.

litigant, party, party to a suit; suitor; plaintiff, defendant, respondent; accused, *accused person*; common informer, *informer*; prosecutor.

Adj. *litigating*, at law with; going to law.

litigated; disputable, arguable.

Vb. *litigate*, go to law, institute legal proceedings, start an action, bring a suit, petition, *request*; prepare a case, prepare a brief, brief counsel; file a claim, contest at law, *claim*; take one to court, make one a party, sue, arraign, impeach, accuse, charge, *indict*; cite, summon; prosecute, bring to justice, bring to trial; advocate, plead, call evidence, *argue*.

try *a case*, hear a cause; examine, cross-examine; rule, find, decide, adjudicate, *judge*; pronounce sentence.

stand *trial*, come before; plead guilty; ask to be tried, hear sentence; defend an action.

Adv. *in litigation*, at law, in court, before the judge; subjudice.

955 Acquittal

N. *acquittal*, favourable verdict; clearance; absolution, discharge; *liberation*; quietus; reprieve, pardon, *forgiveness*; impunity.

Adj. *acquitted*; clear; immune, exempt; *liberated*.

Vb. *acquit*, prove innocent, justify, whitewash, *vindicate*; clear, absolve, exonerate, exculpate; *exempt*; discharge, let go, *liberate*; reprieve, respite, pardon, *forgive*; quash, allow an appeal, *abrogate*.

956 Condemnation

N. *condemnation*, unfavourable verdict, finding of guilty, conviction; damnation, perdition; blacklist, Index, *disapprobation*; *malediction*; doom, sentence, *punishment*; *omen*; death warrant, execution chamber, Death Row; black cap.

Adj. *condemned*, found guilty, made liable; without a case; lost, burning.

Vb. *condemn*, prove guilty; find liable, find against; find guilty, convict, sentence; sentence to death; *reject*; proscribe, outlaw, bar, *make illegal*; blacklist, *disapprove*; damn, excommunicate, *curse*; convict oneself, *be guilty*; plead guilty, confess.

957 Reward

N. *reward*, recompense; deserts, *justice*; recognition, thanks, *gratitude*; tribute, proof of regard, *praise*; award, presentation, prize, crown, cup, pot, shield, certificate, medal, *trophy*; honour; birthday honours, *honours*; *title*; prize money, jackpot; prize fellowship, scholarship, bursary, stipend, exhibition; fee, retainer, payment, emolument, pension, salary, wage, wages, increment, *pay*; productivity bonus, overtime pay, *incentive*; perquisite, perks, expense account; income, turnover, *earnings*; return, profit, *gain*; satisfaction; consideration, *offset*; comeuppance; reparation, *restitution*; bounty, gratuity, golden handshake; commission, rake-off, kickback; tip, baksheesh; *gift*; *offer*; bait, lure, bribe, *incentive*; hush money, blackmail.

Adj. *rewarding*; generous, open-handed, *liberal*; remunerative, *gainful*; promising, *offering*.

Vb. *reward*, recompense; award, present, give a prize, offer a reward; bestow a medal, honour with a title, *honour*; acknowledge, pay tribute, thank, *be grateful*; remunerate, *pay*; satisfy, tip, *give*; tip well, *be liberal*; repay, requite, *retaliate*; compensate, indemnify, make

reparation; offer a bribe, *bribe*.
be *rewarded*, gain a reward, win a prize, get a medal, receive a title; get paid, draw a salary, earn an income, have a gainful occupation, *acquire*; accept payment, *receive*; take a bribe; *deserve*; reap, reap a profit, *gain*.
Adv. *rewardingly*.

958 Punishment

N. *punishment*, sentence; execution of sentence; *reprimand*; discipline; dose, pill, hard lines, trial, visitation, punishing experience, *adversity*; just deserts, meet reward, comeuppance; doom, day of reckoning, divine justice, *justice*; retribution, Nemesis; reckoning, *restitution*; requital, reprisal; penance; self-discipline; hara-kiri, *suicide*; penology.
corporal *punishment*, hiding, beating, thrashing; flogging; slap, smack, rap; blow, buffet, cuff, clout, stroke, stripe, *knock*; third degree, torture, *pain*.
capital *punishment*, extreme penalty, *death*; death sentence, death warrant; execution, *killing*; hanging, drawing and quartering; strangulation, garrotte; hanging, long drop; crucifixion; burning; massacre, mass murder, mass execution, purge, genocide, *slaughter*; martyrdom; illegal execution, lynch law; judicial murder.
penalty, injury, damage, *loss*; task, lines; sentence, penal code, penology; devil to pay; damages, restoration, *restitution*; fine, compulsory payment, *payment*; ransom, *price*; forfeit, deprivation; *detention*; suspension; *restraint*; penal servitude, hard labour, galley service; transportation; expulsion; exile, ban, *exclusion*; reprisal.
punisher; *tyrant*; magistrate, court, law, *judge*; executioner, hangman, Jack Ketch.
Adj. *punitive*, penal; vindictive; *taking*; *painful*.
punishable, liable.
Vb. *punish*, visit, afflict, *hurt*; persecute, make an example of, *be severe*; impose; give one a lesson, chasten, discipline, correct, chastise, castigate; reprimand, strafe, rebuke, *reprove*; impose a penalty, sentence, *condemn*; execute justice, execute a sentence, exact a penalty, exact retribution, settle with, *retaliate*; settle, fix, bring to book, give one what was coming to him, revenge oneself, *avenge*; fine, forfeit, confiscate; demote, degrade, downgrade, suspend, *shame*; pillory, masthead; duck, keelhaul; picket, spread-eagle; *imprison*; transport.
spank, paddle, slap, smack, slipper, paddle; cuff, clout; drub, trounce, beat, belt, strap, leather, lather, larrup, wallop, welt, tan, cane, birch, switch, whack, dust, *strike*.
flog, whip, horsewhip, thrash, hide, belabour, cudgel, *strike*; scourge, lash, flay, flail, flagellate.
torture; *give pain*; put one to torture, thumbscrew, rack, mutilate, kneecap; persecute, *torment*.
execute, punish with death, put to death, kill; lynch, *murder*; dismember; decimate; crucify, impale, flay, flay alive; stone, stone to death; shoot, fusillade, stand against a wall; burn, burn alive, garrotte, strangle; gibbet, hang; hang, draw and quarter; behead, decapitate, guillotine; electrocute; gas; commit genocide, purge, massacre, *slaughter*.
be *punished*, suffer punishment, have it coming to one, catch it; regret it; come to execution; swing.
Int. off with his head! à la lanterne!

959 Means of Punishment

N. *scourge*, birch, cat, rope's end; whip, horsewhip, switch; lash, strap, thong, belt; cane; stick, rod, ferule, cudgel, ruler, *club*; rubber hose, bicycle chain, sandbag.
pillory, stocks; corner; chain, irons, *fetter*, prison house, prison, *gaol*.
instrument *of torture*, rack, thumbscrew, iron boot; Iron Maiden, triangle, wheel, treadmill; torture chamber.
means *of execution*, scaffold, block, gallows, gibbet; cross; stake; hemlock, *poison*; bullet, wall; axe, guillotine, maiden; halter, rope, noose, drop; garrotte; electric chair, hot seat; death chamber, Death Row.

960 Divineness

N. *divineness*, divinity, deity; divine principle; being of God, divine essence, perfection; love, Fatherhood; nirvana; impersonal God, world soul; First Cause, *source*; divine nature, God's ways, Providence.
divine *attribute*, being, existence; perfect being, *perfection*; unity; infinity; presence; wisdom, *knowledge*; power; eternity, *perpetuity*; stability; truth, sanctity, holiness, goodness, justice, mercy; supremacy, sovereignty, majesty, glory, light.
the *Deity*, God, personal god, Supreme Being; Judge of all men, Maker of all things, Creator, Preserver; Allah; Jehovah, ineffable name, I AM; name of God our Father; Great Spirit.
Trinity; Holy Trinity; God the Father, God the Son, God the Holy Ghost.
Holy *Ghost*; Holy Spirit, Spirit of Truth, Dove.
God *the Son*, Word, Son of God, Word made flesh, Incarnate Son; Messiah, Christ; Lamb of God, Son of Man; Holy Infant, Christ Child; Saviour, Redeemer, Friend; Lord, Master; Bread of Life, True Vine; King of Kings, King of Heaven, King of Glory, Prince of Peace.
divine *function*, creation, preservation, mercy, compassion, forgiveness; inspiration, comfort, grace, redemption, salvation.
theophany, divine manifestation, descent, descent to earth, incarnation; transfiguration.
theocracy, divine government, divine dispensation, God's law, Kingdom of God, God's ways, providence.
Adj. *divine*, holy, sacred, sacrosanct, heavenly, celestial; transcendental, sublime, ineffable; religious, spiritual, superhuman, supernatural, transcendent; unearthly; providential.
godlike, divine, superhuman; transcendent, omnipresent, *ubiquitous*; immeasurable, *infinite*; absolute, living; timeless, eternal, everlasting, immortal, *perpetual*; immutable, changeless, *permanent*; almighty, omnipotent, *powerful*; creative, *dynamic*; prescient, providential; omniscient, *knowing*; merciful, *forgiving*; loving; holy; sovereign, *supreme*; authoritative; glorious; incarnate.

deistic, theistic.
redemptive, intercessional, mediatory; messianic.
Adv. *divinely.*

961 Deities in general

N. *deity*, god; Olympian, Olympian deity; idol; petty god, lesser deity; demigod, divine hero, divine king; object of worship, fetish, totem, *idol*; pantheon.
mythic *deity*, Pan, Flora; mother earth, earth mother, Great Mother; fertility god; Pluto; sky god, Jupiter; storm god, wind god; sun god; river god, Neptune; Mars; Cupid, Venus; household gods; *fate*.
Adj. *mythological.*

962 Angel. Saint. Madonna.

N. *angel*, archangel, heavenly host, choir invisible; heavenly hierarchy; cherub; angel of death; guardian angel.
saint, patron saint, saint and martyr, the blessed■ ■■; Church Triumphant.
Madonna, Our Lady, Mother of God; Queen of Heaven.
Adj. *angelic*; cherubic; saintly, glorified, celestial.
Vb. *angelize*; *sanctify.*

963 Devil

N. *Satan*, fallen angel, Prince of this world; serpent, Adversary, Common Enemy, Enemy of mankind; evil genie; King of Hell; spirit of evil.
Mephisto, Mephistopheles, His Satanic Majesty, Old Nick, Old Harry, Old Scratch.
devil, fiend; familiar, imp, imp of Satan, *bad person*; *demon*; malevolent spirit; diabolic hierarchy; fallen angel, lost soul, denizen of Hell; cloven hoof.
diabolism, *inhumanity*; Satanism; devil worship; witchcraft, black magic, Black Mass, *sorcery*.
diabolist, Satanist, devil-worshipper; witch.
Adj. *diabolic*, satanic, fiendish, demoniacal, *malevolent*; infernal, hellish; possessed.
Vb. *diabolize*; possess, bedevil, *bewitch.*

964 Fairy

N. *fairy*, fairy world; fairy folk, little people; fairy being; good fairy, *benefactor*; bad fairy, witch; fairy queen; fairy king, Puck; spirit of air; elemental spirit, sylph; genius; fairy ring, fairy lore, folklore.
elf, elves, brownie; gnome, dwarf; troll; goblin, flibbertigibbet; imp, sprite, hobgoblin; changeling; leprechaun; poltergeist, gremlin; Puck, Hob.
ghost, spirit; visitant, poltergeist; spook, spectre, apparition, phantom, shape, shade, wraith, presence, fetch; *visual fallacy*; control, *spiritualism*; White Lady, Black Shuck.
demon, flibbertigibbet, Friar Rush; imp, familiar, familiar spirit, *devil*; banshee; troll, troll woman; ogre, giant; bugbear, *monster*; ghoul, vampire, werewolf; incubus, succubus, nightmare; fury, harpy; Gorgon.
mythical *being*, angel, *devil*; demon, genie; centaur, satyr, faun; sea nymph, Naiad, water elf; mermaid; Siren; water spirit, *nymph*; *sorcerer*; Green Man; Yeti, Abominable Snowman, Leviathan,

Phoenix.
Adj. *fairylike*, fairy; *lean*; gigantic, *huge*; monstrous, *diabolic*; elvish, impish, Puckish, *maleficent*; magic, *magical*; *imaginary*.
spooky; macabre; weird, uncanny, unearthly, *abnormal*; eerie, supernatural; disembodied, *immaterial*.
Vb. haunt, visit, walk; ghost, gibber.
Adv. *spookishly*, spectrally, uncannily; elfishly, puckishly.

965 Heaven

N. *heaven*, presence of God, kingdom of heaven, heavenly kingdom, kingdom come; Paradise; eternal home, eternal rest, celestial bliss, blessed state; nirvana; earthly Paradise, Holy City, afterlife, eternal life, eternity, *future state*; resurrection; assumption, translation.
mythic *heaven*; Elysium, happy hunting grounds; Earthly Paradise, Eden, *fantasy*.
Adj. *paradisiac*; heavenly, celestial, eternal; beatific, blessed, *happy*; Olympian.

966 Hell

N. *hell*, lower world, nether regions, underworld; grave, limbo, Hades; purgatory; perdition, inferno, Pandemonium; abyss, bottomless pit; place of torment; everlasting fire.
mythic *hell*; realm of Pluto, Hades; river of hell; infernal watchdog; infernal judge; nether gods, Pluto.
Adj. *infernal*, bottomless, *deep*; subterranean, *low*; hellish; Stygian; *diabolic*.

967 Religion

N. *religion*, religious instinct, *humility*; religious feeling, *piety*; *expectation*; religious quest; natural religion; primitive religion, early faith; nature religion; mysticism; yoga; *philosophy*; *worship*; religious cult, state religion, *cult*.
deism, theism; animism, pantheism, polytheism, monotheism.
religious *faith*, faith, *belief*; Christianity; Judaism; Islam; Hinduism; Buddhism; Zen; Taoism.
theology, study of religion; natural theology, religious knowledge, religious learning, divinity; scholastic theology; tradition, deposit of faith; teaching, doctrine, definition, canon; dogma, tenet; articles of faith, credo, *creed*; confession; fundamentalism; higher criticism; comparative religion.
theologian; divinity student, divine; doctor; rabbi, scribe, mufti, mullah; scholastic; psalmist; Bible critic.
religious *teacher*, prophet, inspired writer; guru, *sage*; evangelist, apostle, missionary; Messiah, Invisible Imam; founder of Christianity, Christ; Prophet of God; Confucius.
religionist; *idolater*; pagan, gentile, *heathen*; adherent, believer; militant, believer, *zealot*; Christian; Jew; Muslim, Moslem; dervish; Hindu; Sikh; Mormon, *sect*; *heretic*.
Adj. *religious*, divine, holy, sacred, spiritual; Christian, Moslem, Mosaic; mystic; devout.
theological theosophical, scholastic; doctrinal, dogmatic, canonical.

968 Irreligion

N. *irreligion*; nothing sacred, *impiety*; false religion; disbelief; scepticism, *doubt*; philosophy; lack of faith, infidelity; lapse; apathy.

antichristianity, *opposition*; Satanism; free thinking, free thought, nihilism, *philosophy*; materialism; secularism; *avarice*.

irreligionist; dissenter, atheist, *unbeliever*; rationalist, freethinker; agnostic, sceptic.

heathen, pagan; infidel; gentile; lapsed Christian.

Adj. *irreligious*, without a god, godless, profane; agnostic, sceptical; ungodly, *wicked*; amoral, morally neutral, *indifferent*; secular, mundane, of this world, worldly, *sensual*; lacking faith, faithless, lapsed; *sensual*.

heathenish, unholy, *profane*; unchristian; gentile; heathen, pagan, infidel.

Vb. *be irreligious*, lack faith; *disbelieve*; deny God, blaspheme.

paganize.

969 Revelation

N. *revelation*, apocalypse, *disclosure*; light; inspiration, prophecy; intuition, mysticism; direct communication; divine message, God's word, gospel, gospel message; burning bush, epiphany, incarnation, Word made flesh.

scripture, word of God, inspired text, sacred writings; Holy Scripture, Holy Writ, Bible; Greek version; canon; Old Testament, Major Prophets; New Testament, Revelation, Apocalypse; Apocrypha; psalter, missal; prayer book, Book of Common Prayer; hymn book, *hymn*; Talmud; Higher Criticism; fundamentalism.

non-Biblical *scripture*, Koran; Hindu scripture; Book of Mormon.

Adj. *revelational*, mystic; inspired; apocalyptic; evangelical.

scriptural, sacred, holy; inspired; *authoritative*; Mosaic; gospel, apostolic.

970 Orthodoxy

N. *orthodoxy*, correct opinion, right belief; sound theology; religious truth, pure Gospel, *truth*; primitive faith, early Church, Apostolic age; credo, *creed*; catechism, Church Catechism.

orthodoxism, strict interpretation; fundamentalism; *conformity*; Christian practice, *observance*; Holy Office, *tribunal*; Inquisition; Index, *disapprobation*; *approbation*.

Christendom, Christian world; undivided Church; Christian fellowship; Holy Church, Bride of Christ; Body of Christ, universal Church; Church Militant, visible Church; invisible Church, Church Triumphant.

Catholicism, Scarlet Woman; High Church.

Protestantism, Calvinism; Methodism, *sect*.

Catholic, Orthodox; Roman Catholic, papist; Old Catholic, Anglican, Episcopalian.

Protestant, Anglican, Huguenot; Presbyterian, Baptist, Wesleyan, Quaker, Friend.

church *member*; Christian, disciple of Christ; church people, congregation.

the *orthodox*; evangelical; believer.

Adj. *orthodox*; right-minded, sound, balanced, *judicial*; undivided, *whole*; unswerving, loyal, devout, *obedient*; conventional; precise, strict; intolerant; correct, *accurate*; of faith; authoritative, evangelical, gospel, *genuine*; literal; catholic, universal; held, *credible*; customary, *usual*.

Roman *Catholic*, Catholic, Roman.

Anglican, episcopalian; high.

Protestant; *sectarian*; Presbyterian, Baptist, Wesleyan, Quaker.

Vb. *be orthodox*, believe; *conform*.

Adv. *orthodoxly*.

971 Heterodoxy

N. *heterodoxy*; erroneous opinion, wrong belief, false creed, superstition, *error*; strange doctrine, new teaching; modernism, Higher Criticism; partial truth; heresy.

heresy, heathen theology, gnosticism.

heretic.

Adj. *heterodox*, *different*; nonconformist; less than orthodox, erroneous, *mistaken*; unorthodox.

heretical, heretic; heathen.

Vb. *declare heretical*, anathematize, condemn.

be heretical, be unorthodox.

Adv. *heretically*, unorthodoxly.

972 Sectarianism

N. *sectarianism*, sectionalism, *prejudice*; bias; party spirit; separatism; nonconformity, *dissent*; Calvinism.

schism, division, *quarrel*; separation; religious schism, Great Schism.

church *party*; Catholic; Protestant; Broad Church party.

sect, division, branch, group, faction, *party*; order, brotherhood, *community*; nonconformist sect, chapel; Salvation Army.

non-Christian *sect*; Hindu sect; Pure Land sect, *religious faith*.

sectarian; follower, adherent, devotee; Nonconformist; Puritan, Shaker; Quaker, Friend; Presbyterian, *Protestant*; Mormon; *heretic*.

schismatic; rebel; recusant; dissident, dissenter, nonconformist; wrong believer, *heretic*.

Adj. *sectarian*; clannish, exclusive, *sectional*; episcopalian, *Anglican*; evangelical, *Protestant*; Puritan, Presbyterian, Pharisaic.

schismatical, schismatic; *separate*; nonconformist; recusant; rebellious, rebel, *disobedient*.

Vb. *sectarianize*, follow a sect, *join a party*.

schismatize, commit schism, separate, divide, withdraw, secede; *disobey*.

973 Piety

N. *piety*, goodness, *virtue*; reverence, honour, decent respect, *respect*; affection, kind feeling, *benevolence*; loyalty, conformity, attendance at worship, *observance*; religion, theism; religious feeling, pious sentiment; fear of God, godly fear, *fear*; humility; pious belief, faith, trust, *belief*; devotion, dedication; enthusiasm, fervour, zeal, muscular Christianity; inspiration, exaltation; adoration, *worship*; retreat; mysticism, communion with God, mystic communion, *religion*; *restoration*; act of piety, pious duty, charity, *philanthropy*; pious fiction, tract, sermon; Christian behaviour, Christian life; pilgrimage.

sanctity, holiness; goodness, *virtue*; state of grace, odour of sanctity, *purity*; holy character; *spirituality*; spiritual life; blessed state; enlightenment; rebirth, new birth, *revival*; adoption, *divine function*; dedication.

pietism, show of piety; cant, *sham*; religious mania; tender conscience; *narrow mind*; fundamentalism; *hatred*; *prejudice*; *philanthropy*.

pietist, pious person, real saint, *good person*; martyr; saint; man or woman of prayer, mystic; holy man, fakir, dervish, *ascetic*; hermit, anchorite, *solitary*; monk, nun, religious, *clergy*; devotee, dedicated soul; convert, neophyte; believer, *church member*; pilgrim.

zealot, fanatic, bigot, iconoclast; Puritan; Pharisee, scribe; *sectarian*; evangelical; missionary, *philanthropist*; militant Christian; *tyrant*.

Adj. pious, good, kind, *virtuous*; decent, *respectful*; faithful, true, loyal, devoted, *obedient*; *orthodox*; sincere, *veracious*; pure, otherworldly, spiritual; godly, religious, devout; mystic; holy, sainted, Christian, full of grace.

pietistic, ardent, fervent; inspired; austere, *ascetic*; *unsociable*; earnest, pi, self-righteous; precise, Puritan; Pharisaic, *sectarian*; sanctimonious, *affected*; goody-goody, too good to be true, *virtuous*; evangelical.

sanctified, made holy, dedicated; reverend, holy, sacred, solemn, sacrosanct; sainted; chosen; *liberated*; regenerate, reborn, born again.

Vb. be pious, be holy, wear a halo; mind heavenly things, think of God; fear God, *fear*; have faith, *believe*; *be strong*; humble oneself, *be humble*; go to church, attend divine worship; pray, *worship*; kneel, genuflect, bow, *stoop*; cross oneself; make offering, sacrifice, *offer*; lend to God, *give*; glorify God, *praise*; *thank*; revere, show reverence, *show respect*; hearken, listen, *obey*; preach at, *teach*; set a good example.

become pious, experience religion, get religion; *recant*; reform, repent, receive Christ, *be penitent*; take holy orders, *take orders*; be a pilgrim.

make pious, bring religion to, bring to God, convert, *convince*; *admit*; *purify*; edify, confirm, *strengthen*; inspire, fill with grace, uplift, *make better*; redeem, regenerate, *restore*.

sanctify, hallow, make holy, *honour*; consecrate, dedicate, enshrine, *dignify*; make a saint of, saint, invest with a halo; bless, pronounce a blessing.

974 Impiety

N. impiety; disregard, *disrespect*; lack of piety, lack of reverence; mockery, *ridicule*; scorn, pride, *contempt*; *malediction*; sacrilege, perversion, abuse, *misuse*; sin; materialism; *disapprobation*.

false piety, *falsehood*; solemn mockery, *sham*; hypocrisy, lip service, *duplicity*; cant, *affectation*.

impious person, *malediction*; profane person, gentile, pagan, infidel, unbeliever, *heathen*; *idolater*; atheist, sceptic; reprobate, *bad person*; recidivist; fallen angel, Wicked One, Satan; hypocrite; canter.

Adj. impious, ungodly; recusant; godless, *irreligious*; irreligious, irreverent, without reverence; *lawless*; brazen, bold; hard, unmoved, unfeeling, *cruel*; sinful, impure, reprobate, *wicked*; sanctimonious, *affected*.

profane, unholy; accursed; infidel, pagan, gentile.

Vb. be impious, rebel against God, *be proud*; sin, *be wicked*; swear, blaspheme, *curse*; profane, desecrate, violate, *misuse*; commit sacrilege, defile, sully, *make unclean*; worship false gods; cant, *be affected*; play false, *dissemble*; backslide; *deteriorate*.

975 Worship

N. worship, honour, reverence, homage, respect; holy fear, awe, *fear*; adoration; humility; devotion, *piety*; prayer; retreat, quiet time, communion.

cult, mystique; type of worship, service, *duty*; service of God, supreme worship; inferior worship; false worship.

act of worship, rite; *praise*; hymn-singing, psalm-singing, plainsong, *vocal music*; thanksgiving, blessing, benediction, *thanks*; offering, sacrifice; self-examination; self-denial, self-discipline; keeping fast; pilgrimage, *wandering*.

prayers, private devotion, retreat; prayer, bidding prayer; petition, *request*; suffrage; special prayer, intention; denunciation, *threat*; *malediction*; ban; benediction, grace, *thanks*; collect; Our Father; blessing, rosary; prayer book, missal; call to prayer, *call*.

hymn, song, psalm, religious song, spiritual; processional hymn, recessional; plainsong, descant, *vocal music*; anthem, cantata, motet; response; song of praise, Magnificat; Hosanna; Homeric hymn; psalter.

oblation, collection, *offering*; pew rent; libation, incense, *rite*; dedication; *gratitude*; victim, scapegoat, *substitute*; burnt offering, holocaust; sacrifice, devotion, hecatomb, *slaughter*; human sacrifice, *homicide*; self-sacrifice, suttee, *suicide*.

public worship, common prayer; agape; service, divine service, divine office, mass, matins, evensong, benediction, *church service*; *vocal music*; church, *piety*; assembly; prayer meeting; temple worship, state religion, *religion*.

worshipper, *church member*; devotee; admirer; follower, server, *servant*; *idolater*; caller; supplicant; man or woman of prayer, mystic, visionary; dervish, prophet, *religious teacher*; celebrant, *clergy*; congregation, *church member*; cantor; psalmist; pilgrim, *traveller*.

Adj. worshipping; devout, devoted, *pious*; respectful; fervent; *orthodox*; psalm-singing; mystic.

devotional; solemn, sacred, holy; sacramental, mystic; votive, *offering*.

Vb. worship, honour, revere, venerate, adore, *respect*; *fear*; do worship to, pay homage to, acknowledge; pay divine honours to, make a god of one, deify; kneel to, genuflect, humble oneself; bless, give thanks, *thank*; extol, magnify, glorify, give glory to, *praise*; hymn, anthem, celebrate, *sing*; burn incense before; invoke, address, *speak to*; petition, beseech, intercede, *entreat*; pray, say a prayer; meditate, contemplate, commune with God, *be pious*.

offer worship, celebrate, officiate, minister, *perform ritual*; sacrifice, *give*; sacrifice to, propitiate, appease, *pacify*; vow, *promise*;

live a life of praise; dedicate, consecrate, *sanctify*; enter holy orders, *take orders*; *travel*; go to church, go to chapel, go to meeting, *be pious*; go to service, hear Mass, communicate, take Holy Communion; fast, observe Lent, *starve*; deny oneself, *be ascetic*; *meditate*; chant psalms, carol, *sing*; *praise*.

Int. Alleluia! Hallelujah! Hosanna! Glory be to God! Holy, Holy, Holy; Lord have mercy; Lord, bless us! God save!

976 Idolatry

N. *idolatry*, false worship, superstition, *worship*; *religion*; fetishism, anthropomorphism; image worship; idol worship; hocuspocus, *sorcery*; cult, sacrifice; sun worship; star worship; fire worship; animal worship; snake worship; devil worship; worship of wealth.

deification; hero worship, *respect*; king worship, *worship*.

idol, statue, *sculpture*; image, cult image, fetish, totem pole; golden calf, *deity*; totem; Juggernaut.

idolater; pagan, *heathen*.

Adj. *idolatrous*, pagan, heathen; *diabolic*.

Vb. *idolatrize*; deify, *sanctify*; *praise*.

Adv. *idolatrously*.

977 Sorcery

N. *sorcery*, magic arts; witchcraft; magic lore, *knowledge*; magic skill, *skill*; magic; sympathetic magic, influence, *inducement*; white magic; black magic, black art, necromancy; superstition; voodoo, hoodoo; *divination*; *rite*; magic rite, incantation; ghost dance; coven; Hallowe'en.

spell, charm, hoodoo, curse; evil eye, jinx, influence; fascination, *attraction*; obsession, possession; *frenzy*; incantation, rune; magic sign, pass; magic word, magic formula, open sesame, abracadabra; *lack of meaning*; philtre, love potion (see *magic instrument*).

talisman, charm; cross; *safeguard*; fetish, *idol*; amulet, mascot, lucky charm; horseshoe, black cat; pentagram; swastika; scarab; emblem, flag, relic, *refuge*.

magic instrument, bell, book and candle; magic recipe; philtre, potion; wand, magic ring; magic mirror, magic sword, flying carpet; wishbone.

sorcerer, wise man, seer, soothsayer; Druid; magus; witchdoctor, medicine man, *idolater*; illusionist; enchanter, wizard, warlock; magician; familiar, imp, evil spirit, *devil*; Pied Piper.

sorceress, wise woman, Sibyl; witch, weird sister; hag; succubus; wicked fairy, *fairy*.

Adj. *sorcerous*; magician; *wonderful*; *diabolic*; enchanting; malignant, *maleficent*; occult, esoteric.

magical; otherworldly, supernatural, uncanny, weird; magic.

bewitched, enchanted, fey; spellbound; under the evil eye; cursed.

Vb. *practise sorcery*, cast a nativity, *divine*; do magic; recite a spell, recite an incantation; conjure, invoke; raise spirits; wave a wand; ride a broomstick.

bewitch, witch, charm, enchant, fascinate, *attract*; magic; spellbind; hoodoo, voodoo; overlook, blight, blast, *be maleficent*; curse; taboo, *prohibit*; walk, ghost, haunt.

Adv. *sorcerously*, by means of enchant-

ment.

978 Occultism

N. *occultism*, mysticism, *religion*; secret art, esoteric science, occult lore, alchemy, astrology, spiritualism, magic, *sorcery*; *divination*; *prediction*; clairvoyance, second sight, *vision*; *intuition*; hypnotism; hypnosis, *insensibility*.

psychics, *psychology*; psychic science; ESP; clairvoyance, second sight, *intuition*; psychokinesis; telepathy; precognition.

spiritualism; spirit communication, *sorcery*; *divination*; sitting; spirit manifestation; telekinesis; automatic writing, *writing*; spirit message; control, *ghost*.

occultist, mystic; esoteric; yogi; *sorcerer*; fortune-teller, palmist.

psychic, clairvoyant; telepathist; mind reader; medium; seer, prophet, *oracle*.

psychist, parapsychologist, psychophysicist, psychical researcher.

Adj. *cabbalistic*, esoteric, hermetic, cryptic, *occult*; dark, mysterious, *unknown*; mystic, transcendental, supernatural, *religious*; spooky.

psychical, psychic, fey; telepathic, clairvoyant; mind-reading.

paranormal, supernatural, preternatural.

Vb. *practise occultism*; alchemize, *transform*; *divine*; practise spiritualism; have a control; study spiritualism.

979 The Church

N. *the church*, Christendom; theocracy, *authority*; church government, Vatican; *government*; hierarchy, *order*; papacy; presbytery.

ecclesiasticism; benefit of clergy; Holy Office, *prohibition*.

monasticism, monastic life.

church *ministry*, call, *vocation*; mission; cure; spiritual comfort, spiritual leadership, *philanthropy*; spiritual guidance, confession, absolution, *ministration*; *teaching*.

holy *orders*, orders; apostolic succession; ordination; induction; installation; presentation; appointment, *commission*; translation, elevation, *progression*.

church *office*, *management*; pontificate, papacy, Holy See, Vatican; primacy; see, bishopric; deanery; incumbency, tenure, *possession*.

parish, deanery; presbytery; diocese, bishopric, see; province, *district*.

benefice, incumbency, tenure; living, parsonage; tithe; *property*; patronage, right of presentation.

synod, convocation, general council, *council*; episcopal bench; chapter, vestry; kirk session, presbytery, synod, *tribunal*.

Adj. *ecclesiastical*, infallible, *authoritative*; *orthodox*; apostolic; pontifical, papal, Roman Catholic; patriarchal; episcopal, clerical; episcopalian, presbyterian, *sectarian*; provincial, parochial.

priestly; spiritual; apostolic, pastoral.

Vb. *be ecclesiastical*; frock, ordain, order, consecrate, enthrone; cowl, make a monk of; call, confer, nominate, present; prefer, bestow a living, *give*; translate, *transfer*; elevate, promote; saint, *sanctify*; *take orders*.

Adv. *ecclesiastically*.

980 Clergy

N. *clergy,* hierarchy; clerical order; secular clergy, regular clergy, religious.

cleric, clerical; priest, deacon; divine; Doctor of Divinity; clergyman, servant of God; reverend, father; padre, sky pilot; beneficiary, parson, rector, incumbent, *possessor*; *nonentity.*

pastor, shepherd, minister, parish priest, rector, vicar, perpetual curate, curate; chaplain; penitentiary; spiritual director, spiritual adviser; friar, missionary, *philanthropist*; evangelist.

ecclesiarch, dignitary, *governor*; pope, Supreme Pontiff, Holy Father, Vicar of Christ; cardinal; patriarch, primate, archbishop; prelate, bishop; assistant bishop, 'episcopal curate'; Lords Spiritual; archdeacon, deacon; dean, rural dean; canon, canon regular, canon secular; Superior, abbot, abbess; prior, Grand Prior; elder, presbyter, moderator.

monk, monastic, *celibate*; hermit, Desert Father, *solitary*; Orthodox monk; dervish, fakir, *ascetic*; brother, regular; superior, abbot, prior; novice; lay brother; friar, religious; fraternity, brotherhood, friary; order, *community*; Black Monk, Benedictine, Trappist; teaching order.

nun; recluse; religious, bride of Christ; sister, mother; novice; lay sister; Mother Superior, abbess.

church *officer,* elder, presbyter, deacon, *officer*; priest, chaplain; minister; lay reader; server, altar boy; chorister, choirboy, cantor, *choir*; sidesman or -woman; churchwarden; clerk, beadle, verger; sexton.

priest; prophet, *oracle*; rabbi; imam, mufti; lama, pontiff; Druid; witch doctor.

church *title,* Holy Father; Eminence; Monsignor; Lordship, Lord Spiritual; Most Reverend; parson, rector, vicar; father, brother; mother, sister.

monastery; friary; priory, abbey; cloister, convent, nunnery; hermitage, *retreat*; community house, *abode*; seminary, training school; cell, *chamber.*

parsonage, presbytery, rectory, vicarage; manse; deanery, *abode*; Vatican; close, precincts.

Adj. *clerical,* regular; secular; lay; pastoral; episcopal.

monastic; celibate.

Vb. *take orders;* become a nun; enter a monastery or a nunnery.

Adv. *clerically.*

981 Laity

N. *laity,* lay people; people; cure, charge, parish; flock, sheep, fold; brethren, congregation, society, *church member*; lay brethren, lay community, *community.*

lay *person;* lay rector, lay deacon; lay brother, lay sister; novice; lay reader; elder, deacon, *church officer*; parishioner, *church member.*

Adj. *laical,* parochial; lay; secular; temporal, *irreligious*; profane, unholy.

Vb. *laicize,* secularize, deconsecrate.

982 Ritual

N. *ritual,* procedure, way of doing things, method, *way*; due order, *order*; form, order, liturgy, *practice*; symbolism, *metaphor*; ceremonial, ceremony, *formality*.

ritualism, ceremony.

rite, mode of worship, *cult*; institution, observance, ritual practice, *practice*; form, order, ordinance, rubric, formula, *precept*; ceremony, solemnity, sacrament, mystery, *celebration*; *representation*; rite of passage, initiation, baptism, *reception.*

ministration, performance, *action*; celebration; sermon, address, *teaching*; *lecture*; sacred rhetoric, *oratory*; pastoral care; pastoral epistle, pastoral letter; confession, shrift, absolution, penance.

Christian *rite*; sacrament; baptism, *reception*; First Communion; Holy Communion, Eucharist; *penance*; absolution, *acquittal*; Holy Matrimony, *marriage*; Holy Orders; requiem mass; liturgy, order of service, order of baptism, marriage service, nuptial mass; ordination; ban, bell, book and candle; dedication.

Holy *Communion,* Eucharist, mass; low mass; public mass, communion; preparation, confession; Preface, Great Amen; kiss of peace.

the *sacrament*; real presence, transubstantiation, consubstantiation; altar bread; host; reserved sacrament.

church *service,* office, duty, service, *act of worship*; liturgy, celebration; matins, prime, none, vespers; morning prayer, matins; evening prayer, evensong, benediction; vigil, midnight mass.

ritual *act,* symbolism, *representation*; sprinkling, aspersion; procession, *progression*; *act of worship*; obeisance, homage, *respects*; crossing oneself, *gesture*; kiss of peace.

ritual *object,* cross, crucifix; altar, Lord's table, altar furniture, altar cloth, candle, candlestick; communion wine, communion bread; cup, chalice; cruet; tabernacle; collection plate, salver; incense; holy water; font; wedding garment, wedding ring; relics, sacred relics; shrine, casket, *box*; Holy Sepulchre, *image*; rosary; libation dish, patina; prayer wheel; altar of incense; temple veil.

ritualist; celebrant, minister, *priest*; server.

office-book, ordinal; liturgy; rubric, canon, *precept*; missal; prayer book, Book of Common Prayer, Alternative Service Book; rosary.

hymnal, hymn book, psalter, book of psalms, *hymn.*

holy *day,* feast, feast day, festival, *festivity*; fast day, *fast*; high day, day of observance, day of obligation, *celebration*; sabbath, day of rest, *leisure*; Lord's Day, Sunday; anniversary; Lady Day; Candlemas; Michaelmas; Advent; Christmas, Yuletide, Noel, Nativity, Epiphany, Twelfth Night; Lent, Ash Wednesday, Good Friday; Holy Week, Passion Week; Easter, Easter Sunday; Ascension Day; Whitsun, Pentecost; Trinity Sunday; Passover; Pentecost; Ramadan.

Adj. *ritual,* procedural; formal, solemn, ceremonial; processional, recessional; representational; paschal; unleavened; kosher; blessed.

ritualistic, ceremonious, ceremonial.

Vb. *perform ritual,* say office, celebrate, officiate; lead worship, *offer worship*; christen, confirm, ordain; minister, give communion; sacrifice, bless, give benediction; ban, ban with bell, book and candle; excommunicate; dedicate, consecrate; purify; burn incense; anoint; confess, absolve, pronounce absolution; take communion; bow, kneel, genuflect, pros-

trate oneself; sign oneself; take holy
water; process; fast, flagellate oneself, do
penance.
ritualize, institute a rite; observe, keep, keep
holy.
Adv. *ritually*, ceremonially; symbolically;
liturgically.

983 Canonicals

N. *canonicals*, clerical dress, cloth, clerical
black, *dress*; frock, cassock; cloak, gown,
cloak; robe, cowl, hood; clerical collar;
apron, shovel hat; skullcap; Salvation
Army bonnet.
vestments; cassock, surplice; cope, *robe*;
stole, scarf; *girdle*; mitre, tiara, triple
crown, *regalia*; papal vestment; crook,
staff, *badge of rank*; pectoral, *cross*; episcopal ring.
Adj. *vestmental*; canonical, pontifical.
vestured; hooded, *monastic*; clerical.

984 Temple

N. *temple*, pantheon; shrine; house of God,
tabernacle; place of worship, *worship*;
mosque; house of prayer, oratory; sacred
edifice, pagoda, ziggurat, *edifice*; *doorway*.
holy *place*, holy ground, sacred precinct;
sanctuary; Sanctum, oracle; sacred tomb,
sepulchre, Holy Sepulchre; graveyard,
God's Acre, *cemetery*; place of pilgrimage; Holy City; Mecca.
church, God's house; parish church, chapel
of ease; cathedral, minster; basilica;
abbey; kirk, chapel, tabernacle, temple;
meeting house, house of prayer, oratory;
synagogue, mosque.
altar, sanctuary; altar stone, altar slab; altar
table, altar bread; credence, credence
table, *ritual object*; canopy, altarpiece,
triptych, altar screen, reredos; altar
cloth, altar frontal; altar rails.
church *utensil*, font; chalice, *ritual object*;
pulpit, lectern; bible, prayer book; salver,
collection plate; organ, harmonium; bell,
carillon, *campanology*.
church *interior*, nave, aisle, apse, transept;
chancel, choir, sanctuary; squint; chancel
screen, gallery, organ loft; stall; pew, box
pew; pulpit; lectern; chapel, confessional;
clerestory; calvary, Easter sepulchre;
font; sacristy, vestry; crypt, vault; cross,
crucifix.
church *exterior*, porch; tympanum, *doorway*; tower, steeple, spire, *high structure*;
bell tower, belfry; buttress, *prop*; cloister;
presbytery, *council*; churchyard, lychgate; close.
Adj. *churchlike*; Romanesque, Norman,
Gothic, Early English, Perpendicular,
baroque, Gothic revival.

INDEX

A

abase
  lay waste 160 vb.
  abase 306 vb.
  pervert 650 vb.
  strike at 707 vb.

abate
  shade off 27 vb.
  abate 37 vb.
  subtract 39 vb.
  decompose 51 vb.
  weaken 158 vb.
  moderate 172 vb.
  make smaller
      193 vb.
  shorten 199 vb.
  qualify 463 vb.
  discount 805 vb.
  starve 941 vb.

ability
  intrinsically 5 n.
  ability 155 n.
  influence 173 n.
  possibility 464 n.
  means 624 n.
  utility 635 n.
  skill 689 n.

able, be
  be equal 28 vb.
  be able 155 vb.
  find means
      624 vb.

ablutions
  water 334 n.
  moistening 336 n.
  heater 378 n.
  ablutions 643 n.
  beautification
      838 n.

abnormal
  nonuniform
      17 adj.
  abnormal 84 adj.
  misplaced
      183 adj.
  crazy 498 adj.
  unexpected
      503 adj.
  puzzling 512 adj.
  funny 844 adj.
  wrong 909 adj.
  extramarital
      946 adj.
  spooky 964 adj.

abnormality
  abnormality 84 n.

abode
  district 179 n.
  locality 182 n.
  station 182 n.
  abode 187 n.
  monastery 980 n.
  parsonage 980 n.

abound
  abound 630 vb.
  superabound
      632 vb.

about
  about 33 adv.

abroad
  abroad 59 adv.

abrogate
  nullify 2 vb.
  disable 156 vb.
  weaken 158 vb.
  destroy 160 vb.
  suppress 160 vb.
  counteract
      177 vb.

  negate 528 vb.
  recant 598 vb.
  reject 602 vb.
  relinquish 616 vb.
  make useless
      636 vb.
  stop using
      669 vb.
  command 732 vb.
  liberate 741 vb.
  abrogate 747 vb.
  prohibit 752 vb.
  not observe
      764 vb.
  not retain
      774 vb.
  not pay 800 vb.
  disentitle 911 vb.
  disapprove
      919 vb.
  make illegal
      949 vb.
  acquit 955 vb.

abrogated
  abrogated
      747 adj.

abrogation
  abrogation 747 n.

absence
  nonexistence 2 n.
  simpleness 44 n.
  zero 99 n.
  absence 185 n.
  farness 194 n.
  invisibility 439 n.
  unwillingness
      593 n.
  avoidance 615 n.
  requirement
      622 n.
  nonuse 669 n.
  undutifulness
      913 n.

absence of intellect
  absence of
  intellect 443 n.
  absence of
  thought 445 n.
  unintelligence
      494 n.

absence of thought
  absence of
  intellect 443 n.
  absence of
  thought 445 n.
  inattention
      451 n.
  intuition 471 n.

absent
  nonexistent
      2 adj.
  incomplete
      55 adj.
  misplaced
      183 adj.
  absent 185 adj.
  disappearing
      441 adj.
  unknown 486 adj.
  required 622 adj.
  unprovided
      631 adj.
  unused 669 adj.
  inactive 674 adj.
  lost 767 adj.
  undutiful 913 adj.

absent, be
  be incomplete
      55 vb.
  be excluded
      57 vb.

  be absent 185 vb.
  disappear 441 vb.
  run away 615 vb.
  relinquish 616 vb.
  elude 662 vb.
  be lost 767 vb.
  fail in duty
      913 vb.

absolute
  absolute 32 adj.

absorb
  consume 160 vb.
  destroy 160 vb.
  hold within
      219 vb.
  draw 283 vb.
  absorb 294 vb.
  drink 296 vb.
  eat 296 vb.
  dry 337 vb.
  be credulous
      482 vb.
  superabound
      632 vb.
  appropriate
      781 vb.

abstainer
  abstainer 937 n.

abstract
  shorten 199 vb.
  be concise
      564 vb.
  abstract 587 n.
  select 600 vb.

abstracted
  thoughtful
      444 adj.
  abstracted
      451 adj.
  crazy 498 adj.
  forgetful 501 adj.

abstractedness
  abstractedness
      451 n.

absurd
  disagreeing
      25 adj.
  erroneous
      490 adj.
  absurd 492 adj.
  foolish 494 adj.
  imaginative
      508 adj.
  semantic 509 adj.
  meaningless
      510 adj.
  exaggerated
      541 adj.
  useless 636 adj.
  laughing 830 adj.
  witty 834 adj.
  ridiculous
      844 adj.
  undue 911 adj.

absurd, be
  rampage 61 vb.
  be absurd
      492 vb.
  be foolish 494 vb.
  mean nothing
      510 vb.
  befool 537 vb.
  be capricious
      599 vb.
  waste effort
      636 vb.
  do 671 vb.
  act foolishly
      690 vb.
  amuse oneself
      832 vb.

  be witty 834 vb.
  be ridiculous
      844 vb.
  lose repute
      862 vb.

absurdity
  absurdity 492 n.

abundance
  increase 36 n.
  production 159 n.
  abundance 166 n.
  vegetable life
      361 n.
  plenty 630 n.

academic title
  honours 861 n.
  academic title
      865 n.

academy
  erudition 485 n.
  academy 534 n.

accelerate
  augment 36 vb.
  be early 130 vb.
  be vigorous
      169 vb.
  accelerate
      272 vb.
  impel 274 vb.
  promote 280 vb.
  hasten 675 vb.
  animate 816 vb.

access
  bond 47 n.
  entrance 68 n.
  region 179 n.
  doorway 258 n.
  approach 284 n.
  way in 292 n.
  outlet 293 n.
  passage 300 n.
  access 619 n.

accessible
  near 195 adj.
  open 258 adj.
  accessible
      284 adj.
  admitting
      294 adj.
  communicating
      619 adj.
  easy 696 adj.
  free 739 adj.

accompaniment
  relativeness 9 n.
  addition 38 n.
  speciality 80 n.
  accompaniment
      89 n.
  synchronism
      118 n.
  contiguity 197 n.
  nondesign 613 n.

accompany
  accompany
      89 vb.
  synchronize
      118 vb.
  concur 176 vb.
  be contiguous
      197 vb.
  carry 268 vb.
  follow 279 vb.
  direct 684 vb.
  serve 737 vb.
  take away
      781 vb.
  greet 879 vb.
  court 884 vb.

accompanying
accompanying
89 adj.

accord
be related 9 vb.
be identical
13 vb.
be uniform 16 vb.
resemble 18 vb.
accord 24 vb.
be equal 28 vb.
combine 50 vb.
be in order 60 vb.
conform 83 vb.
conform 83 vb.
concur 176 vb.
harmonize
405 vb.
assent 483 vb.
mean 509 vb.
be expedient
637 vb.
concord 705 vb.

accordingly
accordingly
8 adv.

account
number 86 vb.
estimate 475 vb.
register 543 vb.
pay 799 vb.
account 803 vb.

accountant
enumerator 86 n.
recorder 544 n.
treasurer 793 n.
accountant
803 n.

account book
list 87 n.
record 543 n.
account book
803 n.

account for
account for
153 vb.

accounting
accounting
803 adj.

accounts
accounts 803 n.

accrue
be extrinsic 6 vb.
accrue 38 vb.
approach 284 vb.
be received
777 vb.

accumulation
great quantity
32 n.
increase 36 n.
medley 43 n.
arrangement
62 n.
accumulation
74 n.
collision 274 n.
collection 627 n.
storage 627 n.
store 627 n.
acquisition 766 n.

accumulator
accumulator
74 n.

accuracy
accuracy 489 n.

accurate
adjusted 24 adj.
definite 80 adj.
attentive
450 adj.

careful 452 adj.
discriminating
458 adj.
accurate 489 adj.
interpretive
515 adj.
veracious
535 adj.
perspicuous
562 adj.
descriptive
585 adj.
artless 694 adj.
observant
763 adj.
orthodox 970 adj.

accusable
accusable
923 adj.

accusation
accusation 923 n.

accuse
attribute 153 vb.
inform 519 vb.
divulge 521 vb.
proclaim 523 vb.
retaliate 709 vb.
satirize 846 vb.
curse 894 vb.
blame 919 vb.
dispraise 919 vb.
defame 921 vb.
accuse 923 vb.

accused
accused 923 adj.

accused person
list 87 n.
prisoner 745 n.
vindicator 922 n.
accused person
923 n.
litigant 954 n.

accuser
accuser 923 n.

accusing
accusing 923 adj.

accusingly
accusingly
923 adv.

achieve liberty
separate 46 vb.
escape 662 vb.
revolt 733 vb.
achieve liberty
741 vb.

achromatism
achromatism
421 n.

acoustics
acoustics 393 n.
hearing 410 n.
linguist 552 n.

acquiesce
acquiesce 483 vb.
submit 716 vb.
consent 753 vb.

acquire
bring together
74 vb.
revert 143 vb.
busy oneself
617 vb.
find means
624 vb.
entreat 756 vb.
acquire 766 vb.
change hands
775 vb.
receive 777 vb.
borrow 780 vb.
take 781 vb.

purchase 787 vb.
acquire 802 vb.
be rewarded
957 vb.

acquired
acquired 766 adj.

acquiring
acquiring
766 adj.

acquisition
compensation
31 n.
assemblage 74 n.
reversion 143 n.
transference
267 n.
benefit 610 n.
chase 614 n.
store 627 n.
acquisition 766 n.
gift 776 n.
receiving 777 n.
taking 781 n.
receipt 802 n.

acquit
deliver 663 vb.
liberate 741 vb.
forgive 904 vb.
exempt 914 vb.
justify 922 vb.
acquit 955 vb.

acquittal
escape 662 n.
deliverance
663 n.
liberation 741 n.
mercy 900 n.
forgiveness
904 n.
nonliability 914 n.
vindication 922 n.
innocence 930 n.
legal trial 954 n.
acquittal 955 n.
Christian rite
982 n.

acquitted
acquitted
955 adj.

across
obliquely
215 adv.
across 217 adv.

act
dissemble 536 vb.
act 589 vb.
be affected
845 vb.

act foolishly
act foolishly
690 vb.

acting
representation
546 n.
acting 589 n.

action
event 149 n.
production 159 n.
agency 168 n.
policy 618 n.
action 671 n.
activity 673 n.
effectuation
720 n.
observance
763 n.
celebration
871 n.
ministration
982 n.

active
eventful 149 adj.
stalwart 157 adj.
operative
168 adj.
vigorous 169 adj.
influential
173 adj.
moving 260 adj.
agitated 313 adj.
willing 592 adj.
businesslike
617 adj.
doing 671 adj.
active 673 adj.
labouring
677 adj.
excited 816 adj.

active, be
operate 168 vb.
be vigorous
169 vb.
be active 673 vb.
hasten 675 vb.
exert oneself
677 vb.
behave 683 vb.
withstand
699 vb.
philanthropize
892 vb.

actively
actively 673 adv.

activity
punctuality
130 n.
stimulation
169 n.
vigorousness
169 n.
motion 260 n.
agitation 313 n.
resolution 594 n.
business 617 n.
job 617 n.
instrumentality
623 n.
superfluity 632 n.
action 671 n.
activity 673 n.
haste 675 n.
workshop 682 n.
warm feeling
813 n.

act of worship
act of worship
975 n.
church service
982 n.
ritual act 982 n.

actor
band 74 n.
substitute 145 n.
cinema 440 n.
interpreter 515 n.
speaker 574 n.
actor 589 n.
doer 671 n.
personnel 681 n.
party 703 n.
dance 832 n.
affecter 845 n.

actually
actually 1 adv.
substantially
3 adv.
truly 489 adv.

adagio
adagio 407 adv.

adaptation
adaptation 24 n.

add
conformity 83 n.
accuracy 489 n.

add
augment 36 vb.
add 38 vb.
affix 45 vb.
join 45 vb.
agglutinate 48 vb.
combine 50 vb.
fill 54 vb.
make complete 54 vb.
put in front 64 vb.
place after 65 vb.
do sums 86 vb.
modify 138 vb.
enlarge 192 vb.
transfer 267 vb.
insert 298 vb.
misinterpret 516 vb.
exaggerate 541 vb.

addition
quantity 26 n.
increase 36 n.
increment 36 n.
addition 38 n.
adjunct 40 n.
mixture 43 n.
joining together 45 n.
whole 52 n.
extraneousness 59 n.
sequence 65 n.
numerical result 85 n.
protraction 108 n.
expansion 192 n.
insertion 298 n.
exaggeration 541 n.

additional
extrinsic 6 adj.
increasing 36 adj.
additional 38 adj.
complete 54 adj.
sequential 65 adj.
included 78 adj.
inserted 298 adj.
superfluous 632 adj.

add water
combine 50 vb.
add water 334 vb.
moisten 336 vb.

adhesive
adhesive 47 n.
coherence 48 n.
viscidity 349 n.

adjunct
extrinsicality 6 n.
addition 38 n.
adjunct 40 n.
branch 53 n.
part 53 n.
piece 53 n.
component 58 n.
precursor 66 n.
sequel 67 n.
extremity 69 n.
concomitant 89 n.
expansion 192 n.
hanging object 212 n.

interjection 226 n.
equipment 625 n.

adjust
adjust 24 vb.
equalize 28 vb.
order 60 vb.
regularize 62 vb.
make conform 83 vb.
time 112 vb.
synchronize 118 vb.
modify 138 vb.
moderate 172 vb.
harmonize 405 vb.
be true 489 vb.
rectify 649 vb.
pacify 714 vb.

adjusted
adjusted 24 adj.

admit
add 38 vb.
contain 56 vb.
comprise 78 vb.
introduce 226 vb.
open 258 vb.
enter 292 vb.
admit 294 vb.
receive 777 vb.
take 781 vb.
greet 879 vb.
make pious 973 vb.

admitting
admitting 294 adj.

ad nauseam
ad nauseam 856 adv.

adult
adult 129 n.

adultness
adultness 129 n.

advantage
advantage 34 n.
fair chance 154 n.
power 155 n.
tactics 683 n.
success 722 n.
victory 722 n.
retention 773 n.

adverse
inopportune 133 adj.
presageful 506 adj.
evil 611 adj.
inexpedient 638 adj.
harmful 640 adj.
hindering 697 adj.
opposing 699 adj.
adverse 726 adj.
annoying 822 adj.
unpromising 848 adj.

adversity
affairs 149 n.
ruin 160 n.
pain 372 n.
evil 611 n.
bane 654 n.
difficulty 695 n.
adversity 726 n.
sale 788 n.
sorrow 820 n.
suffering 820 n.

painfulness 822 n.
punishment 958 n.

advertise
predict 506 vb.
communicate 519 vb.
advertise 523 vb.
make important 633 vb.
boast 872 vb.
praise 918 vb.

advertisement
exhibit 517 n.
advertisement 523 n.
broadcast 526 n.
writing 581 n.
inducement 607 n.
request 756 n.
sale 788 n.
boast 872 n.
praise 918 n.

advice
meditation 444 n.
estimate 475 n.
hint 519 n.
conference 579 n.
inducement 607 n.
preparation 664 n.
advice 686 n.
precept 688 n.
aid 698 n.

advisable
circumstantial 8 adj.
fit 24 adj.
opportune 132 adj.
operative 168 adj.
possible 464 adj.
wise 493 adj.
chosen 600 adj.
useful 635 adj.
advisable 637 adj.
used 668 adj.
due 910 adj.

advise
propound 507 vb.
hint 519 vb.
incite 607 vb.
warn 659 vb.
advise 686 vb.

adviser
estimator 475 n.
sage 495 n.
informant 519 n.
teacher 532 n.
motivator 607 n.
warner 659 n.
meddler 673 n.
director 685 n.
adviser 686 n.
expert 691 n.
aider 698 n.
mediator 715 n.
consignee 749 n.

advising
advising 686 adj.

aerate
lighten 318 vb.
gasify 331 vb.
aerate 335 vb.
refrigerate 377 vb.
sanitate 647 vb.

refresh 680 vb.

aeronaut
aeronaut 266 n.

aeronautics
aeronautics 266 n.
aircraft 271 n.
ascent 303 n.
descent 304 n.
plunge 308 n.
sport 832 n.

afar
afar 194 adv.

affairs
affairs 149 n.

affectation
imitation 20 n.
mimicry 20 n.
conformity 83 n.
underestimation 478 n.
sciolism 486 n.
foolery 492 n.
supposition 507 n.
trope 514 n.
sham 537 n.
mental dishonesty 538 n.
neology 555 n.
inelegance 571 n.
conduct 683 n.
wit 834 n.
fashion 843 n.
affectation 845 n.
pride 866 n.
airs 868 n.
contempt 917 n.
prudery 945 n.
false piety 974 n.

affected
imitative 20 adj.
depreciating 478 adj.
dabbling 486 adj.
absurd 492 adj.
figurative 514 adj.
hypocritical 536 adj.
untrue 538 adj.
ornate 569 adj.
inelegant 571 adj.
unskilled 690 adj.
ill-bred 842 adj.
vulgar 842 adj.
fashionable 843 adj.
ridiculous 844 adj.
affected 845 adj.
prideful 866 adj.
vain 868 adj.
modest 869 adj.
ostentatious 870 adj.
unwarranted 911 adj.
prudish 945 adj.
pietistic 973 adj.
impious 974 adj.

affected, be
imitate 20 vb.
show 517 vb.
cant 536 vb.
be busy 673 vb.
behave 683 vb.
be affected 845 vb.
be vain 868 vb.

be ostentatious
870 vb.
be impious
974 vb.
affecter
affecter 845 vb.
affectionately
affectionately
882 adv.
affections
affections 812 n.
affirm
attribute 153 vb.
testify 461 vb.
dogmatize
468 vb.
confute 474 vb.
believe 480 vb.
opine 480 vb.
suppose 507 vb.
mean 509 vb.
manifest 517 vb.
be informed
519 vb.
proclaim 523 vb.
affirm 527 vb.
indicate 542 vb.
phrase 558 vb.
speak 574 vb.
plead 609 vb.
decree 732 vb.
compel 735 vb.
promise 759 vb.
be courageous
850 vb.
affirmation
affirmation
527 n.
affirmative
demonstrating
473 adj.
meaningful
509 adj.
undisguised
517 adj.
informative
519 adj.
affirmative
527 adj.
forceful 566 adj.
affirmatively
affirmatively
527 adv.
affix
affix 45 vb.
afford
have enough
630 vb.
afford 795 vb.
afloat
afloat 270 adv.
after
after 65 adv.
behind 279 adv.
again
twice 91 adv.
again 102 adv.
against
against 235 adv.
age
age 126 n.
helplessness
156 n.
fold 256 n.
insanity 498 n.
health 645 n.
ugliness 837 n.
ageing
ageing 126 adj.
agency
agency 168 n.

instrumentality
623 n.
action 671 n.
agent
producer 159 n.
machinist 625 n.
doer 671 n.
agent 681 n.
consignee 749 n.
agglutinate
agglutinate
48 vb.
aggravate
augment 36 vb.
make violent
171 vb.
give pain 372 vb.
exaggerate
541 vb.
deteriorate
650 vb.
impair 650 vb.
be difficult
695 vb.
make quarrels
704 vb.
miscarry 723 vb.
lose 767 vb.
hurt 822 vb.
aggravate
827 vb.
excite hate
883 vb.
enrage 886 vb.
aggravated
aggravated
827 adj.
aggravatedly
aggravatedly
827 adv.
aggravation
aggravation
827 n.
aggressively
aggressively
707 adv.
agitate
derange 63 vb.
jumble 63 vb.
demolish 160 vb.
force 171 vb.
move 260 vb.
impel 274 vb.
draw 283 vb.
brandish 312 vb.
agitate 313 vb.
blow 347 vb.
cause feeling
369 vb.
distract 451 vb.
gesticulate
542 vb.
frighten 849 vb.
agitated
agitated 313 adj.
agitated, be
be agitated
313 vb.
agitation
agitation 313 n.
agitator
revolutionist
144 n.
violent creature
171 n.
incendiarism
376 n.
speaker 574 n.
motivator 607 n.
reformer 649 n.

troublemaker
658 n.
leader 685 n.
agitator 733 n.
excitant 816 n.
malcontent
824 n.
agrarian
territorial
339 adj.
agrarian 365 adj.
agreeing
agreeing 24 adj.
agreement
identity 13 n.
uniformity 16 n.
similarity 18 n.
agreement 24 n.
equality 28 n.
combination 50 n.
conformity 83 n.
concurrence
176 n.
symmetry 240 n.
melody 405 n.
possibility 464 n.
consensus 483 n.
concord 705 n.
pacification
714 n.
compact 760 n.
agriculture
assemblage 74 n.
causation 151 n.
production 159 n.
fertilizer 166 n.
tree 361 n.
agriculture 365 n.
maturation
664 n.
ahead
before 64 adv.
ahead 278 adv.
aid
addition 38 n.
conduce 151 vb.
strengthening
157 n.
agency 168 n.
influence 173 n.
support 213 n.
support 213 vb.
be behind 233 vb.
promote 280 vb.
elevation 305 n.
elevate 305 vb.
make likely
466 vb.
estimate 475 vb.
assent 483 vb.
inducement
607 n.
incite 607 vb.
instrumentality
623 n.
be instrumental
623 vb.
utility 635 n.
be useful 635 vb.
be expedient
637 vb.
remedy 653 n.
remedy 653 vb.
protection 655 n.
do 671 vb.
facility 696 n.
facilitate 696 vb.
aid 698 n.
aid 698 vb.
cooperate
701 vb.

permission 751 n
give 776 vb.
friendliness
875 n
be courteous
879 vb
kind act 892 n.
be benevolent
892 vb
philanthropy
896 n
approbation
918 n
aider
aider 698 n.
aiding
aiding 698 adj.
aim
place 182 vb.
aim 276 n.
aim at 612 vb.
fire at 707 vb.
threaten 895 vb.
aim at
aim at 612 vb.
pursue 614 vb.
air
rarity 320 n.
gas 331 n.
air 335 n.
ventilation 347 n
wind 347 n.
salubrity 647 n.
aircraft
aircraft 271 n.
ejector 295 n.
air force 717 n.
air force
aeronaut 266 n.
aircraft 271 n.
air force 717 n.
air officer 736 n.
air officer
aeronaut 266 n.
air officer 736 n.
air pipe
orifice 258 n.
respiration 347 n
ventilation 347 n
air pipe 348 n.
airs
affectation
845 n
airs 868 n.
ostentation
870 n
airship
sphere 247 n.
airship 271 n.
gas 331 n.
air force 717 n.
air travel
stopping place
140 n.
motion 260 n.
air travel 266 n.
aircraft 271 n.
goal 290 n.
airy
flying 266 adj.
gaseous 331 adj.
airy 335 adj.
akin
relative 9 adj.
akin 11 adj.
similar 18 adj.
included 78 adj.
near 195 adj.
born 355 adj.
akin, be
be related 9 vb.

be akin 11 vb.
alarmist
false alarm
660 n.
alarmist 849 n.
coward 851 n.
alcoholic drink
stimulant 169 n.
alcoholic drink
296 n.
drunkenness
944 n.
alcoholism
frenzy 498 n.
poison 654 n.
hunger 854 n.
alcoholism 944 n.
alfresco out of doors
alfresco 335 adv.
alive
existing 1 adj.
alive 355 adj.
all
all 52 n.
completeness
54 n.
everyman 79 n.
all along
while 104 adv.
all along 108 adv.
until now
116 adv.
allocution
allocution 578 n.
almost
almost 33 adv.
aloft
aloft 204 adv.
up 303 adv.
alone
unrelated 10 adj.
separate 46 adj.
alone 88 adj.
friendless
878 adj.
unsociable
878 adj.
alphabetically
alphabetically
553 adv.
alpine
alpine 204 adj.
altar
stand 213 n.
altar 984 n.
alterer
alterer 138 n.
although
although 177 adv.
altimetry
altimetry 204 n.
ambush
latency 518 n.
be stealthy
520 vb.
ambush 522 n.
ambush 522 vb.
trap 537 n.
ensnare 537 vb.
danger 656 n.
pitfall 658 n.
be cunning
693 vb.
amendment
compensation
31 n.
interpretation
515 n.
amendment
649 n.

restoration
651 n.
remedy 653 n.
amiable
peaceful 712 adj.
well-bred
843 adj.
amiable 879 adj.
lovable 882 adj.
benevolent
892 adj.
amicably
amicably
875 adv.
amiss
amiss 611 adv.
ammunition
box 189 n.
defence 708 n.
ammunition
718 n.
amnesty
amnesty 501 n.
obliteration
545 n.
peace 712 n.
peace offering
714 n.
forgiveness
904 n.
among
among 43 adv.
amorphism
amorphism 239 n.
amorphous
nonuniform
17 adj.
incomplete
55 adj.
orderless 61 adj.
amorphous
239 adj.
distorted 241 adj.
fluid 330 adj.
unsightly 837 adj.
amphibian
amphibian 360 n.
amuse
please 821 vb.
amuse 832 vb.
be witty 834 vb.
be ridiculous
844 vb.
amused
amused 832 adj.
amusement
pleasure 371 n.
broadcast 526 n.
stage show
589 n.
business 617 n.
trifle 634 n.
easy thing 696 n.
contest 711 n.
enjoyment 819 n.
pleasurableness
821 n.
merriment 828 n.
amusement
832 n.
social gathering
877 n.
amuse oneself
rampage 61 vb.
neglect 453 vb.
be absurd
492 vb.
be foolish 494 vb.
be capricious
599 vb.

busy oneself
617 vb.
be pleased
819 vb.
be cheerful
828 vb.
amuse oneself
832 vb.
be sociable
877 vb.
amusing
amusing 832 adj.
anachronism
anachronism
113 n.
different time
117 n.
untimeliness
133 n.
inexactness
490 n.
anachronistic
anachronistic
113 adj.
anaesthetic
obstetrics 162 n.
moderator 172 n.
anaesthetic
370 n.
drug 653 n.
soporific 674 n.
relief 826 n.
analogue
identity 13 n.
analogue 18 n.
copy 22 n.
compeer 28 n.
adjunct 40 n.
concomitant
89 n.
duality 90 n.
duplication 91 n.
equivocalness
513 n.
actor 589 n.
analytically
analytically
51 adv.
anarchic
anarchic 729 adj.
anarchist
anarchist 61 n.
anarchy
disorder 61 n.
government
728 n.
anarchy 729 n.
nonobservance
764 n.
lawlessness
949 n.
anciently
anciently
122 adv.
anemometry
anemometry
347 n.
an example, be
be an example
23 vb.
influence 173 n.
represent 546 vb.
angel
angel 962 n.
mythical being
964 n.
angelic
angelic 962 adj.
angelize
angelize 962 vb.

anger
helplessness
156 n.
dissent 484 n.
excitation 816 n.
excitable state
817 n.
hatred 883 n.
anger 886 n.
disapprobation
919 n.
angle
angle 242 n.
projection 249 n.
Anglican
Anglican 970 adj.
sectarian
972 adj.
angrily
angrily 886 adv.
angry
furious 171 adj.
frenzied 498 n.
excited 816 adj.
angry 886 adj.
threatening
895 adj.
angry, be
be violent 171 vb.
excrete 297 vb.
be agitated
313 vb.
gaze 433 vb.
gesticulate
542 vb.
be angry 886 vb.
disapprove
919 vb.
angular
oblique 215 adj.
crossed 217 adj.
angular 242 adj.
curved 243 adj.
angular figure
obliquity 215 n.
angular figure
242 n.
angularity
angularity 242 n.
angular measure
obliquity 215 n.
angular measure
242 n.
sailing aid 264 n.
measurement
460 n.
angulated
angulated
242 adj.
animal
fossil 120 n.
young creature
127 n.
animal 360 n.
animal 360 adj.
animal disease
animal disease
646 n.
animal husbandry
assemblage 74 n.
production 159 n.
propagation
162 n.
grassland 343 n.
animal husbandry
364 n.
agriculture 365 n.
animality
animality 360 n.
animate
animate 816 vb.

cheer 828 vb.
anniversary
date 104 n
period 106 n.
anniversary
136 n.
special day
871 n.
anno domini
anno domini
104 adv.
annoyance
annoyance 822 n.
annoying
annoying 822 adj.
anonymous
one 88 adj.
unknown 486 n.
concealed
520 adj.
disguised 520 adj.
anonymous
557 adj.
inglorious
862 adj.
answer
reversion 143 n.
interchange
146 vb.
reason why
151 n.
effect 152 n.
answer 455 n.
answer 455 vb.
counterevidence
462 n.
argue 470 vb.
confutation
474 n.
interpretation
515 n.
correspond
583 vb.
retaliate 709 vb.
witticism 834 n.
be witty 834 vb.
be insolent
873 vb.
answering
answering
455 adj.
anthology
composition 56 n.
literature 552 n.
reading matter
584 n.
textbook 584 n.
anthology 587 n.
poem 588 n.
choice 600 n.
anthropology
zoology 362 n.
anthropology
366 n.
antichristianity
antichristianity
968 n.
anticipation
anticipation
130 n.
antidote
moderator 172 n.
counteraction
177 n.
antidote 653 n.
antiquarian
antiquarian
120 n.
collector 487 n.
interpreter 515 n.
chronicler 544 n.

linguist 552 n.
antiquated
anachronistic
113 adj.
not contemporary
117 adj.
past 120 adj.
antiquated
122 adj.
useless 636 adj.
disused 669 adj.
antiquity
precursor 66 n.
era 106 n.
antiquity 120 n.
archaism 122 n.
oldness 122 n.
unknown thing
486 n.
monument 543 n.
collection 627 n.
apart
apart 46 adv.
apathetic
apathetic
815 adj.
unastonished
860 adj.
ungrateful
903 adj.
aphoristic
aphoristic
491 adj.
apostatize
apostatize
598 vb.
apparently
apparently
440 adv.
appear
be visible 438 vb.
appear 440 vb.
be plain 517 vb.
be disclosed
521 vb.
appearance
modality 7 n.
circumstance 8 n.
similarity 18 n.
beginning 68 n.
data processing
86 n.
changeable thing
147 n.
exteriority 218 n.
view 433 n.
visibility 438 n.
appearance
440 n.
probability 466 n.
ideality 508 n.
manifestation
517 n.
pretext 609 n.
conduct 683 n.
appearing
appearing
440 adj.
applaud
assent 483 vb.
gesticulate
542 vb.
rejoice 830 vb.
honour 861 vb.
congratulate
881 vb.
applaud 918 vb.
applause
gesture 542 n.
rejoicing 830 n.

celebration
871 n.
applause 918 n.
apportion
quantify 26 vb.
sunder 46 vb.
decompose 51 vb.
part 53 vb.
arrange 62 vb.
disperse 75 vb.
bisect 92 vb.
mete out 460 vb.
dispose of
668 vb.
participate
770 vb.
give 776 vb.
apportion 778 vb.
grant claims
910 vb.
apportionment
apportionment
778 n.
appraise
do sums 86 vb.
appraise 460 vb.
appraiser
appraiser 460 n.
approach
relativeness 9 n.
be related 9 vb.
resemble 18 vb.
beginning 68 n.
entrance 68 n.
futurity 119 n.
be to come
119 vb.
event 149 n.
destiny 150 n.
impend 150 vb.
tend 174 vb.
nearness 195 n.
be near 195 vb.
motion 260 n.
navigate 264 vb.
approach 284 n.
approach 284 vb.
convergence
288 n.
arrival 290 n.
access 619 n.
friendship 875 n.
befriend 875 vb.
greet 879 vb.
approaching
approaching
284 adj.
approbation
estimate 475 n.
assent 483 n.
permission 751 n.
repute 861 n.
respect 915 n.
approbation
918 n.
orthodoxism
970 n.
appropriate
dwell 187 vb.
encroach 301 vb.
acquire 766 vb.
appropriate
781 vb.
claim 910 vb.
approvable
approvable
918 adj.
approve
choose 600 vb.
select 600 vb.
permit 751 vb.

consent 753 vb.
be pleased
819 vb.
approve 918 vb.
approved
approved
918 adj.
approving
approving
918 adj.
approvingly
approvingly
918 adv.
apron
apron 223 n.
apt
relevant 9 adj.
apt 24 adj.
special 80 adj.
opportune
132 adj.
plausible 466 adj.
tasteful 841 adj.
aptitude
fitness 24 n.
changeableness
147 n.
ability 155 n.
tendency 174 n.
intelligence
493 n.
learning 531 n.
willingness 592 n.
aptitude 689 n.
aquatics
aquatics 264 n.
arboreal
arboreal 361 adj.
arbour
pavilion 187 n.
arbour 189 n.
cavity 250 n.
screen 416 n.
arc
curve 243 n.
arc 245 n.
archaism
antiquity 120 n.
archaism 122 n.
old man 128 n.
reversion 143 n.
arched
arched 248 adj.
architectural
architectural
187 adj
arena
athletics 157 n.
region 179 n.
meeting place
187 n
horizontality
211 n
slaughterhouse
357 n
training school
534 n
theatre 589 n.
path 619 n.
contest 711 n.
duel 711 n.
racing 711 n.
arena 719 n.
pleasure ground
832 n
argue
disagree 25 vb.
enquire 454 vb.
testify 461 vb.
argue 470 vb.

sophisticate
472 vb.
propound 507 vb.
publish 523 vb.
affirm 527 vb.
confer 579 vb.
dissertate
586 vb.
be irresolute
596 vb.
plead 609 vb.
bicker 704 vb.
be fastidious
857 vb.
vindicate 922 vb.
litigate 954 vb.
guing
arguing 470 adj.
gument
disagreement
25 n.
topic 447 n.
question 454 n.
argument 470 n.
supposition
507 n.
conference 579 n.
dissertation
586 n.
quarrel 704 n.
contention 711 n.
gumentation
argumentation
470 n.
ight
aright 639 adv.
istocracy
superiority 34 n.
social group
366 n.
owner 771 n.
aristocracy
863 n.
istocrat
bigwig 638 n.
master 736 n.
aristocrat 863 n.
proud person
866 n.
med force
band 74 n.
protection 655 n.
attacker 707 n.
armed force
717 n.
mour
covering 221 n.
headgear 223 n.
legwear 223 n.
protection 655 n.
safeguard 657 n.
armour 708 n.
ms
tool 625 n.
arms 718 n.
my
multitude 100 n.
army 717 n.
my officer
soldiery 717 n.
army officer
736 n.
ound
around 225 adv.
range
adjust 24 vb.
compose 56 vb.
order 60 vb.
arrange 62 vb.
modify 138 vb.
produce 159 vb.

place 182 vb.
be careful
452 vb.
make certain
468 vb.
clean 643 vb.
make better
649 vb.
make ready
664 vb.
arranged
arranged 62 adj.
arrangement
relation 9 n.
correlation 12 n.
adaptation 24 n.
subdivision 53 n.
composition 56 n.
order 60 n.
arrangement
62 n.
series 71 n.
assemblage 74 n.
classification
77 n.
regularity 81 n.
production 159 n.
location 182 n.
formation 238 n.
amendment
649 n.
arrest
arrest 742 vb.
take 781 vb.
arrival
beginning 68 n.
aeronautics
266 n.
return 281 n.
approach 284 n.
arrival 290 n.
descent 304 n.
arrive
accrue 38 vb.
happen 149 vb.
be present
184 vb.
travel 262 vb.
voyage 264 vb.
approach 284 vb.
arrive 290 vb.
pass 300 vb.
be visible 438 vb.
appear 440 vb.
climax 720 vb.
arriving
arriving 290 adj.
arrogation
arrogation 911 n.
arsenal
accumulation
74 n.
arsenal 718 n.
art
composition 56 n.
production 159 n.
form 238 n.
art 546 n.
misrepresentation
547 n.
school of painting
548 n.
ornamental art
839 n.
art equipment
pigment 420 n.
art equipment
548 n.
article
estimate 475 n.
publicity 523 n.

reading matter
584 n.
article 586 n.
artisan
producer 159 n.
clothier 223 n.
artist 551 n.
machinist 625 n.
doer 671 n.
artisan 681 n.
expert 691 n.
artist
imitator 20 n.
producer 159 n.
visionary 508 n.
interpreter 515 n.
recorder 544 n.
artist 551 n.
doer 671 n.
artless
simple 44 adj.
amorphous
239 adj.
ignorant 486 adj.
foolish 494 adj.
veracious
535 adj.
plain 568 adj.
inelegant 571 adj.
spontaneous
604 adj.
immature
665 adj.
unprepared
665 adj.
bungled 690 adj.
artless 694 adj.
graceless 837 adj.
ill-bred 842 adj.
vulgar 842 adj.
barbaric 864 adj.
honourable
924 adj.
innocent 930 adj.
artless, be
be artless 694 vb.
be rude 880 vb.
be innocent
930 vb.
artlessly
artlessly 694 adv.
artlessness
artlessness 694 n.
art of war
art of war 713 n.
art style
art style 548 n.
art subject
art subject
548 n.
as before
as before
139 adv.
ascend
be great 32 vb.
grow 36 vb.
be high 204 vb.
be oblique
215 vb.
be in motion
260 vb.
fly 266 vb.
emerge 293 vb.
ascend 303 vb.
lift oneself
305 vb.
leap 307 vb.
be light 318 vb.
be visible 438 vb.
get better
649 vb.

ascending
ascending
303 adj.
ascent
degree 27 n.
increase 36 n.
bond 47 n.
series 71 n.
vertex 208 n.
stand 213 n.
motion 260 n.
progression
280 n.
departure 291 n.
ascent 303 n.
elevation 305 n.
lightness 318 n.
access 619 n.
improvement
649 n.
sport 832 n.
ascetic
philosopher
444 n.
sage 495 n.
severe 730 adj.
poor person
796 n.
abstainer 937 n.
temperate
937 adj.
ascetic 940 n.
ascetic 940 adj.
pietist 973 n.
pietistic 973 adj.
monk 980 n.
ascetically
ascetically
940 adv.
ascetic, be
refuse 755 vb.
be temperate
937 vb.
be ascetic
940 vb.
offer worship
975 vb.
asceticism
asceticism 940 n.
ash
ash 376 n.
coal 380 n.
dirt 644 n.
ask leave
ask leave 751 vb.
ask mercy
knuckle under
716 vb.
deprecate 757 vb.
regret 825 vb.
ask mercy
900 vb.
beg pardon
904 vb.
aspiration
aspiration 847 n.
as promised
as promised
759 adv.
assemblage
joining together
45 n.
combination 50 n.
composition 56 n.
arrangement
62 n.
assemblage 74 n.
convergence
288 n.
acquisition 766 n.

assembled
assembled 74 adj.
assembly
union 45 n.
assembly 74 n.
conference 579 n.
council 687 n.
amusement
832 n.
pageant 870 n.
social gathering
877 n.
public worship
975 n.
assent
agreement 24 n.
accord 24 vb.
concurrence
176 n.
concur 176 vb.
be reasonable
470 n.
believe 480 vb.
assent 483 n.
assent 483 vb.
confess 521 vb.
willingness 592 n.
be willing 592 vb.
submission 716 n.
submit 716 vb.
permit 751 vb.
consent 753 n.
consent 753 vb.
compact 760 n.
approbation
918 n.
approve 918 vb.
assented
assented 483 adj.
assenter
assenter 483 n.
assenting
assenting
483 adj.
assertive
strong 157 adj.
positive 468 adj.
assertive 527 adj.
assiduity
assiduity 673 n.
assign
place 182 vb.
transfer 267 vb.
relinquish 616 vb.
be subject
740 vb.
resign 748 vb.
dower 772 vb.
not retain
774 vb.
assign 775 vb.
give 776 vb.
assimilation
assimilation 18 n.
association
relation 9 n.
mixture 43 n.
union 45 n.
combination 50 n.
group 74 n.
unity 88 n.
accompaniment
89 n.
concurrence
176 n.
life 355 n.
business 617 n.
association
701 n.
corporation
703 n.

society 703 n.
participation
770 n.
friendship 875 n.
sociality 877 n.
assuage
assuage 172 vb.
bring to rest
261 vb.
make inactive
674 vb.
pacify 714 vb.
tranquillize
818 vb.
please 821 vb.
relieve 826 vb.
assume
assume 466 vb.
expect 502 vb.
hope 847 vb.
astray
astray 277 adv.
astride
astride 213 adv.
astronomic
astronomic
316 adj.
astronomy
astronomy 316 n.
telescope 437 n.
gauge 460 n.
map 546 n.
at a discount
at a discount
805 adv.
at a stand
at a stand
261 adv.
athlete
equilibrium 28 n.
athlete 157 n.
bulk 190 n.
rider 263 n.
killer 357 n.
entertainer
589 n.
proficient person
691 n.
contender 711 n.
combatant 717 n.
athletic
athletic 157 adj.
flexible 322 adj.
amused 832 adj.
athletics
athletics 157 n.
motion 260 n.
equitation 262 n.
exercise 677 n.
sport 832 n.
at intervals
at intervals
196 adv.
at last
at last 108 adv.
atmosphere
layer 202 n.
height 204 n.
atmosphere
335 n.
radiation 412 n.
atone
compensate
31 vb.
restore 651 vb.
restitute 782 vb.
be courteous
879 vb.
beg pardon
904 vb.

be penitent
934 vb.
atone 936 vb.
atonement
atonement 936 n.
atoning
atoning 936 adj.
atop
atop 208 adv.
at peace, be
be moderate
172 vb.
concord 705 vb.
be at peace
712 vb.
pacify 714 vb.
be patient
818 vb.
at present
at present
116 adv.
at random
by chance
154 adv.
at random
613 adv.
at rest
at rest 678 adv.
at sea
at sea 338 adv.
at sight
at sight 433 adv.
at sunrise
at sunrise
123 adv.
attack
beginning 68 n.
vigorousness
169 n.
be vigorous
169 vb.
outbreak 171 n.
circumscription
227 n.
collision 274 n.
impulse 274 n.
knock 274 n.
approach 284 n.
approach 284 vb.
ingress 292 n.
burst in 292 vb.
encroach 301 vb.
ascent 303 n.
climb 303 vb.
resolution 594 n.
impairment
650 n.
attempt 666 n.
hindrance 697 n.
attack 707 n.
attack 707 vb.
retaliation 709 n.
fight 711 vb.
battle 713 n.
warfare 713 n.
wage war 713 vb.
weapon 718 n.
victory 722 n.
overmaster
722 vb.
brigandage 783 n.
malediction
894 n.
censure 919 n.
dispraise 919 vb.
detraction 921 n.
indict 923 vb.
attacker
attacker 707 n.

attacking
attacking
707 a
attempt
production 159
experiment
456
experiment
456
be willing 592 v
persevere 595 v
intention 612 n
aim at 612 vb.
attempt 666 n.
attempt 666 vb
undertaking
667
undertake
667
action 671 n.
do 671 vb.
be active 673 v
exertion 677 n.
exert oneself
677
contest 711 n.
contend 711 vb
attempting
attempting
666 a
attempt the
impossible
attempt the
impossible
465
attention
listening 410 n.
intellect 442 n.
thought 444 n.
attention 450 n
carefulness
452
accuracy 489 n
expectation
502
study 531 n.
perseverance
595
assiduity 673 n
completion 720
formality 870 n
attentive
auditory 410 a
thoughtful
444 a
inquisitive
448 a
attentive
450 a
careful 452 adj
knowing 485 ac
accurate 489 a
intelligent
493 a
studious 531 ac
resolute 594 ad
labouring
677 a
observant
763 a
lively 814 adj.
cautious 853 a
fastidious
857 a
courteous
879 a
attentive, be
specify 80 vb.
hear 410 vb.
gaze 433 vb.
watch 436 vb.

axiom
truth 489 n.
axiom 491 n.

B

back
sequential 65 adj.
ending 69 adj.
back 233 adj.

backwards
backwards
281 adv.

bad
inferior 35 adj.
trivial 634 adj.
profitless
636 adj.
bad 640 adj.
imperfect
642 adj.
deteriorated
650 adj.
adverse 726 adj.
disreputable
862 adj.
maleficent
893 adj.
wrong 909 adj.
contemptible
917 adj.
blameworthy
919 adj.
dishonest
925 adj.
heinous 929 adj.
wicked 929 adj.

badge
badge 542 n.
trophy 724 n.
badge of rank
738 n.
trimming 839 n.

badge of rank
badge 542 n.
badge of rank
738 n.
vestments 983 n.

badge of rule
badge 542 n.
badge of rule
738 n.

badly
badly 640 adv.

badness
badness 640 n.

bad person
changed person
142 n.
revolter 733 n.
object of scorn
862 n.
offender 899 n.
wrong 909 n.
bad person
933 n.
impenitence
935 n.
devil 963 n.
impious person
974 n.

bad taste
inaptitude 25 n.
inferiority 35 n.
indiscrimination
459 n.
mistake 490 n.
art 546 n.
inelegance 571 n.

artlessness 694 n.
wit 834 n.
bad taste 842 n.
wrong 909 n.
undueness 911 n.
vice 929 n.
impurity 946 n.

bag
bag 189 n.
carrier 268 n.

ballet
composition 56 n.
ballet 589 n.
dancing 832 n.

ball game
ball game 832 n.

balm
moderator 172 n.
lubricant 329 n.
balm 653 n.
relief 826 n.

band
band 74 n.
classification
77 n.
personnel 681 n.
party 703 n.
formation 717 n.
person of repute
861 n.

bane
destroyer 163 n.
influence 173 n.
resident 186 n.
killer 357 n.
evil 611 n.
badness 640 n.
infection 646 n.
plague 646 n.
insalubrity 648 n.
bane 654 n.
pitfall 658 n.
adversity 726 n.
suffering 820 n.
worry 820 n.
annoyance 822 n.
painfulness 822 n.
hateful object
883 n.
malevolence
893 n.
noxious animal
899 n.
ruffian 899 n.

baneful
baneful 654 adj.

bang
sound 393 n.
loudness 395 n.
be loud 395 vb.
bang 397 n.
bang 397 vb.

bar
bar 953 n.

barbaric
barbaric 864 adj.

bareness
bareness 224 n.

bargain
contract 760 vb.
make terms
761 vb.
bargain 786 vb.
be parsimonious
811 vb.

barrier
exclusion 57 n.
outline 228 n.
barrier 230 n.
defences 708 n.

barter
correlation 12 n.
equivalence 28 n.
interchange
146 n.
transference
267 n.
conditions 761 n.
transfer 775 n.
barter 786 n.

base
inferiority 35 n.
extremity 69 n.
serial place 73 n.
source 151 n.
cellar 194 n.
layer 202 n.
lowness 205 n.
base 209 n.
basis 213 n.
interiority 219 n.
limit 231 n.

basis
prelude 66 n.
base 209 n.
basis 213 n.
preparation
664 n.

basket
basket 189 n.

bastard
bastard 949 adj.

bastardy
bastardy 949 n.

battle
fight 711 n.
battle 713 n.
battleground
719 n.

battleground
battleground
719 n.

bauble
bauble 634 n.
plaything 832 n.
finery 839 n.
bad taste 842 n.

bawd
bawd 947 n.

be
be 1 vb.
be now 116 vb.
live 355 vb.
be true 489 vb.

beachwear
beachwear 223 n.

beam
bond 47 n.
beam 213 n.
cross 217 n.
roof 221 n.
materials 626 n.

bearer
bearer 268 n.
servant 737 n.

bearing
bearing 268 adj.

bearings
bearings 181 n.
direction 276 n.

beast of burden
beast of burden
268 n.
animal 360 n.
mammal 360 n.

beau monde
beau monde
843 n.

beautician
friction 328 n.
cleaner 643 n.

beautician 838 n.

beautification
beautification
838 n.

beautified
beautified
838 adj.

beautiful
pleasant 371 adj.
elegant 570 adj.
excellent 639 adj.
pleasurable
821 adj.
beautiful 836 adj.
beautified
838 adj.
lovable 882 adj.

beautiful, be
be beautiful
836 vb.

beautify
make better
649 vb.
beautify 836 vb.
primp 838 vb.
decorate 839 vb.

beauty
symmetry 240 n.
elegance 570 n.
pleasurableness
821 n.
beauty 836 n.

beauty, a
exceller 639 n.
a beauty 836 n.
favourite 885 n.

beauty parlour
beauty parlour
838 n.

become
become 1 vb.
evolve 311 vb.

become pious
become pious
973 vb.

become small
be small 33 vb.
decrease 37 vb.
be little 191 vb.
become small
193 vb.
be narrow
201 vb.
deteriorate
650 vb.

bed
bed 213 n.
resting place
261 n.

bedecked
bedecked
839 adj.

bedevil
bedevil 63 vb.
destroy 160 vb.
be unintelligible
512 vb.
be difficult
695 vb.

bedim
bedim 414 vb.

befool
befool 537 vb.

before
before 64 adv.
before 114 adv.

before, be
be 1 vb.
come before
64 vb.
be before 114 vb.

eforehand
beforehand
130 adv.

efriend
accord 24 vb.
accompany
89 vb.
patronize 698 vb.
befriend 875 vb.
be sociable
877 vb.

eg
beg 756 vb.
tax 804 vb.
be servile 874 vb.

eggar
idler 674 n.
beggar 758 n.
recipient 777 n.
poor person
796 n.
low fellow 864 n.

eggarly
beggarly 796 adj.

egin
become 1 vb.
come before
64 vb.
begin 68 vb.
repeat 102 vb.
time 112 vb.
revert 143 vb.
cause 151 vb.
start out 291 vb.
be born 355 vb.
appear 440 vb.
be restored
651 vb.
prepare 664 vb.
undertake
667 vb.
work 677 vb.
celebrate 871 vb.

eginner
beginning 68 n.
driver 263 n.
incomer 292 n.
testee 456 n.
ignoramus 488 n.
ninny 496 n.
beginner 533 n.
dupe 544 n.
bungler 692 n.
ingenue 694 n.

eginning
originality 21 n.
increase 36 n.
unfinished 55 adj.
prelude 66 n.
precursory
66 adj.
beginning 68 n.
beginning 68 adj.
repetition 102 n.
new 121 adj.
oldness 122 n.
primal 122 adj.
youth 125 n.
earliness 130 n.
impending
150 adj.
source 151 n.
causal 151 adj.
weak 158 adj.
exiguous 191 adj.
amorphous
239 adj.
arrival 290 n.
appearance
440 n.

curriculum 529 n.
learning 531 n.
preparation
664 n.
immature
665 adj.
celebration
871 n.

beg pardon
beg pardon
904 vb.
atone 936 vb.

behave
do 671 vb.
behave 683 vb.

behaving
behaving 683 adj.

behind
behind 279 adv.

behind, be
be behind 233 vb.
follow 279 vb.

behindhand
behindhand
302 adv.

belief
possibility 464 n.
probability 466 n.
positiveness
468 n.
belief 480 n.
credulity 482 n.
hope 847 n.
religious faith
967 n.
piety 973 n.

believe
think 444 vb.
assume 466 vb.
be certain
468 vb.
believe 480 vb.
be credulous
482 vb.
expect 502 vb.
suppose 507 vb.
take a pledge
759 vb.
hope 847 vb.
be orthodox
970 vb.
be pious 973 vb.

believed, be
be believed
480 vb.

believing
believing 480 adj.

bellicosity
bellicosity 713 n.

belligerency
belligerency
713 n.
enmity 876 n.

belong
be intrinsic 5 vb.
belong 768 vb.

belt
girdle 47 n.
belt 223 n.
loop 245 n.

benefactor
aider 698 n.
patron 702 n.
giver 776 n.
good giver 808 n.
philanthropist
896 n.
benefactor 898 n.
good person
932 n.
fairy 964 n.

benefice
benefice 979 n.

beneficial
good 610 adj.
advisable
637 adj.
beneficial
639 adj.
salubrious
647 adj.
remedial 653 adj.

beneficiary
survivor 41 n.
successor 67 n.
descendant
165 n.
deputy 750 n.
beneficiary 771 n.
recipient 777 n.
rich person
795 n.
hoper 847 n.
dueness 910 n.

benefit
advantage 34 n.
lack of
expectation
503 n.
benefit 610 n.
benefit 610 vb.
good policy
637 n.
do good 639 vb.
be auspicious
725 vb.
acquisition 766 n.

benevolence
carefulness
452 n.
willingness 592 n.
good 610 n.
intention 612 n.
goodness 639 n.
aid 698 n.
leniency 731 n.
permission 751 n.
feeling 813 n.
friendliness
875 n.
courtesy 879 n.
love 882 n.
benevolence
892 n.
philanthropy
896 n.
pity 900 n.
disinterestedness
926 n.
piety 973 n.

benevolent
benevolent
892 adj.

benevolent, be
be benevolent
892 vb.

benevolently
benevolently
892 adv.

bequeath
transfer 267 vb.
possess 768 vb.
dower 772 vb.
bequeath 775 vb.
give 776 vb.
be rich 795 vb.
make rich 795 vb.

besiege
surround 225 vb.
circumscribe
227 vb.
close 259 vb.

besiege 707 vb.

best
great 32 adj.
crowning 34 adj.
supreme 34 adj.
topmost 208 adj.
best 639 adj.
wonderful
859 adj.

betimes
betimes 130 adv.

between
between 226 adv.

bewitch
convert 142 vb.
engross 444 vb.
motivate 607 vb.
subjugate 740 vb.
delight 821 vb.
be beautiful
836 vb.
be wonderful
859 vb.
excite love
882 vb.
be malevolent
893 vb.
curse 894 vb.
diabolize 963 vb.
bewitch 977 vb.

bewitched
bewitched
977 adj.

beyond
beyond 34 adv.
beyond 194 adv.
in front 232 adv.

bias
inequality 29 n.
influence 173 n.
cause thought
444 vb.
engross 444 vb.
positiveness
468 n.
intuition 471 n.
bias 476 n.
bias 476 vb.
error 490 n.
eccentricity
498 n.
opinionatedness
597 n.
caprice 599 n.
motivate 607 vb.
excitability 817 n.
liking 854 n.
dislike 856 n.
boasting 872 n.
injustice 909 n.
sectarianism
972 n.

biased
biased 476 adj.

biased, be
be biased 476 vb.

bibliographical
bibliographical
584 adj.

bicker
disagree 25 vb.
argue 470 vb.
bicker 704 vb.
blame 919 vb.

bicycle
bicycle 269 n.

bifurcate
bifurcate 92 vb.

bifurcation
bifurcation 92 n.

boringly
boringly 833 adv.

born
produced
159 adj.
born 355 adj.

born, be
become 1 vb.
begin 68 vb.
happen 149 vb.
reproduce itself
162 vb.
be born 355 vb.

borrow
result 152 vb.
request 756 vb.
promise 759 vb.
give security
762 vb.
borrow 780 vb.
levy 781 vb.
purchase 787 vb.
credit 797 vb.
be in debt
798 vb.

borrowing
borrowing 780 n.

bosom
bladder 189 n.
bosom 248 n.

botanical
botanical
363 adj.

botanize
botanize 363 vb.

botany
biology 353 n.
botany 363 n.

bought
bought 787 adj.
venal 925 adj.

bourse
bourse 613 n.

bowl
bowl 189 n.

box
box 189 n.
storage 627 n.
treasury 794 n.
ritual object
982 n.

branch
adjunct 40 n.
bond 47 n.
branch 53 n.

brandish
brandish 312 vb.
agitate 313 vb.
show 517 vb.
defy 706 vb.
be ostentatious
870 vb.
boast 872 vb.
threaten 895 vb.

bravely
bravely 850 adv.

brave person
doer 671 n.
brave person
850 n.
good person
932 n.

breadth
quantity 26 n.
greatness 32 n.
measure 178 n.
size 190 n.
breadth 200 n.

break
break 46 vb.
demolish 160 vb.

force 171 vb.
deform 239 vb.
be brittle 325 vb.
pulverize 327 vb.
wound 650 vb.

break in
break in 364 vb.

breathe
be periodic
136 vb.
exude 293 vb.
absorb 294 vb.
oscillate 312 vb.
aerate 335 vb.
breathe 347 vb.
live 355 vb.
smell 389 vb.
cry 403 vb.
be fatigued
679 vb.
show feeling
813 vb.

breed
breed 77 n.

breeder
breeder 364 n.

breed stock
augment 36 vb.
produce 159 vb.
generate 162 vb.
breed stock
364 vb.
mature 664 vb.

breeze
breeze 347 n.

bribe
bribe 607 vb.
offer 754 vb.
give 776 vb.
purchase 787 vb.
pay 799 vb.
reward 957 vb.

bridal party
bridal party
889 n.

bridge
bond 47 n.
series 71 n.
opportunity
132 n.
narrowness
201 n.
crossing 217 n.
passage 300 n.
bridge 619 n.
instrument 623 n.
means of escape
662 vb.

brief
brief 109 adj.

brief span
brief span 109 n.
shortness 199 n.

brigandage banditry
brigandage 783 n.

bring near
bring near
195 vb.
approach 284 vb.

bring together
add 38 vb.
join 45 vb.
combine 50 vb.
compose 56 vb.
arrange 62 vb.
bring together
74 vb.
move 260 vb.
be dense 319 vb.
not discriminate
459 vb.

abstract 587 vb.
store 627 vb.
restore 651 vb.
make ready
664 vb.
command 732 vb.
acquire 766 vb.
take 781 vb.

bring to rest
assuage 172 vb.
place 182 vb.
bring to rest
261 vb.
navigate 264 vb.
pacify 714 vb.
carry through
720 vb.
tranquillize
818 vb.

brittle
small 33 adj.
fragmentary
53 adj.
ephemeral
109 adj.
flimsy 158 adj.
rigid 321 adj.
brittle 325 adj.
powdery 327 adj.
spurious 537 adj.

brittle, be
be brittle 325 vb.
variegate 432 vb.

brittleness
brittleness 325 n.

broad
great 32 adj.
fleshy 190 adj.
large 190 adj.
expanded
192 adj.
broad 200 adj.
tailored 223 adj.

broad, be
grow 36 vb.
expand 192 vb.
be broad 200 vb.
overlie 221 vb.

broadcast
news 524 n.
broadcast 526 n.
stage play 589 n.

broadcaster
broadcaster
526 n.

broadcasting
broadcasting
526 n.

broadways
broadways
200 adv.

brothel
brothel 946 n.

brother or sister to, be
be akin 11 vb.

brown
whitish 422 adj.
brown 425 adj.
red 426 adj.

brownness
brownness 425 n.

brown pigment
brown pigment
425 n.

brute force
strength 157 n.
violence 171 n.
despotism 728 n.
brute force
730 n.

compulsion 735 n.
lawlessness
949 n.

bubble
stimulation
169 n.
sphere 247 n.
swelling 248 n.
commotion 313 n.
be agitated
313 vb.
effervesce
313 vb.
moisture 336 n.
bubble 350 n.
bubble 350 n.
pulpiness 351 n.
bauble 634 n.

bubbly
gaseous 331 adj.
bubbly 350 adj.
excited 816 adj.

building material
edifice 159 n.
housing 187 n.
facing 221 n.
roof 221 n.
building material
626 n.

bulk
piece 53 n.
weakness 158 n.
bulk 190 n.
thickness 200 n.
convexity 248 n.
swelling 248 n.
eating 296 n.
gravity 317 n.

bullion
bullion 792 n.

bunch
bunch 74 n.

bungled
bungled 690 adj.

bungler
bungler 692 n.

bungling
bungling 690 n.

buried
buried 359 adj.

burn
destroy 160 vb.
lay waste 160 vb.
kill 357 vb.
inter 359 vb.
be hot 374 vb.
burn 376 vb.
blacken 423 vb.
embrown 425 vb.
waste 629 vb.
excite 816 vb.

burning
destruction
160 n.
burning 376 n.

burst in
burst in 292 vb.

bus
bus 269 n.

business
relation 9 n.
affairs 149 n.
production 159 n.
topic 447 n.
predetermination
603 n.
intention 612 n.
pursuit 614 n.
business 617 n.
policy 618 n.

carriage
carriage 269 n.
carrier
transferrer 267 n.
carrier 268 n.
courier 524 n.
carry
transfer 267 vb.
carry 268 vb.
carry out
carry out 720 vb.
carry through
make complete
54 vb.
terminate 69 vb.
go on 141 vb.
be vigorous
169 vb.
arrive 290 vb.
be resolute
594 vb.
persevere 595 vb.
be instrumental
623 vb.
perfect 641 vb.
mature 664 vb.
do 671 vb.
carry through
720 vb.
succeed 722 vb.
cart
cart 269 n.
case
case 189 n.
treasury 794 n.
cash down
cash down
799 adv.
casual
extrinsic 6 adj.
irrelevant 10 adj.
accompanying
89 adj.
casual 154 adj.
unintentional
613 adj.
cat
cat 360 n.
hunter 614 n.
caterer
caterer 628 n.
Catholic
Catholic 970 n.
church party
972 n.
Catholicism
Catholicism
970 n.
cattle
beast of burden
268 n.
cattle 360 n.
animal husbandry
364 n.
cattle pen
enclosure 230 n.
cattle pen 364 n.
cauldron
cauldron 189 n.
causal
causal 151 adj.
influential
173 adj.
instrumental
623 adj.
causally
causally 151 adv.
causal means
causal means
151 n.

causation
causation 151 n.
cause
relativeness 9 n.
auspicate 68 vb.
specify 80 vb.
accompany
89 vb.
modify 138 vb.
happen 149 vb.
cause 151 vb.
cause 151 vb.
producer 159 n.
produce 159 vb.
operate 168 vb.
influence 173 n.
promote 280 vb.
reasons 470 n.
lurk 518 vb.
will 590 vb.
predetermine
603 vb.
motivator 607 n.
motive 607 n.
induce 607 vb.
instrumentality
623 n.
be instrumental
623 vb.
be instrumental
623 vb.
caused
caused 152 adj.
cause desire
await 502 vb.
cause desire
854 vb.
excite love
882 vb.
cause discontent
disappoint
504 vb.
displease 822 vb.
cause discontent
824 vb.
sadden 829 vb.
cause dislike
repel 287 vb.
be unpalatable
386 vb.
dissuade 608 vb.
displease 822 vb.
cause discontent
824 vb.
be tedious
833 vb.
cause dislike
856 vb.
sate 858 vb.
excite hate
883 vb.
huff 886 vb.
incur blame
919 vb.
cause doubt
be unlikely
467 vb.
puzzle 469 vb.
cause doubt
481 vb.
be unintelligible
512 vb.
dissuade 608 vb.
be wonderful
859 vb.
defame 921 vb.
cause feeling
cause feeling
369 vb.
itch 373 vb.

causeless
causeless
154 adj.
cause thought
cause thought
444 vb.
caution
delay 131 n.
slowness 273 n.
attention 450 n.
carefulness
452 n.
foresight 505 n.
unwillingness
593 n.
irresolution
596 n.
protection 655 n.
security 762 n.
cowardice 851 n.
caution 853 n.
cautionary
predicting
506 adj.
informative
519 adj.
dissuasive
608 adj.
cautionary
659 adj.
advising 686 adj.
cautious
late 131 adj.
quiescent
261 adj.
slow 273 adj.
vigilant 452 adj.
doubting 469 adj.
foreseeing
505 adj.
taciturn 577 adj.
unwilling 593 adj.
warned 659 adj.
nervous 849 adj.
cowardly 851 adj.
cautious 853 adj.
cautious, be
set off 31 vb.
move slowly
273 vb.
gaze 433 vb.
be careful
452 vb.
make certain
468 vb.
be wise 493 vb.
foresee 505 vb.
be irresolute
596 vb.
seek safety
655 vb.
be nervous
849 vb.
be cowardly
851 vb.
be cautious
853 vb.
cautiously
cautiously
853 adv.
cavalry
rider 263 n.
warhorse 268 n.
war chariot
269 n.
cavalry 717 n.
cavity
receptacle 189 n.
depth 206 n.
head 208 n.
cavity 250 n.

furrow 257 n.
opening 258 n.
orifice 258 n.
tunnel 258 n.
lowering 306 n.
cease
end 69 vb.
time 112 vb.
cease 140 vb.
be unproductive
167 vb.
be quiescent
261 vb.
depart 291 vb.
be taciturn
577 vb.
relinquish 616 vb.
stop using
669 vb.
not act 672 vb.
be inactive
674 vb.
resist 710 vb.
make peace
714 vb.
fail 723 vb.
revolt 733 vb.
deprecate 757 vb.
sell 788 vb.
celebrate
rampage 61 vb.
remind 500 vb.
make important
633 vb.
triumph 722 vb.
be cheerful
828 vb.
rejoice 830 vb.
celebrate 871 vb.
be hospitable
877 vb.
greet 879 vb.
pay one's
respects 879 vb.
congratulate
881 vb.
forgive 904 vb.
respect 915 vb.
applaud 918 vb.
celebration
procession 71 n.
assemblage 74 n.
assembly 74 n.
arrival 290 n.
reception 294 n.
feasting 296 n.
reminder 500 n.
gesture 542 n.
oration 574 n.
victory 722 n.
trophy 724 n.
merriment 828 n.
rejoicing 830 n.
amusement
832 n.
dignification
861 n.
formality 870 n.
pageant 870 n.
celebration
871 n.
congratulation
881 n.
thanks 902 n.
applause 918 n.
holy day 982 n.
rite 982 n.
celebratory
celebratory
871 adj.

celestial
celestial 316 adj.
celibacy
celibacy 890 n.
celibate
unit 88 n.
celibate 890 n.
virgin 945 n.
monk 980 n.
cellar
cellar 189 n.
depth 206 n.
base 209 n.
hiding-place
                        522 n.
storage 627 n.
sink 644 n.
cellular
cellular 189 adj.
cemetery
death 356 n.
cemetery 359 n.
holy place 984 n.
censure
list 87 n.
ridicule 846 n.
slur 862 n.
censure 919 n.
central
median 30 adj.
middle 70 adj.
interior 219 adj.
central 220 adj.
neutral 620 adj.
undeviating
                        620 adj.
important
                        633 adj.
centrality
centrality 220 n.
centralize
centralize 220 vb.
centrally
centrally 220 adv.
centre
essential part
                        5 n.
middle point
                        30 n.
middle 70 n.
focus 76 n.
centre 220 n.
partition 226 n.
objective 612 n.
chief thing 633 n.
cereals
cereals 296 n.
certain
future 119 adj.
unchangeable
                        148 adj.
impending
                        150 adj.
evidential
                        461 adj.
probable 466 adj.
certain 468 adj.
rational 470 adj.
demonstrated
                        473 adj.
believing 480 adj.
known 485 adj.
true 489 adj.
expectant
                        502 adj.
intelligible
                        511 adj.
manifest 517 adj.
necessary
                        591 adj.

successful
                        722 adj.
hoping 847 adj.
certain, be
assume 466 vb.
be certain
                        468 vb.
believe 480 vb.
assent 483 vb.
know 485 vb.
expect 502 vb.
understand
                        511 vb.
take a pledge
                        759 vb.
certainly
positively 32 adv.
certainly 468 adv.
certain quantity
certain quantity
                        100 n.
certainty
destiny 150 n.
evidence 461 n.
probability 466 n.
certainty 468 n.
demonstration
                        473 n.
discovery 479 n.
belief 480 n.
expectation
                        502 n.
foresight 505 n.
intelligibility
                        511 n.
safety 655 n.
easy thing 696 n.
hope 847 n.
cessation
end 69 n.
finality 69 n.
discontinuity
                        72 n.
cessation 140 n.
quiescence 261 n.
deliverance
                        663 n.
inactivity 674 n.
peace 712 n.
chamber
flat 187 n.
retreat 187 n.
chamber 189 n.
storage 627 n.
refuge 657 n.
monastery 980 n.
chance
extrinsicality 6 n.
concomitant
                        89 n.
opportunity
                        132 n.
changeable thing
                        147 n.
event 149 n.
happen 149 vb.
chance 154 n.
chance 154 vb.
probability 466 n.
uncertainty
                        469 n.
fate 591 n.
gambling 613 n.
nondesign 613 n.
prosperity 725 n.
misfortune 726 n.
change
difference 15 n.
differ 15 vb.
make unlike
                        19 vb.

be unequal 29 vb.
fitfulness 137 n.
change 138 n.
change 138 vb.
transition 142 n.
be turned to
                        142 vb.
changeableness
                        147 n.
vary 147 vb.
motion 260 n.
qualification
                        463 n.
changeable
changeable
                        138 adj.
converted
                        142 adj.
changeful
                        147 adj.
changeableness
changeableness
                        147 n.
changeable thing
changeable thing
                        147 n.
waverer 596 n.
tergiversator
                        598 n.
changeably
changeably
                        147 adv.
changed person
changed person
                        142 n.
changeful
changeful
                        147 adj.
change hands
change hands
                        775 vb.
**changeling. See
young creature**
child 127 n.
character
character 5 n.
sort 77 n.
speciality 80 n.
form 238 n.
affections 812 n.
characteristic
characteristic
                        5 adj.
distinctive
                        15 adj.
special 80 adj.
charge
be violent 171 vb.
collide 274 vb.
pursue 614 vb.
charge 707 n.
give battle
                        713 vb.
be courageous
                        850 vb.
charitable, be
be charitable
                        896 vb.
chase
pedestrianism
                        262 n.
following 279 n.
killing 357 n.
cry 403 n.
objective 612 n.
chase 614 vb.
sport 832 n.
chat
rumour 524 n.
chat 579 n.

chatter
empty talk 510 vb.
chatter 576 n.
chat 579 n.
chatterer
chatterer 576 n.
cheap
inferior 35 adj.
spurious 537 adj.
trivial 634 adj.
cheap 807 adj.
cheap, be
be cheap 807 vb.
cheapen
abate 37 vb.
underestimate
                        478 vb.
make useless
                        636 vb.
impair 650 vb.
sell 788 vb.
demonetize
                        792 vb.
discount 805 vb.
cheapen 807 vb.
cheaply
cheaply 807 adv.
cheapness
cheapness 807 n.
cheer
invigorate
                        169 vb.
excite 816 vb.
please 821 vb.
content 823 vb.
relieve 826 vb.
cheer 828 vb.
amuse 832 vb.
give hope 847 vb.
give courage
                        850 vb.
pity 900 vb.
cheerful
content 823 adj.
cheerful 828 adj.
cheerful, be
be pleased
                        819 vb.
be relieved
                        826 vb.
be cheerful
                        828 vb.
rejoice 830 vb.
amuse oneself
                        832 vb.
hope 847 vb.
cheerfully
cheerfully
                        828 adv.
cheerfulness
cheerfulness
                        828 n.
cheering
pleasurable
                        821 adj.
cheering 828 adj.
cheerless
unpleasant
                        822 adj.
cheerless 829 adj.
unpromising
                        848 adj.
chequer
blackness 423 n.
chequer 432 n.
pattern 839 n.
chew
cut 46 vb.
rend 46 vb.
chew 296 vb.
pulverize 327 vb.

chief part
main part 32 n.
chief part 52 n.
size 190 n.

chief thing
essential part
5 n.
chief part 52 n.
chief thing 633 n.

child
child 127 n.
descendant
165 n.
posterity 165 n.
dwarf 191 n.

chilly
chilly 375 adj.

chimney
chimney 258 n.
air pipe 348 n.
furnace 378 n.

choice
superiority 34 n.
separation 46 n.
part 53 n.
precedence 64 n.
opportunity
132 n.
discrimination
458 n.
will 590 n.
willingness 592 n.
choice 600 n.
means 624 n.
chief thing 633 n.
independence
739 n.
liking 854 n.
love 882 n.

choiceless
choiceless
601 adj.

choir
choir 408 n.
church officer
980 n.

choose
will 590 vb.
be willing 592 vb.
choose 600 vb.
desire 854 vb.
be fastidious
857 vb.

choosing
choosing 600 adj.

chosen
superior 34 adj.
separate 46 adj.
future 119 adj.
fated 591 adj.
voluntary
592 adj.
chosen 600 adj.
excellent 639 adj.
beautiful 836 adj.
approved
918 adj.

Christendom
Christendom
970 n.
the church 979 n.

Christian rite
immersion 298 n.
moistening 336 n.
nomenclature
556 n.
wedding 889 n.
penitence 934 n.

Christian rite
982 n.

chromatics
chromatics 420 n.

chronicler
chronicler 544 n.

chronological
chronological
112 adj.

chronologist
chronologist
112 n.

chronology
directory 87 n.
date 104 n.
chronology 112 n.
reference book
584 n.

chronometry
chronometry
112 n.

chum
male 367 n.
chum 875 n.

church
meeting place
187 n.
church 984 n.

church exterior
high structure
204 n.
vertex 208 n.
church exterior
984 n.

church interior
compartment
189 n.
seat 213 n.
window 258 n.
church interior
984 n.

churchlike
churchlike
984 adj.

church member
church member
970 n.
pietist 973 n.
worshipper 975 n.
worshipper 975 n.
laity 981 n.
lay person 981 n.

church ministry
church ministry
979 n.

church office
degree 27 n.
church office
979 n.

church officer
officer 736 n.
servant 737 n.
church officer
980 n.
lay person 981 n.

church party
church party
972 n.

church service
public worship
975 n.
church service
982 n.

church, the
the church 979 n.

church title
church title
980 n.

church utensil
church utensil
984 n.

cinema
motion 260 n.
spectator 436 n.
optical device
437 n.
cinema 440 n.
broadcast 526 n.
photography
546 n.
drama 589 n.
stage play 589 n.
theatre 589 n.
place of
amusement
832 n.

circle
lamina 202 n.
surround 225 n.
outline 228 n.
circle 245 n.
go round 245 vb.
traverse 262 vb.
navigate 264 vb.
fly 266 vb.
circle 309 vb.
rotate 310 vb.
circuit 621 n.
circuit 621 n.
change hands
775 vb.
jewellery 839 n.

circler
circler 309 n.

circuit
run on 71 vb.
deviation 277 n.
circuition 309 n.
circle 309 n.
route 619 n.
circuit 621 n.
circuit 621 vb.

circuition
circuition 309 n.

circuitous
circumjacent
225 adj.
labyrinthine
246 adj.
deviating
277 adj.
circuitous
309 adj.

circularity
circularity 245 n.
rotundity 247 n.

circumjacent
circumjacent
225 adj.

circumscribe
set apart 46 vb.
exclude 57 vb.
make smaller
193 vb.
surround 225 vb.
circumscribe
227 vb.
outline 228 vb.
enclose 230 vb.
limit 231 vb.
close 259 vb.
approach 284 vb.
converge 288 vb.
insert 299 vb.
circle 309 vb.
safeguard 655 vb.
obstruct 697 vb.
defend 708 vb.
restrain 742 vb.
prohibit 752 vb.

circumscribed
circumscribed
227 adj.

circumscription
circumscription
227 n.

circumstance
state 7 n.
circumstance 8 n.
relation 9 n.
degree 27 n.
affairs 149 n.
influence 173 n.
world 316 n.
topic 447 n.
evidence 461 n.

circumstantial
circumstantial
8 adj.
relative 9 adj.

city
city 179 n.
housing 187 n.

civilization
civilization 649 n.

claim
demand 732 vb.
request 756 vb.
possess 768 vb.
appropriate
781 vb.
desire 854 vb.
claim 910 vb.
litigate 954 vb.

class
eliminate 44 vb.
class 62 vb.
group 74 n.
number with
78 vb.
class 533 n.

classification
degree 27 n.
arrangement
62 n.
series 71 n.
classification
77 n.
generality 79 n.
identification
542 n.
community 703 n.
party 703 n.

classificatory
classificatory
77 adj.

classroom
classroom 534 n.
textbook 584 n.

clean
unmixed 44 adj.
orderly 60 adj.
unravel 62 vb.
modernized
121 adj.
new 121 adj.
displace 188 vb.
smooth 253 vb.
empty 295 vb.
rub 328 vb.
aerate 335 vb.
drench 336 vb.
touch 373 vb.
make bright
412 vb.
white 422 adj.
whiten 422 vb.
plain 568 adj.
clean 643 adj.
clean 643 vb.

salubrious
647 adj.
sanitate 647 vb.
make better
649 vb.
restore 651 vb.
refresh 680 vb.
disencumber
696 vb.
decorate 839 vb.
honourable
924 adj.
innocent 930 adj.
pure 945 adj.
cleaner
cleaner 643 n.
worker 681 n.
servant 737 n.
cleaning cloth
cleaning cloth
643 n.
cleaning utensil
cleaning utensil
643 n.
cleanness
cleanness 643 n.
cleanser
lubricant 329 n.
air 335 n.
fat 352 n.
cleanser 643 n.
prophylactic
653 n.
cosmetic 838 n.
cleansing
cleansing 643 n.
cleansing 643 adj.
clergy
questioner 454 n.
pietist 973 n.
worshipper 975 n.
clergy 980 n.
cleric
cleric 980 n.
clerical
ecclesiastical
979 adj.
clerical 980 adj.
vestured 983 adj.
clerical dress. dress
uniform 223 n.
clerically
clerically
980 adv.
climax
culminate 34 vb.
augment 36 vb.
be complete
54 vb.
be high 204 vb.
crown 208 vb.
mature 664 vb.
climax 720 vb.
climb
progress 280 vb.
climb 303 vb.
climber
traveller 263 n.
climber 303 n.
cloak
wrapping 221 n.
cloak 223 n.
screen 416 n.
disguise 522 n.
canonicals 983 n.
clock time
date 104 n.
clock time 112 n.
close
join 45 vb.

become small
193 vb.
make smaller
193 vb.
close 259 vb.
impel 274 vb.
lower 306 vb.
staunch 345 vb.
screen 416 vb.
repair 651 vb.
obstruct 697 vb.
closed
contracted
193 adj.
closed 259 adj.
retentive 773 adj.
close friend
close friend
875 n.
loved one 882 n.
closure
joining together
45 n.
fastening 47 n.
stop 140 n.
contraction
193 n.
interjection
226 n.
barrier 230 n.
closure 259 n.
difficulty 695 n.
hindrance 697 n.
clothier
clothier 223 n.
clothing
clothing 223 n.
badge 542 n.
finery 839 n.
cloud
accumulation
74 n.
powder 327 n.
gas 331 n.
vaporization
333 n.
water 334 n.
air 335 n.
moisture 336 n.
cloud 350 n.
cloud 350 vb.
dimness 414 n.
opacity 418 n.
cloudy
humid 336 adj.
cloudy 350 adj.
dim 414 adj.
semitransparent
419 adj.
club
club 718 n.
scourge 959 n.
clumsy
unapt 25 adj.
unequal 29 adj.
unwieldy 190 adj.
slow 273 adj.
rigid 321 adj.
tactual 373 adj.
mistaken 490 adj.
unintelligent
494 adj.
inexpedient
638 adj.
bad 640 adj.
clumsy 690 adj.
ill-bred 842 adj.
ridiculous
844 adj.
clumsy, be
neglect 453 vb.

blunder 490 vb.
impair 650 vb.
be clumsy
690 vb.
coal
coal 380 n.
coastal
coastal 339 adj.
coat
laminate 202 vb.
coat 221 vb.
line 222 vb.
smooth 253 vb.
make opaque
418 vb.
colour 420 vb.
paint 548 vb.
decorate 839 vb.
be ostentatious
870 vb.
code of duty
code of duty
912 n.
cognize
cognize 442 vb.
cohere
unite with 45 vb.
cohere 48 vb.
concur 176 vb.
be contiguous
197 vb.
transfer 267 vb.
be dense 319 vb.
thicken 349 vb.
coherence
joining together
45 n.
union 45 n.
adhesive 47 n.
coherence 48 n.
arrangement
62 n.
unity 88 n.
contiguity 197 n.
density 319 n.
toughness 324 n.
viscidity 349 n.
cohesive
cohesive 48 adj.
cohesively
cohesively
48 adv.
coil
edging 229 n.
coil 246 n.
circuition 309 n.
difficulty 695 n.
hairdressing
838 n.
pattern 839 n.
coiled
coiled 246 adj.
coinage
small coin 33 n.
coinage 792 n.
coition
coition 45 n.
cold
wintry 124 adj.
cold 375 adj.
cooled 377 adj.
screened 416 adj.
refreshing
680 adj.
inimical 876 adj.
pure 945 adj.
cold, be
be dense 319 vb.
be cold 375 vb.
coldness
coldness 375 n.

collaborator
collaborator
702 n.
colleague
concomitant
89 n.
personnel 681 n.
colleague 702 n.
participator
770 n.
player 832 n.
chum 875 n.
friend 875 n.
collection
accumulation
74 n.
antiquity 120 n.
exhibit 517 n.
collection 627 n.
collectively
collectively
52 adv.
collector
accumulator
74 n.
collector 487 n.
enthusiast 499 n.
patron 702 n.
desirer 854 n.
collide
counteract
177 vb.
navigate 264 vb.
collide 274 vb.
approach 284 vb.
meet 290 vb.
touch 373 vb.
oppose 699 vb.
quarrel 704 vb.
charge 707 vb.
strike at 707 vb.
collision
contrariety 14 n.
disagreement
25 n.
union 45 n.
accumulation
74 n.
ruin 160 n.
violence 171 n.
counteraction
177 n.
collision 274 n.
convergence
288 n.
friction 328 n.
quarrel 704 n.
fight 711 n.
colour
be mixed 43 vb.
mix 43 vb.
modify 138 vb.
coat 221 vb.
light 412 n.
colour 420 n.
colour 420 vb.
variegation
432 n.
painting 548 n.
paint 548 vb.
decorate 839 vb.
coloured
luminous 412 adj.
luminescent
415 adj.
coloured 420 adj.
painted 548 adj.
colourless
insubstantial
4 adj.
weak 158 adj.

weakly 158 adj.
dry 337 adj.
dim 414 adj.
colourless
421 adj.
whitish 422 adj.
unhealthy
646 adj.
unsightly 837 adj.

ombatant
killer 357 n.
contender 711 n.
combatant 717 n.
enemy 876 n.

ombination
agreement 24 n.
a mixture 43 n.
mixture 43 n.
joining together
45 n.
union 45 n.
combination 50 n.
composition 56 n.
assemblage 74 n.
unity 88 n.

ombine
accrue 38 vb.
mix 43 vb.
join 45 vb.
cohere 48 vb.
combine 50 vb.
compose 56 vb.
be one 88 vb.
produce 159 vb.
abstract 587 vb.

ombined
combined 50 adj.

ombustible
heating 376 adj.
combustible
380 adj.

ome after
come after 65 vb.
run on 71 vb.
ensue 115 vb.
be periodic
136 vb.
substitute
145 vb.
be behind 233 vb.
walk 262 vb.
follow 279 vb.
enter 292 vb.

ome before
come first 34 vb.
exclude 57 vb.
be disordered
61 vb.
come before
64 vb.
initiate 68 vb.
accompany
89 vb.
do before 114 vb.
be early 130 vb.
conduce 151 vb.
precede 278 vb.
admit 294 vb.
predict 506 vb.
be important
633 vb.
prepare 664 vb.
direct 684 vb.
facilitate 696 vb.
have a reputation
861 vb.

ome first
come first 34 vb.

ome of age
come of age
129 vb.

come to rest
place oneself
182 vb.
dwell 187 vb.
come to rest
261 vb.
arrive 290 vb.
be inactive
674 vb.
repose 678 vb.

come unstuck
separate 46 vb.
come unstuck
49 vb.
be disordered
61 vb.
be dispersed
75 vb.

comfortable
comfortable
371 adj.
warm 374 adj.
reposeful 678 adj.
easy 696 adj.
facilitated
696 adj.
palmy 725 adj.
rich 795 adj.
happy 819 adj.
pleasurable
821 adj.
content 823 adj.

command
order 60 vb.
influence 173 vb.
attract notice
450 vb.
emphasize
527 vb.
call 542 vb.
will 590 n.
will 590 vb.
requirement
622 n.
directorship
684 n.
direct 684 vb.
advise 686 vb.
precept 688 vb.
warfare 713 n.
dominate 728 vb.
rule 728 vb.
command 732 n.
command 732 vb.
compulsion 735 n.
compel 735 vb.
mandate 746 vb.
desire 854 n.
desire 854 vb.
impose a duty
912 vb.

commanding
commanding
732 adj.

compelling
735 adj.

commandingly
commandingly
732 adv.

command respect
be important
633 vb.
have a reputation
861 vb.
command respect
915 vb.

commendably
commendably
918 adv.

commender
commender
918 n.

commentary
maxim 491 n.
commentary
515 n.

commission
auspicate 68 vb.
transference
267 n.
transfer 267 vb.
message 524 n.
choice 600 n.
select 600 vb.
vocation 617 n.
employ 617 vb.
management
684 n.
authority 728 n.
command 732 n.
commission
746 n.
commission
746 n.
dower 772 vb.
transfer 775 n.
assign 775 vb.
give 776 vb.
dignify 861 vb.
celebration
871 n.
celebrate 871 vb.
duty 912 n.
impose a duty
912 vb.
holy orders
979 n.

commissioned
commissioned
746 adj.

commonalty
commonalty
864 n.

commoner
common man
30 n.
averageness
727 n.
vulgarian 842 n.
commoner 864 n.

common man
common man
30 n.
everyman 79 n.
commoner 864 n.

commotion
turmoil 61 n.
stimulation
169 n.
violence 171 n.
commotion 313 n.
exaggeration
541 n.
overactivity
673 n.
feeling 813 n.
excitation 816 n.
excitable state
817 n.
discontent 824 n.

communalize
communalize
770 vb.

communicate
mean 509 vb.
communicate
519 vb.
divulge 521 vb.
publish 523 vb.
signal 542 vb.

correspond
583 vb.
describe 585 vb.
give 776 vb.

communicating
communicating
619 vb.

community
association
701 n.
association
701 n.
community 703 n.
sect 972 n.
monk 980 n.
laity 981 n.

compact
agreement 24 n.
arrangement
62 n.
inclusion 78 n.
testimony 461 n.
consensus 483 n.
promise 759 n.
compact 760 n.
title deed 762 n.
compromise
765 n.
trade 786 n.

comparative
comparative
27 adj.

comparatively
comparatively
457 adv.

compare
liken 18 vb.
equalize 28 vb.
join 45 vb.
compare 457 vb.
discriminate
458 vb.
figure 514 vb.

compared
compared
457 adj.

comparison
relativeness 9 n.
assimilation 18 n.
degree 27 n.
joining together
45 n.
comparison
457 n.
estimate 475 n.
metaphor 514 n.
trope 514 n.
manifestation
517 n.

compartment
classification
77 n.
place 180 n.
compartment
189 n.
shelf 213 n.
angularity 242 n.
cavity 250 n.
orifice 258 n.

compass point
laterality 234 n.
compass point
276 n.

compeer
compeer 28 n.

compel
make conform
83 vb.
be able 155 vb.
influence 173 vb.

necessitate
591 vb.
induce **607** vb.
motivate **607** vb.
require **622** vb.
dominate **728** vb.
oppress **730** vb.
command **732** vb.
compel **735** vb.
compelling
compelling
735 adj.
compendious
short **199** adj.
compendious
587 adj.
compendium
small quantity
33 n.
combination **50** n.
arrangement
62 n.
list **87** n.
miniature **191** n.
contraction
193 n.
shortening **199** n.
translation **515** n.
conciseness
564 n.
edition **584** n.
description **585** n.
dissertation
586 n.
compendium
587 n.
compensate
correlate **12** vb.
adjust **24** vb.
equalize **28** vb.
compensate
31 vb.
make complete
54 vb.
weigh **317** vb.
compensation
compensation
31 n.
compensatory
compensatory
31 adj.
complete
consummate
32 adj.
whole **52** adj.
complete **54** adj.
revolutionary
144 adj.
destructive
160 adj.
long **198** adj.
symmetrical
240 adj.
sufficient
630 adj.
completed
720 adj.
complete, be
be complete
54 vb.
comprise **78** vb.
carry **268** vb.
superabound
632 vb.
completed
completed
720 adj.
completely
completely
54 adv.

completeness
completeness
54 n.
completion
completion **720** n.
completive
completive
720 adj.
complex
complex **61** adj.
crossed **217** adj.
intricate **246** adj.
uncertain
469 adj.
unclear **563** adj.
complexity
complexity **61** n.
component
intrinsic **5** adj.
adjunct **40** n.
tincture **43** n.
part **53** n.
component **58** n.
component
58 n.
included **78** adj.
accompanying
89 adj.
contents **188** n.
element **314** n.
machine **625** n.
aider **698** n.
society **703** n.
compose
mix **43** vb.
combine **50** vb.
make complete
54 vb.
compose **56** vb.
arrange **62** vb.
bring together
74 vb.
be included
78 vb.
produce **159** vb.
compose music
compose **56** vb.
harmonize
405 vb.
compose music
408 vb.
composing
composing
56 adj.
composition
joining together
45 n.
compound **50** n.
composition **56** n.
order **60** n.
arrangement
62 n.
accumulation
74 n.
assemblage **74** n.
inclusion **78** n.
product **159** n.
structure **326** n.
compound
compound **50** n.
comprehensive
comprehensive
52 adj.
inclusive **78** adj.
general **79** adj.
compression
compression
193 n.
compressive
compressive
193 adj.

compressor
ligature **47** n.
compressor
193 n.
stopper **259** n.
comprise
join **45** vb.
contain **56** vb.
comprise **78** vb.
be general **79** vb.
hold within
219 vb.
possess **768** vb.
compromise
correlation **12** n.
adaptation **24** n.
middle point
30 n.
average out
30 vb.
offset **31** n.
set off **31** vb.
arrangement
62 n.
substitute **145** n.
substitute
145 vb.
interchange
146 vb.
moderation
172 n.
be irresolute
596 vb.
way **619** n.
middle way
620 n.
be halfway
620 vb.
cooperation
701 n.
pacification
714 n.
pacify **714** vb.
laxity **729** n.
be lax **729** vb.
consent **753** n.
compact **760** n.
contract **760** vb.
make terms
761 vb.
compromise
765 n.
compromise
765 vb.
be patient
818 vb.
atonement **936** n.
compulsion
uniformity **16** n.
assemblage **74** n.
cause **151** n.
power **155** n.
necessity **591** n.
resolution **594** n.
no choice **601** n.
labour **677** n.
pacification
714 n.
brute force
730 n.
command **732** n.
compulsion **735** n.
service **740** n.
restraint **742** n.
restriction **742** n.
request **756** n.
conditions **761** n.
tax **804** n.
computerize
computerize
86 vb.

computerized
computerized
86 ad
concave
cellular **189** adj.
low **205** adj.
concave **250** adj.
concave, be
be concave
250 v
concavity
concavity **250** n.
conceal
make unlike
19 v
imitate **20** vb.
contain **56** vb.
modify **138** vb.
transform
142 v
suppress **160** vb.
cover **221** vb.
screen **416** vb.
be unseen
439 v
disappear **441** vb
neglect **453** vb.
mislead **490** vb.
conceal **520** vb.
dissemble **536** vb
obliterate **545** v
store **627** vb.
safeguard **655** vb
defend **708** vb.
be cautious
853 v
concealed
concealed
520 ad
concealment
concealment
520
conceitedly
conceitedly
868 ad
concerning
concerning **9** ad
concise
brief **109** adj.
short **199** adj.
aphoristic
491 ad
concise **564** adj.
taciturn **577** adj
compendious
587 ad
ungracious
880 ad
concise, be
shorten **199** vb.
be concise
564 v
be taciturn
577 v
abstract **587** vb
concisely
concisely
564 ad
conciseness
conciseness
564
concomitant
concomitant
89
concord
agreement **24** n.
a mixture **43** n.
combination **50**
completeness
54
order **60** n.

consensus 483 n.
cooperation
701 n.
concord 705 n.
concord 705 vb.
peace 712 n.
friendliness
875 n.
friendship 875 n.
concordant
concordant
705 adj.
concur
accompany
89 vb.
concur 176 vb.
concord 705 vb.
concurrence
concurrence
176 n.
concurrent
conjunctive
45 adj.
combined 50 adj.
accompanying
89 vb.
concurrent
176 n.
concurrently
concurrently
176 adv.
condemn
kill 357 vb.
confute 474 vb.
judge 475 vb.
curse 894 vb.
blame 919 vb.
dispraise 919 vb.
condemn 956 vb.
punish 958 vb.
declare heretical
971 vb.
condemnation
condemnation
956 n.
condemned
condemned
956 adj.
condensation
increase 36 n.
union 45 n.
coherence 48 n.
contraction
193 n.
centrality 220 n.
condensation
319 n.
thickening 349 n.
refrigeration
377 n.
condiment
tincture 43 n.
food 296 n.
potherb 296 n.
pungency 383 n.
condiment 384 n.
scent 391 n.
preserver 661 n.
conditional
qualifying
463 adj.
uncertain
469 adj.
conditional
761 adj.
conditionally
conditionally
7 adv.
conditions
arrangement
62 n.

period 106 n.
qualification
463 n.
certainty 468 n.
supposition
507 n.
intention 612 n.
requirement
622 n.
mandate 746 n.
compact 760 n.
conditions 761 n.
condolence
lament 831 n.
condolence 900 n.
conduce
conduce 151 vb.
conduct
gait 260 n.
mien 440 n.
practice 605 n.
action 671 n.
conduct 683 n.
etiquette 843 n.
conduct. See route
way 619 n.
conduit
filament 203 n.
cavity 250 n.
furrow 257 n.
tube 258 n.
way in 292 n.
outlet 293 n.
passage 300 n.
water 334 n.
irrigator 336 n.
current 345 n.
conduit 346 n.
access 619 n.
route 619 n.
cone
cone 247 n.
tunnel 258 n.
confer
argue 470 vb.
confer 579 vb.
consult 686 vb.
make terms
761 vb.
conference
assembly 74 n.
listening 410 n.
enquiry 454 n.
class 533 n.
conference 579 n.
advice 686 n.
council 687 n.
cooperation
701 n.
mediation 715 n.
confess
hear 410 vb.
testify 461 vb.
assent 483 vb.
inform 519 vb.
confess 521 vb.
affirm 527 vb.
be truthful
535 vb.
accuse 923 vb.
be guilty 931 vb.
be penitent
934 vb.
do penance
936 vb.
condemn 956 vb.
conform
be uniform 16 vb.
do likewise 20 vb.
conform 83 vb.
change 138 vb.

acquiesce 483 vb.
obey 734 vb.
observe 763 vb.
be in fashion
843 vb.
be servile 874 vb.
be orthodox
970 vb.
conformable
conformable
83 adj.
conformably
conformably
83 adj.
conformance
conformance
24 n.
conformist
conformist 83 n.
conformity
uniformity 16 n.
imitation 20 n.
conformance
24 n.
regularity 81 n.
conformity 83 n.
concurrence
176 n.
credulity 482 n.
habit 605 n.
practice 605 n.
observance
763 n.
sociability 877 n.
right 908 n.
orthodoxism
970 n.
confusedly
confusedly
61 adv.
confusion
medley 43 n.
confusion 61 n.
havoc 160 n.
language 552 n.
confutation
confutation
474 n.
confute
confute 474 vb.
confuted
confuted 474 adj.
confuted, be
be confuted
474 vb.
congratulate
rejoice 830 vb.
congratulate
881 vb.
congratulation
congratulation
881 n.
congratulatory
congratulatory
881 adj.
congregate
cohere 48 vb.
be in order 60 vb.
congregate 74 vb.
be many 100 vb.
be near 195 vb.
approach 284 vb.
converge 288 vb.
meet 290 vb.
burst in 292 vb.
conjecture
empiricism 456 n.
uncertainty
469 n.
opinion 480 n.
conjecture 507 n.

hint 519 n.
conjointly
conjointly 45 adv.
conjunctive
conjunctive
45 adj.
conjuror
conjuror 540 n.
connect
connect 45 vb.
arrange 62 vb.
continue 71 vb.
be contiguous
197 vb.
pass 300 vb.
connotation
connotation
509 n.
consanguinity
relation 9 n.
consanguinity
11 n.
similarity 18 n.
genealogy 164 n.
sonship 165 n.
conscience
warning 659 n.
compulsion 735 n.
fastidiousness
857 n.
conscience 912 n.
consensus
agreement 24 n.
consensus 483 n.
concord 705 n.
consent
accord 24 vb.
concurrence
176 n.
assent 483 n.
assent 483 vb.
endorse 483 vb.
willingness 592 n.
be willing 592 vb.
be induced
607 vb.
be lenient 731 vb.
obey 734 vb.
permission 751 n.
permit 751 vb.
consent 753 n.
consent 753 vb.
content 823 n.
consenting
consenting
753 adj.
consentingly
consentingly
483 adv.
consequently
after 65 adv.
consequently
152 adv.
consignee
band 74 n.
manager 685 n.
consignee 749 n.
deputy 750 n.
recipient 777 n.
treasurer 793 n.
constitute
constitute 56 vb.
be one of 58 vb.
consult
meditate 444 vb.
confer 579 vb.
consult 686 vb.
cooperate
701 vb.
consume
consume 160 vb.

eat 296 vb.
rub 328 vb.
consummate
consummate
32 adj.
complete 54 adj.
contain
contain 56 vb.
comprise 78 vb.
contemporary
present time
116 n.
contemporary
118 n.
contempt
pride 866 n.
insolence 873 n.
scurrility 894 n.
disrespect 916 n.
indignity 916 n.
contempt 917 n.
detraction 921 n.
impiety 974 n.
contemptibility
contemptibility
917 n.
contemptible
contemptible
917 adj.
contemptibly
contemptibly
917 adv.
contemptuously
contemptuously
917 adv.
contend
do likewise 20 vb.
enter 292 vb.
be in difficulty
695 vb.
oppose 699 vb.
resist 710 vb.
contend 711 vb.
give battle
713 vb.
offer oneself
754 vb.
contender
compeer 28 n.
athlete 157 n.
pedestrian 263 n.
rider 263 n.
incomer 292 n.
respondent 455 n.
testee 456 n.
trier 666 n.
hinderer 697 n.
opposites 699 n.
opponent 700 n.
quarreller 704 n.
contender 711 n.
combatant 717 n.
combatant 717 n.
petitioner 758 n.
player 832 n.
enemy 876 n.
contending
contending
711 adj.
content
fill 54 vb.
quiescent
261 adj.
euphoria 371 n.
comfortable
371 adj.
sufficiency 630 n.
filled 630 adj.
suffice 630 vb.
reposeful 678 adj.

pacificatory
714 adj.
pacify 714 vb.
consent 753 vb.
inexcitability
818 n.
inexcitable
818 adj.
enjoyment 819 n.
pleased 819 adj.
please 821 vb.
content 823 n.
content 823 adj.
content 823 n.
cheerfulness
828 n.
cheer 828 vb.
approbation
918 n.
approving
918 adj.
content, be
be complete
54 vb.
have enough
630 vb.
be content
823 vb.
be relieved
826 vb.
contentedly
contentedly
823 adv.
contenting
contenting
823 adj.
contention
contention 711 n.
contents
finite quantity
26 n.
great quantity
32 n.
component 58 n.
bunch 74 n.
contents 188 n.
insides 219 n.
thing transferred
267 n.
property 772 n.
merchandise
790 n.
contest
athletics 157 n.
short distance
195 n.
equitation 262 n.
traction 283 n.
arrival 290 n.
contest 711 n.
sport 832 n.
contiguity
contiguity 197 n.
contiguous
near 195 adj.
contiguous
197 adj.
contiguous, be
extend 178 vb.
be near 195 vb.
be contiguous
197 vb.
touch 373 vb.
contiguously
contiguously
197 adv.
continuance
continuance
141 n.
continue
continue 71 vb.

continue 104 vb.
sustain 141 vb.
continuing
continuing
104 adj.
continuity
uniformity 16 n.
coherence 48 n.
order 60 n.
arrangement
62 n.
sequence 65 n.
continuity 71 n.
accompaniment
89 n.
recurrence 102 n.
perpetuity 110 n.
frequency 134 n.
periodicity 136 n.
continuance
141 n.
production 159 n.
space 178 n.
contiguity 197 n.
motion 260 n.
progression
280 n.
noncompletion
721 n.
continuous
increasing 36 adj.
sequential 65 adj.
continuous
71 adj.
perpetual
110 adj.
periodical
136 adj.
unceasing
141 adj.
contiguous
197 adj.
uncompleted
721 adj.
continuously
continuously
71 adv.
contraception
contraception
167 n.
drug 653 n.
hindrance 697 n.
contract
assent 483 vb.
promise 759 vb.
contract 760 vb.
make terms
761 vb.
bargain 786 vb.
contracted
contracted
193 adj.
contraction
smallness 33 n.
decrease 37 n.
diminution 37 n.
contraction
193 n.
narrowing 201 n.
contractual
agreeing 24 adj.
contractual
760 adj.
contraposition
contraposition
235 n.
contrariety
contrariety 14 n.
contrarily
contrarily 14 adv.

contrary
unrelated 10 adj.
contrary 14 adj.
different 15 adj.
nonuniform
17 adj.
disagreeing
25 adj.
separate 46 adj.
unconformable
84 adj.
counteracting
177 adj.
inverted 216 adj.
opposite 235 adj.
discordant
406 adj.
countervailing
462 adj.
semantic 509 adj.
negative 528 adj.
opposing 699 adj.
quarrelling
704 adj.
contrary, be
be contrary
14 vb.
disagree 25 vb.
counteract
177 vb.
tell against
462 vb.
be equivocal
513 vb.
oppose 699 vb.
be inimical
876 vb.
contrivance
contrivance
618 n.
converge
decrease 37 vb.
unite with 45 vb.
congregate 74 vb.
focus 76 vb.
be near 195 vb.
be contiguous
197 vb.
be narrow
201 vb.
be sharp 251 vb.
collide 274 vb.
approach 284 vb.
converge 288 vb.
convergence
convergence
288 n.
convergent
convergent
288 adj.
converse
notice 450 vb.
communicate
519 vb.
speak 574 vb.
be loquacious
576 vb.
speak to 578 vb.
converse 579 vb.
be sociable
877 vb.
conversely
conversely
462 adv.
conversing
conversing
579 adj.
conversion
conversion 142 n.

convert
make unlike
19 vb.
modify 138 vb.
convert 142 vb.
induce 607 vb.

converted
converted
142 adj.

convertibly
convertibly
142 adv.

convex
cellular 189 adj.
fleshy 190 adj.
expanded
192 adj.
back 233 adj.
rotund 247 adj.
convex 248 adj.

convex, be
expand 192 vb.
round 247 vb.
be convex
248 vb.

convexity
convexity 248 n.

conveyance
conveyance
262 n.

conveyor
conveyor 269 n.

convince
convert 142 vb.
make certain
468 vb.
demonstrate
473 vb.
convince 480 vb.
induce 607 vb.
make pious
973 vb.

convoluted
convoluted
246 adj.

convolution
complexity 61 n.
crossing 217 n.
distortion 241 n.
curvature 243 n.
curve 243 n.
loop 245 n.
convolution
246 n.
lettering 581 n.
circuit 621 n.
difficulty 695 n.

cook
cook 296 vb.
heat 376 vb.
mature 664 vb.

cookery
cookery 296 n.
fat 352 n.
heating 376 n.
preparer 664 n.

cooled
cooled 377 adj.

cooperate
cooperate
701 vb.

cooperation
cooperation
701 n.

cooperative
cooperative
701 adj.

cooperatively
cooperatively
701 adv.

coordinate
coordinate 460 n.

copy
identity 13 n.
uniformity 16 n.
imitation 20 n.
copy 20 n.
copy 22 n.
conform 83 vb.
double 91 vb.
repeat 102 vb.
reproduce 161 vb.
sham 537 n.
photography
546 n.
plan 618 n.
borrow 780 vb.
appropriate
781 vb.
steal 783 vb.

corkscrew. See
twine
meander 246 n.

corporal punishment
knock 274 n.
corporal
punishment
958 n.

corporate
joined 45 adj.
concurrent
176 adj.
cooperative
701 adj.
corporate
703 adj.
sharing 770 adj.

corporation
business 617 n.
association
701 n.
corporation
703 n.
merchant 789 n.

corpse
remainder 41 n.
decay 51 n.
the dead 356 n.
corpse 358 n.

correlate
correlate 12 vb.

correlation
correlation 12 n.

correlative
correlative
12 adj.

correlatively
correlatively
12 adv.

correspond
communicate
519 vb.
communicate
519 vb.
write 581 vb.
correspond
583 vb.
be sociable
877 vb.

correspondence
correspondence
583 n.

correspondent
calligrapher
581 n.
correspondent
583 n.
delegate 749 n.
recipient 777 n.

correspond. See
inform
rumour 524 n.

corroborate
corroborate
461 vb.
make certain
468 vb.
demonstrate
473 vb.
be true 489 vb.
affirm 527 vb.
swear 527 vb.
give security
762 vb.

cosmetic
water 334 n.
unguent 352 n.
scent 391 n.
pigment 420 n.
red pigment
426 n.
balm 653 n.
cosmetic 838 n.

cosmic
cosmic 316 adj.

cosmography
cosmography
316 n.

cost
cost 804 n.
cost 804 n.

council
assembly 74 n.
seniority 126 n.
director 685 n.
advice 686 n.
adviser 686 n.
council 687 n.
corporation
703 n.
consignee 749 n.
jurisdiction
950 n.
tribunal 951 n.
synod 979 n.
church exterior
984 n.

councillor
official 685 n.
councillor 687 n.

counteract
be contrary
14 vb.
set off 31 vb.
disable 156 vb.
weaken 158 vb.
assuage 172 vb.
influence 173 vb.
counteract
177 vb.
be opposite
235 vb.
recoil 275 vb.
tell against
462 vb.
be obstructive
697 vb.
oppose 699 vb.

counteracting
counteracting
177 adj.

counteraction
counteraction
177 n.

counterevidence
counterevidence
462 n.

countervailing
countervailing
462 adj.

counting instrument
counting
instrument 86 n.

country-dweller
country-dweller
864 n.

coupling
coupling 47 n.

courage
vigorousness
169 n.
resolution 594 n.
stamina 595 n.
safety 655 n.
defiance 706 n.
courage 850 n.
rashness 852 n.
disinterestedness
926 n.
drunkenness
944 n.

courageous
manly 157 adj.
defiant 706 adj.
courageous
850 adj.
worshipful
861 adj.
proud 866 adj.
disinterested
926 adj.

courageous, be
face danger
656 vb.
undertake
667 vb.
be courageous
850 vb.

courier
rider 263 n.
traveller 263 n.
bearer 268 n.
speeder 272 n.
courier 524 n.
servant 737 n.

course of time
time 104 n.
course of time
107 n.
conversion 142 n.
affairs 149 n.
destroyer 163 n.
progression
280 n.

court
approach 284 vb.
gaze 433 vb.
pursue 614 vb.
request 756 vb.
desire 854 vb.
befriend 875 vb.
be in love 882 vb.
excite love
882 vb.
court 884 n.
wed 889 vb.

courteous
attentive
450 adj.
well-bred
843 adj.
humble 867 adj.
sociable 877 adj.
courteous
879 adj.
benevolent
892 adj.
respectful
915 adj.
disinterested
926 adj.

reception 294 n.
experiment
456 n.
fitting out 664 n.
attempt 666 n.

decamp
go away 185 vb.
decamp 291 vb.
emerge 293 vb.
disappear 441 vb.
run away 615 vb.
escape 662 vb.
hasten 675 vb.
take away
781 vb.
not pay 800 vb.
fail in duty
913 vb.

decay
extinction 2 n.
decay 51 n.
oldness 122 n.
destroyer 163 n.
death 356 n.
stench 392 n.
dirt 644 n.
ulcer 646 n.
dilapidation
650 n.
blight 654 n.

decease
end 69 n.
decease 356 n.
illness 646 n.

deceive
make unlike
19 vb.
imitate 20 vb.
modify 138 vb.
substitute
145 vb.
outdo 301 vb.
mislead 490 vb.
keep secret
520 vb.
misteach 530 vb.
dissemble 536 vb.
deceive 537 vb.
represent 546 vb.
relinquish 616 vb.
be cunning
693 vb.
fleece 781 vb.
defraud 783 vb.
not pay 800 vb.
flatter 920 vb.
be dishonest
925 vb.

deceiver
deceiver 540 n.

deceiving
deceiving
537 adj.

decelerate
decrease 37 vb.
be moderate
172 vb.
come to rest
261 vb.
decelerate
273 vb.
be inactive
674 vb.

deception
insubstantiality
4 n.
visual fallacy
435 n.
misjudgment
476 n.

concealment
520 n.
disguise 522 n.
falsehood 536 n.
deception 537 n.
cunning 693 n.
stratagem 693 n.
borrowing 780 n.
peculation 783 n.
pretension 845 n.
ostentation
870 n.
boast 872 n.

deceptively
deceptively
537 adv.

decipher
decipher 515 vb.
manifest 517 vb.

declare heretical
declare heretical
971 vb.

decolorize
decolorize
421 vb.

decomposable
decomposable
51 adj.

decompose
simplify 44 vb.
break 46 vb.
disunite 46 vb.
separate 46 vb.
sunder 46 vb.
decompose 51 vb.
class 62 vb.
be dispersed
75 vb.
disperse 75 vb.
be old 122 vb.
make sterile
167 vb.
become small
193 vb.
pulverize 327 vb.
add water
334 vb.
perish 356 vb.
stink 392 vb.
be unclean
644 vb.
deteriorate
650 vb.
deteriorate
650 vb.
impair 650 vb.

decomposed
decomposed
51 adj.

decomposition
decomposition
51 n.

decorate
add 38 vb.
transform
142 vb.
coat 221 vb.
variegate 432 vb.
exaggerate
541 vb.
ornament 569 vb.
make better
649 vb.
beautify 836 vb.
primp 838 vb.
decorate 839 vb.
dignify 861 vb.

decoration
decoration 724 n.

decrease
finite quantity
26 n.
smallness 33 n.
be small 33 vb.
decrease 37 n.
decrease 37 vb.
subtraction 39 n.
disunion 46 n.
series 71 n.
change 138 vb.
be weak 158 vb.
unproductiveness
167 n.
be little 191 vb.
become small
193 vb.
be quiescent
261 vb.
recede 285 vb.
descent 304 n.
descend 304 vb.
disappear 441 vb.
waste 629 n.
scarcity 631 n.
deterioration
650 n.
deteriorate
650 vb.
inactivity 674 n.
be inactive
674 vb.
loss 767 n.

decreasing
decreasing
37 adj.

decree
judgment 475 n.
publication 523 n.
precept 688 n.
decree 732 n.
decree 732 vb.
legislation 948 n.
make legal
948 vb.

decrement
decrement 42 n.

deed
affairs 149 n.
effect 152 n.
contrivance
618 n.
policy 618 n.
important matter
633 n.
attempt 666 n.
deed 671 n.
labour 677 n.
conduct 683 n.
tactics 683 n.
masterpiece
689 n.
fight 711 n.
success 722 n.
prowess 850 n.
thaumaturgy
859 n.

deep
great 32 adj.
low 205 adj.
deep 206 adj.
oceanic 338 adj.
latent 518 adj.
concealed
520 adj.
unclear 563 adj.
felt 813 adj.
infernal 966 adj.

deep, be
be deep 206 vb.
founder 308 vb.

deeply
deeply 206 adv.

defame
cause doubt
481 vb.
misinterpret
516 vb.
shame 862 vb.
not respect
916 vb.
dispraise 919 vb.
defame 921 vb.
accuse 923 vb.

defamer
defamer 921 n.

defeat
be superior
34 vb.
inferiority 35 n.
disperse 75 vb.
stop 140 vb.
ruin 160 n.
destroy 160 vb.
propel 282 vb.
outdo 301 vb.
puzzle 469 vb.
confute 474 vb.
rejection 602 n.
victory 722 n.
defeat 722 vb.
defeat 723 n.
adversity 726 n.
loss 767 n.

defeated
defeated 723 adj.

defeated, be
be defeated
723 vb.

defecation
defecation 297 n.

defect
deficit 55 n.
weakness 158 n.
evil 611 n.
insufficiency
631 n.
defect 642 n.

defence
offset 31 n.
exclusion 57 n.
counteraction
177 n.
repulsion 287 n.
avoidance 615 n.
plot 618 n.
protection 655 n.
defence 708 n.
resistance 710 n.
battle 713 n.
warfare 713 n.
arms 718 n.
weapon 718 n.

defenceless
defenceless
156 adj.

defences
defences 708 n.

defend
screen 416 vb.
safeguard 655 vb.
patronize 698 vb.
defend 708 vb.
wage war 713 vb.
vindicate 922 vb.

defended
defended 708 adj.

defender
defender 708 n.

defending
defending
708 adj.

defensively
defensively
708 adv.

defiance
dissent 484 n.
affirmation
527 n.
negation 528 n.
gesture 547 n.
inaction 672 n.
opposition 699 n.
dissension 704 n.
quarrelsomeness
704 n.
defiance 706 n.
war 713 n.
disobedience
733 n.
refusal 755 n.
courage 850 n.
boast 872 n.
insolence 873 n.
threat 895 n.
accusation 923 n.

defiant
disagreeing
25 adj.
unconformable
84 adj.
dissenting
484 adj.
undisguised
517 adj.
assertive 527 adj.
defiant 706 adj.
disobedient
733 adj.
courageous
850 adj.
insolent 873 adj.
threatening
895 adj.

defiantly
defiantly
706 adv.

deficient
small 33 adj.
inferior 35 adj.
lesser 35 adj.
subtracted
39 adj.
incomplete
55 adj.
deficient 302 adj.
light 318 adj.
unequipped
665 adj.
lost 767 adj.

deficit
deficit 55 n.

definite
definite 80 adj.
intelligible
511 adj.
manifest 517 adj.
informative
519 adj.
assertive 527 adj.
perspicuous
562 adj.

deflect
make oblique
215 vb.
make curved
243 vb.
impel 274 vb.
deflect 277 vb.
repel 287 vb.
mislead 490 vb.
dissuade 608 vb.
parry 708 vb.

deform
destroy 160 vb.
deform 239 vb.
distort 241 vb.
make ugly
837 vb.
blemish 840 vb.

deformed
deformed
241 adj.

deformity
deformity 241 n.
curvature 243 n.
camber 248 n.
ugliness 837 n.

defraud
deceive 537 vb.
misuse 670 vb.
fleece 781 vb.
defraud 783 vb.
not pay 800 vb.
account 803 vb.
be dishonest
925 vb.

defrauder
defrauder 784 n.

defray
patronize 698 vb.
participate
770 vb.
purchase 787 vb.
defray 799 vb.

defy
be present
184 vb.
dissent 484 vb.
affirm 527 vb.
negate 528 vb.
be resolute
594 vb.
face danger
656 vb.
be active 673 vb.
oppose 699 vb.
make quarrels
704 vb.
defy 706 vb.
attack 707 vb.
resist 710 vb.
disobey 733 vb.
be free 739 vb.
be courageous
850 vb.
be ostentatious
870 vb.
boast 872 vb.
be insolent
873 vb.
threaten 895 vb.
accuse 923 vb.

degrading
degrading
862 adj.

degree
relativeness 9 n.
degree 27 n.
greatness 32 n.
superiority 34 n.
series 71 n.
serial place 73 n.
classification
77 n.
situation 181 n.
limit 231 n.
importance
633 n.
army officer
736 n.
apportionment
778 n.
nobility 863 n.

deification
deification 976 n.

deism
deism 967 n.

deistic
deistic 960 adj.

deity
deity 961 n.
idol 976 n.

Deity, the
the Deity 960 n.

dejected
disappointed
504 adj.
inactive 674 adj.
unhappy 820 adj.
discontented
824 adj.
dejected 829 adj.
lamenting
831 adj.
hopeless 848 adj.
humbled 867 adj.
loving 882 adj.

dejected, be
suffer 820 vb.
be discontented
824 vb.
be dejected
829 vb.
despair 848 vb.
be sullen 888 vb.

dejection
adversity 726 n.
sorrow 820 n.
discontent 824 n.
dejection 829 n.
lamentation
831 n.
dullness 835 n.
hopelessness
848 n.
nervousness
849 n.
pity 900 n.

delay
interim 104 n.
protraction
108 n.
looking ahead
119 n.
delay 131 n.
lull 140 n.
slowness 273 n.
negligence 453 n.
unwillingness
593 n.

deliverance
deliverance
663 n.
inaction 672 n.
inactivity 674 n.
tactics 683 n.
caution 853 n.

delegate
interpreter 515 n.
informant 519 n.
speaker 574 n.
agent 681 n.
councillor 687 n.
mediator 715 n.
delegate 749 n.

delight
excite 816 vb.
delight 821 vb.
cheer 828 vb.
amuse 832 vb.

deliver
restore 651 vb.
preserve 661 vb.
deliver 663 vb.

disencumber
696 vb.
aid 698 vb.
defend 708 vb.
liberate 741 vb.
restitute 782 vb.
purchase 787 vb.
relieve 826 vb.

deliverance
extraction 299 n.
restoration
651 n.
safety 655 n.
preservation
661 n.
preserver 661 n.
escape 662 n.
deliverance
663 n.
aid 698 n.
defender 708 n.
liberation 741 n.
restitution 782 n.
purchase 787 n.
relief 826 n.
benefactor 898 n.

demand
require 622 n.
warning 659 n.
demand 732 n.
demand 732 vb.
request 756 n.
request 756 vb.
give terms
761 vb.
appropriate
781 vb.
tax 804 n.
price 804 vb.
torment 822 vb.
regret 825 n.
desire 854 n.
desire 854 vb.
threat 895 n.
threaten 895 vb.

demanding
incomplete
55 adj.
demanding
622 adj.
requesting
756 adj.
desiring 854 adj.

demean oneself
demean oneself
862 vb.
be humble
867 vb.
be servile 874 vb.

demolish
break 46 vb.
decompose 51 vb.
revolutionize
144 vb.
weaken 158 vb.
demolish 160 vb.
force 171 vb.
collide 274 vb.
fell 306 vb.
confute 474 vb.
obliterate 545 vb.
wage war 713 vb.

demon
badness 640 n.
intimidation
849 n.
devil 963 n.
demon 964 n.

demonetize
demonetize
792 vb.

demonstrate
attribute 153 n.
argue 470 vb.
demonstrate
     473 vb.
convince 480 vb.
be true 489 vb.
affirm 527 vb.
be truthful
     535 vb.
have a right
     910 vb.
vindicate 922 vb.

demonstrated
demonstrated
     473 adj.

demonstrating
demonstrating
     473 adj.

demonstration
demonstration
     473 n.

dense
real 1 adj.
substantial 3 adj.
firm 45 adj.
cohesive 48 adj.
complete 54 adj.
assembled 74 adj.
one 88 adj.
multitudinous
     100 adj.
unyielding
     157 adj.
contracted
     193 adj.
thick 200 adj.
formed 238 adj.
closed 259 adj.
weighty 317 adj.
dense 319 adj.
airy 335 adj.
semiliquid
     349 adj.

dense, be
augment 36 vb.
cohere 48 vb.
become small
     193 vb.
make smaller
     193 vb.
centralize 220 vb.
be dense 319 vb.
harden 321 vb.
thicken 349 vb.

density
permanence
     139 n.
stability 148 n.
materiality 314 n.
density 319 n.
opacity 418 n.

denyingly
denyingly
     755 adv.

depart
separate 46 vb.
be excluded
     57 vb.
go away 185 vb.
travel 262 vb.
fly 266 vb.
recede 285 vb.
depart 291 vb.
emerge 293 vb.
die 356 vb.
be unwilling
     593 vb.
relinquish 616 vb.

departing
departing
     291 adj.

departure
departure 291 n.

depend
accompany
     89 vb.
depend 152 vb.
be uncertain
     469 vb.

dependant
inferior 35 n.
successor 67 n.
concomitant
     89 n.
follower 279 n.
auxiliary 702 n.
dependant 737 n.
possessor 771 n.
recipient 777 n.
toady 874 n.

deposal
deposal 747 n.

depose
displace 183 vb.
abase 306 vb.
reject 602 vb.
unthrone 729 vb.
depose 747 vb.
deprive 781 vb.
disentitle 911 vb.

deprecate
qualify 463 vb.
dissent 484 vb.
negate 528 vb.
be unwilling
     593 vb.
dissuade 608 vb.
warn 659 vb.
be active 673 vb.
oppose 699 vb.
resist 710 vb.
revolt 733 vb.
refuse 755 vb.
deprecate 757 vb.
be discontented
     824 vb.
dislike 856 vb.
disapprove
     919 vb.

deprecation
deprecation
     757 n.

deprecatory
dissenting
     484 adj.
negative 528 adj.
unwilling 593 adj.
dissuasive
     608 adj.
cautionary
     659 adj.
refusing 755 adj.
deprecatory
     757 adj.
discontented
     824 adj.
disapproving
     919 adj.

depreciating
depreciating
     478 adj.

depress
dissuade 608 vb.
trouble 822 vb.
cause discontent
     824 vb.
depress 829 vb.

deprive
deprive 781 vb.

depth
quantity 26 n.
degree 27 n.
greatness 32 n.
measure 178 n.
space 178 n.
size 190 n.
gap 196 n.
length 198 n.
lowness 205 n.
depth 206 n.
interiority 219 n.
cavity 250 n.
sailing aid 264 n.
meter 460 n.
imperspicuity
     563 n.

deputize
deputize 750 vb.

deputizing
deputizing
     750 adj.

deputy
inferior 35 n.
substitute 145 n.
intermediary
     226 n.
agent 681 n.
consignee 749 n.
deputy 750 n.

derange
decompose 51 vb.
be disordered
     61 vb.
derange 63 vb.
disperse 75 vb.
enlace 217 vb.
deform 239 vb.
distort 241 vb.
roughen 254 vb.
fold 256 vb.
intrude 292 vb.
agitate 313 vb.
distract 451 vb.
not discriminate
     459 vb.
surprise 503 vb.
harm 640 vb.
impair 650 vb.
hinder 697 vb.
be lax 729 vb.
trouble 822 vb.
frighten 849 vb.

derangement
derangement
     63 n.

derelict
leavings 41 n.
survivor 41 n.
derelict 774 n.
outcast 878 n.
solitary 878 n.

derisive
derisive 846 adj.

dermal
dermal 221 adj.

descend
be inferior 35 vb.
decrease 37 vb.
be oblique
     215 vb.
be in motion
     260 vb.
regress 281 vb.
land 290 vb.
descend 304 vb.
lower 306 vb.
sit down 306 vb.
founder 308 vb.
plunge 308 vb.
weigh 317 vb.

flow 345 vb.
lose repute
     862 vb.

descendant
descendant
     165 n.

descending
descending
     304 adj.

descent
decrease 37 n.
revolution 144 n.
depth 206 n.
incline 215 n.
curvature 243 n.
motion 260 n.
aeronautics
     266 n.
descent 304 n.
plunge 308 n.
deterioration
     650 n.
facility 696 n.
failure 723 n.
sport 832 n.

describe
remind 500 vb.
communicate
     519 vb.
record 543 vb.
represent 546 vb.
write 581 vb.
describe 585 vb.

description
assimilation 18 n.
mimicry 20 n.
indication 542 n.
representation
     546 n.
literature 552 n.
writing 581 n.
reading matter
     584 n.
description 585 n.

descriptive
descriptive
     585 adj.

desert
havoc 160 n.
desert 167 n.
space 178 n.
emptiness 185 n.
dryness 337 n.
land 339 n.
plain 343 n.

deserve
be good 639 vb.
deserve 910 vb.
be rewarded
     957 vb.

deserving
deserving
     910 adj.

desiccation
desiccation
     337 n.

designless
designless
     613 adj.

desire
attraction 286 n.
overstepping
     301 n.
expectation
     502 n.
expect 502 vb.
fantasy 508 n.
will 590 n.
will 590 vb.
be willing 592 vb.
motive 607 n.

intention 612 n.
aim at 612 vb.
require 622 vb.
request 756 n.
request 756 vb.
avarice 811 n.
suffering 820 n.
regret 825 n.
regret 825 vb.
be dejected
829 vb.
desire 854 n.
desire 854 vb.
love 882 n.
be in love 882 vb.
envy 907 n.
envy 907 vb.
be impure
946 vb.
desired
desired 854 adj.
desired object
desired object
854 n.
desirer
desirer 854 n.
desiring
desiring 854 adj.
desirously
desirously
854 adv.
despair
not expect
503 vb.
be disappointed
504 vb.
not act 672 vb.
be dejected
829 vb.
despair 848 vb.
desperado
athlete 157 n.
violent creature
171 n.
fool 496 n.
brave person
850 n.
desperado 852 n.
despise
underestimate
478 vb.
gesticulate
542 vb.
be insensitive
815 vb.
dislike 856 vb.
be fastidious
857 vb.
shame 862 vb.
be proud 866 vb.
be insolent
873 vb.
hate 883 vb.
not respect
916 vb.
despise 917 vb.
disapprove
919 vb.
detract 921 vb.
despising
despising 917 adj.
despotism
despotism 728 n.
dessert
dessert 296 n.
sweet thing
387 n.
destiny
future state
119 n.
futurity 119 n.

destiny 150 n.
cause 151 n.
fate 591 n.
necessity 591 n.
predetermination
603 n.
destroy
nullify 2 vb.
abate 37 vb.
disunite 46 vb.
rend 46 vb.
destroy 160 vb.
displace 183 vb.
deform 239 vb.
navigate 264 vb.
eject 295 vb.
extract 299 vb.
kill 357 vb.
slaughter 357 vb.
tell against
462 vb.
ill-treat 640 vb.
impair 650 vb.
defeat 722 vb.
impoverish
796 vb.
destroyed
destroyed
160 adj.
destroyed, be
be destroyed
160 vb.
destroyer
revolutionist
144 n.
destroyer 163 n.
violent creature
171 n.
flattener 211 n.
bane 654 n.
taker 781 n.
evildoer 899 n.
destruction
extinction 2 n.
separation 46 n.
decomposition
51 n.
finality 69 n.
destruction
160 n.
outbreak 171 n.
violence 171 n.
counteraction
177 n.
ejection 295 n.
extraction 299 n.
friction 328 n.
killing 357 n.
slaughter 357 n.
waste 629 n.
dilapidation
650 n.
impairment
650 n.
revolt 733 n.
inhumanity 893 n.
destructive
revolutionary
144 adj.
destructive
160 adj.
violent 171 adj.
evil 611 adj.
wasteful 629 adj.
harmful 640 adj.
adverse 726 adj.
destructively
destructively
160 adv.
desuetude
desuetude 606 n.

detect
smell 389 vb.
see 433 vb.
detect 479 vb.
be true 489 vb.
understand
511 vb.
disclose 521 vb.
detective
spectator 436 n.
inquisitive person
448 n.
detective 454 n.
informer 519 n.
protector 655 n.
police 950 n.
detector
detector 479 n.
detention
hindrance 697 n.
detention 742 n.
retention 773 n.
penalty 958 n.
deteriorate
be inferior 35 vb.
decrease 37 vb.
decompose 51 vb.
be old 122 vb.
be turned to
142 vb.
be weak 158 vb.
be destroyed
160 vb.
be brittle 325 vb.
be unpractised
606 vb.
waste 629 vb.
be ill 646 vb.
deteriorate
650 vb.
relapse 652 vb.
be unprepared
665 vb.
stop using
669 vb.
be defeated
723 vb.
fail 723 vb.
have trouble
726 vb.
be poor 796 vb.
aggravate
827 vb.
make ugly
837 vb.
be wrong 909 vb.
be wicked
929 vb.
be impious
974 vb.
deteriorated
deteriorated
650 adj.
deterioration
deterioration
650 n.
detract
detract 921 vb.
detracting
detracting
921 adj.
detraction
detraction 921 n.
detractor
detractor 921 n.
deviate
differ 15 vb.
separate 46 vb.
change 138 vb.
vary 147 vb.

make oblique
215 vb.
flank 234 vb.
make angular
242 vb.
be in motion
260 vb.
navigate 264 vb.
move slowly
273 vb.
deviate 277 vb.
recede 285 vb.
diverge 289 vb.
blow 347 vb.
disregard 453 vb.
be diffuse
565 vb.
avoid 615 vb.
circuit 621 vb.
fail 723 vb.
deviating
deviating
277 adj.
deviation
irrelevance 10 n.
difference 15 n.
nonuniformity
17 n.
disunion 46 n.
abnormality 84 n.
nonconformity
84 n.
change 138 n.
displacement
183 n.
distance 194 n.
obliquity 215 n.
laterality 234 n.
curvature 243 n.
meandering
246 n.
motion 260 n.
water travel
264 n.
transference
267 n.
deviation 277 n.
divergence 289 n.
traffic control
300 n.
overstepping
301 n.
shortfall 302 n.
descent 304 n.
visual fallacy
435 n.
inattention
451 n.
error 490 n.
tergiversation
598 n.
circuit 621 n.
devil
monster 933 n.
devil 963 n.
demon 964 n.
mythical being
964 n.
sorcerer 977 n.
devotional
devotional
975 adj.
dextral
dextral 236 adj.
dextrality
dextrality 236 n.
dextrally
dextrally
236 adv.
diabolic
wicked 929 adj.

diabolic 963 adj.
fairylike 964 adj.
infernal 966 adj.
idolatrous 976 adj.
sorcerous 977 adj.

diabolism
diabolism 963 n.

diabolist
diabolist 963 n.

diabolize
diabolize 963 vb.

dialect
speciality 80 n.
unintelligibility 512 n.
language 552 n.
dialect 555 n.
solecism 560 n.
pronunciation 572 n.
speech defect 575 n.

dialectal
dialectal 555 adj.

dictionary
word list 87 n.
commentary 515 n.
dictionary 554 n.
reference book 584 n.
collection 627 n.

die
pass away 2 vb.
end 69 vb.
depart 291 vb.
die 356 vb.
not act 672 vb.
be in love 882 vb.

dieting
dieting 296 n.

differ
be contrary 14 vb.
differ 15 vb.
be unlike 19 vb.
disagree 25 vb.
be unequal 29 vb.
diverge 289 vb.
quarrel 704 vb.

difference
unrelatedness 10 n.
contrariety 14 n.
difference 15 n.
nonuniformity 17 n.
dissimilarity 19 n.
disagreement 25 n.
inequality 29 n.
inequality 29 n.
remainder 41 n.
disunion 46 n.
speciality 80 n.
change 138 n.
divergence 289 n.
variegation 432 n.
discrimination 458 n.

different
contrary 14 adj.
different 15 adj.
nonuniform 17 adj.
dissimilar 19 adj.
inimitable 21 adj.

disagreeing 25 adj.
unequal 29 adj.
superior 34 adj.
separate 46 adj.
extraneous 59 adj.
special 80 adj.
multiform 82 adj.
converted 142 adj.
changeful 147 adj.
heterodox 971 adj.

differentiate
differentiate 15 vb.
make unlike 19 vb.
set apart 46 vb.
specify 80 vb.
compare 457 vb.
discriminate 458 vb.

differentiation
differentiation 15 n.

differently
differently 15 adv.

different time
different time 117 n.

difficult
moot 454 adj.
impracticable 465 adj.
puzzling 512 adj.
unclear 563 adj.
laborious 677 adj.
difficult 695 adj.
hindering 697 adj.

difficult, be
be inexpedient 638 vb.
be difficult 695 vb.
be obstructive 697 vb.
have trouble 726 vb.

difficulty
complexity 61 n.
enigma 525 n.
imperspicuity 563 n.
difficulty 695 n.
obstacle 697 n.
adversity 726 n.
revolter 733 n.
suffering 820 n.
aggravation 827 n.

diffuse
irrelevant 10 adj.
complete 54 adj.
long 198 adj.
veracious 535 adj.
diffuse 565 adj.
inelegant 571 adj.
descriptive 585 adj.
roundabout 621 adj.

diffuse, be
be unrelated 10 vb.
specify 80 vb.

repeat oneself 102 vb.
sophisticate 472 vb.
be diffuse 565 vb.
speak 574 vb.
be loquacious 576 vb.
be tedious 833 vb.

diffusely
diffusely 565 adv.

diffuseness
diffuseness 565 n.

digestive disorders
digestive disorders 646 n.

dignification
dignification 861 n.

dignify
dignify 861 vb.
sanctify 973 vb.

dilapidated
decreasing 37 adj.
decomposed 51 adj.
antiquated 122 adj.
flimsy 158 adj.
weakened 158 adj.
destroyed 160 adj.
brittle 325 adj.
dirty 644 adj.
dilapidated 650 adj.
unsafe 656 adj.
used 668 adj.
beggarly 796 adj.
disreputable 862 adj.

dilapidation
dilapidation 650 n.

dilation
dilation 192 n.

dim
insubstantial 4 adj.
vespertine 124 adj.
cloudy 350 adj.
dark 413 adj.
dim 414 adj.
opaque 418 adj.
semitransparent 419 adj.
colourless 421 adj.
blackish 423 adj.
indistinct 439 adj.
dejected 829 adj.

dim, be
decrease 37 vb.
cloud 350 vb.
be dark 413 vb.
be dim 414 vb.
lose colour 421 vb.
blur 435 vb.
be unseen 439 vb.
disappear 441 vb.

diminuendo
diminuendo 37 adv.

diminution
diminution 37 n.

dimly
dimly 414 adv.

dimness
dimness 414 n.

dim sight
eye 433 n.
vision 433 n.
blindness 434 n.
dim sight 435 n.

dim-sighted
dim-sighted 435 adj.

dim-sighted, be
be dim-sighted 435 vb.

direct
come first 34 vb.
make conform 83 vb.
influence 173 vb.
navigate 264 vb.
precede 278 vb.
educate 529 vb.
indicate 542 vb.
do 671 vb.
direct 684 vb.
rule 728 vb.

directed
directed 276 adj.

directing
directing 684 adj.

direction
tendency 174 n.
bearings 181 n.
laterality 234 n.
contraposition 235 n.
itinerary 262 n.
air travel 266 n.
direction 276 n.
directorship 684 n.

director
superior 34 n.
guide 515 n.
doer 671 n.
director 685 n.
authority 728 n.
master 736 n.

directorship
directorship 684 n.

directory
directory 87 n.
chronology 112 n.
guidebook 519 n.
indication 542 n.
reference book 584 n.

dirt
leavings 41 n.
covering 221 n.
excrement 297 n.
powder 327 n.
powderiness 327 n.
bubble 350 n.
stench 392 n.
opacity 418 n.
obliteration 545 n.
rubbish 636 n.
dirt 644 n.
blemish 840 n.
slur 862 n.

dirty
orderless 61 adj.
travelling 262 adj.

powdery 327 adj.
marshy 342 adj.
bubbly 350 adj.
dim 414 adj.
opaque 418 adj.
black 423 adj.
neglected
　　　453 adj.
negligent 453 adj.
bad 640 adj.
dirty 644 adj.
infectious
　　　648 adj.
beggarly 796 adj.
blemished
　　　840 adj.
dishonest
　　　925 adj.
impure 946 adj.

dirty person
slut 61 n.
dirty person
　　　644 n.

disable
abate 37 vb.
disable 156 vb.
weaken 158 vb.
suppress 160 vb.
make useless
　　　636 vb.
impair 650 vb.
hinder 697 vb.

disaccustom
disaccustom
　　　606 vb.

disagree
be contrary
　　　14 vb.
differ 15 vb.
disagree 25 vb.
be unequal 29 vb.
discord 406 vb.
dissent 484 vb.
mean 509 vb.
cause dislike
　　　856 vb.

disagreeing
disagreeing
　　　25 adj.

disagreement
disagreement
　　　25 n.

disappear
pass away 2 vb.
decrease 37 vb.
be transient
　　　109 vb.
cease 140 vb.
be impotent
　　　156 vb.
go away 185 vb.
regress 281 vb.
recede 285 vb.
decamp 291 vb.
be unseen
　　　439 vb.
disappear 441 vb.
be stealthy
　　　520 vb.
obliterate 545 vb.
be lost 767 vb.

disappearance
disappearance
　　　441 n.

disappearing
disappearing
　　　441 adj.

disappoint
fall short 302 vb.
surprise 503 vb.

disappoint
　　　504 vb.
befool 537 vb.
deceive 537 vb.
not suffice
　　　631 vb.
fail 723 vb.
miscarry 723 vb.
displease 822 vb.
cause discontent
　　　824 vb.
depress 829 vb.
leave no hope
　　　848 vb.
fail in duty
　　　913 vb.

disappointed
disappointed
　　　504 adj.

disappointed, be
be disappointed
　　　504 vb.

disappointing
disappointing
　　　504 adj.

disappointingly
disappointingly
　　　504 adv.

disappointment
disappointment
　　　504 n.

disapprobation
cry 403 n.
estimate 475 n.
dissent 484 n.
gesture 542 n.
rejection 602 n.
hindrance 697 n.
opposition 699 n.
prohibition 752 n.
deprecation
　　　757 n.
discontent 824 n.
odium 883 n.
disrespect 916 n.
indignity 916 n.
disapprobation
　　　919 n.
detraction 921 n.
condemnation
　　　956 n.
orthodoxism
　　　970 n.
impiety 974 n.

disapprove
cry 403 vb.
vociferate
　　　403 vb.
estimate 475 vb.
dissent 484 vb.
gesticulate
　　　542 vb.
reject 602 vb.
oppose 699 vb.
prohibit 752 vb.
refuse 755 vb.
deprecate 757 vb.
be discontented
　　　824 vb.
regret 825 vb.
dislike 856 vb.
make unwelcome
　　　878 vb.
not respect
　　　916 vb.
disapprove
　　　919 vb.
detract 921 vb.
condemn 956 vb.

disapproved
disapproved
　　　919 adj.

disapprover
disapprover
　　　919 n.

disapproving
disapproving
　　　919 adj.

disapprovingly
disapprovingly
　　　919 adv.

disarranged
disarranged
　　　63 adj.

disbelieve
disbelieve 481 vb.
negate 528 vb.
not wonder
　　　860 vb.
be irreligious
　　　968 vb.

disclose
uncover 224 vb.
blunder 490 vb.
manifest 517 vb.
show 517 vb.
inform 519 vb.
disclose 521 vb.
rumour 524 vb.
be truthful
　　　535 vb.
indicate 542 vb.

disclosed
disclosed 521 adj.

disclosed, be
be disclosed
　　　521 vb.

disclosing
disclosing
　　　521 adj.

disclosure
uncovering 224 n.
testimony 461 n.
creed 480 n.
assent 483 n.
manifestation
　　　517 n.
information
　　　519 n.
disclosure 521 n.
publication 523 n.
affirmation
　　　527 n.
veracity 535 n.
indication 542 n.
spontaneity
　　　604 n.
guilt 931 n.
penitence 934 n.
revelation 969 n.

discontent
incompleteness
　　　55 n.
dissent 484 n.
disappointment
　　　504 n.
gesture 542 n.
evil 611 n.
insufficiency
　　　631 n.
danger signal
　　　660 n.
disobedience
　　　733 n.
deprecation
　　　757 n.
sorrow 820 n.
suffering 820 n.
discontent 824 n.
melancholy 829 n.

dislike 856 n.
resentment
　　　886 n.
sullenness 888 n.
disapprobation
　　　919 n.

discontented
discontented
　　　824 adj.

discontented, be
be discontented
　　　824 vb.

discontenting
discontenting
　　　824 adj.

discontinue
be incomplete
　　　55 vb.
discontinue
　　　72 vb.
cease 140 vb.
suppress 160 vb.
distract 451 vb.

discontinuity
discontinuity
　　　72 n.

discontinuous
unrelated 10 adj.
disunited 46 adj.
incomplete
　　　55 adj.
discontinuous
　　　72 adj.
infrequent
　　　135 adj.
fitful 137 adj.
deviating
　　　277 adj.

discontinuous, be
be discontinuous
　　　72 vb.

discontinuously
discontinuously
　　　72 adv.

discord
disagreement
　　　25 n.
misfit 25 n.
medley 43 n.
disorder 61 n.
give pain 372 vb.
sound 393 vb.
nonresonance
　　　400 n.
stridor 402 n.
rasp 402 vb.
discord 406 n.
discord 406 vb.
inelegance 571 n.
dissension 704 n.
make quarrels
　　　704 vb.

discordant
discordant
　　　406 adj.

discount
subtract 39 vb.
decrement 42 n.
earnings 766 n.
portion 778 n.
pay 799 n.
discount 805 n.
discount 805 vb.
cheapness 807 n.

discourteous
violent 171 adj.
clumsy 690 adj.
ill-bred 842 adj.
impertinent
　　　873 adj.

discourteous
880 adj.
sullen 888 adj.
ungrateful
903 adj.
disrespectful
916 adj.
discourtesy
conduct 683 n.
ill-breeding
842 n.
sauciness 873 n.
unsociability
878 n.
discourtesy
880 n.
sullenness 888 n.
contempt 917 n.
discover
come before
64 vb.
initiate 68 vb.
meet with
149 vb.
cause 151 vb.
chance 154 vb.
produce 159 vb.
travel 262 vb.
arrive 290 vb.
cognize 442 vb.
think 444 vb.
discover 479 vb.
believe 480 vb.
manifest 517 vb.
be informed
519 vb.
disclose 521 vb.
pursue 614 vb.
plan 618 vb.
acquire 766 vb.
discovering
discovering
479 adj.
discovery
discovery 479 n.
discreditable
flagrant 32 adj.
bad 640 adj.
discreditable
862 adj.
blameworthy
919 adj.
discriminate
differentiate
15 vb.
set apart 46 vb.
specify 80 vb.
compare 457 vb.
discriminate
458 vb.
know 485 vb.
be wise 493 vb.
name 556 vb.
select 600 vb.
be skilful 689 vb.
have taste
841 vb.
be fastidious
857 vb.
discriminating
discriminating
458 adj.
discrimination
differentiation
15 n.
gastronomy
296 n.
intellect 442 n.
discrimination
458 n.
reasoning 470 n.

judgment 475 n.
sagacity 493 n.
choice 600 n.
skill 689 n.
moral sensibility
814 n.
good taste 841 n.
fastidiousness
857 n.
discursive
discursive
586 adj.
disease
generality 79 n.
helplessness
156 n.
dieting 296 n.
fluid 330 n.
decease 356 n.
insensibility
370 n.
heat 374 n.
insufficiency
631 n.
redundance
632 n.
badness 640 n.
disease 646 n.
dilapidation
650 n.
bane 654 n.
sleep 674 n.
diseased
diseased 646 adj.
disembody
disembody
315 vb.
disencumber
abate 37 vb.
lighten 318 vb.
deliver 663 vb.
disencumber
696 vb.
liberate 741 vb.
take away
781 vb.
relieve 826 vb.
disentitle
disentitle 911 vb.
disguise
dissimilarity 19 n.
covering 221 n.
cloak 223 n.
screen 416 n.
disguise 522 n.
mental dishonesty
538 n.
disguised
disguised 520 adj.
dish
a mixture 43 n.
sequel 67 n.
dish 296 n.
dishonest
unreliable
469 adj.
stealthy 520 adj.
bad 640 adj.
cunning 693 adj.
thieving 783 adj.
discreditable
862 adj.
wrong 909 adj.
dishonest
925 adj.
selfish 927 adj.
wicked 929 adj.
lawbreaking
949 adj.

dishonest, be
disappoint
504 vb.
be false 536 vb.
deceive 537 vb.
apostatize
598 vb.
strike at 707 vb.
not observe
764 vb.
not pay 800 vb.
be dishonest
925 vb.
dishonestly
dishonestly
925 adv.
disinterested
substituted
145 adj.
tutelary 655 adj.
losing 767 adj.
liberal 808 adj.
content 823 adj.
humble 867 adj.
loving 882 adj.
benevolent
892 adj.
philanthropic
896 adj.
disinterested
926 adj.
virtuous 928 adj.
disinterested, be
be humble
867 vb.
be disinterested
926 vb.
atone 936 vb.
disinterestedness
disinterestedness
926 n.
dislike
difference 15 n.
unwillingness
593 n.
be unwilling
593 vb.
opposition 699 n.
resistance 710 n.
tedium 833 n.
be indifferent
855 vb.
dislike 856 n.
dislike 856 vb.
enmity 876 n.
hatred 883 n.
hate 883 vb.
disapprobation
919 n.
disapprove
919 vb.
disliked
disliked 856 adj.
disliking
disliking 856 adj.
dismiss
displace 183 vb.
repel 287 vb.
dismiss 295 vb.
stop using
669 vb.
make inactive
674 vb.
depose 747 vb.
refuse 755 vb.
not retain
774 vb.
disobedience
disobedience
733 n.

disobedient
revolutionary
144 adj.
violent 171 adj.
negative 528 adj.
unwilling 593 adj.
wilful 597 adj.
difficult 695 adj.
opposing 699 adj.
quarrelling
704 adj.
defiant 706 adj.
resisting 710 adj.
anarchic 729 adj.
disobedient
733 adj.
nonobservant
764 adj.
discontented
824 adj.
sullen 888 adj.
undutiful 913 adj.
disrespectful
916 adj.
perfidious
925 adj.
wicked 929 adj.
schismatical
972 adj.
disobey
be contrary
14 vb.
be disordered
61 vb.
negate 528 vb.
oppose 699 vb.
please oneself
729 vb.
disobey 733 vb.
be free 739 vb.
not observe
764 vb.
be insolent
873 vb.
fail in duty
913 vb.
schismatize
972 vb.
disorder
unrelatedness
10 n.
nonuniformity
17 n.
disorder 61 n.
derangement
63 n.
discontinuity
72 n.
fitfulness 137 n.
amorphism 239 n.
negligence 453 n.
badness 640 n.
uncleanness
644 n.
ill-breeding
842 n.
disordered, be
be disordered
61 vb.
disorderly
disorderly 61 adj.
violent 171 adj.
loud 395 adj.
riotous 733 adj.
ill-bred 842 adj.
drunk 944 adj.
disperse
decrease 37 vb.
disunite 46 vb.
separate 46 vb.
decompose 51 vb.

be disordered
61 vb.
jumble 61 vb.
disperse 75 vb.
generalize 79 vb.
destroy 160 vb.
displace 183 vb.
lengthen 198 vb.
move 260 vb.
repel 287 vb.
let fall 306 vb.
waste 629 vb.
defeat 722 vb.
liberate 741 vb.

dispersed, be
be dispersed
75 vb.

dispersion
dispersion 75 n.

displace
subtract 39 vb.
exclude 57 vb.
derange 63 vb.
displace 183 vb.
move 260 vb.
transpose 267 vb.
transpose 267 vb.
land 290 vb.
eject 295 vb.
empty 295 vb.
extract 299 vb.
take 781 vb.
take away
781 vb.

displaced
displaced
183 adj.

displacement
subtraction 39 n.
separation 46 n.
exclusion 57 n.
displacement
183 n.
transference
267 n.
ejection 295 n.
extraction 299 n.
taking 781 n.

displease
displease 822 vb.
cause discontent
824 vb.
depress 829 vb.
cause dislike
856 vb.

dispose of
dispose of
668 vb.
subjugate 740 vb.
possess 768 vb.

dispraise
dispraise 919 vb.

disregard
be deaf 411 vb.
be blind 434 vb.
not think 445 vb.
be incurious
449 vb.
disregard 453 vb.
underestimate
478 vb.
not know 486 vb.
conceal 520 vb.
be taciturn
577 vb.
reject 602 vb.
be unimportant
634 vb.
not act 672 vb.
abrogate 747 vb.

be insensitive
815 vb.
forgive 904 vb.
fail in duty
913 vb.
not respect
916 vb.
hold cheap
917 vb.

disreputable
not nice 640 adj.
vulgar 842 adj.
renowned
861 adj.
disreputable
862 adj.
plebeian 864 adj.
unrespected
916 adj.
disapproved
919 adj.
dishonest
925 adj.
vicious 929 adj.

disrepute
decrease 37 n.
famousness
861 n.
disrepute 862 n.
humiliation 867 n.
odium 883 n.
disrespect 916 n.
disapprobation
919 n.
detraction 921 n.
improbity 925 n.
wickedness 929 n.

disrespect
nonobservance
764 n.
ridicule 846 n.
disrepute 862 n.
undutifulness
913 n.
disrespect 916 n.
disapprobation
919 n.
impiety 974 n.

disrespectful
disrespectful
916 adj.

disrespectfully
disrespectfully
916 adv.

dissemble
imitate 20 vb.
mislead 490 vb.
be equivocal
513 vb.
lurk 518 vb.
be stealthy
520 vb.
conceal 520 vb.
dissemble 536 vb.
deceive 537 vb.
be untrue 538 vb.
misname 557 vb.
plead 609 vb.
be affected
845 vb.
be dishonest
925 vb.
be impious
974 vb.

dissension
difference 15 n.
disagreement
25 n.
disunion 46 n.
stop 140 vb.
argument 470 n.

dissent 484 n.
opposition 699 n.
dissension 704 n.
contention 711 n.
revolt 733 n.
enmity 876 n.
hatred 883 n.

dissent
disagreement
25 n.
disagree 25 vb.
nonconformity
84 n.
argument 470 n.
argue 470 vb.
unbelief 481 n.
disbelieve 481 vb.
dissent 484 n.
dissent 484 vb.
negation 528 n.
negate 528 vb.
unwillingness
593 n.
be unwilling
593 vb.
reject 602 vb.
opposition 699 n.
dissension 704 n.
quarrel 704 vb.
defy 706 vb.
refuse 755 vb.
dislike 856 vb.
disapprove
919 vb.
sectarianism
972 n.

dissentient
dissentient 484 n.

dissenting
dissenting
484 adj.

dissertate
dissertate
586 vb.

dissertation
composition 56 n.
arrangement
62 n.
accumulation
74 n.
commentary
515 n.
diffuseness 565 n.
oration 574 n.
reading matter
584 n.
dissertation
586 n.

dissertator
dissertator 586 n.

dissimilar
different 15 adj.
nonuniform
17 adj.
dissimilar 19 adj.
unequal 29 adj.

dissimilarity
dissimilarity 19 n.

dissimilarly
dissimilarly
19 adv.

dissuade
revert 143 vb.
moderate 172 vb.
cause doubt
481 vb.
dissuade 608 vb.
warn 659 vb.
advise 686 vb.
hinder 697 vb.
prohibit 752 vb.

deprecate 757 vb.
cause discontent
824 vb.
depress 829 vb.
frighten 849 vb.

dissuasion
dissuasion 608 n.

dissuasive
dissuasive
608 adj.

distance
difference 15 n.
futurity 119 n.
range 178 n.
distance 194 n.
length 198 n.
exteriority 218 n.
rear 233 n.
propulsion 282 n.
avoidance 615 n.

distant
dissimilar 19 adj.
extraneous
59 adj.
alone 88 adj.
distant 194 adj.
exterior 218 adj.
invisible 439 adj.

distant, be
be distant
194 vb.
recede 285 vb.
avoid 615 vb.

distinctive
distinctive
15 adj.
separate 46 adj.
discriminating
458 adj.

distort
make unlike
19 vb.
break 46 vb.
modify 138 vb.
transform
142 vb.
force 171 vb.
shorten 199 vb.
make oblique
215 vb.
deform 239 vb.
distort 241 vb.
crinkle 246 vb.
draw 283 vb.
misinterpret
516 vb.
misteach 530 vb.
be false 536 vb.
exaggerate
541 vb.
misrepresent
547 vb.
impair 650 vb.
pervert 650 vb.
misuse 670 vb.
make ugly
837 vb.

distorted
distorted 241 adj.

distortion
distortion 241 n.

distract
derange 63 vb.
distract 451 vb.

distracted
distracted
451 vb.

distressing
distressing
822 adj.

district
subdivision 53 n.
district 179 n.
place 180 n.
locality 182 n.
abode 187 n.
housing 187 n.
political
organization
728 n.
parish 979 n.
disunion
disunion 46 n.
disunite
disunite 46 vb.
unstick 49 vb.
decompose 51 vb.
part 53 vb.
discontinue
72 vb.
disperse 75 vb.
disable 156 vb.
weaken 158 vb.
demolish 160 vb.
displace 183 vb.
doff 224 vb.
open 258 vb.
soften 322 vb.
make useless
636 vb.
wound 650 vb.
deliver 663 vb.
disencumber
696 vb.
be lax 729 vb.
not retain
774 vb.
divorce 891 vb.
disunited
disunited 46 adj.
disused
disused 669 adj.
diver
depth 206 n.
descent 304 n.
diver 308 n.
gravity 317 n.
diverge
separate 46 vb.
be dispersed
75 vb.
disperse 75 vb.
bifurcate 92 vb.
make angular
242 vb.
deviate 277 vb.
diverge 289 vb.
divergence
divergence 289 n.
divergent
divergent
289 adj.
dividing line
dividing line 92 n.
divination
equal chance
154 n.
astronomy 316 n.
divination 506 n.
hermeneutics
515 n.
nondesign 613 n.
sorcery 977 n.
occultism 978 n.
spiritualism
978 n.
divine
divine 506 vb.
divine 960 adj.
practise sorcery
977 vb.

practise
occultism 978 vb.
divine attribute
divine attribute
960 n.
divine function
deliverance
663 n.
propitiation
936 n.
divine function
960 n.
sanctity 973 n.
divinely
divinely 960 adv.
divineness
divineness 960 n.
diviner
diviner 506 n.
divorce
separation 46 n.
unit 88 n.
parentage 164 n.
nonretention
774 n.
not retain
774 vb.
divorce 891 n.
divorce 891 vb.
divorced
divorced 891 adj.
divulge
divulge 521 vb.
publish 523 vb.
speak 574 vb.
accuse 923 vb.
do
cause 151 vb.
be able 155 vb.
produce 159 vb.
operate 168 vb.
be instrumental
623 vb.
be useful 635 vb.
do 671 vb.
be active 673 vb.
exert oneself
677 vb.
behave 683 vb.
deal with 683 vb.
carry out 720 vb.
be successful
722 vb.
observe 763 vb.
celebrate 871 vb.
do one's duty
912 vb.
do before
do before 114 vb.
do business
do business
617 vb.
do 671 vb.
trade 786 vb.
doctor
substitute 145 n.
resident 186 n.
cover 221 vb.
animal husbandry
364 n.
psychologist
442 n.
insanity 498 n.
mender 651 n.
cure 651 vb.
doctor 653 n.
doctor 653 vb.
preserve 661 vb.
adviser 686 n.
minister to
698 vb.

relieve 826 vb.
doctrinaire
doctrinaire 468 n.
narrow mind
476 n.
theorist 507 n.
do easily
do easily 696 vb.
be successful
722 vb.
win 722 vb.
doer
producer 159 n.
doer 671 n.
busy person
673 n.
agent 681 n.
manager 685 n.
political party
703 n.
doff
decrease 37 vb.
unstick 49 vb.
doff 224 vb.
open 258 vb.
excrete 297 vb.
be plain 517 vb.
disclose 521 vb.
relinquish 616 vb.
stop using
669 vb.
dog
dog 360 n.
hunter 614 n.
protector 655 n.
doggerel
doggerel 588 n.
dogmatize
dogmatize
468 vb.
do good
be useful 635 vb.
be expedient
637 vb.
do good 639 vb.
make better
649 vb.
be auspicious
725 vb.
be benevolent
892 vb.
be virtuous
928 vb.
doing
operative
168 adj.
doing 671 adj.
observant
763 adj.
do law
do law 953 vb.
do likewise
do likewise 20 vb.
dome
roof 221 n.
curve 243 n.
cone 247 n.
sphere 247 n.
dome 248 n.
domestic
clothier 223 n.
domestic 737 n.
keeper 744 n.
dominate
be able 155 vb.
prevail 173 vb.
dominate 728 vb.
do one's duty
do one's duty
912 vb.

doorkeeper
doorway 258 n.
doorkeeper 259 n.
servant 737 n.
doorway
entrance 68 n.
lobby 189 n.
threshold 229 n.
front 232 n.
rear 233 n.
doorway 258 n.
stopper 259 n.
way in 292 n.
outlet 293 n.
access 619 n.
church exterior
984 n.
temple 984 n.
do penance
do penance
936 n.
do sums
do sums 86 vb.
double
dual 90 adj.
dual 90 adj.
double 91 adj.
double 91 vb.
repeat 102 vb.
doubt
philosophy 444 n.
dubiety 469 n.
be uncertain
469 n.
doubt 481 n.
doubt 481 vb.
dissent 484 n.
not know 486 vb.
unwillingness
593 n.
be nervous
849 vb.
jealousy 906 n.
be jealous
906 vb.
irreligion 968 n.
doubtfully
doubtfully
481 adv.
doubting
doubting 469 adj.
dower
dower 772 n.
dower 772 vb.
down
down 304 adv.
downy
downy 254 adj.
soft 322 vb.
do wrong
be biased 476 vb.
harm 640 vb.
ill-treat 640 vb.
oppress 730 vb.
do wrong 909 vb.
be illegal 949 vb.
drag on
drag on 108 vb.
drain
gap 196 n.
tunnel 258 n.
lake 341 n.
drain 346 n.
cleanser 643 n.
sink 644 n.
drama
composition 56 n.
broadcast 526 n.
literature 552 n.
poem 588 n.
drama 589 n.

amusement
832 n.

dramatic
dramatic 589 adj.

dramatist
author 584 n.
dramatist 589 n.

dramatize
dramatize
589 vb.

dramaturgy
dramaturgy
589 n.

draught
draught 296 n.
fluid 330 n.
pungency 383 n.

draught horse
draught horse
268 n.

draw
draw 28 n.
synchronism
118 n.
stop 140 vb.
move 260 vb.
navigate 264 vb.
transpose 267 vb.
draw 283 vb.
attract 286 vb.
extract 299 vb.
victory 722 n.

drawing
dynamic 155 adj.
drawing 283 adj.

draw money
draw money
792 vb.

drench
fill 54 vb.
destroy 160 vb.
overlie 221 vb.
flow out 293 vb.
immerse 298 vb.
encroach 301 vb.
soften 322 vb.
drench 336 vb.
flow 345 vb.
superabound
632 vb.
clean 643 vb.
sate 858 vb.

drenched
drenched 336 adj.

dress
dress 223 n.
dress 223 vb.
equipment 625 n.
decorate 839 vb.
canonicals 983 n.

dressed
dressed 223 adj.

dressing
adjunct 40 n.
dressing 223 n.
appearance
440 n.

drink
assuage 172 vb.
empty 295 vb.
drink 296 vb.
have enough
630 vb.
revel 832 vb.
toast 871 vb.
be sociable
877 vb.
get drunk 944 vb.

drinking
drinking 296 n.

driver
driver 263 n.
carrier 268 n.
speeder 272 n.
passing along
300 n.
domestic 737 n.

drug
mouthful 296 n.
anaesthetic
370 n.
pungency 383 n.
drug 658 n.
poison 654 n.
drug-taking
944 n.

drugged
drugged 944 adj.

druggist
druggist 653 n.

drug oneself
drug oneself
944 vb.

drug-taking
drug-taking
944 n.

drum
drum 409 n.

drunk
foolish 494 adj.
intemperate
938 adj.
drunk 944 adj.

drunkard
drinking 296 n.
madman 499 n.
reveller 832 n.
sensualist 939 n.
drunkard 944 n.

drunk, be
be drunk 944 vb.

drunken
disorderly 61 adj.
feeding 296 adj.
sensual 939 adj.
drunken 944 adj.

drunkenness
drunkenness
944 n.

dry
weak 158 adj.
unproductive
167 adj.
make smaller
193 vb.
absorb 294 vb.
powdery 327 adj.
aerate 335 vb.
dry 337 adj.
dry 337 vb.
staunch 345 vb.
hot 374 adj.
burn 376 vb.
heat 376 vb.
sanitate 647 vb.
preserve 661 vb.
make insensitive
815 vb.

dry, be
be dry 337 vb.
be hot 374 vb.

dryer
dryer 337 n.

dryness
dryness 337 n.

dual
dual 90 adj.
double 91 adj.

duality
duality 90 n.

dubiety
dubiety 469 n.

due
advisable
637 n.
just 908 adj.
due 910 adj.

due, be
be right 908 vb.
be due 910 vb.
be one's duty
912 vb.

duel
slaughter 357 n.
duel 711 n.

dueness
dueness 910 n.

duet
duet 407 n.

dull
tedious 833 adj.
dull 835 adj.

dull, be
be dull 835 vb.

dullness
dullness 835 n.

duly
duly 910 adv.

dunce
ignoramus 488 n.
dunce 496 n.

dupe
weakling 158 n.
credulity 482 n.
ignoramus 488 n.
ninny 496 n.
dupe 539 n.
loser 723 n.
unlucky person
726 n.
sufferer 820 n.

duped, be
be duped 539 vb.

duplicate
analogue 18 n.
duplicate 22 n.
duplication 91 n.
reproduction
161 n.
record 543 n.
image 546 n.
representation
546 n.
script 581 n.

duplication
duplication 91 n.

duplicity
appearance
440 n.
concealment
520 n.
duplicity 536 n.
deception 537 n.
sham 537 n.
mental dishonesty
538 n.
cunning 693 n.
affectation
845 n.
perfidy 925 n.
false piety 974 n.

durability
durability 108 n.

duty
bond 47 n.
liability 175 n.
necessity 591 n.
motive 607 n.
needfulness
622 n.
labour 677 n.

obedience 734 n.
promise 759 n.
right 908 n.
dueness 910 n.
duty 912 n.
cult 975 n.

dwarf
small animal
33 n.
dwarf 191 n.

dwarfish
dwarfish 191 adj.

dwell
stay 139 vb.
be stable 148 vb.
be situated
181 vb.
place oneself
182 vb.
be present
184 vb.
dwell 187 vb.
live 355 vb.

dweller
dweller 186 n.

dwelling
dwelling 187 n.
canopy 221 n.
tunnel 258 n.

dying
extinct 2 adj.
ephemeral
109 adj.
ageing 126 adj.
dying 356 adj.
sick 646 adj.

dynamic
dynamic 155 adj.
operative
168 adj.
vigorous 169 adj.
godlike 960 adj.

E

ear
ear 410 n.

earliness
earliness 130 n.

early
instantaneous
111 adj.
anachronistic
113 adj.
matinal 123 adj.
early 130 adj.
timely 132 adj.
ill-timed 133 adj.
speedy 272 adj.

early, be
be unconformable
84 vb.
time 112 vb.
misdate 113 vb.
be before 114 vb.
look ahead
119 vb.
be early 130 vb.
precede 278 vb.
arrive 290 vb.
err 490 vb.
foresee 505 vb.
deceive 537 vb.
be unprepared
665 vb.
acquire 766 vb.
possess 768 vb.
take 781 vb.
hope 847 vb.

earnings
increment 36 n.
earnings 766 n.
receiving 777 n.
taking 781 n.
pay 799 n.
receipt 802 n.
reward 957 n.

earth sciences
earth sciences 316 n.

earthwork
antiquity 120 n.
small hill 204 n.
earthwork 248 n.
tomb 359 n.
signpost 542 n.
monument 543 n.
fort 708 n.

easily
easily 696 adv.

easy
possible 464 adj.
intelligible 511 adj.
easy 696 adj.

easy, be
be easy 696 vb.

easy thing
trifle 634 n.
easy thing 696 n.
victory 722 n.

eat
abate 37 vb.
absorb 294 vb.
eat 296 vb.
taste 381 vb.
waste 629 vb.
have enough 630 vb.
prosper 725 vb.
fleece 781 vb.
be hungry 854 vb.
be sociable 877 vb.
gluttonize 942 vb.

eater
eater 296 n.
reveller 832 n.
glutton 942 n.

eating
eating 296 n.

eccentricity
eccentricity 498 n.

ecclesiarch
ecclesiarch 980 n.

ecclesiastical
ecclesiastical 979 adj.

ecclesiastical, be
be ecclesiastical 979 vb.

ecclesiastical court
ecclesiastical court 951 n.

ecclesiastically
ecclesiastically 979 adv.

ecclesiasticism
ecclesiasticism 979 n.

economical
economical 809 adj.
parsimonious 811 adj.
cautious 853 adj.
temperate 937 adj.

fasting 941 adj.

economize
economize 809 vb.

economy
diminution 37 n.
provision 628 n.
preservation 661 n.
restriction 742 n.
prohibition 752 n.
gain 766 n.
economy 809 n.
parsimony 811 n.
temperance 937 n.
asceticism 940 n.

eddy
coil 246 n.
water travel 264 n.
vortex 310 n.
eddy 345 n.
pitfall 658 n.

edge
adjunct 40 n.
extremity 69 n.
nearness 195 n.
contiguity 197 n.
roof 221 n.
outline 228 n.
edge 229 n.
limit 231 n.
laterality 234 n.
projection 249 n.
shore 339 n.

edging
filament 203 n.
garment 223 n.
edging 229 n.
coil 246 n.
trimming 839 n.

edible
edible 296 adj.
soft 322 adj.
clean 643 adj.

edifice
adjunct 40 n.
composition 56 n.
accumulation 74 n.
edifice 159 n.
house 187 n.
high structure 204 n.
structure 326 n.
temple 984 n.

edition
variant 15 n.
duplicate 22 n.
subdivision 53 n.
repetition 102 n.
reproduction 161 n.
miniature 191 n.
letterpress 582 n.
edition 584 n.
amendment 649 n.

educate
inform 519 vb.
educate 529 vb.
motivate 607 vb.

education
education 529 n.
civilization 649 n.

educational
influential 173 adj.
demonstrating 473 adj.

informative 519 adj.

educational
pedagogic 532 adj.
scholastic 534 adj.

effect
relativeness 9 n.
remainder 41 n.
sequence 65 n.
sequel 67 n.
end 69 n.
event 149 n.
effect 152 n.
product 159 n.
instrumentality 623 n.
completion 720 n.

effectuation
effectuation 720 n.

effervesce
be violent 171 vb.
effervesce 313 vb.
bubble 350 vb.
be hot 374 vb.
crackle 397 vb.
hiss 401 vb.
be excited 816 vb.

egotist
egotist 927 n.

egress
motion 260 n.
wandering 262 n.
departure 291 n.
egress 293 n.
excretion 297 n.
passage 300 n.
gas 331 n.
current 345 n.
escape 662 n.
means of escape 662 n.

eject
abate 37 vb.
subtract 39 vb.
eliminate 44 vb.
disunite 46 vb.
exclude 57 vb.
render few 101 vb.
substitute 145 vb.
destroy 160 vb.
displace 183 vb.
externalize 218 vb.
make concave 250 vb.
transpose 267 vb.
impel 274 vb.
propel 282 vb.
eject 295 vb.
extract 299 vb.
reject 602 vb.
clean 643 vb.
stop using 669 vb.
depose 747 vb.
prohibit 752 vb.
not retain 774 vb.
deprive 781 vb.
make unwelcome 878 vb.
be rude 880 vb.

ejection
ejection 295 n.

ejector
ejector 295 n.

elapse
end 69 vb.
continue 104 vb.
elapse 107 vb.

elapsing
elapsing 107 adj.

elastic
regressive 281 adj.
rare 320 adj.
flexible 322 adj.
soft 322 adj.
elastic 323 adj.

elastic, be
soften 322 vb.

elasticity
elasticity 323 n.

elastic - tensile etc.
adj. bounce, be
be elastic 323 vb.

elation. See mania
psychopathy 498 n.

electorate
list 87 n.
estimator 475 n.
electorate 600 n.

electricity
electricity 155 n.
radiation 412 n.
metrology 460 n.

electronics
electronics 155 n.
microelectronics 191 n.
mechanics 625 n.

elegance
elegance 570 n.

elegant
apt 24 adj.
elegant 570 adj.
well-made 689 adj.
witty 834 adj.
tasteful 841 adj.

elegant, be
be elegant 570 vb.
be affected 845 vb.

element
element 314 n.

elevate
augment 36 vb.
bring together 74 vb.
cause 151 vb.
strengthen 157 vb.
produce 159 vb.
place 182 vb.
displace 183 vb.
enlarge 192 vb.
make higher 204 vb.
make vertical 210 vb.
support 213 vb.
form 238 vb.
move 260 vb.
impel 274 vb.
promote 280 vb.
draw 283 vb.
elevate 305 vb.
lighten 318 vb.
celebrate 871 vb.

dishonest
925 adj.

equivocal, be
be contrary
14 vb.
liken 18 vb.
vary 147 vb.
tell against
462 vb.
be uncertain
469 vb.
sophisticate
472 vb.
be unintelligible
512 vb.
be equivocal
513 vb.
misinterpret
516 vb.
dissemble 536 vb.
be diffuse
565 vb.
be irresolute
596 vb.
tergiversate
598 vb.
avoid 615 vb.
not observe
764 vb.
be witty 834 vb.
be dishonest
925 vb.

equivocalness
equivocalness
513 n.

era
date 104 n.
era 106 n.
chronology 112 n.
antiquity 120 n.
past time 120 n.
oldness 122 n.
literature 552 n.

erotic
erotic 882 adj.
sensual 939 adj.

err
err 490 vb.
be foolish 494 vb.
misinterpret
516 vb.

erroneous
unreal 2 adj.
irrelevant 10 adj.
impossible
465 adj.
unreliable
469 adj.
illogical 472 adj.
erroneous
490 adj.
absurd 492 adj.
imaginary
508 adj.

error
unrelatedness
10 n.
deviation 277 n.
inattention
451 n.
unreliability
469 n.
misjudgment
476 n.
ignorance 486 n.
sciolism 486 n.
error 490 n.
lack of
expectation
503 n.
fantasy 508 n.

deception 537 n.
inexpedience
638 n.
defect 642 n.
imperfection
642 n.
heterodoxy 971 n.

eruct
eruct 295 vb.

erudition
erudition 485 n.

escape
separate 46 vb.
go away 185 vb.
navigate 264 vb.
speeding 272 vb.
recession 285 n.
recede 285 vb.
departure 291 n.
decamp 291 vb.
egress 293 n.
emerge 293 vb.
disappearance
441 n.
disappear 441 vb.
plead 609 vb.
avoidance 615 n.
run away 615 vb.
safety 655 n.
be safe 655 vb.
seek safety
655 vb.
danger 656 n.
escape 662 n.
escape 662 vb.
deliverance
663 n.
deliver 663 vb.
parry 708 vb.
triumph 722 vb.
be free 739 vb.
achieve liberty
741 vb.
undutifulness
913 n.
fail in duty
913 vb.
be exempt
914 vb.

escaped
escaped 662 adj.

escape notice
escape notice
451 vb.
be forgotten
501 vb.
be modest
869 vb.

escaper
escaper 662 n.

essence
essence 1 n.
essential part
5 n.
main part 32 n.
simpleness 44 n.
goodness 639 n.

essential part
essence 1 n.
substance 3 n.
essential part
5 n.
concomitant
89 n.
centre 220 n.
life 355 n.
spirit 442 n.
chief thing 633 n.
affections 812 n.

established
established
148 adj.

estate
territory 179 n.
possession 768 n.
estate 772 n.

estimate
class 62 n.
cognize 442 vb.
meditate 444 vb.
experiment
456 n.
discrimination
458 n.
discriminate
458 vb.
measurement
460 n.
appraise 460 vb.
estimate 475 n.
estimate 475 vb.
expectation
502 n.
expect 502 vb.
interpretation
515 n.
report 519 n.
affirmation
527 n.
literature 552 n.
article 586 n.
intention 612 n.
advice 686 n.
account 803 n.
tax 804 n.
price 804 vb.
be cautious
853 n.
approbation
918 n.

estimator
estimator 475 n.

et cetera
et cetera 97 adv.

eternal, be
last 108 vb.
be eternal
110 vb.
go on 141 vb.
be remembered
500 vb.

ethical
right 908 adj.
ethical 912 adj.
virtuous 928 adj.

ethnic
ethnic 11 adj.
parental 164 adj.
human 366 adj.

etiquette
conformity 83 n.
practice 605 n.
good taste 841 n.
etiquette 843 n.
formality 870 n.
right 908 n.

etymology
linguist 552 n.
linguistics 552 n.
etymology 554 n.
grammar 559 n.

eunuch
nonconformist
84 n.
eunuch 156 n.
male animal
367 n.

euphoria
softness 322 n.
decease 356 n.

euphoria 371 n.
health 645 n.
repose 678 n.
palmy days
725 n.
wealth 795 n.
happiness 819 n.
content 823 n.

evening
end 69 n.
period 106 n.
evening 124 n.
regular return
136 n.
obscuration
413 n.
half-light 414 n.

event
reality 1 n.
juncture 8 n.
irrelevance 10 n.
futurity 119 n.
occasion 132 n.
event 149 n.
effect 152 n.
chance 154 n.
arrival 290 n.
certainty 468 n.
disclosure 521 n.
narrative 585 n.
necessity 591 n.
evil 611 n.
nondesign 613 n.
completion 720 n.
adversity 726 n.

eventful
eventful 149 adj.

eventual
circumstantial
8 adj.
future 119 adj.
eventual 149 adj.
caused 152 adj.

eventually
eventually
149 adv.
in the future
150 adv.

everyman
everyman 79 n.

evidence
evidence 461 n.
evidence 461 vb.
probability 466 n.
make likely
466 vb.
demonstration
473 n.
demonstrate
473 vb.
assent 483 n.
accuracy 489 n.
supposition
507 n.
mean 509 vb.
be intelligible
511 vb.
exhibit 517 n.
manifestation
517 n.
manifest 517 vb.
untruth 538 n.
indication 542 n.
indicate 542 vb.
trace 543 n.
accusation 923 n.
legal trial 954 n.

evidential
evidential
461 adj.

penalty 958 n.
exclusive of
exclusive of
  57 adv.
excrement
leavings **41** n.
excrement **297** n.
fluid **330** n.
moisture **336** n.
stench **392** n.
dirt **644** n.
excrete
emit **295** vb.
empty **295** vb.
excrete **297** vb.
make flow
  345 vb.
excretion
excretion **297** n.
excretory
excretory
  297 adj.
excusing
excusing **609** adj.
execute
kill **357** vb.
execute **958** vb.
exemplify
exemplify **83** vb.
interpret **515** vb.
exempt
qualify **463** vb.
deliver **663** vb.
liberate **741** vb.
permit **751** vb.
relieve **826** vb.
exempt **914** vb.
acquit **955** vb.
exempt, be
escape **662** vb.
fail in duty
  913 vb.
be exempt
  914 vb.
exercise
athletics **157** n.
teaching **529** n.
hygiene **647** n.
civilization **649** n.
exercise **677** n.
exertion
exertion **677** n.
exert oneself
be vigorous
  169 vb.
be attentive
  450 vb.
be careful
  452 vb.
search **454** vb.
be resolute
  594 vb.
persevere **595** vb.
attempt **666** vb.
be active **673** vb.
exert oneself
  677 vb.
exhibit
accumulation
  74 n.
spectacle **440** n.
exhibit **517** n.
advertisement
  523 n.
label **542** n.
collection **627** n.
market **791** n.
plaything **832** n.
fashion **843** n.
pageant **870** n.

exhibitor
exhibitor **517** n.
exhume
exhume **359** vb.
exiguous
exiguous **191** adj.
lean **201** adj.
existence
existence **1** n.
cause **151** n.
materiality **314** n.
life **355** n.
appearance
  440 n.
truth **489** n.
divine attribute
  960 n.
existing
existing **1** adj.
exorbitant
exorbitant
  32 adj.
violent **171** adj.
huge **190** adj.
surpassing
  301 adj.
exaggerated
  541 adj.
redundant
  632 adj.
harmful **640** adj.
intolerable
  822 adj.
expand
be great **32** vb.
augment **36** vb.
grow **36** vb.
be large **190** vb.
expand **192** vb.
lengthen **198** vb.
be broad **200** vb.
jut **249** vb.
eat **296** vb.
expanded
expanded
  192 adj.
expansion
expansion **192** n.
expect
look ahead
  119 vb.
assume **466** vb.
expect **502** vb.
foresee **505** vb.
intend **612** vb.
prepare **664** vb.
hope **847** vb.
not wonder
  860 vb.
impose a duty
  912 vb.
expectant
attentive
  450 adj.
expectant
  502 adj.
foreseeing
  505 adj.
warned **664** adj.
hoping **847** adj.
unastonished
  860 adj.
expectantly
expectantly
  502 adv.
expectation
futurity **119** n.
looking ahead
  119 n.
destiny **150** n.
probability **466** n.

dubiety **469** n.
expectation
  502 n.
prediction **506** n.
hope **847** n.
religion **967** n.
expected
expected **502** adj.
expedient, be
accord **24** vb.
answer **455** vb.
answer **455** vb.
suffice **630** vb.
be useful **635** vb.
be expedient
  637 vb.
advise **686** vb.
expediently
expediently
  637 adv.
expend
waste **629** vb.
lose **767** vb.
pay **799** vb.
expend **801** vb.
expended
expended
  801 adj.
expending
expending
  801 adj.
expenditure
waste **629** n.
loss **767** n.
purchase **787** n.
payment **799** n.
expenditure
  801 n.
cost **804** n.
experiment
modify **138** vb.
calculation of
chance **154** n.
listening **410** n.
be curious
  448 vb.
enquiry **454** n.
enquire **454** vb.
experiment
  456 n.
experiment
  456 vb.
demonstration
  473 n.
discover **479** vb.
gambling **613** n.
gamble **613** vb.
preparation
  664 n.
attempt **666** n.
attempt **666** vb.
litigation **954** n.
experimental
experimental
  456 adj.
experimentally
experimentally
  456 adv.
experimenter
experimenter
  456 n.
expert
superior **34** n.
old man **128** n.
powerful **155** adj.
mariner **265** n.
seamanlike
  265 adj.
instructed
  485 adj.
knowing **485** adj.

planner **618** n.
bigwig **633** n.
matured **664** adj.
doer **671** n.
adviser **686** n.
expert **689** adj.
expert **691** n.
lawyer **953** n.
expert, be
know **485** vb.
be expert **689** vb.
explosive
destroyer **163** n.
propellant **282** n.
ejector **295** n.
fireworks **415** n.
pitfall **658** n.
explosive **718** n.
expressive
meaningful
  509 adj.
expressive
  511 adj.
expropriation
expropriation
  781 n.
expulsive
expulsive **295** adj.
extempore
at present
  116 adv.
extempore
  604 adv.
extend
be great **32** vb.
fill **54** vb.
continue **104** vb.
extend **178** vb.
be large **190** vb.
be distant
  194 vb.
be contiguous
  197 vb.
be long **198** vb.
superabound
  632 vb.
extensive
extensive **32** adj.
comprehensive
  52 adj.
inclusive **78** adj.
universal **79** adj.
spacious **178** adj.
extenuate
qualify **463** vb.
plead **609** vb.
extenuate
  922 vb.
exterior
extrinsic **6** adj.
separate **46** adj.
extraneous
  59 adj.
exterior **218** n.
appearing
  440 n.
exterior, be
be exterior
  218 vb.
exteriority
exteriority **218** n.
externalize
externalize
  218 vb.
externally
externally
  218 adv.
extinct
extinct **2** adj.
past **120** adj.

disappearing
441 adj.

extinction
extinction 2 n.
destruction
160 n.
death 356 n.

extinguish
abate 37 vb.
suppress 160 vb.
moderate 172 vb.
extinguish
377 vb.

extinguisher
moderator 172 n.
extinguisher
377 n.

extra
inequality 29 n.
increment 36 n.
extra 40 n.
component 58 n.
pleonasm 565 n.
superfluity 632 n.
safeguard 657 n.
receipt 802 n.
price 804 n.

extract
subtract 39 vb.
produce 159 vb.
displace 183 vb.
uncover 224 vb.
pierce 258 vb.
draw 283 vb.
eject 295 vb.
empty 295 vb.
extract 299 vb.
elevate 305 vb.
manifest 517 vb.
provide 628 vb.
deliver 663 vb.
use 668 vb.
acquire 766 vb.
levy 781 vb.
take 781 vb.

extracted
extracted
299 adj.

extraction
subtraction 39 n.
displacement
183 n.
transference
267 n.
extraction 299 n.
deliverance
663 n.

extractor
extractor 299 n.

extramarital
extramarital
946 adj.

extraneous
extrinsic 6 adj.
unrelated 10 adj.
disagreeing
25 adj.
additional 38 adj.
separate 46 adj.
nonadhesive
49 adj.
excluded 57 adj.
extraneous
59 adj.
discontinuous
72 adj.
unconformable
84 adj.
unusual 84 adj.
unstable 147 adj.
exterior 218 adj.

interjacent
226 adj.
travelling
262 adj.
hindering
697 adj.
ridiculous
844 adj.
wonderful
859 adj.
unsociable
878 adj.

extraneousness
extraneousness
59 n.

extremely
extremely 32 adv.
eminently 34 adv.

extremity
adjunct 40 n.
remainder 41 n.
completeness
54 n.
extremity 69 n.
vertex 208 n.
edge 229 n.
limit 231 n.
rear 233 n.
goal 290 n.

extricable
extricable
663 adj.

extrinsic
extrinsic 6 adj.
unrelated 10 adj.
additional 38 adj.
separate 46 adj.
extraneous
59 adj.
exterior 218 adj.

extrinsicality
extrinsicality 6 n.

extrinsically
extrinsically
6 adv.

extrinsic, be
be extrinsic 6 vb.
be exterior
218 vb.

exude
exude 293 vb.
emit 295 vb.
excrete 297 vb.
be wet 336 vb.
flow 345 vb.

eye
screen 416 n.
eye 433 n.
surveillance
452 n.

eyeglass
eyeglass 437 n.

eyesore
deformity 241 n.
painfulness 822 n.
eyesore 837 n.
blemish 840 n.

F

fable
fantasy 508 n.
empty talk 510 n.
fable 538 n.
exaggeration
541 n.
narrative 585 n.

face
face 232 n.

form 238 n.
dome 248 n.
protuberance
249 n.
feature 440 n.

face danger
be resolute
594 vb.
face danger
656 vb.
undertake
667 vb.
be in difficulty
695 vb.
withstand
699 vb.
defy 706 vb.
resist 710 vb.
be courageous
850 vb.
be rash 852 vb.

facilitate
make possible
464 vb.
be intelligible
511 vb.
interpret 515 vb.
tempt 607 vb.
facilitate 696 vb.
give scope
739 vb.
permit 751 vb.

facilitated
facilitated
696 adj.

facility
possibility 464 n.
intelligibility
511 n.
skill 689 n.
facility 696 n.
aid 698 n.
acquisition 766 n.

facing
adhesive 47 n.
facing 221 n.
smoother 253 n.
art equipment
548 n.
building material
626 n.
ornamental art
839 n.

fail
be inferior 35 vb.
lose a chance
133 vb.
cease 140 vb.
be impotent
156 vb.
be unproductive
167 vb.
blunder 490 vb.
be disappointed
504 vb.
be useless
636 vb.
attempt 666 vb.
be clumsy
690 vb.
be unskilful
690 vb.
not complete
721 vb.
fail 723 vb.
have trouble
726 vb.
lose repute
862 vb.

fail in duty
fail in duty
913 vb.

failure
stop 140 n.
helplessness
156 n.
impotence 156 n.
ruin 160 n.
propagation
162 n.
shortfall 302 n.
negligence 453 n.
mistake 490 n.
disappointment
504 n.
lost labour 636 n.
bungling 690 n.
noncompletion
721 n.
failure 723 n.
misfortune 726 n.

faintly
faintly 396 adv.

faintness
faintness 396 n.

fair chance
opportunity
132 n.
fair chance
154 n.
possibility 464 n.

fairy
sea nymph 338 n.
fairy 964 n.
sorceress 977 n.

fairylike
fairylike 964 adj.

fake
make unlike
19 vb.
copy 20 vb.
corroborate
461 vb.
fake 536 vb.
deceive 537 vb.
predetermine
603 vb.
plot 618 vb.
indict 923 vb.

fall short
be small 33 vb.
be inferior 35 vb.
be incomplete
55 vb.
be impotent
156 vb.
be short 199 vb.
fall short 302 vb.
be disappointed
504 vb.
disappoint
504 vb.
not suffice
631 vb.
be imperfect
642 vb.

false
imitative 20 adj.
unattested
462 adj.
erroneous
490 adj.
false 536 adj.
deceiving
537 adj.
spurious 537 adj.
untrue 538 adj.
affected 845 adj.
perfidious
925 adj.

false alarm
insubstantial
thing 4 n.
false alarm
660 n.

false, be
misteach 530 vb.
be false 536 vb.
be untrue 538 vb.
exaggerate
541 vb.
misrepresent
547 vb.
indict 923 vb.
be dishonest
925 vb.

false charge
censure 919 n.
false charge
923 n.

falsehood
imitation 20 n.
improbability
467 n.
error 490 n.
ideality 508 n.
empty talk 510 n.
misteaching
530 n.
falsehood 536 n.
deception 537 n.
untruth 538 n.
liar 540 n.
misrepresentation
547 n.
improbity 925 n.
false piety 974 n.

falsely
falsely 536 adv.

false money
false money
792 n.
nonpayment
800 n.

false piety
false piety 974 n.

family
family 11 n.
group 74 n.
parentage 164 n.
posterity 165 n.
inhabitants
186 n.
social group
366 n.
community 703 n.
nobility 863 n.

famousness
famousness
861 n.

fantasy
insubstantial
thing 4 n.
rara avis 84 n.
absence 190 n.
visual fallacy
435 n.
appearance
440 n.
misjudgment
476 n.
error 490 n.
fantasy 508 n.
narrative 585 n.
sleepiness 674 n.
happiness 819 n.
pleasurableness
821 n.
aspiration 847 n.
hopelessness
848 n.

desire 854 n.
prodigy 859 n.
mythic heaven
965 n.

farm
assemblage 74 n.
place 180 n.
house 187 n.
enclosure 230 n.
soil 339 n.
farm 365 n.
workshop 682 n.
joint possession
770 n.

farmer
accumulator
74 n.
producer 159 n.
dweller 186 n.
settler 186 n.
farmer 365 n.
preparer 664 n.
worker 681 n.
servant 737 n.
participator
770 n.
possessor 771 n.
country-dweller
864 n.

farm tool
sharp edge 251 n.
conveyor 269 n.
farm tool 365 n.

farness
farness 194 n.

fashion
generality 79 n.
conformity 83 n.
modernism 121 n.
clothier 223 n.
dressing 223 n.
practice 605 n.
beauty 836 n.
fashion 843 n.
affectation
845 n.
repute 861 n.

fashionable
modern 121 adj.
usual 605 adj.
personable
836 adj.
tasteful 841 adj.
fashionable
843 adj.
reputable
861 adj.
proud 866 adj.
showy 870 adj.

fashionably
fashionably
843 adv.

fast
asceticism 940 n.
fast 941 n.
holy day 982 n.

fastening
fastening 47 n.
legwear 223 n.
sharp point
251 n.
perforator 258 n.
stopper 259 n.
nippers 773 n.
jewellery 839 n.
trimming 839 n.

fastidious
attentive
450 adj.
careful 452 adj.

discriminating
458 adj.
narrow-minded
476 adj.
accurate 489 adj.
capricious
599 adj.
clean 643 adj.
improving
649 adj.
severe 730 adj.
observant
763 adj.
discontented
824 adj.
tasteful 841 adj.
fastidious
857 adj.

fastidious, be
be capricious
599 vb.
select 600 vb.
be discontented
824 vb.
have taste
841 vb.
be fastidious
857 vb.

fastidiousness
fastidiousness
857 n.

fasting
fasting 941 n.
fasting 941 adj.

fat
cookery 296 n.
fat 352 n.

fatalist
fatalist 591 n.

fate
finality 69 n.
future state
119 n.
destiny 150 n.
effect 152 n.
chance 154 n.
influence 173 n.
philosophy 444 n.
certainty 468 n.
expectation
502 n.
fate 591 n.
nondesign 613 n.
mythic deity
961 n.

fated
impending
150 adj.
certain 468 adj.
fated 591 adj.
predetermined
603 adj.

fatigue
helplessness
156 n.
weakness 158 n.
pain 372 n.
imperfection
642 n.
use 668 vb.
misuse 670 vb.
sleepiness 674 n.
work 677 vb.
fatigue 679 n.
fatigue 679 vb.
difficulty 695 n.
oppress 730 vb.
suffering 820 n.
trouble 822 n.
dejection 829 n.
depress 829 vb.

tedium 833 n.
be tedious
833 vb.
impose a duty
912 vb.

fatigued
fatigued 679 adj.

fatigued, be
be fatigued
679 vb.

fatiguing
fatiguing 679 adj.

fatty
fatty 352 adj.

favourite
superior 34 n.
weakling 158 n.
attraction 286 n.
person 366 n.
actor 589 n.
bigwig 633 n.
exceller 639 n.
exceller 639 n.
prosperous
person 725 n.
a beauty 836 n.
desired object
854 n.
person of repute
861 n.
pride 866 n.
sociable person
877 n.
favourite 885 n.
good person
932 n.

favour. See badge
indication 542 n.

fear
expectation
502 n.
expect 502 vb.
motive 607 n.
avoidance 615 n.
danger signal
660 n.
defeat 723 n.
excitation 816 n.
fear 849 n.
fear 849 vb.
cowardice 851 n.
dislike 856 n.
dislike 856 vb.
wonder 859 n.
wonder 859 vb.
honour 861 vb.
respect 915 n.
respect 915 vb.
piety 973 n.
be pious 973 vb.
worship 975 n.
worship 975 vb.

fearing
fearing 849 adj.

feasting
feasting 296 n.

feature
outline 228 n.
face 232 n.
form 238 n.
feature 440 n.
identification
542 n.

feeble
repeated 102 adj.
feeble 567 adj.

feebleness
feebleness 567 n.

feed
enlarge 192 vb.
feed 296 vb.

vitalize 355 vb.
groom 364 vb.
refresh 680 vb.
be hospitable
877 vb.

feeding
feeding 296 adj.

feel
meet with
149 vb.
have feeling
369 vb.
opine 480 vb.
feel 813 vb.
be excited
816 vb.
suffer 820 vb.

feeler
limb 53 n.
filament 203 n.
protuberance
249 n.
feeler 373 n.
nippers 773 n.

feeling
crowd 74 n.
sense 369 n.
sentient 369 adj.
intuition 471 n.
opinion 480 n.
knowledge 485 n.
vigour 566 n.
spontaneous
604 adj.
conduct 683 n.
liberation 741 n.
affections 812 n.
with affections
812 adj.
feeling 813 n.
feeling 813 adj.
excitation 816 n.
excited 816 adj.
excitable state
817 n.
love 882 n.
benevolence
892 n.

feelingly
feelingly 813 adv.

feel pain
feel pain 372 vb.
cry 403 vb.
suffer 820 vb.

feel pride
seek repute
861 vb.
feel pride 866 vb.
be vain 868 vb.

fell
demolish 160 vb.
flatten 211 vb.
strike 274 vb.
fell 306 vb.

felt
felt 813 adj.

female
abnormality 84 n.
adult 129 n.
adultness 129 n.
grown-up
129 adj.
weak 158 adj.
female 368 n.
female 368 adj.

female animal
female animal
368 n.

fence
surroundings
225 n.

partition 226 n.
circumscription
227 n.
edge 229 n.
fence 230 n.
stopper 259 n.
screen 416 n.
protection 655 n.
shelter 657 n.

fertilized
fertilized 162 adj.

fertilizer
propagation
162 n.
fertilizer 166 n.
agriculture 365 n.

fervent
forceful 566 adj.
active 673 adj.
hasty 675 adj.
fervent 813 adj.
lively 814 adj.
excited 816 adj.
loving 882 adj.

festivity
meal 296 n.
rejoicing 830 n.
festivity 832 n.
pageant 870 n.
celebration
871 n.
social gathering
877 n.
holy day 982 n.

fetid
unsavoury
386 adj.
odorous 389 adj.
fetid 392 adj.
unclean 644 adj.
unpleasant
822 adj.

fetter
tie 45 vb.
fastening 47 n.
halter 47 n.
stopper 259 n.
safeguard 657 n.
make inactive
674 vb.
encumbrance
697 n.
hinder 697 vb.
subjection 740 n.
restraint 742 n.
fetter 742 vb.
fetter 743 n.
take 781 vb.
pillory 959 n.

few
inconsiderable
33 adj.
few 101 n.
infrequent
135 adj.
scarce 631 adj.

few, be
decrease 37 vb.
be few 101 vb.

fewness
fewness 101 n.

fibre
cable 47 n.
ligature 47 n.
fibre 203 n.
textile 217 n.
textile 217 n.
skin 221 n.
convolution
246 n.
hair 254 n.

texture 326 n.
materials 626 n.

fibrous
narrow 201 adj.
fibrous 203 adj.

fiery
violent 171 adj.
fiery 374 adj.
luminous 412 adj.

fifth and over
fifth and over
96 adj.

fight
turmoil 61 n.
strike 274 vb.
withstand
699 vb.
quarrel 704 n.
attack 707 vb.
fight 711 n.
fight 711 vb.
battle 713 n.
give battle
713 vb.
go to war
713 vb.
be courageous
850 vb.
be inimical
876 vb.
anger 886 n.

figurative
compared
457 adj.
semantic 509 adj.
figurative
514 adj.
occult 518 adj.
ornate 569 adj.
rhetorical
569 adj.
descriptive
585 adj.

figure
figure 514 vb.

filament
small thing 33 n.
narrowness
201 n.
thinness 201 n.
filament 203 n.
hair 254 n.

filial
filial 165 adj.

fill
be great 32 vb.
fill 54 vb.
bring together
74 vb.
be many 100 vb.
stow 182 vb.
load 188 vb.
enlarge 192 vb.
make smaller
193 vb.
overstep 301 vb.
replenish 628 vb.
suffice 630 vb.
superabound
632 vb.
sate 858 vb.

filled
filled 630 adj.

film
film 440 n.
photography
546 n.

finality
completeness
54 n.
finality 69 n.

period 106 n.
future state
119 n.
evening 124 n.
ruin 160 n.
decease 356 n.
completion 720 n.

finally
after 65 adv.
finally 69 adv.

finance
finance 792 n.

find means
cause 151 vb.
find means
624 vb.

find useful
find useful
635 vb.
use 668 vb.

finery
clothing 223 n.
headgear 223 n.
loop 245 n.
plumage 254 n.
finery 839 n.
ostentation
870 n.

finger
finger 373 n.
nippers 773 n.

finite quantity
finite quantity
26 n.
small quantity
33 n.
measurement
460 n.

fire
fire 374 n.
burning 376 n.
kindle 376 vb.
furnace 378 n.
fire 380 vb.
light 412 n.
luminary 415 n.
redness 426 n.
signal 542 n.
celebration
871 n.

firearm
propellant 282 n.
bang 397 n.
chase 614 n.
firearm 718 n.

fire at
demolish 160 vb.
shoot 282 vb.
fire at 707 vb.
give battle
713 vb.

fireworks
fireworks 415 n.

firm
firm 45 adj.
full 54 adj.
strong 157 adj.

first
first 68 adj.
fundamental
151 adj.

fish
fish 360 n.

fish food
fish food 296 n.
fish 360 n.

fishing boat
fishing boat
270 n.

fit
fit 24 adj.

advisable
637 adj.

right 908 adj.

fitful
nonuniform
17 adj.
discontinuous
72 adj.
fitful 137 adj.
unstable 147 adj.

fitfully
fitfully 137 adv.

fitfulness
fitfulness 137 n.

fitness
relevance 9 n.
fitness 24 n.
occasion 132 n.
ability 155 n.
tendency 174 n.

fitting out
fitting out 664 n.

five
five 96 n.

fixed
uniform 16 adj.
equal 28 adj.
firm 45 adj.
immemorial
122 adj.
unceasing
141 adj.
fixed 148 adj.
strong 157 adj.
located 182 adj.
deep 206 adj.
interior 219 adj.
still 261 adj.
habitual 605 adj.

fix the time
fix the time
104 vb.

fixture
identity 13 n.
permanence
139 n.
fixture 148 n.

flag
cross 217 n.
shipping 270 n.
flag 542 n.
regalia 738 n.

flagrant
flagrant 32 adj.

flank
flank 234 vb.

flash
agitation 313 n.
fire 374 n.
flash 412 n.
glimmer 414 n.
luminary 415 n.

flat
uniform 16 adj.
flat 187 n.
chamber 189 n.
low 205 adj.
flat 211 adj.
smooth 253 adj.

flatten
demolish 160 vb.
suppress 160 vb.
make smaller
193 vb.
flatten 211 vb.
straighten
244 vb.
smooth 253 vb.
strike 274 vb.
fell 306 vb.

flattener
flattener 211 n.

flatter
repeat 102 vb.
influence 173 vb.
assent 483 vb.
mean nothing
510 vb.
be false 536 vb.
befool 537 vb.
exaggerate
541 vb.
misrepresent
547 vb.
induce 607 vb.
be cunning
693 vb.
minister to
698 vb.
be lenient 731 vb.
delight 821 vb.
please 821 vb.
honour 861 vb.
make conceited
868 vb.
be servile 874 vb.
pay one's
respects 879 vb.
excite love
882 vb.
pet 884 vb.
praise 918 vb.
flatter 920 vb.
be dishonest
925 vb.

flatterer
flatterer 920 n.

flattering
flattering
920 adj.

flatteringly
flatteringly
920 adv.

flattery
conformity 83 n.
assent 483 n.
empty talk 510 n.
lack of meaning
510 n.
falsehood 536 n.
exaggeration
541 n.
misrepresentation
547 n.
inducement
607 n.
cunning 693 n.
pleasurableness
821 n.
servility 874 n.
courtesy 879 n.
endearment
884 n.
praise 918 n.
flattery 920 n.

fleece
fleece 781 vb.
defraud 783 vb.
impoverish
796 vb.
overcharge
806 vb.
be parsimonious
811 vb.

fleecy
smooth 253 adj.
fleecy 254 adj.

fleshy
fleshy 190 adj.

flexible
conformable
83 adj.
flexible 322 adj.
tractable
696 adj.

flimsy
insubstantial
4 adj.
flimsy 158 adj.
imperfect
642 adj.

flog
strike 274 vb.
flog 958 vb.

floor-cover
floor-cover 221 n.

florid
florid 420 adj.
variegated
432 adj.
splendid 836 adj.
ornamented
839 adj.
showy 870 adj.

flourish
flourish 610 vb.

flow
be violent 171 vb.
be in motion
260 vb.
move slowly
273 vb.
burst in 292 vb.
flow out 293 vb.
rotate 310 vb.
liquefy 332 vb.
flow 345 vb.
sound faint
396 vb.
be diffuse
565 vb.
superabound
632 vb.
be active 673 vb.

flower
flower 361 n.

flowing
furrowed 257 adj.
fluid 330 adj.
flowing 345 adj.
redundant
632 adj.

flow out
flow out 293 vb.

fluctuate
be unequal 29 vb.
vary 147 vb.
fluctuate 312 vb.
be agitated
313 vb.

fluctuation
fluctuation 312 n.

fluid
nonadhesive
49 adj.
changeable thing
147 n.
unstable 147 adj.
amorphous
239 adj.
soft 322 adj.
fluid 330 n.
fluid 330 adj.
liquefied 332 n.
water 334 n.
watery 334 n.
moisture 336 n.
humid 336 adj.
flowing 345 adj.

fluidity
fluidity 330 n.

flute
stridor 402 n.
flute 409 n.

fly
ride 262 vb.
fly 266 vb.
decamp 291 vb.
ascend 303 vb.
be light 318 vb.

flying
flying 266 adj.
aviational
271 adj.

focus
union 45 n.
assemblage 74 n.
focus 76 n.
focus 76 vb.
place 180 n.
locality 182 n.
abode 187 n.
meeting place
187 n.
centre 220 n.
convergence
288 n.
objective 612 n.
society 703 n.
arena 719 n.
market 791 n.
social round
877 n.

fold
joint 45 n.
derangement
63 n.
jumble 63 vb.
duplication 91 n.
receptacle 189 n.
become small
193 vb.
make smaller
193 vb.
invert 216 vb.
garment 223 n.
enclose 230 vb.
angularity 242 n.
curvature 243 n.
make curved
243 vb.
convolution
246 n.
crinkle 246 vb.
roughness 254 n.
roughen 254 vb.
notch 255 vb.
fold 256 n.
fold 256 vb.
groove 257 vb.
rotate 310 vb.

folded
folded 256 adj.

foliage
branch 53 n.
foliage 361 n.
greenness 429 n.

follow
do likewise 20 vb.
be inferior 35 vb.
come after 65 vb.
accompany
89 vb.
ensue 115 vb.
be late 131 vb.
happen 149 vb.
result 152 vb.
be near 195 vb.
be behind 233 vb.
walk 262 vb.

move slowly
273 vb.
follow 279 vb.
pursue 614 vb.
obstruct 697 vb.
court 884 vb.
follower
imitator 20 n.
retinue 67 n.
concomitant
89 n.
follower 279 n.
dependant 737 n.
following
sequence 65 n.
posteriority
115 n.
motion 260 n.
following 279 n.
following 279 adj.
pursuit 614 n.
pursuing 614 adj.
folly
insubstantial
thing 4 n.
ignorance 486 n.
absurdity 492 n.
folly 494 n.
deception 537 n.
merriment 828 n.
rashness 852 n.
food
food 296 n.
life 355 n.
materials 626 n.
refreshment
680 n.
subvention 698 n.
sociability 877 n.
food content
food content
296 n.
fool
misfit 25 n.
ignoramus 488 n.
fool 496 n.
madman 499 n.
entertainer
589 n.
bungler 692 n.
humorist 834 n.
laughingstock
846 n.
foolery
foolery 492 n.
folly 494 n.
whim 599 n.
revel 832 n.
wit 834 n.
ridicule 846 n.
ostentation
870 n.
foolish
ageing 126 adj.
weak 158 adj.
mindless 443 adj.
misjudging
476 adj.
credulous
482 adj.
absurd 492 adj.
foolish 494 adj.
crazy 498 adj.
gullible 539 adj.
trivial 634 adj.
ridiculous
844 adj.
foolish, be
not discriminate
459 vb.
misjudge 476 vb.

be absurd
492 vb.
be foolish 494 vb.
be insane 498 vb.
mean nothing
510 vb.
impair 650 vb.
foot
foot 209 n.
conveyance
262 n.
finger 373 n.
footed
footed 209 adj.
footwear
footwear 223 n.
fop
people of taste
841 n.
fop 843 n.
affecter 845 n.
aristocrat 863 n.
proud person
866 n.
vain person
868 n.
for a long time
for a long time
108 adv.
force
derange 63 vb.
be vigorous
169 vb.
force 171 vb.
open 258 vb.
burst in 292 vb.
misuse 670 vb.
compel 735 vb.
not observe
764 vb.
forced, be
be forced 591 vb.
have no choice
601 vb.
forceful
keen 169 adj.
assertive 527 adj.
forceful 566 adj.
eloquent 574 adj.
lively 814 adj.
forcefully
forcefully
566 adv.
foregoing
foregoing
120 adj.
foreigner
foreigner 59 n.
dweller 186 n.
native 186 n.
settler 186 n.
wanderer 263 n.
incomer 292 n.
egress 293 n.
outcast 878 n.
foremost
foremost 278 adj.
foresee
see 433 vb.
assume 466 vb.
be wise 493 vb.
expect 502 vb.
foresee 505 vb.
intend 612 vb.
foreseeing
foreseeing
505 adj.
foresight
priority 114 n.
anticipation
130 n.

thought 444 n.
carefulness
452 n.
knowledge 485 n.
sagacity 493 n.
foresight 505 n.
prediction 506 n.
policy 618 n.
preparation
664 n.
caution 853 n.
forestry
forestry 361 n.
botany 363 n.
agriculture 365 n.
gardener 365 n.
for ever
for ever 110 adv.
forget
be inattentive
451 n.
not know 486 n.
forget 501 vb.
obliterate 545 vb.
relinquish 616 vb.
be unskilful
690 vb.
make peace
714 vb.
be lenient 731 vb.
forgive 904 vb.
fail in duty
913 vb.
exempt 914 vb.
forgetful
inattentive
451 adj.
negligent 453 adj.
ignorant 486 adj.
forgetful 501 adj.
ungrateful
903 adj.
forgive
abate 37 vb.
put off 131 vb.
disregard 453 vb.
forget 501 vb.
be lenient 731 vb.
liberate 741 vb.
be patient
818 vb.
be humble
867 vb.
be benevolent
892 vb.
pity 900 vb.
show mercy
900 vb.
forgive 904 vb.
exempt 914 vb.
acquit 955 vb.
forgiven
forgiven 904 adj.
forgiveness
amnesty 501 n.
peace offering
714 n.
leniency 731 n.
liberation 741 n.
benevolence
892 n.
mercy 900 n.
forgiveness
904 n.
nonliability 914 n.
acquittal 955 n.
forgiving
forgetful 501 adj.
lenient 731 adj.
benevolent
892 adj.

pitying 900 adj.
forgiving 904 adj.
godlike 960 adj.
forgivingly
forgivingly
904 adv.
forgotten
forgotten
501 adj.
forgotten, be
be forgotten
501 vb.
form
modality 7 n.
similarity 18 n.
mould 23 n.
sort 77 n.
make conform
83 vb.
modify 138 vb.
convert 142 vb.
produce 159 n.
receptacle 189 n.
outline 228 n.
form 238 n.
form 238 vb.
structure 326 n.
appearance
440 n.
feature 440 n.
represent 546 vb.
art style 548 n.
sculpt 549 vb.
plan 618 vb.
way 619 n.
use 668 vb.
fashion 843 n.
formal
regulated 83 adj.
slow 273 adj.
inelegant 571 adj.
well-bred
843 adj.
affected 845 adj.
formal 870 adj.
courteous
879 adj.
formal dress
formal dress
223 n.
formality
floor-cover 221 n.
formal dress
223 n.
gait 260 n.
marching 262 n.
etiquette 843 n.
pretension 845 n.
title 865 n.
formality 870 n.
celebration
871 n.
courtesy 879 n.
ritual 982 n.
formation
band 74 n.
group 74 n.
production 159 n.
formation 238 n.
art 546 n.
sculpture 549 n.
formation 717 n.
formative
such 7 adj.
productive
159 adj.
formative
238 adj.
formed
formed 238 adj.

former
former 120 adj.

formerly
long ago 108 adv.
formerly 120 adv.
anciently
122 adv.

formication
formication
373 n.

fort
edifice 159 n.
vertex 208 n.
barrier 230 n.
refuge 657 n.
fort 708 n.

fortification
basket 189 n.
summit 208 n.
incline 215 n.
projection 249 n.
window 258 n.
fortification
708 n.
art of war 713 n.

forward
forward 280 adv.

fossil
fossil 120 n.
archaism 122 n.
organism 353 n.
corpse 358 n.

foul play
duplicity 536 n.
trap 537 n.
trickery 537 n.
evil 611 n.
contrivance
618 n.
deed 671 n.
cunning 693 n.
attack 707 n.
injustice 909 n.
wrong 909 n.
foul play 925 n.
wickedness 929 n.
lawbreaking
949 n.

founder
be deep 206 vb.
descend 304 vb.
founder 308 vb.
weigh 317 vb.
perish 356 vb.
fail 723 vb.
have trouble
726 vb.

four
four 95 adj.

fraction
quantity 26 n.
fraction 98 n.

fractional
fractional 98 adj.

fragmentary
fragmentary
53 adj.
incomplete
55 adj.
fractional 98 adj.
exiguous 191 n.
imperfect
642 adj.

fragrance
fragrance 391 n.

fragrant
pleasant 371 adj.
odorous 389 adj.
fragrant 391 adj.

fragrant, be
be fragrant
391 vb.

frail
frail 929 adj.
unchaste 946 adj.

frame
basket 189 n.
layer 202 n.
base 209 n.
hanger 212 n.
frame 213 n.
structure 326 n.
preparation
664 n.

free
original 21 adj.
volitional
590 adj.
free 739 adj.
nonliable 914 adj.

free, be
be unconformable
84 vb.
will 590 vb.
behave 683 vb.
dominate 728 vb.
be free 739 vb.
live single 890 vb.
be exempt
914 vb.

freedom
unrelatedness
10 n.
originality 21 n.
opportunity
132 n.
freedom 739 n.
permission 751 n.
dueness 910 n.
nonliability 914 n.

freely
freely 739 adv.

free person
free person
739 n.

frenzied
frenzied 498 adj.

frenzy
commotion 313 n.
spasm 313 n.
frenzy 498 n.
fantasy 508 n.
lack of meaning
510 n.
illness 646 n.
restlessness
673 n.
excitation 816 n.
excitable state
817 n.
desire 854 n.
spell 977 n.

frequency
continuity 71 n.
recurrence 102 n.
frequency 134 n.

frequent
many 100 adj.
multitudinous
100 adj.
repeated 102 adj.
frequent 134 adj.
usual 605 adj.

friction
diminution 37 n.
subtraction 39 n.
energy 155 n.
slowness 273 n.
collision 274 n.

powderiness
327 n.
friction 328 n.
touch 373 n.
stridor 402 n.
difficulty 695 n.
hindrance 697 n.

friend
concomitant
89 n.
auxiliary 702 n.
colleague 702 n.
friend 875 n.
sociable person
877 n.
sociality 877 n.
kind person
892 n.
benefactor 898 n.

friendless
separate 46 adj.
alone 88 adj.
defenceless
156 adj.
friendless
878 adj.

friendliness
friendliness
875 n.

friendly
assenting
483 adj.
aiding 698 adj.
corporate
703 adj.
concordant
705 adj.
pacificatory
714 adj.
friendly 875 adj.
sociable 877 adj.
benevolent
892 adj.

friendly, be
combine 50 vb.
assent 483 vb.
concord 705 vb.
pacify 714 vb.
be friendly
875 vb.
be sociable
877 vb.
forgive 904 vb.

friendship
relation 9 n.
band 74 n.
accompaniment
89 n.
concord 705 n.
peace 712 n.
friendship 875 n.
sociality 877 n.
social round
877 n.
love 882 n.
benevolence
892 n.

frighten
unman 156 vb.
weaken 158 vb.
dismiss 300 vb.
dissuade 608 vb.
raise the alarm
660 vb.
hinder 697 vb.
defeat 722 vb.
oppress 730 vb.
displease 822 vb.
depress 829 vb.
frighten 849 vb.

cause dislike
856 vb.
be wonderful
859 vb.
humiliate 867 vb.
threaten 895 vb.

frightening
frightening
849 adj.

front
precedence 64 n.
prelude 66 n.
beginning 68 n.
nearness 195 n.
exteriority 218 n.
front 232 n.
preceding 278 n.

frontal
preceding 64 adj.
first 68 adj.
near 195 adj.
exterior 218 adj.
frontal 232 adj.
opposite 235 adj.
opposing 699 adj.

frostily
frostily 375 adv.

fruit
fruit 296 n.
plant 361 n.

fruitful, be
grow 36 vb.
be many 100 vb.
reproduce itself
162 vb.
be fruitful
166 vb.
expand 192 vb.
abound 630 vb.
superabound
632 vb.
be useful 635 vb.
get better
649 vb.
be successful
722 vb.
prosper 725 vb.

fuel
fossil 120 n.
sources of energy
155 n.
propellant 282 n.
gas 331 n.
oil 352 n.
heater 378 n.
fuel 380 n.
materials 626 n.

full
firm 45 adj.
full 54 adj.
assembled 74 adj.
multitudinous
100 adj.
dense 319 adj.
filled 630 adj.
redundant
632 adj.

fumigator
fumigator 380 n.

function
agency 168 n.
operate 168 vb.
function 617 n.
function 617 vb.
use 668 vb.
do 671 vb.
serve 737 vb.
deputize 750 vb.
jurisdiction
950 n.

fundamental
intrinsic 5 adj.
beginning 68 adj.
fundamental
151 adj.
generative
162 adj.

funds
funds 792 n.

funeral
bed 213 n.
funeral 359 n.
weeper 831 n.

funereal
funereal 359 adj.
black 423 adj.
lamenting
831 adj.

funny
dramatic 589 adj.
amusing 832 adj.
witty 834 adj.
funny 844 adj.

furious
destructive
160 adj.
furious 171 adj.
excited 816 adj.
excitable 817 adj.
angry 886 adj.

furnace
outbreak 171 n.
chimney 258 n.
ejector 295 n.
cookery 296 n.
gas 331 n.
fire 374 n.
burning 376 n.
furnace 378 n.
pitfall 658 n.
workshop 682 n.

furrow
receptacle 189 n.
gap 196 n.
cavity 250 n.
concavity 250 n.
roughness 254 n.
furrow 257 n.
wave 345 n.

furrowed
furrowed 257 adj.

future
unborn 2 adj.
subsequent
115 adj.
future 119 n.
impending
150 adj.
possible 464 adj.
unknown 486 adj.

future state
sequel 67 n.
finality 69 n.
future state
119 n.
destiny 150 n.
reproduction
161 n.
life 355 n.
the dead 356 n.
fantasy 508 n.
revival 651 n.
heaven 965 n.

futurity
time 104 n.
posteriority
115 n.
different time
117 n.
futurity 119 n.
destiny 150 n.

possibility 464 n.

G

gain
increment 36 n.
extra 40 n.
growth 152 n.
product 159 n.
incentive 607 n.
benefit 610 n.
flourish 610 vb.
provision 628 n.
utility 635 n.
find useful
635 vb.
triumph 722 vb.
prosper 725 vb.
gain 766 n.
gain 766 vb.
booty 785 n.
sell 788 vb.
wealth 795 n.
get rich 795 vb.
debt 798 n.
receipt 802 n.
reward 957 n.
be rewarded
957 vb.

gainful
profitable
635 adj.
gainful 766 adj.
rewarding
957 adj.

gait
gait 260 n.
equitation 262 n.
pedestrianism
262 n.
slowness 273 n.
leap 307 n.

gale
turmoil 61 n.
storm 171 n.
storm 171 n.
vortex 310 n.
commotion 313 n.
weather 335 n.
rain 345 n.
gale 347 n.
pitfall 658 n.
excitable state
817 n.

galley
galley 270 n.

gamble
chance 154 vb.
be tentative
456 vb.
divine 506 vb.
suppose 507 vb.
gamble 613 vb.
endanger 656 vb.
face danger
656 vb.
attempt 666 vb.
speculate 786 vb.
amuse oneself
832 vb.
be rash 852 vb.

gambler
gambler 613 n.

gambling
gambling 613 n.

gambling game
gambling game
832 n.

gaming-house
gaming-house
613 n.

gaol
gaol 743 n.
pillory 959 n.

gaoler
gaoler 744 n.

gap
disunion 46 n.
discontinuity
72 n.
weakness 158 n.
emptiness 185 n.
short distance
195 n.
gap 196 n.
depth 206 n.
partition 226 n.
valley 250 n.
notch 255 n.
furrow 257 n.
opening 258 n.
defect 642 n.

garden
seedbed 151 n.
arbour 189 n.
enclosure 230 n.
flower 361 n.
wood 361 n.
botany 363 n.
garden 365 n.
heater 378 n.
fragrance 391 n.

gardener
gardener 365 n.

garment
adjunct 40 n.
garment 223 n.

gas
fluid 330 n.
gas 331 n.
air 335 n.
fuel 380 n.
stench 392 n.

gaseous
gaseous 331 adj.

gaseousness
gaseousness
331 n.

gasify
gasify 331 vb.
vaporize 333 vb.

gastronomy
gastronomy
296 n.
gluttony 942 n.

gauge
prototype 23 n.
counting
instrument 86 n.
altimetry 204 n.
horizontality
211 n.
velocity 272 n.
direction 276 n.
hygrometry
336 n.
testing agent
456 n.
gauge 460 n.
gauge 460 vb.
estimate 475 vb.
indicator 542 n.
recording
instrument 544 n.

gaze
gaze 433 vb.
be curious
448 vb.

be attentive
450 vb.
gesticulate
542 vb.
be rude 880 vb.
court 884 vb.

gem
rock 339 n.
exceller 639 n.
gem 839 n.

genealogy
heredity 5 n.
consanguinity
11 n.
series 71 n.
breed 77 n.
list 87 n.
antiquity 120 n.
genealogy 164 n.
nobility 863 n.

general
comprehensive
52 adj.
inclusive 78 adj.
general 79 adj.
typical 83 adj.
one 88 adj.
spacious 178 adj.
broad 205 adj.
indiscriminate
459 adj.
known 485 adj.
inexact 495 adj.
usual 610 adj.

general, be
be general 79 vb.

generality
average 30 n.
whole 52 n.
completeness
54 n.
inclusion 78 n.
generality 79 n.
conformity 83 n.
social group
366 n.
indiscrimination
459 n.
inexactness
495 n.

generalize
generalize 79 vb.

generally
on an average
30 adv.
greatly 32 adv.
generally 79 adv.

generate
be akin 11 vb.
mix 43 vb.
unite with 45 vb.
initiate 68 vb.
cause 151 vb.
generate 162 vb.
make fruitful
166 vb.
emit 295 vb.
vitalize 355 vb.

generative
productive
159 adj.
reproduced
161 adj.
generative
162 adj.
prolific 166 adj.
female 368 adj.

generic
generic 77 adj.

genetic
genetic 5 adj.

reverted 143 adj.
inherited 152 adj.
parental 164 adj.
filial 165 adj.
with affections
812 adj.

genitalia
genitalia 162 n.

genteel
well-bred
843 adj.
genteel 863 adj.

genuine
inimitable 21 adj.
certain 468 adj.
genuine 489 adj.
orthodox 970 adj.

geographic
geographic
316 adj.

geometry
geometry 460 n.

gerontology
gerontology
126 n.

gesticulate
distort 241 vb.
move 260 vb.
hint 519 vb.
gesticulate
542 vb.
be mute 573 vb.
speak 579 vb.
behave 683 vb.
command 732 vb.

gesture
mimicry 20 n.
distortion 241 n.
motion 260 n.
knock 274 n.
agitation 313 n.
hint 519 n.
gesture 542 n.
language 552 n.
voicelessness
573 n.
speech 574 n.
conduct 683 n.
command 732 n.
feeling 813 n.
affectation
845 n.
sauciness 873 n.
ritual act 982 n.

get angry
go mad 498 vb.
show feeling
813 vb.
be excitable
817 vb.
be rude 880 vb.
get angry 886 vb.
be irascible
887 vb.
threaten 895 vb.

get better
grow 36 vb.
change 138 vb.
progress 280 vb.
tergiversate
598 vb.
flourish 610 vb.
find useful
635 vb.
get better
649 vb.
be restored
651 vb.
be honourable
924 vb.

be penitent
934 vb.

get drunk
be complete
54 vb.
drink 296 vb.
revel 832 vb.
be intemperate
938 vb.
get drunk 944 vb.

get healthy
get healthy
645 vb.

get rich
flourish 610 vb.
prosper 725 vb.
gain 766 vb.
get rich 795 vb.
economize
809 vb.

ghost
immateriality
315 n.
the dead 356 n.
corpse 358 n.
visual fallacy
435 n.
appearance
440 n.
fantasy 508 n.
intimidation
849 n.
ghost 964 n.
spiritualism
978 n.

giant
athlete 157 n.
giant 190 n.
tall creature
204 n.

gift
extra 40 n.
thing transferred
267 n.
voluntary work
592 n.
incentive 607 n.
benefit 610 n.
subvention 698 n.
offer 754 n.
acquisition 766 n.
transfer 775 n.
gift 776 n.
receiving 777 n.
no charge 807 n.
liberality 808 n.
reward 957 n.

gifted
intelligent
493 adj.
gifted 689 adj.

gild
colour 420 vb.
gild 428 adj.

girdle
girdle 47 n.
compressor
193 n.
strip 203 n.
wrapping 221 n.
belt 223 n.
surroundings
225 n.
loop 245 n.
vestments 983 n.

give
attribute 153 vb.
provide 628 vb.
permit 751 vb.
consent 753 vb.
offer 754 vb.

dower 772 vb.
assign 775 vb.
give 776 vb.
apportion 778 vb.
defray 799 vb.
pay 799 vb.
expend 801 vb.
cheapen 807 vb.
be liberal 808 vb.
content 823 vb.
reward 957 vb.
be pious 973 vb.
offer worship
975 vb.
be ecclesiastical
979 vb.

give bail
give bail 762 vb.

give battle
fight 711 vb.
give battle
713 vb.

give courage
strengthen
157 vb.
incite 607 vb.
aid 698 vb.
animate 816 vb.
cheer 828 vb.
give courage
850 vb.

give hope
evidence 461 vb.
be likely 466 vb.
predict 506 vb.
give hope 847 vb.
cause desire
854 vb.

given
given 776 adj.
uncharged
807 adj.

give pain
cause feeling
369 vb.
give pain 372 vb.
touch 373 vb.
hurt 822 vb.
torture 958 vb.

giver
giver 776 n.

give scope
sustain 141 vb.
facilitate 696 vb.
be lax 729 vb.
give scope
739 vb.
liberate 741 vb.
permit 751 vb.
be liberal 808 vb.

give security
promise 759 vb.
contract 760 vb.
give security
762 vb.
borrow 780 vb.

give terms
require 622 vb.
pacify 714 vb.
liberate 741 vb.
request 756 vb.
contract 760 vb.
give terms
761 vb.
bargain 786 vb.
impose a duty
912 vb.

giving
giving 776 n.
giving 776 adj.

glimmer
glimmer 414 n.
hint 519 n.

glove
glove 223 n.

glow
heavens 316 n.
fire 374 n.
glow 412 n.
glow-worm
415 n.
redness 426 n.

glow-worm
flash 412 n.
glow 412 n.
glimmer 414 n.
glow-worm
415 n.
visual fallacy
435 n.

glutton
destroyer 163 n.
eater 296 n.
sensualist 939 n.
glutton 942 n.

gluttonize
gluttonize
942 vb.

gluttonous
gluttonous
942 adj.

gluttonously
gluttonously
942 adv.

gluttony
gluttony 942 n.

glyptic
glyptic 549 adj.

goal
extremity 69 n.
focus 76 n.
stopping place
140 n.
resting place
261 n.
air travel 266 n.
direction 276 n.
goal 290 n.
objective 612 n.
completion 720 n.

go away
go away 185 vb.

godlike
godlike 960 adj.

God the Son
God the Son
960 n.

go mad
go mad 498 vb.
be excitable
817 vb.
be in love 882 vb.

gong
campanology
407 n.
gong 409 n.
signal 542 n.

good
good 610 n.
good 610 adj.
utility 635 n.
profitable
635 adj.
safe 655 adj.
prosperity 725 n.

good, be
be superior
34 vb.
be wise 493 vb.
be good 639 vb.
be skilful 689 vb.

have a reputation
861 vb.
be virtuous
928 vb.
good giver
good giver 808 n.
goodness
superiority 34 n.
importance
633 n.
utility 635 n.
goodness 639 n.
health 645 n.
skill 689 n.
good taste 841 n.
good person
exceller 639 n.
benefactor 898 n.
honourable
person 924 n.
good person
932 n.
pietist 973 n.
good policy
fitness 24 n.
occasion 132 n.
substitute 145 n.
possibility 464 n.
choice 600 n.
good 610 n.
utility 635 n.
good policy
637 n.
use 668 n.
good taste
discrimination
458 n.
elegance 570 n.
civilization 649 n.
beauty 836 n.
good taste 841 n.
etiquette 843 n.
fastidiousness
857 n.
sociability 877 n.
courtesy 879 n.
purity 945 n.
go on
go on 141 vb.
go round
go round 245 vb.
go smoothly
go smoothly
253 vb.
go to sea
go to sea 264 vb.
go to war
be violent 171 vb.
quarrel 704 vb.
attack 707 vb.
fight 711 vb.
go to war
713 vb.
governance
governance
728 n.
governed, be
be governed
728 vb.
government
influence 173 n.
nation 366 n.
government
728 n.
master 736 n.
commission
746 n.
the church 979 n.
governmental
governmental
728 adj.

governor
director 685 n.
leader 685 n.
governor 736 n.
person of rank
863 n.
ecclesiarch 980 n.
graceless
graceless 837 adj.
gradatim
gradatim
273 adv.
gradational
gradational
27 adj.
grade
graduate 27 vb.
grade 73 vb.
graduate
graduate 27 vb.
continue 71 vb.
grade 73 vb.
gauge 460 vb.
grammar
differentiation
15 n.
decomposition
51 n.
arrangement
62 n.
sequel 67 n.
extremity 69 n.
assemblage 74 n.
time 104 n.
course of time
107 n.
past time 120 n.
linguist 552 n.
linguistics 552 n.
word 554 n.
grammar 559 n.
grammatical
grammatical
559 adj.
gramophone
sound 393 n.
musical piece
407 n.
gramophone
409 n.
hearing aid
410 n.
record 543 n.
recording
instrument 544 n.
grant claims
grant claims
910 vb.
grass
grass 361 n.
grassland
space 178 n.
soil 339 n.
grassland 343 n.
grass 361 n.
stock farm 364 n.
farm 365 n.
grateful
content 823 adj.
grateful 902 adj.
approving
918 adj.
grateful, be
be content
823 vb.
congratulate
881 vb.
be grateful
902 vb.
reward 957 vb.

gratefully
gratefully
902 adv.
gratitude
congratulation
881 n.
gratitude 902 n.
approbation
918 n.
reward 957 n.
oblation 975 n.
grave clothes
wrapping 221 n.
robe 223 n.
grave clothes
359 n.
gravity
substantiality
3 n.
quantity 26 n.
inequality 29 n.
energy 155 n.
power 155 n.
bulk 190 n.
size 190 n.
materiality 314 n.
gravity 317 n.
redundance
632 n.
encumbrance
697 n.
graze
graze 296 vb.
grease
lubricate 329 vb.
grease 352 vb.
great
great 32 adj.
superior 34 adj.
supreme 34 adj.
increasing 36 adj.
abnormal 84 adj.
many 100 adj.
powerful 155 adj.
strong 157 adj.
influential
173 adj.
large 190 adj.
plenteous
630 adj.
important
633 adj.
worshipful
861 adj.
noble 863 adj.
proud 866 adj.
great, be
be great 32 vb.
grow 36 vb.
be many 100 vb.
greater number
finite quantity
26 n.
main part 32 n.
advantage 34 n.
chief part 52 n.
part 53 n.
plurality 97 n.
greater number
100 n.
power 155 n.
greatly
substantially
3 adv.
greatly 32 adv.
on the whole
52 adv.
completely
54 adv.
infinitely 103 adv.

greatness
greatness 32 n.
great quantity
finite quantity
26 n.
great quantity
32 n.
chief part 52 n.
crowd 74 n.
multitude 100 n.
abundance 166 n.
contents 188 n.
bulk 190 n.
plenty 630 n.
redundance
632 n.
funds 792 n.
wealth 795 n.
greedy
greedy 854 adj.
green
vegetal 361 adj.
green 429 adj.
unhealthy
646 adj.
greenness
greenness 429 n.
green pigment
green pigment
429 n.
greet
approach 284 vb.
cry 403 vb.
notice 450 vb.
gesticulate
542 vb.
speak to 578 vb.
be friendly
875 vb.
be hospitable
877 vb.
greet 879 vb.
show respect
915 vb.
grey
colourless
421 adj.
whitish 422 adj.
grey 424 adj.
painted 548 adj.
greyness
greyness 424 n.
groom
groom 364 n.
groove
cut 46 vb.
make concave
250 vb.
fold 256 vb.
groove 257 vb.
wound 650 vb.
decorate 839 vb.
grounded
grounded
723 adj.
group
subdivision 53 n.
group 74 n.
classification
77 n.
self 80 n.
certain quantity
100 n.
contemporary
118 n.
animal 360 n.
social group
366 n.
grow
grow 36 vb.
congregate 74 vb.

come of age
129 vb.
change 138 vb.
be turned to
142 vb.
result 152 vb.
reproduce itself
162 vb.
expand 192 vb.
ascend 303 vb.
vegetate 361 vb.

grown-up
grown-up
129 adj.
manly 157 adj.
matured 664 adj.

grow old
pass time 104 vb.
last 108 vb.
be old 122 vb.
grow old 126 vb.
be weak 158 vb.
deteriorate
650 vb.
be ugly 837 vb.

growth
conversion 142 n.
growth 152 n.
product 159 n.
propagation
162 n.
expansion 192 n.
evolution 311 n.

guide
magnet 286 n.
guide 515 n.
guidebook 519 n.
teacher 532 n.
directorship
684 n.
director 685 n.

guidebook
guidebook 519 n.

guilt
intention 612 n.
badness 640 n.
wrong 909 n.
wickedness 929 n.
guilt 931 n.
penitence 934 n.
lawbreaking
949 n.

guiltily
guiltily 931 adv.

guiltless
guiltless 930 adj.

guilty
bad 640 adj.
wrong 909 adj.
wicked 929 adj.
guilty 931 adj.
lawbreaking
949 adj.

guilty act
overstepping
301 n.
disobedience
733 n.
wrong 909 n.
vice 929 n.
guilty act 931 n.

guilty, be
be guilty 931 vb.
condemn 956 vb.

gulf
entrance 68 n.
gap 196 n.
narrowness
201 n.
curve 243 n.
cavity 250 n.

open space
258 n.
way in 292 n.
gulf 340 n.
access 619 n.

gullible
credulous
482 adj.
foolish 494 adj.
gullible 539 adj.

gun
gun 718 n.

H

habit
uniformity 16 n.
average 30 n.
order 60 n.
continuity 71 n.
generality 79 n.
regularity 81 n.
recurrence 102 n.
tradition 122 n.
regular return
136 n.
permanence
139 n.
phrase 558 n.
habit 605 n.
use 668 n.
conduct 683 n.
possession 768 n.
fashion 843 n.
intemperance
938 n.

habitual
orderly 60 adj.
general 79 adj.
immemorial
122 adj.
frequent 134 adj.
habitual 605 adj.
inducing 607 adj.
businesslike
617 adj.
doing 671 adj.

habitually
habitually
605 adv.

habituate
habituate 605 vb.

habituated
habituated
605 adj.

habituation
habituation
605 n.

habitu
habitu´e
605 N.

haemorrhage
outflow 293 n.
haemorrhage
297 n.

hair
sequel 67 n.
filament 203 n.
hanging object
212 n.
weaving 217 n.
wig 223 n.
front 232 n.
laterality 234 n.
loop 245 n.
coil 246 n.
prickle 251 n.
hair 254 n.

softness 322 n.
texture 326 n.

hairdressing
838 n.
trimming 839 n.

hairdressing
hairdressing
838 n.

hairless
hairless 224 adj.

hairwash
hairwash 838 n.

hairy
fibrous 203 adj.
sharp 251 adj.
hairy 254 adj.
textural 326 adj.

half-light
half-light 414 n.

halfway, be
be moderate
172 vb.
lie between
226 vb.
be neutral
601 vb.
be halfway
620 vb.
be middling
727 vb.
compromise
765 vb.

halt
terminate 69 vb.
halt 140 vb.
come to rest
261 vb.
be obstructive
697 vb.
resist 710 vb.
restrain 742 vb.

halter
halter 47 n.
loop 245 n.
fetter 743 n.

hammer
hammer 274 n.
pulverizer 327 n.
tool 625 n.
club 718 n.

handed
handed 373 adj.

handle
handle 213 n.
tool 625 n.

hang
come unstuck
49 vb.
be periodic
136 vb.
vary 147 vb.
be high 204 vb.
hang 212 vb.
be curved 243 vb.
jut 249 vb.
be in motion
260 vb.
fly 266 vb.
descend 304 vb.
oscillate 312 vb.

hanger
hanger 212 n.
prop 213 n.
dryer 337 n.
tool 625 n.

hanging
nonadhesive
49 adj.
weak 158 adj.
hanging 212 adj.

hanging object
extremity 69 n.
hanging object
212 n.
bed 213 n.
covering 221 n.
jewellery 839 n.

happen
be 1 vb.
happen 149 vb.
result 152 vb.
chance 154 vb.
be present
184 vb.
appear 440 vb.

happening
happening
149 adj.
casual 154 adj.

happiness
happiness 819 n.

happy
good 610 adj.
prosperous
725 adj.
happy 819 adj.
pleasurable
821 adj.
content 823 adj.
cheerful 828 adj.
enamoured
882 adj.
paradisiac
965 adj.

hard
past 120 adj.
strong 157 adj.
hard 321 adj.
resolute 594 adj.
severe 730 adj.
thick-skinned
815 adj.
unkind 893 adj.
pitiless 901 adj.

harden
strengthen
157 vb.
be dense 319 vb.
harden 321 vb.
thicken 349 vb.
mature 664 vb.
make insensitive
815 vb.

hardening
hardening 321 n.

hardness
stability 148 n.
strength 157 n.
covering 221 n.
straightness
244 n.
quiescence 261 n.
density 319 n.
hardness 321 n.
toughness 324 n.
inelegance 571 n.
resolution 594 n.
obstinacy 597 n.
severity 730 n.
moral insensibility
815 n.
inhumanity 893 n.
pitilessness
901 n.
impenitence
935 n.

hard task
impossibility
465 n.
undertaking
667 n.

hard task 695 n.

harm
be inexpedient
638 vb.
harm 640 vb.
impair 650 vb.
hurt 822 vb.
be malevolent
893 vb.
do wrong 909 vb.

harmful
harmful 640 adj.

harmonic
harmonic
405 adj.

harmonious
harmonious
405 adj.

harmonize
harmonize
405 vb.

harp
harp 409 n.

haste
crowd 74 n.
vigorousness
169 n.
speeding 272 n.
velocity 272 n.
commotion 313 n.
nonpreparation
665 n.
activity 673 n.
haste 675 n.
excitability 817 n.
rashness 852 n.

hasten
be early 130 vb.
cause 151 vb.
move 260 vb.
accelerate
272 vb.
move fast
272 vb.
progress 280 vb.
incite 607 vb.
pursue 614 vb.
be busy 673 vb.
hasten 675 vb.
be rash 852 vb.

hastily
hastily 675 adv.

hasty
brief 109 adj.
furious 171 adj.
speedy 272 adj.
negligent 453 adj.
unwise 494 adj.
unprepared
665 adj.
hasty 675 adj.
excitable 817 adj.
rash 852 adj.

hate
dislike 856 vb.
hate 883 vb.
be malevolent
893 vb.
be revengeful
905 vb.

hated
hated 883 adj.

hateful
not nice 640 adj.
disliked 856 adj.
disreputable
862 adj.
hateful 883 adj.

hateful object
enemy 876 n.

hateful object
883 n.

hating
hating 883 adj.

hatred
contrariety 14 n.
prejudice 476 n.
dissension 704 n.
phobia 849 n.
dislike 856 n.
enmity 876 n.
hatred 883 n.
resentment
886 n.
malevolence
893 n.
jealousy 906 n.
pietism 973 n.

haunt
appear 440 vb.
haunt 964 vb.
bewitch 977 vb.

have a reputation
be remembered
500 vb.
do 671 vb.
have a reputation
861 vb.
command respect
915 vb.
be praised
918 vb.

have a right
have a right
910 vb.

have enough
be complete
54 vb.
have enough
630 vb.
climax 720 vb.
afford 795 vb.

have feeling
have feeling
369 vb.

have leisure
pass time 104 vb.
not act 672 vb.
have leisure
676 vb.
repose 678 vb.
amuse oneself
832 vb.

have luck
have luck 725 vb.

have no choice
have no choice
601 vb.

have no repute
have no repute
862 vb.

have no smell
have no smell
390 vb.

have rank
have rank 73 vb.

have taste
be elegant
570 vb.
have taste
841 vb.

have trouble
feel pain 372 vb.
be in difficulty
695 vb.
have trouble
726 vb.
lose 767 vb.
suffer 820 vb.

havoc
disorder 61 n.

revolution 144 n.
havoc 160 n.
destroyer 163 n.
uncovering 224 n.
impairment
650 n.
terror tactics
707 n.
spoliation 783 n.

head
head 208 n.
skin 221 n.
face 232 n.
rear 233 n.
dome 248 n.
intellect 442 n.

headgear
headgear 223 n.

health
vitality 157 n.
euphoria 371 n.
goodness 639 n.
health 645 n.
salubrity 647 n.

healthily
healthily 647 adv.

healthy
ageing 126 adj.
athletic 157 adj.
strong 157 adj.
vigorous 169 adj.
undamaged
641 adj.
healthy 645 adj.
restored 651 adj.

healthy, be
be vigorous
169 vb.
be healthy
645 vb.
be salubrious
647 vb.

hear
hear 410 vb.
be curious
448 vb.
be attentive
450 vb.
be mindful
450 vb.
be informed
519 vb.
consent 753 vb.

heard, be
be heard 410 vb.

hearing
sound 393 n.
hearing 410 n.
exam 454 n.

hearing aid
sound 393 n.
megaphone
395 n.
hearing aid
410 n.
publicity 523 n.
telecommunication
526 n.

heat
summer 123 n.
make violent
171 vb.
harden 321 vb.
liquefy 332 vb.
weather 335 n.
dryness 337 n.
dry 337 vb.
heat 374 n.
heat 376 vb.
glow 412 vb.
whiteness 422 n.

excite 816 vb.
excitable state
817 n.
excite love
882 vb.

heated
violent 171 adj.
hot 374 adj.
heated 376 adj.

heater
sources of energy
155 n.
cauldron 189 n.
heating 376 n.
heater 378 n.

heathen
religionist 967 n.
heathen 968 n.
impious person
974 n.
idolater 976 n.

heathenish
heathenish
968 adj.

heating
increase 36 n.
stimulation
169 n.
liquefaction
332 n.
atmosphere
335 n.
desiccation
337 n.
heat 374 n.
heating 376 n.
heating 376 adj.
heater 378 n.

heaven
future state
119 n.
destiny 150 n.
life 355 n.
death 356 n.
heaven 965 n.

heavens
heavens 316 n.

height
quantity 26 n.
degree 27 n.
greatness 32 n.
superiority 34 n.
measure 178 n.
hugeness 190 n.
size 190 n.
height 204 n.
verticality 210 n.
elevation 305 n.

heinous
accusable
923 adj.
heinous 929 adj.
guilty 931 adj.

hell
future state
119 n.
depth 206 n.
death 356 n.
hell 966 n.

hellhag
hellhag 899 n.

helplessness
helplessness
156 n.

hem
be contiguous
197 vb.
hem 229 vb.
limit 231 vb.
flank 234 vb.
decorate 839 vb.

hence
consequently
152 adv.
hence 153 adv.

henceforth
henceforth
119 adv.

heraldic
heraldic 542 adj.

heraldry
cross 217 n.
centre 220 n.
colour 420 n.
orange 427 n.
heraldry 542 n.
monument 543 n.
regalia 738 n.
ornamental art
839 n.
honours 861 n.
nobility 863 n.

herdsman
accumulator
74 n.
herdsman 364 n.
leader 685 n.
servant 737 n.

here
here 184 adv.

here and there
here and there
101 adv.

heredity
heredity 5 n.
consanguinity
11 n.
recurrence 102 n.
reversion 143 n.
reproduction
161 n.
influence 173 n.
organism 353 n.
deterioration
650 n.
affections 812 n.

heresy
unbelief 481 n.
heresy 971 n.

heretic
nonconformist
84 n.
unbeliever 481 n.
religionist 967 n.
heretic 971 n.
schismatic 972 n.
sectarian 972 n.

heretical
heretical 971 adj.

heretical, be
be heretical
971 vb.

heretically
heretically
971 adv.

hermeneutics
hermeneutics
515 n.

heterodox
heterodox
971 adj.

heterodoxy
heterodoxy 971 n.

hider
hider 522 n.

hiding-place
hiding-place
522 n.

high
enormous 32 adj.
great 32 adj.
high 204 adj.

topmost 208 adj.
vertical 210 adj.
elevated 305 adj.
proud 866 adj.

high, be
be superior
34 vb.
grow 36 vb.
be large 190 vb.
be high 204 vb.
crown 208 vb.
ascend 303 vb.
climb 303 vb.

high land
narrowness
201 n.
high land 204 n.
vertex 208 n.
verticality 210 n.
horizontality
211 n.
prominence
249 n.
roughness 254 n.
ascent 303 n.
elevation 305 n.
land 339 n.
plain 343 n.
pitfall 658 n.

high structure
accumulation
74 n.
edifice 159 n.
bulk 190 n.
high structure
204 n.
vertex 208 n.
projection 249 n.
view 433 n.
church exterior
984 n.

high water
high water 204 n.

hinder
add 38 vb.
derange 63 vb.
jumble 63 vb.
halt 140 vb.
disable 156 vb.
counteract
177 vb.
interfere 226 vb.
retard 273 vb.
weigh 317 vb.
be inattentive
451 vb.
disappoint
504 vb.
avoid 615 vb.
be useless
636 vb.
impair 650 vb.
be difficult
695 vb.
hinder 697 vb.
resist 710 vb.
restrain 742 vb.
prohibit 752 vb.

hindered
hindered 697 adj.

hinderer
hinderer 697 n.

hindering
hindering
697 adj.

hindrance
inferiority 35 n.
exclusion 57 n.
complexity 61 n.
derangement
63 n.

protraction
108 n.
delay 131 n.
stop 140 n.
destruction
160 n.
counteraction
177 n.
interjection
226 n.
estimate 475 n.
unwillingness
593 n.
dissuasion 608 n.
avoidance 615 n.
safeguard 657 n.
difficulty 695 n.
hindrance 697 n.
failure 723 n.
disobedience
733 n.
restraint 742 n.
fetter 743 n.
undutifulness
913 n.

hint
look 433 n.
gaze 433 vb.
notice 450 n.
evidence 461 n.
knowledge 485 n.
sciolism 486 n.
reminder 500 n.
remind 500 vb.
supposition
507 n.
propound 507 vb.
latency 518 n.
imply 518 vb.
hint 519 n.
hint 519 vb.
disclosure 521 n.
divulge 521 vb.
gesture 542 n.
indication 542 n.
indicate 542 vb.
speak low 573 vb.
speak 574 vb.
incite 607 vb.
warning 659 n.
warn 659 vb.
advice 686 n.
advise 686 vb.
command 732 vb.

hire
hire 780 vb.
purchase 787 vb.

hiss
hiss 401 vb.
ululate 404 vb.

hitch
disappointment
504 n.
evil 611 n.
difficulty 695 n.
hitch 697 n.
failure 723 n.

hoarse
muted 396 adj.
nonresonant
400 adj.
hoarse 402 adj.
vocal 572 adj.
vocal 572 adj.
voiceless 573 adj.

hold cheap
be inattentive
451 vb.
disregard 453 vb.
underestimate
478 vb.

reject 602 vb.
be unimportant
634 vb.
oppose 699 vb.
defy 706 vb.
ridicule 846 vb.
be indifferent
855 vb.
not respect
916 vb.
hold cheap
917 vb.
detract 921 vb.

hold court
judge 475 vb.
hold court
950 n.

hold within
hold within
219 vb.

Holy Communion
Holy Communion
982 n.

holy day
anniversary
136 n.
special day
871 n.
holy day 982 n.

Holy Ghost
Holy Ghost
960 n.

holy orders
celibate 890 n.
holy orders
979 n.

holy place
holy place 984 n.

home
family 11 n.
origin 68 n.
focus 76 n.
source 151 n.
territory 179 n.
place 180 n.
home 187 n.
resting place
261 n.
goal 290 n.
refuge 657 n.

homicide
homicide 357 n.
poisoning 654 n.
revolt 733 n.
cruel act 893 n.
oblation 975 n.

honour
elevate 305 vb.
be auspicious
725 vb.
decorate 839 vb.
honour 861 vb.
respect 915 vb.
approve 918 vb.
reward 957 vb.
sanctify 973 vb.

honourable
simple 44 adj.
careful 452 adj.
veracious
535 adj.
artless 694 adj.
observant
763 adj.
well-bred
843 adj.
reputable
861 adj.
just 908 adj.
ethical 912 adj.

honourable
924 adj.
disinterested
926 adj.
virtuous 928 adj.
pure 945 adj.
honourable, be
keep faith
763 vb.
be just 908 vb.
be honourable
924 vb.
be virtuous
928 vb.
be innocent
930 vb.
honourable person
person of repute
861 n.
honourable
person 924 n.
good person
932 n.
honours
decoration 724 n.
honours 861 n.
title 865 n.
reward 957 n.
hope
looking ahead
119 n.
look ahead
119 vb.
probability 466 n.
overestimation
477 n.
belief 480 n.
expectation
502 n.
expect 502 vb.
persevere 595 vb.
motive 607 n.
relief 826 n.
cheerfulness
828 n.
be cheerful
828 vb.
hope 847 n.
hope 847 vb.
desire 854 n.
desire 854 vb.
hopefully
hopefully
847 adv.
hopeless
depreciating
478 adj.
expectant
502 adj.
inexpectant
503 adj.
disappointed
504 adj.
nonactive
672 adj.
unhappy 820 adj.
dejected 829 adj.
hopeless 848 adj.
nervous 854 adj.
cowardly 851 adj.
hopelessness
hopelessness
848 n.
hoper
hoper 847 n.
hoping
hoping 847 vb.
horizontal, be
lengthen 198 vb.
be low 205 vb.

be horizontal
211 vb.
sit down 306 vb.
repose 678 vb.
horizontality
horizontality
211 n.
horizontally
horizontally
211 adv.
horn
horn 409 n.
hors-d'oeuvres
hors-d'oeuvres
296 n.
horse
conveyance
262 n.
horse 268 n.
animal 360 n.
horticultural
horticultural
365 adj.
hospitable, be
feed 296 vb.
offer 754 vb.
give 776 vb.
be liberal 808 vb.
amuse 832 vb.
be in fashion
843 vb.
desire 854 vb.
celebrate 871 vb.
be friendly
875 vb.
be hospitable
877 vb.
hospital
abode 187 n.
bed 213 n.
lunatic asylum
498 n.
hygiene 647 n.
hospital 653 n.
hot
dry 337 adj.
hot 374 adj.
heated 376 adj.
white 422 adj.
red 426 adj.
fervent 813 adj.
excited 816 adj.
hot, be
grow 36 vb.
exude 293 vb.
emit 295 vb.
excrete 297 vb.
effervesce
313 vb.
be hot 374 vb.
shine 412 vb.
be excited
816 vb.
house
edifice 159 n.
place 180 n.
house 187 n.
housing
district 179 n.
inhabitants
186 n.
housing 187 n.
expansion 192 n.
surroundings
225 n.
road 619 n.
sink 644 n.
how
how 619 adv.
hue
tincture 43 n.

hue 420 n.
huff
hurt 822 vb.
cause discontent
824 vb.
be rude 880 vb.
huff 886 vb.
huge
enormous 32 adj.
stalwart 162 adj.
huge 190 adj.
tall 204 adj.
fairylike 964 adj.
hugeness
hugeness 190 n.
human
human 366 adj.
humankind
precursor 66 n.
palaeology 120 n.
parentage 164 n.
life 355 n.
mammal 360 n.
humankind 366 n.
humble
depreciating
478 adj.
submitting
716 adj.
humble 867 adj.
modest 869 adj.
courteous
879 adj.
respectful
915 adj.
disinterested
926 adj.
humble, be
be unseen
439 vb.
relinquish 616 vb.
knuckle under
716 vb.
be humble
867 vb.
be modest
869 vb.
be servile 874 vb.
be courteous
879 vb.
show respect
915 vb.
be disinterested
926 vb.
be pious 973 vb.
humbled
humbled 867 adj.
humbled, be
be humbled
867 vb.
humid
watery 334 adj.
humid 336 adj.
rainy 345 adj.
humiliate
abate 37 vb.
abase 306 vb.
disappoint
504 vb.
be unimportant
634 vb.
cause discontent
824 vb.
ridicule 846 vb.
shame 862 vb.
humiliate 867 vb.
not respect
916 vb.
hold cheap
917 vb.

humiliation
humiliation 867 n.
humility
inferiority 35 n.
underestimation
478 n.
submission 716 n.
modesty 869 n.
servility 874 n.
courtesy 879 n.
respect 915 n.
disinterestedness
926 n.
penitence 934 n.
religion 967 n.
piety 973 n.
worship 975 n.
humorist
imitator 20 n.
deceiver 540 n.
dramatist 589 n.
entertainer
589 n.
humorist 834 n.
affecter 845 n.
hundred
hundred 96 n.
hunger
eating 296 n.
dryness 337 n.
rapacity 781 n.
hunger 854 n.
fasting 941 n.
gluttony 942 n.
hungry
dry 337 adj.
taking 781 adj.
hungry 854 adj.
fasting 941 adj.
gluttonous
942 adj.
hungry, be
eat 296 vb.
excrete 297 vb.
be unsatisfied
631 vb.
be poor 796 vb.
be hungry 854 vb.
starve 941 vb.
hunt
eject 295 vb.
detect 479 vb.
hunt 614 vb.
attack 707 vb.
frighten 849 vb.
be inimical
876 vb.
defame 921 vb.
hunter
concomitant
89 n.
rider 263 n.
killer 357 n.
hunter 614 n.
hurt
harm 640 vb.
excite 816 vb.
hurt 822 vb.
huff 886 vb.
punish 958 vb.
hybrid
hybrid 43 n.
nonconformist
84 n.
hygiene
cleansing 643 n.
hygiene 647 n.
prophylactic
653 n.
protection 655 n.

think 444 vb.
be inattentive
451 vb.
suppose 507 vb.
imagine 508 vb.
be false 536 vb.
be untrue 538 vb.
describe 585 vb.
plan 618 vb.
hope 847 vb.

imitate
liken 18 vb.
resemble 18 vb.
imitate 20 vb.
conform 83 vb.
show 517 vb.
dissemble 536 vb.
fake 536 vb.
gesticulate
542 vb.
represent 546 vb.
act 589 vb.
be affected
845 vb.
satirize 846 vb.

imitation
imitation 20 n.

imitative
imitative 20 adj.

imitatively
imitatively
20 adv.

imitator
imitator 20 n.
conformist 83 n.
deceiver 540 n.
actor 589 n.
humorist 834 n.

immaterial
insubstantial
4 adj.
immaterial
315 adj.
rare 320 adj.
mental 442 adj.
psychic 447 adj.
spooky 964 adj.

immateriality
immateriality
315 n.

immature
unreal 2 adj.
incomplete
55 adj.
beginning 68 adj.
new 121 adj.
young 125 adj.
early 130 adj.
amorphous
239 adj.
sour 388 adj.
unhabituated
606 adj.
imperfect
642 adj.
immature
665 adj.
unskilled 690 adj.
uncompleted
721 adj.

immemorial
lasting 108 adj.
perpetual
110 adj.
former 120 adj.
immemorial
122 adj.
permanent
139 adj.
parental 164 adj.

worshipful
861 adj.

immerse
immerse 298 vb.
drench 336 vb.

immersion
immersion 298 n.

impair
abate 37 vb.
subtract 39 vb.
break 46 vb.
derange 63 vb.
modify 138 vb.
disable 156 vb.
weaken 158 vb.
lay waste 160 vb.
influence 173 vb.
deform 239 vb.
distort 241 vb.
infiltrate 292 vb.
encroach 301 vb.
waste 629 vb.
make insufficient
631 vb.
make useless
636 vb.
harm 640 vb.
make unclean
644 vb.
impair 650 vb.
misuse 670 vb.
meddle 673 vb.
be clumsy
690 vb.
hinder 697 vb.
make ugly
837 vb.
blemish 840 vb.
disentitle 911 vb.

impairment
impairment
650 n.

impassive
inert 170 adj.
still 261 adj.
unfeeling 370 adj.
incurious 449 adj.
inattentive
451 adj.
indiscriminating
459 adj.
unintelligible
512 adj.
nonactive
672 adj.
inactive 674 adj.
impassive
815 adj.
inexcitable
818 adj.
indifferent
855 adj.
unkind 893 adj.
pitiless 901 adj.
pure 945 adj.

impel
be vigorous
169 vb.
move 260 vb.
transpose 267 vb.
impel 274 vb.
propel 282 vb.
repel 287 vb.
insert 298 vb.
fell 306 vb.
lower 306 vb.
motivate 607 vb.
be active 673 vb.
attack 707 vb.

impelling
impelling 274 adj.

impend
impend 150 vb.

impending
future 119 adj.
impending
150 adj.
approaching
284 adj.
arriving 290 adj.
probable 466 adj.
expected 502 adj.
preparatory
664 adj.
threatening
895 adj.

impenitence
impenitence
935 n.

impenitent
obstinate
597 adj.
impenitent
935 adj.

impenitent, be
be obstinate
597 vb.
be impenitent
935 vb.

impenitently
impenitently
935 adv.

imperfect
inferior 35 adj.
fragmentary
53 adj.
incomplete
55 adj.
crippled 158 adj.
deformed
241 adj.
deficient 302 adj.
inelegant 571 adj.
bad 640 adj.
imperfect
642 adj.
immature
665 adj.
bungled 690 adj.
uncompleted
721 adj.
blemished
840 adj.
frail 929 adj.

imperfect, be
not suffice
631 vb.
be imperfect
642 vb.
be middling
727 vb.

imperfection
imperfection
642 n.

imperfectly
imperfectly
642 adv.

imperspicuity
imperspicuity
563 n.

impertinent
impertinent
873 adj.
discourteous
880 adj.
disrespectful
916 adj.

impiety
misuse 670 n.
undueness 911 n.
disrespect 916 n.
wickedness 929 n.

irreligion 968 n.
impiety 974 n.

impious
impious 974 adj.

impious, be
be impious
974 vb.

impious person
impious person
974 n.

implant
implant 298 vb.
cultivate 365 vb.

imply
be intrinsic 5 vb.
evidence 461 vb.
make likely
466 vb.
mean 509 vb.
imply 518 vb.

impolitely
impolitely
880 adv.

importance
importance
633 n.

important
substantial 3 adj.
relative 9 adj.
great 32 adj.
superior 34 adj.
supreme 34 adj.
crucial 132 adj.
eventful 149 adj.
fundamental
151 adj.
influential
173 adj.
meaningful
509 adj.
important
633 adj.
best 639 adj.
hasty 675 adj.
directing 684 adj.
noteworthy
861 adj.

important, be
come first 34 vb.
influence 173 vb.
be important
633 vb.

importantly
importantly
633 adv.

important matter
reality 1 n.
needfulness
622 n.
important matter
633 n.

impose a duty
command 732 vb.
compel 735 vb.
impose a duty
912 vb.

impossibility
impossibility
465 n.

impossible
unapt 25 adj.
prodigious 32 adj.
excluded 57 adj.
unusual 84 adj.
unthought
445 adj.
impossible
465 adj.
improbable
467 adj.

unbelieved
481 adj.
difficult **695** adj.
prohibiting
752 adj.
refused **755** adj.
unpromising
848 adj.

impossible, be
be impossible
465 vb.

impossibly
impossibly
465 adv.

impostor
imitator **20** n.
substitute **145** n.
sciolist **488** n.
ambush **522** n.
hider **522** n.
sham **537** n.
impostor **540** n.
bungler **692** n.
affecter **845** n.
boaster **872** n.
usurper **911** n.

impotence
impotence **156** n.

impotent
impotent **156** adj.
crippled **158** adj.
weak **158** adj.
unproductive
167 adj.
unimportant
634 adj.
useless **636** adj.
nonactive
672 adj.
unskilful **690** adj.

impotent, be
be impotent
156 vb.
be lax **729** vb.

impoverish
abate **37** vb.
defeat **722** vb.
not retain
774 vb.
assign **775** vb.
fleece **781** vb.
impoverish
796 vb.

impracticable
closed **259** adj.
impracticable
465 adj.

impress
be vigorous
169 vb.
influence **173** vb.
attract **286** vb.
cause feeling
369 vb.
cause thought
444 vb.
attract notice
450 vb.
surprise **503** vb.
motivate **607** vb.
subjugate **740** vb.
feel **813** vb.
impress **816** vb.
delight **821** vb.
sadden **829** vb.
frighten **849** vb.
be wonderful
859 vb.
command respect
915 vb.

impressed
impressed
813 adj.

impressible
impressible
814 adj.

impressive
great **32** adj.
prodigious **32** adj.
influential
173 adj.
striking **369** adj.
forceful **566** adj.
notable **633** adj.
felt **813** adj.
impressive
816 adj.
frightening
849 adj.
wonderful
859 adj.
worshipful
861 adj.
proud **866** adj.
respected
915 adj.

imprison
hold within
219 vb.
circumscribe
227 vb.
enclose **230** vb.
close **259** vb.
safeguard **655** vb.
subjugate **740** vb.
imprison **742** vb.
retain **773** vb.
seclude **878** vb.
punish **958** vb.

imprisoned
imprisoned
742 adj.

improbability
improbability
467 n.

improbable
prodigious **32** adj.
unusual **84** adj.
improbable
467 adj.
uncertain
469 adj.
erroneous
490 adj.
unexpected
503 adj.
wonderful
859 adj.

improbity
improbity **925** n.

improved
improved
649 adj.

improvement
improvement
649 n.

improving
improving
649 adj.

improvise
imagine **508** vb.
represent **546** vb.
orate **574** vb.
improvise **604** vb.
be unprepared
665 vb.

improviser
improviser **604** n.

impulse
energy **155** n.
influence **173** n.

spurt **272** n.
impulse **274** n.
propulsion **282** n.
lowering **306** n.
agitation **313** n.
gesture **542** n.
desire **854** n.

impure
undisguised
517 adj.
not nice **640** adj.
unclean **644** adj.
free **739** adj.
vulgar **842** adj.
disreputable
862 adj.
erotic **882** adj.
sensual **939** adj.
impure **946** adj.

impure, be
desire **854** vb.
be intemperate
938 vb.
be impure
946 vb.

impurely
impurely **946** adv.

impurity
impurity **946** n.

inaction
helplessness
156 n.
inertness **170** n.
nonuse **669** n.
inaction **672** n.
inactivity **674** n.

inactive
inactive **674** adj.

inactive, be
be inactive
674 vb.

inactively
inactively
170 adv.

inactivity
inactivity **674** n.

in addition
in addition
38 adv.

in adversity
in adversity
726 adv.

inadvertently
inadvertently
451 adv.

in aid of
in aid of **698** adv.

in and out
in and out
246 adv.

inaptitude
inaptitude **25** n.
impotence **156** n.
inexpedience
638 n.

in a state of, be
be in a state of
7 vb.

inattention
changeableness
147 n.
changeable thing
147 n.
blindness **434** n.
absence of
thought **445** n.
attention **450** n.
inattention
451 n.
negligence **453** n.
mistake **490** n.

folly **494** n.
visionary **508** n.
restlessness
673 n.
bungling **690** n.
noncompletion
721 n.
moral insensibility
815 n.
wit **834** n.
rashness **852** n.
indifference
855 n.
rudeness **880** n.
improbity **925** n.

inattentive
inattentive
451 adj.

inattentive, be
be inattentive
451 vb.

in at the death
in at the death
357 adv.

inborn capacity or tendency
heredity **5** n.

incendiarism
incendiarism
376 n.

incentive
stimulant **169** n.
sharp point
251 n.
impulse **274** n.
incentive **607** n.
shekels **792** n.
discount **805** n.
excitant **816** n.
reward **957** n.
reward **957** n.

incidentally
incidentally
132 adv.

incite
make violent
171 vb.
impel **274** vb.
incite **607** vb.
hasten **675** vb.
advise **686** vb.
excite **816** vb.
give courage
850 vb.

incline
high land **204** n.
lowness **205** n.
incline **215** n.
ascent **303** n.
descent **304** n.

included
included **78** n.

included, be
be included
78 vb.

including
including **78** adv.

inclusion
inclusion **78** n.

inclusive
extensive **32** adj.
comprehensive
52 adj.
complete **54** adj.
composing
56 adj.
inclusive **78** adv.

in cold blood
in cold blood
815 adv.

incombustibility
incombustibility
377 n.

incombustible
incombustible
377 adj.

incomer
incomer 292 n.

in comfort
in comfort
371 adv.

incoming
extraneous
59 adj.
incoming 292 adj.
flowing 345 adj.

in common
in common
770 adv.

incomplete
incomplete
55 adj.
amorphous
239 adj.
deficient 302 adj.
insufficient
631 adj.
imperfect
642 adj.
uncompleted
721 adj.

incomplete, be
be incomplete
55 vb.
be unprepared
665 vb.

incompletely
incompletely
55 adv.

incompleteness
incompleteness
55 n.

inconsiderable
inconsiderable
33 adj.
lesser 35 adj.
little 191 adj.
unimportant
634 adj.

in control
in control
684 adv.

increase
finite quantity
26 n.
greatness 32 n.
increase 36 n.
addition 38 n.
adjunct 40 n.
continuity 71 n.
series 71 n.
crowd 74 n.
conversion 142 n.
growth 152 n.
production 159 n.
propagation
162 n.
stimulation
169 n.
expansion 192 n.
ascent 303 n.
redundance
632 n.
improvement
649 n.
gain 766 n.
aggravation
827 n.

increasing
increasing 36 adj.

incredibly
incredibly
481 adv.

increment
increment 36 n.
remainder 41 n.
accumulation
74 n.
gain 766 n.

incur a duty
be liable 175 vb.
busy oneself
617 vb.
undertake
667 vb.
direct 684 vb.
promise 759 vb.
be in debt
798 vb.
incur a duty
912 vb.

incur blame
be imperfect
642 vb.
displease 822 vb.
cause discontent
824 vb.
cause dislike
856 vb.
be wonderful
859 vb.
lose repute
862 vb.
shame 862 vb.
excite hate
883 vb.
incur blame
919 vb.

incuriosity
incuriosity 449 n.

incurious
incurious 449 adj.

incurious, be
be incurious
449 vb.

in danger, be
be in danger
656 vb.

in debt, be
be in debt
798 vb.

indebted
indebted 798 adj.
nonpaying
800 adj.

in deduction
in deduction
39 adv.

in defiance of
in defiance of
25 adv.

independence
independence
739 n.

independent
unconformable
84 adj.
governmental
728 adj.
independent
739 adj.
unwedded
890 adj.

indicate
relate 9 vb.
come before
64 vb.
specify 80 vb.
orientate 276 vb.
point to 276 vb.

attract notice
450 vb.
evidence 461 vb.
predict 506 vb.
mean 509 vb.
manifest 517 vb.
show 517 vb.
inform 519 vb.
indicate 542 vb.
direct 684 vb.
dignify 861 vb.

indicating
indicating
542 adj.

indication
indication 542 n.

indicator
degree 27 n.
indicator 542 n.
warning 659 n.

indict
indict 923 vb.
litigate 954 vb.

indifference
indifference
855 n.

indifferent
unrelated 10 adj.
inert 170 adj.
moderate
172 adj.
quiescent
261 adj.
incurious 449 adj.
inattentive
451 adj.
negligent 453 adj.
inexpectant
503 adj.
irresolute
596 adj.
choiceless
601 adj.
neutral 620 adj.
nonactive
672 adj.
inactive 674 adj.
lax 729 adj.
independent
739 adj.
apathetic
815 adj.
impassive
815 adj.
inexcitable
818 adj.
bored 833 adj.
indifferent
855 adj.
disliking 856 adj.
unastonished
860 adj.
unsociable
878 adj.
discourteous
880 adj.
wicked 929 adj.
irreligious
968 adj.

indifferent, be
be incurious
449 vb.
disregard 453 vb.
dissent 484 vb.
not know 486 vb.
negate 528 vb.
be neutral
601 vb.
relinquish 616 vb.
not act 672 vb.
submit 716 vb.

not retain
774 vb.
be insensitive
815 vb.
be indifferent
855 vb.
be insolent
873 vb.

in difficulties
in difficulties
695 adj.

in difficulty, be
be in difficulty
695 vb.

indignity
annoyance 822 n.
ridicule 846 n.
slur 862 n.
humiliation 867 n.
sauciness 873 n.
rudeness 880 n.
anger 886 n.
resentment
886 n.
scurrility 894 n.
indignity 916 n.
contempt 917 n.
reproach 919 n.
calumny 921 n.
accusation 923 n.

indiscriminate
mixed 43 adj.
indiscriminate
459 adj.
designless
613 adj.

indiscriminating
indiscriminating
459 adj.

indiscrimination
indiscrimination
459 n.

indissoluble
indissoluble
319 adj.

indistinct
indistinct
439 adj.

indivisible
indivisible 52 adj.

indoor game
indoor game
832 n.

induce
cause 151 vb.
influence 173 vb.
induce 607 vb.
aid 698 vb.
request 756 vb.

induced
induced 607 adj.

induced, be
be induced
607 vb.

inducement
conversion 142 n.
causation 151 n.
influence 173 n.
attraction 286 n.
inattention
451 n.
inducement
607 n.
cooperation
701 n.
offer 754 n.
gift 776 n.
trade 786 n.
purchase 787 n.
excitation 816 n.
courage 850 n.

liking 854 n.
sorcery 977 n.

inducing
inducing 607 adj.

industrious
unyielding
157 adj.
vigorous 169 adj.
attentive
450 adj.
careful 452 adj.
studious 531 adj.
persevering
595 adj.
industrious
673 adj.
labouring
677 adj.

in earshot
in earshot
410 adv.

inebriate
invigorate
169 vb.
inebriate 944 vb.

ineffectuality
ineffectuality
156 n.

inelegance
inelegance 571 n.

inelegant
unapt 25 adj.
unclear 563 adj.
inelegant 571 adj.
clumsy 690 adj.
dull 835 adj.
graceless 837 adj.
vulgar 842 adj.

inequality
unrelatedness
10 n.
difference 15 n.
dissimilarity 19 n.
disagreement
25 n.
inequality 29 n.
superiority 34 n.
changeableness
147 n.
weakness 158 n.
distortion 241 n.
bias 476 n.
injustice 909 n.

inert
weakened
158 adj.
inert 170 adj.
quiescent
261 adj.
latent 518 adj.
irresolute
596 adj.
nonactive
672 adj.
inactive 674 adj.
apathetic
815 adj.
inexcitable
818 adj.

inert, be
be inert 170 vb.
be quiescent
261 vb.
lurk 518 vb.
not act 672 vb.

inertness
inertness 170 n.

inexact
general 79 adj.
deviating
277 adj.

negligent 453 adj.
indiscriminating
459 adj.
inexact 490 adj.
interpretive
515 adj.
clumsy 690 adj.

inexactness
inexactness
490 n.

in exchange
in exchange
146 adv.

inexcitability
inexcitability
818 n.

inexcitable
inexcitable
818 adj.

inexpectant
inexpectant
503 adj.

inexpedience
inexpedience
638 n.

inexpedient
unapt 25 adj.
ill-timed 133 adj.
unwise 494 adj.
rejected 602 adj.
useless 636 adj.
inexpedient
638 adj.
harmful 640 adj.
unused 669 adj.
hindering
697 adj.
discreditable
862 adj.
undue 911 adj.

inexpedient, be
be inexpedient
638 vb.

inexpressible
unspeakable
32 adj.
unusual 84 adj.
inexpressible
512 adj.
wonderful
859 adj.

infantine
infantine 127 adj.

infantry
pedestrian 263 n.
infantry 717 n.

in fashion, be
be in fashion
843 vb.

infection
excretion 297 n.
badness 640 n.
sink 644 n.
uncleanness
644 n.
infection 646 n.
insalubrity 648 n.
impairment
650 n.
poison 654 n.
poisoning 654 n.
pitfall 658 n.

infectious
mixed 43 adj.
influential
173 adj.
transferable
267 adj.
unclean 644 adj.
infectious
648 adj.

inferior
extrinsic 6 adj.
different 15 adj.
dissimilar 19 adj.
unequal 29 adj.
inconsiderable
33 adj.
inferior 35 n.
inferior 35 adj.
low 205 adj.
back 233 adj.
human 366 adj.
insufficient
631 adj.
nonentity 634 n.
unimportant
634 adj.
bad 640 adj.
imperfect
642 adj.
loser 723 n.
defeated 723 adj.
unlucky person
726 n.
middling 727 adj.
dependant 737 n.
servant 737 n.
subject 740 adj.
poor person
796 n.
commoner 864 n.
lower classes
864 n.
plebeian 864 adj.

inferior, be
be unlike 19 vb.
be unequal 29 vb.
be inferior 35 vb.
descend 304 vb.
not suffice
631 vb.
obey 734 vb.
be subject
740 vb.
have no repute
862 vb.

inferiority
inferiority 35 n.

infernal
infernal 966 adj.

infiltrate
be mixed 43 vb.
pervade 184 vb.
introduce 226 vb.
infiltrate 292 vb.
infuse 298 vb.
descend 304 vb.
be wet 336 vb.
irrigate 336 vb.

infinite
absolute 32 adj.
many 100 adj.
multitudinous
100 adj.
infinite 103 adj.
spacious 178 adj.
huge 190 adj.
godlike 960 adj.

infinitely
infinitely 103 adv.

infinity
quantity 26 n.
greatness 32 n.
infinity 103 n.
perpetuity 110 n.
space 178 n.
divine attribute
960 n.

in flight
in flight 266 adv.

influence
relativeness 9 n.
be related 9 vb.
greatness 32 n.
superiority 34 n.
component 58 n.
come before
64 vb.
modify 138 vb.
conversion 142 n.
convert 142 vb.
causation 151 n.
cause 151 n.
cause 151 vb.
effect 152 n.
power 155 n.
agency 168 n.
operate 168 vb.
be vigorous
169 vb.
influence 173 n.
influence 173 vb.
tendency 174 n.
tend 174 vb.
pervade 184 vb.
transference
267 n.
transfer 267 vb.
evidence 461 vb.
bias 476 vb.
convince 480 vb.
latency 518 n.
teach 529 vb.
habituate 605 vb.
inducement
607 n.
motivator 612 n.
motivate 607 vb.
plot 618 vb.
instrumentality
623 n.
be instrumental
623 vb.
bigwig 633 n.
be important
633 vb.
improvement
649 n.
make better
649 vb.
troublemaker
658 n.
action 671 n.
do 671 vb.
manage 684 vb.
director 685 n.
cunning 693 n.
aid 698 n.
be successful
722 vb.
authority 728 n.
dominate 728 vb.
subjugate 740 vb.
excitation 816 n.
excite 816 vb.
impress 816 vb.
prestige 861 n.

influential
influential
173 adj.

influentially
influentially
173 adv.

inform
interpret 515 vb.
inform 519 vb.
disclose 521 vb.
divulge 521 vb.
publish 523 vb.
educate 529 vb.
indicate 542 vb.

in rebuttal
in rebuttal
474 adv.
in reply
in reply 455 adv.
in return
in return 31 adv.
insalubrious
sealed off
259 adj.
deadly 357 adj.
warm 374 adj.
inexpedient
638 adj.
harmful 640 adj.
unclean 644 adj.
insalubrious
648 adj.
dangerous
656 adj.
impure 946 adj.
insalubrity
insalubrity 648 n.
insane
disarranged
63 adj.
mindless 443 adj.
unintelligent
494 adj.
insane 498 adj.
insane, be
be absurd
492 vb.
be foolish 494 vb.
be insane 498 vb.
be in love 882 vb.
insanity
insanity 498 n.
in search of
in search of
454 adv.
insect
insect 360 n.
dirt 644 n.
bane 654 n.
noxious animal
899 n.
insensibility
helplessness
156 n.
weakness 158 n.
inertness 170 n.
quiescence 261 n.
insensibility
370 n.
ignorance 486 n.
fantasy 508 n.
illness 646 n.
nervous disorders
646 n.
inaction 672 n.
sleep 674 n.
sluggishness
674 n.
fatigue 679 n.
moral insensibility
815 n.
occultism 978 n.
insensible
impotent 156 adj.
inert 170 adj.
still 261 adj.
slow 273 adj.
insensible
370 adj.
ignorant 486 adj.
sick 646 adj.
remedial 653 adj.
nonactive
672 adj.
inactive 674 adj.

apathetic
815 adj.
impassive
815 adj.
drugged 944 adj.
insensible, be
be impotent
156 vb.
be insensible
370 vb.
be insensitive
815 vb.
insensitive, be
be insensible
370 vb.
be incurious
449 vb.
be insensitive
815 vb.
keep calm
818 vb.
not wonder
860 vb.
inseparably
inseparably
45 adv.
insert
add 38 vb.
mix 43 vb.
affix 45 vb.
join 45 vb.
fill 54 vb.
place 182 vb.
load 188 vb.
hold within
219 vb.
cover 221 vb.
line 222 vb.
introduce 226 vb.
enter 292 vb.
admit 294 vb.
insert 298 vb.
inserted
inserted 298 adj.
insertion
insertion 298 n.
inside
inside 219 adv.
inside, be
be inside 219 vb.
insides
insides 219 n.
insipidity
insipidity 382 n.
in small compass
in small compass
191 adv.
insolence
insolence 873 n.
insolent
defiant 706 adj.
anarchic 729 adj.
authoritarian
730 adj.
rash 852 adj.
proud 866 adj.
vain 868 adj.
insolent 873 adj.
unwarranted
911 adj.
disrespectful
916 adj.
despising 917 adj.
insolent, be
defy 706 vb.
be free 739 vb.
be proud 866 vb.
be insolent
873 vb.
be rude 880 vb.
hate 883 vb.

be undue 911 vb.
not respect
916 vb.
accuse 923 vb.
insolently
insolently
873 adv.
insolent person
insolent person
873 n.
rude person
880 n.
insolvency
insolvency 800 n.
inspection
inspection 433 n.
instant
small quantity
33 n.
date 104 n.
brief span 109 n.
instant 111 n.
instantaneity
instantaneity
111 n.
instantaneous
instantaneous
111 adj.
instantaneously
instantaneously
111 adv.
instead
instead 145 adv.
instructed
instructed
485 adj.
instrument
inferior 35 n.
dupe 544 n.
contrivance
618 n.
instrument 623 n.
means 624 n.
tool 625 n.
nonentity 634 n.
agent 681 n.
aider 698 n.
auxiliary 702 n.
government
728 n.
dependant 737 n.
slave 737 n.
toady 874 n.
instrumental
instrumental
623 adj.
mechanical
625 adj.
useful 635 adj.
used 668 adj.
aiding 698 adj.
instrumental, be
conduce 151 vb.
be instrumental
623 vb.
minister to
698 vb.
be subject
740 vb.
be servile 874 vb.
instrumentalist
instrumentalist
408 n.
instrumentality
instrumentality
623 n.
instrument of
torture
compressor
193 n.
pain 372 n.

instrument of
torture 959 n.
insubstantial
unreal 2 adj.
insubstantial
4 adj.
inconsiderable
33 adj.
incomplete
55 adj.
not one 99 adj.
transient 109 adj.
powerless
156 adj.
flimsy 158 adj.
weak 158 adj.
shallow 207 adj.
immaterial
315 adj.
rare 320 adj.
brittle 325 adj.
airy 335 adj.
shadowy 414 adj.
imaginary
508 adj.
insufficient
631 adj.
trivial 634 adj.
unimportant
634 adj.
insubstantiality
insubstantiality
4 n.
insubstantial thing
nonexistence 2 n.
insubstantial
thing 4 n.
small quantity
33 n.
brief span 109 n.
ineffectuality
156 n.
weak thing 158 n.
lightness 318 n.
transparency
417 n.
sham 537 n.
nonentity 634 n.
vain person
868 n.
insufficiency
insufficiency
631 n.
insufficient
unequal 29 adj.
small 33 adj.
inferior 35 adj.
fragmentary
53 adj.
incomplete
55 adj.
powerless
156 adj.
unproductive
167 adj.
short 199 adj.
deficient 302 adj.
disappointing
504 adj.
insufficient
631 adj.
inexpedient
638 adj.
imperfect
642 adj.
unskilful 690 adj.
discontenting
824 adj.
disapproved
919 adj.

insufficiently
insufficiently
631 adv.

insular
insular 344 adj.

in sum
in sum 587 adv.

in suspense
in suspense
469 adv.

intact
intact 52 adj.
complete 54 adj.
perfect 641 adj.
undamaged
641 adj.

intellect
intellect 442 n.
thought 444 n.
idea 446 n.
knowledge 485 n.
intelligence
493 n.
intention 612 n.

intellectual
philosopher
444 n.
reasoner 470 n.
erudition 485 n.
intellectual
487 n.
sage 495 n.

intelligence
head 208 n.
intellect 442 n.
discrimination
458 n.
intelligence
493 n.
wit 834 n.

intelligent
intelligent
493 adj.

intelligibility
intelligibility
511 n.

intelligible
simple 44 adj.
orderly 60 adj.
positive 468 adj.
known 490 adj.
sane 497 adj.
semantic 509 adj.
intelligible
511 adj.
manifest 517 adj.
veracious
535 adj.
perspicuous
562 adj.
easy 696 adj.

intelligible, be
be intelligible
511 vb.
interpret 515 vb.
be plain 517 vb.
speak plainly
568 vb.
be easy 696 vb.
impress 816 vb.

intelligibly
intelligibly
511 adv.

intemperance
intemperance
938 n.

intemperate
selfish 927 adj.
intemperate
938 adj.
sensual 939 adj.

drunken 944 adj.

intemperate, be
overstep 301 vb.
superabound
632 vb.
please oneself
729 vb.
be intemperate
938 vb.
be sensual
939 vb.
be impure
946 vb.

intemperately
intemperately
938 adv.

intend
be mindful
450 vb.
expect 502 vb.
will 590 vb.
be willing 592 vb.
be resolute
594 vb.
predetermine
603 vb.
intend 612 vb.
pursue 614 vb.
plan 618 vb.
attempt 666 vb.
promise 759 vb.
hope 847 vb.
desire 854 vb.

intended
intended 612 adj.

intending
intending
612 adj.

intention
destiny 150 n.
expectation
502 n.
will 590 n.
predetermination
603 n.
intention 612 n.
business 617 n.
plan 618 n.
promise 759 n.
aspiration 847 n.
liking 854 n.

inter
inter 359 vb.

interchange
correlation 12 n.
correlate 12 vb.
equalization 28 n.
equivalence 28 n.
compensation
31 n.
offset 31 n.
union 45 n.
derangement
63 n.
jumble 63 vb.
change 138 n.
modify 138 vb.
substitution
145 n.
substitute
145 vb.
interchange
146 n.
interchange
146 vb.
displacement
183 n.
displace 183 vb.
inversion 216 n.
invert 216 vb.

be in motion
260 vb.
move 260 vb.
transference
267 n.
transpose 267 vb.
deflect 277 vb.
transfer 775 vb.
assign 775 vb.
barter 786 n.
trade 786 vb.

interchanged
interchanged
146 adj.

interest
interest 798 n.

interfere
discontinue
72 vb.
interfere 226 vb.

interim
interim 104 n.
period 106 n.
transience 109 n.
lull 140 n.
interval 196 n.
repose 678 n.

interior
intrinsic 5 adj.
included 78 adj.
interior 219 adj.

interiority
interiority 219 n.

interjacency
interjacency
226 n.

interjacent
interjacent
226 adj.

interjection
irrelevance 10 n.
discontinuity
72 n.
interjection
226 n.
insertion 298 n.

interjector
interjector 226 n.

interlocution
interlocution
579 n.

interlocutor
interlocutor
579 n.

intermediary
joining together
45 n.
intermediary
226 n.
informant 519 n.
messenger 524 n.
speaker 574 n.
mediator 715 n.
consignee 749 n.

intermediate
intermediate
104 adj.

interment
interment 359 n.

in terms
in terms 558 adv.

interpret
copy 20 vb.
unravel 62 vb.
specify 80 vb.
account for
153 vb.
hear 410 vb.
answer 455 vb.
reason 470 vb.

be intelligible
511 vb.
interpret 515 vb.
manifest 517 vb.
teach 529 vb.
parse 559 vb.
dissertate
586 vb.
facilitate 696 vb.

interpretation
imitation 20 n.
transformation
138 n.
reason why
151 n.
attribution 153 n.
listening 410 n.
answer 455 n.
estimate 475 n.
discovery 479 n.
connotation
509 n.
intelligibility
511 n.
metaphor 514 n.
interpretation
515 n.
hint 519 n.
indication 542 n.
literature 552 n.

interpreted
interpreted
515 adj.

interpreter
interpreter 515 n.

interpretive
interpretive
515 adj.

interrogate
hear 410 vb.
be curious
448 vb.
interrogate
454 vb.

interrogation
interrogation
454 n.

interval
incompleteness
55 n.
interval 196 n.
interiority 219 n.
concavity 250 n.

in the act
in the act
671 adv.

in the future
in the future
150 adv.

in the trough
in the trough
209 adv.

in threes
in threes 93 adv.

in time
in time 107 adv.

intimidation
intimidation
849 n.

intolerable
exorbitant
32 adj.
bad 640 adj.
intolerable
822 adj.
disliked 856 adj.

intoxicating
intoxicating
944 adj.

in trade
in trade 786 adv.

in transit
in transit
267 adv.
intricate
mixed 43 adj.
intricate 246 adj.
difficult 695 adj.
intrinsic
existing 1 adj.
substantial 3 adj.
intrinsic 5 adj.
inimitable 21 adj.
simple 44 adj.
joined 45 adj.
combined 50 adj.
component
58 adj.
included 78 adj.
fundamental
151 adj.
interior 219 adj.
interior 219 adj.
habitual 605 adj.
with affections
812 adj.
intrinsicality
intrinsicality 5 n.
intrinsically
intrinsically
5 adv.
intrinsic, be
be 1 vb.
be intrinsic 5 vb.
contain 56 vb.
be one of 58 vb.
be included
78 vb.
accompany
89 vb.
conduce 151 vb.
introduce
introduce 226 vb.
intrude
interfere 226 vb.
intrude 292 vb.
encroach 301 vb.
meddle 673 vb.
obstruct 697 vb.
intruder
intruder 59 n.
intuit
intuit 471 vb.
intuition
intellect 442 n.
absence of
intellect 443 n.
absence of
thought 445 n.
empiricism 456 n.
reasoning 470 n.
intuition 471 n.
sophistry 472 n.
judgment 475 n.
belief 480 n.
knowledge 485 n.
intelligence
493 n.
conjecture 507 n.
supposition
507 n.
necessity 591 n.
spontaneity
604 n.
occultism 978 n.
psychics 978 n.
intuitive
intuitive 471 adj.
intuitively
intuitively
471 adv.

inutility
inutility 636 n.
inversely
inversely 216 adv.
inversion
inversion 216 n.
invert
be contrary
14 vb.
bedevil 63 vb.
derange 63 vb.
modify 138 vb.
revert 143 vb.
revolutionize
144 vb.
demolish 160 vb.
invert 216 vb.
make curved
243 vb.
navigate 264 vb.
lower 306 vb.
inverted
inverted 216 adj.
inverted, be
be inverted
216 vb.
invigilate
scan 433 vb.
invigilate 452 vb.
manage 684 vb.
invigorate
augment 36 vb.
cause 151 vb.
strengthen
157 vb.
operate 168 vb.
invigorate
169 vb.
promote 280 vb.
vitalize 355 vb.
cultivate 365 vb.
cause feeling
369 vb.
incite 607 vb.
mature 664 vb.
refresh 680 vb.
animate 816 vb.
cheer 828 vb.
invisibility
invisibility 439 n.
invisible
inconsiderable
33 adj.
small 33 adj.
minute 191 adj.
distant 194 adj.
shadowy 414 adj.
invisible 439 adj.
disappearing
441 adj.
neglected
453 adj.
unknown 486 adj.
unintelligible
512 adj.
latent 518 adj.
inglorious
862 adj.
invisibly
invisibly 439 adv.
involuntary
involuntary
591 adj.
unintentional
613 adj.
invulnerable
strong 157 adj.
unyielding
157 adj.
sealed off
259 adj.

certain 468 adj.
salubrious
647 adj.
invulnerable
defended 708 adj.
**invulnerable. See
fixed**
unchangeable
148 adj.
irascibility
irascibility 887 n.
irascible
violent 171 adj.
wilful 597 adj.
capricious
599 adj.
quarrelling
704 adj.
contending
711 adj.
sensitive 814 adj.
excitable 817 adj.
ungracious
880 adj.
angry 886 adj.
irascible 887 adj.
sullen 888 adj.
irascible, be
be excitable
817 vb.
be irascible
887 vb.
iridescent
mixed 43 adj.
changeful
147 adj.
iridescent
432 adj.
irrelevance
irrelevance 10 n.
irrelevant
irrelevant 10 adj.
unapt 25 adj.
misplaced
183 adj.
deviating
277 adj.
absurd 492 adj.
prolix 565 adj.
unimportant
634 adj.
irreligion
irreligion 968 n.
irreligionist
irreligionist
968 n.
irreligious
negligent 453 adj.
irreligious
968 adj.
impious 974 adj.
laical 981 adj.
irreligious, be
be irreligious
968 vb.
irresolute
changeful
147 adj.
impotent 156 adj.
weak 158 adj.
doubting 469 adj.
irresolute
596 adj.
tergiversating
598 adj.
choiceless
601 adj.
neutral 620 adj.
lax 729 adj.
nervous 849 adj.

cowardly 851 adj.
irresolute, be
conform 83 vb.
vary 147 vb.
be uncertain
469 vb.
doubt 481 vb.
be irresolute
596 vb.
tergiversate
598 vb.
be capricious
599 vb.
be neutral
601 vb.
be cowardly
851 vb.
irresolutely
irresolutely
596 adv.
irresolution
irresolution
596 n.
irrigate
irrigate 336 vb.
make flow
345 vb.
cultivate 365 vb.
irrigator
irrigator 336 n.
island
projection 249 n.
land 339 n.
island 344 n.
itch
itch 373 vb.
itinerary
itinerary 262 n.
way 619 n.

J

jacket
wrapping 221 n.
jacket 223 n.
jealous
opposing 699 adj.
loving 882 adj.
jealous 906 adj.
envious 907 adj.
selfish 927 adj.
jealous, be
contend 711 vb.
be jealous
906 vb.
jealousy
jealousy 906 n.
jerkily
jerkily 313 adv.
jersey
jersey 223 n.
jewellery
jewellery 839 n.
job
job 617 n.
join
accord 24 vb.
add 38 vb.
mix 43 vb.
join 45 vb.
agglutinate
48 vb.
combine 50 vb.
make complete
54 vb.
compose 56 vb.
bring together
74 vb.
produce 159 vb.

join a party
make smaller
193 vb.
hang 212 vb.
cross 217 vb.
introduce 226 vb.
close 259 vb.
implant 298 vb.
repair 651 vb.
join a party
accrue 38 vb.
unite with 45 vb.
be included
78 vb.
assent 483 vb.
join a party
703 vb.
sectarianize
972 vb.
joined
joined 45 adj.
joining together
joining together
45 n.
joint
joint 45 n.
bond 47 n.
fastening 47 n.
gap 196 n.
pivot 213 n.
angularity 242 n.
projection 249 n.
joint possession
store 627 n.
association
701 n.
joint possession
770 n.
lands 772 n.
journal
journal 523 n.
book 584 n.
reading matter
584 n.
joy
vigorousness
169 n.
pleasure 371 n.
excitation 816 n.
joy 819 n.
pleasurableness
821 n.
cheerfulness
828 n.
rejoicing 830 n.
jubilant
pleased 819 adj.
jubilant 828 adj.
rejoicing 830 adj.
hoping 847 adj.
judge
cause 151 vb.
notice 450 vb.
answer 455 vb.
discriminate
458 vb.
appraise 460 vb.
make certain
468 vb.
judge 475 vb.
will 590 vb.
choose 600 vb.
mediate 715 vb.
decree 732 vb.
officer 736 n.
have taste
841 vb.
be cautious
853 vb.
be just 908 vb.
law officer 950 n.

hold court
950 vb.
judge 952 vb.
try a case
954 vb.
punisher 958 n.
judgment
judgment 475 n.
judicatory
judicatory
951 adj.
judicial
discriminating
458 adj.
judicial 475 adj.
sane 497 adj.
tasteful 841 adj.
orthodox 970 adj.
jumble
mix 43 vb.
jumble 63 vb.
impair 650 vb.
jumper
jumper 307 n.
dance 832 n.
juncture
juncture 8 n.
degree 27 n.
event 149 n.
**junket. See dairy
product**
milk 296 n.
jurisdiction
authority 728 n.
law 948 n.
jurisdiction
950 n.
legal process
954 n.
jurisdictional
jurisdictional
950 adj.
jurisprudence
jurisprudence
948 n.
jurisprudential
jurisprudential
953 adj.
jurist
jurist 953 n.
jury
estimator 475 n.
jury 952 n.
just
equal 28 adj.
moderate
172 adj.
rational 470 adj.
judicial 475 adj.
wise 493 adj.
choiceless
601 adj.
neutral 620 adj.
free 739 adj.
indifferent
855 adj.
just 908 adj.
honourable
924 adj.
disinterested
926 adj.
virtuous 928 adj.
legal 948 adj.
just, be
discriminate
458 vb.
be just 908 vb.
grant claims
910 vb.
be honourable
924 vb.

be virtuous
928 vb.
justice
equality 28 n.
judgment 475 n.
no choice 601 n.
indifference
855 n.
justice 908 n.
probity 924 n.
disinterestedness
926 n.
virtue 928 n.
legality 948 n.
reward 957 n.
punishment
958 n.
justify
plead 609 vb.
forgive 904 vb.
justify 922 vb.
jut
jut 249 vb.
juxtapose
connect 45 vb.
bring near
195 vb.
juxtapose 197 vb.
compare 457 vb.

K

keen
keen 169 adj.
keenness
keenness 169 n.
keep calm
keep calm
818 vb.
be courageous
850 vb.
not wonder
860 vb.
keeper
concomitant
89 n.
doorkeeper 259 n.
surveillance
452 n.
collector 487 n.
teacher 532 n.
protector 655 n.
manager 685 n.
defender 708 n.
retainer 737 n.
servant 737 n.
keeper 744 n.
consignee 749 n.
keep faith
obey 734 vb.
keep faith
763 vb.
keep secret
not know 486 vb.
keep secret
520 vb.
be mute 573 vb.
be taciturn
577 vb.
retain 773 vb.
be cautious
853 vb.
kept woman
loved one 882 n.
kept woman
947 n.
key
key 405 n.

kick
kick 274 vb.
strike at 707 vb.
kill
abate 37 vb.
disable 156 vb.
destroy 160 vb.
kill 357 vb.
hinder 697 vb.
execute 958 vb.
killer
killer 357 n.
killing
death 356 n.
killing 357 n.
capital
punishment
958 n.
kill oneself
perish 356 vb.
kill oneself
357 vb.
kind act
benefit 610 n.
aid 698 n.
liberality 808 n.
courteous act
879 n.
kind act 892 n.
kindle
make violent
171 vb.
kindle 376 vb.
fire 380 vb.
make bright
412 vb.
kind person
kind person
892 n.
philanthropist
896 n.
benefactor 898 n.
good person
932 n.
kinsman
kinsman 11 n.
knave
deceiver 540 n.
trickster 540 n.
tergiversator
598 n.
low fellow 864 n.
ruffian 899 n.
knave 933 n.
knock
end 69 n.
ruin 160 n.
knock 274 n.
propulsion 282 n.
touch 373 n.
gesture 542 n.
evil 611 n.
lunge 707 n.
corporal
punishment
958 n.
know
meet with
149 vb.
have feeling
369 vb.
see 433 vb.
cognize 442 vb.
discriminate
458 vb.
be certain
468 vb.
discover 479 vb.
know 485 vb.
be wise 493 vb.
memorize 500 vb.

latrine
vessel 189 n.
cleansing 643 n.
latrine 644 n.

latrine. See compartment
chamber 189 n.

laugh
be loud 395 vb.
cry 403 vb.
gesticulate
542 vb.
laugh 830 vb.

laugher
laugher 830 n.

laughing
laughing 830 adj.

laughingstock
misfit 25 n.
nonconformist
84 n.
fool 496 n.
crank 499 n.
dupe 539 n.
laughingstock
846 n.

laughter
loudness 395 n.
cry 403 n.
gesture 542 n.
merriment 828 n.
laughter 830 n.
festivity 832 n.
ridicule 846 n.

law
rule 81 n.
necessity 591 n.
vocation 617 n.
precept 688 n.
compulsion 735 n.
restraint 742 n.
law 948 n.

law agent
consignee 749 n.
law agent 953 n.

lawbreaking
lawbreaking
949 n.
lawbreaking
949 adj.

lawcourt
lawcourt 951 n.

lawless
riotous 733 adj.
rascally 925 adj.
lawless 949 adj.
impious 974 adj.

lawlessness
lawlessness
949 n.

law officer
messenger 524 n.
officer 736 n.
law officer 950 n.
notary 953 n.

lawyer
reasoner 470 n.
adviser 686 n.
lawyer 953 n.

lax
weak 158 adj.
inert 170 adj.
negligent 453 adj.
irresolute
596 adj.
lax 729 adj.
lenient 731 adj.
nonobservant
764 adj.
indifferent
855 adj.

benevolent
892 adj.
pitying 900 adj.
frail 929 adj.

lax, be
sustain 141 vb.
disregard 453 vb.
qualify 463 vb.
be lax 729 vb.
be lenient 731 vb.
give scope
739 vb.
liberate 741 vb.
permit 751 vb.
not observe
764 vb.
compromise
765 vb.
be patient
818 vb.
please 821 vb.
be intemperate
938 vb.

laxity
laxity 729 n.

layer
series 71 n.
compartment
189 n.
layer 202 n.
horizontality
211 n.
basis 213 n.
covering 221 n.

layered
layered 202 adj.

lay person
beginner 533 n.
lay person 981 n.

lay waste
lay waste 160 vb.
make sterile
167 vb.
be violent 171 vb.
uncover 224 vb.
waste 629 vb.
impair 650 vb.
attack 707 vb.
wage war 713 vb.
rob 783 vb.
be malevolent
893 vb.

lazy
slow 273 adj.
negligent 453 adj.
profitless
636 adj.
lazy 674 adj.

leader
living model 23 n.
superior 34 n.
precursor 66 n.
concomitant
89 n.
navigator 265 n.
motivator 607 n.
leader 685 n.
governor 736 n.
person of repute
861 n.
philanthropist
896 n.

lean
weak 158 adj.
weakly 158 adj.
exiguous 191 adj.
long 198 adj.
lean 201 adj.
deformed
241 adj.
legged 262 adj.

underfed 631 adj.
shapely 836 adj.
fasting 941 adj.
fairylike 964 adj.

leap
be curved 243 vb.
gait 260 n.
be in motion
260 vb.
walk 262 vb.
spurt 272 n.
emerge 293 vb.
overstep 301 vb.
ascent 303 n.
ascend 303 vb.
tumble 304 vb.
leap 307 n.
leap 307 vb.
oscillate 312 vb.
agitation 313 n.
be agitated
313 vb.
flow 345 vb.
ballet 589 n.
pursue 614 vb.
racing 711 n.
be excited
816 vb.
rejoice 830 vb.
children's games
832 n.
sport 832 n.
dance 832 vb.

leaping
leaping 307 n.

learn
be tentative
456 vb.
know 485 vb.
memorize 500 vb.
understand
511 vb.
be informed
519 vb.
learn 531 vb.
get better
649 vb.
prepare oneself
664 vb.
be expert 689 vb.
be penitent
934 vb.

learner
learner 533 n.

learning
erudition 485 n.
remembrance
500 n.
curriculum 529 n.
learning 531 n.
preparation
664 n.
subjection 740 n.

lease
assign 775 vb.
lease 779 vb.

leaven
cookery 296 n.
lifter 305 n.
leaven 318 n.
bubble 350 n.

leave no hope
leave no hope
848 vb.

leave over
leave over 41 vb.

leavings
leavings 41 n.

lecherous
lecherous
946 adj.

lecture
lecture 529 n.
rostrum 534 n.
oration 574 n.
dissertation
586 n.
inducement
607 n.
ministration
982 n.

left, be
be left 41 vb.
outlast 108 vb.
live 355 vb.
persevere 595 vb.
be superfluous
632 vb.

leg
limb 53 n.
stand 213 n.
leg 262 n.

legal
necessary
591 adj.
preceptive
688 adj.
permitted
751 adj.
just 908 adj.
due 910 adj.
legal 948 adj.

legal, be
be legal 948 vb.

legality
legality 948 n.

legally
legally 948 adv.

legal process
warrant 732 n.
legal process
954 n.

legal trial
listening 410 n.
enquiry 454 n.
experiment
456 n.
advice 686 n.
law 948 n.
legal trial 954 n.

legged
legged 262 adj.

legislation
management
684 n.
precept 688 n.
decree 732 n.
legislation 948 n.

legwear
legwear 223 n.

leisure
interim 104 n.
opportunity
132 n.
lull 140 n.
slowness 273 n.
inaction 672 n.
inactivity 674 n.
leisure 676 n.
repose 678 n.
resignation 748 n.
pleasurableness
821 n.
amusement
832 n.
holy day 982 n.

leisurely
ageing 126 adj.
tranquil 261 adj.
slow 273 adj.
nonactive
672 adj.

inactive 674 adj.
lazy 674 adj.
leisurely 676 adj.
reposeful 678 adj.
free 739 adj.

lend
aid 698 vb.
assign 775 vb.
lend 779 vb.
credit 797 vb.

lender
lender 779 n.

lending
lending 779 n.
lending 779 adj.

length
quantity 26 n.
greatness 32 n.
measure 178 n.
size 190 n.
distance 194 n.
length 198 n.
depth 206 n.

lengthen
augment 36 vb.
continue 71 vb.
spin out 108 vb.
enlarge 192 vb.
lengthen 198 vb.
make thin
        201 vb.
be diffuse
        565 vb.

lengthening
lengthening
        198 n.

leniency
leniency 731 n.

lenient
moderate
        172 adj.
lax 729 adj.
lenient 731 adj.
permitting
        751 adj.
inexcitable
        818 adj.
content 823 adj.
amiable 879 adj.
benevolent
        892 adj.
pitying 900 adj.
forgiving 904 adj.

lenient, be
be moderate
        172 vb.
pacify 714 vb.
be lax 729 vb.
be lenient 731 vb.
permit 751 vb.
consent 753 vb.
give 776 vb.
be patient
        818 vb.
show mercy
        900 vb.
forgive 904 vb.
exempt 914 vb.
extenuate
        922 vb.

lenitive
lenitive 172 adj.

less
less 35 adv.

lesser
small 33 adj.
lesser 35 adj.

let fall
be deep 206 vb.
move 260 vb.
insert 298 vb.

let fall 306 vb.
make flow
        345 vb.
be clumsy
        690 vb.

letter
list 87 n.
indication 542 n.
letter 553 n.
lettering 581 n.
print-type 582 n.

lettering
unintelligibility
        512 n.
letter 553 n.
lettering 581 n.

letterpress
letterpress 582 n.

levy
beg 756 vb.
request 756 vb.
levy 781 vb.
tax 804 vb.
claim 910 vb.

liability
liability 175 n.

liable
tending 174 vb.
liable 175 adj.
probable 466 adj.
vulnerable
        656 adj.
subject 740 adj.
guilty 931 adj.

liable, be
be liable 175 vb.
be in danger
        656 vb.

liar
liar 540 n.
exaggeration
        541 n.
boaster 872 n.

liberal
plenteous
        630 adj.
giving 776 adj.
expending
        801 adj.
liberal 808 adj.
prodigal 810 adj.
ostentatious
        870 adj.
benevolent
        892 adj.
rewarding
        957 adj.

liberal, be
superabound
        632 vb.
give 776 vb.
expend 801 vb.
be liberal 808 vb.
be hospitable
        877 vb.
reward 957 vb.

liberality
giving 776 n.
liberality 808 n.
sociability 877 n.
benevolence
        892 n.

liberally
liberally 808 adv.

liberate
disunite 46 vb.
exclude 57 vb.
revert 143 vb.
extract 299 vb.
restore 651 vb.
deliver 663 vb.

give scope
        739 vb.
liberate 741 vb.
permit 751 vb.
not retain
        774 vb.
exempt 914 vb.
acquit 955 vb.

liberated
disunited 46 adj.
nonadhesive
        49 adj.
free 739 adj.
liberated 741 adj.
not retained
        774 adj.
acquitted
        955 adj.
sanctified
        973 adj.

liberation
separation 46 n.
exclusion 57 n.
transference
        267 n.
escape 662 n.
deliverance
        663 n.
facility 696 n.
laxity 729 n.
freedom 739 n.
liberation 741 n.
permission 751 n.
loss 767 n.
nonretention
        774 n.
nonliability 914 n.
acquittal 955 n.

libertine
libertine 947 n.

libido
libido 854 n.
love 882 n.
unchastity 946 n.

library
accumulation
        74 n.
erudition 485 n.
library 584 n.

lie between
lie between
        226 vb.
obstruct 697 vb.

life
existence 1 n.
substance 3 n.
vitality 157 n.
blood 330 n.
organism 353 n.
life 355 n.
restlessness
        673 n.
cheerfulness
        828 n.

lifelike
lifelike 18 adj.

lifter
lifter 305 n.

lift oneself
be high 204 vb.
ascend 303 vb.
lift oneself
        305 vb.

ligature
ligature 47 n.

light
insubstantial
        4 adj.
unequal 29 adj.
small 33 adj.
morning 123 n.

weak 158 adj.
ascending
        303 adj.
light 318 adj.
rare 320 adj.
bubbly 350 adj.
light 412 n.
glimmer 414 n.
lighting 415 n.
luminary 415 n.
whiteness 422 n.
variegation
        432 n.
metrology 460 n.
spurious 537 adj.
trivial 634 adj.
beauty 836 n.
revelation 969 n.

light, be
be unequal 29 vb.
be small 33 vb.
decrease 37 vb.
become small
        193 vb.
fly 266 vb.
be light 318 vb.

light contrast
light contrast
        412 n.

lighten
abate 37 vb.
make smaller
        193 vb.
lighten 318 vb.

lighter
burning 376 n.
furnace 378 n.
lighter 380 n.
torch 415 n.

lighting
light 412 n.
lighting 415 n.

light-minded
light-minded
        451 adj.

lightness
lightness 318 n.

likely, be
tend 174 vb.
be possible
        464 vb.
be likely 466 vb.
be reasonable
        470 vb.
give hope 847 vb.

liken
liken 18 vb.

liking
liking 854 n.

limb
adjunct 40 n.
limb 53 n.
extremity 69 n.
propeller 264 n.

limit
finite quantity
        26 n.
separation 46 n.
completeness
        54 n.
entrance 68 n.
extremity 69 n.
specify 80 vb.
region 179 n.
place 180 n.
farness 194 n.
contiguity 197 n.
summit 208 n.
horizontality
        211 n.

surroundings
225 n.
partition 226 n.
circumscribe
227 vb.
outline 228 n.
edge 229 n.
hem 229 vb.
limit 231 n.
limit 231 vb.
gauge 460 n.
signpost 542 n.
mark 542 vb.
hinder 697 vb.
completion 720 n.
restriction 742 n.
apportionment
778 n.
apportion 778 vb.

limited
comparative
27 adj.
limited 231 adj.

line
strengthen
157 vb.
load 188 vb.
enlarge 192 vb.
line 198 n.
strip 203 n.
cover 221 vb.
overlay 221 vb.
line 226 vb.
put between
226 vb.
straightness
244 n.
insert 298 vb.
repair 651 vb.

linguist
antiquarian
120 n.
collector 487 n.
interpreter 515 n.
linguist 552 n.

linguistic
semantic 509 adj.
linguistic 552 adj.

linguistics
source 151 n.
form 238 n.
formation 238 n.
meaning 509 n.
hermeneutics
515 n.
linguistics 552 n.
etymology 554 n.
dialect 555 n.
grammar 559 n.

lining
adjunct 40 n.
contents 188 n.
covering 221 n.
wrapping 221 n.
lining 222 n.
interjection
226 n.
hair 254 n.
stopper 259 n.
insertion 298 n.
softness 322 n.
warm clothes
376 n.
materials 626 n.

liquefaction
liquefaction
332 n.

liquefied
liquefied 332 adj.

liquefy
pass away 2 vb.

abate 37 vb.
come unstuck
49 vb.
decompose 51 vb.
be dispersed
75 vb.
destroy 160 vb.
deform 239 vb.
soften 322 vb.
liquefy 332 vb.
make flow
345 vb.
be hot 374 vb.
heat 376 vb.
disappear 441 vb.
waste 629 vb.

list
all 52 n.
arrangement
62 n.
class 62 vb.
continue 71 vb.
band 74 n.
specify 80 vb.
statistics 86 n.
number 86 vb.
list 87 n.
list 87 vb.
chronology 112 n.
contents 188 n.
meal 296 n.
death roll 356 n.
question 454 n.
record 543 n.
register 543 vb.
description 585 n.
compendium
587 n.
abstract 587 vb.
accounts 803 n.
account 803 vb.
honours 861 n.

listed
listed 87 adj.

listener
listener 410 n.

listening
listening 410 n.

literal
literal 553 adj.
written 581 adj.

literary
interpretive
515 adj.
literary 552 adj.
descriptive
585 adj.
poetic 588 adj.

literature
culture 485 n.
interpretation
515 n.
literature 552 n.
writing 581 n.
reading matter
584 n.

litigant
litigant 954 n.

litigate
quarrel 704 vb.
command 732 vb.
indict 923 vb.
litigate 954 vb.

litigated
litigated 954 adj.

litigating
litigating 954 adj.

litigation
litigation 954 n.

little
small 33 adj.

infantine 127 adj.
weak 158 adj.
little 191 adj.
short 199 adj.
light 318 adj.

little, be
be small 33 vb.
be little 191 vb.

littleness
littleness 191 n.

live
be 1 vb.
pass time 104 vb.
live 355 vb.

lively
vigorous 169 adj.
leaping 307 adj.
agitated 313 adj.
alive 355 adj.
forceful 566 adj.
active 673 adj.
lively 814 adj.
excitable 817 adj.
cheerful 828 adj.
proud 866 adj.

livery
uniform 223 n.
livery 542 n.
badge of rank
738 n.

live single
live single 890 vb.

living model
living model 23 n.

load
stow 182 vb.
load 188 vb.
transpose 267 vb.
insert 298 vb.
make heavy
317 vb.
be dense 319 vb.
store 627 vb.
hinder 697 vb.

lobby
entrance 68 n.
lobby 189 n.
access 619 n.

locality
district 179 n.
place 180 n.
locality 182 n.
abode 187 n.
near place 195 n.

located
located 182 adj.

location
addition 38 n.
arrangement
62 n.
bearings 181 n.
location 182 n.
nearness 195 n.
discovery 479 n.

lockup
lockup 743 n.

locomotive
locomotive 269 n.
traction 283 n.

loincloth
loincloth 223 n.

long
great 32 adj.
lasting 108 adj.
long 198 adj.
narrow 201 adj.
prolix 565 adj.

long ago
long ago 108 adv.

long, be
be long 198 vb.

long duration
time 104 n.
period 106 n.
course of time
107 n.
long duration
108 n.
perpetuity 110 n.
age 126 n.
life 355 n.
habit 605 n.

longitudinal
longitudinal
198 adj.

long measure
long measure
198 n.
measurement
460 n.
metrology 460 n.

longwise
longwise 198 adv.

look
look 433 n.
attention 450 n.
gesture 542 n.

look after
be mindful
450 vb.
look after
452 vb.
safeguard 655 vb.
preserve 661 vb.
manage 684 vb.

look ahead
look ahead
119 vb.
foresee 505 vb.
be cautious
853 vb.

look along
look along
198 vb.

look back
be unconformable
84 vb.
look back 120 vb.
be late 131 vb.
retrospect
500 vb.

looking ahead
looking ahead
119 n.

loop
halter 47 n.
outline 228 n.
curve 243 n.
loop 245 n.
orifice 258 n.
circuition 309 n.
vortex 310 n.
jewellery 839 n.

loose woman
woman 368 n.
bad person
933 n.
loose woman
947 n.

loquacious
informative
519 adj.
disclosing
521 adj.
diffuse 565 adj.
speaking 574 adj.
loquacious
576 adj.
conversing
579 adj.

loquacious, be
mean nothing
510 vb.
inform 519 vb.
publish 523 vb.
be diffuse
565 vb.
speak 574 vb.
be loquacious
576 vb.
converse 579 vb.
be obstructive
697 vb.

loquaciously
loquaciously
576 adv.

loquacity
loquacity 576 n.

lorry
lorry 269 n.

lose
decrease 37 vb.
relinquish 616 vb.
fail 723 vb.
lose 767 vb.
sell 788 vb.

lose a chance
be late 131 vb.
lose a chance
133 vb.
act foolishly
690 vb.
fail 723 vb.
lose 767 vb.

lose colour
change 138 vb.
be dim 414 vb.
lose colour
421 vb.
disappear 441 vb.

loser
bungler 692 n.
loser 723 n.
unlucky person
726 n.
laughingstock
846 n.
object of scorn
862 n.

lose repute
be inferior 35 vb.
lose repute
862 vb.
incur blame
919 vb.
be dishonest
925 vb.

losing
losing 767 adj.

loss
decrease 37 n.
deficit 55 n.
unproductiveness
167 n.
absence 185 n.
outflow 293 n.
evil 611 n.
waste 629 n.
inutility 636 n.
impairment
650 n.
failure 723 n.
loss 767 n.
nonownership
769 n.
debt 798 n.
loss of right
911 n.
penalty 958 n.

loss of right
conversion 142 n.

loss of right
911 n.

lost
lost 767 adj.

lost, be
be lost 767 vb.

lost labour
unproductiveness
167 n.
shortfall 302 n.
absurdity 492 n.
folly 494 n.
lost labour 636 n.

lost labour
bungling 690 n.
failure 723 n.

loud
great 32 adj.
violent 171 adj.
sounding 393 adj.
loud 395 adj.
resonant 404 adj.
strident 402 adj.
ululant 409 adj.
ornate 569 adj.
rhetorical
569 adj.
frightening
849 adj.
approving
918 adj.

loud, be
sound 393 vb.
be loud 395 vb.
bang 397 vb.
resound 399 vb.
shrill 402 vb.
vociferate
403 vb.
be heard 410 vb.
deafen 411 vb.
proclaim 523 vb.
emphasize
527 vb.
voice 572 vb.
be obstructive
697 vb.
be angry 886 vb.

loudly
loudly 395 adv.

loudness
loudness 395 n.

lovable
lovable 882 adj.

lovableness
lovableness
882 n.

love
maternity 164 n.
concord 705 n.
feeling 813 n.
moral sensibility
814 n.
be pleased
819 vb.
liking 854 n.
desire 854 vb.
wonder 859 n.
wonder 859 vb.
honour 861 vb.
friendship 875 n.
be friendly
875 vb.
love 882 n.
love 882 vb.
court 884 vb.
pet 884 vb.
benevolence
892 n.
jealousy 906 n.

approbation
918 n.
approve 918 vb.
disinterestedness
926 n.

love affair
love affair 882 n.
illicit love 946 n.

loved one
loved one 882 n.

love emblem
love emblem
882 n.
love token 884 n.

love god
love god 882 n.

love-making
love-making
882 n.
wooing 884 n.

love-nest
love-nest 882 n.

lover
concomitant
89 n.
patron 702 n.
desirer 854 n.
lover 882 n.
nubility 889 n.
libertine 947 n.

lovers
lovers 882 n.

love token
love emblem
882 n.
love token 884 n.

loving
friendly 875 adj.
loving 882 adj.
caressing
884 adj.
benevolent
892 adj.
jealous 906 adj.
godlike 960 adj.

low
small 33 adj.
short 199 adj.
low 205 adj.
undermost
209 adj.
lowered 306 adj.
infernal 966 adj.

low, be
be small 33 vb.
be low 205 vb.
descend 304 vb.

lower
abate 37 vb.
suppress 160 vb.
be low 205 vb.
impel 274 vb.
draw 283 vb.
immerse 298 vb.
lower 306 vb.
plunge 308 vb.
weigh 317 vb.
obliterate 545 vb.

lower classes
lower classes
864 n.

lowered
lowered 306 adj.

lowering
lowering 306 n.

low fellow
low fellow 864 n.
ruffian 899 n.
knave 933 n.

lowness
lowness 205 n.

loyalty
submission 716 n.
loyalty 734 n.
service 740 n.
observance
763 n.
love 882 n.
respect 915 n.
probity 924 n.

lubricant
smoother 253 n.
lubricant 329 n.
oil 352 n.
silencer 396 n.

lubricate
smooth 253 vb.
soften 322 vb.
rub 328 vb.
lubricate 329 vb.
grease 352 vb.
facilitate 696 vb.

lubricated
lubricated
329 adj.

lubrication
lubrication 329 n.
unctuousness
352 n.

lull
discontinuity
72 n.
interim 104 n.
period 106 n.
delay 131 n.
lull 140 n.
interval 196 n.
quiescence 261 n.
repose 678 n.
refreshment
680 n.
peace 712 n.
pacification
714 n.

luminary
luminary 415 n.

luminescent
luminescent
415 adj.

luminous
luminous 412 adj.
florid 420 adj.
white 422 adj.
obvious 438 adj.
noteworthy
861 adj.

lunatic asylum
lunatic asylum
498 n.
hospital 653 n.
shelter 657 n.

lunge
lunge 707 n.

lurk
be inert 170 vb.
be low 205 vb.
wander 262 vb.
be dark 413 vb.
be dim 414 vb.
be unseen
439 vb.
disappear 441 vb.
escape notice
451 vb.
lurk 518 vb.
be stealthy
520 vb.
ambush 522 vb.
avoid 615 vb.
be safe 655 vb.
seek safety
655 vb.

M

machine
component 58 n.
causal means
151 n.
electronics 155 n.
sources of energy
155 n.
production 159 n.
instrument 623 n.
instrumentality
623 n.
means 624 n.
machine 625 n.

machinist
machinist 625 n.

maculation
maculation 432 n.

madman
violent creature
171 n.
fool 496 n.
madman 499 n.
sick person
646 n.
ruffian 899 n.

Madonna
Madonna 962 n.

magical
extraneous
59 adj.
instrumental
623 adj.
wonderful
859 adj.
fairylike 964 adj.
magical 977 adj.

magic instrument
magic instrument
977 n.

magistracy
magistracy 952 n.

magnet
traction 283 n.
magnet 286 n.
incentive 607 n.

magniloquence
magniloquence
569 n.

main part
main part 32 n.
part 53 n.
greater number
100 n.
redundance
632 n.
chief thing 633 n.
undueness 911 n.

make angular
cross 217 vb.
make angular
242 vb.
make curved
243 vb.

make appetizing
taste 381 vb.
make appetizing
385 vb.
delight 821 vb.
cause desire

make better
unravel 62 vb.
modify 138 vb.
transform
142 vb.
influence 173 vb.
be attentive
450 vb.
benefit 610 vb.
do good 639 vb.
purify 643 vb.
make better
649 vb.
restore 651 vb.
make rich 795 vb.
be benevolent
892 vb.
make pious
973 vb.

make bright
smooth 253 vb.
make bright
412 vb.
illuminate 415 vb.
be transparent
417 vb.
clean 643 vb.
beautify 836 vb.

make certain
corroborate
461 vb.
testify 461 vb.
make certain
468 vb.
demonstrate
473 vb.
discover 479 vb.
endorse 483 vb.
safeguard 655 vb.
take a pledge
759 vb.
give security
762 vb.
be cautious
853 vb.

make complete
augment 36 vb.
add 38 vb.
make complete
54 vb.
pervade 184 vb.
crown 208 vb.
carry through
720 vb.

make concave
disable 156 vb.
be deep 206 vb.
make concave
250 vb.
pierce 258 vb.
transpose 267 vb.
descend 304 vb.
lower 306 vb.

make conceited
make conceited
868 vb.

make conform
make uniform
16 vb.
make conform
83 vb.
modify 138 vb.

make curved
make curved
243 vb.

make enemies
make enemies
876 vb.

make extrinsic
make extrinsic
6 vb.

externalize
218 vb.

make flow
liquefy 332 vb.
make flow
345 vb.
purify 643 vb.

make fruitful
make fruitful
166 vb.
cultivate 365 vb.

make heavy
make heavy
317 vb.

make higher
augment 36 vb.
make higher
204 vb.
elevate 305 vb.

make illegal
disentitle 911 vb.
make illegal
949 vb.
condemn 956 vb.

make important
be attentive
450 vb.
discriminate
458 vb.
manifest 517 vb.
emphasize
527 vb.
exaggerate
541 vb.
make important
633 vb.

make impossible
exclude 57 vb.
make impossible
465 vb.
negate 528 vb.
be difficult
695 vb.

make inactive
make inactive
674 vb.

make insensitive
make insensitive
815 vb.
be indifferent
855 vb.

make insufficient
shorten 199 vb.
make insufficient
631 vb.
be parsimonious
811 vb.

make legal
do 671 vb.
manage 684 vb.
decree 732 vb.
permit 751 vb.
grant claims
910 vb.
make legal
948 vb.

make likely
evidence 461 vb.
make likely
466 vb.

make mad
derange 63 vb.
make violent
171 vb.
distract 451 vb.
make mad
498 vb.
excite love
882 vb.

make mute
abate 37 vb.

silence 394 vb.
make mute
573 vb
hinder 697 vb.
restrain 742 vb.

make oblique
make oblique
215 vb
deflect 277 vb.

make opaque
bedim 414 vb.
screen 416 vb.
make opaque
418 vb
variegate 432 vb.

make peace
cease 140 vb.
make peace
714 vb
be content
823 vb
befriend 875 vb.

make pious
make pious
973 vb

make possible
make possible
464 vb
facilitate 696 vb.
permit 751 vb.
offer 754 vb.

make quarrels
make quarrels
704 vb

make ready
time 112 vb.
predestine
150 vb
dress 223 vb.
start out 291 vb.
find means
624 vb
provide 628 vb.
make ready
664 vb
defend 708 vb.

make rich
make rich 795 vb

make round
make curved
243 vb
make round
245 vb

make sane
make sane
497 vb

make smaller
make smaller
193 vb

make sterile
unman 156 vb.
lay waste 160 vb.
make sterile
167 vb
make useless
636 vb

make terms
accord 24 vb.
do business
617 vb
cooperate
701 vb
consent 753 vb.
contract 760 vb.
make terms
761 vb
bargain 786 vb.

make thin
abate 37 vb.
make smaller
193 vb

lengthen 198 vb.
make thin
    201 vb.
laminate 202 vb.
be temperate
    937 vb.
make ugly
deform 239 vb.
mark 542 vb.
impair 650 vb.
make ugly
    837 vb.
blemish 840 vb.
make unclean
thicken 349 vb.
bedim 414 vb.
decolorize
    421 vb.
blacken 423 vb.
variegate 432 vb.
mark 542 vb.
make unclean
    644 vb.
impair 650 vb.
misuse 670 vb.
make ugly
    837 vb.
blemish 840 vb.
shame 862 vb.
defame 921 vb.
debauch 946 vb.
be impious
    974 vb.
make uniform
make uniform
    16 vb.
equalize 28 vb.
simplify 44 vb.
join 45 vb.
order 60 vb.
regularize 62 vb.
make conform
    83 vb.
gauge 460 vb.
make unlike
make unlike
    19 vb.
exclude 57 vb.
make unwelcome
make unwelcome
    878 vb.
make useless
disable 156 vb.
make useless
    636 vb.
stop using
    669 vb.
make inactive
    674 vb.
make vertical
make vertical
    210 vb.
elevate 305 vb.
make violent
make violent
    171 vb.
make wicked
misteach 530 vb.
pervert 650 vb.
make wicked
    929 vb.
malcontent
dissentient 484 n.
opponent 700 n.
revolter 733 n.
malcontent
    824 n.
moper 829 n.
weeper 831 n.
rude person
    880 n.

misanthrope
    897 n.
disapprover
    919 n.
male
abnormality 84 n.
adult 129 n.
adultness 129 n.
grown-up
    129 adj.
athlete 157 n.
manly 157 adj.
violent creature
    171 n.
person 366 n.
male 367 n.
male 367 adj.
master 736 n.
male animal
male animal
    367 n.
malediction
word 554 n.
badness 640 n.
discontent 824 n.
hatred 883 n.
malediction
    894 n.
threat 895 n.
reproach 919 n.
detraction 921 n.
condemnation
    956 n.
impiety 974 n.
impious person
    974 n.
prayers 975 n.
maleficent
evil 611 adj.
maleficent
    893 adj.
wicked 929 adj.
fairylike 964 adj.
sorcerous
    977 adj.
malevolence
malevolence
    893 n.
malevolent
inimical 876 adj.
hating 883 adj.
resentful 886 adj.
malevolent
    893 adj.
revengeful
    905 adj.
detracting
    921 adj.
wicked 929 adj.
diabolic 963 adj.
malevolent, be
harm 640 vb.
ill-treat 640 vb.
oppress 730 vb.
be inimical
    876 vb.
hate 883 vb.
resent 886 vb.
be malevolent
    893 vb.
curse 894 vb.
be revengeful
    905 vb.
bewitch 977 vb.
malevolently
malevolently
    893 adv.
mammal
beast of burden
    268 n.
mammal 360 n.

hunter 614 n.
manage
arrange 62 vb.
look after
    452 vb.
motivate 607 vb.
undertake
    667 vb.
deal with 683 vb.
manage 684 vb.
deputize 750 vb.
management
superiority 34 n.
arrangement
    62 n.
agency 168 n.
inspection 433 n.
vocation 617 n.
action 671 n.
conduct 683 n.
management
    684 n.
government
    728 n.
commission
    746 n.
church office
    979 n.
manager
superior 34 n.
spectator 436 n.
manager 685 n.
master 736 n.
consignee 749 n.
man and boy
man and boy
    106 adv.
mandate
job 617 n.
precept 688 n.
command 732 n.
mandate 746 n.
permit 751 n.
conditions 761 n.
jurisdiction
    950 n.
mania
attention 450 n.
prejudgment
    476 n.
mania 498 n.
desire 854 n.
alcoholism 944 n.
manifest
uncovered
    224 adj.
open 258 adj.
visible 438 adj.
be visible 438 vb.
appearing
    440 adj.
appear 440 vb.
evidence 461 n.
demonstrate
    473 vb.
discover 479 vb.
manifest 517 adj.
manifest 517 vb.
disclose 521 vb.
well-known
    523 adj.
show feeling
    813 vb.
manifestation
inspection 433 n.
visibility 438 n.
appearance
    440 n.
demonstration
    473 n.
discovery 479 n.

manifestation
    517 n.
disclosure 521 n.
publicity 523 n.
veracity 535 n.
indication 542 n.
signal 542 n.
representation
    546 n.
ostentation
    870 n.
manifestly
manifestly
    517 adv.
manliness
manliness 850 n.
manly
manly 157 adj.
man or woman of action
doer 671 n.
many
plural 97 adj.
many 100 adj.
infinite 103 adj.
frequent 134 adj.
redundant
    632 adj.
many, be
grow 36 vb.
be many 100 vb.
reproduce 161 vb.
reproduce itself
    162 vb.
be fruitful
    166 vb.
abound 630 vb.
superabound
    632 vb.
map
arrangement
    62 n.
statistics 86 n.
situation 181 n.
distortion 241 n.
itinerary 262 n.
sailing aid 264 n.
world 316 n.
guidebook 519 n.
map 546 n.
plan 618 n.
marching
marching 262 n.
marginal
marginal 229 adj.
lateral 234 adj.
marine
seafaring
    264 adj.
seamanlike
    265 adj.
marine 270 adj.
marine life
marine life 360 n.
mariner
traveller 263 n.
water travel
    264 n.
mariner 265 n.
circler 309 n.
director 685 n.
naval man 717 n.
mark
make uniform
    16 vb.
class 62 vb.
make conform
    83 vb.
limit 231 vb.
mark 542 vb.
name 556 vb.

select 600 vb.
intend 612 vb.
blemish 840 vb.
shame 862 vb.

marked
marked 542 adj.

market
focus 76 n.
meeting place
187 n.
way in 292 n.
exhibit 517 n.
trade 786 n.
market 791 n.
finance 792 n.

marriage
misfit 25 n.
mixture 43 n.
coition 45 n.
union 45 n.
interiority 219 n.
promise 759 n.
compact 760 n.
love affair 882 n.
wooing 884 n.
marriage 889 n.
Christian rite
982 n.

marriageable
grown-up
129 adj.
marriageable
889 adj.

married
joined 45 adj.
married 889 adj.

marry
join 45 vb.
not retain
774 vb.
assign 775 vb.
marry 889 vb.

marsh
desert 167 n.
lowness 205 n.
horizontality
211 n.
softness 322 n.
moisture 336 n.
lake 341 n.
marsh 342 n.
plain 348 n.
semiliquidity
349 n.
dirt 644 n.
uncleanness
644 n.
pitfall 658 n.
difficulty 695 n.

marshy
soft 322 adj.
humid 336 adj.
marshy 342 adj.
semiliquid
349 adj.
pulpy 351 adj.
dirty 644 adj.
insalubrious
648 adj.

master
superior 34 n.
director 685 n.
authority 728 n.
master 736 n.
taker 781 n.

masterpiece
product 159 n.
exceller 639 n.
perfection 641 n.
deed 671 n.

masterpiece
689 n.
success 722 n.

matchmaker
joining together
45 n.
intermediary
226 n.
matchmaker
889 n.

material
real 1 adj.
substantial 3 adj.
material 314 adj.
sensuous 371 adj.
tactual 373 adj.
sensual 939 adj.

materiality
materiality 314 n.

materialize
materialize
314 vb.

materials
materials 626 n.

maternity
maternity 164 n.
woman 368 n.

mathematics
quantity 26 n.
mathematics
86 n.
reasoning 470 n.

matinal
matinal 123 adj.

matrimonial
matrimonial
889 adj.

matrimonially
matrimonially
889 adv.

matter
substantiality
3 n.
matter 314 n.
universe 316 n.
solid body 319 n.

maturation
maturation
664 n.

mature
augment 36 vb.
grow 36 vb.
be complete
54 vb.
be turned to
142 vb.
impend 150 vb.
reproduce itself
162 vb.
soften 322 vb.
perfect 641 vb.
get better
649 vb.
make better
649 vb.
mature 664 vb.
carry through
720 vb.

matured
matured 664 adj.

maw
maw 189 n.

maxim
certainty 468 n.
premise 470 n.
judgment 475 n.
creed 480 n.
maxim 491 n.
lack of meaning
510 n.

affirmation
527 n.
phrase 558 n.
conciseness
564 n.
precept 688 n.

meal
meal 296 n.
provision 628 n.
festivity 832 n.

mean
specify 80 vb.
mean 509 vb.
be equivocal
513 vb.
imply 518 vb.
indicate 542 vb.
represent 546 vb.
be important
633 vb.

meander
meander 246 vb.
deviate 277 vb.
circle 309 n.
flow 345 vb.

meandering
meandering
246 n.

meaning
substance 3 n.
relation 9 n.
identity 13 n.
contrariety 14 n.
differentiation
15 n.
accuracy 489 n.
meaning 509 n.
interpretation
515 n.
linguistics 552 n.
etymology 554 n.
word 554 n.
chief thing 633 n.

meaningful
evidential
461 adj.
meaningful
509 adj.
intelligible
511 adj.
indicating
542 adj.
important
633 adj.

meaningless
insubstantial
4 adj.
absurd 492 adj.
semantic 509 adj.
meaningless
510 adj.
unimportant
634 adj.

mean nothing
reason badly
472 vb.
be absurd
492 vb.
be foolish 494 vb.
mean nothing
510 vb.
be unintelligible
512 vb.
be loquacious
576 vb.
boast 872 vb.

means
opportunity
132 n.
causal means
151 n.

contrivance
618 n.
instrumentality
623 n.
means 624 n.
materials 626 n.
good policy
637 n.
estate 772 n.
funds 792 n.
wealth 795 n.

means of escape
outlet 293 n.
ascent 303 n.
pretext 609 n.
contrivance
618 n.
means 624 n.
safety 655 n.
safeguard 657 n.
means of escape
662 n.

means of execution
killer 357 n.
furnace 378 n.
means of
execution 959 n.

measure
do sums 86 vb.
measure 178 n.
size 190 n.
navigate 264 vb.
plunge 308 vb.
weigh 317 vb.
metrology 460 n.
measure 460 vb.

measured
measured
460 adj.

measurement
finite quantity
26 n.
quantity 26 n.
degree 27 n.
arrangement
62 n.
inclusion 78 n.
numeration 86 n.
size 190 n.
long measure
198 n.
depth 206 n.
navigation 264 n.
measurement
460 n.
estimate 475 n.
accuracy 489 n.

meat
insides 219 n.
meat 296 n.
corpse 358 n.

mechanical
dynamic 155 adj.
instrumental
623 adj.
mechanical
625 adj.

mechanics
data processing
86 n.
mechanics 625 n.

meddle
be vigorous
169 vb.
counteract
177 vb.
interfere 226 vb.
be curious
448 vb.
busy oneself
617 vb.

impair 650 vb.
do 671 vb.
meddle 673 vb.
be clumsy
690 vb.
hinder 697 vb.
obstruct 697 vb.
mediate 715 vb.
meddler
meddler 673 n.
meddling
meddling 673 adj.
median
median 30 adj.
inconsiderable
33 adj.
middle 70 adj.
general 79 adj.
typical 83 adj.
not bad 639 adj.
imperfect
642 adj.
middling 727 adj.
mediate
interfere 226 vb.
be instrumental
623 vb.
be at peace
712 vb.
pacify 714 vb.
mediate 715 vb.
deprecate 757 vb.
forgive 904 vb.
mediation
mediation 715 n.
mediator
moderator 172 n.
intermediary
226 n.
instrument 623 n.
pacifist 712 n.
mediator 715 n.
signatory 760 n.
matchmaker
889 n.
**mediatory.
propotiatory**
mediatory
715 adj.
medical
fertilized 162 adj.
medical 653 adj.
medical art
medical art
653 n.
aid 698 n.
medicine
draught 296 n.
medicine 653 n.
meditate
meditate 444 vb.
notice 450 vb.
enquire 454 vb.
estimate 475 vb.
suppose 507 vb.
offer worship
975 vb.
meditation
meditation 444 n.
medley
nonuniformity
17 n.
medley 43 n.
piece 53 n.
confusion 61 n.
accumulation
74 n.
bunch 74 n.
chequer 432 n.

meet
synchronize
118 vb.
meet with
149 vb.
converge 288 vb.
meet 290 vb.
meeting place
focus 76 n.
meeting place
187 n.
goal 290 n.
meet with
meet with
149 vb.
result 152 vb.
chance 154 vb.
discover 479 vb.
megaphone
megaphone
395 n.
hearing aid
410 n.
telecommunication
526 n.
melancholic
melancholic
829 adj.
melancholy
psychopathy
498 n.
suffering 820 n.
melancholy 829 n.
tedium 833 n.
sullenness 888 n.
melodious
pleasant 371 adj.
melodious
405 adj.
musical 407 adj.
musicianly
408 adj.
vocal 572 adj.
pleasurable
821 adj.
melody
agreement 24 n.
sound 393 n.
melody 405 n.
music 407 n.
concord 705 n.
memorize
memorize 500 vb.
memory
thought 444 n.
memory 500 n.
storage 627 n.
famousness
861 n.
mender
mender 651 n.
mental
immaterial
315 adj.
mental 442 adj.
knowing 485 adj.
diseased 646 adj.
mental dishonesty
mental dishonesty
538 n.
Mephisto
Mephisto 963 n.
merchandise
accumulation
74 n.
product 159 n.
equipment 625 n.
store 627 n.
property 772 n.
sale 788 n.

merchandise
790 n.
merchant
intermediary
226 n.
transferrer 267 n.
agent 681 n.
merchant 789 n.
minter 792 n.
merchant ship
merchant ship
270 n.
mercy
mercy 900 n.
forgiveness
904 n.
merriment
enjoyment 819 n.
merriment 828 n.
rejoicing 830 n.
amusement
832 n.
festivity 832 n.
wit 834 n.
merry
lively 814 adj.
happy 819 adj.
pleased 819 adj.
merry 828 adj.
amusing 832 adj.
witty 834 adj.
affected 845 adj.
sociable 877 adj.
message
information
519 n.
message 524 n.
telecommunication
526 n.
signal 542 n.
messenger
precursor 66 n.
omen 506 n.
informant 519 n.
publicizer 523 n.
messenger 524 n.
postal
communications
526 n.
officer 736 n.
delegate 749 n.
deputy 750 n.
metaphor
comparison
457 n.
connotation
509 n.
metaphor 514 n.
interpretation
515 n.
latency 518 n.
literature 552 n.
ritual 982 n.
metaphorically
metaphorically
514 adv.
meteor
meteor 316 n.
luminary 415 n.
mete out
mete out 460 vb.
meter
altimetry 204 n.
gas 331 n.
meter 460 n.
detector 479 n.
metrical
numerable
86 adj.
metrical 460 adj.

metrology
metrology 460 n.
microelectronics
counting
instrument 86 n.
electronics 155 n.
microelectronics
191 n.
microorganism
small animal
33 n.
microorganism
191 n.
organism 353 n.
animal 360 n.
plant 361 n.
insalubrity 648 n.
microscope
microscope
437 n.
microscopy
microscopy
191 n.
middle
middle point
30 n.
median 30 adj.
middle 70 n.
middle 70 adj.
focus 76 n.
interim 104 n.
centre 220 n.
central 220 adj.
interjacency
226 n.
intermediary
226 n.
interjacent
226 adj.
middle age
middle point
30 n.
middle age 126 n.
adultness 129 n.
middle classes
middle classes
864 n.
middle point
middle point
30 n.
middle way
620 n.
middle way
middle point
30 n.
middle 70 n.
moderation
172 n.
middle way
620 n.
compromise
765 n.
indifference
855 n.
middling
median 30 adj.
inconsiderable
33 adj.
typical 83 adj.
middling 727 adj.
plebeian 864 adj.
middling, be
be middling
727 vb.
midnight
midnight 124 n.
lateness 131 n.
darkness 413 n.
midstream, be
be midstream
620 vb.

midway
midway 70 adv.

mien
form 238 n.
mien 440 n.
gesture 542 n.
conduct 683 n.

militarist
militarist 717 n.

milk
milk 296 n.

mimicry
mimicry 20 n.
disguise 522 n.
acting 594 n.
satire 846 n.
ostentation
870 n.

mindful, be
be mindful
450 vb.
remember
500 vb.
be cautious
853 vb.

mindless
mindless 443 adj.
unthinking
445 adj.

mineral
object 314 n.
mineral 354 n.

mineralogy
rock 339 n.
mineralogy 354 n.

miniature
small thing 33 n.
miniature 191 n.
record 543 n.

minister to
concur 176 vb.
look after
452 vb.
be instrumental
623 vb.
doctor 653 vb.
work 677 vb.
minister to
698 vb.
obey 734 vb.
serve 737 vb.
philanthropize
892 vb.

ministration
church ministry
979 n.
ministration
982 n.

mint
produce 159 vb.
mint 792 vb.

minter
minter 792 n.

minute
minute 191 adj.
indistinct
439 adj.

minuteness
minuteness
191 n.

mirror
reflection 412 n.
mirror 437 n.

misanthrope
enemy 876 n.
shrew 887 n.
celibate 890 n.
misanthrope
897 n.
disapprover
919 n.

misanthropic
misanthropic
897 adj.

misanthropically
misanthropically
897 adv.

misanthropize
misanthropize
897 vb.

misanthropy
misanthropy
897 n.

miscarry
pass away 2 vb.
reproduce itself
162 vb.
be unproductive
167 vb.
fall short 302 vb.
be clumsy
690 vb.
be in difficulty
695 vb.
miscarry 723 vb.
have trouble
726 vb.

misdate
misdate 113 vb.

misfit
unrelatedness
10 n.
dissimilarity 19 n.
misfit 25 n.
discontinuity
72 n.
nonconformist
84 n.
displacement
183 n.
bungler 692 n.
loser 723 n.

misfortune
untimeliness
133 n.
event 149 n.
chance 154 n.
ruin 160 n.
disappointment
504 n.
evil 611 n.
badness 640 n.
deterioration
650 n.
failure 723 n.
misfortune 726 n.

misinterpret
transform
142 vb.
distort 241 vb.
misjudge 476 vb.
blunder 490 vb.
mean nothing
510 vb.
misinterpret
516 vb.
be false 536 vb.

misinterpretation
misinterpretation
516 n.

misinterpreted
misinterpreted
516 adj.

misjudge
mistime 133 vb.
not think 445 vb.
misjudge 476 vb.
underestimate
478 vb.
not know 486 vb.
blunder 490 vb.
err 490 vb.

be foolish 494 vb.
not understand
512 vb.
misinterpret
516 vb.

misjudging
misjudging
476 adj.

misjudgment
misjudgment
476 n.

mislead
derange 63 vb.
deflect 277 vb.
blind 434 vb.
puzzle 469 vb.
mislead 490 vb.
misteach 530 vb.
befool 537 vb.
deceive 537 vb.
motivate 607 vb.
obstruct 697 vb.

mismatch
mismatch 25 vb.

misname
misname 557 vb.

misnamed
misnamed
557 adj.

misnomer
name 556 n.
misnomer 557 n.

misplace
derange 63 vb.
misplace 183 vb.
lose 767 vb.

misplaced
misplaced
183 adj.

misrepresent
make unlike
19 vb.
distort 241 vb.
sophisticate
472 vb.
misinterpret
516 vb.
misteach 530 vb.
be false 536 vb.
misrepresent
547 vb.
satirize 846 vb.
detract 921 vb.

misrepresentation
misrepresentation
547 n.

misrepresented
misrepresented
547 adj.

missile
speeder 272 n.
missile 282 n.
ammunition
718 n.
missile weapon
718 n.

missile weapon
rocket 271 n.
missile 282 n.
propellant 282 n.
missile weapon
718 n.

mistake
mistake 490 vb.
absurdity 492 n.
misinterpretation
516 n.
misteaching
530 n.
solecism 560 n.
bungling 690 n.

failure 723 n.
guilty act 931 n.

mistaken
misjudging
476 adj.
mistaken 490 adj.
unwise 494 adj.
misinterpreted
516 vb.
misteaching
530 adj.
heterodox
971 adj.

misteach
misteach 530 vb.

misteaching
misteaching
530 n.
misteaching
530 adj.

mistime
derange 63 vb.
misdate 113 vb.
mistime 133 vb.

misuse
consume 160 vb.
force 171 vb.
sophisticate
472 vb.
waste 629 n.
waste 629 vb.
ill-treat 640 vb.
impairment
650 n.
pervert 650 vb.
use 668 n.
misuse 670 n.
misuse 670 vb.
bungling 690 n.
be unskilful
690 vb.
be severe 730 vb.
prodigality 810 n.
cruel act 893 n.
impiety 974 n.
be impious
974 vb.

mix
abate 37 vb.
add 38 vb.
mix 43 vb.
join 45 vb.
combine 50 vb.
compose 56 vb.
jumble 63 vb.
modify 138 vb.
weaken 158 vb.
infiltrate 292 vb.
infuse 298 vb.
rotate 310 vb.
agitate 313 vb.
impair 650 vb.

mixed
ethnic 11 adj.
different 15 adj.
mixed 43 adj.
combined 50 adj.
component
58 n.
multiform 82 adj.
abnormal 84 adj.
spurious 537 adj.

mixed, be
be mixed 43 vb.
be one of 58 vb.
be included
78 vb.
be turned to
142 vb.
cooperate
701 vb.

ixture
mixture 43 n.
union 45 n.
combination 50 n.
composition 56 n.
confusion 61 n.
middle 70 n.
weakness 158 n.
draught 296 n.
liquefaction 332 n.
imperfection 642 n.
impairment 650 n.
type of marriage 889 n.

ixture, a
a mixture 43 n.
compound 50 n.
product 159 n.
dish 296 n.

mnemonics
mnemonics 500 n.

odality
modality 7 n.

oderate
abate 37 vb.
disunite 46 vb.
moderate 172 adj.
moderate 172 vb.
retard 273 vb.
qualify 463 vb.
depreciating 478 adj.
dissuade 608 vb.
avoid 615 vb.
moderate 620 vb.
reformer 649 n.
make better 649 vb.
middling 727 adj.
be lenient 731 vb.
free person 739 n.
restrain 742 vb.
inexcitable 818 adj.
relieve 826 vb.
indifference 855 n.
temperate 937 adj.

oderate, be
be moderate 172 vb.
be temperate 937 vb.

oderately
moderately 172 adv.

oderation
average 30 n.
diminution 37 n.
weakness 158 n.
moderation 172 n.
counteraction 177 n.
qualification 463 n.
underestimation 478 n.
avoidance 615 n.
middle way 620 n.
peace 712 n.
pacification 714 n.

peace offering 714 n.
averageness 727 n.
leniency 731 n.
inexcitability 818 n.
relief 826 n.
temperance 937 n.

moderator
substitute 145 n.
moderator 172 n.
quietude 261 n.
anaesthetic 370 n.
balm 653 n.
remedy 653 n.
pacifist 712 n.
peace offering 714 n.
mediator 715 n.

modern
present 116 adj.
synchronous 118 adj.
modern 121 adj.
progressive 280 adj.
fashionable 843 adj.

modernism
present time 116 n.
modernism 121 n.
fashion 843 n.

modernist
modernist 121 n.

modernize
modernize 121 vb.

modernized
modernized 121 adj.

modest
plain 568 adj.
unwilling 593 adj.
avoiding 615 adj.
artless 694 adj.
middling 727 adj.
nervous 849 adj.
cowardly 851 adj.
inglorious 862 adj.
humble 867 adj.
modest 869 adj.
pure 945 adj.

modest, be
be nervous 849 vb.
be humble 867 vb.
be modest 869 vb.

modestly
modestly 869 adv.

modesty
modesty 869 n.

modify
mix 43 vb.
modify 138 vb.
transform 142 vb.
influence 173 vb.
qualify 463 vb.

moisten
mix 43 vb.
disperse 75 vb.
emit 295 vb.
let fall 306 vb.

add water 334 vb.
moisten 336 vb.
flow 345 vb.
make unclean 644 vb.

moistening
moistening 336 n.

moisture
moisture 336 n.
rain 345 n.
bubble 350 n.
obfuscation 416 n.

monastery
quarters 187 n.
retreat 187 n.
monastery 980 n.

monastic
unwedded 890 adj.
monastic 980 adj.
vestured 983 adj.

monasticism
monasticism 979 n.

monetary
monetary 792 adj.

money
quid pro quo 145 n.
incentive 607 n.
means 624 n.
acquisition 766 n.
money 792 n.
wealth 795 n.
payment 799 n.

moneyed
moneyed 795 adj.

monk
celibate 890 n.
virgin 945 n.
monk 980 n.

monster
violent creature 171 n.
tyrant 730 n.
intimidation 849 n.
hellhag 899 n.
monster 933 n.
demon 964 n.

monument
antiquity 120 n.
edifice 159 n.
small hill 204 n.
earthwork 248 n.
obsequies 359 n.
tomb 359 n.
reminder 500 n.
monument 543 n.
trophy 724 n.

moon
evening 124 n.
moon 316 n.
luminary 415 n.

moot
moot 454 adj.
uncertain 469 adj.

moper
moper 829 n.

moral insensibility
incuriosity 449 n.
indiscrimination 459 n.
sluggishness 674 n.
moral insensibility 815 n.

inexcitability 818 n.
lack of wonder 860 n.
purity 945 n.

morals
right 908 n.
morals 912 n.
virtue 928 n.

moral sensibility
life 355 n.
sensibility 369 n.
discrimination 458 n.
imagination 508 n.
interpretation 515 n.
persuadability 607 n.
feeling 813 n.
moral sensibility 814 n.
painfulness 822 n.
pride 866 n.
love 882 n.
irascibility 887 n.

morbidly
morbidly 646 adv.

morning
beginning 68 n.
period 106 n.
morning 123 n.
earliness 130 n.
regular return 136 n.
ascent 303 n.
light 412 n.

motion
degree 27 n.
changeable thing 147 n.
displacement 183 n.
motion 260 n.
water travel 264 n.
velocity 272 n.
progression 280 n.
way 619 n.
action 671 n.
activity 673 n.

motivate
cause 151 vb.
influence 173 vb.
propound 507 vb.
motivate 607 vb.
be important 633 vb.
dispose of 668 vb.
do 671 vb.
manage 684 vb.
make quarrels 704 vb.
cause desire 854 vb.

motivator
motivator 607 n.

motive
causation 151 n.
power 155 n.
influence 173 n.
motive 607 n.
plot 618 n.
activity 673 n.

mottled
whitish 422 adj.
mottled 432 adj.
marked 542 adj.

mould
mould 23 n.

mouthful
mouthful 296 n.
savouriness
385 n.

move
derange 63 vb.
operate 168 vb.
displace 183 vb.
move 260 vb.
propel 282 vb.
be active 673 vb.

move fast
elapse 107 vb.
be transient
109 vb.
be violent 171 vb.
be in motion
260 vb.
travel 262 vb.
walk 262 vb.
navigate 264 vb.
move fast
272 vb.
progress 280 vb.
decamp 291 vb.
pass 300 vb.
outdo 301 vb.
run away 615 vb.
seek safety
655 vb.
be active 673 vb.
hasten 675 vb.

move slowly
move slowly
273 vb.

moving
dynamic 155 adj.
moving 260 adj.
travelling
262 adj.
flying 266 adj.
progressive
280 adj.
active 673 adj.

multiform
unrelated 10 adj.
different 15 adj.
nonuniform
17 adj.
dissimilar 19 adj.
mixed 43 adj.
multiform 82 adj.
many 100 adj.
changeful
147 adj.
variegated
432 adj.

multiformity
multiformity
82 n.

multitude
quantity 26 n.
greatness 32 n.
great quantity
32 n.
band 74 n.
crowd 74 n.
plurality 97 n.
multitude 100 n.
abundance 166 n.
safety 655 n.
army 717 n.

multitudinous
great 32 adj.
assembled 74 adj.
multitudinous
100 adj.
frequent 134 adj.
filled 630 adj.

murder
destroy 160 vb.
murder 357 vb.
oppress 730 vb.
execute 958 vb.

murderer
murderer 357 n.

murderous
furious 171 adj.
murderous
357 adj.
cruel 893 adj.
guilty 931 adj.

music
combination 50 n.
composition 56 n.
arrangement
62 n.
sound 393 n.
melody 405 n.
music 407 n.
pleasurableness
821 n.

musical
adjusted 24 adj.
musical 407 adj.

musical, be
be musical
408 vb.

musical instrument
blowing 347 n.
musical
instrument 409 n.

musical note
degree 27 n.
series 71 n.
interval 196 n.
ascent 303 n.
roll 398 n.
resonance 399 n.
stridor 402 n.
musical note
405 n.

musical piece
musical piece
407 n.

musical skill
production 159 n.
melody 405 n.
music 407 n.
musical skill
408 n.

musician
concomitant
89 n.
producer 159 n.
musician 408 n.
interpreter 515 n.
proficient person
691 n.

musicianly
musicianly
408 adj.

mutatis mutandis
mutatis mutandis
138 adv.

mute
weaken 158 vb.
silencer 396 n.
mute 396 vb.
sound dead
400 vb.
mute 409 n.

make mute
573 vb.

mute, be
decrease 37 vb.
cease 140 vb.
be silent 394 vb.
be mute 573 vb.
be taciturn
577 vb.

muted
muted 396 adj.

mythical being
mythical being
964 n.

mythic deity
mythic deity
961 n.

mythic heaven
mythic heaven
965 n.

mythic hell
mythic hell 966 n.

mythological
mythological
961 adj.

N

name
class 62 vb.
auspicate 68 vb.
specify 80 vb.
word 554 n.
name 556 n.
name 556 vb.
misnomer 557 n.
misname 557 vb.
dignify 861 vb.

named
named 556 adj.

named, be
be named 556 vb.

namely
namely 80 adv.

naming
naming 556 adj.

narrative
maxim 491 n.
remembrance
500 n.
information
519 n.
report 519 n.
fable 538 n.
record 543 n.
literature 552 n.
narrative 585 n.
dramaturgy
589 n.

narrator
informant 519 n.
chronicler 544 n.
author 584 n.
narrator 585 n.

narrow
small 33 adj.
little 191 adj.
contracted
193 adj.
narrow 201 adj.
fibrous 203 adj.
tall 204 adj.
shallow 207 adj.
restraining
742 adj.

narrow, be
decrease 37 vb.
become small
193 v
be narrow
201 v
converge 288 vb

narrowing
narrowing 201 n

narrow mind
narrow mind
476
ignoramus 488
obstinate perso
597
enemy 876 n.
pietism 973 n.

narrow-minded
narrow-minded
476 a
unwise 494 adj.

narrowness
narrowness
201

nation
consanguinity
11
native 186 n.
nation 366 n.
community 703
independence
739

national
ethnic 11 adj.
national 366 ad

native
earliness 130 n
native 186 n.
native 186 adj.
subject 737 n.
commoner 864

nautical personne
nautical
personnel 265 n
naval man 717
naval officer
736

naval man
nautical
personnel 265 n
naval man 717

naval officer
nautical
personnel 265 n
naval man 717
naval officer
736

navigate
vary 147 vb.
be in motion
260
navigate 264 v
retard 273 vb.
orientate 276 v
deflect 277 vb.
draw 283 vb.
approach 284 v
start out 291 v
pass 300 vb.
direct 684 vb.

navigation
navigation 264 n

navigator
navigator 265 n
director 685 n.

navy
shipping 270 n.
navy 717 n.

nay
nay 528 adv.

not think
  not think 445 vb.
not understand
  not understand
    512 vb.
not use
  not use 669 vb.
not wonder
  not wonder
    860 vb.
nourishing
  nourishing
    296 adj.
novel
  ideality 508 n.
  reading matter
    584 n.
  novel 585 n.
now, be
  be 1 vb.
  be now 116 vb.
noxious animal
  creepy-crawly
    360 n.
  bane 654 n.
  noxious animal
    899 n.
  knave 933 n.
nubility
  nubility 889 n.
nucleonics
  nucleonics 155 n.
nullify
  nullify 2 vb.
  not be 4 vb.
  abate 37 vb.
  destroy 160 vb.
number
  quantity 26 n.
  part 53 n.
  specify 80 vb.
  number 85 n.
  number 86 vb.
  list 87 vb.
  measure 460 vb.
number with
  add 38 vb.
  number with
    78 vb.
numerable
  numerable
    86 adj.
numeration
  numeration 86 n.
numerical
  numerical 85 adj.
numerical element
  subtraction 39 n.
  numerical
    element 85 n.
  fraction 98 n.
  changeable thing
    147 n.
numerical operation
  increase 36 n.
  subtraction 39 n.
  numerical
    operation 86 n.
numerical result
  numerical result
    85 n.
nun
  spinster 890 n.
  virgin 945 n.
  nun 980 n.
nurse
  obstetrics 162 n.
  nurse 653 n.
nymph
  vegetable life
    361 n.

mythical being
    964 n.

O

oath
  testimony 461 n.
  oath 527 n.
  recantation
    598 n.
  promise 759 n.
obedience
  obedience 734 n.
obedient
  orderly 60 adj.
  willing 592 adj.
  submitting
    716 adj.
  obedient 734 adj.
  serving 737 adj.
  subject 740 adj.
  restrained
    742 adj.
  observant
    763 adj.
  inexcitable
    818 adj.
  servile 874 adj.
  amiable 879 adj.
  obliged 912 adj.
  trustworthy
    924 adj.
  virtuous 928 adj.
  legal 948 adj.
  orthodox 970 adj.
  pious 973 adj.
obediently
  obediently
    734 adv.
obeisance
  curvature 243 n.
  obeisance 306 n.
  submission 716 n.
  servility 874 n.
  courteous act
    879 n.
  respects 915 n.
obey
  be inferior 35 vb.
  conform 83 vb.
  acquiesce 483 vb.
  be willing 592 vb.
  obey 734 vb.
  serve 737 vb.
  be subject
    740 vb.
  observe 763 vb.
  be servile 874 vb.
  do one's duty
    912 vb.
  be pious 973 vb.
obfuscation
  obfuscation
    416 n.
object
  substance 3 n.
  product 159 n.
  object 314 n.
objective
  extremity 69 n.
  focus 76 n.
  centre 220 n.
  limit 231 n.
  goal 290 n.
  motive 607 n.
  objective 612 n.
  chase 614 n.
  attempt 666 n.
  aspiration 847 n.

desired object
    854 n.
object of scorn
  nonentity 634 n.
  poor person
    796 n.
  object of scorn
    862 n.
  contemptibility
    917 n.
  bad person
    933 n.
oblation
  oblation 975 n.
obligatory
  necessary
    591 adj.
  compelling
    735 adj.
  conditional
    761 adj.
  obligatory
    912 adj.
obliged
  obliged 912 adj.
oblique
  unequal 29 adj.
  unequal 29 adj.
  low 205 adj.
  oblique 215 adj.
  crossed 217 adj.
  distorted 241 adj.
  angular 242 adj.
  curved 243 adj.
  directed 276 adj.
  deviating
    277 adj.
  occult 518 adj.
oblique, be
  be unequal 29 vb.
  be oblique
    215 vb.
  be inverted
    216 vb.
  cross 217 vb.
  be in front
    232 vb.
  be behind 233 vb.
  make angular
    242 vb.
  navigate 264 vb.
  deviate 277 vb.
  ascend 303 vb.
  tumble 304 vb.
  be agitated
    313 vb.
obliquely
  obliquely
    215 adv.
obliquity
  obliquity 215 n.
obliterate
  nullify 2 vb.
  subtract 39 vb.
  exclude 57 vb.
  revolutionize
    144 vb.
  destroy 160 vb.
  eject 295 vb.
  rub 328 vb.
  disappear 441 vb.
  forget 501 vb.
  conceal 520 vb.
  obliterate 545 vb.
  clean 643 vb.
  restrain 742 vb.
  abrogate 747 vb.
  prohibit 752 vb.
  forgive 909 vb.
  disapprove
    919 vb.

obliterated
  obliterated
    545 adj.
obliteration
  obliteration
    545 n.
oblivion
  extinction 2 n.
  anachronism
    113 n.
  inattention
    451 n.
  negligence 453 n.
  error 490 n.
  oblivion 501 n.
  desuetude 606 n.
  ingratitude 903 n.
  undutifulness
    913 n.
obscuration
  obscuration
    413 n.
obsequies
  obsequies 359 n.
observance
  conformity 83 n.
  obedience 734 n.
  consent 753 n.
  observance
    763 n.
  duty 912 n.
  probity 924 n.
  orthodoxism
    970 n.
  piety 973 n.
observant
  observant
    763 adj.
observe
  conform 83 vb.
  obey 734 vb.
  observe 763 vb.
  do one's duty
    912 vb.
obsessed
  obsessed 450 adj.
obstacle
  counteraction
    177 n.
  prop 213 n.
  barrier 230 n.
  closure 259 n.
  solid body 319 n.
  impossibility
    465 n.
  lost labour 636 n.
  inexpedience
    638 n.
  defect 642 n.
  pitfall 658 n.
  obstacle 697 n.
  opposition 699 n.
obstetrics
  sequel 67 n.
  obstetrics 162 n.
  contraction
    193 n.
  medical art
    653 n.
obstinacy
  obstinacy 597 n.
obstinate
  unconformable
    84 adj.
  lasting 108 adj.
  permanent
    139 adj.
  unchangeable
    148 adj.
  unyielding
    157 adj.

inimitable 21 adj.
simple 44 adj.
combined 50 adj.
whole 52 adj.
special 80 adj.
one 88 adj.
infrequent
135 adj.
one, be
join 45 vb.
be one 88 vb.
on edge
on edge 254 adv.
one of, be
constitute 56 vb.
be one of 58 vb.
be included
78 vb.
be included
78 vb.
enter 292 vb.
one's duty, be
be one's duty
912 vb.
on foot
on foot 262 adv.
on land
on land 339 adv.
on loan
on loan 779 adv.
onlookers
onlookers 436 n.
on record
on record
543 adv.
on stage
on stage 589 adv.
on terms
on terms
761 adv.
on the move
on the move
260 adv.
on the raw
on the raw
814 adv.
on the spot
on the spot
184 adj.
on the stocks
on the stocks
721 adv.
on the whole
on the whole
52 adv.
on trial
on trial 454 adv.
opacity
opacity 418 n.
opaque
unlit 413 adj.
dim 414 adj.
opaque 418 adj.
unclear 563 adj.
open
break 46 vb.
cut 46 vb.
disunite 46 vb.
separate 46 vb.
sunder 46 vb.
be weak 158 vb.
force 171 vb.
expanded
192 adj.
spaced 196 adj.
space 196 n.
broad 200 adj.
uncover 224 vb.
open 258 adj.
open 258 vb.
enter 292 vb.

admit 294 vb.
empty 295 vb.
evolve 311 vb.
make flow
345 vb.
manifest 517 vb.
disclosed 521 adj.
disclose 521 vb.
easy 696 adj.
liberate 741 vb.
not retain
774 vb.
opener
opener 258 n.
ingress 292 n.
extractor 299 n.
discovery 479 n.
instrument 623 n.
opening
receptacle 189 n.
garment 223 n.
opening 258 n.
openly
openly 258 adv.
open space
room 178 n.
place 180 n.
open space
258 n.
plain 343 n.
open thew door to
open
permit 751 vb.
operate
computerize
86 vb.
operate 168 vb.
influence 173 vb.
move 260 vb.
impel 274 vb.
touch 373 vb.
motivate 607 vb.
function 617 vb.
be instrumental
623 vb.
be useful 635 vb.
use 668 vb.
do 671 vb.
deal with 683 vb.
be successful
722 vb.
operative
operative
168 vb.
instrumental
623 vb.
doing 671 adj.
opine
opine 480 vb.
suppose 507 vb.
affirm 527 vb.
opinion
philosophy 444 n.
idea 446 n.
positiveness
468 n.
estimate 475 n.
bias 481 n.
opinion 480 n.
supposition
507 n.
vote 600 n.
conduct 683 n.
opinionatedness
opinionatedness
597 n.
opponent
dissentient 484 n.
hinderer 697 n.
opponent 700 n.
revolter 733 n.

malcontent
824 n.
enemy 876 n.
disapprover
919 n.
opportune
circumstantial
8 adj.
opportune
132 adj.
opportunely
opportunely
132 adv.
opportunity
opportunity
132 n.
fair chance
154 n.
possibility 464 n.
facility 696 n.
scope 739 n.
oppose
be contrary
14 vb.
counteract
177 vb.
dissent 484 vb.
negate 528 vb.
be unwilling
593 vb.
be obstructive
697 vb.
oppose 699 vb.
quarrel 704 vb.
defy 706 vb.
attack 707 vb.
resist 710 vb.
disobey 733 vb.
restrain 742 vb.
deprecate 757 vb.
be discontented
824 vb.
be inimical
876 vb.
opposing
opposing 699 adj.
opposite
contrary 14 adj.
separate 46 adj.
inverted 216 adj.
frontal 232 adj.
back 233 adj.
opposite 235 adj.
directed 276 adj.
opposing 699 adj.
opposite, be
be contrary
14 vb.
be in front
232 vb.
be opposite
235 vb.
orientate 276 vb.
opposites
opposites 699 n.
opposition
contrariety 14 n.
counteraction
177 n.
contraposition
235 n.
qualification
463 n.
doubt 481 n.
unbelief 481 n.
dissent 484 n.
dissentient 484 n.
unwillingness
593 n.
hindrance 697 n.
opposition 699 n.

dissension 704 n.
resistance 710 n.
adversity 726 n.
disobedience
733 n.
deprecation
757 n.
enmity 876 n.
censure 919 n.
antichristianity
968 n.
oppress
suppress 160 vb.
be violent 171 vb.
be biased 476 vb.
pursue 614 vb.
ill-treat 640 vb.
misuse 670 vb.
meddle 673 vb.
rule 728 vb.
oppress 730 vb.
compel 735 vb.
subjugate 740 vb.
levy 781 vb.
rob 783 vb.
torment 822 vb.
frighten 849 vb.
shame 862 vb.
be proud 866 vb.
be insolent
873 vb.
be inimical
876 vb.
be malevolent
893 vb.
despise 917 vb.
oppressive
oppressive
730 adj.
optical device
optical device
437 n.
optics
electronics 155 n.
range 178 n.
optics 412 n.
vision 433 n.
optical device
437 n.
optimistic
optimistic
477 adj.
optionally
optionally
600 adv.
oracle
certainty 468 n.
sage 495 n.
oracle 506 n.
latency 518 n.
preacher 532 n.
psychic 978 n.
priest 980 n.
orange
orange 427 n.
orange 427 adj.
orate
orate 574 vb.
oration
lecture 529 n.
diffuseness 565 n.
oration 574 n.
allocution 578 n.
reading matter
584 n.
oratory
style 561 n.
oratory 574 n.
ministration
982 n.

orbit
orbit 245 n.

orchestra
band 74 n.
orchestra 408 n.
musical
instrument 409 n.

order
uniformity 16 n.
adjust 24 vb.
order 60 n.
order 60 vb.
arrangement
62 n.
regularity 81 n.
list 87 n.
regular return
136 n.
permanence
139 n.
carefulness
452 n.
habit 605 n.
practice 605 n.
plan 618 n.
plan 618 vb.
peace 712 n.
the church 979 n.
ritual 982 n.

orderless
orderless 61 adj.

orderly
adjusted 24 adj.
orderly 60 adj.
arranged 62 adj.
regular 81 adj.
regulated 83 adj.
careful 452 adj.
businesslike
617 adj.
planned 618 adj.
clean 643 adj.

organ
air pipe 348 n.
organ 409 n.

organic
organic 353 adj.

organism
prototype 23 n.
composition 56 n.
arrangement
62 n.
origin 68 n.
fossil 120 n.
insides 219 n.
matter 314 n.
structure 326 n.
organism 353 n.
life 355 n.

orientate
navigate 264 vb.
orientate 276 vb.

orifice
entrance 68 n.
maw 189 n.
gap 196 n.
circle 245 n.
cavity 250 n.
orifice 258 n.
way in 292 n.
outlet 293 n.
air pipe 348 n.

origin
prototype 23 n.
origin 68 n.
seedbed 151 n.
source 151 n.
propagation
162 n.
genealogy 164 n.
home 187 n.

base 209 n.
element 314 n.
life 355 n.

original
unrelated 10 adj.
original 21 adj.
first 68 adj.
new 121 adj.
unwonted
606 adj.

originality
originality 21 n.

ornament
repetition 102 n.
equivocalness
513 n.
trope 514 n.
figure 514 vb.
exaggeration
541 n.
solecism 560 n.
style 561 n.
imperspicuity
563 n.
ornament 569 n.
ornament 569 vb.
elegance 570 n.
ornamentation
839 n.
decorate 839 vb.
affectation
845 n.

ornamental
ornamental
839 adj.

ornamental art
ornamental art
839 n.

ornamentation
ornamentation
839 n.

ornamented
ornamented
839 adj.

ornate
figurative
514 adj.
diffuse 565 adj.
ornate 569 adj.
ornamented
839 adj.
affected 845 adj.

orthodox
conformable
83 adj.
regulated 83 adj.
evidential
461 adj.
positive 468 adj.
believing 480 adj.
habitual 605 adj.
orthodox 970 adj.
pious 973 adj.
worshipping
975 adj.
ecclesiastical
979 n.

orthodox, be
believe 480 vb.
be orthodox
970 vb.

orthodoxism
orthodoxism
970 n.

orthodoxly
orthodoxly
970 adv.

orthodox, the
the orthodox
970 n.

orthodoxy
orthodoxy 970 n.

oscillate
correlate 12 vb.
be periodic
136 vb.
vary 147 vb.
be weak 158 vb.
walk 262 vb.
voyage 264 vb.
deviate 277 vb.
leap 307 vb.
oscillate 312 vb.
be agitated
313 vb.
roll 398 vb.
be irresolute
596 vb.
show feeling
813 vb.
be drunk 944 vb.

oscillating
oscillating
312 adj.

oscillation
oscillation 312 n.

ostensible
ostensible
609 adj.

ostensibly
ostensibly
609 adv.

ostentation
insubstantial
thing 4 n.
aeronautics
266 n.
spectacle 440 n.
foolery 492 n.
manifestation
517 n.
publicity 523 n.
duplicity 536 n.
falsehood 536 n.
exaggeration
541 n.
magniloquence
569 n.
inelegance 571 n.
deed 671 n.
defiance 706 n.
trophy 724 n.
prodigality 810 n.
ornamentation
839 n.
fashion 843 n.
affectation
845 n.
pride 866 n.
airs 868 n.
vanity 868 n.
ostentation
870 n.
boasting 872 n.

ostentatious
ostentatious
870 adj.

ostentatious, be
be ostentatious
870 vb.

outbreak
revolution 144 n.
havoc 160 n.
outbreak 171 n.
egress 293 n.
voidance 295 n.
revolt 733 n.

outcast
nonconformist
84 n.
ejection 295 n.

outcast 878 n.

outdo
be unequal 29 n.
be superior
34 vb.
be early 130 vb.
be distant
194 vb.
outstrip 272 vb.
outdo 301 vb.
deceive 537 vb.
endanger 656 vb.
be cunning
693 vb.
contend 711 vb.
defeat 722 vb.
overmaster
722 vb.
humiliate 867 vb.

outflow
outflow 293 n.

outgoing
outgoing 293 adj.
flowing 345 adj.

outlast
continue 104 vb.
outlast 108 vb.
be stable 148 vb.
resist 710 vb.

outlet
gap 196 n.
orifice 258 n.
outlet 293 n.
drain 346 n.
blowing 347 n.

outline
region 179 n.
size 190 n.
distance 194 n.
frame 213 n.
exteriority 218 n.
surroundings
225 n.
outline 228 n.
outline 228 vb.
edging 229 n.
enclosure 230 n.
limit 231 n.
form 238 vb.
circle 245 n.
go round 245 vb.
shore 339 n.
representation
546 n.
represent 546 vb.
describe 585 vb.
abstract 587 vb.

outlined
outlined 228 adj.

outstrip
be superior
34 vb.
do before 114 vb.
outstrip 272 vb.
precede 278 vb.
progress 280 vb.
approach 284 vb.
outdo 301 vb.
hasten 675 vb.
take 781 vb.

overactivity
overactivity
673 n.

overcharge
overcharge
806 vb.

overcoat
overcoat 223 n.
warm clothes
376 n.

overestimation
overestimation
477 n.

over five
over five 96 n.

overhanging
overhanging
204 adj.

overlay
overlay 221 vb.

overlie
overlie 221 vb.

overlying
overlying 221 vb.

overmaster
be strong 157 vb.
prevail 173 vb.
attack 707 vb.
overmaster
722 vb.
dominate 728 vb.
subjugate 740 vb.
take 781 vb.
frighten 849 vb.
humiliate 867 vb.

over one hundred
over one hundred
96 n.

overrate
augment 36 vb.
overstep 301 vb.
misjudge 476 vb.
overrate 477 vb.
be credulous
482 vb.
err 490 vb.
misinterpret
516 vb.
advertise 523 vb.
exaggerate
541 vb.
make important
633 vb.
bargain 786 vb.
praise 918 vb.
flatter 920 vb.

overrated
overrated
477 adj.

overstep
be great 32 vb.
be superior
34 vb.
flank 234 vb.
pass 300 vb.
overstep 301 vb.
exaggerate
541 vb.
superabound
632 vb.
be clumsy
690 vb.
not observe
764 vb.
be intemperate
938 vb.

overstepping
overstepping
301 n.

overturning
overturning
216 n.

owed
owed 798 adj.

owner
owner 771 n.

P

pacification
pacification
714 n.

pacificatory
pacificatory
714 adj.

pacifist
quietude 261 n.
pacifist 712 n.

pacify
assuage 172 vb.
induce 607 vb.
concord 705 vb.
pacify 714 vb.
mediate 715 vb.
compromise
765 vb.
tranquillize
818 vb.
content 823 vb.
be courteous
879 vb.
ask mercy
900 vb.
atone 936 vb.
offer worship
975 vb.

paganize
paganize 968 vb.

pageant
procession 71 n.
assemblage 74 n.
pageant 870 n.

pain
pain 372 n.
cry 403 n.
evil 611 n.
badness 640 n.
illness 646 n.
adversity 726 n.
suffering 825 n.
painfulness 822 n.
corporal
punishment
958 n.

pained
pained 372 adj.
suffering 820 adj.

painful
sentient 369 adj.
painful 372 adj.
paining 822 adj.
punitive 958 adj.

painfully
painfully 32 adv.

painfulness
painfulness 822 n.

paining
paining 822 adj.

painkiller. See drug
antidote 653 n.

paint
compose 56 vb.
colour 420 vb.
represent 546 vb.
paint 548 vb.
decorate 839 vb.

painted
painted 548 adj.

painting
mimicry 20 n.
composition 56 n.
production 159 n.
colour 420 vb.
art 546 n.
representation
546 n.
painting 548 n.

pair
combine 50 vb.
pair 90 vb.

palaeology
palaeology 120 n.

palmy
tranquil 261 adj.
peaceful 712 adj.
palmy 725 adj.

palmy days
palmy days
725 n.

pang
spasm 313 n.
pang 372 n.
rheumatism
646 n.
suffering 820 n.

panting
panting 679 adj.

paper
lamina 202 n.
art equipment
548 n.
stationery 581 n.
bookbinding
584 n.
paper 626 n.

paper money
paper money
792 n.

paradisiac
paradisiac
965 adj.

paragon
prototype 23 n.
superior 34 n.
exceller 639 n.
paragon 641 n.
proficient person
691 n.
a beauty 836 n.
prodigy 859 n.
person of repute
861 n.
pride 866 n.
good person
932 n.

parallel
relative 9 adj.
parallel 214 adj.
lateral 234 adj.
symmetrical
240 adj.
directed 276 adj.

parallel, be
be equal 28 vb.
be parallel
214 vb.

parallelism
parallelism 214 n.

paranormal
paranormal
978 adj.

parentage
consanguinity
11 n.
kinsman 11 n.
precursor 66 n.
origin 68 n.
cause 151 n.
source 151 n.
attribution 153 n.
producer 159 n.
propagation
162 n.
parentage 164 n.
master 736 n.

parental
parental 164 adj.

parish
parish 979 n.

parliament
parliament 687 n.
authority 728 n.
lawcourt 951 n.

parliamentary
parliamentary
687 adj.

parry
deflect 277 vb.
repel 287 vb.
screen 416 vb.
sophisticate
472 vb.
avoid 615 vb.
obstruct 697 vb.
parry 708 vb.
retaliate 709 vb.
resist 710 vb.

parse
parse 559 vb.

parsimonious
careful 452 adj.
insufficient
631 adj.
retentive 773 adj.
economical
809 adj.
parsimonious
811 adj.
selfish 927 adj.
temperate
937 adj.

parsimonious, be
make insufficient
631 vb.
not pay 800 vb.
economize
809 vb.
be parsimonious
811 vb.
starve 941 vb.

parsimoniously
parsimoniously
811 adv.

parsimony
insufficiency
631 n.
parsimony 811 n.
unsociability
878 n.
selfishness 927 n.

parsonage
house 187 n.
parsonage 980 n.

part
degree 27 n.
part 53 n.
part 53 vb.
incompleteness
55 n.
component 58 n.
bisection 92 n.
fraction 98 n.
trifle 634 n.
portion 778 n.

partially
partially 33 adv.

participate
be equal 28 vb.
be one of 58 vb.
mete out 460 vb.
be instrumental
623 vb.
do 671 vb.
be active 673 vb.
behave 683 vb.
cooperate
701 vb.

participate
     770 vb.
give 776 vb.
apportion 778 vb.
defray 799 vb.
feel 813 vb.
be sociable
     877 vb.
pity 900 vb.
participation
participation
     770 n.
participator
participator
     770 n.
particularism
particularism
     80 n.
particulars
particulars 80 n.
partition
separation 46 n.
middle 70 n.
dividing line 92 n.
gap 196 n.
summit 208 n.
centrality 220 n.
partition 226 n.
barrier 230 n.
limit 231 n.
obstacle 697 n.
partly
partly 53 adv.
part of speech
adjunct 40 n.
name 556 n.
part of speech
     559 n.
party
part 53 n.
assemblage 74 n.
prejudice 476 n.
dissent 484 n.
dissentient 484 n.
association
     701 n.
party 703 n.
sect 972 n.
pass
connect 45 vb.
change 138 vb.
be turned to
     142 vb.
cross 217 vb.
be in motion
     260 vb.
traverse 262 vb.
navigate 264 vb.
pass 300 vb.
overstep 301 vb.
flow 345 vb.
passage
union 45 n.
entrance 68 n.
change 138 n.
transition 142 n.
gap 196 n.
narrowness
     201 n.
shallowness
     207 n.
open space
     258 n.
motion 260 n.
wandering 262 n.
transference
     267 n.
passage 300 n.
overstepping
     301 n.
access 619 n.

bridge 619 n.
pass away
pass away 2 vb.
pass
ageing 126 adj.
passing
moving 260 adj.
travelling
     262 adj.
passing 300 adj.
passing along
motion 260 n.
conveyance
     262 n.
passing along
     300 n.
pass time
pass time 104 vb.
elapse 107 vb.
past
extinct 2 adj.
past 120 adj.
antiquated
     122 adj.
olden 122 adj.
unwonted
     606 adj.
past, be
come before
     64 vb.
elapse 107 vb.
be past 120 vb.
cease 140 vb.
happen 149 vb.
pastor
preacher 532 n.
teacher 532 n.
pastor 980 n.
pastries
pastries 296 n.
past time
precedence 64 n.
time 104 n.
long duration
     108 n.
priority 114 n.
different time
     117 n.
past time 120 n.
newness 121 n.
possibility 464 n.
paternity
old man 128 n.
paternity 164 n.
male 367 n.
path
passage 300 n.
path 619 n.
pathology
pathology 646 n.
medical art
     653 n.
patience
leniency 731 n.
feeling 813 n.
moral insensibility
     815 n.
patience 818 n.
caution 853 n.
forgiveness
     904 n.
patient
slow 273 adj.
lenient 731 adj.
patient 818 adj.
cautious 853 adj.
pitying 900 adj.
forgiving 904 adj.
patient, be
be lenient 731 vb.
permit 751 vb.

be patient
     818 vb.
be courteous
     879 vb.
forgive 904 vb.
patriot
patriot 896 n.
benefactor 898 n.
patriotic
patriotic 896 adj.
patriotism
patriotism 896 n.
patron
intermediary
     226 n.
onlookers 436 n.
witness 461 n.
assenter 483 n.
enthusiast 499 n.
protector 655 n.
aider 698 n.
patron 702 n.
combatant 717 n.
master 736 n.
deputy 750 n.
security 762 n.
participator
     770 n.
desirer 854 n.
friend 875 n.
kind person
     892 n.
benefactor 898 n.
commender
     918 n.
patronize
patronize 698 vb.
pattern
crossing 217 n.
textile 217 n.
edging 229 n.
curve 243 n.
notch 255 n.
pattern 839 n.
pause
be discontinuous
     72 vb.
wait 131 vb.
pause 140 vb.
be quiescent
     261 vb.
decelerate
     273 vb.
arrive 290 vb.
pavilion
pavilion 187 n.
arbour 189 n.
paving
base 209 n.
basis 213 n.
paving 221 n.
smoothness
     253 n.
building material
     626 n.
pawnshop
pawnshop 779 n.
pay
compensate
     31 vb.
employ 617 vb.
keep faith
     763 vb.
earnings 766 n.
give 776 vb.
restitute 782 vb.
draw money
     792 vb.
pay 799 n.
pay 799 vb.

expenditure
     801 n.
expend 801 vb.
grant claims
     910 vb.
do one's duty
     912 vb.
reward 957 n.
reward 957 vb.
paying
paying 799 adj.
payment
offset 31 n.
part 53 n.
incentive 607 n.
security 762 n.
gift 776 n.
funds 792 n.
payment 799 n.
expenditure
     801 n.
accounts 803 n.
tax 804 n.
dueness 910 n.
penalty 958 n.
pay one's respects
pay one's
respects 879 vb.
pay too much
pay too much
     806 vb.
peace
quietude 261 n.
concord 705 n.
peace 712 n.
peace offering
     714 n.
palmy days
     725 n.
peaceful
inert 170 adj.
moderate
     172 adj.
concordant
     705 adj.
peaceful 712 adj.
submitting
     716 adj.
obedient 734 adj.
inexcitable
     818 adj.
content 823 adj.
amiable 879 adj.
peacefully
peacefully
     712 adv.
peace offering
argument 470 n.
peace offering
     714 n.
peculation
peculation 783 n.
pedagogic
pedagogic
     532 adj.
pedestrian
pedestrian 263 n.
passing along
     300 n.
pedestrianism
pedestrianism
     262 n.
pedlar
traveller 263 n.
seller 788 n.
pedlar 789 n.
penalty
decrease 37 n.
decrement 42 n.
labour 677 n.
compulsion 735 n.

restraint 742 n.
nonobservance
764 n.
loss 767 n.
restitution 782 n.
pay 799 n.
nonpayment
800 n.
cost 804 n.
price 804 n.
tax 804 n.
mercy 900 n.
penalty 958 n.
penance
penitence 934 n.
penance 936 n.
asceticism 940 n.
Christian rite
982 n.
pendency
pendency 212 n.
pending, be
continue 104 vb.
be pending
131 vb.
penitence
penitence 934 n.
penitent
penitent 934 n.
ascetic 940 n.
penitent, be
be wise 493 vb.
confess 521 vb.
tergiversate
598 vb.
get better
649 vb.
regret 825 vb.
be penitent
934 vb.
become pious
973 vb.
penitently
penitently
934 adv.
people of taste
sensibility 369 n.
collector 487 n.
enthusiast 499 n.
people of taste
841 n.
perfect
consummate
32 adj.
supreme 34 adj.
unmixed 44 adj.
whole 52 adj.
complete 54 adj.
elegant 570 adj.
be elegant
570 vb.
best 639 adj.
excellent 639 adj.
perfect 641 adj.
perfect 641 vb.
clean 643 adj.
preserved
661 adj.
mature 664 vb.
skilful 689 adj.
completed
720 adj.
carry through
720 vb.
beautiful 836 adj.
shapely 836 adj.
approvable
918 adj.
virtuous 928 adj.
innocent 930 adj.
pure 945 adj.

perfection
prototype 23 n.
superiority 34 n.
completeness
54 n.
summit 208 n.
symmetry 240 n.
goodness 639 n.
perfection 641 n.
preparedness
664 n.
skill 689 n.
completion 720 n.
beauty 836 n.
desired object
854 n.
virtues 928 n.
innocence 930 n.
purity 945 n.
divine attribute
960 n.
perfectionist
narrow mind
476 n.
trier 666 n.
perfectionist
857 n.
perfectly
perfectly
641 adv.
perfidious
perfidious
925 adj.
perfidy
latency 518 n.
falsehood 536 n.
deception 537 n.
mental dishonesty
538 n.
untruth 538 n.
tergiversation
598 n.
sedition 733 n.
nonobservance
764 n.
enmity 876 n.
undutifulness
913 n.
perfidy 925 n.
perforated
perforated
258 adj.
perforation
perforation
258 n.
insertion 298 n.
indication 542 n.
wound 650 n.
perforator
perforator 258 n.
perform ritual
drench 336 vb.
name 556 vb.
offer worship
975 vb.
perform ritual
982 vb.
period
part 53 n.
time 104 n.
period 106 n.
brief span 109 n.
periodicity 136 n.
regular return
136 n.
limit 231 n.
labour 677 n.
periodic
continuous
71 adj.
periodic 106 adj.

periodical
discontinuous
72 adj.
regular 81 adj.
repeated 102 adj.
continuing
104 adj.
frequent 134 adj.
periodical
136 adj.
unstable 147 adj.
oscillating
312 adj.
periodically
periodically
136 adv.
periodic, be
come after 65 vb.
be periodic
136 vb.
periodicity
periodicity 136 n.
perish
pass away 2 vb.
be destroyed
160 vb.
perish 356 vb.
kill oneself
357 vb.
permanence
permanence
139 n.
permanent
uniform 16 adj.
perpetual
110 adj.
antiquated
122 adj.
permanent
139 adj.
unchangeable
148 adj.
godlike 960 adj.
permission
ability 155 n.
ingress 292 n.
assent 483 n.
facility 696 n.
laxity 729 n.
leniency 731 n.
permission 751 n.
consent 753 n.
nonliability 914 n.
approbation
918 n.
permit
stay 139 vb.
opener 258 n.
ingress 292 n.
credential 461 n.
be possible
464 vb.
make possible
464 vb.
assent 483 n.
acquiesce 483 vb.
assent 483 vb.
label 542 n.
instrument 623 n.
protection 655 n.
facilitate 696 vb.
be lax 729 vb.
be lenient 731 vb.
warrant 732 n.
give scope
739 vb.
mandate 746 n.
commission
746 n.
permit 751 n.
permit 751 vb.

consent 753 vb.
give 776 vb.
be patient
818 vb.
dueness 910 n.
grant claims
910 vb.
nonliability 914 n.
exempt 914 vb.
approve 918 vb.
permitted
permitted
751 adj.
permitting
permitting
751 adj.
perpetual
existing 1 adj.
continuous
71 adj.
infinite 103 adj.
continuing
104 adj.
lasting 108 adj.
perpetual
110 adj.
permanent
139 adj.
unceasing
141 adj.
unchangeable
148 adj.
renowned
861 adj.
godlike 960 adj.
perpetually
perpetually
134 adv.
perpetuate
perpetuate
110 vb.
sustain 141 vb.
stabilize 148 vb.
perpetuity
existence 1 n.
continuity 71 n.
infinity 103 n.
time 104 n.
neverness 105 n.
long duration
108 n.
perpetuity 110 n.
permanence
139 n.
continuance
141 n.
immateriality
315 n.
divine attribute
960 n.
perseverance
perseverance
595 n.
persevere
continue 71 vb.
stay 139 vb.
go on 141 vb.
stand firm
594 vb.
persevere 595 vb.
be obstinate
597 vb.
pursue 614 vb.
be active 673 vb.
exert oneself
677 vb.
work 677 vb.
hope 847 vb.
persevering
persevering
595 adj.

persistently
persistently
595 adv.

person
self 80 n.
unit 88 n.
object 314 n.
person 366 n.

personable
personable
836 adj.

personnel
component 58 n.
band 74 n.
list 87 n.
power 155 n.
resident 186 n.
mariner 265 n.
aeronaut 266 n.
person 366 n.
means 624 n.
personnel 681 n.
party 703 n.
domestic 737 n.

perspicuity
perspicuity 562 n.

perspicuous
perspicuous
562 adj.

persuadability
persuadability
607 n.

pertinently
pertinently
24 adv.

pervade
be 1 vb.
fill 54 vb.
be general 79 vb.
prevail 173 vb.
pervade 184 vb.
lie between
226 vb.
pass 300 vb.

pervert
derange 63 vb.
modify 138 vb.
convert 142 vb.
harm 640 vb.
pervert 650 vb.
misuse 670 vb.
make insensitive
815 vb.
make wicked
929 vb.

pet
look after
452 vb.
tempt 607 vb.
patronize 698 vb.
be lenient 731 vb.
pet 884 vb.
philanthropize
892 vb.

petitioner
petitioner 758 n.

philanthropic
philanthropic
896 adj.

philanthropist
visionary 508 n.
volunteer 592 n.
reformer 649 n.
worker 681 n.
keeper 744 n.
xenophile 875 n.
kind person
892 n.
philanthropist
896 n.
benefactor 898 n.

good person
932 n.
zealot 973 n.
pastor 980 n.

philanthropize
philanthropize
892 vb.

philanthropy
generality 79 n.
voluntary work
592 n.
subvention 698 n.
gift 776 n.
giving 776 n.
benevolence
892 n.
philanthropy
896 n.
disinterestedness
926 n.
pietism 973 n.
piety 973 n.
church ministry
979 n.

philosopher
immateriality
315 n.
philosopher
444 n.
enquirer 454 n.
reasoner 470 n.
intellectual
487 n.
sage 495 n.
theorist 507 n.

philosophic
philosophic
444 adj.

philosophy
existence 1 n.
philosophy 444 n.
enquiry 454 n.
reasoning 470 n.
estimate 475 n.
creed 480 n.
opinion 480 n.
morals 912 n.
religion 967 n.
antichristianity
968 n.
irreligion 968 n.

phobia
psychopathy
498 n.
phobia 849 n.
dislike 856 n.

photograph
enlarge 192 vb.
record 543 vb.
photograph
546 vb.

photography
imitation 20 n.
copy 22 n.
duplicate 22 n.
miniature 191 n.
astronomy 316 n.
optics 412 n.
darkness 413 n.
achromatism
421 n.
camera 437 n.
optical device
437 n.
cinema 440 n.
recorder 544 n.
photography
546 n.
picture 548 n.
print 582 n.

phrase
part 53 n.
composition 56 n.
commentary
515 n.
word 554 n.
phrase 558 n.
phrase 558 vb.
style 561 n.
show style
561 vb.
ornament 569 n.

phrasemonger
phrasemonger
569 n.

phraseological
phraseological
558 adj.

physics
physics 314 n.

piano
piano 409 n.

picture
assimilation 18 n.
copy 22 n.
miniature 191 n.
outline 228 n.
spectacle 440 n.
representation
546 n.
picture 548 n.
book 584 n.
edition 584 n.

piece
small quantity
33 n.
small thing 33 n.
remainder 41 n.
piece 53 n.
incompleteness
55 n.
bulk 190 n.
strip 203 n.
powder 327 n.
soil 339 n.
portion 778 n.

piecemeal
piecemeal 53 adv.

pied
pied 432 adj.

pierce
cut 46 vb.
make concave
250 vb.
pierce 258 vb.
strike 274 vb.
shoot 282 vb.
enter 292 vb.
empty 295 vb.
infuse 298 vb.
insert 298 vb.
pass 300 vb.
kill 357 vb.
give pain 372 vb.
mark 542 vb.
ill-treat 640 vb.
wound 650 vb.
strike at 707 vb.

pierce. See break
sunder 46 vb.

pietism
pietism 973 n.

pietist
pietist 973 n.

pietistic
pietistic 973 adj.

piety
progression
280 n.
meditation 444 n.
offering 776 n.

feeling 813 n.
religion 967 n.
piety 973 n.
public worship
975 n.
worship 975 n.

pig
pig 360 n.

pigment
facing 221 n.
pigment 420 n.

pillar
verticality 210 n.
hanger 212 n.
pillar 213 n.

pillory
hanger 212 n.
seat 213 n.
penance 936 n.
pillory 959 n.

pious
honourable
924 adj.
pious 973 adj.
worshipping
975 adj.

pious, be
be honourable
924 vb.
be pious 973 vb.
offer worship
975 vb.
worship 975 vb.

pistol
propellant 282 n.
pistol 718 n.

pitfall
depth 206 n.
invisibility 439 n.
latency 518 n.
ambush 522 n.
trap 537 n.
bane 654 n.
danger 656 n.
pitfall 658 n.
stratagem 693 n.
threat 895 n.

pitiable
distressing
822 adj.
lamenting
831 adj.
pitiable 900 adj.

pitiless
destructive
160 adj.
resolute 594 adj.
obstinate
597 adj.
severe 730 adj.
cruel 893 adj.
malevolent
893 adj.
pitiless 901 adj.
revengeful
905 adj.

pitiless, be
destroy 160 vb.
slaughter 357 vb.
be severe 730 vb.
be insensitive
815 vb.
be malevolent
893 vb.
be pitiless
901 vb.
be impenitent
935 vb.

pitilessness
pitilessness
901 n.

pity
bond 47 n.
leniency 731 n.
be sensitive
814 vb.
relieve 826 vb.
lamentation
831 n.
lament 831 vb.
benevolence
892 n.
pity 900 n.
pity 900 vb.
forgiveness
904 n.
disinterestedness
926 n.

pitying
pitying 900 adj.

pivot
joint 45 n.
influence 173 n.
pivot 213 n.
centre 220 n.
extractor 299 n.
lifter 305 n.
rotator 310 n.
tool 625 n.
chief thing 633 n.

place
arrange 62 vb.
put in front
64 vb.
specify 80 vb.
region 179 n.
place 180 n.
situation 181 n.
locality 182 n.
place 182 vb.
enclosure 230 n.
open space
258 n.
aim 276 vb.
orientate 276 vb.
discover 479 vb.

place after
place after 65 vb.

place of amusement
meeting place
187 n.
place of
amusement
832 n.

place oneself
be in order 60 vb.
have rank 73 vb.
place oneself
182 vb.
dwell 187 vb.
be quiescent
261 vb.
travel 262 vb.
enter 292 vb.
appropriate
781 vb.

plague
badness 640 n.
plague 646 n.
blight 654 n.

plain
uniform 16 adj.
simple 44 adj.
space 178 n.
lowness 205 n.
horizontality
211 n.
open space
258 n.
land 339 n.
plain 343 n.

soft-hued
420 adj.
meaningful
509 adj.
semantic 509 adj.
intelligible
511 adj.
figurative
514 adj.
undisguised
517 adj.
informative
519 adj.
assertive 527 adj.
veracious
535 adj.
perspicuous
562 adj.
feeble 567 adj.
plain 568 adj.
elegant 570 adj.
inelegant 571 adj.
prosaic 588 adj.
artless 694 adj.
free 739 adj.
tedious 838 adj.
tasteful 841 adj.
plebeian 864 adj.
disrespectful
916 adj.
detracting
921 adj.

plain, be
result 152 vb.
be visible 438 vb.
be plain 517 vb.
be disclosed
521 vb.

plainly
plainly 568 adv.

plainness
plainness 568 n.

plan
prototype 23 n.
incompleteness
55 n.
arrangement
62 n.
arrange 62 vb.
statistics 86 n.
cause 151 n.
production 159 n.
produce 159 vb.
outline 228 n.
think 444 vb.
be wise 493 vb.
foresight 505 vb.
foresee 505 vb.
prediction 506 n.
suppose 507 vb.
representation
546 n.
represent 546 vb.
compendium
587 n.
predetermine
603 vb.
intention 612 n.
intend 612 vb.
plan 618 n.
plan 618 vb.
find means
624 vb.
preparation
664 n.
prepare 664 vb.
undertaking
667 n.
tactics 683 n.
deal with 683 vb.

be cunning
693 vb.
art of war 713 n.
warfare 713 n.
desire 854 vb.

planet
circler 309 n.
planet 316 n.

planned
planned 618 adj.

planner
planner 618 n.

planning
planning 618 n.

plant
young plant
127 n.
source 151 n.
vessel 189 n.
microorganism
191 n.
filament 203 n.
prop 213 n.
coil 246 n.
vegetable 296 n.
plant 361 n.

plate
plate 189 n.
horizontality
211 n.

plausible
plausible 466 adj.

player
hunter 614 n.
player 832 n.

playgoer
playgoer 589 n.

play music
shrill 402 vb.
play music
408 vb.

plaything
jumper 307 n.
bauble 634 n.
plaything 832 n.

plead
plead 609 vb.
avoid 615 vb.
justify 922 vb.

pleasance
pleasance 187 n.

pleasant
pleasant 371 adj.
sweet 387 adj.
fragrant 391 adj.

please
enjoy 371 vb.
please 821 vb.
content 823 vb.
cheer 828 vb.

pleased
assenting
483 adj.
pleased 819 adj.
content 823 adj.
jubilant 828 adj.
amused 832 adj.

pleased, be
enjoy 371 vb.
gaze 438 vb.
show feeling
813 vb.
be pleased
819 vb.
be content
823 vb.
rejoice 830 vb.
feel pride 866 vb.
boast 872 vb.
greet 879 vb.

congratulate
881 vb.

please oneself
will 590 vb.
be obstinate
597 vb.
please oneself
729 vb.
oppress 760 vb.
disobey 733 vb.
be free 739 vb.
permit 751 vb.
be intemperate
938 vb.
be illegal 949 vb.

pleasurable
pleasurable
821 adj.

pleasurableness
pleasurableness
821 n.

pleasure
pleasure 371 n.
joy 819 n.
sensualism 939 n.

pleasure ground
abode 187 n.
pleasance 187 n.
arena 719 n.
pleasure ground
832 n.

plebeian
inferior 35 adj.
general 79 adj.
ill-bred 842 adj.
inglorious
862 adj.
plebeian 864 adj.
humble 867 adj.

pledged
pledged 762 adj.

plenitude
plenitude 54 n.

plenteous
plenteous
630 adj.

plenty
greatness 32 n.
great quantity
32 n.
productiveness
166 n.
feasting 296 n.
vegetable life
361 n.
store 627 n.
plenty 630 n.
redundance
632 n.
prosperity 725 n.
wealth 795 n.
cheapness 807 n.
liberality 808 n.
pleasurableness
821 n.

pleonasm
pleonasm 565 n.

pleonastic
pleonastic
565 adj.

plot
combination 50 n.
combine 50 vb.
concurrence
176 n.
concur 176 vb.
latency 518 n.
secrecy 520 n.
be stealthy
520 vb.
fake 536 vb.

deception 537 n.
deceive 537 vb.
predetermination
603 n.
plot 618 n.
plot 618 vb.
overactivity
673 n.
cunning 693 n.
stratagem 693 n.
be cunning
693 vb.
cooperation
701 n.
cooperate
701 vb.
sedition 733 n.
compact 760 n.

plumage
filament 203 n.
skin 221 n.
plumage 254 n.
wing 266 n.
softness 322 n.
trimming 839 n.

plunge
be inferior 35 vb.
decrease 37 vb.
be destroyed
160 vb.
suppress 160 vb.
motion 260 n.
aquatics 264 n.
navigate 264 vb.
swim 264 vb.
fly 266 vb.
enter 292 vb.
immersion 298 n.
immerse 298 vb.
descent 304 n.
descend 304 vb.
tumble 304 vb.
lowering 306 n.
lower 306 vb.
plunge 308 n.
plunge 308 vb.
be wet 336 vb.
measure 460 vb.
ablutions 643 n.
defeat 722 vb.

plural
plural 97 adj.

plurality
plurality 97 n.

pneumatics
pneumatics
335 n.

pocket
pocket 189 n.
garment 223 n.
opening 258 n.
treasury 794 n.

poem
subdivision 53 n.
composition 56 n.
literature 552 n.
reading matter
584 n.
description 585 n.
narrative 585 n.
poem 588 n.

poet
author 584 n.
poet 588 n.
dramatist 589 n.

poetic
poetic 588 adj.

poetize
poetize 588 vb.

poetry
composition 56 n.

ideality 508 n.
reading matter
584 n.
poetry 588 n.

point to
point to 276 vb.
indicate 542 vb.
direct 684 vb.

poison
nucleonics 155 n.
gas 331 n.
unsavouriness
386 n.
radiation 412 n.
infection 646 n.
prophylactic
653 n.
poison 654 n.
weapon 718 n.
means of
execution 959 n.

poisoning
poisoning 654 n.

poisonous plant
plant 361 n.
poisonous plant
654 n.

polarity
polarity 14 n.
duality 90 n.

police
protector 655 n.
police 955 n.

police enquiry
police enquiry
454 n.

policy
mathematics
86 n.
topic 447 n.
policy 618 n.
action 671 n.
deed 671 n.
conduct 683 n.
tactics 683 n.
management
684 n.

**political
organization**
political
organization
728 n.

political party
association
701 n.
political party
703 n.
government
728 n.

polygamist
polygamist 889 n.

pony
pony 268 n.

poop
poop 233 n.
laterality 234 n.

poor
uncovered
224 adj.
necessitous
622 adj.
unprovided
631 adj.
unimportant
634 adj.
deteriorated
650 adj.
dilapidated
650 adj.
unprosperous
726 adj.

not owning
769 adj.
poor 796 adj.
nonpaying
800 adj.

poor, be
have trouble
726 vb.
be poor 796 vb.
not pay 800 vb.
starve 941 vb.

poorly reasoned
poorly reasoned
472 adj.
feeble 567 adj.

poor person
slut 61 n.
wanderer 263 n.
nonentity 634 n.
unlucky person
726 n.
poor person
796 n.
low fellow 864 n.

**poor person. See
native**
dweller 186 n.

porosity
porosity 258 n.

porous
porous 258 adj.

portion
finite quantity
26 n.
degree 27 n.
part 53 n.
piece 53 n.
fraction 98 n.
meal 296 n.
provisions 296 n.
participation
770 n.
portion 778 n.

**position of
authority**
official 685 n.
position of
authority 728 n.
law officer 950 n.

positive
evidential
461 adj.
positive 468 adj.
narrow-minded
476 adj.
believing 480 adj.
affirmative
527 adj.
assertive 527 adj.
obstinate
597 adj.

positively
positively 32 adv.

positiveness
positiveness
468 n.
narrow mind
476 n.
affirmation
527 n.
opinionatedness
597 n.

possess
be present
184 vb.
dwell 187 vb.
dispose of
668 vb.
possess 768 vb.
appropriate
781 vb.

possessed
located 182 adj.
possessed
768 adj.

possessing
possessing
768 adj.

possession
presence 184 n.
use 668 n.
possession 768 n.
church office
979 n.

possessively
possessively
768 adv.

possessor
resident 186 n.
possession 768 n.
participator
770 n.
possessor 771 n.
dueness 910 n.
cleric 980 n.

possibility
existence 1 n.
opportunity
132 n.
conversion 142 n.
fair chance
154 n.
ability 155 n.
liability 175 n.
life 355 n.
possibility 464 n.
probability 466 n.
expectation
502 n.
supposition
507 n.
latency 518 n.
sufficiency 630 n.
facility 696 n.
hope 847 n.

possible
unreal 2 adj.
future 119 adj.
powerful 155 adj.
liable 175 adj.
accessible
284 adj.
possible 464 adj.
probable 466 adj.
rational 470 adj.
credible 480 adj.
latent 518 adj.
easy 696 adj.

possible, be
be possible
464 vb.
be likely 466 vb.

possibly
actually 1 adv.
by chance
154 adv.
possibly 464 adv.

**postal
communications**
transferrer 267 n.
courier 524 n.
message 524 n.
postal
communications
526 n.
correspondence
583 n.

posteriority
posteriority
115 n.

posterity
kinsman 11 n.

survivor 41 n.
sequence 65 n.
successor 67 n.
posteriority
115 n.
futurity 119 n.
effect 152 n.
posterity 165 n.

post meridiem
post meridiem
124 adv.

post-obit
post-obit
356 adv.

potentate
potentate 736 n.
person of rank
863 n.

potherb
potherb 296 n.

pottery
product 159 n.
receptacle 189 n.
formation 238 n.
brittleness 325 n.
soil 339 n.
pottery 376 n.
sculpture 549 n.
building material
626 n.

poultry
meat 296 n.
poultry 360 n.

poverty
smallness 33 n.
inferiority 35 n.
decrease 37 n.
piece 53 n.
extremity 69 n.
necessity 591 n.
evil 611 n.
needfulness
622 n.
scarcity 631 n.
uncleanness
644 n.
deterioration
650 n.
dilapidation
650 n.
adversity 726 n.
nonownership
769 n.
poverty 796 n.
asceticism 940 n.

powder
small thing 33 n.
leavings 41 n.
remainder 41 n.
powder 327 n.
dirt 649 n.
divine attribute
960 n.

powderiness
powderiness
327 n.

powdery
minute 191 adj.
brittle 325 adj.
powdery 327 adj.
dry 337 adj.

power
greatness 32 n.
power 155 n.
strength 157 n.
agency 168 n.
instrumentality
623 n.
utility 635 n.
brute force
730 n.

powerful
great 32 adj.
powerful 155 adj.
strong 157 adj.
vigorous 169 adj.
vigorous 169 adj.
influential
173 adj.
instrumental
623 adj.
useful 635 adj.
compelling
735 adj.
godlike 960 adj.

powerfully
powerfully
155 adv.

powerless
powerless
156 adj.
weak 158 adj.
inert 170 adj.

practice
conformity 83 n.
eating 296 n.
expectation
502 n.
connotation
509 n.
practice 605 n.
business 617 n.
way 619 n.
use 668 n.
action 671 n.
conduct 683 n.
precept 688 n.
observance
763 n.
etiquette 843 n.
formality 870 n.
rite 982 n.
ritual 982 n.

practise occultism
practise
occultism 978 vb.

practise sorcery
deprecate 757 vb.
practise sorcery
977 vb.

praise
overrate 477 vb.
description 585 n.
rejoicing 830 n.
rejoice 830 vb.
honours 861 n.
thanks 902 n.
respect 915 vb.
praise 918 n.
praise 918 vb.
flatter 920 vb.
reward 957 n.
be pious 973 vb.
act of worship
975 n.
offer worship
975 vb.
worship 975 vb.
idolatrize 976 vb.

praised, be
be praised
918 vb.

prayers
prayers 975 n.

preacher
preacher 532 n.

precede
come before
64 vb.
be before 114 vb.
do before 114 vb.

be in front
232 vb.
walk 262 vb.
precede 278 vb.
motivate 607 vb.

precedence
superiority 34 n.
addition 38 n.
precedence 64 n.
priority 114 n.
seniority 126 n.
anticipation
130 n.
front 232 n.
preceding 278 n.
importance
633 n.
authority 728 n.

preceding
superior 34 adj.
supreme 34 adj.
additional 38 adj.
precedence 64 n.
preceding 64 adj.
precursory
66 adj.
priority 114 n.
prior 114 adj.
foregoing
120 adj.
frontal 232 adj.
motion 260 n.
preceding 278 vb.
progression
280 n.
preparatory
664 adj.

precept
prototype 23 n.
rule 81 n.
traffic control
300 n.
maxim 491 n.
commentary
515 n.
advice 686 n.
precept 688 n.
decree 732 n.
conditions 761 n.
right 908 n.
code of duty
912 n.
legislation 948 n.
office-book
982 n.
rite 982 n.

preceptive
preceptive
688 adj.

precursor
precedence 64 n.
precursor 66 n.
beginning 68 n.
example 83 n.
priority 114 n.
morning 123 n.
earliness 130 n.
paternity 164 n.
native 186 n.
settler 186 n.
front 232 n.
traveller 263 n.
preceding 278 n.
the dead 356 n.
messenger 524 n.
preacher 532 n.
preparer 664 n.
director 685 n.

precursory
precursory
66 adj.

predestine
predestine
150 adj.
necessitate
591 vb.
predetermine
603 vb.
intend 612 vb.

predetermination
predetermination
603 n.

predetermine
predestine
150 adj.
prejudge 476 vb.
foresee 505 vb.
predetermine
603 vb.
motivate 607 vb.
intend 612 vb.
plan 618 vb.
prepare 664 vb.
decree 732 vb.

predetermined
predetermined
603 adj.

predicament
circumstance 8 n.
complexity 61 n.
crisis 132 n.
foolery 492 n.
necessity 591 n.
evil 611 n.
danger 656 n.
predicament
695 n.
adversity 726 n.
painfulness 822 n.
hopelessness
848 n.

predict
look ahead
119 vb.
predestine
150 adj.
foresee 505 vb.
predict 506 vb.
be truthful
535 vb.
indicate 542 vb.
warn 659 vb.
give hope 847 vb.
be cautious
853 vb.
threaten 895 vb.

predicting
predicting
506 adj.

prediction
looking ahead
119 n.
destiny 150 n.
weather 335 n.
appearance
440 n.
probability 466 n.
expectation
502 n.
foresight 505 n.
prediction 506 n.
policy 618 n.
warning 659 n.
occultism 978 n.

predominate
predominate
34 vb.
cause 151 vb.
prevail 173 vb.
weigh 317 vb.
motivate 607 vb.

be important
633 vb.
overmaster
722 vb.
dominate 728 vb.
prejudge
prejudge 476 vb.
prejudgment
prejudgment
476 n.
prejudice
race 11 n.
exclusion 57 n.
prejudice 476 n.
belief 480 n.
insanity 498 n.
exaggeration
541 n.
predetermination
603 n.
bellicosity 713 n.
affections 812 n.
warm feeling
813 n.
pride 866 n.
friendliness
875 n.
hatred 883 n.
injustice 909 n.
sectarianism
972 n.
pietism 973 n.
prelude
prelude 66 n.
beginning 68 n.
premise
premise 470 n.
premise 470 vb.
preparation
arrangement
62 n.
prelude 66 n.
beginning 68 n.
futurity 119 n.
looking ahead
119 n.
anticipation
130 n.
production 159 n.
thought 444 n.
foresight 505 n.
learning 531 n.
predetermination
603 n.
provision 628 n.
preparation
664 n.
exercise 677 n.
war measures
713 n.
caution 853 n.
preparatory
precursory
66 adj.
future 119 adj.
impending
150 adj.
businesslike
617 adj.
preparatory
664 adj.
prepare
arrange 62 vb.
auspicate 68 vb.
begin 68 vb.
be strong 157 vb.
foresee 505 vb.
educate 529 vb.
train 529 vb.
plan 618 vb.
warn 659 vb.

prepare 664 vb.
be cautious
853 vb.
prepared
early 130 adj.
impending
150 adj.
tending 174 adj.
on the spot
184 adj.
formed 238 adj.
vigilant 452 adj.
expectant
502 adj.
willing 592 adj.
predetermined
603 adj.
habituated
605 adj.
planned 618 adj.
warned 659 adj.
prepared 664 adj.
expert 689 adj.
defended 708 adj.
warring 713 adj.
cautious 853 adj.
preparedness
adultness 129 n.
carefulness
452 n.
preparedness
664 n.
completion 720 n.
prepare oneself
look ahead
119 vb.
expect 502 vb.
learn 531 vb.
store 627 vb.
prepare oneself
664 vb.
undertake
667 vb.
preparer
preparer 664 n.
presageful
presageful
506 adj.
presence
existence 1 n.
generality 79 n.
space 178 n.
presence 184 n.
interiority 219 n.
interjacency
226 n.
approach 284 n.
arrival 290 n.
utility 635 n.
divine attribute
960 n.
present
existing 1 adj.
present 116 adj.
synchronous
118 adj.
modern 121 adj.
present, be
be 1 vb.
accrue 38 vb.
happen 149 vb.
be present
184 vb.
dwell 187 vb.
be near 195 vb.
arrive 290 vb.
watch 436 vb.
present time
existence 1 n.
time 104 n.

instantaneity
111 n.
present time
116 n.
synchronism
118 n.
futurity 119 n.
modernism 121 n.
newness 121 n.
presence 184 n.
preservation
separation 46 n.
permanence
139 n.
storage 627 n.
protection 655 n.
preservation
661 n.
defence 708 n.
preserve
set apart 46 vb.
sustain 141 vb.
drench 336 vb.
dry 337 vb.
season 383 vb.
store 627 vb.
sanitate 647 vb.
safeguard 655 vb.
preserve 661 vb.
retain 773 vb.
preserved
preserved
661 adj.
preserver
preserver 661 n.
preserving
preserving
661 adj.
press
press 582 n.
press, the
the press 523 n.
prestige
greatness 32 n.
superiority 34 n.
influence 173 n.
importance
633 n.
prosperity 725 n.
credit 797 n.
prestige 861 n.
pride 866 n.
approbation
918 n.
pretension
duplicity 536 n.
unskilfulness
690 n.
pretension 845 n.
preterite
preterite 120 adj.
pretext
reason why
151 n.
testimony 461 n.
reasons 475 n.
sophistry 472 n.
mental dishonesty
538 n.
pretext 609 n.
stratagem 693 n.
ostentation
870 n.
vindication 922 n.
prevail
predominate
34 vb.
cause 151 vb.
be able 155 vb.
prevail 173 vb.
be wont 605 vb.

motivate 607 vb.
price
equivalence 28 n.
statistics 86 n.
list 87 n.
quid pro quo
145 n.
appraise 460 vb.
goodness 639 n.
demand 732 vb.
account 803 vb.
price 804 n.
price 804 vb.
penalty 958 n.
priced
priced 804 adj.
prickle
prickle 251 n.
roughness 254 n.
pride
greatness 32 n.
overestimation
477 n.
pride 866 n.
vanity 868 n.
insolence 873 n.
unsociability
878 n.
contempt 917 n.
prideful
prideful 866 adj.
priest
priest 980 n.
ritualist 982 n.
priestly
priestly 979 adj.
primal
beginning 68 adj.
secular 106 adj.
past 120 adj.
primal 122 adj.
fundamental
151 adj.
primp
primp 838 vb.
print
copy 20 vb.
composition 56 n.
compose 56 vb.
reproduction
161 n.
reproduce 161 vb.
form 238 n.
publicity 523 n.
publish 523 vb.
mark 542 vb.
record 543 vb.
printing 550 n.
engrave 550 vb.
writing 581 n.
print 582 n.
print 582 vb.
printed
printed 582 adj.
printer
engraver 551 n.
printer 582 n.
printing
mould 23 n.
photography
546 n.
representation
546 n.
printing 550 n.
print 582 n.
print-type
print-type 582 n.
prior
existing 1 adj.
original 21 adj.
preceding 64 adj.

hindrance 697 n.
command 732 n.
restraint 742 n.
prohibition 752 n.
illegality 949 n.
ecclesiasticism
979 n.

projecting
projecting
249 adj.

projection
layer 202 n.
high land 204 n.
horizontality
211 n.
prop 213 n.
shelf 213 n.
edge 229 n.
projection 249 n.
land 339 n.

prolific
increasing 36 adj.
multitudinous
100 adj.
productive
159 adj.
generative
162 adj.
prolific 166 adj.
vigorous 169 adj.
diffuse 565 adj.
plenteous
630 adj.
rich 795 adj.

prolix
prolix 565 adj.

prominence
convexity 248 n.
prominence
249 n.
elevation 305 n.

promise
oath 527 n.
affirm 527 vb.
intention 612 n.
intend 612 vb.
undertaking
667 n.
undertake
667 vb.
promise 759 n.
promise 759 vb.
compact 760 n.
contract 760 vb.
security 762 n.
give security
762 vb.
debt 798 n.
duty 912 n.
incur a duty
912 vb.
offer worship
975 vb.

promised
promised 759 adj.

promising
promising
847 adj.

promissory
promissory
759 adj.

promote
augment 36 vb.
tend 174 vb.
promote 280 vb.
elevate 305 vb.
make better
649 vb.
aid 698 vb.
dignify 861 vb.

be ecclesiastical
979 vb.

pronunciation
linguistics 552 n.
etymology 554 n.
dialect 555 n.
pronunciation
572 n.
speech 574 n.
speech defect
575 n.

prop
bond 47 n.
stabilizer 148 n.
receptacle 189 n.
hanger 212 n.
prop 213 n.
rear 233 n.
projection 249 n.
leg 262 n.
carrier 268 n.
sail 270 n.
hardness 321 n.
pretext 609 n.
refuge 657 n.
church exterior
984 n.

propagation
propagation
162 n.

propel
move 260 vb.
send 267 vb.
impel 274 vb.
strike 274 vb.
propel 282 vb.
eject 295 vb.
eject 295 vb.
elevate 305 vb.
let fall 306 vb.
blow 347 vb.
lapidate 707 vb.

propellant
propellant 282 n.

propeller
limb 53 n.
propeller 264 n.
aircraft 271 n.
propellant 282 n.

property
thing transferred
267 n.
means 624 n.
equipment 625 n.
store 627 n.
independence
739 n.
possession 768 n.
joint possession
770 n.
property 772 n.
wealth 795 n.
benefice 979 n.

prophylactic
hygiene 647 n.
prophylactic
653 n.

propitiation
propitiation
936 n.

propound
propound 507 vb.
affirm 527 vb.
advise 686 vb.
offer 754 vb.

proprietary
proprietary
772 adj.

propulsion
energy 155 n.
influence 173 n.

impulse 274 n.
propulsion 282 n.
ejection 295 n.
lowering 306 n.
agitation 313 n.
tool 625 n.
aid 698 n.

propulsive
propulsive
282 adj.

pro rata
pro rata 778 adv.

prosaic
plain 568 adj.
prosaic 588 adj.
inexcitable
818 adj.

prose
plainness 568 n.
reading matter
584 n.
prose 588 n.

prosody
assimilation 18 n.
recurrence 102 n.
tempo 405 n.
prosody 588 n.

prospectively
prospectively
119 adv.

prosper
progress 280 vb.
arrive 290 vb.
enjoy 376 vb.
flourish 610 vb.
do good 639 vb.
get better
649 vb.
be active 673 vb.
succeed 722 vb.
prosper 725 vb.
be profitable
766 vb.
gain 766 vb.
get rich 795 vb.
be content
823 vb.
have a reputation
861 vb.
be sensual
939 vb.

prosperity
prosperity 725 n.

prosperous
opportune
132 adj.
presageful
506 adj.
beneficial
639 adj.
successful
722 adj.
prosperous
725 adj.
acquiring
766 adj.
rich 795 adj.
happy 819 adj.
promising
847 adj.

prosperously
prosperously
725 adv.

prosperous person
progression
280 n.
victor 722 n.
prosperous
person 725 n.
rich person
795 n.

prostitute
prostitute 947 n.

protection
parentage 164 n.
parentage 164 n.
barrier 230 n.
reception 294 n.
screen 416 n.
surveillance
452 n.
surveillance
452 n.
storage 627 n.
hygiene 647 n.
protection 655 n.
preservation
661 n.
management
684 n.
aid 698 n.
defence 708 n.
detention 742 n.
security 762 n.

protector
concomitant
89 n.
doorkeeper 259 n.
nautical
personnel 265 n.
protector 655 n.
warner 659 n.
manager 685 n.
aider 698 n.
patron 702 n.
defender 708 n.
armed force
717 n.
soldier 717 n.
keeper 744 n.
friend 875 n.
benefactor 898 n.

Protestant
Protestant 970 n.
Protestant
970 adj.
church party
972 n.
sectarian 972 n.
sectarian
972 adj.

Protestantism
Protestantism
970 n.

prototypal
prototypal
23 adj.

prototype
originality 21 n.
prototype 23 n.
rule 81 n.
example 83 n.
form 238 n.
idea 446 n.
comparison
457 n.
gauge 460 n.
prediction 506 n.
plan 618 n.
paragon 641 n.

protracted
protracted
108 adj.

protraction
protraction
108 n.

protuberance
face 232 n.
angularity 242 n.
protuberance
249 n.
odour 389 n.

proud
  narrow-minded
      476 adj.
  defiant 706 adj.
  proud 866 adj.
  insolent 873 adj.
  despising 917 adj.
proud, be
  walk 262 vb.
  defy 706 vb.
  seek repute
      861 vb.
  be proud 866 vb.
  boast 872 vb.
  be insolent
      873 vb.
  despise 917 vb.
  be impious
      974 vb.
proud person
  proud person
      866 n.
  insolent person
      873 n.
proved, be
  be proved 473 vb.
provender
  provender 296 n.
proverbially
  proverbially
      491 adv.
provide
  fill 54 vb.
  support 213 vb.
  drink 296 vb.
  feed 296 vb.
  foresee 505 vb.
  find means
      624 vb.
  store 627 vb.
  provide 628 vb.
  suffice 630 vb.
  preserve 661 vb.
  make ready
      664 vb.
  offer 754 vb.
  sell 788 vb.
  be hospitable
      877 vb.
provided
  provided 463 adv.
provider
  provider 628 n.
  preparer 664 n.
provincial
  regional 179 adj.
  provincial
      187 adj.
provision
  adjunct 40 n.
  extra 40 n.
  accumulation
      74 n.
  contents 188 n.
  transference
      267 n.
  cookery 301 n.
  provisions 296 n.
  means 624 n.
  store 627 n.
  provision 628 n.
  restoration
      651 n.
  preservation
      661 n.
  fitting out 664 n.
  subvention 698 n.
  funds 792 n.
  accounts 803 n.

provisioning
  provisioning
      628 adj.
provisions
  provisions 296 n.
  provision 628 n.
prow
  prow 232 n.
  protuberance
      249 n.
prowess
  deed 671 n.
  prowess 850 n.
prude
  people of taste
      841 n.
  affecter 845 n.
  disapprover
      919 n.
  prude 945 n.
prudery
  underestimation
      478 n.
  severity 730 n.
  pretension 845 n.
  fastidiousness
      857 n.
  modesty 869 n.
  prudery 945 n.
prudish
  prudish 945 adj.
psychic
  psychic 442 adj.
  intuitive 471 adj.
  psychic 978 n.
psychical
  psychical 978 adj.
psychics
  psychics 978 n.
psychist
  psychist 978 n.
psychologist
  psychologist
      442 n.
psychology
  psychology 442 n.
  insanity 498 n.
  therapy 653 n.
  psychics 978 n.
psychopathy
  psychopathy
      498 n.
publication
  hearing aid
      410 n.
  prediction 506 n.
  manifestation
      517 n.
  disclosure 521 n.
  publication 523 n.
  broadcast 526 n.
  call 542 n.
  warning 659 n.
  ostentation
      870 n.
publicity
  generality 79 n.
  overestimation
      477 n.
  knowledge 485 n.
  manifestation
      517 n.
  information
      519 n.
  publicity 523 n.
  news 524 n.
  broadcasting
      526 n.
  teaching 529 n.
  rostrum 534 n.

  exaggeration
      541 n.
  correspondence
      583 n.
  excitant 816 n.
  famousness
      861 n.
  ostentation
      870 n.
  boasting 872 n.
publicizer
  publicizer 523 n.
publicly
  publicly 523 adv.
public worship
  public worship
      975 n.
publish
  attract notice
      450 vb.
  manifest 517 vb.
  communicate
      519 vb.
  divulge 521 vb.
  publish 523 vb.
  rumour 524 vb.
  print 582 vb.
  correspond
      583 vb.
  boast 872 vb.
published
  published
      523 adj.
published, be
  be published
      523 vb.
publishing
  publishing
      523 adj.
puffing
  puffing 347 adj.
pugilism
  defence 708 n.
  pugilism 711 n.
  pugilist 717 n.
  sport 832 n.
pugilist
  pugilist 717 n.
pulpiness
  pulpiness 351 n.
pulpy
  pulpy 351 adj.
pulverize
  pulverize 327 vb.
pulverizer
  pulverizer 327 n.
punctuality
  punctuality
      130 n.
punctuation
  joining together
      45 n.
  bond 47 n.
  discontinuity
      72 n.
  question 454 n.
  punctuation
      542 n.
  grammar 559 n.
pungency
  pungency 383 n.
pungent
  keen 169 adj.
  hot 374 adj.
  tasty 381 adj.
  pungent 383 adj.
  savoury 385 adj.
  unsavoury
      386 adj.
  sour 388 adj.
  odorous 389 adj.

  fetid 392 adj.
  felt 813 adj.
  ungracious
      880 adj.
pungent, be
  be pungent
      383 vb.
punish
  exclude 57 vb.
  strike 274 vb.
  eject 295 vb.
  give pain 372 vb.
  retaliate 709 vb.
  be severe 730 vb.
  tax 804 vb.
  shame 862 vb.
  make unwelcome
      878 vb.
  reprove 919 vb.
  make illegal
      949 vb.
  punish 958 vb.
punishable
  punishable
      958 adj.
punished, be
  be punished
      958 vb.
punisher
  punisher 958 n.
punishment
  judgment 475 n.
  retaliation 709 n.
  deposal 747 n.
  suffering 820 n.
  intimidation
      849 n.
  revenge 905 n.
  reprimand 919 n.
  vindication 922 n.
  legal trial 954 n.
  condemnation
      956 n.
  punishment
      958 n.
punitive
  prohibiting
      752 adj.
  atoning 936 adj.
  punitive 958 adj.
purchase
  transference
      267 n.
  requirement
      622 n.
  deliverance
      663 n.
  deliver 663 vb.
  aid 698 n.
  patronize 698 vb.
  acquisition 766 n.
  acquire 766 vb.
  borrow 780 vb.
  trade 786 n.
  purchase 787 n.
  purchase 787 vb.
  expend 801 vb.
purchaser
  purchaser 787 n.
pure
  elegant 570 adj.
  tasteful 841 adj.
  modest 869 adj.
  unwedded
      890 adj.
  honourable
      924 adj.
  virtuous 928 adj.
  temperate
      937 adj.
  pure 945 adj.

purgative
ejector 295 n.
cleanser 648 n.
purgative 658 n.

purify
eliminate 44 vb.
exclude 57 vb.
make sterile
167 vb.
moderate 172 vb.
empty 300 vb.
purify 648 vb.
sanitate 652 vb.
make better
649 vb.
make pious
973 vb.

purity
cleanness 648 n.
good taste 841 n.
modesty 869 n.
celibacy 890 n.
probity 929 n.
virtue 933 n.
innocence 935 n.
temperance
942 n.
purity 950 n.
sanctity 973 n.

purple
red 426 adj.
purple 431 adj.

purpleness
purpleness 431 n.

purposely
purposely
612 adv.

pursuant to
pursuant to
614 adv.

pursue
accompany
89 vb.
be behind 233 vb.
follow 279 vb.
be mindful
450 vb.
enquire 454 vb.
search 454 vb.
aim at 612 vb.
pursue 614 vb.
be severe 730 vb.
desire 854 vb.
be in love 882 vb.
court 884 vb.
not respect
916 vb.
defame 921 vb.

pursuing
pursuing 614 adj.

pursuit
sequence 65 n.
motion 260 n.
approach 284 n.
search 454 n.
discovery 479 n.
pursuit 614 n.

pushcart
pushcart 269 n.

put between
add 38 vb.
discontinue
72 vb.
put between
226 vb.
insert 298 vb.
mediate 715 vb.

put in front
put in front
64 vb.

put off
put off 131 vb.

puzzle
distract 451 vb.
puzzle 469 vb.
mean nothing
510 vb.
be unintelligible
512 vb.
be difficult
695 vb.
defeat 722 vb.
trouble 822 vb.
be wonderful
859 vb.

puzzled
puzzled 512 adj.

puzzling
puzzling 512 adj.

Q

quadruple
augment 36 vb.

quake
quake 849 vb.

qualification
adjunct 40 n.
change 138 n.
limit 231 n.
counterevidence
462 n.
qualification
463 n.
doubt 481 n.
dissent 484 n.
negation 528 n.
mental dishonesty
538 n.
unwillingness
593 n.
pretext 609 n.
means of escape
662 n.
resistance 710 n.
conditions 761 n.
nonliability 914 n.
disapprobation
919 n.
vindication 922 n.

qualify
limit 231 vb.
discriminate
458 vb.
qualify 463 vb.
doubt 481 vb.
dissent 484 vb.
negate 528 vb.
resist 710 vb.
give terms
761 vb.

qualifying
qualifying
463 adj.

quantify
quantify 26 vb.

quantitative
quantitative
26 adj.

quantity
quantity 26 n.
degree 27 n.
greatness 32 n.
store 627 n.

quarrel
differ 15 vb.
disagreement
25 n.
disagree 25 vb.
turmoil 61 n.
argument 470 n.
dissent 484 n.
interlocution
579 n.
quarrel 704 n.
quarrel 704 vb.
contention 711 n.
fight 711 n.
fight 711 vb.
war 713 n.
discontent 824 n.
be discontented
824 vb.
enmity 876 n.
be inimical
876 vb.
anger 886 n.
resent 886 vb.
reproach 919 vb.
litigation 954 n.
schism 972 n.

quarreller
quarreller 704 n.

quarrelling
quarrelling
704 adj.

quarrelsomeness
quarrelsomeness
704 n.

quarters
place 180 n.
quarters 187 n.
resting place
261 n.

quaternity
quaternity 95 n.

question
topic 447 n.
curiosity 448 n.
question 454 n.
empiricism 456 n.
uncertainty
469 n.

questionable, be
be questionable
454 vb.

questioner
questioner 454 n.

quid pro quo
quid pro quo
145 n.

quiescence
quiescence 261 n.

quiescent
permanent
139 adj.
weak 158 adj.
inert 170 adj.
located 182 adj.
quiescent
261 adj.
insensible
370 adj.
silent 394 adj.
latent 518 adj.
nonactive
672 adj.
inactive 674 adj.
apathetic
815 adj.
inexcitable
818 adj.

quiescent, be
be pending
131 vb.
stay 139 vb.
cease 140 vb.
be inert 170 vb.
be moderate
172 vb.
be quiescent
261 vb.
lurk 518 vb.
not act 672 vb.
be inactive
674 vb.
be unsociable
878 vb.

quietude
order 60 n.
moderation
172 n.
quietude 261 n.
wind 347 n.
death 356 n.
inexcitability
818 n.
pleasurableness
821 n.
content 823 n.
lack of wonder
860 n.
seclusion 878 n.

R

rabble
crowd 74 n.
rabble 864 n.

race
race 11 n.
breed 77 n.
genealogy 164 n.
posterity 165 n.
humankind 366 n.

racing
pedestrianism
262 n.
aquatics 264 n.
speeding 272 n.
gambling 618 n.
chase 614 n.
racing 711 n.
sport 832 n.

radiate
emit 295 vb.
oscillate 312 vb.
radiate 412 vb.

radiating
radiating 412 adj.

radiation
electronics 155 n.
nucleonics 155 n.
ejection 295 n.
oscillation 312 n.
star 316 n.
radiation 412 n.
invisibility 439 n.
broadcasting
526 n.
photography
546 n.
poison 654 n.

raft
raft 270 n.
safeguard 657 n.

railway
crossing 217 n.
train 269 n.
railway 619 n.

rain
storm 171 n.
descent 304 n.
descend 304 vb.
water 334 n.
weather 335 n.
moistening 336 n.
moisture 336 n.
be wet 336 vb.

rain 345 n.
rain 345 n.
abound 630 vb.

rainy
violent 171 adj.
humid 336 adj.
rainy 345 adj.

raise the alarm
signal 542 vb.
raise the alarm
660 vb.

ram
ram 274 vb.
propellant 282 n.
pulverizer 327 n.
club 718 n.

rampage
rampage 61 vb.
be violent 171 vb.
be agitated
313 vb.
be loud 395 vb.
be active 673 vb.
bicker 704 vb.
charge 707 vb.
be excitable
817 vb.
rejoice 830 vb.
celebrate 871 vb.
be angry 886 vb.
dispraise 919 vb.

range
degree 27 n.
ability 155 n.
range 178 n.
distance 194 n.
breadth 200 n.
visibility 438 n.
function 617 n.
scope 739 n.

rank, person of
person of repute
861 n.
person of rank
863 n.

rapacity
rapacity 781 n.

rape
coition 45 n.
rape 946 n.

rapping
rapping 397 adj.

rara avis
rara avis 84 n.

rare
small 33 adj.
light 318 adj.
rare 320 adj.
airy 335 adj.

rarefy
be dispersed
75 vb.
make thin
201 vb.
rarefy 320 vb.

rarity
insubstantiality
4 n.
smallness 33 n.
thinness 201 n.
lightness 318 n.
rarity 320 n.
air 335 n.

rascally
rascally 925 adj.

rash
furious 171 adj.
speedy 272 adj.
inattentive
451 adj.
negligent 453 adj.

indiscriminating
459 adj.
unwise 494 adj.
spontaneous
604 adj.
enterprising
667 adj.
hasty 675 adj.
defiant 706 adj.
excitable 817 adj.
courageous
850 adj.
rash 852 adj.
insolent 873 adj.
irascible 887 adj.

rash, be
prejudge 476 vb.
be obstinate
597 vb.
gamble 613 vb.
face danger
656 vb.
hasten 675 vb.
be courageous
850 vb.
be rash 852 vb.

rashly
rashly 852 adv.

rashness
rashness 852 n.

rasp
breathe 347 vb.
hiss 401 vb.
rasp 402 vb.
ululate 404 vb.
discord 406 vb.

ratio
ratio 85 n.

rational
relevant 9 adj.
mental 442 adj.
plausible 466 adj.
rational 470 adj.
true 489 adj.
wise 493 adj.

reading matter
subdivision 53 n.
list 87 n.
information
519 n.
journal 528 n.
literature 552 n.
writing 581 n.
reading matter
584 n.
novel 590 n.

ready-made
ready-made
664 adj.

real
real 1 adj.

reality
reality 1 n.
substantiality
3 n.
event 149 n.
truth 489 n.
chief thing 633 n.

rear
contrariety 14 n.
sequence 65 n.
sequel 67 n.
extremity 69 n.
distance 194 n.
rear 233 n.
contraposition
235 n.
doorway 258 n.
following 279 n.

rearward
after 65 adv.

rearward
233 adv.
behind 279 adv.

reason
relate 9 vb.
cognize 442 vb.
think 444 vb.
discriminate
458 vb.
assume 466 vb.
reason 470 vb.
demonstrate
473 vb.
judge 475 vb.
suppose 507 vb.
interpret 515 vb.

reasonable, be
accord 24 vb.
be certain
468 vb.
be reasonable
470 vb.
be proved 473 vb.
assent 483 vb.
be wise 493 vb.
be intelligible
511 vb.

reasonably
reasonably
470 adv.

reason badly
reason badly
472 vb.
misjudge 476 vb.
be credulous
482 vb.
hope 847 vb.

reasoner
reasoner 470 n.

reasoning
relevance 9 n.
conformance
24 n.
sequence 65 n.
mathematics
86 n.
intellect 442 n.
philosophy 444 n.
thought 444 n.
discrimination
458 n.
reasoning 470 n.
demonstration
473 n.
judgment 475 n.
teaching 529 n.
legal trial 954 n.

reasons
reasons 470 n.

reason why
reason why
151 n.
attribution 153 n.
motive 607 n.
intention 612 n.

recant
revert 143 vb.
opine 480 vb.
disbelieve 481 vb.
negate 528 vb.
recant 598 vb.
reject 602 vb.
abrogate 747 vb.
resign 748 vb.
not retain
774 vb.
be penitent
934 vb.
become pious
973 vb.

recantation
recantation
598 n.

recede
decrease 37 vb.
revert 143 vb.
recede 285 vb.
avoid 615 vb.
be defeated
723 vb.

receding
receding 285 adj.

receipt
means 624 n.
earnings 766 n.
estate 772 n.
credit 797 n.
payment 799 n.
receipt 802 n.

receive
admit 294 vb.
give security
762 vb.
acquire 766 vb.
receive 777 vb.
take 781 vb.
acquire 802 vb.
be rewarded
957 vb.

received
received 802 adj.

received, be
be received
777 vb.

receiver
receiver 777 n.
taker 781 n.
treasurer 793 n.

receiving
increment 36 n.
receiving 777 n.
receiving 777 adj.
wealth 795 n.

receptacle
bunch 74 n.
receptacle 189 n.
handle 213 n.
covering 221 n.
wrapping 221 n.
enclosure 230 n.
storage 627 n.
arsenal 718 n.

reception
identity 13 n.
combination 50 n.
inclusion 78 n.
energy 155 n.
transference
267 n.
ingress 292 n.
reception 294 n.
receiving 777 n.
approbation
918 n.
Christian rite
982 n.
rite 982 n.

recession
motion 260 n.
regression 281 n.
recession 285 n.
departure 291 n.
eddy 345 n.
defeat 723 n.

recipient
recipient 189 adj.
beneficiary 771 n.
recipient 777 n.

recoil
correlate 12 vb.
separate 46 vb.

recoiling

reversion 143 n.
revert 143 vb.
counteraction
177 n.
counteract
177 vb.
recoil 275 n.
recoil 275 vb.
return 281 n.
regress 281 vb.
recession 285 n.
recede 285 vb.
repulsion 287 n.
ascent 303 n.
ascend 303 vb.
elasticity 323 n.
be elastic 323 vb.
tergiversation
598 n.
avoidance 615 n.
retaliation 709 n.
retaliate 709 vb.
dislike 856 vb.
hate 883 vb.

recoiling
recoiling 275 adj.

record
copy 22 n.
remainder 41 n.
arrangement
62 n.
class 62 n.
bunch 74 n.
list 87 n.
chronology 112 n.
time 112 vb.
fossil 120 n.
death roll 356 n.
listening 410 n.
answer 455 n.
evidence 461 n.
testimony 461 n.
information
519 n.
broadcast 526 n.
classroom 534 n.
indicate 542 vb.
record 543 n.
record 543 vb.
represent 546 vb.
phrase 558 n.
script 581 n.
writing 581 n.
write 581 vb.
reading matter
584 n.
reference book
584 n.
biography 585 n.
description 585 n.
narrative 585 n.
describe 585 vb.
compendium
587 n.
abstract 587 vb.
collection 627 n.
title deed 767 n.
account book
803 n.
legal trial 954 n.

recorded
recorded 543 adj.

recorder
chronologist
112 n.
recorder 544 n.
calligrapher
581 n.
narrator 585 n.
keeper 744 n.
magistracy 952 n.

recording
chronological
112 adj.
recording
543 adj.

recording
instrument
hearing aid
410 n.
broadcasting
526 n.
recording
instrument 544 n.

recoup
recoup 31 vb.
progress 280 vb.
retrieve 651 vb.
retaliate 709 vb.
acquire 766 vb.

rectify
adjust 24 vb.
regularize 62 vb.
modify 138 vb.
plan 618 vb.
perfect 641 vb.
rectify 649 vb.
repair 651 vb.
be just 908 vb.

recumbency
recumbency
211 n.

recuperation
recuperation
651 n.

recur
recur 134 vb.
go on 141 vb.

recurrence
heredity 5 n.
recurrence 102 n.
periodicity 136 n.
reversion 143 n.
reproduction
161 n.
resonance 399 n.

red
fiery 374 adj.
luminous 412 adj.
florid 420 adj.
red 426 adj.
personable
836 adj.
angry 886 adj.

redden
colour 420 vb.
redden 426 vb.
show feeling
813 vb.
be humbled
867 vb.
be modest
869 vb.

redemptive
redemptive
960 adj.

redness
redness 426 n.

red pigment
pigment 420 n.
red pigment
426 n.

redundance
redundance
632 n.

redundant
great 32 adj.
remaining 41 adj.
full 54 adj.
diffuse 565 adj.
plenteous
630 adj.

redundant
632 adj.
liberal 808 adj.
intemperate
938 adj.

redundantly
redundantly
632 adv.

reference book
directory 87 n.
guidebook 519 n.
reference book
584 n.

referral
referral 9 n.

reflection
contrariety 14 n.
copy 22 n.
recoil 275 n.
reflection 412 n.
visual fallacy
435 n.
image 546 n.

reformer
reformer 649 n.

reformism
reformism 649 n.

refresh
augment 36 vb.
strengthen
157 vb.
invigorate
169 vb.
refrigerate
377 vb.
make better
649 vb.
revive 651 vb.
refresh 680 vb.
aid 698 vb.
relieve 826 vb.
amuse 832 vb.

refreshed
refreshed
680 adj.

refreshed, be
be refreshed
680 vb.

refreshing
lenitive 172 adj.
pleasant 371 adj.
refreshing
680 adj.
relieving 826 adj.
amusing 832 adj.

refreshment
lull 140 n.
strengthening
157 n.
water travel
264 n.
pleasure 371 n.
revival 651 n.
repose 678 n.
refreshment
680 n.
aid 698 n.
pleasurableness
821 n.
relief 826 n.
amusement
832 n.

refrigerate
moderate 172 vb.
harden 321 vb.
blow 347 vb.
render insensible
370 vb.
be cold 375 vb.
refrigerate
377 vb.

redundant
632 adj.
liberal 808 adj.

preserve 661 vb.
refresh 680 vb.

refrigeration
refrigeration
377 n.

refrigerator
cabinet 189 n.
provisions 296 n.
air 335 n.
ventilation 347 n.
ice 375 n.
refrigeration
377 n.
refrigerator
379 n.
preserver 661 n.

refuge
resting place
261 n.
hiding-place
522 n.
protection 655 n.
refuge 657 n.
fort 708 n.
talisman 977 n.

refusal
dissent 484 n.
negation 528 n.
unwillingness
593 n.
rejection 602 n.
hitch 697 n.
resistance 710 n.
prohibition 752 n.
refusal 755 n.
deprecation
757 n.
retention 773 n.
nonpayment
800 n.
disapprobation
919 n.

refuse
exclude 57 vb.
put off 131 vb.
repel 287 vb.
be deaf 411 vb.
dissent 484 vb.
negate 528 vb.
be unwilling
593 vb.
reject 602 vb.
hinder 697 vb.
oppose 699 vb.
resist 710 vb.
prohibit 752 vb.
refuse 755 vb.
retain 773 vb.
be parsimonious
811 vb.

refused
refused 755 adj.

refusing
refusing 755 adj.

regalia
headgear 223 n.
loop 245 n.
badge 542 n.
regalia 738 n.
jewellery 839 n.
vestments 983 n.

region
range 178 n.
space 178 n.
region 179 n.
situation 181 n.
world 316 n.
land 339 n.
political
organization
728 n.

regional
regional 179 adj.
register
list 87 vb.
register 543 vb.
account 803 vb.
registration
gramophone
409 n.
registration
543 n.
regress
decrease 37 vb.
repeat oneself
102 vb.
revert 143 vb.
be inverted
216 vb.
navigate 264 vb.
retard 273 vb.
regress 281 vb.
recede 285 vb.
arrive 290 vb.
fall short 302 vb.
descend 304 vb.
flow 345 vb.
deteriorate
650 vb.
relapse 652 vb.
regression
regression 281 n.
regressive
regressive
281 adj.
regret
reversion 143 n.
be impotent
156 vb.
remembrance
500 n.
disappointment
504 n.
be disappointed
504 vb.
be unwilling
593 vb.
abrogate 747 vb.
sorrow 820 n.
suffer 825 vb.
be discontented
824 vb.
regret 825 n.
regret 825 vb.
be dejected
829 vb.
lament 831 vb.
desire 854 n.
desire 854 vb.
dislike 856 vb.
pity 900 n.
disapprove
919 vb.
penitence 934 n.
be penitent
934 vb.
regretted
regretted
825 adj.
regretting
regretting
825 adj.
regular
orderly 60 adj.
arranged 62 adj.
regular 81 adj.
periodical
136 adj.
unceasing
141 adj.
unchangeable
148 adj.

symmetrical
240 adj.
habitual 605 adj.
regularity
regularity 81 n.
regularize
regularize 62 vb.
regular return
recurrence 102 n.
regular return
136 n.
regulated
regulated 83 adj.
reject
leave over 41 vb.
exclude 57 vb.
repel 287 vb.
eject 295 vb.
dissent 484 vb.
disappoint
504 vb.
negate 528 vb.
vote 600 vb.
reject 602 vb.
be unsatisfied
631 vb.
not use 669 vb.
oppose 699 vb.
refuse 755 vb.
not observe
764 vb.
be discontented
824 vb.
dislike 856 vb.
hate 883 vb.
not respect
916 vb.
despise 917 vb.
disapprove
919 vb.
condemn 956 vb.
rejected
rejected 602 adj.
rejection
rejection 602 n.
rejoice
vociferate
403 vb.
be pleased
819 vb.
be content
823 vb.
be cheerful
828 vb.
rejoice 830 vb.
revel 832 vb.
celebrate 871 vb.
boast 872 vb.
rejoicing
rejoicing 830 n.
rejoicing 830 adj.
rejoinder
interchange
146 n.
rejoinder 455 n.
negation 528 n.
retaliation 709 n.
sauciness 873 n.
vindication 922 n.
accusation 923 n.
legal trial 954 n.
relapse
reversion 143 n.
revert 143 vb.
tergiversation
598 n.
tergiversate
598 vb.
deterioration
650 n.

deteriorate
650 vb.
relapse 652 n.
relapse 652 vb.
relate
relate 9 vb.
connect 45 vb.
attribute 153 vb.
related, be
be related 9 vb.
be akin 11 vb.
be one of 58 vb.
be included
78 vb.
accompany
89 vb.
result 152 vb.
be important
633 vb.
relation
circumstance 8 n.
relation 9 n.
correlation 12 n.
similarity 18 n.
fitness 24 n.
union 45 n.
bond 47 n.
association
701 n.
relative
relative 9 adj.
akin 11 adj.
correlative
12 adj.
comparative
27 adj.
included 78 adj.
numerable
86 adj.
attributed
153 adj.
relatively
relatively 9 adv.
relativeness
relativeness 9 n.
relevance
relevance 9 n.
relevant
relevant 9 adj.
apt 24 adj.
typical 83 adj.
rational 470 adj.
demonstrating
473 adj.
important
633 adj.
relief
moderation
172 n.
recuperation
651 n.
escape 662 n.
deliverance
663 n.
refreshment
680 n.
liberation 741 n.
relief 826 n.
hope 847 n.
condolence 900 n.
relieve
abate 37 vb.
assuage 172 vb.
remedy 653 vb.
deliver 663 vb.
refresh 680 vb.
disencumber
696 vb.
liberate 741 vb.
be lost 767 vb.

tranquillize
818 vb.
please 821 vb.
content 823 vb.
relieve 826 vb.
cheer 828 vb.
relieved, be
escape 662 vb.
be content
823 vb.
be relieved
826 vb.
be cheerful
828 vb.
hope 847 vb.
relieving
relieving 826 adj.
relievo
relievo 249 n.
religion
philosophy 444 n.
news 524 n.
religion 967 n.
piety 973 n.
public worship
975 n.
idolatry 976 n.
occultism 978 n.
religionist
religionist 967 n.
religious
immaterial
315 adj.
religious 967 adj.
cabbalistic
978 adj.
religious faith
belief 480 n.
religious faith
967 n.
non-Christian
sect 972 n.
religious teacher
sage 495 n.
interpreter 515 n.
religious teacher
967 n.
worshipper 975 n.
relinquish
separate 46 vb.
cease 140 vb.
depart 291 vb.
disregard 453 vb.
dissent 484 vb.
negate 528 vb.
be irresolute
596 vb.
tergiversate
598 vb.
be neutral
601 vb.
relinquish 616 vb.
not use 669 vb.
be lax 729 vb.
abrogate 747 vb.
resign 748 vb.
refuse 755 vb.
not retain
774 vb.
give 776 vb.
divorce 891 vb.
fail in duty
913 vb.
relinquished
relinquished
616 adj.
relinquishment
relinquishment
616 n.
remainder
difference 15 n.

remainder 41 n.
part 53 n.
piece 53 n.
numerical result
  85 n.
fewness 101 n.
antiquity 120 n.
effect 152 n.
superfluity 632 n.

remaining
remaining 41 adj.

remarkable
remarkable
  32 adj.
notable 633 adj.

remarkably
remarkably
  32 adv.

remedial
lenitive 172 adj.
counteracting
  177 adj.
salubrious
  647 adj.
restorative
  651 adj.
remedial 653 adj.
successful
  722 adj.
relieving 826 adj.

remedy
a mixture 43 n.
moderator 172 n.
counteract
  177 vb.
plant 361 n.
answer 455 n.
contrivance
  618 n.
means 624 n.
recuperation
  651 n.
remedy 653 n.
remedy 653 vb.
precept 688 n.

remember
repeat 102 vb.
repeat oneself
  102 vb.
think 444 vb.
be mindful
  450 vb.
remember
  500 vb.
understand
  511 vb.
register 543 vb.
honour 861 vb.
celebrate 871 vb.

remembered
remembered
  500 adj.

remembered, be
be remembered
  500 vb.

remembering
remembering
  500 adj.

remembrance
remainder 41 n.
past time 120 n.
reversion 143 n.
remembrance
  500 n.
loquacity 576 n.
biography 585 n.
narrative 585 n.
celebration
  871 n.

remind
remind 500 vb.

hint 519 vb.
warn 659 vb.

reminder
reminder 500 n.

removed
removed 194 adj.

rend
rend 46 vb.

render few
abate 37 vb.
render few
  101 vb.
weaken 158 vb.
destroy 160 vb.
empty 295 vb.
extract 299 vb.

render insensible
assuage 172 vb.
render insensible
  370 vb.
make inactive
  674 vb.
make insensitive
  815 vb.
relieve 826 vb.
frighten 849 vb.

renowned
renowned
  861 adj.

reoccur
reoccur 102 vb.

repair
adjunct 40 n.
join 45 vb.
variegate 432 vb.
amendment
  649 n.
make better
  649 vb.
rectify 649 vb.
repair 651 n.
repair 651 vb.
preserve 661 vb.

repeat
be identical
  13 vb.
liken 18 vb.
do likewise 20 vb.
accord 24 vb.
augment 36 vb.
conform 83 vb.
number 86 vb.
double 91 vb.
repeat 102 vb.
sustain 141 vb.
reproduce 161 vb.
notice 450 vb.
answer 455 vb.
memorize 500 vb.
remind 500 vb.
mean 509 vb.
be intelligible
  511 vb.
advertise 523 vb.
emphasize
  527 vb.
describe 585 vb.
habituate 605 vb.

repeated
repeated 102 adj.

repeatedly
repeatedly
  102 adv.

repeat oneself
repeat oneself
  102 vb.
recur 134 vb.
be diffuse
  565 vb.
be tedious
  833 vb.

repel
influence 173 vb.
repel 292 vb.
dismiss 295 vb.
parry 708 vb.
defeat 722 vb.
refuse 755 vb.
cause dislike
  856 vb.
excite hate
  883 vb.

repellent
repellent 287 adj.
resisting 710 adj.
disliked 856 adj.

repentant
repentant
  934 adj.

repetition
identity 13 n.
uniformity 16 n.
mimicry 20 n.
copy 22 n.
continuity 71 n.
conformity 83 n.
duplication 91 n.
repetition 102 n.
future state
  119 n.
frequency 134 n.
continuance
  141 n.
reproduction
  161 n.
roll 398 n.
answer 455 n.
remembrance
  500 n.
affirmation
  527 n.
diffuseness 565 n.
vigour 566 n.
perseverance
  595 n.
habituation
  605 n.
tedium 833 n.

replace
replace 182 vb.

replenish
drink 296 vb.
store 627 vb.
replenish 628 vb.
suffice 630 vb.
restore 651 vb.

report
evidence 461 n.
estimate 475 n.
report 519 n.
broadcast 526 n.
record 543 n.
speech 574 n.
description 585 n.

reportedly
reportedly
  519 adv.

repose
cease 140 vb.
pause 140 vb.
quietude 261 n.
be quiescent
  261 vb.
come to rest
  261 vb.
sit down 306 vb.
euphoria 371 n.
inaction 672 n.
not act 672 vb.
sleep 674 vb.
be inactive
  674 vb.

leisure 676 n.
have leisure
  676 vb.
repose 678 n.
repose 678 vb.

refreshment
  680 n.
be refreshed
  680 vb.
be free 739 vb.
keep calm
  818 vb.
amusement
  832 n.
be sociable
  877 vb.

reposeful
reposeful 678 adj.

represent
make extrinsic
  6 vb.
resemble 18 vb.
imitate 20 vb.
outline 228 vb.
form 238 vb.
darken 413 vb.
gauge 460 vb.
evidence 461 vb.
be true 489 vb.
imagine 508 vb.
mean 509 vb.
figure 514 vb.
show 517 vb.
indicate 542 vb.
record 543 vb.
represent 546 vb.
paint 548 vb.
describe 585 vb.
act 589 vb.

representation
similarity 18 n.
imitation 20 n.
mimicry 20 n.
copy 22 n.
substitute 145 n.
appearance
  440 n.
manifestation
  517 n.
indication 542 n.
record 543 n.
representation
  546 n.
painting 548 n.
picture 548 n.
sculpture 549 n.
description 585 n.
acting 589 n.
drama 589 n.
dramaturgy
  589 n.
stage play 589 n.
rite 982 n.
ritual act 982 n.

represented
represented
  546 adj.

representing
representing
  546 adj.

reprimand
warning 659 n.
humiliation 867 n.
reprimand 919 n.
punishment
  958 n.

reproach
scurrility 894 n.
reproach 919 n.
accusation 923 n.
guilt 931 n.

reprobate
name 556 vb.
curse 894 vb.
cuss 894 vb.
not respect
916 vb.
despise 917 vb.
reprobate 919 vb.

reproduce
copy 20 vb.
augment 36 vb.
repeat 102 vb.
produce 159 vb.
reproduce 161 vb.

reproduced
reproduced
161 adj.

reproduce itself
grow 36 vb.
be mixed 43 vb.
produce 159 vb.
reproduce 161 vb.
reproduce itself
162 vb.
be fruitful
166 vb.

reproduction
imitation 20 n.
copy 22 n.
reproduction
161 n.
propagation
162 n.

reprove
dissuade 608 vb.
warn 659 vb.
deprecate 757 vb.
curse 894 vb.
reprove 919 vb.
accuse 923 vb.
punish 958 vb.

reptile
serpent 246 n.
reptile 360 n.
bane 654 n.
noxious animal
899 n.

repulsion
energy 155 n.
influence 173 n.
recoil 275 n.
repulsion 287 n.
refusal 755 n.

reputable
reputable
861 adj.
respected
915 adj.
approved
918 adj.
honourable
924 adj.

repute
greatness 32 n.
importance
633 n.
trophy 724 n.
repute 861 n.
respect 915 n.
probity 924 n.

repute, person of
broadcaster
526 n.
bigwig 633 n.
prosperous
person 725 n.
officer 736 n.
person of repute
861 n.
favourite 885 n.

request
topic 447 n.
enquire 454 vb.
remind 500 vb.
propound 507 vb.
affirm 527 vb.
inducement
607 n.
requirement
622 n.
require 622 vb.
demand 732 n.
demand 732 vb.
ask leave 751 vb.
offer 754 n.
offer oneself
754 vb.
request 756 n.
request 756 vb.
deprecation
757 n.
borrow 780 vb.
claim 910 vb.
litigation 954 n.
litigate 954 vb.
prayers 975 n.

requesting
requesting
756 adj.

require
be incomplete
55 vb.
send 267 vb.
fall short 302 vb.
qualify 463 vb.
necessitate
591 vb.
require 622 vb.
be unsatisfied
631 vb.
not suffice
631 vb.
demand 732 vb.
beg 756 vb.
request 756 vb.
give terms
761 vb.
purchase 787 vb.
be poor 796 vb.
be discontented
824 vb.
desire 854 vb.

required
required 622 adj.

requirement
offset 31 n.
deficit 55 n.
shortfall 302 n.
qualification
463 n.
necessity 591 n.
requirement
622 n.
waste 629 n.
chief thing 633 n.
imperfection
642 n.
completion 720 n.
request 756 n.
conditions 761 n.
purchase 787 n.
poverty 796 n.
desire 854 n.
desired object
854 vb.

resemble
correlate 12 vb.
resemble 18 vb.
imitate 20 vb.
accord 24 vb.
be equal 28 vb.

reproduce 161 vb.
taste 381 vb.
appear 440 vb.

resent
be discontented
824 vb.
regret 825 vb.
dislike 856 vb.
be inimical
876 vb.
hate 883 vb.
resent 886 vb.
be revengeful
905 vb.

resentful
resentful 886 adj.

resentment
dissension 704 n.
feeling 813 n.
moral sensibility
814 n.
annoyance 822 n.
discontent 824 n.
regret 825 n.
dislike 856 n.
humiliation 867 n.
enmity 876 n.
hatred 883 n.
resentment
886 n.
malevolence
893 n.
revengefulness
905 n.
jealousy 906 n.
wrong 909 n.

resident
resident 186 n.

residing
residing 187 adj.

resign
cease 140 vb.
regress 281 vb.
depart 291 vb.
tergiversate
598 vb.
relinquish 616 vb.
have leisure
676 vb.
be lax 729 vb.
resign 748 vb.
not retain
774 vb.

resignation
disunion 46 n.
cessation 140 n.
relinquishment
616 n.
leisure 676 n.
laxity 729 n.
resignation 748 n.
nonliability 914 n.

resigning
resigning 748 adj.

resin
viscidity 349 n.
resin 352 n.

resinous
resinous 352 adj.

resist
cease 140 vb.
be violent 171 vb.
oppose 699 vb.
withstand
699 vb.
parry 708 vb.
retaliate 709 vb.
resist 710 vb.
contend 711 vb.
give battle
713 vb.

triumph 722 vb.
revolt 733 vb.
refuse 755 vb.

resistance
protraction
108 n.
strike 140 n.
counteraction
177 n.
obstinacy 597 n.
dissuasion 608 n.
hindrance 697 n.
opposition 699 n.
defence 708 n.
resistance 710 n.
disobedience
733 n.
revolt 733 n.
refusal 755 n.

resisting
resisting 710 adj.

resolute
unchangeable
148 adj.
unyielding
157 adj.
volitional
590 adj.
resolute 594 adj.
persevering
595 adj.
obstinate
597 adj.
intending
612 adj.
attempting
666 adj.
active 673 adj.
completive
720 adj.
unbeaten
722 adj.
courageous
850 adj.

resolute, be
gesticulate
542 vb.
will 590 vb.
be resolute
594 vb.
choose 600 vb.
intend 612 vb.
attempt 666 vb.
fight 711 vb.
be successful
722 vb.
be insensitive
815 vb.
be cheerful
828 vb.
take courage
850 vb.

resolutely
resolutely
594 adv.

resolution
stability 148 n.
vitality 157 n.
vigorousness
169 n.
limit 231 n.
attention 450 n.
gesture 542 n.
will 590 n.
resolution 594 n.
perseverance
595 n.
obstinacy 597 n.
intention 612 n.
assiduity 673 n.
courage 850 n.

manliness 850 n.

resonance
resonance 399 n.

resonant
sounding 393 adj.
loud 395 adj.
rolling 398 adj.
resonant 399 adj.
melodious
405 adj.
speaking 574 adj.

resound
repeat oneself
102 vb.
recoil 275 vb.
rotate 310 vb.
sound 393 vb.
be loud 395 vb.
resound 399 vb.

respect
obeisance 306 n.
look after
452 vb.
assent 483 vb.
make important
633 vb.
fear 849 n.
fear 849 vb.
repute 861 n.
honour 861 vb.
friendliness
875 n.
courtesy 879 n.
be courteous
879 vb.
love 882 n.
love 882 vb.
respect 915 n.
respect 915 vb.
approbation
918 n.
approve 918 vb.
piety 973 n.
worship 975 n.
worship 975 vb.
deification 976 n.

respected
respected
915 adj.

respectful
fearing 849 adj.
courteous
879 adj.
respectful
915 adj.
pious 973 adj.
worshipping
975 adj.

respectfully
respectfully
915 adv.

respects
courteous act
879 n.
respects 915 n.
ritual act 982 n.

respiration
outlet 293 n.
reception 294 n.
excretion 297 n.
oscillation 312 n.
respiration 347 n.
life 355 n.
loudness 395 n.
cry 403 n.
fatigue 679 n.

respiratory disease
respiration 347 n.
respiratory
disease 646 n.

respondent
exam 454 n.
respondent 455 n.
testee 456 n.
interlocutor
579 n.

resting place
resting place
261 n.

restitute
restitute 782 vb.

restitution
compensation
31 n.
offset 31 n.
reversion 143 n.
restoration
651 n.
remedy 653 n.
peace offering
714 n.
restitution 782 n.
payment 799 n.
dueness 910 n.
vindication 922 n.
atonement 936 n.
reward 957 n.
penalty 958 n.
punishment
958 n.

restlessness
restlessness
673 n.

restoration
equalization 28 n.
compensation
31 n.
duplication 91 n.
repetition 102 n.
conversion 142 n.
reversion 143 n.
strengthening
157 n.
reproduction
161 n.
improvement
649 n.
restoration
651 n.
deliverance
663 n.
refreshment
680 n.
acquisition 766 n.
restitution 782 n.
dignification
861 n.
piety 973 n.

restorative
salubrious
647 adj.
improving
649 adj.
restorative
651 adj.
remedial 653 adj.
refreshing
680 adj.

restore
adjust 24 vb.
augment 36 vb.
make complete
54 vb.
double 91 vb.
repeat 102 vb.
modify 138 vb.
transform
142 vb.
revert 143 vb.
reproduce 161 vb.
replace 182 vb.

restore 651 vb.
remedy 653 vb.
deliver 663 vb.
refresh 680 vb.
aid 698 vb.
restitute 782 vb.
animate 816 vb.
make pious
973 vb.

restored
restored 651 adj.

restored, be
be restored
651 vb.

restoring
restoring 782 adj.

restrain
abate 37 vb.
exclude 57 vb.
halt 140 vb.
moderate 172 vb.
make smaller
193 vb.
limit 231 vb.
retard 273 vb.
qualify 463 vb.
dissuade 608 vb.
not suffice
631 vb.
hinder 697 vb.
be severe 730 vb.
compel 735 vb.
restrain 742 vb.
abrogate 747 vb.
prohibit 752 vb.
retain 773 vb.
tranquillize
818 vb.
be temperate
937 vb.

restrained
small 33 adj.
moderate
172 adj.
circumscribed
227 adj.
quiescent
261 adj.
hindered 697 adj.
subjected
740 adj.
restrained
742 adj.
temperate
937 adj.

restraining
restraining
742 adj.

restraint
diminution 37 n.
delay 131 n.
cessation 140 n.
helplessness
156 n.
contraception
167 n.
moderation
172 n.
moderator 172 n.
counteraction
177 n.
slowness 273 n.
protection 655 n.
hindrance 697 n.
severity 730 n.
compulsion 735 n.
subjection 740 n.
restraint 742 n.
prohibition 752 n.
sale 788 n.
price 804 n.

temperance
937 n.
legal process
954 n.
penalty 958 n.

restriction
restriction 742 n.

result
ensue 115 vb.
happen 149 vb.
result 152 vb.

retain
join 45 vb.
tie 45 vb.
cohere 48 vb.
prevail 173 vb.
remember
500 vb.
persevere 595 vb.
store 627 vb.
preserve 661 vb.
restrain 742 vb.
refuse 755 vb.
possess 768 vb.
retain 773 vb.
take 781 vb.
be parsimonious
811 vb.
caress 884 vb.
be selfish 927 vb.

retained
retained 773 adj.

retainer
concomitant
89 n.
bearer 268 n.
retainer 737 n.
toady 874 n.

retaliate
correlate 12 vb.
compensate
31 vb.
revert 143 vb.
interchange
146 vb.
recoil 275 vb.
answer 455 vb.
quarrel 704 vb.
attack 707 vb.
retaliate 709 vb.
be severe 730 vb.
pay 799 vb.
avenge 905 vb.
be just 908 vb.
blame 919 vb.
reward 957 vb.
punish 958 vb.

retaliation
retaliation 709 n.

retaliatory
retaliatory
709 adj.

retard
abate 37 vb.
halt 140 vb.
shorten 199 vb.
bring to rest
261 vb.
retard 273 vb.
hinder 697 vb.
restrain 742 vb.

retention
retention 773 n.

retentive
retentive 773 vb.

reticent
reticent 520 adj.
taciturn 577 adj.
cunning 693 adj.
cautious 853 adj.

reticular
reticular 217 adj.

retinue
retinue 67 n.
procession 71 n.
band 74 n.
concomitant
89 n.
rear 233 n.
follower 279 n.
retainer 737 n.

retreat
retreat 187 n.
chamber 189 n.
hiding-place
522 n.
refuge 657 n.
seclusion 878 n.
monastery 980 n.

retrieve
recoup 31 n.
revert 143 vb.
counteract
177 vb.
retrieve 651 vb.
acquire 766 vb.
possess 768 vb.
appropriate
781 vb.
restitute 782 vb.
claim 910 vb.

retrospect
look back 120 vb.
turn back 281 vb.
retrospect
500 vb.
describe 585 vb.
regret 825 vb.

retrospective
retrospective
120 adj.
antiquated
122 adj.
reverted 143 adj.
regressive
281 adj.
ignorant 486 adj.
regretting
825 adj.

retrospectively
retrospectively
120 adv.

return
return 281 n.
arrival 290 n.
departure 291 n.
ingress 292 n.
circuition 309 n.
tergiversation
598 n.

revel
eat 296 vb.
foolery 492 n.
rejoicing 830 n.
rejoice 830 vb.
revel 832 n.
revel 832 vb.
pageant 870 n.
celebrate 871 vb.
sociability 877 n.
be hospitable
877 vb.
be sociable
877 vb.
be intemperate
938 vb.
sensualism 939 n.
drunkenness
944 n.
get drunk 944 vb.

revelation
knowledge 485 n.
truth 489 n.
prediction 506 n.
revelation 969 n.

revelational
revelational
969 adj.

reveller
reveller 832 n.

revenge
compensation
31 n.
quarrel 704 n.
retaliation 709 n.
severity 730 n.
resentment
886 n.
revenge 905 n.
jealousy 906 n.
punishment
958 n.

revengeful
revengeful
905 adj.

revengeful, be
be revengeful
905 vb.

revengefulness
revengefulness
905 n.

reversibly
reversibly
143 adv.

reversion
start 68 n.
reversion 143 n.
revolution 144 n.
destruction
160 n.
inversion 216 n.
recoil 275 n.
regression 281 n.
return 281 n.
relapse 652 n.
abrogation 747 n.

revert
revert 143 vb.

reverted
reverted 143 adj.

revival
newness 121 n.
reproduction
161 n.
life 355 n.
pungency 383 n.
revival 651 n.
refreshment
680 n.
relief 826 n.
sanctity 973 n.

revive
convert 142 vb.
strengthen
157 vb.
reproduce 161 vb.
vitalize 355 vb.
get healthy
645 vb.
revive 651 vb.
doctor 653 vb.

revolt
rampage 61 n.
revolution 144 n.
be violent 171 vb.
opposition 699 n.
withstand
699 vb.
resistance 710 n.
resist 710 vb.

go to war
713 vb.
revolt 733 n.
revolt 733 vb.
achieve liberty
741 vb.
be discontented
824 vb.
cause discontent
824 vb.
fail in duty
913 vb.
lawlessness
949 n.

revolter
revolter 733 n.

revolution
disorder 61 n.
change 138 n.
reversion 143 n.
revolution 144 n.
destruction
160 n.
ruin 160 n.
outbreak 171 n.
overturning
216 n.
lowering 306 n.
obliteration
545 n.
revolt 733 n.

revolutionary
revolutionary
144 adj.
destructive
160 adj.
violent 171 adj.

revolutionist
revolutionist
144 n.

revolutionize
revolutionize
144 vb.

reward
compensation
31 n.
offset 31 n.
compensate
31 vb.
increment 36 n.
extra 40 n.
incentive 607 n.
inducement
607 n.
bribe 607 vb.
subvention 698 n.
retaliation 709 n.
trophy 724 n.
resignation 748 n.
acquisition 766 n.
earnings 766 n.
gift 776 n.
giving 776 n.
give 776 vb.
pay 799 n.
pay 799 vb.
receipt 802 n.
honours 861 n.
celebrate 871 vb.
thanks 902 n.
thank 902 vb.
justice 908 n.
reward 957 n.
reward 957 vb.

rewarded, be
be rewarded
957 vb.

rewarding
gainful 766 adj.
rewarding
957 adj.

rewardingly
rewardingly
957 adv.

rhetorical
rhetorical
569 adj.

rheumatism
rheumatism
646 n.

rich
powerful 155 adj.
monetary
792 adj.
rich 795 adj.
ornamented
839 adj.

rich, be
abound 630 vb.
superabound
632 vb.
bequeath 775 vb.
be rich 795 vb.

rich person
prosperous
person 725 n.
minter 792 n.
rich person
795 n.
upper class
863 n.
proud person
866 n.

ride
ride 262 vb.
start out 291 vb.
break in 364 vb.

rider
rider 263 n.

ridicule
imitate 20 vb.
copy 22 n.
be superior
34 vb.
confutation
474 n.
underestimate
478 vb.
unbelief 481 n.
disbelieve 481 vb.
foolery 492 n.
be absurd
492 vb.
misinterpretation
516 n.
misinterpret
516 vb.
befool 537 vb.
misrepresentation
547 n.
reject 602 vb.
laughter 830 n.
laugh 830 vb.
wit 834 n.
be witty 834 vb.
be ridiculous
844 vb.
affectation
845 n.
ridicule 846 n.
ridicule 846 vb.
shame 862 n.
sauciness 873 n.
be insolent
873 vb.
rudeness 880 n.
disrespect 916 n.
indignity 916 n.
not respect
916 vb.
contempt 917 n.
despise 917 vb.

disapprobation
919 n.
reproach 919 n.
calumny 921 n.
detract 921 vb.
impiety 974 n.
ridiculous
unusual 84 adj.
absurd 492 adj.
foolish 499 adj.
inelegant 571 adj.
laughing 830 adj.
ridiculous
844 adj.
ridiculous, be
be absurd
492 vb.
be foolish 499 vb.
amuse 837 vb.
be ridiculous
844 vb.
ridiculousness
ridiculousness
844 n.
rig
rig 270 n.
right
fit 24 adj.
advisable
637 adj.
right 908 n.
right 908 adj.
dueness 910 n.
dueness 910 n.
due 910 adj.
probity 929 n.
virtuous 928 adj.
right, be
be right 908 vb.
rightly
rightly 908 adv.
rightly served, be
be rightly served
709 vb.
rigid
unconformable
84 adj.
impotent 156 adj.
unyielding
157 adj.
straight 244 adj.
still 261 adj.
dense 319 adj.
rigid 321 adj.
tough 324 adj.
brittle 325 adj.
obstinate
597 adj.
restraining
742 adj.
rioter
anarchist 61 n.
rioter 733 n.
riotous
disorderly 61 adj.
violent 171 adj.
anarchic 729 adj.
riotous 733 adj.
excitable 817 adj.
intemperate
938 adj.
lawless 949 adj.
rite
practice 605 n.
act of worship
975 n.
oblation 975 n.
sorcery 977 n.
rite 982 n.
ritual
order 60 n.

formality 870 n.
celebration
871 n.
ritual 982 n.
ritual 982 adj.
ritual act
social gathering
877 n.
ritual act 982 n.
ritualism
ritualism 982 n.
ritualist
ritualist 982 n.
ritualistic
ritualistic
982 adj.
ritualize
ritualize 982 vb.
ritually
ritually 982 adv.
ritual object
small box 189 n.
cross 217 n.
water 334 n.
ritual object
982 n.
altar 984 n.
church utensil
984 n.
road
housing 187 n.
crossing 217 n.
paving 221 n.
limit 231 n.
traffic control
300 n.
road 619 n.
instrument 623 n.
building material
626 n.
facility 696 n.
rob
lay waste 160 vb.
take away
781 vb.
rob 783 vb.
robber
robber 784 n.
robe
robe 223 n.
vestments 983 n.
rock
solid body 319 n.
hardness 321 n.
rock 339 n.
mineral 354 n.
rocket
aeronautics
266 n.
rocket 271 n.
roll
periodicity 136 n.
impulse 274 n.
sound 393 n.
loudness 395 n.
faintness 396 n.
roll 398 n.
roll 398 vb.
resound 399 vb.
play music
408 vb.
call 547 vb.
rolling
rolling 398 adj.
Roman Catholic
Roman Catholic
970 adj.
ecclesiastical
979 adj.
roof
dwelling 187 n.

high structure
204 n.
vertex 208 n.
beam 213 n.
roof 221 n.
dome 248 n.
projection 249 n.
building material
626 n.
room
greatness 32 n.
advantage 34 n.
inclusion 78 n.
room 178 n.
emptiness 185 n.
interval 196 n.
storage 627 n.
scope 739 n.
rostrum
stand 213 n.
publicity 523 n.
rostrum 534 n.
oratory 574 n.
rotary
periodical
136 adj.
rotary 310 adj.
rotate
be periodic
136 vb.
twine 246 vb.
round 247 vb.
propel 282 vb.
circle 309 vb.
rotate 310 vb.
agitate 313 vb.
rotation
continuity 71 n.
regular return
136 n.
revolution 144 n.
motion 260 n.
circuition 309 n.
rotation 310 n.
planet 316 n.
ballet 589 n.
rotator
rotator 310 n.
rotund
round 245 adj.
rotund 247 adj.
convex 248 adj.
tubular 258 adj.
rotundity
circularity 245 n.
rotundity 247 n.
rough
nonuniform
17 adj.
discontinuous
72 adj.
amorphous
239 adj.
convex 248 adj.
projecting
249 adj.
sharp 251 adj.
rough 254 adj.
textural 326 adj.
flowing 345 adj.
pungent 383 adj.
difficult 695 adj.
rough, be
be rough 254 vb.
roughen
jut 249 vb.
roughen 254 vb.

notch 255 vb.
roughness
nonuniformity
17 n.
inequality 29 n.
discontinuity
72 n.
roughness 254 n.
agitation 313 n.
texture 326 n.
wave 345 n.
difficulty 695 n.
round
curved 243 adj.
round 245 adj.
rotund 247 adj.
round 247 vb.
roundabout
circuitous
309 adj.
roundabout
621 n.
round about
621 adv.
round and round
round and round
310 adv.
route
water travel
264 n.
air travel 266 n.
direction 276 n.
route 619 n.
row
be in motion
260 n.
row 264 n.
rowing boat
rowing boat
270 n.
rub
abate 37 vb.
subtract 39 vb.
uncover 224 vb.
smooth 253 vb.
collide 274 vb.
pulverize 327 vb.
rub 328 vb.
give pain 372 vb.
touch 373 vb.
obliterate 545 vb.
clean 643 vb.
wound 650 vb.
rubbing
rubbing 328 n.
rubbish
leavings 41 n.
piece 53 n.
confusion 61 n.
accumulation
74 n.
sham 537 n.
waste 629 n.
rubbish 636 n.
dirt 644 n.
derelict 774 n.
outcast 878 n.
rude, be
disregard 453 vb.
reject 602 vb.
torment 822 vb.
humiliate 867 vb.
be insolent
873 vb.
make unwelcome
878 vb.
be rude 880 vb.
not respect
916 vb.
despise 917 vb.

scent
scent 391 n.

schism
disagreement
25 n.
tergiversation
598 n.
relinquishment
616 n.
dissension 704 n.
revolt 733 n.
undutifulness
913 n.
schism 972 n.

schismatic
dissentient 484 n.
tergiversator
598 n.
revolter 733 n.
undutifulness
913 n.
schismatic 972 n.

schismatical
schismatical
972 adj.

schismatize
schismatize
972 vb.

scholar
antiquarian
120 n.
scholar 487 n.
sage 495 n.
learning 531 n.
learner 533 n.
linguist 552 n.
bookperson
584 n.
expert 691 n.

scholastic
scholastic
534 adj.

school
edifice 159 n.
curriculum 534 n.
school 534 n.
amendment
649 n.

school of painting
art 546 n.
school of painting
548 n.
sculpture 549 n.
artist 551 n.

science
physics 314 n.
science 485 n.

science of forces
energy 155 n.
science of forces
157 n.

sciolism
sciolism 486 n.

sciolist
sciolist 488 n.

scission
scission 46 n.

scope
opportunity
132 n.
influence 173 n.
range 178 n.
ingress 292 n.
facility 696 n.
laxity 729 n.
scope 739 n.
permit 751 n.
trade 786 n.
liberality 808 n.

scourge
scourge 959 n.

screen
separation 46 n.
canopy 221 n.
shade 221 n.
headgear 223 n.
partition 226 n.
stopper 259 n.
refrigerate
377 n.
darken 413 vb.
screen 416 n.
screen 416 vb.
opacity 418 n.
make opaque
418 vb.
eye 433 n.
blind 434 vb.
dim sight 435 n.
be unseen
439 vb.
concealment
520 n.
conceal 520 vb.
disguise 522 n.
pretext 609 n.
safeguard 655 vb.
shelter 657 n.
defences 708 n.
defend 708 vb.

screened
screened 416 adj.

script
speech sound
393 n.
lack of meaning
510 n.
identification
542 n.
symbology 542 n.
record 543 n.
phrase 558 n.
script 581 n.

scriptural
scriptural
969 adj.

scripture
scripture 969 n.

sculpt
sculpt 549 vb.

sculptor
sculptor 551 n.

sculpture
copy 22 n.
composition 56 n.
production 159 n.
high structure
204 n.
formation 238 n.
relievo 249 n.
art 546 n.
image 546 n.
sculpture 549 n.
ornamental art
839 n.
idol 976 n.

scurrility
slang 555 n.
quarrel 704 n.
quarrelsomeness
704 n.
insolence 873 n.
rudeness 880 n.
scurrility 894 n.
disrespect 916 n.
reproach 919 n.
detraction 921 n.

seafaring
seafaring
264 adj.
marine 270 adj.
oceanic 338 adj.

sea god
mariner 265 n.
sea god 338 n.

sealed off
sealed off
259 adj.

seamanlike
seamanlike
265 adj.

sea nymph
sea nymph 338 n.

search
be curious
448 vb.
search 454 n.
search 454 vb.
discovery 479 n.
discover 479 vb.
pursuit 614 n.
pursue 614 vb.
attempt 666 vb.
request 756 vb.
take 781 vb.

season
cook 296 vb.
season 383 vb.
spice 384 vb.
make appetizing
385 vb.
preserve 661 vb.

seasonal
periodic 106 adj.
seasonal 136 adj.
territorial
339 adj.
celebratory
871 adj.

seat
seat 213 n.

seclude
set apart 46 vb.
exclude 57 vb.
eject 295 vb.
disappear 441 vb.
conceal 520 vb.
sanitate 647 vb.
imprison 742 vb.
seclude 878 vb.

secluded
closed 259 adj.
tranquil 261 adj.
invisible 439 adj.
latent 518 adj.
concealed
520 adj.
secluded 878 adj.

seclusion
seclusion 878 n.

secrecy
invisibility 439 n.
secrecy 520 n.
symbology 542 n.
taciturnity 577 n.
caution 853 n.

secret
unknown thing
486 n.
unintelligibility
512 n.
latency 518 n.
information
519 n.
secrecy 520 n.
secret 525 n.
trap 537 n.
writing 581 n.

secretly
secretly 520 adv.

secret service
secret service
454 n.

sect
classification
77 n
party 703 n.
religionist 967 n.
Protestantism
970 n
sect 972 n.

sectarian
classificatory
77 adj
nonconformist
84 n
unconformable
84 adj.
biased 476 adj.
dissentient 484 n.
dissenting
484 adj
auxiliary 702 n.
sectional 703 adj.
Protestant
970 adj
sectarian 972 n.
sectarian
972 adj
zealot 973 n.
pietistic 973 adj.
ecclesiastical
979 adj

sectarianism
sectarianism
972 n.

sectarianize
sectarianize
972 vb

sectional
excluding 57 adj.
biased 476 adj.
sectional 703 adj.
sectarian
972 adj

secular
secular 106 adj.

secured
secured 762 adj.

security
offset 31 n.
list 87 n.
thing transferred
267 n
credential 461 n.
testimony 461 n.
prisoner 745 n.
promise 759 n.
compact 760 n.
security 762 n.
paper money
792 n
debt 798 n.

sedition
disorder 61 n.
dissent 484 n.
reformism 649 n.
activity 673 n.
sedition 733 n.
perfidy 925 n.

see
see 433 vb.
watch 436 vb.
cognize 442 vb.
be mindful
450 vb
detect 479 vb.
know 485 vb.
be wise 493 vb.
imagine 508 vb.
understand
511 vb.

seedbed
origin 68 n.

seedbed 151 n.
abundance 166 n.
seeing
seeing 433 adj.
seek refuge
dwell 187 vb.
navigate 264 vb.
seek safety
655 vb.
seek refuge
657 vb.
seek repute
seek repute
861 vb.
be praised
918 vb.
seek safety
gamble 613 vb.
seek safety
655 vb.
seek refuge
657 vb.
prepare 664 vb.
be cautious
853 vb.
seldom
seldom 135 adv.
select
subtract 39 vb.
set apart 46 vb.
extract 299 vb.
discriminate
458 vb.
select 600 vb.
self
intrinsicality 5 n.
no imitation
21 n.
group 74 n.
self 80 n.
subjectivity
315 n.
spirit 442 n.
selfish
unthinking
445 adj.
avaricious
811 adj.
greedy 854 adj.
vain 868 adj.
selfish 927 adj.
selfish, be
be parsimonious
811 vb.
be selfish 927 vb.
selfishly
selfishly 927 adv.
selfishness
selfishness 927 n.
sell
provide 628 vb.
offer 754 vb.
request 756 vb.
not retain
774 vb.
assign 775 vb.
trade 786 vb.
sell 788 vb.
overcharge
806 vb.
seller
traveller 263 n.
speaker 574 n.
worker 681 n.
servant 737 n.
seller 788 n.
pedlar 789 n.
tradespeople
789 n.
semantic
semantic 509 adj.

semiliquid
semiliquid
349 adj.
semiliquidity
semiliquidity
349 n.
semitransparency
semitransparency
419 n.
semitransparent
semitransparent
419 adj.
send
disperse 75 vb.
displace 183 vb.
move 260 vb.
send 267 vb.
admit 294 vb.
emit 295 vb.
pass 300 vb.
give 776 vb.
take away
781 vb.
seniority
seniority 126 n.
sense
sense 369 n.
feeling 813 n.
sensibility
weakness 158 n.
liability 175 n.
sensibility 369 n.
moral sensibility
814 n.
sensitive
attentive
450 adj.
receiving 777 adj.
feeling 813 adj.
sensitive 814 adj.
excitable 817 adj.
tasteful 841 adj.
irascible 887 adj.
sensitive, be
have feeling
369 vb.
feel 813 vb.
be sensitive
814 vb.
sensual
material 314 adj.
sensuous 371 adj.
feeling 813 adj.
intemperate
938 adj.
sensual 939 adj.
lecherous
946 adj.
irreligious
968 adj.
sensual, be
be sensual
939 vb.
sensualism
sensualism 939 n.
sensualist
sensualist 939 n.
sensually
sensually
939 adv.
sensuous
sensuous 371 adj.
pleasurable
821 adj.
sentient
sentient 369 adj.
feeling 813 adj.
impressible
814 adj.
sensitive 814 adj.

separate
different 15 adj.
separate 46 adj.
separate 46 vb.
nonadhesive
49 adj.
fragmentary
53 adj.
extraneous
59 adj.
discontinuous
72 adj.
unassembled
75 adj.
be dispersed
75 vb.
recede 285 vb.
diverge 289 vb.
cultivate 365 vb.
schismatical
972 adj.
separately
separately
46 adv.
separation
unrelatedness
10 n.
separation 46 n.
noncoherence
49 n.
decomposition
51 n.
derangement
63 n.
discontinuity
72 n.
dispersion 75 n.
unity 88 n.
destruction
160 n.
farness 194 n.
gap 196 n.
partition 226 n.
divergence 289 n.
liberation 741 n.
seclusion 878 n.
schism 972 n.
sequel
adjunct 40 n.
remainder 41 n.
sequence 65 n.
sequel 67 n.
end 69 n.
extremity 69 n.
continuity 71 n.
posteriority
115 n.
lateness 131 n.
effect 152 n.
abundance 166 n.
hanging object
212 n.
rear 233 n.
eddy 345 n.
thought 444 n.
remembrance
500 n.
tergiversation
598 n.
amendment
649 n.
regret 825 n.
wit 834 n.
sequence
relativeness 9 n.
addition 38 n.
adjunct 40 n.
order 60 n.
sequence 65 n.
continuity 71 n.

posteriority
115 n.
futurity 119 n.
effect 152 n.
near place 195 n.
line 198 n.
following 279 n.
pursuit 614 n.
sequential
sequential 65 adj.
serial place
circumstance 8 n.
degree 27 n.
average 30 n.
order 60 n.
serial place 73 n.
prestige 861 n.
series
increase 36 n.
decrease 37 n.
coherence 48 n.
all 52 n.
arrangement
62 n.
retinue 67 n.
series 71 n.
accumulation
74 n.
group 74 n.
sort 77 n.
continuance
141 n.
following 279 n.
serious
wise 493 adj.
forceful 566 adj.
plain 568 adj.
inexcitable
818 adj.
serious 829 adj.
dull 835 adj.
ungracious
880 adj.
angry 886 adj.
sullen 888 adj.
serious, be
be truthful
535 vb.
be serious
829 vb.
seriousness
seriousness
829 n.
serpent
serpent 246 n.
servant
inferior 35 n.
mariner 265 n.
aeronaut 266 n.
animal husbandry
364 n.
spectator 436 n.
instrument 623 n.
nonentity 634 n.
worker 681 n.
official 685 n.
auxiliary 702 n.
officer 736 n.
servant 737 n.
commoner 864 n.
worshipper 975 n.
serve
be inferior 35 vb.
follow 279 vb.
busy oneself
617 vb.
be useful 635 vb.
minister to
698 vb.
obey 734 vb.
serve 737 vb.

be servile 874 vb.

service
service 740 n.
servility 874 n.

servile
willing 592 adj.
obedient 734 adj.
subject 740 adj.
subjected
　　　　740 adj.
inglorious
　　　　862 adj.
servile 874 adj.
courteous
　　　　879 adj.
respectful
　　　　915 adj.
flattering
　　　　920 adj.

servile, be
obey 734 vb.
be subject
　　　　740 vb.
be servile 874 vb.
flatter 920 vb.

servilely
servilely 874 adv.

servility
servility 874 n.

serving
inferior 35 adj.
aiding 698 adj.
serving 737 adj.
subjected
　　　　740 adj.

servitude
submission 716 n.
compulsion 735 n.
servitude 740 n.
detention 742 n.
servility 874 n.

set apart
differentiate
　　　　15 vb.
set apart 46 vb.
exclude 57 vb.
be one 88 vb.
space 196 vb.
discriminate
　　　　458 vb.
select 600 vb.

set off
set off 31 vb.

settler
foreigner 59 n.
settler 186 n.
egress 293 n.

severable
severable 46 adj.

severally
severally 80 adv.

severe
regulated 83 adj.
strong 157 adj.
operative
　　　　168 adj.
vigorous 169 adj.
narrow-minded
　　　　476 adj.
severe 730 adj.
restraining
　　　　742 adj.
paining 822 adj.
serious 829 adj.
fastidious
　　　　857 adj.
ungracious
　　　　880 adj.
unkind 893 adj.
pitiless 901 adj.
unjust 909 adj.

ascetic 940 adj.

severe, be
dominate 728 vb.
be severe 730 vb.
restrain 742 vb.
prohibit 752 vb.
give terms
　　　　761 vb.
be pitiless
　　　　901 vb.
do wrong 909 vb.
impose a duty
　　　　912 vb.
punish 958 vb.

severely
severely 730 adv.

severity
severity 730 n.

shade
shade 221 n.
headgear 223 n.
curtain 416 n.
screen 416 n.

shade off
shade off 27 vb.

shadowy
amorphous
　　　　239 adj.
dark 413 adj.
shadowy 414 adj.
screened 416 adj.
uncertain
　　　　469 adj.
imaginary
　　　　508 adj.
puzzling 512 adj.

shallow
insubstantial
　　　　4 adj.
inconsiderable
　　　　33 adj.
near 195 adj.
shallow 207 adj.
exterior 218 adj.
inattentive
　　　　451 adj.
trivial 634 adj.

shallowness
shallowness
　　　　207 n.

sham
mimicry 20 n.
copy 22 n.
misfit 25 n.
disguise 522 n.
duplicity 536 n.
sham 537 n.
inelegance 571 n.
stratagem 693 n.
lament 831 n.
flattery 920 n.
pietism 973 n.
false piety 974 n.

shame
hinder 697 vb.
shame 862 vb.
humiliate 867 vb.
be rude 880 vb.
not respect
　　　　916 vb.
despise 917 vb.
defame 921 vb.
debauch 946 vb.
punish 958 vb.

shapely
symmetrical
　　　　240 adj.
shapely 836 adj.

sharing
sharing 770 adj.

sharp
violent 171 adj.
sharp 251 adj.
hairy 254 adj.
notched 255 adj.
pungent 383 adj.
forceful 566 adj.
felt 813 adj.

sharp, be
be sharp 251 vb.

sharp edge
sharp edge 251 n.
smoother 253 n.
roughness 254 n.
pulverizer 327 n.
farm tool 365 n.
tool 625 n.
axe 718 n.
sidearms 718 n.

sharpen
invigorate
　　　　169 vb.
make violent
　　　　171 vb.
sharpen 251 vb.
animate 816 vb.

sharpener
sharpener 251 n.

sharpness
sharpness 251 n.

sharp point
fastening 47 n.
extremity 69 n.
angularity 242 n.
protuberance
　　　　249 n.
sharp point
　　　　251 n.
perforator 258 n.
bane 654 n.
sidearms 718 n.
spear 718 n.
weapon 718 n.
nippers 773 n.

sheep
sheep 360 n.

shekels
shekels 792 n.

shelf
compartment
　　　　189 n.
shelf 213 n.

shelter
station 182 n.
dwelling 187 n.
retreat 187 n.
stable 187 n.
projection 249 n.
goal 290 n.
screen 416 n.
hiding-place
　　　　522 n.
protection 655 n.
shelter 657 n.
defences 708 n.

shine
grow 36 vb.
vary 147 vb.
recoil 275 vb.
oscillate 312 vb.
be agitated
　　　　313 vb.
shine 412 vb.
illuminate 415 vb.
blur 435 vb.
be visible 438 vb.
be beautiful
　　　　836 vb.
be ostentatious
　　　　870 vb.

ship
layer 202 n.
vertex 208 n.
prow 232 n.
poop 233 n.
water travel
　　　　264 n.
transport 267 n.
carrier 268 n.
ship 270 n.
aircraft 271 n.
speeder 272 n.
follower 279 n.
traction 283 n.
warship 717 n.

shipping
shipping 270 n.

shirt
shirt 223 n.

shoot
shoot 282 n.
fell 306 vb.
kill 357 vb.
fire at 707 vb.

shooter
shooter 282 n.

shop
shop 791 n.

shore
edge 229 n.
limit 231 n.
laterality 234 n.
shore 339 n.

short
small 33 adj.
incomplete
　　　　55 ad
brief 109 adj.
dwarfish 191 adj
short 199 adj.
thick 200 adj.
low 205 adj.
deformed
　　　　241 ad
concise 564 adj.
compendious
　　　　587 ad

short, be
be short 199 vb.

short distance
draw 28 n.
small quantity
　　　　33 n
short distance
　　　　195 n
interval 196 n.
shortness 199 n.
narrowness
　　　　201 n
straightness
　　　　244 n
contest 711 n.

shorten
shade off 27 vb.
abate 37 vb.
subtract 39 vb.
cut 46 vb.
sunder 46 vb.
make smaller
　　　　193 vb
shorten 199 vb.
smooth 253 vb.
cultivate 370 vb.
neglect 453 vb.
be concise
　　　　564 vb
abstract 587 vb.
impair 650 vb.

shortener
shortener 199 n.

shortening
diminution 37 n.
subtraction 39 n.
decrement 42 n.
scission 46 n.
contraction
193 n.
shortening 199 n.
conciseness
564 n.
compendium
587 n.

shortfall
smallness 33 n.
inferiority 35 n.
decrement 42 n.
incompleteness
55 n.
shortfall 302 n.
requirement
622 n.
insufficiency
631 n.
scarcity 631 n.
defect 642 n.
imperfection
642 n.
noncompletion
721 n.
debt 798 n.

shortly
shortly 199 adv.

shortness
shortness 199 n.

show
open 258 vb.
attract notice
450 vb.
detect 479 vb.
interpret 515 vb.
show 517 vb.
be truthful
535 vb.
indicate 542 vb.
dramatize
589 vb.
be ostentatious
870 vb.

show feeling
show feeling
813 vb.
be excited
816 vb.
be excitable
817 vb.
be pleased
819 vb.

show mercy
be moderate
172 vb.
safeguard 655 vb.
be lenient 731 vb.
show mercy
900 vb.
forgive 904 vb.
be just 908 vb.
exempt 914 vb.

shown
obvious 438 adj.
appearing
440 adj.
shown 517 adj.
disclosed 521 adj.
dramatic 589 adj.
offering 754 adj.

show respect
stoop 306 vb.
make important
633 vb.
honour 861 vb.
greet 879 vb.

pay one's
respects 879 vb.
show respect
915 vb.
be pious 973 vb.

show style
phrase 558 vb.
show style
561 vb.
be elegant
570 vb.

showy
appearing
440 adj.
manifest 517 adj.
ornate 569 adj.
splendid 836 adj.
ornamented
839 adj.
vulgar 842 adj.
fashionable
843 adj.
prideful 866 adj.
proud 866 vb.
showy 870 adj.

shrew
violent creature
171 n.
quarreller 704 n.
shrew 887 n.
hellhag 899 n.
defamer 921 n.

shrill
blow 347 vb.
be loud 395 vb.
shrill 402 vb.

sibilant
sibilant 401 adj.
vocal 572 adj.

sibilation
sibilation 401 n.

sick
orderless 61 adj.
lean 201 adj.
dying 356 adj.
frenzied 498 adj.
sick 646 adj.
suffering 820 adj.

sick person
list 87 n.
helplessness
156 n.
weakling 158 n.
transferrer 267 n.
sick person
646 n.
sufferer 820 n.

side arms
sharp edge 251 n.
sharp point
251 n.
sidearms 718 n.

sideways
broadways
200 adv.
sideways
234 adv.

sign
endorse 483 vb.
sign 542 vb.
spell 553 vb.
write 581 vb.

signal
signal light 415 n.
manifestation
517 n.
communicate
519 vb.
message 524 n.
telecommunication
526 n.

signal 542 n.
signal 542 vb.
warning 659 n.
danger signal
660 n.
greet 879 vb.

signal light
signal light 415 n.
signal 542 n.

signatory
witness 461 n.
assenter 483 n.
promise 759 n.
signatory 760 n.

significantly
significantly
509 adv.

signpost
itinerary 262 n.
sailing aid 264 n.
direction 276 n.
visibility 438 n.
gauge 460 n.
signpost 542 n.

silence
abate 37 vb.
stop 140 n.
disable 156 vb.
destruction
160 n.
quietude 261 n.
bring to rest
261 vb.
silence 394 n.
silence 394 vb.
mute 396 vb.
deafness 411 n.
secrecy 520 n.
obliterate 545 vb.
voicelessness
573 n.
make mute
573 vb.
taciturnity 577 n.
make insensitive
815 vb.
wonder 859 n.

silencer
silencer 396 n.
nonresonance
400 n.
mute 409 n.

silent
still 261 adj.
silent 394 adj.
nonresonant
400 adj.
deaf 411 adj.
taciturn 577 adj.
wondering
859 adj.

silent, be
cease 140 vb.
be quiescent
261 vb.
be silent 394 vb.
wonder 859 vb.

silly talk
absurdity 492 n.
silly talk 510 n.

similar
relative 9 adj.
correlative
12 adj.
uniform 16 adj.
similar 18 adj.
agreeing 24 adj.
equal 28 adj.
equivalent 28 adj.
included 78 adj.
repeated 102 adj.

parallel 214 adj.
symmetrical
240 adj.
harmonious
405 adj.
semantic 509 adj.

similarity
relativeness 9 n.
correlation 12 n.
uniformity 16 n.
similarity 18 n.
mimicry 20 n.
copy 22 n.
conformance
24 n.
equivalence 28 n.
conformity 83 n.
appearance
440 n.
comparison
457 n.
consensus 483 n.
representation
546 n.
word 554 n.

similarly
similarly 18 adv.

simple
simple 44 adj.
artless 694 adj.
easy 696 adj.

simpleness
simpleness 44 n.

simplification
simplification
44 n.

simplify
simplify 44 vb.
decompose 51 vb.

simply
simply 44 adv.

simulating
simulating 18 adj.

sing
vociferate
403 vb.
ululate 404 vb.
harmonize
405 vb.
sing 408 vb.
voice 572 vb.
rejoice 830 vb.
offer worship
975 vb.
worship 975 vb.

singly
singly 88 adv.

sinistral
sinistral 237 adj.

sinistrality
sinistrality 237 n.

sinistrally
sinistrally
237 adv.

sink
receptacle 189 n.
vessel 189 n.
base 209 n.
cavity 250 n.
lake 341 n.
drain 346 n.
stench 392 n.
storage 627 n.
badness 640 n.
sink 644 n.
insalubrity 648 n.
wickedness 929 n.

sit down
sit down 306 vb.

situated
situated 181 adj.

relieve 826 vb.
smoother
smoother 253 n.
smoothness
smoothness
253 n.
snaky
snaky 246 adj.
snow
snow 375 n.
snuff out
snuff out 413 vb.
sober
moderate
172 adj.
temperate
937 adj.
ascetic 940 adj.
sober 943 adj.
sober, be
be temperate
937 vb.
be sober 943 vb.
soberly
soberly 943 adv.
sober person
abstainer 937 n.
ascetic 940 n.
sober person
943 n.
sobriety
moderation
172 n.
temperance
937 n.
sobriety 943 n.
sociability
sociability 877 n.
sociable
accessible
284 adj.
corporate
703 adj.
free 739 adj.
liberal 808 adj.
cheerful 828 adj.
friendly 875 adj.
sociable 877 adj.
amiable 879 adj.
benevolent
892 adj.
sociable, be
unite with 45 vb.
meet 290 vb.
be cheerful
828 vb.
rejoice 830 vb.
be in fashion
843 vb.
be friendly
875 vb.
be sociable
877 vb.
greet 879 vb.
sociable person
incomer 292 n.
reveller 837 n.
beau monde
843 n.
friend 875 n.
sociable person
877 n.
sociably
sociably 877 adv.
social evil
social evil 946 n.
social gathering
assembly 74 n.
conference 579 n.
festivity 832 n.

social gathering
877 n.
social group
social group
366 n.
community 703 n.
sociality
sociality 877 n.
social round
festivity 832 n.
social round
877 n.
society
band 74 n.
group 74 n.
society 703 n.
sociology
anthropology
366 n.
vocation 622 n.
reformism 649 n.
nurse 653 n.
safety 655 n.
benevolence
892 n.
sociology 896 n.
soft
unstable 147 adj.
weak 158 adj.
lenitive 172 adj.
soft 322 adj.
elastic 323 adj.
marshy 342 adj.
pulpy 351 adj.
comfortable
371 adj.
unsavoury
386 adj.
irresolute
596 adj.
submitting
716 adj.
impressible
814 adj.
soft drink
soft drink 296 n.
water 334 n.
soften
conform 83 vb.
be weak 158 vb.
weaken 158 vb.
assuage 172 vb.
soften 322 vb.
soft-hued
soft-hued
420 adj.
softness
softness 322 n.
soil
leavings 41 n.
piece 53 n.
shallowness
207 n.
covering 221 n.
soil 339 n.
farm 365 n.
materials 626 n.
sold, be
be published
523 vb.
be sold 788 vb.
soldier
aeronaut 266 n.
descent 304 n.
defender 708 n.
soldier 717 n.
brave person
850 n.
soldiery
soldiery 717 n.

solecism
inexactness
490 n.
mistake 490 n.
misinterpretation
516 n.
neology 555 n.
misnomer 557 n.
grammar 559 n.
solecism 560 n.
inelegance 571 n.
pronunciation
572 n.
solid body
substance 3 n.
coherence 48 n.
bulk 190 n.
gravity 317 n.
solid body 319 n.
blood 330 n.
semiliquidity
349 n.
solidifying
solidifying
319 adj.
soliloquist
soliloquist 580 n.
soliloquize
soliloquize
580 vb.
soliloquizing
soliloquizing
580 adj.
soliloquy
oration 574 n.
soliloquy 580 n.
solitary
nonconformist
84 n.
unit 88 n.
wanderer 263 n.
free person
739 n.
solitary 878 n.
celibate 890 n.
misanthrope
897 n.
ascetic 940 n.
pietist 973 n.
monk 980 n.
solution
solution 332 n.
somehow
somehow
153 adv.
sometimes
sometimes
134 adv.
somewhere
somewhere
180 adv.
sonship
sonship 165 n.
sophism
sophism 472 n.
sophist
sophist 472 n.
sophistical
sophistical
472 adj.
sophisticate
sophisticate
472 vb.
sophistry
discontinuity
72 n.
argument 470 n.
sophistry 472 n.
inexactness
490 n.
absurdity 492 n.

folly 494 n.
fantasy 508 n.
lack of meaning
510 n.
equivocalness
513 n.
misteaching
530 n.
falsehood 536 n.
deception 537 n.
wit 834 n.
soporific
moderator 172 n.
lenitive 172 adj.
anaesthetic
370 n.
insensible
370 adj.
drug 653 n.
soporific 674 n.
soporific 674 adj.
relief 826 n.
tedious 833 adj.
sorcerer
alterer 138 n.
sage 495 n.
oracle 506 n.
conjuror 540 n.
doctor 653 n.
prodigy 859 n.
mythical being
964 n.
sorcerer 977 n.
occultist 978 n.
sorceress
sorceress 977 n.
sorcerous
sorcerous
977 adj.
sorcerously
sorcerously
977 adv.
sorcery
conversion 142 n.
power 155 n.
influence 173 n.
eye 433 n.
knowledge 485 n.
sleight 537 n.
instrumentality
623 n.
badness 640 n.
excitation 816 n.
thaumaturgy
859 n.
love 882 n.
diabolism 963 n.
idolatry 976 n.
sorcery 977 n.
occultism 978 n.
spiritualism
978 n.
sorrow
evil 611 n.
bane 654 n.
adversity 726 n.
sorrow 820 n.
painfulness 822 n.
discontent 824 n.
dejection 829 n.
pity 900 n.
sort
character 5 n.
degree 27 n.
group 74 n.
sort 77 n.
sorting
sorting 62 n.
sound
sound 393 n.
sound 393 vb.

loudness 395 n.
be heard 410 vb.
radiation 412 n.
metrology 460 n.
indication 542 n.
voice 572 n.

sound dead
sound faint
396 vb.
sound dead
400 vb.

sound faint
be small 33 vb.
blow 347 vb.
sound faint
396 vb.
roll 398 vb.
cry 403 vb.
sing 408 vb.
speak low 573 vb.

sounding
sounding 393 adj.

sour
keen 169 adj.
painful 372 adj.
pungent 383 adj.
unsavoury
386 adj.
sour 388 adj.
unpleasant
822 adj.
discontented
824 adj.
hateful 883 adj.
irascible 887 adj.
sullen 888 adj.

sour, be
be sour 388 vb.

source
origin 68 n.
young creature
127 n.
reversion 143 n.
source 151 n.
attribution 153 n.
genitalia 162 n.
propagation
162 n.
parentage 164 n.
outflow 293 n.
stream 345 n.
flower 361 n.
plant 361 n.
connotation
509 n.
store 627 n.
divineness 960 n.

sources of energy
sources of energy
155 n.

sourness
sourness 388 n.

sovereign
sovereign 736 n.
beneficiary 771 n.
aristocrat 863 n.

space
quantity 26 n.
greatness 32 n.
grade 73 vb.
inclusion 78 n.
infinity 103 n.
space 178 n.
district 179 n.
size 190 n.
distance 194 n.
space 196 n.
open space
258 n.
open 258 vb.
air 335 n.

plain 343 n.

spaced
spaced 196 adj.

spaceship
space travel
266 n.
spaceship 271 n.
follower 279 n.
satellite 316 n.
detector 479 n.

space travel
space travel
266 n.

spacious
extensive 32 adj.
great 32 adj.
unassembled
75 adj.
spacious 178 adj.
recipient 189 adj.
large 190 adj.
expanded
192 adj.
broad 200 adj.
telluric 316 adj.

spank
spank 958 vb.

sparingly
sparingly
809 adv.

spasm
fitfulness 137 n.
revolution 144 n.
violence 171 n.
impulse 274 n.
spasm 313 n.
pang 372 n.
frenzy 498 n.
gesture 542 n.
illness 646 n.
nervous disorders
646 n.
activity 673 n.
feeling 813 n.
excitation 816 n.
fear 849 n.

spatial
spatial 178 adj.

speak
cry 403 vb.
inform 519 vb.
divulge 521 vb.
publish 523 vb.
affirm 527 vb.
voice 572 vb.
speak 574 vb.
converse 579 vb.

speaker
informant 519 n.
preacher 532 n.
phrasemonger
569 n.
speaker 574 n.
actor 589 n.
motivator 607 n.

speaking
speaking 574 adj.

speak low
sound faint
396 vb.
speak low 573 vb.

speak plainly
be plain 517 vb.
divulge 521 vb.
affirm 527 vb.
speak plainly
568 vb.
be artless 694 vb.

speak to
orate 574 vb.
speak to 578 vb.

entreat 756 vb.
greet 879 vb.
worship 975 vb.

spear
sharp point
251 n.
spear 718 n.

special
characteristic
5 adj.
unrelated 10 adj.
different 15 adj.
nonuniform
17 adj.
original 21 adj.
special 80 adj.
unconformable
84 adj.
unusual 84 adj.
one 88 adj.
semantic 509 adj.
indicating
542 adj.
possessed
768 adj.

special day
anniversary
136 n.
important matter
633 n.
amusement
832 n.
festivity 832 n.
special day
871 n.
wedding 889 n.

speciality
reality 1 n.
temperament 5 n.
unrelatedness
10 n.
differentiation
15 n.
variant 15 n.
nonuniformity
17 n.
disunion 46 n.
speciality 80 n.
nonconformity
84 n.
unity 88 n.
tendency 174 n.
materiality 314 n.
qualification
463 n.
connotation
509 n.
phrase 558 n.
style 561 n.
independence
739 n.

specially
specially 80 adv.

specify
differentiate
15 vb.
specify 80 vb.
inform 519 vb.
indicate 542 vb.
name 556 vb.
describe 585 vb.

spectacle
spectacle 440 n.
exhibit 517 n.
classroom 534 n.
image 546 n.
stage set 589 n.
stage show
589 n.
beauty 836 n.
prodigy 859 n.

pageant 870 n.

spectator
traveller 263 n.
listener 410 n.
spectator 436 n.
inquisitive person
448 n.
witness 461 n.
broadcasting
526 n.
playgoer 589 n.

speculate
lend 779 vb.
speculate 786 vb.
purchase 787 vb.

speculative
experimental
456 adj.
speculative
613 adj.
dangerous
656 adj.
trading 786 adj.
rash 852 adj.

speech
mimicry 20 n.
tradition 122 n.
cry 403 n.
affirmation
527 n.
language 552 n.
voice 572 n.
speech 574 n.
stage play 589 n.

speech defect
repetition 102 n.
unintelligibility
512 n.
dialect 555 n.
neology 555 n.
solecism 560 n.
inelegance 571 n.
pronunciation
572 n.
speech defect
575 n.
drunkenness
944 n.

speech sound
speech sound
393 n.
letter 553 n.
spoken letter
553 n.
word 554 n.
voice 572 n.

speeder
speeder 272 n.

speeding
speeding 272 n.
racing 711 n.

speedy
brief 109 adj.
transient 109 adj.
instantaneous
111 adj.
speedy 272 adj.
active 673 adj.
hasty 675 adj.

spell
spell 553 vb.
incentive 607 n.
instrument 623 n.
malevolence
893 n.
malediction
894 n.
spell 977 n.

spelling
spelling 553 n.

sphere
part 53 n.
bisection 92 n.
swelling 248 n.
plaything 832 n.
spice
spice 384 vb.
spin out
spin out 108 vb.
spinster
woman 368 n.
spinster 890 n.
spirit
insubstantial
thing 4 n.
essential part
5 n.
self 80 n.
subjectivity
315 n.
life 355 n.
spirit 442 n.
intuition 471 n.
affections 812 n.
spiritualism
interpreter 515 n.
ghost 964 n.
spiritualism
978 n.
splendid
splendid 836 adj.
spoken letter
spoken letter
553 n.
spoliation
havoc 160 n.
taking 781 n.
spoliation 783 n.
spontaneity
spontaneity
604 n.
spontaneous
brief 109 adj.
intuitive 471 adj.
involuntary
591 adj.
voluntary
592 adj.
spontaneous
604 adj.
unintentional
613 adj.
unprepared
665 adj.
artless 694 adj.
independent
739 adj.
spookishly
spookishly
964 adv.
spooky
insubstantial
4 adj.
spooky 964 adj.
cabbalistic
978 adj.
sporadically
sporadically
75 adv.
sport
athletics 157 n.
aquatics 264 n.
snow 375 n.
chase 614 n.
exercise 677 n.
contention 711 n.
contest 711 n.
pugilism 711 n.
sport 832 n.

spouse
concomitant
89 n.
old woman 128 n.
male 367 n.
woman 368 n.
colleague 702 n.
loved one 882 n.
spouse 889 n.
spring
spring 123 n.
spurious
simulating 18 adj.
substituted
145 adj.
erroneous
490 adj.
false 536 adj.
spurious 537 adj.
untrue 538 adj.
ostentatious
870 adj.
boastful 872 adj.
unwarranted
911 adj.
dishonest
925 adj.
perfidious
925 adj.
spurt
increase 36 n.
brief span 109 n.
vigorousness
169 n.
spurt 272 n.
progression
280 n.
haste 675 n.
stability
uniformity 16 n.
equilibrium 28 n.
durability 108 n.
permanence
139 n.
stability 148 n.
power 155 n.
quiescence 261 n.
resolution 594 n.
obstinacy 597 n.
divine attribute
960 n.
stabilize
stabilize 148 vb.
stabilizer
stabilizer 148 n.
stable
stable 187 n.
chamber 189 n.
edge 229 n.
enclosure 230 n.
air travel 266 n.
goal 290 n.
cattle pen 364 n.
storage 627 n.
shelter 657 n.
workshop 682 n.
stable, be
stay 139 vb.
be stable 148 vb.
stagecoach
stagecoach
269 n.
stagehand
stagehand 589 n.
stage manager
producer 159 n.
exhibitor 517 n.
stage manager
589 n.
stage play
composition 56 n.

vocal music
407 n.
lecture 529 n.
narrative 585 n.
stage play 589 n.
ridiculousness
844 n.
stage set
rear 233 n.
spectacle 440 n.
stage set 589 n.
pageant 870 n.
stage show
medley 43 n.
uncovering 224 n.
spectacle 440 n.
stage show
589 n.
stalwart
stalwart 157 adj.
fleshy 190 adj.
broad 200 adj.
healthy 645 adj.
stamina
strength 157 n.
vigorousness
169 n.
resolution 594 n.
stamina 595 n.
obstinate person
597 n.
courage 850 n.
stammer
repeat oneself
102 vb.
lengthen 198 vb.
move slowly
273 vb.
be unintelligible
512 vb.
be ungrammatical
560 vb.
voice 572 vb.
be mute 573 vb.
stammer 575 vb.
be clumsy
690 vb.
show feeling
813 vb.
be drunk 944 vb.
stammering
stammering
575 adj.
stand
cabinet 189 n.
base 209 n.
stand 213 n.
lifter 305 n.
stand firm
stay 139 vb.
be stable 148 vb.
affirm 527 vb.
stand firm
594 vb.
persevere 595 vb.
be obstinate
597 vb.
withstand
699 vb.
defend 708 vb.
resist 710 vb.
wage war 713 vb.
be successful
722 vb.
suffer 820 vb.
hope 847 vb.
be courageous
850 vb.
take courage
850 vb.

stand trial
stand trial
954 vb.
star
group 74 n.
star 316 n.
island 344 n.
luminary 415 n.
signpost 542 n.
seclusion 878 n.
start
start 68 n.
reversion 143 n.
departure 291 n.
universe 316 n.
start out
start out 291 vb.
starve
decrease 37 vb.
be temperate
937 vb.
be ascetic
940 vb.
starve 941 vb.
offer worship
975 vb.
state
state 7 n.
circumstance 8 n.
whole 52 n.
concomitant
89 n.
event 149 n.
situation 181 n.
affections 812 n.
station
station 182 n.
abode 187 n.
stationery
recording
instrument 544 n.
stationery 581 n.
paper 626 n.
statistical
statistical 86 adj.
statistics
statistics 86 n.
report 519 n.
map 546 n.
plan 618 n.
staunch
dry 337 vb.
staunch 345 vb.
repair 651 vb.
doctor 653 vb.
obstruct 697 vb.
stay
stay 139 vb.
go on 141 vb.
be stable 148 vb.
prevail 173 vb.
place oneself
182 vb.
be quiescent
261 vb.
steal
copy 20 vb.
subtract 39 vb.
intrude 292 vb.
encroach 301 vb.
ensnare 537 vb.
take 781 vb.
take away
781 vb.
steal 783 vb.
be undue 911 vb.
stealing
stealing 783 n.
stealthily
stealthily
520 adv.

stealthy
  stealthy 520 adj.
stealthy, be
  be stealthy
        520 vb.
steer for
  steer for 276 vb.
stench
  odour 389 n.
  stench 392 n.
  uncleanness
        644 n.
stenographer
  stenographer
        581 n.
still
  fixed 148 adj.
  smooth 253 adj.
  still 261 adj.
stimulant
  cause 151 n.
  stimulant 169 n.
  impulse 274 n.
  pungency 383 n.
  incentive 607 n.
  tonic 653 n.
  refreshment
        680 n.
  excitant 816 n.
stimulation
  stimulation
        169 n.
stink
  stink 392 vb.
  be unclean
        644 vb.
  deteriorate
        650 vb.
stock farm
  place 180 n.
  animal 360 n.
  cattle 360 n.
  stock farm 364 n.
  farm 365 n.
  workshop 682 n.
stoop
  be low 205 vb.
  be horizontal
        211 vb.
  be oblique
        215 vb.
  make curved
        243 vb.
  descend 304 vb.
  stoop 306 vb.
  knuckle under
        716 vb.
  be servile 874 vb.
  greet 879 vb.
  show respect
        915 vb.
  be pious 973 vb.
stop
  equilibrium 28 n.
  stop 140 n.
  quiescence 261 n.
  inaction 672 n.
  difficulty 695 n.
  hitch 697 n.
  defeat 723 n.
  failure 723 n.
stopper
  moderator 172 n.
  covering 221 n.
  stopper 259 n.
  safeguard 657 n.
  retention 773 n.
stopping place
  stopping place
        140 n.

stop using
  stop using
        669 vb.
storage
  separation 46 n.
  assemblage 74 n.
  bunch 74 n.
  room 178 n.
  location 182 n.
  cellar 189 n.
  chamber 189 n.
  provisions 296 n.
  gas 331 n.
  lake 341 n.
  agriculture 365 n.
  farm tool 365 n.
  hiding-place
        522 n.
  storage 627 n.
  preservation
        661 n.
  arsenal 718 n.
  emporium 791 n.
  treasury 794 n.
store
  great quantity
        32 n.
  join 45 vb.
  set apart 46 vb.
  bring together
        74 vb.
  data processing
        86 n.
  source 151 n.
  case 189 n.
  receptacle 189 n.
  vat 189 n.
  excavation 250 n.
  emit 295 vb.
  water 334 n.
  irrigator 336 n.
  stream 345 n.
  agriculture 365 n.
  cultivate 365 vb.
  coal 380 n.
  mnemonics 500 n.
  conceal 520 vb.
  dictionary 554 n.
  store 627 n.
  store 627 vb.
  provision 628 n.
  provide 628 vb.
  plenty 630 n.
  redundance
        632 n.
  safeguard 655 vb.
  preserve 661 vb.
  preparation
        664 n.
  make ready
        664 vb.
  nonuse 669 n.
  not use 669 vb.
  workshop 682 n.
  acquire 766 vb.
  joint possession
        770 n.
  retain 773 vb.
  purchase 787 vb.
  merchandise
        790 n.
  funds 792 n.
  treasury 794 n.
  wealth 795 n.
  economy 809 n.
  economize
        809 vb.
stored
  stored 627 adj.
storm
  storm 171 n.

commotion 313 n.
  powder 327 n.
  weather 335 n.
  rain 345 n.
  gale 347 n.
  loudness 395 n.
stow
  add 38 vb.
  fill 54 vb.
  stow 182 vb.
  load 188 vb.
  insert 298 vb.
straight
  simple 44 adj.
  orderly 60 adj.
  continuous
        71 adj.
  symmetrical
        240 adj.
  straight 244 adj.
  directed 276 adj.
  undeviating
        620 adj.
straight, be
  be straight
        244 vb.
  orientate 276 vb.
  steer for 276 vb.
straighten
  straighten
        244 vb.
straightness
  straightness
        244 n.
straight on
  straight on
        244 adv.
stratagem
  trickery 537 n.
  pretext 609 n.
  contrivance
        618 n.
  plot 618 n.
  tactics 683 n.
  stratagem 693 n.
stratification
  stratification
        202 n.
stray
  be dispersed
        75 vb.
  wander 262 vb.
  stray 277 vb.
  recede 285 vb.
  be inattentive
        451 vb.
  be uncertain
        469 vb.
  err 490 vb.
  be in danger
        656 vb.
  be free 739 vb.
stream
  great quantity
        32 n.
  outbreak 171 n.
  motion 260 n.
  approach 284 n.
  ingress 292 n.
  outflow 293 n.
  climber 303 n.
  water 334 n.
  stream 345 n.
  plenty 630 n.
strength
  durability 108 n.
  power 155 n.
  strength 157 n.
  vigorousness
        169 n.
  toughness 324 n.

stamina 595 n.
strengthen
  augment 36 vb.
  accrue 38 vb.
  empower 155 vb.
  strengthen
        157 vb.
  invigorate
        169 vb.
  support 213 vb.
  harden 321 vb.
  be tough 324 vb.
  corroborate
        461 vb.
  restore 651 vb.
  safeguard 655 vb.
  aid 698 vb.
  defend 708 vb.
  animate 816 vb.
  aggravate
        827 vb.
  make pious
        973 vb.
strengthening
  strengthening
        157 n.
strident
  loud 395 adj.
  strident 402 adj.
  discordant
        406 adj.
  vocal 572 adj.
stridor
  stridor 402 n.
strike
  affix 45 vb.
  strike 140 n.
  disable 156 vb.
  demolish 160 vb.
  be vigorous
        169 vb.
  pierce 258 vb.
  slowness 273 n.
  strike 274 n.
  propel 282 vb.
  kill 357 vb.
  render insensible
        370 vb.
  dissent 484 n.
  relinquishment
        616 n.
  ill-treat 640 vb.
  wound 650 vb.
  hitch 697 n.
  strike at 707 vb.
  resistance 710 n.
  fight 711 n.
  revolt 733 vb.
  fast 941 n.
  flog 958 vb.
  spank 958 vb.
strike at
  collide 274 vb.
  strike at 707 vb.
  contend 711 vb.
  fight 711 n.
striking
  striking 369 adj.
strip
  strip 203 n.
stripe
  furrow 257 n.
  stripe 432 n.
  pattern 839 n.
stripper
  stripper 224 n.
strong
  great 32 adj.
  unmixed 44 adj.
  lasting 108 adj.
  powerful 155 adj.

substitute 145 n.
rear 233 n.

such
such 7 adj.
circumstantial
8 adj.

suddenly
suddenly 130 adv.

suffer
meet with
149 vb.
feel pain 372 vb.
be resolute
594 vb.
stand firm
594 vb.
persevere 595 vb.
be in difficulty
695 vb.
resist 710 vb.
knuckle under
716 vb.
have trouble
726 vb.
feel 813 vb.
suffer 820 vb.
be dejected
829 vb.
lament 831 vb.
weep 831 vb.
be courageous
850 vb.
resent 886 vb.

sufferer
weakling 158 n.
unlucky person
726 n.
recipient 777 n.
sufferer 820 n.

suffering
pain 372 n.
frenzied 498 adj.
perseverance
595 n.
evil 611 n.
badness 640 n.
difficulty 695 n.
in difficulties
695 adj.
adversity 726 n.
poverty 796 n.
feeling 813 n.
feeling 813 adj.
suffering 820 n.
suffering 820 adj.
painfulness 822 n.
melancholy 829 n.
dejected 829 adj.

suffice
be equal 28 vb.
fill 54 vb.
conform 83 vb.
be able 155 vb.
support 213 vb.
suffice 630 vb.
be useful 635 vb.
be expedient
637 vb.
be good 639 vb.
be middling
727 vb.
be free 739 vb.
observe 763 vb.
sate 858 vb.

sufficiency
completeness
54 n.
plenitude 54 n.
possibility 464 n.
sufficiency 630 n.

redundance
632 n.
utility 635 n.
completion 720 n.
independence
739 n.
observance
763 n.
wealth 795 n.

sufficient
complete 54 adj.
powerful 155 adj.
provisioning
628 adj.
sufficient
630 adj.
useful 635 adj.
not bad 639 adj.
contenting
823 adj.

suicide
suicide 357 n.
burning 376 n.
punishment
958 n.
oblation 975 n.

suit
suit 223 n.

sullen
unconformable
84 adj.
unwilling 593 adj.
obstinate
597 adj.
quarrelling
704 adj.
discontented
824 adj.
melancholic
829 adj.
serious 829 adj.
ugly 837 adj.
unsociable
878 adj.
ungracious
880 adj.
angry 886 adj.
irascible 887 adj.
sullen 888 adj.
malevolent
893 adj.
unkind 893 adj.
threatening
895 adj.

sullen, be
distort 241 vb.
gesticulate
542 vb.
be unwilling
593 vb.
quarrel 704 vb.
be discontented
824 vb.
be dejected
829 vb.
make ugly
837 vb.
dislike 856 vb.
be rude 880 vb.
hate 883 vb.
be angry 886 vb.
be irascible
887 vb.
be sullen 888 vb.
threaten 895 vb.
disapprove
919 vb.

sullenly
sullenly 888 adv.

sullenness
sullenness 888 n.

summer
summer 123 n.
heat 374 n.

summery
summery 123 adj.

summit
superiority 34 n.
superiority 34 n.
completeness
54 n.
extremity 69 n.
serial place 73 n.
attic 189 n.
height 204 n.
high land 204 n.
high structure
204 n.
summit 208 n.
limit 231 n.
sharp point
251 n.
ascent 303 n.
perfection 641 n.
completion 720 n.

sun
morning 123 n.
sun 316 n.
luminary 415 n.

sunder
sunder 46 vb.
decompose 51 vb.
part 53 vb.
disperse 75 vb.
do sums 86 vb.
bisect 92 vb.
demolish 160 vb.
force 171 vb.
shorten 199 vb.
make quarrels
704 vb.

super
super 639 adj.

superabound
superabound
632 vb.

superfluity
superfluity 632 n.

superfluous
additional 38 adj.
exaggerated
541 adj.
pleonastic
565 adj.
wasteful 629 adj.
plenteous
630 adj.
superfluous
632 adj.
useless 636 adj.
intemperate
938 adj.

superfluous, be
make complete
54 vb.
be superfluous
632 vb.
be useless
636 vb.
waste effort
636 vb.

superior
extrinsic 6 adj.
different 15 adj.
dissimilar 19 adj.
inimitable 21 adj.
unequal 29 adj.
great 32 adj.
superior 34 n.
superior 34 adj.
older 126 adj.
strong 157 adj.

surpassing
301 adj.
necessary
591 adj.
bigwig 633 n.
important
633 adj.
notable 633 adj.
excellent 639 adj.
improved
649 adj.
director 685 n.
successful
722 adj.
master 736 n.
noteworthy
861 adj.

superior, be
be extrinsic 6 vb.
be unlike 19 vb.
be unequal 29 vb.
be great 32 vb.
be superior
34 vb.
abate 37 vb.
come before
64 vb.
influence 173 vb.
be high 204 vb.
crown 204 vb.
outstrip 272 vb.
outdo 301 vb.
be good 639 vb.
be skilful 689 vb.
defeat 722 vb.
overmaster
722 vb.
succeed 722 vb.
win 722 vb.
have a reputation
861 vb.

superiority
superiority 34 n.

supine
impotent 156 adj.
low 205 adj.
supine 215 adj.
inverted 216 adj.
quiescent
261 adj.
lowered 306 adj.

supplicatory
supplicatory
756 adj.

support
sustain 141 vb.
stabilize 148 vb.
strengthen
157 vb.
operate 168 vb.
moderate 172 vb.
support 213 n.
support 213 vb.
carry 268 vb.
elevate 305 vb.
tool 625 n.
suffice 630 vb.
safeguard 655 vb.
preserve 661 vb.
aid 698 vb.
retention 773 n.
retain 773 vb.
hope 847 n.

supported, be
be supported
213 vb.

supporting
supporting
213 adj.

taking
subtraction 39 n.
decrement 42 n.
separation 46 n.
reversion 143 n.
restoration
651 n.
compulsion 735 n.
acquisition 766 n.
possession 768 n.
taking 781 n.
taking 781 adj.
stealing 783 n.
punitive 958 adj.

talisman
omen 506 n.
indication 542 n.
nondesign 613 n.
preserver 661 n.
jewellery 839 n.
talisman 977 n.

tall
large 190 adj.
long 198 adj.
tall 204 adj.
legged 262 adj.

tall creature
giant 190 n.
tall creature
204 n.

tamed
tamed 364 adj.

tapering
tapering 251 adj.

tardily
tardily 131 adv.

taste
tincture 43 n.
absorb 294 vb.
eat 296 vb.
pleasure 371 n.
enjoy 371 vb.
taste 381 n.
taste 381 vb.
make appetizing
385 vb.
experiment
456 vb.
discrimination
458 n.
be pleased
819 vb.
liking 854 n.

tasteful
agreeing 24 adj.
elegant 570 adj.
beautiful 836 adj.
personable
836 adj.
tasteful 841 adj.
fashionable
843 adj.
pure 945 adj.

tastefully
tastefully
841 adv.

tasteless
unmixed 44 adj.
weak 158 adj.
still 261 adj.
tasteless 382 adj.
unsavoury
386 adj.
feeble 567 adj.
deteriorated
650 adj.
tedious 833 adj.
dull 835 adj.

tasty
edible 296 adj.
pleasant 371 adj.
tasty 381 adj.
pungent 383 adj.
savoury 385 adj.

tavern
focus 76 n.
tavern 187 n.
chamber 189 n.
servant 737 n.

tax
decrement 42 n.
exclusion 57 n.
demand 732 n.
demand 732 vb.
gift 776 n.
borrowing 780 n.
taking 781 n.
levy 781 vb.
pay 799 vb.
payment 799 n.
receipt 802 n.
tax 804 n.
tax 804 vb.

teach
convert 142 vb.
admit 294 vb.
break in 364 vb.
argue 470 vb.
judge 475 vb.
convince 480 vb.
show 517 vb.
inform 519 vb.
publish 523 vb.
teach 529 vb.
orate 574 vb.
habituate 605 vb.
depress 829 vb.
be pious 973 vb.

teacher
scholar 487 n.
sage 495 n.
interpreter 515 n.
lecture 529 n.
teacher 532 n.
director 685 n.
adviser 686 n.
expert 691 n.
master 736 n.

teaching
mimicry 20 n.
conversion 142 n.
visibility 438 n.
argument 470 n.
culture 485 n.
metaphor 514 n.
information
519 n.
teaching 529 n.
class 533 n.
habituation
605 n.
vocation 617 n.
preparation
664 n.
art of war 713 n.
church ministry
979 n.
ministration
982 n.

tearfully
tearfully 831 adv.

tedious
identical 13 adj.
repeated 102 adj.
long 198 adj.
prolix 565 adj.
feeble 567 adj.
plain 568 adj.
redundant
632 adj.
fatiguing 679 adj.
annoying 822 adj.

discontenting
824 adj.
cheerless 829 adj.
serious 829 adj.
tedious 833 adj.
dull 835 adj.

tedious, be
be diffuse
565 vb.
be loquacious
576 vb.
fatigue 679 vb.
trouble 822 vb.
be serious
829 vb.
depress 829 vb.
be tedious
833 vb.
be dull 835 vb.
sate 858 vb.

tedium
recurrence 102 n.
repetition 102 n.
diffuseness 565 n.
bane 654 n.
moral insensibility
815 n.
tedium 833 n.
dullness 835 n.
satiety 858 n.

telecommunication
electronics 155 n.
reception 294 n.
ejector 295 n.
sound 393 n.
hearing aid
410 n.
publication 523 n.
message 524 n.
telecommunication
526 n.
signal 542 n.
recording
instrument 544 n.

telescope
astronomy 316 n.
telescope 437 n.
detector 479 n.

tell against
tell against
462 vb.

telluric
telluric 316 adj.

temperament
temperament 5 n.
state 7 n.
composition 56 n.
tendency 174 n.
habit 605 n.
affections 812 n.

temperance
moderation
172 n.
will 590 n.
avoidance 615 n.
restraint 742 n.
prohibition 752 n.
refusal 755 n.
inexcitability
818 n.
virtues 928 n.
temperance
937 n.
asceticism 940 n.
sobriety 943 n.
purity 945 n.

temperate
moderate
172 adj.
feeding 296 adj.
resolute 594 adj.

restrained
742 adj.
inexcitable
818 adj.
disinterested
926 adj.
virtuous 928 adj.
temperate
937 adj.
ascetic 940 adj.
fasting 941 adj.
sober 943 adj.
pure 945 adj.

temperate, be
be moderate
172 vb.
avoid 615 vb.
be insensitive
815 vb.
be modest
869 vb.
be virtuous
928 vb.
be temperate
937 vb.
starve 941 vb.
be sober 943 vb.

temple
edifice 159 n.
house 187 n.
high structure
204 n.
temple 984 n.

tempo
tempo 405 n.

tempt
attract 286 vb.
attract notice
450 vb.
distract 451 vb.
ensnare 537 vb.
tempt 607 vb.
cause desire
854 vb.
excite love
882 vb.
make wicked
929 vb.

tend
go on 141 vb.
conduce 151 vb.
tend 174 vb.
point to 276 vb.
approach 284 vb.
be likely 466 vb.
choose 600 vb.
be useful 635 vb.
desire 854 vb.

tendency
temperament 5 n.
modality 7 n.
continuity 71 n.
continuance
141 n.
ability 155 n.
tendency 174 n.
liability 175 n.
direction 276 n.
probability 466 n.
bias 476 n.
willingness 592 n.
choice 600 n.
habit 605 n.
intention 612 n.
aptitude 689 n.
affections 812 n.
liking 854 n.
love 882 n.

tending
tending 174 adj.

tentative, be
move slowly
273 vb.
touch 373 vb.
be blind 434 vb.
be careful
452 vb.
enquire 454 vb.
search 454 vb.
be tentative
456 vb.
be uncertain
469 vb.
not know 486 vb.
attempt 666 vb.
be clumsy
690 vb.
be in difficulty
695 vb.
make terms
761 vb.
be cautious
853 vb.

tergiversate
tergiversate
598 vb.

tergiversating
tergiversating
598 adj.

tergiversation
tergiversation
598 n.

tergiversator
tergiversator
598 n.

terminate
make complete
54 vb.
terminate 69 vb.
time 112 vb.
cease 140 vb.
destroy 160 vb.
be resolute
594 vb.
carry through
720 vb.

territorial
territorial
339 adj.

territory
territory 179 n.
enclosure 230 n.
air travel 266 n.
political
organization
728 n.
lands 772 n.

terror tactics
terror tactics
707 n.

testee
testee 456 n.

testify
testify 461 vb.
affirm 527 vb.
swear 527 vb.
take a pledge
759 vb.

testimony
testimony 461 n.
certainty 468 n.
affirmation
527 n.
oath 527 n.
legal trial 954 n.

testing agent
testing agent
456 n.

textbook
cookery 296 n.
curriculum 529 n.

classroom 534 n.
literature 552 n.
textbook 584 n.
anthology 587 n.

textile
piece 53 n.
product 159 n.
fibre 203 n.
textile 217 n.
roughness 259 n.
texture 326 n.
materials 626 n.
pattern 839 n.

textural
textural 326 adj.

texture
fibre 203 n.
texture 326 n.
pattern 839 n.

thank
rejoice 830 vb.
honour 861 vb.
thank 902 vb.
grant claims
910 vb.
praise 918 vb.
be pious 973 vb.
worship 975 vb.

thanks
rejoicing 830 n.
celebration
871 n.
thanks 902 n.
dueness 910 n.
praise 918 n.
act of worship
975 n.
prayers 975 n.

thaumaturgy
thaumaturgy
859 n.

theatre
compartment
189 n.
seat 213 n.
view 433 n.
cinema 440 n.
theatre 589 n.
place of
amusement
832 n.

theocracy
theocracy 960 n.

theologian
theologian 967 n.

theological
theosophical
theological
967 adj.

theology
creed 480 n.
theology 967 n.

theophany
theophany 960 n.

theorist
theorist 507 n.

therapy
assembly 74 n.
gerontology
126 n.
dieting 296 n.
water 334 n.
psychology 442 n.
insanity 498 n.
representation
546 n.
pathology 646 n.
hygiene 647 n.
therapy 653 n.
advice 686 n.

thermometry
thermometry
374 n.

thick
fleshy 190 adj.
short 199 adj.
thick 200 adj.
fibrous 203 adj.

thicken
thicken 349 vb.

thickening
thickening 349 n.

thickness
thickness 200 n.

thick-skinned
thick-skinned
815 adj.

thief
incomer 292 n.
thief 784 n.
offender 899 n.

thieving
thieving 783 adj.

thievishness
thievishness
783 n.

thing transferred
thing transferred
267 n.

think
cognize 442 vb.
think 444 vb.
be attentive
450 vb.
reason 470 vb.
imagine 508 vb.
be dejected
829 vb.

thinness
thinness 201 n.

thoroughbred
thoroughbred
268 n.
speeder 272 n.

thought
production 159 n.
intellect 442 n.
thought 444 n.
idea 446 n.
attention 450 n.
wisdom 493 n.
supposition
507 n.

thoughtful
thoughtful
444 adj.
ideational
446 adj.
attentive
450 adj.
wise 493 adj.

threat
destiny 150 n.
limit 231 n.
incentive 607 n.
intention 612 n.
danger 656 n.
warning 659 n.
defiance 706 n.
adversity 726 n.
demand 732 n.
compulsion 735 n.
request 756 n.
conditions 761 n.
intimidation
849 n.
boast 872 n.
boasting 872 n.
insolence 873 n.
malediction
894 n.

scurrility 894 n.
threat 895 n.
prayers 975 n.

threaten
impend 150 vb.
predict 506 vb.
dissuade 608 vb.
intend 612 vb.
endanger 656 vb.
warn 659 vb.
defy 706 vb.
demand 732 vb.
compel 735 vb.
request 756 vb.
frighten 849 vb.
boast 872 vb.
threaten 895 vb.

threatening
threatening
895 adj.

threateningly
threateningly
895 adv.

three
three 93 n.
three 93 adj.

threshold
threshold 229 n.

through
through 623 adv.

throughout
throughout
54 adv.
while 104 adv.
widely 178 adv.
aloft 204 adv.

thrower
thrower 282 n.

thus
thus 8 adv.

thus far
thus far 231 adv.

tie
relate 9 vb.
add 38 vb.
tie 45 vb.
bring together
74 vb.
stabilize 148 vb.
produce 159 vb.
place 182 vb.
wear 223 vb.
repair 651 vb.
fetter 742 vb.
restrain 742 vb.

tied
tied 45 adj.

tighten
tighten 45 vb.
fill 54 vb.
strengthen
157 vb.
make smaller
193 vb.
support 213 vb.
close 259 vb.
harden 321 vb.

time
time 104 n.
fix the time
104 vb.
course of time
107 n.
chronometry
112 n.
time 112 vb.
space 178 n.
measure 460 vb.

timekeeper
timekeeper 112 n.

timely
  apt 24 adj.
  chronological
          112 adj.
  timely 132 adj.
  important
          633 adj.
  advisable
          637 adj.

tincture
  tincture 43 n.
  component 58 n.
  tendency 174 n.

tipsy
  tipsy 944 adj.

title
  name 556 n.
  decoration 724 n.
  master 736 n.
  honours 861 n.
  title 865 n.
  formality 870 n.
  reward 957 n.

title deed
  record 543 n.
  compact 760 n.
  title deed 762 n.
  dueness 910 n.

toady
  beggar 758 n.
  toady 874 n.
  flatterer 920 n.

to and fro
  to and fro
          312 adv.

toast
  drink 296 vb.
  toast 871 n.
  be sociable
          877 vb.
  pay one's
  respects 879 vb.
  show respect
          915 vb.
  applaud 918 vb.

tobacco
  air pipe 348 n.
  tobacco 383 n.
  poison 654 n.
  drug-taking
          944 n.

to come, be
  be to come
          119 vb.
  impend 150 vb.

together
  together 74 adv.

tomb
  edifice 159 n.
  box 189 n.
  high structure
          204 n.
  small hill 204 n.
  covering 221 n.
  excavation 250 n.
  resting place
          261 n.
  death 356 n.
  tomb 359 n.
  monument 543 n.

tonic
  stimulant 169 n.
  soft drink 296 n.
  tonic 653 n.

too far
  too far 194 adv.

tool
  opportunity
          132 n.
  causal means
          151 n.

influence 173 n.
handle 213 n.
instrument 623 n.
means 624 n.
tool 625 n.

tooth
  tooth 251 n.
  notch 260 n.
  eater 296 n.
  pulverizer 327 n.
  nippers 773 n.

toothed
  toothed 251 adj.

topic
  topic 447 n.
  question 454 n.
  supposition
          507 n.
  meaning 509 n.
  chief thing 633 n.

topical
  topical 447 adj.
  supposed 507 adj.

topmost
  great 32 adj.
  supreme 34 adj.
  high 204 adj.
  topmost 208 adj.
  important
          633 adj.
  completive
          720 adj.

torch
  filament 203 n.
  fire 374 n.
  lighter 380 n.
  torch 415 n.

torment
  harm 640 vb.
  ill-treat 640 vb.
  oppress 730 vb.
  excite 816 vb.
  torment 822 vb.
  frighten 849 vb.
  cause dislike
          856 vb.
  enrage 886 vb.
  torture 958 vb.

torture
  give pain 372 vb.
  interrogate
          454 vb.
  ill-treat 640 vb.
  oppress 730 vb.
  compel 735 vb.
  torment 822 vb.
  torture 958 vb.

to rule
  in order 60 adv.
  to rule 81 adv.

to the amount of
  to the amount of
          26 adv.

to the quick
  to the quick
          369 adv.

touch
  union 45 n.
  connect 45 vb.
  operate 168 vb.
  contiguity 197 n.
  be contiguous
          197 vb.
  transference
          267 n.
  impulse 274 n.
  collide 274 vb.
  texture 326 n.
  touch 373 n.
  touch 373 vb.

be tentative
          456 vb.
use 668 vb.
endearment
          884 n.

tough
  cohesive 48 adj.
  strong 157 adj.
  hard 321 adj.
  tough 324 adj.
  unsavoury
          386 adj.
  uncooked
          665 adj.

tough, be
  be tough 324 vb.

toughness
  toughness 324 n.

towards
  straight on
          244 adv.
  towards 276 adv.

toxic
  destructive
          160 adj.
  fluid 330 adj.
  deadly 357 adj.
  unsavoury
          386 adj.
  fetid 392 adj.
  harmful 640 adj.
  unclean 644 adj.
  diseased 646 adj.
  toxic 648 adj.
  baneful 654 adj.

trace
  remainder 41 n.
  effect 152 n.
  concavity 250 n.
  furrow 257 n.
  odour 389 n.
  identification
          542 n.
  label 542 n.
  trace 543 n.

tractable
  tractable
          696 adj.

traction
  energy 155 n.
  transport 267 n.
  traction 283 n.
  extraction 299 n.

trade
  correlate 12 vb.
  union 45 n.
  interchange
          146 vb.
  transference
          267 n.
  ingress 292 n.
  vocation 617 n.
  do business
          617 vb.
  provide 628 vb.
  assign 775 vb.
  trade 786 n.
  trade 786 vb.
  sell 788 vb.
  market 791 vb.
  pay 799 vb.

tradespeople
  tradespeople
          789 n.

trading
  trading 786 adj.

tradition
  tradition 122 n.

traffic control
  timekeeper 112 n.
  crossing 217 n.

traffic control
          300 n.
indicator 542 n.
access 619 n.
road 619 n.
route 619 n.

train
  produce 159 vb.
  train 269 n.
  experiment
          456 vb.
  train 529 vb.
  habituate 605 vb.
  railway 619 n.
  make ready
          664 vb.

trainer
  trainer 532 n.

training school
  training school
          534 n.
  monastery 980 n.

tram
  tram 269 n.

tranquil
  moderate
          172 adj.
  tranquil 261 adj.
  comfortable
          371 adj.
  reposeful 678 adj.
  peaceful 712 adj.
  impassive
          815 adj.
  inexcitable
          818 adj.
  pleasurable
          821 adj.

tranquillize
  tranquillize
          818 vb.

transfer
  add 38 vb.
  subtract 39 vb.
  disunite 46 vb.
  sequence 65 n.
  displace 183 vb.
  move 260 vb.
  transference
          267 n.
  transfer 267 vb.
  carry 268 vb.
  following 279 n.
  admit 294 vb.
  eject 295 vb.
  pass 300 vb.
  relinquishment
          616 n.
  depose 747 vb.
  security 762 n.
  acquisition 766 n.
  nonretention
          774 n.
  transfer 775 n.
  assign 775 vb.
  gift 776 n.
  giving 776 n.
  expropriation
          781 n.
  be exempt
          914 vb.
  be ecclesiastical
          979 n.

transferable
  transferable
          267 n.

transference
  transference
          267 n.

transferred
transferred
775 adj.
transferrer
transferrer 267 n.
transform
transform
142 vb.
revolutionize
144 vb.
influence 173 vb.
make better
649 vb.
pervert 650 vb.
practise
occultism 978 vb.
transformation
nonconformist
84 n.
transformation
138 n.
conversion 142 n.
transference
267 n.
improvement
649 n.
beautification
838 n.
transience
transience 109 n.
transient
circumstantial
8 adj.
inconsiderable
33 adj.
elapsing 107 adj.
transient 109 adj.
unstable 147 adj.
short 199 adj.
dying 356 adj.
disappearing
441 adj.
uncertain
469 adj.
transient, be
be transient
109 vb.
pass 300 vb.
disappear 441 vb.
transiently
transiently
109 adv.
transition
transition 142 n.
passage 300 n.
translate
transform
142 vb.
transpose 267 vb.
be deaf 411 vb.
translate 515 vb.
phrase 558 vb.
translation
copy 22 n.
transference
267 n.
translation 515 n.
spelling 558 n.
phrase 558 n.
transparency
thinness 201 n.
covering 221 n.
window 258 n.
transparency
417 n.
optical device
437 n.
perspicuity 562 n.
materials 626 n.

transparent
insubstantial
4 adj.
narrow 201 adj.
undimmed
412 adj.
transparent
417 adj.
intelligible
511 adj.
disclosing
521 adj.
perspicuous
562 adj.
transparent, be
be transparent
417 vb.
be visible 438 vb.
be disclosed
521 vb.
disclose 521 vb.
transport
motion 260 n.
air travel 266 n.
transport 267 n.
passage 300 n.
transpose
jumble 63 vb.
modify 138 vb.
interchange
146 vb.
replace 182 vb.
transpose 267 vb.
empty 295 vb.
infuse 298 vb.
make flow
345 vb.
trap
adhesive 47 n.
enclosure 230 n.
velocity 272 n.
ambush 522 n.
trap 537 n.
incentive 607 n.
chase 619 n.
pitfall 663 n.
stratagem 693 n.
defences 708 n.
bomb 718 n.
travel
travel 262 vb.
emerge 293 vb.
offer worship
975 vb.
traveller
foreigner 59 n.
precursor 66 n.
traveller 263 n.
aeronaut 266 n.
thing transferred
267 n.
spectator 436 n.
enquirer 454 n.
detector 479 n.
reveller 832 n.
worshipper 975 n.
travelling
travelling
262 adj.
traverse
traverse 262 vb.
voyage 264 vb.
treasurer
accumulator
74 n.
provider 628 n.
consignee 749 n.
receiver 777 n.
minter 792 n.
treasurer 793 n.
pay 799 n.

accountant
803 n.
treasury
accumulation
74 n.
box 189 n.
storage 627 n.
treasurer 793 n.
treasury 794 n.
treaty
conference 579 n.
peace 712 n.
pacification
714 n.
treaty 760 n.
conditions 761 n.
treble
augment 36 vb.
treble 94 adj.
treble 94 vb.
trebly
trebly 94 adv.
tree
nest 187 n.
tall creature
204 n.
tree 361 n.
triality
triality 93 n.
tribunal
certainty 468 n.
council 687 n.
jurisdiction
950 n.
tribunal 951 n.
orthodoxism
970 n.
synod 979 n.
trickery
trickery 537 n.
trickster
trickster 540 n.
avoider 615 n.
expert 691 n.
slyboots 693 n.
defrauder 784 n.
knave 933 n.
trier
trier 666 n.
trifle
insubstantial
thing 4 n.
small quantity
33 n.
minuteness
191 n.
shallowness
207 n.
trifle 634 n.
trimming
hanging object
212 n.
edging 229 n.
trimming 839 n.
Trinity
Trinity 960 n.
triplication
triplication 94 n.
triumph
defy 706 vb.
triumph 722 vb.
subjugate 740 vb.
boast 872 vb.
be praised
918 vb.
trivial
trivial 634 adj.
trope
trope 514 n.
trophy
badge 542 n.

monument 543 n.
objective 612 n.
elite 639 n.
trophy 724 n.
acquisition 766 n.
gift 776 n.
booty 785 n.
receipt 802 n.
desired object
854 n.
honours 861 n.
celebration
871 n.
reward 957 n.
tropical disease
tropical disease
646 n.
trouble
recur 134 vb.
agitate 313 vb.
give pain 372 vb.
be inexpedient
638 vb.
harm 640 vb.
meddle 673 vb.
fatigue 679 vb.
be difficult
695 vb.
hinder 697 vb.
impress 816 vb.
trouble 822 vb.
frighten 849 vb.
enrage 886 vb.
troublemaker
troublemaker
658 n.
trousers
trousers 223 n.
true
real 1 adj.
evidential
461 adj.
plausible 466 adj.
certain 468 adj.
true 489 adj.
veracious
535 adj.
vindicable
922 adj.
trustworthy
924 adj.
true, be
be 1 vb.
be 1 vb.
be proved 473 vb.
be true 489 vb.
be truthful
535 vb.
truly
actually 1 adv.
imitatively
20 adv.
positively 32 adv.
truly 489 adv.
truthfully
535 adv.
trustworthy
certain 468 adj.
genuine 489 adj.
wise 493 adj.
veracious
535 adj.
safe 655 adj.
observant
763 adj.
cautious 853 adj.
reputable
861 adj.
friendly 875 adj.
trustworthy
924 adj.

truth
reality 1 n.
power 155 n.
certainty 468 n.
demonstration
473 n.
truth 489 n.
information
519 n.
disclosure 521 n.
veracity 535 n.
vindication 922 n.
probity 924 n.
orthodoxy 970 n.

truthful, be
be true 489 vb.
confess 521 vb.
be truthful
535 vb.
be artless 694 vb.
be honourable
924 vb.

truthfully
truthfully
535 adv.

try a case
enquire 454 vb.
hold court
950 vb.
try a case
954 vb.

tube
cylinder 247 n.
cavity 250 n.
tube 258 n.
conduit 346 n.

tubular
tubular 258 adj.

tumble
come unstuck
49 vb.
be weak 158 vb.
be destroyed
160 vb.
be inverted
216 vb.
fly 266 vb.
collide 274 vb.
enter 292 vb.
tumble 304 vb.
be brittle 325 vb.
deteriorate
650 vb.
be in danger
656 vb.
fail 723 vb.
miscarry 723 vb.

tune
musical note
405 n.
tune 407 n.

tunnel
excavation 250 n.
tunnel 258 n.
bridge 619 n.

turmoil
turmoil 61 n.
havoc 160 n.
violence 171 n.
knock 274 n.
commotion 313 n.
loudness 395 n.
discord 406 n.
activity 673 n.
quarrel 704 n.
fight 711 n.
anarchy 729 n.
revolt 733 n.

turn back
be inverted
216 vb.

turn round
277 vb.
turn back 281 vb.
recede 285 vb.
depart 291 vb.
pass 300 vb.
circle 309 vb.
tergiversate
598 vb.
parry 708 vb.
submit 716 vb.

turned to, be
be turned to
142 vb.

turn round
navigate 264 vb.
turn round
277 vb.
tergiversate
598 vb.
run away 615 vb.

tutelary
tutelary 655 adj.

twenty and over
twenty and over
96 n.

twice
twice 91 adv.

twine
distort 241 vb.
be curved 243 vb.
make curved
243 vb.
twine 246 vb.
rotate 310 vb.
decorate 839 vb.

type of marriage
type of marriage
889 n.
illicit love 946 n.

type size
type size 582 n.

typical
uniform 16 adj.
general 79 adj.
regular 81 adj.
typical 83 adj.
usual 605 adj.
middling 727 adj.

tyrant
violent creature
171 n.
bane 654 n.
tyrant 730 n.
malcontent
824 n.
ruffian 899 n.
usurper 911 n.
monster 933 n.
punisher 958 n.
zealot 973 n.

U

ubiquitous
existing 1 adj.
comprehensive
52 adj.
general 79 adj.
universal 79 adj.
influential
173 adj.
ubiquitous
184 adj.
godlike 960 adj.

ugliness
ugliness 837 n.

ugly
inelegant 571 adj.

unpleasant
822 adj.
ugly 837 adj.
disliked 856 adj.

ugly, be
be ugly 837 vb.

ulcer
ulcer 646 n.
wound 650 n.
bane 654 n.

ululant
ululant 404 adj.

ululate
ululate 404 vb.

ululation
ululation 404 n.

unadmitted
unadmitted
484 adj.

unanimously
unanimously
483 adv.

unapt
unapt 25 adj.

unassembled
unassembled
75 adj.

unastonished
unastonished
860 adj.

unastonishing
unastonishing
860 adj.

unattested
unattested
462 adj.

unbeaten
unbeaten
722 adj.

unbelief
unbelief 481 n.

unbelieved
unbelieved
481 adj.

unbeliever
unbeliever 481 n.
irreligionist
968 n.

unbelieving
unbelieving
481 adj.

unborn
unborn 2 adj.

unceasing
unceasing
141 adj.

uncertain
casual 154 adj.
causeless
154 adj.
topical 447 adj.
moot 454 adj.
experimental
456 adj.
indiscriminate
459 adj.
unattested
462 adj.
improbable
467 adj.
uncertain
469 adj.
arguing 470 adj.
ignorant 486 adj.
uninstructed
486 adj.
mistaken 490 adj.
puzzled 512 adj.
puzzling 512 adj.
unclear 563 adj.

speculative
613 adj.
unsuccessful
723 adj.

uncertain, be
be pending
131 n.
change 138 vb.
be uncertain
469 vb.
doubt 481 vb.
not know 486 vb.
not understand
512 vb.
be irresolute
596 vb.
be halfway
620 vb.
be in danger
656 vb.
be inactive
674 vb.
be in difficulty
695 vb.

uncertainty
uncertainty
469 n.

uncertified
uncertified
469 adj.

unchangeable
unchangeable
148 adj.

uncharged
uncharged
807 adj.

unchaste
unchaste 946 adj.

unchastity
unchastity 946 n.

unclean
unclean 644 adj.
insalubrious
648 adj.
ugly 837 adj.
disreputable
862 adj.

unclean, be
decompose 51 vb.
be unclean
644 vb.

uncleanness
uncleanness
644 n.

unclear
unclear 563 adj.

uncompleted
uncompleted
721 adj.

unconditional
complete 54 adj.
unconditional
739 adj.
permitted
751 adj.

unconfined
unconfined
739 adj.

unconformable
unconformable
84 adj.

unconformable, be
be unconformable
84 adj.

unconformably
unconformably
84 adv.

uncooked
uncooked
665 adj.

uncover
abate 37 vb.
subtract 39 vb.
disunite 46 vb.
demolish 160 vb.
laminate 202 vb.
uncover 224 vb.
empty 295 vb.
extract 299 vb.
manifest 517 vb.
disclose 521 vb.
deprive 781 vb.
fleece 781 vb.
take 781 vb.

uncovered
uncovered
224 adj.

uncovering
uncovering 224 n.

unctuous
unctuous 352 adj.

unctuousness
unctuousness
352 n.

undamaged
undamaged
641 adj.

under
under 205 adv.

underestimate
abate 37 vb.
disregard 453 vb.
misjudge 476 vb.
underestimate
478 vb.
err 490 vb.
misinterpret
516 vb.
bargain 786 vb.
not respect
916 vb.
hold cheap
917 vb.
detract 921 vb.

underestimation
underestimation
478 n.

underfed
underfed 631 adj.

undermost
undermost
209 adj.

under shelter
under shelter
655 adj.

understand
discover 479 vb.
know 485 vb.
be wise 493 vb.
imagine 508 vb.
mean 509 vb.
understand
511 vb.
interpret 515 vb.
be informed
519 vb.
not wonder
860 vb.
be friendly
875 vb.

undertake
begin 68 vb.
be tentative
456 vb.
intend 612 vb.
attempt 666 vb.
undertake
667 vb.
do 671 vb.
promise 759 vb.
contract 760 vb.

be courageous
850 vb.

undertaking
calculation of
chance 154 n.
production 159 n.
vigorousness
169 n.
progression
280 n.
intention 612 n.
gambler 613 n.
danger 656 n.
attempt 666 n.
undertaking
667 n.
deed 671 n.
mandate 746 n.
promise 759 n.
compact 760 n.
trade 786 n.
courage 850 n.

under the sun
under the sun
316 adv.

undervalued
undervalued
478 adj.

under way
under way
264 adv.

underwear
compressor
193 n.
hanger 212 n.
prop 213 n.
underwear 223 n.

undevelopment
undevelopment
665 n.

undeviating
undeviating
620 adj.

undimmed
undimmed
412 adj.

undisguised
undisguised
517 adj.

undisputed
undisputed
468 adj.

undue
inexpedient
638 adj.
undue 911 adj.

undue, be
please oneself
729 vb.
oppress 730 vb.
appropriate
781 vb.
be undue 911 vb.

undueness
undueness 911 n.

undulatory
undulatory
246 adj.

unduly
unduly 911 adv.

undutiful
undutiful 913 adj.

undutifulness
undutifulness
913 n.

unentitled
unentitled
911 adj.

unequal
unrelated 10 adj.
different 15 adj.

nonuniform
17 adj.
dissimilar 19 adj.
unequal 29 adj.
numerable
86 adj.
fitful 137 adj.
weighty 317 adj.
clumsy 690 adj.
unjust 909 adj.

unequal, be
be unequal 29 vb.
predominate
34 vb.

unequipped
unequipped
665 adj.

unevenly
unevenly 29 adv.

unexpected
unexpected
503 adj.

unexpectedly
unexpectedly
503 adv.

unfearing
unfearing
850 adj.

unfeeling
unfeeling 370 adj.

unfeeling person
unfeeling person
815 n.

unfinished
unfinished 55 adj.

unfortunate
evil 611 n.
unsuccessful
723 adj.
unfortunate
726 adj.
unhappy 820 adj.
hopeless 848 adj.

ungracious
concise 564 adj.
plebeian 864 adj.
prideful 866 adj.
ungracious
880 adj.
unkind 893 adj.

ungrammatical
ungrammatical
560 adj.

ungrammatical, be
be ungrammatical
560 vb.

ungrateful
forgetful 501 adj.
ungrateful
903 adj.

ungrateful, be
be ungrateful
903 vb.

unguent
lubricant 329 n.
unguent 352 n.
cosmetic 838 n.

unhabituated
unhabituated
606 adj.

unhappy
unhappy 820 adj.
discontented
824 adj.
melancholic
829 adj.
lamenting
831 adj.
nervous 849 adj.

unhealthy
weakly 158 adj.

colourless
421 adj.
imperfect
642 adj.
unhealthy
646 adj.

uniform
identical 13 adj.
uniformity 16 n.
uniform 16 adj.
similar 18 adj.
agreeing 24 adj.
equal 28 adj.
simple 44 adj.
cohesive 48 adj.
indivisible 52 adj.
orderly 60 adj.
continuous
71 adj.
regular 81 adj.
one 88 adj.
repeated 102 adj.
unchangeable
148 adj.
uniform 223 n.
symmetrical
240 adj.
smooth 253 adj.
tranquil 261 adj.
coloured 420 adj.
indiscriminate
459 adj.
accurate 489 adj.
livery 542 n.
inexactable
818 adj.
tedious 833 adj.
formality 870 n.

uniform, be
be uniform 16 vb.
repeat oneself
102 vb.

uniformist
uniformist 16 n.

uniformity
uniformity 16 n.

uniformly
uniformly 16 adv.

unimportance
unimportance
634 n.

unimportant
unimportant
634 adj.

unimportant, be
be unimportant
634 vb.

uninstructed
uninstructed
486 adj.

unintelligence
unintelligence
494 n.

unintelligent
unintelligent
494 adj.

unintelligibility
unintelligibility
512 n.

unintelligible
unintelligible
512 adj.

unintelligible, be
be unintelligible
512 vb.

unintentional
unintentional
613 adj.

union
addition 38 n.
mixture 43 n.

union 45 n.
coherence 48 n.
combination 50 n.
accompaniment
89 n.
concurrence
176 n.
contiguity 197 n.
interjacency
226 n.
convergence
288 n.
association
701 n.

unit
whole 52 n.
component 58 n.
unit 88 n.

unite with
unite with 45 vb.
generate 162 vb.
love 882 vb.
wed 889 vb.
debauch 946 vb.

unity
identity 13 n.
originality 21 n.
simpleness 44 n.
coherence 48 n.
combination 50 n.
whole 52 n.
completeness
54 n.
speciality 80 n.
unity 88 n.
association
701 n.
divine attribute
960 n.

universal
comprehensive
52 adj.
unassembled
75 adj.
universal 79 adj.
ubiquitous
184 adj.
usual 605 adj.

universe
substantiality
3 n.
whole 52 n.
arrangement
62 n.
generality 79 n.
universe 316 n.

unjust
unjust 909 adj.

unkind
harmful 640 adj.
unkind 893 adj.
selfish 927 adj.

unknown
unconformable
84 adj.
unusual 84 adj.
new 121 adj.
unknown 486 adj.
unintelligible
512 adj.
latent 518 adj.
disguised 520 adj.
inglorious
862 adj.
secluded 878 adj.
cabbalistic
978 adj.

unknown thing
unknown thing
486 n.
secret 525 n.

unlike, be
be unlike 19 vb.

unlikely, be
chance 154 vb.
be unlikely
467 vb.
cause doubt
481 vb.
not expect
503 vb.
be untrue 538 vb.

unlit
unlit 413 adj.

unlucky person
unlucky person
726 n.

unman
unman 156 vb.

unmeant
unmeant 510 adj.

unmixed
unmixed 44 adj.

unpalatable, be
be unpalatable
386 vb.

unpleasant
painful 372 adj.
unsavoury
386 adj.
fetid 392 adj.
unpleasant
822 adj.

unpossessed
unpossessed
769 adj.

unpractised, be
be unpractised
606 vb.

unprepared
unprepared
665 adj.

unprepared, be
be unprepared
665 vb.

unproductive
unproductive
167 adj.

unproductive, be
be unproductive
167 vb.

unproductiveness
unproductiveness
167 n.

unpromising
unpromising
848 adj.

unprosperous
unprosperous
726 adj.

unprovided
unprovided
631 adj.

unravel
simplify 44 vb.
disunite 46 vb.
unravel 62 vb.
straighten
244 vb.
smooth 253 vb.
evolve 311 vb.
deliver 663 vb.
disencumber
696 vb.
liberate 741 vb.

unreadily
unreadily
665 adv.

unreal
unreal 2 adj.
erroneous
490 adj.

supposed 507 adj.

unrelated
unrelated 10 adj.

unrelated, be
be unrelated
10 adj.

unrelatedly
unrelatedly
10 adv.

unrelatedness
unrelatedness
10 n.

unreliability
unreliability
469 n.

unreliable
unreliable
469 adj.

unrepented
unrepented
935 adj.

unrespected
unrespected
916 adj.

unsafe
unsafe 656 adj.

unsatisfied, be
be unsatisfied
631 vb.

unsavouriness
unsavouriness
386 n.

unsavoury
tasteless 382 adj.
unsavoury
386 adj.
sour 388 adj.
unpleasant
822 adj.
unwanted
855 adj.
disliked 856 adj.

unseen, be
be unseen
439 vb.
disappear 441 vb.
lurk 518 vb.
have no repute
862 vb.

unsharpened
unsharpened
252 adj.

unsightly
amorphous
239 adj.
deformed
241 adj.
unsightly 837 adj.

unskilful
unskilful 690 adj.

unskilful, be
be unskilful
690 vb.

unskilfulness
unskilfulness
690 n.

unskilled
immature
665 adj.
unskilled 690 adj.
artless 694 adj.

unsociability
unsociability
878 n.

unsociable
unconformable
84 adj.
alone 88 adj.
reticent 520 adj.
independent
739 adj.

inimical 876 adj.
unsociable
878 adj.
ungracious
880 adj.
sullen 888 adj.
unkind 893 adj.
misanthropic
897 adj.
pietistic 973 adj.

unsociable, be
be quiescent
261 vb.
be stealthy
520 vb.
be fastidious
857 vb.
make enemies
876 vb.
be unsociable
878 vb.
be sullen 888 vb.
live single 890 vb.

unspeakable
unspeakable
32 adj.

unstable
unequal 29 adj.
unstable 147 adj.
weak 158 adj.
uncertain
469 adj.
irresolute
596 adj.
capricious
599 adj.
unsafe 656 adj.

unstick
unstick 49 vb.

unsubstantially
unsubstantially
4 adv.

unsuccessful
unsuccessful
723 adj.

unsuccessfully
unsuccessfully
723 adv.

unthanked
unthanked
903 adj.

unthinking
mindless 443 adj.
unthinking
445 adj.
incurious 449 adj.
inattentive
451 adj.
negligent 453 adj.
unwise 494 adj.

unthought
unthought
445 adj.

unthrone
unthrone 729 vb.

until now
until now
116 adv.
retrospectively
120 adv.

untimeliness
untimeliness
133 n.

untrue
untrue 538 adj.

untrue, be
be untrue 538 vb.

untruth
equivocalness
513 n.

virtuous 928 adj.
pure 945 adj.
pietistic 973 adj.
pious 973 adj.
virtuous, be
behave 683 vb.
be modest
     869 vb.
be honourable
     924 vb.
be virtuous
     928 vb.
be innocent
     930 vb.
virtuously
virtuously
     928 adv.
viscid
viscid 349 adj.
viscidity
viscidity 349 n.
visibility
prominence
     249 n.
inspection 433 n.
visibility 438 n.
appearance
     440 n.
manifestation
     517 n.
prestige 861 n.
visible
lifelike 18 adj.
impending
     150 adj.
seeing 433 adj.
visible 438 adj.
appearing
     440 adj.
intelligible
     511 adj.
manifest 517 adj.
shown 517 adj.
disclosed 521 adj.
visible, be
be inside 219 vb.
jut 249 vb.
approach 284 vb.
emerge 293 vb.
make bright
     412 vb.
see 433 vb.
be visible 438 vb.
appear 440 vb.
attract notice
     450 vb.
be intelligible
     511 vb.
be plain 517 vb.
be disclosed
     521 vb.
visibly
at sight 433 adv.
visibly 438 adv.
apparently
     440 adv.
vision
vision 433 n.
occultism 978 n.
visionary
spectator 436 n.
crank 499 n.
visionary 508 n.
avoider 615 n.
reformer 649 n.
hoper 847 n.
philanthropist
     896 n.
visit
recur 134 vb.

be present
     184 vb.
dwell 187 vb.
travel 262 vb.
arrive 290 vb.
enter 292 vb.
scan 433 vb.
visit 877 vb.
visual fallacy
insubstantial
thing 4 n.
dimness 414 n.
vision 433 n.
visual fallacy
     435 n.
appearance
     440 n.
error 490 n.
fantasy 508 n.
deception 537 n.
incentive 607 n.
ghost 964 n.
vitality
vitality 157 n.
vigorousness
     169 n.
blood 330 n.
health 645 n.
vitalize
vitalize 355 vb.
vocal
sounding 393 adj.
literal 553 adj.
vocal 572 adj.
speaking 574 adj.
vocalist
vocalist 408 n.
entertainer
     589 n.
vocal music
repetition 102 n.
cry 403 n.
vocal music
     407 n.
voice 572 n.
poem 588 n.
stage play 589 n.
act of worship
     975 n.
hymn 975 n.
public worship
     975 n.
vocation
motive 607 n.
vocation 617 n.
conduct 683 n.
duty 912 n.
church ministry
     979 n.
vocative
vocative 578 adj.
vociferate
vociferate
     403 vb.
rejoice 830 vb.
greet 879 vb.
threaten 895 vb.
voice
sound 393 n.
speech sound
     393 n.
sound 393 vb.
cry 403 n.
spoken letter
     553 n.
neologize 555 vb.
voice 572 n.
voice 572 vb.
speech 574 n.
speak 574 vb.
conduct 683 n.

voiceless
silent 394 adj.
voiceless 573 adj.
stammering
     575 adj.
taciturn 577 adj.
voicelessly
voicelessly
     573 adv.
voicelessness
voicelessness
     573 n.
voidance
voidance 295 n.
volitional
volitional
     590 adj.
voluntary
volitional
     590 adj.
voluntary
     592 adj.
spontaneous
     604 adj.
uncharged
     807 adj.
desired 854 adj.
voluntary work
will 590 n.
voluntary work
     592 n.
vocation 617 n.
undertaking
     667 n.
gift 776 n.
no charge 807 n.
amusement
     832 n.
kind act 892 n.
volunteer
volunteer 592 n.
worker 686 n.
philanthropist
     896 n.
vomit
vomit 295 vb.
be ill 646 vb.
dislike 856 vb.
vomiting
vomiting 295 adj.
vortex
coil 246 n.
vortex 310 n.
commotion 313 n.
eddy 345 n.
gale 347 n.
activity 673 n.
vote
statistics 86 n.
substitution
     145 n.
enquiry 454 n.
experiment
     456 vb.
judgment 475 n.
judge 475 vb.
affirmation
     527 n.
vote 600 n.
vote 600 vb.
patronize 698 vb.
government
     728 n.
decree 732 n.
freedom 739 n.
mandate 746 n.
commission
     746 vb.
legislation 948 n.
voyage
voyage 264 vb.

vulgar
inferior 35 adj.
indiscriminating
     459 adj.
feeble 567 adj.
inelegant 571 adj.
unwonted
     606 adj.
artless 694 adj.
graceless 837 adj.
ornamented
     839 adj.
vulgar 842 adj.
derisive 846 adj.
disreputable
     862 adj.
plebeian 864 adj.
showy 870 adj.
cursing 894 adj.
wrong 909 adj.
vicious 929 adj.
vulgarian
upstart 121 n.
ignoramus 488 n.
vulgarian 842 n.
commoner 864 n.
detractor 921 n.
vulgarize
vulgarize 842 vb.
vulnerability
vulnerability
     656 n.
vulnerable
defenceless
     156 adj.
liable 175 adj.
probable 466 adj.
imperfect
     642 adj.
vulnerable
     656 adj.
unprepared
     665 adj.
accusable
     923 adj.
frail 929 adj.

W

wage war
fight 711 vb.
wage war 713 vb.
be inimical
     876 vb.
wait
pass time 104 vb.
wait 131 vb.
pause 140 vb.
be in motion
     260 vb.
be quiescent
     261 vb.
await 502 vb.
be irresolute
     596 vb.
not act 672 vb.
be inactive
     674 vb.
walk
be in motion
     260 vb.
walk 262 vb.
move slowly
     273 vb.
emerge 293 vb.
wander
be dispersed
     75 vb.

be in motion
 260 vb.
wander 262 vb.
stray 277 vb.
wanderer
foreigner 59 n.
nonconformist
 84 n.
displacement
 183 n.
wanderer 263 n.
rotator 310 n.
idler 674 n.
beggar 758 n.
low fellow 864 n.
outcast 878 n.
wandering
wandering 262 n.
deviation 277 n.
act of worship
 975 n.
war
disagreement
 25 n.
destroyer 163 n.
vocation 617 n.
dissension 704 n.
war 713 n.
revolt 733 n.
war chariot
war chariot
 269 n.
warfare
slaughter 357 n.
poisoning 654 n.
quarrel 704 n.
contention 711 n.
fight 711 n.
warfare 713 n.
weapon 718 n.
warhorse
warhorse 268 n.
warlike
powerful 155 adj.
violent 171 adj.
active 673 adj.
quarrelling
 704 adj.
defiant 706 adj.
attacking
 707 adj.
contending
 711 adj.
warlike 713 adj.
courageous
 850 adj.
boastful 872 adj.
insolent 873 adj.
warm
summery 123 adj.
warm 374 adj.
warm clothes
warm clothes
 376 n.
war measures
war measures
 713 n.
warm feeling
restlessness
 673 n.
warm feeling
 813 n.
warn
foresee 505 vb.
predict 506 vb.
hint 519 vb.
signal 542 vb.
dissuade 608 vb.
warn 659 vb.
advise 686 vb.
defy 706 vb.

threaten 895 vb.
reprove 919 vb.
warned
warned 659 adj.
warned, be
be warned
 659 vb.
warner
warner 659 n.
warning
precursor 66 n.
omen 506 n.
hint 519 n.
dissuasion 608 n.
warning 659 n.
danger signal
 660 n.
advice 686 n.
intimidation
 849 n.
threat 895 n.
warrant
precept 688 n.
warrant 732 n.
mandate 746 n.
permit 751 n.
security 762 n.
legal process
 954 n.
warring
warring 713 adj.
warship
sailing ship
 270 n.
ship 270 n.
warship 717 n.
waste
decrease 37 n.
abate 37 vb.
decrement 42 n.
dispersion 75 n.
disperse 75 vb.
disable 156 vb.
consume 160 vb.
destroy 160 vb.
destroy 160 vb.
lay waste 160 vb.
desert 167 n.
make sterile
 167 vb.
outflow 293 n.
reception 294 n.
require 622 vb.
waste 629 n.
waste 629 vb.
make insufficient
 631 vb.
redundance
 632 n.
deterioration
 650 n.
impair 650 vb.
use 668 n.
dispose of
 668 vb.
use 668 vb.
misuse 670 n.
misuse 670 vb.
loss 767 n.
lose 767 vb.
expend 801 vb.
prodigality 810 n.
be prodigal
 810 vb.
be rash 852 vb.
be intemperate
 938 vb.
wasted
wasted 629 adj.
waste effort
fall short 302 vb.

attempt the
impossible
 465 vb.
be foolish 494 vb.
waste 629 vb.
be superfluous
 632 vb.
waste effort
 636 vb.
misuse 670 vb.
be busy 673 vb.
be inactive
 674 vb.
act foolishly
 690 vb.
fail 723 vb.
wasteful
destructive
 160 adj.
wasteful 629 adj.
superfluous
 632 adj.
watch
be impotent
 156 vb.
be present
 184 vb.
see 433 vb.
watch 436 vb.
acquiesce 483 vb.
not act 672 vb.
water
fluid 330 n.
fluidity 330 n.
water 334 n.
lake 341 n.
waterfall
sources of energy
 155 n.
high water 204 n.
outflow 293 n.
descent 304 n.
moistening 336 n.
waterfall 345 n.
conduit 346 n.
water travel
motion 260 n.
water travel
 264 n.
watery
fluid 330 adj.
watery 334 adj.
humid 336 adj.
wave
increase 36 n.
periodicity 136 n.
outbreak 171 n.
high water 204 n.
shallowness
 207 n.
convolution
 246 n.
swelling 248 n.
roughness 254 n.
furrow 257 n.
oscillation 312 n.
commotion 313 n.
water 334 n.
ocean 338 n.
wave 345 n.
pitfall 658 n.
waverer
waverer 596 n.
way
itinerary 262 n.
policy 618 n.
way 619 n.
means 624 n.
conduct 683 n.
compromise
 765 n.

fashion 843 n.
ritual 982 n.
way in
way in 292 n.
weak
small 33 adj.
inferior 35 adj.
ephemeral
 109 adj.
impotent 156 adj.
powerless
 156 adj.
weak 158 adj.
inert 170 adj.
moderate
 172 adj.
little 191 adj.
narrow 201 adj.
brittle 325 adj.
watery 334 adj.
irresolute
 596 adj.
unhealthy
 646 adj.
unsafe 656 adj.
lax 729 adj.
cowardly 851 adj.
frail 929 adj.
weak, be
be impotent
 156 vb.
be weak 158 vb.
be imperfect
 642 vb.
be ill 646 vb.
be fatigued
 679 vb.
be wicked
 929 vb.
weaken
abate 37 vb.
mix 43 vb.
modify 138 vb.
disable 156 vb.
unman 156 vb.
weaken 158 vb.
demolish 160 vb.
moderate 172 vb.
rarefy 320 vb.
add water
 334 vb.
qualify 463 vb.
impair 650 vb.
weakened
weakened
 158 adj.
weakling
helplessness
 156 n.
weakling 158 n.
male 367 n.
ninny 496 n.
sick person
 646 n.
unlucky person
 726 n.
coward 851 n.
weakly
weakly 158 adj.
weakness
decrease 37 n.
transience 109 n.
old age 126 n.
impotence 156 n.
weakness 158 n.
brittleness 325 n.
female 368 n.
feebleness 567 n.
irresolution
 596 n.
defect 642 n.

ill health 646 n.
illness 646 n.
impairment
650 n.
vulnerability
656 n.
sluggishness
674 n.
failure 723 n.
laxity 729 n.
vice 929 n.

weak thing
insubstantial
thing 4 n.
weak thing 158 n.
brittleness 325 n.

wealth
euphoria 371 n.
good 615 n.
means 624 n.
plenty 630 n.
prosperity 725 n.
independence
739 n.
estate 772 n.
money 792 n.
wealth 795 n.

weapon
destroyer 163 n.
perforator 258 n.
hammer 274 n.
protection 655 n.
safeguard 657 n.
defence 708 n.
weapon 718 n.
intimidation
849 n.
threat 895 n.

wear
wear 223 vb.
show 517 vb.
be ostentatious
870 vb.

weather
lowering 306 n.
weather 335 n.
indicator 542 n.

weave
mix 43 vb.
tie 45 vb.
combine 50 vb.
compose 56 vb.
produce 159 vb.
weave 217 vb.

weaving
weaving 217 n.

wed
be akin 11 vb.
unite with 45 vb.
combine 50 vb.
choose 600 vb.
promise 759 vb.
be in love 882 vb.
excite love
882 vb.
court 884 vb.
wed 889 vb.

wedding
wedding 889 n.

weep
cry 403 vb.
weep 831 vb.

weeper
weeper 831 n.

weigh
be unequal 29 vb.
grow 36 vb.
load 188 vb.
descend 304 vb.
lower 306 vb.
founder 308 vb.

weigh 317 vb.
measure 460 vb.
hinder 697 vb.
oppress 730 vb.

weighing
weighing 317 n.

weightily
weightily
317 adv.

weighty
substantial 3 adj.
unequal 29 adj.
great 32 adj.
strong 157 adj.
large 190 adj.
weighty 317 adj.
dense 319 adj.
hindering
697 adj.
annoying 822 adj.

welcomed
welcomed
877 adj.

well
well 615 adv.
expediently
637 adv.

well-bred
orderly 60 adj.
tasteful 841 adj.
well-bred
843 adj.
genteel 863 adj.
courteous
879 adj.

well-known
known 485 adj.
manifest 517 adj.
well-known
523 adj.

well-made
well-made
689 adj.

wet, be
swim 264 vb.
exude 293 vb.
plunge 308 vb.
be wet 336 vb.

wheel
edge 229 n.
wheel 245 n.
rotator 310 n.
tool 625 n.

when
when 104 adv.

while
while 104 adv.
between 226 adv.

whim
bias 476 n.
foolery 492 n.
eccentricity
498 n.
whim 599 n.
wit 834 n.

white
unmixed 44 adj.
colourless
421 adj.
white 422 adj.
clean 643 adj.
pure 945 adj.

whiten
colour 420 vb.
decolorize
421 vb.
lose colour
421 vb.
whiten 422 vb.
clean 643 vb.

show feeling
813 vb.

whiteness
whiteness 422 n.

white thing
white thing
422 n.

whiting
whiting 422 n.
cleanser 643 n.

whitish
whitish 422 adj.

whole
finite quantity
26 n.
quantity 26 n.
great quantity
32 n.
consummate
32 adj.
simple 44 adj.
whole 52 n.
whole 52 adj.
completeness
54 n.
complete 54 adj.
inclusion 78 n.
inclusive 78 adj.
generality 79 n.
universal 79 adj.
numerical result
85 n.
unity 88 n.
strong 157 adj.
spacious 178 adj.
form 238 n.
universe 316 n.
structure 326 n.
association
701 n.
orthodox 970 adj.

wholly
greatly 32 adv.
wholly 52 adv.
generally 79 adv.

whopper
whopper 190 n.

whopping
whopping 32 adj.
large 190 adj.

why wherefore
whence how how
come cui bono
why 153 adv.

wicked
bad 640 adj.
difficult 695 adj.
wrong 909 adj.
dishonest
925 adj.
wicked 929 adj.
guilty 931 adj.
impenitent
935 adj.
lawbreaking
949 adj.
irreligious
968 adj.
impious 974 adj.

wicked, be
deteriorate
650 vb.
behave 683 vb.
be wicked
929 vb.
be guilty 931 vb.
be impious
974 vb.

wickedly
wickedly 929 adv.

wickedness
wickedness 929 n.

widely
widely 178 adv.

widow
widow 891 vb.

widowed
widowed 891 adj.

widowed, be
be widowed
891 vb.

widowhood
widowhood
891 n.

widows' weeds
formal dress
widowhood
891 n.

wig
wig 223 n.
hairdressing
838 n.

wilful
wilful 597 adj.
capricious
599 adj.
rash 852 adj.
malevolent
893 adj.

will
intellect 442 n.
will 590 n.
will 590 vb.
be willing 592 vb.
resolution 594 n.
be resolute
594 vb.
choose 600 vb.
predetermination
603 n.
freedom 739 n.
be free 739 vb.
desire 854 n.

willing
vigorous 169 adj.
assenting
483 adj.
studious 531 adj.
willing 592 adj.
resolute 594 adj.
induced 607 adj.
intending
612 adj.
instrumental
623 adj.
attempting
666 adj.
active 673 adj.
tractable
696 adj.
obedient 734 adj.
consenting
753 adj.
cheerful 828 adj.
courageous
850 adj.

willing, be
will 590 vb.
be willing 592 vb.
undertake
667 vb.
be active 673 vb.
exert oneself
677 vb.
minister to
698 vb.
obey 734 vb.
consent 753 vb.
offer oneself
754 vb.